THE OXFORD HISTORY OF POETRY IN ENGLISH

General Editor
PATRICK CHENEY

Coordinating Editors
ROBERT R. EDWARDS
LAURA L. KNOPPERS
STEPHEN REGAN
VINAY DHARWADKER

Dedicated to the Beloved Memory of
Michael O'Neill
1953–2018
Professor of English, University of Durham, United Kingdom
Founding Coordinating Editor, OHOPE,
Great Romantics Scholar and Distinguished British Poet

THE OXFORD HISTORY OF POETRY IN ENGLISH

The Oxford History of Poetry in English (*OHOPE*) is designed to offer a fresh, multi-voiced, and comprehensive analysis of 'poetry': from Anglo-Saxon culture through contemporary British, Irish, American, and Global culture, including English, Scottish, and Welsh poetry, Anglo-American colonial and post-colonial poetry, and poetry in Canada, Australia, New Zealand, the Caribbean, India, Africa, Asia, and other international locales. *OHOPE* both synthesises existing scholarship and presents cutting-edge research, employing a global team of expert contributors for each of the fourteen volumes.

1. *Medieval Poetry: c. 670–1100*
2. *Medieval Poetry: 1100–1400*
3. *Medieval Poetry: 1400–1500*
4. *Sixteenth-Century British Poetry*
5. *Seventeenth-Century British Poetry*
6. *Eighteenth-Century British Poetry*
7. *Romantic Poetry*
8. *Victorian Poetry*
9. *Modern British and Irish Poetry: Twentieth Century to Today*
10. *American Poetry: First Encounters to 1865*
11. *American Poetry: 1865–1939*
12. *American Poetry: 1939–present*
13. *Poetry in Canada, Australia, New Zealand, and Oceania*
14. *Poetry in Asia, Africa, and the Caribbean*

The Oxford History of Poetry in English

Medieval Poetry: 1400–1500

Volume 3

Edited by
JULIA BOFFEY
AND
A. S. G. EDWARDS

Great Clarendon Street, Oxford, OX2 6DP,
United Kingdom

Oxford University Press is a department of the University of Oxford.
It furthers the University's objective of excellence in research, scholarship,
and education by publishing worldwide. Oxford is a registered trade mark of
Oxford University Press in the UK and in certain other countries

© The several contributors 2023

The moral rights of the authors have been asserted

All rights reserved. No part of this publication may be reproduced, stored in
a retrieval system, or transmitted, in any form or by any means, without the
prior permission in writing of Oxford University Press, or as expressly permitted
by law, by licence or under terms agreed with the appropriate reprographics
rights organization. Enquiries concerning reproduction outside the scope of the
above should be sent to the Rights Department, Oxford University Press, at the
address above

You must not circulate this work in any other form
and you must impose this same condition on any acquirer

Published in the United States of America by Oxford University Press
198 Madison Avenue, New York, NY 10016, United States of America

British Library Cataloguing in Publication Data

Data available

Library of Congress Control Number: 2023930629

ISBN 978–0–19–883968–2

DOI: 10.1093/oso/9780198839682.001.0001

Printed and bound by
CPI Group (UK) Ltd, Croydon, CR0 4YY

Links to third party websites are provided by Oxford in good faith and
for information only. Oxford disclaims any responsibility for the materials
contained in any third party website referenced in this work.

General Editor's Preface

The Oxford History of Poetry in English (*OHOPE*) aims to offer a fresh, multi-voiced, and comprehensive survey of its vast and complicated topic: from Anglo-Saxon poetry through contemporary British, Irish, American, and Global poetry, including English, Scottish, and Welsh poetry, Anglo-American colonial and post-colonial poetry, and poetry in Canada, Australia, New Zealand, the Caribbean, India, Africa, Asia, and other locales.

By 'poetry in English', we mean, quite simply, *poetry written in the English language*: Old English, Middle English, Early Modern English, Modern English. 'English' poetry certainly emerges in Anglo-Saxon England, around the sixth century CE; but, as 'poetry in English' develops, it extends beyond the geographical boundaries of England. Today, poetry in English is planetary. While *OHOPE* necessarily limits the coverage if not the scope simply to come into existence, hopefully the Series will join other international projects in the world-service of 'poetry'.

What do we mean by 'poetry'? While we believe that most readers will know what we mean, the topic is intricate, so much so that a quick definition proves elusive. For example, the *Oxford English Dictionary* (*OED*) offers six major definitions, with seven sub-definitions, bringing the total to thirteen. The definitions range from 'Imaginative or creative literature in general; fable, fiction', to 'The art or work of a poet', and can include even 'A treatise on the art of poetry', or, '*figurative*. Something comparable to poetry in its beauty or emotional impact; a poetic quality of beauty and intensity of emotion; the poetic quality *of* something.' The earliest attested use of the word 'poetry' traces to the 1380s, in contexts that emphasize the contested truth claims of figurative representation. In Chaucer's *House of Fame*, one of the rivalrous authorities on the Troy story 'seyde that Omer made lyes, / Feynynge in hys poetries' (1477–8). The ending of *Troilus and Criseyde* includes a valediction for 'the forme of olde clerkis speche / In poetrie' (5.1854–5). John Trevisa's translation of Ranulf Higden's *Polychronicon* (finished in 1387) connects idolatry and poetry: 'Of þe bryngynge forþ of mawmetrie com wel nyh al þe feyninge of poetrie' (2.279). In the 1390s, by contrast, Chaucer's Clerk sees poetry as an authoritative, illustrious tradition embodied in 'Frauncheys Petrak, the lauriat poete, / ... whos rethorike sweete / Enlumyned al Ytaille of poetrie' (*Canterbury Tales* IV.31–3). Intriguingly, none of the *OED* definitions speak of metre, let alone rhyme, and there is no suggestion that poetry includes different 'kinds' (or forms or genres). The recent and authoritative *Princeton Encyclopedia of Poetry and Poetics* (2012), perhaps wisely, does not include an entry on 'poetry' itself. Because poetry remains such an elusive concept—and can include language in distinct metres (such as iambic pentameter) and rhymes (such as the 'Shakespearean' sonnet, rhyming *abab cdcd efef gg*, or three quatrains and a couplet)—we might remain content simply to open the concept up, and let the volumes in the Series speak on their own.

Yet *OHOPE* does proceed through a general rubric. We have encouraged our contributors to address their project through the following formula: *poetry as poetry*—rather than say, poetry *as context* or *in context*. The goal is to highlight the art of poetry itself, as it unfolds historically in time, across idioms, forms, nations, and so forth. Yet we do not think such a goal at odds with context, nor should it be. Each volume is thus free to situate poetry historically, ideologically, as the editors see fit.

Precisely because 'Poetry in English' spans some fifteen centuries, develops in four major historical 'languages' (Old, Middle, Early Modern, Modern), spread across multiple nations (ever-changing), and includes countless poets, both men and women, the fourteen-volume *Oxford History of Poetry in English* cannot succeed in mapping the full terrain. That has never been the goal. In keeping with the Press's Oxford Series template, the volumes remain necessarily selective: no satisfactorily comprehensive 'coverage' is possible, or perhaps desirable. Each volume does the best it can to remain representative, and fair.

We believe that *OHOPE* fills a gap in the available scholarship and criticism. At present, there is no authoritative history of poetry in English covering British, Irish, American, and Global poetry from the medieval through the modern eras. Readers might like to know that the origins to the present history evidently began with Alexander Pope. In the eighteenth century, Pope *conceived* of a history of 'British' poetry, but it took Thomas Warton to begin writing one, which he left unfinished at his death, still at work on the English Renaissance. Accordingly, the first to complete a comprehensive *History of British Poetry* was W. J. Courthope, who published a six-volume, single-authored work between 1895 and 1905. Other histories followed: in 1947, Herbert Grierson and J. C. Smith coauthored a one-volume *Critical History of English Poetry* (Oxford); in 1961, James Reeves published *A Short History of English Poetry from 1340–1940* (New York); in 1962, Kenneth Hopkins published *English Poetry: A Short History* (London); and in 1981, G. S. Fraser produced *A Short History of English Poetry* (Shepton Mallet). Between 1977 and 1981, Routledge began a *History of English Poetry*, but evidently the series was never completed; only three volumes are in print: *Old English and Middle English Poetry*, edited by Derek A. Pearsall; *Restoration and Eighteenth Century Poetry 1660–1780*, edited by Eric Rothstein; and *Poetry of the Romantic Period*, edited by J. R. de J. Jackson. In 1994, Carl Woodring, working with James Shapiro as Associate Editor, published *The Columbia History of British Poetry*, a one-volume edited collection beginning with Old English Poetry and ending in 1990. In 2010, the most recent attempt at such a history appeared, edited by the late Michael O'Neill, *The Cambridge History of English Poetry*, another single-volume collection, covering England, Scotland, Ireland, and Wales, with all chapters devoted to a single author or a small group of authors.

As for histories of American poetry, in 1993 Jay Parini published an edited *Columbia History of American Poetry*, making Columbia the first press to print a history of poetry combining 'British' and 'American'—anticipating the present *Oxford History*, yet on a much-reduced scale, minus Global poetry, and now thirty years from its publication date. Earlier histories in American poetry include Horace Gregory and Marya Zaturenska's 1946 *History of American Poetry 1900–1940* (Harcourt Brace) and Donald Barlow Stauffer's 1974 *Short History of American Poetry* (Dutton). No histories of Global poetry in English exist. Consequently, the field remains wide open for a comprehensive history that includes Global, American, and British and Irish poetry, medieval to modern.

The target audience for *OHOPE* is similarly complex, to include the general reader of poetry, students at several levels (upper-division secondary school, undergraduate, graduate), teachers at all levels, literary critics, and textual scholars—effectively, anyone interested in poetry in English. Each chapter aims to meet the primary criterion required for this readership: a combination of both a general orientation to its topic and a fresh approach and contribution to the field. A comprehensive bibliography will be printed at the back of each volume.

Moreover, each volume aims to feature a stable set of chapters. Not simply will there be chapters on major poets ('Milton'), but each volume aims to include chapters on the following topics, geared to the particular era or century it covers:

- The nature of authorship and literary career, as well as the role of the poet in society.
- Imitation and intertextuality.
- Prosody, poetics, and the nature of literary theory.
- Figuration and allusiveness.
- Modes of representation (e.g., allegory, ekphrasis, and blazon during the Renaissance).
- Genre, mode, and form.
- Translation.
- The material production and circulation of poetry (manuscript, performance, print), including the role of patronage.

OHOPE pays significant attention to such major cultural vectors as religion/theology, politics/nationalism, race/class, and gender/sexuality. However, the goal will be unusual in today's critical climate: to connect such vectors to the *matter of poetry* itself; to discuss 'history' and the 'material' insofar as it allows for the historicisation of poetry *as an art*. Above all, *The Oxford History of Poetry in English* aims to provide an authoritative, useful helpmeet for enjoying and embracing one of the seminal achievements of world-art.

Patrick Cheney

Acknowledgements

The Oxford History of Poetry in English has had a long history. Formally, it began on 16 April 2008, when Andrew McNeillie, then Senior Commissioning Editor of Literature at the Press, invited Patrick Cheney to be General Editor of the Series. The history continued when Penn State University offered its support—in particular, when the Head of the English Department at the time, Robin Schulze, offered financial and administrative support. Cheney then appointed four Coordinating Editors to manage the wide range of coverage for the Series, and we remain indebted to their early work and support: along with Professor Schulze, Robert R. Edwards, Laura L. Knoppers, and Robert Caserio. The Penn State team produced a detailed proposal to the Press, which in turn produced a series of readers' reports, including recommendations for revision, one of which was to widen leadership of the project. At this point, a new set of Coordinating Editors was appointed: along with Professor Edwards for Medieval and Professor Knoppers for Early Modern (now at the University of Notre Dame), Michael O'Neill of the University of Durham for Modern British and Irish, Langdon Hammer of Yale for American, and Vinay Dharwadker of the University of Wisconsin for Global. A revised proposal then went to Press readers, to whom again we remain grateful. When Professor O'Neill passed away in 2018, his colleague at Durham, Stephen Regan, was appointed Coordinating Editor of Modern British and Irish. Recently as well, Professor Hammer has stepped down, and new appointments are underway. We wish to express our gratitude to all these early begetters of *The Oxford History of Poetry in English* (*OHOPE*).

OHOPE is dedicated to the memory of Michael O'Neill, who sadly passed away on 21 December 2018. Not merely was Michael a distinguished Romantics scholar and British poet, but he was a Coordinating Editor of the Modern British and Irish unit of *OHOPE*, for which he provided expert, collegial leadership.

The editors of Volume 3 would like to express their gratitude to Professor Robert R. Edwards of the Department of English at Penn State, for his advice and support. They thank Rachel Addison for her astute copyediting and Mark Ajin Millet, Integra Project Manager, and Aimee Wright, Senior Project Editor of Oxford University Press, for their efficient handling of this volume. We are grateful to all the contributors for their work. This volume is dedicated to the memory of Derek Pearsall (1931-2021), scholar, teacher, and friend.

Contents

List of Abbreviations   xv
List of Contributors   xvii
Editorial Note   xix

1. Introduction   1
   Julia Boffey & A. S. G. Edwards

PART I CONTEXTS

2. Contexts of English Poetry 1400–1500   13
   David Rundle
3. Literary Traditions: Continuity and Change   28
   James Simpson
4. Translation into English   46
   Marco Nievergelt
5. Literary Language   61
   Jenni Nuttall
6. Verse Forms and Prosody   76
   Eric Weiskott
7. Authorship   91
   Robert J. Meyer-Lee

PART II TRANSMISSION

8. Poetic Manuscripts   111
   Julia Boffey & A. S. G. Edwards
9. Poetry in Print   127
   Siân Echard
10. Verse Outside Books   140
    Julia Boffey

PART III TOPICS AND GENRES

11. Biblical Paraphrase and Poems of Religious Instruction   159
    Takami Matsuda
12. Saints' Lives and Miracles of the Virgin   178
    Cynthia Turner Camp

13. Religious Lyrics and Carols 194
    Christiania Whitehead

14. The Poetry of Religious and Moral Drama 213
    Tamara Atkin

15. Science and Information 238
    A. S. G. Edwards

16. Conduct Poetry 264
    Matthew Giancarlo

17. Love Visions and Love Poetry 282
    Rory G. Critten

18. Chronicle and History 300
    Andrew Galloway

19. Fictions of Antiquity 326
    Venetia Bridges

20. Fictions of Britain 341
    Aisling Byrne

21. Fictions of Christendom and Other Late Romances 355
    Phillipa Hardman

22. Popular Tales 371
    Ben Parsons

23. Occasional Poetry, Popular Poetry, and the Robin Hood Tradition 385
    Helen Phillips

PART IV POETS

24. John Lydgate 407
    Robert R. Edwards

25. Thomas Hoccleve 424
    Sebastian Langdell

26. Robert Henryson 442
    Joanna Martin

27. William Dunbar 461
    Pamela M. King

PART V CONTINUITY AND CHANGE

28. Transitions: After the Fifteenth Century 481
    Jane Griffiths

Bibliography 501
Manuscript Index 551
Index 555

List of Abbreviations

BL:	British Library.
BodL:	Bodleian Library.
CUL:	Cambridge University Library.
DIMEV:	Linne Mooney et al., *A Digital Index of Middle English Verse* (online).
EETS:	Early English Text Society; cited by series (e.s., o.s., s.s.), volume number(s) and date(s).
e.s.:	extra series.
MED:	*Middle English Dictionary*, ed. Robert E. Lewis, et al. (Ann Arbor, MI, 1952–2001).
MET:	Middle English Texts (Heidelberg), cited by series number.
MS(S):	manuscript(s).
NIMEV:	J. Boffey and A. S. G. Edwards, *A New Index of Middle English Verse*. London, 2005.
ODNB:	H. C. G. Matthew and Brian Harrison (eds). *Oxford Dictionary of National Biography*. Oxford, 2004 (also online, with supplements).
o.s.:	original series.
s.s.:	supplementary series.
STC:	A. W. Pollard and G. R. Redgrave, revised and enlarged by W. A. Jackson, and F. S. Ferguson, completed by Katharine F. Pantzer, *A Short-Title Catalogue of Books Printed in England, Scotland, & Ireland and of English Books Printed Abroad 1475–1640*. 2nd edn. 3 vols. London, 1976–91.
STS:	Scottish Text Society, cited by series, volume number(s) and date(s).
Wing:	Donald G. Wing, *A Short-Title Catalogue of Books, 1641–1700*. 3 vols. 2nd edn. New York, 1994.

List of Contributors

Tamara Atkin *Queen Mary University of London*

Julia Boffey *Queen Mary University of London*

Venetia Bridges *Durham University*

Aisling Byrne *University of Reading*

Cynthia Turner Camp *University of Georgia*

Rory G. Critten *University of Lausanne*

Siân Echard *University of British Columbia*

A. S. G. Edwards *University of Kent*

Robert R. Edwards *Pennsylvania State University*

Andrew Galloway *Cornell University*

Matthew Giancarlo *University of Kentucky*

Jane Griffiths *University of Oxford*

Phillipa Hardman *University of Reading*

Pamela M. King *Glasgow University*

Sebastian Langdell *Baylor University*

Joanna Martin *University of Nottingham*

Takami Matsuda *Keio University*

Robert J. Meyer-Lee *Agnes Scott College*

Marco Nievergelt *Ecole Pratique des Hautes Etudes Paris*

Jenni Nuttall *University of Oxford*

Ben Parsons *University of Leicester*

Helen Phillips *Cardiff University*

David Rundle *University of Kent*

James Simpson *Harvard University*

Eric Weiskott *Boston College*

Christiania Whitehead *University of Lausanne*

Editorial Note

All *OHOPE* volumes work from the Series Style Guide, a modified version of the one used by Oxford University Press for humanities publications. Individual *OHOPE* volumes may further modify the Style Guide according to needs—for instance, the need to print and translate Old and Middle English in Volumes 1–3, or of early modern Scots in Volume 4. Because of the linguistic diversity of poetry in Middle English, the editors of Volume 3 have followed the judgement of contributors in matters of quotation and orthography.

Where feasible, then, the standard editions of all authors have been quoted and cited. Primary texts are cited in full in the footnotes on their first occurrence, with abbreviated citations thereafter. Secondary texts are cited in full in the footnotes on their first occurrence in each chapter, and in abbreviated form thereafter.

When difficult words or phrases appear in quotations from primary texts, explanatory glosses are provided.

Quotations from Classical authors generally come from the Loeb Classical Library. For convenience, all Greek words quoted in the texts are transliterated. All Latin quotations are translated into English.

References to NIMEV numbers (see *List of Abbreviations*) identify the primary sources for texts cited. Early printed editions are identified by reference to STC numbers (see *List of Abbreviations*).

Each *OHOPE* volume concludes with a detailed, alphabetised Bibliography, combining primary and secondary sources mentioned in the individual chapters.

CHAPTER 1
Introduction

Julia Boffey & A. S. G. Edwards

Most of the poets that immediately succeeded Chaucer seem rather relapsing into barbarism than availing themselves of those striking ornaments which his judgement and imagination have disclosed. They seem to have been insensible to his vigour of versification, and to his flights of fancy. It was not indeed likely that a poet should soon arise equal to Chaucer ... His successors, however, approach him in no degree of proportion.[1]

Thomas Warton's judgement, in his *History of English Poetry* (1775), established a critical stance towards the poetry of the fifteenth century that was to hold sway for the next two centuries. It was one that saw the poetry of this period as embodying a significant decline from the standards of poetic excellence established by Chaucer. It was not until the latter half of the twentieth century that it was possible to see the beginnings of a new appreciation of the qualities of the poetry of the fifteenth century, an appreciation that over the past fifty years has grown to a spate of radical reassessments of its intrinsic merits and historical importance. This volume seeks to consolidate this new sense of the achievements of the age.

It is appropriate to begin, like Warton, with Chaucer. In the last book of the *Confessio Amantis*, written towards the end of the fourteenth century, Gower claimed that 'the lond fulfild is overal' with Chaucer's songs.[2] With a proper sense of periodization Chaucer died in October 1400. His death thereby served to create a clear division in the literary history of English poetry. Fifteenth-century poetry was to be crucially shaped by the range of its attempts to mirror and modify Chaucer's achievements. Little more than a decade after Chaucer's death Thomas Hoccleve, who may well have known him, assessed his poetic significance. He was 'the firste fyndere (*inventor*) of our fair langage', 'the honour of Englissh tonge', 'flour of eloquence / Mirour of fructuous entendement (*edifying meaning*)'. He was both 'maistir' (*master*) and 'fadir' (*father*).[3] Hoccleve's acclaim set the parameters for what was to be the historical and exemplary sense of Chaucer's importance over the course of the fifteenth century and beyond.[4] But its terms of reference, with Chaucer as the source of what came to be thought of as a specifically English poetic tradition, accommodates only part of the full range of fifteenth-century poetic production. While Chaucer's influence was

---

[1] Thomas Warton, *History of English Poetry*, revised by Richard Price, 3 vols. (London, 1824), 2.269.
[2] *Confessio Amantis*, 8.2943–7, in G. C. Macaulay (ed.), *The English Works of John Gower*, 2 vols., EETS, e.s. 81, 82 (London, 1900–1901), 2.466.
[3] Thomas Hoccleve, 'The Regiment of Princes', in F. J. Furnivall (ed.), *Hoccleve's Works*: III. *The Regiment of Princes*, EETS, e.s. 72 (London, 1897), 1958–67.
[4] See Caroline Spurgeon, *Five Hundred Years of Chaucer Criticism and Allusion, 1375–1900*, 3 vols. (Cambridge, 1925), 1.14–65 for a detailed record of such references to Chaucer. The literature on Chaucer's influence on fifteenth-century poetry is extensive. Seth Lerer, *Chaucer and His Readers: Imagining the Author in Late-Medieval England* (Princeton, NJ, 1993) remains the most suggestive account; see also Derek Pearsall, 'The English Chaucerians', in D. S. Brewer (ed.), *Chaucer and Chaucerians* (London, 1966), 201–39.

widely and powerfully felt, its reverberations generated diverse effects, variously inflected by factors of time, occasion, and place, across the landscape of fifteenth-century verse writing. Other earlier poetic traditions, some with lineages stretching well back beyond Chaucer's lifetime, continued to generate response through the course of the century.

If the date of Chaucer's death might seem to constitute a reassuringly firm point of literary-historical reference, there were few indications of such stability in the real world of fifteenth-century England, as David Rundle demonstrates (Chapter 2). 'England', 'English', and 'Englishness' were complicated terms in the islands of Britain.[5] In Scotland, a separate country with its own king, both 'Inglis' (early Scots, a distinct form of English) and Gaelic were in use. Wales, under English rule since the late thirteenth century, had its own flourishing traditions of writing in Welsh; and the principality's charged relations with the English crown were briefly invigorated in the opening decades of the fifteenth century under its prince Owain Glyndŵr, who led an ultimately unsuccessful rebellion before his death c1415. In Ireland, largely Gaelic-speaking, English flourished only in the area of the 'Pale', immediately around Dublin. These parts of Britain remained in uneasy relationship with England through the century. And their own distinct literary cultures, especially that of Scotland, show limited response to the expanding literary activity in England.

For those considering themselves English, the century began with a usurpation and ensuing efforts to consolidate the new Lancastrian dynasty inaugurated by Henry IV (1399–1413). These troubled years were also dominated by anxieties about religious orthodoxy, with popular dissemination of Wycliffite ideas prompting Lollard support for movements such as the rebellion led by John Oldcastle in 1414. This rebellion and other manifestations of Lollardy were attacked in verse of different kinds, notably by Thomas Hoccleve.

The desire to promote religious stability was to a degree undercut by various forms of political disorder both outside and within England. The uncertainties arising from this found expression in both short poems and longer works. Lancastrian successes in the Hundred Years' War against France—Henry V's victory at Agincourt in 1415, which produced a range of verse responses; the 1420 Treaty of Troyes which established an English right to the French throne, an event celebrated by Lydgate at the end of his *Siege of Thebes*—brought no lasting stability. By the 1430s, with French forces invigorated after the collapse of the siege of Orleans, and the withdrawal of Burgundian support for Henry VI, the English cause was dramatically weakened. The end of the Hundred Years' War, with French victory at the Battle of Castillon in 1453, saw the loss of all English territory in France, including the long-held territory of Gascony; only Calais remained under English control. That such significant events received only intermittent commentary in verse suggests the weight of their impact.

Political cataclysms at some further distance from English interests and Britain's borders also provoked little in the way of significant verse. The seizure of Constantinople in 1453, and the 1480 siege of the island of Rhodes, for example—two reminders of the strength of the Ottoman empire and its potential threat, not just to Christianity itself, but to western culture—do not seem to have been marked by poetic responses.

This may have been because of the weight of internal preoccupations. The shadow of usurpation lay over the century from its beginning. Its implications for English poetry were marked by Gower in a revision of the prologue to *Confessio Amantis* which changed its dedicatee from Richard II to Henry IV. The reign of Henry IV prompted various literary

---

[5] For the place of England, Ireland, Scotland, and Wales in the wider global context, see Christopher Allmand (ed.), *The New Cambridge Medieval History, Volume VII: c.1415–c.1500* (Cambridge, 1998).

expressions of the need for order and stability, detectable among some of the political poems in BodL MS Digby 102. The death of Henry V in 1422 created further instability, with his successor, Henry VI, the last Lancastrian king, only an infant. Henry VI's reign was long but fractured by conflicts arising from competing Lancastrian and Yorkist claims to the crown in the course of the so-called Wars of the Roses. Henry was deposed by the Yorkist Edward IV in 1461. He reclaimed the throne in 1470, but at his death in 1477 was again replaced by Edward. The shifting allegiances and troubles of these decades are reflected in anonymous short poems and carols whose support for one or other faction is occasionally subsumed in a more heartfelt wish for 'concorde & unite'.[6] The reign of Edward IV was followed by the accession of another Yorkist, Richard III. His death in 1485 at the Battle of Bosworth opened the way for Henry VII's inauguration of a new Tudor dynasty, albeit one whose status continued to be marked by periodic unrest with the emergence of different claimants to the throne. Such concern with disorder in Henry's reign finds expression in one of Skelton's earliest poems, an elegy on the death of Henry Percy, fourth earl of Northumberland, killed by rebels in 1489.[7]

The implications of these domestic events for the production and transmission of poetry were necessarily contingent on policy and moment. A number of works commissioned or patronized in court circles in the early decades of the century evidently constituted responses to the new Lancastrian regime, variously lauding and warning those at its heart. In these circles, and for poets like Lydgate and Hoccleve, discussed by Sebastian Langdell and Robert R. Edwards (Chapters 24 and 25), the ethical aspects of Chaucer's poetry, together with its Englishness, made it a powerful touchstone. Some choices of both poetic matter and form look to Chaucer's models. Among works offering commentary on contemporary events and advice to England's rulers, Lydgate's *Troy Book* (commissioned in 1412 by the future Henry V) responds to Chaucer's *Troilus and Criseyde* (a manuscript of which the king owned); and Hoccleve's *Regiment of Princes* (completed in 1411 and dedicated to the future king) includes directions to remember the 'fresch lyflynesse' of Chaucer's 'persone'.[8] Both of these works employ forms given English currency by Chaucer, pentameter couplets and rhyme royal stanzas respectively. On occasions, the use of Chaucerian models was not without its ironies. Later in the century in Scotland, at a time of tense relations between England and its northern neighbour (c1477), Blind Hary's nationalistic poetic history *The Wallace* would use iambic pentameter and eight- and nine-line stanzas based on Chaucerian models for his own nationalist ends, as Andrew Galloway shows (Chapter 18).[9]

Not all early fifteenth-century poetic commentators on Lancastrian rule felt under the shadow of Chaucer's influence to the same extent. The anonymous author of *The Crowned King*, writing close to the date of Henry V's Agincourt campaign in 1415, couched his advice to the king in the form of a dream vision in alliterative metre.[10] The choice of form and metre places him at a distance from court-affiliated Lancastrian commentators. Doubtless regional factors were an element in decisions about how to respond to the increasing availability of manuscripts of Chaucer's writings.

---

[6] See the selection of poems in R. H. Robbins (ed.), *Historical Poems of the XIVth and XVth Centuries* (New York, 1959), 189–227. The quotation is taken from the refrain line in poem no. 79, 'Reconciliation of Henry VI and the Yorkists (1458)'.
[7] Macaulay (ed.), *The English Works of John Gower*, 1.1–34.
[8] A. Erdmann and E. Ekwall (eds), *Lydgate's Siege of Thebes*, 2 vols., EETS, e.s. 108, 125 (London, 1911, 1930), and Furnivall (ed.), *Hoccleve's Works: III*, 4993–5 (180).
[9] Anne McKim (ed.), *The Wallace: Blind Harry* (Edinburgh, 2003).
[10] In Helen Barr (ed.), *The Piers Plowman Tradition* (London, 1993), 205–10.

Some of the verse that emerged in the course of the century was, as already noted, directly prompted by political and military events both abroad and at home. John Page's *Siege of Rouen* offers an unusual first-hand perspective on a military event of 1418–19 in the Hundred Years' War. The *Libelle of Englyshe Polycye*, originating at a slightly later point in the context of the 'werre in Fraunce', presents distinctive political and economic commentary on current events through its analyses of England's trade relations with various countries in the 1430s.[11] Its contemporary appeal to a wide social spectrum is evidenced by the large number of surviving manuscript copies. But it is rare for such poetic voices to achieve distinctive expression about historical matters, present or past. Most often, verse depictions of political events and historical characters are shaped, with varying degrees of explicitness, by faction, individual or regional, and constitute what we would now term propaganda.

There were wider literary consequences to the extended war with France. At the beginning of the fifteenth century England still had a trilingual culture, with French and Latin in fairly widespread use alongside, or (in some contexts) in preference to English. Although this remained the case, the continuing war with France imbued this situation with new complexities. Domestic hostility to the French language may have been a factor in the growth of Anglophone literary culture from the later fourteenth century, one that found expression in a developing sense of a distinctive literary English, as explored here by Jenny Nuttall (in Chapter 5). But at the same time the English presence in France must have exposed some English people to French poetic forms, while the presence in England of noble French prisoners and their households (newly visible after Agincourt and the taking of prisoners for ransom) probably gave French literary culture an increased palpable presence in England. The debt owed by Chaucer and Gower to French models and forms anyway constituted a powerful precedent. The continuing 'anglicization' of French genres and verse forms in the fifteenth century, and the taste for works in French, was thus perhaps at once admiring and a statement of English cultural assertion. This double-edged phenomenon found expression most obviously in forms of what may be broadly thought of as 'courtly' poetry, as discussed by Rory G. Critten (Chapter 17). The bodies of poetry in both French and English associated with Charles of Orleans, resident in England under house arrest for nearly three decades after his capture at Agincourt, are significant products of this complex set of cultural relationships.[12]

There were other Continental literary influences in this period of a less definable kind. The translation into English verse of Latin texts from either the classical past or from the Italian Renaissance, considered here by Marco Nievergelt (Chapter 4), was infrequent and often derivative. Duke Humfrey of Gloucester's associations with Italian humanism are well documented, as is his role in vernacular verse translation of various kinds including this one (on which see A. S. G. Edwards, Chapter 15) and Lydgate's *Fall of Princes* (on which see Robert R. Edwards, Chapter 24). But Lydgate's work is not a direct ('humanist') translation of Boccaccio's Latin, but is based on an early fifteenth-century French prose version of it. Nor is it clear whether another unique Middle English verse rendering, of Boccaccio's *De mulieribus claris*, is a direct translation of the Latin.[13] Few English

---

[11] Joanna Bellis (ed.), *John Page's 'The Siege of Rouen'*, MET 51 (Heidelberg, 2015), and George Warner (ed.), *The Libelle of Englyshe Polycye: A Poem on the Use of Sea-Power, 1436* (Oxford, 1926).

[12] Mary-Jo Arn (ed.), *Fortunes Stabilnes: Charles of Orleans' English Book of Love* (Binghamton, NY, 1994); Mary-Jo Arn and John Fox (eds), *Poetry of Charles d'Orléans and His Circle: A Critical Edition of BnF MS. fr. 25458* (Turnhout, 2010).

[13] Janet Cowen (ed.), *On Famous Women: The Middle English Translation of Boccaccio's 'De Mulieribus Claris'*, MET 52 (Heidelberg, 2015).

poets actually ventured to Italy in the fifteenth century. Osbern Bokenham and John Capgrave, members of the Augustinian order, are notable exceptions, but their Italian travels seem to have made little impression on their hagiographic writings. The direct influence of Latin humanism on English poetry of the fifteenth century seems to have been limited. It probably achieved its most distinctive expression in the anonymous translation of part of Claudian's *De consulatu Stilichonis*, that survives in a single manuscript done for Richard, duke of York, composed uniquely in blank verse with the Latin original on facing pages.[14]

The forms of political, economic, and social change which invited poetic experimentation did so in part by expanding the range of environments hospitable to poetic production. Courtly environments—English and Scottish, royal and aristocratic—nonetheless remained pre-eminent nodes of poetic production and consumption throughout the century. The presence of educated and wealthy readers, the possibilities of patronage and preferment, and the availability of skilled scribes and illuminators to record texts in material form must all have contributed to the concentration of poetic energy in these milieux. Much of Hoccleve's occasional poetry was produced in the ambit of the Lancastrian court, based in Westminster and London; in the second half of the century, the poet George Ashby was employed in the signet office and in the service of Margaret of Anjou before his commitment to the Fleet prison.[15] Beyond royal circles, the patronage of a number of aristocratic families can be associated with surviving poems. Lydgate responded to commissions for members of the Beauchamp and Stafford families; Walton's verse translation of Boethius's *Consolation of Philosophy* was undertaken for Elizabeth Berkeley, one of a family of major literary patrons in Gloucestershire. Poetry also flourished in the households of some lesser knights, such as Sir Miles Stapleton of Norfolk, to whom John Metham dedicated *Amoryus and Cleopes*.[16]

The characteristics of court poetry from this period are various. Features of 'courtliness' might include reference to both the general tastes and specific commissions of noble patrons, and allusions to their lineage or the events in which they were involved: Richard Holland's *Buke of the Howlat*, produced mid-century, is dedicated to Elizabeth, wife of Archibald Douglas, earl of Moray.[17] The earliest surviving printed poem by a contemporary poet was a lament for the death of Jasper Tudor, earl of Pembroke, published in 1496.[18] Poems emanating from court environments might also include circumstantial details about particular occasions. The range of William Dunbar's late fifteenth-century output for the Scottish court of James IV indicates something of the occasional variety that might be required,[19] and Dunbar's command of a range of forms and voices illustrates the resourcefulness useful to a court poet, as Pamela M. King shows (Chapter 27). For serious court occasions, allusions to Chaucerian precedents seem to have been appropriate: rhyme royal and ballade stanzas, and (for shorter pieces) variations of English versions of French fixed forms, retained a lengthy cachet.

---

[14] Ewald Flügel, 'Eine mittelenglische Claudian-Übersetzung (1445) (Brit. Mus. Add. Ms. 11814)', *Anglia*, 28 (1905), 255–99, 421–38.
[15] Mary Bateson (ed.), *George Ashby's Poems*, EETS, e.s. 76 (London, 1899).
[16] See Derek Pearsall, *John Lydgate* (London, 1970), 166–8; Mark Science (ed.), John Walton, *Boethius: De Consolatione Philosophiae*, EETS, o.s. 170 (London, 1927); H. Craig (ed.), *The Works of John Metham*, EETS, o.s. 132 (London, 1916).
[17] Ralph Hanna (ed.), Richard Holland, *The Buke of the Howlat*, STS, 5th series, 12 (Woodbridge, 2014).
[18] STC 14477.
[19] Priscilla Bawcutt (ed.), *The Poems of William Dunbar*, 2 vols. (Glasgow, 1998).

The 'courtly' forms and subject matter of verse produced in royal and noble circles were, however, more widely influential. In lesser households, whether those of provincial members of the gentry class, or of the urban elite, or of important ecclesiasts, such verse served a range of educative and recreational purposes. Household reading in these contexts sometimes also comprehended more obviously instructive poems, a number of which had a wide circulation, and included verse instructions on conduct or piety, and fictional narratives and saints' lives promoting exemplary behaviour. Such collections, which include both works by identifiable fourteenth and fifteenth century poets as well as much anonymous verse, are discussed below by Edwards and Boffey (Chapter 8).

Prosperous urban households were also increasingly significant sites of poetic production and use. Here, as in the more rural contexts just invoked, verse served a variety of functions, from the instruction of children and apprentices to the devotional needs of mixed secular communities. Lydgate's *Bycorne and Chichevache*, written for performance in a London merchant's household, offers what was evidently considered a comic take on household dynamics.[20] Civic fraternities in towns and cities were important to poetic production, whether directly as sponsors of verse marking specific occasions, or more diffusely in relation to social connections informing networks of patronage.

Monastic houses, schools, and ecclesiastical establishments in all parts of Britain remained important cultural centres hospitable to verse production. The long list of named poets working in such environments includes Henry Bradshaw and John Lydgate, members of the Benedictine order; John Audelay, Osbern Bokenham, John Capgrave, John Hardyng, John Walton, and Andrew Wyntoun, all Augustinians, and James Ryman, a Franciscan friar. In collections surviving from these environments, English verse sometimes keeps company with Latin and French material. Schools, colleges, inns of court, and government departments were other communities hospitable to literary production. Some, possibly much of the anonymous poetry surviving from such environments is perhaps to be associated with the diffuse 'precariat' of those with loose affiliations to religious houses or ecclesiastical or academic establishments.

Some institutionally sponsored poetry, originating in communities of this kind or with civic bodies, served occasional purposes that included single notable events such as the London sheriffs' feast for which Lydgate provided *The Mumming at Bishopswood*, or royal entries to London and other cities, or the completion of buildings or monuments.[21] But in other instances verse was needed for occasions which came round at regular intervals, as with annual performances of religious plays, and the texts provided for these would have been subject to change and adaptation over time. Civic authorities were the sponsoring agents for some of this drama, especially in urban centres such as York and Coventry, as Tamara Atkin demonstrates (Chapter 14); and religious communities and ecclesiastical households (like that of Archbishop Morton in the 1490s at Lambeth Palace, home to Henry Medwall) were other important centres of play production. The survival of fifteenth-century material of this kind was enhanced by a growing wish to record and preserve it in the context of civic records and chronicles. In the case of Medwall's plays, survival was made more likely by the fact of their transmission into print, a factor which also contributed to the preservation of his name as author;[22] this and other implications of the appearance

---

[20] Henry Noble MacCracken (ed.), *The Minor Poems of John Lydgate: Part I: Religious Poems; Part II: Secular Poems*, 2 vols., EETS, e.s. 107 and 192 (London, 1911, 1934), 2.433–8.
[21] MacCracken (ed.), *Minor Poems of John Lydgate*, 2.668–71.
[22] STC 17778 and 17779; Alan H. Nelson (ed.), *The Plays of Henry Medwall* (Cambridge, 1980).

of print culture in England in the last quarter of the fifteenth century are discussed by Siân Echard (Chapter 9).

The authors of occasional poetry may not always be identifiable by name, but they can sometimes be attached to place, and to historical moment, from the internal evidence of what they wrote or from the context in which their writings have survived. But a very large quantity of fifteenth-century poetry is nonetheless both anonymous and resistant to localization. The origins of many of the lyrics, carols, charms, comic poems, and short narratives, discussed by Helen Phillips (Chapter 23), and a variety of other kinds of verse loosely categorizable as 'popular', discussed by Ben Parsons (Chapter 22), are impossible to pin down to particular places or contexts and sometimes even to date within a century. Much of this material enjoyed very wide geographical transmission; some of it, such as songs and carols on the holly and the ivy, may have come into being well before the fifteenth century and would remain in circulation well beyond it.[23] Such materials find broader expression and survival in other forms, as illustrated in Julia Boffey's discussion of 'Verse Outside Books' (Chapter 10).

Unsurprisingly, the topics of fifteenth-century poetry are multifarious. The increasing tendency to record and preserve texts of all kinds means that a wide range of material has survived, and from different parts of Britain. More of the 'popular' verse likely to have enjoyed an essentially oral circulation was recorded in written form in the fifteenth century than had been the case in earlier centuries, giving a material posterity to songs and charms and comic narratives. Utilitarian poems, considered here by A. S. G. Edwards (Chapter 15) similarly begin to survive in greater numbers from this period, whether in the form of lengthy verse treatises on topics like masonry and alchemy, or snappier stanzas on health or the weather. But at the heart of much fifteenth-century poetry remain topics that had informed the verse writing of earlier periods. History, both ancient and more recent, made its way into the narratives and chronicles examined here by Venetia Bridges and by Andrew Galloway (Chapters 18 and 19 respectively). The versifying of Christian teaching and narrative is discussed by Takami Matsuda (Chapter 11), hagiography by Cynthia Turner Camp (Chapter 12), and the religious lyric by Christiana Whitehead (Chapter 13). In terms of secular writing, the familiar 'matters' of romance are explored by Aisling Byrne (Chapter 20) and Phillipa Hardman (Chapter 21).

Some new and specific religious preoccupations are discernible, however. Forms of hagiographical and devotional writing received new impetus, in part through the emergence of individual saints' lives by Lydgate, Bokenham, and Capgrave, and also through Lydgate's extremely popular *Life of Our Lady*. Some new emphases are also apparent in the shorter poems discussed here by Christiania Whitehead (Chapter 13). The range of verse here, including the poems of BodL MS Digby 102, the anthology of works associated with John Audelay, James Ryman's collection of carols, and other groups of shorter lyrics and prayers in anonymous collections, reflects a new intensity of engagement with individual pious practice. Lydgate's short religious lyrics contrive this intensity in part by their notably dense texture of liturgical allusion and quotation, a feature also of the burdens and refrains of some popular anonymous carols.

Against the backdrop of spiritual anxieties and political volatility, some of the century's poetry seems also to be preoccupied with reflections on the private self in the public world. Hoccleve's *Series* famously encapsulates these worries, perceptible also in Ashby's

---

[23] Richard L. Greene (ed.), *The Early English Carols*, 2nd edn. (Oxford, 1977), 82–4.

Prisoner's Reflections and (sometimes less explicitly) in poems offering advice on conduct, as discussed by Matthew Giancarlo (Chapter 16).[24] Rory G. Critten (Chapter 17) shows how the private self's capacity to negotiate human relationships comes to the fore in some of the century's dream visions and love lyrics, forms of writing in which the world of courtly sociability presents opportunities for exploring aspects of behaviour and community.

Perhaps the most notable strand of the century's poetic concerns is its focus on a literary tradition of writing in English, a new phenomenon made possible by the late fourteenth-century burgeoning of English poetry of different kinds. This was not a monolithic tradition, as James Simpson makes clear (Chapter 3), and it accommodated a variety of forms and conventions, but for poetic writing it offered new vistas of creative possibility, both for composition in the native tongue and for reflections about the making and functions of poetry.

Chaucer was inevitably a pervasive shaping presence in poetic writings throughout this period, both explicitly and implicitly. Some poetic practitioners silently appropriated phrases, lines, or passages from his works, while others drew on Chaucerian topoi or aspects of style. Still others turned to Chaucer's works to provide more complex forms of inspiration: as Rory G. Critten (Chapter 17) and Joanna Martin (Chapter 26) demonstrate, works such as the anonymous *Flower and the Leaf* and Robert Henryson's *Testament of Cresseid* both emulate and interrogate Chaucerian models.[25]

The presence of works by Chaucer and Gower in the literary manuscripts accessible to fifteenth-century readers naturally gave prominence to poetic forms with their imprimatur. Pentameter couplets, ballade and rhyme royal stanzas, lyrics shaped on the models of French fixed forms, all became increasingly popular choices for post-fourteenth-century poets, whether for stately long poems or more ephemeral shorter pieces. Alliterative poetry retained its own special prestige, however, as Eric Weiskott shows (Chapter 6): the continuing circulation of *Piers Plowman* and of works in a Langlandian tradition gave alliterative poetry a profile that extended beyond those midland and northerly regions of England with which scholarship has traditionally associated it. Early sixteenth-century poets working in both England and Scotland considered here by Jane Griffiths (Chapter 28)—pre-eminently Skelton and Douglas—were familiar with alliterative forms as well as with the range of those employed by Chaucer. Alliteration continued in wide use as an element of rhymed verse, especially in dramatic texts. And tail-rhyme, ballade and rhyme royal stanzas, tetrameter couplets, and traditional 'ballad' stanzas were employed across a range of works.

One effect of the growing status of English, explored here by Robert Meyer-Lee (Chapter 7), was a new sense of the idea of the author and, by association, of the authorial corpus. The presence of large bodies of work by Chaucer and Gower, primarily fourteenth-century poets but most widely read in fifteenth-century manuscript copies in which various of their works were assembled, must have given prominence to this idea. Thomas Hoccleve's autograph compilations of his own shorter poems are significant early fifteenth-century instances of the impulse to form single-author collections. Other assemblages include collections of the short poems of Lydgate and John Audelay and of the lyric corpora associated with Charles of Orleans and James Ryman.

---

[24] J. A. Burrow (ed.), *Thomas Hoccleve's Complaint and Dialogue*, EETS, o.s. 313 (Oxford, 1999); Bateson (ed.), *George Ashby's Poems*, 1–12.
[25] Derek Pearsall (ed.), *The Floure and the Leafe, The Assembly of Ladies, The Isle of Ladies* (Kalamazoo, MI, 1990); Denton Fox (ed.), *The Poems of Robert Henryson* (Oxford, 1981), 111–31.

A widespread growth in vernacular manuscript transmission in both manuscript and printed forms took place over the course of the century. It found expression in new forms of transmission, both of author collections and of single works, and also of regional compilations of distinct kinds that reflected the interests of individuals or individual households (Julia Boffey and A. S. G. Edwards discuss these developments in Chapter 8). The emergence of print enabled a further widening of such processes of transmission, as illustrated in Siân Echard's discussion here (Chapter 9). Some works of Chaucer achieved a separate identity in print that they had not enjoyed in manuscript, for example, while the appeal of other works popular in manuscript was further extended. The widening availability of poetic texts was naturally coterminous with widening audiences: those who read and heard English verse must have come to recognize its new variety of forms, and to understand and appreciate their associations.

To return to Thomas Warton and his assertions about the 'barbarism' of fifteenth-century writing. In the last half century literary history and literary criticism have, for the first time, shaken off the view of the literary achievements of the fifteenth century that he so influentially advanced, a view that for too long impeded its appropriate study. Poets such as Lydgate and Hoccleve have risen from dismissive footnotes to become the subjects of full-length studies exploring different aspects of their literary achievements. The importance of a range of other figures, including John Audelay, Osbern Bokenham, and James Ryman, has been brought into focus. The misleadingly dubbed 'Scottish Chaucerians', James I, Robert Henryson, and William Dunbar, are now assessed with a proper sense of their individual distinctiveness. Such critical rehabilitation has been undertaken in the light of a growing understanding of the significance of related social, cultural, and political questions of patronage and of the forms in which literary texts were transmitted. For the fuller appreciation of both the contexts and complexities of fifteenth-century poetry we have to thank a range of modern scholars whose names figure prominently in the following chapters, including John Burrow, Douglas Gray, Richard Green, David Lawton, Derek Pearsall, and A. C. Spearing (many of their works are listed here in the Bibliography). We hope that we and our fellow contributors have profited from the examples that they have given, and that future generations of readers of fifteenth-century verse will profit equally from the essays assembled here.

The poetry and poetic developments covered in this volume are framed by the reigns of the first Lancastrian and the first Tudor king, Henry IV (1399–1413) and Henry VII (1485–1509). The years between 1400 and 1500 saw the consolidation of traditions of poetry in English that had begun to take shape in the fourteenth century, and the development of a new canon of English verse in part shaped by the past but also demonstrating distinct forms of innovation. The essays here thus explore the combinations of tradition and innovation significant to fifteenth-century poetic production, mapping the range of surviving texts and their particular features onto the contours of history and social change, and outlining the characteristics of the different environments in which these texts came into being. The volume's chronological coverage takes in the formation of an influential English poetic canon in both manuscript and early printed forms. It aims to situate this canon in the range of energetic experimentation discernible in the poetry of this century, and in the light of the important innovation of print as a medium for its dissemination.

The volume is constructed in five sections, the first of which covers historical and literary contexts relevant to the creation of poetry 1400–1500 and matters significant to poetic form and style (this includes reference to the oeuvres of Chaucer and Gower, significant for fifteenth- and early sixteenth-century readers). Next comes a section devoted to the material production, transmission, performance, and audiences of poetry. The third section comprises chapters dealing with the poetic topics and genres characteristic of the period. In the fourth section are chapters on especially important poets, John Lydgate, Thomas Hoccleve, Robert Henryson, and William Dunbar. A final section contains an essay on transitions, taking in poets whose work straddles the late fifteenth and the early sixteenth century, and whose achievements provide a point of connection with *The Oxford History of Poetry in English*, Volume 4.

PART I
CONTEXTS

CHAPTER 2
Contexts of English Poetry 1400–1500

David Rundle

If history was solely as narrated by late medieval chronicles like *The Brut* in England or Walter Bower's *Scotichronicon*—as a march of conflicts and conspiracies that decide the fate of kings and their realms—then, for many in the fifteenth century, history was elsewhere. This was not for want of events historians deemed worth recording: across Scotland and England, of the nine monarchs who died in that hundred years only three did so at home in their bed; the majority were either assassinated or ended their days on military campaign. There were, in both countries, repeated outbursts of civil strife. It was also the century that saw England manage to both win and lose an empire. There were wars but, all the more, there were rumours of wars. For the majority of the population of the island of Britain, who lived on the land or in communities no larger than villages, these events, if they heard of them at all, would have sounded like distant thunder.

For sure, wars could not be fought without men being turned into soldiers, and the bonds of service that saw tenants and servants become retainers to a lord could entail some of them being required to take up arms. If they returned from battle, they might regale family and friends with tales of what had happened. Others might hear of some of the developments on their trips into the local town, if that was one of the occasions when an English royal proclamation was announced. Monarchical government impinged on the localities through its quotidian reach—the coinage, for instance, or the administration of justice, though the latter in fifteenth-century England was notorious for being skewed by lords and their henchmen. Even for the minority who lived in towns, life was shaped less around regnal years than by the cycle of market days and the seasons. When thought was given to a grander sweep of time, it was one in which kings were small figures painted into the depiction of 'Doom', the 'Last Judgement', as often displayed on the wall of the parish church.

This was a world with low life expectancy and sharp social contrasts. It was also one far from universal literacy and from ubiquitous and instantaneous news—and from this vernacular poetry drew some of its power. To understand its limitations and its potential in the societies of fifteenth-century Britain, this chapter will be divided into three sections. We will consider the omnipresence of death, and some of its economic and social impact. We will also survey the range of languages available, and the possibilities for being educated in them. We will, finally, turn to the locations in which poetry was to be found, both on the page and—all the more importantly—in people's mouths.

The Shadow of Death

Timor mortis conturbat me. Several late-medieval vernacular poems take as their refrain this line from the liturgy of the Office of the Dead, the most famous being William Dunbar's 'Lament for the Makars'.[1] One glosses the Latin: 'This is in Englis tong to say / The drede of deth does distrowlyt* (*disquiets*) me' (97–8).[2] The poet opens by saying 'this is the song of my old age'. The speaker, then, was one of the lucky ones: individuals could live to advanced years, even beyond the Biblically-allotted three score and ten, but many more died young, even though infant mortality was low compared to other parts of Europe.[3] For those men who had been born into wealth or who had become a monk at one of England's better-provided houses, if they survived until they were twenty-five, they could then have reasonable hope of living into their later forties or early fifties, but the prospect for most women and those of lower birth was not so favourable.[4] Moreover, as the poems suggest, hope could be offset by fear at the capriciousness with which people could be taken from the community. The verses' message of the enormity of death, which we should fear but which we should also look beyond, thinking on the afterlife, was a perennial staple of Christian morality. It had particular resonance, however, in the fifteenth century, living in the shadow of the second global pandemic, known as the Black Death. The bubonic plague reached Italy from Asia in 1347, arriving in southern England and Ireland during the summer of the following year, with Wales, northern England, and Scotland succumbing by mid-1349.[5] Certainty about mortality rates is impossible, but between a third and a half of the population were killed in this one outbreak.

The Black Death, though, was not a single event: plague returned repeatedly, in both the later fourteenth century and the fifteenth. There were national outbreaks in 1400, 1407, 1413, 1434, 1438–9, 1464, 1471, 1479, and 1485.[6] Even in years when it did not have as wide a reach, it could have a deadly impact. For example, in 1457, nearly a fifth of the monks of Christ Church, Canterbury died from it. The house's chronicler records 'this year there was a grave pestilence in the city of Canterbury and various places in the kingdom of England'.[7] Moreover, the Black Death did not stalk the country alone; there were other diseases that similarly terrified fifteenth-century England. In 1427, 'a rheumatic illness known as "the mure"', tentatively identified as a virulent strain of influenza, 'so infected the old along with the young that a great number were led to the grave'.[8] In 1485, itself a plague year,

---

[1] 'I that in heill wes and gladnes'; see Priscilla Bawcutt (ed.), *The Poems of William Dunbar*, 2 vols. (Glasgow, 1998), 1.94–7. On Dunbar, see Chapter 27.

[2] NIMEV 3743; Richard L. Greene, 'A Middle English "Timor Mortis" Poem', *Modern Language Review*, 28 (1933), 234–8.

[3] On mortality rates, admittedly for a later period, see E. A. Wrigley, R. S. Davies, J. E. Oeppen, and R. S. Schofield, *English Population History from Family Reconstitution 1580–1837* (Cambridge, 1997), 198–353.

[4] M. A. Jonker, 'Estimation of Life Expectancy in the Middle Ages', *Journal of the Royal Statistical Society. Series A (Statistics in Society)*, 146 (2003), 105–117; John Hatcher, 'Mortality in the Fifteenth Century: Some New Evidence', *The Economic History Review*, n.s. 49 (1986), 19–38.

[5] For an introduction, see Rosemary Horrox, *The Black Death* (Manchester, 1994), and, for recent emphasis on a global perspective, see Monica Green (ed.), *Pandemic Disease in the Medieval World: Rethinking the Black Death* [The Medieval Globe, i] (Kalamazoo, MI, 2014), available at the Scholars at WMU website.

[6] J. L. Bolton, *The Medieval English Economy 1150–1500* (London, 1980), 6.

[7] Hatcher, 'Mortality', 28; the quotation is from William George Searle (ed.), *Christ Church Canterbury*, Cambridge Antiquarian Society, Octavo publications 34 (Cambridge, 1902), 67.

[8] Quotation from Henry T. Riley (ed.), *Annales Monasterii S. Albani*, 2 vols., Rolls Series 28 (London, 1870–1), 1.19; for brief comment, see Kathleen Pribyl, *Farming, Famine and Plague: The Impact of Climate in Late Medieval England* (Cham, 2017), 232.

parts of England were struck with a new mystery illness so severe that, at Westminster, the coronation of the new king, Henry VII, was postponed. Being nearly entirely confined to England and not to other parts of Europe, it is remembered as *sudor anglicus* ('the English sweat') or 'the sweating sickness', but its pathology remains debated.[9] What is known is that, in contrast to the Black Death, those it affected were more often well-to-do men rather than women or the poor.

What was the cumulative impact of these outbreaks on society? It certainly seems that England in the early fourteenth century was overpopulated for its level of agricultural production, and famine hit in 1315–7. Following the mid-century collapse in numbers, the repeated visitation of epidemics slowed the recovery in population, the size of which continued to be below pre-1348 levels not just for decades but for centuries, only rising to similar figures in the mid- or late eighteenth century. It is also undoubtedly the case that in the plague's aftermath, the numbers in some villages declined to the extent that they were unsustainable and abandoned.[10] This trend was exacerbated by the transfer of farmland from arable to pasture (which required fewer workers). For some, these developments were an opportunity. In the immediate aftermath of the arrival of the Black Death, the transformation from a situation where labour was plentiful and land scarce held potential for those peasants who survived the trauma and were able or willing to migrate. Yet, for a society which believed in the virtue of stasis, with each in their allotted place, this was an unsettling consequence; the attempt, in reaction, to return to the *status quo ante* created tensions that overflowed into the unrest that centred on the Peasants' Revolt of 1381, providing a theme for *Piers Plowman*. That year was by no means the end of discontent, and even in some of the more ostensibly political rebellions of the fifteenth century, like those of 1450, there were some elements of wider social grievance. So, for instance, the cathedral close of Salisbury in 1450 was attacked for a similar reason that some Cambridge colleges had been a target in 1381—because of their association with written records which were perceived to be a force for suppression.[11]

In addition to a tradition of dissent, the second half of the fifteenth century found new cause for complaint. Some of those who bettered themselves through becoming pasture farmers did so by adopting uncultivated strips of formerly common land as their own, marking out their territory by erecting hedges or fences. The processes came to be called engrossing and enclosing, and invited harsh criticism. The most famous literary response appeared in 1516 in Thomas More's *Utopia*, where the fashion for turning land over to flocks was said to impoverish and to create man-eating sheep.[12] Thomas More did not start the backlash: since the 1480s, there had been riots against enclosures in towns like York and Coventry.[13] The discontented often presented themselves as 'the commons' rising against injustice, and, as with Jack Cade's Rebellion of 1450, they had their own poetic

---

[9] John L. Flood, '"Safer on the Battlefield than in the City": England, the "Sweating Sickness", and the Continent', *Renaissance Studies*, 17 (2003), 147–76. For a recent attempt at identification, see Paul Heyman, Leopold Simons, and Christel Cochez, 'Were the English Sweating Sickness and the Picardy Sweat Caused by Hantaviruses?', *Viruses*, 6 (2014), 151–71.

[10] Christopher Dyer, *Deserted Villages Revisited* (Hatfield, 2010).

[11] I. M. W. Harvey, *Jack Cade's Rebellion* (Oxford, 1991), 124–6; Roger Chartier, 'Jack Cade, the Skin of a Dead Lamb, and the Hatred for Writing', *Shakespeare Studies*, 34 (2006), 77–89; Susan Crane, 'The Writing Lesson of 1381', in B. Hanawalt (ed.), *Chaucer's England* (Minneapolis, MI, 1992), 201–21.

[12] George M. Logan, Robert M. Adams, and Clarence H. Miller (eds), Thomas More, *Utopia* (Cambridge, 1995), 62–4.

[13] Christian D. Liddy, 'Urban Enclosure Riots: Risings of the Commons in English Towns, 1480–1525', *Past & Present*, 226 (2015), 41–77.

manifestations, to which we will turn later.¹⁴ Rebels, that is to say, were often suspicious of the written word but they also used some forms of it as a weapon.

To go beyond these observations and attempt to sense further the impact of mortality upon cultural activities would be to draw inference from our own (recently developed) assumptions about what the psychological effect of a pandemic may be. In the next section, we will see that it may have had some expression far from the narrowly economic but, before we discuss that, we should consider the languages in which the peoples of Britain expressed themselves. In doing this, we will need to reflect on what constituted 'England' in this century.

Languages and Learning

Constance, 1417: a General Council of the Church was gathered in the lake-side city, bringing together clerics from across Western Christendom. They had deeply serious matters to discuss: the most pressing was the need to end the schism during which rival popes claimed the tiara; there was also the need to repress heresy—a matter about which the English had some knowledge, though the main threat was perceived to be the Hussite Reformation in Bohemia; and there was a desire to reform the church's governance. The assembled ecclesiasts, however, also found time to argue over the organization of their own meetings. The original plan had been to divide representation into four parts by geographical area or *natio*: Italy, Germany, France, and England. The belated arrival of delegates from Iberia created the need for a rethink: the simple solution was to have five *nationes*, but the French objected that such an increase was unnecessary, as the *Anglica natio* did not deserve to be given an autonomous role. The French pointed out England's small size, both physically, relative to other European kingdoms, and in ecclesiastical structure—it was home to merely two archdioceses. Of those, the province of York oversaw only three dioceses, 'at least in obedience to the King of England, for the rest are in the kingdom of Scotland and are not subjects of the Most Serene King of England or obedient to him, and are not—nor do they want to be—of the English nation'; of the other, the province of Canterbury, the orator said 'a large part is in Wales'.¹⁵ It was also claimed that of all the dioceses in Ireland, only two acknowledged obedience to the English king.¹⁶

It fell to Thomas Polton, bishop of Chichester, to respond to this attack.¹⁷ His strategy was to shift definition so he talked of 'the English or British nation'. This allowed him to refute the French swipe about the Scottish bishops for 'they can in no way deny that Scotland is part of Britain, admittedly not as great as England (as much is known to the whole world) and they even have the same language as the English'.¹⁸ More generally, however, it was to

---

¹⁴ See p. 27 below.
¹⁵ Hermann von der Hardt (ed.), *Magnum oecumenicum Constantiense Concilium de universali Ecclesiae reformatione*, 6 vols. (Frankfurt, 1697–1700), 5 (1699), col. 68. The sees of Scotland had, in fact, been absolved of any English overlordship by Pope Celestine III in 1192.
¹⁶ von der Hardt (ed.), *Magnum oecumenicum Constantiense Concilium*, 5, col. 70; the orator claims there were forty-eight dioceses, but the Synod of Kells in 1152 had established thirty-six dioceses, which had been reduced by mergers to thirty-four by this date.
¹⁷ On Polton's speech, see J.-P. Genet, 'English Nationalism: Thomas Polton at the Council of Constance', *Nottingham Medieval Studies*, 28 (1984), 60–78; Robert N. Swanson, '*Gens secundum cognationem et collectionem ab alia distincta*? Thomas Polton, Two Englands, and the Challenge of Medieval Nationhood', in Gabriela Signori and Birgit Studt (eds), *Das Konstanzer Konzil als europäisches Ereignis: Begegnungen, Medien und Rituale* (Ostfildern, 2014), 57–87.
¹⁸ von der Hardt (ed.), *Magnum oecumenicum Constantiense Concilium*, 5, col. 87.

Polton's purpose in this debate over Council organization to emphasize not the similarities between the parts of *Britannia* but their diversity. In particular, he belittled the French for having just one language, while Britain (Polton claimed) has five: 'English (which the English and Scots have in common), Welsh, Irish, Gascon and Cornish, and thus [this *natio*] can with all justice represent as many nations as it has different languages.'[19]

Polton's list understates and misrepresents. It forgets the Gaelic of the Scottish Highlands; it mentions the Occitan of the English-controlled lands of Gascony but shows restraint in failing to note that the English king's newly conquered subjects in Normandy spoke French. His speech does serve to remind of us of four significant features of England in the fifteenth century. First, that solipsistic solecism in evidence in more recent times, by which the English assume 'British' is all about them, was already in play, even if in reality English royal control was weak or non-existent. Scotland was determinedly independent and quite where one kingdom ended and the other began was a repeated matter of dispute: for instance, the town of Berwick was at the time that Polton spoke in English hands, only to return in 1461 to Scottish control previously seen in the early fourteenth century, with this reversed again by the campaign of Richard, duke of Gloucester (soon to be Richard III) in 1482. Meanwhile, Wales may have been subdued by the English in the later thirteenth century but, as the revolt of Owain Glyndŵr demonstrated, some of its people were not resigned to peaceable subservience. At the same time, Polton's words also make clear that the lands the kings of England claimed for themselves were not confined to the island of *Britannia*. In neighbouring *Hibernia* or Ireland, undeniably, English control was yet more limited than it was in Wales, being mainly confined to 'the pale' around Dublin. For some monarchs, however, of much greater concern was the tradition of the English crown claiming rights on the mainland of Europe: Polton's own master, Henry V, emulated his great-grandfather, Edward III, in pressing his proclaimed rights to not only the Plantagenet inheritance of Aquitaine but also the crown of France itself. Henry's remarkably successful Blitzkrieg, begun in 1415, saw swathes of northern France, including Paris, fall to English rule, but the attempts to hold onto those lands, and the domestic consequences that ensued, were to define English politics for the following decades, poisoning them with a stench of failure. By the mid-1450s, the holdings in France had been ignominiously reduced to a patch of land around Calais, and the subsequent kings 'of England and France' had at least to make some show of seeking to reverse this decline.

Just as what constituted fifteenth-century England in a political sense did not map neatly onto geography as defined either by classical knowledge or by our own latter-day expectations, so too the fortunes of the English language were not coterminous with the boundaries of the English *regnum*. If we were to accept Polton's repeated assertion that *lingua Anglicana* was the language used north of the border and so describe Older Scots as a form of Middle English, we would need to concede that a keynote of British identity was diversity not solely between languages but also within English, varying in dialect across the island, including within the counties of England. However, during the course of the fifteenth century London English seems increasingly to have established itself as a norm for written language in southern England and the Midlands. This process was strengthened by William Caxton's introduction to Westminster of the German invention of printing. What is more, an 'English-speaking' area did not necessarily mean it solely employed that vernacular. This is exemplified by a mid-fifteenth century manuscript where a set of five English lines of verse

---

[19] von der Hardt (ed.), *Magnum oecumenicum Constantiense Concilium*, 5, col. 93.

are a mere marginal addition to a book whose main contents is the late fourteenth-century *Pascon agun Arluth*, a poem on Christ's passion which is the premier witness to the poetic tradition in the last of the languages mentioned by Polton: Cornish.[20]

Such cohabitation, where English sometimes had to play a minor role, was not confined to the Celtic fringe of Britain. It had greater significance in the presence of the two supranational languages which were central to English culture. The more localized of these was French. It had obvious use in diplomatic correspondence with those continental authorities conversant in it, not just the kingdom of France but also the duchies of Burgundy and Brittany. Burgundy, for much of the century, incorporated not only the lands around Dijon but also the towns of the southern Low Countries (including Bruges, home to William Caxton for several decades in the mid-century). There was also a tradition of its use in the domestic bureaucracy or royal bureaucracy, and so it was known to a clerk like Thomas Hoccleve, though its role substantially declined in the following decades. Where it did not die was in the law courts, where an antiquated form was the accepted language of England's common law. It also had a poetic presence, and not solely through the works of an émigré like the royal prince Charles d'Orléans, who whiled away his long-term captivity following Agincourt composing verses in both English and French.[21] An incidental demonstration of an ongoing Francophone presence appears in one of the poems with the refrain of '*timor mortis*' mentioned above, where the author contrasts their moral message with fashionable love songs, one in English ('Herte myne ...') and one in French ('*Ma bell amour ...*').[22]

The importance of French was overshadowed by the language which bound England to the rest of western Europe, that used in the Mass and for communication across Christendom—including by Polton at the Council of Constance: Latin. It was also a major element of royal administration and, at least in the office of the privy seal from the 1430s, was used increasingly at the expense of any vernacular.[23] Its professional applications were complemented by its prestige as a literary language. In prose, it was deployed in various idioms, with there being a particular early fifteenth-century fashion for a florid style seen, for instance, in the first full biography of Henry V.[24] It was also a vehicle for poetic expression, in the hands of authors like John Whethamstede, abbot of St Albans (d. 1465), or among the so-called *grex poetarum* ('flock of poets') that orbited around the court of Henry VII at the end of the century.[25] Latin verses could, indeed, be used to add stature to English poetry, as when Caxton commissioned the immigrant scholar Stefano Surigone to write an epitaph for Geoffrey Chaucer.[26] More fundamentally, knowledge of the Latin language was the measure by which it was judged whether someone was 'lettred' or not—or, as we would put it, literate.

---

[20] The manuscript is BL MS Harley 1782, with the English added at the foot of col. 3v.
[21] Mary-Jo Arn, *Charles d'Orléans in England (1415–1440)* (Woodbridge, 2000).
[22] Greene, '"Timor Mortis" Poem', 235.
[23] Gwilym Dodd, 'Trilingualism in the Medieval English Bureaucracy: The Use—and Disuse—of Languages in the Fifteenth-Century Privy Seal Office', *Journal of British Studies*, 51 (2012), 253–83.
[24] On the florid style generally, see E. F. Jacob, '"Florida Verborum Venustas": Some Early Signs of Euphuism in England', *Bulletin of the John Rylands Library*, 18 (1933), 264–90; on the *Vita et Gesta Henrici V* (attributed to 'Ps-Elmham') and its influence, see David Rundle, 'The Unoriginality of Tito Livio Frulovisi's *Vita Henrici Quinti*', *English Historical Review*, 123 (2008), 1109–31.
[25] David R. Carlson, 'The Civic Poetry of Abbot John Whethamstede of St Albans (+1465)', *Mediaeval Studies*, 61 (1999), 205–42.
[26] David R. Carlson, 'Chaucer, Humanism and Printing: The Conditions of Authorship in Fifteenth-Century England', *University of Toronto Quarterly*, 64 (1995), 274–88; Alexandra Gillespie, *Print Culture and the Medieval Author: Chaucer, Lydgate, and their Books, 1473–1557* (Oxford, 2006), 70–2.

Our own concept of literacy is broad and widening; official definitions include within it numeracy, and it has come to be used metaphorically, as in the phrase 'computer literacy'. If we pare it back, however, to its essentials as suggested by its etymology from the Latin *litterae* for letters, it involves the skills of reading and writing, which we might assume are inseparable twins. In medieval and early modern Europe, however, an inability to write did not necessarily imply that one had not learnt to read, and this particularly applied to girls. On the other hand, the most basic witness to having held a pen, signing one's name, may not denote any wider facility at writing. These should serve as a warning that any bald figures given for literacy rates will be overly bold estimates, but it has been suggested that by 1500 about 3% of the adult population of England had some ability to write, comprising 5% of men and 1% of women.[27] Those capable of some level of reading are likely to have been more than double that figure, but there was substantial geographical variation, dependent on the availability of education.

There is one way in which our latter-day perceptions of literacy are more confined for those of the later Middle Ages. In our societies' aspirations for universal literacy, we aim to ensure proficiency in a single language. In post-classical Europe, *literatus* did not retain its Roman meaning of being learned in both Latin and Greek, but it did imply an expectation for being at least bilingual: it assumed that one was educated in Latin and could transfer that skill to the vernacular which one heard at home. The most likely route, then, to becoming fully literate was by having a schoolmaster who was capable of explicating Latin grammar. In doing so, a teacher in the fifteenth-century would use English sentences to introduce elements of Latin and, in the process, help the child also understand that English too was a language with a grammatical structure.[28]

The availability of schoolmasters was not uniform across England. In the last years of the fourteenth century, there were some complaints that there were too many teachers. The claim had anticlerical intentions, asserting that the social order was being disrupted by the low-born receiving education and thus being able to rise up the ecclesiastical hierarchy:

> Now mot ich soutere his sone setten to schole ...
> So of that begger's brol a bychop to worthen.
>
> (Now might each cobbler set his son to school ...
> So of the beggar's brat a bishop is made).[29]

Contrariwise, in the decades that immediately followed, there were grumblings that the numbers of schoolmasters had declined. Whatever the fluctuations in the early fifteenth century, the year 1440, when the royal initiative of Eton College gained its charter, was to prove the beginning of a sustained increase: a further forty endowed schools were established before the end of the century.[30] Those schools joined existing foundations

---

[27] Adam Fox, *Oral and Literate Culture in England* (Oxford, 2000), 18, employing and glossing the figures provided by David Cressy, *Literacy and the Social Order: Reading and Writing in Tudor and Stuart England* (Cambridge, 1980). For a general discussion, see R. A. Houston, *Literacy in Early Modern Europe: Culture and Education, 1500–1800*, 2nd ed. (Oxford, 2013).

[28] Nicholas Orme, *Medieval Schools* (New Haven, CT, 2006), 86–127.

[29] 'Piers the Plowman's Crede', lines 744–8, in James M. Dean (ed.), *Six Ecclesiastical Satires* (Kalamazoo, MI, 1991).

[30] Orme, *Medieval Schools*, 218–50; J. M. W. Willoughby (ed.), *The Libraries of Collegiate Churches*, Corpus of British Medieval Library Catalogues, 15 (London, 2013).

which survived any decline and they were supplemented by other routes to learning: individual schoolmasters could establish a classroom, while some monastic communities took seriously a commitment to educating those children who lived near them. Even with this range, however, the provision was patchy. Most counties had at least one endowed school by the end of our period and the practice of boarding extended their catchment areas, but the numbers for which they catered were small. While gender denied schooling for girls, place of birth defined access to education for many boys.

Whatever their reputation in more recent centuries, schools like Eton could act as motors of social mobility. There was no equivalent in England of Scotland's 1496 Act of Parliament, which stipulated that all lairds and freeholders should send their sons to school 'to obtain perfect Latin' and then study law.[31] That statute hints at the increase in educational institutions that occurred north as well as south of the border (and among the Scottish schoolmasters is counted the poet Robert Henryson at Dunfermline); it may also imply that, at this point, its clientele was largely drawn from those of lesser status than the nobility.[32] It was certainly common practice for the statutes establishing an endowed school, wherever it was in Britain, to require that the classroom should include 'poor students', and so there was some truth to the claim, quoted in the previous paragraph, that education created possibilities for boys born into low status, usually allowing a career in the church. For the founders, their acts of charity had a double benefit: not only was it a good deed in its own right (on which God might look benignly), but it also provided young voices to say or sing masses in which prayers were made for their benefactors and their families. These schools, that is to say, were also chantries, intended to assist the souls of those who had established them through the terrors of purgatory. How far did the insistent presence and capriciousness of death play on those minds which hatched the plans to erect new educational institutions? It is impossible to fully discern their motives—it must be said that such acts of philanthropy were not an invention of the post-pandemic era, nor does the chronology for their establishment fit snugly with the pattern of the plague's virulence; but, as we have seen, that was not the only threat which was feared and the timing of the wider fashion for chantries is suggestive.

There were other new foundations which were chantries with an educational element. Indeed, some of the schools, following the fourteenth-century precedent set by William of Wykeham, bishop of Winchester, were established simultaneously with a university college: thus, Henry VI endowed, alongside Eton, King's College, Cambridge, and, in the following decades, a successor to Wykeham as bishop of Winchester, William Waynflete (himself a former headmaster of Eton), founded two schools, one in his Lincolnshire hometown from which he took his surname and the other in Oxford, with the intention that both should act as feeders to his addition to the constituency of the University of Oxford, Magdalen College. This is not to suggest that all Oxbridge colleges opened in our period fitted this pattern of a double foundation. Moreover, not all students taking a degree had to be a member of a college: many were associated with less permanent structures, run by an individual or small group of dons.[33]

---

[31] Elizabeth Ewan, 'Schooling in the Towns, c.1400–c.1560', in R. D. Anderson (ed.), *The Edinburgh History of Education in Scotland* (Edinburgh, 2015), 39–56; John Durkan, *Scottish Schools and Schoolmasters, 1560–1633* (Woodbridge, 2013), 3–44.

[32] On Henryson, see Chapter 26 below.

[33] J. I. Catto, 'The Triumph of the Hall in Fifteenth-Century Oxford', in Ralph Evans (ed.), *Lordship and Learning: Studies in Memory of Trevor Aston* (Woodbridge, 2004), 209–23.

Both English universities were growing in the fifteenth century, but the expansion in higher education was greater elsewhere. By the end of the century, Scotland had three universities, all of them new foundations (St Andrews, 1413, Glasgow 1450/1, Aberdeen, 1495). It is also the case that, in the lands under the control of the English king, there had been a brief increase in the number of universities, with one established in the crown's French domain, at Caen (1432; after the loss of Normandy, it was refounded by Charles VII). Like schools, all these were male preserves and, in contrast to those places of secondary education, they set a particular expectation on the boys that entered them, usually in their early teens: the students were required to live in Latin, not just reading and writing in it but also using it for after-dinner conversation (only in the sixteenth century was an alternative allowed in new colleges, and that was Greek). This culture defined their library resources, their reading and their own literary productions; some, like John Shirwood, later bishop of Durham (d. 1493), turned their hand to Latin poetry but it must be said that they were only a small minority, prose compositions in Latin being rather more frequent.[34] It is also the case that if a figure like Magdalen's founder, Waynflete, was to be addressed in verse, it was in Latin: his first Oxford schoolmaster, John Anwykyll, had his printed Latin grammar prefaced by Latin elegiacs from the pen of an immigrant poet, Pietro Carmeliano.[35] None of this means, however, that those whose learning reached degree level always spurned vernacular literature. To cite just one example, Thomas Chaundler, warden of Oxford's New College and chancellor of that university, composed plays and dialogues in Latin but he also owned at least one manuscript in English, BL MS Harley 43, John Walton's early fifteenth-century verse translation of Boethius's *De consolatione philosophiae*, which he glossed in Latin.

The universities were not the only institutions of higher education in England. While they had faculties for the internationally recognized codes of canon and civil law, they did not dabble in the legal system of common law used in most of the king's courts. For training in that, a young man would have to go to London and to one of the various establishments known as the Inns of Court and the Inns of Chancery. As we have already noted, the main language required for this was a form of French, though Latin was also necessary for some of the essential texts on which the law was based. As with university graduates, this does not mean that common lawyers insistently ignored vernacular literature throughout their lives: Thomas Urswick, who was at Gray's Inn in the 1440s, owned at his death in 1479 both a copy of Jean Froissart's *Chroniques* in French and a manuscript of Chaucer's *Canterbury Tales*.[36]

The formal structures of education that have been outlined in the preceding paragraphs were not the only sources of learning. The child of an aristocratic family, for instance, was unlikely to be sent to a school—the master would come to the household rather than vice versa, and other children may have been allowed to join the classroom (thus the origin of the particular English meaning of a 'private school').[37] Scotland's 1496 Education Act might imply a concern that this did not happen often enough or that its quality was considered

---

[34] Shirwood wrote an epitaph to John Southwell, seneschal to George Neville, bishop of Exeter, which was recently rediscovered in a manuscript of Oxford provenance; it is now in Princeton University Library, MS Taylor 22; the poem is edited by Don C. Skemer, 'Words Not Written in Stone: John Shirwood's Epitaph for a Canon of Exeter Cathedral', in Colum P. Hourihane (ed.), *Manuscripta illuminata: Approaches to Understanding Medieval and Renaissance Manuscripts* (Princeton, NJ, 2014), 108–43.

[35] David R. Carlson, 'The Occasional Poetry of Pietro Carmeliano', *Aevum*, 61 (1987), 495–502 (at 497–8).

[36] J. M. Manly and Edith Rickert, *The Text of the Canterbury Tales*, 8 vols. (Chicago, 1940), 1.616–7.

[37] Nicholas Orme, *From Childhood to Chivalry: The Education of the English Kings and Aristocracy 1066–1530* (London, 1984).

wanting. In the early sixteenth century, scholars both sides of the border complained that the nobility were more interested in hunting than in books.[38] This did not stop aristocrats being seen as suitable targets for authors' importunings for patronage, as we shall see in the next section: some may have considered themselves too grand for book-learning, but that did not place them above book-owning.

For those lower down the social scale who did not have the opportunity of going to school, learning was through apprenticeship or on the job. For some skills or for running a workshop, a certain familiarity with the written word would have been an advantage or sometimes a necessity, and so this was the impulse to what is now known as pragmatic literacy.[39] Detailed information like business accounts may need to be remembered only for a short time. A traditional format for such ephemeral written records was the wax tablet; few survive from medieval England, though one set was found in a rubbish pit in York, with late fourteenth-century writing both in Latin and in English verse.[40] By the time those tablets were incised and discarded, a significant change had occurred: the availability of paper as a writing surface, alongside parchment. It was not an indigenous product: introduced into Mediterranean Christian culture from Islamic Spain in the late twelfth and early thirteenth centuries, the technology became more widespread, but, apart from the 1490s when there was for a decade or so a paper mill near Hertford, none was produced in the British Isles until the later 1580s.[41] Instead, it was continually imported from mainland Europe. Even with the costs that trade entailed, it was cheaper than parchment, and so catered for a market for whom thrift was a consideration. There was never the intensity of record-keeping that developed in, say, Florence (where literacy rates were higher) but the ability to compile a book on paper did allow the possibility that the information recorded would not only be professional but could be for private reflection or entertainment.[42]

Even when we amplify the definition of literacy by moving beyond the *literati* to those with some pragmatic engagement with writing, our focus remains upon a minority of the population. This does not mean, however, that vernacular poetry was beyond the majority's reach. A textual community encompasses not only those who can create, write, and read texts, but those also who heard them spoken or viewed them as performances. Texts come down to us as shapes drawn on a page but we have a duty to give them their voice.

Poetry's Living Places

London, 1406 or 1407: looking back to those years from the mid-century, John Shirley, a scribe responsible for the circulating of many poems in the English vernacular, transcribed a short *Moral Balade* by the poet and royal tutor Henry Scogan.[43] The opening announces

---

[38] Durkan, *Scottish Schools*, 23; Cathy Curtis, 'Richard Pace's *De fructu* and Early Tudor Pedagogy', in Jonathan Woolfson (ed.), *Reassessing Tudor Humanism* (London, 2002), 43–77.

[39] M. B. Parkes, 'The Literacy of the Laity', in David Daiches and Anthony Thorlby (eds), *Literature and Western Civilization: The Medieval West* (London, 1973), 555–77.

[40] Michelle P. Brown, 'The Role of the Wax Tablet in Medieval Literacy: A Reconsideration in Light of a Recent Find from York', *British Library Journal*, 20 (1994), 1–16.

[41] Allan Stevenson, 'Tudor Roses from John Tate', *Studies in Bibliography*, 20 (1967), 15–34; R. L. Hills, *John Tate, England's First Papermaker* (London, 1993); for the use of imported paper in England, see Orietta da Rold, *Paper in Medieval England* (Cambridge, 2020).

[42] Erik Kwakkel, 'A New Type of Book for a New Type of Reader: The Emergence of Paper in Vernacular Book Production', *The Library*, 7th ser., 4 (2003), 219–48.

[43] NIMEV 2464; on Shirley, see Margaret Connolly, *John Shirley: Book Production and the Noble Household in Fifteenth-Century England* (Aldershot, 1998). The 'Moral Balade' is in W. W. Skeat (ed.), *Chaucerian and*

that the author is sending 'this litel tretys ... writen with myn owne hand full rudely' to its intended recipients, whom Shirley identified as the four sons of Henry IV. The title he provides, however, also explains the occasion for which it was a written: 'a souper ... in the Vyntre in London, at the hous of Lowys Johan'. In other words, Scogan emphasizes his work's written status, but its first outing to the world was a performance, over dinner, in the house of Lewis Johan, a merchant of Welsh extraction, in London's Vintry ward, just north of the Thames, opposite Southwark.[44]

It was, then, not only those who were born too low to read and write who could enjoy a reading of poetry. This is a truth of which we are already aware, if we care to remember the famous frontispiece of a copy of Chaucer's *Troilus and Criseyde* made in the first decades of the fifteenth century.[45] It depicts a double scene, with courtiers, male and female, leaving the city and then sitting *en plein air*, listening to the poet who stands before them in a portable pulpit, declaiming his work. We might think that the presence of the image undermines its content: surely such a lavish illumination was intended to be seen; it is mute and so could not be heard. Yet, its silence was no bar to its being the object of a shared experience. The volume in which it sits is of such a size (at 315 x 220mm, a royal quarto), that two or three viewers could have looked at it together, then passed it along to others in a large group. That is to say, the book itself, and with it any images it contained, could be performative. It played on more sense than just vision; it was made to be touched and, indeed, smelt, but it was also an invitation to hearing. What has been called aurality was an important element in the life of a medieval text.[46]

There are a couple of ways in which the *Troilus* frontispiece may misdirect. First, its al fresco setting, complete with pulpit, should not be taken to suggest that readings were most often a fair-weather picnic pursuit. Shirley's stated timing and location of the performance of Scogan's *Balade*, at dinnertime and indoors, was closer to the norm. The precedent for such events may have been monastic meals but, at those, the monks were expected to eat in silence while one of their brothers read out an improving Latin text. It may be that, in a secular context, the works chosen were not solely ones of vernacular literature or, if they were, they might, like John Gower's *Confessio amantis*, move between English and Latin.[47] Perhaps no works were more appropriate for these readings than poetry, with its metre's invitation to listen to the words spoken aloud. The main difference from monastic practice was that these 'lectures' functioned as an entertainment designed to act as a spur to conversation or debate.

The second issue with the *Troilus* image is that it conjures up an audience which, while mixed in gender, is homogeneous in social standing. In contrast, Shirley's assumption that it was plausible that the royal princes would gather with a merchant host to hear Scogan's

---

Other Pieces ... Being a Supplement to the Complete Works of Geoffrey Chaucer (Oxford, 1897), xli–iii, 237–44. For discussion, see M. Newman Hallmundsson, 'Chaucer's Circle: Henry Scogan and his Friends', *Medievalia et Humanistica*, n.s. 10 (1981), 129–39; J. D. Burnley, 'Scogan, Shirley's Reputation and Chaucerian Occasional Verse', in G. Lester (ed.), *Chaucer in Perspective: Middle English Essays in Honour of Norman Blake* (Sheffield, 1999), 28–46.

[44] On Johan, see A. D. Carr, 'Sir Lewis John—a Medieval London Welshman', *Bulletin of the Board of Celtic Studies*, 22 (1966–8), 260–70.

[45] Cambridge, Corpus Christi College, MS 61. For recent discussion, see Joyce Coleman, 'Where Chaucer Got His Pulpit: Audience and Intervisuality in the *Troilus and Criseyde* Frontispiece', *Studies in the Age of Chaucer*, 32 (2010), 103–28.

[46] The term is Joyce Coleman's; see her classic introduction to the topic, *Public Reading and the Reading Public in Late Medieval England and France* (Cambridge, 1996).

[47] Joyce Coleman, 'Lay Readers and Hard Latin: How Gower May Have Intended the *Confessio Amantis* to be Read', *Studies in the Age of Chaucer*, 24 (2002), 209–35.

poem (and perhaps fall into discussion afterwards) provides an important corrective. It should encourage us to rein in our natural tendency to want to compartmentalize: scholarship writes in terms of 'courtly culture' and 'civic culture', as it does of 'monastic culture'. Seen from the viewpoint of the verses, however, the world was not so segregated; texts travelled between these locales. In fact, it may be in their ability to foster interaction between these different cultures that the success of vernacular poems lay.

To talk of 'the court' is no more to signify a single location than it does when we discuss 'the civic'. It is most often employed to designate the community around the monarch, wherever they were, but other princes could also 'hold court'. In part, this was a political and quasi-legal role, with the noble showing good lordship to those who lived in their area of influence, but it could also see their castles or palaces as hubs of cultural activity. This was particularly possible when the king was a minor or absent, as was repeatedly the case in both Scotland and England. So, during the long minority of Henry VI, from 1422 until 1437, the king's uncles (two of the princes who had, earlier in the century, been at the supper with Lewis Johan), John, duke of Bedford, regent in France, and Humfrey, duke of Gloucester, protector in England, acted as cultural patrons. Royal birth, however, was not an essential to acting in that role: Richard Beauchamp, earl of Warwick (1382–1439), was one of England's most substantial landowners to whom his tenants looked for 'good lordship'—when, that is, he was not abroad either on pious pilgrimage or bloody campaigning—and who had the wherewithal to finance both eye-catching events, like a joust at Guînes, near Calais, and more permanent memorials, including his chantry chapel in Warwick, for which he left a bequest and which was built in the years after his death.[48] His sometime secretary was, incidentally, John Shirley.[49]

Courts, in this century as earlier, were hives of hybridity: they took their strength from the eclecticism of the activities that they could licence.[50] With that also came a cavalcade of characters. There was more than a whiff of the menagerie about a court, sometimes literally, given that, alongside the animals needed for hunting, there was a royal tradition of keeping lions, leopards, and other exotic animals. It was within this context that patronage of letters and the learned took place. Those who produced literature included princely captives, not only Charles d'Orléans, whom we have already noted, but also James I of Scotland, who was held in England from a few days before he became king in 1406 until 1424, and who penned *The Kingis Quair* probably in the months before his return to his homeland. The aristocratic author, however, was a rare beast, particularly when it came to penning poetry. Edward IV's brother-in-law, Anthony Woodville, Earl Rivers (d. 1483), may have been responsible for some short verses, but nothing as sustained as his prose *Dictes and*

---

[48] For his political significance, see Christine Carpenter, *Locality and Polity: A Study of Warwickshire Landed Society, 1401–1499* (Cambridge, 1992) and her 'The Beauchamp Affinity: a Study of Bastard Feudalism at Work', *English Historical Review*, 95 (1980), 514–32. For the joust and Beauchamp's play on his association with Guy of Warwick, see Yin Liu, 'Richard Beauchamp and the Uses of Romance', *Medium Ævum*, 74 (2005), 271–8. For the significance of his chantry chapel and its monument to the earl, see Julian Munby, 'Richard Beauchamp's Funeral Car', *Journal of the British Archaeological Association*, 155 (2002), 278–87; Linda Monckton, 'Fit for a King? The Architecture of the Beauchamp Chapel', *Architectural History*, 47 (2004), 25–52, and Alexandra Buckle, 'Fit for a King: Music and Iconography in Richard Beauchamp's Chantry Chapel', *Early Music*, 38 (2010), 3–20.

[49] See Connolly, *John Shirley*, and also Ryan Perry, 'The Clopton Manuscript and the Beauchamp Affinity: Patronage and Reception Issues in a West Midlands Reading Community', in Wendy Scase (ed.), *Essays in Manuscript Geography: Vernacular Manuscripts of the English West Midlands from the Conquest to the Sixteenth Century* (Turnhout, 2007), 131–59.

[50] For the concept of hybridity in earlier centuries, see Malcolm Vale, *The Princely Court* (Oxford, 2001).

Sayings of the Philosophers.[51] There certainly does not seem to have been the communal habit of sharing love poems which became a feature of the court of Edward's grandson, Henry VIII. Instead, a noble figure most often delegated the production of literary works to others, as can be shown by the example of one prince just mentioned: Humfrey, duke of Gloucester.

Humfrey was more addicted to books than many of his peers in the secular nobility. He amassed a library of probably over 600 volumes, ranging across at least four languages, the fourth being Hebrew, though (given the ban on Jews in England) there was probably nobody in his entourage who could decipher its shapes. There were also at least a few manuscripts in his household in another language, Greek, since one of his secretaries, Antonio Beccaria, produced some Latin versions of some prose works composed in that language.[52] That translator's place of origin, Verona, reminds us that another part of the hybridity of the court was its ability to be an international meeting place. Humfrey employed at least two other 'aliens' as secretaries, one being from Normandy, and the other, like Beccaria, an Italian, Tito Livio Frulovisi from Ferrara, who, when receiving English naturalization, was termed the duke's 'poet and orator'.[53] His compositions included a verse epic celebrating his master's military exploits, written in Latin.[54] The English-born writers who addressed a prince took their place among a wider range of characters.

The example of Beccaria and his study of Greek also serves to highlight two other important factors. First, the books that gravitated around a court were not all the property of a single person. This was not only because there could be both employees with their own learned interests and attendant lords with their own means but also because a court may be made up of multiple households. So, the leading women, the king's consort or the dowager queen, would have their own servants, as would the heir to the throne. To give an example of each as it impinges on English poetry: from soon after her arrival in England in 1445 and for a decade and a half following, Henry VI's wife, Margaret of Anjou, had as one of her clerks George Ashby, who, incidentally, moved into the role from the service of Humfrey, not a friend to Margaret.[55] In the very last years of the century, Henry VII's younger son, later to be Henry VIII, had as his tutor John Skelton, who addressed his charge in Latin verses.[56] Courts were bookish places because they were expressions of more than one identity and homes to more than one person's belongings.

The second point can build on this insight: princes were not in full control of the texts that entered their household. When Humfrey's secretary, Beccaria, produced his translations, he dedicated them to the duke, but that does not mean he had been positively enjoined to undertake them by his master. This situation pertained all the more to authors from outside the court who might send their works to a potential patron speculatively, in the hope that the time and expense they had outlaid would receive some return from the

---

[51] On Woodville's poems, see Omar Khalaf, 'An Unedited Fragmentary Poem by Anthony Woodville, Earl Rivers in Oxford, Bodleian Library, MS Bodley 264', *Notes and Queries*, n.s. 58 (2011), 487–90.

[52] David Rundle, 'From Greenwich to Verona: Antonio Beccaria, St Athanasius and the Translation of Orthodoxy', *Humanistica*, 5 (2010), 109–19.

[53] For Dreu Malfourni, a canon of Lisieux, see Jenny Stratford, *The Bedford Inventories* (London, 1993), 29, 38.

[54] Cristina Cocco (ed.), *Tito Livio Frulovisi, Hunfreidos* (Florence, 2014).

[55] On Ashby see Robert J. Meyer-Lee, 'Laureates and Beggars in Fifteenth-Century English Poetry: The Case of George Ashby', *Speculum*, 79 (2004), 688–726.

[56] For Skelton's service to the future Henry VIII, see Aysha Pollnitz, *Princely Education in Early Modern Britain* (Cambridge, 2015), 43–9, and David R. Carlson, 'The Latin Writings of John Skelton', *Studies in Philology*, 88 (1991), 1–125 (at 42).

lord. It was certainly possible for an author to be snubbed, either not being able to make the presentation or not receiving what they considered due recompense.[57] Over time, a noble's reputation for generosity (or otherwise) would develop, affecting future attempts to seek their patronage. There was, however, a burden of expectation on any prince that they would act virtuously, showing their appreciation of learning and the learned. In short, it was difficult for a noble to reject all literary advances and so book ownership was, for any lord, an occupational hazard.

The arrival of manuscripts at court reminds us that its hybridity thrived on its hosting of outsiders, and its association with literature dependent on interactions with those beyond its walls. So, among those who addressed Humfrey, duke of Gloucester, there were representatives of monastic culture, most notable of them being John Lydgate.[58] There were also those involved in royal administration: Thomas Hoccleve was a clerk of the privy seal, some of whose poems are addressed to members of the nobility.[59] This takes us into an urban setting, though not quite the city where Humfrey had attended that dinner with Lewis Johan: London was physically and legally separate from Westminster, the city of royal government (and Southwark, residence of prisoners and prostitutes, was a separate jurisdiction).

Both England and Scotland were under-urbanized in comparison to, say, the Low Countries or northern Italy. Nor was the fifteenth century a golden age of British towns: most had only a few hundred inhabitants and, for most of the larger ones, their population was in decline. By 'large' is meant between 4000 and 10,000 inhabitants: in the early sixteenth century, nineteen English and three Scottish towns fell into that bracket, while Norwich and Edinburgh were a little above the upper number, and Westminster-London, at about 40,000, was the nearest the whole of Britain had to a metropolis (Paris had more than double the population size).[60] The range of activities associated with the twin cities by the Thames ensured that literacy levels were higher there than in most English communities, and that reading habits were fed by an infrastructure of book production and book trade.[61] The absence of a university encouraged that trade to show a special interest in the provision of vernacular works. Such a focus was enhanced when the printing press was introduced to England, with William Caxton making the shrewd business decision to seek as broad a market as was possible in a society with limited literacy.[62] A corollary was that the learned needed to look to the mainland of Europe to import Latin printed books, but that trade was also channelled through London and Westminster, with Caxton himself involved in it.[63]

We have already sensed how Westminster-London could act as an arena for not only the dissemination of poetry but also its composition and its performance. Its concentration of royal government and commercial significance made it unique, but smaller cities also had

---

[57] For an example from just outside our period, see David Rundle, 'Filippo Alberici, Henry VII and Richard Fox: the English Fortunes of a Little-Known Italian Humanist', *Journal of Warburg and Courtauld Institutes*, 68 (2005), 137–55.

[58] On Lydgate, see Chapter 24 below.

[59] On Hoccleve, see Chapter 25 below.

[60] Maurice Keen, *English Society in the Later Middle Ages 1348–1500* (Harmondsworth, 1990), 87–8; Elizabeth Ewan, 'Hamperit in ane hony came': Sights, Sounds and Smells in the Medieval Town', in Edward J. Cowan and Lizanne Henderson (eds), *A History of Everyday Life in Medieval Scotland* (Edinburgh, 2011), 109–44 (at 109).

[61] C. Paul Christianson, *A Directory of London Stationers and Book Artisans 1300–1500* (New York, 1990).

[62] On print, see Chapter 9 below.

[63] M. T. W. Payne, 'Caxton the Businessman: A New Glimpse', *The Library*, 7th ser., 17 (2016), 103–14; Holly James-Maddocks, 'Illuminated Caxtons and the Trade in Printed Books', *The Library*, 7th ser., 22 (2021), 291–315.

their bustle, as, for instance, William Dunbar reminds us in his vivid depiction of Edinburgh.[64] That latter city was of obvious national importance, while others had a regional hinterland, like York, or created international links through their ports, as did Norwich across the North Sea or Bristol looking towards Europe's western seaboard. Indeed, for both its administrative and trading role, Westminster-London was dependent on the existences of other nodal points across England. For instance, the coinage was minted not only at the Tower of London but also in places like York, Canterbury, and Calais.[65] For the dissemination of information and the running of justice, county towns were essential; some of those had another role in the country's ecclesiastical structure, as the seat of a bishop and thus being a cathedral city. There were many ways in which other urban centres could sustain a culture which could include the presence of poetry.

Recourse was made to verse on special occasions, as when the city of York employed pageants to welcome Henry VII in 1486 and demonstrate loyalty to a king suspicious of its association with the previous régime.[66] It was also, however, part of the fabric of the yearly cycle in some towns, where mystery plays were performed.[67] The presence of poetry was not always a reflection of city government or conventional piety; it could also be oppositional and out of the control of the city fathers. This returns us to a theme on which we touched early in this chapter: the association of protest and poems. Just as towns were centres for the spreading of messages from those in authority, they could also be deployed by those resisting the established structures of power. So, poems of protest were sometimes posted in a public place: during Coventry's enclosure riot of 1496, for example, 'seditious bills' were found pinned to the church door, one with a poem beginning: 'The cyte is bond that shuld be fre! / The right is holden fro þe Cominalte!'[68]

Why express such an attitude in verse? Presumably because when a literate person read it to the others congregated around the door, it was easily memorable. Such jingles took their force from being performed not once but repeatedly: their intention was to move from written to spoken. In other cases, beyond the political and more widely than the urban, poems like ballads or lullabies were inventions of an oral culture which were only belatedly, if ever, transferred to written record. We have seen that English was only one among several languages in use in Britain, and much of the time it was not the most prestigious. We have also noted how rare the talent of writing was. Neither of these factors, however, limited the importance of poetry. On the contrary, the paradox is that the rarity of the ability to read text on the pages rendered some forms of vernacular poetry all the more powerful.

---

[64] See his 'Quhy will ye, merchantis of renoun', in Bawcutt (ed.), *The Poems of William Dunbar*, 1.174–6.
[65] Bolton, *Medieval English Economy*, 73.
[66] C. E. McGee, 'Politics and Platitudes: Sources of Civic Pageantry, 1486', *Renaissance Studies*, 3 (1989), 29–34; Emma Cavell, 'Henry VII, The North of England, and the First Provincial Progress of 1486', *Northern History*, 39 (2002), 187–207.
[67] On drama see Chapter 14 below.
[68] NIMEV 3322; Rossell Hope Robbins (ed.), *Historical Poems of the XIVth and XVth Centuries* (New York, 1959), no. 25, 63–4.

CHAPTER 3
Literary Traditions

Continuity and Change

James Simpson

In his *Regiment of Princes* (1412), Thomas Hoccleve describes Chaucer (c1342–1400) as 'the firste fyndere of our fair langage'.[1] This claim does not mean, as was implausibly claimed in the late nineteenth century, that Chaucer somehow invented, or at least massively restructured, the English language itself.[2] Hoccleve is rather using a technical term, derived from the rhetorical concept of *inventio* (Latin *invenire*, to find).[3] *Inventio* is the capacity to find poetic matter, where 'finding' is as much a psychological as an investigative capacity. The rhetorical concept derives from legal rhetorical practice, where *inventio* embraces the investigative 'circumstances' of an action under forensic examination (why, what, who, when, how, and where);[4] it also embraces psychological meditation on those circumstances so as to invent a plausible case (*'excogitatio rerum verarum aut veri similium quae causam probabilem reddant'*).[5] This intensely psychological feature of invention, drawn originally from legal practice, is extended by later medieval writers of poetic treatises to embrace the inner conception, or mental *archetypus*, of a literary work, prior to any execution.[6] Invention, then, is a matter of two things: the poet's psychological projection of the idea of a literary work; and of the poet's dressing that idea with an appropriate, plausible narration.

Hoccleve's description of Chaucer as 'finder' extends Chaucer's achievement from poetic conception to poetic execution: Chaucer is 'the firste fyndere *of our fair langage*' (my emphasis). Hoccleve uses the term 'finder' here, that is, to include both Chaucer's capacity to 'find' poetic matter and also his capacity to embellish that matter through the

---

[1] Thomas Hoccleve, in Charles R. Blyth (ed.), *The Regiment of Princes* (Kalamazoo, MI, 1999), line 4978. In 1463, George Ashby used the same key phrase with regard to Chaucer, Gower, and Lydgate, and with the same extension to stylistic embellishment: 'Embelysshing oure englisshe tendure algate, / *Firste finders* to our consolacion / Off Fresshe, douce englisshe and formacion / Of newe balades'. See Mary Bateson (ed.), *George Ashby's Poems*, EETS, e.s. 76 (London, 1899), 3–6, my emphasis. See also MED, 'fyndere', sense 2(b): 'one who creates literary works; author, writer'.

[2] For which claims, see Christopher Cannon, *The Making of Chaucer's Language: A Study of Words* (Cambridge, 1998), 12–3.

[3] Compare Chaucer's description of Pythagoras as the 'firste finder' of the art of song in *The Book of the Duchess*, 1168. All citations from the works of Chaucer will be cited in the text, and are taken from Larry D. Benson (general ed.), *The Riverside Chaucer*, 3rd edn. (Boston, MA, 1987).

[4] For the origins and diffusion of the *circumstantiae*, see Rita Copeland and Ineke Sluiter (eds), *Medieval Grammar and Rhetoric: Language Arts and Literary Theory, AD 300–1475* (Oxford, 2009), 49, and Index of Latin Terms, *inventio*.

[5] 'Invention is the discovery of valid or seemingly valid arguments to render one's cause plausible'. Cicero, in H. Hubbell (ed.), *De inventione: De optimo genere oratorum* (Cambridge, MA, 1949), 1.7.9, 18–9.

[6] See Geoffrey of Vinsauf, *Poetria Nova* (c1202): 'If a man has a house to build, his impetuous hand does not rush into action. The measuring line of his mind first lays out the work, and he mentally outlines the successive steps in a definite order. The mind's hand shapes the entire house before the body's hand builds it. Its mode of being is archetypal before it is actual' (translation from Margaret F. Nims (trans.), *Poetria Nova of Geoffrey of Vinsauf* (Toronto, 1967), 17). Chaucer adapts this passage precisely in *Troilus and Criseyde*, 1.1065–71.

resources of what rhetoricians called '*ornatus*' (*ornament*),[7] so as to produce 'fair' language.[8] Elsewhere in the *Regiment*, Hoccleve praises Chaucer for his *ornatus*, but also for his philosophical depth: Chaucer is both 'flour of eloquence', *and* 'mirour of fructuous entendement' (i.e., *a model of fruitful judgement*).[9] By Hoccleve's account, then, Chaucer does at least three things for the first time: he enlarges the available matters for English poetic writing by his 'finding'; embellishes that matter in new ways; and manifests a profound philosophical depth.

Hoccleve's praise of Chaucer as 'finder' is in substance true. From what is plausibly Chaucer's first published work, *The Book of the Duchess* (c1369), Chaucer opens up extraordinary new potentialities for poetic making in English. Already in that work, we can see the following possibilities found and expanded: access to Classical Latin and contemporary French poetic sources; a dynamic mixing of the written and textual on the one hand, with the oral, the lyric and the spontaneous on the other; a represented narrator; a distinction between a narratorial and an authorial voice, such that a text can come to be significantly 'about' the narrator; a correlative appeal to the reader to exercise interpretative choice and discrimination.

As if that set of advances were insufficient, we observe in what is plausibly Chaucer's next ambitious work, *The House of Fame* (c1370s), a freakishly precocious poetic talent extending the ambitions of *inventio* yet further. The narrative of this poem is itself fundamentally *about* poetic 'finding', or rhetorical *inventio*. Here Chaucer enormously expands the potential range of poetic matters, or what he calls 'tidings', now incorporating not only courtly matter, but also news of a very much wider range of experiential, class, and gender experience, which will, in turn, elicit a much wider range of rhetorical resources. In particular, Chaucer generates this ambitious 'finding', which will not be exhausted for the rest of his career, through an act of reading: as he reads Virgil's *Aeneid*, he listens his way sympathetically into the female voice (of Dido), with Ovid's help.[10]

Further, in *The House of Fame* Chaucer absorbs and distinguishes his own poetic project from that of Dante, whose *Commedia*, along with the other great Italian vernacular works by Petrarch and Boccaccio, Chaucer would seem to have encountered in his trip to Florence—probably his first to Italy—in 1373. Unlike Dante, Chaucer will consciously restrict his poetic matter to earthly experience. Chaucer's will not be the poetry of transcendental truth, but rather of 'fals and soth compouned' (*House of Fame*, 1029), with all the interpretative challenges for the reader that such a mix involves.

In his next dream poem, *The Parliament of Fowls* (c1378), Chaucer also devised a new metrical form for English poetry: the five-stress, seven-line stanza rhyming *ababbcc* (later to become known as 'rhyme royal'); and by the mid-1380s, in *The Legend of Good Women*, he will have initiated another new metrical form of his own devising, the five-stress rhyming couplet (later to be known as the heroic couplet). Both of these five-stress forms

---

[7] For Chaucer's reception of these rhetorical terms, see James Simpson, '"Gaufred, deere maister soverain": Chaucer and Rhetoric', in Suzanne Akbari and James Simpson (eds), *The Oxford Handbook to Chaucer* (Oxford, 2020), 126–46.
[8] For correlative evidence that Hoccleve is using 'finder' rhetorically, and that he understands rhetorical finding to include embellishment, see Lydgate's praise of Chaucer as the writer who 'fonde the floures firste of Retoryke' (in Joseph A. Lauritis, Ralph A. Klinefelter, and Vernon F. Gallagher (eds), *A Critical Edition of John Lydgate's Life of Our Lady* (Pittsburgh, PA, 1961), 2.1635 (my emphasis).
[9] Blyth (ed.), *The Regiment of Princes*, 1962–3.
[10] For the generative connection to the voice of suffering women by Chaucer as he shapes a vernacular poetics, see especially Jill Mann, *Feminizing Chaucer* (Woodbridge, 2002). For the fertile adoption of an Ovidian perspective across Chaucer's career, see James Simpson, 'Chaucer as a European Writer', in Seth Lerer (ed.), *The Yale Companion to Chaucer* (New Haven, CT, 2005), 55–86.

permitted a much more resonant verse form than the standard four-stress rhyming couplet that had been used to translate French poetry throughout the fourteenth century, and that had been used by Chaucer himself in both *The Book of the Duchess* and *The House of Fame*.[11]

By the mid-1380s, then, Chaucer has staked out, or 'found', poetic territories in English of a very remarkable kind. He has invented a new narratorial presence, new stylistic ranges, and new metrical forms for poetry in English. He will spend the rest of his career working within this capacious set of possibilities. And, so literary history has had it until relatively recently, fifteenth-century English poetic history is thus determined: a history of slavish and insubstantial imitation of Chaucer's project follows, until, with regard to lyric poetry at least, a new set of lyric possibilities opened up in the 1530s.[12] Already in Thomas Warton's view, stated in his otherwise brilliant *The History of English Poetry from the Close of the Eleventh to the Commencement of the Eighteenth Centuries* (1774–81), the tone is set, one way or another, for criticism until the later twentieth century. For Warton, the history of fifteenth-century poetry was, for the most part, a wasteland: after the spring of Chaucer, he says, we expect summer, but 'winter returns with redoubled horrors ... Most of the poets that immediately succeeded Chaucer, seem rather relapsing into barbarism, than availing themselves of those striking ornaments which his judgment and imagination had disclosed'.[13]

In this chapter I will not diminish the exceptional quality and achievement of Chaucer's poetic finding and rhetorical embellishment across his career. On the contrary, that set of claims will remain firmly in place. As we look, however, to the ways in which English poets of the late fourteenth century continued to inflect poetic making in the century to follow, I take issue with Hoccleve's claim for Chaucer both as the *only* 'first finder' and as the *first* such finder. Here I will instead attempt to delineate a set of vectors that drive poetic writing in English from the late fourteenth into the fifteenth century. Instead of focusing on Chaucer's projects alone, and instead of giving Chaucer exclusive priority, I isolate, in addition to Chaucer, the following three, roughly contemporary bodies of work (here named by the phrase that best characterizes their influence), each of which significantly influenced poetic writing in English in the following century: the Gower-tradition, the *Piers Plowman* tradition, and historical alliterative poetry. Each of these *corpora* produces accomplished fifteenth-century 'finder-poets', who extend the range of possible matters for poetry in English, and who exploit poetic language in distinctive ways.

The story of prose would of course be different, and would include extraordinary writing by women writers, such as Julian of Norwich, as well, of course, as the influence of

---

[11] These Chaucerian metrical innovations are adopted by fifteenth-century religious poets who work within only very restricted areas of Chaucer's *oeuvre*. See, for example, Karen A. Winstead (ed.), John Capgrave, *Life of St Katharine* (Kalamazoo, MI, 1999). The work (c1445), 8624 lines, in rhyme royal stanzas, divided into five books, is formally indebted to Chaucer.

[12] For the largest scale characteristics of criticism of fifteenth-century English poetry, and the cultural forces driving them, see James Simpson, *Reform and Cultural Revolution, 1350–1547* (Oxford, 2002), 34–51.

[13] Thomas Warton, *The History of English Poetry from the Close of the Eleventh to the Commencement of the Eighteenth Centuries*, 3 vols. (London, 1774–81), 2.51. For a collection of such statements from later twentieth-century critics, see David Lawton, 'Dullness and the Fifteenth Century', *ELH*, 54 (1987), 761–99 (at 761). See also the Oedipal account of early fifteenth-century English poets and 'father' Chaucer by Seth Lerer, *Chaucer and his Readers: Imagining the Author in Late-Medieval England* (Princeton, NJ, 1993), 23.

Chaucer's own voluminous prose works.[14] My four bodies of work, further, by no means exhaust the list of great late fourteenth-century poets: the *Gawain*-poet is indisputably a very remarkable writer, but without fifteenth-century influence. It should also be mentioned, correlatively, that certain kinds of fifteenth-century poetry have no substantial fourteenth-century precedent, such as the improperly maligned and relatively small body of 'aureate' poetry,[15] or the remarkable examples of dramatic poetry of largely fifteenth-century cycle plays (especially that of the so-called 'Wakefield Master'). In four sections I define, then, the inventive posture of relevant fourteenth-century writers; I also delineate the ways fifteenth-century poets adapted late fourteenth-century *corpora*, starting with reception of Chaucer.

Before we approach our specific *corpora*, we need, however, to delineate the basic inventive postures of vernacular poets, and the historical conditions of those postures, in the fifteenth century. Nicholas Watson has supplied a rich typology of such positioning for medieval English writing, which include the *pastoral* (in the ecclesiastical sense), where writers speak down to those in need of instruction; the *communal*, where a writer speaks as one among equals; and the *patronal*, speaking up to a patron of higher status, where poets use their expertise to inform a readership of 'social superiors of what they wish or need to know'.[16]

For both political and religious historical reasons, fifteenth-century English poets wrote within significantly more constrained circumstances than late fourteenth-century poets. From the 1399 coup d'état by Henry Bolingbroke, England experienced five further violent seizures of the crown (1460 by Edward IV; 1470 by Henry VI (briefly reclaiming his crown); 1471 by Edward IV (again); 1483 by Richard III; and 1485 by Henry VII). Poets found themselves writing within less than wholly legitimate, stable régimes, and often to young and inexperienced kings or future kings (e.g., to the future Henry V before he assumed the crown in 1413, or to the mentally enfeebled Henry VI). And from 1401 England was also subject to a much more aggressive religious policy against the newly-defined Lollard 'heresy', with two draconian pieces of legislation, the 1401 statute *Concerning the Burning of Heretics*, and the English Church's own complementary legislation issued in 1409, known as Arundel's *Constitutions*.[17]

For these historical reasons, and because the English vernacular had become, thanks to later fourteenth-century writers, a vehicle for consequential, public, attention-worthy discourse, fifteenth-century poets wrote for the most part with a much tighter relation to centres of power, with the promise and bane of laureateship coming into focus for political

---

[14] For the histories of Middle English prose, see A. S. G. Edwards (ed.), *A Companion to Middle English Prose* (Woodbridge, 2004).

[15] Properly defined as an extraordinarily mannered, Latinate style designed for religious subjects, probably in response to the plain English of Lollard, and used for translation of theological material. See James Simpson, 'John Lydgate', in Larry Scanlon (ed.), *The Cambridge Companion to Medieval Literature* (Cambridge, 2009), 205–16 (at 212–5).

[16] Nicholas Watson, *Balaam's Ass: Vernacular Theology Before the English Reformation* (Philadelphia, PA, 2022), Ch. 10. I am grateful to Nicholas Watson for sharing this work with me prior to publication.

[17] Available in, respectively, T. E. Tomlins, et al. (eds), *Statutes of the Realm*, 11 vols. (London, 1810–28; rpt. 1963), 2 Henry IV, c. 15, 2. 125–8, and David Wilkins (ed.), *Concilia Magnae Britanniae et Hiberniae*, 4 vols. (London, 1737), 3.314–9.

authors, and the bane of censorship coming into sharp focus for authors of religious matter.[18] Accordingly, whereas fourteenth-century poets had written on the communal model, their fifteenth-century counterparts often wrote on the patronal model. This much more intimate relation with powerful and courtly patrons entails a very significant narrowing of the social, and therefore the corresponding rhetorical, range of Chaucer's *oeuvre* (there is, for example, no significant bourgeois, Chaucer-inspired tradition in fifteenth-century English poetry).[19] Within that narrower social ambit of largely courtly topics and readers, however, fifteenth-century poets creatively exploit the set of late fourteenth-century *corpora*, to which we now turn.

The Chaucer Tradition

The range of Chaucer's poetic *oeuvre* is astonishing. It embraces elegy (both lyrics and longer narratives with inset lyrics),[20] romance, tragedy, hagiography, petitionary poetry (both secular and religious), fabliau, satire, exemplary moral narrative, and animal fable. Plenty of individual works by fifteenth-century poets exploit Chaucerian possibilities, but only one, very large fifteenth-century poetic *corpus*, that of Lydgate, takes shape fundamentally within the range of possibilities opened by Chaucer.

Chaucer was acclaimed before he died. Precisely given that incipient fame, it was essential for early fifteenth-century poets to enlist Chaucer's reputation by way of promoting their own work. Throughout his career, the Benedictine monk John Lydgate (c1370–1449/50) evokes Chaucer's name, and defines especially his rhetorical achievement.[21] Rhetorically brilliant, exceptionally wide in his range, generous and generative,[22] and,

---

[18] For the tighter relation of fifteenth-century poets to patrons, see Robert J. Meyer-Lee, *Poets and Power from Chaucer to Wyatt* (Cambridge, 2007), 3–4 and *passim*. For post-Arundelian religious censorship, see Nicholas Watson, 'Censorship and Cultural Change in Late-Medieval England: Vernacular Theology, the Oxford Translation Debate, and Arundel's Constitutions of 1409', *Speculum*, 70 (1995), 822–64.

[19] There are some rare exceptions: *The Tale of Beryn*, for which see John M. Bowers (ed.), *The Canterbury Tales: Fifteenth-Century Continuations and Additions* (Kalamazoo, MI, 1992), 79–164, and John Metham's *Amoryus and Cleopes* (1448–9), for which see the edition by Stephen F. Page (ed.), *Amoryus and Cleopes* (Kalamazoo, MI, 1999).

[20] For the literary Ovidian mode of 'elegy' as applied to late medieval and early modern poetry in English, see Simpson, *Reform and Cultural Revolution*, 121–90.

[21] Some examples: Lauritis et al. (eds), *Lydgate's Life of Our Lady*, 2.1628–37; Henry Bergen (ed.), *Troy Book*, EETS, e.s. 97, 103, 106 (London, 1906, 1908, 1910), 2.4677–723; 3.560–4, 4197–4263; 4.3519–39; Axel Erdmann (ed.), *Siege of Thebes*, EETS, e.s. 108 (London, 1911), 4501–25; Henry Bergen (ed.), *Fall of Princes*, EETS, e.s. 121, 122, 123, (Oxford, 1924–7)), 1.246–357, 1795–1806, 3.3855–64. For a full set of explicit references to Chaucer by Lydgate, see David R. Carlson, 'The Chronology of Lydgate's Chaucer References', *The Chaucer Review*, 38 (2004), 246–54. For discussion, see Derek Pearsall, *John Lydgate* (London, 1970), 65–7, and Lois Ebin, *Illuminator, Makar, Vates: Visions of Poetry in the Fifteenth Century* (Lincoln, NE, 1988), 1–18.

[22] See especially Bergen (ed.), *Troy Book*, 5.3519–26:

> For he þat was gronde of wel-seying,
> In al hys lyf hyndred no makyng,
> My maister Chaucer, þat founde ful many spot;
> Hym liste nat pinche nor gruche at euery blot,
> Nor meue hym silf to parturbe his reste
> (I haue herde telle), but seide alweie þe best,
> Suffring goodly of his gentilnes
> Ful many thing enbracid with rudnes.

above all, gone and lamented: thus the emphases of Lydgatian praise of 'master' Chaucer. The correlative posture for those left behind is due modesty, and a recognition of stumbling inadequacy:

> Ther is no makyng to his equipollent*; *equal*
> We do but halt*, whoso taketh hede, *limp*
> That medle of making*, withouten any drede. *engage in writing poetry*
> Whan we wolde his (*i.e. Chaucer's*) stile counterfet,
> We may al day oure colour* grynde and bete, (fig.) *literary skill*
> Tempere oure azour and vermyloun:
> But al I holde but presumpcioun.[23]

Should we, however, take Lydgate at his word? Might we rather be able to redescribe this posture of stumbling ineptitude as a modesty *topos* produced by a much closer relation to centres of political power?[24]

Chaucer has only two poems that can with any confidence be connected with a patron, his first and his last: the *Book of the Duchess* (c1369) has evident connections with John of Gaunt, duke of Lancaster; and what is apparently Chaucer's last poem, the witty 'Complaint to his Purse' (1399), which is explicitly addressed to the newly-crowned son of John of Gaunt, King Henry IV. The rest of Chaucer's entire *oeuvre* stands detached from any named or imagined patron, with the possible exception of Queen Anne, allusively referred to in the F Prologue to the *Legend of Good Women* (496–7).

The situation with Lydgate is dramatically different, and the difference informs every aspect of his poetry. Lydgate wrote for royalty, the upper nobility, the metropolitan elite, and for ecclesiastical patrons of the highest rank.[25] His *Fall of Princes* contains an account of Chaucer's patronage by aristocrats that is in fact misleading with regard to Chaucer: like Virgil, Dante, and Petrarch, Lydgate says 'Support of princes fond hem ther dispense' (3.3864). The *Fall of Princes*, commissioned by Humfrey, duke of Gloucester (uncle to Henry VI), is itself punctuated by thanks or calls for generous payment (e.g., 2.156, 3.74). Lydgate's final envoy sends the poem off to the duke 'with hand shaking / Of hool affeccioun knelyng on my knee' (9.3599–600).

We have, then, a new configuration of poetic making in post-Chaucerian, Lancastrian England (i.e., from 1399), in which powerful patrons are active agents in the production of poetry (or represented at least as such), and in which poets are much more closely dependent on such patronage.[26] That new configuration, coupled with, or perhaps produced by, the new political conditions of nervous régimes with less than iron-cast legitimacy, has led critics to describe early Lancastrian poets as sycophantic mouthpieces for official lines.[27] In what remains of this section, I resist this argument by defining the early Lancastrian patron-poet relationship through the lens of Chaucerian reception. Chaucer's is

---

[23] Bergen (ed.), *Troy Book*, 2.4712–8.
[24] See Lawton, 'Dullness and the Fifteenth Century'.
[25] For a survey of the wide and generally very elite range of those patrons, see Derek Pearsall, *John Lydgate (1371–1449): A Bio-bibliography* (Victoria, BC, 1997).
[26] John, duke of Bedford, even had images of Lancastrian vernacular poets worked into his magnificent devotional book, *The Bedford Hours* (1414), for which see Sylvia Wright, 'The Author Portraits in the Bedford Psalter Hours: Gower, Chaucer and Hoccleve', *British Library Journal*, 18 (1992), 190–201.
[27] A case most subtly prosecuted by Paul Strohm, *England's Empty Throne: Usurpation and the Language of Legitimation 1399–1422* (New Haven, CT, 1998), and Paul Strohm, 'Hoccleve, Lydgate and the Lancastrian Court', in David Wallace (ed.), *The Cambridge History of Medieval English Literature* (Cambridge, 1999), 640–61.

an enabling presence in all cases, and, in some genres at least, the occasion for exceptionally powerful admonition to Lancastrian rulers. I exemplify the case with three different genres. Lydgate is the prime example.

Derek Pearsall has made the plausible case that Lydgate's entire set of poetic projects can be described as a set of responses to, and attempts to overtake, equivalent works by Chaucer.[28] The kinds of case I will make now could, then, be made from almost any one of Lydgate's works. For the purposes of this chapter, I restrict myself to three texts exemplifying genres in which Lydgate excelled: elegy; tragedy; and animal fable. In each, Chaucerian positioning enables the Lancastrian voice to operate in a matrix of poetic making different from that of Chaucer.

Lydgate's elegiac *Temple of Glass* (?1420) consists of 1403 lines, in which the narrative is written in five-stress rhyming couplets, while the voices of the lovers and their own patron Venus are presented in rhyme royal stanzas.[29] The dreamer-narrator falls asleep and finds himself 'ravysshid in spirit' to a temple of glass 'on a craggy roche / Like ise ifrore [*frozen*]' (16–20). There he witnesses iconographic images of true lovers (e.g., Dido, Alceste, Griselde, Palamon ('as Chaucer tellith us' (110)), plus three living figures in particular: (i) a woman who makes a complaint before Venus about being locked in unhappy marriage and unable to communicate with the man she loves; (ii) the goddess Venus, who answers the woman with both sympathy and encouragement; and (iii) 'a man that welke al solitarie, / That as me semed for hevines and dole / Him to complein' (550–2). Hearing the complaint of the male, Venus makes 'a ful bihest: / Perpetuelli, by confirmacioun, / Whiles that thei lyve, of oon affeccioun / Thei shal endure' (1323–6). Each of the human voices in the poem is subject to powerful constraint: the dreamer-narrator starts under conditions of melancholy (going to sleep with 'thought, constreint, and grevous hevines, / For pensifhede and for heigh distres' (1–2); the woman lover can express herself only to Venus; and the male lover walks in solitary grief before presenting his petition to Venus. With exquisite tact and daring, the poem creates the conditions of intensely sympathetic, confidential expression and emotional relief of sorts.

The *Temple of Glass* is, clearly, saturated with Chaucerian references: the temple evokes the 'temple [*of Venus*] ymade of glas' in *The House of Fame* (120); the grieving courtly lovers, both female and male, evoke the narrative of *The Book of the Duchess*; and the iconographic lovers depicted evoke *The Parlement of Foules* (284–94), no less than the specific lovers mentioned are drawn from memorable Chaucerian narratives. The presentation of love's predicaments through bureaucratic textual and theatrical protocols evokes Chaucer's searing 'Complaint to Pity'.[30]

More to the point, the Chaucerian resources *liberate* the poem's suffering aristocratic voices: the poet's own suffering, dreaming, observant narratorial presence obliquely frees the painfully constrained voices of the courtly represented by the narrator. The psychological state of the Lydgatian narrator, that is, allows entry into a poetic world made of both classical (Ovidian) and vernacular (Chaucerian) materials; in that intimate and trusting space, patronal voices are permitted to voice intimate sufferings. The poet's voice is sympathetically proximate and adjacent to both lovers, and to Chaucer. He facilitates the lovers' propitious approach to a higher 'patron', the goddess Venus, from whose 'privité' nothing 'mai be concelid' (795).

---

[28] Derek Pearsall, 'Chaucer and Lydgate', in Ruth Morse and Barry Windeatt (eds), *Chaucer Traditions: Studies in Honour of Derek Brewer* (Cambridge, 1990), 39–53.

[29] John Lydgate, 'The Temple of Glass', in Julia Boffey (ed.), *Fifteenth-Century English Dream Visions: An Anthology* (Oxford, 2003), 15–89.

[30] For the bureaucratic protocols of Lydgate's elegiac poetry, see Simpson, *Reform and Revolution*, 175–85.

Lydgate is not the only fifteenth-century poet to work within Chaucerian elegiac possibilities. The essential characteristic such poets share is making the poet's poetic finding part of the poem's own narrative. Thus James I, King of Scotland (1394–1437), who was captured in 1407 and remained a prisoner in England until 1424, himself seems to have written a delightfully optimistic text within elegiac conditions. *The Kingis Quair* (1379 lines in five-stress, rhyme royal stanzas, a Chaucerian metre named thus for the fact that King James used it) narrates James' imprisonment.[31] It seems, however, to have been composed immediately after his release from prison and marriage to Joan Beaufort in 1424, and before his return to Scotland, where he was assassinated in 1437.

The poem opens with an account of the sleepless, mentally unsettled king picking up Boethius's *Consolation* in an almost random way. He calls the *Consolation* by the title 'Boece' (16), which is the title Chaucer had given his translation of Boethius' work; this possible reference to Chaucer's translation would be wholly appropriate, since James' act of invention is mediated wholly by Chaucerian example: one thinks most obviously of the *Parlement of Foules*, whose initial reading experience (15–84) invokes a long sequence of otherworldly voyages (Cicero's Scipio, Virgil's Dido, Dante's pilgrim) so as to inflect the new voyage about to be made by Chaucer's narrator. And just as Chaucer's narrator reflects deeply on the *Somnium Scipionis* before sleeping, before going on to effectively rewrite the authoritative text, with significantly new emphases in the dream experience that follows, so too does James rewrite the texts that prompt his act of poetic invention: not only Boethius' *Consolation*, but also, especially, 'The Knight's Tale' (cf. *Kingis Quair* 204–305 with 'Knight's Tale' 1062-111). James does not dream initially, but is inspired to write the poem that we now read, which then includes a narrative of an astral journey, in which James experiences a much more optimistic account of Fortune than Boethius or 'The Knight's Tale' would allow.

James' is an act of distinctively Chaucerian *inventio*, 'This mater new in my mynd rolling' (54). Many of the features of the Chaucerian poetic are found here: access to and adaption of Classical Latin and now contemporary English (i.e., Chaucerian) poetic sources; a represented narrator; texts played through dream experience, which involves a correlative appeal to the reader to exercise interpretative choice and discrimination. James sends his finished text off to 'my maisteris dere, / Gowere and Chaucere' (1373–4), which, along with poems by Lydgate and Hoccleve especially,[32] signal the existence of something that had not confidently existed prior to the early fifteenth century: a poetic tradition—a passing on—of named poets. There are other elegiac poets working in Chaucerian mode who claim attention, but space forbids more than notational reference.[33]

Chaucerian models also inspired something quite different and distinctive in fifteenth-century vernacular poetry in English: large scale, tragic, *romans antiques*. Again, Lydgate demands attention. In his *Siege of Thebes* (1421–2), Lydgate's initial circumstantial positioning (his 'finding') is brilliantly productive, both with regard to Chaucer and to Lydgate's own patrons. Lydgate finds himself riding among the Canterbury pilgrims, who are now returning to London, just as Chaucer had promised they would (General Prologue, 794). Chaucer himself, though, is not named until line 4501. He is, textually, vividly present to the narrator (his words ' ... never shal appallen in my mynde / But alwey fressh ben in my memoyré' (44–5)). But he is physically absent from his own pilgrimage. That the intense praise of Chaucer, indeed, is in the past tense marks him out as now dead: Chaucer 'sothly

---

[31] James I of Scotland, 'The Kingis Quair', in Boffey (ed.), *Fifteenth-Century English Dream Visions*, 90–157.
[32] By Lydgate, especially *The Complaint of the Black Knight*, *The Temple of Glass*, *Troy Book*, *The Siege of Thebes*, and *Fall of Princes*; by Hoccleve, especially *The Regiment of Princes*.
[33] E.g. Derek Pearsall (ed.), *Floure and the Leafe, The Assembly of Ladies, The Isle of Ladies* (Kalamazoo, MI, 1990).

hadde most of excellence / In rethorike and in eloquences' (41–2, my emphasis); he is the honour 'of wel seyinge first in oure language' (47). It falls to the pilgrim Lydgate to begin the first tale on return to London, which he duly does, in a 4716-line tale delivered in five-stress couplets (Chaucer's invention).

In Chaucer's outward journey from London, the Knight had told the first tale; he had also interrupted the Monk's tragedies (7.2767). On the way back, the Monk Lydgate enters the field of tale-telling first, whence Chaucer's Monk had been chased, and he does so with deliberate aim. The Knight had told a small part of the story of Thebes, translated from Boccaccio's invented portion of the *Teseida* dealing with the lovers Palemone and Arcita; Lydgate opens the Chaucerian story up, by giving the pilgrims the vast Theban prequel to 'The Knight's Tale': Lydgate tells the story of Thebes from its founding by Amphion, through the narrative of Oedipus, to the civil war between Eteocles and Polinices, into which the Argives are drawn for the best reasons and with the worst results, right up to the very point of the *beginning* of the Knight's narrative, with Theseus and the Theban women.

Lydgate does very much the same with Chaucer's treatment of the story of Thebes as he does with Chaucer's treatment of the other great catastrophe narrative of late medieval Europe, that of Troy. Whereas Chaucer had, again following Boccaccio, written a deeply poignant, enclosed narrative of love inset within the Trojan War (i.e., *Troilus and Criseyde*), keeping the larger war at bay, Lydgate writes the large, dark prequel to Chaucer's narrative in his *Troy Book* (1412–20). For both Troy and Thebes, that is, Lydgate opens up Chaucer's narratives to reveal how those detailed, partitioned Chaucerian narratives rhyme with the larger, darker movement of catastrophic history of which they are a part. Lydgate gives us the whole picture in both cases.

In both cases, too, Lydgate writes as a monk to his secular, aristocratic audience. This is not to say that Lydgate primarily moralizes his narratives of polytheistic societies with specifically Christian doctrine. So far from doing that, Lydgate keeps all the gods, polytheistic or the Christian God, out of the story.[34] Lydgate writes as a monk insofar as he writes with a powerful machine of *inventio* at his disposal: the monastic library, with 'an hundred' books 'in [his] celle' (*Canterbury Tales* 7.1971–2), from which he draws the wisdom of ancient societies to address contemporary predicaments. Lydgate emphasizes ethical virtues in his delivery, but not the penitential ethics of Christianity: instead he elucidates the Cardinal Virtue of Prudence, the capacity to see from the present, by reference to the past, into the future, and to judge whether or not an action will be manageable (e.g., 2796–2812, 2891–8, 2952–62, 3442–4).[35] This is the ethics of practical but successful action in the world.

Lydgate's audience of aristocratic male rulers was possessed of another ethical system for practical action in the world, that of chivalric ethics, which principally promoted the need to accrue honour and avoid shame. Throughout both the *Troy Book* and the *Siege of Thebes*, Lydgate represents headstrong male aristocrats making all the wrong, stupid moves under the impulse of honour accumulation and shame avoidance (e.g., *Troy Book* 2.2305–68, 2.3295–318; *Siege of Thebes* 2922–40).

Whereas Chaucer's Canterbury pilgrimage heads *away* from the city, Lydgate's heads back there, and so it well might in the early 1420s: after the premature death of Henry

---

[34] See James Simpson, 'Human Prudence Versus the Emotion of the Cosmos: War, Deliberation and Destruction in the Late Medieval Statian Tradition', in Andrew Lynch et al. (eds), *Emotions and War* (London, 2015), 98–116.

[35] For the Ciceronian sources of Prudential theory and its later medieval diffusion, see James Simpson, '"Dysemol daies and Fatal houres": Lydgate's *Destruction of Thebes* and Chaucer's *Knight's Tale*', in Helen Cooper and Sally Mapstone (eds), *The Long Fifteenth Century: Essays in Honour of Douglas Gray* (Oxford, 1997), 15–33.

V in August 1422, Parliament determined that governance of England should be shared between John, duke of Bedford and his brother Humfrey, duke of Gloucester. Civil war, which had already afflicted and terribly weakened France from 1407, is the threat that haunts (and visited) England throughout the fifteenth century. In 1422 Lydgate urgently and confidently addresses his narrative of Thebes to his Lancastrian patrons, implicitly urging them to avoid the fate of Thebes with its warring princely brothers, urging them to avoid replicating the fate the Argives. He speaks from the position of learned *clericus* to dangerously powerful soldiers.

The only other fifteenth-century poet to take on Chaucer's *roman antique* material is Robert Henryson (d. c1490). Henryson, writing from an entirely different social environment in Scotland, positions himself wholly differently from fifteenth-century English poets. In his darkly intense *Testament of Cresseid* (written probably in the 1470s) his inventive posture is not as advisor to patrons, but as deeply reflective, private, trenchant reader. The poem's power derives partly from its commitment to seeing Chaucer's Criseyde through to her end, where Chaucer had her move painfully out of the picture. The poem's power also derives from the way in which the appalling fate of Cresseid undoes, and exposes the vacuity of, key elegiac poetic resources. As an abandoned leper suffering from a hideous venereal disease, Cresseid delivers, for example, a piercing, rhetorically expert, inset *planctus* (407–69),[36] which is unimaginable without the precedent of the inset complaints in Chaucer's *Troilus and Criseyde* (e.g., 1.400–20, 3.820–40, and 5.638–44). So far from persuading anyone that she is the victim of Fortune, however, Cresseid's complaint serves only to highlight the failure of that lyric tradition to meet this situation. The only intelligible, human sound worth making is, by the estimation of an old leper lady, the noise of the clapper soliciting alms, making 'vertew of ane neid' (478, a horribly shrunken version of Theseus' identical claim in 'the Knight's Tale' (1.3042)). From this collapse of intelligence, the poem must edge back to some kind of fit human judgement. Judgement comes not, however, from the gods: their savage legal 'sentence' beggars any poetic 'sentence'; neither does it come from the poet: 'Sen scho is deid I speik of hir no moir' (616) is his final disclaimer; and neither does the epitaph Troylus' has inscribed on Cresseid's tomb invest Cresseid's terrible fate with human sense: Cresseid, 'Sumtyme countit the flour of womanheid, / Under this stane, lait lipper, lyis deid' (607–8). The only human 'sentence' on Cresseid, and so the only really intelligible comment on her situation, is made by Cresseid herself. Crucially, it is not a judgement, but an accusation:

> Thocht* sum be trew*, I wait* richt few ar they;   *Though, faithful, know*
> Quha findis treuth*, lat him his lady ruse*;   *fidelity, praise*
> Nane but my self as now I will accuse.
> (572–4)

So in both these genres, the elegiac and the tragic, Lydgate and other fifteenth-century poets in English position themselves productively with regard to their master Chaucer, to his matter, and, in the English cases, to their patrons. The kinds of case made here about the enabling presence of Chaucer for the fifteenth-century Chaucerian Lydgate could be made for many other genres. Thus both Lydgate and, again, Henryson exploit Chaucerian potential with the animal fable. Lydgate's brilliant and understudied *Churl and the Bird* (of uncertain date), along with Henryson's powerfully corrosive, bleak *Morall Fabillis*

---

[36] Robert Henryson, 'The Testament of Cresseid', in Denton Fox (ed.), *The Poems of Robert Henryson* (Oxford, 1981).

(2975 lines in rhyme royal stanzas)[37] are the key examples, since they bear all the Chaucerian rhetorical hallmarks (both of *inventio* and *ornatus*) that Chaucer deploys in his own animal fables (especially 'The Nun's Priest's Tale' and 'The Manciple's Tale'), no less than meta-poetic reflection on the use of rhetorical persuasion when addressing the powerful. The *Churl and the Bird* is strikingly forthright about the position of the Chaucerian poet, since the implicit aristocrat in that poem is pictured as deaf to wisdom. The poem ends with the clever bird (i.e., court poet) abjuring the value of speaking to obtuse patrons at all: 'I cast me nevir hensforth, my lyvyng, / Aforn a cherl anymore to syng!' (363–4).[38]

The Gower Tradition

Readers familiar with scholarship on 'English Chaucerians' will perhaps be surprised that I have not discussed Thomas Hoccleve (c1367–1426) in any detail under the aegis of Chaucer. To be sure, Hoccleve praises Chaucer and depends on his name to generate his own poetic identity.[39] But even as he does so in the *Regiment of Princes* (1412), he also praises 'my maistir Gower' (1975). In this section I focus on the understudied influence of John Gower (1330–1408), and in particular his *Confessio amantis* (1390–3). Hoccleve is much more, I suggest, a Gowerian than a Chaucerian.

Gower's *Confessio amantis* pretends to be what it is not. It pretends, that is, to be an extended penitential confession, in which the failed lover Amans details his errancy across eight books, devoted in turn to each of the seven deadly sins (Books 1–6 and 8). One of the giveaways of this extended literary feint is the confessor figure—Venus's priest Genius—to whom Amans confesses his lover's sins. Genius is a figure with a long and rich intellectual history;[40] Gower merges four key functions of the Genius figure: a tutelary figure; a conscience figure; a psychological representative of *ingenium*, or imagination, situated between the senses and reason; and a force of sexual desire (thus 'priest of Venus'). Through Genius, Gower angles the entire force of the *Confessio* away from penitential ethics, and turns it instead to matters concerned with love.

That turn towards amorous desire, however, is itself not the whole story: the stories told by Genius to instruct Amans consistently involve *political* issues. The second giveaway of the structure of the whole book is that Book 7 seems to fit neither penitential nor amatory concerns. Book 7 is devoted to the education of the king, especially in the practical sciences. Genius, however, resolves the amatory and the political. In his adjacency to reason, Genius reveals that the psyche is itself a political realm, potentially subject to the tyrant Cupid. The 'political' health of the politic body requires commerce between the abstract force of reason and the desires of the body, just as the ruler of a well-ordered body politic requires dialogue with his people. In the psyche, that mediating figure is Genius himself, whereas in the body politic the mediator is royal council and Parliament. By the end of the poem, Amans is taught, by a cannily subtle pedagogy, to abandon his obsessive pursuit of amatory

---

[37] Robert Henryson, 'Morall Fabillis', in Fox (ed.), *The Poems of Robert Henryson*.
[38] Citation from *The Churl and the Bird*, in Henry Noble MacCracken (ed.), *The Minor Poems of John Lydgate*, EETS, e.s. 107, o.s. 192 (London, 1911, 1934), 2.468–85. For analysis of this brilliant poem, see James Simpson, '"For al my body ... weieth nat an unce": Empty Poets and Rhetorical Weight in Lydgate's *Churl and the Bird*', in Larry Scanlon and James Simpson (eds), *John Lydgate: Poetry, Culture, and Lancastrian England* (Notre Dame, IN, 2006), 129–46.
[39] Blyth (ed.), *Regiment of Princes*, 1863–7.
[40] Jane Chance Nitzsche, *The Genius Figure in Antiquity and the Middle Ages* (New York, 1975).

desire. Instead he regains his proper name, 'John Gower' (8.2321), integrated as he is both personally and as a citizen in the larger body politic.[41]

Gower's inventive posture for this work is exceptionally fertile. Genius as the imagination is the storehouse of images and of narrative: he remembers stories from multiple sources (upwards of eighty of them across the *Confessio* as a whole), frequently from Ovid; as a priest of Venus and confessor, he produces ironic structures, pretending to be based on penitential ethics, when in fact the stories are often an occasion for Amans to indulge his fantasy of erotic satisfaction. But that pretence is also ultimately ironic: Genius as imagination mediates between the senses and reason, to each of which he is psychologically adjacent. The overall drift of the work is away from erotic concerns and towards the political, or, rather, towards understanding the place of the whole body in the political. The reader experiences the drift of the poem, and is educated through that experience.

There are two presiding authorial geniuses, as it were, behind the poem: Ovid and Aristotle. Ovid supplies the posture of the lover-poet giving voice to repressed desire, and also supplies much of the poetic matter of the poem. Aristotle, by contrast, ultimately supplies the poem's fundamental philosophical and structural coordinates: beneath the movement of this text lies an Aristotelian philosophical ground, where the soul is most fully itself when embodied. As an embodied soul, the soul must recognize the whole body, of which it is a part, in any formulation of rule; and as the soul strives to attain its fullest form, so too must it undergo a process of 'enformacion' (to use Gower's term) though teaching and reading.[42] The poem so produced is what might be called a 'person-shaped' poem: the text reaches its own fullest form as the soul of the ideal reader is brought to its own fullest 'form'. The essential sciences within which the poem works are the practical sciences in what was known as the Aristotelian scheme of the division of philosophy: ethics (i.e., governance of the self); economics (i.e., governance of the household); and politics (i.e., governance of the polis).[43] The political order is modelled on the self: the king learns how to govern the polis by governance of his own body in the first instance.[44] Every romance narrative in the *Confessio* is implicitly 'economic', insofar as each addresses governance of the household, including marriage (e.g., Florent (1.1407), Constance (2.587–1612), and especially Apollonius of Tyre (8.271–2008)); many other exemplary narratives of household mismanagement (e.g., Phoebus and Cornide (3.783–817) also point to the broader issue of political governance by exposing household, 'economic' mismanagement.

That discursive structure illuminates Hoccleve's poetic project. Hoccleve's *oeuvre* is distinctive for its sharply focused, extended autobiographical accents. We find nothing comparable in late fourteenth-century writing. His *Male regle* (1405) (448 lines in rhyme royal stanzas), for example, presents itself as a comically self-demeaning portrait of youthful excess; the *Regiment of Princes* (1412) (5463 lines in mostly rhyme royal stanzas) begins with a 2016-line report of a conversation between Hoccleve and an old man, in which the Hoccleve figure complains of his terror of bankruptcy; and the *Series* (c1420) (an extended *prosimetrum* consisting of seven miscellaneous texts) begins with a searing complaint about social alienation after a period of mental instability, followed by a dialogue between Hoccleve and a friend in which the dangers of publication are candidly addressed.

---

[41] For this argument in full, see James Simpson, *Sciences and the Self in Medieval Poetry: Alan of Lille's Anticlaudianus and John Gower's Confessio amantis* (Cambridge, 1995), 134–299.
[42] Simpson, *Sciences and the Self*, 168–72.
[43] Simpson, *Sciences and the Self*, 219–29.
[44] Elizabeth Porter, 'Gower's Ethical Microcosm and Political Macrocosm', in Alastair Minnis (ed.), *Gower's 'Confessio amantis': Responses and Reassessments* (Cambridge, 1983), 135–62.

Hoccleve represents himself as painfully unabsorbed by a social fabric. He may have learned from Chaucer how long prologues by socially ill-integrated figures (e.g., the Wife of Bath, the Pardoner) serve to invest the matter that follows with the presence of that unabsorbed voice: 'the Wife of Bath's Tale' is inescapably also about its speaker. But the larger structure of Hoccleve's works points rather to Gower, not Chaucer, as the poetic and discursive model. Just as Gower reveals the powerful interrelations of the ethical, the economic, and the political, Hoccleve works within that discursive frame, and accentuates, more than any other later Middle English poet (except perhaps the author of *Winner and Waster* (1353)), the realm of the economic, in the sense of the concern of the household. What might look like 'merely' household concerns are, in fact, the concerns of a major institution in late medieval England;[45] Hoccleve's 'autobiographical' material is better described as 'economic' material.

And in the poetic terrain mined most deeply by Gower, economic material points irresistibly to the political. The 'economic' is the place to 'find' the poetic matter of the political, since economic balance is dependent on the higher science of politics. This is certainly true of Hoccleve's widely copied *Regiment*.[46] The very structure of the poem reveals its discursive relations: a 3447-line work in the Mirror for Princes tradition (offering advice for good rulership to a king) is preceded by a 2016-line Prologue, focused on the economic fragility of Hoccleve's household. The two areas—the economic and the political—are not at all unrelated: Hoccleve is impecunious in part because the royal household is badly managed, with irregular payments and unjust exploitation of scribes' work.

The resonance between the personal and the political is in fact much more pronounced: Hoccleve's striking account of a personified mental depression, or 'Thought', sucking the 'fresschest of my blod' (90) reveals the unruly political dangers that await kings of mismanaged realms. The young Prince is taught that his régime is dependent on his respecting the irrepressible, unruly bodies of his orthodox subjects. The advice that pertains to a king does not pertain to his subjects. Thus the king should not talk too much: 'it is fair and honurable, / A kyng from mochil speeche him refreyne'. He should instead, advises Hoccleve, be sparing in his speech, since 'mochil clap wole his estate desteyne [*damage*]' (2416–22). The subject, by contrast, must absolutely speak up, even if indirectly, so as to make the monarch listen. This is definitely 'patronal' poetry, but poetry in which the patron is guided to recognize that his interests overlap with those of his proxy-subject, the writing poet.

This Gowerian discursive tradition, transmitted through Hoccleve, passes to another Lancastrian poet, George Ashby (b. 1385?, d. 1475), who found himself in prison with time on his hands in 1463, when he wrote his *Prisoner's Reflections* (350 lines in rhyme royal stanzas), and *The Active Policy of a Prince* (918 lines in rhyme royal stanzas). Like Hoccleve, Ashby claims both Chaucer and Gower as his 'masters', and adds Lydgate (*Active Policy*, 1–7); and, like Hoccleve in the *Regiment*, Ashby encourages Prince Edward to pay the wages of his men in the *Active Policy* (296); in particular he should pay 'suche as be makers. / These may exalt your name and werkes' (613–4).[47]

---

[45] See David Starkey, 'The Age of the Household: Politics, Society and the Arts c.1350—c.1550', in Stephen Medcalf (ed.), *The Later Middle Ages* (London, 1981), 225–90.

[46] It survives in forty-five manuscripts, making it one of the most widely copied vernacular poems of the fourteenth and fifteenth centuries; see Nicholas Perkins, *Hoccleve's 'Regiment of Princes': Counsel and Constraint* (Cambridge, 2001).

[47] See Meyer-Lee, *Poets and Power from Chaucer to Wyatt*, 139–68, and Sebastian Sobecki, *Last Words: The Public Self and the Social Author in Late Medieval England* (Oxford, 2019), 159–91.

The *Piers Plowman* Tradition

Between at least 1377 (possibly from the late 1360s) and the mid-1380s,[48] a London-based poet from the West Midlands produced an extraordinary alliterative poem that exists in three, possibly four different versions. The poet has been named 'William Langland', but in my view that name is likely not a proper, biographical name. It is, rather, a thematized concept that will generate a poem. It is, to refer back to the rhetorical concept with which I began this essay, a place of poetic invention. Even if, as a note to an early manuscript has it, the poet's real name was Willielm[us] de Langlond,[49] the deeper possibilities of the name are exemplified by the poetic structure that emerges from it.

What, that is, if we were to regard that name as meaning 'the will [or desire] of the long land'? Immediately we would find ourselves in a poetic tradition of satirical, 'uplandish' poetry; in a theological tradition of '*longanimitas*' ('*long-suffering*') prompted by two Pauline epistles (2 Corinthians 6.6 and Galatians 5.22); and in a monastic tradition of the '*voluntas communis*' ('common will'), according to which model the monk is to suppress his 'proper' will, and to submit himself instead to the 'common will' of the monastery. Langland takes that monastic tradition out of the cloister.

The inventive posture of the Gower-tradition is to trace the trajectory whereby the voice of the narrator moves from a pathological personification of one part of the psyche (e.g., 'Amans', 'Thought') to recovering the proper name (e.g., 'John Gower', 'Thomas Hoccleve') of the full self that constructively reincorporates the previously pathological element. The *Piers Plowman* trajectory remains, by contrast, wholly within, and fulfilling the potential of, the personified name. 'Will Langland' wants to efface the distinction between author and reader, to bring every reader into the newly-imagined vernacular Church, the Barn of Unity, which brings the will of the long land to fulfilment.

That hugely ambitious project involves, as it must, a set of political, theological, and, most importantly, ecclesiological trajectories. Each is focused intently on the question of work and payment. The unfulfilled will, as desire, comes into sharp focus in economic discourse, as Langland creates a dramatic dialogue between Conscience and Mede, or Profit (Passus B. 2–4); those issues lead directly to payment in the world, as Langland imagines real-life wage payment scenes in England's post-Plague world of unruly labour relations (Passus B. 5–7); the collapse of those labour relations prompts an intense theological enquiry as to the nature and grounds of salutary payment from God, in which the will animates, and is informed by, a series of educational figures—Thought, Wit, Study, Imaginatif, and Conscience—who each contribute to the issue of proper reward from increasingly profound psychological depths (Passus B. 8–14); and that enquiry prepares the way for the poem's magnificent but doomed ecclesiological narrative, in which the historical grounds, the rebuilding, and the inherent strife of the Church militant—the sorting house of proper payment and reward—are all imagined. Here the vernacular Pope Piers Plowman is responsible for the distribution of spiritual reward within the 'Barn of Holy Church' (Passus B. 15–20).

---

[48] For the sequence, and therefore the dating, of the different versions of *Piers Plowman*, see Ralph Hanna, 'The Versions and Revisions of *Piers Plowman*', in Andrew Cole and Andrew Galloway (eds), *The Cambridge Companion to 'Piers Plowman'* (Cambridge, 2013), 33–49.

[49] For the scholarship around Langland's name, and a broader argument for the case made here, see James Simpson, 'The Power of Impropriety: Authorial Naming in *Piers Plowman*', in Kathleen M. Hewett-Smith (ed.), *William Langland's 'Piers Plowman': A Book of Essays* (New York, 2001), 145–65.

English poetry had seen nothing like this discursive sweep, and the looser, satirical, non-courtly exercise of alliterative diction and metre that it involves. Langland shapes a poetic 'ornatus', or style, that is just as capable of capturing the most corporeal aspects of empirical reality with Breughelesque particularity as it is of abstract but urgent scholastic argument. Langland's English confidently invades and enlivens territories previously guarded by scholastic and institutional Latinity.

After *Piers Plowman*, neither would English poetry see anything of the scale or vitality, both poetic and intellectual, of the late fourteenth-century poem. That said, there is most definitely a very late fourteenth- and early fifteenth-century *Piers Plowman* tradition, in which poets with different agendas adroitldeploy satirical strategies they have learned from *Piers Plowman*, even if they apply those strategies within a very much narrower discursive range.[50] Thus both *Piers the Plowman's Creed* (850 alliterative lines, certainly written after 1393 and probably before 1400), and *Mum and the Sothsegger* (?1409, 1751 alliterative lines, though acephalous and atelous), for example, are finely sensitive to the perils of articulating dangerous truths. Each manoeuvres cunningly to authorize and project its own truth-telling voice, by apparently innocent consultation of all the sources of institutional counsel that should transmit the truth. As each of these sources manifestly fails to deliver said counsel, so too does each poem engage in authority distributions of inverse relation: sources of institutional authority *lose* authority to precisely the same degree that the poems themselves *gain* it. *Mum* applies this tactic to the situation of Parliament (like another alliterative poem in the *Piers Plowman* tradition, *Richard the Redeles*, written very early in the reign of Henry IV), whereas *Piers the Plowman's Creed* is a rare example of proto-Lollard poetic polemic against the mendicant orders.

It is no doubt significant that this tradition seems to recede after the first decade of the fifteenth century. Its voice is, in Watson's typology, very much communal, projecting texts from one equal to many others. In the realm of religious discourse, that voice came under significant threat with Arundel's *Constitutions* (issued 1409). Communal Lollard discourse, no less than pastoral discourse that sought to open dialogue with Lollard, was, for the most part, written in non-literary prose.[51] Both forms of discourse were under hostile surveillance and repression.

All the more remarkable and interesting, then, is John Audelay's brilliant poem *Marcolf and Solomon* (c?1414, 1013 lines, in stanzas of thirteen lines, eight alliterative rhyming lines, followed by a five-line rhyming sequence with three- and four-stress lines). As is often the case for literature produced under menacing conditions, the poet's voice fragments, eludes confident detection, and creates discursive fluidity.[52] Audelay exploits a traditional discursive position, that of the fool, Marcolf, who writes to a wise man, Solomon. The poem is written in the voice of Marcolf, on behalf of 'homle [homely] hosbondusmen' (68) (a communal voice), but it manages to create escape routes as it broaches dangerous territory: Marcolf is not so much making this complaint as asking the wise man, Salomon, to pass it on to official audiences. Marcolf's voice is a kind of funnel, though which scraps of reported speech, including prophecy and official legislation, flow. The

---

[50] For the fifteenth-century texts of this tradition, see Helen Barr (ed.), *The Piers Plowman Tradition* (London, 1993).

[51] For post-Arundel theological discourse, see Watson, 'Censorship and Cultural Change', and Vincent Gillespie, 'Chichele's Church: Vernacular Theology in England after Thomas Arundel', in Vincent Gillespie and Kantik Ghosh (eds), *After Arundel: Religious Writing in Fifteenth-Century England* (Turnhout, 2011), 3–42.

[52] For *Marcolf and Solomon*, see Susanna Greer Fein (ed.), *John the Blind Audelay* (Kalamazoo, MI, 2009), item 2.

poem's voice and audience is fragmented: both often change, without warning, within the same stanza. 'Marcolf' displays detailed knowledge of *Piers Plowman*, since the poem is brimming with citations of the earlier text. And like *Piers Plowman*, this poem's constantly shifting audience finally forms one audience: a Church from which no one is irredeemably excluded.[53]

Historical Alliterative Poetry

The astonishing efflorescence of alliterative poetry in the last half of the fourteenth century begins, so far as we can tell, with the crisply intelligent debate-poem *Winner and Waster* (1353) and the romance *William of Palerne* (1350s). We should not properly call this body of poetry a 'regional tradition', since it is neither regionally specific nor, as a body of poetry, a tradition in any but a very weak sense. On the contrary, it is geographically and generically diverse; and the connections of many individual alliterative poems are most productively made with works in the same genre in non-alliterative metres. This body of work is not chronologically concentrated, or at least not so far as the evidence permits. We cannot, for example, as we can with our other *corpora*, confidently match certain poems of the late fourteenth century with fifteenth-century followers.[54] From the evidence of both vocabulary and metre we can, however, distinguish a largely North-Midland from a more southern group of texts. The northern texts deploy a more specific poetic vocabulary; they also observe metrical norms with greater regularity than the more southern group. The more southern group (i.e., the texts discussed in the previous section) are also, despite the marked differences, all in the broad genre of satire. Among the northern texts, one genre is represented with a certain strength, that of historical narrative, either classical or Arthurian.

I therefore turn here to the more 'classical' alliterative texts, and in particular to the historical narratives, starting with the (?) late fourteenth-century *Destruction of Troy*. Possibly fifteenth-century texts within this field are *The Wars of Alexander* (1350–1450), and *The Alliterative Morte Arthure* (4346 lines, probably composed around 1400, and copied between 1420–40).[55] I do not dwell on another exceptionally accomplished body of alliterative poetry, that of the *Gawain*-poet (?1390s), with which one might associate the no less accomplished *St Erkenwald* (late fourteenth century), since those poems have no fifteenth-century followers.

The author of the *Destruction of Troy* (14,044 alliterative lines, and therefore the longest alliterative poem of this period) was a certain Master John Clerk of Whalley in Lancashire, the site of a Cistercian Abbey.[56] The text makes reference to *Troilus and Criseyde*, and must also therefore postdate c1385; it must also, I think, predate 1400, since a passage in the *Siege*

---

[53] See James Simpson, 'Saving Satire after Arundel: John Audelay's *Marcolf and Solomon*', in Ann Hutchison and Helen Barr (eds), *Text and Controversy from Wyclif to Bale, Essays in Honour of Anne Hudson* (Turnhout, 2005), 387–404.

[54] Thorlac Turville-Petre, *Description and Narration in Middle English Alliterative Poetry* (Liverpool, 2018), 1–3.

[55] John J. Thompson, *Robert Thornton and the London Thornton Manuscript* (Woodbridge, 1987), 2–5.

[56] Observed from the initial letters of the chapter headings (forming an acrostic of the author's title, name and place), by Thorlac Turville-Petre, 'The Author of the *Destruction of Troy*', *Medium Ævum*, 57 (1988), 264–9.

of *Jerusalem* (also pre-1400) seems evidently drawn from the *Destruction*.⁵⁷ It survives in a single sixteenth-century manuscript.⁵⁸

Almost everything that has been said about Lydgate's *Troy Book* above can be said about the *Destruction*. Like the *Troy Book*, it is a translation of Guido delle Colonne's *Historia destructionis Troiae* (1287), and like the *Troy Book* it unfolds the larger, specifically medieval Troy narrative, from the prior destruction of Troy through the second, more well-known destruction, through to the catastrophic return of the victorious Greeks to their homeland.⁵⁹ And, like the *Troy Book* again, it presents history as badly made by aristocrats in committees. This is not a providential, Virgilian history of increasingly manifest destiny: it is instead a tragic narrative of militarist adventurisms going horribly and avoidably wrong.

The Destruction of Troy is a patronal text, directed at non-metropolitan English nobility and gentry, so as both to connect them to larger Mediterranean histories, and to offer urgent lessons from those distant histories that had immediate import for the conduct of late medieval international war. The Prologue to one of these Western, alliterative poems, *The Wars of Alexander*, reveals the kind of intimate, patronal, household world implied by many historical alliterative texts (though wholly absent from the *Piers Plowman* tradition):⁶⁰

> When folk ere festid and fed, fayn wald thai here
> Sum farand thinge eftir fode to fayn[en] thare hertis,
> Or thai ware fourmed on fold or thaire fadirs other ...
> Sum covettis & has comforth to carpe & to lestyn
> Of curtaissy, of knyghthode, of craftis of armys,
> Of kyngis that has conquirid & ovircomyn landis ...
> And I forthwith yow all ettillis to schewe
> Of ane emperoure the aghefullest that ever armys haunted;
> That was the athill Alexsandire, as the buke tellis ...
> I sall rehers, & ye will, renkis, rekyn your tongis,
> A remnant of his rialte, & rist quen us likis.

(When guests have been well feasted, they eagerly wish to hear some suitable [narrative] to please their hearts, about times before they or their parents existed ... Some people are delighted to speak and to hear about courtliness, about knighthood and martial skill, about kings who have conquered territories ... And I, in your company, intend to present [the story of] an emperor, the most awesome who ever practised warfare. That was the noble Alexander, as the text relates ... I shall relate, if you permit me, lords, and if you govern your tongues, some part of his magnificence; we can pause when we please.)

---

⁵⁷ For the relationship between the *Siege of Jerusalem* and the *Destruction*, see Mary Hamel (ed.), *Morte Arthure, A Critical Edition* (New York, 1984), 54–5. For the allusion to *Troilus and Criseyde* in the *Destruction*, see C. David Benson, 'A Chaucerian Allusion and the Date of the Alliterative *Destruction of Troy*', *Notes and Queries*, n.s. 21 (1974), 206–7.

⁵⁸ C. A Luttrell, 'Three North-West Midland Manuscripts', *Neophilologus*, 42 (1958), 38–50.

⁵⁹ For a larger presentation of the text, including a synopsis of the plot, see James Simpson, 'The Other Book of Troy: Guido delle Colonne's *Historia destructionis Troiae* in Fourteenth- and Fifteenth-Century England', *Speculum*, 73 (1998), 397–423.

⁶⁰ Hoyt Duggan and Thorlac Turville-Petre (eds), *The Wars of Alexander*, EETS, s.s. 10 (Oxford, 1989), lines 1–22.

The poets of *The Destruction of Troy*, *The Wars of Alexander*, and *The Alliterative Morte Arthur* are not lightweight minstrels; they entertain, but with solid, extended matter drawn from 'authentic' historical books; they treat their larger than life militarist heroes with immense, not to say spectacular, rhetorical respect; they draw no attention to themselves as a presence in the narration or their audience as interpretative readers. Above all, they unflinchingly relate tragic matter: each text points to the brutal downward turn of Fortune's wheel.[61] Each of these matters (Trojan, Alexandrian, Arthurian) also has fifteenth-century histories in non-alliterative prose traditions.[62]

We have considered four corpora of late fourteenth-century poetry, and followed the fortune of each into the fifteenth century. The fate of these different *corpora* through and beyond the fifteenth century is determined by many factors, notably the centralization of literary language and production in London, accelerated by the introduction of print and then by dispersal of monastic libraries; and the cataclysmic ructions of religious change from the 1530s, both institutional and theological. Chaucer, Gower, and the secular poetry of Lydgate fared well, especially Chaucer. The *Piers Plowman* tradition survived but in shadow form, as its theology of works was officially repudiated. The alliterative historical tradition did not survive as a living tradition.

---

[61] See Alex Mueller, *Translating Troy: Provincial Politics in Alliterative Romance* (Columbus, OH, 2013).

[62] Thus, for Troy, for example: William Caxton, *The Recuyell of the Historyes of Troye, translated by William Caxton*, ed. H. Oskar Sommer, 2 vols. (London, 1894), originally published from Bruges 1473–4, as the first printed book published in English. For Alexander, *The Prose Life of Alexander*, ed. J. S. Westlake, EETS, o.s. 143 (London, 1913), found in Lincoln Cathedral MS 91 (c1420 x 40). And for Arthur: William Caxton, *Caxton's Malory*, ed. James W. Spisak, 2 vols. (Berkeley, CA, 1983), originally published in print in 1485.

CHAPTER 4
Translation into English

Marco Nievergelt

The medieval understanding of translation is notoriously fluid and capacious, and includes a range of textual activities that modern readers would likely define as instances of adaptation, creative emulation, or rewriting, as opposed to 'translation' in the narrow sense.[1] This makes it difficult to categorize a large group of texts that are not translations in the strict, modern sense. In the case of specifically *literary* translation, such difficulties also highlight the discrepancy between modern and medieval literary aesthetics, and divergent attitudes towards authorship, notions of literary invention, and originality of thought and expression. Any discussion of the perceived 'literary value' of late medieval verse translations will necessarily have to take such problems into account.[2]

This fluid and nebulous nature of medieval ideas of translation, however, also highlights its central importance in fifteenth-century textual, literary, and intellectual culture. The present chapter therefore pursues two rather different aims. On the one hand, it is intended to provide a balanced descriptive survey of the thematic, generic, formal, and expressive range of fifteenth-century poetic translations into English, within their specific cultural, literary, and socio-political contexts. On the other hand, the chapter also aims to shed light on the more elusive but imaginatively central importance of the *idea* of translation for the development of fifteenth-century English poetry, poetics, and literary culture. It is not coincidental that some of the most influential fifteenth-century English poets such as John Lydgate and Thomas Hoccleve were also engaged in several major translation projects throughout their respective careers (see further Chapters 24 and 25). Like many other fifteenth-century poets, Hoccleve and Lydgate engaged in translation not so much as an alternative to producing original poetic compositions, but rather as an active means to forge their own, distinctive poetic styles in English. As much as involving a simple 'transfer' of texts from one language into another, then, *translatio* was a habit of mind that infused poetic activity as a whole during the fifteenth century, and enabled a dialogic, critical, appropriative, or confrontational engagement with various kinds of cultural difference.

Translation and Cultural Transition, c1380–1425

Like much else in the history of fifteenth-century English literature, the evolution of translation was substantially shaped by developments occurring during the final decades of the fourteenth century. The period between c1380 and 1425 saw 'a previously unparalleled

---

[1] Among seminal discussions of medieval translation, see especially Roger Ellis (ed.), *The Medieval Translator: The Theory and Practice of Translation in the Middle Ages* (Cambridge, 1989); and Rita Copeland, *Rhetoric, Hermeneutics, and Translation in the Middle Ages* (Cambridge, 1991).

[2] For a detailed overview of literary translation into English until 1550, see especially Roger Ellis (ed.), *Oxford History of Literary Translation into English. Vol. 1: to 1550* (Oxford, 2008), henceforth cited as Ellis, *OHLTE*.

increase in the production of translations' from both Latin and French.³ A variety of factors contributed to this rapid acceleration, and for the purposes of the present analysis it will be useful to identify five different ones. Firstly, the history of fifteenth-century translation was deeply shaped by the production of the Wycliffite Bible, in English prose, from the 1380s onwards. While there was nothing intrinsically heterodox or subversive in Bible translation as such at the close of the fourteenth century,⁴ the condemnations of John Wycliff and his followers created a climate of pervasive suspicion, triggering an extended and acrimonious debate over the legitimacy of vernacular translations of biblical, religious, theological, and ecclesiological texts in early fifteenth-century Oxford.⁵ This clearly had an adverse effect on the development of translations of religious texts,⁶ although official policy largely failed in its attempt to curb the circulation of the Wycliffite Bible itself, which survives in about 250 manuscripts, making it the most widely read translation of the fifteenth century as a whole.

Secondly, during the 1380s and 90s John Trevisa undertook the first extensive programme of translation into English in post-Conquest Britain, at the behest of his patron, Thomas, Lord Berkeley.⁷ Moving in the same circles as the scholars responsible for the 'Wycliffite' Bible, Trevisa chose prose as his medium, emphasizing its greater truth-value. As is declared by his semi-fictional patron figure in the *Dialogue between a Lord and a Clerk*, in the prologue to Trevisa's translation of Ranulph Higden's *Polychronicon* (1387): 'for comynliche prose is more clere than ryme, more easy and more pleyn to know and to understonde'.⁸ Observations of this kind eventually led to the establishment of prose as the dominant medium for translations during the fifteenth century.⁹

As a third factor, political, dynastic, and administrative developments equally facilitated the unprecedented increase in translation activity during the period between c1380 and 1425. Translations into English were encouraged, and later actively promoted, by the Ricardian and early Lancastrian courts. Although English rulers never pursued a systematic programme of vernacularization that could rival that of Charles V of France (reigning 1364–80),¹⁰ in the context of early Lancastrian efforts of dynastic legitimation it becomes possible to speak of an actual language policy.¹¹ Beyond this, the development of English as a language in regular administrative use, eventually leading to the rise of 'Chancery

---

³ Roger Ellis, 'The Translator: Introduction', in Ellis, *OHLTE*, 95–7 (at 96).

⁴ David Lawton, 'The Bible', in Ellis, *OHLTE*, 193–233 (at 199–202, 217–24).

⁵ See further Anne Hudson, 'The Debate on Bible Translation, Oxford 1401', *English Historical Review*, 90 (1975), 1–18; Nicholas Watson, 'Censorship and Cultural Change in Late-Medieval England: Vernacular Theology, the Oxford Translation Debate, and Arundel's Constitutions of 1409', *Speculum*, 70 (1995), 822–64.

⁶ For a detailed discussion of the long-term effects of this culture of censorship, see Kantik Ghosh and Vincent Gillespie (eds), *After Arundel: Religious Writing in Fifteenth-Century England* (Turnhout, 2011).

⁷ Traugott Lawler, 'On the Properties of John Trevisa's Major Translations', *Viator*, 14 (1983), 267–88; David Fowler, *The Life and Times of John Trevisa, Medieval Scholar* (Seattle, WA, 1995); John Trevisa, in Ronald Waldron (ed.), 'Trevisa's Original Prefaces on Translation: A Critical Edition', in Edward D. Kennedy, Ronald Waldron, and Joseph S. Wittig (eds), *Medieval English Studies Presented to George Kane* (Wolfeboro, NH, 1988), 285–95.

⁸ In Jocelyn Wogan-Browne, Nicholas Watson, Andrew Taylor, and Ruth Evans (eds), *The Idea of the Vernacular: An Anthology of Middle English Literary Theory, 1280–1520* (Philadelphia, PA, 1999), 130–8 (at 134).

⁹ Lawler, 'On the Properties of John Trevisa's Major Translations'; Fowler, *The Life and Times of John Trevisa*; Waldron, 'Trevisa's Original Prefaces'.

¹⁰ For a useful discussion of differences in literary and cultural sponsorship of the French and English courts in the period, with particular attention to translation and commentary, see Alastair J. Minnis, *Translations of Authority in Middle English Literature: Valuing the Vernacular* (Cambridge, 2009), 1–4, 17–37.

¹¹ John H. Fisher, 'A Language Policy for Lancastrian England', *PMLA*, 107 (1992), 1168–80; Derek Pearsall, 'The Idea of Englishness in the Fifteenth Century', in Helen Cooney (ed.), *Nation, Court and Culture: New Essays on Fifteenth-Century Poetry* (Dublin, 2001), 15–27.

English',[12] equally heightened the prestige of the vernacular and facilitated intensified translation activity throughout the fifteenth century.

Fourthly, the history of translation during the fifteenth century was also shaped by broader political circumstances, particularly the protracted war with France. The modern tendency to view linguistic choices through the prism of national identity, however, is misleading on many counts in this case.[13] Since the Hundred Years War itself had been triggered by an English king's claim to the French crown, all English kings from Edward III to Henry VI continued to represent themselves as Kings of France. This created opportunities for a range of complex processes of cultural appropriation and accommodation,[14] and many translations from French into English produced during the first quarter of the century—a time of spectacular English military successes in France—therefore participate in a larger effort of political legitimation on the part of the new Lancastrian dynasty. In parallel, francophone and specifically Parisian literary fashions continued to dominate English court culture throughout the late fourteenth and fifteenth centuries. The influence of francophone culture persisted into the Tudor period, albeit in mutated form, sustained by a complex web of Anglo-continental relations and alliances, particularly with important figures linked to the Duchy of Burgundy.[15]

A final, strictly literary factor that helped to accelerate the emergence of English as a literary language was the legacy of Geoffrey Chaucer. Crucially, early readers viewed Chaucer as an eminent translator—a '*grant translateur*', as Eustache Deschamps put it in 1385[16]— and this shaped the subsequent evolution of literary translation into English. Translations by Hoccleve and Lydgate are famously explicit about their debts to their master,[17] but Chaucerian features also characterize a much wider range of verse translations, as will be seen below. Chaucer's trademark verse form, the seven-line rhyme royal stanza (*ababbcc*), proved particularly popular.

Religious and Devotional Poetry

The repression of religious heterodoxy by the authorities, together with the Oxford translation debate, made the translation of religious materials a hazardous undertaking in the period. Furthermore, the gradual rise of prose as the preferred vehicle for religious instruction had an adverse effect on the translation of religious verse during this period: not

---

[12] See John H. Fisher, 'Chancery and the Emergence of Standard Written English in the Fifteenth Century', *Speculum*, 52 (1977), 870–99; and Malcolm Richardson, 'Henry V, the English Chancery, and Chancery English', *Speculum*, 55 (1980), 726–50; Seth Lerer, 'Chancery, Caxton, and the Making of English Prose', in Seth Lerer (ed.), *Inventing English: A Portable History of the Language* (New York, 2007), 115–28. The term 'Chancery English' remains problematic and disputed.

[13] Pearsall, 'The Idea of Englishness in the Fifteenth Century'.

[14] See especially Ardis Butterfield, *The Familiar Enemy: Chaucer, Language, and Nation in the Hundred Years War* (Oxford, 2009), and Joanna Bellis, *The Hundred Year War in Literature, 1337–1600* (Cambridge, 2016).

[15] Marie-Rose Thielmans, *Bourgogne et Angleterre, relations politiques et économiques entre les Pays-Bas bourguignons et l'Angleterre 1435–1467* (Brussels, 1966); Gordon Kipling, *The Triumph of Honour: Burgundian Origins of the Elizabethan Renaissance* (Leiden, 1977). Specifically on translations from French, see A. E. B. Coldiron, 'Translation's Challenge to Critical Categories: Verses from French in the Early English Renaissance', *The Yale Journal of Criticism*, 16 (2003), 315–44; Coldiron, 'A Survey of Verse Translations from French Printed Between Caxton and Tottel', in Ian F. Moulton (ed.), *Reading and Literacy: in the Middle Ages and Renaissance* (Turnhout, 2004), 63–84.

[16] See Barry Windeatt, 'Geoffrey Chaucer', in Ellis, *OHLTE*, 137–48.

[17] See further e.g. David R. Carlson, 'The Chronology of Lydgate's Chaucer References', *The Chaucer Review*, 38 (2004), 246–54; and John M. Bowers, 'Thomas Hoccleve and the Politics of Tradition', *The Chaucer Review*, 36 (2002), 352–69.

only the 'Wycliffite' Bible was written in prose, but so were many of the most popular state-sponsored religious classics of the century intended to supplant it, such as Nicholas Love's translation of the pseudo-Bonaventuran *Mirror of the Life of our Blessed Lord Jesus Christ*.[18]

The smaller number of religious verse translations that were produced at the time often seized on older and more traditional sources that were immune to potential accusations of heresy. Saints' lives, many of which were redacted in verse, became particularly popular around the middle of the century (see further Chapter 12). Many of these focused on female saints and were written for female patrons and female readers.[19] John Lydgate played a particularly important role in popularizing the genre, beginning with the widely circulated *Life of our Lady* (1409–22?), running to around 6000 lines, and the much shorter *Life of St Margaret* (1426), both in rhyme royal.[20] While not translations in the strict sense, but rather adaptations of traditional narratives compiling a range of sources, both poems are characterized by an interest in specifically feminine saintly qualities. This ideal of feminized sainthood also served as a foundation to construct a new, distinctive ideal of poetic inspiration.[21] Lydgate's female saints' lives thus helped to popularize a new form of self-consciously literary religious poetry in English, using verse to render an affectively powerful hagiographical narrative and to promote orthodox devotional practices and reading habits.[22]

These and other popular saints' lives by Lydgate helped to spark a wider trend for the genre that was particularly pronounced in East Anglia (see further Chapter 12). Among the most notable translations in this later tradition it is worth signalling those of John Capgrave and Osbern Bokenham. Both were Augustinian friars, and both benefitted from the patronage of members of the East Anglian gentry and aristocracy, particularly women. Bokenham is responsible for a remarkable collection of female saints' lives in verse, the *Legendys of Hooly Wummen* (1443–7), written in a mixture of different Chaucerian verse forms, alternating rhyme royal and the eight-line stanza form of the 'Monk's Tale',[23] as well as a much larger, recently rediscovered collection of saints' lives in a mixture of verse and prose.[24]

John Capgrave translated a total of four saints' lives into English, two of which are in verse, produced during an earlier phase of his prolific writing career. The *Life of St Norbert* (1420–40) runs to 4109 lines in rhyme royal,[25] while the *Life of St Katharine* (mid- to

---

[18] Michael G. Sargent (ed.), *Nicholas Love's Mirror of the Blessed Life of Jesus Christ: a Critical Edition* (New York, 1992). A useful list of didactic prose treatises is provided as an Appendix in Watson, 'Censorship and Cultural Change'.

[19] A. S. G. Edwards, 'Fifteenth-Century English Collections of Female Saints' Lives', *The Yearbook of English Studies*, 33 (2003), 131–41.

[20] NIMEV 2574 and 439. See respectively John Lydgate, in Joseph A. Lauritis, Vernon F. Gallagher, and Ralph A. Klinefelter (eds), *A Critical Edition of John Lydgate's Life of Our Lady* (Pittsburgh, PA, 1961); and Henry Noble MacCracken (ed.), *The Minor Poems of John Lydgate: Part I, the Religious Poems*, EETS, e.s. 107 (London, 1911), 173–92.

[21] Amanda Walling, 'Feminizing Aureation in Lydgate's *Life of Our Lady* and *Life of Saint Margaret*', *Neophilologus*, 101 (2017), 321–36.

[22] See further Robert J. Meyer-Lee, 'The Emergence of the Literary in John Lydgate's *Life of Our Lady*', *JEGP*, 109.3 (2010), 322–34; Katherine K. O'Sullivan, 'John Lydgate's *Lyf of Our Lady*: Translation and Authority in Fifteenth-Century England', *Mediaevalia*, 26 (2005), 169–201.

[23] Osbern Bokenham, in Mary S. Serjeantson (ed.), *Legendys of Hooly Wummen*. EETS, o.s. 206 (London, 1938).

[24] Simon Horobin, 'A Manuscript Found in the Library of Abbotsford House and the Lost Legendary of Osbern Bokenham', *English Manuscript Studies 1100–1700*, 14 (2008), 132–62. For the first two volumes of the edition, in progress, see Simon Horobin (ed.), *Osbern Bokenham: Lives of Saints*. Vols. I, II, EETS, o.s. 356, 359 (Oxford, 2020, 2022).

[25] NIMEV 1805, in Cyril Smetana (ed.), *The Life of St Norbert* (Toronto, 1977).

late 1440s) adopts the same verse form but stretches to some 8000 lines organized into five books, perhaps in imitation of Chaucer's *Troilus and Criseyde* or some of Lydgate's saints' lives.[26] *Katharine* is in many ways a poem of epic proportions, not only for its length, intricacy, and ambition, but also because of the breadth of its subject matter, its continuously shifting register, its abundant use of popular romance tradition, and its multivalent understanding of the principle of *translatio*.[27] Both the verse lives of Katharine and Norbert also provide further examples of how the new vogue of verse hagiography sought to establish its literary credentials by adopting an unmistakeably Chaucerian aesthetic.[28]

Alongside such extended lives of individual saints, religious verse of very different kinds continued to be translated. Much religious poetry in translation consists of shorter, often occasional, and anecdotal verses included within larger works or miscellanies. Among such shorter works we find a large corpus of short verses, couplets, or tags embedded in preaching manuals and sermons,[29] and an even larger number of translations of short devotional lyrics, from Passion and Annunciation lyrics to prayers or complaints.[30] Many of these translations adopted the aureate poetic style popularized by Lydgate, which gradually became the dominant stylistic register for religious poetry in the fifteenth century. But the adoption of an aureate style in this period was far more than a strictly aesthetic and stylistic choice, and often signalled a desire to buttress the authority of the official ecclesiastical establishment and its spiritual prerogatives by using a heavily latinate register and deliberately convoluted syntax, as in this anonymous fifteenth-century Marian lyric, added to an older manuscript, BL MS Add. 20059 (fols 99–100):

> By the spectable* splendure of hir fulgent* face   *virtuous, shining*
> My sprete* was ravesshed and in my body sprent*;   *spirit; leapt*
> Inflamed was my hert with gret solace
> Of the luciant corruscall resplendent*.   *shining shimmering resplendent one*
>
> Then this curious cumpany incontinent*   *immediately*
> Withe the seraphynnes in their solemnyté
> Solemply sang this subsequent*:   *as follows*
>   Ecce virgo, radix Jesse.[31]   *Behold a virgin, root of Jesse*

By creating a high degree of verbal complexity and conceptual density, the aureate style was thus used to signal the rarefied nature of the religious experience itself, often suggesting that a doctrinally appropriate understanding of spiritual rapture was dependent on effective clerical guidance, mediation, and exposition.[32] John Audelay makes precisely this point in *Marcolf and Solomon*, in a passage that describes an ecstatic vision of the Trinity while reminding readers of their dependence on the clarifications of a 'clerke':

---

[26] NIMEV 6, in Carl Horstmann (ed.), *The Life of St Katharine of Alexandria*, EETS, o.s. 100 (London, 1893).
[27] Nicholas Watson, 'Theories of Translation', in Ellis, *OHLTE*, 76–8.
[28] See further Karen A. Winstead, 'John Capgrave and the Chaucer Tradition', *The Chaucer Review*, 30 (1996), 389–400.
[29] On sermons see especially Alan J. Fletcher, *Preaching, Politics and Poetry in Late-Medieval England* (Dublin, 1998); Fletcher, 'The Lyric in the Sermon', in Thomas G. Duncan (ed.), *A Companion to the Middle English Lyric* (Cambridge, 2005), 189–209.
[30] For an indicative overview, including many translations, see Peter Revell, *Fifteenth-Century English Prayers and Meditations: A Descriptive List of Manuscripts in the British Library* (New York, 1975).
[31] NIMEV 3391; Karen Saupe (ed.), *Middle English Marian Lyrics* (Kalamazoo, MI, 1997), 113–15, lines 41–8.
[32] See Christiania Whitehead, 'The Middle English Religious Lyric', in Duncan (ed.), *A Companion to the Middle English Lyric*, 96–119 (117–19); Gillespie 'Religious Writing', in Ellis, *OHLTE*, 234–83 (254).

I se, sothlé, in the sune* knyt thre maner kynde,	*son*
His clerté* and his clerenes, what clerke can declare*	*brightness, explain*
Bohold the hete in thi hert, and have hit in mynd.³³	

The vast majority of these materials, often short and anonymous, survive in miscellanies, and are often difficult to place in a precise context, exemplifying the challenges involved in mapping religious translations not associated with major individual authors or prominent patrons. But some major authors too were involved in producing such shorter occasional verse, a case in point being Thomas Hoccleve's translation of the 'Lament of the Virgin' from a French source, one of the popular allegorical *Pèlerinage*-poems by the French Cistercian Guillaume de Deguileville, active between 1331 and c1358–60.³⁴ Recent work has highlighted the complex transmission history of Hoccleve's translation, symptomatic for the wider difficulty of tracing the circulation and reception for this kind of religious verse.³⁵

Moral, Allegorical, and Courtly Verse

The complex transmission history of Hoccleve's 'Lament' needs to be placed within the wider context of the English reception of Deguileville's *Pèlerinages*. The popularity of the *Pèlerinages* trilogy is in turn part of a wider surge of interest in allegorical poetry during the period between c1380–1440, presenting moral and didactic instruction in the form of extended fictional verse narratives. The earliest Deguileville translation in English was Chaucer's rendering of the 'ABC prayer', an embedded lyric from the earliest poem in Deguileville's allegorical trilogy, the *Pèlerinage de vie humaine* (two versions, 1331 and 1355 respectively), and possibly produced for Blanche of Lancaster.³⁶ Chaucer's translation is found inserted into a later, complete prose translation of the first version of the *Pèlerinage de vie humaine* by an anonymous translator, *The Pilgrimage of the Life of the Manhode*, usually dated to the first third of the fifteenth century.³⁷

Chaucer's prayer is also conspicuous through its 'absent presence' in a later verse translation of the second, much expanded redaction of Deguileville's *Pèlerinage de vie humaine* (c1355),³⁸ John Lydgate's *Pilgrimage of the Life of Man* (1426).³⁹ Although Lydgate explicitly celebrates the literary merits of Chaucer's prayer in this section of his translation, the two complete manuscripts of Lydgate's *Pilgrimage of the Life of Man* both feature an extended gap that was designed to accommodate Chaucer's 'ABC' but was never filled. Beyond its unmistakable Chaucerian affiliations, Lydgate's *Pilgrimage of the Life of Man* is also shaped by a set of larger, broadly propagandist agendas—religious, cultural, and political.

---

[33] NIMEV 947, in Susanna Fein (ed.), *Poems and Carols (Oxford, Bodleian Library MS Douce 302)* (Kalamazoo, MI, 2009), lines 858–60. While the poem is generally treated as an original composition featuring alliterative diction and Audelay's trademark thirteen-line stanza, the relation of Audelay's poem to the wider oral tradition of Solomon and Marcolf dialogues and any potential written sources remains to be more closely examined. For further discussion of Audelay's poetry, see Chapter 13.

[34] NIMEV 2428. Guillaume de Deguileville, in J. J. Stürzinger (ed.), *Le pèlerinage de vie humaine* (London, 1893), and in J. J. Stürzinger (ed.), *Le pèlerinage de l'âme* (London, 1895); and J. J. Stürzinger (ed.), *Le pèlerinage Jhésucrist* (London, 1897).

[35] Josephine Houghton 'Deguileville and Hoccleve Again', *Medium Ævum*, 82 (2013), 260–8.

[36] NIMEV 239. Helen Phillips, 'Chaucer and Deguileville: The ABC in Context', *Medium Ævum*, 62 (1993), 1–19; Kathryn L. Lynch, 'Dating Chaucer', *The Chaucer Review*, 42 (2007), 1–22.

[37] Avril Henry (ed.), *The Pilgrimage of the Lyfe of the Manhode*, 2 vols., EETS, o.s. 288 and 292 (Oxford, 1985 and 1988).

[38] Graham R. Edwards and Philippe Maupeu (eds and trans), *Le livre du pèlerin de vie humaine* (Paris, 2015).

[39] NIMEV 4265; Frederick J. Furnivall and Katharine B. Locock (eds), *The Pilgrimage of the Life of Man*, 3 vols., EETS, o.s. 78, 83 and 92 (London, 1899–1904).

On the one hand, it has been argued that Lydgate harnessed the powerfully visual quality of Deguileville's pilgrimage allegory to elaborate a sophisticated theory about the legitimate use of religious imagery.[40] On the other hand, Lydgate's translation of Deguileville's pious moral allegory must also be seen in a more strictly political context, as part of Anglo-French hostilities. As is suggested by the extended, heavily militaristic dedication to the commander of the English forces in France, Thomas Montague (lines 122–79),

> ... my lord
> Of Salysbvry, the noble manly knyght
> Wych in Fravnce, for the kynges Ryht,
> In the werre hath meny day contunyd,
> Whom God & grace han ful wel ffortunyd,
> In thenpryses* which he hath vndertake.   *deeds*
> (123-7)

Lydgate's translation participates in a larger Lancastrian attempt to affirm its hold on francophone literary culture, supplementing military aggression with a project of cultural and linguistic appropriation.

The vogue for this kind of francophone allegorical poetry in England more broadly was ultimately triggered by the hugely influential and ever-controversial *Roman de la Rose*, completed by Jean de Meun in the 1270s, and partially translated by Geoffrey Chaucer roughly a century later.[41] Because of its perceived misogyny, at the start of the fifteenth century the *Rose* also came to be at the heart of a sustained literary controversy involving Christine de Pizan, Jean Gerson, the Col brothers, and Jean de Montreuil (1401–3).[42] Christine de Pizan had already begun confronting the underlying antifeminism of the courtly tradition before the beginning of the *querelle* proper, notably with the *Epistre au dieu d'Amours* (1399), a fictional letter ostensibly authored by Cupid himself. Christine's poem was translated into English rhyme royal as *The Letter of Cupid* by Thomas Hoccleve in 1402, making it Hoccleve's earliest datable work.[43] The translation is revealing in terms of Hoccleve's early literary aspirations, which are both distinctly Francophile and strongly Chaucerian, echoing Chaucer's defence of virtuous female heroines in the *Legend of Good Women* and elsewhere. But Hoccleve's handling of the gender politics in the poem appears awkward and inconclusive: where Christine confidently occupies her authorial position to denounce the latent antifeminism of the courtly tradition, Hoccleve's letter lacks a clearly identifiable authorial position, referring to a wide range of discordant viewpoints, and even relapsing into conventional misogynist stereotypes.[44]

---

[40] Shannon Gayk, *Image, Text, and Religious Reform in Fifteenth-Century England* (Cambridge, 2010), 87–95.

[41] Guillaume de Lorris and Jean de Meun, in Félix Lecoy (ed.), *Le Roman de la Rose*, 3 vols. (Paris, 1965–70); and (NIMEV 2092), Charles Dahlberg (ed.), *The Romaunt of the Rose by Geoffrey Chaucer* (Norman, OK, 1999). On the reception of the *Rose* and its tradition in England see Julia Boffey, 'English Dream Poems of the Fifteenth Century and Their French Connections', in Donald Maddox and Sara Sturm-Maddox (eds), *Literary Aspects of Courtly Culture: Selected Papers from the Seventh Triennial Congress of the International Courtly Literature Society* (Cambridge, 1994), 113–21; and Philip Knox, *The Romance of the Rose and the Making of Fourteenth-Century English Literature* (Oxford, 2021).

[42] Christine de Pizan et al., in David F. Hult (ed. and trans.), *The Debate of the 'Romance of the Rose'* (Chicago, IL, 2010).

[43] Both Christine's original and Hoccleve's translation (NIMEV 666) are edited in Thelma S. Fenster and Mary C. Erler (eds), *Poems of Cupid, God of Love: Christine de Pizan's Epistre au dieu d'Amours and Dit de la Rose; Thomas Hoccleve's The Letter of Cupid* (Leiden, 1990).

[44] Catherine Batt, 'The *Epistre au dieu d'Amours* and *The Letter of Cupid*: Christine de Pizan, Thomas Hoccleve, and Vernacular Poetics', in Catherine Batt, Jonathan Hsy, and René Tixier (eds), *'Booldly bot meekly': Essays on the Theory and Practice of Translation in the Middle Ages in Honour of Roger Ellis* (Turnhout, 2018), 427–44; Rory G. Critten, 'Imagining the Author in Late Medieval England and France: The Transmission and Reception

A similar discomfort with Christine's strong female authorial persona and with her unmistakable feminist agenda can be discerned in a later English translation of her *Epistre Othéa à Hector* (1400) by Stephen Scrope, as the *Epistle of Othea* (c1440), rendering the verse portion in rhyming couplets, accompanied by extensive allegorical interpretations in prose as in Christine's original.[45] Spoken in the voice of Othea herself—goddess of female wisdom and prudence—Christine's poem consists of an extended fictional letter sent to a teenage Hector, comprising an extended selection of short didactic narratives drawn from classical mythology and allegorized with the assistance of scripture, the church fathers, and pagan philosophers. Scrope offers a close, meticulous translation, but clearly obscures the role of Christine as a female author, and reduces Christine's emphasis on women as wise counsellors and advisers in her exemplary allegorical stories.[46] Christine de Pizan's works continued to enjoy considerable popularity well into the sixteenth century, when several were printed.[47]

Among further allegorical poems of substantial length it is worth signalling *Reson and Sensuallyte* (c1408–12), an incomplete poem of some 7000 lines in rhyming couplets, whose manuscript attribution to Lydgate is highly dubious.[48] The poem is a translation of Évrart de Conty's *Eschéz Amoureux* (1375–8),[49] another direct response to the *Roman de la Rose* that takes the form of an allegorized chess game. In pitching the rational intellect squarely against sensual pleasure, Conty had sought to convey a much stronger moral message in his response to the slippery, playful, and ultimately evasive *Rose*. The English translation, by contrast, eschews any such schematic imbalance, transforming the poem from a moral allegory into a more ambitious philosophical speculation whose overall tenor remains to be more fully explored. Almost completely neglected by modern critics, the poem has recently been read as an exploration of the natural potentialities of the higher, immaterial intellect, but also as a poem that highlights the productive affinity between irrational sensual pleasure and poetic creativity.[50]

The philosophical concerns of *Reson and Sensuallyte* fit within the larger interest in self-knowledge and introspection that underpins much allegorical poetry of the period, often shaped by the lasting influence of Boethius's *Consolation of Philosophy*.[51] Such Boethian concerns also provide the context for John Walton's translation of the *Consolation of Philosophy* (1410), a version that survives in twenty-three manuscripts and several extracts, and thus was circulated more widely than Chaucer's own prose *Boece* (see further Chapter 15). The translation, likely produced at the behest of Elizabeth Berkeley—daughter of Trevisa's

---

of Christine de Pizan's *Epistre au dieu d'Amours* and Thomas Hoccleve's *Letter of Cupid*', *Studies in Philology*, 112 (2015), 680–97.

[45] See Christine de Pizan, in Renate Blumenfeld-Kosinski and Earl Jeffrey Richards (eds and trans), *Othea's Letter to Hector* (Toronto, 2017), and (NIMEV 2766) Stephen Scrope, in Curt F. Bühler (ed.), *The Epistle of Othea*, EETS, o.s. 264 (Oxford, 1970).

[46] For more details on the context and significance of this translation, produced in the circle of Sir John Fastolf, Stephen Scrope, and William Worcester, see further Daniel Wakelin, *Humanism, Reading, and English Literature 1430–1530* (Oxford, 2007), 93–125.

[47] Danielle Buschinger, 'Le Livre des faits d'armes et de chevalerie de Christine de Pizan et ses adaptations anglaise et haut-alémanique', *Comptes rendus des séances de l'Académie des Inscriptions et Belles-Lettres*, 155.2 (2011), 1073–92.

[48] NIMEV 3746; Ernst Sieper (ed.), *Reson and Sensuallyte*, 2 vols., EETS, e.s. 84, 89 (London, 1901).

[49] Gregory Heyworth and Daniel E. O'Sullivan, with Frank Coulson (eds), *Les Eschéz d'Amours: A Critical Edition of the Poem and its Latin Glosses* (Leiden, 2013).

[50] See respectively Kellie Robertson, *Nature Speaks: Medieval Literature and Aristotelian Philosophy* (Philadelphia, PA, 2017), 295–310; and Samuel F. McMillan, 'Trailing an Unreasonable Rose: Authorship in John Lydgate's *Reson and Sensuallyte*', *Modern Philology*, 116 (2018), 95–120.

[51] H. F. Stewart, E. K. Rand, and S. J. Tester (eds and trans), *Theological Tractates*, Loeb Classical Library 74 (Cambridge, MA, 1973), 130–435.

patron Thomas Berkeley—is poetically skilful and elegant, and switches from the eight-line stanza borrowed from Chaucer's 'Monk's Tale', used in the first three books, to rhyme royal for books four and five, underscoring the tonal transition to loftier subject matter for the two final books.[52] Walton's translation is notable also for the wide and diverse range of responses in its manuscripts, including some meticulously close commentary, topical as well as allegorical interpretations, occasional humanist marginal references, and the presence of several extracts in other manuscripts.[53]

Alain Chartier's incomplete *Traité de l'espérance* (1430) also participates in this Boethian wave, as does his *Quadrilogue invectif* (1422).[54] Both were translated into English prose, and Chartier's work remained popular with English readers throughout the century.[55] In the present context the most significant English rendering of Chartier's work is undoubtedly Richard Roos's translation of the *Belle Dame Sans Merci* (*BDSM*, c1424).[56] Chartier's original is again part of the tradition of Jean de Meun's *Roman de la Rose*, and circulated so widely throughout Europe that it has been called 'the most important single poem of its century'.[57] Stretching to some 856 lines and organizing the narrative into one hundred separate stanzas of *huitains* (eight-line stanzas), the *BDSM* managed to combine the narrative element of allegory with the more static and meditative tone of the first-person love lyric. Chartier's *BDSM* effectively traces the lover's futile efforts to woo the lady, and ends with the lover's death, an event that may or may not be meant ironically. The fact of the lover's death and the presumed cruelty of the 'merciless' lady (*sans merci*, i.e., 'without mercy') became the object of an extended literary debate among readers and imitators, whose creative responses were often appended to manuscripts of the *BDSM*, developing into a fully-fledged literary *querelle* that echoes and explicitly references the earlier *Querelle de la Rose* (1401–3).[58]

Strikingly, Richard Roos decided to reproduce Chartier's formal choices in his translation of the *BDSM*: not only did he maintain the structure of one hundred eight-line stanzas—albeit extending his lines from tetrameter to the more current pentameter—but he managed to produce a poem whose fluidity and elegance truly lives up to its original. Yet Roos also supplements the poem with a more self-consciously 'English' prologue and epilogue, both written in Chaucerian rhyme royal. This alternation of quintessentially French and English stanza forms is symptomatic of Roos's complex aims in translating the poem,

---

[52] NIMEV 1597; Mark Science (ed.), *Boethius 'De Consolatione Philosophiae'*, EETS, o.s. 170 (London, 1927); Ian R. Johnson, 'Walton's Sapient Orpheus', in Alastair J. Minnis (ed.), *The Medieval Boethius: Studies in the Vernacular Translations of 'De Consolatione Philosophiae'* (Cambridge, 1987), 139–68.

[53] Wakelin, *Humanism, Reading, and English Literature*, 9–16; A. S. G. Edwards, 'Reading John Walton's Boethius in the 15th and 16th Centuries', in Mary Flannery and Carrie Griffin (eds), *Spaces for Reading in Late Medieval England* (London, 2016), 35–49.

[54] J. C. Laidlaw (ed.), *The Poetical Works of Alain Chartier* (Cambridge, 1974).

[55] See M. S. Blayney (ed.), *Fifteenth-Century English Translations of Alain Chartier's Le Traite de l'Esperance and Le Quadrilogue Invectif*, 2 vols., EETS, o.s. 270, 281 (Oxford, 1974 and 1980). On the fortunes of Chartier in England, see Julia Boffey, 'The Early Reception of Chartier's Works in England and Scotland', and Catherine Nall, 'William Worcester reads Alain Chartier: Le *Quadrilogue invectif* and its English Readers', both in Emma Cayley and Ashby Kinch (eds), *Chartier in Europe* (Cambridge, 2008), 105–18 and 135–48 respectively.

[56] NIMEV 1086; For an edition see Dana M. Symons (ed.), *Chaucerian Dream Visions and Complaints* (Kalamazoo, MI, 2004), 201–74.

[57] William Calin, *The French Tradition and the Literature of Medieval England* (Toronto, 1994), 250. On the European reception of Chartier's work, see further Ashby Kinch, 'Chartier's European Influence', and Joan McRae, 'A Community of Readers: The Quarrel of the *Belle Dame Sans Mercy*', in Daisy Delogu, Emma Cayley, and Joan E. McRae (eds), *A Companion to Alain Chartier (c.1385–1430): Father of French Eloquence* (Leiden, 2015), 279–302; 200–22.

[58] Joan E. McRae (ed.), *Alain Chartier: The Quarrel of the Belle Dame Sans Mercy* (London, 2004); and in her 'A Community of Readers'.

combining a tribute to the leading courtly poet of fifteenth-century France with the desire to transplant his fine poetic art to a very different, more conservative cultural climate in England, while also affirming the newly found literary dignity of the English language. The result is a poem that maintains the grace and elegance of the original, but moderates the darker and more subversive implications of Chartier's version, celebrating courtly aesthetics instead of interrogating them through subtle and at times bitter irony, and thus affirming the high cultural value of francophone courtly traditions in an English context.[59]

A similarly complex interlacing of French and English literary sensibilities is found in Charles d'Orléans's poetic output, which includes poetry in both languages, and is more fully discussed elsewhere in this volume (see Chapter 17). Produced during an extended period of captivity in England, between 1415 and 1440, the corpus of Charles's poetry is gathered in two separate manuscripts, both commissioned by Charles himself in the late 1430s. Most but not all of Charles's English poems in BL MS Harley 682 are adaptations of the French poems preserved in Paris, Bibliothèque nationale de France MS fr. 25458, making this a rare, indeed unique case of 'self-translation', although the exact details and chronology of Charles's composition–and–translation process remain unclear.[60] Despite its uniqueness, Charles's work shares many characteristics with Roos's translation of the *BDSM*: we again find a combination of lyric poetry and narrative allegory; an emotionally powerful account of a personal experience of amorous disappointment and disillusion with the courtly ethos; and a movement between quintessentially French, strictly codified poetic forms (*formes fixes*) and freer English courtly verse. Where the French collection is discontinuous and open-ended, leaving the door open to further possibilities of continuation and reconfiguration after Charles's return to France, the English collection strives to attain formal and narrative closure, as if to signal the completion of an important major phase in the life of its culturally and linguistically mobile author.[61]

Romance, Exemplary History, and Statecraft

Romance too was a quintessentially French literary form, originally designating little more than a text written in 'romauns' language—i.e., in French. Insular Britain provided a particularly fruitful ground for the growth and development of the romance genre, ever since the days of Henry II and Eleanor of Aquitaine. Insular sources in Anglo-Norman French were frequently translated into English throughout the thirteenth and fourteenth centuries, and translation activity carried on throughout the fifteenth century and into Tudor times. The fifteenth century was the great age of the prose romance, culminating with Caxton's printing of a range of chivalric classics including several romances, but the translation of romances into English verse also continued, albeit in attenuated form, and declining more rapidly after the middle of the century.[62]

---

[59] On the political and cultural context of the translations, see further Ashby Kinch, 'A Naked Roos: Translation and Subjection in the Middle English "La Belle Dame Sans Mercy"', *JEGP*, 105 (2006), 415–45.

[60] See Jean-Claude Mühlethaler (ed.), *Charles d'Orléans, Ballades et rondeaux* (Paris, 1996) and Mary-Jo Arn (ed.), *Fortunes Stabilnes: Charles of Orleans's English Book of Love* (Binghamton, NY, 1994).

[61] See further Mary-Jo Arn (ed.), *Charles d'Orléans in England* (Cambridge, 2000), and more recently Rory Critten, 'Locating Charles d'Orléans: In France, England and out of Europe', *New Medieval Literatures*, 20 (2020), 174–215.

[62] Helen Cooper, 'Romance after 1400', in David Wallace (ed.), *The Cambridge History of Medieval English Literature* (Cambridge, 1999), 690–719; Rosalind Field, 'Romance', in Ellis, *OHLTE*, 296–331 (at 323–7).

Many verse romances discussed more fully elsewhere in this volume are in fact translations of one kind or another (see further Chapters 19, 20, 21). This included a spate of Charlemagne romances in verse adapted from French and Latin sources, produced across the late fourteenth and early fifteenth century. Difficult to date and contextualize, such translations of French *chansons de geste* lack any strictly literary ambition, but provide precious indications of contemporary popular attitudes to cultural difference and national identity, particularly in the context of ongoing Anglo-French hostilities and the renewed, if fitful, crusading enthusiasm in this period (see further Chapter 21).[63] Crusading ideals are indeed conspicuous in many verse romances copied during the period, notably those included in two remarkable manuscripts produced by Robert Thornton during the 1430s (see further Chapter 8), although many of these items were first translated or composed in the previous century.

English verse translations of Arthurian materials were comparatively rare, and only achieved very limited circulation. They include Henry Lovelich's monumental *History of the Holy Grail* and *Merlin* (c1450), jointly running to almost 50,000 lines of rhyming couplets, surviving in a single manuscript and based on the French prose *Estoire del Saint Graal* but replacing the source's focus on mystical contemplation with a new emphasis on warfare against the infidel;[64] and the incomplete couplet *Lancelot of the Laik* in Middle Scots,[65] a rare insular retelling of the amorous intrigue as recounted in the French prose *Lancelot*. The only comparable Arthurian translation into English is the *Stanzaic Morte Arthur*, dating from c1400 (see further Chapter 20).[66] We also find several non-cyclical romances translated from francophone sources, many of which display 'Chaucerian' features of one kind of another, such as the rhyme royal *Romans of Partenay* (1500?),[67] *Partonope of Blois* (c1420),[68] in octosyllabic couplets and with a conspicuously Chaucerian narrator,[69] or the couplet *Lyfe of Ipomydon*, based on Hugh de Rotelande's twelfth-century Anglo-Norman romance.[70]

Romances of antiquity proved particularly popular at the start of the century, and are discussed more fully elsewhere (see Chapter 19). It is worth stressing, however, that many of the most popular works in these genres were in fact 'translations'. This included both Lydgate's popular *Troy Book* (between 1412 and 1420),[71] based upon Guido delle

---

[63] Phillipa Hardman and Marianne Ailes (eds), *The Legend of Charlemagne in Medieval England: The Matter of France in Middle English and Anglo-Norman Literature* (Cambridge, 2017).

[64] NIMEV 842.5, in Frederick J. Furnivall (ed.), *The History of the Holy Grail by Henry Lovelich*, 5 vols., EETS, e.s. 20, 24, 28, 30, 95 (London, 1874–1905); and NIMEV 2312, in E. A. Kock (ed.), *Henry Lovelich's Merlin*, 3 vols., EETS, e.s. 93, 112, and o.s. 185 (London, 1904, 1913, 1932).

[65] NIMEV 3466; Alan Lupack (ed.), *Lancelot of the Laik and Sir Tristrem* (Kalamazoo, MI, 1994).

[66] NIMEV 1994; P. F. Hissiger (ed.), *Le Morte Arthur: A Critical Edition* (The Hague, 1975).

[67] NIMEV 819.5; W. W. Skeat (ed.), *The Romans of Partenay or of Lusignen*, EETS, o.s. 22 (London, 1866).

[68] NIMEV 4132; A.Trampe Bödtker (ed.), *The Middle English Versions of Partonope of Blois*, EETS, e.s. 109 (London, 1912).

[69] See further Barry Windeatt, 'Chaucer and Fifteenth-Century Romance: *Partonope of Blois*', in Ruth Morse and Windeatt (eds), *Chaucer Traditions* (Cambridge, 1990), 62–80; Brenda Hosington, 'Partonopeu de Blois and its Fifteenth-Century English Translation: a Medieval Translator at Work', in Roger Ellis (ed.), *The Medieval Translator: Volume II* (London, 1991), 231–52.

[70] NIMEV 2142; Eugen Kölbing (ed.), *Ipomedon, in drei englischen Bearbeitungen* (Breslau, 1889). See further Jordi Sánchez-Martí, 'Reading Romance in Late Medieval England: The Case of the Middle English *Ipomedon*', *Philological Quarterly*, 83.1 (2004), 13–39.

[71] NIMEV 2516; Henry Bergen (ed.), *Lydgate's Troy Book*, 4 vols., EETS, e.s. 97, 103, 106, 126 (London, 1906, 1908, 1910, 1935).

Colonne's *Historia destructionis Troiae*,⁷² and his *Fall of Princes* (1431–8),⁷³ a translation of Boccaccio's *De casibus virorum illustrium* via Laurent de Premierfait's earlier French translation, *Des cas des nobles hommes et femmes* from 1409,⁷⁴ as well as Thomas Hoccleve's *Regiment of Princes* (1410–12),⁷⁵ 'translating' three main sources: Giles of Rome's *De regimine principum*;⁷⁶ Jacob de Cessolis's moralized *Book of Chess*;⁷⁷ and the hugely popular *Secretum secretorum*⁷⁸ (see further Chapters 24 and 25). Many of these translated romances of antiquity emphasize the historical and exemplary significance of events from the pagan past, as opposed to their legendary, romantic, or supernatural elements, and are thus best viewed as works of 'history'.⁷⁹

These classical romances fit within the larger trend that saw the growth in popularity of broadly didactic literature on chivalry, kingship, governance, and domestic conduct (see further Chapter 16). This tradition in turn included several translations, such as the *Secrees of Old Philisoffres*, a verse translation of the hugely popular *Secretum secretorum* in rhyme royal, and by far the most successful of its many English adaptations with twenty-two surviving witnesses.⁸⁰ The translation was begun by Lydgate in the late 1440s at the behest of Henry VI, and was completed by his self-appointed disciple Benedict Burgh after Lydgate's death. Rivalling the pan-European success of the *Secretum*, we find Vegetius's *De Re Militari*,⁸¹ surviving in two fifteenth-century English translations: one into prose, produced in 1408 for Thomas Berkeley,⁸² and a second translation into rhyme royal, *Knyghthode and Bataile*, characterized by its distinctly classicizing interests.⁸³ Another avatar of the *Secretum* is Caxton's prose translation of Christine de Pizan's *Livre des faits et d'armes et de chevalerie*, *The book of fayytes of armes and of chyualrye* ([1489]; STC 7269),⁸⁴ which had rendered extended portions of Vegetius's treatise in French.⁸⁵

---

⁷² For an English translation, see Guido delle Colonne, in Mary Elizabeth Meek (trans.), *Historia destructionis Troiae* (Bloomington, IN, 1974).
⁷³ NIMEV 1168; Henry Bergen (ed.), *Lydgate's Fall of Princes*, 4 vols., EETS, e.s. 121–4 (London, 1924, 1927).
⁷⁴ Vittore Branca (ed.), *Tutte le opere di Giovanni Boccaccio*, 10 vols. (Milan, 1964–1998), 9: *De casibus virorum illustrium*; Patricia M. Gathercole (ed.), *Laurent de Premierfait's 'Des cas des nobles hommes et femmes': Book I, translated from Boccaccio. A Critical Edition Based on 6 Manuscripts*, (Chapel Hill, NC, 1968).
⁷⁵ NIMEV 2229; Frederick J. Furnivall (ed.), *Hoccleve's Works: The Regement of Princes and Fourteen Minor Poems*, EETS, e.s. 72 (London, 1897).
⁷⁶ No full critical edition is available. For an edition of Trevisa's Middle English prose translation, see David C. Fowler, Charles F. Briggs, and Paul G. Remley (eds), *The Governance of Kings and Princes: John Trevisa's Middle English Translation of the 'De Regimine Principum' of Aegidius Romanus* (New York, 1997).
⁷⁷ No full critical edition is available, but see Jacob de Cessolis, in W. H. Williams (ed. and trans.), *Book of Chess* (New York, 2008).
⁷⁸ Multiple Latin versions are available, on which see Catherine Gaullier-Bougassas, Margaret Bridges, and Jean-Yves Tilliette (eds), *Trajectoires européennes du 'Secretum secretorum' du Pseudo-Aristote (XIIIe–XVIe siècle)* (Turnhout, 2015).
⁷⁹ Field, 'Romances', in Ellis, *OHLTE*, especially 315–9.
⁸⁰ NIMEV 935; R. Steele (ed.), *Lydgate and Burgh's Secrees of Old Philisoffres*, EETS, e.s. 66 (London, 1894). For other versions, see Mahmoud Manzalaoui (ed.), *Secretum Secretorum: Nine English Versions*, EETS, o.s. 276 (Oxford, 1977).
⁸¹ M. D. Reeve (ed.), Vegetius, *Epitoma Rei Militaris* (Oxford, 2004).
⁸² Geoffrey Lester (ed.), *The Earliest English Translation of Vegetius' 'De re militari'*, MET 21 (Heidelberg, 1988).
⁸³ NIMEV 3185; R. Dyboski and Z. M. Arend (eds), *Knyghthode and Bataile: A XVth Century Verse Paraphrase of Flavius Vegetius Renatus' Treatise 'De re militari'*, EETS, o.s. 201 (London, 1935). See further Daniel Wakelin, 'The Occasion, Author and Readers of *Knyghthode and bataile*', *Medium Ævum*, 73 (2004), 260–72; and his *Humanism, Reading and English Literature*, 19–22.
⁸⁴ Christine de Pizan, in Sumner Willard and Charity Cannon Willard (eds), *The Book of Deeds of Arms and of Chivalry* (University Park, PA, 1999).
⁸⁵ See further Christopher Allmand, 'Translations', in *The De Re Militari of Vegetius: The Reception, Transmission and Legacy of a Roman Text in the Middle Ages* (Cambridge, 2011), 148–96 (at 185–93).

Humanist Translations and Italian Poets

Humanism is widely understood as a cultural programme hinging on the recovery of original Greek and Latin texts from antiquity, and it may seem counterintuitive to view late medieval vernacular translations as somehow contributing to the growth of humanism in the strict sense. Nonetheless, there is substantial evidence to suggest that Britain's fifteenth-century 'humanists' had more than a passing interest in contemporary translations into English, even as they reinterpreted rather different, earlier forms of classicism found in the generation of Geoffrey Chaucer and John Walton.[86]

Frequently invoked as the father of English humanism, Humfrey, duke of Gloucester, youngest brother of King Henry V, was heavily invested in the ideal of cultural *translatio*, and was the dedicatee of numerous translations during the second quarter of the fifteenth century, some of which he personally commissioned (see further Chapter 2).[87] The majority of these translations, however, rendered Greek or Italian texts into Latin, and only two were translations into English, both in verse. They were Lydgate's translation of Boccaccio's *De casibus* as the *Fall of Princes*, already discussed; and *On Husbondrie* (c1442–3), a translation of Palladius's widely read prose treatise on agriculture, the *Opus agriculturae* or *De re rustica*.[88] The translation has been variously read as a practical guide to agriculture; a self-consciously humanist exercise in classicizing scholarship; a reflection of Humfrey's own desire for a retreat from the active life to a world of 'georgic' culture and agriculture; and a meditation on political governance, stability, and power, figured as a process of carefully managed agricultural growth (see further Chapter 15).[89]

The work of another major classical author, Claudian's *De consulatu Stilichonis*, is the source of a selective translation into unrhymed English verse, internally dated to 1445.[90] The original is a panegyric on Claudian's patron, Stilicho, congratulating the latter on his appointment as consul, and the relevant extracts of the original Latin are included on facing pages in the single surviving manuscript of the English translation. The dedication to Richard, duke of York, suggests that the latter's achievements ought to be viewed as broadly analogous with those of the Roman general, although the text does not elaborate on the details of the implied analogy. The question of authorship remains disputed: Osbern Bokenham is a likely candidate, but the work has also been attributed to the author of the *De re rustica* translation, and it has been suggested that the same author may also be responsible for *Knyghthode and Bataile*, already mentioned.[91] Regardless of the question of authorship, all three translations display a distinctively humanist interest in classical

---

[86] Wakelin, *Humanism, Reading, and English Literature*, 1–22.
[87] Alessandra Petrina, *Cultural Politics in Fifteenth-Century England: The Case of Humphrey, Duke of Gloucester* (Leiden, 2004).
[88] NIMEV 654; Robert H. Rodgers (ed.), *Palladius Rutilius Taurus Aemilianus: Opera* (Leipzig, 1975).
[89] Mark Liddell (ed.), *The Middle English Translation of Palladius' De Re Rustica* (Berlin, 1896). See further Alessandra Petrina, 'The Middle English Translation of Palladius's *De Agricultura*', in René Tixier et al. (eds), *The Medieval Translator 8* (Turnhout, 2003), 317–28; and in her *Cultural Politics in Fifteenth-Century England*; and A. S. G. Edwards, 'Duke Humfrey's Middle English Palladius Manuscript', in Jenny Stratford (ed.), *The Lancastrian Court: Proceedings of the 2001 Harlaxton Symposium* (Donington, 2003), 68–78.
[90] NIMEV 1526; E. Flügel, 'Eine mittelenglische Claudian-Übersetzung (1445) (Brit. Mus. Add. Ms. 11814)', *Anglia*, 28 (1905), 255–99, 421–38.
[91] A. S. G. Edwards, 'The Middle English Translation of Claudian's *De Consulatu Stilichonis*', in Alastair J. Minnis, *Middle English Poetry: Texts and Traditions: Essays in Honour of Derek Pearsall* (York, 2001), 267–78; Livia Visser-Fuchs, "Honour is the Reward of Virtue': The Claudian Translation Made for Richard, Duke of York, in 1445', *The Ricardian*, 18 (2008), 66–82; Wakelin, *Humanism, Reading, and English Literature*, 70–80.

authors, marking an important moment in the slow metamorphosis of classicizing interests during the fifteenth century.

Given the modern reputation of Francis Petrarch, considered together with Dante and Boccaccio one of Italy's three most eminent vernacular poets from the Middle Ages, it may appear surprising that early English translators were attracted almost exclusively by his Latin.[92] Petrarch's seminal collection of love lyrics in the vernacular—the *Rime Sparse* or *Rerum vulgarium fragmenta*, often known more simply as the *Canzoniere*[93]—helped to spark the European vogue for Petrarchan sonnet sequences during the sixteenth century, but appears to have been largely ignored by English readers until the time of Thomas Wyatt, with the notable exception of Chaucer's precocious—and unacknowledged—translation of a single sonnet as the 'Canticus Troili' in his *Troilus and Criseyde* (1. 400–20, cf. *Canzoniere* 132). This interest in Petrarch as a Latinist, however, is consonant with the wider patterns of early European responses to Petrarch's reputation as that of a pioneering humanist intellectual.[94] Two substantial English Petrarch translations were produced during the fifteenth century, both of which are dialogues and survive in single manuscripts. The first is a prose *Dialogue Between Reason and Adversity*, an abridgement of the *De remediis utriusque Fortunae*.[95] More relevant in the present context is the second, later translation into English verse (c1477–87) of Petrarch's *Secretum*.[96] The *Secretum* is an introspective spiritual dialogue between the author/narrator-figure, Franciscus, and St Augustine of Hippo, moderated by Truth personified (*Veritas*). The English translator turns Petrarch's prose into rhyming couplets, but only the first of the original three days of the dialogue has come down to us in the single surviving manuscript. The translation encapsulates the transitional and hybrid nature of much early English humanism: while the poem is clearly marked by a new kind of classicizing aesthetic and a conspicuously aureate diction, it also draws inspiration from far more traditional forms of moral didacticism, Boethian dialogue, and the introspective spiritual monologue in the tradition of St Augustine.

Boccaccio has already featured in the preceding account, providing the ultimate source for Lydgate's *Fall of Princes* with the *De casibus virorum illustrium*. Boccaccio's companion piece to the *De casibus*, the *De mulieribus claris*,[97] which rehearses lives of noble women, was also translated into English rhyme royal stanzas, albeit much reduced in size (from 106 to twenty-one lives), around the middle of the fifteenth century.[98] Although the translation is in many ways derivative and heavily Lydgatean in style, it survives in a single manuscript witness characterized by a striking humanist *mise en page* that was highly unusual and precocious for vernacular texts in England.[99] But also Boccaccio's

---

[92] On English translations of their work, see more broadly Karla Taylor, 'Writers of the Italian Renaissance', in Ellis, *OHLTE*, 390–406.

[93] Mark Musa (ed. and trans.), *Petrarch: The Canzoniere, or Rerum vulgarium fragmenta* (Bloomington, IN, 1999).

[94] Alessandra Petrina, 'The Humanist Petrarch in Medieval and Early Modern England', *Journal of Anglo-Italian Studies*, 12 (2013), 45–62.

[95] F. N. M. Diekstra (ed.), *A Dialogue Between Reason and Adversity: A Late Middle English Version of Petrarch's De Remediis* (Assen, 1968).

[96] DIMEV 2129; Edward Wilson and Daniel Wakelin (eds), *A Middle English Translation from Petrarch's Secretum*, EETS, o.s. 351 (Oxford, 2018).

[97] Virginia Brown (ed. and trans.), *Giovanni Boccaccio: Famous Women* (Cambridge, MA, 2001).

[98] NIMEV 2642; Janet Cowen (ed.), *On Famous Women: The Middle English Translation of Boccaccio's 'De Mulieribus Claris'. Edited from London, British Library, MS Additional 10304*, MET 52 (Heidelberg, 2015); Gustav Schleich (ed.), *Die mittelenglische Umdichtung von Boccaccios 'De claris mulieribus'* (Leipzig, 1924).

[99] Wakelin, *Humanism, Reading, and English Literature*, 60–1.

Italian work—unlike Petrarch's—was translated into English, although this is far from being indicative of broader trends: only a single one of Boccaccio's one hundred tales from the *Decameron*—The Tale of Tancredi, Ghismunda, and Guiscardo (*Decameron* 4.1)—was translated into English rhyme royal on two occasions, and continued to increase in popularity during the following century.[100] But the popularity of the tale in England is part of a wider, pan-European phenomenon,[101] and once more highlights the nearly total lack of any direct engagement with Italian literature by English translators in the generations between Chaucer and Thomas Wyatt.[102] It is also symptomatic that both translations were made at one or even two removes from Boccaccio's original, via Leonardo Bruni's Latin prose *Fabula Tancredi* (c1436–8),[103] possibly along with a French adaptation of the *Decameron*, although the exact relation among these different versions remains debated.[104] The cultural distance from Boccaccio's original is also reflected in the rather different ideological affinities of the English translations. Banester's slightly earlier version (c1472?) provides a telling illustration of the difficulty of transplanting Boccaccio's early humanist values and ideals to English soil: instead of affirming the priority of acquired nobility of spirit over inherited nobility, as the original had done, Banester's translation turns the story into a cautionary tale about the dangers of unbridled youthful passion and generational conflict. The later version, by contrast, attempts to balance Banester's moralizing approach with the humanist emphasis on personal virtue found in Boccaccio's original.

As is well exemplified by these last few examples, then, translation during the fifteenth century served a wide range of cultural and intellectual ends that reach far beyond the desire to merely reproduce foreign texts in a native idiom. By pushing both readers and translators to engage not only in textual interpretation and reinterpretation, but also prompting them to consider and reconsider ethical, spiritual, political, and cultural ideals—past and present, foreign and domestic—the very act of *translatio* plays a fundamental role in enabling the construction of English language, poetry, cultural identity, and political self-understanding throughout the fifteenth century. Translation therefore becomes the means to forge an expanding network of cultural, intellectual, and emotional connections between authors, readers, and historical subjects across time and space, and between multiple languages and very different, often conflicting forms of discourse and textuality.

---

[100] NIMEV 4082 (by Gilbert Banester) and 3258; Herbert G. Wright (ed.), *Early English Versions of the Tales of Guiscardo and Ghismonda and Titus Gisippus from the Decameron*, EETS, o.s. 205 (London, 1937). See also Herbert G. Wright, *Boccaccio in England: From Chaucer to Tennyson* (London, 1957), 123–33.

[101] Federico Poletti, 'Fortuna letteraria e figurativa della "Ghismonda" (*Dec.* IV, 1) fra Umanesimo e Rinascimento', *Studi sul Boccaccio*, 32 (2004), 101–44.

[102] Taylor, 'Writers of the Italian Renaissance'.

[103] Transcription available in Maria Luisa Doglio, *L'exemplum nella novella latina del Quattrocento* (Turin, 1975), 150–63.

[104] Alessandra Petrina, 'Boccaccio in Kent: le peregrinazioni di Guiscardo e Ghismonda', in Giuseppe Sertoli, Carla Vaglio Marengo, Chiara Lombardi (eds), *Comparatistica e intertestualità: Studi in onore di Franco Marenco* (Alessandria, 2010), 217–26.

CHAPTER 5
Literary Language

Jenni Nuttall

Inventing Literary English

Most of the conventions by which poets diverged from everyday linguistic norms in the fifteenth century were inherited from verse written in English in the thirteenth and fourteenth centuries.[1] Poetry organizes its language into metrical patterns of stressed and unstressed syllables, creating lines which, in the forms of verse written in English and Scots in these centuries, were also shaped by alliteration, rhyme, or alliteration and rhyme in concert in the case of stanzaic-alliterative verse. Such metrical and formal constraints might lead to the use of other verbal licences.[2] Poets could add to the language, inventing words to meet the demands of metre, rhyme, and alliteration. They might borrow words, most often from French, or coin new English words modelled on equivalents in French or Latin.[3] They also derived new vocabulary from the pre-existing resources of English, converting words from one grammatical class to another or by adding prefixes or suffixes to existing elements. Depending on their formal constraints, authors might draw on poetic diction (for example the synonyms for common words which appear in alliterative verse), or deploy formulaic phrases chosen more for rhyme or alliteration than for their full semantic import.[4] Poetic language also had licence to be notably ornate or stylized. Poets decorated their verse with rhetorical schemes, both intentional deviations from everyday usage, such as syntactical inversions, and also purposefully created patterns of sound such as alliteration, parallelism, or repetition.

Despite this tradition of poetic language, the swift popularity of Chaucer's poetry after his death in 1400 marked a moment at which literary English supposedly came of age, at least according to the testimonies of fifteenth-century poets.[5] For Thomas Hoccleve, Chaucer did not so much transform the language of English poetry as invent it from scratch. In the *Regiment of Princes* (written 1410–11), Hoccleve praises Chaucer as the 'firste fyndere of our fair langage' (4978), *fyndere* meaning 'inventor' or 'originator'.[6] This

---

[1] On poetry's licences, see Nicolette Zeeman, 'The Schools Give a License to Poets', in Rita Copeland (ed.), *Criticism and Dissent in the Middle Ages* (Cambridge, 1996), 151–80.

[2] For an introduction to medieval English poetry's language, see N. F. Blake, *The English Language in Medieval Literature* (London, 1977). See also N. F. Blake, 'The Literary Language', in N. F. Blake (ed.), *1066–1476*, vol. 2, in Richard M. Hogg (ed.), *The Cambridge History of the English Language* (Cambridge, 1992), 500–41. For an overview of literary style in the fifteenth century, see A. S. G. Edwards, 'Poetic Language in the Fifteenth Century', in Corinne Saunders (ed.), *A Companion to Medieval English Poetry* (Chichester, 2010), 520–37.

[3] On English's contacts with other languages and on variation within English in this period, see J. D. Burnley, 'Lexis and Semantics', in N. F. Blake (ed.), *1066–1476*, vol. 2, in Hogg (ed.), *The Cambridge History of the English Language*, 409–99 (409–61).

[4] For an overview of alliterative verse's formulaic phrases and diction, see John Finlayson, 'Alliterative Narrative Poetry: The Control of the Medium', *Traditio*, 44 (1988), 419–51.

[5] Praise for Chaucer's linguistic skill is surveyed by Joanna Bellis, '"Fresch Anamalit Termes": The Contradictory Celebrity of Chaucer's Aureation', in Isabel Davis and Catherine Nall (eds), *Chaucer and Fame: Reputation and Reception* (Cambridge, 2015), 143–63 (at 144–9).

[6] Thomas Hoccleve, in Charles R. Blyth (ed.), *The Regiment of Princes* (Kalamazoo, MI, 1999), 185.

claim of *ex nihilo* creation is itself an invention to a considerable degree. What were once hailed as Chaucer's own innovations have been shown to be continuations, exaggerations, or extensions of 'the *general* practice of the literary language that Chaucer's English simply joined'.[7] Yet passages posthumously praising Chaucer nevertheless claimed that his language was both distinctive and superlative. Chaucer's acquaintance Henry Scogan lamented a friend who 'in his langage was so curyous' (66), that is ingenious, skilful, artistic, or sophisticated.[8] In his translation of Boethius's *Consolation of Philosophy*, completed in 1410, the Augustinian canon John Walton named Chaucer as 'floure of rethoryk / In Englisshe tong' (Prologue, 33–4), the model of a rhetorician.[9]

Though Chaucer did not invent literary English, his style was thus perceived as markedly different to what had gone before. Alongside many continuities with earlier practice, Chaucer broke with literary tradition both by eschewing previously common features of poetic English and by introducing techniques from French verse. Chaucer avoided certain clichés of earlier style, using them only ironically or comically. The adjective *hende*, for example, used widely in romances to mean 'pleasant' or 'gracious', is not applied to characters in Chaucer's own romances but reserved almost exclusively for the character of Nicholas in 'the Miller's Tale' fabliau in order to mock the uncritical ubiquity of its earlier usage.[10] Chaucer simultaneously developed a high style of allusions to classical and historical figures along with rhetorical schemes and tropes.[11] Also noteworthy was his stylistic variety, his juxtaposition of high and low styles in close proximity. Chaucer's classical allusions and examples coexist with his talent for capturing the contours of contemporary speech in his characters' dialogue.[12] His fabliaux provide a route by which 'cherles termes' (*Canterbury Tales*, 1.3917) enter literary language, not just lower-class speech but also obscenities such as the notorious *swyven* which some scribes primly censored.[13]

Chaucer's formal innovations also had consequences for the language of his verse, just as they did for his fellow Ricardian poet John Gower. The regularity of their syllable-counted iambic verse required the syllabification of final *-e* after this feature had become optional and perhaps old-fashioned in everyday speech, as well as careful selection between variants depending on their syllable-count or stress pattern.[14] Unlike the majority of verse written in English in the thirteenth and fourteenth centuries, Gower and Chaucer tended not to match the length of their syntactic units to that of the line, but, following their French models, made frequent use of enjambment, where a verse line ends with a syntactical unit not yet completed. To meet the demands of complex rhyme-schemes, they had more inversion and dislocation in their syntax, where earlier poets made use of pleonastic phrasing or padded out lines with tags or filler phrases.[15] All this gives an impression of seemingly effortless metrical fluency, yet requires a very firm control of orthography, vocabulary, and grammar.

---

[7] Christopher Cannon, *The Making of Chaucer's English: A Study of Words* (Cambridge, 1998), 65 (his italics).
[8] Kathleen Forni (ed.), *The Chaucerian Apocrypha: A Selection* (Kalamazoo, MI, 2005), 149.
[9] John Walton, in Mark Science (ed.), *Boethius: De consolatione philosophiae*, EETS, o.s. 170 (London, 1927), 2.
[10] E. Talbot Donaldson, 'Idiom of Popular Poetry in the *Miller's Tale*', in his *Speaking of Chaucer* (London, 1970), 13–29 (at 17–19).
[11] For Chaucer's rhetoric, see Amanda Holton, *The Sources of Chaucer's Poetics* (Aldershot, 2008).
[12] Simon Horobin, *Chaucer's Language*, 2nd edn. (Basingstoke, 2013), 128–51.
[13] See Larry D. Benson (general ed.), *The Riverside Chaucer* (Boston, MA, 1987), 78. On decorum and vulgarity in Chaucer, see David Burnley and Graham Williams, 'Language', in Peter Brown (ed.), *A New Companion to Chaucer* (Hoboken, NJ, 2019), 227–42 (at 232–3).
[14] On the careful craftsmanship of Chaucer's metre and rhyme, see the brief comments in Burnley and Williams, 'Language', 230–2.
[15] G. H. Roscow, *Syntax and Style in Chaucer's Poetry* (Cambridge, 1981).

While those celebrating Chaucer's poetic style downplayed its continuities with earlier English verse, they thus articulated the ground-breaking effect of Chaucer's linguistic and formal choices *in toto*. Hoccleve memorializes Chaucer in the *Regiment* as both 'the honour of Englisshe tonge' and 'floure of eloquence' (1959 and 1962). Chaucer's works offered 'ornat endytyng / That is to al this land enlumynyng' (1973–4), while his death deprived England 'of the swetnesse / Of rethorik' (2084–5). Hoccleve's phrasing echoes Chaucer's Clerk's description of Petrarch 'whos rethorike sweete / Enlumyned al Ytaille of poetrie' (*Canterbury Tales*, 4.32–3).[16] The verb *enluminen*, as well as suggesting that such verse enlightens its readers, also asserts that it has the power to make the vernaculars of Italy and England illustrious, not inferior or subordinate but equally worthy of praise.

Lydgate and Aureation

Building on the posthumous praise of Scogan, Walton, and Hoccleve, John Lydgate particularized this account of Chaucer's literary innovation, and, in doing so, created an important model of the causes and effects of the Chaucerian high style. In Book 2 of the *Troy Book*, Lydgate describes what is supposedly missing from his own English in comparison to Chaucer's, though in fact he enumerates features of literary language which he himself valued and which would, through his influence, become characteristic of much fifteenth-century verse. He professes that 'Of rethorik ... I haue no flour / Nor hewes riche, stonys nor perre' (2.4726–7), that is he lacks both flowers and colours (i.e., figures of speech and thought), and jewels or pearls.[17] Such imagery suggests that poets ornament their verse with exquisite language as if with precious gems, whether their jewels are rhetorical figures or individual words.

Lydgate's own academic training as a young Benedictine monk took place during the revival of Anglo-Latin rhetoric teaching in Oxford in the last decades of the fourteenth century and the first years of the fifteenth, when tutors returned to the study of early medieval arts of poetry and rhetoric.[18] These earlier works catalogued and exemplified rhetorical schemes and tropes which could be used by those writing Latin prose in letters, treatises, or sermons. They also offered analyses of literary language, particularly the capacity of words and figures to decorate or illuminate verse. Alongside sweetness of content and colouring of style, Matthew of Vendôme names '*verba polita*' (polished words) as the third element which creates a poem's flavour and elegance.[19] Just as an object shines more because of '*alicuius margarite vel emblematis*' (some pearl or inlay), Matthew writes in his *Ars versificatoria* that '*similiter sunt quedam dicciones que sunt quasi gemmarum vicarie, ex quarum artificiosa positione totum metrum videtur festivari*' (similarly, there are some expressions which are, as it were, substitutes for jewels; from skillful positioning of these the whole meter will seem to be celebrating).[20] Alan of Lille's account of rhetoric's powers in his

---

[16] Benson (ed.), *Riverside Chaucer*, 137.

[17] John Lydgate, in Henry Bergen (ed.), *Lydgate's Troy Book*, 4 vols., EETS, e.s. 97, 103, 106, 127 (London, 1906, 1908, 1910, 1935), 1.279.

[18] Martin Camargo, 'Chaucer and the Oxford Renaissance of Anglo-Latin Rhetoric', *Studies in the Age of Chaucer*, 34 (2012), 173–207, and 'The Late Fourteenth-Century Renaissance of Anglo-Latin Rhetoric', *Philosophy and Rhetoric*, 45 (2012), 107–33.

[19] Matthew of Vendôme, '*Ars versificatoria*', in Franco Munari (ed.), *Mathei Vindocinesis: Opera*, 3 vols. (Rome, 1977–88), 3.165. Translation from Matthew of Vendôme, in Roger Parr (trans.), *Ars versificatoria: The Art of the Versemaker* (Milwaukee, WI, 1981), 79.

[20] Munari (ed.), *Mathei Vindocinesis: Opera*, 3.139 (Parr (trans.), *Ars versificatoria*, 64).

Anticlaudianus, a poem which describes an ideal education in terms similar to these early medieval arts, likewise describes beautiful, illuminated language:

> Assunt Rethoricae cultus floresque colorum,
> verba quibus stellata nitent et sermo decorem
> induit, et multa splendescit clausula luce.
> Has sermonis opes, cultus et sidera verbi
> copia Rethoricae iactat iuvenisque loquelam
> pingit et in vario praesignit verba colore.

(At hand also are the elegances of Rhetoric and its flowers of speech, through which words shine like stars, a discourse acquires dignity, and a final phrase gives out a brilliant light. The bounty of Rhetoric casts forth these riches of speech, these graces and brilliants of language, adorns the young man's speaking and dignifies his words with a variety of colours.)[21]

Such an education left Lydgate well placed not only to follow Chaucer in developing a high style for English verse but also to theorize the evolution of English as a literary language. Lydgate does not transpose the techniques of rhetoric exemplified by Matthew and others directly into English poetry, but he borrows their celebration of poetic language as decorated and illuminated.

In Book Three of his *Troy Book*, Lydgate expands on his account of Chaucer's supposed transformation of literary English, describing English's evolution from supposedly crude and simple to praiseworthy and eloquent:

For he owre Englishe gilte with his sawes*,	*words*
Rude and boistous* firste be olde dawes*,	*humble, days*
That was ful fer from al perfeccioun,	
And but of litel reputacioun,	
Til that he cam, and, þoruȝ* his poetrie,	*through*
Gan oure tonge firste to magnifie,	
And adourne it with his elloquence ...	
(3.4237–43)[22]	

The choice of words in these lines is itself designed to act out such a transformation, though scrutinizing their vocabulary reveals that Lydgate, just like Chaucer, draws on centuries of word borrowing to create this supposed renovation of English. For the sake of contrast, Lydgate begins with words derived from Old English: *sawes*, *gilte*, and the archaic plural *dawes*. *Boistous* and *rude*, which were perhaps no longer recognizably French by the time Lydgate was writing, at least to monolingual speakers, were in use in thirteenth-century Anglo-Norman and borrowed by 1300, showing the long embedding of French-derived words in English vocabulary. Lydgate then shifts gears from the third line of this quotation to include polysyllabic words, generally in rhyme position, producing the feminine rhyming characteristic of courtly verse. Yet the majority of these words are in use in Anglo-Norman and already borrowed into fourteenth-century English. *Poetrie* and *elloquence*

---

[21] Alan of Lille, in Winthrop Wetherbee (ed. and trans.), *Literary Works*, Dumbarton Oaks Medieval Library, 22 (Cambridge, MA, 2013), 450–1.
[22] Bergen (ed.), *Lydgate's Troy Book*, 2.516–17.

had arrived more recently as a result of Ricardian translation of Latin texts in the 1380s and 1390s. Only one word here, *adourne*, is, as far as we can tell, first used in English by Chaucer (though *aourner* and *adonare* would be familiar from French and Latin), appearing in the opening phrase of the proem to Book Three of *Troilus and Criseyde*. As with Chaucer's supposed transformation of English, Lydgate's lexical ornamentation develops and exaggerates tendencies already present within literary language.

In theorizing his own poetics, Lydgate builds on the twelfth-century representations of verse as ornamented, jewelled, gleaming, and illuminated by decorative words and figures which he encountered in his rhetorical education. He describes his fear in the Prologue of the *Troy Book* that his pen lacks 'aureat lycour' (31).[23] Such liquid is not the black ink of everyday writing but an imagined golden fluid which would create the style and rhetoric demanded by his source, Guido delle Colonne's *Historia destructionis Troiae*. This golden writing literalizes Hoccleve's image of Chaucer's illumination of English verse and becomes a vital trope of Lydgate's poetics. In the *Life of our Lady*, a biography of the Virgin, Lydgate testifies that Chaucer was first 'to distille and rayne / The golde dewe dropes of speche and eloquence / Into our tunge' (2.1632–4).[24] Though putatively describing Chaucer's innovation, this account of literary inspiration conveys Lydgate's own poetic aspirations. Lydgate's golden dewdrops project an analogy between Mary's conception of Jesus through the Holy Spirit and the granting of poetic inspiration and linguistic skill, as Robert Meyer-Lee explains:

> like Christ's possession of eternal divinity, the poem possesses a quality divinely bestowed upon its mortal author, the 'grace' that was 'shede' into his 'penne', which in turn is evident in—that is, signified by—the seminally illumined 'golde dewe drops of speche and eloquence' that are the manifestations of discursive grace.[25]

Varieties of Aureation

Lydgate repeats similar figurations of literary language in other poems, whether in describing Chaucer's skill or when appealing for help from muses or divinities because his own style is supposedly lacking.[26] Such passages, confessing what is purportedly missing from Lydgate's verse, show him aspiring to eloquence, sweetness, harmony, and the skilful use of rhetorical colours and flowers (that is, figures of speech and thought).[27] Lydgate is more evaluative than descriptive and does not fully articulate what distinguishes this aureate style. Nonetheless, the adjective *aureate* gives the modern critical term *aureation* which,

---

[23] Bergen (ed.), *Lydgate's Troy Book*, 1.2. On what Lydgate means by the term, see John Norton-Smith (ed.), *John Lydgate: Poems* (Oxford, 1966), 192–5.

[24] In Joseph A. Lauritis, Ralph A. Klinefelter, and Vernon F. Gallagher (eds), *A Critical Edition of John Lydgate's Life of Our Lady* (Pittsburgh, PA, 1961), 426 (punctuation altered). See also Bergen (ed.), *Lydgate's Troy Book*, 1.279 (2.4697–700).

[25] Robert J. Meyer-Lee, 'The Emergence of the Literary in John Lydgate's *Life of Our Lady*', JEGP, 109 (2010), 322–48 (at 328–9). On Lydgate's aureate poetics, see also Andrea Denny-Brown, 'Charles d'Orléans' Aureation', in R. D. Perry and Mary-Jo Arn (eds), *Charles D'Orléans' English Aesthetic: The Form, Poetics, and Style of Fortunes Stabilnes* (Cambridge, 2020), 211–35 (at 219–23).

[26] For further discussion, see Amanda Walling, 'Feminizing Aureation in Lydgate's *Life of Our Lady* and *Life of Saint Margaret*', *Neophilologus*, 101 (2017), 321–36.

[27] For an in-depth study of the attitudes and assumptions about poetry and language that underpin Lydgate's poetics and those of his fifteenth-century successors, see Lois A. Ebin, *Illuminator, Makar, Vates: Visions of Poetry in the Fifteenth Century* (Lincoln, NE, 1988).

in its narrowest definition, is 'the use of (mainly Latin) loans that have hardly been assimilated into the language'.[28] It does not begin with Lydgate: there are proto-aureate passages in Chaucer's various Marian invocations and Hoccleve's religious poems that also have diction which we might label as 'aureate'.[29] Within these lyrics are new words which, as far as we can tell, Hoccleve introduces into English. He is the first to use *intercession*, in this case simply transferring a common concept familiar as Latin *intercessio* and French *intercession*.[30] A trilingual audience might hardly have been conscious of this as a new word in English. More unfamiliar might be *flagicioun* ('an urgent demand or incitement', from Latin *flagitare*) and *exaudicioun* ('the granting of a prayer', from Latin *exauditio*, found in the Vulgate Bible and Augustine's *City of God*, perhaps also inspired by the French verb *exaucer*).[31] Such polysyllabic coinages are often nouns, recognizable by their suffixes, used for ease of rhyme in stanzas which require several rhymes on the same sound.

Hoccleve also coins adjectives which appear within the line and are not driven by the need for rhyme or the desire to display Latinate diction at the line end. In his 'Mother of God', he constructs a comparison which drives him to borrow from a Latin technical register. Just as it is only our eyes, rather than the rest of our body, which are 'perceptible of light', so Mary was the only virgin to have the power to gestate divinity.[32] *Perceptible* derives from Latin *perceptibilis*, found in academic writing in relation to the action of the senses. Words like *exaudition* and *perceptible* would have been decipherable by educated trilingual readers, while a less learned audience might have found these words exotic and solemnizing. Importantly, Hoccleve does not simply decorate his verse with Latinate coinages, but also produces new words from the available native elements of English. Our sins, for example, are *cloudeful* because they obscure our virtue.[33] Through both Latinate and vernacular coinages, Hoccleve defamiliarizes the potentially clichéd and formulaic language of prayer, creating verse whose conventional gestures of devotion are reanimated by the introduction of novel vocabulary.

This literary fashion for polysyllabic, barely assimilated words is transmitted from one generation to another and moves outwards from its courtly and metropolitan origins to wider communities of readers and writers through the fifteenth century. It is not one style but many styles, sharing some features but differing in others, each poet creating their own particular literary idiolect. One can see such variation in the Middle English translation of Guillaume de Deguileville's *Pèlerinage de l'âme*, completed in 1410 or 1413. Though predominantly in prose, the *Pylgremage of the Sowle* versifies the various complaints, letters, charters, and angels' songs which are inset in the allegorical narrative.[34] One of these verse inserts was written by Hoccleve, and the others have thus been tentatively attributed to him, though they may equally represent the work of an anonymous versifier moving in Lancastrian literary circles. In one manuscript of the *Pylgremage*, a mid-fifteenth-century copy whose scribes can be associated with Lincolnshire, the original work is supplemented

---

[28] Sara María Pons-Sanz, *The Language of Early English Literature: From Cædmon to Milton* (Basingstoke, 2014), 60.
[29] For example, the invocations to Mary in the *Prioress's Prologue* and *Second Nun's Prologue*, as well as some of the vocabulary of his *ABC*, a translation of a French Marian prayer.
[30] Thomas Hoccleve, in Frederick J. Furnivall and I. Gollancz (eds) and Jerome Mitchell and A. I. Doyle (rev. eds), *Hoccleve's Works: The Minor Poems*, EETS, e.s. 61 and 93, reprinted in one vol. (London, 1970), 276.
[31] Furnivall and Gollancz (eds), *Hoccleve's Works*, 279 and 44.
[32] Furnivall and Gollancz (eds), *Hoccleve's Works*, 287.
[33] Furnivall and Gollancz (eds), *Hoccleve's Works*, 55.
[34] Rosemarie Potz McGerr (ed.), *The Pilgrimage of the Soul. Vol. 1: A Critical Edition of the Middle English Dream Vision* (New York, 1990).

both with further lyric insertions and, in three cases, with extra stanzas added to the original poems.³⁵ Comparing the stanzas composed in the first decades of the fifteenth century with these later additions shows how these fashionable features could be adapted and exaggerated. In the following example from this manuscript from an angelic song in honour of the Purification of the Virgin, the first stanza was written by the original versifier while the second and third are the additions:

> Honourid be þou blessid lady bright:
> By thi persone enlumyned is nature;
> Of heuen blisse augmented is þe light
> By presence of so faire a creature.
> Thi worthynesse passes al mesure,
> ffor vnto thyne estate imperiale
> No preisynge is that may be peregale*.   *equal*
>
> What nedid þe birth with oute synne
> To haue purificacione,
> Bot with meknesse agayn to wynne
> That Adames preuaricacion
> Deseruyd, and hadd pryuacioun*   *was removed*
> ffro blisse; bot þat humylite
> Our restauracioun agayn shuld be?
>
> The gates were sparred* of paradyse   *locked*
> To vs by Eues transgressione:
> By mayde mary, princesse of price,
> There is now appericione.
> She is now oure proteccioun:
> This blissed lucifere orient
> Detaynes lucifere occident.
>   (8–21)³⁶

The first stanza is carefully syllable-counted with features which differentiate it from prose and everyday speech. Syntactical inversion accommodates the demands of metre and rhyme, as does the shifting of stress to French patterns in words like *per<u>sone</u>*, *na<u>ture</u>*, *me<u>sure</u>*, and trisyllabic *crea<u>ture</u>*.³⁷ Despite these literary features, the poet's aim is not to exclude ordinary language: there is a mix of everyday and formal lexis (both *bright* and *enlumyned* for example). The poet uses native abstract nouns (*worthynesse*, *preisynge*) alongside Latinate words. None of the borrowings in this stanza have been coined by the author; rather they are already in English having been borrowed from Latin (*enlumyned*, *augmented*, *imperiale*) and French (*peregale*).

By contrast, the additions were likely written by a cleric with less interest in or knowledge of the principles of versification which underpin Ricardian and Lancastrian courtly verse and with a different impulse about poetic lexis, producing a much more ostentatious aureate style. Though the second and third stanzas have similar amounts of syntactical inversion to the first, they are metrically less regular and less carefully syllable-counted. The aureate diction generally takes the form of polysyllabic nouns (conspicuous by their

---

³⁵ P. D. Roberts, 'Some Unpublished Middle English Lyrics and Stanzas in a Victoria Public Library Manuscript', *English Studies*, 54 (1973), 105–18.
³⁶ Roberts, 'Unpublished Middle English Lyrics', 111.
³⁷ On stress shifts like these, see Roger Lass, 'Phonology and Morphology', in Blake (ed.), *1066–1476*, 23–155 (at 89).

suffixes *-ation* and *-cio(u)n*) and adjectives used in rhyme position. The poet constructs some learned wordplay, contrasting Mary as the eastern morning star, 'lucifere orient', who keeps prisoner or holds back 'lucifere occident', the devil. The word *appericione*, meaning an opening or unclosing (here the gates of hell) appears only in surgical texts before this date and so may well represent a direct coinage modelled on Latin *apertionem*, a noun of action deriving from *aperire*, 'to open'. In these stanzas, aureation is much less one part of a larger poetic project to create eloquent, smoothly controlled verse and much more an end in itself. The added stanzas showcase individual items of aureate diction, emphasized by feminine rhyme, presenting polysyllabic words to be deciphered with reference to a reader's own clerical training.

At their most extreme, some experiments in aureation produce an avant garde poetics which fuses English and Latin. A lyric like '*Te deum laudamus*' shows how stylized and *recherché* such texts can become, though the eclecticism of its literary language suggests that its attribution to Lydgate is doubtful.[38] The poem partly quotes and partly amplifies the *Te deum*, a fourth-century hymn, combining macaronic writing with ornamental alliteration and noticeably Latinate English diction within the constraints of a refrained octave stanza rhyming *ababbcbc*. Here one stanza of the poem expands three lines of the Latin hymn via a mixture of quotation, expansion of the Latin, and translation into English:

> *Tibi omnis chorus angelorum,*
> With the principal Ierarchyes of the pretence,
> *Tibi* coriously *cantant celi celorum,*
> *Cherubyn et Seraphyn* in thy precious presence;
> Incessauntly syngyng this solempne sentence,
> *Sanctus! Sanctus! tu summus Sanctus!*
> Lord God of hostis, omnipotence,
> *Te laudat omnis spiritus.*
>
> (9–16)

As well as alternating lines of Latin and English, this stanza also combines the two languages within a single line, an English adverb qualifying an otherwise Latin verb phrase in line 11. In the English lines, aureate borrowings (*ierarchyes, incessauntly, omnipotence*) translate and expand the original Latin text.

This stanza illustrates the variety of methods by which Latin and English might be hybridized, an approach which was very fashionable in the middle of the century. A fellow East Anglian poet, John Metham, praised Lydgate posthumously for his 'bokys endytyd wyth termys of retoryk, / And half chongyd Latyne' (*Amoryus and Cleopes*, 2194–5).[39] Metham's presentation of Lydgate's literary diction as Latin only partly assimilated into English is sometimes cited in order to disparage Lydgate's verse, but Metham intends this very much as a compliment. It was not, though, to everyone's taste, and could be criticized as clerical self-indulgence taking delight in obscure and learned terms in sermons, letters, or treatises which many in congregations could not understand. The vice characters in the

---

[38] In H. N. McCracken (ed.), *The Minor Poems of John Lydgate*, EETS, e.s. 107 (London, 1911), 22. This poem is also discussed by Pons-Sanz, *Language of Early English Literature*, 60–2.

[39] Stephen Page (ed.), *Amoryus and Cleopes* (Kalamazoo, MI, 1999), 98.

East Anglian morality play *Mankind* mock the 'Englysch Laten' (124) spoken by the personification Mercy who is, as Mischief says, 'all to-gloryede in yowr termys' (773) ('too elaborate in his language').[40]

Such Latin-English hybrids were not however merely motivated by fashion or pretention, but also represent a reaction to Lollard demands for translation of religious materials into English accessible to all. Aureation thus in part emerged 'as a lexical manifestation of reform orthodoxy'.[41] As one part of their response to Wycliffite calls for ecclesiastical reform, churchmen were motivated to produce various kinds of devotional material to meet the needs of an enthusiastic and curious laity. As Vincent Gillespie writes, '[t]he membrane between the registers and lexis of clerical Latin and those of the English vernacular seems to have become increasingly permeable in the early fifteenth century. Aureation created a lexical and stylistic bridge between the Latin language of formal theology and the vulgar tongue of vernacularity'.[42] It permitted authors to write in a vernacular which was not the same as the plainer styles of Lollard translation, producing an English which remained a special, elite register requiring clerical mediation of its content.

While ecclesiastical reform offers one point of origin for aureation, it is in truth a style (or set of related styles) whose motivations and causations are multifaceted and not yet fully mapped out. Scholarly studies, often concentrating on the vocabulary of a single poet or a small group of poets, have disagreed as to whether aureate borrowings are generally technical or scientific terms from French and Latin coined in English to fill a lexical gap or whether such diction is borrowed for 'strictly artistic, rhetorical ends', if such a distinction can be made.[43] There is similar disagreement as to the particular registers of Latin and French which provide the lexical sources of aureation. A narrower focus on aureate Marian texts suggests that the majority of terms were borrowed from or modelled on the Latin of the liturgy, hymnody and other devotional registers, as well as from the Vulgate Bible.[44] Yet elements of the aureate style diffuse widely in the fifteenth century, far beyond this more restricted definition. Particular sources of aureate diction may thus depend on the education, linguistic abilities, and professions of individual poets, as well as on the subject matter of the texts they translated and composed.

Likewise, it is not possible to generalize about the effect of aureate diction on English vocabulary. Some words were purely nonce-words, one-offs coined for a specific purpose which did not catch on more broadly, yet others became key parts of the English still in use today for abstract discussion. The purposes and functions of aureation are thus various rather than uniform. Pamela Gradon has demonstrated how aureation increases semantic density and specificity in some passages, while in other lines semantic precision is diluted, with learned polysyllabic words chosen more for the sake of sound than for their referent.[45] Yet, as Northrop Frye writes in relation to Lydgate's aureate diction, even such vagueness has significance, gesturing at 'that region of thought where ideas give out and symbols

---

[40] Kathleen M. Ashley and Gerard NeCastro (eds), *Mankind* (Kalamazoo, MI, 2010), 17, 37.
[41] Vincent Gillespie, 'Chichele's Church: Vernacular Theology in England after Thomas Arundel', in Vincent Gillespie and Kantik Ghosh (eds), *After Arundel: Religious Writing in Fifteenth-Century England* (Turnhout, 2011), 36 (fn. 79). See also the brief comments in Vincent Gillespie, 'Religious Writing', in Roger Ellis (ed.), *The Oxford History of Literary Translation in English, Volume One: To 1500* (Oxford, 2008), 234–83 (at 234–9, 254).
[42] Vincent Gillespie, 'Vernacular Theology', in Paul Strohm (ed.), *Middle English: Oxford Twenty-First Century Approaches to Literature* (Oxford, 2007), 401–20 (at 418).
[43] Norton-Smith (ed.), *John Lydgate: Poems*, 194.
[44] Douglas Gray defines aureation more narrowly than I have done here and hence argues for a restricted set of linguistic sources in his *Later Medieval English Literature* (Oxford, 2008), 130–2. For commentary on the often contradictory definitions of aureation, see Denny-Brown, 'Charles d'Orléans' Aureation?', 214–15.
[45] Pamela Gradon, *Form and Style in Early English Literature* (London, 1971), 347–60.

begin'.⁴⁶ For Frye, the function of a celebrated example of the aureate style such as Dunbar's *Ane Ballat of Our Lady* is not so much the particularizing of meaning but rather the invocation of language's 'capacity for expressing the artificial, using that word in its old-fashioned laudatory sense' (that is things which are man-made, technically skilful or ingenious).⁴⁷ Dunbar's Marian hymn of praise, which deploys aureate diction and other types of lexical invention to create lines of verse each with two or three internal rhymes (e.g., 'Implore, adore, thow, indeflore', 55), represents human language at its most strikingly crafted in praise of the Virgin. Frye suggests that we might see such artifice as 'a stimulus to contemplation' rather than as ostentatious, trivializing, or merely aesthetic.⁴⁸

Beyond Marian Aureation

Whatever aureation's origins, the neologisms which distinguish the aureate style became a dominant feature of fifteenth-century versification. Inspired by Chaucer's supposed invention of English as a literary language, translators exercised their poetic licence to coin new words and to draw on the linguistic resources of French and Latin. Though not usually considered 'aureate' texts, the lexical creativity of these works expands the vocabulary of English in the service of poetry. Such translations thus complicate any straightforward account of widening vernacular access to Latin and French materials. Works in Latin and French were translated into English, but that same English required knowledge of specialized registers of French and Latin, or indeed knowledge of the source text itself, to decode it (though the surrounding English would give some clue to the meaning of the word). This polysyllabic, neologistic style was thus not prompted by a desire to communicate the meaning of a source in as simple a fashion as possible. Neologisms appear even when a word was not prompted by a translation's source material. The style of *On husbondrie*, a Middle English verse-translation of Palladius's guide to agriculture, *De re rustica*, is not plain and practical, as we might expect from a work of instruction, but has a considerable amount of formal and lexical ornamentation. The translator not only invents English neologisms modelled on the technical terms of his source, but also coins words when there is no prompt for such neologism in the source text.⁴⁹

Similar lexical choices are found in the vocabulary of mid-century English verse-translations of French texts. The *Liber proverbiorum* (also sometimes called the *Summum sapientiae*), a translation of an early fourteenth-century Anglo-Norman collection of proverbs, was made, as its epilogue makes clear, for a queen of England who, in the period in which the translation was written, must have been a French noblewoman (either Joan of Navarre, Catherine of Valois, or Margaret of Anjou).⁵⁰ The same poet also translated a French romance by Couldrette, *Mélusine* or *Le Roman de Parthenay*, which was completed in 1401, into rhyme royal as the *Romans of Partenay*. Both texts are ornamented with fashionable aureate diction, suggesting that the purpose of these translations is to update the form and language of pre-existing texts. In the *Liber proverbiorum*'s prologue,

---

⁴⁶ Northrop Frye, 'Intoxicated with Words', in Robert D. Denham (ed.), *Northrop Frye's Uncollected Prose* (Toronto, 2015), 61–74 (at 69).
⁴⁷ Frye, 'Intoxicated with Words', 70. The text of Dunbar's lyric can be found in Priscilla Bawcutt (ed.), *The Poems of William Dunbar*, 2 vols. (Glasgow, 1998), 16.
⁴⁸ Frye, 'Intoxicated with Words', 72.
⁴⁹ Daniel Wakelin, *Humanism, Reading, and English Literature 1430–1530* (Oxford, 2007), 47.
⁵⁰ Information about these texts can be found in Jenni Nuttall, 'Margaret of Anjou as Patron of English Verse?: The *Liber Proverbiorum* and the *Romans of Partenay*', *Review of English Studies*, n.s. 67 (281) (2016), 636–59.

for example, we find *ficte* ('fictional, man-made', from Latin *fictus*), *antiquious* ('ancient', modelled on Latin *antiquus* or perhaps combining French *antique* with the suffix *–ious*) and *impressure* ('impression', from French *impressure*).⁵¹ Works like *Partenay* and the *Liber* could have easily read in their original language by a French queen and her francophone household. Moreover, their rarefied neologisms would not have helped her or her attendants to learn English of an everyday sort: their diction would often need a knowledge of French and Latin to decipher it. Rather like the porous boundaries between clerical Latin and the vernacular, translations such as *Partenay* and the *Liber proverbiorum* bear witness to a literary culture impelled to synthesize the three main languages of medieval England and to decorate English with elite new coinages, ones which celebrated the sophistication of this Anglo-French court culture.

The neologistic diction found in *Liber proverbiorum* and *Partenay* also emerges in fifteenth-century historiography. John Hardyng was an administrator and soldier who, having retired to an Augustinian priory, worked on various versions of his history of Britain and its legendary Trojan founders, the first completed in 1457 for Henry VI and later versions intended for Richard, duke of York and subsequently for Edward IV. Hardyng's description of Priam's building of Troy, followed by a stanza in which he steers his narrative back towards Anchises, father of Aeneas, illustrates how conspicuous diction sits alongside elements which have become second nature in mid-fifteenth-century versification:

So brode he made Troy and in longitude	
Thre days jornays it was on horse to ryde	
With walles stronge and toures grete multitude	
And yates therto ful strongly fortyfyde.	
Never cyté was so gretly edyfiede*	*built*
Of marbre clere, fresshe of dyverse coloure	
Of whiche the walles were murifyde*	*walled*
Two hundre cubits with many rial toure.	
This longeth nought I say to my matere	
It is so ferre and longe degrecioun*	*digression*
Wherfore fro it I wille agayn refere	
To Anchises, fro whom I made egrecioun*	*a departure*
That fadyr was by alle repetycioun	
To Eneas as cronyclers expreme*	*express*
Who gat Ascanyus by disposicioun	
Of God above by ought that men can deme.	
(2.137–52).⁵²	

Hardyng's verse imitates Chaucerian and Lydgatian forms and styles, even if his verse is not always as metrically regular as his predecessors. He maps his sentences onto the stanza as a unit, fitting his content into the frame of his chosen rhyme-scheme through inversions of usual word order and the fluid piling up of clause on clause. The chronicle also exhibits features which could be labelled as aureate, most particularly polysyllabic words borrowed from Latin and French creating feminine rhyming.

Some of the polysyllabic words in these stanzas are already in English (*longitude*, *multitude*, *fortified*, *edified*) and create a somewhat pretentious effect, with near-synonyms appearing for the sake of rhyme (first *degrecioun*, 'digression', and then *egrecioun*, i.e., a

---

⁵¹ Nuttall, 'Margaret of Anjou', 652, 653.
⁵² In Sarah Peverley and James Simpson (eds.), *John Hardyng: Chronicle, Edited from British Library MS Lansdowne 204: Volume 1* (Kalamazoo, MI, 2015).

departure from his subject matter), as do Latinate words chosen for the same reason in place of plainer alternatives (*edified* rather than *built*, for example). Some of the words in these stanzas are likely to be Hardyng's own coinages (e.g., *murified*, 'encased' or literally 'enwalled', presumably based on French *murer*, 'to wall', or *expreme*, 'to express', modelled on Latin *exprimere*). One suspects that these two coinages are likewise created for ease of rhyme as the stanza-form constrains him towards the end of each verse. These polysyllabic rhyme-words have become the fifteenth-century equivalent of the poetic formulae and tags which helped earlier Middle English poets to meet the demands of versification. Nevertheless, even though some of his diction may be redundant or showy, Hardyng confidently draws on Latin and French to expand his vocabulary, though we might not necessarily think of him as a clerical or learned author. As well as coining many new words modelled on Latin equivalents, Hardyng also takes lexical items directly from French, such as *assemblement* ('a host or army'), *broudur* ('embroidery', from *broudure*), *felonement* ('treacherously'), *fraterne* ('fraternal'), and *regence* ('sovereignty').[53] Such lexis anticipates a trilingual readership unconcerned by the boundaries between French and English, and able to interpret neologisms with ease.

Strange English, Strange Scots

In addition to his lexical inventiveness, Hardyng also sporadically bends the spelling or sound of existing English words in order to fit into the rhyme-pattern of his stanzas. To rhyme with *feete* and *mete*, for example, he uses the variant spelling *behete* rather than the more usual *behight* or *behot* (meaning 'a promise', from the verb *behoten*).[54] Elsewhere he rhymes *assigned* with *benyngned*, a variant form of the adjective *benign*.[55] Writing before the spelling and morphology of English was fully standardized, Hardyng made use of this freedom, at least where licenced by the need for rhyme, to distort English in this small-scale way. Poets and their readers tolerated or perhaps even delighted in a literary language which was artificial, stylized, and notably strange.

Such strangeness appears not only in the Chaucerian and Lydgatian traditions but also in alliterative poetry. *The Buke of the Howlat*, a comic poem in which an owl dissatisfied with his appearance has his request for better plumage debated by a council of birds, was written by Richard Holland, a Scottish cleric, between 1447 and 1452.[56] It is the oldest surviving alliterative poem in Scots, composed in the thirteen-line stanza which became popular north of the border having been used earlier in England for narrative. This stanza-form, combining dense alliteration and rhyme, often has, in its fourteenth-century examples, additional wordplay, punning, and consonance. To write in this form was to participate in a tradition of demanding verse-forms which strained language almost to breaking point, distortions which both poets and readers seem to have enjoyed. In some stanzas, Holland imitates earlier works which use a single consonant rhyme for the first eight lines of a stanza with only the vowels differentiating the *ababababa* rhyme (612–24 and 885–92). The

---

[53] These examples are from the second version of Hardyng's chronicle: H. Ellis (ed.), *The Chronicle of John Hardyng* (London, 1812), 169, 347, 287, 371, 158, 97, 98, 317, 421.
[54] Ellis (ed.), *Chronicle of John Hardyng*, 268.
[55] Ellis (ed.), *Chronicle of John Hardyng*, 211.
[56] See Ralph Hanna (ed.), *The Buke of the Howlat*, STS, 5th series, 12 (Woodbridge, 2014).

Howlat delights in linguistic experiment, having a passage of mock Gaelic mixed with pidgin Scots as spoken by a highland bard at a banquet the birds hold mid-poem (794–819). Like Hardyng, Holland employs verbal licences to create some of his rhymes. Ralph Hanna, who has recently edited the text, gives, *inter alia*, the examples of singular *duke* instead of the expected plural *dukis* (299), *deir* for superlative *deirest* (439) and, most extraordinarily, *citharist* (757), where the word for the player of a *cithara* becomes a name for the instrument itself in a musical catalogue.[57] Holland also makes use of southern English spellings and word forms, drawn from his reading of Chaucer and other poets. The verbal licences which Holland exploits can be paralleled in earlier poems as 'occasional variants' but are by no means the 'universal forms that Holland makes them'.[58] Holland's language is thus 'exuberant in its variousness and pursuit of parallel forms', an artificial hybrid differing from his own everyday speech, a literary language marking out its own special status.[59]

We might compare the strangeness of Holland's literary Scots with what Ardis Butterfield has described as the 'experimental English' of Charles, duke of Orleans, the French nobleman who spent twenty-five years in England as a prisoner following his capture at the battle of Agincourt in 1415.[60] During this lengthy imprisonment, Charles both translated French verse written in his younger days into English and wrote a considerable amount of verse in his newly acquired language. Charles's English poems exhibit 'startling colloquialisms and radical neologisms', alongside idiosyncrasies and what we might perceive as errors in grammar and spelling.[61] Butterfield sees this 'rough English' as a product of 'contact between English and French in the fifteenth century—a place full of pressure, radical redefinition and cultural uncertainty'.[62] More broadly, fifteenth-century poetry in English registers similarly experimental and unstable contact between English and Latin and between English and Scots, as well as between spoken and written language and between learned and unlettered discourses. Chaucer bequeaths to the fifteenth century not a stable hierarchy of low, middle, and high styles, but radical mixtures of informal and formal, oral and textual, everyday and artificial.

Not everyone shared this enthusiasm for mixed or hybrid languages, with some poets creating fantasies of purification through aureation. Just as Chaucer was said to have invented literary English at the start of the century, so by the first decade of the sixteenth century Lydgate could be imagined to have completed a process of purifying English of its humble origins. In his *Pastime of Pleasure* (first printed in 1509), Stephen Hawes, groom of the chamber to Henry VII, celebrates how classical authors conveyed knowledge by eloquent rhetoric: 'Vyrgyll ... and also Tullyus [i.e., Cicero]' educated their readers with 'latyn pure, swete and delycyous' (1161–2).[63] In Hawes's account, Lydgate inherits this pure Latinity from Virgil and Cicero and was thus able to infuse Latin vocabulary into English, displacing less elevated terms:

---

[57] Hanna (ed.), *Buke of the Howlat*, 50.
[58] Hanna (ed.), *Buke of the Howlat*, 22.
[59] Hanna (ed.), *Buke of the Howlat*, 23.
[60] Ardis Butterfield, 'Rough Translation: Charles d'Orléans, Lydgate and Hoccleve', in Emma Campbell and Robert Mills (eds), *Rethinking Translation: Ethics, Politics, Theory* (Cambridge, 2012), 204–25 (at 223).
[61] Butterfield, 'Rough Translation', 215. For discussion of Charles's English, see Mary-Jo Arn, 'Charles of Orleans and the Poems of BL MS, Harley 682', *English Studies*, 74 (1993), 222–35, and, more recently, Jeremy J. Smith, 'Charles d'Orléans and His Finding of English', in Perry and Arn (eds), *Charles D'Orléans' English Aesthetic*, 182–210.
[62] Butterfield, 'Rough Translation', 224.
[63] See William Edward Mead (ed.), *The Pastime of Pleasure*, EETS, o.s. 173 (London, 1928), 49.

> From whens my mayster Lydgate deryfyde* *derived*
> The depured* rethoryke in englysshe language, *purified*
> To make our tongue so clerely puryfyed
> That the vyle termes shoulde nothynge arage*, *enrage*
> As lyke a pye* to chattre in a cage, *magpie*
> But for to speke with Rethoryke formally
> In the good ordre withouten vylany.
>
> (1163–9)⁶⁴

Hawes imagines that Lydgate has purified the vernacular in a manner which is not only lexically but socially exclusive. English is purged of terms which are *vyle* (that is, morally offensive but also worthless or low in status) so that rhetoric can proceed without *vylany*, freed from anything shameful or churlish. In this theorization, aureation does not coexist with other registers but drives them out to create a pure Latin-English hybrid. Yet while Hawes privileges rhetorical schemes and tropes, order, decorum, and Latinate diction, his verse is not as carefully syllable-counted and its metre not as smoothly alternating as Chaucer's or Lydgate's. Hawes's word order in these lines is largely without inversion or dislocation and he cannot resist the contrastingly homely image of a magpie chattering, despite his praise of purified, elevated language.⁶⁵ For Hawes, aureate diction becomes the key signifier of social acceptability, rendering other elements of versification and poetic technique less indexical.

Hawes's claims of purification, however much they suit his own purpose, do not reflect the variousness of fifteenth-century literary English, a linguistic heterogeneity which increases as the century progress. John Skelton's poetry mixes aureate diction with informal speech, proverbs, insults and innuendos, snatches of songs, and parodies of and quotations from other languages in works in which high, middle, and low registers jostle.⁶⁶ Scottish *makars* compose poems famed for their aureation, such as Dunbar's *Ballad of our Lady* or his *Goldyn Targe*, yet embrace vulgarity and obscenity in their flytings.⁶⁷ Gavin Douglas, in the prologue of his translation of Virgil's *Aeneid* (completed in 1509), sets out what he must do to create the 'fowth' (Prologue, 120) or plenitude of language needed to convey Virgil's meaning fully. Though versifying in Scots, what he calls 'our awyn language' (111), Douglas will also, if necessary, select some word of 'bastard Latyn, French or Inglys' (117) or pronounce some words 'as nyghtbouris doys' (114), as his English neighbours do, that is, he will borrow a word from those languages (creating a 'bastard' hybrid lexis) or borrow spellings, stress-patterns, or variants from other dialects or languages.⁶⁸ Douglas is though careful to say that he doesn't do this because 'our tong is in the selwyn skant' (119), i.e., is in itself lacking, thereby acknowledging the capaciousness and variety already available within literary Scots by 1500.⁶⁹ Considering the Scottish *makars* in 1952, the poet Edwin

---

⁶⁴ Mead (ed.), *Pastime of Pleasure*, 49.

⁶⁵ On Hawes's own language, see Seth Lerer, 'The Rhetoric of Fame: Stephen Hawes's Aureate Diction', *Spenser Studies*, 5 (1984), 169–84.

⁶⁶ Greg Waite, 'Skelton and the English Language', in Sebastian Sobecki and John Scattergood (eds.), *A Critical Companion to John Skelton* (Cambridge, 2018), 139–62.

⁶⁷ Studies of the *makars'* diction can be found in Bengt Ellenberger, *The Latin Element in the Vocabulary of the Earlier Makars, Henryson and Dunbar*, Lund Studies in English, 51 (Lund, 1977), and Arne Zettersten, 'On the Aureate Diction of William Dunbar', in Michael Chesnutt et al. (eds), *Essays Presented to Knud Schibsbye: On his 75th Birthday 29 November 1979* (Copenhagen, 1979), 51–68. The range and diversity of Dunbar's language is outlined by Priscilla Bawcutt, *Dunbar the Makar* (Oxford, 1992), 347–82.

⁶⁸ Gavin Douglas, in David F. C. Coldwell (ed.), *Virgil's Aeneid*, 4 vols., STS, 3rd series, 25, 27, 28, 30 (Edinburgh, 1957–64), 2.6.

⁶⁹ The diverse vocabulary of Douglas's 'Palice of Honour' is discussed in Priscilla Bawcutt (ed.), *The Shorter Poems of Gavin Douglas*, STS, 5th series, 2 (Edinburgh, 1967), xlv-l.

Morgan saw their literary language as 'a brilliant, optimistic, zealous, unhappy, and premature attempt to produce what England successfully developed later in the next century—an instrument of expression that would fuse what was most valued and accessible in popular speech with an immense body of reference-extending terms'.[70] Yet, just as the critical stock of this century's poetry has risen, so too we might now revise Morgan's opinion of the literary language of Scots poetry, and indeed earlier assessments of fifteenth-century literary language as a whole. These literary languages were, in their own terms, successful and productive fusions of the energies of spoken and written English and Scots with borrowings from French and Latin, not purified and refined but eclectic and inventive.

---

[70] Edwin Morgan, 'Dunbar and the Language of Poetry', *Essays in Criticism*, 11 (1952), 138–56 (at 143).

CHAPTER 6
Verse Forms and Prosody

Eric Weiskott

This chapter describes the checklist of vernacular metrical options available to a fifteenth-century poet writing in English, with an emphasis on the internal diversity in metrical tradition and the diversity of traditions. The choice of a verse form might be, for various reasons, overdetermined by circumstances, but this chapter, for the sake of exposition, envisages a situation in which all options are open synoptically. The three major English verse forms are treated in order of historical attestation: alliterative verse and its offshoots, tetrameter and other four-stress forms, and pentameter. Of these, tetrameter accounts for the largest proportion of poetic output. A majority of the texts discussed in Part III of this volume are in tetrameter, with particular concentrations in practical and didactic treatises (Chapters 11 and 15–16), religious lyrics (Chapter 13), drama (Chapter 14), and romance (Chapters 19–22).

From the perspective of verse form, the history of poetry in English has had four phases. In the first and longest phase, from the beginnings of insular writing to *c*1200, alliterative verse was the single available form of poetry in English. In the second phase, to *c*1550, poets writing in English could choose from among several metres. In the third phase, to *c*1930, the 'iambic' (alternating-stress) pentameter invented by Geoffrey Chaucer eclipsed other metres in the hierarchy of verse forms. In the fourth (and, logically, the final) phase of metrical history, 'free' (unmetered) verse forms have dramatically displaced the cultural authority of metre: contemporary metered poetry in English must accept, or else labour to resist, strong connotations of aesthetic conservatism.

Diversity is a Chaucerian theme and keyword, from Chaucer's vision of 'a compaignye / Of sondry folk' (*Canterbury Tales*, 1.24–5) to the apostrophe to the work at the end of *Troilus and Criseyde*: 'And for ther is so gret diversite / In Englissh and in writyng of oure tonge …' (5.1793–4).[1] Yet it was the fifteenth century, not the fourteenth, in which poets working in English had the greatest diversity of verse forms from which to choose. The pentameter line did not begin to circulate until the beginning of the fifteenth century, with the copying of manuscripts of Chaucer's *Canterbury Tales*, *Parliament of Fowls*, *Troilus and Criseyde*, and lyrics; by the end of the sixteenth century, pentameter was the normative form of English drama, epic, and lyric. In between, pentameter, the form of Thomas Hoccleve's and others' poetry, was joined by two other metrical traditions. These were the alliterative metre, the form of *Mum and the Sothsegger*, a social satire influenced by William Langland's *Piers Plowman*; and tetrameter, the form of most of John Audelay's lyrics. Among the less common or more experimental verse forms attested in English in the fifteenth century, two merit special comment: tail rhyme, and, around the edges of the category 'poetry', the alliterating prose of the *Jack Upland* series of polemical treatises.

---

[1] Geoffrey Chaucer, 'The Canterbury Tales', in Larry D. Benson (general ed.), *The Riverside Chaucer*, 3rd edn. (Boston, MA, 1987). See Emily Steiner, '*Piers Plowman*, Diversity, and the Medieval Political Aesthetic', *Representations*, 91 (2005), 1–25 (at 19–20).

These metres had, by the fifteenth century, divergent histories, and poets handled them variously. Verse forms carried political and social meanings, but these cannot be mechanically extrapolated from the choice of form. One and the same form will signify differently when employed in different cultural contexts and turned to different literary effects. The study of prosody therefore is—or should be—part of cultural studies. The fifteenth century, a time of unprecedented formal diversity for poetry in English, requires that the cultural work of metre always be borne in mind. As David Lawton influentially observed (with reference only to pentameter), fifteenth-century poetry's reputation for 'dullness' masks the subtlety of its political and social stances.[2] What is needed is a theoretical framework for analysing the historically mediated relationship between literary form and social placement. Such is provided by Pierre Bourdieu's theory of the literary field, defined as 'the space of literary *prises de position* that are possible in a given period in a given society', where *prises de position* 'arise from the encounter between particular agents' dispositions (their *habitus*, shaped by their social trajectory) and their position in a field of positions'.[3] Metrical traditions go into the shaping of the ever-shifting 'literary *prises de position* that are possible', or what Bourdieu equivalently terms 'the *space of possibles*'.[4] Metrical tradition, as it were, forms the space of possibles; literary history is the record of actual position-taking. The fifteenth century was a time of expansion and realignment in the English literary field. Positions staked then had far-reaching consequences for literary history. Without the fifteenth century, William Shakespeare surely would have written his plays in tetrameter.

Fifteenth-century poetry in English had no prosody, if by *prosody* is meant an explicit theory of versification. In contrast to the study of Latin prosody, taught to every grammar-school boy down the ages, fifteenth-century literature in English corresponded to no academic subject. The very first treatises of English poetics lay far in the future. They would begin with George Gascoigne's *Certayne Notes of Instruction Concerning the Making of Verse or Ryme in English* (1575), itself a partial and distorting representation of what poets do. The time lag between poetic practice and literary theory means that one must reconstruct medieval English verse forms without the benefit of 'indigenous' systemic thinking, of the sort that one always has to hand for later periods of English literature, and for Latin. Metaliterary passages from within poems in English, such as the *Gawain* poet's allusion to a narrative 'With lel letteres loken' (*Sir Gawain and the Green Knight*, 35; 'enclosed in loyal learning/letters/writing'), often taken to refer to alliteration, are not sufficiently specific to be helpful for metrical scholarship.[5]

The historiography of English literature has endowed the subject of verse form with a teleological narrative that must be bracketed if we are to recover a sense of metrical cultures as they appeared to contemporaries. Alliterative verse is, for us, a 'lost tradition', having exited literary culture in the sixteenth century. But it was not yet lost for fifteenth-century poets.[6] The eventual triumph of pentameter, and, relatedly, its immediate and enduring association with London and the royal court, have meant that students of premodern poetry in English can bypass alliterative metre and tetrameter, proceeding directly from

---

[2] David Lawton, 'Dullness and the Fifteenth Century', *ELH*, 54 (1987), 761–99.
[3] Pierre Bourdieu, 'The Field of Cultural Production, or: The Economic World Reversed', trans. Richard Nice, *Poetics*, 12 (1983), 311–56 (at 311).
[4] Bourdieu, 'Field of Cultural Production', 313.
[5] Israel Gollancz (ed.), and Mabel Day and M. S. Serjeantson (intro.), *Sir Gawain and the Green Knight*, EETS, o.s. 210 (London, 1940). See Derek Pearsall, *Old English and Middle English Poetry* (London, 1977), 153–4, and Ian Cornelius, *Reconstructing Alliterative Verse: The Pursuit of a Medieval Meter* (Cambridge, 2017), 27–8.
[6] John Scattergood, *The Lost Tradition: Essays on Middle English Alliterative Poetry* (Dublin, 2000).

Chaucer to Hoccleve and John Lydgate; Thomas Wyatt and Henry Howard, earl of Surrey; Shakespeare and John Milton. But in the first half of the fifteenth century, Chaucer's interventions had not yet permeated literary culture beyond the southeast and East Anglia. Pentameter was, however temporarily, a local metre.

In this chapter, stressed syllables are underlined in quotations of verse. Single lines are accompanied by matching graphic notation, where 'S' represents a metrically stressed syllable, 'x' represents a metrically unstressed syllable, and parentheses denote an optional element. Thus a normative line of pentameter, with optional feminine ending, is xSxSxSxSxS(x).

Alliterative Verse and Alliterating Stanzaic Verse

Fifteenth-century poems in (unrhymed) alliterative verse and alliterating stanzaic verse are nearly all anonymous. This situation may be incidental, due to the precarious conditions of the survival of this form of poetry. Anonymity may equally be a by-product of the cultural work that poets asked the alliterative metre to perform. Alliterative poetics emphasizes universalist themes of community, penance, and salvation.[7] It is patrons, more than authors, who count in this poetic tradition. Indulging in a commonplace humility topos, the poet of *William of Palerne* represents himself as a reluctant translator obliging his patron, Humphrey de Bohun, earl of Hereford and Essex. A fifteenth-century example is the 'narrator' of the *Ireland Prophecy* (NIMEV 366.5/2834.3/3557.55), a Yorkist political prophecy of the 1450s, who emerges only and precisely to endorse the poem's formal work, e.g., 'I highte yow þe soothe' (80b; 'I swear to you the truth of this').[8]

The anonymity of most alliterative verse contributes to difficulties of dating.[9] For example, does *St Erkenwald* belong in this volume of the *Oxford History of Poetry in English*, or the previous one?[10] Extant only in BL MS Harley 2250 (1477), the poem is sometimes ascribed to the *Gawain* poet. In all, there are over thirty alliterative and alliterating stanzaic poems certainly or plausibly from the fifteenth century. They are listed in the subsections that follow.

The alliterative tradition was a clerkly tradition.[11] Although not all alliterative poets were clerics by any means, the poetry's penitential focus and degraded authors/narrators speak to the pressure of clerical social trajectories on literary practice.

Alliterative Metre in the Fifteenth Century

The form and genealogy of Middle English alliterative verse have posed a severe challenge to historical understanding. Technical studies from Thomas Cable and Hoyt N. Duggan in the 1980s and 1990s demonstrated that alliterative verse possessed a rigorous metrical

---

[7] See David Lawton, 'The Unity of Middle English Alliterative Poetry', *Speculum*, 58 (1983), 72–94.
[8] Eric Weiskott, '*The Ireland Prophecy*: Text and Metrical Context', *Studies in Philology*, 114 (2017), 245–77.
[9] See Ralph Hanna, 'Alliterative Poetry', in David Wallace (ed.), *The Cambridge History of Medieval English Literature* (Cambridge, 1999), 488–512 (at 494–7), and Cornelius, *Reconstructing Alliterative Verse*, 100–3.
[10] See David Lawton, 'Literary History and Scholarly Fancy: The Date of Two Middle English Alliterative Poems', *Parergon*, 18 (1977), 17–25 (at 18–19).
[11] See A. V. C. Schmidt, *The Clerkly Maker: Langland's Poetic Art* (Cambridge, 1987), and Alex Mueller, *Translating Troy: Provincial Politics in Alliterative Romance* (Columbus, OH, 2013), 206–28.

structure.[12] Cable and Duggan each discovered that unstressed syllables were regulated in the 'b-verse' (second half) of the long line of fourteenth-century alliterative poems. Their metrical models partly agree and partly conflict. However, neither scholar prescribed norms for scansion of post-1400 poems. Because metrical traditions change over time, the consensus view of fourteenth-century alliterative metre requires adjustment for the fifteenth century.

The consensus view, first articulated by Cable and refined by him and by other researchers, is this. The b-verse (1) contains exactly one 'long dip' (sequence of two or more unstressed syllables), (2) contains exactly two 'lifts' (stressed syllables), and (3) ends with a 'short dip' (single unstressed syllable). These three requirements are independent of one another. The licit metrical patterns for the b-verse can be expressed graphically: (x)Sx … xSx or x … xS(x)Sx. These two patterns stand in free variation. An instance of the first is *Mum and the Sothsegger* 1b: 'fro couetous peuple' (xSxxSx: 'from covetous people').[13] An instance of the second is *Mum and the Sothsegger* 2b: 'and at his heeste eke' (xxxSxSx: 'and also at his command'). No pithy formalization appears possible for the 'a-verse' (first half) of the line, which remains a metrical *terra incognita*. Even the count of stresses is disputed.[14] Cable's initial insight is still the most satisfying for its simplicity: in the a-verse, a great many patterns are permitted, but not the b-verse patterns. The fourteenth-century a-verse and b-verse stand in a relation of metrical asymmetry. That is, those metrical patterns allowable in one half of the line are disallowed in the other.

Fifteenth-century alliterative b-verses show overwhelming support for requirements (1) and (2), while requirement (3) had by then relaxed into a tendency. The acceptable b-verse patterns thus became (x)Sx … xS(x) or x … xS(x)S(x). From the three requirements in the b-verse, and from the associated principle of asymmetry, fifteenth-century alliterative poets derived a kaleidoscopic variety of formal effects across literary genres and social terrain.

The *Piers Plowman* Tradition

Langland's shadowy biographical existence and intense 'consciousness of blameworthiness' precluded celebrations of the author like those surrounding Chaucer in the fifteenth century.[15] Nevertheless, *Piers Plowman* inspired a school of imitators. This is represented by a quintet of poems with interlinked themes: (in conjectural chronological order) *Richard the Redeless*, *Piers the Plowman's Creed*, *Mum and the Sothsegger*, *Crowned King*,

---

[12] Hoyt N. Duggan, 'The Shape of the B-Verse in Middle English Alliterative Poetry', *Speculum*, 61 (1986), 564–92, and 'Final -e and the Rhythmic Structure of the B-Verse in Middle English Alliterative Poetry', *Modern Philology*, 81 (1988), 119–45; and Thomas Cable, 'Middle English Meter and its Theoretical Implications', *Yearbook of Langland Studies*, 2 (1988), 47–69, 'Standards from the Past: The Conservative Syllable Structure of the Alliterative Revival', *Tennessee Studies in Literature*, 31 (1989), 42–56, and *The English Alliterative Tradition* (Philadelphia, PA, 1991), 66–84.

[13] Mabel Day and Robert Steele (eds), *Mum and the Sothsegger*, EETS, o.s. 199 (London, 1936).

[14] Cf. Hoyt N. Duggan, 'Extended A-Verses in Middle English Alliterative Poetry', *Parergon*, 18 (2000), 53–76 (two to four stresses); Noriko Inoue, 'A New Theory of Alliterative A-Verses', *Yearbook of Langland Studies*, 18 (2004), 107–32 (exactly two); Nicolay Yakovlev, 'The Development of Alliterative Metre from Old to Middle English' (DPhil Thesis, University of Oxford, 2008), 172–80 (two or three); Inoue and Myra Stokes, 'The Caesura and the Rhythmic Shape of the A-Verse in the Poems of the Alliterative Revival', *Leeds Studies in English*, n.s. 40 (2009), 1–26 (exactly two); and Cornelius, *Reconstructing Alliterative Verse*, 114–21 (two to four). Yakovlev 'Development of Alliterative Metre', 163–7, further argues that, like the b-verse, the a-verse must not end in a long dip.

[15] Hanna, 'Alliterative Poetry', 511.

and *Death and Life*. The first four are from the turn of the fifteenth century; the last cannot be dated. The *Parliament of the Three Ages*, an allegorical debate, possibly belongs here, but it too is undatable.

Poems of the *Piers Plowman* tradition share with their exemplar a less formal, more experimental vocabulary and metrical style than fourteenth-century alliterative romances. This is particularly true of the *Creed*, whose author had a keen ear for Langland's eccentricities.[16] In contravention of the three requirements enumerated above, b-verses in *Mum and the Sothsegger* might have no final dip: 'þough his hoode be on' (1473b; xxSxS); or two long dips: 'and euer þe lenger þe bettre' (1616b; xxxxSxxSx); or three lifts: 'I holde þaym halfe a-masid' (1726b; xSxxSxSx; 'I consider them half mad'). Poets of the *Piers Plowman* tradition sought 'an open style and middle ground for English verse'.[17]

Political Prophecies

Also showing influence from *Piers Plowman* are a number of alliterative political prophecies. The *Ireland Prophecy* and *Vision of William Banastre* (NIMEV 1967.8), two Yorkist poems, are securely fifteenth-century. So are 'And fifty Christian barons full bold shall be brittened to death' (NIMEV 308.5), 'In May when mirth moves upon loft' (NIMEV 1507.5), and 'In the season of summer surely who likes' (NIMEV 1564), three shorter prophecies extant in fifteenth-century manuscripts and evidently alluding to fifteenth-century events. The *Prophecies of St Thomas of Canterbury* is probably also from this century.

Intersection of the traditions of alliterative verse and political prophecy accelerated in the fifteenth century. The genre is enigmatic, trading in heraldic cognizances, coded animal symbolism, retrodictions, and conveniently vague predictions. While just as topical and satirical as the poems of the *Piers Plowman* tradition narrowly construed, the alliterative prophecies aspire to a stateliness of style rather associated with romance. 'In May', a dream vision/prophecy on the Council of Basel, has the following representative lines: 'Then schal a breton hym boun[e] / ouer þe brad streme / & care to paleys / & þer a court hold' (45–6; 'Then a Briton shall go over the broad [*sc.* English] channel and go to the palace and hold court there').[18] The vivacious verbs *boune* 'prepare oneself' and *care* 'travel', used colorlessly and interchangeably to mean 'go', typify alliterative romance, as does the postponement of the verb in verse 46b. The inverted syntax of alliterative b-verses has a metrical rationale: a b-verse *& þer hold a court*, with prose syntax, would have two long dips and no final dip (xxSxxS).[19] This scansion counts the unwritten inflectional -*e* of the infinitive verb *hold* (<OE *healdan*), as expected in this metrical tradition.

---

[16] See Cornelius, *Reconstructing Alliterative Verse*, 104–26.

[17] Cornelius, *Reconstructing Alliterative Verse*, 126 (of *Piers the Plowman's Creed* only).

[18] V. J. Scattergood, *Politics and Poetry in the Fifteenth Century, 1399–1485* (New York, 1971), 391–2. Scattergood, *Political and Poetry*, 221, discusses the poem briefly. In verse 45a, for Scattergood's *bound* 'set a boundary', nonsensical in context, I read *boune* as 'go'. (*bound* 'leap' is not attested until the sixteenth century.) I thank Celia Smithmier for discussing 'In May' with me.

[19] Another plausible prose rendition, *& hold a court þer* (xSxxSS), would have three lifts by the principle that verse-final function words receive metrical stress.

Romances?

Did fifteenth-century poets compose (unrhymed) alliterative romances? The fragmentary textual record makes it impossible to be certain. With *St Erkenwald*, the *Alliterative Morte Arthure*, *Chevalere Assigne*, *Destruction of Troy*, *King Alisaunder*, and *Wars of Alexander* are all usually grouped together with *Gawain* in the late fourteenth century, but any or all of them may be later. Metrical history and literary history are hopelessly entangled. Neither domain supports deductions about the other.

The metrical styles of these six poems tend towards the ornate though not necessarily the punctilious (by the lights of the *Gawain* metre). A tic of the *Morte Arthure* poet's is b-verses with two long dips, e.g., 'to the populle that theme heres' (11b; xxSxxxSx; 'to the people who hear them')—if these are not scribal errors.[20] The *Destruction of Troy* follows 'different rules' from other unrhymed poems by making b-verse short dips optional.[21] A difference of date, style, or social context could account for this. Like *Death and Life*, the *Destruction of Troy* is extant only in a single, postmedieval manuscript.

Alliterating Stanzaic Poetry

In the late fourteenth century, a new form of alliterating poetry in rhymed thirteen-line stanzas emerged. The stanzas have eight or nine long lines followed by a 'wheel', or 'bob' and wheel, and the rhyme scheme is often *ababababcdccd* or *ababababcdddc*. Fifteenth-century examples are *De tribus regibus mortuis*, also known as *Three Dead Kings*, ascribed to Audelay;[22] possibly the brilliant *Awntyrs off Arthure*; many passages from English drama; and several poems in Scots, beginning with Richard Holland's *Buke of the Howlat*.[23] These poems stand in 'an expanded field of variance' with the unrhymed poems.[24] Variance encompassed geographical, linguistic, generic, and metrical dimensions. Taken one by one, lines from the rhyming poems can be subjected to the same principles of scansion as those from the unrhymed poems. The rhyming and unrhymed poems share sources, themes, vocabulary, poetic syntax, and manuscript contexts. Yet the embedding of alliterative rhythms in stanzaic forms inevitably nudges readerly expectations away from a 'horizontal' accounting of a-verses and b-verses, dips and lifts, towards a 'vertical' accounting of beats and rhymes that is characteristic of accentual-syllabic metres. The old unrhymed alliterative verse is in its element at a comfortable trot; the new alliterating stanzaic verse wants to gallop. We see in these poems, as Ian Cornelius argues, one kind of metre in the process of becoming another kind.[25]

---

[20] Edmund Brock (ed.), *Morte Arthure*, EETS, o.s. 8 (London, 1865). For the view that certain metrically asystematic verses in the unique text of the poem are textually corrupt, see Ralph Hanna and Thorlac Turville-Petre, 'The Text of the *Alliterative Morte Arthure*: A Prolegomenon for a Future Edition', in Susanna Fein and Michael Johnston (eds), *Robert Thornton and his Books: Essays on the Lincoln and London Thornton Manuscripts* (Woodbridge, 2014), 131–55 (at 136–7).

[21] Kristin Lynn Cole, '*The Destruction of Troy*'s Different Rules: The Alliterative Revival and the Alliterative Tradition', *JEGP*, 109 (2010), 162–76.

[22] Ad Putter, 'The Language and Metre of *Pater Noster* and *Three Dead Kings*', *Review of English Studies*, n.s. 55 (2004), 498–526, places the poem in the fourteenth century.

[23] Thorlac Turville-Petre, '"Summer Sunday", "De Tribus Regibus Mortuis", and "The Awntyrs off Arthure": Three Poems in the Thirteen-Line Stanza', *Review of English Studies*, n.s. 25 (1974), 1–14 (at 12–14), provides a checklist.

[24] Cornelius, *Reconstructing Alliterative Verse*, 133.

[25] Cornelius, *Reconstructing Alliterative Verse*, 130–46.

Here is a representative quatrain from *De tribus*:

> Þre <u>kyng</u>ys þer <u>come</u>   <u>trew</u>le I <u>tolde</u>,
> With <u>don</u>yng and <u>tryffy</u>lyng   and <u>tal</u>is þai <u>telde</u>.
> Vche a <u>wy</u> þat þer <u>was</u>   wroȝt as þai <u>wold</u>.
> Þese <u>wod</u>is and þese <u>was</u>tis   þai <u>wal</u>tyn al to <u>w[e]lde</u>.
> (18–21)[26]

(There came three kings, to reckon truly; they carried on with clamour and jesting and tales. Every man of them did as he liked. They wanted to rule over all the woods and the barren lands here.)

The b-verses follow the three independent requirements discovered by Cable and Duggan, e.g., 19b (xSxxSx). Yet each a-verse has two content words, never three as in a substantial minority of a-verses in the unrhymed poems. Three of the four a-verses, all but 20a, have metrical patterns acceptable in the b-verse, violating the principle of asymmetry. Hyperalliteration (*aabb* in line 18 and *aaaa* in lines 20 and 21) is a third indication that the half-lines have coalesced into a single balanced line of four beats. A further indication is what might be called 'rhythm rhyme' between 18b and 20b and between 19b and 21b, aligned with the end rhymes. The thirteen-line alliterating stanza is beautiful, but it affords a different beauty from passages of unrhymed alliterative long lines.

Tetrameter and Other Four-Stress Metres

Of the three major metrical traditions, tetrameter and associated four-stress verse forms have received by far the least scholarly attention. To an extent, the neglect is understandable. Tetrameter is neither mysterious, like alliterative verse, nor favoured by canonical authors, like pentameter. Yet tetrameter was quite securely the predominant mode for poetry in English in the fifteenth century—just as it had been in the fourteenth century.

A Metrical Family

Iambic tetrameter, the form of Chaucer's *Book of the Duchess*, stands at one end of a spectrum of four-stress metres. At the other end of the spectrum from tetrameter lies purely accentual four-stress metre, in which the count of syllables does not matter. Metres towards that end of the spectrum have many, interchangeable names in scholarship, including 'four-beat metre', 'strong-stress metre', and 'template metre'. Members of this metrical family share the count of four, i.e., they are accentual, but they count syllables, i.e., they are syllabic, to different degrees. In the fifteenth century, rhyme in all these metres was mandatory. The simplest scheme, couplets, was the most common. The normative form of a line of iambic tetrameter, with an optional feminine ending, is xSxSxSxS(x). That is, the line is comprised of eight alternating weak and strong metrical positions of one syllable apiece (or the equivalent through elision). Four-stress template metre could be represented this

---

[26] John Audelay, '*De tribus regibus mortuis*', in Ella Keats Whiting (ed.), *The Poems of John Audelay*, EETS, o.s. 184 (London, 1931).

way: (x(x ...))S(x(x ...))S(x(x ...))S(x(x ...))S(x). That is, the line is comprised of eight alternating weak and strong metrical positions, with no constraints on the number of syllables in weak positions. Unlike alliterative metre and pentameter, tetrameter and four-stress template metre do not have a 'caesura' (midline break).

Even when four-stress verse alliterates heavily, it can be distinguished from alliterative verse with reference to the structural principles introduced in the previous section.[27] Tetrameter has a different lineage. It arose in the twelfth century as a significant prosodic innovation—the first syllable-counting metre in English—through the influence of French octosyllables and Latin 'rhythmical' (accentual) tetrameter. By the fifteenth century, it was the standard form for poems in English. Rather than superficially introduce the many varieties of tetrameter verse, the following subsections annotate at length two representative examples, situated for illustrative purposes at opposite ends of the tetrameter/template metre spectrum.

A Lyric Tradition

Tetrameter is the default form of fifteenth-century lyric poems and songs in English, whether secular or religious. These include, for example, nearly all the short poems in BL, MS Digby 102 and most of those in Audelay's manuscript, BodL MS Douce 302. The association between lyric and song in late medieval Britain means that tetrameter lyrics are octosyllabic or nearly so. A fourteenth-century example is the twice-remembered 'lay' (*Book of the Duchess*, 471, referring to lines 475–86) spoken by Chaucer's sorrowful knight.[28] Chaucer's use of tetrameter makes plain the influence of the French lyric tradition on (tetrameter) lyrics in English.

Here are the burden and first two stanzas of Audelay's carol 'Childhood' ('*Cantalena de puericia*'):

> And <u>God</u> wold <u>graunt</u> me <u>my</u> pra<u>yer</u>,
> A <u>child</u> aʒene I <u>wold</u> I <u>were</u>.
>
> Fore <u>pride</u> in <u>herte</u> he <u>hat</u>is alle <u>one</u>;
> <u>Wor</u>chip ne <u>reuerens</u> <u>kep</u>is he <u>non</u>;
> Ne <u>he</u> is <u>wroþ</u> with no <u>mon</u>;
>   In <u>charete</u> is <u>alle</u> his <u>chere</u>.
>
> He <u>wot</u> <u>neuer</u> wat <u>is</u> en<u>vy</u>;
> He <u>wol</u> vche <u>mon</u> fard <u>wele</u> him <u>by</u>;
> He <u>couetis</u> <u>noʒt</u> vn<u>laufully</u>,
>   Fore <u>chere</u> <u>stons</u> is <u>his</u> tre<u>soure</u>.
>   (1–10)[29]

(If God would grant me my prayer, I'd wish to be a child again. For he entirely hates a prideful heart; he has no truck with deference or respect for social rank; nor is he angry

---

[27] See also, with reference to fourteenth-century poetry in English, Thomas Cable, 'Foreign Influence, Native Continuation, and Metrical Typology in Alliterative Lyrics', in Judith Jefferson and Ad Putter (eds), *Approaches to the Metres of Alliterative Verse* (Leeds, 2009), 219–34.
[28] See Ardis Butterfield, 'Lyric and Elegy in *The Book of the Duchess*', *Medium Ævum*, 60 (1991), 33–60.
[29] John Audelay, 'Childhood', in Whiting (ed.), *Poems of John Audelay*.

with any man; his manner is wholly set on love. He does not know at all what envy is; he wants each man to fare well by him; he covets nothing unlawfully, for cherry pits are his treasure.)

The poem is strongly octosyllabic. Its 'metrical phonology' (metrically marked vocabulary) may be less linguistically conservative than the scansions here assume. For example, line 3 *hatis* may scan as a single syllable (S?) and line 4 *reuerens* may scan as two syllables, the first stressed, with -*e*-² discounted after *u/v* (Sx?). It is not possible to be definitive. Metre and metrical phonology inflect and redefine one another in the mind and in history. This is true of all metered poetry, but the situation is acute for four-stress metres in English, since the possibilities for rhythmical variation within a four-beat frame are legion. The passage supplies no evidence for the metrical significance of historical -*e*. Line 2 *aȝene* (xS; <OE *ongeanes*), 3 *pride* (S; <OE *prytu*), and 3 *herte* (S; <OE *heorte*) show either forms without -*e* or else elision of -*e* with the following vowel or *h*-. In the case of line 1 *graunt* (S; inf.), 4 *reuerens* (S(x)x; <OF *reverence*), and 10 *stons* (S), where elision is not a possibility, spelling and metre both suggest forms without historical -*e*. The evidence of end rhyme also points to the insignificance of final -*e* in this poem's metre. Words with and without historical -*e* rhyme together: 3 *one* (with -*e*: <OE *ana*)/4 *non* (without: <OE *nan*)/5 *mon* (without: <OE *man*); 7 *envy* (with: <OF *envie*)/8 *by* (without: <OE *bi*)/9 -*ly* (with: <OE -*lice*). Alliteration adorns most lines, e.g., lines 3 (*h*), 5 (*w*), and 6 (*ch*), but it is not organized into the elaborate repeated patternings of alliterative verse or alliterating stanzaic verse. Line 5 defeats iambic scansion, in that it shows only seven syllables, with clashing stress between *wroþ* and *with* (xSxSSxS). A final -*e* is not etymologically justified in *wroþ* (S; <OE *wraþ*), though a form with unetymological -*e*, modelled on *wratthe* 'wrath' (<OE *wræþþu*), is conceivable. Tetrameter drives home the truth that '[t]here is a constitutive gap between linguistic givens and metrical systems, and hence always more than one way of correlating language to metre'.³⁰ Scanning this poetry involves repeated missteps and readjustments.

A Dramatic Tradition

If crisp tetrametric verse like Audelay's 'Childhood' places interpretive burdens on the reader or listener, who must intuit the metre from the language and the metrical value of language from the metre, then poetry in template metre exacerbates these. Here is the opening of the banns of the *Croxton Play of the Sacrament*:

Primus Vexillator   Now þe Father and þe Sune and þe Holy Goste,
That all þis wyde worlde hat wrowght,
Save all thes semely, bothe leste and moste,
And bryn[g]e yow to þe blysse þat he hath yow to bowght!
We be ful purposed with hart and with thowght
Off our mater to tell þe entent,
Off þe marvellys þat wer wondursely wrowght
Off þe holi and blyssed Sacrament.

(1–8)³¹

---

³⁰ Ian Cornelius, 'The Accentual Paradigm in Early English Metrics', *JEGP*, 114 (2015), 459–81 (at 481).
³¹ Norman Davis (ed.), *Non-Cycle Plays and Fragments*, EETS, s.s. 1 (London, 1970).

(Now the Father and the Son and the Holy Ghost, who has created this whole wide world, please save all these worthy folk, both the least and the most of them, and bring you all to the bliss to which He has redeemed you! With heart and with thought, we fully intend to tell the substance of our story, of the marvels that were wondrously accomplished by the holy and blessed Sacrament.)

Reading these lines with attention to metre is a taxing experience. Does the grammatically justified *-e* of the weak adjective *wyde* (line 2) contribute an unstressed syllable to the metre, as it would in Chaucer's verse? Do the inflectional *-e*'s of the subjunctives *Save* (line 3) and *brynge* (line 4) extend the long dips in which they appear? (What principle, if any, constrains the length of long dips here?) Is there elision between *þe* and *entent* in line 6? (Is elision generally in force in this play, or only after the definite article?) On which function word does the second metrical stress fall in line 7: *þat* or *wer*? (Does the alliteration on *w* in this line factor in?)

These questions ideally would be adjudicated through a sample scansion of lines from throughout the play and through setting the *Croxton Play* into its metrical-historical context: a mapping of the positions in the literary field available to the playwright. In this text, it transpires that the flexibility of four-stress metre is a tool of characterization. When, 700 lines in, Jesus speaks, he does so in a sparer metre—and more ornamented stanza form (*ababbcbccdcd*)—than the 'vexillators' (standard-bearers): 'Oh ye merveylows Jewys, / Why ar ye to yowr kyng onkynd, / And [I] so bytterly bowt yow to my blysse?' (719–21; 'Oh you astonishing Jews, why are you unkind to your King—and I redeemed you to my bliss so painfully?'). This modulation, like Shakespeare's later use of tetrameter for incantations and spells in his blank-verse plays, brings metrical form into the foreground of the playgoing or reading experience. Lines 719 and 720 are iambic, counting the unwritten inflectional *-e* of plural *merveylows* (SxSxSxS/xSxSxSxS). The difficult rhyme *Jewys/blysse* works only if both words scan as monosyllables (S not Sx). Because alliteration is not mandatory, it too is available for special effects. Alliteration in lines 4 and 721 highlights the connection between Christ's suffering (*bytterly*) and humankind's redemption (*blysse, bow(gh)t*) in Christian theology.

Pentameter

Pentameter was still, in the fifteenth century, very much Chaucer's metre. Chaucer had invented it in the 1380s under influence from Italian and French decasyllabic poetry, an idiosyncratic lineage generating what must have seemed, at the time, an idiosyncratic English metre.[32] Associated with pentameter for Chaucer, and so for his successors, was the rhyme royal stanza form (*ababbcc*) that Chaucer also invented. This was the form of the *Parliament of Fowls* and *Troilus and Criseyde*. Pentameter made a small splash during Chaucer's lifetime in his immediate social circle, in the verse of his friends John Clanvowe, John Gower, and Henry Scogan. In the fifteenth century, Hoccleve, Lydgate, and a sequence of younger writers picked up the new metre and ran with it. In the process, they

---

[32] See Martin J. Duffell, '"The craft so long to lerne": Chaucer's Invention of the Iambic Pentameter', *The Chaucer Review*, 34 (2000), 269–88, and *Chaucer's Verse Art in its European Context* (Tempe, AZ, 2018), especially 179–97 and 211–26, and Robert P. Stockwell and Donka Minkova, 'The Partial-Contact Origins of English Pentameter Verse: The Anglicization of an Italian Model', in Dieter Kastovsky and Arthur Mettinger (eds), *Language Contact in the History of English* (Frankfurt, 2001), 337–62.

(not Chaucer) forged 'the central English meter, whose dominance' since the mid fifteenth century 'gives it the claim to be an epochal form, coterminous with bourgeois culture.'[33]

While accentual-syllabic, like tetrameter, pentameter is more than tetrameter + a foot.[34] In pentameter, overlaying the syllable pairs visible to classicizing foot-based scansion are two 'cola' (sub-line units), divided by a caesura. Pentameter inherits cola and caesurae from its Italian and French precursors. To these features, Chaucer and most later practitioners in English added iambic rhythm, familiar from English tetrameter and from Latin accentual metres. Pentameter's structure thus refers to four language traditions, English, French, Italian, and Latin. The normative form of a line of pentameter, with an optional feminine ending, is xSxSxSxSxS(x). That is, the line is comprised of ten alternating weak and strong metrical positions of one syllable apiece (or the equivalent through elision). Most of the time, the caesura falls after the fourth metrical position (xSxS|xSxSxS(x)), the fifth (xSxSx|SxSxS(x)), or the sixth (xSxSxS|xSxS(x)). In the fifteenth century, rhyme was mandatory in pentameter verse. Fifteenth-century poets did not have the option of writing in blank verse, a form that would be invented by Surrey c1540. Chaucer's two favoured rhyme schemes, couplets and rhyme royal, remained standard for fifteenth-century pentameter poets.

Hoccleve

Historically, biographically, and metrically, Hoccleve bridges Chaucer and the so-called Chaucerians. Hoccleve, Clerk of the Privy Seal, shared with his 'worthi maister Chaucer' (*Regiment of Princes*, 4983) a career as a middling bureaucrat.[35] This placement was possible only in London. It afforded both men social proximity to the royal court in the absence of aristocratic status or high-ranking religious vocation. Hoccleve's scribal and authorial activities provide the most direct connection between the circulation of Chaucer's texts and the circulation of Chaucer's metres. Hoccleve's hand has been identified in corrections and insertions in the Hengwrt manuscript of the *Canterbury Tales*. Simon Horobin contends that Hoccleve supervised the production of both the Hengwrt and Ellesmere manuscripts, patching in his own pentameters to finish couplets and link tales in Hengwrt. If so, he was 'Chaucer's first editor.'[36] Hoccleve worked to make the phenomenon of fifteenth-century Chaucerians possible by purveying Chaucer's texts and adapting Chaucer's metre. He adds a second layer of French style onto Chaucer's prosody, writing lines that have ten syllables (or eleven with feminine ending) but non-iambic accentual rhythms, like French decasyllabic verse. An example from the *Regiment of Princes* is line 34: 'I destitut was of joye and good hope' (xSxxS|xSxSSx). Here, instead of occupying only the even-numbered metrical positions as typical in Chaucer's verse, stresses appear in odd positions: the fifth (*was*), seventh (*joy-*), and ninth (*good*). This scansion assumes elision between *joye* (<OF *joie*)

---

[33] Antony Easthope, 'Problematizing the Pentameter', *New Literary History*, 12 (1981), 475–92 (at 488). The full quotation reads 'whose dominance *since the Renaissance* gives it the claim ...' (emphasis mine). This specification intrudes the conventional medieval/modern periodization into a differently ordered metrical history.

[34] See Derek Attridge, *The Rhythms of English Poetry* (London, 1982), 123–44.

[35] Thomas Hoccleve, 'The Regiment of Princes', in Frederick J. Furnivall (ed.), *Hoccleve's Works*: III. *The Regiment of Princes*, EETS, e.s. 72 (London, 1897).

[36] Simon Horobin, 'Thomas Hoccleve: Chaucer's First Editor?', *The Chaucer Review*, 50 (2015), 228–50. See also Sebastian J. Langdell, *Thomas Hoccleve: Religious Reform, Transnational Politics, and the Invention of Chaucer* (Liverpool, 2018), 64–99, and Sonja Drimmer, *The Art of Allusion: Illuminators and the Making of English Literature, 1403–1476* (Philadelphia, PA, 2019), 69–80.

and *and*. In such lines, the principle of alternating stress recedes from Hoccleve's metrical practice. It is not clear whether the same scansional expectations apply as to the iambic lines. The underlined syllables are rhythmically, but arguably not metrically, prominent.

Other Early Chaucerians

Apart from two special cases discussed below, the other pentameter poets active between 1400 and 1440 are John Walton, Lydgate, the anonymous author of the *Libelle of Englyshe Polycye* (NIMEV 3491), James I of Scotland, and Charles d'Orléans. The early pentameter tradition shows a strong regional bias towards the southeast. Like Clanvowe, Gower, Chaucer, and Hoccleve, all these men lived, worked, or were imprisoned in or near London. The anonymous *Libelle of Englyshe Polycye* extends the connections between pentameter and the civil service. The alignment between its politics and those of the office of the Privy Seal suggest that the author was a senior civil servant under Henry VI.[37] Sebastian Sobecki identifies him as Richard Caudray, who served on the king's council.[38]

These poets' metrical styles develop in several new directions the organizational logic of Chaucer's pentameter. Lydgate prioritized the caesura over a count of ten, a reinterpretation that allows for 'broken-backed' lines with one syllable deleted after the caesura. Such lines are allowable in Lydgate's metrical system because, while they have nine syllables instead of ten, they respect the division of the line into cola. An example is *Siege of Thebes* 112: '3if nedë be / Sparë not to blowe' (xSxS|SxSxSx; 'If need be, don't hold back from farting').[39] The royal prisoners James I and Charles d'Orléans came to Chaucer's pentameter through the mediation of other language traditions: respectively, Scots and French.

A Problem: *London Lickpenny*

What is the metrical form of this poem? Once ascribed to Lydgate but now considered anonymous, *London Lickpenny* survives in two late sixteenth-century manuscripts. The text in BL MS Harley 542 shows a mixture of tetrameter and pentameter lines in 'Monk's Tale' stanzas (*ababbcbc*). BL MS Harley 367 gives a version in tetrameter in rhyme royal. Both manuscripts are associated with the antiquarian John Stow. One early editor, Ferdinand Holthausen, emended the poem heavily in the conviction that pentameter has priority in the poem's textual transmission.[40] Later editors usually print one manuscript text or the other, lightly emended. Unless we are dealing with authorial revision, or scribal corruption in the archetype as total as Holthausen conjectured, there are two possible scenarios. A scribe either suppressed the pentameter in a mixed-metre poem or interposed it in a tetrameter poem. Either conclusion would be significant for metrical history. Further study is needed.

---

[37] See Sebastian Sobecki, 'Bureaucratic Verse: William Lynwood, the Privy Seal, and the Form of *The Libelle of Englyshe Polycye*', *New Medieval Literatures*, 12 (2011), 251–88.

[38] Sebastian Sobecki, *Last Words: The Public Self and the Social Author in Late Medieval England* (Oxford, 2019), 101–26.

[39] John Lydgate, 'Siege of Thebes', in Axel Erdmann (ed.), *Lydgate's Siege of Thebes*, 2 vols., EETS, e.s. 108 and 125 (London, 1911 and 1930). See Maura Nolan, 'Performing Lydgate's Broken-Backed Meter', in Susan Yager and Elise E. Morse-Gagné (eds), *Interpretation and Performance: Essays for Alan Gaylord* (Provo, UT, 2013), 141–59.

[40] F. Holthausen, 'London Lickpenny', *Anglia*, 43 (1919), 61–8.

An Exception: 'Quixley'

The one early fifteenth-century pentameter poet not operating in the southeast or East Anglia is 'Quixley', translator of Gower's decasyllabic Anglo-Norman/French *Traitié pour les amantz marietz* into English. R. F. Yeager identifies him as Robert de Quixley, prior of Nostell, Yorkshire.[41] Like Hoccleve, Quixley observes strict decasyllabism and shows a willingness to mismatch linguistic and metrical stress in multisyllabic words. The first line of his preface to the translation runs: 'Who þat liste loke in þis litel tretice' (SxxS|xSxSxSx; 'Whoever would like to peruse this little treatise').[42] Social connections between the Augustinian priories of Nostell and St Mary Overie, Southwark, where Gower lived and was buried, may have helped a manuscript of the *Traitié* travel far from the metropolis.[43]

Chaucerians, 1440–1500

After c1440, pentameter ascended to the top of the hierarchy of English verse forms. The roll call of pentameter poets grows longer and longer from this point to the early twentieth century, as the pentameter tradition annexes more and more cultural territory.[44] Named late fifteenth-century pentameter poets in English or Scots include Osbern Bokenham, John Metham, George Ashby, Robert Henryson, and William Dunbar. The first three crafted pentameters so complex they now require dedicated historical study to appreciate. Metham's line, the most complex of all, 'poses a unique problem' in English historical metrics.[45] The last two are Scottish and reasserted Chaucer's metrical style.[46] This is the rare context in which the label 'Scottish Chaucerians' fits. In general, the categorization conceals the different local meanings accruing to pentameter in Scotland, where, for example, alliterating stanzaic verse remained vital for longer. As Bourdieu writes: 'a *prise de position* changes, even when it remains identical, whenever there is change in the universe of options that are simultaneously offered for producers and consumers to choose from'.[47]

Forms of Experimentation

Two less common but notable forms for poetry in English attested in the fifteenth century are tail rhyme, as in the *Avowynge of Arthur* and other romances, and the form of the *Jack Upland* series. The first is accentual-syllabic, like tetrameter and pentameter. The second resists classification. These two forms stretch the limits of the field of poetry in English as it existed in the fifteenth century, though they are not experimental in the modern sense since they have precedents in pre-1400 poetry.

---

[41] R. F. Yeager (ed. and trans.), *John Gower: The French Balades* (Kalamazoo, MI, 2011), 157–63.

[42] 'Quixley', translation of John Gower's *Traitié pour les amantz marietz* (NIMEV 4105), in Henry Noble MacCracken, 'Quixley's Ballades Royal (? 1402)', *Yorkshire Archaeological Journal*, 20 (1909), 33–50.

[43] Yeager (ed. and trans.), *John Gower*, 162.

[44] See Kristin Hanson, 'From Dante to Pinsky: A Theoretical Perspective on the History of the Modern English Iambic Pentameter', *Rivista di Linguistica*, 9 (1996), 53–97.

[45] Nicholas Myklebust, 'The Problem of John Metham's Prosody', in Ad Putter and Judith A. Jefferson (eds), *The Transmission of Medieval Romance: Metres, Manuscripts and Early Prints* (Cambridge, 2018), 149–69 (at 159).

[46] See Duffell, *Chaucer's Verse Art*, 243–53.

[47] Bourdieu, 'Field of Cultural Production', 313.

Tail rhyme is a catch-all term, referring to rhyming stanzaic forms with lines of different lengths. Typically the basic line is tetrameter, mixed with trimeters and/or dimeters that form bobs and wheels. Tail rhyme evoked romance, as parodied in Chaucer's 'Tale of Sir Thopas'. Chaucer's Host's term for it, 'rym dogerel' (*Canterbury Tales*, 7.925), is pejorative. *The Avowynge of Arthur* opens this way:

> He that made us on the mulde,
> And fair fourmet the folde,
> Atte His will, as He wold,
> The see and the sande ...
> (1–4)[48]

(He who created us out of dust, and beautifully formed the world, at will, as He wished, the sea and the sand ...)

Tetrameter (lines 1 and 3) alternates with trimeter (line 2) and dimeter (line 4), in a pattern repeated four times per stanza.

By contrast, the form of the *Upland* series (*Jack Upland, Friar Daw's Reply*, and *Upland's Rejoinder*) is a problem for historical poetics. Syntactically and lexically, it is prose, and it lacks any apparent metrical structure. Yet the consistent use of alliteration segments the prose into lines. Here is the opening of *Friar Daw's Reply* (asterisks mark alliterating words): 'Who shal graunten to myn eyen a *strong *streme of teres / To *wailen and to *wepyn the *sorwyng of *synne? / For *charite is *chasid and flemed out of londe' (1–3).[49] Is this poetry? The problem is analogous to the equally controversial case, from the tenth century, of Ælfric's saints' lives.[50] A fourteenth-century composition eliciting similar ambivalence from modern scholars is John Gaytryge's *Lay Folks' Catechism*. All these texts share an ambition to disseminate religious teaching, in an English made plain, among a readership or listenership constructed as excluded from Latin learning.[51] In each case, the connection with the alliterative tradition is palpable but difficult to specify. Perhaps the most cogent response to the form of the *Upland* series would be to repeat Cornelius's subtle argument regarding the *Lay Folks' Catechism*: Gaytryge 'disassembled' alliterative metre, 'stripping it of everything that could get in the way of ... efficient, un-ornamented communication'.[52] Alliterative metre haunts the prose work, as a position not quite taken.

Retrospect

If the English Reformation was a cataclysm in religious, literary, and political history,[53] for metrical history it was a non-event. Like the Tudor dynasty, the suite of metres discussed

---

[48] Thomas Hahn (ed.), *Sir Gawain: Eleven Romances and Tales* (Kalamazoo, MI, 1995).
[49] James M. Dean (ed.), *Six Ecclesiastical Satires* (Kalamazoo, MI, 1991).
[50] Cf. N. F. Blake, 'Rhythmical Alliteration', *Modern Philology*, 67 (1969), 118–24 (119 on the *Upland* series); Sherman M. Kuhn, 'Was Ælfric a Poet?' *Philological Quarterly*, 52 (1973), 643–62; Thomas A. Bredehoft, 'Ælfric and Late Old English Verse', *Anglo-Saxon England*, 33 (2004), 77–107; and Rafael J. Pascual, 'Ælfric's Rhythmical Prose and the Study of Old English Metre', *English Studies*, 95 (2014), 803–23.
[51] In other words, they are all works of vernacular theology. For the term, see Nicholas Watson, 'Censorship and Cultural Change in Late-Medieval England: Vernacular Theology, the Oxford Translation Debate, and Arundel's Constitutions of 1409', *Speculum*, 70 (1995), 822–64.
[52] Ian Cornelius, 'The Lay Folks' Catechism, Alliterative Verse, and Cursus', *Review of English Studies*, n.s. 70 (2018), 14–36 (at 28).
[53] See James Simpson, *Reform and Cultural Revolution* (Oxford, 2002), and 'Trans-Reformation English Literary History', in Kristen Poole and Owen Williams (eds), *Early Modern Histories of Time: The Periodizations of Sixteenth- and Seventeenth-Century England* (Philadelphia, PA, 2019), 88–101.

in this essay survived the Reformation. With respect to the major and minor metrical options, the literary field that confronted Wyatt and Surrey was largely the same one in which the poet of the *Ireland Prophecy* had manoeuvered.[54] Verse forms were durably installed, transporting the experiences and sensibilities of one century into the next. The traditional periodization of postclassical European history into 'medieval' and 'modern', breaking at the year 1500 for England, inappropriately subdivides the continuous histories of alliterative verse, tetrameter, and pentameter.

The early fifteenth century marked a high point for prosodic variety in English, bringing to fruition a developmental trend that began in the twelfth century, when poets first transposed syllabic metres from French and Latin into English. Before c1930, the field of English prosody continually consolidated the state of play already in effect by c1450, whereby pentameter, the courtly metre, outranked other verse forms. The intrusion of explicit vernacular prosodic discourse in the 1570s and 1580s rendered that state of play newly intelligible but did not change it. Spiritually, though not by direct influence, the twentieth-century free verse revolution returned Anglophone poetics to the experimental openness of the period before centralization of the pentameter tradition.

---

[54] One noteworthy metrical difference between the fifteenth and sixteenth centuries is blank verse. A second is the resurgence, in the sixteenth century, of septenary, a.k.a. 'fourteeners' (xSxSxSxSxSxSxSxS(x)), and the related form known as 'poulter's measure' (hexameter, xSxSxSxSxSxS(x), alternating with septenary). See O. B. Hardison, Jr., *Prosody and Purpose in the English Renaissance* (Baltimore, MD, 1989), 148–70 and 206–10. Septenary had been widely used in the thirteenth and fourteenth centuries. See Derek Pearsall, 'The Metre of the *Tale of Gamelyn*', in Putter and Jefferson (eds), *The Transmission of Medieval Romance*, 33–49.

CHAPTER 7
Authorship

Robert J. Meyer-Lee

Authorship, Literary History, and the Fifteenth Century

Until relatively recently, the organization of most literary histories featured a chronology of authors, usually divided into categories of major and minor, grouped by schools, periods, and genres, and calibrated with similarly construed political histories organized regnally. Accordingly, among the waves of self-scrutiny that washed over the field of literary study in the second half of the twentieth century, the theoretical troubling of the concept of authorship was no small one. Standard literary histories began to seem ideologically problematic, with the putatively self-evident figure of the canonical author understood to be a primary suspect in this regard. The consequent suspension of this figure's paradigmatic status helped, then, to spur a thoroughgoing rethinking of the bases of literary history, which eventually led to the emergence of the sort of alternative organizations evident in, for example, the turn-of-the-millennium Cambridge and Oxford and multivolume English literary histories. Of the thirty-one chapters in the volume of the former series devoted to the period between the Conquest and the Reformation, only five have titles that refer to authors (including the chapters on *Piers Plowman* and William Caxton); tellingly outnumbering these are the six chapters comprising the section on 'institutional productions', which include, for example, 'Classroom and Confession' and 'Medieval Literature and Law'.[1] (This present literary history is comparable, with just four of twenty-eight chapters titled after authors.) Even more dramatically, of the ten chapters in the parallel Oxford volume, only two named individuals appear in titles, and these are the first chapter's John Leland (the early sixteenth-century producer, not at all coincidentally, of the first author-centric English literary history) and the second chapter's John Lydgate (d. 1449), the very poet who in earlier accounts of literary history served as the defining foil for the greatness of the authors who came both before and after him.[2]

During this same time, however, the concept of authorship scarcely faded from view. Indeed, with a half-century having now elapsed since Michel Foucault's 'What Is an Author?' and Roland Barthes's 'The Death of the Author',[3] one may confidently conclude that the mid-twentieth-century decentralizing of the author led to voluminous investigation of this very concept, in which specific authors figure as significantly as they ever did, if not exactly in the same fashion. Following Foucault, Barthes, and many others, authorship has been no longer conceived merely as the creative activity of singular, uniquely gifted human beings who in turn serve as the ultimate source of their texts' meaning. It is

---

[1] David Wallace (ed.), *The Cambridge History of Medieval English Literature* (Cambridge, 1999).
[2] James Simpson, *Reform and Cultural Revolution* (Oxford, 2002).
[3] Michel Foucault, 'What Is an Author?', in Donald F. Bouchard (ed.), Donald F. Bouchard and Sherry Simon (trans), *Language, Counter-Memory, Practice: Selected Essays and Interviews*, (Ithaca, NY, 1977), 113–38; Roland Barthes, 'The Death of the Author', in Stephen Heath (trans.), *Image-Music-Text* (New York, 1977), 142–8.

now understood to be a discursively constituted, institutionally maintained, bibliographically transmitted, and ideologically freighted gravitational force that lends a text coherence and authority. So reconfigured, authorship has become an ideal object of study for a field that has undergone so many changes during this period. It especially lends itself to the shift in interest towards questions of hermeneutic indeterminacy, socio-political valence, material and institutional underpinnings and transmission, and ideological complicity and resistance, at the cost of traditional concerns with, say, artistic unity or literary greatness.

For medievalists, this reconfiguration of the idea of authorship has been, mostly, a happy turn of events. For as many commentators have pointed out, the postmodern critique of authorship comes full circle, so to speak, and aligns in several ways with premodern concepts and practices. In the Latin Middle Ages, an *auctor* was rather transparently understood as an instance of institutionally produced and transmitted textual meaning and value. As Vincent Gillespie has summarized, drawing on the seminal work of Alistair Minnis—and casting a sidelong glance at Barthes's 'Death':

> If a saying is given authority because contemporary readers deem it worthy of imitation, if it is validated by the approval and resonance that it finds in the context of their own value systems and thought worlds, then its author is nothing more than a named personification of their estimation of its value, projected onto the saying in the process of their interpretation of it.[4]

The academic prologues whose literary theoretical importance Minnis has so well taught us to see represent only the most formalized apparatus for the widespread medieval habit of conceiving authorship in textual and institutional terms, a habit that medievalists have found readily amenable to Foucauldian analysis.[5]

Moreover, in a manuscript culture, authorship was in practice no singular creative event but, quite saliently to everyone involved, a dispersed activity of an array of temporally and spatially distributed agents. St Bonaventure's division of this activity into the four roles of *scriptor, compilator, commentator,* and *auctor* (to which one may incrementally add others, such as *illuminator* or *translator*) has become the standard account to cite in this regard.[6] Although in this account the first three roles are positioned as supplementary to the fourth, they are so in subtle and overlapping ways, and ultimately the role designated by *auctor* wholly depends upon on its mediation by the others.[7] Hence, while Barthes (not coincidentally) revives the term *scriptor* to denominate modern writers who are no longer

---

[4] Vincent Gillespie, 'Authorship', in Marion Turner (ed.), *A Handbook of Middle English Studies* (Malden, MA, 2013), 137–54; A. J. Minnis, *Medieval Theory of Authorship: Scholastic Literary Attitudes in the Later Middle Ages*, Reissued 2nd edn. (Philadelphia, PA, 2010). Other helpful overviews of the topic, especially as it bears on vernacular poetry, include Anthony Bale, 'From Translator to Laureate: Imagining the Medieval Author', *Literature Compass*, 5 (2008), 918–34; Graham D. Caie, '"I do not wish to be called auctour, but the pore compilatour": The Plight of the Medieval Vernacular Poet', *Miscelánea*, 29 (2004), 9–21; Robert R. Edwards, *Invention and Authorship in Medieval England* (Columbus, OH, 2017), xi–xxxviii; and Andrew Taylor, 'Vernacular Authorship and the Control of Manuscript Production', in Michael Johnston and Michael Van Dussen (eds), *The Medieval Manuscript Book: Cultural Approaches* (Cambridge, 2015), 199–213.

[5] Hence, for example, Jocelyn Wogan-Browne, Nicholas Watson, Andrew Taylor, and Ruth Evans (eds), *The Idea of the Vernacular: An Anthology of Middle English Literary Theory, 1280–1520* (University Park, PA, 1999); and Alexandra Gillespie, *Print Culture and the Medieval Author: Chaucer, Lydgate, and Their Books 1473–1557* (Oxford, 2006) both begin with an epigraph taken from Foucault's 'What Is an Author?'.

[6] This account occurs at the end of the prologue to Bonaventure's commentary on Peter Lombard's *Sentences*. For Minnis's widely cited translation of the passage and comments thereon, see *Medieval Theory*, 94–5. *The Idea of the Vernacular* pairs this passage with Foucault as a complementary second opening epigraph. For the role of artists in the production of a text's meaning, value, and authority in books of English provenance, see, e.g., Sonja Drimmer, *The Art of Allusion: Illuminators and the Making of English Literature, 1403–1476* (Philadelphia, PA, 2019). For the relation of translation to authorship, the seminal study is Rita Copeland, *Rhetoric, Hermeneutics, and Translation in the Middle Ages: Academic Traditions and Vernacular Texts* (Cambridge, 1991).

[7] See, e.g., J. A. Burrow, *Medieval Writers and Their Work: Middle English Literature 1100–1500* (Oxford, 1982), 29–31.

deluded by the myth of the Author—those who understand their writing to be 'a tissue of quotations' and their 'only power' to be 'to mix writings, to counter the ones with the others'—numerous medievalists have shown, in effect, that this describes fairly well the actual practices of medieval producers of texts.[8]

Barthes makes no distinction between authors of poetry and those of prose, moving without pause from Honoré de Balzac to Stéphane Mallarmé, while Foucault ranges across the literary and non-literary alike, from Homer to Freud. This broad applicability to text types also resonates with medieval thinking and practice. The conception of authorship that Minnis documents was in no way bound to specific textual categories. Rooted in a fundamentally rhetorical understanding of all writing, the idea applied equally to, say, the prose historians Josephus and Guido delle Colonne on the one hand, and epic poets Virgil and Statius on the other, each of whom appears on pillars in Lady Fame's court in Chaucer's most sustained meditation on *auctors* and *auctoritee*, the *House of Fame* (1429–85).[9]

It would thus seem safe to assume that for the poetry of fifteenth-century England, in a manuscript culture that conceived of authors as personifications of authority that readers, copyists, annotators, etc. themselves bestowed upon texts, the idea of the author that Barthes and Foucault sought to demystify—the author as a unique, expressive human agent who serves as the presiding genius of a work—does not apply. And yet, one of most the striking features of the best-known poetry of this period is that it contains representations of authors, including especially self-representations, that may prod us towards that very idea, or at least some provisional, incipient version of it. Perhaps most famous in this regard are the lines of verse accompanying the portrait of Chaucer in the *Regiment of Princes* (c1411), Thomas Hoccleve's *Fürstenspiegel* for Prince Henry of Monmouth.[10] In a section exhorting the prince to pay heed to counsel, and having just further advised that, nonetheless, a king should not hold councils on 'holy dayes' (4964; 185), Hoccleve digresses to make notice of, for the fourth and final time in the poem, his esteemed poetic precursor:

> The firste fyndere* of our fair langage   *originator*
> Hath seid, in cas semblable*, and othir mo*,   *similar writings*
> So hyly wel that it is my dotage*   *folly*
> For to expresse or touche any of tho.
> Allas, my fadir fro the world is go,
> My worthy mastir Chaucer – him I meene;
> Be thow advocat for him, hevenes queene.
>
> ...
>
> Althogh his lyf be qweynt*, the resemblance   *extinguished*
> Of him hath in me so fresh lyflynesse
> That to putte othir men in remembrance
> Of his persone, I have heere his liknesse
> Do make, to this ende, in soothfastnesse*,   *authentically*
> That they that han* of him lost thoght and mynde   *have*
> By this peynture may ageyn him fynde.
> (4978–98)

---

[8] Barthes, 'Death', 146. In addition to the studies cited above, for consonant notices of medieval practices of text production, see, e.g., Matthew Fisher, *Scribal Authorship and the Writing of History in Medieval England* (Columbus, OH, 2012).

[9] Larry D. Benson (general ed.), *The Riverside Chaucer* (Boston, MA, 1987), 365–6; all quotations from Chaucer will be taken from this edition.

[10] Charles R. Blyth (ed.), *Thomas Hoccleve: The Regiment of Princes* (Kalamazoo, MI, 1999), from which all quotations will be taken. Among the many perceptive analyses of this passage and Hoccleve's other eulogies of Chaucer in the *Regiment*, see David Lawton, *Voice in Later Medieval English Literature: Public Interiorities* (Oxford, 2017), 183–94; Ethan Knapp, *The Bureaucratic Muse: Thomas Hoccleve and the Literature of Late Medieval England* (University Park, PA, 2001), 107–27; and Sebastian J. Langdell, *Thomas Hoccleve: Religious Reform, Transnational Poetics, and the Invention of Chaucer* (Liverpool, 2018), *passim*.

Here, Chaucer is plainly no mere name attached to an abstract textual authority. Rather, Hoccleve emphasizes his 'fresh lyflynesse'—the memory of the flesh-and-blood, historically specific man whose 'liknesse' he wishes to transmit to his own readers, a man who authored works 'So hyly wel' that Hoccleve considers it 'dotage' to attempt to follow in his wake.

Moreover, by referring to Chaucer's poetic accomplishments with the phrase 'cas semblable'—i.e., writings that address matters similar to those Hoccleve is addressing—Hoccleve at the same time points back at himself: what I am doing right now, he insinuates, is akin to what Chaucer just accomplished in recent memory. Of course, we know, as Hoccleve certainly did, that the closest that Chaucer actually ever came to writing something akin to the *Regiment* was, say, the *Melibee*. This difference between Hoccleve's representation of Chaucer and Chaucer's actual work hence underscores how Hoccleve refashions Chaucer into the sort of author that Hoccleve is claiming to be.[11] In an advice-to-princes poem that features a 2016-line introductory dramatization of a rambling conversation between Hoccleve and an old man that recounts, among other things, the genesis of the very poem that we are reading, the attention that Hoccleve gives to Chaucer as an author cannot help but redound upon himself. Indeed, Hoccleve goes out of his way to versify this reflexive relationship by staging the poem's initial naming of Chaucer as prompted by a doubled naming of himself, in response to the old man's query about his identity:

> 'What shal I calle thee, what is thy name?'
> 'Hoccleve, fadir myn, men clepen* me.'   *call*
> 'Hoccleve, sone?' 'Ywis*, fadir, that same.'   *Yes*
> 'Sone, I have herd or* this men speke of thee; *before*
> Thow were aqweyntid with Chaucer, pardee* –   *surely*
> God have his soule, best of any wight*!   *person*
> Sone I wole holde* thee that I have hight'.   *keep my promise*
>   (1863–9)

While it would be wrong to characterize these relays of authorial namings as Hoccleve's self-representation as the singular presiding genius behind the *Regiment* (much of the text, as Hoccleve enthusiastically acknowledges, is in fact a tissue of quotations), the importance to the poem of an idea of the author as the specific living human agent from whom the work proceeds nonetheless seems unmistakable. To be sure, this is not to suggest any straightforward identity between the actual Hoccleve and the one who voices, and is represented within, the *Regiment*. As A. C. Spearing and others have shown, the relation between these two remains shifting and blurred, and this is a calculated literary strategy. But since an enticement towards such a straightforward identity is part of this very strategy, the idea of the actual Hoccleve remains a crucial and—for English poetry—rather unprecedented element of the poem. As Spearing acknowledges,

> In Hoccleve's work ... autography [i.e., discourse involving an unstable, ambiguous relation between first-person speaker and flesh-and-blood author] begins to merge into what we would call autobiography: his textual 'I,' much more than

---

[11] The most in-depth consideration of this point is Langdell, *Thomas Hoccleve*.

the various first persons of Chaucer's poems, corresponds stably to a single imaginable person, and that person ... corresponds to the Hoccleve of documentary record.[12]

Yet, as unprecedented as this is, and despite the many other ways that Hoccleve's body of work is peculiar, this general mode of authorial self-representation—one that invokes the living, historical specificity of the first-person authorial speaker—is not merely idiosyncratic. Rather, in the years that follow it crops up repeatedly in fifteenth-century English poetry. The self-representation of Hoccleve's contemporary John Lydgate was entirely comparable, at least in this respect. And indeed it was Lydgate, rather than Hoccleve, who was more influential in this respect, judging from the dissemination of his manuscripts and explicit borrowings from and citations of his work. But however the habit spread, one of its effects is that, while we know the names of a relatively small number of English poets before the fifteenth century (tellingly, we remain more-or-less stymied about the certain identities of two of the most important late-fourteenth poets, i.e., the *Gawain*-poet and Langland), rather suddenly after 1400 we have named English authors aplenty, and often because those authors are careful to inscribe verifiable identities into their verse in some fashion. And they do so, as in the above example by Hoccleve—and as Lydgate even more frequently does—in respect to named poetic predecessors, especially Chaucer. In this way, fifteenth-century poets for the first time textualized an English poetic tradition, which is to say that it is in this century that an incipient idea of English literary history as a sequence of greater and lesser authors—that is, the idea that has only recently been eclipsed—is first recorded.[13] Authorship as a concept, therefore, is not just an important consideration in the study of fifteenth-century poetry in a general, literary critical sense, but it also represents one of this century's most crucial and influential areas of literary innovation.

As one might suspect, the question of why English poets regularly began to represent themselves and their predecessors in this fashion after 1400 does not possess a single or simple answer. The most obvious reason—that Hoccleve, Lydgate, and other poets mentioned herein, inspired by the brilliance of the Ricardians, were imitating Chaucer's practice in, say, the *House of Fame* or the 'Man of Law's Introduction', and Gower's practice in the *Confessio Amantis*—surely holds to some degree. Yet not only do those scarce instances of self-naming contrast with the relative frequency we encounter in the fifteenth century, but the nature of those instances also differs in important respects. Ricardian self-namings are embedded within a manifest fiction often involving allegory, dream vision, or both, and teeter upon an intractably ambiguous relation between first-person speaker and author. This practice contrasts strikingly with much fifteenth-century self-naming, as illustrated by Hoccleve's declaration of his actual, current authorship vis-à-vis Chaucer's actual, past authorship. There were contemporary French writers well known to Hoccleve and Lydgate, moreover, who engaged in much more prominent and spectacular experiments in authorial self-representation, poets such as Guillaume de Machaut (d. 1377) and, especially, Christine de Pizan (d. c1430), behind both of whom lay the *Roman de*

---

[12] A. C. Spearing, *Medieval Autographies: The 'I' of the Text* (Notre Dame, IN, 2012), 145. Sebastian Sobecki, *Last Words: The Public Self and the Social Author in Late Medieval England* (Oxford, 2019), helpfully provides the term *indexical* to denote the sort of authorial self-representation illustrated so strikingly by Hoccleve.

[13] This point about fifteenth-century poetry, especially that of Hoccleve and Lydgate in respect to Chaucer, has frequently been made. See, e.g., Edwards, *Invention*, 149–96; Stephanie Trigg, *Congenial Souls: Reading Chaucer from Medieval to Postmodern* (Minneapolis, MN, 2002), 74–108; Seth Lerer, *Chaucer and His Readers: Imagining the Author in Late-Medieval England* (Princeton, NJ, 1993); and my *Poets and Power from Chaucer to Wyatt* (Cambridge, 2007).

la Rose.¹⁴ In addition, Lydgate was plainly familiar with the innovations of some of the Italian authors who had influenced Chaucer, and both poets would have been shaped by the evolving trends in the Latin commentary tradition that Minnis has shown to have been the bedrock of late medieval conceptions of authorship. Numerous other sources may be adduced, such as (to name just a few) the tradition of history writing, the legacy of Boethius, and Augustine's *Confessions*.

Recalling Foucault, we must in addition acknowledge the many social, political, and institutional forces determining conceptions of authorship, such as, to list just some notable ones at the beginning of the century, the politics of the Lancastrian usurpation and subsequent intra-dynastic Lancastrian conflict, the gradual incursion of the English language into situations that were before the exclusive reserve of French or Latin, and the impetus given that incursion by the resumption of the war with France and religious controversies that, in part, were fought over and in English. More broadly over the course of the century, but perhaps no less influential, were the growth of literacy across ever wider social spheres and an expansion in the size and importance of the gentry, for whom book ownership became a mark of their class status. And likely both an effect and cause of these broader changes, the production of manuscripts containing English poetry accelerated briskly in the period, culminating at the end of the century, of course, in the books of English verse printed by William Caxton, who quite evidently capitalized on a pre-existing market. All these factors have received due attention, and, as with the aforementioned literary influences, this list is in no way comprehensive.¹⁵

Hence, as tempting as it might be to accept at face value Hoccleve's establishment of Chaucer as a point of origin for all that came afterward, the conventions of fifteenth-century authorial self-representation clearly had myriad sources, ones that, furthermore, held varying degrees of influence and intersected in different ways for different poets, and even for the same poet in different works. The prompting inspirations for Hoccleve's self-representation in the *Series* (completed 1421), for example, are not identical to those of the *Regiment*, and, accordingly, those works' respective authorial poses differ in important ways; and both poses, and corresponding influences, differ from Lydgate's self-representation in, say, the *Siege of Thebes* (*c*1421). Nonetheless, despite the manifold forms in which it appears, running through the century is a convention in which the proximity of a living, historically specific author to the first-person narrator is conveyed in some fashion, appearing regularly, if by no means universally, in many kinds of literary works, composed by a diverse set of writers, in various institutional and regional contexts. Across England and Scotland, by the end of this period, as Anthony Bale observes, 'the author has become he who defines and promotes himself as such: this is far from those earlier medieval writers, for whom the insertion of authorial identity in the text was playful, hidden or anxious'.¹⁶

---

¹⁴ See, e.g., Stephanie A. Viereck Gibbs Kamath, *Authorship and First-Person Allegory in Late Medieval France and England* (Cambridge, 2012).

¹⁵ The bibliography on the topics mentioned in this paragraph is immense. In addition to consulting the relevant chapters in the present volume, readers might begin with the chapters grouped under the heading 'Before the Reformation' in Wallace (ed.), *Cambridge History*.

¹⁶ Bale, 'From Translator to Laureate', 931. Bale cites Margery Kempe's *Book* as a further example of this new conception of authorship, which suggests its broad dissemination. See also Rory G. Critten, *Author, Scribe, and Book in Late Medieval English Literature* (Cambridge, 2018), who calls attention to the 'self-publishing pose' textualized by Hoccleve, Kempe, John Audelay, and Charles d'Orléans.

In the second section of this chapter, I describe some notable instances of fifteenth-century authorial poses to provide a sense of the variety of incarnations of this convention; I point out their distinguishing features, review their institutional circumstances, and note their means of transmission. First, however, I must clarify that I do not mean to suggest that poetry incorporating this convention was the principal sort of verse written in this period or necessarily the verse of the most literary historical importance. Rather, much verse—perhaps the major part—continued to be produced that contained or was transmitted with only the most perfunctory nods to the historical existence of its author, or, more commonly, possessed no such nods whatsoever, that is, was wholly anonymous not just in fact but also in what we might call narrational ethos.[17]

In particular, for various reasons both practical and literary, certain genres of Middle English verse were especially resistant to the incursion of this convention—for example, romance, satire, drama, and both religious and secular lyric (inasmuch as those may be distinguished). To consider just a single instance, the satirical and religious short poems preserved in BodL MS Digby 102 possess a consistent, powerful voice, but essential to these poems' literary strategy is that this voice comes across as depersonalized. Much like the *Regiment* and perhaps written at about the same time,[18] these poems direct moral, political, and spiritual exhortations at an imagined audience that is socially broad but politically graded, ramping up to those holding positions of civil and ecclesiastical power and, at times, specifically directed at the king, as in the following stanza from poem thirteen, 'Dede is worchyng'. After encouraging the 'you' of these lines (probably a recently crowned Henry V) in the conflict with France, the poet rather bellicosely advises,

> Stuffe ȝoure castels in eche coost,
> Warnestor* and folk þeder sende,   *military provision*
> So mow ȝe abate ȝoure enemys bost,   *may you humble your enemy*
> But not in trete* in wast* to spende*.   *treaty; futilely; employ*
> Wheþer ȝe assayle or defende,
> On see, on land, God ȝow spede*:   *make you succeed*
> Wiþ word of wynd mad neuere were* ende,   *war*
> But dent* of swerd endid þe dede.   *blow*
> (121–8)

The authority of this voice rests not upon any specificity but on the fiction of its speaking for the general good sense of the king's subjects; the voice is, as Helen Barr describes, 'common, communal and consensual'.[19] Accordingly, the imperative mood of this stanza is quite typical; in contrast, the first-person pronoun—when not attached to, say, Christ—appears sparingly and fleetingly, as in the opening of poem three, 'Treuth, reste and pes':

---

[17] Sobecki, *Last Words*, 5–7, provides the salutatory reminder, however, that many of the poems that we take as exhibiting this ethos may be anonymous merely because the author assumed his readers knew his identity. Nevertheless, that, say, Hoccleve's authorship of the *Regiment* also likely went without saying to his immediate audience suggests that often the decision to include one's name within the body of a poem, or not, was a literarily meaningful one.

[18] Helen Barr favours 1413–14 but acknowledges the difficulty of certain dating; see Helen Barr (ed.), *The Digby Poems* (Exeter, 2009), 6–18. Citations of the poems are from this edition.

[19] Barr (ed.), *Digby Poems*, 55.

For drede ofte my lippes Y steke*,	seal
For false reporters that trouthe mys famed*;	slandered
Ʒut charitee chargeth* me to speke:	orders
Þouȝ trouþe be drede*, he nys not ashamed,	afraid
Trouþe secheþ non hernes ther los* is lamed,	corners where reputation
Trouþe is worschiped at euery des*.	dais

(1–6)

Here the speaker, with his sealed lips, becomes imaginatively embodied just enough to create the impression that the conventional wisdom that fills these poems plausibly represents the real views of real people. But it is the collective force of the general, not the particular, that this embodiment seeks to marshal, and thus self-reference, by the fourth line, has evaporated into the proverbial. The result is that the Digby poems are very nearly literally a tissue of quotations, in the sense that their authority rests precisely on the reproduction of the expected, but the expected tuned in extraordinary application to the topics of the moment. They are, as Barr puts it, 'an echo chamber of the already said', uttered by the voice of 'a weathered sage who speaks timeless wisdom' with 'a very timely edge'.[20]

The very similarities between the Digby poems and portions of the *Regiment* in aims, tone, and matter underscore, therefore, the vast differences in the ideas of authorship that they attach to their respective narrating voices. With the benefit of hindsight, we know that the conventions of the Digby poems in this respect would eventually yield to those incipiently present in the *Regiment*. By the end of the sixteenth century, in Edmund Spenser's *Faerie Queene*—with its combination of romance, allegory, and satire; its public and political aims; and its address to a hierarchically organized readership with the sovereign at the top—we encounter the very features that had in Middle English poetry typically lent themselves to an ethos of anonymity, but are now married to one of English literary history's grandest assertions of authorial individuality. While at the beginning of the fifteenth century the readers of the *Regiment* and the Digby poems, obviously, would have perceived no such teleology, over the course of the next hundred years assertions of authorial individuality evolved into a well-established convention for marking off one sort of verse—the kind that we have come associate with the adjective *literary*—from another, which we might label *popular* or, as Bale puts it, the 'sub-literary'.[21] Thus, although important works of poetry in English—as other chapters in this volume attest—continued to be produced throughout the century with little to no interest in an idea of authorship like that of the *Regiment*, that idea possesses a distinctive literary historical significance, in that the very notion of English literary history that has come down to us is pendant upon it. The rest of this chapter considers some of the more typical or striking forms that this idea of authorship took.

Authorial Poses

In accounting for these forms, we might begin by considering the institutional circumstances or regions where Middle English verse was produced. We might, for example, adduce royal patronage as a determining institutional circumstance and consider Hoccleve and Lydgate in this light. Yet we would then have to put aside the determining

---

[20] Barr (ed.), *Digby Poems*, 59. For an incisive account of the nuances of the poet's language, including an analysis of the quoted lines from poem three, see Matthew Giancarlo, 'Troubling the New Constitutionalism: Politics, Penitence, and the Dilemma of Dread in the Digby Poems', *JEGP*, 110 (2011), 78–104.

[21] Bale, 'From Translator to Laureate', 923.

circumstances of the other institutions in which these poets wrote (e.g., the civil service for Hoccleve, the Benedictine monastery for Lydgate), those other of these poets' authorial poses that were not as related to royal patronage, and the other poets, like John Metham (fl. 1449), who assume poses that resemble those related to royal patronage but were textualized outside of those circumstances.[22] Similarly, we might call attention to East Anglia as an especially fertile region of fifteenth-century verse production, home to a complexly interlinked network of writers, patrons, and book producers. And, indeed, the authorial poses of the identifiable poets who were resident in this region—Lydgate, Metham, Osbern Bokenham (d. c1467), Benedict Burgh (d. 1483), John Capgrave (d. 1464)—do share some features.[23] But again we confront important differences among these writers' home institutions, differences among the poses taken up in these writers' various works, other poets outside of this group who assume similar poses, and, in this case, the central role of Lydgate's influence and, accordingly, the fact of Lydgate's poetic activities elsewhere (for example, in London and Paris).[24] As important as institutional and regional contexts are, therefore, they turn out not to be the most helpful organizational frameworks, since authorial poses circulated through and were shaped by literary influences that cut across institutional and geographical borders, with poets adopting different poses according to different literary purposes.

Alternatively, we might provide more concrete grounding to the analysis of poses by beginning with specific manuscripts, considering, say, the producers, features, and circulation of those manuscripts that especially encode an idea of the author as historically specific. And, certainly, there are some crucial manuscripts to spotlight in this regard. For example, the manuscripts collecting poetry by Lydgate and Chaucer either directly produced by John Shirley (d. 1456) or copied from ones produced by him present that poetry in ways that place strong emphasis on those poets' historical identities as authors. Shirley's famously chatty rubrics (however fanciful they might be) seemed designed to function as something like modern book-jacket author biographies, linking the value and authority of specific poems with the concrete individuality of (in Lydgate's case) a living author, as in this instance from BL MS Add. 29729:

Here begyneth a balade which Iohn Lydgate the Monke of Bery wrott & made at þe commanundement of þe Quene Kateryn as in here sportes she walkyd by the medowes that were late mowen in the monthe of Iulij.[25]

In addition, there are those manuscripts copied or otherwise organized by the poets themselves that feature solely (or almost solely) their work. These include a trio of manuscripts

---

[22] For Metham, see, in particular, the final fifteen stanzas or so of the romance *Amoryus and Cleopes* (1449) in Hardin Craig (ed.), *The Works of John Metham* (London, 1916), 2107–211; 77–81. Over the course of these stanzas, Metham lauds by name his patron Sir Miles Stapleton; Stapleton's wife's cousin William de la Pole, duke of Suffolk; Henry VI; Chaucer; and Lydgate; and then concludes by naming himself and recording his place of birth and lineage.

[23] For a consideration of one slice of this literary network, see Anthony Bale, 'A Norfolk Gentlewoman and Lydgatian Patronage: Lady Sibylle Boys and her Cultural Environment', *Medium Ævum*, 78 (2009), 394–413. The *Book of Margery Kempe*, of course, was also a product of this environment.

[24] Another environment quite conducive to poses of authorial individuality was the prison, as well demonstrated by Joanna Summers, *Late-Medieval Prison Writing and the Politics of Autobiography* (Oxford, 2004).

[25] Quoted from H. N. MacCracken (ed.), *The Minor Poems of John Lydgate, Part II: The Secular Poems*, EETS o.s. 192 (London, 1934), 809. For Shirley, the place to begin is Margaret Connolly, *John Shirley: Book Production and the Noble Household in Fifteenth-Century England* (Aldershot, 1998). For a sceptical view regarding the reliability of Shirley's rubrics, see Julia Boffey and A. S. G. Edwards, '"Chaucer's Chronicle", John Shirley, and the Canon of Chaucer's Shorter Poems', *Studies in the Age of Chaucer*, 20 (1998), 201–18.

copied by Hoccleve that seem designed to collect together his short poems, the sole surviving manuscript of poetry by John Audelay (fl. 1426), and the holograph containing the *Active Policy of a Prince* and its appendix of sorts, the *Dicta & opiniones diversorum philosophorum*, by George Ashby (d. 1475).[26] Yet, as important testimony as these manuscripts provide for an emerging idea of fifteenth-century Middle English authorship, they represent the proverbial drop in the ocean compared to the total number of manuscripts produced during the period containing Middle English verse. In contrast with the codicological innovations of poets across the Channel—who were considerably more sophisticated in this regard—the vast majority of English manuscripts, including those containing works by the presumably well-known personages of Chaucer and Lydgate, do not emphasize authorship in any way close to the manner that Shirley's do.[27] Indeed, many (probably most) leave no trace of identifiable authorship whatsoever, with the sole exception of those moments in which poets themselves somehow textualize their own authorial specificity. It is therefore those moments—what I have been referring to as the textualization of authorial poses—that provide the most ready focal point for considering the emergent fifteenth-century idea of English poetic authorship.

By the term *pose*, moreover, I should make clear that I do not mean to suggest any necessary element of duplicity. Instead, I mean to emphasize the performative nature of this sort of authorship, the way in which poets constitute it (however consciously) by drawing on a potpourri of pre-existing literary resources, which comprise a sort of script that each poet assembles and acts out in his particular manner as shaped by his particular institutional circumstances. There is no falseness or artificiality to these poses because there is no authorship that exists outside or prior to these scripts and performances thereof. To be sure, there may be discrepancies between the textualized details of a given performance of authorship and its extra-textual circumstances (as with, perhaps, some of Shirley's rubrics), but as modern theorists have argued about gender, a misrepresentative performance does not point to a more authentic, non-performative identity but rather to the constructedness and fluidity of the category of personal identity itself.[28] Since the emergent fifteenth-century idea of English authorship involved precisely the concept of *author* as a dimension of personal identity, it is the textualized performances of this identity, whatever their degree of factual accuracy, that constitute this idea's social reality and primary historical record.

These textualized performances or authorial poses all feature a declared or implied identity between author and first-person speaker, and they all associate this author/speaker with a biological, historically specific person. Some make this association definitive through self-naming or the supplying of other, localizing detail; others hint strongly at it but leave it—for one reason or another—at arm's length, so to speak. Broadly, the poses divide between those in which the author/speaker plays some sort of mediating role between the matter of the poem and its readers, and those in which the author/speaker

---

[26] For the Hoccleve holographs, see J. A. Burrow and A. I. Doyle (eds), *Thomas Hoccleve: A Facsimile of the Autograph Verse Manuscripts*, EETS, s.s. 19 (Oxford, 2002). For the Audelay manuscript, see Susanna Fein (ed.), *John the Blind Audelay, Poems and Carols (Oxford, Bodleian Library MS Douce 302)* (Kalamazoo, MI, 2009). That the sole surviving manuscript of Ashby's *Active Policy* and *Dicta* is a holograph has recently been demonstrated by Sobecki, *Last Words*, 162–81.

[27] For this point, see A. S. G. Edwards, 'Fifteenth-Century Middle English Verse Author Collections', in A. S. G. Edwards, Vincent Gillespie, and Ralph Hanna (eds), *The English Medieval Book: Studies in Memory of Jeremy Griffiths* (London, 2000), 101–12; and Taylor, 'Vernacular Authorship'.

[28] See, e.g., Judith Butler, *Gender Trouble: Feminism and the Subversion of Identity* (New York, 1990). Cf. Edwards's characterization of authorship as performative, *Invention*, xv.

himself *is* the matter (i.e., the protagonist)—or at least a prominent element of it. Admittedly, however, even this relatively straightforward distinction becomes in many instances difficult to sustain, as the constitution of the mediating voice may itself become the subject of a work, and, conversely, a speaker may use the subject of himself as a vehicle to ruminate upon countless other topics. The bipartite structure of the *Regiment of Princes*, in fact, illustrates vividly both the distinction and the difficulty of sustaining it. On the one hand, while the subject of the poem's long preamble is manifestly Hoccleve himself and how he came to write the poem that we are reading, over the course of the dramatized dialogue with the old man, Hoccleve takes the opportunity to address many other topics, for example, to decry the fashion of the excessive 'sleeves encombrous' (466) that may prevent a lord's man from effectively defending his lord during a street ambush. On the other hand, while Hoccleve's role in the subsequent advice text proper is ostensibly simply to convey the wisdom of authoritative political sources to Prince Henry, this mediation, as we have already seen, at times quite unmistakably points back at itself, taking the person of the mediator as one of its primary topics. Nevertheless, since this distinction between author-as-topic and author-as-mediator was apparent enough to Hoccleve for him to divide his poem formally between the two, we may utilize it here to survey some of the century's most typical or noteworthy poses. Yet let me reiterate that if a poet left behind even a modest quantity of verse—say, a poet such as Ashby—that verse very likely exhibits a variety of authorial poses (and hence Lydgate's immense body of writings exhibits a dizzying array). Similarly, no genre of poetry necessarily correlates with any kind of pose, although some genres—and some poets—do have tendencies in this respect. Hence, while I must limit the description below to a few poses of a few poets, this should not be understood to represent the limits of the practice of any of those poets or others whom I do not mention.

The author-as-mediator pose that Hoccleve assumes in the advice-text section of the *Regiment* provides an example of what turned out to be one of the most pervasive and influential types of authorial poses in fifteenth-century Middle English poetry. We may designate this pose as that of the author as laureate, since it imagines an authorial ideal that corresponds to that which Francis Petrarch sought to enact in his 1341 laureation address in Rome.[29] This pose's primary characteristic is a triangulation of political authority, typically as embodied in the person of a sovereign; literary (and sometimes also cultural, intellectual, moral, or spiritual) authority as denoted by a tradition signalled in some fashion, often by reference to specific past authors; and the living, first-person poet-narrator who addresses the sovereign as the mouthpiece of literary tradition. Although this pose is plainly evident in, and was widely disseminated through, Hoccleve's Chaucer eulogy quoted above, for Middle English poets it was Lydgate who provided the most paradigmatic and influential examples of it across a career that frequently involved writing for royal patrons.

Lydgate's mammoth 36,365-line *Fall of Princes*—completed in 1439 and surviving in thirty-nine manuscripts and in extracts in dozens more—perhaps most completely realizes this pose (although other works, and in particular the 1420 *Troy Book*, are similarly noteworthy in this respect).[30] Despite being a translation, via a French intermediary, of Boccaccio's *De casibus virorum illustrium*, the *Fall* prominently features a first-person representation of the historically specific Lydgate, who appears throughout as engaging in a

---

[29] See Ernest Hatch Wilkins, *Studies in the Life and Works of Petrarch* (Cambridge, MA, 1955), 300–13.
[30] For the *Fall*, the place to begin is Nigel Mortimer, *John Lydgate's 'Fall of Princes': Narrative Tragedy in Its Literary and Political Contexts* (Oxford, 2005).

kind of dialogue with the author whom he calls 'Bochas'. The latter functions as no mere nominal *auctor* but is rather represented as a flesh-and-blood writer, in conversation, for example, with 'Frauncets Petrak, the laureat poete' in the prologue to Book Eight.[31] At the same time, Lydgate explicitly departs from his source at the end of each chapter to supply a moralizing envoy directly addressed to his reader. This reader, most immediately, is Duke Humfrey of Gloucester, who, as Lydgate tells us in the prologue to Book Two, requested that, after each 'tragedie', Lydgate should

> At the eende sette a remedie,
> With a lenvoie conueied be resoun*,   *reasonably*
> And afftir that, with humble affeccioun,
> To noble pryncis lowli* it directe,   *humbly*
> Bi othres fallyng thei myht themsilff correcte.
>   (2.150–4)

In this way, the very structure and *modus operandi* of the *Fall* enacts the triangulation of the laureate pose: Lydgate serves as the focal point between, on the one hand, the laureate literary tradition figured by 'Bochas' and, on the other hand, the political authority figured by Humfrey and more generally extending to the 'noble pryncis' to which the work's wisdom is ceaselessly recommended. This same triangulation, moreover, appears in more pointed, miniature formations throughout the work, perhaps most revealingly in the prologue to Book One. Here Lydgate bewails the deaths of Seneca, Cicero, Petrarch, and, most of all, his 'maistir Chaucer', for whom he goes on to provide a rather complete bibliography (1.246–357). He then mentions that 'these poetis' were held 'in gret deynte' by 'pryncis in euery regioun' (1.358–60), which quickly takes him to the 'prynce ful myhti off puissaunce, / A kyngis sone and vncle to the kyng / Henry the Sexte' (1.373–75) and Humfrey's commissioning of the present work, which Lydgate declares he will humbly undertake despite 'Hauyng no colours but onli whit & blak' (1.465). This last remark, of course, punningly calls attention to the historical person of Lydgate and his frequent self-description as a monk of Bury, in his habit of white and black. Hence here in the final stanza of the prologue Lydgate unmistakably completes the triangulation among literary tradition (Chaucer), political authority (Humfrey), and himself.

Writing some quarter-of-a-century later, George Ashby textualized what was plainly intended to be a similar kind of pose, but under rather different circumstances. At the beginning of *Active Policy of a Prince*, Ashby names 'Maisters Gower, Chauucer & Lydgate' as 'Primier poetes of this nacion' and thereby invokes the English literary tradition with the first two lines of this *Fürstenspiegel* (and realizes in fact the recently deceased Lydgate's implied, notional claim to be part of that tradition).[32] At the head of the fourth stanza, the author then names himself, claiming that he, 'George Asshby' does not intend any 'comparison' to his predecessors' 'excellent enditing' (22–3), the very comparison, obviously, that his close imitation of their (and especially Lydgate's) self-authorizing gestures beckons. After several more stanzas of apologizing for his inadequacies (which enables him to embody his voice further through mention of his 'decrepit age' of 'Right nygh at mony yeres of foure score' [64–5]), he turns next to his royal addressee:

---

[31] Henry Bergen (ed.), *Lydgate's Fall of Princes*, EETS, e.s. 121–4 (London, 1924–7), 8.61.
[32] Mary Bateson (ed.), *George Ashby's Poems*, EETS, e.s. 76 (London, 1899), 1–2. For studies of Ashby, in addition to Sobecki, *Last Words*, see Summers, *Prison Writing*, 142–69, and my *Poets and Power*, 139–68.

> Right & myghty prince and my right goode Lorde,
> Linially comyn of blode royal,
> Bothe of Faders & moders of recorde*,   *as officially recorded*
> Occupying by grace celestial
> Thaier Roiaulmes, with grace especial
> To whom be al honnour and reuerence,
> Dewe to youre high estate and excellence,
>
> I mene, to youre highnesse Edwarde by name,
> Trewe sone & heire to the high maiestie
> Of oure liege lorde Kynge Henry & dame
> Margarete, the Quene ...
>   (85–95)

These lines complete the laureate pose triangulation, in which Ashby embodies a literary tradition culminating in Lydgate that speaks to political authority figured here by Prince Edward, son of 'King Henry [VI] & dame / Margarete [of Anjou], the Quene'. Yet, in their plainly belaboured insistence on the legitimacy of Edward's claim to the throne (in, e.g., 'Right ... prince', 'Linially comyn', and 'Trewe sone & heire'), these lines also provide a pointed example of the vicissitudes to which this pose is subject.[33]

When Humfrey commissioned Lydgate's *Fall* sometime after May 1431, Lydgate had long been established as the country's most famous and authoritative living poet, writing from a position of some political and economic independence as a Benedictine monk, whose range of patrons included royalty, nobility, gentry, civic authorities, and ecclesiastical leaders. When Ashby wrote the *Active Policy*, he was almost certainly virtually unknown as a poet. He rather would have been recognized as a scribe with over four decades of service to the Lancastrians, most recently as Margaret's signet clerk, and hence entirely dependent, politically and economically, on his patron. When Lydgate wrote the above lines about the envoys he was including for Humfrey, the latter—as regent of England while both nine-year-old Henry VI and Humfrey's older brother John of Bedford were in France—was the *de facto* ruler of the country. When Ashby wrote the above lines about Edward's true lineage (if we accept Sebastian Sobecki's argument for the period between the Battle of Towton [March 1461] and the beginning of Ashby's imprisonment in mid-1462),[34] Henry and Margaret's forces had just suffered a devastating defeat at the hands of Edward of York, prior to which this latter Edward had declared himself the true king of England; and Henry, Margaret, and their son Edward had fled to Scotland, apparently leaving Ashby behind. Consequently, after his long service to the Lancastrians, Ashby had suddenly found himself unemployed and no doubt a person of some suspicion to the victorious Yorkists. For whatever reason, Ashby chose this profoundly inauspicious moment to fashion a pose as laureate. He carefully produced a copy of his advice text (CUL MS Mm. 4. 42), which is its only surviving witness, for the prince whom he still wanted to believe would inherit the throne, and he presumably did so without any assurance that that prince would even ever see the poem. If Lydgate's *Fall* represents the closest fifteenth-century English approximation of an actual laureate performance as Petrarch imagined it, Ashby's *Active Policy* illustrates how a laureate pose may serve in desperate straits as a poetic device for imagining the world other than how it is.

---

[33] In her edition, Bateson emends the first line of this passage to insert 'high' after the line-initial 'Right', but there is no manuscript support for this extra-metrical addition; instead, 'Right' here is adjectival, meaning 'true'.
[34] Sobecki, *Last Words*, 184–91.

Another sort of author-as-mediator pose resembles the laureate one in some respects but aligns more straightforwardly with the identity of churchman that so many of the Middle English poets in this period also held. What is notable about this version of the pose—which we may call that of the sacerdotal author—is that it should resemble the laureate one at all, since its basic function of conveying spiritually edifying matter to its readers is one that had been accomplished by a long tradition of Middle English writing (as in, say, the homiletic verse in the Vernon manuscript) without the sort of authorial self-representational strategies that emerged in this century. Because neither the matter of this writing nor the addressee required any special figuration as concrete individuals, neither did the first-person speaker, when there even was one.

We can readily see in the codex of religious verse by Audelay both what had been the earlier norm in this respect and how fifteenth-century poetry departed from it. In lines such as the following from the *Epilogue to the Counsel of Conscience*,

Thus in this Gospel wretyn I fynd,	
He that lovys here rust and pese*,	*rest and peace*
He is Godis child without lese*,	*lie*
And he that sterys debate* with his males*,	*discord; evil intentions*
Thai be chylder* of the Fynd*,[35]	*children; Fiend*

the 'I' seems wholly akin to that of the Digby 102 poems, serving as a kind of placeholder for a generic voice of spiritual authority, one that conveys the wisdom of the 'Gospel' to an equally generic reader. Yet just a few lines later, the above 'I' materializes as the voice of the flesh-and-blood Audelay specifically. Conventionally approaching his conclusion by asking God to grant him his 'payne' and 'purgatory / Out of this word (*world*) or (*before*) that I dy', the speaker next localizes the scene of writing, telling us, 'As I lay seke in my langure, / In an abbay here be west, / This boke I made with gret dolour' (482–4; 145). He then concludes, in a formulation that he has already used at four points earlier in the codex:

Mervel ye not of this making*	*poetry writing*
Fore I me excuse—hit* is not I;	*it*
This was the Hole Gost wercheng,	
That sayd these wordis so faithfully,	
...	
Beware, seris*, I youe pray,	*Take heed, sirs*
Fore I mad this with good entent,	
In the reverens of God Omnipotent.	
Prays fore me that beth present—	
My name is Jon the Blynd Awdlay.	
(495–7)	

What has occurred here, as it does throughout the codex, is a conjoining of two ordinary conventions—homiletic exhortation and penitential request for prayer—that together effect a departure from what had been the norm. The generic voice of spiritual authority becomes that of Audelay specifically, lying in bed blind and sick, and what he mediates is not only Christian truths but also the personalized inspiration of the 'Hole Gost'. And while his implied readership still appears to be all inclusive, since the subsequent Latin

---

[35] Fein (ed.), *Poems and Carols*, 464–8, 145.

colophon identifies him as '*capellanum*' or chaplain (146), we may suspect that he also has a more specific individual in mind—his employer, Lord Lestrange of Knockin.[36]

In several instances of Lydgate's religious verse, as we might expect, the resemblance between laureate and sacerdotal pose is more obviously marked, as in, for example, his long hagiographical work, the *Lives of Saints Edmund and Fremund* (composed 1434–6), an epic account of the life of the saint to which his abbey is devoted (as well as of the life of that saint's nephew), written in commemoration of a visit by, and for presentation to, a young Henry VI.[37] Although it is not certain that Audelay knew of Lydgate's verse, the latter's influence is readily on display elsewhere. To mention just examples in the hagiographical vein, the Augustinian friar Capgrave's lengthy *Life of Saint Katherine* (from 1445) and the thirteen female saints' lives that Capgrave's confrere Bokenham collected in BL MS Arundel 327, and which are now known as *Legendys of Hooly Wummen* (from 1447), clearly respond to the precedent of Lydgate's authorial pose—the former in a loosely emulative manner and the latter in a rather complex, ambivalent sort of dialogue.[38] By the early sixteenth century this hagiographical author-as-mediator pose had migrated into print, unmistakably visible in, for instance, Benedictine monk Henry Bradshaw's epic *Life of Saint Werburge* (written 1513), especially as it is framed in Richard Pynson's 1521 print.[39] That print begins with a six-stanza lyric eulogy, by one 'J. T.', to the recently deceased Bradshaw, lauding him by name as, among other epithets, 'the styrpe (*stock*) of eloquence'[40] and containing in its first two stanzas an acrostic of his name; and the print concludes with three *balades*, the first two of which celebrate Bradshaw at least as much as Werburge. Bradshaw himself, in his 'Go forth, litell boke' finale, submits his poem for 'pardon' first 'To all auncient poetes' and next

... to all other / whiche present* nowe be,   *contemporary*
Fyrst to maister Chaucer and Ludgate sentencious*,   *full of wisdom*
Also to preignaunt* Barkley nowe beyng religious*,   *imaginative*; *bound by vow*
To inuentiue Skelton and poet laureate.

(2.2020–6)

In this way, Bradshaw's embodied presence within the text becomes defined not just vis-à-vis recent English authorial precedents but also by Bradshaw's living, noteworthy contemporaries Alexander Barclay (d. 1552) and John Skelton (d. 1529) (both of whose work was also, probably not coincidentally, printed by Pynson). By the turn of the century, a religious work as ambitious as the 5500-line *Werburge* almost inevitably featured

---

[36] Several commentators have suggested that Audelay's codex obliquely responds to Lestrange's notorious and bloody assault on Sir John Trussell on Easter Sunday, 1417, while the latter was performing his devotions in a London church—an event at which Audelay was present. See, e.g., Critten, *Author*, 111–46.

[37] See A. S. G. Edwards, 'John Lydgate's *Lives of Ss Edmund and Fremund*: Politics, Hagiography and Literature', in Anthony Bale (ed.), *St Edmund, King and Martyr: Changing Images of a Medieval Saint* (Woodbridge, 2009), 133–44.

[38] See Karen A. Winstead (ed.), *John Capgrave: The Life of Saint Katherine* (Kalamazoo, MI, 1999); and Mary S. Serjeantson (ed.), *Legendys of Hooly Wummen*, EETS, o.s. 206 (London, 1939). For Capgrave, the place to begin is Karen A. Winstead, *John Capgrave's Fifteenth Century* (Philadelphia, PA, 2007); for Bokenham, Alice Spencer, *Language, Lineage and Location in the Works of Osbern Bokenham* (Newcastle upon Tyne, 2013). Bokenham was the first to formulate in verse the triumvirate of Chaucer, Gower, and Lydgate (with Ashby the second to do so), but a subtle note of critique seems to creep into these ostensible celebrations. Simon Horobin's comments on his recently identified translation of the complete *Legenda aurea* by Bokenham (Edinburgh, Advocates Library, Abbotsford MS) suggest that this larger collection does not contain the same emphasis on Bokenham's authorship; see 'Politics, Patronage, and Piety in the Work of Osbern Bokenham', *Speculum*, 82 (2007), 932–49.

[39] STC 3506. Bradshaw's *Werburge* has been the topic of increasing attention; see, e.g., Cynthia Turner Camp, *Anglo-Saxon Saints' Lives as History Writing in Late Medieval England* (Cambridge, 2015), 102–32.

[40] Carl Horstman (ed.), *The Life of Saint Werburge of Chester*, EETS, o.s. 88 (London, 1887), 23, 2.

this sort of authorial pose, in contrast with, say, the elusive authorial identity behind *Piers Plowman* a century before.

Of course, *Piers Plowman* falls into the category of poetry in which the first-person narrator is also an important focus of the matter of the poem, and admittedly this category was through the fifteenth century more resistant to straightforward identifications between historical author and first-person narrator/protagonist. In this kind of poetry, as *Piers Plowman* well illustrates, the narrator/protagonist serves to some degree as a paradigmatic figure with whom the reader is meant to identify, and any element that we would now call autobiographical is subject to fictionalization in order to fit into expected literary conventions and to further its paradigmatic purposes. For these reasons, the thematic energy of the author/narrator identification may depend on that identification being simultaneously palpable and loose. In King James I's *Kingis Quair* (likely written 1423-4), for example, the incarcerated first-person narrator seems initially to insert himself into a version of the narrative of Chaucer's 'Knight's Tale', complete with allusions to Boethius, although this protagonist is imprisoned without a rival. The poem then segues into a dream vision resembling the *House of Fame* by way of Lydgate's *Temple of Glas*, and concludes, as did James's own story of imprisonment (if not his subsequent life), rather more optimistically than its sources. Although James in his 'Go litill tretise' envoy names 'Gowere and Chaucere' as his 'maisteris dere', 'Superlatiue as poetis laureate' (1373-6), he himself is only named, in the poem's sole surviving witness, in a late fifteenth-century scribal colophon and sixteenth-century opening rubric, which has led some to argue for an unknown author impersonating James.[41] Although recent scholarship tends to accept James's authorship as more likely than not, that there exists any uncertainty at all suggests both the continued resistance of the author-as-protagonist pose to unambiguous historical concretization and, conversely, the emergence of the thematic importance of the historically specific author (again, in contrast with *Piers Plowman* or, say, *Pearl*)—so much so that, even if one supposes the author were not James, one would have to acknowledge that the actual author wished to create this impression.[42]

Not surprisingly, it is Hoccleve who supplied the century's most thorough infusion of an author-as-protagonist pose with a representation of historically specific authorship. In particular, Hoccleve reworked the genre of first-person penitential verse in a manner that infuses its conventional matter—the spiritually broken interiority of a paradigmatic speaker—with unprecedented specificity. For example, the poem that Hoccleve entitled '*la male regle de T. Hoccleue*'[43] (1405-6) self-consciously makes use of this genre in order to accomplish something other than penance—namely, begging. At least in part because the latter activity, for rather practical reasons, necessitates the reader's knowledge of the author's identity in a way that a poem directed towards God does not, *La male regle* by its conclusion comes as close to autobiography as anything to that point written in Middle English verse. Following the cue of its title's confession of the author's 'unruly life', the poem

---

[41] Julia Boffey (ed.), *The Kingis Quair* in *Fifteenth-Century English Dream Visions: An Anthology* (Oxford, 2003). For the authorship question, see Julia Boffey, 'Chaucerian Prisoners: The Context of the *Kingis Quair*', in Julia Boffey and Janet Cowen (eds), *Chaucer and Fifteenth-Century Poetry* (London, 1991), 84–102; and Summers, *Prison Writing*, 60–89.

[42] Many of these same points may be made about the sequence of Middle English poems that Mary-Jo Arn in her edition has christened *Fortunes Stabilnes*, which, as most now accept, was authored by Charles, duke of Orléans between 1420 and 1440 while in English captivity. See Mary-Jo Arn (ed.), *Fortunes Stabilnes: Charles of Orlean's English Book of Love* (Binghamton, NY, 1994).

[43] This is the rubric in the holograph San Marino, CA, Huntington Library MS HM 111.

initially focuses on elaborating this confession, albeit to a personified 'helthe' rather than to God. As it proceeds, this confession accrues increasingly localizing detail, until at about midway through the speaker recalls going 'Hoom to the Priuee Seel',[44] a reference to Hoccleve's professional identity as Privy Seal clerk that cements the first-person speaker to a historically specific author in a way that decisively limits that speaker's paradigmatic status, if not simply dissipates it. Later the speaker mentions his workplace again (308), refers to his coworkers 'Prentys and Arondel' (321), and names himself in a rather odd moment in which Hoccleve as author addresses Hoccleve as protagonist: 'Bewaar, Hoccleue, I rede (*advise*) thee therfore, / And to a mene reule (*moderate behaviour*) thow thee dresse' (351–2). Here author-as-mediator and author-as-protagonist are simultaneously distinct and fused, and both are the historically specific Hoccleve, a fact that the speaker makes sure we do not miss when he remarks, 'Ey, what is me, þat to myself thus longe / Clappid (*jabbered*) haue I' (393–4). That the result of all this is something new in Middle English verse is cast into stark relief when Hoccleve's autograph copy of the poem is compared with the extracts that survive as a freestanding *balade* in Canterbury Cathedral Archives Register O.[45] In the latter, an unknown writer has carefully selected and recrafted nine stanzas of *La male regle* in order to fashion a more conventional moral/penitential poem—substituting, for example, 'ther fore' for line 351's 'Hoccleue'. The result is a lyric with a first-person voice akin to that of the roughly contemporary Digby poems, only in this instance we can see just how much authorial specificity was considered not only unnecessary but in fact an obstacle to a poem's purpose.

Although Hoccleve would later go on to write the tour-de-force of author-as-protagonist poetry that we now call the *Series*, Middle English poets in the rest of the century did not much follow him in this respect—Ashby's *A Prisoner's Reflections* (c1464), with its echoes of the *Series*, being a telling exception. In the next century, however, authors plainly working within the Lydgatean tradition more readily conjoined the poses of author-as-mediator and author-as-protagonist. For example, in the first dozen years of the century, Stephen Hawes, a groom of Henry VII's privy chamber, produced three separate narrative poems in the prologues of which he quite explicitly assumes a laureate pose, as an author who 'gladly wolde folowe the makynge of Lydgate'.[46] At the same time, each narrative features an allegorically named first-person protagonist who is explicitly, though inconsistently, conflated with the author who introduces himself in the prologue (as signalled through, e.g., self-referential passages).[47] *The Garlande or Chapelet of Laurell* (published in 1523) by John Skelton, Hawes's contemporary in the Tudor court, pushes this conjoining to its

---

[44] Roger Ellis (ed.), '*My Compleinte' and Other Poems* (Exeter, 2001), 188, 69.

[45] For an edition of this extract and accompanying discussion, see David Watt, 'Thomas Hoccleve's *La Male Regle* in the Canterbury Cathedral Archives', *Opuscula: Short Texts of the Middle Ages and Renaissance*, 2 (2012), 1–11.

[46] Florence W. Gluck and Alice B. Morgan (eds), *Stephen Hawes: The Minor Poems*, EETS, o.s. 271 (London, 1974), *The Conforte of Louers*, 21. Hawes completed this poem 1510–11. The other two poems are *The Example of Vertu* (1503–4) and the much longer *Pastime of Pleasure* (1505–6). For Hawes, the place to begin is A. S. G. Edwards, *Stephen Hawes* (Boston, MA, 1983). See also Antony J. Hasler, *Court Poetry in Late Medieval England and Scotland: Allegories of Authority* (Cambridge 2011), 108–44.

[47] While each poem at various points clearly associates the first-person narrator/protagonist with Hawes, *The Example of Vertu* and the *Pastime of Pleasure* also recount, in first-person, that protagonist's death. And near the end of *The Example of Vertu* the protagonist Vertu is also associated with Henry VII, as the speaker, having just recounted his marriage to Clennes, refers to the union of Henry and Elizabeth of York, the 'rede rose and the whyte in maryage', as 'all clennes and vertuous courage'; Gluck and Morgan (eds), *Hawes: Minor Poems*, 2089–91.

extremist point of conflation, as it relates a story in which a first-person laureate author is the hero of a triumphal narrative precisely because of his achievements as the former.[48]

John Milton, of course, would later compose the definitive English epic that conjoins author-as-mediator with author-as-protagonist, and in the process definitively establish the concept of English literary history as a sequence of great authors. Yet, as this chapter has shown, it is Hoccleve's witty, idiosyncratic, and rather abject petition to Henry IV's treasurer Lord Furnival for his belated £10 annuity that stands behind this august tradition. And this at once underscores the importance of the fifteenth century to the very concept of English literary history and provides a salutary reminder that an author's textualization as a flesh-and-blood person is not inevitable but rather, as Foucault taught us, a strategic discursive construct that organizes the meaning of a text towards some end, however lofty or pragmatic that may be.

---

[48] See the edition in John Scattergood (ed.), *The Complete English Poems of John Skelton*, rev. edn. (Liverpool, 2015), 274–315. For a reading of another work of Skelton's that directly considers Barthes's relevance, see James Simpson, 'Killing Authors: Skelton's Dreadful *Bouge of Court*', in Kathleen Tonry and Shannon Gayk (eds), *Form and Reform: Reading the Fifteenth Century* (Columbus, OH, 2011), 180–96.

PART II
TRANSMISSION

CHAPTER 8
Poetic Manuscripts

Julia Boffey & A. S. G. Edwards

The fifteenth century saw a massive increase in the volume of production of vernacular poetic manuscripts. These range from copies made to the highest standards by trained scribes and artists to informal compilations made by individuals for their own purposes. Between (and sometimes within) these possible models lies a range of categories, created from a variety of motives to satisfy the needs of different readers, both individual and institutional.

Various factors shaped the sudden increase in demand for manuscripts of English verse in the early fifteenth century. This period saw the developed transmission of the poetic writings of the late fourteenth-century. It saw the growing circulation of the works of William Langland, John Gower, and Geoffrey Chaucer, all of whose substantial English poems were frequently copied in the fifteenth century. This period also saw the emergence and dissemination of the new kinds of poetic collection which provide the focus of this chapter. But against the patterns of innovation described here it is worth noting the continuity of copying of popular earlier works: for example, the *Prick of Conscience*, the most frequently copied surviving verse work in Middle English, and the very popular *South English Legendary*, were frequently copied for new audiences over the course of the century.[1]

The copying and dissemination of Chaucer's works after his death in 1400, particularly of his longest and most widely circulating work, the *Canterbury Tales*, provide a helpful starting point for a consideration of manuscript production. Probably very shortly after Chaucer's death, the Ellesmere manuscript of this poem was created (now San Marino, CA, Huntington Library, MS EL 26 C 9). This is among the most sumptuous manuscripts of fifteenth-century English poetry. Its preparation drew on the skills of an accomplished scribe, several illustrators who prepared marginal pictures of the pilgrims, and various decorators, who had to coordinate the preparation of a large work (over 230 parchment leaves) in a number of verse forms, some of which required different page layouts, and which also included lengthy prose texts in the form of Melibee and 'The Parson's Tale'. There were no precedents or parallels for the preparation of such a finely produced manuscript of a work of Middle English poetry by a single author.

That the challenges of producing such a manuscript were so triumphantly met was in part a consequence of the site of Ellesmere's production. All the evidence suggests that it was made in London, which had the largest pool of artisans necessary for the

---

[1] NIMEV 4019 and 3428. See further Robert E. Lewis and Angus McIntosh, *A Descriptive Guide to the Manuscripts of the Prick of Conscience* (Oxford, 1982) who record 115 manuscripts, a figure updated to 118 in Ralph Hanna and Sarah Woods (eds), *Richard Morris's 'Prick of Conscience'*, EETS, o.s. 342 (Oxford, 2013), 378-82; and Manfred Görlach, *The Textual Tradition of the South English Legendary*, Leeds Texts and Monographs, n.s. 6 (Leeds, 1974), viii–x, who records sixty-two manuscripts in various forms. In both cases further manuscripts can be added to those recorded.

production of manuscript books: scribes, parchment makers, limners, artists, binders, and stationers, both native and foreign.[2] During the early fifteenth century the availability of such resources, together with the accessibility of manuscripts of London-based poets like Chaucer and Gower, established the city as the centre for the production of literary works.

The apparent patterns of such production have been inferred chiefly through the establishment of scribal corpora which can be associated with the metropolis. This method underpinned the research of Ian Doyle and Malcolm Parkes who first established the importance of London for vernacular poetic book production at the beginning of the fifteenth century.[3] They identified a number of scribes, sometimes copying alone, sometimes in collaboration. These scribes prepared early manuscripts of the works of Chaucer, Gower, and others.[4] They also worked in shifting associations with other figures in the book trade, particularly limners and artists. The irregular patterns of connections between these various book artisans suggests that metropolitan book production was shaped by loose, unsystematic associations designed for specific manuscripts rather than through the kinds of organized scriptoria that have been identified in monastic houses, for example, in earlier periods.

Such loose forms of commercial collaboration seem to have been a response to the emergence of the new demand for manuscripts of poetic works in the vernacular. The actual dynamics of such production are less clear. Was it a wholly bespoke trade, dependent on commissions? If so, how were such commissions made and executed? How would a commissioner know what he or she wanted, and to whom would they specify their desires both for text and for form of production? These questions cannot be answered: no contract survives setting out terms and costs at this time.[5] The economic, social, and practical dynamics of manuscript production cannot be confidently established. It is possible that the stationer was the crucial middleman in linking personnel, in establishing levels of production (such as decoration and illustration), and in making available the necessary exemplars. Historically the stationer seems to have been the mediating figure who brought together potential purchasers with appropriate artisans.[6] But assumptions about the extent and continuity of the stationer's role cannot be supported by much hard evidence. And the apparent proximity of different book artisans at particular sites in London may have led to loose ad hoc collaborations, at least in the London area.[7] There is some evidence that suggests that not all poetic manuscripts were necessarily bespoke, and that some may have been produced

---

[2] See further C. Paul Christianson, 'The Rise of London's Book-Trade', in Lotte Hellinga and J. B. Trapp (eds), *The Cambridge History of the Book in Britain, Volume III: 1400–1557* (Cambridge, 1999), 128–47, and his *A Directory of London Stationers and Book Artisans 1300–1500* (New York, 1990).

[3] A. I. Doyle and M. B. Parkes, 'The Production of Early Copies of the *Canterbury Tales* and the *Confessio Amantis* in the Early Fifteenth Century', in M. B. Parkes and Andrew G. Watson (eds), *Medieval Scribes, Manuscripts and Libraries: Essays Presented to N. R. Ker* (London, 1978), 163–210.

[4] After Doyle and Parkes there has been subsequent work on London scribes in the early fifteenth century by Linne R. Mooney and Estelle Stubbs, *Scribes and the City: London Guildhall Clerks and the Dissemination of Middle English Literature 1375–1425* (York, 2013). Their identifications and conclusions remain controversial and have not gained general acceptance; see further, Lawrence Warner, *Chaucer's Scribes* (Cambridge, 2018).

[5] A little information does exist later in the century. For example, the late fifteenth-century scribe William Ebesham gives details of his per-page rates for copying a manuscript for the Pastons; see A. I. Doyle, 'The Work of a Late Fifteenth-Century Scribe, William Ebesham', *Bulletin of the John Rylands Library*, 39 (1957), 298–325.

[6] The role of stationers in the provision of Oxford books in the fourteenth century is discussed by M. B. Parkes, 'The Provision of Books', reprinted in P. R. Robinson (ed.), *Pages from the Past: Medieval Writing Skills and Manuscript Books* (Aldershot, 2013), 407–83, especially 465–70. On the development of the role of the stationer in London in the later Middle Ages, see Peter M. W. Blayney, *The Stationers' Company and the Printers of London 1501–1557*, 2 vols. (Cambridge, 2013), 1.1–14.

[7] See the discussion by C. Paul Christianson, 'London's Late Medieval Manuscript-Book Trade', in Jeremy Griffiths and Derek Pearsall (eds), *Book Production and Publishing in Britain, 1375–1475* (Cambridge, 1989), 87–108.

speculatively, as least as the book trade developed.[8] This may indicate the emergence of new kinds of individual entrepreneurship in manuscript production over time, establishing patterns that meant that by the end of the fifteenth century, and the advent of printing, a purchaser would have been able to buy printed books on sale from various outlets.

What is clear is that there was a steady widening of possibility in the production of poetic manuscripts in London as well as an increase in numbers. One distinctive aspect of this was a new focus on the production of single works. While it initially drew on later fourteenth-century works, Chaucer's *Canterbury Tales* and *Troilus and Criseyde*, Gower's *Confessio Amantis* and Langland's *Piers Plowman*, it rapidly extended to works by contemporary poets. Thomas Hoccleve's *Regiment of Princes* was copied in London before 1413, very shortly after its completion, and other copies made there are close to it in time.[9] The career of John Lydgate (c1375–1449), significantly represents this tendency: his major works, his *Troy Book*, *Siege of Thebes*, *Life of Our Lady*, and *Fall of Princes*, all enjoyed wide contemporary circulation as single works in manuscripts often of demonstrably metropolitan production, some of high quality.[10]

But the production of copies of Lydgate's works also serves as a reminder that it was possible to produce manuscripts of a high standard and textual authority outside London as well as within it. Lydgate was for many years resident at the Benedictine Abbey in Bury St Edmunds, and this seems to have been an important site for the production of his works. It was under the auspices of the Abbot there, William Curteys, that Lydgate was commissioned to create his *Lives of Saints Edmund and Fremund*;[11] Edmund was the patron saint of the Abbey. This was composed in the mid 1430s to mark a visit to Bury by the young king, Henry VI. The event was commemorated by the production of a remarkably elaborate manuscript, now BL MS Harley 2278, which contains 120 miniatures, as well as other decoration. It is one of the most imposing pieces of book production of the first half of the fifteenth century, a poem presented in a material form fit for presentation to a king.[12]

This was not a one-off. Evidently the designs for the miniatures were retained in Bury and subsequently employed in the production of further deluxe illustrated copies of Lydgate's poem. These copies were made by a scribe in the 1450s and 1460s who also transcribed other elaborately illustrated and decorated manuscripts of works by Lydgate, particularly of his *Fall of Princes*, composed in the 1430s, as well as manuscripts of works by others.[13] While it is not possible to establish whether the Abbey itself or some other organization in Bury was responsible for such production, the evidence suggests an energetic, high-level regional production centre with access to affluent audiences, in operation for several decades and particularly focused on a local poet.

Other local centres for the production of poetic manuscripts seem to have existed elsewhere in East Anglia. For example, the Augustinian friar, John Capgrave, who spent most

---

[8] See, for example, the discussion by A. S. G. Edwards and Derek Pearsall, 'The Manuscripts of the Major English Poetic Texts', in Griffiths and Pearsall (eds), *Book Production and Publishing in Britain*, 257–78 (at 265–8).
[9] NIMEV 2229; see Kathleen L. Scott, *Later Gothic Manuscripts, 1390–1490*, 2 vols. (London, 1996), 2.158–60, 160–2.
[10] NIMEV 2516, 3928, 2574, 1168.
[11] NIMEV 3440.
[12] For a facsimile of the manuscript see A. S. G. Edwards (intro.), *The Life of St Edmund King and Martyr: A Facsimile of British Library MS Harley 2278* (London, 2004).
[13] See Kathleen L. Scott, 'Lydgate's *Lives of SS Edmund and Fremund*: a Newly Located Manuscript in Arundel Castle', *Viator*, 13 (1982) 335–66, and A. S. G. Edwards, 'McGill MS 143 and the Composition of Lydgate's *Fall of Princes*', *Florilegium*, 33 (2019 for 2016), 45–62. Joseph Grossi, 'Cloistered Lydgate, Commercial Scribe: British Library Harley 2255 Revisited', *Medieval Studies*, 72 (2010), 313–61, discusses this scribe's likely involvement in the copying of a collection of Lydgate's shorter poems.

of his career in the region, made holograph presentation copies of his own writings and organized their wider circulation by other scribes.[14] A number of his verse works were clearly either made for or owned early by various religious or religious houses. *The Life of St Norbert* was made by Capgrave for John Wingale, abbot of the Premonstratensian house of West Dereham, near Capgrave's birthplace of Lynn (now King's Lynn). The surviving manuscripts of his *Life of St Katherine* also had a significant East Anglian readership.[15]

Another Augustinian, Osbern Bokenham, resident at Clare in Suffolk, composed saints' lives for local nobility there, naming several local individuals and families in the dedications to his *Legends of Holy Women*, a collection of female saints' lives, composed between 1443 and 1447.[16] This survives in a manuscript copied in Cambridge in 1447 on behalf of Bokenham's acquaintance, Friar Thomas Burgh (BL Arundel 327); it may have been made for a house of women religious, perhaps the Franciscan nuns of Denny, Cambridgeshire.[17] A much fuller English legendary, rendered variously by Bokenham into verse and prose, survives in the form of a manuscript now at Abbotsford House in Scotland.[18] Like Lydgate and Capgrave, when Bokenham worked for local audiences he used local resources in the production of manuscript copies of his poems. The Abbotsford legendary may have been undertaken for Cecily Neville. One of the scribes of the Abbotsford manuscript, probably local to Clare, in Suffolk, or a lay clerk attached to the Augustinian house there, also copied the unique surviving manuscript (in BL MS Add. 11814) of a verse translation of Claudian, *De consulatu Stilichonis* for her husband Richard, duke of York and lord of Clare Castle.[19] These manuscripts suggest a standard of production available locally at East Anglian centres, probably monastic, that demonstrates the high levels of competence available outside London.

Such examples also show the extent to which East Anglia in particular swiftly developed the capacity to create poetic manuscripts to a high standard. This was a wealthy area, with a number of important religious houses and a population that included magnates, aristocrats, and wealthy gentry families, and with tastes and resources that could accommodate the commissioning of literary works and of manuscripts. One of the earliest and most substantial collections of Chaucer's works, CUL MS Gg. 4. 27, dating probably from the 1420s, appears on the evidence of its dialect to have been produced in East Anglia.[20] The circumstances and location of its production cannot now be clearly established. But the size of the manuscript (over 500 leaves), and its quality, with numerous illuminated borders and some illustration, indicate the scale of the undertaking.

---

[14] For details of Capgrave's holograph manuscripts and their early circulation, see Peter J. Lucas, *From Author to Audience: John Capgrave and Medieval Publication* (Dublin, 1997), particularly 19–58.

[15] NIMEV 1805 and 6; for details of the latter, see Lucas, *From Author to Audience*, 15, 18. In one manuscript, BL Arundel 168, it is combined with Lydgate's *Life of Our Lady* and verse lives of female saints, perhaps for a house of female religious in Norfolk; see A. S. G. Edwards, 'Fifteenth-Century English Collections of Female Saints' Lives', *Yearbook of English Studies*, 33 (2003), 131–41 (at 136-5).

[16] Some of the lives are separately indexed in NIMEV (see index under 'Bokenham') but a number more have come to light recently in the Abbotsford manuscript (Edinburgh, Advocates Library).

[17] For discussion see A. S. G. Edwards, 'The Circulation and Audience of Bokenham's *Legendys of Hooly Wummen*', in A. J. Minnis (ed.), *Late Medieval Religious Texts and their Transmission* (Cambridge, 1994), 157–67.

[18] See Simon Horobin (ed.), *Osbern Bokenham: Lives of Saints*, I and II, EETS, o.s. 356, 359 (Oxford, 2020, 2022).

[19] NIMEV 1526; A. S. G. Edwards, 'The Middle English Translation of Claudian's *De Consulatu Stilichonis*', in A. J. Minnis (ed.), *Middle English Poetry: Texts and Traditions. Essays in Honour of Derek Pearsall* (Woodbridge, 2001), 267–78.

[20] M. B. Parkes and Richard Beadle (intro.), *The Poetical Works of Geoffrey Chaucer: A Facsimile of Cambridge University Library MS Gg. 4. 27*, 3 vols. (Norman, OK, 1979–80), and see Scott, *Later Gothic Manuscripts*, 2.143–7.

Aspects of the local patterns of East Anglian manuscript production that centred on religious houses seem to have been replicated in other parts of England in relation to the works of individual authors, if not always generating manuscripts of the high quality evident in some of the Capgrave and Bokenham collections. BodL MS Douce 302, a manuscript of the poems of John Audelay, chaplain to Lord Richard Lestrange and later chantrist at the Augustinian house of Haughmond in Shropshire, was produced under some form of authorial supervision in 1426 at the abbey, perhaps by Audelay's fellows on his behalf (he was blind).[21] Towards the very end of the fifteenth century, in 1492, the poems of James Ryman were assembled and copied together in a manuscript that is now CUL MS Ee. 1. 12, evidently by Ryman and two others who worked at his Franciscan house in Canterbury.[22] Carols associated with both these authors occur in small numbers in other manuscripts, perhaps transmitted orally as songs; in Ryman's case at least one of the poems travelled some distance and was known to someone in Norfolk who copied it onto some empty space in a business document.[23]

As suggested by these examples of manuscripts made in religious houses, regional production seems to have limited the circulation of certain writings. Some works produced in secular households had similarly limited transmission. For example, John Metham's *Amoryus and Cleopes*, a romance, was written c1440 for Sir Miles Stapleton of Ingham, Norfolk, to whose household the author was probably attached.[24] It survives in only one manuscript, Princeton, NJ, University Library MS Garrett 141. The Norfolk dialectal forms of its scribe, who also copied a prose devotional work for Stapleton (the *Privity of Privities*, now New Haven, CT, Beinecke Library, MS Takamiya 38) suggest local production, probably undertaken with no intention of circulation beyond Stapleton's household or circle.[25]

On the other hand, some secular works produced under provincial auspices seem to have had more complex patterns of circulation, as demonstrated by John Hardyng's *Chronicle*.[26] The first version of Hardyng's work was composed by 1457, by which time Hardyng himself was a long-term resident at the Augustinian priory of South Kyme in Lincolnshire. It survives in a single high-quality copy, BL MS Lansdowne 204, that may have been produced in in this locality,[27] possibly designed for presentation to Henry VI, whom Hardyng had served in various capacities. Subsequently Hardyng began work on a revised version of the chronicle intended first for presentation to Richard, duke of York, and then (after Richard's death in 1460) for his heir Edward IV. The revised versions had a much wider circulation than

---

[21] Ella Keats Whiting (ed.), *The Poems of John Audelay*, EETS o.s .184 (Oxford, 1931); Susanna Fein (ed.), '*My Wyl and My Wrytyng*': *Essays on John the Blind Audelay*' and Susanna Fein (ed.), *John the Blind Audelay: Poems and Carols (Oxford, Bodleian Library MS Douce 302)* (Kalamazoo, MI, 2009).

[22] Julius Zupitza, 'Die Gedichte de Franziskaners Jakob Ryman', *Archiv für das Studium der neueren Sprachen und Literaturen*, 89 (1892), 167–338, and 'Anmerkungen zu Jacob Rymans Gedichten. II Tiel', *Archiv für das Studium der neueren Sprachen und Literaturen*, 93 (1894), 369–98; Karl Reichl, 'James Ryman's Lyrics and the Ryman Manuscript: A Reappraisal', in Lucia Kornexl and Ursula Lenker (eds), *Bookmarks from the Past: Studies in Early English Language and Literature in Honour of Helmut Gneuss* (Frankfurt am Main, 2003), 195–227; Susanna Fein, 'John Audelay and James Ryman', in Julia Boffey and A. S. G. Edwards (eds), *A Companion to Fifteenth-Century Poetry* (Cambridge, 2013), 127–41.

[23] John Scattergood, 'Two Unrecorded Poems from Dublin, Trinity College Library MS 490', *Review of English Studies*, n.s. 38 (1987), 44–9, reprinted in *Manuscripts and Ghosts: Essays on the Transmission of Medieval and Early Renaissance Literature* (Dublin, 2006), 269–77; Richard Beadle and Anthony Smith, 'A Carol by James Ryman in the Holkham Archives', *Review of English Studies*, n.s. 71 (2020), 850–66.

[24] NIMEV 3320.

[25] See Parkes and Richard Beadle (introd.), *Poetical Works: Geoffrey Chaucer*, 3.63–4.

[26] NIMEV 710.

[27] Scott, *Later Gothic Manuscripts*, 2.206, suggests 'Lincolnshire or Eastern England (Kings Lynn?, Cambridge?'; see also 2.218.

the first one. Hardyng may not have completed this version before his death in 1465.[28] It survives in a variety of textual forms in twelve copies, with provenances that suggest a range of sites of production, some of which were likely metropolitan. The fate of Hardyng's work, and especially the extent of textual variation across surviving copies, point to the complicatedly fluid patterns of transmission to which a work was subject once beyond authorial control and in the hands of those concerned to transmit it commercially.

The extent of such commercial activity is not always easy to establish. Its complexities are suggested by the activities of Thomas Hoccleve. As a clerk employed at Westminster in a government office, the Privy Seal, Hoccleve had advanced scribal skills, and his familiarity with different business documents is evident in a formulary copied in his own hand (BL MS Add. 24062).[29] He also produced holograph anthologies of his own poems.[30] One of these, Durham University Library MS Cosin V. iii. 9, was made for presentation to Joan Beaufort, countess of Westmorland. But the other holographs, San Marino, CA, Huntington Library MSS HM 111 and HM 744, were not necessarily intended for circulation. They may have been Hoccleve's own personal copies, perhaps retained so that they might be used as exemplars if and when required. Other presentation manuscripts in Hoccleve's hand may also once have existed. His longest and most widely circulating work was his *Regiment of Princes,* extant in more than forty manuscripts, on occasion combined with other of his works. This does not survive in a copy in Hoccleve's hand.[31] On the evidence of poems evidently written to accompany presentation volumes, Hoccleve may have copied manuscripts of his works for Edward, duke of York and John, duke of Bedford. Some of these *Regiment* manuscripts are high-quality copies, such as BL MSS Arundel 38 and Royal 17 D VI, both of which have presentation miniatures associated with the poem's dedicatee, Prince Henry of Lancaster.[32] Hoccleve's situation was unusual. He was a professional scribe, whose working life was spent in the offices of the Privy Seal. But he has also been directly associated, at least occasionally, with the commercial copying of poetic manuscripts, in the collaborative configurations identified by Doyle and Parkes. Even so, it is not possible to connect all of the holograph manuscripts of his own works with motives of commercial transmission. He seems to have ranged over the multiple potentialities of scribal activity, personal, professional, and commercial, in ways that have few parallels in the fifteenth century.[33]

The example of Stephen Dodesham points to other complexities of motive in scribal activity and to the challenge of interpreting the evidence of surviving manuscripts. Dodesham seems to have begun his career as a scribe working within commercial environments, seemingly in London, where he copied several manuscripts of Lydgate's *Siege of Thebes,* and

---

[28] A. S. G. Edwards, 'The Manuscripts and Texts of the Second Version of John Hardyng's Chronicle', in Daniel Williams (ed.), *England in the Fifteenth Century. Proceedings of the 1986 Harlaxton Symposium* (Woodbridge, 1987), 75–84.

[29] For biographical details, see J. A. Burrow, *Thomas Hoccleve,* Authors of the Middle Ages: English Writers of the Late Middle Ages, 4 (Aldershot, 1994).

[30] *Thomas Hoccleve: A Facsimile of the Autograph Verse Manuscripts,* J. A. Burrow and A. I. Doyle (intro.), EETS, s.s. 19 Oxford, 2002).

[31] The suggestion that BL MS Royal 17 D XVIII is an autograph presentation copy of *The Regiment of Princes,* advanced by Linne R. Mooney, 'A Holograph Copy of Thomas Hoccleve's *Regiment of Princes*', *Studies in the Age of Chaucer,* 33 (2011), 263–96, has not been generally endorsed.

[32] See Scott, *Later Gothic Manuscripts,* 2.158–60.

[33] The closest is perhaps the figure of George Ashby (b. 1385?, d. 1475), who was a clerk of the signet and left holograph copies of his poems in CUL MS Mm. 4. 42; see further, John Scattergood, 'The Date and Composition of George Ashby's Poems', *Leeds Studies in English,* n.s. 21 (1990), 167–76.

other Middle English works in verse and prose.[34] Subsequently he became a Carthusian monk and other manuscripts in his hand are associated with his order's houses at Witham (Somerset) and Sheen.[35] In overall terms Dodesham was among the most prolific of fifteenth-century scribes. Over twenty manuscripts survive in his hand in verse and prose, Middle English and Latin, in various scripts, from the various contexts of his scribal activity. His example is unlikely to be typical of the copying of verse texts in English. But it does suggest some of the ramifications which complicate efforts to understand it.

Other copyists raise further questions about the links between personal and commercial production. London was an important centre of production, the residence of many scribes employed in civic, government, and legal business, some of whom may have taken on other scribal tasks on a freelance basis; it also had significant markets in the form of literate residents and an affluent transient population. In addition to its body of professional scribes, it was home to other identifiable copyists of indeterminate status. John Shirley, attached in the early decades of the fifteenth century to the retinue of Richard Beauchamp, earl of Warwick, and from the early 1430s until his death in 1456 resident in London, was one of these. Shirley's activities did much to promote the transmission of English poetry, especially of works in the Chaucerian tradition, notably those by Lydgate.[36] Shirley's position in the service of Beauchamp, which entailed much travel between England and France, gave him access to the kinds of social verse produced in courtly circles. His own earliest manuscript anthologies (BL MS Add. 16165 and Cambridge, Trinity College MS R. 3. 20) include some of Chaucer's minor poems, Lydgate's *Temple of Glass*, and other of his shorter poems, French lyrics attributed to William de la Pole, duke of Suffolk, and some Middle English prose works (including Chaucer's *Boece*). In verse prologues to BL MS Add. 16165 and another, now lost, collection Shirley talks of his labour in searching out and copying the contents of his manuscripts, and requests that readers return the books to him, as if he lent them out.[37] He also praises Chaucer and speaks in sufficiently familiar terms of Lydgate to suggest that he might have known him and have had some means of access to Lydgate's works (his later manuscripts, Cambridge, Trinity College MS R. 3. 20 and BodL MS Ashmole 59, include much Lydgate, with a greater focus on devotional and religious verse). Although Shirley's earliest compilation, BL MS Add. 16165, may have been made for circles associated with Beauchamp, his later ones do not have an identifiable audience. They may have been intended for circulation within London, perhaps initially among other residents of the precincts of St Bartholomew's hospital, where Shirley lived. The extent to which he was in any sense a 'publisher', distributing texts with any commercial motive, is unclear.[38]

Whatever Shirley's motivation in preparing his manuscripts, there are indications that some of them became available to scribes both within and outside London. Some reached the hands of an anonymous London scribe, the so-called 'Hammond scribe', whose hand

---

[34] On his copying of the *Siege of Thebes* see A. S. G. Edwards, 'Beinecke 661 and Early Fifteenth-Century Manuscript Production', *Beinecke Studies in Early Manuscripts, Yale University Library Gazette*, 66, supplement, (1991), 181–96.

[35] For a full assessment of Dodesham's career see A. I. Doyle, 'Stephen Dodesham of Witham and Sheen', in P. R. Robinson and Rivkah Zim (eds), *Of the Making of Books: Medieval Manuscripts, their Scribes and Readers: Essays Presented to M. B. Parkes* (Aldershot, 1997), 94–115.

[36] For details of Shirley's life, and the contents of his manuscript anthologies, see Margaret Connolly, *John Shirley: Book Production and the Noble Household in Fifteenth-Century England* (Aldershot, 1998).

[37] NIMEV 1426, 2598; see Connolly, *John Shirley*, 206–11.

[38] For discussion of a variety of views, and arguments for his possible commercial motives, see A. S. G. Edwards, 'John Shirley, John Lydgate, and the Motives of Compilation', *Studies in the Age of Chaucer*, 38 (2016), 245–54.

has been identified in at least thirteen manuscripts.[39] This scribe's affiliations and activities are characteristic of much late fifteenth-century London manuscript production. As well as literary anthologies including many works by Lydgate, he was also involved in copying the *Canterbury Tales*, the *Regiment of Princes*, *Piers the Plowman's Creed*,[40] pious verse and prose, and medical, heraldic, and documentary materials. Opportunities for scribal work of many kinds must have been available in London, and the Hammond scribe's connections with John Vale, secretary to Sir Thomas Cook, a London mayor, suggest that he may have held a position in a London household.[41] Like Hoccleve, or the Richard Frampton who copied the alliterative *Siege of Jerusalem* as well as serving as some kind of government clerk,[42] or the scribe of the poems in BodL MS Digby 102 who seems also to have worked for the Brewers' Company, the Hammond scribe worked in more than one context.[43]

In contrast to these London compilations, another manuscript with Shirley connections, BL MS Harley 7333, has scribal notes and signatures that indicate that at least some portions of it were copied at the abbey of St Mary de Pratis in Leicester, a house of Augustinian canons.[44] This is a large-format parchment manuscript of over 200 leaves, copied in a series of booklets in the years after c1450–60 by at least four scribes. It has rubrics that often insistently recall Shirley's characteristic idiom, and traces of his distinctive orthography are preserved in some items. The fifteenth-century verse in the volume includes Hoccleve's *Regiment of Princes*, Benedict Burgh's *Cato Minor* and *Cato Major*,[45] and poems by Lydgate, along with the *Canterbury Tales* and selections from *Confessio Amantis*, as well as the prose *Brut*. While it is not possible to determine how an exemplar might have been transmitted from Shirley to provincial hands, the manuscript is an indication of the intersections between regional and metropolitan manuscript production, and of the ways that texts could travel.

The example of the dissemination of Shirley's texts outside London needs to be set against instances where poems copied in the metropolis did not achieve wider circulation. Henry Lovelich's translations of the romances *Merlin* and *The History of the Holy Grail* survive only in Cambridge, Corpus Christi College MS 80.[46] They seem to have been copied in London 'at þe instaunce' (fol. 127) of a fellow member of the London Skinners' Company, the London mayor Henry Barton, and were also annotated by a London scribe, John Cok (coincidentally a resident of the precinct at St Bartholomew's hospital, like Shirley).[47] They were presumably copied with a specific audience in mind, most probably among members of the Skinners' company. A limited coterie audience of this kind, and the

---

[39] Eleanor P. Hammond, 'Two British Museum Manuscripts (Harley 2251 and Adds 34360): A Contribution to the Bibliography of John Lydgate', *Anglia*, 28 (1905), 1–28 and 'A Scribe of Chaucer', *Modern Philology*, 27 (1929–30), 27–33. See also A. I. Doyle, 'An Unrecognized Piece of *Piers the Ploughman's Creed* and Other Work by its Scribe', *Speculum*, 34 (1959), 428–36. Manuscripts showing the influence of Shirley's exemplars are discussed by Connolly, 172–8.

[40] NIMEV 663.

[41] See Margaret Lucille Kekewich, Colin Richmond, Anne F. Sutton, Livia Visser-Fuchs, and John L. Watts, *The Politics of Fifteenth-Century England: John Vale's Book* (Stroud, 1995), 107–12, where it is suggested that the Hammond scribe worked for, or is possibly to be identified with, the stationer John Multon.

[42] NIMEV 1583.

[43] M. B. Parkes, 'Richard Frampton: A Commercial Scribe, c.1390–c.1420', in Robinson (ed.), *Pages from the Past*, 113–24; Simon Horobin, 'The Scribe of Bodleian Manuscript Digby 102 and the Circulation of the C-Text of *Piers Plowman*', *Yearbook of Langland Studies*, 24 (2010), 89–112.

[44] Connolly, *John Shirley*, 173–5.

[45] NIMEV 3955, 854.

[46] NIMEV *842.5, 231.

[47] See Carol M. Meale, '"Gode Men / Wiues Maydnes and Alle Men": Romance and its Audiences', in Carol M. Meale (ed.), *Readings in Medieval English Romance* (Cambridge, 1994), 209–25 (at 217–19).

subject matter and considerable length of the translations (*Merlin* runs to 27,852 lines in couplets; *The Holy Grail* survives as a fragment of 11,892 lines, also in couplets) may well have played a part in their apparently restricted circulation. The example of Lovelich is a cautionary reminder of the factors that could limit manuscript transmission even within the metropolis.

BL MS Harley 7333 may serve to suggest the resources located in the religious establishments of provincial environments, but secular environments outside London were also important to the circulation of poetic manuscripts. In some cases, as for instance with the examples of East Anglian manuscript production discussed above, interconnected circles within both secular and religious establishments seem to have contributed to the flourishing of textual production. But noble and gentry households in the regions were especially significant nodes in the processes by which texts were acquired and multiplied. The extent to which the commissioning and ownership of a manuscript necessarily reflects the site of its production is unclear, however. For example, the fine copy of Lydgate's *Troy Book* made for Sir Thomas Chaworth of Wiverton in Nottinghamshire (now BL MS Cotton Augustus A IV) seems to have been produced in London, as were other of Chaworth's books.[48] So too was the sumptuously illustrated copy of the *Troy Book* owned by the MP for Somerset and Dorset William Carent of Toomer (now Manchester, John Rylands University Library, MS Eng. 1), one of a number of English books he owned.[49] It seems likely that the various copies of Lydgate's *Fall of Princes* owned by the Nevilles, Percies, and other northern families also made their way from London to the borders.[50] During the fifteenth century clear lines of commercial transmission for verse works (and others) were established from the metropolis to outlying regions.

Poetic manuscripts produced in regional secular contexts, probably made for readers of the gentry class, are often characterized by production values rather lower than those of metropolitan manuscripts. Some of these are nonetheless quite extensive compilations, produced by individuals or groups of people with ready access to exemplars and at least some scribal training.[51] In BodL MS Ashmole 61 the romances *Sir Isumbras*, *The Erle of Tolous*, *Lybeaus Desconus*, *Sir Cleges*, and *Sir Orfeo* accompany popular tales such as *The Sinner's Lament* and *The Adulterous Falmouth Squire*, lives of Saints Eustace and Margaret, and works of popular piety such as *The Northern Passion*; the collection also includes instructions on proper behaviour for children, on courtesy, and on purchasing land.[52] The single scribe, who signs himself as 'Rate', seems likely to have been a guild member from Leicester, making a compendium for his immediate circle, and conscious of a responsibility to offer moral guidance to its younger members. The manuscript has fairly low production values and the sequences of texts at times lack evidence of controlling design. A rather more carefully organized production probably produced professionally in the Leicester area is

---

[48] See Thorlac Turville-Petre, 'Some Medieval English Manuscripts in the North-East Midlands', in Derek Pearsall (ed.), *Manuscripts and Readers in Fifteenth-Century England: The Literary Implications of Manuscript Study* (Cambridge, 1983), 125–41 (at 133).

[49] See for example New Haven, CT, Beinecke Library MS 283, a sumptuous copy of Lydgate's *Life of Our Lady*.

[50] For some discussion see A. S. G. Edwards, 'Northern Magnates and their Books', *Textual Cultures*, 7 (2012), 176–86 and the references cited there.

[51] For an overview see Julia Boffey and John J. Thompson, 'Anthologies and Miscellanies: Production and Choice of Texts', in Griffiths and Pearsall (eds), *Book Production and Publishing in Britain*, 279–315.

[52] NIMEV 1184, 1681, 1690, 1890, 1907, and 3868; NIMEV 172, 2052; NIMEV 211 and 2673. See George Shuffelton (ed.), *Codex Ashmole 61: A Compilation of Popular Middle English Verse* (Kalamazoo, MI, 2008) and Lynne S. Blanchfield, 'Rate Revisited: the Compilation of the Narrative Works in MS Ashmole 61', in Jennifer Fellows, Rosalind Field, Gillian Rogers, and Judith Weiss (eds), *Romance Reading on the Book: Essays on Medieval Narrative Presented to Maldwyn Mills* (Cardiff, 1996), 208–20.

CUL MS Ff. 2. 38.[53] Roughly contemporary with MS Ashmole 61, and with some contents in common with that compilation, and one shared paper stock, it was made by a scribe writing in a dialect similar to Rate's. Although its contents have a similar flavour to those of MS Ashmole 61, this seems to have been commissioned rather than made by a single household member for domestic use. One further difference between the two is that Rate's compendium is a long, narrow book, the format used for business manuscripts such as those probably used by Rate in his working life; CUL MS Ff. 2. 38, in contrast, is of a size and shape more conventional for literary collections.[54]

Some of these single codices are of substantial size and offer evidence of elaborate patterns of compilation and internal organization. The two manuscripts copied by Robert Thornton of East Newton, near Helmsley in Yorkshire, in the middle of the century, Lincoln Cathedral MS 91 and BL MS Add. 31042, have been extensively studied. These large collections, including both verse and prose, have often been seen as the consequence of forms of 'antiquarian' interest in vernacular writing. They certainly reflect a sustained search for a range of materials, including substantial verse works, some unique (the *Alliterative Morte Arthure*, for example),[55] and some careful patterns of assemblage in which cognate works are grouped together. The contents of the Lincoln manuscript, which include verse romances and medical texts, suggest that this was perhaps a book for practical and diverting family or household use; the London manuscript, with a more spiritual focus, perhaps catered for different communal needs.[56] Thornton copied both manuscripts himself, making some interventions into what he copied, and at times responding ingeniously to the difficulties caused by the unpredictable supply of exemplars. The ornamentation of the manuscripts seems to have been partly his own work but may also have been outsourced to professionals in a nearby local centre such as York. The exemplars which Thornton used seem to have come from a range of sources, not all immediately adjacent to his place of residence: his text of the verse *Three Kings of Cologne*, for example, contains linguistic forms characteristic of Scottish English.[57]

The range of materials in collections like those of Thornton and Rate is reflected to lesser degrees in other regional compilations. BL MS Harley 5396 (part IV) with popular comic and pious tales, instructions for children, and some carols and verse prayers, has been connected with the household of a Northampton merchant.[58] Also connected with Northampton is Dublin, Trinity College MS 432, including historical notes and poems, popular tales, and texts evidently prepared for performance, which looks to have been

---

[53] Michael Johnston, 'Two Leicestershire Romance Codices: Cambridge, University Library MS Ff. 2. 38 and Oxford, Bodleian Library MS Ashmole 61', *Journal of the Early Book Society*, 15 (2012), 84–99.

[54] Ralph Hanna notes an approximate standard size of 275/290 mm x 185 mm for parchment manuscripts; see 'The Sizes of Middle English Books ca.1390–1430', *Journal of the Early Book Society*, 18 (2015), 181–91; on the 'holster book' format of Ashmole 61, see Gisela Guddat-Figge, *Catalogue of Manuscripts Containing Middle English Romances* (Munich, 1976), 30–6.

[55] NIMEV 2322.

[56] Derek Brewer and A. E. B. Owen (introd.), *The Thornton Manuscript (Lincoln Cathedral MS 91)* (London, 1975); John J. Thompson, *Robert Thornton and the London Thornton Manuscript: British Library Additional 31042* (Cambridge, 1987). See most recently Susanna Fein and Michael Johnston (eds), *Robert Thornton and his Books: Essays on the Lincoln and London Thornton Manuscripts* (Woodbridge, 2014).

[57] NIMEV *854.3; H. N. MacCracken, 'Lydgatiana III: The Three Kings of Cologne', *Archiv für das Studium der neueren Sprachen und Literaturen*, 129 (1912), 50–68 (who also argues that this poem is likely to be the earliest Scots example of the use of rhyme royal).

[58] Bradford York Fletcher and A. L. Harris, 'A Northampton Poetic Miscellany of 1455–56', *English Manuscript Studies 1100–1700*, 7 (1998), 216–35.

copied by a practised scribe.⁵⁹ Edinburgh, National Library of Scotland, Advocates' MS 19. 3. 1 seems to have been copied in the north-east Midlands, mostly by a scribe named Richard Heege.⁶⁰ Its contents include various verse romances and religious verse, including William Lichfield's *Complaint of God*, parts of Lydgate's *Life of Our Lady*, and the *Vision of Tundale*.⁶¹ Another of these more modest compilations is New Haven, CT, Beinecke Library MS 365, the so-called 'Book of Brome', which includes a unique mystery play, *Abraham and Isaac*, a fragmentary verse life of St Margaret, pious and didactic tales such as *Owayne Miles*, rules of conduct, and a garbled extract from Chaucer's 'Lak of Steadfastness'.⁶² These were all copied by a trained scribe. Subsequently, Robert Melton of Stuston in Suffolk, who may have originally commissioned the copying of these items, added various household accounts and other documentary materials.⁶³

The amalgam of the literary, devotional, pragmatic, and the simply utilitarian is reflected in other compilations that contain significant and variegated amounts of verse. One such is BodL MS Tanner 407, compiled by Robert Reynes of Acle in Norfolk between the 1470s and 1490s. It includes formulae concerning land transactions; charms, recipes, proverbs and prayers; accounts of local church matters, of taxes, and of family events.⁶⁴ Among the verse contents are a life of St Anne, a poem recounting two miracles of the Virgin, and some extracts from dramatic performances: pageants of the Nine Worthies, a speech made by a character called Delight, and an epilogue to a church play.⁶⁵ Reynes was a church warden and an alderman in a local parish guild, roles in which he would have witnessed or been still more directly involved in pageants and plays.⁶⁶

Related to these compilations of material for family or household use are manuscripts compiled by individuals as holdalls for more miscellaneous contents. Often serving primarily as repositories for information, collections of these kinds sometimes include verse. New Haven, CT, Beinecke Library MS 163 (also known as the Wagstaffe miscellany), compiled by John Whittocksmead of Wiltshire (d. 1482), an MP and a gentleman of some local standing, is an encyclopaedic mixture of English and Latin, with texts on legal matters, spiritual instruction, hunting, horse medicine, and herbs.⁶⁷ Although much of this is in prose, the compilation contains verse hymns and prayers, a charm, and a long poem on hawking.⁶⁸ BL MS Harley 1735, partly copied by John Crophill (d. c1485), bailiff of the priory of Benedictine nuns at Wix in Essex and a medical practitioner, includes among much medical and other practical information in Crophill's hand a short verse lunary, a herbal, and

---

⁵⁹ See further Raluca Radulescu, 'Vying for Attention: The Contents of Dublin, Trinity College, MS 432', in Margaret Connolly and Raluca Radulescu (eds), *Insular Books: Vernacular Manuscript Miscellanies in Late Medieval Britain* (London, 2015), 121–42.

⁶⁰ Phillipa Hardman (intro.), *The Heege Manuscript: A Facsimile of National Library of Scotland MS 19. 3. 1*, Leeds Texts and Monographs, NS 16 (Leeds, 2000).

⁶¹ NIMEV 2714, 2574, 1724.

⁶² NIMEV 786, 2673, 1767, 576, 3190.

⁶³ Described in Barbara Shailor, *Catalogue of Medieval and Renaissance Manuscripts in the Beinecke Rare Book and Manuscript Library Yale University, Volume II: MSS 25–500* (Binghamton, NY, 1897), 210–14.

⁶⁴ Cameron Louis (ed.), *The Commonplace Book of Robert Reynes of Acle: An Edition of Tanner MS 407* (New York, 1980).

⁶⁵ NIMEV 3207, 3119, 1929.5, 3666, 1927, 2380; all transcribed in Louis (ed.), *Commonplace Book*.

⁶⁶ For discussion of the Tanner and Beinecke manuscripts see Carol M. Meale, 'Amateur Book Production and the Miscellany in Late Medieval East Anglia: Tanner 407 and Beinecke 365', in Connolly and Radulescu (eds), *Insular Books*, 156–73.

⁶⁷ See further, George Keiser, 'Practical Books for the Gentleman', in Lotte Hellinga and J. B. Trapp (eds), *The Cambridge History of the Book in Britain, III: 1400–1557* (Cambridge, 1999), 470–94 (at 474–7); M. Laing, 'John Whittokesmede as Parliamentarian and Horse Owner in Yale University Library, Beinecke MS 163', *SELIM: Journal of the Spanish Society for Medieval English Language and Literature*, 17 (2010), 1–72.

⁶⁸ NIMEV 1727, 2119, 242.5, 3693.

a comic poem on alewives.[69] Manuscripts of this sort, for which the term 'personal compilation' seems preferable to 'commonplace book' or 'miscellany', typically include business notes and memoranda, bits of practical and pious instruction, and items of local interest, as well as songs, tales, and verse of other kinds.[70]

Not all of these manuscripts are single-scribe productions on the models of Rate's book or Robert Thornton's two compilations: scribal labour might be on hand from family clerks or from other sources, and could involve collaborations of more or less organized kinds. Aberystwyth, National Library of Wales, MS Brogyntyn ii. 1 (formerly Porkington 10), which from its contents appears to be an assemblage of materials for collective entertainment and instruction, was produced by no less than sixteen scribes, working in a milieu somewhere in the West Midlands.[71]

More extensive, both in scale, period of compilation and number of scribes is the so-called 'Findern Anthology' (CUL MS Ff. 1.6).[72] This seems to have been a household assemblage made by a Derbyshire family to which material was added over some decades. It includes various works by Chaucer, selections from Gower's *Confessio Amantis*, poems by Lydgate, Benedict Burgh, Richard Roos, and John Clanvowe, and a large number of unique lyrics, possibly composed by members of the Findern family. It is mainly written in a large number of informal hands. It seems an ad hoc compilation of a local, amateur kind, created in part because of the simple availability of texts, at least some of which may have been compositions made by those who also read the manuscript. It was evidently shaped by the circumstances of availability rather than by any overall design or more systematic motives. What is striking is its exclusive interest in verse texts, chiefly lyric.

The Findern manuscript might be categorized as a household compilation, drawing on a range of locally accessible resources. A more ambitious regional household assemblage is BodL MS Arch. Selden. B. 24, which was prepared in Scotland in the last decade of the fifteenth century. The quality of its production, with frequent illuminated borders and an opening historiated initial, may reflect the status of its commissioner, Henry, 3rd Lord Sinclair (d. 1513). Much of the manuscript, an exclusively verse collection that includes works by Chaucer, Lydgate, Hoccleve, and others, seems to have been copied by a scribe who copied other manuscripts for Sinclair and may have been a household clerk.[73] It acquired a distinctively regional identity by the addition to its English contents of a number of Scots poems. The assortment of items in this manuscript suggests a deliberate statement about the capacity of Scots verse to hold its own against the Chaucerian tradition as established

---

[69] NIMEV 1171, 3754, 870.8; James K. Mustain, 'A Rural Medical Practitioner in Fifteenth-Century England', *Bulletin of the History of Medicine*, 46 (1972), 469–76; R. H. Robbins, 'John Crophill's Ale-Pots', *Review of English Studies*, n.s. 20 (1969), 181–9, and 'Medical Manuscripts in Middle English', *Speculum*, 45 (1970), 393–415 (at 411–13).

[70] For discussion of the related categories associated with such assemblages see Julia Boffey and A. S. G. Edwards, 'Towards a Taxonomy of Middle English Manuscript Assemblages', in Connolly and Radulescu (eds), *Insular Books*, 263–80.

[71] See Daniel Huws, 'Porkington 10 and its Scribes', in Fellows, Field, Rogers, and Weiss (eds), *Romance Reading on the Book*, 188–207.

[72] Richard Beadle and A. E. B. Owen (intro), *The Findern Manuscript: Cambridge University Library MS Ff. i. 6* (London, 1978). See also Joanna Martin (ed.), *The Findern Manuscript: A New Edition of the Unique Poems* (Liverpool, 2020).

[73] See Julia Boffey and A. S. G. Edwards (intro.), *Bodleian Library MS. Arch. Selden. B. 24: A Facsimile* (Cambridge, 1997), 9–12; and further, Julia Boffey, 'Bodleian Library MS Arch. Selden. B. 24 and Definitions of the "Household Book"', in A. S. G. Edwards, Ralph Hanna, and Vincent Gillespie (eds), *The Medieval English Book: Studies in Memory of Jeremy Griffiths*, (London, 2000), 125–34.

south of the border, as well an affirmation of familial literary association: it includes the unique copy of *The Kingis Quair* by James I,[74] who was related to Henry Sinclair.

While family connections may have ensured that exemplars of *The Kingis Quair* and other Scottish poems were available to the compilers of this manuscript, these individuals must also have had access to a range of older English poems. The Scottish circulation of Chaucer's works is attested by the inclusion of his lyric 'Truth' in another late fifteenth-century Scottish manuscript, CUL Kk. 1. 5 (part VI).[75] Gower's *Confessio* was also evidently available to Scots poets.[76] As noted at the start of this chapter and as further demonstrated by a number of the compilations discussed thus far, the verse contents of many fifteenth-century manuscripts were fourteenth-century works (in some cases even older ones: some moral and proverbial lyrics had a very long medieval life). It is not uncommon to find poems by Chaucer or Gower, or anonymous fourteenth-century romances or works such as *The Prick of Conscience*, rubbing shoulders with more up-to-date compositions.

Poems could travel over time, and they could also travel geographically. Just as Chaucer and Gower acquired fifteenth-century Scottish audiences, so Langland's *Piers Plowman* made its way to Ireland, where it was copied in the early fifteenth century in a Hiberno-English dialect in a manuscript, now BodL Douce 104, unique among manuscripts of this work in having an extended programme of illustrations.[77] The circulation of individual texts was not always closely confined to their place of origin. The alliterative romance *The Awyntrs off Arthure*,[78] probably originating somewhere around Carlisle in the north-west of England, survives in one fifteenth-century manuscript localized to that region (Princeton, NJ, University Library, MS Taylor 9, known as the Ireland-Blackburne MS), another more likely from the west midlands (BodL MS Douce 324), and one made in London by a metropolitan scribe who also worked on a collection of civic documents for the Guildhall Library (London, Lambeth Palace Library, MS 491, part I). It also made its way to Yorkshire to be included in one of Robert Thornton's compilations (Lincoln Cathedral Library MS 91). The movement of texts must have relied on individuals who transported them from place to place, sometimes serendipitously but on other occasions prompted by specific requests. Particular communities, whether religious houses, secular households, or other forms of association, must have served as informal hubs for the loan and exchange of manuscripts, and offered connections to wider networks of supply.

Compilers and commissioners sourcing poems for inclusion in a manuscript must have acted on a variety of impulses, ranging from the simple—what happened to be locally available or recommended by friends—to the more complicated searching out of works known about by hearsay and felt to be especially desirable for particular contingencies. Certain collocations of poetic works seem to have had an influential circulation. Lydgate's *Siege of Thebes*, for instance, not unsurprisingly, accompanies the *Canterbury Tales* (to which it purports to be an addition) in five manuscripts, and Lydgate's own *Troy Book* in three.

---

[74] NIMEV 1215.
[75] NIMEV 809; See Emily Wingfield, '*Lancelot of the Laik* and the Literary Manuscript Miscellany in 15th- and 16th-century Scotland', in Connolly and Radulescu (eds), *Insular Books*, 209–20.
[76] Joanna M. Martin, 'Responses to the Frame Narrative of John Gower's *Confessio Amantis* in Fifteenth- and Sixteenth-Century Scottish Literature', *Review of English Studies*, n.s. 60 (2009), 561–77.
[77] See Derek Pearsall (intro.) and Kathleen L. Scott (catalogue of the illustrations), *Piers Plowman. A Facsimile of Bodleian Library Oxford MS Douce 104* (Cambridge, 1992).
[78] NIMEV 1566.

Some identical runs of works occur in collections of short poems, which must often have been transmitted in single quires or on bifolia. Warminster, Longleat House MS 30 and San Marino, CA, Huntington Library MS HM 142 are twin repertories of devotional and instructive verse, including poems by Lydgate, Richard de Caistre's hymn, some prayers from the *Speculum Christiani*, and Maidstone's verse paraphrase of the Penitential Psalms. Both were copied by a Dutch scribe named 'T. Werken' who worked extensively in England for William Gray, chancellor of Oxford in 1441 before moving abroad and then returning to England to become bishop of Ely in 1454.[79] Two extensive runs of Lydgate's shorter poems, in BL MS Lansdowne 699, and Leiden, University Library MS Vossius Germ. Gall. Q. 9, present the same items, in the same order, perhaps copied (by different scribes) from a common exemplar.[80] And other compilations preserve what seem to have been influential clusters of Lydgate's short poems, circulating on bifolia or in single quires.[81] London, Lambeth Palace Library, MS 344 and BodL MS Hatton 73, similarly, have identical runs of contents: short religious and moral poems, mainly by Chaucer and Lydgate, preceding the latter's *Life of Our Lady*.[82] In the case of Charles of Orleans's English poems, surviving as a body only in BL MS Harley 682, it seems that another manuscript, copied from this one, once existed: fragments remain in the form of CUL MS Add. 2585 (one leaf) and two leaves pasted into BodL MS Hearne's Diaries 38, fols. 261–4.[83]

These duplicate manuscripts suggest patterns of production in which scribes worked to order through intermediaries, probably stationers, who may have maintained an archive of exemplars for distribution.[84] In other contexts, prospective owners or scribes must have made their own selections from multiple available exemplars, sometimes dipping in and out of these and thus not reproducing exactly the copy from which they worked.

Illustration on any scale seems to have been an infrequent aspect of manuscript production for verse texts. One obvious factor was expense. Another was the availability of artists. A third was the accessibility of appropriate models. The Ellesmere manuscript of the *Canterbury Tales* with its systematic programme of marginal illustrations of all the pilgrims found no imitators. Curiously, the evidence of the most sustained illustrative patterns of decoration comes from provincial environments. As noted above, Lydgate's *Lives of Saints Edmund and Fremund* and his *Fall of Princes* survive in extensively illustrated copies made in Bury St Edmunds.[85] The elaborately illustrated copy of his *Pilgrimage of the Life of Man* in BL MS Cotton Tiberius A VII seems to have been produced in East Anglia.[86] The single

---

[79] On Werken see R. A. B. Mynors, 'A Fifteenth-century Scribe: T. Werken', *Transactions of the Cambridge Bibliographical Society*, 1 (1949–53), 97–104, and Dan Mosser, 'Longleat House MS 30, T. Werken, and Thomas Betson', *Journal of the Early Book Society*, 15 (2012), 319–31(with comparative tables of the contents of both manuscripts; as Mosser notes, MS HM 142 includes some further items that might once have been present in MS Longleat 30).

[80] J. A. Van Dorsten, 'The Leyden Lydgate Manuscript', *Scriptorium*, 14 (1960), 315–25.

[81] See Grossi, 'Cloistered Lydgate', and Julia Boffey, 'Short Texts in Manuscript Anthologies: The Minor Poems of John Lydgate in Two Fifteenth-Century Collections', in Stephen G. Nichols and Siegfried Wenzel (eds), *The Whole Book: Cultural Perspectives on the Medieval Miscellany* (Ann Arbor, MI, 1996), 69–82.

[82] H. N. MacCracken, 'Notes Suggested by a Chaucer Codex', *Modern Language Notes*, 23 (1908), 212–14. See further, in relation to the text of *The Life of Our Lady* in these manuscripts, George R. Keiser, 'Serving the Needs of Readers: Textual Division in Some Late-Medieval English Texts', in Richard Beadle and A. J. Piper (eds), *New Science out of Old Books: Studies in Manuscripts and Early Printed Books in Honour of A. I. Doyle* (Aldershot, 1995), 207–26.

[83] Simon Horobin, 'Charles d'Orléans, Harley 682, and the London Booktrade', in R. D. Perry and Mary-Jo Arn (eds), *Charles d'Orléans's English Aesthetic* (Cambridge, 2020), 245–64.

[84] Margaret Connolly, 'Compiling the Book', in Alexandra Gillespie and Daniel Wakelin (eds), *The Production of Books in England 1350–1500* (Cambridge, 2011), 129–49. On London stationers, see Christianson, *A Directory of London Stationers and Book Artisans*.

[85] See Scott, 'Lydgate's *Lives of SS Edmund and Fremund*'.

[86] NIMEV 4265; Scott, *Later Gothic Manuscripts*, 2.251–3.

copy of Langland's *Piers Plowman* with a programme of illustration was made in the fifteenth century in Ireland.[87] Only in the cases of Lydgate's *Troy Book* and Gower's *Confessio Amantis* is there evidence that artists drew, albeit to varying degrees, on the availability in London of models for illustration for verse works.[88]

Perhaps the growing appeal of rhyme royal as a verse form for longer works may have served to limit the commercial attractiveness of illustration. The seven-line stanza made it straightforward to arrive at an easily calculable page design, often four spaced stanzas to a page, and overall volume size. The pragmatics of book production in terms of both calculable work rates and relative expense may have significant factors in the production of verse texts. The manuscript of Henry Lovelich's romance translations seems to have been planned to accommodate illustration, but the fact that this was never supplied may have been connected with the financial outlay that might have been involved.

Beyond the long poems of Lydgate, instances of illustrated fifteenth-century verse texts are thus few and scattered. Some copies of Hoccleve's *Regiment of Princes* have portraits of Chaucer at the point where is name is invoked in the text.[89] Programmed combinations of verse texts and images were evidently produced for *The Desert of Religion*, a devotional compilation, and for some copies of Stephen Scrope's translation of Christine de Pizan's *Epistle of Othea*, in which sections of both verse and prose accompany illustrations.[90] Apart from these, the provision of illustration with verse texts seems to have been a matter of practical necessity, whether in supplying visual prompts to accompany devotional verse, as with *Arma Christi* poems,[91] or in clarifying particular forms of information. The maps in some copies of Hardyng's *Chronicle*, for example, and the illustrations provided with some alchemical and medical poems, come into this category.[92]

By the end of the fifteenth century print was established as an alternative to manuscript production. Although the only significant centre for the production of printed books was London, there were existing means of sending them extensively beyond the metropolis. Fifteenth-century poetic works did not feature significantly in this new form of textual transmission. A number of Lydgate's major works, his *Life of our Lady*, *Siege of Thebes*, and *Fall of Princes*, and some of his shorter poems, were printed. These last, including *The Temple of Glass*, the *Churl and the Bird*, *Horse Sheep and Goose*, and *Stans puer ad mensam*,[93] achieved for the first time a separate identity as freestanding works, whereas in manuscript they survive only as parts of larger collections.

But if print offered new opportunities for the circulation of Lydgate the same possibility was not extended to other verse produced in the fifteenth century. Printers were chiefly attracted by the opportunities presented by the works of Chaucer, whose *Canterbury Tales* was the first substantial poem printed by Caxton (he followed this with the first

[87] See Pearsall and Scott, *Piers Plowman*.
[88] See Lesley Lawton, 'The Illustration of Late Medieval Secular Texts', in Pearsall (ed.), *Manuscripts and Readers*, 41–69, and Jeremy Griffiths, '*Confessio Amantis*: The Poem and its Pictures' in A. J. Minnis (ed.), *Gower's Confessio Amantis: Responses and Reassessments* (Cambridge, 1983), 163–77. The short poem *Parce mihi domine* (NIMEV 561) is prefaced with an illustration in two manuscripts, both of London provenance (BodL MS Douce 322 and Cambridge, Trinity College MS R. 3. 21).
[89] See Derek Pearsall, *The Life of Geoffrey Chaucer* (Oxford, 1992), 284–305.
[90] On the *Desert* (NIMEV 672), see Anne Mouron, '*The Desert of Religion*: A Textual and Visual Compilation', in Marleen Cré, Diana Denissen and Denis Renevey (eds), *Late Medieval Devotional Compilations in England* (Turnhout, 2020), 385–409, and on the *Epistle* (NIMEV 2700.66), see Scott, *Later Gothic Manuscripts*, 2.263–6.
[91] L. H. Cooper and A. Denny-Brown (eds), *The 'Arma Christi' in Medieval and Early Modern Culture, With a Critical Edition of 'O Vernicle'* (Farnham, 2014).
[92] Alfred Hiatt, 'Beyond a Border: The Maps of Scotland in John Hardyng's *Chronicle*', in Jenny Stratford (ed.), *The Lancastrian Court: Proceedings of the 2001 Harlaxton Symposium* (Donington, 2003), 78–94. On alchemical manuscripts, see this volume, Chapter 15.
[93] NIMEV 851, 2784, 658, 2233.

editions of Chaucer's *Troilus and Criseyde*, *House of Fame*, and *Parliament of Fowls*). Caxton's contemporaries and successors were largely content to follow his lead and ignore much fifteenth-century poetry. Printing does not seem to have offered attractions as a launching pad for new verse. Only the remarkable *Epitaffe on the moste noble & valyaunt Iasper late duke of Beddeforde* ([1496]; STC 14477) by one 'Smerte', Skelton's *Bowge of Court* ([1499?]; STC 22597) and William of Tours, *Contemplation of Sinners* (1499; STC 5643), the earliest printed verse work by a Scot, can be noted in the final decade of the century.

CHAPTER 9
Poetry in Print

Siân Echard

The John Rylands Library in Manchester owns a copy of Richard Pynson's 1492 printing of Chaucer's *Canterbury Tales* (STC 5084).[1] This is not the first printing of the *Tales*, as will be made clear in what follows, but this particular copy is a good place to begin this chapter, because of how the book ends. Pynson's printing lacked Chaucer's *Retraction*, though earlier (and some later) printings included this final part of the text.[2] Pynson finished his text on the recto of the page, and set his printer's mark in the middle of the then-blank verso. In this particular copy, however, the printer does not have the last word. On the verso, a sixteenth-century owner, one Robert Maykin, has written an ownership inscription above Pynson's mark. He may or may not also be responsible for the doodles of horses that appear beside and below the mark; the more finished of the doodles bears a close resemblance to some of the horses in the woodcuts found in early illustrated copies of the *Tales*. The recto of this opening, opposite the page bearing Pynson's mark, the ownership notes, and the horses, is filled with a handwritten copy of the missing 'Retraction', taken from Caxton's 1483 printing (STC 5083) and signed at the end by Robert Saham, a chaplain from Bury St Edmunds in the early sixteenth century.[3]

The Rylands copy, like many other early printed books, witnesses the permeable manuscript/print boundary in this period of English printing,[4] and reminds us as well that owners have their own ideas about what their books should look like, and what they should contain. The last quarter of the fifteenth century saw the coexistence of two systems of textual production in England. One, the manuscript tradition described in Chapter 8 of this collection, was fully developed; the other, the print tradition to be traced in this chapter, was new, and relied, in this period of its infancy, on manuscript for its source materials and also for many of its ways of framing and delivering poetry. Manuscript became print in this period, but as both the doodles and the hand-written 'Retraction' in the Rylands

---

[1] This copy is JRL 10002. Dates for early print are often conjectural, as not all printers indicate date of issue in their colophons, and printing errors can also cause confusion. Two resources that are helpful in working with early print are the *English Short Title Catalogue*, which lists items published mainly in the British Isles, and usually in English, from 1473 to 1800; and *Early English Books Online*, a database of texts from the STC, with scanned page images. The STC is available online for free through the British Library, and many universities hold subscriptions to EEBO. Throughout this chapter, I indicate the *STC* number in parentheses, so that readers can locate the printing in question.

[2] Between 1532 and 1721, however, the Retraction did not appear in printed editions of the *Canterbury Tales*; see Megan L. Cook, '"Here taketh the maker of this book his leve": The *Retraction* and Chaucer's Works in Tudor England', *Studies in Philology*, 113 (2016), 32–54 (at 34).

[3] See Alexandra Gillespie, *Print Culture and the Medieval Author: Chaucer, Lydgate, and their Books 1473–1557* (Oxford, 2006), 92. She does not discuss the horse doodles.

[4] Another copy of Pynson's 1492 edition, now in the University of London, also illustrates the communication between manuscript and print. As Daniel W. Mosser shows, this copy was glossed by hand shortly after it was printed, and those glosses may be traced to a now-lost, fifteenth-century manuscript exemplar, He concludes that 'The producers and consumers of fifteenth-century books ... did not necessarily perceive these objects as being so different as we might', 'The Manuscript Glosses of the *Canterbury Tales* and the University of London's Copy of Pynson's [1492] Edition: Witness to a Lost Exemplar', *The Chaucer Review*, 41 (2007), 360–92 (at 370).

Canterbury Tales indicate, print could also once again become manuscript. Printers staged various interventions that attempted to claim, control, and market the texts they produced, but—and this was of course true in manuscript culture as well—once a book made its way into the hands of readers, anything could happen.

English Poetry in Early Print: An Overview

The first book printed in English was neither poetry, nor printed in England, nor even particularly English. William Caxton's *Recuyell of the Historyes of Troye* (STC 15375) was his own translation of a French text by Raoul Lefèvre, and it was printed around 1473, probably in Bruges or Ghent. However, by 1476, Caxton had moved his operations to England, and while prose translations continued to be part of his output, he also produced editions of English poetry. Indeed, his earliest major undertaking after the move was his first edition of Geoffrey Chaucer's *Canterbury Tales* (STC 5082). This was a big book, a folio of 374 leaves. Also around 1476, he produced another poetic text, John Lydgate's *Stans puer ad mensam* (STC 17030), a quarto of four leaves. This is a pamphlet-like production that might have been intended for collection with similar small pieces of printing into a *Sammelband*, a collection of separately printed pieces bound together at some later point.[5] These two types of printing typify Caxton's poetry editions. Between 1476 and 1484, his output included shorter works by Lydgate and Chaucer in quarto: Lydgate's *The Churl and the Bird* (STC 17008, 17009); *Horse, Goose and Sheep* (STC 17018, 17019); and *The Temple of Glass* (STC 17032); and Chaucer's *Anelida and Arcite* (STC 5090) and *The Parliament of Fowls* (STC 5091). He also produced folio-sized printings of works by Chaucer—*The House of Fame* (STC 5087), *Troilus and Criseyde* (STC 5094) and the 1483 edition of *The Canterbury Tales* mentioned above; Lydgate's *Life of Our Lady* (STC 17023); and John Gower's *Confessio Amantis* (STC 12142).[6] He also printed *The Court of Sapience* (STC 17015), which would later sometimes be attributed to Lydgate. But while there is no doubt that Caxton was essential in transmitting the work of the triumvirate of Middle English laureate poets (Chaucer, Gower, and Lydgate), it is important not to lose sight of everything else that he published. Most of Caxton's output was prose, rather than verse. His first book, as already noted, was his prose translation from a French original, and he continued to be a prolific printer of his own translations.[7] As will be discussed further below, the second, 1483 edition of the *Canterbury Tales* has woodcuts, but Caxton's first illustrated book was the encyclopaedic prose text, the *Mirror of the World*, which he printed in 1481 and again in 1491 (STC 24762, 24763). Other illustrated books included his translation of Aesop's beast fables (1484, STC 175). Nicholas Orme has suggested that some early, small-format English books might have been intended for children, and also notes the rise, as printing develops, in books aimed at young students. While Orme is writing primarily about the second generation of English printers, one can easily see how texts like Lydgate's *Stans*

---

[5] Gillespie discusses the production of *Sammelbände* by early English printers in *Print Culture and the Medieval Author*, and in 'Poets, Printers, and Early English Sammelbände', *Huntington Library Quarterly*, 67 (2004), 189–214.

[6] He also printed *The Pilgrimage of the Soul* (1483, STC 6473), a work that was often attributed to Lydgate, though in fact it was an English translation of Guillaume de Deguileville's *Pèlerinage de l'âme*.

[7] For a recent discussion of Caxton's translation practices, see Anne E. B. Coldiron, *Printers without Borders: Translation and Textuality in the Renaissance* (Cambridge, 2015). She notes (at 35) that about three-quarters of Caxton's output consisted of translation, most of it from the French, and most of it his own work.

puer, or Benedict Burgh's English verse translations of Cato's *Distichs*, set below the original Latin lines (printed by Caxton in 1476, 1477, and 1483: STC 4851, 4850, and 4852), or illustrated encyclopaedias and beast fables, might also appeal to an educational market.[8] In other words, Caxton's output of Middle English verse was part of a larger project of using the new medium of print to bring educational works, classical texts, and continental texts, as well as English poetry, to a broader audience.

Caxton's immediate successor was his assistant, Wynkyn de Worde. Originally from the Low Countries,[9] he came to England to work for Caxton quite early,[10] and took over the printing business when Caxton died in 1492. Some of the books de Worde printed were set up from Caxton's earlier editions, but de Worde also greatly expanded Caxton's list, printing almost 1000 separate titles, many of which were illustrated. Martha Driver notes that 'Plentiful, if not always beautiful, illustration, provided in ingeniously economical ways, seems to have been one key to de Worde's success';[11] increasing the number and types of titles he printed might well have been another. De Worde's prolific production means that he printed far more verse than Caxton did, but it also means that, as with Caxton, we need to be careful not to over-emphasize his production of laureate texts. Like Caxton, de Worde printed works by Chaucer and Lydgate (though not by Gower), repeating texts Caxton had already printed, such as, for Chaucer, the *Canterbury Tales* (1498, STC 5085), *Troilus and Criseyde* (1517, STC 5095), and *The Parliament of Fowls* (1530, STC 5092); and for Lydgate, *The Churl and the Bird* (1494 and 1510; STC 17011, 17012), *Horse, Goose and Sheep* (three times: STC 17020, 17021, 17022), *Stans puer ad mensam* (c1510 and 1520, STC 17030.5, 17030.7), and *The Temple of Glass* (three times, STC 17032a, 17033, 17033.7). He printed Lydgate texts Caxton had not, such as the *Siege of Thebes* (1497, STC 17031), the anonymous *Assembly of Gods* attributed, in one edition, to Lydgate (1498, STC 17005),[12] and the *Virtue of the Masse* (1500, 1520; STC 17037.5, 17038). He also printed such popular medieval verse romances as *Bevis of Hampton*, *Guy of Warwick*, and *Sir Eglamour of Artois*, all around 1500 and all surviving today only in fragments (STC 1987, 12541, 7541). More verse romances followed in the years after 1500, including *Generydes* in 1506 and 1518 (STC 11721.5, 11721.7), *Richard Coeur de Lion* in 1509 and 1528 (STC 21007, 21008), *Sir Degore* in 1513 (STC 6470), and *Capystranus* in 1515 (STC 14649). There are also short verse pieces like the *Little Gest of Robin Hood* from 1506 (STC 13689) and *How the plowman learned his pater noster* (1510, STC 20034). That is, de Worde's verse output included many texts that could be classed as popular, rather than laureate. A little later in his career, de Worde printed *Undo Youre Dore* (STC 23111.5, c1520), also known as *The Squire of Low Degree*, a somewhat unconventional romance with more emphasis on dialogue and economic factors, and less on knightly adventuring, than is typical in the genre. Julia Boffey and A. S. G. Edwards argue that de Worde's interest in this text, at a time when

---

[8] Nicholas Orme, *Medieval Children* (New Haven, CT, 2001), 293–7. Caxton's 1483 printing of the Cato includes two small woodcuts of a master instructing students.

[9] There has been some doubt over de Worde's exact origins; N. F. Blake in the *ODNB* (latest online version 3 January 2008) notes that while the 1496 letters of denization say de Worde originated from the duchy of Lorraine, neither Woerth-sur-Sauer nor Wörth am Rhein were part of the duchy at that time. In *William Caxton and Early Printing in England* (London, 2010), 134–5, Lotte Hellinga says that de Worde came from Woerden in Holland.

[10] The first record of de Worde's presence in England is a deed from 1480; see James Moran, *Wynkyn de Worde: Father of Fleet Street*, 2nd revised edn. (London, 1976), 12.

[11] Martha Driver, *The Image in Print: Book Illustration in Late Medieval England and its Sources* (London, 2004), 34.

[12] The two printings of the *Assembly of Gods* in 1500—STC 17006 and 17007—lack the attribution to Lydgate found in the 1498 printing. De Worde also printed *The Court of Sapience* (STC 17015), which, as noted above, was sometimes attributed to Lydgate.

conventional romance seemed to have been losing its appeal to his fellow printers, is one of his attempts to 'develop new markets for verse texts'.[13]

In addition to publishing Middle English verse, de Worde also published the works of contemporary poets such as John Skelton, whose satirical poem *The Bowge of Court* he printed in 1499 (STC 22597). He seems to have collaborated quite closely with Stephen Hawes, printing *The Example of Virtue* and the *Pastime of Pleasure* in 1509 (STC 12945, 12948), and the *Conforte of Lovers* in 1515 (STC 12942.5). A. S. G. Edwards has argued that the woodcuts for the *Example of Virtue* and the *Pastime of Pleasure* were produced specifically for these printings—as we will see below, it was common for early printers to use, and reuse, generic woodcuts to illustrate many of their texts, so the care with which illustration and text are integrated in de Worde's printings of Hawes is striking.[14] While much of de Worde's production falls outside the chronological limits of this volume, and while, like Caxton, he printed a great deal of prose, his importance in transmitting English verse, both old and new, in the first generations of print, cannot be underestimated.

Another significant printer, whose career runs roughly parallel to de Worde's (and indeed they were occasional collaborators as well as competitors), is Richard Pynson, who like de Worde came to the English book trade via the continent; in his case, from Normandy. He functioned in the newly-created role of King's Printer from 1506, and much of his output was legal printing, but he also printed other kinds of books, including both medieval and Tudor verse. His Chaucer editions included the 1492 *Canterbury Tales* with which this chapter opened (and he printed the *Tales* again in 1526, STC 5086), and *Troilus and Criseyde* (STC 5096) and *The House of Fame* (STC 5088), both perhaps in 1526. In the case of Lydgate, like Caxton and de Worde he printed the *Temple of Glass* in 1503 (STC 17033.3). He also added another piece to the Lydgate canon by printing *The Fall of Princes*, first in 1494 and then again in 1527 (STC 3175, 3176).

Pynson also printed popular and romance texts. I have already mentioned de Worde's *Little Gest of Robin Hood*, but it was Pynson who was responsible for the first printing of a Robin Hood text, in 1500 (STC 13688). Like de Worde, he printed both *Guy of Warwick* and *Bevis of Hampton*, and while two of these printings survive only in fragments (STC 12540, 1987.5), his 1503 illustrated printing of *Bevis* (STC 1988) not only survives, but set the pattern for illustrated versions of *Bevis* for several subsequent centuries.[15] Pynson produced substantial editions of sixteenth-century poetry; in his case, the works of Alexander Barclay. *The Castle of Labour*, a verse translation from a French original which Pynson printed in 1505 and again c 1528 (STC 12380, 12382), has been attributed to Barclay (de Worde also printed it, in 1506 and 1512; STC 12381 and 12381.4), and Barclay was certainly the author of a popular verse translation of Sebastian Brant's *Narrenschiff*, in English *The Ship of Fools*, which Pynson printed in 1509 (STC 3545). In that same year, Wynkyn de Worde published the prose translation of Brant's work by Henry Watson (STC 3547). And finally, with *The epitaffe of the most noble [and] valyaunt Iasper late duke of Beddefore* (STC 14477) in 1496, Pynson printed the first contemporary verse in English.

---

[13] Julia Boffey and A. S. G. Edwards, 'The *Squire of Low Degree* and the Penumbra of Romance Narrative in the Early Sixteenth Century', in Elizabeth Archibald, Megan G. Leitch, and Corinne Saunders (eds), *Romance Rewritten: The Evolution of Middle English Romance. A Tribute to Helen Cooper* (Cambridge, 2018), 229–40 (at 240).

[14] A. S. G. Edwards, *Stephen Hawes* (Boston, 1983), 21–3.

[15] I discuss Pynson's printing and its influence in *Printing the Middle Ages* (Philadelphia, PA, 2008), 60–96. For an overview of the early printing of romance in England, see Carol M. Meale, 'Caxton, de Worde, and the Publication of Romance in England', *The Library* 6th series, 14 (1992), 283–98.

Another second-generation printer was Julian Notary, whose primary focus was religious printing, largely in Latin. He printed three short pieces by Chaucer (*The Complaint of Mars, the Complaint of Venus*, and the 'Envoy to Bukton') together some time around 1500 (STC 5089), and while it survives only in a fragment, we know he printed *Bevis of Hampton* in 1510 (STC 1988.2). The first Scottish printers also contributed to the early print history of verse in English (and Scots). Androw Myllar and Walter Chepman, who established a press in Edinburgh in 1508, printed works by Lydgate (*The Complaint of the Black Knight*, STC 17014.3); by Scottish writers such as William Dunbar (*The Ballad of Bernard Stewart*, STC 7347; *The flyting of Dunbar and Kennedy*, STC 7348; *The Goldyn Targe*, STC 7349; and *The tua mariit wemen and the wedo*, STC 7350), Robert Henryson (*The Traitie of Orpheus*, STC 13166), and Richard Holland (*Buke of the Howlat*, STC 13594); anonymous romances such as *Golagrus and Gawain* (STC 11984), *Sir Eglamour of Artois* (STC 7542), and the anonymous *Book of Good Counsel to the Scots King* (STC 3307), a translation in Scots verse of *De regimine principum*. English verse continues to appear on the lists of later printers such as Thomas Berthelet, Robert Wyer, John Rastell, and Robert Copland, and while their productions lie chronologically outside the scope of this volume, many continued to draw on texts produced in this first age of print.

Authorship and Authority

As the overview of early printing of verse has already indicated, the first English printers did much to lay the groundwork for establishing the canon(s) of medieval verse, though definitive efforts such as the first deliberate collection of works by Chaucer (Thomas Godfray's printing of William Thynne's *Workes of Geffray Chaucer* in 1532, STC 5068), are still in the future. Many of the moves made by early printers had to do with establishing textual authority in ways that did not always depend solely on the invocation of an author. Indeed, the activity that is most prominent in much of the paratextual material in early printings is often that of the printer himself, as his own processes of selecting and framing text are foregrounded. As illustrations of this kind of activity, we can consider Caxton's 1483 printings of Chaucer's *Canterbury Tales* and Gower's *Confessio Amantis*, both of which show the printer addressing his imagined readers directly, and framing both his activity, and their reading experience.

The 1483 *Tales* is, as noted above, Caxton's second printing of the text. The first printing is a straightforward affair. There is no front matter, and little in the layout to allow easy navigation of what is, after all, a long text. The text is printed in a single column, with the occasional centred textual link; as is common in early print (and in manuscript production too), spaces have been left for large capitals, filled in by hand in some copies, but otherwise there is very little to help readers find their way through the text. Chaucer is named at the end of 'The Parson's Tale', though in an odd formulation that links author and character, perhaps leading a reader to imagine them as dual conduits for the narrative: '*Explicit Tractatus Galfrydi Chaucer de Penitencia vt dicitur pro fabula Rectoris*' (Here ends Geoffrey Chaucer's treatise concerning penitence, told as the story of the Parson, fol. 371). But when Caxton prints the *Tales* again in 1483, much has changed. The order of the tales differs from the order in the 1477 printing.[16] The book is now an illustrated edition,

---

[16] The question of the correct order for the *Tales* is one of very long standing. There is a helpful overview in Larry D. Benson, 'The Order of *The Canterbury Tales*', *Studies in the Age of Chaucer*, 3 (1981), 77–120. For a useful table comparing the tale order in Caxton's editions, see Eleanor Prescott Hammond, 'On the Order of the Canterbury Tales: Caxton's Two Editions', *Modern Philology*, 3 (1905), 161–2.

as discussed further below. It is much easier for a reader to navigate, since, in addition to the visual punctuation provided by the woodcuts, it also has running titles throughout, and more variation in the layout of the individual tales, with some now set in stanzas. And the work now has a long proem by Caxton, in which he outlines how he came to print this book, and gives a sense of how he understands the function of writing in general, Chaucer in particular, and the place of print in this textual universe.

The proem begins by asserting that great thanks and honour should be given to the 'clerkes/ poetes/ and historiographs' (a ii r) who have written about wisdom, the saints, history, and great deeds and acts up to the present day. These people have, Caxton says, made it possible for us to 'haue knowleche of many thynges/ of whom we shold not haue knowen/ yf they had not left to vs theyr monumentis wreton (*written*)' (sig. aii). An author is one who preserves and transmits important knowledge, but an author's work survives because of the physical objects—the written monuments, as Caxton calls them—that contain that work. The proem is in fact quite preoccupied with the very nature of books, referring to the 'beauteuous volumes' (a ii r), at this point still most likely to be written manuscripts, of Chaucer's work, before moving into Caxton's explanation for why he is printing the *Tales* a second time. He relates that, after his first edition appeared, a gentleman told him that the printed text did not accord with 'the book that Gefferey Chaucer had made' (a ii v), an opinion he bases upon his knowledge of a manuscript owned by his father. This book is, the gentleman says, 'very trewe/ and accordynge vnto hys (that is, Chaucer's) owen first book by hym made'. Caxton promises to print a new edition, according to this copy, in order, he says, 'to satysfye thauctour/ where as to fore (*before*) by ygnouraunce I erryd in hurting and dyffamyng his book in dyuerce (*many*) places in setting in somme thynges that he neuer sayd ne made/ and leuyng out many thynges that he made whyche ben requisyte (*are necessary*) to be sette in it' (sig. aii verso).

There is an interesting idea of what constitutes Chaucer's 'book' in this passage. On the one hand, there is a single, physical copy whose qualities, if true, would match modern desires as a suitable manuscript base text for a critical edition: the gentleman's father's copy has a good text, and close proximity to an authorial original. On the other hand, however, there is also an idea of the book that seems to inhere in the author himself; the 'book' that Caxton apologizes for hurting and defaming is not this particular base text, since he did not have access to it, but rather an idea of the author's intentions for his book. Chaucer is the 'first auctour/ and maker of this book'. Again, the book is the notional, original *Canterbury Tales*, rather than any particular physical copy. And there is a further intervenor in the author-book relationship as Caxton imagines it, and that is the printer himself. Defending himself against the gentleman's complaints, Caxton notes that his first edition was printed 'accordyng to my copye/ and by me was nothyng added ne mynusshyd (*taken away*)' (sig. aii verso). So, while the copy was faulty, Caxton's own actions were not. Indeed, the printer is, to return to the preamble to the proem, a maker of monuments, and texts (and authors) survive only if those monuments do, and only if they are up to their important task.

The 1483 *Tales*, then, are delivered to readers with a proem that proclaims this edition as corrective and restorative, in relation to the author's original intentions. Lotte Hellinga has pointed out that Caxton did not replace his apparently faulty first text. Instead, he collated and corrected it against the new copy, and in fact his editing hand was quite light. She argues that the changes to layout and tale-order suggest an emphasis on completeness, rather than on 'establishing the author's actual words'.[17] We need also to remember that the proem is partly a marketing exercise: Caxton needs to persuade people who may already own a copy of his earlier edition that it is worth spending money for a new one. The woodcuts, and the general improvements in navigation provided by the enhanced layout, would be one reason a buyer might pick up this edition, but these are not the things Caxton mentions in his pitch. Instead, he argues that the 1483 *Tales* give a reader closer access to Chaucer's book, and thus, perhaps, to Chaucer himself, the book's first 'maker'.

In the same year that he printed his second edition of the *Canterbury Tales*, Caxton also printed John Gower's *Confessio Amantis*. This was the first printing of Gower's work, and there would not be another until Thomas Berthelet's in 1532 (STC 12143). Like the second *Canterbury Tales*, this is a big book with a layout that facilitates navigation. The text is printed in two columns, with generous space left for initials. Some quite large spaces at the beginning of books may perhaps have been intended for illustrations, but this is not an illustrated copy (nor would Berthelet's be). There are running titles for the book divisions. Gower's Latin verses are printed as prose, and verses, glosses, and speaker markers are all printed in the text column. Where medieval manuscripts of the *Confessio* often used colour to distinguish the parts of the text, rendering Latin in red (or, sometimes, black underlined in red), Caxton uses white space, centring small features like the speaker markers, and often, though not always, setting glosses or verses apart with blank lines. Caxton's most significant contribution to navigating Gower's text, however, comes in the front matter. After a short preamble, he produces a printed table of contents, running for thirteen pages. He outlines the purpose of the table in his preamble: 'by cause there been comprysed therin dyuers (*many*) hystoryes and fables towchyng euery matere/ I haue ordeyned a table here folowynge of al suche hystoryes and fables where and in what book and leef they stande in as here after foloweth' (sig. aii). Caxton's presentation of Chaucer in the proem to the 1483 *Tales* included specific commentary about the poet's style. He writes that Chaucer, 'for his ornate wrytyng in our tongue maye wel haue the name of a laureate poete', and while his Chaucer is, like Gower, a conduit for 'many a noble historye', he is also presented, in a way that Gower is not, as a literary stylist, one who 'comprehended hys maters in short/ quyck and hye sentences/ eschewing prolyxyte/ casting away the chaf of superfluyte/ and shewing the pyked grayn of sentence/ vtteryd by crafty and sugred (*sweet*) eloquence' (sig. aii). The much shorter introduction to Gower's poem, by contrast, focuses on the content rather than the style of the work.

The table of contents, then, reinforces Caxton's framing of Gower's text as a collection of stories, a compilation from many sources (an idea echoed in his description of the book as having been 'maad and compyled by Johan Gower' (sig. aii). A table of contents is not an innovation unique to print: many medieval manuscripts of long Latin texts feature *capituli* at the outset, and there are several *Confessio* manuscripts with similar finding aids, including two with tables of contents.[18] It is also not unusual for Caxton to provide a table of contents for his printed books. What is unusual is the decision to do this for a verse text. Caxton's tables are generally found in his prose printings. Norman Blake has suggested

---

[17] Lotte Hellinga, 'Manuscripts in the Hands of Printers', in J. B. Trapp (ed), *Manuscripts in the Fifty Years after the Invention of Printing* (London, 1983), 3–11 (at 7).

[18] The manuscripts with tables of contents are Princeton University Library, Taylor Collection, MS 5 and Oxford, Magdalen College MS 213. The Magdalen table is particularly relevant because it appears to have been added near the point of production, and the manuscript is dated to the end of the fifteenth century; that is, it might well overlap with the beginning of the print era. See my 'Pre-Texts: Tables of Contents and the Reading of John Gower's *Confessio Amantis*', *Medium Ævum*, 66 (1997), 270–87.

that the table might have appealed to Caxton because Gower's Latin glosses had already done much of the organizational work.[19] Certainly there is a close relationship between the glosses and the entries in Caxton's tables, though the printer does not echo every gloss, and nor does he make use of every detail even from those glosses on which he is clearly drawing.

There are two small but telling details in Caxton's preamble that give further insight into how Gower's bilingual poem is framed for Caxton's audience. He opens by writing that 'This book is intituled confessio amantis/ that is to saye in englysshe the confession of the louer' (sig. aii). As was the case in the proem to the 1483 *Tales*, the physical book is presented in such a way as to indicate a notional book that lies behind or beneath. There is a book with the title *Confessio Amantis*, and that is the book John Gower compiled, but that is not necessarily *this particular* book, which is, rather, Caxton's realization of Gower's book. That is, early printers often show awareness of the work being done by printers, work that lies between the idea of a book and a printer's presentation of it. The innocuous phrase 'to saye in englysshe' is the key: Caxton translates the Latin title, and his table of contents, in addition to packaging the poem as a collection of stories, effectively translates the Latin interpretive and navigational framework Gower provided for his text. One can read the table as a collaboration between printer and author, as Caxton makes accessible both the poem as a whole, and parts of the poem that might be less readily available to the audience. Caxton, unlike Berthelet, preserves Gower's extensive Latin end matter, and so might fairly be said to have transmitted Gower's text without the kind of injury to the author for which he apologized in the proem to the 1483 *Tales*. At the same time, Gower was clear in his own presentation of his work that his deployment of Latin was a stylistic choice, and the Latin framework, while it does provide navigational pathways, thanks to the common practices of manuscript production, also interacts with the English text in complex ways. Caxton's version of the *Confessio* is silent on these matters, and instead presents the work as a compilation whose built-in interpretive framework is translated and to some degree flattened by the table.

As noted above, neither de Worde nor Pynson seems to have printed Gower's *Confessio*, but their printings of the *Canterbury Tales* offer further instances of the intersection of print with ideas about authorship and authority. I have already discussed the lack of Chaucer's 'Retraction' in Pynson's printing, and the decision of one sixteenth-century owner/reader to supplement that lack. Because Pynson's text ends with 'The Parson's Tale' (and without the Explicit to that tale that names Chaucer), the poet's presence in this printing is perhaps somewhat subdued, although, like Caxton in the 1483 printing, Pynson provides the running title 'The Tale of Chaucer' for 'Melibee'. Pynson also uses Caxton's proem, which begins, as we have seen, with praise of Chaucer's poetic abilities. There are some interesting edits towards the end of the proem that shift the perception of poet and printer somewhat, however. Pynson removes Caxton's story about securing a new copy of the *Tales*, and adjusts the language about the relationship between the author and the print. Describing his perplexity at the variations in the 'bookes' that he has seen of the *Tales*—referring here to manuscript books—Caxton writes that he has 'dylygently ouersen (*supervised*) and duly examined [his own printing] to thende (*with the goal*) that it be made acordyng vnto his (i.e. Chaucer's) owen makyng'. In Pynson's hands, this section reads, 'Whiche boke diligently ouirsen (*supervised*) and duely examined by the politike reason (*sound judgement*)

---

[19] N. F. Blake, *Caxton: England's First Publisher* (London, 1976), 117.

and ouirsight of my worshipful master William Caxton according to the entent and effecte of the seid Geffrey Chaucer and by a copy of the seid master Caxton purpos to imprent' (sig. ai). Caxton is, in this version, the guarantor of direct access to Chaucer's 'intent', a word whose substitution for 'makyng' shifts the poet away from the maker/compiler model of, say, a figure like Gower. Caxton's textual authority is heightened through reference to his judiciousness (his 'politic reason'), and it is Caxton, rather than Chaucer, who is Pynson's 'worshipful master'. Caxton worried about injuring Chaucer and his text; Pynson is concerned to give credit to Caxton. And yet, Pynson closes the proem—which is still almost verbatim Caxton's, apart from the omissions and slight changes I have discussed—with the word 'By Richard Pynson' (the 1483 proem ended 'By Wylliam Caxton'), thus overwriting his master even as he praises him.

Pynson printed the *Tales* again in 1526 (STC 5086), and the paratexts are further developed along the lines suggested by the 1492 printing. There is a title page, that reads 'Here begynneth the boke of Caunterbury tales/ dilygently and truely corrected/ and newly printed'—foregrounding both the technology that can produce 'new' printings, and the textual activity of the printer. The proem now has a title, 'The proheme of the printer' (sig. ai verso), and the General Prologue is titled 'The prologe of the author' (sig. aii); these titles face each other at the top of the verso and recto of the first opening, creating a visual parallel between printer and poet. This printing does include the Retraction, introduced by the reference to 'The Parson's Tale' as the *tractatus* of Geoffrey Chaucer, but the final word is Pynson's, as this copy (unlike either the 1483 or 1492 printings) has a complete colophon: 'Thus endeth the boke of Caunterbury tales. Imprinted at London in fletestrete / by me Rycharde Pynson / printer vnto the kynges noble grace ... ' (sig. yiii verso).

Wynkyn de Worde also printed the *Canterbury Tales*, in his case in 1498 (STC 5085). He worked largely, though not exclusively, from Caxton's 1483 printing, and used Caxton's woodcuts (Pynson's edition was illustrated too, but his cuts, while clearly modelled on Caxton's, were not the exact same blocks). He provided a title page, that reads 'The boke of Chaucer named Caunterbury tales'. Martha Driver writes that de Worde was 'the main pioneer' of the title page in England, printing the first book to have a title page, the prose *The Chastising of God's Children*, in 1493.[20] As title pages developed, printers could use images to suggest something of the contents to potential purchasers; Pynson, for example, puts one of the pilgrim portrait woodcuts on the title page of his 1526 edition of the *Tales*. There is no image on the title page for de Worde's *Canterbury Tales*, but the few words of the title establish the author/book relation. De Worde prints Caxton's proem, including the account of the gentleman's book that sparked Caxton's second edition. He does not sign the proem as if it were his own, as Pynson had done, but below Caxton's 'By Wylliam Caxton', he sets 'His soule in heuen won' (sig. aii verso). The main text of Caxton's proem, as de Worde presents it, ends with an appeal to readers to 'remembre the soule of the sayde Gefferey Chaucer fyrste auctour and maker of this boke' (sig. aii verso). Thus de Worde's addition of the statement about Caxton's soul links the book's 'first author' with its first printer, underlining the link between the two.

Two of de Worde's innovations in his printing can be found in 'The Tale of Sir Thopas'. First, he designates it as 'Chaucers tale ... of Syre Thopas' (sig. rii), something Caxton did not do. Second, he sets 'Thopas' so as to emphasize the tail rhymes, something none of the other printings discussed here have done. Some manuscript copies of the *Canterbury*

---

[20] Driver, *The Image in Print*, 77, 82.

Tales mark out the rhyme-scheme in 'Thopas' with bracketing and/or layout, and de Worde's practice here is one of the pieces of evidence used by scholars to demonstrate that his printing is not simply a repeat of Caxton's 1483 edition.[21] In addition to providing evidence about de Worde's sources, the layout is important because it evokes a reading practice dependent on manuscript tradition; that is, readers of de Worde's printed book can draw parallels with their experience (if they have such experience, of course) of manuscript books.

I opened this essay with an instance of print/manuscript overlap in a copy of the 1492 Pynson printing of the *Tales*. Some printings of Gower and Chaucer discussed in this section of this essay provide further evidence of just how permeable the print/manuscript boundary could be.[22] BodL MS Hatton 51 is a copy of John Gower's *Confessio Amantis* that was copied from Caxton's edition of the *Confessio*, thus reversing the usual relationship between manuscript and print. Manuscript practice influences this copy from a printed text, however, in that the copyist used red ink, as was common in manuscript copies, for the Latin text, and bracketed many of the couplets in red (a feature, as noted above, of some manuscript treatments of 'Sir Thopas' as well).[23] The British Library's copy of Caxton's printing of the *Confessio* offers another kind of technological intersection, as at some point in the seventeenth or early eighteenth century, someone added an engraving of the famous portrait of Gower as an archer, drawn originally from BL MS Cotton Tiberius A IV, thus enhancing print with a technology that in its turn depends on manuscript. Similarly, in the eighteenth century a full-length portrait of Chaucer was added as a frontispiece to a copy of Caxton's first edition of the *Tales*, also now in the British Library.[24] The portrait resembles the drawing of the poet in the plate labelled 'The Progenie of Geffrey Chaucer', created by John Speed for the 1598 printing of Chaucer's *Workes*. A hand-coloured version of that engraving is also found bound into a manuscript containing Chaucer's works, CUL MS Gg. 4. 27. What these instances all show is that, even well beyond the period dealt with in this volume, the boundaries between different ways of conveying text (and image) are porous.

---

[21] Thomas Garbáty collated de Worde's *Thopas* with Caxton's 1483 printing of the *Tales* to challenge the then-accepted view that de Worde's printing was entirely dependent on Caxton: 'Wynkyn de Worde's "Sir Thopas" and Other Tales', *Studies in Bibliography*, 31 (1978), 57–67. More recently, Satoko Tokunaga notes that some manuscripts make prominent display of the tail-rhymes in 'Sir Thopas', and goes on to argue that 'In early print history, no editors before (and even after) de Worde went to such trouble to arrange the composition of the page, and it is therefore most likely that de Worde learned such a layout from the manuscript tradition'; 'Wynkyn de Worde's Lost Manuscript of the *Canterbury Tales*: With New Light on HRC MS 46', *The Chaucer Review*, 50 (2015), 30–54 (at 37). The treatment of tail-rhyme in manuscripts of 'Sir Thopas' is discussed in Jessica Brantley, 'Reading the Forms of *Sir Thopas*', *The Chaucer Review* 47 (2013), 416–38; Aditi Nafde, 'Laughter Lines: Reading the Layouts of *The Tale of Sir Thopas*', *Pecia*, 16 (2015), 143–51; and Rhiannon Purdie, 'The Implications of Manuscript Layout in Chaucer's *Tale of Sir Thopas*', *Forum for Modern Language Studies*, 41 (2005), 263–74.

[22] There is an overview in N.F. Blake, 'Manuscript to Print', in Jeremy Griffiths and Derek Pearsall (eds), *Book Production and Publishing in Britain 1375–1475* (Cambridge, 1989), 403–32.

[23] For a recent discussion of Hatton 51, see Aditi Nafde, 'Gower from Print to Manuscript: Copying Caxton in Oxford, Bodleian Library, MS Hatton 51', in Martha Driver, Derek Pearsall, and R. F. Yeager (eds), *John Gower in Manuscripts and Early Printed Books* (Cambridge, 2020), 189–200. Hand-copying from print continued well into the seventeenth century; for example, Caxton's edition of *The Court of Sapience* might be the source copied by John Stow in 1558 in his manuscript collection of English verse, now BL MS Add. 29729; see N. F. Blake, *William Caxton and English Literary Culture* (London, 1991), 296.

[24] Maidie Hilmo discusses the added portraits in 'The Clerk's Unscholarly Bow: Seeing and Reading Chaucer's Clerk from the Ellesmere MS to Caxton', *Journal of the Early Book Society*, 10 (2007), 71–105 (at 79, 89). Discussions of the tradition of Chaucer portraiture include Martha W. Driver, 'Mapping Chaucer: John Speed and the Later Portraits', *The Chaucer Review*, 36 (2002), 228–49; Megan L. Cook discusses the Speed portrait in *The Poet and the Antiquaries* (Philadelphia, PA, 2019), 34–8.

Image and Text

The addition of author portraits to early printed copies of the works of Chaucer and Gower speaks to a desire to picture the poets, a desire that is a logical extension of the interest in the poet/poem/book relationship I have been tracing in early printings of English verse. The addition of images to verse in early print extended beyond visual reference to an author figure. There are two quite different types of illustrations in early printings of English verse. Some, like the illustrations de Worde provided for the works of Stephen Hawes, or the woodcuts in Richard Pynson's 1503 printing of *Bevis of Hampton*, or the *Canterbury Tales* pilgrim portraits to be discussed shortly, were clearly made to order, to suit the poems they were to illustrate. Others were generic, and the same cut could be reused often. There is some overlap between the two categories. For example, Caxton's 1483 printing of the *Tales* included, at the end of the *General Prologue*, an image of the pilgrims and their host seated together around a dinner table. Wynkyn de Worde used the same cut, twice, in his 1498 *Tales*, but he also used it in his 1498 and 1500 printings of the *Assembly of Gods*. Wynkyn de Worde's 1517 printing of *Troilus and Criseyde* made use of what Martha Driver has called factotum images, standard cuts of men and women that could be assembled in various combinations, and stand in for any number of characters.[25]

Sometimes this kind of routine reuse can, serendipitously, frame texts in ways that might affect how readers apprehend them, creating what Driver calls 'networks of meaning across a variety of contexts'.[26] For example, the image of a crowned lion surrounded by animals on the title page of two of de Worde's printings of Lydgate's *Horse, Goose and Sheep* was probably part of a series of illustrations for the beast-epic of Reynard the Fox,[27] and so the cut visually 'sorts' Lydgate's poem into the category of beast narrative. The title-page for de Worde's 1507 printing of the *Jousts of the Month of May* (STC 3543) features a generic cut of knights tilting. This poem records jousts organized by Charles Brandon at the court of Henry VII. Brandon and his set, which would come to include Prince Henry, were keen participants in tournaments. The visual alignment of these real men with the romance knights, whose exploits the generic tournament cuts often illustrated, might have performed a welcome linking of the two groups.

In addition to the reuse of woodcuts, the copying of cuts was common, and that practice, too, could participate in certain kinds of framing and potential meaning-making. The text-specific cuts in Pynson's 1509 printing of Barclay's version of *The Ship of Fools* were copied from the French version that had been printed in Paris in 1497, and those cuts in their turn were copied from a Latin edition printed in Basel in the same year.[28] There are many ways in which this book declares its European and humanist credentials. The Latin dedication is printed in humanist type (a typeface based on the writing of the Italian humanists of the early Renaissance), followed, in black letter (an older typeface, based on medieval Gothic script), by Pynson's account of the text's origins and his printing of it. Throughout, Latin is printed in humanist type and English in black letter; the glosses match the type of the text. The Latin and French originals lying behind Pynson's recut illustrations add another element that links this English book—whose final words locate it firmly in England, in

---

[25] Driver, *Image in Print*, 61–2.
[26] Driver, *Image in Print*, 3.
[27] Edward Hodnett uses to this cut (no. 1288 in his catalogue) as evidence that de Worde must have printed Reynard before 1500, pointing to the reappearance of the series in an early seventeenth-century printing of the text; *English Woodcuts 1480–1535* (Oxford, 1973), 15.
[28] Hodnett, *English Woodcuts*, 41–2.

'Flete Strete … / At the George: in Richade [sic] Pynsonnes place' (folium cclxxiiii)—to a wider world.

While it was de Worde who accelerated the illustration of books, both prose and verse, Caxton did produce some illustrated books, and one of them, as already noted, was the 1483 printing of the *Tales*. There are twenty-three blocks used to produce the forty-seven illustrations found throughout the text; apart from the feast cut already discussed, these are all individual portraits of the pilgrims.[29] Some of them, such as the portrait of the Knight, are quite generic in appearance, and indeed, this proves to be one of the easiest cuts to replace. For example, while de Worde uses many of Caxton's cuts for his 1498 printing, his knight is a different cut that he inherited from Caxton, one used in the former's 1483 *Game and Play of the Chess* (STC 4921). Richard Pynson's cuts were copied from Caxton's, but he added scrolls behind his pilgrims, and while most of these are not filled in, the one behind the Knight reads 'The knyght'—a redundant label that is surely not necessary as the Knight is (unlike some of the other pilgrims) instantly recognizable in the woodcut. The only other pilgrim with lettering on his scroll in the Clerk. It has been pointed out that the bow and arrows carried by Caxton's Clerk are improbable accoutrements for the scholar from Oxford, but Pynson retained these in his copied block. Perhaps Pynson labelled his Clerk in order to avoid confusion, although the fact that the scroll reads 'The Sclerts' is not helpful.[30] David Carlson suggests that Caxton's Clerk cut might have been designed for a yeoman and misplaced.[31] Whatever the source of the confusing details in the illustration, the Caxton cut and its reappearance in Pynson's printing are a reminder that error, or carelessness, or a lack of ability on the part of an artist, can have persistent and lasting effects.

While their details may be at times confusing, the cuts in the printings of the *Tales* by Caxton, de Worde, and Pynson all serve to help a reader navigate through Chaucer's long poem. In Caxton's printing, they occur in the General Prologue and then again to introduce individual tales. While later printings are less likely to illustrate both the Prologue and the rest of the text, the cuts continue to function as a visual guide. They can also create ways of understanding the poem that, while perhaps not deliberate, might nevertheless be meaningful. Caxton uses the same cut for the Franklin, Merchant, and Summoner, and for the Parson and the Doctor. Pynson's Franklin is also his Shipman, and so on: all of the early printings of the *Tales* reuse some blocks. Would a reader notice these repetitions, and if so, would they matter? At times the repetition seems intentional. For example, while Caxton does not identify 'Sir Thopas' as Chaucer's tale, as de Worde would do in 1498, he uses the same cut to introduce both 'Thopas' and 'Melibee' (and the latter is titled 'The Tale of Chaucer'). This figure does not look much like the Chaucer-pilgrim as he describes himself, nor does it look like the manuscript and print portraits discussed above. He does,

---

[29] David R. Carlson, 'Woodcut Illustrations of the *Canterbury Tales*, 1483–1602', *The Library*, 6th series, 19 (1997), 25–67 (at 26).

[30] Hilmo, 'The Clerk's Unscholarly Bow', discusses this portrait at length. Stephen Orgel writes that the banner reads 'The Scients', referring to the Liberal Arts, and argues that it responded to a 'felt necessity' created by the bow: 'Textual Icons: Reading Early Modern Illustrations', in Jonathan Sawday and Neil Rhodes (eds), *The Renaissance Computer: Knowledge Technology in the First Age of Print* (London, 2000), 64. However, while the banner might have been intended to read 'The Scients', it clearly does not.

[31] Carlson, 'Woodcut Illustrations', 29. Carlson argues, at 26, that the very specific details of some of the illustrations suggest that the woodcuts were derived from a programme of manuscript illustration, though the cuts tailored for other early printings suggest a specific visual source was not a necessary precondition for woodcuts with close links to the text they illustrate.

however, frame 'Chaucer's' contributions, in books that are clearly interested in the idea of the author.

(Broken) Transmission

As the overview at the beginning of this essay illustrated, the first generations of print did a great deal to transmit medieval English poetry to new audiences. It is important to note finally, however, that there were significant gaps in this transmission. *Piers Plowman* was not printed until 1550 (STC 19906, 19907, 19907a), and the printer's prologue, which discusses the metrical form and refers to the 'darcke' nature of the language, makes clear that it had by that time become somewhat strange. John Gower's *Confessio Amantis*, as we have seen, was printed by Caxton, and later by Thomas Berthelet (in 1532 and again in 1554), but the rest of his work had to wait until the nineteenth and early twentieth centuries to see print. When one considers how important his trilingual accomplishments clearly were to Gower, it is striking that his early print history muted that aspect of his *oeuvre*. Romances like *Guy of Warwick*, *Richard Coeur de Lyon*, and *Bevis of Hampton* did receive early print attention, and indeed *Bevis* continued to be printed in something very much like its medieval form into the early eighteenth century. But many romances were not printed at all in the early period; works like *Sir Gawain and the Green Knight* or the *Alliterative Morte Arthure*, now considered central to the romance canon, had no immediate post-medieval print presence. In some cases this neglect can be explained by the fact that a medieval poem might have survived in only a single manuscript copy, and as early print depended on manuscript, if that copy was not in circulation, the text could not be printed. Whether by accident or by design, a significant amount of medieval English verse did not make its way into the hands of early print readers, and when we consider the general decline in the printing of many medieval texts after the sixteenth century (Chaucer is a notable exception), we can see that the chains of transmission are often frayed, or broken entirely. Print brought English verse to new centuries and new readers, but some things were left behind.

CHAPTER 10
Verse Outside Books

Julia Boffey

Opportunities for encountering English verse in the fifteenth century need not always have involved scrutiny of a written copy in what we would now recognize as a book. Verse was declaimed or sung to listeners, inscribed on buildings and many portable artefacts, painted on hangings, and impressed onto items of food. Even when copied (or by the end of the century, printed) on parchment or paper, it was not always in a codex, but sometimes occupied space on a roll, or on a single sheet. This essay will outline some of the ways in which fifteenth-century poetry was transmitted in forms that did not involve books, reaching its audiences in a variety of other ways.[1]

Situations in which verse reached listeners rather than readers would have included a range of dramatic performances, from large-scale civic plays and pageants to smaller court or domestic entertainments where communities or families were gathered together (see Chapters 14, 22, 23). In some contexts, especially in religious communities or educational establishments, formal 'prelection', with a designated speaker reading from a book, perhaps serially over the course of several days, seems a possibility.[2] Other contexts probably warranted arrangements of other kinds, involving household or community members or occasional itinerant visitors, and the performance of materials that ranged from the instructive to the more readily entertaining: romances, popular narratives, ballads, and songs and carols of many kinds, some on topical themes.[3] Much of this material, circulating orally without the need for written copies, must have been lost. Written survivals tend to have been preserved in household miscellanies or through incorporation into other works such as prose histories. Some poems on contemporary events remained in oral circulation for many years and survive only in very late written copies. 'The Hunting of the Cheviot', a contemporary celebration of fifteenth-century hostilities on the border between England and Scotland, remained in a minstrel's repertoire almost a century later, and in the form of the broadside ballad *Chevy Chase* had a still longer life.[4]

---

[1] For relevant discussion and examples, see Douglas Gray, *Later Medieval English Literature* (Oxford, 2008), 106–22.

[2] See Joyce Coleman, 'Aurality', in Paul Strohm (ed.), *Middle English: Oxford Twenty-First Century Approaches to Literature* (Oxford, 2007), 68–85, for discussion of prelection, and *Public Reading and the Reading Public in Late Medieval England and France* (Cambridge, 2005), 72, for a review of arguments about the decline of public reading.

[3] Adam Fox, *Oral and Literate Culture in England 1500–1700* (Oxford, 2000), contains much that is relevant to the later Middle Ages.

[4] 'The Hunting of the Cheviot' is in BodL MS Ashmole 48; see A. Taylor, *The Songs and Travels of a Tudor Minstrel: Richard Sheale of Tamworth* (Woodbridge, 2012). A copy of *Chevy Chase* is preserved in the Percy Folio manuscript, BL MS Add. 27879; see J. W. Hales and F. J. Furnivall (eds), *Bishop Percy's Folio Manuscript: Ballads and Romances*, 3 vols. (London, 1867–8), 2.7.

Topical poems posted in public locations in the form of handbills must have necessitated forms of communal reading in order for their contents to be widely comprehensible.[5] By no means all bystanders would have been literate, and some surely must have relied on intermediaries to read aloud or summarize the substance of what was posted. A 'Balat set uppone the yates of Caunterbury' in 1460, recorded in a version of the prose *Brut* chronicle, advocates support for Yorkist lords who had returned from exile under Henry VI in terms which are a curious mix of plain speaking and macaronic allusiveness, and would surely have needed some explication for most of those encountering it:

Tempus* ys come falshede to dystroy,	*Time*
Tempus eradicandi* the wedes fro the corne,	*Time to be eradicated*
Tempus cremandi the breres that trees noye,	*Time to be burnt*
Tempus evellendi* the fals hunter with his horne.[6]	*Time to be brought down*
(49–52)	

Another pro-Yorkist poem makes pointed reference to the letters making up the names of Edward IV and his chief supporters, using these to form a mnemonic device:

Yerly be þe morowe in a somer-tyde*,	*early on a summer morning*
I sawe in a strete in london as I went,	
A gentyl-woman sittyng in chepe-syde,	
Syt wirkyng vpon a vestiment.	
She set xij letteris* in order on a rowe,	*twelve letters*
Þat I might right wele vnderstande,	
Þorought* þe grace of god it shal be knowe,	*through*
Þese xij letters shall saue all Inglande.	
A litel while if þat ye wol dwelle	
And yeue audience* all vnto me,	*listen*
What letters þei were, I shal you telle:	
Þei were drawen out* of þe a b c.[7]	*taken from*
(1–12)	

The London street scene invoked here suggests contexts in which one reader paraphrased or interpreted for others the content of posted materials.

The dual possibilities of spoken and written transmission are frequently invoked in forms of verse likely to have featured in social occasions. These would have included romances such as *The Sege of Melayne*:

---

[5] See V. J. Scattergood, *Politics and Poetry in the Fifteenth Century* (London, 1971), 25–6, 30–1; Wendy Scase, *Literature and Complaint in England, 1272–1553* (Oxford, 2007), 83–169. For verses posted in Coventry, see NIMEV 466, 1665, 3322.

[6] NIMEV 1544. Rossell Hope Robbins (ed.), *Historical Poems of the XIVth and XVth Centuries* (New York, 1959), 207–10 (the manuscript, untraced at the time of this edition, is now BodL MS Lyell 34); and see Scase, *Literature and Complaint*, 139–40.

[7] NIMEV 700; Robbins (ed.), *Historical Poems*, 218–21.

> All werthy men that luffes* to here   *love*
> Off chevallry that byfore us were
>   That doughty* weren of dede,   *bold*
> Off Charlles of Fraunce, the heghe kinge of alle
> That ofte sythes* made hethyn men for to falle   *times*
>   That styffely* satte one stede*.   *upright, horse*
> This geste* es sothe*, wittnes the buke,   *story, true*
> The ryghte lele* trouthe whoso will like   *honest*
>   In cronekill for to rede ...[8]   *chronicle*
>   (1–9)

This address takes in both those who 'here' and those with access to 'the buke ... for to rede'. The single surviving copy of *The Sege of Melayne*, in BL MS Add. 31042, may well have been made by its Yorkshire scribe Robert Thornton with household use and reading aloud in mind.[9] Another collection of entertaining and instructive material, now BodL MS Ashmole 61, was compiled by a scribe who seems to have specially adapted some of the contents to the needs of an assembled listening company, introducing features such as opening pleas for attention.[10]

Poems were a part of many social occasions, from presentations of gifts to celebratory feasts where elaborate table decorations and *tableaux vivants*, or 'sotelties', sometimes combined visual display with appropriately pitched verse.[11] It is not easy to imagine the material forms taken by poems in these events, since the texts that survive are transcriptions evidently made for the record. In the case of poems accompanying gifts, the words to be declaimed as the presentation took place were perhaps read aloud from single sheets or rolls that would later serve as exemplars. Lydgate's 'Ballade on a New Year's Gift of an Eagle, Presented to King Henry VI' is described in one manuscript as 'gyven vn to þe kyng Henry ye vj and to his moder þe qweene Kateryne sittyng at þe mete (*dining*) vpon þe yeris day (*New Year's Day*) in þe Castell of Hertford', which seems to indicate that a physical copy was handed over with the gift.[12] Similarly, some accounts of banquet 'sotelties' make reference to the provision of 'scripture' or written words accompanying the *tableaux*. At the coronation banquet for Henry VI in 1432, for example, one display depicted the king's dual Anglo-French ancestry: 'A sotelte, Saint Edward and Seint Lowes armed in cote armours (*tunics with heraldic colours*) bryngyng yn bitwene hem the Kyng in his cote armour with this scripture suyng (*following*): Loo here twoo kynges righte perfit and right good.'[13] Somehow the 'scripture' or written copy of the poem was a part of the

---

[8] NIMEV 234; 'The Siege of Milan' in A. Lupack, *Three Middle English Charlemagne Romances* (Kalamazoo, MI, 1990), 109.

[9] See Susanna Fein and Michael Johnston (eds), *Robert Thornton and his Books. Essays on the Lincoln and London Thornton Manuscripts* (Woodbridge, 2014), especially Fein, 'The Contents of Robert Thornton's Manuscripts', 13–65, and George R. Keiser, *Robert Thornton: Gentleman, Reader and Scribe*, 67–108 (especially 74–6).

[10] George Shuffelton, 'Is There a Minstrel in the House? Domestic Entertainment in Late Medieval England', *Philological Quarterly*, 87 (2008), 51–76 (at 58), and (ed.), *Codex Ashmole 61: A Compilation of Popular Middle English Verse* (Kalamazoo, MI, 2008); Karl Reichl, 'Orality and Performance', in Raluca L. Radulescu and Cory James Rushton (eds), *A Companion to Medieval Popular Romance* (Cambridge, 2009), 132–49. Douglas Gray, *Simple Forms. Essays on Medieval English Popular Literature* (Oxford, 2015), covers many works that circulated orally; minstrel performance of popular romances is discussed at 90–2.

[11] See the section on 'Occasional Verse', in Rossell Hope Robbins (ed.), *Secular Lyrics of the XIVth and XVth Centuries*, 2nd edn. (Oxford, 1955), 85–119.

[12] NIMEV 3604; Henry Noble MacCracken (ed.), *The Minor Poems of John Lydgate*, 2 vols., EETS, e.s. 107 and o.s. 192 (London, 1911 and 1934), 2.649.

[13] NIMEV 1929; MacCracken (ed.), *Minor Poems*, 2.623. See Robert Epstein, 'Eating their Words: Food and Text in the Coronation Banquet of Henry VI', *Journal of Medieval and Early Modern Studies*, 36 (2006), 355–77;

display. The tenor of such verse presumably depended on the nature of the occasion. We might suppose that stanzas declaimed at a feast would have been rousing and celebratory, but this was not always so: the 'sotelties' that marked John Morton's installation as bishop of Ely in 1479 were sobering, reminding the new bishop, and the assembled company, of their mortality.[14]

Most of the categories of verse discussed so far, disseminating news or particular opinions, sung or spoken aloud in contexts of social diversion or ceremony, were probably not expected to take striking material form unless designed for presentation or display. But for certain categories of verse surviving outside books, the material on which the words were registered was itself important to whatever meaning those words conveyed. Poems inscribed, painted, or incised on portable artefacts of various kinds, or on the fabric or contents of buildings, once constituted a large corpus. Many have disappeared, whether as a result of deliberate acts of destruction or simply in the course of time, but those that survive offer opportunities to consider how meaning could be generated by conjunctions of poems with a variety of host artefacts and environments.[15]

At their simplest, snippets of verse on material objects could remind users of the identities of their makers or donors. The pearl sword still among the civic insignia of Bristol, given to the city by Sir John Welles, a member of the Grocers' Company who was mayor of London in 1431–2, is inscribed with the words 'Jon Wellis of London Grocer & Meyr / To Bristow gave this swerd feir'.[16] Engraved on the inner side of an early fifteenth-century gold ring excavated in the nineteenth century at the site of the Benedictine nunnery of Godstow, near Oxford, is a lover's motto: 'Most in mynd and in myn hert, / Lothest from you ferto depart'.[17] Easily memorable verse on household items could remind users of moral precepts or nuggets of wisdom: a wooden and silver-gilt fifteenth-century mazer bowl, used for drinking wine, carries around its rim the proverbial couplet 'Resun bad [that] I Shulde writ / th[i]nk micul + spek lite' (*Reason commanded me to write 'think a lot and say little'*).[18]

The space available for text on objects of these kinds must have necessarily limited the choice of verse employed.[19] Short verse prayers and charms, and short devotional poems, were appropriate choices, and well known because easily memorized.[20] Verse

---

Claire Sponsler, *The Queen's Dumbshows. John Lydgate and the Making of Early Theater* (Philadelphia, PA, 2014), 147–66; Heather Blatt, *Participatory Reading in Late-Medieval England* (Manchester, 2018), 111–17.

[14] DIMEV 5633; see Anne Brannen, 'Intricate Subtleties: Entertainment at Bishop Morton's Installation Feast', *REED Newsletter*, 22:2 (1997), 2–11.

[15] A. S. G. Edwards, 'Middle English Inscriptional Verse Texts', in John Scattergood and Julia Boffey (eds), *Texts and their Contexts: Papers from the Early Book Society* (Dublin, 1997), 26–43, collects together much information.

[16] NIMEV 1796.5; M. E. Williams, *Civic Treasures of Bristol* (Bristol, 1984), 45.

[17] DIMEV 3550.5; now British Museum AF.1075. See 'The Godstow Ring', in R. Marks and P. Williamson (eds), *Gothic Art for England, 1400–1557* (London, 2003), 371. Other ring inscriptions, possibly fifteenth-century, include NIMEV 3892.5 and DIMEV 6173.5.

[18] NIMEV 2796.5; now New York, Metropolitan Museum of Art, Cloisters Collection 55.25. See T. B. Husband and J. Hayward (intros.), *The Secular Spirit: Life and Art at the End of the Middle Ages* (New York, 1975), 43–4. For the proverb, see B. J. and H. W. Whiting, *Proverbs, Sentences and Proverbial Phrases from English Writings Mainly Before 1500* (Cambridge, MA, 1968), M791 and T207. Other inscriptions on portable items, possibly fifteenth-century, include NIMEV 1426.2 (a slate bearing information about horse medicine); NIMEV 938 and 942 (inscriptions recorded on mazers).

[19] Some ambitious projects were nevertheless undertaken: in 1414 the French poet Charles of Orleans had both text and music of one of his songs, '*Madame je suis plus joyeulx*', embroidered with pearls on the sleeves of a garment. See Mary-Jo Arn (ed.), *Fortunes Stabilnes: Charles of Orleans's English Book of Love* (Binghamton, NY, 1994), note 21.

[20] Scholarship on medieval charms in England and Europe is extensive: see most recently D. C. Skemer, *Binding Words: Textual Amulets in the Middle Ages* (Philadelphia, PA, 2006). Studies of particular relevance to Middle English verse charms include R. H. Robbins, 'Medical Manuscripts in Middle English', *Speculum*, 45 (1970), 393–415; D. Gray, 'Notes on Some Middle English Charms', in B. Rowland (ed.), *Chaucer and Middle English*

charms in particular must have had an extensive oral circulation; their popularity can be gauged from the numbers of written copies that survive, and the contexts in which these were copied—often collections of handy items made for household use. Robert Thornton, the fifteenth-century Yorkshire scribe whose copies of romances for family reading have already been mentioned, included two verse charms against toothache in a section of one of his manuscripts devoted to medical remedies.[21] Copies of other fifteenth-century verse charms invoke an assortment of divinities, saints, and biblical episodes against the dangers of sickness (toothache, infection, worms), the challenges presented by thieves and rats, and a variety of other less specific perils.[22] As with much popular material, these texts were notably open to variation: a charm for staunching blood that begins by recalling Jesus's baptism in the river Jordan survives in a number of shapes and sizes, some more carefully versified than others:

> Ihesu that was in bedelem* borne   *Bethlehem*
> & bapty3ed in flem iorden*   *the river Jordan*
> thou command the blode of thys man
> (here name hym) that hyt stynte* & stoned* ageyn   *cease, stop flowing*
>
> Cryst þat was born in bedlem
> And bapty3ed in flem Iordan
> þat flod was wod*   *raging*
> þu sesedyst hys mod*   *calmed its anger*
> so sesy* þy blod.[23]   *stop*

Some surviving copies of charms include instructions indicating that these should be carried or worn about the person, or lodged in specific places. A charm 'Against the Night Goblin', invoking the protection of 'Sent Iorge, our lady kny3th' (*St George, Mary's knight*), indicates that it was to be written 'in a bylle (*document*)' and hung in a horse's mane.[24] Late medieval criticism of popular magic inveighed against such practices:

> Ther ben somme that make wrytynges and breuettys (*written documents*) full of crosses and other wrytynges. And sayen that alle they that bere (*carry*) suche breuettys on them may not perysshe in fyre ne in water: ne in other peryllous place: And ther ben also somme breuettis and wrytynges whyche they doo bynde vpon certeyn persones for to hele them of somme sekenesses and maladyes: And for admonycyon (*despite warning*) ne

---

Studies in Honour of Rossell Hope Robbins (Kent, OH, 1974), 56–71; T. M. Smallwood, 'Conformity and Originality in Middle English Charms', in J. Roper (ed.), *Charms, Charmers and Charming. International Research on Verbal Magic* (London, 2009), 87–99, and 'The Transmission of Charms in English, Medieval and Modern', in J. Roper (ed.), *Charms and Charming in Europe* (Basingstoke, 2004), 11–31; L. T. Olsan. 'The Corpus of Charms in the Middle English Leechcraft Remedy Books', in Roper (ed.), *Charms, Charmers and Charming*, 214–37.

[21] The charms in Thornton's manuscript are NIMEV 1292 and NIMEV 3709, fol. 176r.

[22] See the section on 'Charms', in Robbins (ed.), *Secular Lyrics*, 58–61

[23] NIMEV 624. Of the many versions recorded, the two here are from San Marino, CA, Huntington Library, MS HM 1086, fol. 176v (see R. Hanna, 'The Index of Middle English Verse and Huntington Library Collections: A Checklist of Addenda', *Papers of the Bibliographical Society of America*, 74 (1980), 235–58 (at 241)), and Cambridge, Trinity College MS O. 9. 26, fol. iv\`. See further T. M. Smallwood, '"God Was Born in Bethlehem ...": The Tradition of a Middle English Charm', *Medium Ævum*, 58 (1989), 206–25.

[24] NIMEV 2903, in BodL MS Rawlinson C 506, fol. 297; Robbins (ed.), *Secular Lyrics*, 61. For maximum efficacy, some prose charms were evidently to be written on edible materials and consumed: see K. S. Hindley, 'Eating Words and Burning Them: The Power of Destruction in Medieval English Charm Texts', in C. Kühne-Wespi, P. Oschema and J. F. Quack (eds), *Zerstörung von Geschriebenem: historische und transkulturelle Perspektiven* (Berlin, 2019), 359–72.

for predycacyon (*preaching*) ne for excom*m*ynycacyon (*excommunication*) that may be doo to them they will not leue it.²⁵

But even this writer proceeds to make an exclusion for 'symple people' who can be forgiven if they acted in ignorance; the wearing or carrying of spiritually instructive rather than apotropaic texts was not vigorously proscribed.

The practice mentioned here of binding written material onto the human body is attested in the survival of late medieval 'birthing girdles', long rolls of parchment or paper, to be bound around the bodies of women in childbirth, on which prayers and charms, occasionally in English verse, were inscribed, often alongside images. One vellum roll nearly six feet long (New Haven, CT, Beinecke Library, MS Takamiya 56), includes in its programme of combined texts and images six rhyming English lines on the number of drops of Christ's blood at the crucifixion, and two verse prayers on the elevation of the host.²⁶ The lines on Christ's blood are a version of a short poem found in another birthing girdle (London, Wellcome Library, MS 632) as well as in a variety of non-roll manuscript contexts. In the two rolls the lines are copied as continuous prose, without any attempt to mark rhymes or divisions between verse lines:

> The nomber off the droppys
> of blodde of ihe*s*u all I wyll re-
> herce* in generall. Ffyve hun-   *report*
> dred thowsande for to tell
> And . vij .* and fourty mylle   *seven*
> thowsande welle. Ffyve hun-
> dred also grete and smale.
> Here ys the nomber off
> them all.
>   (Beinecke, MS Takamiya 56)

In MS Takamiya 56 the elevation prayers are similarly dissolved into prose lines.

Conjunctions of images and texts for prayerful meditation are found in other kinds of roll. A series of Middle English verse prayers attached to images of Christ's wounds and the instruments of the Passion, the *arma Christi*, survives in ten rolls. Starting with the Veronica cloth, a relic of the crucifixion (hence its opening words, 'O Vernicle'), and invoking up to twenty-three further items such as hammer and nails, sponge, and crown of thorns, this series of devotions was relatively widely transmitted, and appears to have been considered especially appropriate for copying in roll form.²⁷ English verse translations of the 'Fifteen Oes', variant forms of a sequence of rhyme royal stanzas each beginning with the

---

²⁵ G. de Roye (trans. W. Caxton), *The Doctrinal of Sapience* (1489; STC 21431), sig. [Av] (quoted in Skemer, *Binding Words*, 134–5); see the edition by J. Gallagher, *MET* (Heidelberg, 1993), 55.

²⁶ NIMEV 3443, and M. Morse, 'Two Unpublished English Elevation Prayers in Takamiya 56', *Journal of the Early Book Society*, 16 (2013), 269–77 and '"Thys moche more ys oure lady mary longe": Takamiya 56 and the English Birth Girdle Tradition', in S. Horobin and L. Mooney (eds), *Middle English Texts in Transition. A Festschrift Dedicated to Toshiyuki Takamiya on his 70th Birthday* (Woodbridge, 2014), 199–219. At least one printed birth girdle survives (c1520; STC 14547.5): see Joseph J. Gwara and Mary Morse, 'A Birth Girdle Printed by Wynkyn de Worde', *The Library*, 7th series, 13 (2012), 33–62.

²⁷ 'O Vernicle' is NIMEV 2577. Important studies include R. H. Robbins, 'The *Arma Christi* Rolls', *Modern Language Review*, 34 (1939), 415–21 and A. E. Nichols, '"O Vernicle": Illustrations of an *Arma Christi* Poem', in M. V. Hennessy (ed.), *Tributes to Kathleen L. Scott. English Medieval Manuscripts: Readers, Makers and Illuminators* (London, 2009), 139–69. Among the essays in L. H. Cooper and A. Denny-Brown (eds), *The 'Arma Christi' in Medieval and Early Modern Culture, With a Critical Edition of 'O Vernicle'* (Farnham, 2014), see especially the edition of 'O Vernicle' by A. E. Nichols, 308–91, and R. G. Newhauser and A. G. Russell, 'Mapping Virtual Pilgrimage in an Early Fifteenth-Century *Arma Christi* Roll', 83–112.

words 'O Jhesu', itemizing and prompting meditation on images relevant to Christ's sufferings, form part of the content of some rolls.²⁸ The depiction of a woman owner in the illustrations to one of these may suggest a particular female interest in prayers copied in this form.²⁹

The manner in which larger rolls were used remains a matter of debate. Would a roll have been suspended from a nail or hook and viewed as long wall-hanging, or rather gradually unfurled as a viewer worked through a programme of private devotions? The survival of at least one carrying bag suggests that some were designed to be portable rather than kept in a permanent location on display.³⁰ But contexts where public, collective reading was envisaged must have dictated different kinds of use. An alliterative hymn to St Katherine, copied on a roll slightly larger than most of the *arma Christi* or prayer rolls, and including acrostics (one spelling out 'katerina' and another the name of the poem's likely author, 'Ricardus spaldyng') may have been made for a parish guild of St Katherine in Stamford, Lincolnshire. Its final stanza prays for collective protection:

> I grete þe*, most gracyous to governe hem* al   *greet you, them*
> Þat geder* þe to hir giyld*, hem for to gyde*.   *gather, guild, guide*
> Fe[n]d vs*, feer* fa[i]þful, þat vs no foly fal*   *defend us, friends, befall*
> For [f]eynthed* and freelte* we feel vs besyde.³¹   *weakness, frailty*
> (267–70)

In serving a communal purpose, and celebrating St Katherine's life, this roll functioned rather differently from talismanic girdles or devotional rolls offering programmes for private prayer.

Larger rolls opened possibilities of public display to be exploited for various ends, and proved ideal vehicles for illustrating fifteenth-century claims to the English crown, whether Henry VI's title as king of both England and France, or rival Yorkist and Lancastrian versions of the descent of English kings.³² The provision of verse on some of these genealogical rolls may owe something to the propaganda campaign instigated in France by John, duke of Bedford, regent during the minority of Henry VI. Bedford commissioned from the French poet Laurence Calot a poem on Henry VI's title to the crown, to be displayed throughout northern France; for England, in turn, Richard Beauchamp, earl of Warwick, commissioned from John Lydgate a translation of Calot's poem. Although it survives only in a

---

²⁸ NIMEV 2470 is in New York, Morgan Library & Museum, MS M 486; NIMEV 2469 in New York, Columbia University Library, MS Plimpton Add. 4 and New Haven, CT, Beinecke Library, MS Takamiya 112.

²⁹ The image is in Morgan MS M 486. See further D. C. Skemer, 'Amulet Rolls and Female Devotion in the Late Middle Ages', *Scriptorium*, 55 (2001), 197–227; M. A. Edsall, '*Arma Christi* Rolls or Textual Amulets? The Narrow Roll Format Manuscripts of "O Vernicle"', *Magic, Ritual, and Witchcraft*, 9 (2014), 178–209. Wider use is suggested by C. F. Bühler, 'Prayers and Charms in Certain Middle English Scrolls', *Speculum*, 39 (1964), 270–8, and by New York, Morgan Library & Museum, MS G 39, a roll containing Latin prayers, some invoking the protection of saints against the plague, copied and illustrated c1500 by a canon at the Premonstratensian Abbey of Coverham in North Yorkshire.

³⁰ Edsall, '*Arma Christi* Rolls'; Sarah Noonan, 'Private Reading and the Rolls of the *Symbols of the Passion*', *Journal of the Early Book Society*, 15 (2012), 289–301; K. S. Hindley, 'The Power of Not Reading: Amulet Rolls in Medieval England', in S. G. Holz, J. Peltzer, and M. Shirota (eds), *The Roll in England and France in the Late Middle Ages: Form and Content*, Materiale Textkulturen, 28 (Berlin and Boston, MA, 2019), 289–306. San Marino, CA, Huntington Library, MS 26054 was kept in a small silk bag: images and a description are available through the Digital Scriptorium at https://digital-scriptorium.org/. Portability may have been an element in the design of the late fourteenth-century roll copy of the 'Stations of Rome' (NIMEV 1172) in Chicago, Newberry Library, MS 32; see Jeanne Krochalis, 'The Newberry Stations of Rome', in Hennessy (ed.), *Tributes to Kathleen L. Scott*, 129–37.

³¹ NIMEV 1813; R. Kennedy (ed.), *Three Alliterative Saints' Hymns*, EETS, o.s. 321 (Oxford, 2003), 1–9. The roll is approximately 1630mm long and 280mm wide.

³² M. Lamont, '"Genealogical History" and the English Roll', in *Medieval Manuscripts, Their Makers and Users: A Special Issue of Viator in Honor of Richard and Mary Rouse* (Turnhout, 2011), 245–61, notes that over seventy English genealogical rolls survive from the fifteenth century.

manuscript anthology, Lydgate's poem invites readers to 'see' an outline of the family relationships, and must at some point have accompanied a visual representation of Lancastrian genealogy:

Verily, liche as* ye may se,	*just as*
The pee-degre* doth hit specifie,	*pedigree*
The figure, lo, of the genelagye*,	*genealogy*
How that God list for her purchace*	*wished to provide for them*
Thurgh his power and benigne grace,	
An heir of peas by iust* successioun,	*just*
This ffigure* makith clere demonstracioun.[33]	*image*
(123–9)	

Probably somehow associated with this poem, Lydgate's 'Verses on the Kings of England', a handy rhyme royal condensation of the English royal line from William the Conqueror onwards, was widely transmitted: invitingly malleable, it survives in different versions in nearly forty fifteenth- and sixteenth-century manuscript copies, and in early printed editions that include a single-sheet broadside.[34] Although not itself surviving in roll form, this poem clearly had some connection to another verse account of the kings of England extant in six rolls as well as in a number of codices.[35] In this poem, as the comparison below illustrates, the content of each of Lydgate's rhyme royal stanzas is recast in the form of a series of couplets:

[Lydgate:] The Sext Herry*, brouht foorth in al vertu,	*sixth Henry*
Bi iust title, born bi enheritaunce.	
Aforn provided*, bi grace of Crist Ihesu,	*previously appointed*
To wer too* crownys in Yngland & in Fraunce,	*two*
To whom God hath yovyn* souereyn suffisaunce	*given*
Of vertuous liff, and chose hym for his knyht,	
Long to reioissh* and regne heer in his riht*.	*rejoice, right*
(204–10)	

[Anonymous:] The vj^{te}* Harry broght forth in vertu,	*sixth*
Afore provyded by grace of Crist Ihesu,	
By iust titull borne by enheritaunce	
To were ij. crownys in Englond, Fraunce,	
Furst crownyd at Westmynstr þe viij* yer aftur his reigne,	*eighth*
And sithen* crownyd at Paris substaunce*,	*afterwards, ?in the flesh*
Ryally resceyued* for lord and sovereyne,	*royally received*
A rightfull kynge of England and Fraunce.	
Of whom our Lord hath yeve* suffisaunce*	*given, sufficiency*
Of vertuos lyve and chose him for his knyght,	
Now Lord him sende suche gouernaunce,	
Long to reiose and regne in his right.	
(181–92)	

---

[33] NIMEV 3808; MacCracken (ed.), *Minor Poems*, 2.613–22; J. W. McKenna, 'Henry VI of England and the Dual Monarchy: Aspects of Royal Political Propaganda', *Journal of the Warburg and Courtauld Institutes*, 28 (1965), 145–62.

[34] NIMEV 3632 and 882; MacCracken (ed.), *Minor Poems*, 2.710–16 (an expanded version, with stanzas on kings before William the Conqueror). The lost broadside text survives in the form of a twentieth-century transcription in BodL MS Firth d. 14.

[35] NIMEV 444; MacCracken (ed.), *Minor Poems*, 2.717–22; L. R. Mooney, 'Lydgate's "Kings of England" and Another Verse Chronicle of the Kings', *Viator*, 20 (1989), 255–89.

Roll versions of this poem also depict the pedigree, often with other illustrations, and two retain signs of being hung up for display.[36] In one case the stanzas on English kings are interwoven with the pedigree of the English family whose members commissioned the roll: the Sudeleys and Botelers of Sudeley Castle in Gloucestershire.[37] Family commissions of this sort were not unusual. Over the course of years from the fifteenth to the early sixteenth century, various members of the Percy family, earls of Northumberland, commissioned a roll displaying a Latin genealogy of the Kings of England, another that amalgamates an illustrated genealogy of English kings with a prose chronicle of the Percy family, and one more depicting kings of England from William the Conqueror to Henry VIII alongside a verse chronicle of the house of Percy, dedicated to the fifth earl.[38] The anonymous author of this chronicle, probably a household clerk, noting the difficulty of confirming an accurate family pedigree, and insisting that 'Soo liberall a lynage, a stoke so reuerent, / Soo prepotent a progenie of noble bloode discendid, / Oght to be regestrid, rembryd and pennyd' (12–14), works through family history from the Conquest onwards, signalling military successes, marriages, and deaths in capably handled rhyme royal stanzas. He speaks, it seems, to viewers of the poem:

> In this Roole* ȝe þat schall herre reede*, *roll, read here*
> Beholde and considere þe noble discent
> Of þis vth Erle. Marke it well in dede.
> His progenitours in mynde if ȝe will imprent* *have in your mind*
> It schall apper cler and also euident
> Of the grettest blode he is commyn*, ȝe can tell ... *come*
> (295–300)

But he also signals deeds for which there is no space in 'this lytyll booke' (304), as if roll format, with its emphasis on the visual, was only one option for the future transmission of his work.

Fifteenth-century manuscript anthologies preserve the texts of other poems originally designed for portable display. Some of these may have originally been included in tapestries, others represented on painted cloth hangings.[39] Lydgate's poem on the *Life of St George* is introduced in its earliest surviving witness as 'þe devyse (*account*) of a steyned halle (*tapestry, painted cloth*) of þe lyf of saint George ymagyned by daun (*sir*) Iohan þe Munk of Bury Lydegate'. Produced for a feast held by the London company of Armourers, the poem begins (like the alliterative hymn to St Katherine discussed above) with a stanza addressing spectators:

> O yee folk þat heer present be,
>   Wheeche of þis story shal haue Inspeccioun*, *be able to witness*
> Of Saint George yee may beholde and see
>   His martirdome, and his passyon*; *death*

---

[36] Mooney, 'Lydgate's "Kings of England"', supplies further details and lists of the manuscripts.
[37] New York Public Library, MS Spencer 193; D. Winkless, 'Medieval Sudeley. Part II etc.', *Family History*, 10 (1977), 21–39.
[38] BodL MSS Marshall 135 and Bodley Rolls 5; Alnwick Castle MS 79. The text in the last is edited by A. S. G. Edwards, 'A Verse Chronicle of the House of Percy', *Studies in Philology*, 105 (2008), 226–44.
[39] No Middle English verse survives in medieval tapestries, but the currency of tapestry verse is illustrated in the stanzas of French and Latin woven into a series of tapestries on the war of Troy acquired by Henry VII in 1486 (V&A Museum number 6-1887); see T. P. Campbell, *Tapestry in the Renaissance. Art and Magnificence* (New York, 2002), 55–64. Eleanor Prescott Hammond, 'Two Tapestry Poems by Lydgate: the *Life of St George* and the *Falls of Seven Princes*', *Englische Studien*, 43 (1910–11), 10–26, discusses the possibility that some of Lydgate's poems may have been conceived as tapestry poems.

>   And how he is protectour and patroun
>   Þis hooly martir, of knighthood loodsterre*,   loadstar
>   To Englisshe men booþe in pees and werre.⁴⁰
>   (lines 1–7)

The text of the poem, presented with one or more cloth hangings displaying images, may have been either painted on the cloth or attached to it in the form of a written copy, in the way that the texts of 'sotelties' must have been attached to table displays; on the specific occasion of the feast the poem was probably declaimed as well. Lydgate's connections with the civic elite probably lie behind his provision of text for the 'deuise' of *Bycorne and Chychevache*, scripted for some form of display in the house of 'a werþy citeseyn of London'. For this, a fat beast well fed with patient husbands, a thin one whose diet is patient wives, and representative men and women who confirm the nature of marriage as 'a double cheyne', were somehow 'pourtrayed'; the earliest witness preserves prompts between the groups of stanzas, indicating the different voices taking part, as if delivery in this case might have involved both a *compère* ('an ymage in poete-wyse') and other speakers taking different roles.⁴¹

Images and text seem to have functioned jointly here, with the paintings supplying visual details that could serve as reminders of whatever was 'pourtrayed' in live performance. Much of the success of a rendition would have depended on the presence of one or more speakers whose gestures could have directed audience interpretation. The survival from the very late fifteenth century of some stanzas devised by the young Thomas More to accompany a series of painted images supplies a useful analogy. More's poem, produced 'in his youth', for his father's London house, consists of eight English rhyme royal stanzas appropriate to depictions of the ages of man and the 'triumphs' of death, fame, time, and eternity; it is rounded off with a Latin stanza. In the single surviving witness, the collected edition of More's works printed in 1557 (STC 18076), the introduction mentions 'a goodly hangyng of fyne paynted clothe, with nyne pageauntes, and verses ouer euery of those pageauntes'; rubrics between stanzas describe what each image or 'pageaunt' represented. The stanza spoken by 'Manhod', for example, accompanied a depiction of 'a goodly freshe yonge man rydyng vppon a goodly horse, hauynge an hawke on his fyste, and a brase of grayhowndes folowynge hym'.⁴² The term 'pageaunte' used here of these images suggests the interesting quasi-dramatic nature of the display.⁴³

Tapestries and painted cloths may be portable items, but the places in which they were displayed were often significant to their meaning. Lydgate's *Life of St George* was an apt choice for display in the Armourers' hall, since St George was the company's patron saint; and the merchant household for which *Bycorne and Chichevache* was devised would have included both men and women alert to marital 'acorde ... and stryves'. Much of the

---

⁴⁰ NIMEV 2592; MacCracken (ed.), *Minor Poems*, 1.145–54; J. Floyd, 'St George and the "Steyned Halle": Lydgate's Verses for London Armourers', in L. Cooper and A. Denny-Brown (eds), *Lydgate Matters: Poetry and Material Culture in the Fifteenth Century* (Basingstoke, 2008), 139–64; Sponsler, *The Queen's Dumbshows*, 67–75, 82–8.

⁴¹ MacCracken (ed.), *Minor Poems*, 2.433–8. Sponsler, *The Queen's Dumbshows*, 88–93, discusses the possibilities of quasi-dramatic performance.

⁴² A. S. G. Edwards, Katherine Gardiner Rodgers, and Clarence H. Miller (eds), *The Yale Edition of the Complete Works of St Thomas More. Volume 1, English Poems, The Life of Pico, The Last Things* (New Haven, 1997), xvii–xxi, 3–7.

⁴³ Martha W. Driver, 'Pageants Reconsidered', in Carol M. Meale and Derek Pearsall (eds), *Makers and Users of Medieval Books: Essays in Honour of A. S. G. Edwards* (Cambridge, 2014), 34–47.

fifteenth-century verse copied or inscribed outside the context of a manuscript book was conceived for display in a specific location, even if it was not necessarily going to remain a permanent part of it. A number of Lydgate's shorter poems fall into this category, evidently designed for display alongside images or statuary in ecclesiastical or monastic environments. His version of *De profundis clamavi*, a prayer based on Psalm 130, commissioned by William Curteys, Lydgate's abbot at Bury St Edmunds, 'At his chirche to hang it on the wal' (168), combines lines on the psalm's significance with a verse translation in which each stanza is preceded by a couplet from the Latin original.[44] 'A Prayer to St Thomas of Canterbury' ends with a stanza addressing the poem as a 'litle Table' (*tablet*), to be copied for display.[45] Two prayers on Christ's passion must have accompanied images of some kind, the first recommending that devout spectators 'To-fore his cros ... shal the see, / Onys aday this compleynt ffor to reede (115–16), the second exhorting them 'Erly on morwe, and toward nyght also, / First and last, looke on this ffygure ... My bloody woundis, set here in picture' (1–5).[46]

As these poems suggest, many words, as well as many images, were present in English parish churches. One form of presenting texts was to affix them to 'litle Tables', of the kind mentioned by Lydgate: portable framed wooden boards, suitable for hanging near images or memorials.[47] No Middle English verse has survived in its original 'table' form, but manuscript copies of the Lydgate poems discussed above, and of some epitaphs to be hung at tombs, indicate that it once existed.[48] And certain items now lost remained available beyond the end of the fifteenth century to be recorded by antiquaries. A rhyme royal life of St Walstan written on vellum affixed to three wooden boards, once present at the home of the saint's shrine in Bawburgh church, Norfolk, survives in the form of a copy made in 1658.[49] Tables recorded from Stone Priory in Staffordshire offered a version of the lives of St Wulfhad and St Ruffin and a history of the Stafford family, both in couplets, and (possibly not in verse) a list of lords who came to England with William the Conqueror.[50] Medieval visitors to the priory of Worksop Abbey in Nottinghamshire could orient themselves and learn about its history from tables bearing Middle English rhyme royal stanzas directing the gaze to the monuments of notable benefactors: 'Thomas on the north-side is

---

[44] NIMEV 1130; MacCracken (ed.), *Minor Poems*, 1.77–84.

[45] NIMEV 3115; MacCracken (ed.), *Minor Poems*, 1.140–4.

[46] NIMEV 2081 and 702; MacCracken (ed.), *Minor Poems*, 1.216–21, and 250–2. See also C. Cornell, '"Purtreture" and "Holsom Stories": John Lydgate's Accommodation of Image and Text in Three Religious Lyrics', *Florilegium*, 10 (1988–91), 167–78.

[47] See Richard Marks, 'Picturing Word and Text in the Late Medieval Parish Church', in Linda Clark, Maureen Jurkowski, and Colin Richmond (eds), *Image, Text and Church, 1380–1600. Essays for Margaret Aston* (Toronto, 2009), 162–203 (especially 164–72), and M. Van Dussen, 'Tourists and *Tabulae* in Late-Medieval England', in F. Somerset and N. Watson (eds), *Truth and Tales: Cultural Mobility and Medieval Media* (Columbus OH, 2015), 238–54. Survivals from Glastonbury and York Minster illustrate what such tables may have been like: see Jeanne Krochalis, '*Magna Tabula*: The Glastonbury Tablets', *Arthuriana* 15 (1997), 93–118, and 16 (1998), 41–27; Vincent Gillespie, 'Medieval Hypertext: Image and Text from York Minster', in P. R. Robinson and Rivkah Zim (eds), *Of the Making of Books: Medieval Manuscripts, their Scribes and Readers. Essays Presented to M. B. Parkes* (Aldershot, 1997), 206–29.

[48] See for example 'O deth hough better ys the mynde of the' (NIMEV 2411), evidently displayed at the tomb of Ralph, Lord Cromwell, in Tattershall church; H. N. MacCracken, 'A Meditation upon Death, for the Tomb of Ralph, Lord Cromwell (c.1450), Lord Treasurer of England', *Modern Language Notes*, 26 (1911), 85–6.

[49] NIMEV 242; See M. R. James, 'Lives of St Walstan', *Norfolk Archaeology Society Papers* 19 (1917), 238–67; the transcription is in London, Lambeth Palace MS 935, article 8.

[50] NIMEV *1219.5 and 193; for the first of these, edited from BL MS Cotton Nero C XII, fols. 183–8, see C. Horstmann (ed.), *Altenglische Legenden*, neue folge (Henninger, 1881), 308–14; and for NIMEV 193, John Caley, Henry Ellis, the Rev. Bulkeley Bandinel (eds), Sir William Dugdale, *Monasticon Anglicanum*, 6 vols. (London, 1830), 6 (i).230–31. Both are discussed by Gordon Hall Gerould, 'The Legend of St Wulfhad and St Ruffin at Stone Priory', *PMLA*, 32 (1917), 323–37, and '"Tables" in Medieval Churches', *Speculum*, 1 (1926), 439–40.

layde / In a tumbe of alabaster ... Thomas Nevill treasorer of England, / Aboven the quere (*choir*) is tumulate (*entombed*).'[51] The author (named as Pigott) must have written to order, compressing informative content into the fifteenth century's favourite stanza form.

Texts were also present as more permanent fixtures of pre-reformation parish churches in wall-paintings and stained glass, on lecterns, fonts, carved screens, and painted cloths, and on funerary monuments. The shared bank of medieval iconographic traditions informing visual as well as other communicative media made for a fluid relationship between text and image. Poems on certain topics would have readily called to mind familiar images (a crucifix or a *pietà*, for example), just as by the reverse process certain images would have called to mind particular configurations of words (Christ's words on the cross, perhaps, or a Marian lament). These relationships have been productively explored in relation to medieval drama and in manuscript contexts, most recently with reference to the copiously captioned illustrations in the Carthusian miscellany that is now BL MS Add. 37049, for which the term 'imagetext' usefully encapsulates the combination of visual and verbal associations evoked.[52]

Of the many forms of 'imagetext' surviving in the stained glass, wall paintings, and furnishings of parish churches, some made their point with no need for words, simply including labels naming the figures depicted, or quoting relevant phrases from Biblical or other sources.[53] On occasion, though, verse was put to use. In glass once at the church of SS Peter and Paul, Heydon, Norfolk, Mary was depicted upbraiding blasphemers with words similar to those of 'A lamentacioun of our lady for sweryng' copied in a mid-fifteenth century miscellany.[54] The (still visible) donor figure in a wall painting of the coronation of the Virgin in St Mary's Church, Boughton, Oxfordshire, begs 'Leuedy (*Lady*) for this Joyzes five (*five joys*), led me the way of clene lyue (*sinless life*)', using a version of a couplet that appears in a number of manuscripts, including one of Robert Thornton's anthologies (Lincoln Cathedral MS 91).[55] The early fifteenth-century glazing of a window in the north aisle of the church of All Saints, North Street, York, depicts the Fifteen Tokens of Doom in a series of images accompanied by extracts from the anonymous northern poem *The Prick of Conscience*, in a combination made specially for local patrons (members of the Hessle and Henrysson familes) who are also represented in the glass.[56] In some other locations, widely circulating anonymous poems, often of some antiquity, were put to use. 'Erthe upon erthe', extant in many manuscript copies, accompanies paintings on one of the walls of the guild chapel in Stratford-upon-Avon, together with a well-known mortality lyric, 'Whoo soo hym be thowgh'.[57]

---

[51] NIMEV 4071; Dugdale, *Monasticon Anglicanum*, 6(i).123–5 (Dugdale transcribed a copy made in 1587, now BL MS Lansdowne 205, fols. 167v-69).

[52] M. D. Anderson, *Drama and Imagery in English Medieval Churches* (Cambridge, 1963); Jessica Brantley, *Reading in the Wilderness: Private Devotion and Public Performance in Late Medieval England* (Chicago, 2007).

[53] On labels in glass, see Christopher Woodforde, *The Norwich School of Glass-Painting in the Fifteenth* Century (London, 1950), 193–201, and Richard Marks, *Stained Glass in England during the Middle Ages* (Abingdon, 1993), 17–20.

[54] NIMEV 158.4; Rosemary Woolf, *English Religious Lyric in the Middle Ages* (Oxford, 1968), 397(the manuscript, Dublin, Trinity College MS 432, is erroneously described as the Book of Brome).

[55] NIMEV 2099; Roger Rosewell, *Medieval Wall Paintings* (Woodbridge, 2008), 280.

[56] NIMEV 3428; Ralph Hanna and Sarah Woods (eds), *Richard Morris's 'Prick of Conscience'*, EETS, o.s. 342 (Oxford, 2013): the extracts come from part five, lines 3966–6416; see also Sue Powell, 'All Saints' Church, North Street, York: Text and Image in the *Pricke of Conscience* Window', in Nigel J. Morgan (ed.), *Prophecy, Apocalypse and the Day of Doom*, Harlaxton Medieval Studies, 12 (Donington, 2004) 292–316.

[57] NIMEV 704 etc. and 4129; Linne R. Mooney, 'Verses upon Death and Other Wall Paintings Surviving in the Guild Hall, Stratford-upon-Avon', *Journal of the Early Book Society*, 3 (2000), 182–90, and Kate Giles, Antony

Death's approach features in many combinations of word and image that appear outside books.[58] A depiction of the 'three living and the three dead', a confrontation between gaily dressed young men and grinning skeletons frequently represented in wall painting, survives in the church of Holy Trinity, Wensley, North Yorkshire, with three monorhymed English lines.[59] The 'dance of death', a macabre pageant in which a personified Death invites into his dance representatives from different social levels and walks of life, was disseminated to fifteenth-century English readers especially effectively through Lydgate's *Danse Macabre*. Lydgate's poem was translated into English c1426 from French stanzas accompanying murals in the Church of Holy Innocents in Paris. He had apparently seen the original—his version refers to the 'exawmple / whiche that at Parise I fownde depict / Ones on a walle' (18–20)—and in different versions of his translation new victims were introduced, to exemplify the point that 'Deth spareth not low ne hye degre' (9).[60] The text was further revised to accompany images 'artificially and richly painted' on boards attached to the cloister walls of the Pardon churchyard near St Paul's Cathedral in London.[61] Other traces of the dance survive in wall-paintings elsewhere: those in the Guild Chapel at Stratford-upon-Avon, recently made more accessible in the course of restoration, preserve images seemingly close to those of the Pardon churchyard.[62] A variation on the dance of death motif featured a skeleton's encounter with a 'gallant', a fashionably-dressed and carefree young man, a scene once represented with stanzas of text in the Hungerford Chapel at Salisbury Cathedral.[63]

The passage of time inevitably means that many of these survivals are fragmentary, often obscuring the amount of text present. Furthermore, a good deal of the surviving verse consists simply of couplets or small extracts from longer poems.[64] For purposes requiring more substantial verse inscriptions, Lydgate's pre-eminence in the fifteenth century made him an attractive choice. Extracts from his *Testament*, 'A Lamentacioun of Our Lady Maria', and 'Ballade at the Reverence of Our Lady' were incorporated into the decorative programme commissioned by John Clopton (d. 1497) for the chantry chapel of Holy Trinity Church,

---

Masinton, and Geoff Arnott, 'Visualizing the Guild Chapel, Stratford-upon-Avon: Digital Models as Research Tools in Buildings Archaeology', *Internet Archaeology* at https://intarch.ac.uk/journal/issue32/1/toc.html.

[58] Douglas Gray, *Themes and Images in the Medieval Religious Lyric* (London, 1972), 176–220; Kenneth Rooney, *Mortality and Imagination: The Life of the Dead in Medieval English Literature* (Turnhout, 2011).

[59] See Rosewell, *Medieval Wall Paintings*, 346–7, and E. Carleton-Williams, 'Mural Paintings of the Three Living and Three Dead in England', *Journal of the British Archaeological Association*, 3rd series, 7 (1942), 31–40. Versions of similar lines (NIMEV 1270) accompany images in the fourteenth-century De Lisle Psalter, BL MS Arundel 83, fol. 127, and Taymouth Hours, BL MS Yates Thompson 13, fol. 179v. Robert Henryson's short poem, 'The Thre Deid Pollis' (NIMEV 2551) deals with the same theme.

[60] NIMEV 2590, 2591; Florence Warren and Beatrice White (eds), *The Dance of Death*, Early English Text Society, o.s. 181 (1931). For the wider context, see Sophie Oosterwijk and S. Knöll (eds), *Mixed Metaphors: The Danse Macabre in Medieval and Early Modern Europe* (Newcastle upon Tyne, 2011).

[61] Charles Lethbridge Kingsford (ed.), *John Stow, A Survey of London*, 2 vols. (Oxford, 1908), 1.327 (the cloister was demolished in 1549); Amy Appleford, *Learning to Die in London, 1380–1540* (Philadelphia, PA, 2015), 83–97; Blatt, *Participatory Reading*, 142–52.

[62] W. Puddephat, 'The Mural Paintings of the Dance of Death in the Guild Chapel of Stratford-upon-Avon', *Transactions of the Birmingham Archaeological Society* 76 (1958), 29–35; Mooney, 'Verses upon Death'; Kate Giles and Jonathan Clark, 'The Archaeology of the Guild Buildings of Shakespeare's Stratford-upon-Avon', in J. R. Mulryne (ed.), *The Guild and Guild Buildings of Shakespeare's Stratford: Society, Religion, School and Stage*, (Farnham, 2012), 135–70. See also Sophie Oosterwijk, 'Of Corpses, Constables and Kings: The *Danse Macabre* in Late Medieval and Renaissance Culture', *Journal of the British Archaeological Association*, 157 (2004), 61–90 (surviving depictions are discussed at 70–1 and note 43).

[63] NIMEV 143.8; Gray, *Themes and Images*, 207; M. Hicks, 'Chantries, Obits and Almshouses: The Hungerford Foundations, 1325–1478', in C. M. Barron and C. Harper-Bill (eds), *The Church in Pre-Reformation* Society (Woodbridge, 1985), 123–42.

[64] See, for example, NIMEV 1703, 2099, 3565.5.

Long Melford, Suffolk;⁶⁵ unaccompanied by specific images, the texts here make their point as part of a larger architectural design.

For particular commissions text could be produced to order. A seventeenth-century account of lost medieval windows in the cloister at Peterborough Abbey, illustrating the role of St Wulstan in its founding, noted that 'Every window had at the bottom the explanation of the History thus in Verse', preserving a transcription of these rough site-specific couplets.⁶⁶ At Carlisle, the lives of Saints Cuthbert, Anthony Hermit, and Augustine, represented in images painted in the late fifteenth century on the back of the choir screens, were expounded in fifty-six couplets, based on relevant parts of the Latin *Legenda Aurea*. Evidence that models for some of the illustrations to St Cuthbert's life came from a manuscript borrowed from Durham Priory suggests that some energy went into the plans for this multimedia programme.⁶⁷

Some commemorative poems are so short that they barely constitute verse, but others are more ambitious, incorporating details of place, date, and patron or donor.⁶⁸ The rebuilding of the Chapel of St Mary Magdalen at Holloway, near Bath in Somerset, instigated under John Cantlow, prior of Bath Abbey in the 1490s, was commemorated in a fashionably aureate inscription on the porch wall:

Thys chapell floryschyd with formosyte spectabyll*	*notable beauty*
In the honowre of M Magdalen prior Cantlow hath edyfyde*.	*built*
Desyring yow to pray for him with yowre pryers delectabyll*	*pleasing prayers*
That sche will inhabit* him in hevyn ther euyr to abyde.⁶⁹	*lodge*

At Carlisle, some time after the construction of the Prior's Tower in the 1490s, roof beams were embellished with couplets commemorating Simon Senhouse, prior from 1494–1521, with a stanza reminding spectators to 'Remember man þe gret pre-emynance / Geven unto ye by God omnipotente', and to show appropriate 'kindness' in return.⁷⁰ Verse of this kind was produced for secular as well as for sacred spaces. At Abingdon in 1458, a 'table' set in place to commemorate the building of bridges in the locality was inscribed with a 100-line poem, in four-line alliterative stanzas, the work of a local man named Richard Formande whose name appears in a concluding rebus. The stanzas incorporate much local detail, especially about labour and costs ('An C. pownde and xv. li. was truly payed / Be the hondes of Iohn Huchyns and Banbery also', 63–4), but they also occasionally recall the

---

⁶⁵ NIMEV 2464, 4099, 99; MacCracken (ed.), *Minor Poems*, I.329–62, 324–9, 254–60; J. B. Trapp, 'Verses by Lydgate at Long Melford', *Review of English Studies*, n.s. 6 (1955), 1–11, and David Griffith, 'A Newly Identified Verse Item by John Lydgate at Holy Trinity Church, Long Melford, Suffolk', *Notes and Queries*, n.s. 58 (2011), 364–7.

⁶⁶ NIMEV 1823.55; Simon Gunton, *The History of the Church of Peterburgh* (London, 1686), 103–12, and Dugdale, *Monasticon Anglicanum*, 1.377; Marks, *Stained Glass*, 90.

⁶⁷ NIMEV 1197–1197.8; Charles Gordon Vernon Harcourt, *Legends of Saint Augustine, Saint Antony, and Saint Cuthbert Painted on the Back of Stalls in Carlisle Cathedral* (Carlisle, 1868), 1–36. Edmund Colledge, 'Caxton's Additions to the *Legendi Sancti Augustiniani*', *Augustiniana*, 34 (1984), 198–212, and 'The Augustine Screen in Carlisle Cathedral', *Augustiniana*, 36 (1986), 65–99; Bertram Colgrave, 'The St Cuthbert Paintings on the Carlisle Cathedral Stalls', *Burlington Magazine*, 23 (1938), 17–19.

⁶⁸ See for example DIMEV 2829.5 (Addlethorpe, Lincs), a porch inscription; DIMEV 4393.5 (Tickhill, Yorks), an inscription in stained glass asking for prayers for local people who paid for the window.

⁶⁹ NIMEV 3584.5; the Rev. J. Nightingale, *Beauties of England and Wales*, 19 vols. in 26 parts (London, 1801–15), 13 (i).388.

⁷⁰ NIMEV 2806.77; J. H. Martindale, 'Notes on the Deanery, Carlisle', *Cumberland and Westmoreland Antiquarian and Archaeological Society Transactions*, series 2, 7 (1907) 185–206.

idiom of alliterative poems like *Piers Plowman* ('Of all Werkys in this Worlde that ever were wrought / Holy chirche is chefe', 1–2; 'It was a solace to see in a somer sesoun', 43).[71]

Verse represented in domestic contexts, in glass or painted onto walls and beams, seems mostly to have tended to the proverbial. An early sixteenth-century manuscript made for members of the Percy family records an extensive programme of verse in different parts of the family's houses at Leconfield and Wressle in East Yorkshire. Although the dates at which the words were incorporated into the decorative schemes of each room are not clear, they are likely to represent a fashion for interior decoration that was present in the fifteenth century, even if not now widely visible.[72] At Launceston Priory in Cornwall the decoration of the walls of the dining hall used by visitors and lay-workers incorporated improving proverbial couplets, while in Cheshire, Humphrey Newton, born in 1466, had an alphabetical list of versified proverbs known as the 'ABC of Aristotle' hanging in his house, perhaps for the instruction and edification of his children: 'These byn gode prouerbes to set in þe bordere of þe halle: **a** To amerus to aunterous and angure þe not to oft …' (*Don't be too amorous or too adventurous or get angry too often*).[73] Among surviving examples of medieval graffiti, some scrappy lines incised on a pillar in the church of St Mary the Virgin at Great Bardfield, Essex, look like a half-remembered extract from this same poem: 'Be noȝt to bold ne to bustusne[s] bost noȝt to mych' (*Don't be too bold or too brutish, and don't boast too much*).[74] Graffiti elsewhere that are sufficiently extensive to count as verse include some lines on 'The abuses of the age', from the church of St Lawrence, Ridgewell, Essex, echoing a poem surviving in at least fifteen manuscript copies made between the fourteenth and sixteenth centuries;[75] and the words of a fragmentary love poem, beginning 'With wiel my herte is wa', not attested in any other witnesses, from St John's Church, Duxford, Cambridgeshire.[76]

Like graffiti, the range of verse epitaphs chosen by individuals for inscription on tombs and memorial brasses offers a revealing glimpse of favoured modes and forms, and evidence of the increasing use of English (rather than Latin or French) in such contexts. Many of these inscriptions have disappeared altogether; some were recorded by antiquaries like John Stow and John Weever; others survive in more and less intact forms in the churches for which they were commissioned.[77] A large number of survivals are simply couplets: 'Erth

---

[71] NIMEV 2619.2; Ralph Hanna, '*The Bridges at Abingdon*: An Unnoticed Alliterative Poem', in Michael Calabrese and Stephen H. A. Shepherd (eds), *Yee? Baw for Bokes. Essays on Medieval Manuscripts and Poetics in Honor of Hoyt N. Duggan* (Los Angeles, CA, 2013), 31–44.

[72] BL, MS Royal 18 D II, fols. 195v–211v, in Ewald Flügel (ed.), 'Kleinere Mitteilungen aus Handschriften', *Anglia*, 14 (1892), 463–97; see also Blatt, *Participatory Reading*, 130–42. For proverbs in late fifteenth- and early sixteenth-century domestic glass, see Woodforde, *The Norwich School of Glass-Painting*, 199–201.

[73] Rossell Hope Robbins, 'Wall Verses at Launceston Priory', *Archiv für das Studium der neueren Sprachen und Literaturen*, 200 (1963), 338–43 (the priory does not survive but the verses were recorded in the fifteenth century in BodL MS Bodley 315); Newton's poem, NIMEV 3793, is copied in BodL MS Lat. misc. c. 66, fol. 26v; see Deborah Youngs, *Humphrey Newton (1466–1536): An Early Tudor Gentleman* (Woodbridge, 2008), 27.

[74] DIMEV 770; George G. Coulton, 'Medieval Graffiti, Especially in the Eastern Counties', *Cambridge Antiquarian Society Communications* 19 (1914–15), 53–62 (at 57). On graffiti generally see Violet Pritchard, *English Medieval Graffiti* (Cambridge, 1967), and Matthew Champion, *Medieval Graffiti: The Lost Voices of England's Churches* (London, 2015).

[75] NIMEV 1820; Pritchard, *English Medieval Graffiti*, 75–6.

[76] NIMEV 4206; R. M. Wilson, *The Lost Literature of Medieval England*, 2nd edn. (London, 1970), 179.

[77] Stow, *Survey of London*; John Weever, *Ancient Funerall Monuments within the United Monarchie of Great Britaine* (London, 1631), STC 25223. See also Gray, *Themes and Images*, 200–6, and 'A Middle English Epitaph', *Notes and Queries*, n.s. 8 [206] (1961), 132–5 (at 135: 'the majority of the rough verses that are used as inscriptions on tombs have no literary value. The sentiments are trite, the language awkward, the metre limping'); David Griffith, 'English Commemorative Inscriptions: Some Literary Dimensions', in Caroline M. Barron and Clive Burgess (eds), *Memory and Commemoration in Medieval England*, Harlaxton Medieval Studies, 20 (Donington, 2010), 251–70. Epitaphs were sometimes displayed on 'tables', of the sort discussed above.

my bodye I giue to the / On my sowle Iesu haue pite', from a brass in Great Ormsby church, Norfolk; 'God þat sittyth in Trinite / On the Soule of John Todenham have Mercy et Pite', from a memorial brass in the church of St John Maddermarket in Norwich.[78] Sometimes the intention to produce verse is present but not fully realised, as in an epitaph of 1473 commemorating Piers and Elizabeth Jon in the church of St Edward the Confessor in Romford, Essex:

> Her vndyr this ston lyes Piers Ion
> And Elizabeth his wyff lyeth him hard by
> On whos sowlys Iesu haue mercy
> Besech yow for cherite
> Sey a Pater Noster* and an Aue* *Our Father, Ave*
> The whych decessyd* the on and twentyth of Septembre *who died*
> In the yer of owr Lord God, on thowsand four hundred seuenty and thre.[79]

In practice, though, these inscriptions manage capably enough to insert details of the individual(s) commemorated into handy strings of couplets or single seven- or eight-line stanzas. As today, existing models could be tweaked to be made appropriate to specific cases: many examples start 'Here lies graven/idolven under this stone ....'[80] There were clearly some special favourites. A single rhyme royal stanza beginning 'Farewel my frends the tide abideth no man' is recorded in a number of churches and must have been widely known.[81] Another, beginning 'Such as ye be, such wer we / Such as we be, such shall ye be' is recorded in multiple locations.[82]

These last examples illustrate some of the favourite themes. Variations on 'Such as ye be, such wer we' are common, with occasional reminders that the living should 'make a mirror' of the commemorated dead.[83] Versions of 'Erthe upon erthe' and 'Whoso him bethought', two of the poems incorporated in the wall paintings in the Guild Chapel at Stratford-upon-Avon, are put to service.[84] The Latin phrase *Timor mortis conturbat me* (the fear of death confounds me) is incorporated into lines of Middle English in several epitaphs.[85] Allusion is made to the 'abuses of the age', sometimes with criticism of greedy executors and thoughtless children.[86] Pleasingly site-specific reference is often made to features of the church surroundings that have been supported by the benevolence of those commemorated. A verse inscription in the church of Barton Turf, Norfolk, for example, details gifts to the church made by Thomas and Margery Amys in 1445; and a long epitaph for Thomas Knolles recorded from the church of St Antolin in London recalls that 'His Fader & he to this Chyrch / Many good dedys they did wyrch (*work*)', before adding the reminder 'Example by him ye may see / That this world is but vanitie'.[87]

Epitaphs such as these fulfilled functions that had little to do with the aesthetic appreciation of artfully crafted poetry: they invited prayer for the souls of the departed, registered

---

[78] DIMEV 1168 (from 1440), DIMEV 1616.5 (c1440).
[79] NIMEV 1211.9; Weever, *Ancient Funeral Monuments*, 650.
[80] See the range from NIMEV 1205 to NIMEV 1211.9.
[81] NIMEV 765; Gray, 'A Middle English Epitaph'.
[82] NIMEV 3220.7.
[83] DIMEV 6581.
[84] NIMEV 702.5 and 4129.
[85] NIMEV 2066.5.
[86] NIMEV 2068.5, 1206.5, 2818.2.
[87] NIMEV 1187.5 and 1285.5; DIMEV 5808. Gifts made by John and Alice Spycer are similarly noted in the church of Burford, Oxfordshire (1437; NIMEV 1341.5) by Roger and Johane Hunt, Great Linford, Bucks (1473; NIMEV 1206.4); by Henry Nottingham, Holme next the Sea, Norfolk (1405; DIMEV 1799); by Joan and Johane Caxton, Canterbury (1485; NIMEV 2766.6).

acts of family and local piety, and enhanced their surroundings with reminders of the essentials of Christian teaching. The extent to which they were read and comprehended by all those who encountered them is moot. An inscription recorded at the very end of the fifteenth century on a brass in All Saints' Church, Spofforth, North Yorkshire, anticipates a range of reading skills on the part of beholders:

> With humble prayer I beseche The,
> That this scripture* shall here or see,   *writing*
> To say *De Profundos**, if thou letter'd be*,   *Psalm 130, if you can read*
> For ye saules* of Jane, my wiefe, and me,   *souls*
> Thomas Middleton, sometymes man of lawe*,   *formerly a lawyer*
> Under this stone are laid full lawe.
> Yf thou be unlerned and cannot reed
> For our soules and all Christen sowles med*,   *benefit*
> Say a *Pater Noster** and a *Crede**.[88]   *Our Father, creed*

Even the 'unlerned' seem to have been expected to recognize the invitation to intercessory prayer.

Much of the verse considered in this chapter functioned in combination with something else, whether a funeral monument, a building, a painted image, or a social event. It was in many cases expressly functional, in some cases offering conjunctions of words thought to afford protection, in others inviting readers to 'see' or 'remember' significant topics, or commemorating specific actions and individuals. In some circumstances it may not have been 'read', or even 'heard', but (as with charms) used in applied ways. Although mostly in formal terms undistinguished, it usefully reflects some of the characteristic features of fifteenth-century verse composition, underlining the predilection for rhyme royal and *ballade* stanzas, for instance, or the taste for polysyllabic rhyme words ('suffisaunce' / 'governaunce', and 'spectabyll' / 'delectabyll' are just two examples from the extracts quoted here), or the enduring popularity of alliteration. The material considered in this chapter is of course just a small portion of a larger world of verse that has not survived, much of it never recorded in written form. It nonetheless holds suggestive clues about the role of verse in fifteenth-century life, and about its prevalence and significance in a variety of contexts.

---

[88] DIMEV 6731.3; the inscription was recorded in the seventeenth century; Roger Dodsworth and John William Clay (eds), *Yorkshire Church Notes, 1619–1631*, Yorkshire Archaeological Society, Record Society Series 34 (Leeds, 1904), 96. Thomas Midleton, of Kirkby Overblow (d. *c*1492) married Joan, daughter of Sir William Plumpton.

PART III
TOPICS AND GENRES

CHAPTER 11
Biblical Paraphrase and Poems of Religious Instruction

Takami Matsuda

Biblical Paraphrases After Arundel

Continuation and change characterize English religious writings as we move from the end of the fourteenth century to the period after the Arundel Constitutions (1409). Nicholas Watson pointed out that 'vigorous copying of earlier works continues' and 'translation and compilation are key fifteenth-century modes'.[1] The impact of the Arundel Constitutions in restricting the composition, translation, and reading of vernacular scriptural and theological texts has been an issue among the students of fifteenth-century religious writings.[2] Watson regarded them as effectively coercive, restricting the extent of lay knowledge within the so-called Pecham's syllabus, issued by John Pecham, Archbishop of Canterbury, in 1281. The syllabus assigned the minimum doctrines the laity should know, which consisted of the Articles of Faith, the Ten Commandments, the Works of Mercy, the Seven Deadly Sins, the Seven Virtues, and the Sacraments. Now 'Pecham's *minimum* necessary for the laity to know if they are to be saved has been redefined as the maximum they may hear, read, or even discuss'.[3] Vincent Gillespie rather differently emphasizes the importance of Arundel's reformist successor, Henry Chichele, the archbishop from 1414 to 1443. After the Council of Constance (1414–8) whose 'publicly expressed purpose' was 'reformation of the institutional church in head and members',[4] Chichele's church became 'passionately interested in orthodox reform, and in the exploitation of the vernacular as a medium of orthodox, but still imaginative and inventive, texts suitable for the growing lay audience for vernacular books of religion'.[5]

In the later Middle Ages, translation in a broad sense of the word was understood as a process not just of conveying the literal meaning, but of elucidating the hidden layers of meanings and significance, i.e., *sententia*, of the text. The standard rendering of the Bible into the vernacular was a selective paraphrase that sometimes rearranged the scriptural text, usually adding glosses and apocryphal matter and expanding it with commentary and *allegoria*. The translator is therefore a commentator, compiler, and preacher at the same time.[6] In this respect, the Wycliffite version, verbatim translation of the Bible with

---

[1] Nicholas Watson, '"A Clerke schulde haue it of kinde for to kepe counsell"', in Vincent Gillespie and Kantik Ghosh (eds), *After Arundel: Religious Writing in Fifteenth-Century England* (Turnhout, 2011), 581–82.
[2] David Lawton, 'Voice after Arundel', in Gillespie and Ghosh (eds), *After Arundel*, 135–36.
[3] Nicholas Watson, 'Censorship and Cultural Change in Late-Medieval England: Vernacular Theology, the Oxford Translation Debate, and Arundel's Constitutions of 1409', *Speculum*, 70 (1995), 828.
[4] Vincent Gillespie, 'Chichele's Church: Vernacular Theology in England after Thomas Arundel', in Gillespie and Ghosh (eds), *After Arundel*, 12.
[5] Gillespie, 'Chichele's Church', 42.
[6] Cf. Ian Johnson, 'Prologue and Practice: Middle English Lives of Christ', in Roger Ellis (ed.), *The Medieval Translator: The Theory and Practice of Translation in the Middle Ages* (Cambridge, 1989), 70–3;

no glosses by followers of John Wyclif, was an exception and did not hinder the continued popularity of biblical paraphrases. The Wycliffite Bible, especially the Later version in which the heavily literal translation of the Early version is rendered more idiomatic, circulated widely throughout the fifteenth century, extant in some 250 manuscripts. As Ralph Hanna points out, the Wycliffite translation is not 'an oppositional force' to the strong indigenous tradition of vernacular biblical narrative, but rather helped to consolidate it.[7]

While uncensored and amateur access to theology in the vernacular was restricted after Arundel, there was a new concern with the education of the clergy, resulting in the production of Latin pastoral manuals often with macaronic elements.[8] The purpose they served was not to stimulate originality in relation to theology and ecclesiology, but to provide a secure channel to orthodoxy, functioning in the same way as Nicholas Love's *Mirror of the Blessed Life of Jesus Christ*, which conformed to the tradition of biblical paraphrase with orthodox commentary.[9]

In such a religious milieu, in which restriction paralleled a renewed interest in the instruction of the laity, verse biblical paraphrases continued to play a major role in promulgating not only biblical but more broadly catechetical knowledge among the laity. There was an objection to rendering the divine text into verse, as in Edmund of Abingdon's *Speculum Ecclesie*, which criticizes rhymed versions of the Pater Noster: 'for God him-self made hit; and þerfore he doþ gret schome and gret vnreuerrence to God þat takeþ him to Rymede wordes & queynte, and leueþ þe wordes and þe preyere þat he vs tauhte'.[10] But '[v]erse was still regarded as a maid of all work'[11] and as the manner of telling changes with the intended audience, the verse paraphrase was one positive way to render the word of God explicable, and more memorable.

In terms of indigenous tradition, we should bear in mind that biblical paraphrases of the fifteenth century come in the wake of giant enterprises of the previous century. *Cursor Mundi*, whose origin probably predates its earliest extant manuscripts of the first quarter of the fourteenth century, was still being edited and copied at the beginning of the fifteenth century as an 'open compilation', the work of different compilers 'into which separate poems were dropped and spliced'.[12] We also have a number of *temporale* narratives from the late thirteenth-century *South English Legendary*, that circulated independently in the following two centuries. To the later compilers, the *South English Legendary* 'was an open text, one that not merely could, but should be improved, adapted, and suited to local use'.[13]

Ian Johnson, *The Middle English Life of Christ: Academic Discourse, Translation, and Vernacular Theology* (Turnhout, 2013), 19.

[7] Ralph Hanna, 'English Bible Texts before Lollardry and their Fate', in Fiona Somerset, Jill C. Havens, and Derrick G. Pitard (eds), *Lollards and Their Influence in Late Medieval England* (Woodbridge, 2003), 153. Also see James H. Morey, *Book and Verse: A Guide to Middle English Biblical Literature* (Urbana, IL, 2000), 26: 'The critical difference lay precisely between translating Scripture verbatim, with no glosses, and selectively paraphrasing and rearranging Scripture, usually, but not always, with traditional exegesis and apocryphal additions'.

[8] Watson, '"A Clerke schulde haue it of kinde for to kepe counsell"', 580. Also cf. Gillespie, 'Chichele's Church', 22.

[9] Morey, *Book and Verse*, 43.

[10] Carl Horstman (ed.), *Yorkshire Writers: Richard Rolle of Hampole, an English Father of the Church and His Followers*, 2 vols. (London, 1895–96), 1.251; also quoted in Morey, *Book and Verse* 19.

[11] Douglas Gray, *Later Medieval English Literature* (Oxford, 2008), 339.

[12] Morey, *Book and Verse*, 100. On the evolution of *Cursor Mundi*, see John J. Thompson, 'Textual Instability and the Late Medieval Reputation of Some Middle English Religious Literature', *Text: Transactions of the Society for Textual Scholarship*, 5 (1991), 182–7; *The Cursor Mundi: Poem, Texts and Contexts*, Medium Ævum Monographs, 19 (Oxford, 1998).

[13] Thomas R. Liszka, 'The *South English Legendaries*', in Heather Blurton and Jocelyn Wogan-Browne (eds), *Rethinking the South English Legendaries* (Manchester, 2011), 41.

The massive Vernon manuscript, which was perhaps completed in the first decade of the fifteenth century,[14] is also an open compilation. It includes large portions of the *Northern Homily Cycle* and the *South English Legendary* as well as independent biblical narratives, so that the manuscript as a whole is, as David Lawton explains, a kind of a vernacular bible, or what the late fourteenth century envisaged as biblical literature in English.[15] The Vernon manuscript often includes early specimens of some biblical narratives which became more widely disseminated in the fifteenth century. For example, *La Estorie del Evangelie* (*The Story of Gospels*), the metrical life of Christ in 'four-stressed accentual line', appears in the Vernon manuscript with some rich miniatures. It was presumably first composed in Norfolk in the late thirteenth century as an independent poem, but was adapted as excerpts in the *South English Legendary* and *Northern Passion*, reworked with added Latin quotations, or carefully abridged for consistency well into the fifteenth century.[16] It is based on a gospel harmony with some additions from other sources. For example, there are short exemplary episodes apparently based on the bestiary, beginning:

> For a wis man seiz þat bestis be
> Hert ant neddre ant ern, þis þre
> Þat changiz þere lif þoruut þere kinde,
> For þus of hem iwrite we finde.
>   (65–8)[17]

Also, the Middle English version of Robert Grosseteste's *Chateau d'amour*, Richard Maidstone's *Penitential Psalms*, and the *Charter of Christ* make their first appearances in the Vernon manuscript; they would be disseminated widely in fifteenth-century manuscripts.[18]

The *South English Legendary* and *Cursor Mundi* continued to grow and diversify in the fifteenth century; about half of the extant manuscripts were produced after 1400. Some biblical narratives originally composed in the fourteenth century, or earlier, are extant only in fifteenth-century manuscripts. The stanzaic *Quatrefoil of Love*, the life of Christ and Mary set within the 'love-rune' tradition, which consists of 520 alliterative lines with bob and wheel, was probably composed in the middle of the fourteenth century, but it survives only in two fifteenth-century manuscripts.[19] It is not surprising that English biblical literature as a whole survives most in fifteenth-century manuscripts.[20]

Old Testament Paraphrases

The Middle English Metrical Paraphrase of the Old Testament stands out by its length. It is 18,372 lines in twelve-lines rhymed stanzas which, though composed around 1380 in Yorkshire, is extant in two mid-fifteenth-century manuscripts. The work paraphrases the

---

[14] Wendy Scase, '2.2 Date and Provenance', in Wendy Scase (ed.), *The Vernon Manuscript: A Facsimile Edition of Oxford, Bodleian Library MS. Eng. Poet. A. 1*, Bodleian Digital Texts, 3 (Oxford, 2011).
[15] David Lawton, 'The Bible', in Roger Ellis (ed.), *The Oxford History of Literary Translation in English: Volume 1 To 1550* (Oxford, 2008), 216–7.
[16] Celia Millward (ed.), *La Estorie del Evangelie: A Parallel-Text Edition*, MET 30 (Heidelberg, 1998), 56, 80; NIMEV 3194; see also Morey, *Book and Verse*, 205–8.
[17] Quoted from London, Dulwich College MS 22 (c1300), the earliest extant manuscript of *Estoire* (Millward, 92). Also see Morey, *Book and Verse*, 206n.
[18] Lawton, 'The Bible', 216.
[19] Israel Gollancz and Magdalene M. Weale (eds), *The Quatrefoil of Love*, EETS, o.s. 195 (London, 1935); NIMEV 1453; also see Morey, *Book and Verse*, 313–4.
[20] Morey, *Book and Verse*, 26.

Old Testament from Genesis as far as to 4 Kings, and then Tobias, Esther, Judith, and Job, excising non-narrative materials (such as Leviticus on Mosaic Law) and ending with two episodes of martyrdom from 2 Machabees. Although it relies silently on the Old French metrical paraphrase of the Old Testament and makes occasional uses of the previous Middle English versions including *Cursor Mundi*, it is the most sustained paraphrase into Middle English of Peter Comestor's *Historia Scholastica* (c1170), arguably the most popular biblical narrative in the late Middle Ages, whose influence on Middle English biblical narratives is pervasive.[21]

The *Paraphrase*-poet is aware of its great length ('This buke is of grett degré', 13) but declares that it was set in a paraphrase by 'the maystur of storyse' (i.e., Peter Comester) to present the important highlights of the Bible, especially narrative matters:

> For sympyll men soyn forto se,
> settes yt thus in this schort assyse;
> And in moyr schort maner
> is my mynd forto make yt,
> That men may lyghtly leyre
> to tell and undertake yt.
>   (19–24)

(For the uneducated men to understand quickly, [Comester] sets it thus in this short paraphrase; it is my intention to make it even shorter, so that men can easily learn to recite and understand it.)

Towards the end, he again specifies that he has translated it 'in Ynglysch lawd men forto lere! / Insampyll may men here se / to be trew in trowyng' ('in English for the uneducated men to learn! Men may here see examples to be faithful in belief', 17744–6). This is however not just a narrative paraphrase, as it is also stated that 'all wer fygurs fayr to fald / how commyng of Crist myght be kawn' ('all were attractive figures to tell how the coming of Christ might be perceived', 31–2). Also, the poet relates the biblical stories to the present to arouse the interest of contemporary readers in the teachings drawn from the Bible, so that it becomes what its editor describes as a 'romantic Scripture: a holy text that becomes at once ancient history and present reality'.[22]

---

[21] Michael Livingston (ed.), *The Middle English Metrical Paraphrase of the Old Testament* (Kalamazoo, MI, 2011), 5–7; NIMEV 944; Morey, *Book and Verse*, 146. On Peter Comester, see James H. Morey, 'Peter Comestor, Biblical Paraphrase, and the Medieval Popular Bible', *Speculum*, 68 (1993), 6–35, especially 35. *Historia* served not only as the basis of thirteenth- and fourteenth-century English biblical paraphrases including *Cursor Mundi* and the translation of Ranulf Higden's *Polychronicon*, but was also the source of several other biblical paraphrases including *Genesis and Exodus*, the early fourteenth-century verse rendering that goes as far as to the death of Moses (NIMEV 2072), the *History of the Patriarks*, the fifteenth-century prose paraphrase of the Genesis (Mayumi Taguchi (ed.), *The Historye of the Patriarks*, MET 42 [Heidelberg, 2010]) and *Old Testament History* in verse (NIMEV 3973), the *temporale* narrative of the *South English Legendary* which survive in ten late fourteenth- and fifteenth-century manuscripts in whole or part. Morey claims that '[a]bridging the *Historia* was a popular fifteenth-century pastime' ('Peter Comestor', 8, n.6) while Lawton suggests that '[i]t may be that in England Comestor's interest in linear salvation history militated against more typological systems pairing Old and New Testaments as their structural principle. The most popular work of the latter kind in fourteenth-century Europe, *Speculum humane salvationis*, was not translated into English until c1420, and only one manuscript survives. It too is indebted to Comestor' (Lawton, 'The Bible', 212).

[22] Livingston, *Middle English Metrical Paraphrase*, 40–1.

Another notable Old Testament narrative is the *Storie of Asneth*, which is an apocryphal spin-off of the story of Joseph, triggered by parts of Genesis (41.45 and 50) that report Joseph's marriage to Asneth, daughter of Potiphar. It consists of 933 lines in heavily alliterating rhyme royal stanzas, originally composed in West Midland dialect, and is extant in one early fifteenth-century manuscript.[23] Opening with a *chanson d'aventure* framework in which the narrator says he undertook the translation from Latin at the request of a lady (La Bele), the poem focuses on Asneth's gradual change of feeling towards Joseph that culminates in their marriage, with the biblical story of Joseph in the background.

The poem can be read as a conversion narrative of an independent woman. Asneth is first against the arranged marriage but when she actually meets Joseph and finds him respectable, decides to impose harsh penance for seven days on herself, which is approved by an angel and wins over Joseph. After the marriage, calling herself a handmaid, she helps Joseph well and prudently in his absence, taking over his administrative role. It also has an element of conduct literature for young women, promoting for a noble readership a 'mixed life' in which a married life is compatible with piety.[24]

Penitential Monologues

The sections of the Old Testament that can offer a best model for devotional practice are paraphrases of the Book of Job and the Penitential Psalms. They both belong to a larger 'trend for the English versification of key liturgical texts coupled with devotional gloss'.[25]

The *Pety Job* ('the little Job'), so entitled in manuscripts as it is an abridgement of the Job story, is the lament and complaint of Job, which uses Job's questionings to initiate meditation on the state of the self and the world.[26] The poem, extant in two verse versions, is structured as a continuous penitential monologue, although in some manuscripts each stanza is headed by the corresponding Latin verse from the Office of the Dead. One version consists of 418 four-stress lines in eight-line stanzas and is preserved in BodL MS Digby 102, an orthodox penitential miscellany compiled in the first quarter of the fifteenth century.[27] As the last item in the so-called 'Digby 102 Poems', similar in its orthodox and practical religious orientation to the series of religious lyrics in the Vernon manuscript, this version ends with a final explicit warning to those in office or in power, reminding the reader of the sternness of the God that judges every action and movement (even the twinkling of an eye), let alone 'Benefice, auauncement, house or londe, / The leste bargayn þat he dede bye' (417–8).

The other version, 684 irregular four-stress verses in twelve-line stanzas with a complex rhyme scheme, is extant in five manuscripts, all of the fifteenth century, erroneously attributed to Richard Rolle in some.[28] With each stanza ending with 'Parce mihi, Domine!'

---

[23] Russell A. Peck (ed.), *Heroic Women from the Old Testament in Middle English Verse* (Kalamazoo, MI, 1991), 16; NIMEV 367; Morey, *Book and Verse*, 159.

[24] Cathy Hume, '*The Storie of Asneth*: A Fifteenth-century Commission and the Mystery of its Epilogue', *Medium Ævum*, 82 (2013), 46–8.

[25] Annie Sutherland, *English Psalms in the Middle Ages 1300–1450* (Oxford, 2015), 39.

[26] It is also known as the *Nine Lessons of the Dirige* because it paraphrases the nine lessons (passages) from the Book of Job used in the Matins of the Office of the Dead (*Dirige* being the first word in the antiphon) followed by a paraphrase of responses after the last lesson. The nine lessons are: (1) Job 7.16–21, (2) Job 10.1–7, (3) Job 10.8–12, (4) Job 13.22–8, (5) Job 14.1–6, (6) Job 14.13–6, (7) Job 17.1–3, 11–25, (8) Job 19.20–7, and (9) Job 10.18–22 (Morey, *Book and Verse*, 168).

[27] NIMEV 251; Helen Barr (ed.), *The Digby Poems* (Exeter, 2009), 304–27 (the manuscript is described at 1–2).

[28] Susanna Greer Fein (ed.), *Moral Love Songs and Laments* (Kalamazoo, MI, 1998), 289–359; NIMEV 1854.

as a refrain, the voice of Job gradually moves, along the nine lessons, from personal utterance of regret and repentance of sin to a call for mercy and divine aid. As in the version in Digby 102, the poem meditates successively on the mutability of life, contempt for the body, and the dread of approaching death and the doom, touching upon a number of popular motifs of death and mutability such as signs of death and false executors. It expresses the call to mercy more persistently than does the Digby 102 version, ending with a prayer to avoid hell. Though the poem has a dramatic and narrative value as a penitential monologue of the suffering Job, it is also a performative text, in that 'reading becomes an activity pursued solely for spiritual improvement' just as the lessons from the Office of the Dead are expected to do in the Primers.[29] It has a powerful appeal to the mind uneasily balancing itself between divine reliance and self-negation.

Another verse handling of the story of Job is the *Metrical Life of Job*, preserved in one fifteenth-century manuscript. This is the retelling of the plight of Job, corresponding only to the narrative frame at the beginning and the end of the Book of Job (1–2, 42), disregarding the dialogue section almost entirely.[30] It tells how Job was repeatedly persecuted by 'this tortuose serpent, oure ancient enemy of hell' (43), with such added details as Job rewarding minstrels with scabs that miraculously turn into gold, and the anger and rebuke of Job's wife for his action. Job's patience and his belief in providence are duly emphasized.

The Penitential Psalms also provide, like the *Pety Job*, a penitential monologue closely linked to private prayer. As a book for private prayer and meditation, the Psalter gradually gave way to the Book of Hours but the Psalms always remained central to lay devotion; they provided the core text for the office of the Virgin Mary, while the seven Penitential Psalms (6, 31, 37, 50, 101, 129, 142 in the Vulgate) were a standard component of the Book of Hours. The Penitential Psalms were found especially suitable for private devotion because David's emotional utterances move from repentance of sin to assurance of pardon.[31] Also, since each of the seven Psalms correspond to the seven deadly sins—wrath, pride, gluttony, lechery, avarice, envy, and sloth in that order—they can serve a didactic purpose.[32]

In the fifteenth century, there are two verse paraphrases, one attributed to Richard Maidstone (d. 1396), a Carmelite friar and an Oxford theologian, extant in twenty-seven manuscripts including partial versions, and the second to the Franciscan friar, Thomas Brampton (c1414), extant in six manuscripts,[33] containing stanzas apparently directed towards Henry V.[34] Although their rhyme schemes differ, both create from the Penitential Psalms one long poem of eight-line stanzas, each stanza paraphrasing and commenting on an individual verse. These formal similarities suggest the possible influence of

---

[29] Fein, *Moral Love Songs*, 294.

[30] G. N. Garmonsway and R. R. Raymo, 'A Middle English Metrical Life of Job', in Arthur Brown and Peter Foote (eds), *Early English and Norse Studies Presented to Hugh Smith in Honour of his Sixtieth Birthday* (London, 1963), 78; NIMEV 2208.

[31] Annie Sutherland, 'Performing the Penitential Psalms in the Middle Ages', in Almut Suerbaum and Manuele Gragnolati (eds), *Aspects of the Performative in Medieval Culture* (Berlin, 2010), 17–21.

[32] Michael P. Kuczynski, *Prophetic Song: The Psalms as Moral Discourse in Late Medieval England* (Philadelphia, PA, 1995), 135.

[33] Valerie Edden (ed.), *Richard Maidstone's Penitential Psalms, ed. from Bodl. MS Rawlinson A 389*, MET 22 (Heidelberg, 1990); NIMEV 1961; Morey, *Book and Verse*, 177–80; James R. Kreuzer, 'Thomas Brampton's Metrical Paraphrase of the Seven Penitential Psalms: A Diplomatic Edition of the Version in MS Pepys 1584 and MS Cambridge University Ff 2. 38 with Variant Readings from All Known Manuscripts', *Traditio*, 7 (1951), 359–403; NIMEV 1591; Morey, *Book and Verse*, 180–2.

[34] Lynn Staley, 'The Penitential Psalms: Conversion and the Limits of Lordship', *Journal of Medieval and Early Modern Studies*, 37 (2007), 245–7.

Maidstone's version on Brampton's.³⁵ Both versions seem pro-ecclesiastical, asking for 'sustained meditative reading and engagement', and 'eager to associate the devotional material provided by their texts with the liturgical and sacramental practices of the church'.³⁶

In Maidstone's paraphrase, each stanza is preceded by the Latin text which is translated in the first half of the stanza, to be followed by the explicatory supplementary material in the later half. In Brampton, however, although in each stanza translation is followed by gloss as in Maidstone, it is not accompanied with the Vulgate text, so that the paraphrase claims a self-conscious poetic identity independent of the Psalms.³⁷ The speaker often asks for mercy in a straightforward and sometimes almost audacious plea, expressing personal anxiety more readily than Maidstone. It vividly recalls moral failings ('My woundis be Rotyn and festirith with in / Because of onwise gouernaunce', 35.3–4) as well as duties of the clergy ('Preestys perfyte in ther leuyng / Schulden telle þe peple þe ry3t waye', 96.1–2).³⁸ Both versions were probably read alongside other devotional and catechetical materials in Middle English and Latin in the same manuscript, including the *Pety Job*.³⁹ They share with the *Pety Job* the dramatic individuality that makes them performative texts. Understanding that 'David's words speak to the present, to the souls of individuals and collective soul of society', both Maidstone and Brampton recover from the Psalms 'not only the passions but also the moral teachings latent in David's poetry'.⁴⁰

As the verse paraphrase of an individual psalm, Psalm 50, one of the Penitential Psalms typically understood as an expression of David's penitence following his adultery with Bathsheba, seems to have been especially popular, being a routine reading for private devotion and also included in the Matins of the Office of the Dead.⁴¹ 'Haue mercy on me' (240 lines, c1400) is a verse paraphrase of Psalm 50 in the fifteenth-century London Thornton Manuscript, BL MS Add. 31042, that fulfills the same penitential function as Maidstone's version.⁴² We may also note that six of the twenty-seven manuscripts of Maidstone's *Penitential Psalms* contain only this Psalm.⁴³

Passion Narratives

The verse life of Christ retained its popularity throughout the Middle Ages.⁴⁴ One characteristic of the lives of Christ as a genre is the accepted variety in the manner of telling, to

---

³⁵ Sutherland, *English Psalms*, 39–40; Staley, 'The Penitential Psalms', 224.
³⁶ Sutherland, 'Performing the Penitential Psalms', 25.
³⁷ Sutherland, *English Psalms*, 49. Cf. Francis Leneghan, 'Introduction: A Case Study of Psalm 50.1–3 in Old and Middle English', in Tamara Atkin and Francis Leneghan (eds), *The Psalms and Medieval English Literature: From the Conversion to the Reformation* (Cambridge, 2017), 29.
³⁸ Cf. Sutherland, 'Performing the Penitential Psalms', 26.
³⁹ The Wheatley manuscript contains Richard Maidstone's *Penitential Psalms* followed immediately by a prose version of the *Pety Job*. The manuscripts of Brampton's paraphrase, Cambridge, Magdalene College, MS Pepys 1584 and CUL MS Ff. 2. 38, also contain the *Pety Job*. See Sutherland, *English Psalms*, 39.
⁴⁰ Kuczynski, *Prophetic Song*, 135.
⁴¹ On the popularity of the Psalm 50, see Leneghan, 'Introduction', 3–30; John J. Thompson, 'Literary Associations of an Anonymous Middle English Paraphrase of Vulgate Psalm L', *Medium Ævum*, 57 (1988), 38–55; Morey, *Book and Verse*, 191–2.
⁴² Susanna Greer Fein, '*Haue Mercy of Me* (Psalm 51): An Unedited Alliterative Poem from the London Thornton Manuscript', *Modern Philology*, 86 (1989), 223–41; NIMEV 990.
⁴³ Edden, *Richard Maidstone*, 12–20.
⁴⁴ On the account of Middle English lives of Christ up to the end of the fifteenth century, see Elizabeth Salter, *Nicholas Love's 'Myrrour of the Blessed Lyf of Jesu Christ'*, Analecta Cartusiana, 10 (Salzburg, 1974), 73–118.

achieve various combinations of narrative and commentary or of didacticism and devotion. The tradition of gospel harmonies existed in Middle English prose, for example as *Oon of Foure*, the translation of mid-twelfth-century Clement of Llanthony's *Unum ex Quattuor*, and the fifteenth-century *Pepysian Gospel Harmony*. Translators worked as compilers who, as Ian Johnson maintains, combined and harmonized 'four different but equally authoritative evangels' that 'accord in sentence but differ in telling'.[45] They chose the mode accordingly in view of the intended readers to fulfill the common function of instructing the laity in the words and works of Christ and of 'stirring the soul affectively towards the love of God by a sympathetic rendering of Christ's life and particularly His Passion'.[46]

Other than the sections of the *South English Legendary* that circulated independently,[47] there are several verse lives of Christ extant in fifteenth-century manuscripts. The *Stanzaic Life of Christ* consists of 10,840 octosyllabic lines grouped in four-line stanzas, extant in three fifteenth-century manuscripts.[48] Probably composed at St Werburgh's Abbey, Chester, it is a *compilatio* encyclopaedic in its scope that deals with the events from the Conception to Pentecost. It is based on Ranulf Higden's *Polychronicon*, whose Books Two to Four summarize biblical history, with the addition of material from the *Legenda Aurea* which replaces *Polychronicon* as the main source in the later part of the poem.[49]

The author insists on naming the authorities:

> So þat no fable, in good fay,
> Þat fals ys, shal he fynde non,
> But thyng þat trewe ys & verray,
> And wyttnesse names wryten þere-on.
>
> (25-8)

Authorities are often named in the Latin headings that group the stanzas. There are repeated references to Peter Comestor's *Historia Scholastica* as well as to such major names as Augustine, Gregory, and Bernard of Clairvaux. The text is interspersed with key Latin phrases which are almost always followed by the Middle English translation.[50] The Latin functions as a supplementary 'safety net', added to legitimize and strengthen the English text.[51] It is an expository work set in a liturgical framework. Familiarity with major episodes is taken for granted but examples of miracles and apocryphal legends are often given in detail, such as the events leading to the death of Pilate (6433–816) taken from the *Legenda Aurea*. It elucidates main doctrinal issues relating to the life of Christ, such as different meanings of Christ's tears (5621–60), the significance of three days between the death and the Resurrection, and Jesus's ten appearances between the Resurrection and the Ascension. It also includes basic catechetical and encyclopaedic materials including vices and virtues,

---

[45] Johnson, 'Prologue and Practice', 73; also see Johnson, *The Middle English Life of Christ*, 76.
[46] Johnson, *The Middle English Life of Christ*, 8.
[47] There are at least twelve poems dealing with the life of Chrit that were a part of the *South English Legendary* but also circulated independently. See O. S. Pickering, 'The *Temporale* Narratives of the *South English Legendary*', *Anglia*, 91 (1973), 425–55.
[48] Frances A. Foster (ed.), *A Stanzaic Life of Christ Compiled from Higden's Polychronicon and the Legenda Aurea Edited from MS. Harley 3909*, EETS, o.s. 166 (London, 1926). Morey, *Book and Verse*, 256–62; NIMEV 1755.
[49] Foster (ed.), *A Stanzaic Life of Christ*, xiv–xvii.
[50] Cf. 'ffor write Latyn may I not spar / to sich as han vnderstongyng, / but after þe Latyn I wil declar / In Englisch, lewide to haue likyng' (5565–8).
[51] Johnson n, *The Middle English Life of Christ*, 84; Johnson, 'Prologue and Practice', 82.

the ages of man, the four elements and complexions of man, the structure of the heavens, and finally ends with an exposition on love.

The *Metrical Life of Christ* survives in one mid-fifteenth-century manuscript as 5519 lines in couplets.[52] The extant version narrates the life of Christ from the Nativity to the Ascension, followed by the Pentecost and the dispersal of the Apostles, as well as the imprisonment and release of Joseph of Arimathea, the destruction of Jerusalem, and the Assumption of Mary.

A predilection for miracles and 'grete meruayle to se' (201) is prominent throughout, not only in relation to Christ's Ministry. Seven miracles surrounding the Nativity are recounted and the account of Christ's life in manhood is literally a succession of miracles. He performed miracles every day and 'His miracles were so mony & fale, / Might no man telle alle by tale' (1548–9). Miraculous episodes after the Ascension, such as the vernicle and Joseph of Arimathea's deliverance from prison, and the cure of Vespasian from wasps, are also narrated in detail. The life of Mary is also carefully followed, as in the details about her life in Egypt and her last days spent teaching maidens in the temple (4836–53). On the other hand, there is a significant lack of doctrinal content; the Sermon on the Mount and parables are omitted though the Credo is included, jointly composed by the twelve Apostles (4058–121). In contrast to the *Stanzaic Life of Christ*, the poem gives the overall impression of a preference for a continuous dramatic narrative punctuated by miracles and apocryphal episodes.

Another Passion narrative that is conscious of lay readers is Walter Kennedy's *Passioun of Christ*.[53] Walter Kennedy (c1455—c1518) came from a powerful aristocratic family, attended Glasgow University and was a parson of Douglas.[54] This is the longest (1715 lines in rhyme royal stanza) of his six surviving poems, extant in a single manuscript, BL MS Arundel 285, a miscellany of devotional works in Middle Scots compiled around 1500. The poem mentions as its source 'Lendulphus' (196), the encyclopaedic *Vita Christi* by the Carthusian monk Ludolphus of Saxony (d. 1377), which was a widely disseminated devotional text in the fifteenth-century.[55] The *Passioun of Christ* begins with the observation that although people nowadays read deeds of ancient heroes and nine worthies, the remembrance of the Passion is the only narrative that profits the soul. He will tell it in English in simple language:

> In proceß I think als commonly,
> For till exclud all curiosite,
> Maist plane terms with deligence to spy,
> Quhilk may be tane with small deficulte,
> (57–60)

---

[52] Walter Sauer (ed.), *The Metrical Life of Christ ed. from MS BM Add. 39996*, MET 5 (Heidelberg, 1977); NIMEV 123, 130, 311, 315, 1579, 2365, 3845.3; Morey *Book and Verse*, 252–6. Some lines are missing toward the beginning, as the extant version abruptly begins with a reference to the Three Kings of Cologne (Magi).

[53] Nicole Meier (ed.), *The Poems of Walter Kennedy*, STS, 5th series, 6 (Woodbridge, 2008), 17–82; J. A. W. Bennett (ed.), *Devotional Pieces in Verse and Prose from MS Arundel 285 and MS Harleian 6919*, STS, 3rd series, 23 (Edinburgh, 1955), 7–63; NIMEV 1040; William A. Ringler, Jr (ed.), *Bibliography and Index of English Verse in Manuscript 1501–1558* (London, 1992), TM508; Morey, *Book and Verse*, 288–9.

[54] Meier, *The Poems of Walter Kennedy*, xv–xvii.

[55] R. James Goldstein, '"Betuix pyne and faith": The Poetics of Compassion in Walter Kennedy's *Passioun of Crist*', *Studies in Philology*, 110 (2013), 495. Kennedy is also indebted to the *Meditationes vitae Christi* by a Franciscan of San Gimignano, Johannes Caulibus (also a major source for *Vita Christi*) as well as to *Legenda Aurea*. On the sources of the *Passioun of Christ*, see Meier (ed.), *The Poems of Walter Kennedy*, xl–lxii.

The narrative begins with the creation of Man and the Fall, followed by the debate of Four Daughters on human fate (Psalms 85 (Vulg. 84).8–14), that ends in the decision of God to sacrifice his son as a ransom. Being recounted within the framework of salvation history, as is *Meditationes Vitae Christi*, the debate as well as the decision to save mankind by Christ's death needs to come before the narrative of the Passion.[56] The events in the life of Christ which then follow are apportioned to the canonical hours as in the *Stanzaic Life of Christ*. This section narrates a sequence of events from the Annunciation to the Last Supper and his Arrest, and, following the Hours of the Cross, proceeds from the Agony in the Garden (Compline) to the Burial (second Compline), ending with the sequence of events from the Resurrection to Pentecost.[57]

Kennedy does not make use of prayers found in *Vita Christi*, nor discuss theological matters or name authorities, but he inserts two 'planctus Mariae' into his narrative, first as a doctrinal dialogue between Mary and the Cross after the Crucifixion (1093–1162) and then as a dramatic monologue at the Deposition (1240–81). These, especially the latter, provide a figure of identification to readers in the affective framework and enable them to see Christ's suffering through Mary's eyes, by the interchange of details of Christ's lacerated body and Mary's lament ending each time with 'full wa is me!'[58] Such affective scenes, along with dramatic scenes of the Passion, visually stimulate compassion, but the poem also inculcates repentance and moral improvement through meditation. It urges the performance of compassion in the tradition of affective piety but also functions as a pragmatic didactic text that leads the reader to repentance.[59]

There are shorter Passion narratives that go beyond the simple combination of narrative and exposition; some of them retain a certain 'romance-like' character as in *Resurrection and Apparitions*[60] and the *Story of Resurrection*.[61] On the other hand, *A Remembraunce of the Passioun of Our Lord Jesu Criste*, 400 lines in quatrains extant in one mid-fifteenth-century manuscript, narrates events of the Passion from the Scourging to the Deposition in considerable, graphic detail.[62] It is a penitential poem in which the narrative is flanked by a rather long prologue and epilogue that emphasize the love of God and divine mercy. There are also several versions of a poem that recounts events of the Passion using the Hours of the Cross format.[63]

Paraphrases of the *Gospel of Nicodemus* and the *Charter of Christ*

The sequence of events from the Harrowing of Hell to the Destruction of Jerusalem, as is narrated in the *Gospel of Nicodemus*, was popular as an independent narrative poem.[64]

---

[56] Meier (ed.), *The Poems of Walter Kennedy*, xliii.
[57] Meier (ed.), *The Poems of Walter Kennedy*, xliv–xlv.
[58] Meier (ed.), *The Poems of Walter Kennedy*, lxx–lxxi.
[59] Goldstein, '"Betuix pyne and faith"', 494.
[60] Carl Horstman, 'Nachträge zu den Legenden. 7. Romanze von Christi Auferstehung aus Ms. Ashmol. 61, fol. 138', *Archiv für das Studium der neueren Sprachen und Literatur*, 79 (1887), 441–7; NIMEV 3980; Morey, *Book and Verse*, 308–9.
[61] O. S. Pickering, 'An Unpublished Middle English Resurrection Poem', *Neuphilologische Mitteilungen*, 74 (1973), 269–82; NIMEV 2685; Morey, *Book and Verse*, 309.
[62] R. H. Bowers (ed.), *Three Middle English Religious Poems* (Gainesville, FL, 1963), 33–43; NIMEV 2613; Morey, *Book and Verse*, 279–80.
[63] NIMEV 701; Morey, *Book and Verse*, 284–5.
[64] The episode is treated within a larger framework of the life of Christ, for example in the *Cursor Mundi* and the *Stanzaic Life of Christ*. There is however only one manuscript of the *South English Legendary* that incorporates the

A verse translation of the Harrowing of Hell section of the *Gospel of Nicodemus* had already been composed in the thirteenth-century,[65] and there are also several later versions.

The Stanzaic Version of the Gospel of Nicodemus, extant in four late fourteenth- or fifteenth-century manuscripts with some variations (1812 lines in the longest version), is comprised of both the Acts of Pilate and the Descent of Christ into Hell, narrating a sequence of events of the Passion from the accusation of the Jews to the Resurrection and the Ascension, as well as the account of the Harrowing of Hell by Leucius and Karinus, and Pilate's letter to Emperor Claudius reporting the death and resurrection of Christ.[66] C. W. Marx points out that dialogues, such as the dispute between Christ and Pilate, are changed into sustained speeches by Christ, and because all four manuscripts include the *Pricke of Conscience* and are mostly didactic and instructional in their contents, this version was 'used for instructional purposes in the manner of homiletic and legendary texts as well as popularizing treatises on doctrine'.[67]

The Harrowing of Hell and the Destruction of Jerusalem,[68] which survives in a single manuscript of the second quarter of the fifteenth-century, extends the narrative to the destruction of Jerusalem, following 'a tradition of continuations of the Gospels of Nicodemus into post-ascension history, up to and including the destruction of Jerusalem', as does the Old English prose translation.[69] After the Harrowing of Hell, it narrates the warning to the Jews to repent, the illness and cure of Vespasian, and the destruction of Jerusalem by his son Titus, and the final release of Joseph of Arimathea. The dismay of Jews and the altercation among the devils, especially of the master of hell and Satan, as well as other details of the harrowing are vividly narrated.

The *Devil's Parliament*, composed in the first half of the fifteenth-century, exists in two versions, the later and longer version (504 lines) perhaps being a revision of the earlier one (442 lines).[70] The narrative is organized around the two parliaments held by the devils in hell and belongs to the tradition of the 'Devil's version of the life of Christ', that describes the Devil's bemusement over the figure of Jesus, and his belated realization of Christ's identity.[71] The first parliament debates the identity of Mary's child, narrating his birth, failed attempts on his life, and prophecies of the birth of Christ. After Jesus reaches manhood and the bid to tempt him fails, the second parliament is summoned. This consists of the Devil's account of the miracles and ministry of Jesus, as well as of the Crucifixion by the Jews at the instigation of the Devil, but the devils are at loss as to the whereabouts of Jesus's soul. Then follows the Harrowing of Hell, in which the debate between Christ and Lucifer takes

Harrowing of Hell and Destruction of Jerusalem. Marx conjectures that it was 'too extensive to be incorporated into a text like the *Ministry and Passion* and would have overbalanced it': C. W. Marx, 'The *Gospel of Nicodemus* in Old English and Middle English', in Zbigniew Izydorczyk (ed.), *The Medieval Gospel of Nicodemus: Texts, Intertexts, and Contexts in Western Europe* (Tempe, AZ, 1997), 233.

[65] William Henry Hulme (ed.), *The Middle-English Harrowing of Hell and Gospel of Nicodemus*, EETS, e.s. 100 (London, 1907), 2–23; NIMEV 185, 1850.5; Morey, *Book and Verse*, 217.

[66] Hulme (ed.), *The Middle-English Harrowing of Hell*, 22–136; NIMEV 512; Morey, *Book and Verse*, 217–9.

[67] Marx, 'The *Gospel of Nicodemus*', 239–40.

[68] C. W. Marx (ed.), *The Devil's Parliament and the Harrowing of Hell and Destruction of Jerusalem*, MET 25 (Heidelberg, 1993), 115–76; NIMEV 3706: Morey, *Book and Verse*, 226–8.

[69] Marx (ed.), *The Devil's Parliament*, 124. Marx points out that it was 'designed specifically as a *temporale* collection' of the *South English Legendary*, probably 'to supplement a separate, now lost, *sanctorale* volume' (Marx (ed.), *The Devil's Parliament*, 116). The composition dates back to c1270–85 when *Ministry and Passion*, one of the other *South English Legendary* texts to which it is closely affiliated, was also composed (Marx (ed.), *The Devil's Parliament*, 119). Cf. O. S. Pickering (ed.), *The South English Ministry and Passion, ed. from St John's College, Cambridge, MS B.6.*, MET 16 (Heidelberg, 1984), 64.

[70] Marx (ed.), *The Devil's Parliament*, 34; NIMEV 3992; Morey, *Book and Verse*, 224–5.

[71] C. W. Marx, *The Devil's Rights and the Redemption in the Literature of Medieval England* (Cambridge, 1995), 126.

place, revealing the identity of Christ as God and his purpose in coming to hell, followed by that between Lucifer and Hell admitting the inability to stop Christ. In the later version, the debate touches upon the question of the redemption of Lucifer, who asks Christ to help him to regain the bliss he lost through his pride (325–36).

The sequence of events is consistently narrated by the Devil up to the Harrowing of Hell, so that the reader can see the Devil's misunderstanding more clearly.[72] Marx points out that while the earlier version is 'conceived around the theme of the deception of the Devil', the later version was not only enlivened by switching the consistent third person narrative into the mixture of the third and first person, but was conceived more readily as 'a verse sermon or Lent reading' with a reference to Lent in the additional stanza (489–92).[73]

The Devil's Parliament refers to the 'bargeyn' or the agreement prepared for mankind—those who ask for grace and amend their error shall be in the kingdom of God (later version, 380–4). This is also the theme of the Middle English *Charters of Christ*, in which Christ deeds the bliss of heaven to those who follow his commandments.[74] The charter exists in both short and long versions which are different in their function. The Short Charter, approximately thirty-four lines in couplets that survives in eighteen fifteenth- and sixteenth-century manuscripts, basically consists of the text of the charter itself in which the 'dispositive nature of the legal document' is used 'to contain the affective qualities of the Passion'.[75] On the other hand, the Long Charter, which exists in three versions (ranging from 234 to 618 lines) in a total of eighteen manuscripts, all of the fifteenth century, has an element of biblical narrative as it recounts the details of the Passion and the lamentation of Mary with references to the events before and after.[76] By specifying the commandments humanity is required to follow and referring to the quatrefoil of love (B version, 202–8), the longer version is more plainly didactic. Also, the staple metaphor of the body of Christ as the parchment on which the deed is written, common to all charters, is more fully developed, with images of the Passion (such as Christ's skin stretched on the Cross as the parchment on a frame), more readily inviting an affective response.

Allegory and Catechism

Watson points out that in vernacular theological production in the fifteenth century, there is a shift of interest to such genres and modes as 'hagiography, pastoralia, *vitae Christi*, compilation, preaching, and urban drama' alongside the continuing transmission of earlier works. He argues that this shift can be 'understood as a positive development: as the result of a process of emergence, not as a response to constraint'. In case of pastoralia, it signalled, as Arundel's Constitutions decreed, the return of pastoral teaching to the laity to Pecham's syllabus and renewed 'interest in the principles underlying pastoral instruction'.[77] In the context of this 'positive development', we have seen that catechetical materials are sometimes embedded into a biblical narrative or that a liturgical frame works to highlight

---

[72] Marx (ed.), *The Devil's Parliament*, 47; cf. Marx, *The Devil's Rights*, 132.
[73] Marx (ed.), *The Devil's Parliament*, 35.
[74] Marx, *The Devil's Rights*, 137–8.
[75] Laura Ashe, 'The 'Short Charter of Christ': An Unpublished Longer Version, from Cambridge University Library, MS Add. 6686', *Medium Ævum*, 72 (2003), 32–48 (at 37).
[76] Ashe, 'The "Short Charter of Christ"', 35. Most of versions of the *Charters of Christ* are edited in Mary Caroline Spalding, *The Middle English Charters of Christ* (Bryn Mawr, PE, 1914). For the Long Charter, see NIMEV 1718 (A version), 4154 (B version), 1174 (C version); Morey, *Book and Verse*, 272–3.
[77] Watson, '"A Clerke schulde haue it of kinde for to kepe counseill"', 581.

the significance of major events in the life of Christ, contributing to the diversity in this genre. In this respect, biblical paraphrase and writings of religious instruction supplement each other with the same aim of educating the laity, combining devotion and teaching.

Robert Grosseteste's *Chateau d'amour*, composed in Anglo-Norman around 1230–53 is such a combination of a biblical narrative and the exposition of catechism in the framework of salvation history. It was written in response to the Fourth Lateran Council (1215), which commanded every Christian to confess sins in their entirety at least once a year to his/her priest. As the priest in turn needs to be properly educated for the task and be able to preach to the laity in vernacular, there was a growth of *pastoralia* to aid him in the care for the souls.[78] Like Walter Kennedy's *Passioun of Christ*, it narrates how it was necessary for the God to become man and die to redeem mankind, using the allegory of Four Daughters of God to make its point. Robert Grosseteste (c1170–1253) lectured in theology in Oxford and was the reforming bishop of Lincoln. Gillespie notes that 'his pastoral constitutions for Lincoln diocese, promulgated in 1239, fed directly Pecham's provincial decrees in the 1280s and therefore into Arundel's constitutions in 1409'. Not surprisingly, his writings were 'systematically and energetically reclaimed by the orthodox reformers of the early fifteenth century as an example of episcopal zeal and idealism'.[79]

Chateau d'amour is extant in two translations in Middle English, respectively known as *A Castle of Love* and *Myrour of Lewed Men*.[80] *A Castle of Love*, composed in the West Midlands about 1300 but first recorded in the Vernon manuscript, is the more complete of the two versions.[81] The poem is punctuated by catechetical exposition. After the sequence of events leading to the Expulsion from Paradise is narrated, it introduces the allegory of the Four Daughters of God, in which the king's son who willingly suffers punishment for a misbehaved servant stands for Christ who dies for humanity (575–80). The poem also expounds the body of Mary, from which Christ is born (660), allegorically as the Castle of Love, listing seven virtues as against seven vices. Humanity, beset with the three enemies of man, invokes Mary, who is the closed door (Ezekiel 44.1–3) to be opened. After the birth of Christ, the issue of the Devil's right to possess the descendants of Adam and divine redemption, also part of the *Devil's Parliament*, is introduced.[82] Miracles are recounted as testimonies that Christ is God and man at the same time. After the Crucifixion and the Harrowing of Hell, the poem ends with the promise of the return of Jesus at the Last Judgement, which is in turn described in some details along with the fifteen signs of the Doomsday.

The *Myrour of Lewed Men*, which was composed by an unidentified monk of the Cistercian abbey of Sawley in a north-east Midlands dialect during the second half of the fourteenth century, is extant in a single early fifteenth-century manuscript.[83] This is a free,

---

[78] For a succinct survey of pastoralia after the Fourth Lateran Council, see Leonard E. Boyle, 'The Fourth Lateran Council and Manuals of Popular Theology', in Thomas J. Heffernan (ed.), *The Popular Literature of Medieval England* (Knoxville, TN, 1985), 30–43.

[79] Gillespie, 'Chichele's Church', 20.

[80] There are also two partial translations, both of the section on the Four Daughters of God. All four versions are edited in Kari Sajavaara (ed.), *The Middle English Translations of Robert Grosseteste's Chateau d'Amour* (Helsinki, 1967); NIMEV 1677, 1879, 3270, 4145; Morey, *Book and Verse*, 95–7.

[81] Sajavaara (ed.), *Chateau d'Amour*, 159–60.

[82] Marx, *The Devil's Rights*, 77–8.

[83] Robert R. Raymo, 'Works of Religious and Philosophical Instruction', in Albert E. Hartung (ed.), *A Manual of the Writings in Middle English 1050–1500*, 11 vols. (New Haven, CT, 1986), 7.2255–378, 2467–582 (at 2338); Also cf. Sajavaara (ed.), *Chateau d'Amour*, 175.

somewhat condensed paraphrase, that expresses its didactic policy more clearly. The translator's prologue says that 'Here begynnes a romance of Englische ... of al that a lewed man has nede for to knawe for hele of soule', containing much that seems 'spedeful to edificacion and swettenes of deuocion and lering of lewed men'.[84] This version assigns more lines to catechetical matters, with a long discussion of the Decalogue.

Grosseteste also composed a pastoral handbook in Latin entitled *Templum Domini* which 'enjoyed a resurgence of popularity in early fifteenth-century English clerical miscellanies'.[85] Its first chapters were translated into English verse (784 lines in eight-line stanzas) and survive in one fifteenth-century manuscript.[86] It expounds three theological and four cardinal virtues through the allegory of the body as a temple. The idea goes back to 1 Corinthians 6.19 where it is said the body is the temple of the Holy Spirit. *Templum Domini* identifies two temples, corporeal and spiritual, which are used to display the hierarchy of faculties that constitute the exemplary body and soul. The corporeal temple is composed out of the physical organs of the body (kidney as foundation, breast as walls, and head as roof), each corresponding to one of four cardinal virtues. The spiritual temple is constructed out of three theological virtues: the foundation of faith, the four walls of hope, and the roof of love.[87]

Allegorical poems dealing with catechetical matters feature in some numbers in fifteenth-century religious poetry. The *Desert of Religion* is a devotional poem of Carthusian origin, totalling some 940 lines in rhyming couplets, extant in three fifteenth-century manuscripts from the north of England, presumably also written in response to Pecham's syllabus for a monastic audience. The poem consists of twenty *passus*, each dealing with one item of Pecham's syllabus such as the Creed and the Ten Commandments, as well as the Five Wits, the Fourteen Pains of Hell and Fourteen Joys of Heaven, seven deadly sins, and seven virtues.[88] It is based on the late fourteenth-century *Speculum vitae*, the popular Middle English verse translation of *Somme le Roi* (*A Survey for a King*), a treatise on vices and virtues compiled around 1279 by Dominican Friar Laurent at the request of Philip III of France for education of his children.[89] The most notable feature of this poem is its unique paratext in which illustration and text are juxtaposed. Each *passus* consists of one opening of two facing pages, dealing with an allegorical tree in the forest. The verso page is a combination of a verse describing the tree and an illustration of an inhabitant of the desert, famous hermits that include Paul, Anthony, Mary of Egypt, Mary Magdalen, and Richard Rolle, as well as anonymous monks and nuns. The figure often speaks about his or her experience in the desert, or the same information is conveyed by the verse lines that frame the figure. The facing recto page depicts the tree diagram that schematizes the verse

---

[84] Sajavaara (ed.), *Chateau d'Amour*, 320.
[85] Gillespie, 'Chichele's Church', 20.
[86] Roberta D. Cornelius, *The Figurative Castle: A Study in the Mediaeval Allegory of the Edifice with Especial Reference to Religious Writings* (Bryn Mawr, PA, 1930), 91–122; NIMEV 967.
[87] Christiania Whitehead, *Castles of the Mind: A Study of Medieval Architectural Allegory* (Cardiff, 2003), 24–7.
[88] Walter Hübner, 'The Desert of Religion', *Archiv für das Studium der neueren Sprachen und Literatur*, 126 (1911), 58–74; NIMEV 672; A. McGovern-Mouron, 'The *Desert of Religion* in British Library Cotton Faustina B VI, pars II', in James Hogg (ed.), *The Mystical Tradition and the Carthusians*, Analecta Cartusiana, 130: 9 (Salzburg, 1996), 150–1. The three manuscripts (BL MSS Add. 37049, Cotton Faustina B VI, Part II, and Stowe 39) differ in the quality of illustration as well as in some details of the text, and therefore give the reader slightly different orientations. McGovern-Mouron (151) succinctly comments, 'the Additional manuscript may be described as "devotional", the Stowe manuscript as "didactic" and the Cotton manuscript as "contemplative"'.
[89] Hope Emily Allen, 'The Desert of Religion: Addendum', *Archiv für das Studium der neueren Sprachen und Literatur*, 127 (1911), 388–90. On *Somme le Roi*, see Edith Brayer and Anne-Françoise Leurquin-Labie (eds), *La Somme le Roi par Frère Laurent* (SATF, Paris, 2008).

together with added inscriptions. This visual presentation engages the reader in a more self-conscious, therefore performative act of devotional reading.[90]

Speculum misericordie (*The Mirror of Mercy*) is another example of religious allegory. It is 976 four-stress lines in eighty-one stanzas, extant only in one mid-fifteenth-century manuscript. The dialect of the poem shows both Midland and Northern features.[91] After the *chanson d'aventure* opening of May morning, the young knight who despairs of salvation meets the Lady Discretio and her seven maidens (virtues) of whom she is 'Moder & Maysteresse' (190). The sinner confesses his transgressions as the seven deadly sins, which are countered one by one by corresponding virtues, illustrated by notorious biblical figures (such as proud Nebuchadnezzar cited by Humility). In the end, the sinner pleads for mercy, confessing his unworthiness with reference to the Ten Commandments and Works of Mercy, and after stanzas on general confession, utters a litany of the Blessed Virgin, Angels, Apostles, Confessors, and Virgins. Then, with the reassurance from Discretio and her maidens, the sinner finally commends his soul to God and dies. By simple personification allegory, the poem illustrates seven vices and their remedies, but as such contents could also be central to a penitential manual as in Chaucer's 'Parson's Tale', it understandably ends with encouragement of confession performed in an orthodox liturgical context.

Literature of Religious Instruction

John Mirk's *Instructions for Parish Priests* is an example of religious verse with a more narrowly practical function. The work, 1934 lines in octosyllabic couplets, was originally written in West Midland dialect and is extant in seven manuscripts. John Mirk, canon and later prior of the Augustinian abbey of Lilleshall in Shropshire, probably composed it in the late 1380s as a free translation of William of Pagula's *Oculus sacerdotis* (*Priest's Eye*), an early fourteenth-century manual for parish priests that would aid them in hearing confession and preaching.[92] The *Instructions* is a pedagogic work on the duties of parish priests. Starting with admonition to priests themselves for righteous living, the treatise emphasizes the need to teach parishioners how to confess and receive communion at Easter (urging them to believe in the sacraments) and to behave properly in church. It discusses what priests should bear in mind at baptism, confirmation, marriage, and extreme unction, while encouraging practical leniency in enjoining fairly light penance with Purgatory in mind. In the course of the work, Mirk deals with the contents of Pecham's syllabus, the teaching of which was again emphasized through the 1357 injunctions of John Thoresby, archbishop of York, which were translated into Middle English by John Gaytryge as *The*

---

[90] Jessica Brantley, *Reading in the Wilderness: Private Devotion and Public Performance in Late Medieval England* (Chicago, 2007), 79–109. One of the MSS, BL MS Add. 37049 (fols. 46–66v), is available as digital facsimile on the British Library website.
[91] Rossell Hope Robbins, 'The *Speculum misericordie*', *PMLA*, 54 (1939), 935–66; NIMEV 1451.
[92] Gillis Kristensson (ed.), *John Mirk's Instructions for Parish Priests Edited from MS Cotton Claudius A II and Six Other Manuscripts* (Lund, 1974); Edward Peacock (ed.), *Instructions for Parish Priests by John Myrc*, revised edn., EETS, o.s. 31 (London, 1902); NIMEV 961; On the dialects of the manuscripts, see Kristensson (ed.), *Instructions for Parish Priests*, 57–62. See David B. Foss, 'John Mirk's Instructions for Parish Priests', *Studies in Church History*, 26 (1989), 131–40 for a summary of its contents.

Lay Folks' Catechism.[93] That the section on catechism circulated independently in one fifteenth-century manuscript is an indication of its practical usefulness for parish priests.[94]

Virtues of the Mass[95] is the title given to a group of some ten poems, found mostly in fifteenth-century manuscripts, that enumerate temporal benefits to be gained from properly observing mass: if you attend a mass, you shall not go hungry, not become blind, and venial sins will be forgiven. Lydgate and Audelay also composed poems on this subject and there are similar passages in Mirk's *Instructions for Parish Priests*.[96] Many of them refer to Augustine as an authority, but they are of varying length with different prologues and epilogues that reflect the context of composition. For example, the version preserved in BL MS Cotton Titus A XXXI, urges laymen to follow the example of the worthies, mentioning Godfrey of Bouillon, Charlemagne, and Arthur, who always prayed before the image of Mary and willingly attended mass.[97]

Debates and Dialogues

The debate or dialogue remained popular throughout the Middle Ages as a medium for elementary religious instruction, and the diversity of topics in this genre is a distinct feature of fifteenth-century religious poetry.

Death and Life was composed in alliterative long lines, probably in the first decade of the fifteenth century although it is recorded only in the mid-seventeenth-century Percy Folio manuscript.[98] It is a debate between Lady Death and Lady Life in two fitts in a dream vision, possibly inspired by *Piers Plowman*.[99] In the first fitt, the splendid Lady Life is attacked by the ugly vicious Lady Death, who is presented as a macabre figure similar to the dead in the Three Living and the Three Dead motif or the ghost of Guinevere's mother in the first part of the alliterative *Awntyrs off Arthure*, but the assault is halted by Sir Countenance who is sent in answer to Life's prayer to God for mercy. In the second fitt, where the debate takes place, Life rebukes Death for senseless destruction while Death defends her actions as a natural consequence of original sin. Death triumphantly enumerates the names of those she has conquered, beginning with Adam and Eve, but as she names Christ as one of

---

[93] Susan Powell, 'John Audelay and John Mirk: Comparisons and Contrasts', in Susanna Fein (ed.), *My Wyl and My Wrytyng: Essays on John the Blind Audelay* (Kalamazoo, MI, 2009), 87–8. Susan Powell (ed.), *John Mirk's Festial Edited from British Library MS Cotton Claudius A. II*, 2 vols., EETS, o.s. 334–5 (Oxford, 2009, 2011), 1. xxvi–xxvii. It is suggested that Mirk is attentive to gendered needs of wives and husbands, especially in the version in BL, MS Royal 17 C XVII. See Beth Allison Barr, 'Gendering Pastoral Care: John Mirk and His *Instructions for Parish Priests*', in J. S. Hamilton (ed.), *Fourteenth Century England, IV* (Woodbridge, 2006), 93–108.

[94] Klaus Bitterling, 'An Abstract of John Mirk's "Instructions for Parish Priests"', *Notes and Queries*, n.s. 24 (1977), 146–8.

[95] NIMEV 333, 957, 1986, 1988, 2323, 2373, 3268, 3426.55, 3427, 3573, 4244, 4276. See Raymo, 'Works of Religious Instruction', 2354–5.

[96] Henry Noble MacCracken (ed.), *The Minor Poems of John Lydgate*, Part I, EETS, e.s. 107 (Oxford, 1911), 87–115; NIMEV 4246; John the Blind Audelay, 'Virtues of the Mass', in Susanna Fein (ed.), *Poems and Carols (Oxford, Bodleian Library MS Douce 302)* (Kalamazoo, MI, 2009), 80–91. In *Instructions for Parish Priests*, the passage appears in the context of the priest administering the Communion. Those who see the priest pass carrying the Eucharist receive those benefits: Kristensson (ed.), *John Mirk's Instructions for Parish Priests*, 85 (lines 314–29).

[97] Thomas Frederick Simmons (ed.), *The Lay Folks Mass Book*, EETS, o.s. 71 (London, 1879), 148–54; NIMEV 957; Raymo, 'Works of Religious Instruction', 2353[198].

[98] Joseph M. P. Donatelli (ed.), *Death and Liffe* (Cambridge, MA, 1989); John W. Conlee (ed.), *Middle English Debate Poetry: A Critical Anthology* (East Lansing, MI, 1991), 139–65; NIMEV 603.

[99] Conlee (ed.), *Middle English Debate Poetry*, 140; see also Donatelli (ed.), *Death and Liffe*, 26–8 on the influence of *Piers Plowman*.

them, both Death and Life remove their crowns and fall to their knees. Life recounts how Christ vanquished Death and harrowed hell. Life resurrects the dead who are now 'fairer by 2 ffold then they before were' (449) and leads them away. The theme of the poem is the redemption of mankind by Christ rather than the struggle between the two natural forces of the world. In this sense, there is an element of the Passion narrative in the later part of fitt two where the Harrowing of Hell is narrated.

The body and soul dialogue, a genre that remained current in English verse from the time of the Old English *Soul and Body* onwards, also betrays a new development in the fifteenth century. One fifteenth-century version in rime royal stanzas is found in Aberystwyth, National Library of Wales, Brogyntyn MS ii. 1 (formerly MS Porkington 10).[100] This is a translation of the enormously popular twelfth-century Latin debate poem, *Dialogus inter Corpus et Animam*, which is done more faithfully than the earlier Middle English version, *Desputisoun bitwen þe Bodi and þe Soule*.[101] The dialogue takes place in the short interval between death and the ravishing of the soul by demons, and the body (or more precisely, the mortal part of the soul that includes senses and appetitive aspects) and the soul accuse each other for their sorry plight, only to realize that it is now too late to make amends or indeed to lament.[102] We can observe the tendency to simplify or ignore more sophisticated theological arguments.[103] Doctrinal passages in the Latin version are edited to make a hortatory poem on the dreadful consequences of the unrepentant death; however, the translator's original prologue and epilogue dwell on divine mercy to the repentant to adjust the balance. Still, the debate admits no grey area between heaven and hell; it does not mention any possibility of salvation via Purgatory. It is structured around the balanced awakening of justice and mercy or fear and hope, conforming at a fundamental level to the didactic demand for dualism in the homiletic literature on death.

Another example of this genre, or a rather an offshoot from it, is the *Disputacion bitwyx the Body and Wormes* in BL MS Add. 37049, the only debate which takes place not before the separation of the body and the soul but after the body is interred.[104] Just as in the Old English *Soul and Body I*, the body is harassed by the assault by a troop of worms (107–13) from which the body learns that mutability is the essential nature of man and finally comes to recognize the worms as the messengers of death and ultimate decay, as well as the embodiment of the earthly and mutable nature of man and physical beauty. This recognition leads to a resolution to bear the present ordeal meekly in the hope of coming to final bliss 'þorow þe mene & þe mediacione / Of our blissed Lord, our verry patrone' (201–2). The debate ends as the body gains hope and offers reconciliation to the worms.

The *Disputacioun betwyx þe Body and Wormes* is the only example in the body and soul tradition in which the debate achieves an understanding and acceptance of the opponent's

---

[100] J. O. Halliwell (ed.), *Early English Miscellanies in Prose and Verse* (London, 1855), 12–40; NIMEV 3330. On the body and soul dialogue, see Francis Lee Utley, 'Dialogues, Debates, and Catechisms', in Albert E. Hartung (ed.), *A Manual of the Writings in Middle English 1050–1500*, 11 vols. (New Haven, CT, 1972), 3.669–745, 829–902 (at 691–6). A digital facsimile of the manuscript is available on the National Library of Wales webpages.

[101] *Desputisoun bitwen þe Bodi and þe Soule*, also known as *Als I lay in a winteris nyt*, is extant in seven manuscripts from the late thirteenth to the early fifteenth century; Conlee (ed.), *Middle English Debate Poetry*, 20–49; NIMEV 351.

[102] On the nature of the body in the body and soul dialogue, see Elizabeth Robertson, 'Kissing the Worm: Sex and Gender in the Afterlife and the Poetic Posthuman in the Late Middle English "A Disputacion betwyx the Body and Wormes"', in Jane E. Burns and Peggy McCracken (eds), *From Beasts to Souls: Gender and Embodiment in Medieval Europe* (Notre Dame, IN, 2013), 122–3.

[103] The tendency is more consistently observed with regard to the *Desputisoun*: Robert W. Ackerman, 'The Debate of the Body and the Soul and Parochial Christianity', *Speculum*, 37 (1962), 541–65.

[104] Conlee (ed.), *Middle English Debate Poetry*, 50–62; NIMEV 1563.

view. The poem starts with the repellent image of the corpse gnawed by worms and is accompanied throughout with illustrations of worms and the decomposed female corpse in the grave apparently done by the scribe; however, it ends with an affirmation of the importance of trust in divine mercy. Although nothing is said about the fate of the separated soul, the positive outcome of the debate suggests that it is in the purgatorial rather than infernal condition.

Another debate which exemplifies diversity in this genre is *Complaint of God* by William Lichfield (1380s—c1448), who was rector of All Hallows-the-Great in Dowgate, a London ward that 'contained a cluster of halls of artisan and merchants guilds'.[105] The debate is extant in three manuscripts widely different in length and detail as well as in two editions by Wynkyn de Worde. In the version in London, Lambeth Palace MS 853, the *Complaint* is composed of five units, each consisting of two paired complaints and responses (four eight-line stanzas), for the total of 640 lines, dealing with such subjects as sins of the flesh, the wasteful use of wealth, the abuse of natural reason, unholy oaths, and the need to attain charity with contrition, confession, and penance.[106] It is suggested that the originality of the debate lies in the fact that the man is a 'representative not of humankind as a whole, but of urban merchant class' who is not ignorant of his religious duty and quite ready to repent, but postpones it all the time.[107]

In the mid-fifteenth-century manuscript Winchester College MS 33, there are two dialogues. *Lucidus and Dubius* appears to be unfinished, but it is a free adaptation in verse dialogue of 650 lines of a part of the questions in Book One of the *Elucidarium* (c1100), a popular Latin compendium of theology attributed to Honorius Augustodunensis, with a few additions from Book Two.[108] It is important as the only verse rendering of the *Elucidarium* in Middle English.

Occupacyon and Ydelnes, which immediately follows *Lucidus and Dubius* in the same manuscript, appears somewhat like a mini-morality play or 'a Tudor interlude *avant la lettre*' as it involves more than two characters and some dramatic actions.[109] Occupation denounces Idleness, who is characterized as a frivolous youth and puts him to study with Doctrine, a master of divinity who then instructs him in the basic theology of salvation supported by conventional scriptural and liturgical allusions. Idleness finally converts and changes his name to Cleanness when he hears Doctrine speaks of the mercy of the Virgin. As Beadle observes, its edifying content is suited to be a school play though we have no explicit evidence to link this specifically to a repertoire performed in the college hall at Winchester and its theme and teaching can be said to be applicable to all Christians rather than to youth only.[110]

---

[105] Amy Appleford and Nicholas Watson, 'Merchant Religion in Fifteenth-Century London: The Writings of William Lichfield', *The Chaucer Review*, 46 (2011), 208.

[106] Appleford and Watson, 'Merchant Religion', 217. The poem is edited in Frederick J. Furnivall, (ed.), *Political, Religious, and Love Poems*, EETS, o.s. 15 (London, 1866; re-edited 1903), 190–232; NIMEV 2714.

[107] Appleford and Watson, 'Merchant Religion', 219.

[108] B. S. Lee, 'Lucidus and Dubius: A Fifteenth-Century Theological Debate and its Sources', *Medium Ævum*, 45 (1976), 80–4. The poem is transcribed in Norman Davis (ed.), *Non-Cycle Plays and the Winchester Dialogues: Facsimiles of Plays and Fragments in Various Manuscripts and the Dialogues in Winchester College MS 33* (Leeds, 1979), 179–91; NIMEV 3352.5; Utley, 'Dialogues, Debates, and Catechisms', 742–3 [73].

[109] Richard Beadle, '*Occupation and Idleness*', *Leeds Studies in English*, n.s 32 (2001), 7. It is edited in 15–47; NIMEV 3430.5.

[110] Beadle, 'Occupation and Idleness', 7–9.

The *Debate between Mercy and Righteousness* is extant in four fifteenth-century manuscripts which differ rather considerably from one another.[111] The debate is between a sinner who despairs of mercy (personified as Righteousness) and Mercy who counsels, with the refrain 'mercy passes righteousness', that forgiveness is granted to all who seek it and are willing to undergo penance. The theme often treated by the Four Daughters of God is presented here in the simplified debate between Justice and Mercy, to warn against the sin of despair.

As the above survey of representative poems shows, there is a considerable variety in the narrative and non-narrative verse designed for religious instruction in the fifteenth century. The Old Testament paraphrases, the Passion narratives of varying scope, as well as the Post-Resurrection narratives based on the *Gospel of Nicodemus* flourished in variety. They indicate that a strong indigenous tradition of biblical paraphrases, as attested in continuous copying of the *South English Legendary*, was enriched by incorporating catechetical materials into narrative, sometimes making use of a liturgical framework. There was also a strong continuing tradition of penitential monologues that achieved a distinct personal voice that can be appropriated by individual readers.

A renewed interest in *pastoralia* gave birth to the literature of religious instruction that treats catechism in a new guise. Notable fifteenth-century features in this respect can be the innovative use of religious allegory as a vehicle to convey the content of Pecham's syllabus and imaginative debate poems, which are sometimes mini-dramas, on various religio-moral subjects.

Biblical paraphrases and writings of religious instruction are not totally separate genres in terms of their function. Catechism is often incorporated into a biblical narrative or a debate as a commentary or a distinct section so that devotion and teaching combine to work towards the single aim of making the reader engage in interiorizing the text, in other words, to render the text performative in the service of the individual self. The fifteenth century is an age of expansion rather than innovation, but the considerable diversity we can witness gives a remarkable breath to the longer religious poetry of the century.

---

[111] Conlee (ed.), *Middle English Debate Poetry*, 201–9 (from MS Lambeth 853); Auvo Kurvinen, 'Mercy and Righteousness', *Neuphilologische Mitteilungen*, 73 (1972), 181–91 (from Aberystwyth, National Library of Wales MS Brogyntyn ii.1); Joyce Bazire, '"Mercy and Justice": The Additional 31042 Version', *Leeds Studies in English*, n.s. 16 (1985), 259–71; Joyce Bazire, 'Mercy and Justice', *Neuphilologische Mitteilungen*, 83 (1982), 178–91(from Chichester, West Sussex Record Office, PAR/59/9 Churchwardens' accounts); NIMEV560.

CHAPTER 12
Saints' Lives and Miracles of The Virgin

Cynthia Turner Camp

The fifteenth century saw an explosion of verse saints' legends. While stories about exceptionally holy individuals—the superheroes of the medieval church—had been popular in English since at least the tenth century, in the fifteenth these tales became sites of intense stylistic experimentation. Hagiography (saints' lives) and Marian miracles appear in nearly every stanza form, and range in length from a few hundred lines to thousands;[1] their formal abundance accompanies an equivalent diversity in the way poets treat their subject matter, as they turned legends into vehicles for devotion and doctrinal exposition as well as entertainment. This essay therefore ranges widely across the century, from its best-known poets to little studied texts, to demonstrate how recurring impulses within this formal variety affect the theological significance of the holy stories these poems tell.

These legends are both narrative and poetry, an observation self-evident but nevertheless critical for understanding how they proliferated.[2] On the one hand, the tortures, temptations, and wonders of saints' lives and Marian miracles had always invited lively storytelling, and both earlier and fifteenth-century writers prioritized linear progression and character development, features of other narrative genres like romance and chronicle. On the other hand, plot stability from version to version—George always kills the dragon, Katherine argues down the philosophers, Mary extends grace to the undeserving—also made these legends attractive playgrounds for poetic inventiveness, much as jazz standards invite fresh arrangements by talented musicians. Poets found in saints' legends a suitable venue for developing a sophisticated, self-consciously ambitious poetic style; in so doing, they often elevate their verse to the transcendent level of the literary.[3]

It is in their prologues and envoys that fifteenth-century poets reflect on their literary goals. Osbern Bokenham, an Augustinian friar writing in the 1440s, frequently uses his prologues to analyse the poetry he and his contemporaries produced. In the Prologue to his 'Life of St Margaret' (NIMEV 2651), Bokenham clearly distinguishes between subject matter and formal play. Following the Aristotelian *accessus* tradition,[4] Bokenham differentiates the material cause, 'The matere wych I wil of wryte' (73), from the formal cause, the

---

[1] The best resource for identifying poetic saints' lives is still Charlotte D'Evelyn and Frances A. Foster, 'Saints' Legends', in J. Burke Severs (ed.), *A Manual of the Writings in Middle English, 1050–1500*, 11 vols. (New Haven, CT, 1970), 2.410–57, 553–649. For an updated bibliography, see John Scahill, *Middle English Saints' Legends*, vol. 8 of Annotated Bibliographies of Old and Middle English Literature (Cambridge, 2005). For Marian legends, consult Thomas D. Cooke with Peter Whiteford and Nancy Mohr McKinley, 'Pious Tales: Miracles of the Virgin', in Albert E. Hartung (ed.), *A Manual of the Writings in Middle English, 1050–1500*, vol. 9 (New Haven, CT, 1993), 3177–258, 3501–51.
[2] Saints' lives also appeared more frequently in prose in the fifteenth century; see Oliver Pickering, 'Saints' Lives', in A. S. G. Edwards (ed.) *A Companion to Middle English Prose*, (Cambridge, 2004), 249–69.
[3] Robert J. Meyer-Lee, 'The Emergency of the Literary in John Lydgate's *Life of Our Lady*', *JEGP*, 109 (2010), 322–48; Catherine Sanok, 'Saints' Lives and the Literary After Arundel', in Vincent Gillespie and Kantik Ghosh (eds), *After Arundel: Religious Writing in Fifteenth-Century England* (Brepols, 2011), 269–86; Robert J. Meyer-Lee and Catherine Sanok (eds), *The Medieval Literary: Beyond Form* (Cambridge, 2018).
[4] On this tradition see A. J. Minnis and A. B. Scott (eds), *Medieval Literary Theory and Criticism c1100–c1375: The Commentary Tradition* (Oxford, 1988).

way in which he writes.[5] The material cause is 'the lyf of blyssyd Margarete' (75), the standard storyline of her life, tortures, and death. Bokenham's 'forme of procedyng' (83), his manner of writing, he defines against other poets' choices, revealing how fifteenth-century poets perceived their formal decisions. It is 'artificyal' (83), the product of verbal expertise that attends to set guidelines. It could have been 'poetycal' (84), following the precepts of Geoffrey of Vinsauf's *Poetria nova* (*New Poetry*, c1200); 'Enbelshyd wyth colours of rethoryk' (89), deploying elaborated rhetorical devices; or a 'crafty werk' (98), skilful artistry in words. Elsewhere Bokenham speaks of writers' 'kunnyng' (10,529) and ability to 'endyten [*compose*] ... copyously' (10,530) and their 'conceytes craftely to dilate' (1402), their experience in the ways of rhetorical colours and narrative elaboration which allows them to enlarge upon their subject matter, often via metaphor or pleonism. Bokenham refers to this battery of poetic options as a 'hey (high) style', a term that encompasses stanza form, rhetorical embellishments, and lexical register, and is frequently characterized by polysyllabic words (especially in rhyme positions), convoluted syntax, and extended metaphors.

While any fifteenth-century poet could elevate their poetry via a tonal shift, many writers developed their ambitious style partially in response to Chaucer, even as their poetic decisions had an un-Chaucerian, fifteenth-century flavour. That imitation occurred partly through the stanza forms of rhyme royal, the stanza of Chaucer's saints' lives and secular hagiographies in the *Canterbury Tales*, and the eight-line 'Monk's Stanza', the form Chaucer used for his Marian poem 'An ABC'. Moreover, Chaucer was hailed by fifteenth-century poets as the model of formally embellished verse, and to imitate his rhyme schemes and (supposed) style was to participate in a courtly school of English poetry.[6] Under the pen of Benedictine monk John Lydgate and his imitators, 'high style' evolved into full aureation, involving grandiloquent Latinate terms, wrought alliteration, and densely packed appositional epithets.[7] Other poets, like John Capgrave (fl. 1430–64), also an Augustinian friar, resisted this flamboyance while still engaging sophisticated rhetoric to convey doctrinal complexity.[8] Fifteenth-century 'high style', as Jennifer Nuttall discusses in this volume, encompasses the range of possibilities through which poets legitimized their verse through post-Chaucerian courtly poetics.

This chapter centres on fifteenth-century legends' formal variety, often but not necessarily characterized by this 'high style'. As the first section details, saints' lives and miracles continued to be written in older styles: couplets, quatrains, and tail rhyme schemes that foreground brisk, event-driven narrative and employ snappy dialogue.[9] These poems coexisted with the ornamented poetic styles of the post-Chaucerian writers as well as a trio of

---

[5] Quotations from Bokenham's *Legendys* are from Mary S. Serjeantson (ed.), *Legendys of Hooly Wummen by Osbern Bokenham*, EETS, o.s. 206 (London, 1938).

[6] Joanna Bellis, '"Fresch anamalit termes": The Contradictory Celebrity of Chaucer's Aureation', in Isabel Davis and Catherine Nall (eds), *Chaucer and Fame: Reputation and Reception* (Cambridge, 2015), 143–63; Heather Blurton and Hannah Johnson, 'Reading the *Prioress's Tale* in the Fifteenth Century: Lydgate, Hocclleve, and Marian Devotion', *The Chaucer Review*, 50 (2015), 134–58; Seth Lerer, *Chaucer and His Readers: Imagining the Author in Late-Medieval England* (Princeton, NJ, 1993).

[7] For a still useful, narrow definition of aureation, see Derek Pearsall, *John Lydgate* (London, 1970), 262–3, 268–71.

[8] Shannon Gayk, '"Ete this book": Literary Consumption and Poetic Invention in John Capgrave's *Life of St Katherine*', in Shannon Gayk and Kathleen Tonry (eds), *Form and Reform: Reading Across the Fifteenth Century* (Columbus, OH, 2011), 88–109.

[9] For discussion see Anne B. Thompson, *Everyday Saints and the Art of Narrative in the South English Legendary* (Aldershot, 2003); Eva von Contzen, *The Scottish Legendary: Towards a Poetics of Hagiographic Narration* (Manchester, 2016).

legends written in demanding, formally ambitious rhymed alliterative stanzas. Also characteristic of fifteenth-century legends, and discussed in the second section, is framing matter: the prologues, epilogues, envoys, and prayers that address both saint and reader to govern the verse's impact. A third characteristic of many lives, addressed in section three, is their length. Whereas most earlier legends appeared as short epitomes in coherent if constantly evolving collections like the *South English Legendary*, fifteenth-century lives are longer, sometimes running to thousands of lines in imitation of chronicles and the expansive Latin legends circulating since the eleventh century. The fourth section returns to the 'high style' to consider those few legends that, in their attempts to elevate the saint through opulent metaphors and eloquent petitions, reimagine the foundational principles of the legend itself.

This plethora of formal opportunities, all used to tell the same holy stories, helps show how Bokenham's sharp distinction between 'matere' and 'forme', or between subject and style, breaks down. Style and subject matter are inseparable.[10] The poet's stylistic decisions—elevating descriptions of the saints' perfections via transcendent language, relating their earthly deeds through vigorous storytelling—inform the nature of the holiness on display, and vice-versa. Amidst this poetic creativity that elevates the legend to rhetorical heights suitable to its holy subject, poets stretch the idea of narrative, based on the recounting of events in linear sequence, into new forms. The fifteenth century was an age of narrative as well as poetic innovation, invited by the heavenly perfections of Mary and the saints.

Narrating Holiness

Although narrative elements typical of earlier legends persist through the fifteenth century, the ambition of the century's poets shaped not only literary style but also the depiction of holiness. To oversimplify somewhat, those poets who incorporate narrative features from the literature of entertainment—foregrounding the rapid unfolding of plot, heightened attention to deeds, and the emotional engagement of characters—frequently portray the saint's holiness as stemming from their actions on earth. Those 'crafty clerk[es]' (Bokenham, *Legendys*, 85) who emphasize lexical elaboration, employ extended metaphors, and use complex stanza forms develop a poetic of stasis, a transcendent 'idiom free from the possibility of temporal decay'.[11] This elevated register functions to exalt the saint much as a shrine embellishes the holy relics it contains, depicting the saint's holiness as proceeding from their immutable heavenly perfection.[12]

As was true of earlier legends, many lives and miracle stories known from fifteenth-century manuscripts employ lively dialogue and the vigorous narration of action as a way of 'heightening the enjoyment of the stories of the saints without betraying the didactic kernel of the genre'.[13] This is especially true of lives written in couplets and tail rhyme, the latter being firmly associated with romance by the late fourteenth century.[14] Frequently circulating alongside romances in manuscripts, these legends tend to develop dynamic

---

[10] See the discussions in Christopher Cannon, 'Form', in Paul Strohm (ed.), *Oxford Twenty-First Century Approaches to Literature: Middle English* (Oxford, 2007), 177–90; Amanda Walling, 'Feminizing Aureation in Lydgate's *Life of Our Lady* and Life of Saint Margaret', *Neophilologus*, 101 (2017), 321–36.

[11] Lerer, *Chaucer and His Readers*, 24.

[12] See further Robyn Malo, *Relics and Writing in Late Medieval England* (Toronto, 2013), especially 68–80.

[13] von Contzen, *Scottish Legendary*, 19.

[14] For tail-rhyme legends see Rhiannon Purdie, *Anglicising Romance: Tail-Rhyme and Genre in Medieval English Literature* (Cambridge, 2008), 58–9.

characters who are, if not imitable, certainly sympathetic. This is a feature of Marian miracles, where fallible human characters invite the readers' identification. In the tail rhyme version of the Marian miracle 'Theophilus' found in BodL MS Rawlinson poet. 225 (after 1450), Theophilus is cast as a courteous, generous, chivalric hero; the wicked knight of the fragmentary Marian legend in the Lincoln Thornton manuscript (Lincoln Cathedral MS 91, c1435) is convicted by a friar's preaching; and the lord and his lady in the miracle of the jealous wife, found in BodL MS Ashmole 61 (c1500) alongside romances and didactic verse, are caught up in a *fabliau* plot turned tragic until Mary intervenes.[15] These legends' quick rhymes propel the action forwards and encourage snappy dialogue. In Ashmole 61's couplet 'Life of Margaret', Margaret's expressions of faith are simplified, and she gives sharp responses to her persecutors: '"After you"' she tells those who advise her to convert, '"I wyll not do. / Bot go your wey," sche seyd, "me fro"' (242–3; '*I will not act as you want. But go away from me', she said*).[16] The couplet 'Life of Katherine', appearing too in late-fifteenth-century witnesses alongside didactic poems and romances, develops the converted soldier Porphiry in the mould of a romance hero, albeit a misplaced one. When Porphiry fights the tyrant's men, Katherine intervenes, explaining that he cannot fight and be a martyr too:

> 'Parfory, let be þy fyghtyng!' sche seyde,
> 'Yf þou wylt wyth me martyrd be,
> Fyghtynge þou muste leue, y telle the.'[17]
> (262–4)

('Porphry, stop your fighting!' she said. 'If you want to be martyred with me, you must stop fighting, I tell you'.)

The poet's unique inclusion of this episode depicts a 'humanisation of the holy';[18] Porphiry wishes to preserve his life through his martial training, while Katherine's exasperation at his misplaced motivation appears in her imperatives and the final half-line's pleonastic emphasis on her speech. The saints' bold responses give these virgins a verbal agency (and in Katherine's case, a momentary failing of patience) that is recognizably human.

Sanctity is also portrayed as a development with which the reader can sympathize in the couplet 'Life of Christopher' from the Lincoln Thornton manuscript as well as the tail-rhyme 'Life of Anne' (c1400), an ambitious narrative that begins with Mary's conception and continues through Jesus's infancy. The 'matere' of the Christopher account already lends itself to a story of personal progress, as Christopher converts from a lordless wild man to a God-fearing ferryman and preacher. Still, the poet's 'forme', his descriptions of the world through which Christopher moves, locates Christopher's holiness in action taken or rejected: the landscapes over which he travels, the terrifying storm through which he carries the infant Jesus, the physical blandishments of the women who attempt to seduce him (130–5, 305–12, 1711–12).[19] The tail-rhyme 'Anne', uniquely found in Minneapolis,

---

[15] The Theophilus story (NIMEV 1883) is in Beverley Boyd (ed.), *The Middle English Miracles of the Virgin* (San Marino, CA, 1964), 68–87. The Lincoln Thornton miracle (NIMEV 1722) is in Carl Horstmann (ed.), *Altenglische Legenden: Neue Folge* (Heilbronn, 1881), 503–4. The version in Ashmole 61 (NIMEV 1987) is in George Shuffelton (ed.), *Codex Ashmole 61: A Compilation of Popular Middle English Verse* (Kalamazoo, MI, 2008), item 22.
[16] NIMEV 2673; Shuffelton (ed.), *Codex Ashmole 61*, item 37.
[17] NIMEV 227; Horstmann (ed.), *Altenglische*, 260–4.
[18] von Contzen, *Scottish Legendary*, 175.
[19] NIMEV 1990; Horstmann (ed.), *Altenglische*, 454–66.

MN, Minnesota University Library MS Z.822.N.81, similarly develops the human elements of social and marital struggle. The poet heightens the emotional cost of childlessness in Anne and Joachim's speeches, and Anne's welcoming of Joachim at the city gate highlights her joy at their reunion:

> Scho halsed hym fast about þe neke
> & kyssed hym sayand, I ne reke
>   On lyf I haue 30w here.
> I was a wedow in my lyfe,
> Now loue I god I am a wyfe;
>   Lo goddes help ay es nere.[20]
>   (268–73)

(She hugged him tightly around the neck and kissed him, saying, 'I had no idea! I have you here alive! I was a widow in my life; now, as I love God, I am a wife. Lo, God's help is always near'.)

The staccato clauses capture Anne's elation at Joachim's return and her transformation from widow to wife. While the power of God's goodness is the main point, these versions' dialogue and narrative pacing accentuate the saints' human emotions and challenges.

Action-based storytelling also appears in those legends that use the newer stanza forms of rhyme royal and Monk's Stanza, but as Eva von Contzen observes of Lydgate's verse, 'the dynamics of narration are systematically deemphasized and reduced'.[21] The shorter stanza lengths encourage a different narrative pacing, and a different use of dialogue. In Lydgate's 'Life of St Margaret' and 'Life of St George',[22] for example, the narrative moves swiftly through the rhyme royal stanzas, as is equally true of Bokenham's lives of virgin martyrs (written in various rhyme schemes). However, these poets minimize attention to the saint's action in the world, and therefore their identities' contingent elements. Both poets, maintaining stanza integrity, give their characters long set speeches ideal for theological exposition or extended prayers rather than brief, emotionally impactful outbursts, as Bokenham's 'Life of St Anne' demonstrates. Meeting Joachim at the gate,

> & a-non she gan hym halsen & kysse,
> No ioye wenynge þat she myht mysse
> Syth she hym hadde, & þus she gan crye:
> 'Welkecome, dere spouse, & god gramercy!
> I was a wedowe, now I am non.
> I was also bareyn and repreuable,
> But nowe bareynesse is from me gon,
> And to conceyuyn I am made able

---

[20] NIMEV 208; Roscoe E. Parker (ed.), *The Middle English Stanzaic Versions of the Life of Saint Anne*, EETS, o.s. 174 (London, 1928), 1–89.

[21] Eva von Contzen, 'Narrating Vernacular Sanctity: The *Scottish Legendary* as a Challenge to the "literary turn" in Fifteenth-Century Hagiography', in von Contzen and Anke Bernau (eds), *Sanctity as Literature in Late Medieval Britain* (Manchester, 2015), 172–90 (at 173).

[22] Henry Noble MacCracken (ed.), *The Minor Poems of John Lydgate*, 2 vols., EETS, e.s. 107, o.s. 192 (London, 1911, 1934), 1.173–92 (NIMEV 439), 145–54 (NIMEV 2592).

> Be goddes prouidence eterne & stable;
> & for his goodenesse shewyd vnto me
> Magnyfyed mot euere his name be.'[23]
> (1969-79)

(Right away Anne began to hug and kiss him, thinking that she would lack no joy since she had him, and she began to cry out: 'Welcome, dear spouse, and thank God! I was a widow, now I am not. I was also barren and disgraced. But now barrenness is gone from me and I am made able to conceive by God's eternal and stable providence. And may his name be ever magnified for his goodness shown unto me.')

While she still hugs and kisses Joachim, Anne's speech includes only one line welcoming her husband, despite being twice as long as the version in the tail-rhyme 'Anne'; the remainder glorifies God for removing her barrenness. This balance elevates Anne as an example of 'goddes prouidence eterne & stable' but decentres her personal joy—and the preceding trials.

By characterizing these saints less as human actors and more as manifestations of spiritual truths, these poets engage a poetic of saintly stasis in which 'forme' and 'matere' coincide. The dilation and *amplificatio* that delay the narrative emphasize the saints' eternal, unchanging glories. Passages 'Enbelshyd wyth colours of rethoryk' (Bokenham, 89; *decorated with rhetorical devices*) establish the saint as an unchanging intercessor, and the saint's transcendence is encapsulated in common metaphors, visible throughout my examples below: lapidary ones of heavenly impassibility, floral ones of spiritual fecundity, light ones of divine illumination. The legends of Christopher, Katherine, and Theophilus foreground the protagonist's development into spiritual uprightness, often through extensive use of direct speech; the poetic of saintly stasis, on the other hand, constructs the saint through extended ekphrasis as persisting 'wyth o chere in contenaunce perseuerently' (Bokenham, 4227; *steadfastly with a singular expression in conduct*), persisting in heavenly perfection even when undergoing earthly trials.

Although others too develop this poetic of saintly stasis, the technique characterizes Lydgate's saints' lives, as evident in his 'Life of Giles'.[24] Completely eschewing dialogue, Lydgate identifies the French abbot as 'Laumpe and lanterne of perfeccyoun' (174) and pauses regularly to expound upon his abstemiousness, discretion, and humility. Even in moments when the narrative appears to progress, Lydgate's formal technique constructs Giles' sanctity as unchanging. When the deer feeds the hermit Giles, Lydgate details its movements in a full stanza:

> Thus of costom the hynde kept þi tyme
> At serteyn houris duryng ful thre yeer,
> Wente in pasture gresyng fro the pryme,
> Toward mydday she kam with ful glad cheer,
> Of God provided to be thy vytayller,
> With a repast of hir mylk most soote,
> She was thy cook, she was thy boteleer,
> Ageyn the constreynt of hunger to de boote.
> (105-112)

---

[23] NIMEV 1414; Serjeantson (ed.), *Legendys of Hooly Wummen*, 54-5.
[24] NIMEV 2606; MacCracken, *Minor Poems*, 1.161-73.

(Thus the deer had the habit of keeping to your time of particular [monastic] hours for a full three years. Going to graze in the pasture from prime, at midday she gladly came; provided by God to be your provisioner with a feast of sweet milk, she was your cook, she was your cupbearer, providing you with relief from the distress of hunger.)

Without using highly Latinate terms, Lydgate dilates the miracle through pleonastic epithets describing the deer and repetition of time markers ('serteyn houris', 'fro the pryme', 'Toward mydday'). These and verbs of motion ('wente', 'kam') do not move the narrative forwards, however; they pause it, dwelling on the deer's 'costom' over the 'ful thre yeer' that it aids Giles. Just as the deer loops from pasture to hovel in the near-endless cycle of monastic prayer, the Monk's stanza rhymes interlace aurally and Lydgate's anastrophic syntax circles back on itself, emphasizing Giles' immovability in saintly perfection.

This poetic of stasis can be detected earlier, in the alliterative tradition. The three alliterating lives of John the Baptist, John the Evangelist, and Katherine, all dating from c1400, similarly elevate their saints via the alliterative line's abundant vocabulary.[25] The stanzaic form—fourteen-line rhyming stanzas in strong stress alliterative verse, divided into an octave and sestet via rhyme scheme and meter—provides a formal complexity appropriate to the elevated praise these legends deploy.[26] In Richard Spalding's *Life of St Katherine*, she, like Giles, is a 'lanterne to leche hem below' (3; *a lantern to redeem those below*), illuminating her petitioners with heavenly aid. John the Baptist's virtues are listed, again like Giles's, in the stanza that honours his birth:

> Blissid be þou, Baptist, to many folk a frende;
> Oure Jewel of Joy, jugged be lawe;
> Faythful in frestyng, oure foos fro vs fende;
> Solace to the sory, s[e]kir in thy sawe,
> Serteyn to synful, socour þow sende
> At þe dredeful day whennes bemes schul blowe,
> Þou þat mylde Mary helde in hir h[e]nde,
> First whan þou were born, as clerkes wele knowe.
> (71–8)

(Blessed are you, Baptist, a friend to many people; our jewel of joy, adjudicated by the law; faithful [one] under testing, defend us from our foes; you who are secure in your faith, who gives solace to the wretched and are trustworthy to sinners, send aid at the fearful day when trumpets will blow, you whom gentle Mary held in her hand as soon as you were born, as learned men know well.)

The narrative pauses between John's naming in line 70 and Mary's cradling of the infant in line 77 for this praise passage that recalls Latin prayers in its grammatically imprecise petitioning imperatives. The richness of the alliterative vocabulary adds aural depth to the octave through the strings of terms used for both saint and sinners, while those words— 'Jewel', 'Faythful', 'Solace', 'Serteyn'—convey John's eternal permanence.

---

[25] Ruth Kennedy (ed.), *Three Alliterative Saints' Hymns: Late Middle English Stanzaic Poems*, EETS, o.s. 321 (Oxford, 2003). For St Katherine (NIMEV 1813), see 1–9, and St John the Baptist (NIMEV 528), 19–23. St John the Evangelist (NIMEV 2608), 10–18, is discussed below, 190–91.

[26] As argued by Ruth Kennedy, 'Strong-Stress Metre in Fourteen-Line Stanza Forms', *Parergon*, 18 (2000), 127–55.

The desire to glorify the saint through poetic eloquence recurs across the century, popularized by Lydgate but not limited to him and his followers. The broad availability of an elevated poetic highlights the wide range of narrative and poetic possibilities open to hagiographers. Even as certain stanza forms lent themselves to different narrative pacings, poets could mix ornate vocabulary and snappy dialogue within the same poem. These extensive options in turn invited varied portrayals of holiness; whether the saint was depicted as a transcendent intercessor to be petitioned for aid or a glorified but ultimately human individual with whose trials the reader might commiserate was, largely, a function of poetic style. A writer's formal decisions were not only driven by literary ambition or audience engagement: they also carried doctrinal weight.

The Narrative Framed

These poets' literary concerns are often visible in the paratexts that proliferated across fifteenth-century literature. Prologues, prohemes, envoys, and other framing devices operate as sites of negotiation through which the reader passes into or out of the narrative and in which the poet strives to legitimize the text.[27] These transitional literary spaces also possess illocutionary force; the poet can speak directly to the audience, guiding their engagement with the poem, and to the saint, requesting aid. In this dual-voiced address, hagiographic paratexts can differ from their secular counterparts, which address earthly readers only. When they invoke saints for poetic assistance, these prologues and closing prayers assert the text's poetic and spiritual efficacy, the saint's aid visible in the poet's eloquence.

Written in a literary context in which title pages were non-existent and authorial attribution not always evident, prologues provide 'vehicles for their writers to define various degrees of vocational and intellectual authority and some proprietary claim on the works'.[28] In both devotional and secular work, they were frequently sites for situating the work within a Chaucerian tradition through the humility *topos*, and prologues and envoys were also occasions for eulogizing the poem's patrons. Bokenham does both extensively as part of his authorial self-representation.[29] In his prologues he laments that he lacks the 'cunnyng and eloquens' of those 'fyrsh [fresh] rethoryens, / Gowere, Chauncere, and now Lytgate' (1401, 1403–4), and his Proluctorye to the 'Life of St Mary Magdalene' (NIMEV 3508) does not simply praise the poem's patron, Isabella Bourgchier, Countess of Eu and sister to Richard, duke of York: it narrates the entire commission process. As Robert Meyer-Lee discusses in this volume, devotional poets create for themselves a sacerdotal authorial pose by positioning themselves as purveyors of spiritual wisdom within a literary and/or political economy. For Bokenham, that economy is grounded in Chaucer and his patrons.

Addressing the reader through this sacerdotal authorial pose, these poets frequently use their paratexts to exhort their readers directly. Thomas Hoccleve (fl. 1402–26) establishes Mary as the ideal path to 'The blisse of heuene' (2) in his sole Marian miracle, the rhyme royal legend (variably titled) that explains the rosary's origin.[30] The poem's three-stanza prologue characterizes Mary's spiritual authority so the reader will adopt this prayer.

---

[27] See further Gérard Genette and Marie Maclean, 'Introduction to the Paratext', *New Literary History*, 22 (1991), 261–72.
[28] Andrew Galloway, 'Middle English Prologues', in David F. Johnson and Elaine Treharne (eds), *Readings in Medieval Texts: Interpreting Old and Middle English Literature* (Oxford, 2005), 288–305 (at 291).
[29] A. C. Spearing, *Medieval Autographies: The 'I' of the Text* (Notre Dame, IN, 2012), 209–56.
[30] NIMEV 4122; Roger Ellis (ed.), *'My Compleinte' and Other Poems, by Thomas Hoccleve* (Exeter, 2001), 88–92.

Given the 'malice / Of the feend' (10–11) and the peril of 'this slipir (*treacherous*) lyf' (17), the devout reader is in need of a 'guyde' (2) to attain heaven. A further series of protection metaphors—Mary is a 'seur (*sure*) sheeld' (10) and a 'Staf of confort' (18)—construct Mary as the ideal 'mediatrice (*mediatrix*) / For our offenses mercy to purchace' (8–9). As a result, Hoccleve urges the reader to do 'seruice, honour, and plesance' (20) to 'þat lady free' (19), characterizing his poem as a 'remembrance' (20) of the glories due to Mary. Hoccleve thereby introduces his miracle story as a praise-poem lauding Mary while simultaneously emphasizing her efficacy as an intercessor, urging his readers to honour Mary via the rosary to win her mediating grace.

The ends of poems too are sites of paratextual additions, the poet sending the text to the reader through last words that encourage an ideal reception. The closing prayer was a *de rigueur* feature of fifteenth-century saints' lives; typically intercessory in mode, the prayer leads the reader out of the narrative in a devotional mindset. The other dominant closing paratext was the envoy. In both devotional and secular verse, as Jennifer Nuttall shows, the envoy was often distinguished by a change in rhyme scheme or a heading, which developed from 'go little book' and humility *topoi* to become a formally heightened expression of the poet's artistry.[31] When saints' lives merge the envoy's form with the closing prayer's devotional purpose, the envoy's function shifts from simple humility to prayerful request for poetic aid. Lydgate's one-stanza envoy to his 'Life of Giles' addresses the saint 'Tween hope & dred' (362) that he might 'Thynk on þi man þat laboureth to compile / This lytel dete' (363–4; *Think on your man who worked to compile this little ditty*), using the language of humility to invoke Giles's intercessory blessing. This shift in addressee transforms the envoy into a prayer, sending the poem to a heavenly rather than earthly patron to seek spiritual aid.

Whether they occur as opening or closing paratexts, the prayer's utterance possesses a locutionary power different from the legend's narrative or even the address to patrons. Whereas the address to earthly patrons showcases the poet's artistic achievements *in hope of* receiving the patron's approval, when addressed to heavenly patrons such requests demonstrate that the saint's blessing *has already been* received. Spalding's alliterative *Life of St Katherine* daringly performs this shift. Although most lives of Katherine give her an intercessory death-scene prayer in direct speech, Spalding replaces it with a mere four lines of reported speech (165–8). Instead, Spalding provides an intercessory prayer voiced by himself, in the three closing stanzas that include an acrostic on the saint and poet's names (225–66). The acrostic encodes Spalding and Katherine's close affiliation to transfer intercessory capacity from saint to author. Lydgate, in turn, imagines himself as a conduit through which the saint's heavenly powers manifest on the page.[32] When, in the opening stanzas of his 'Life of Anne', Lydgate beseeches the 'first moeuer' (1; *first mover*) for divine 'licour aureate' (14; *golden liquid*) to help him with his life of Jesus's grandmother because 'my wit is to (*too*) bareyne, / My mynde derk' (8–9), he transforms the humility *topos* into a prayerful request for poetic assistance.[33] By asking God for help crafting a suitably worthy poem for Anne, in a stylistically heightened, at times fully aureate register that displays his artistic capacity, Lydgate's prayer becomes proof of heavenly approbation: the poem's style

---

[31] Jenni Nuttall, 'Lygate and the Lenvoy', *Exemplaria*, 30 (2018), 35–48.

[32] Meyer-Lee, 'Emergence of the Literary'; Cynthia Turner Camp, *Anglo-Saxon Saints' Lives as History Writing in Late Medieval England* (Cambridge, 2015), 203–4; Anke Bernau, 'Lydgate's Saintly Poetics', in Eva von Contzen and Bernau (eds), *Sanctity as Literature in Late Medieval Britain* (Manchester, 2015), 151–71.

[33] NIMEV 3671; MacCracken, *John Lydgate: Minor Poems*, 1.130–3.

is so transcendent that Lydgate could only have crafted these exquisite stanzas with divine aid.

These writers' stylistic achievements in turn authorize their spiritual and artistic probity. Their poetry performs the saints' grace, while also partaking in their timeless perfection. The prayerful paratexts integrate the elevated stylistic elements of the 'forme' irreducibly to the poem's spiritual 'matere': this heightened poetic style is not only suitable to the saint's heavenly glories, but it is the product of them. Hagiographic paratexts can thereby assert a poem's claims to a literary eminence not as readily available to secular poetry, as they allow the poet to imagine the saint as manifesting within the verses' eloquence.

The Narrative Expanded

Fifteenth-century legends are additionally characterized by sheer length: some dozen massive saints' lives run to thousands of lines. These legends attain this scope partially via dilatory elaboration, but more commonly by emulating chronicle history, so increasing the legend's narrativity. As chronicles depend on the linear unfolding of events to impose meaning on the past, so long legends frequently position their holy subjects precisely within space and time to establish their historico-spiritual significance.[34] Almost always written by monks or friars and often supporting an institutional agenda, these capacious lives' devotional task is coupled with a fascination with historical facticity and an adjudication of textual sources. Poetic legitimation in these lives frequently stems not from saintly aid in the composition process but from carefully documenting textual transmission.

The two earliest such lives exemplify many features of this sub-set of legends: the *Wilton Chronicle* (c1425), as the life of the early English nun-saint Edith is entitled by its modern editors, and the *Metrical Life of St Cuthbert* (by 1425) about the conversion-era Northumbrian bishop.[35] Both are written by anonymous poets affiliated with the institutions about which they write, the Wilton poet perhaps a priest attached to the nunnery, the Cuthbert poet likely a member of Durham Abbey.[36] Both translate (with additions) these saints' standard Latin *vitae et miracula*; and both are extremely long, the *Metrical Cuthbert* running to over 8000 lines and the *Wilton Chronicle* to nearly 5000 lines. Furthermore, both poets construct their lives as historical accounts as much as, or more than, devotional texts. The Wilton poet hangs his translation of Edith's Latin *vita* upon a chronicle superstructure that positions her life within England's history, while the Cuthbert poet carefully details his sources (17–58). Both write in couplets, the standard form for verse chronicles before the mid-fifteenth century, the Cuthbert poet also 'chaung[ing] my stile' (4157) to tail rhyme for Book Three's miracle stories; and neither include the extended paratexual prayers that characterize fifteenth-century legends.

Although neither appears to have influenced other writers, these legends' strategies are echoed in other long lives, particularly those written about English saints, suggesting that

---

[34] This is the general argument of Camp, *Anglo-Saxon Saints' Lives*.
[35] For the former, NIMEV 243, see Mary Dockray-Miller (ed.), *Saints Edith and Æthelthryth: Princesses, Miracle Workers, and Their Late Medieval Audience. The Wilton Chronicle and the Wilton Life of St Æthelthryth* (Brepols, 2009), 37–333. For the latter, NIMEV 2879, see J. T. Fowler (ed.), *The Life of St Cuthbert in English Verse*, Surtees Society, 88 (Edinburgh, 1891).
[36] Dockray-Miller, *Saints Edith and Æthelthryth*, 8–9; Christiania Whitehead, 'Regional, and with Attitude: The Middle English Metrical *Life of St Cuthbert*', in Catherine Batt and René Tixier (eds), *Boolldly bot meekly: Essays on the Theory and Practice of Translation in the Middle Ages in Honour of Roger Ellis* (Turnhout, 2018), 115–32 (at 117).

monastic poets valued these features. Many such works promoted institutional causes. *Robert of Knaresborough* (by 1450) was written partly to connect the hermit to the Trinitarian Order, who claimed Robert as their predecessor,[37] and the one collection of Marian miracles set in England (c1496) is a (spurious) account of the foundation of the Walsingham shrine, printed by Richard Pynson, and designed to encourage pilgrimage.[38] Henry Bradshaw's *Life of Werburge* (1513, printed 1521) integrates history, *vita*, and *miracula* to champion Chester Abbey's monastic privileges within a multi-book, rhyme royal poem indebted to Lydgate.[39] That poet's two double saints' lives, *Edmund and Fremund* (after 1434) and *Alban and Amphibal* (1439), were commissioned by monastic patrons, the latter by Abbot John Whethamstede of St Alban's Abbey and the former by Lydgate's own abbot, William Curteys, as a gift for the young King Henry VI.[40] While these lives exemplify the poetic of stasis in aid of literary aspirations, they attend to each monastic house's political motivations through their attention to the past.[41]

Beyond this documentary functionality, many writers seem genuinely curious about the time and place in which their saintly subjects lived. In the opening lines of his 'Life of Wenefrede' and 'Life of St Audrey' (Etheldreda) in his *Lives of the Saints*, Bokenham nods to this desire just to refuse its tendency towards lengthy genealogy and geographic description (Melrose, Abbotsford House Library, Abbotsford Legendary, fols. 214v, 117v).[42] The poet of the *Wilton Audrey*, a companion to the *Wilton Chronicle*, embraces both: the poem's opening 110 lines detail Etheldreda's genealogy and the seven kingdoms of conversion-era England, neither necessary to the story.[43] Similarly, the prologue to William Hatfield's *Life of St Ursula* (c1510), printed by Wynkyn de Worde, begins with Maxentius and Conan Meriadoc, uniquely among Middle English Ursula legends, to situate her life within the *Brut*'s narrative of early British history.[44] Unlike the Wilton poet, however, Hatfield rejects this chronicle account in favour of Ursula's standard *Legenda Aurea* narrative.[45] In this instance, historical curiosity might encourage Hatfield to reference the *Brut*, but the weight of tradition leads him to reject it.

As part of this concern with facticity, these legends often discuss their sources precisely. These considerations reveal the poet's investment in if not modern historical accuracy then a medieval version of it: reference to ancient, established textual traditions to authenticate the legend's veracity. Such citation practices preoccupy the Cuthbert poet as well as Laurence Wade, whose rhyme royal *Life of Thomas Becket* (1497) opens with a prose incipit that details his sources and who peppers his poem with

---

[37] NIMEV 3677; Joyce Bazire (ed.), *The Metrical Life of St Robert of Knaresborough*, EETS, o.s. 228 (London, 1953).

[38] NIMEV 2664.5; *Of this chapel se here the fundacyon* ([c1496]; STC 25001).

[39] STC 3506; Carl Horstmann (ed.), *The Life of St Werburge of Chester by Henry Bradshaw*, EETS, o.s. 88 (London, 1887). Bradshaw also wrote the rhyme royal *Life of St Radegunde* printed by Pynson ([c1525]; STC 3507).

[40] NIMEV 3748; J. E. van der Westhuizen (ed.), *John Lydgate: The Life of Saint Alban and Saint Amphibal* (Leiden, 1974). NIMEV 5422; Anthony Bale and A. S. G. Edwards (eds), *John Lydgate's Lives of Ss Edmund & Fremund and the Extra Miracles of St Edmund*, MET 41 (Heidelberg, 2009).

[41] Camp, *Anglo-Saxon Saints' Lives*, 190–206; Walling, 'Feminizing Aureation', in Catherine Sanok, *New Legends of England: Forms of Community in Late Medieval Saints' Lives* (Philadelphia, PA, 2018), 193–202.

[42] An edition by Simon Horobin is in progress; see *Osbern Bokenham: Lives of* Saints, vols. I, II, EETS, o. s. 356, 359 (Oxford, 2020, 2022). I cite the manuscript by folio in advance of completion of that edition.

[43] Dockray-Miller (ed.), *Saints Edith and Æthelthryth*, 335–405.

[44] Edmund Hatfield, *Here begynneth ye lyf of Saynt Ursula after ye cronycles of englonde* ([c1510]; STC 24541.3), A.ii.r–v.

[45] William Marx, 'St Ursula and the Eleven Thousand Virgins: The Middle English *Legenda Aurea* Tradition', in Jane Cartwright (ed.), *The Cult of St Ursula and the 11000 Virgins* (Cardiff, 2016), 143–62 (at 156–60).

references to the 'auctor' and 'his autentyke processe' (*his reliable account*).⁴⁶ This concern for authenticity finds its fullest articulation in Capgrave's *Life of St Katherine* (c1445). The prologue tells an elaborate story about Capgrave's source, identifying its original writer as an eyewitness to Katherine's martyrdom then tracing the text's movement from Greece to England, a journey that includes a visionary book-eating experience and twelve years of language training (Prol. 47–231).⁴⁷ Whether or not the narrative is fictitious, Capgrave's extended story about textual transmission exposes this anxiety about credibility.⁴⁸

The question of textual legitimacy looms large across fifteenth century legends. Whereas Lydgate, Spalding, and others authenticate their poems' efficacy through the prayerful sacerdotal pose, as shown earlier, for poets like Capgrave veracity could be demonstrated by citing authorities. For Bokenham, on the other hand, 'experience me tawt (*taught*) the soth (*truth*) to seyn' (Abbotsford Legendary, fol. 217r), as he provides personal backstories about his pilgrimages to the shrines of St Margaret (105–22) and St Winifred (Abbotsford Legendary, fols. 116v–117r) and how he gathered additional material for these legends. Fifteenth-century poets therefore had diverse options for authenticating their texts: noble or monastic patronage, saintly assistance, attempted historical accuracy, or a combination thereof.

The Narrative Suspended

Engaging other narrative genres, like chronicle and romance, was not the only way poets expanded their legendary 'matere'. Some poets elaborated their lives by adapting from non-narrative genres of worship and edification, thereby *decreasing* the legend's narrativity. Saints were honoured regularly in church services, so the language of prayer, praise, and spiritual exposition from sermons and the liturgy offered itself naturally to Middle English writers. These discursive registers of adoration and petition already inform the poetic of stasis, as Middle English poets borrowed imagery from hymns to elevate their poetic style. Some lives in the most formally elevated registers of aureation and the rhymed alliterative stanza, however, display a more wholesale integration of these non-narrative discursive modes with the event-based storytelling of saints' lives. In so doing, they reconfigure the boundaries of what a Middle English legend might entail, a 'life' becoming a meditation on the saint's eternal significance. Yet these poems never abandon the hagiographic storyline to transform into purely hymn-like devotional utterances. Rather, they stretch the concept of narrative, sometimes near its breaking point, without rejecting the linear account of the saints' deeds.

Only a handful of ambitious poets attempt to completely blur the line between storytelling and direct spiritual edification. Lydgate is the master of this technique. His saints' lives frequently prioritize elaboration of holy virtues over narrative continuity, and the impact of the liturgy is visible, for example, in the 'Life of Giles' passage discussed above, where the deer cycles between field and hermitage according to the monastic hours. The

---

⁴⁶ Carl Horstmann (ed.), 'Thomas Beket, Epische Legende, von Laurentius Wade (1497)', *Englische Studien*, 3 (1880), 409–69. This was inadvertently omitted from NIMEV; it should be NIMEV 2601.
⁴⁷ NIMEV 6; Karen A. Winstead (ed.), *The Life of Saint Katherine, by John Capgrave* (Kalamazoo, MI, 1999).
⁴⁸ Shannon Gayk, '"Ete this book"'; Auvo Kurvinen, 'The Source of Capgrave's *Life of St Katharine of Alexandria*', *Neuphilologische Mitteilungen*, 61 (1960), 268–324.

most ambitious example of this approach is his *Life of Our Lady*, integrating aureate praise, liturgical structures, and theological exposition within the storyline of Mary's life.[49]

Instead of turning to Lydgate for examples, I conclude by examining similar narrative suspensions in two anonymous poems, one in alliterative stanzas and one in rhyme royal. The alliterative 'Life of John the Evangelist' appears in Robert Thornton's manuscript, Lincoln Cathedral MS 91, paired in its gathering with two prose tracts by Walter Hilton and one attributed to Richard Rolle.[50] The rhyme royal 'Life of St Anne' in Cambridge, Trinity College MS R. 3. 21 opens a sequence of Lydgate's Marian poetry, including his Marian miracle the 'Legend of Dan Joos'.[51] Both poems are stylistically demanding, 'John the Evangelist' working in the stanzaic complexity of rhymed alliteration and 'Anne' operating in a Lydgatean mode through its metrical form, elevated style, and doctrinally weighty metaphors. Each participates in the discursive modes of the hymn and the sermon, respectively, to shape the 'matere' of their lives.

The alliterative 'John the Evangelist' is situated firmly within the language of worship. The entire poem is addressed to the Evangelist in apostrophe, like Latin and English hymns, and lauds his spiritual powers. The poem's modern editor has accordingly labelled the poem a 'hymn'. The opening and closing stanzas construct John as an exalted intercessor; as a 'gete or gem dere and gente, / As jasper, þe jowell of gentill perry' (15–16; *jet or valued and noble gem, like jasper, the jewel of noble precious stones*) who is 'lugede in lyghte' (5; *lodged in light*), John is characterized through gemological and light-filled metaphors. His virginity, like that of virgin martyrs, is established as eternally stable in the fifth stanza's sestet:

> Forthi was þou chosen, chaste as a childe;
> Oure cheftane He chose the, vnchangide of chere.
> Thi chere was full chaste
> Fro werkes all waste,
> Noghte assentand to syn.
> Full gude was thi gaste;
> Na filthe had defaste
> The, verray virgyn.
>
> (63–70)

(You were chosen accordingly, pure as a child. Our leader chose you, unchanging in bearing. Your behaviour was entirely chaste, separate from all worthless works, never assenting to sin. Your spirit was entirely good, no impurity had defiled you, true virgin.)

The alliteration on *ch* that carries over lines 63–5, as well as the repetition of 'chere' and 'chaste' in the sestet's first line, ties John's virginity to his immutability. As 'verray virgyn', John is both truly chaste and completely, wholly above sin, the sestet expanding on the previous lines to embrace all aspects of John's 'gude ... gaste'.

These hymn-like elements notwithstanding, the poem is fully narrative, deploying both thematic and structural elements that foreground John's holy deeds within the world.

---

[49] Joseph A. Lauritis, R. A. Klinefelter, and V. F. Gallagher (eds), *A Critical Edition of John Lydgate's Life of Our Lady* (Pittsburgh, PA, 1961). See further Meyer-Lee, 'Emergence'.

[50] NIMEV 2608; Kennedy, *Three Alliterative Saints' Hymns*, lxix, 10–18.

[51] NIMEV 2392; Parker (ed.), *Middle English Stanzaic Versions*, 90–109. The rhyme royal 'Life of Anne' also appears in Manchester, Chetham's Library 8009, following a verse account of the Assumption of the Virgin.

Although the poet emphasizes John's stable spiritual perfection, he insists that such perfection is only visible in John's actions, again through verbal repetition that links octave to sestet:

> And by thi werkes I wate þat þou was worthi.
> Wele worthi þou ware
> For thi werkes ay-whare
> And dedis by-dene.
>
> (22–5)

(And through your works I know that you were worthy. You were entirely, utterly worthy on account of your works and deeds everywhere.)

From stanzas 3 through 18, the poem retells John's life from his birth and relationship with Jesus to his exile on Patmos and conversion efforts. While the poet eulogizes some virtues, like his virginity, the poem does relate several episodes that display John's merits in action: his resurrection of a boy (185–92), his transformation of stones into gems (173–82), and his successful trial by poison (220–32). Like strongly narrative legends, the poem includes passages of direct address, both longer set speeches and shorter dialogue. The poem develops these features of strong narrativity to recount John's life within the second-person worshipful discourse of the hymn and the alliterative line's rich descriptive ability.

The rhyme royal 'Anne' is even less narrative than 'John the Evangelist'. Stylistically informed by Lydgate—one early reader attributed it to him—the poem is only partly an account of Anne's life. While incipits and colophons in the manuscripts clearly mark the legend as a 'life', the poem is driven by its theologically weighty metaphors rather than storytelling.[52] It only begins recounting standard legendary material (Joachim and Anne's virtues) thirty-nine stanzas into the poem, and it does so incompletely. The poet narrates Joachim and Anne's childlessness, the accusation by the temple priest, and Joachim's escape to the country, but the angels' proclamation to Joachim, told in reported speech, segues without pause into metaphors of praise at Mary's conception. The narrative never returns to Anne's storyline. Her parents' meeting at the city gate is never recounted, and Mary's childhood is related obliquely and out of sequence. Her presentation at the temple is given three lines (561–3) and her time there invoked via *occupatio* and the ineffability *topos* (603–16), but only after the poet has told of the Annunciation and Mary's marriage to Joseph (514–58).

Rather than providing a linear retelling of Anne's life, the poem offers a homiletic exposition on Anne's spiritual significance within salvation history's figural patterning. The poem accomplishes this via cascading metaphors, as the first one demonstrates:

> She ys forsoth that blessyd hygh erthe syne
>   Of the whyche the heuynly potter hath made
>   Of the most swete shoure of hys dewe dyuyne;
>   The pot of oure hope whiche shall neuer fade
>   The son of god conceued vs to glade

---

[52] Parker (ed.), *Middle English Stanzaic Versions*, 90, 93n, 109.

> In oure nature hath brought forth incarnate,
> Whyche of the hygh influence was create.
>
> (134–40)

(She is truly that blessed, elevated clay from which the heavenly potter, using the sweetest showers of his divine dew, has made the pot of our hope which will never fade. [The potter] has brought forth, in our nature, the incarnate son of God, conceived to comfort us, who was created from that elevated influx.)

Describing Anne's role in the mystery of the Incarnation, the conceit pictures Jesus's grandmother as the earthly clay from which was created Jesus, imagined as a divinely imbued pot, through the in-flooding of 'dewe dyuyne'. The poet heightens the theological mystery by characterizing Anne herself as paradoxically 'blessyd hygh erthe', and this figure deepens the affective connection between the reader and Anne: if Jesus is made 'In *oure* nature' of Anne's 'hygh erthe' (emphasis added), then the reader too partakes of Anne's privileged material substance.

The poem's extended metaphors, which continue in this vein, originate in the sermon tradition, here taking on a worshipful cast. They first appear in a sermon on Anne, written in the early twelfth century by Osbert of Clare, prior of Westminster Abbey, and they also figure in the English liturgy.[53] The poem is clear about its homiletic roots—it directly addresses its audience as 'Most dere brethern' gathered on 'thys day' (106) to 'halow and worshyp' (108) Anne's 'festfull memory' (109), and it refers to its source as 'the verrey pleyne Omely' (421; *true complete homily*)—but it is not a sermon itself. Rather, its aureate style transforms Osbert's ingenious metaphors into an extended poetic meditation on Anne and Mary's roles in the salvation plan. The earthly enactment of that plan emerges as the poem recounts Anne's life (not present in Osbert's sermon), but because the poem centres around her theological significance, her earthly actions are not retold in full.

While the 'John the Evangelist' and 'Anne' poets do narrate events from their saints' lives, a linear recounting of the legend is secondary, taking a back seat to the language of praise and doctrinal exposition. These poems, like Lydgate's *Life of Our Lady*, envision a 'life' not as a linearly organized sequence of episodes but as the saint's significance within a spiritual landscape that encompasses both earthly events and heavenly perfections. The saints' actions provide a framework around which the poet weaves theological explication that positions the saint within the divine design. Working partly within the non-narrative 'forme' of sermons and hymns, these poems' rhetorically ambitious poetic registers transform the 'matere' of a saint's life from a series of events to content more meditative than was typical in earlier legends.

The experimentation of poets working across the century finds its most imposing articulation in these legends, but such interplay between 'form' and 'matere' holds true for all poetic lives and miracles. While Marian miracles tend to be recounted in brisk narration that heightens the protagonist's destitution and therefore Mary's grace, saints' lives invite a more expansive approach to poetic elaboration, whether poets choose a lively, event-based, and dialogue-heavy narrative style, an extended account that prioritizes facticity and historical events, a 'high style' that partakes of the poetic of stasis, or a combination

---

[53] Sherry Reames, 'Origins and Affiliations of the Pre-Sarum Office for Anne in the Stowe Breviary', in John Haines and Randall Rosenfeld (eds), *Music and Medieval Manuscripts: Paleography and Performance* (Farnham, 2004), 349–68. The sermon is in Dom A. Wilmart, 'Les compositions d'Osbert de Clare en l'honneur de sainte Anne', in *Auteurs spirituels et textes dévots du moyen age Latin* (Paris, 1932), 261–86 (at 270–6).

thereof. The saintly subject matter is not an unchangeable ground upon which poets experiment with their verse; rather, the nature of sanctity itself was reconfigured through formal play. At the same time, saints' sempiternal perfection enabled poets to stretch their verse towards new literary heights. Liturgically inspired meditations, action-driven storytelling, authorial self-representation, and historically informed narrative all find their place within this collection of texts that showcase poets' ambition, inventiveness, and creativity aided by and serving their holy subjects.

CHAPTER 13
Religious Lyrics and Carols

Christiania Whitehead

Fifteenth-century religious lyrics range in tone and subject-matter from aureate addresses to Mary, Queen of Heaven, to affective laments over the obduracy of humankind, and from pastoral songs of joy at the nativity, to poignant lullabies to the Christ child helplessly foreseeing his tragic future. A majority utilize the carol form, consisting of an initial burden, repeated at the end of each stanza, whilst others adopt the fashionable poetic forms of rhyme royal and ballade, creatively combine alliteration with aureation and rhyme, or experiment with entirely new stanzaic forms such as Audelay's thirteen-line stanza. While some of these lyrics possess the traits conventionally associated with the classical, Renaissance, and Romantic lyric corpus, including a 'song-like' quality and a personal voice preoccupied with feeling,[1] the way the term has been used by anthology editors and scholars of medieval religious verse since the early twentieth century has tended to incorporate a far broader range of styles and forms of short poem.[2] Short poems building on liturgical phrases, interacting with Latin, indistinguishable from prayer, or, conversely, organizing and transmitting very basic doctrinal facts, have all found their way into modern anthologies of medieval poetry under the rubric of 'lyric', and by now the term seems so entrenched that it would be unhelpful to disavow it. Their presence helps us appreciate that the majority of medieval religious lyrics are primarily *instrumental* pieces of writing. Their easily-memorized rhymes and rhythms make them effective tools with which to teach, meditate, or gain remission from sins, recited prayerfully in front of an image. But their first-person voice is a world away from the closeted interiority of later lyric verse, instead ventriloquizing Christ's or Mary's pleas to mankind, or offering the generic Christian reader a script with which to make an acceptable contribution to that divine conversation.

In what follows, I shall explore the forms and subjects of a range of fifteenth-century religious lyrics and carols in relation to some of their most noteworthy authors and manuscript settings, tracing a broadly chronological path through the textual landscape. While, on the face of it, this may seem to give less prominence to key themes than has traditionally been the case (complaints of Christ, songs of religious love-longing), it *does* have the advantage of bringing other, frequently occluded, issues to attention. Twentieth-century

---

[1] Jonathan Culler, *Theory of the Lyric* (Boston, 2015).
[2] See E. K. Chambers and Frank Sidgwick (eds), *Early English Lyrics* (London, 1907), discussed by Julia Boffey and Christiania Whitehead, 'Introduction', in Julia Boffey and Christiania Whitehead (eds), *Middle English Lyrics: New Readings of Short Poems* (Cambridge, 2018), 1–11 (at 2); Carleton Brown (ed.), *Religious Lyrics of the XIVth Century* (Oxford, 1924); Carleton Brown (ed.), *Religious Lyrics of the XVth Century* (Oxford, 1939); R. L. Greene (ed.), *The Early English Carols*, 2nd edn. (Oxford, 1977); Douglas Gray (ed.), *English Medieval Religious Lyrics*, rev. edn. (Exeter, 1992); Thomas G. Duncan (ed.), *Medieval English Lyrics, 1200–1400* (London, 1995); Thomas G. Duncan (ed.), *Late Medieval English Lyrics and Carols, 1400–1530* (London, 2000); John C. Hirsh (ed.), *Medieval Lyric: Middle English Lyrics, Ballads and Carols* (Malden, MA, 2005); Rosemary Woolf, *The English Religious Lyric in the Middle Ages* (Oxford, 1968); Douglas Gray, *Themes and Images in the Medieval Religious Lyric* (London, 1972); Ingrid Nelson, *Lyric Tactics: Poetry, Genre and Practice in Later Medieval England* (Philadelphia, PA, 2017).

anthologies have sometimes created an impression of the bareness and anonymity of these short poems. However, quite a number of fifteenth-century religious lyrics *do* have a connection to a named author, most notably John Lydgate, John Audelay, and James Ryman. In addition, the greater visibility of the manuscript setting that has come about through recent trends in editorial practice has enabled us to gain a better sense of these poems, enhancing our understanding of their purpose from the texts and illustrations they sit alongside.[3] Many of the manuscripts which preserve significant numbers of fifteenth-century religious lyrics were produced and utilized in monastic milieux, continuing older patterns of preservation. Others, a product of newer currents, were assembled in gentry households to provide their members with spiritually edifying reading. Religious poems find their way alongside secular ones into commercially-produced London collections. Finally, carols are found clustered in a small number of institutional manuscripts associated with cathedrals, major religious houses, and college and royal chapels.[4] We begin with an example of monastic manuscript production, a sequence of twenty-five religious lyrics, probably by a single Benedictine author, apparently composed in London during the reign of Henry V (1413–22).

The Admonitory Poetics of Digby 102

Written in the shadow of the Lollard controversy, the poems of BodL MS Digby 102 make little impression on present-day poetic taste and have generally been excluded from modern anthologies of medieval religious verse.[5] Fervently committed to the ecclesiastical institution (reconvening itself under Archbishops Arundel (1399–1414) and Chichele (1414–43) as a hotbed of reform orthodoxy),[6] these poems proceed by admonition, excoriating the clergy for corrupt practice and urging the laity to confess and do penance, from a misanthropic perspective that takes an exceptionally low view of humanity, positioning it as wilfully vicious. The severity of the narratorial voice infects the characterization of Christ. Even though there is an antecedent tradition of versifying the Good Friday Reproaches (the liturgical reproaches addressed by Christ to mankind in the run-up to the Passion), the Digby author produces an unusually harsh version of this monologue (No. 10, NIMEV 2091). Rather than inciting pity, Christ threatens vengeance against his deficient church in elemental terms: 'Man, I can do þe erþe to shake, / Wiþ flood and drowtes, distroye ȝoure wele … Fyre and thonder fro heuene make; / Nes non fro my strokes may stele' (183–4, 187–8).[7] This bias towards retaliation resurfaces in No. 21 (NIMEV 2763), a

---

[3] See Susanna Fein (ed.), *John the Blind Audelay, Poems and Carols (Oxford, Bodleian Library, MS Douce 302)* (Kalamazoo, MI, 2009); Susanna Fein, David Raybin, and Jan Ziolowski (eds and trans), *The Complete Harley 2253 Manuscript*, 3 vols. (Kalamazoo, MI, 2014–15).

[4] A wealth of information on lyric manuscripts is embedded in the endnotes to Greene (ed.), *Early English Carols*, and Gray (ed.), *English Medieval Religious Lyrics*. See further, Julia Boffey, 'Middle English Lyrics and Manuscripts', in Thomas G. Duncan (ed.), *A Companion to the Middle English Lyric* (Cambridge, 2005), 1–18; Julia Boffey, 'Audelay's Carol Collection', in Susanna Fein (ed.), *My Wyl and my Wrytyng: Essays on John the Blind Audelay* (Kalamazoo, MI, 2009), 218–29 (at 223–4).

[5] Other items in the manuscript include an incomplete C text of *Piers Plowman*, a metrical paraphrase of the *Seven Penitential Psalms* by Richard of Maidstone, and *The Debate between the Body and Soul*. For a brief description of the manuscript, see Helen Barr (ed.), *The Digby Poems* (Exeter, 2009), 1.

[6] The seminal essay collection on fifteenth-century ecclesial reform is Vincent Gillespie and Kantik Ghosh (eds), *After Arundel: Religious Writing in Fifteenth-Century England* (Turnhout, 2011).

[7] Barr (ed.), *Digby Poems*, 180.

metrical paraphrase of the Beatitudes,[8] in which each blessing uttered by Christ (blessed are the poor in spirit, the meek etc.) is offset by an equivalent curse from Deuteronomy.[9] These parallels have a deadening effect upon Christ's mercifulness and amorousness towards man, so often the subject of vernacular lyrics, casting him instead as a financier invested in achieving a meticulous balance between punishment and reward. Even when the focus of the Digby poems turns towards Christ's love for mankind and his pleas for man's love in exchange (No. 17, NIMEV 3279), reprising petitions that have a long devotional history, it is remarkable how quickly the voice of love distorts towards a coerciveness we would now associate with marital abuse: if you love me, I'll seat you in heaven; if you won't love me, I'll return hate for hate and chase you with hell-hounds. Whatever your choice, you are unable to escape my lordship (137–60).

The Digby author's tendency to dwell on the stricter, more accusatory aspects of Christ presumably stems from the fraught religious climate of the early fifteenth century. While it remains a matter of dispute whether or not individual poems refer directly to Oldcastle's Rebellion (1414), a Lollard uprising against Henry V and Archbishop Arundel headed by Sir John Oldcastle,[10] nonetheless anxiety about heresy lurks beyond the perimeters of the texts, enforcing an emphasis on the transubstantive character of the Eucharist and the necessary mediation of priests to hear confession and bestow penance. No. 23 (NIMEV 1389), a vernacular rendition of a hymn by Thomas Aquinas venerating the Eucharist, comes as close as we get to registering this undercurrent of heterodoxy, interpolating an extra stanza insisting on the importance of priests in performing the sacrament (65–72). The appropriation of Aquinas's hymn to fight a contemporary battle offers a clue to the make-up of the poetic voice, which turns out to be overwhelmingly impersonal, formed from liturgical and scriptural elements and the axioms of wisdom literature.[11] Helen Barr has remarked on how difficult this voice is to question, posturing as it does as an expression of 'time-worn common sense'.[12] The tightly regulated form of these lyrics, largely consisting in an eight-line stanza which rhymes *abababab* without refrain, or *ababbcbc* with refrain, adds to the certitude of this stance—there are no stray elements, excess feet, or slithering moments of enjambment here. However, that posture also imposes limits on the figurative and lexical capacities of the poetry. Little is here that we have not seen before: such images as there are fail to arouse the imagination, instead, the poet makes repeated play with the commonplace binaries of 'pyne' and 'bliss', 'loue' and 'drede', 'body' and 'soule', and 'pyne' and 'mede', driving them before him from poem to poem. One poem alone seems to circumvent these limits. Following straight after No. 19 (NIMEV 1508), a conventional Complaint of Christ, No. 20 (NIMEV 3484) works as a parody in which the Body complains noisily that Christ has absconded with his feminine spouse, the Soul. In the comedy that follows, the Soul adopts many of the traits of the wayward wife of fabliau fame, conspiring with Christ to beat and humiliate the Body, and refusing to recognize its lordship over her: 'comeþ she hom in wraþþe ful hete ... Casteþ me doun, and doþ me bete, / And tredeþ on me and makeþ debate' (77, 79–80).[13] Developed at length, this allegory makes an ingenious contribution to Body/Soul debate poetry and the *Sawles Warde* textual tradition. Condoning the

---

[8] Matthew 5.1–20.
[9] Deuteronomy 27–8.
[10] Barr (ed.), *Digby Poems*, 7–10, disagrees with this, reading the poems as more generalized criticisms.
[11] The 'dirige' of the Office of the Dead, and the 'learn to die' textual tradition also inform certain poems.
[12] Barr (ed.), *Digby Poems*, 60.
[13] Barr (ed.), *Digby Poems*, 275.

Soul's spiritual adultery and bullishness towards her spouse, it also hints at an unorthodox appreciation of gender, possibly the only glint of rebellion within the whole rigorously controlled sequence.

Elsewhere, rebellion gets short shrift. On the contrary, the Digby poems are notable for the way they interlace many of the themes of religious lyric with episodes of political patriotism. No. 12 (NIMEV 910), 'God saue oure kyng and saue the croune', vindicates Henry V's divinely-held kingship and calls for loyalty and unity within the body politic, while Nos. 13 and 15 (NIMEV 3924 and 4070) moot unity at home as a prerequisite to success in the wars against France, stressing England's historic right to the French crown (No. 13, 113–20). Here, the incontestable poetic voice which morphs imperceptibly into God's voice at many points within the sequence, is requisitioned to uphold the national cause. No. 12 lights on the crown as an emblem of social and moral unity, while elsewhere the Digby author underlines reception of the Eucharist as the source of ecclesial unity. Within the idiosyncratic arc of these religio-political poems, the two begin to look barely distinguishable from one another.

Lydgate and Literary Devotion

Written during the same decades and within the same parameters of orthodoxy, John Lydgate's Benedictine lyrics, extant in numerous manuscripts, have garnered a much more appreciative modern critical response.[14] Like the Digby author, Lydgate celebrates the centrality of the Eucharist in fifteenth-century religious life ('A Procession of Corpus Christi', NIMEV 3606), and praises Henry VI as the champion of the church ('A Defence of Holy Church', NIMEV 2219).[15] Unlike the Digby author, he is also extremely invested in the efficacy of images (a Wycliffite bone of contention), arguing their reliability as accurate likenesses ('The Image of Our Lady', NIMEV 490), and setting them in motion in relation to his poems, so that the combination of the two—the recitation of the right words, in the right state of mind, in front of the right image—becomes spiritually generative, awarding the performer a set period of remission from purgatory.

Lydgate ploughs several of the same furrows as other fifteenth-century religious poets, but he also does some things differently. Singularly, he brings his immersion in Chaucer's poetry, and his conscious formation of himself as a post-Chaucerian writer, to his composition of devotional verse, encircling many of his main subjects in Chaucerian literary frames and couching them in Chaucer's most reverential poetic forms. On numerous occasions, Lydgate utilises the rhyme royal stanza (*ababbcc*) introduced to English verse by Chaucer,

---

[14] These manuscripts vary in kind and function, from BL MS Harley 2255, a collection of mostly religious poems intended for Lydgate's abbot, William Curteys, to Cambridge, Trinity College, MS R. 3. 20, and BodL MS Ashmole 59, commercial productions by the well-known scribe John Shirley, pairing Lydgate's poetry with ballades and roundels by Chaucer, Hoccleve, Gower, and others. Cambridge, Trinity College, MS R. 3. 21, is a later anthology which convenes Lydgate's lyrics and translations in the context of other catechetical and eucharistic materials, suggesting their active use in a paraliturgical context. See Boffey, 'Middle English Lyrics', 5; A. S. G. Edwards, 'Fifteenth-Century Middle English Verse Author Collections', in A. S. G. Edwards, Vincent Gillespie and Ralph Hanna (eds), *The English Medieval Book: Studies in Memory of Jeremy Griffiths* (London, 2000), 101–12 (at 104).

[15] I use the poem titles provided in Henry Noble MacCracken (ed.), *The Minor Poems of John Lydgate*, 2 vols., EETS, e.s. 107, o.s. 192 (London, 1911, 1934).

rightly noting its association with sonorous religious narrative in the *Canterbury Tales*.¹⁶ And on several others, he opts for Chaucer's much rarer eight-line stanza (*ababbcbc*), probably principally influenced by his *ABC to the Virgin*, where the capacious decasyllabic lines terminating in French-derived feminine rhymes (*socour, errour, debonayre, adversaire*), formally mimic the elevated subject of address.¹⁷

In 'The Fifteen Joys and Sorrows of Mary' (NIMEV 447), Lydgate opens by picturing himself leafing through a 'contemplatiff' book between midnight and dawn (5), subsequently using the textual meditations and images that he finds there as springboards for his own verse.¹⁸ The correlation with the bookish openings of Chaucer's dream-visions is not hard to see. The same poem (along with several others)¹⁹ closes with an *envoye*, addressing his composition and releasing it for hypothetical correction in words which closely paraphrase Chaucer's famous stanza from the close of *Troilus and Criseyde*:

> Goo litil tretys! And meekly me excuse,
> To alle tho that shal the seen or reede;
> Giff* any man thy rudenesse list accuse   *if*
> Make no diffence, but with lowlheede
> Pray hym refourne*, wher as he seeth neede.²⁰   *amend*
> (309–13)

In fact, it transpires that the influence of the closing apostrophes of *Troilus and Criseyde* runs even deeper. 'An Epistle to Sibille', a metrical paraphrase of Proverbs 31, praising the wife of noble character, closes with a suit to 'wyves ... wydowes ... And godely maydens yonge and fresshe of face' (127–8) to grant the poet grace, subtly evoking *Troilus and Criseyde*, V. 1772–8 and 1835–41.²¹ Similarly, 'A Ballade at the Reverence of our Lady, Qwene of Mercy' (NIMEV 99) opens by rejecting classical tales of erotic love in a series of measured exclamations: 'Lo, here the fin of the errour and the weere! / Lo, here of loue the guerdoun and greuaunce' (5–6) which amalgamate *Troilus and Criseyde*, 5.1828–34 and 1849–55.²² The positioning here is significant: it would seem that Lydgate's praise of Mary, and his religious verse more generally, begin where *Troilus and Criseyde* stops. His religious poetry self-consciously proposes itself as the celestial antidote to the tragedy and disillusionment suffered by the earthly lovers.²³ What is the effect of infusing these orthodox religious poems with such frequent Chaucerian echoes? On the one hand, it is possible to regard it as a bid for superiority: Lydgate requisitions Chaucer's literary effects to address a higher Christian subject matter. However, on the other it also has the inevitable side-effect of diffusing and distracting us from the devotional intention of the poems. When a petition to Mary is explicitly situated in relation to a Chaucerian classical romance or a dream-vision, we start to respond to it on *literary* terms, evaluating its intertextuality. The transparency of its gaze towards heaven, and the artlessness of its memorialization of the gospel, is lost.

---

¹⁶ It is used for the Man of Law's, Clerk's, Prioress's, and Second Nun's Tales. Elsewhere it is used in a more secular and classicizing frame for *Anelida and Arcite*, *The Parliament of Fowls*, and *Troilus and Criseyde*.
¹⁷ Geoffrey Chaucer, 'An ABC', in Larry D. Benson (general ed.), *The Riverside Chaucer*, 3rd edn. (Boston, MA, 1987), 637. Elsewhere, Chaucer uses the eight-line stanza only for the Monk's Tale.
¹⁸ MacCracken (ed.), *Minor Poems*, 1.268–79. See Mary Wellesley, 'Textual Lyricism in Lydgate's *Fifteen Joys and Sorrows of Mary*', in Boffey and Whitehead (ed.), *Middle English Lyrics*, 122–37.
¹⁹ For example, 'Cristes Passioun', NIMEV 2081 (113–20); 'An Epistle to Sibille', NIMEV 3321 (134–40).
²⁰ MacCracken (ed.), *Minor Poems*, 1.279.
²¹ MacCracken (ed.), *Minor Poems*, 1.18.
²² MacCracken (ed.), *Minor Poems*, 1.254.
²³ Robert Henryson's *Testament of Cresseid* offers another kind of sequel to the poem. See Chapters 3 and 26.

It is of a piece with the Chaucerian inflections of Lydgate's religious verse that he should also give singular weight to the individual circumstances surrounding the composition of these poems, undermining the universality of their sentiment (*'Benedic Anima Mea Domino'*, NIMEV 2572: at Windsor while the king is at Evensong; *'Gaude virgo Mater Christi'*, NIMEV 464: in bed at night in London),[24] and to the 'I'-voice's feelings as he writes. In 'The Fifteen Joys and Sorrows of Mary', halfway through the poem, Lydgate pauses to ponder the effect that inscribing Mary's sorrows has upon his own emotions: 'Of dreedful herte tremblyng in euery membre, / My penne quakyng whan I gan to write' (171–2).[25] Emotion breeds emotion, it seems, and while this is indubitably a key component of late medieval religiosity it also means that our readerly attention remains divided between the observation of Mary's anguish and Lydgate's empathetic distress. The poet intrudes himself between us and the object of devotional contemplation, creating a *mediated* poetics. Furthermore, in confiding to the reader his troubled feelings about his subject matter, the 'I'-voice creates an additional relationship within the poem: a horizontal bond of confessionalism between reader and writer which arguably exercises a stronger affective pull than the reader's much more distant apprehension of Mary.

As can be seen, Mary looms very large in Lydgate's devotional *oeuvre*. In addition to composing *The Life of Our Lady*, a compendious verse-hagiography (NIMEV 2574), he returns several times to her joys and sorrows—a way of reshaping her life-narrative as a series of emotionally oppositional 'stills'—translates hymns and salutations to her, and repeatedly eulogizes her posthumous exaltation as Queen of Heaven. Many of these eulogies show Lydgate at his most stylistically accomplished, apostrophizing her in rhyme royal via a series of figures derived from the liturgy and Old Testament: 'chambyr and closet clennest of chastyte ... O closid gardeyn ... cristallyn welle ... fructifying olyve ... redolent cedyr' ('Ballade at the Reverence of our Lady, Qwene of Mercy', 34–9).[26] Later, in the same poem, the lexical field of reference changes, and she is eulogized as a succession of birds and precious stones: 'O trest turtyl ... O curteys columbe ... O ruby ... O stedfast dyamaunt' (78–87).[27] Effectively, these addresses render the posthumous Mary as a figure of encyclopaedic moral amplitude, identifying her as the prime referent behind the poetic language of the scriptures and the natural world in all its categories. This is a wonderful way of conveying Mary's spiritual fecundity and the infinitude of her mercy. It is also a way of maintaining her at a level of unbroken metaphoric textuality, very different from Christ's continual plea to fifteenth-century readers to comprehend the *unmetaphorical* starkness of his broken body and blood.

With Mary's metaphoricity retained in mind, it is worth enquiring about the way in which Lydgate's *textual* images of Mary ('Celestial cipresse ... Charboncle of charite', 'To Mary the Queen of Heaven', NIMEV 2791, 9, 11)[28] work in relation to his evocation of *material* images likely to have been present before the reader in the form of a manuscript illumination or a statue or crucifix. Both work in tandem insofar as both convey Lydgate's confidence in the ability of visual objects authentically to reproduce the nature and channel the thaumaturgical power of Christ and his Mother. However, whereas physical images generally serve as the start or endpoint of a devotional lyric—a chance discovery of an image of a pietà in a book generating extended verbal veneration ('The

---

[24] MacCracken (ed.), *Minor Poems*, 1.288.
[25] MacCracken (ed.), *Minor Poems*, 1.274.
[26] MacCracken (ed.), *Minor Poems*, 1.256.
[27] MacCracken, (ed.), *Minor Poems*, 1.258.
[28] MacCracken, (ed.), *Minor Poems*, 1.285.

Fifteen Joys and Sorrows of Mary', 1–14), a completed poem being affixed to the crucifix it addresses ('Cristes Passioun', 113–14)—his textual images show a much greater capacity for unbounded amplitude and aestheticism. Mary is not just one literal image, of a bereaved woman, she is every type of image: tree, plant, bird and gem, all effortlessly controlled and set in harmonious relation through Lydgate's formidable formal skills. Doctrinally, Lydgate is an apologist for images, but his most penetrating arguments are implicit ones, demonstrated through the visualizing virtuosity of his verse.

Lydgate's interest in amplitude also carries over into his metrical translations. Like several other religious poets, he contributes to the pastoral and educational agendas consequent upon Archbishop Chichele's vision of a renewed English church by translating select psalms, prayers, and hymns from the liturgy (*Pater Noster, Ave Maria, Te Deum* etc.). His method, which is broadly representative of much fifteenth-century translation of this type, bears analysis. In '*Benedic Anima Mea Domino*', a metrical translation of Psalm 103, Lydgate converts each verse of the psalm into his hallmark eight-line stanza, beginning with a relatively faithful translation which then opens out into explication and Christological elaboration. Not only is the psalm text expanded in this way, its teleology is also fundamentally altered by the addition of a loose refrain occupying the last two lines of each stanza, emphasizing God's mercy and fervently requesting its application to the 'I' voice:

> And late þy mercy beon oure proteccyoun
> For oþer saufconduyt haue I noon for me ...
> (151–2)

> Nowe, good lorde, of mercy sheed þy lyght
> Myn hert tenlumyne þat boughtest me so deer.[29]
> (159–60)

The psalm is recast as a circular series of petitions for mercy, its linear narrative extension hauled back time and time again to the single truth of God's mercifulness, while the devotional 'I'-voice is made a much stronger presence, appropriating the content of the psalm to address its own spiritual situation. '*Deus in Nomine Tuo Saluum me Fac*' (NIMEV 951), Lydgate's free translation of Psalm 53, offers an additional example; here, a two-line variable refrain at the end of each stanza focuses on the 'I'-voice's ongoing need to reform itself in response to what it learns from the psalm: 'On hit to be remembred well y aught, / Which may me mende, whyll y haue tyme & space' (23–4).[30] 'The *Pater Noster* Translated' (NIMEV 2711) works somewhat differently. While each line of the prayer once again opens out into an expository eight-line stanza, in this case the closing refrain (line 8) repeats the opening of the prayer: '*O pater noster qui es in celis!*', while the sixth line of each stanza operates as an additional internal refrain, driving home the effect of the prayer upon the devil: 'The fende confusyd with all hys wyles.'[31] By means of these two refrains, the Lord's Prayer is effectively reassembled as God's militant action against the devil, rendering it a far more oppositional piece of writing.

---

[29] MacCracken (ed.), *Minor Poems*, 1.6.
[30] MacCracken, (ed.), *Minor Poems*, 1.11.
[31] MacCracken, (ed.), *Minor Poems*, 1.18–20.

John Audelay and the Liturgical Sequence

While Lydgate's religious lyrics reappear flexibly in a range of different manuscripts, the poems and prayers of his contemporary, John Audelay, concentrate themselves within one codex, BodL MS Douce 302 (c1426), creating a sizeable anthology periodically signed with Audelay's name, which has some claim to be considered the earliest Middle English author collection, although the poet's role in the actual production of the manuscript remains unclear.[32] In his later years, Audelay operated as a chantry priest at Haughmond Augustinian Abbey in Shropshire, having spent the majority of his religious career as chaplain to the aristocratic Lestrange household situated close by. His poetry collection bears the impress of both situations, containing salutations and meditations that might be read privately by lay people in the course of the mass, carols designed for festive performance within a secular household, and metrical prayers and exhortations (including material in Latin) that must have been intended principally for the Augustinian community.[33] The mix of audiences apparently envisaged within the anthology is paralleled by its wide range of poetic genres and forms. Poems of pastoral instruction shaped around catechetical numerology rub shoulders with prayers to the sacrament of the altar, verse sermons, visions, versifications of the Passion, *memento mori* pieces, and more dramatic and prophetic outbursts, using the mouthpiece of a rustic fool to excoriate clerical corruption and admonish preachers to return to the truth of scripture ('Marcolf and Solomon', NIMEV 947 etc.). Audelay experiments with many different stanza types, sometimes matching them to a specific genre: his salutations, for example, often deploy a nine-line stanza (*ababcdddc*) incorporating shortened fifth and ninth lines.[34] However, his most characteristic form is the thirteen-line stanza (*ababbcbcdeeed*), conducted in octo- or decasyllabic metre, where shortened ninth and thirteenth rhyming lines bracket three longer lines rhyming on the same sound.[35] On occasion, he also brings alliteration into play, colouring the admonitory content with a more oral and 'native' overlay.[36]

Like Lydgate's religious poems, much if not all of this material seems to have been intended for use *in church* rather than a private devotional setting: before an image or altar, with the purpose of gaining remission from sin, or to enrich participation in the liturgy. And, as with Lydgate's poems, translation is an integral part of the anthology, turning Latin liturgical prose and hymnody into vernacular stanzas, generally rounded off by a Latin refrain ('Song of the Magnificat', NIMEV 2271; 'Paternoster', NIMEV 3445; 'Seven Hours of the Cross', NIMEV 623). Also like Lydgate, but much more prominently and independently, Audelay's poems come accompanied by paratextual instructions for their use, mostly in couplet form. Here, however, the main emphasis is on the *order* in which they should be read:

---

[32] Fein (ed.), *Poems and Carols*, 1–3.
[33] Susanna Fein, 'English Devotions for a Noble Household: The Long Passion in Audelay's *Counsel of Conscience*', in Gillespie and Ghosh (eds), *After Arundel*, 325–42 (at 330–1).
[34] For example, 'Salutation to Saint Winifred' (NIMEV 1084), 'Salutation to Saint Bridget' (NIMEV 1058).
[35] Susanna Fein, 'The Early Thirteen-Line Stanza: Style and Metrics Reconsidered', *Parergon*, 18 (2000), 97–126.
[36] The principal example here is 'Marcolf and Solomon'. Several poems in the fourth section of the anthology, 'Over-Hippers and Skippers', 'Paternoster', and 'Three Dead Kings' (NIMEV 2736.11, 3445, 2677), also pair alliterative metre with a thirteen-line stanza; however, it remains uncertain whether these poems are Audelay's own compositions.

> I pray you, serys, pur charyté,
> When ye had red this, treuly,
> Then redis this Passion,
> What Cryst sofyrd* fore synful mon.[37]   *suffered*
>   ('Instructions for Reading 2', 1–4)

This emphasis on order, often linking together three or four items, such as a Middle English Salutation to Christ's Body at the time of its levation, and a subsequent Prayer for Pardon (NIMEV 4052), with two Latin Prose and Verse Prayers,[38] draws the majority of the poetry in the manuscript together into short *quasi-liturgical sequences*. This, to my mind, is what is unique about Audelay: his innate tendency to perceive poetry as a liturgical adjunct, and to phrase it sequentially.

Rory Critten notes that the couplets of instruction accompanying these texts personalize what are otherwise often conventional and impersonal poems.[39] Audelay's persona, however, is characterized very differently from the Chaucerian look-alike who haunts the borders of Lydgate's religious poems. Inhabiting not only short paratexts but also the final stanzas of several longer poems ('Dread of Death', NIMEV 693), together with two entire poems ('Audelay's Epilogue to the Counsel of Conscience', NIMEV 1200; 'Audelay's Conclusion', NIMEV 1210), Audelay constructs himself as a deathbed figure, straitened in all his senses, a prophetic voice channelling the words of the Holy Spirit,[40] and a penitential example to readers, demonstrating how to overcome the lures of the world:

> Herfore Y have dyspysed this worlde,
> And have overcomen alle erthely thyng.
> My ryches in heven with dede and worde
> I have ypurchest* in my levyng,   *bought*
> With good ensampul to odur* gefyng.   *others*
> Loke in this book; here may ye se
> Hwatt* ys my wyl and my wrytyng.   *what*
> All odur by me war for to be![41]
>   ('Audelay's Conclusion', 27–34)

This focus on Audelay's *exemplary* function may make us question how literally we should take these apparent self-disclosures. The deathbed subject-position is also somewhat conventional in fifteenth-century religious writing, as we shall see shortly. The decision to convene this anthology around the choices of a single 'authorial' voice, who makes his presence felt through internal and external interventions, is nonetheless an unprecedented one, marking a sharp shift in the possibilities of fifteenth-century religious verse.

The Fifteenth-Century Carol

The manuscript of Audelay's poems, BodL Douce 302, divides into four mini-anthologies, to some degree differentiated by the generic forms of Audelay's verse. The third mini-anthology, a group of twenty-five carols, has a good claim to be regarded as the earliest surviving collection of this genre, although a few individual examples appear in late

---

[37] Fein (ed.), *Poems and Carols*, 103.
[38] Fein, (ed.), *Poems and Carols*, 77–80.
[39] Rory Critten, *Author, Scribe and Book in Late Medieval English Literature* (Cambridge, 2018), 127.
[40] 'Audelay's Epilogue', 482–507.
[41] Fein (ed.), *Poems and Carols*, 224–5.

fourteenth-century manuscripts.⁴² As we learnt earlier, Richard Leighton Greene defines the carol as a lyric form, 'intended or at least suitable for singing, made up of uniform stanzas and provided with a burden which begins the piece and is to be repeated after each stanza',⁴³ and it seems probable that it originated as a song which accompanied dancing.⁴⁴ Although over half the late medieval carols which survive treat convivial themes associated with the Christmas season, the genre is not purely a festive one. This is well illustrated by Douce 302; here, the first five carols present catechetical subjects ('The Ten Commandments', NIMEV 304; 'The Seven Deadly Sins', NIMEV 858, etc.), before turning to a short micro-sequence cued to the Days of Christmas (25–9 December; NIMEV 3877, 3057, 2929, 601). The remainder of the collection shifts back and forth between religious and more societal subjects, interspersing devotions to St Anne and Mary (NIMEV 3244, 536), and a carol crying out for God's mercy from the deathbed (NIMEV 693), with praise of Henry VI (NIMEV 822), and endorsement of the conservative social and female sexual estates ('Virginity of Maids', 'Chastity of Wives', NIMEV 1595, 1630).⁴⁵ The spread of topics gives a good sense of the *variety* available to the genre: its brisk rhythm and easy burdens enable it to function as a successful pedagogic device fixing catechetical lists in the memory; its confident communal voice makes it a capable vehicle for social propaganda, while its form also has the potential to carry more intimate moments of self-loathing and existential fear:

> Here is cause of gret mournyng –
> Of myselfe nothyng I se,
> Save filth, unclennes, vile stynkyng –
> *Passio Christi conforta me.*   *Passion of Christ, fortify me*
> Ladé, helpe! Jhesu, mercé!
> *Timor mortis conturbat me.*⁴⁶   *Fear of death confounds me*
>   ('Dread of Death', 25–30)

Here we see that Audelay's distinctive tendency to interpolate his 'I'-persona into his poetry also permeates his carols. Elsewhere in the collection, idiosyncratically he follows an initial quatrain (*abab*) with a short, two-stress fifth line rhyming with the burden. This two-stress line, situated at the heart of the stanza, is the place from which he makes contact with his audience, deploying a personal voice to add extra conviction to otherwise conventional precepts: 'Leve ye me' ('Ten Commandments'), 'I say thee so' ('Seven Deadly Sins', NIMEV 858), 'I say, allegate' ('Four Estates', NIMEV 1588).⁴⁷

The spread of tones and functions throughout Audelay's carol collection is reflected in the dual instructions provided for their reception. An instructional couplet at the beginning of the section requests 'syrus' to sing these carols at Christmas, while the last stanza of the final carol to St Francis exhorts the same 'seris' to read reverently (NIMEV 44, 73–4).⁴⁸ The compilers of Douce 302 seem to have judged the carol suitable for both public performance and private readerly reflection, at this stage at least.

The fifteenth-century repertories of carols which succeed Douce 302 were probably put to similar uses, although the presence of musical notation in many of these manuscripts

---

⁴² For example, the preaching notebook of the Franciscan, John Grimestone: Edinburgh, Advocates' MS 18. 7. 21 (1372).
⁴³ Greene (ed.), *Early English Carols*, xi.
⁴⁴ Karl Reichl, 'The Middle English Carol', in Duncan (ed.), *Companion*, 150–70 (at 151–2).
⁴⁵ Boffey observes that these carols were not all necessarily by Audelay, noting analogues in other carol repertories: 'Carol Collection', 221–3.
⁴⁶ Fein (ed.), *Poems and Carols*, 206.
⁴⁷ Fein, (ed.), *Poems and Carols*, 175, 176, 190.
⁴⁸ Fein, (ed.), *Poems and Carols*, 175, 209.

indicates that public performance often took the upper hand.[49] While this notation remains independent of liturgical melody, these notated carols sometimes sit alongside liturgical music and Latin offices, suggesting that they were sung in abbeys, royal chapels, and cathedrals as a vernacular supplement to Latin hymns.[50] A couple of collections *without* music show close links with religious houses: BL MS Sloane 2593 was probably compiled at Bury St Edmunds Abbey, while CUL MS Ee.1.12, a collection of 121 carols composed after 1492, includes a colophon identifying their author as 'Frater Jacobus Ryman', a member of the Franciscan community at Canterbury.[51] Further collections including carols mixed in with other kinds of texts seem to have been designed as household miscellanies of a more or less pious character.[52]

Although carols were not the only medieval religious poems to bridge the linguistic divide between Latin and Middle English by utilizing macaronic forms of expression, they seem to have done so much more consistently than any other kind of poem. It is interesting to explore the variety of ways in which this works, and the insights it provides into how the two languages were evaluated within the carol corpus. In a carol such as *'Enixa est puerpera'* (NIMEV 61, 2645), in which the stanza quatrains consist of alternating lines of Latin and English, the languages remain relatively separate from one another:

> Lady, flour of alle thing,
>   *Rosa sine spina*,   *rose without thorn*
> That barist Jhesu, Heuyn King,
>   *Gracia diuina* ...   *by divine grace*
> Of al wymmen thou art beste,
>   *Felix fecundata*;   *happy fruitfulness*
> To al wery thou art reste,
>   *Mater honorata*.[53]   *esteemed mother*
>   (4–8, 13–16)

Each language rhymes with itself (thing/king; *spina/diuina*), and the English lines form an intelligible narrative in their own right, the Latin simply offering explanatory embellishment. Here, one might get away with only understanding English. However, more often the two languages show a much closer degree of integration. A majority of macaronic carols are furnished with a burden couplet in which an English tetrameter line rhymes with

---

[49] See BodL MS Arch. Selden. B. 26 (Worcester Cathedral?); BL MS Egerton MS 3307 (College of St George, Windsor, or Meaux Abbey, Beverley); BL MS Add. 5665 (Exeter Cathedral); BL MS Add. 5465 (Chapel Royal). BodL, MS Eng. poet e.1 (Beverley Minster? Daniel Wakelin however argues for a provenance in Norfolk on the basis of scribal dialect: 'The Carol in Writing: Three Anthologies from Fifteenth-Century Norfolk', *Journal of the Early Book Society*, 9 (2006), 25–49 (at 28)). Boffey, 'Carol Collection', 223–4.

[50] E.g., BL Egerton 3307, containing processional music for Holy Week, English carols, and Latin *cantillenae* with polyphonic musical settings; BodL Arch. Selden. B. 26 containing Latin and English carols and antiphons with music; Cambridge, Trinity College, MS O. 3. 58, a six-foot vellum roll containing Latin masses. Shelley Batt Archambo, 'The Development of the English Carol through the Fifteenth Century', *Choral Journal*, 27.3 (1986), 28–31.

[51] Fol. 80. The manuscript contains forty-five further religious poems by Ryman; Greene (ed.), *Early English Carols*, 306–7, 321. Poems by Ryman, or at least associated with his name, also appear in other manuscripts: John Scattergood, 'Two Unrecorded Poems from Trinity College, Dublin, MS 490', *Review of English Studies*, n.s. 38 (1987), 46–9; Richard Beadle and Anthony Smith, 'A Carol by James Ryman in the Holkham Archives', *Review of English Studies*, n.s. 71 (2020), 850–66.

[52] BL MS Add. 31042 (one of two manuscripts compiled by the Yorkshire gentleman Robert Thornton); Oxford, Balliol College MS 354 (copied by the London grocer Richard Hill); Edinburgh, National Library of Scotland, Advocates' MS 19. 3. 1 (mostly copied by Richard Heege).

[53] Greene (ed.), *Early English Carols*, 191A. NIMEV 61 and 2645.

a similar Latin line: 'Jhesus, almyghty Kyng of Blys, / *Assumpsit carnem virginis* (*took flesh by the Virgin*)'; 'Joy we all now yn this feste, / For *verbum caro factum est* (*the word is made flesh*; NIMEV 340)'.[54] Even more closely melded together, a *Terribilis mors* lyric in Balliol 354 (NIMEV 1444) gives the first half of each stanza line in Latin and the second in English:

> *Christus se ipsum*, whan he shuld dye,   Christ himself
> *Patri suo* his manhode did crye: to his father
> '*Respice me, Pater*, that is so hye,   look upon me, father
> *Terribilis mors conturbat me*'.[55]   dreadful death confounds me
> (18–21)

As Elizabeth Archibald notes, here, even Christ uses macaronics.[56] In all these instances, significant skill is required to conform Latin and English at the level of rhyme and metre, keeping the stress system consistent across the two languages, and some Latinity is necessary to make full sense of them. These requirements indicate a sophisticated milieu of composition and initial reception, most probably within a monastic or cathedral environment. The melding of Latin and English also tells us something about the way both languages were regarded. Occasionally Latin might be downgraded to supplementary ornament, but more often the two languages were placed in a balance, the one complementing and completing the other, with the Latin lines or half-lines (often lifted from the liturgy or lectionary) opening out into substantive vernacular continuations. The somewhat overlooked carol corpus reveals then that, at the end of the Middle Ages, Latin and English were perceived to harmonize, not simply at the level of doctrine and sentiment but also of form. *Both* were deemed fundamental to the full narration of the Christian story.

As well as being a focus of Latinity, the burden, sung initially and then repeated at the end of each stanza, also brings other qualities to the fifteenth-century carol. Greene has analysed its semi-independent character, noting that a single burden might be shared between several carols, perhaps losing one line in the process and gaining another, or switching from Latin into the vernacular.[57] This characteristic draws carols together into loose flows, but at the same time it makes it problematic for us to posit a meaningful connection between the stanza and burden within a particular composition, despite their possible connection through rhyme. Similar disjunctures occur where a pre-existent lyric is turned into a carol through the later addition of a burden. The tendency of the burden to embody communal sentiment and, often, to compel merriment ('What cher? Gud cher, gud cher, gud cher! / Be mery and glad this gud New Yere'; NIMEV 1873),[58] brings far-reaching changes of tone to otherwise sober texts.[59] Karl Reichl remarks upon the way in which Ryman's vernacular adaptation of one of the penitential psalms into carol form (psalm 51, NIMEV 2476) shifts it into a more sprightly register.[60] Here, the references to 'Mary's son' in the refrain and burden effectively remedy the confessions of moral shortcoming that determine the original psalmic voice:

---

[54] Greene (ed.), *Early English Carols*, 23A, 23B; NIMEV 340.
[55] Thomas G. Duncan (ed.), *Medieval English Lyrics and Carols* (Cambridge, 2013), 2.88; NIMEV 1444.
[56] Elizabeth Archibald, 'Macaronic Poetry', in Corinne Saunders (ed.), *A Companion to Medieval Poetry* (Oxford, 2010), 277–88 (at 283).
[57] Greene (ed.), *Early English Carols*, clx–clxxii.
[58] Greene (ed.), *Early English Carols*, 120; NIMEV 1873.
[59] Wakelin discusses some instances of this transformation in 'Carol in Writing', 37.
[60] Karl Reichl, 'James Ryman's Lyrics and the Ryman Manuscript: A Reappraisal', in Lucia Kornexl and Ursula Lenker (eds), *Bookmarks from the Past* (Frankfurt, 2003), 195–227 (at 217–21).

> Thou shalt not, Lorde, despise but know
> A contrite hert and meked lowe;
> Lorde, fro thy face thou me not throw,
>   *Fili Marie virginis.*   *Son of the Virgin Mary*
> Of thy mercy lete vs not mys,
>   *Fili Marie virginis.*[61]

Whether or not burden and stanza achieve a close degree of 'fit', there is always the potential for tension between the stasis of the burden—repeating the same prayer or declaration ad infinitum—and the teleology of the stanzaic progression. Sometimes this can work to undermine the certitude of the narrative outcome. The 'Carol to St Stephen' in Balliol 354 (NIMEV 4012) details Stephen's martyrdom, using the manner of his death to establish his efficacy as a heavenly intercessor in the final stanza. However, the remorselessness with which both refrain *and* burden continue to repeat '*Lapidaverunt Stephanum*' (they stoned Stephen), even after his theoretical apotheosis, means that we are left with a strong impression of the stoning as an ongoing, unredeemed atrocity.[62] The strain between burden and stanza is also exploited to interesting effect in the important sub-category of lullaby carols. In these female-voiced carols Mary is shown alternately conversing with the infant Christ and lulling him to sleep.[63] The scenario sounds innocent enough, but in fact these dialogues are fraught with tension, for the infant Christ turns out to have a precocious knowledge of what awaits him on the cross, making the reassurances of the answering burden seem increasingly inadequate and questionable:

> 'Dole it is to se,
>   Her shall I be
>   Hang upon the rode,
> With baleis to-bete*,   *beaten with scourges*
> My woundes to-wete*,   *streaming*
>   And yeffe* my flesche to bote*'.   *give, as ransom*
>
> 'Lullay, my chyld, and wepe no more,
>   Slepe and be now styll;
> The Kyng of Blyse thi fader ys,
>   As it was hys wyll.'[64]
>   ('This endrys nyght', 40–5; NIMEV 3596)

Does Mary understand that what awaits Christ is part of God's greater plan ('hys wyll'), or can she see no further than the miracle of the Annunciation? The same ironies attend the well-known 'Coventry carol' (NIMEV 2551.8), in which the lullaby-burden of the mothers of Bethlehem is offset by a stanzaic timescale veering from the anguished anticipation of their children's slaughter to its aftermath in the final stanza.[65] Consistently, it seems, the innocence of the nursery is set against acts of adult violence in order to deliver the greatest possible affective reaction.

Several lullaby carols position the dialogue between Mary and the Christchild as the product of a meditative vigil or dream vision. A late fourteenth-century Franciscan carol,

---

[61] Greene (ed.), *Early English Carols*, 276.
[62] Greene (ed.), *Early English Carols*, 100.
[63] Kathleen Palti, 'Singing Women: Lullabies and Carols in Medieval England', *JEGP*, 110 (2011), 359–82, explores the implications of the female voice.
[64] Duncan (ed.), *Medieval English Lyrics*, 2.66.
[65] Duncan (ed.), *Medieval English Lyrics*, 2.68.

several times recopied in the fifteenth century, opens 'Als I lay upon a nith, / Alone in my longging, / Me thouthe *I sau* a wonder sith, / A maiden child rokking' (NIMEV 352),[66] while a fifteenth-century carol, with several variants, lays more emphasis upon the sense of sound: 'This endres nyght, / About mydnyght, / As I me lay for to sclepe, / *I hard* a may / Syng lullay' (NIMEV 3597).[67] The presence of a meditating or sleeping 'I'-voice suggests that these carols construct themselves as Christian counterparts to the poetic dream-vision of secular love. It also removes Mary and the Christchild out of the field of historical time (despite initial appearances, we are not in a Life of Christ) and into the field of visionary time (a time out of time, as it were) in which a baby can converse intelligently with its mother, and see forwards into the future as well as backwards. The same mediated approach can be discerned in various carols in which Mary is encountered as *pietà*, lamenting the dead Christ laid across her lap. 'Sodenly afraide', one of the better-known such (NIMEV 4189), sketches the state of distressed semi-consciousness in which the narrator becomes cognizant of Mary's grief in its opening burden:

> Sodenly afraide,
> Half wakyng, half slepyng,
> And gretly dismayde –
> A wooman sate weepyng.[68]
>
> (1–4)

This, it would seem, is the psychological state required to gain full access to the sentiment appropriate to Christ's death. Like the lullaby carols, the encounter with Mary as *pietà* takes place in a compacted temporality outside historical time in which past and present intersect. On the one hand, Christ's wounds are still bleeding—he has only just died (27–8); on the other, Mary looks *through* time to the contemporary 'I'-persona and addresses him directly: 'On me she caste hir ey, / said, "See, man, thy brothir!"' (32), identifying herself as an affective model for the present age: '"Who cannot wepe, / come lern at me"' (31). Her visionary status is finally cemented by the way in which she takes leave of the narrator: '… with that word, / she vanysht away' (41). Visionary stature is disconcertingly akin to ghostliness, it would seem.

Carthusian Poems and Images

Having considered some key Benedictine and Augustinian lyric collections, and touched on Franciscan productions in passing, we will close with a poetry manuscript from a more reclusive religious order: the renowned northern Carthusian miscellany, BL MS Add. 37049 (c1460–70).[69] This extraordinary codex reiterates several themes we have already encountered, while also contributing some new ideas.

First, Add. 37049 continues the preoccupation with images that we encountered earlier in Lydgate's religious poetry. However, whereas Lydgate describes physical images and illuminations *in words*, positioning his poems as responses to them, Add. 37049 juxtaposes

---

[66] Greene (ed.), *Early English Carols*, 149. My italics.
[67] Greene (ed.), *Early English Carols*, 146B. My italics.
[68] Duncan (ed.), *Medieval English Lyrics*, 2.74.
[69] A digital facsimile of the manuscript is available on the British Library website. For a book length study, see Jessica Brantley, *Reading in the Wilderness* (Chicago, 2007).

poems and images alongside one another on the manuscript page, crafting a multimedia space in which both participate equally in the devotional programme. This complexity is often lost in modern anthologies in which the poem is reproduced but not the image. So, for example, the poetic diptych 'O man kynde' spoken by Christ (NIMEV 2507), creating the human response 'Jesu, my love, my joy, my reste' (NIMEV 1735), on fol. 24r, is clarified by reference to the images above the texts. A bloodied Christ presents a gigantic externalized heart containing a horizontal side wound, while an image of a monk kneeling before the heart brings specificity to the human reply.[70] Close attention to the manuscript page also uncovers a second verse to 'Jesu, my love', enumerating the drops of Christ's blood shed at the crucifixion, uniformly omitted from anthologies.[71] In this specific manuscript context then, attentiveness towards both text and image exposes these poems as Carthusian tools directed towards the devotion to Christ's wounds and blood.

Another useful example comes shortly after. Fols 25v–26r contain an eleven-stanza version of 'In a tabernakil of a towre',[72] in which the Virgin Mary makes yet another visionary appearance to a nocturnal 'I'-persona: 'As I stode musyng on the mone' (2). The vision arises from the poet's meditation on a statue of Mary as Queen of Heaven on the side of a tower—a clear indication of the power of architectural statuary to grant contemplative insight—and takes the form of an extended love-lament in which the Virgin sues for the love of mankind, appropriating idioms from the Song of Songs normally associated with Christ:[73]

> I take the ful fayne, *I clyppe, I kysse,*
>   *Quia amore langueo ...*   *Because I languish for love*
> *Nowe man, have mynde on me* forever,
> Loke on thy love thus languysshyng;
> Late us never fro other dissevere ...
>   (71–2, 89–91. My italics)

Both italicized phrases are conventionally spoken by Christ himself in lyric verse. Once again, this poem is accompanied by several telling images in Add. 37049. Its initial stanzas run alongside an image of the Virgin and Child in an architectural frame, with a kneeling Carthusian monk at the base. Superficially, the Virgin is portrayed in accordance with the *fin' amor* approach taken by the poem: shapely and elegant, with long golden hair. However, her depiction *with* the infant Christ (who doesn't feature in the poem) places obvious restrictions on the devotional imaginary, substantially curtailing her ability to resonate as a romantic love-object. The second half of the poem is set alongside a very different depiction of the Virgin: the iconic name MARY inscribed in a tree, followed by a prose note, purportedly by St Bridget, exhorting readers to dread the power of Mary's name. Here again, these visual accompaniments fundamentally modify the way we react to the written text. While the poem takes a sensual tone, depicting Mary as a woman languishing for love, this visual context encourages a much more *cerebral* response, deflecting the reader

---

[70] A variant of 'O man kynde' (NIMEV 2504), with a different human response, and the image of a kneeling layman, can be found on fol. 20.
[71] The second verse of 'Jesu, my love' is omitted from both Brown (ed.), *XVth Century Religious Lyrics*, 67, and Gray (ed.), *English Medieval Religious Lyrics*, 46B.
[72] This version varies in parts from Duncan (ed.), *Medieval English Lyrics*, 2.73, NIMEV 1460.
[73] Song of Songs 2.5, 5.8.

towards the abstract, graphological devotion to the Name of Mary, a fifteenth-century parallel to the cult of the Name of Jesus.[74] In sum, both illustrations act to *curb* the romanticism of Mary's poetic monologue within a Carthusian devotional milieu.

The Carthusian monk on fol. 25v not only kneels prayerfully before the tabernacled statue of Mary, he is also accompanied by a speech scroll inscribed with a devotional couplet. Such small-scale visualizations of poetic speech proliferate throughout the manuscript, most notably at fol. 19, where Mary, the crucified Christ, God the Father, an angel, a devil, and personifications of Death and Man's Soul are depicted surrounding the bed of a dying man. Each participant voices a couplet defining their relation to the fate of Man's Soul in a scroll rising vertically from their mouth. Essentially, the page offers the viewer a poetic psychodrama, using a visual technique not much different from a contemporary graphic verse novel. The same tactic can be discerned at fols. 28v–29r, where a poem recounting the seven ages of man is broken down into a series of speech scrolls issuing from the mouths of the protagonists: an angel, a devil, and seven temporal personifications of humankind. In all these instances we see an emphasis on the *voiced* poem, on poetry as dramatic conversation, and on poetry as a natural corollary to the vivification of images (part of a theology of images, as it were). These possibilities offer new, relatively uncharted ways of thinking about fifteenth-century poetics.[75] It is also worth reflecting on the relation of the short poems in speech scrolls uttered by devotional meditators to the 'main' poem on the page: do they pick up the same stress system and rhyme scheme or generate their own form? Should we view them as poetic glosses to the main text or as potentially independent verse prayers?[76]

Second, carrying across from Audelay's fascination with the didactic potential of his own deathbed and the Digby poet's dour preoccupation with the Office of the Dead, Add. 37049 is notable for the number and variety of its treatments of death. We have already mentioned the psychodrama surrounding the deathbed at fol. 19. At fol. 31v, 'The Dawnce of Makabre' (NIMEV 2589), a twelve-stanza poem describing the way in which death levels out the hierarchies of human society, is followed by an illustration of a transi tomb (an effigy of a beautiful woman on the upper slab set above an 'X-ray' image into the tomb showing her decaying skeleton), followed in turn by an eight-line poem in which the corpse from the preceding image speaks to draw attention to the lessons to be learnt from its decay. Fols. 33r–v contain a poetic disputation between the body and the worms who devour it (NIMEV 1563). Fol. 38v, rather similar to fol. 19, adds verse scrolls to a depiction of the protagonists around a human deathbed (which, in this instance, includes a Carthusian monk).[77] Elsewhere, images of Death piercing the side of a dying man with his spear recur several times,[78] forming an obvious counterpoint to the visual emphasis on the salvific

---

[74] The devotion to the Name of Jesus also figures extensively in Add. 37049: see, for example, fol. 23, displaying an image of the Name accompanied by a short poem describing how St Edmund Rich was instructed in a vision to write 'Jesus Nazarene' nightly upon his forehead; fol. 37, displaying a seated image of Richard Rolle, with 'IHU' inscribed on his breast.

[75] See, however, Brantley, *Reading in the Wilderness*, 211–58, 278–90.

[76] The long poem, *The Desert of Religion* (NIMEV 672; fols. 46–66v) is accompanied by many images of eremitic and monastic meditators, some of whom utter devotional quatrains.

[77] The presence of the monk is spiritual rather than physical. Carthusian monks could not literally have attended deathbeds other than in their monasteries. See also fol. 19v, a verse allegory of a man pursued by a unicorn symbolizing death taken from *Barlam and Josephat* (NIMEV 491), and fol. 69r, a poem on death including extracts from the *Prick of Conscience* (NIMEV 3428). Elsewhere, an extract from *Horologium sapientiae* explains how man should learn to die. It is interesting to observe how extracts from fourteenth-century prose texts are dexterously collated to construct a fifteenth-century poetry miscellany focused around death.

[78] Fols. 38v–43.

capabilities of Christ's side-wound and heart. As the manuscript progresses, the opposing destinations available to the dead take centre stage: images and poetic and prose texts show saved souls being escorted to heaven and damned souls committed to hell.[79] Earlier, an image of dead souls being drawn up in a basket from purgatorial flames while monks perform deeds of mercy and celebrate mass accompanies verses on the relief of souls from purgatory (fol. 24r).

Collectively, these examples suggest a strong strain of late fifteenth-century religious poetry directed towards the moment of death and its aftermath. They show the deathbed as a particular hub of poetic contention over the destiny of the soul, and bring colour and drama to that debate by stressing the violent binary between worldly beauty and posthumous corruption. Most importantly, these examples placed in their manuscript context indicate that the Carthusians saw themselves (and wanted others to see them) as remote providers of deathbed services, shifting dead souls from purgatory to heaven, and weighting the balance in favour of dying men's salvation through their intercessions and offices.[80]

The Rollean Miscellany

As well as continuing and extending preoccupations already encountered in the religious poetry of Lydgate and Audelay, Add. 37049 also contributes something distinctively new to our survey: a fascination with the fourteenth-century Yorkshire hermit Richard Rolle (d. 1349), which laces through the entire manuscript.[81] This would not be relevant to an essay on poetry were it not for the fact that it is precisely Rolle's work as a devotional poet, his distinctive posture of 'sitting and singing', and his claim to hear and reproduce the structures of heavenly song, which engages the interest of the compiler. Images of Rolle recur at different points in the manuscript, depicting him both as a sleeping visionary acting out his most popular vernacular treatise, *Ego dormio (et cor meum vigilat)*, and as someone who 'sits and sings', fired by the Name of Jesus inscribed on his breast. At fol. 30v, where he sleeps, he is shown experiencing a vision of the Virgin and Child and participating in a poetic exchange with them: a scroll issuing from Rolle's hand declaims 'I slepe and my hert wakes to the', answered by a scroll from Virgin and Child pronouncing 'If thou my trewe lufer wil be' (NIMEV 1367.8). The rhyme ('the'/'be') places the hermit and Virgin in linguistic harmony with one another (it should be said that the Virgin plays a much stronger role in this fifteenth-century imagining of Rolle than she does in his original treatises). At fol. 37r, where Rolle sits and sings, a poem to the right of this image self-reflexively voices his reception and translation of heavenly song into lyric poetry:

> Whils I satte in a chapel in my prayere
> A heuenly sound to me drew nere
> For þe sange of sanges I felt in me
> And my þought turned into luf dyte
> Of þe heuenly and sweetest armony

---

[79] Fols. 70v forwards.

[80] In doing so, they place themselves within a strong northern eremitic tradition emphasizing these deathbed abilities. See, for example, the Life of St Godric of Finchale.

[81] We should note, however, that BodL MS Douce 302 includes a prose treatise by Rolle in its final section, focused on the end of life.

>   Þe whilk I toke in mynde delitabylly.
>   Þerfore, I sytt and syng of luf langyng ...[82]

A very similar image of Rolle recurs part way through the long poem, *The Desert of Religion* (fol. 52v), accompanied by a couplet from one of his songs of 'love-longing to Jesus'. Rolle's poetry insinuates itself into later (and dryer) religious verse, injecting it with his charisma, and physically and formally displays its harmonious resonance with divine song. When 'aungeles songe' appears as a series of independent lyric items towards the end of the manuscript, its inclusion needs to be viewed with these Rollean precedents held in mind.[83]

Once again, we need to consider these Rollean tags within their Carthusian manuscript milieu. Add. 37049 demonstrates the degree to which a northern Carthusian house modelled its spirituality upon the meditative example of Rolle, and on specific texts by him, in the fifteenth century. The manuscript foregrounds Rolle's performance of devotional songs, drawing his inspiration from the angels, and this in turn seems to become both the inspiration and justification for the poetic work of the miscellany as a whole. While it would be an exaggeration to argue that Rolle's poetic practice underwrites fifteenth-century religious poetry in its entirety, nonetheless his lyrics and meditations *do* reappear, intertwined with more contemporary religious poems and devotions, in other key miscellanies, including several intended for audiences outside the monastery.[84] An account of fifteenth-century religious lyric poetry is incomplete without a consideration of Rolle's poetic reception.

Conclusion

While the fifteenth century opens on a religio-political poetic note, channelling the post-Wycliffite church's zeal for penitence and orthodox reform, it quickly broadens to encompass many other kinds of religious sentiment. The stanzaic translation of scriptural poems and hymns plays a seminal role in poetic output, pressing to the fore the relation between Latin and the vernacular, explored from a different angle in the vogue for macaronic verse. Poetry's alignment to prayer, the divine office, and the celebration of mass are also central—in effect, religious lyrics often seem to have been envisaged principally as a private supplement to public participation in the liturgy. At times, these types of poems are given a curiously literary tint—harnessing Chaucer's characteristic tropes and apostrophes to a more ecclesiastical purpose. The Virgin Mary also becomes a locus for extravagant literariness, inspiring an ornate poetry founded entirely upon metaphor.

The newest religious form of the fifteenth century, the carol, directs our attention towards the possibilities and limitations of employing a repetitive burden within a communal and musical context of performance. At the other end of the spectrum, poetry also emerges from the extraordinarily withdrawn circumstances of the Carthusian regime,

---

[82] NIMEV 4076. For an excellent analysis of this two-page opening, see Katherine Zieman, 'Compiling the Lyric: Richard Rolle, Textual Dynamism and Devotional Song in London, British Library, Additional MS 37049', in Boffey and Whitehead (eds), *Middle English Lyrics*, 158–73.

[83] See fols. 70v–1, 71r–v, 74v–5, 76, 76r–v, 77r, songs of angels by Thomas Hoccleve, from Deguileville's *Pilgrimage of the Soul* (NIMEV 233, 263, 1242, 1243, 1246, 1248, 1249); 77v, a full-page image of the nine orders of angels; 78–9, a Dionysian tract on the angelic orders.

[84] See, for example, Lincoln Cathedral Library, MS 91, one of two manuscripts compiled by the Yorkshire landowner, Robert Thornton, intertwining Rollean items with contemporary devotions to the five wounds, the *arma Christi*, and seven joys of Mary, alongside other devotional prose pieces.

compensating for the strictures of reclusion by participating in ingenious textual performances, intersecting with images, and adopting a distinctively visionary format. Some of these preoccupations continue into the Protestant sixteenth century, the penitential 'I'-persona gaining an ever-stronger hold over the poetics of religious commonplace. Others do not: the easy traffic with images, in particular, is irrevocably damaged by Tudor iconoclasm, leading ultimately to the visually duplicitous panoramas of Spenser's religious allegory. Manuscript gives way to print, and with it, the opportunity to admire the eccentric collocations of Douce 302 and Add. 37049, and consider the religious lyric under a wholly individual lenses. Much is gained, but something is also lost.

CHAPTER 14
The Poetry of Religious and Moral Drama

Tamara Atkin

> ANIMA. *Hanc amaui et exquisiui:*   *This have I loved and sought*
> Fro my youghte thys haue I sowte
> To haue to my spowse most specyally,
> For a louer of yowr schappe am I wrowte*.   *created*
> Aboue all hele* and bewty þat euer was sowght   *health*
> I haue louyde Wysdom as for my light,
> For all goodness wyth hym ys brought*.   *Because all goodness comes with him*
> In wysdom I was made all bewty bryghte.[1]

These are the first lines given to Anima (i.e., the Soul) in the fifteenth-century play *Wisdom*. Like many characters from medieval English drama, her words are adapted from the Bible (*Wisdom* 8.2, 7.10, and 7.11). But her words do more than translate the biblical text; they seek to embody its authority. Adopting an eight-line or ballade stanza that rhymes *ababbcbc*, Anima uses a form that by the fifteenth century had come to be associated with serious, moral, and often Marian authority.[2] It is a form used elsewhere in medieval English drama, notably by the character Mercy in the morality play *Mankind*, and in *Wisdom* it is used, at different points, for all of the speaking characters with the exception of Lucifer. Typically, the play's speeches that assume this form are one or more stanzas in length, but at its opening, Anima and Wisdom share stanzas in a way that formally echoes the marriage between them:

> ANIMA. O endles Wysdom, how may I haue knowynge*   *knowledge*
> Off þi Godhede incomprehensyble?
> WYSDOM. By knowynge of yowrsylff 3e* may haue felynge   *through self-knowledge*
> Wat Gode ys in yowr sowle sensyble.
> The more knowynge of yowr selff passyble*,   *The more you know yourself*
> þe more veryly 3e xall* God knowe.   *you shall*
> (*Wisdom*, 93–8)

As Anima learns though this catechism-like sequence of questions and answers, knowledge of self and God are inseparable; Anima's allegorical marriage to Wisdom is therefore also one that binds her to Christ. The distribution of stanzas between these two characters consequently emphasizes their marriage as the play's sustaining metaphor.

---

[1] NIMEV 1440; *Wisdom*, 17–24, in Mark Eccles (ed.), *The Macro Plays*, EETS, o.s. 262 (Oxford, 1969).
[2] This verse form does not have a name in Middle English and the term 'ballade' is not universally accepted by modern critics. Its widespread use for English poetry can be traced to Chaucer, who perhaps conceived it as an adaptation of the Italian *ottava rima* stanza used for the *Teseida* and *Filostrato*. He makes use of it for the *Monk's Tale* as well as the Marian lyric the *ABC*, and it subsequently became a popular choice for Marian verse. Its moral associations are set out by Vincent Gillespie in 'Moral and Penitential Lyrics', in Thomas G. Duncan (ed.), *A Companion to the Middle English Lyric* (Cambridge, 2005), 68–96.

The ballade is not the only stanza form used in this play, and the *Wisdom*-playwright experiments with a range of different forms—from tail-rhyme to twelve-line stanzas—in ways that underpin the play's moral and theological message about the union between the human soul and Christ, and the various ways Lucifer works to undermine this relationship.[3] Neither arbitrary, nor even purely aesthetic, poetry is therefore integral to this play's meaning. The intention of this chapter is to reframe discussion of medieval English drama in ways that emphasize its status as poetry, and to show how its poetic forms contribute to its dramatic effects. The chapter therefore begins with two assumptions: that the surviving corpus of medieval drama should be understood as primarily a fifteenth-century cultural phenomenon; and that it should be read as poetry.[4] Before proceeding, these assumptions require further consideration. The medieval drama that survives covers an expansive array of forms and genres. It includes, but is not limited to, biblical drama, saint and miracle plays, moralities, and secular interludes. The category of drama might also be expanded to include texts with no known performance history, but which nonetheless seem to have been intended for performative engagement. However, while generally understood as a product of the fifteenth century, the extant texts preserved in manuscript and print are only rarely dateable to that century, and performance records often indicate traditions that stretch back to the fourteenth century and forwards through the sixteenth century.

The Witnesses

Of the so-called mystery plays, only BL MS Add. 35290, the sole witness to the full cycle of plays from York, can be dated squarely to the fifteenth century, and it is usually accepted that the main scribe's work on the manuscript took place between 1463 and 1477.[5] However, a cycle of plays being performed to celebrate the annual festival of Corpus Christi is first recorded in York as early as 1377 and references recur in the city's archives until at least as late as 1580.[6] Twenty-four of the twenty-five plays that make up the Chester cycle survive only in manuscripts copied between 1591 and 1604 from a single, now lost exemplar,

---

[3] On the relationship between verse form and meaning in *Wisdom*, see Eleanor Johnson, *Staging Contemplation: Participatory Theology in Middle English Prose, Verse, and Drama* (Chicago, IL, 2018), 139–68.

[4] In the discussion that follows, the following editions are used as standard. For York (NIMEV 1273), Richard Beadle (ed.), *The York Plays: A Critical Edition of the York Corpus Christi Play as Recorded in British Library Additional MS 35290*, 2 vols., EETS, s.s. 23–4 (Oxford, 2009 and 2013). For *Everyman* (c1515; STC 10604), Clifford Davidson, Martin W. Walsh, and Ton J. Broos (eds), *Everyman and its Dutch Original, Elckerlijc* (Kalamazoo, MI, 2007). For the Croxton *Play of the Sacrament* and the Brome *Abraham and Isaac* (NIMEV 786), Norman Davis (ed.), *Non-Cycle Plays and Fragments*, EETS, s.s. 1 (Oxford, 1970). For *The Castle of Perseverance* (NIMEV 917), *Mankind* (NIMEV 3495), and *Wisdom* (NIMEV 1440), Mark Eccles (ed.), *The Macro Plays*, EETS, o.s. 262 (Oxford, 1969). For Chester (NIMEV 716), R. M. Lumiansky and David Mills (eds), *The Chester Mystery Cycle*, 2 vols., EETS, s.s. 3 and 9 (Oxford, 1974 and 1986). For the Digby *Mary Magdalen* (NIMEV 1291), Donald C. Baker, John L. Murphy, and Louis B. Hall Jr. (eds), *The Late Medieval Religious Plays of Bodleian MSS Digby 133 and E Museo 160*, EETS, o.s. 283 (Oxford, 1982). For *Fulgens and Lucrece*, Alan H. Nelson (ed.), *The Plays of Henry Medwall* (Cambridge, 1980). For N-Town (NIMEV 2321), Stephen Spector (ed.), *The N-Town Play: Cotton MS Vespasian D.8*, 2 vols., EETS, s.s. 11–12 (Oxford, 1991). For Towneley (NIMEV 715), Martin Stevens and A. C. Cawley (eds), *The Towneley Plays*, 2 vols., EETS, s.s. 13–14 (Oxford, 1994). For *Henry VI's Triumphal Entry into London* (NIMEV 3799), see Henry Noble MacCracken (ed.), *The Minor Poems of John Lydgate*, 2 vols., EETS, e.s. 107, o.s. 192 (London, 1911, 1934), 2.630–48. All citations will be to these editions (unless otherwise specified), with line numbers given parenthetically within the text.

[5] On the dating of this manuscript, see Beadle (ed.), *The York Plays*, 1.xii–xviii.

[6] Systematic record-keeping of the civic records began in York in the 1370s, and the A/Y Memorandum Book, begun during the first half of 1377, contains a list of rents for the previous year that includes a payment for a place where three Corpus Christi pageant wagons were kept. See York, City Archives, A/Y Memorandum Book, fol. 4v. The last recorded performance took place at Whitsun 1569, though a further performance was mooted

itself a copy from unknown sources.[7] Critics disagree about the extent to which these witnesses preserve the features an earlier fifteenth-century version of the cycle.[8] Only the Chester *Antichrist* in Aberystwyth, National Library of Wales, MS Peniarth 399 is generally accepted as a fifteenth-century artefact. Two other manuscripts contain the Towneley and N-Town plays. These are often referred to as mystery cycles but are in fact compilations of plays of varied origins and auspices. Until the last century, it was assumed that San Marino, CA, Huntington Library, MS HM 1, which preserves the Towneley plays, was a fifteenth-century witness to a series of pageants performed annually by the craft guilds of Wakefield.[9] But over the last twenty years, the consensus has shifted and the manuscript is now regarded as containing a collection of texts originally performed alone or in short sequences in various locations in the West Riding of Yorkshire, and copied down by a chancery clerk writing during the reign on the Catholic Queen Mary I.[10] Like Towneley, the N-Town plays were once associated with a specific place: in this case, Coventry. However, they are now similarly understood as a compilation, copied down in in East Anglia in the years between 1460 and 1520 and preserved as BL MS Cotton Vespasian D VIII.[11]

Other witnesses to cycle drama are fragmentary. Of the Coventry Corpus Christi plays, only two pageants survive: the Weavers' *Presentation/Doctors*, which is extant in a sixteenth-century version prepared by Robert Croo;[12] and the Shearmen and Taylors' *Infancy of Jesus*, the original copy of which was lost in the fire in the Birmingham Free Library in 1879.[13] Like the Shearmen and Taylors' play, the original manuscripts of single pageants from Norwich and Newcastle have been lost, though records for a Newcastle

in April 1579. See Alexandra F. Johnston and Margaret Rogerson (eds), *Records of Early English Drama: York*, 2 vols. (Toronto, 1979), 1.390.

[7] They are: San Marino, CA, Huntington Library, MS HM 2; BL MS Add. 10305; BL MS Harley 2013; BodL MS Bodley 175; and BL MS Harley 2124.

[8] As Sheila Christie has summarized, 'David Mills and those who follow him … see continuity between scriptural dramatic activity evident in Chester during the fifteenth century and the extant cycle of the sixteenth century, whereas Lawrence Clopper and those of his scholarly lineage argue for a clear break between the fifteenth-century Corpus Christi play and the sixteenth-century Whitsun plays'. Sheila Christie, 'The Chester Cycle', in Thomas Betteridge and Greg Walker (eds), *The Oxford Handbook of Tudor Drama* (Oxford, 2012), 21–35 (at 21). For more on the difficulty in dating the Chester cycle, see Matthew Sergi, 'Un-Dating the Chester Plays: A Reassessment of Lawrence Clopper's "History and Development" and MS Peniarth 399', in Tamara Atkin and Laura Estill (eds), *Early British Drama in Manuscript* (Turnhout, 2019), 71–102.

[9] See, for instance, the work of A. C. Cawley and Martin Stevens in their edition and facsimile of the plays: *The Towneley Plays* and *The Towneley Cycle: A Facsimile of Huntington MS HM 1* (San Marino, CA, 1976).

[10] The manuscript was re-dated by Malcom Parkes in 2002. See https://reed.utoronto.ca/malcolm-parkes-letter/ (accessed 11 October 2019). On the consequences of this re-dating, see, for instance, Garrett P. J. Epp, '"Corectyd & not playd": An Unproductive History of the Towneley Plays', *Research Opportunities in Renaissance Drama*, 43 (2004), 38–53; Alexandra F. Johnston, 'The Towneley Plays: Huntington Library MS HM 1', in Atkin and Estill (eds), *Early British Drama in Manuscript*, 55–70; and Barbara D. Palmer, 'Recycling the "Wakefield Cycle": The Records', *Research Opportunities in Renaissance Drama*, 41 (2002), 88–130.

[11] The manuscript's unusual piecemeal construction was first considered by Peter Meredith in 'A Reconsideration of Some Textual Problems in the N-Town Manuscript (BL MS Cotton Vespasian D VIII)', *Leeds Studies in English*, n.s. 9 (1977), 35–50; and 'Manuscript, Scribe and Performance: Further Looks at the N-Town Manuscript', in Paula Neuss (ed.), *Aspects of Early English Drama* (Cambridge, 1983), 109–28. The broader implications of his findings inform discussion like Alan J. Fletcher, 'The N-Town Plays', in Richard Beadle (ed.), *The Cambridge Companion to Medieval English Theatre* (Cambridge, 1994), 163–88; and Douglas Sugano, '"The game wel pleyd in good a-ray": The N-Town Playbooks and East Anglian Games', *Comparative Drama*, 28 (1994), 221–34.

[12] Coventry, City Record Office, Accession 11/2. An earlier, 119-line fragment of the same pageant is Coventry, City Record Office, Accession 11/1. For further discussion of these playbooks, see Pamela M. King, 'The Coventry Playbooks', in Atkin and Estill (eds), *Early British Drama in Manuscript*, 33–54.

[13] This text was twice transcribed and edited before the manuscript was lost. See Thomas Sharp (ed.), *The Pageant of the Sheremen and Taylors* (Coventry, 1817), and *A Dissertation on the Pageants or Dramatic Mysteries Anciently Performed at Coventry* (Coventry, 1825).

cycle go back at least as far as the middle of the fifteenth century.[14] In contrast, it is unclear whether the *Abraham and Isaac* pageants that survive from Northampton and Brome were ever part of larger series. Both are preserved in fifteenth-century witnesses: Brome in New Haven, CT, Beinecke Library, MS 365, a modest vernacular miscellany; and Northampton in Dublin, Trinity College, MS 432, a largely political miscellany thought to have been copied in 1461.[15] *The Killing of the Children* in BodL MS Digby 133 seems also to have functioned as a stand-alone text, though one that can be dated to the following century.[16]

Of the extant corpus of biblical drama, then, only a handful of witnesses can be dated to the fifteenth century. That said, the relationship between any manuscript copy of a text and its composition is always fraught, and this is especially true of drama, where recurrent performance can explain both an extended gap between the writing of a play and the production of a surviving witness and the likelihood that any such witness will reflect the sorts of changes inevitable when a play is performed over decades or even centuries. Consequently, it is important—though not always possible—to know the precise relationship between witnesses and performance. In the case of the York 'Register', the manuscript is an official copy that functioned to assist the Corporation in the management of the pageants. Guild copies, like the Coventry Weavers' *Presentation/Doctors* or the Chester *Antichrist*, were clearly intended to enable performance and were demonstrably used as production scripts. The late full-cycle manuscripts of the Chester plays, by contrast, appear to be antiquarian projects undertaken to preserve records of local performance before they passed out of living memory. And sometimes, the texts neither record a past performance nor enable a future one, but seem instead to have been copied to be read. Thus Joe Stadolnik has argued the Brome *Abraham* was written down 'to enrich the mixture of devotional and narrative reading material' found elsewhere in the Book of Brome.[17] A similar case might be made for the two biblical 'plays' *Christ's Burial* and *Christ's Resurrection* preserved in BodL MS e Museo 160, an early sixteenth-century manuscript of miscellaneous materials thought to have been used in the instruction of Carthusian lay brethren.[18] There is no evidence that these meditative plays were ever performed, though the case for the Carthusian practice of performative reading is now well established.[19]

So far, I have only accounted for the material witnesses to biblical drama, and when it comes to the surviving corpus of morality and saint plays the extant texts similarly comprise a mixture of fifteenth-century and post-medieval artefacts. While records suggest that hagiographic drama may have once represented the most widespread form of religious entertainment, the surviving texts are few, and seem mostly to reflect a once rich East Anglian tradition. The same Digby manuscript that contains *The Killing of the Children* also preserves the sole extant copies of *The Conversion of St Paul* and *Mary Magdalen*, as well as an incomplete copy of the morality play *Wisdom*. These plays were copied by different scribes and seem to have circulated independently before being included in BodL MS Digby 133. *The Conversion of St Paul* and *Mary Magdalen* have been dated to the early sixteenth century, but the copy of *Wisdom*, though thought to be in the same hand as *The Killing of the Children*, is somewhat earlier, perhaps belonging to the final decade

---

[14] For a discussion of the manuscript situation, see Davis (ed.), *Non-Cycle Plays*, xxii–xlvii.

[15] A codicological account of their different auspices is given in Joe Stadolnik, 'The Brome *Abraham and Isaac* and Impersonal Compilation', in Atkin and Estill (eds), *Early British Drama in Manuscript*, 19–32.

[16] The date 1512 appears on fols. 146, 146v, and 157v.

[17] Stadolnik, 'The Brome Abraham and Isaac', 24.

[18] Laviece Ward, 'The E Museo 160 Manuscript: Writing and Reading as Remedy', in James Hogg (ed.), *The Mystical Tradition and the Carthusians* (Salzburg, 1995), 68–86.

[19] Jessica Brantley, *Reading in the Wilderness: Private Devotion and Public Performance in Late Medieval England* (Chicago, IL, 2007).

of the fifteenth century.[20] All three plays, however, bear the initials of Miles Blomfylde, a sixteenth-century East Anglian antiquarian, though he can hardly be attributed with assembling the volume in its present form; early foliation suggests that the pamphlets containing *The Conversion of St Paul*, *The Killing of the Children*, and *Wisdom* were all added between 1616 and 1634, when Kenelm Digby's library was bequeathed to the Bodleian.[21] Another East Anglian play, the Croxton *Play of the Sacrament,* completes the record of full-text saint and miracle plays, and it too is a late survivor. Though it treats a miracle purported to have taken place in 1461, the manuscript copy may be as late as the middle of the sixteenth century.[22]

Together with Digby 133, the Macro manuscript Washington DC, Folger Shakespeare Library, MS V.a.354 is considered the major surviving compilation of East-Anglian non-cycle drama. In addition to preserving the only full copy of *Wisdom*, it contains two further examples of the morality genre: *The Castle of Perseverance* and *Mankind*. So-called after its eighteenth-century owner, Rev. Cox Macro (d. 1767), the manuscript contains two plays (*Mankind* and *Wisdom*) copied by Thomas Hyngham, a fifteenth-century monk from the Benedictine abbey at Bury St Edmunds.[23] The copy of *The Castle* is older still. Usually dated to around 1440, it is clear the scribe was working from an earlier manuscript, and internal references in the text make it possible to date the play to the first quarter of the fifteenth century. These three plays, then, would seem to identify morality drama as a fifteenth-century genre, and that is certainly the line adopted by a number of twentieth-century critics.[24] More recently, however, the dominance of the morality genre has been shown to be overstated, and the surviving examples may be less representative of fifteenth-century dramatic culture than they are unique articulations of the kinds of human concerns found in a range of contemporary texts.[25]

Finally, we need also to consider those plays that survive as printed texts. These include the morality *Everyman*, but as a translation and adaptation from the Dutch *Elckerlijc* identified on the title page of the two complete sixteenth-century editions as 'a tretyse ... in maner of a morall playe' (1528?, STC 10606 and 1535?, STC 10606.5), its status as an original piece of English drama is certainly questionable. Also printed were two plays by Henry Medwall, often described as the earliest named vernacular dramatist.[26] *Nature*,

---

[20] On the scribes and dating of BodL MS Digby 133, see Donald C. Baker and John L. Murphy, 'The Late Medieval Plays of MS Digby 133: Scribes, Dates, and Early History', *Research Opportunities in Renaissance Drama*, 10 (1967), 153–66 and Baker, Murphy, and Hall (eds), *The Digby Plays*, 10, lxiv. Milla Cozart Riggio rejects the evidence for a common hand for *The Killing of the Children* and *Wisdom*. See Milla Cozart Riggio (ed.), *The Play of Wisdom: Its Texts and Contexts* (New York, 1998), 75.

[21] On the piecemeal assembly of MS Digby 133, see Baker, Murphy, and Hall (eds), *Late Medieval Religious Plays*, xi–xv.

[22] See Tamara Atkin, 'Playbooks and Printed Drama: A Reassessment of the Date and Layout of the Manuscript of the Croxton *Play of the Sacrament*', *Review of English Studies*, n.s. 60 (2009), 194–205.

[23] See Richard Beadle, 'Monk Hyngham's Hand in the Macro Manuscript', in Richard Beadle and A. J. Piper (eds), *New Science out of Old Books: Studies in Manuscripts and Early Printed Books in Honour of A. I. Doyle* (Aldershot, 1995), 315–41. On the post-medieval afterlife of this manuscript, see Gail McMurray Gibson, 'The Macro Manuscripts and the Making of the Morality Play', *The Papers of the Bibliographical Society of America*, 113 (2019), 255–95; and Gail McMurray Gibson, 'The Macro Play in Georgian England', in Atkin and Estill (eds), *Early British Drama in Manuscript*, 311–28.

[24] See, for instance, W. A. Davenport, *Fifteenth-Century English Drama* (Cambridge, 1982) and Robert Potter, *The English Morality Play: Origins, History, and Influence of a Dramatic Tradition* (London, 1975). I exclude from this discussion of witnesses to English moralities *The Pride of Life*, a corrupt Anglo-Irish text, though see Davenport, *Fifteenth-Century English Drama*, 15–20.

[25] As Pamela M. King has argued, 'the identification of the genre has been retrospective and depends largely on the perceived influence of these plays on the more abundantly surviving Tudor interlude'. Pamela M. King, 'Morality Plays', in Beadle (ed.) *The Cambridge Companion to Medieval English Theatre*, 240–64 (at 240).

[26] Nelson (ed.), *The Plays of Henry Medwall*, 1.

which loosely draws on *Reson and Sensuallyte* (c1430) also owes a debt to the morality play and dramatizes the battle between the forces of good and evil over the soul of mankind.[27] It was printed by William Rastell around 1530 (STC 17779) but was probably written and perhaps performed during the final decade of the fifteenth century, during which time Medwall was employed by the archbishop of Canterbury, John Morton. Medwall's other play, *Fulgens and Lucrece*, can be dated to the same period, though was printed slightly earlier; John Rastell's edition is usually dated between 1512 and 1516 (STC 17778), making it the first play to be printed in English. Based on Buonaccorso da Montemagno's Latin treatise *De vera nobilitate* (on true nobility), it is the first surviving play on a secular subject, and an early example of English humanism.[28] One surviving copy, now in the Huntington Library, bears the inscription and annotations of the same Miles Blomfylde who once owned three of the Digby plays. Here, then, is one early user who clearly had an interest in the shared dramatic nature of these otherwise very different texts.

Dramatic Poetry

As this survey indicates, the extant medieval dramatic corpus is perhaps best considered a product of the fifteenth century that has, in a great number of instances, gone through various stages of transmission before being recorded in its surviving texts. But to what extent should it be considered poetry? On one level, this is a straightforward question to answer. All medieval drama is drama in verse and as a whole it makes use of a range of different verse forms. While it remains uncertain whether such poetic variation 'reflects extreme sensitivity of ear in the mediaeval audience, or the craftsman's private delight, or devotional decoration for the glory of God, or simply flamboyant contemporary taste', medieval playwrights were undoubtedly interested in poetic experimentation.[29] Moreover, though we cannot know how contemporary audiences responded to such experiments, the scribes who copied dramatic texts seem to have been alive to poetic variety. The rhyme braces—also called 'rhyme brackets' or 'tie lines'—that appear in many dramatic manuscripts serve to draw attention to rhyming lines, albeit that the final effect may have been to highlight the idea of verse rather than any specific form.[30] At the same time, while it remains true that the majority of fifteenth-century plays survive as stand-alone texts or copied into manuscripts comprised only of drama, the inclusion of some plays in manuscript anthologies of fifteenth-century verse would seem to suggest that at certain points in their receptive history, some plays were understood by some people as a examples of a chiefly poetic—rather than a performative—genre.[31]

---

[27] W. Roy Mackenzie, 'A Source for Medwall's *Nature*', *PMLA*, 29 (1914), 189–99.
[28] See, for instance, Daniel Wakelin, *Humanism, Reading, and English Literature 1430–1530* (Oxford, 2007).
[29] Avril Henry, 'The Dramatic Functions of Rhyme and Stanza Patterns in *The Castle of Perseverance*', in O. S. Pickering (ed.), *Individuality and Achievement in Middle English Poetry* (Cambridge, 1997), 147–83 (at 183). See also: Richard Collier, *Poetry and Drama in the York Corpus Christi Play* (Hamden, CT, 1979); O. S. Pickering, 'Poetic Style and Poetic Affiliation in the *Castle of Perseverance*', *Leeds Studies in English*, n.s. 29 (1998), 275–91.
[30] On rhyme bracing as a codicological feature of manuscripts containing Middle English verse, see Daniel Sawyer, 'Codicological Evidence of Reading in Late Medieval England, with Particular Reference to Practical Pastoral Verse' (DPhil Thesis, University of Oxford, 2016, 205–25). See also his *Reading English Verse in Manuscript c.1350–c.1500* (Oxford, 2020). Dramatic manuscripts that use rhyme bracing include: Beinecke MS 365, BL MS Add. 35290, BL MS Cotton Vespasian D VIII, Folger MS V.a.354, Huntington MS HM1, Dublin, Trinity, College, MSS 432, and 652. Occasional use of rhyme bracketing is also found in BodL MS Digby 133.
[31] Plays that occur in non-dramatic miscellanies include the Brome and Northampton plays of *Abraham and Isaac*. I exclude here fifteenth-century playtexts that were subsequently incorporated into manuscript compilations.

Despite the purposeful use of different poetic forms by medieval playwrights—and the attention drawn to them by medieval scribes—the *poetry* of fifteenth-century drama has sustained little critical attention, with recent scholarship overwhelmingly concerned with aspects of historical performance.[32] This emphasis is perhaps a natural consequence of—and driver for—the success of the *Records of Early English Drama* project, but the lasting legacy of damning assessments by such well-regarded and influential critics as Derek Pearsall have hardly helped:

> ... of the mystery cycles it must be said that, though they contain some of what is good in the religious verse of the [fifteenth] century, they contain more of what is bad, and that whatever interest these plays have from the point of view of theatre, social history or theology, little of that interest derives from any use of language that might be called effectively poetic.[33]

Medieval drama, in Pearsall's assessment, can reveal much about historical theatrical, social, and religious practice, but poetic it is not. One recent practical study of medieval drama has even gone so far as to suggest that since the primary function of dramatic verse is to generate performance, medieval playtexts tend to privilege words' 'extra-verbal coding of cues over their verbal significance'.[34] In this appraisal, it is not that the poetry of medieval drama is ineffective, but rather that its purpose is to facilitate extra-verbal action. If such conclusions highlight the entwined nature of 'poetry' and 'drama' in the extant texts, the aim of this chapter is to suggest this interdependence created for fifteenth-century writers, unique *poetic* opportunities. In the words of A. C. Spearing, 'it is precisely because its quality as literary language cannot be separated from its theatrical qualities that the former should not be overlooked in any attempt at overall judgment'.[35]

The remainder of this chapter offers a series of case studies that compare the treatment of similar episodes and themes across different plays, showing how a range of writers and communities used dramatic poetry to respond to political, economic, and social change. The first considers the treatment of a single biblical episode, the Abraham and Isaac story, as an example of the various approaches taken by those who attempted to dramatize biblical narrative by using poetry as their dominant communicative tool. The second explores the productive exchange of secular and religious tropes through a comparison of John Lydgate's *Triumphal Entry of Henry VI* with the Entry into Jerusalem pageants from the York, Chester, and N-Town mystery plays. It shows how such plays capitalized on audience understanding of certain poetic and dramatic modes in ways that suggest a high level of poetic 'literacy'. A third compares the treatment of sacramental theology, particularly penance, in *Mankind*, *Everyman*, the Digby *Magdalen*, and the Croxton *Play*. In so doing, it demonstrates the ways that dramatic poetry engaged with important elements of orthodox religious teaching. The final case study treats the use of subplots in the Towneley *Second Shepherds' Play*, the Croxton *Play of the Sacrament*, and *Fulgens and Lucres* and suggests that like poetic form itself, these episodes are often integral to the overall meaning and

---

[32] See, for instance, Philip Butterworth and Katie Normington (eds), *Medieval Theatre Performance: Actors, Dancers, Automata and Their Audiences* (Cambridge, 2017); Jody Enders (ed.), *A Cultural History of Theatre in the Middle Ages* (London, 2019); Pamela M. King (ed.), *The Routledge Research Companion to Early Drama and Performance* (London, 2017), and Pamela M. King, Meg Twycross, and Greg Walker (eds), '"The Best Pairt of our Play": Essays Presented to John J. McGavin', in *Medieval English Theatre*, 37–38 (2016–17).

[33] Derek Pearsall, *Old English and Middle English Poetry* (London, 1977), 252.

[34] Matthew Sergi, *Practical Cues and Social Spectacle in the Chester Plays* (Chicago, 2020).

[35] A. C. Spearing, *Medieval to Renaissance in English Poetry* (Cambridge, 1985), 142.

effect. Together, these comparative readings show how fifteenth-century dramatists drew on a rich and often shared heritage to produce new and at times surprising forms.

Abraham and Isaac

Of the six surviving medieval plays that dramatize the biblical story of Abraham and Isaac, only Chester begins with the episode, recorded in Genesis 14, in which King Melchisedek of Salem offers bread and wine to Abraham.[36] Though he makes little more than a fleeting appearance in the Bible, Melchisedek's significance in medieval thought lay in his actions, which were interpreted as a type of eucharistic offering.[37] It is this understanding that John Lydgate invokes in his *Procession of Corpus Christi*:

> Remembreþe eeke* in youre Inwarde entente*   *also; in your mind*
> Melchysedec, þat offred bred and wyne,
> In fygure oonly of þe sacrament.[38]

Using 'Inwarde entente' the reader is invited to see Melchisedek figurally, as a priest offering the Eucharist. In Chester, the reader-viewer is lead to a similar interpretation, but in the place of Lydgate's compressed explanation an Expositor explains the significance of the scene over four eight-line tail-rhyme stanzas. He concludes:

> By Abraham understand I maye
> the Father of heaven, in good faye*;   *faith*
> Melchysedecke, a pryest to his paye*   *of His liking*
> to minister that sacramente
> that Christe ordayned the foresayde daye
> in bred and wyne to honour him aye.
> This signifyeth, the sooth to saye*,   *the truth be told*
> Melchysedeck his presente*.   *Melchidesek's offerings*
>   (Chester, 4.137–44)

Of all medieval drama, the Chester plays are most closely associated with presenters, of which the *Abraham* Expositor is just one example. Such figures occur in no fewer than five out of twenty-four plays, and their function and meaning have been the source of extended scholarly debate.[39] As Michelle M. Butler has summarized, 'while early work on Chester argued that the presenters were an unsophisticated technique and thus indicative

---

[36] The six different plays to dramatize the story of Abraham and Isaac are from York, Chester, Towneley, N-Town, Brome, and Northampton; in this section I consider examples from York, Chester, and Brome.

[37] Hence his place in the canon of the mass, where his offering is linked to those of Abel and Abraham: '*Supra quæ propitio ac sereno vultu respicere digneris, et accepta habere sicut accepta habere dignatus es munera pueri tui justi Abel, et sacrificium patriarchæ nostri Abrahæ, et quod tibi obtulit summus sacerdos tuus Melchisedech, sanctum sacrificium, immaculatam hostiam*' (Upon which vouchsafe to look with a propitious and serene countenance, and to accept them, even as thou didst vouchsafe to accept the gifts of thy righteous servant Abel, and the sacrifice of our Patriarch Abraham, and that which thy High Priest Melchisedech offered to thee, a holy sacrifice, an immaculate host).

[38] NIMEV 3606; Lydgate, *Procession of Corpus Christi*, 17–19, in MacCracken (ed.), *Minor Poems*, 1.35–43.

[39] See for instance, David Mills, 'Brought to Book: Chester's Expositor and His Kin', in Philip Butterworth (ed.), *The Narrator, the Expositor, and the Prompter in European Medieval Theatre* (Turnhout, 2007), 307–25; Charlotte Steenbrugge, *Drama and Sermon in Late Medieval England: Performance, Authority, Devotion* (Kalamazoo, MI, 2017), especially 67–86; and Melissa Walter, 'Performance Possibilities for the Chester Expositor, 1532–1575', *Comitatus*, 31 (2000), 175–95.

of the oldest parts of the cycle, more recent work has argued that Expositors were incorporated into the cycle during early sixteenth-century revision.[40] Irrespective of when this figure was added, his effect is to sanction a particular, orthodox reading of the episode: the bread and wine are to be interpreted as sacramental symbols. The sacramental meaning of Melchisedek's offering is emphasized by the interlocking *aaabcccb* rhyme scheme which spans the four stanzas of this speech. The *b*-rhyme in stanza one becomes the *c*-rhyme in stanza two, the *c*-rhyme in stanza two becomes the *a*-rhyme in stanza three, and the *b*-rhyme in stanza two becomes the *b*-rhyme in stanza four; in the final stanza the *a*- and *c*-rhymes are the same. The result is that certain rhymes are repeated across these four stanzas. 'Sacramente' (124, 140) is linked with 'veremente' (117), 'testamente' (118), 'good intente' (119), 'commandemente' (128), and 'presente' (144), so that the significance of Melchisedek's actions is performed through the rhyme pattern of the Expositor's speech. Meaning here has not been left to chance. Two further interventions by the Expositor in the same play (4.194–208 and 4.460–75) are similarly prescriptive; the circumcision (Genesis 17.1–14) is explained as a type of baptism, while Abraham's willingness to sacrifice Isaac (Genesis 22.1–13) is taken to prefigure the Incarnation. The allegorical exegesis encouraged by the play's Expositor consequently extends the typological equation of Isaac with Christ that is a feature of all medieval Abraham plays to mount an explicitly sacramental interpretation of its version of this Old Testament story. His concerted effort to fix meaning perhaps reflects anxiety about vernacular religious writing after Arundel,[41] but it might also explain why the cycle had become problematic to stage by the 1570s; by then, the prevailing Protestant view held that the bread and wine offered by Melchisedek was 'not to make a sacrifice, but to refresh Abraham and his seruants'.[42]

In contrast to the sacramental focus of the Chester play, the other plays, which omit the Melchisedek episode, centre on Abraham and Isaac and their typological significance. Rosemary Woolf first highlighted the importance of typology in shaping dramatic treatment of Genesis 22, and the influence of her work, especially on late-twentieth-century criticism, cannot be underestimated.[43] While subsequent critics have cautioned against the overuse of typology as an interpretative key to understanding medieval dramatizations of the sacrifice of Isaac,[44] attending to the episode's typological significance does provide explanations for some otherwise baffling details. For instance, where other versions stick to the biblical account in which a ram is sacrificed instead of Isaac, in Chester a lamb is used. The lamb as a symbol of Christ would have been so well known as to require no further explanation, but still the Angelus Secundus explains that 'God hath sent by mee in faye / a lambe that is both good and gaye' (4.433–4). Abraham's binding of Isaac and

---

[40] Michelle M. Butler, 'The Borrowed Expositor', *Early Theatre*, 9.2 (2006), 73–90 (at 73).

[41] Archbishop Thomas Arundel's anti-Wycliffite Constitutions were promulgated in 1411. Among other things, they restricted the use of the vernacular for religious writing. On Arundel and his effect on religious writing, see Vincent Gillespie and Kantik Ghosh (eds), *After Arundel: Religious Writing in Fifteenth-Century England* (Turnhout, 2011).

[42] William Perkins, *A Reformed Catholike; Or, A Declaration Shewing How Neere We May Come to the Present Church of Rome In Sundrie Points Of Religion: And Wherein We Must Euer Depart From Them* (1598; STC 19736), sig. O1v.

[43] Rosemary Woolf, 'The Effect of Typology on the English Medieval Plays of Abraham and Isaac', *Speculum*, 32 (1957), 805–25. This argument was given fuller expression in her subsequent monograph *The English Mystery Plays* (London, 1972), especially 145–53. On the influence of her work, see, for instance, Walter E. Meyers, 'Typology and the Audience of the English Cycle Plays', in Hugh T. Keenan (ed.), *Typology and English Medieval Literature* (New York, 1992), 261–73; and Pamela Sheingorn, 'Typology and the Teaching of Medieval Drama', in Richard Emmerson (ed.), *Approaches to Teaching Medieval English Drama* (New York, 1990), 90–100.

[44] Arnold Williams, 'Typology and the Cycle Plays: Some Criteria', *Speculum*, 43 (1968), 677–84.

his subsequent covenant with God thus prefigure but are ultimately replaced by 'the Lamb of God ... who taketh away the sin of the world' (John 1.29). Similarly, in the York *Abraham and Isaac*, Abraham describes his much loved son as 'of eelde to reken right / Thyrty ȝere and more sumdele' (10.81–2). While the Bible does not specify Isaac's age at the time of Abraham's offering, he is commonly portrayed as a child, and in all other extant plays Isaac's youthfulness is implied; as if to emphasize his childish innocence, in N-Town Isaac is described as a 'swete' or 'dere childe' no fewer than eight times over the course of the 264-line play. The York depiction of Isaac as a man who has attained his majority, whose age is given as thirty years and more, not only makes his willingness to do his father's bidding the actions of a grown man, but also makes explicit the equation of Isaac with Christ, who was understood to be a similar age when he died on the cross (see Luke 3.23). In this, the dramatist follows an exegetical tradition that can be traced back to Josephus, and which was widely disseminated in the Middle Ages through the writings of Petrus Comestus.[45] The effect is to emphasize the doctrinal significance of the binding of Isaac as an event that prefigures Christ's atoning sacrifice:

> Fadir, I am euere at youre wille,
> As worthy is withowten trayne*;   *deception*
> Goddis comaundement to fulfille
> Awe* all folke for to be fayne*.   *Ought; glad*
> (*York*, 10.101–4)

Here, the rhyme scheme emphasizes the equation of paternal and divine authority; Isaac's submission to his father's will is also a fulfilment of God's commandment. Moreover, the *b*-line pairing of 'trayne' (treachery) with 'fayne' (happy, joyful), points towards the eschatological significance of the episode; the fate of 'all folke' hangs in the balance. Quite clearly, the typological meaning of the sacrifice as a prefiguration of the Passion is stressed by making these lines those of a man rather than a child.

In the Brome version of the episode, while the typological interpretation can be inferred, the play's primary interest is in the human dimension of the story, in particular the emotional responses of its protagonists.[46] As has long been noted, the central dialogue between Abraham and Isaac (105–315) is closely paralleled in the Chester *Abraham and Isaac* (229–420), though the relationship between the two versions remains contested.[47] Regardless of which is earlier, the psychological realism of Brome is striking when compared to Chester. Where Chester has Isaac say:

> Marye*, father, God forbydde   *Indeed*
> but you doe your offeringe*.   *but that you do your offering*

---

[45] Minnie E. Wells, 'The Age of Isaac at the Time of the Sacrifice', *Modern Language Notes*, 54 (1939), 579–82. As Richard Beadle has noted, the decision to follow this approach may have been suggested by the appearance of the same motif in the *Middle English Metrical Paraphrase of the Old Testament*, which is the source for some of the pageant. See Richard Beadle, 'The Origins of Abraham's Preamble in the York Play of *Abraham and Isaac*', *Yearbook of English Studies*, 11 (1981), 178–87.

[46] Isaac as a type of Christ is suggested, for instance, in the requirement that he carry the faggot to be used for his sacrifice (*Brome*, 116).

[47] See, for instance, Margaret D. Fort, 'The Metres of the Brome and Chester *Abraham and Isaac* Plays', *PMLA*, 41 (1926), 832–39; Carrie A. Harper, 'A Comparison Between the Brome and Chester Plays of *Abraham and Isaac*', in Agnes Irwin, *Studies in English and Comparative Literature Presented to Agnes Irwin* (Boston, 1910), 31–73; and J. Burke Severs, 'The Relationship Between the Brome and Chester Plays of *Abraham and Isaac*', *Modern Philology*, 42 (1945), 137–51.

> Father, at home your sonnes you shall fynde
> that you muste love by course of kynde*. *nature*
> Be I once out of your mynde,
> your sorrowe may sonne cease.
> But yet you must doe Godes byddinge.
> Father, tell my mother for nothinge.
> (*Chester*, 4.315–22)

In Brome we find:

> Nay, nay fader. God forbade
> That euer ʒe schuld greve hym for me*. *That ever you should do anything that might anger him on my account.*
>
> ʒe haue other chyldryn, on or too,
> The wyche ʒe schuld love wyll be kynd*; *whom it is nature's will that you should love*
>
> I prey ʒow, fader, make ʒe no woo*, *do not grieve*
> For, be I onys ded and fro ʒow goo*, *gone from you*
> I schall be sone owt of ʒoure mynd.
>
> Therefor doo owre Lordys byddyng,
> And wan I am ded, than prey for me;
> But, good fader, tell ʒe my moder nothyng,
> Sey þat I am in another cuntré dwellyng.
> (*Brome*, 196–206).

Both plays contrast the path sanctioned by God ('Godes byddinge'/ 'owre Lordys byddyng') with an unpermitted course ('God fobydde'/ 'God forbade'). The effect in both plays is to stress the importance of Abraham's obedience, but in Brome the pathos of the situation is heightened by making Isaac voice the implicit but irreconcilable tension between Abraham's love for his son and his duty to God. Chester's Isaac tells his father simply that God forbids all but the required sacrifice, but the Brome Isaac makes the more emotionally complex assertion that God has forbidden any action that will anger Him on his account. And while Chester includes Isaac's pathetic plea that Abraham not tell Sarah what he has done, in Brome he goes further, supplying his father with an alternative account for his absence ('Sey þat I am in another cuntré dwellyng'). In this dramatization of the episode, Isaac's love for his father is at least as important as his father's love for him.

While Brome and Chester are closely similar in their treatment of the dialogue between Abraham and Isaac, in their final sections they are quite different. After the angel's intervention, Chester ends with the Expositor's gloss of the action and the announcement by a messenger that the next play will be about Balaam. The Brome version includes extended treatment of the substitute sacrifice of a ram (316–14), before concluding with a short didactic epilogue delivered by a Doctor (435–65). This section announces its separateness from the rest of the action through its distinct metrical scheme, but it diverges from the tone of the preceding text in other ways too. In her treatment of the passage, Rosemary Woolf suggested that it 'turns the play into an exemplum for parents who grieve excessively for the death of their children'; David Mills subsequently refuted this interpretation, arguing instead that, following Origen, the passage should be understood 'as a general example of Man's need of patience before the demands of God'.[48] Their different readings offer two possible responses to thirteen problematic lines at the heart of the Doctor's speech. For while the epilogue begins and ends with the conventional exhortation to follow God's commandments, the middle section confronts the reader with some difficult questions:

Trowe ȝe, sorys*, and God sent an angell	sirs
And commawndyd ȝow ȝoure chyld to slayn,	
Be ȝowre trowthe ys ther ony of ȝow	
That eyther wold groche or stryve thereageyn*?	complain or work against it?
How thyngke ȝe now, sorys, therby?	
I trow ther be thre ore a fowr or moo*;	more
And thys women that wepe so sorowfully	
Whan that hyr chyldryn dey them froo*,	die and leave them
As nater woll, and kynd*;	As happens in nature
Yt ys but folly, I may wyll awooe*,	avow
To groche aȝens God or to greve* ȝow	grieve
For ȝe schall neuer se hym myschevyd*, wyll I know	harmed
Be land nor watyr, haue thys in mynd.	

(Brome, 443–55)

Adopting a technique borrowed from contemporary sermons, the Doctor engages his audience rhetorically: What would you do if God sent an angel and commanded you to kill your child?[49] The answer he gives offers cold comfort: death is natural, it is nature's will, and to 'groche' against God is folly since His will is unavoidable. The word 'groche' occurs here twice and four times in the epilogue as a whole. Derived from the Old French *groucier* (to murmur) it survives in modern usage as the verb 'grudge'. In the quoted passage, the first time it is used it means something like 'to complain' or 'find fault'; in the second stanza its meaning is closer to a hardened protest, as in 'to oppose' or 'withstand'. Obedience may be the moral lesson the Doctor seeks to teach, but he does so by emphasizing its linguistic opposite; rather than highlight the virtue of patience, the epilogue stresses the sin of 'grucching'.

The recurring use of 'grucchen' in the Doctor's speech also reveals retrospectively its centrality to the preceding action and perhaps indicates the particular function of repetition and restatement in dramatic poetry, where the primary mode of reception is likely to have been aural rather than read.[50] The word is first used by Abraham, immediately after he has received the instruction to sacrifice his son, 'Lord, I am sore aferd / To groche ony thing aȝens ȝowre wyll' (79–80); it occurs next to express Isaac's acceptance of his fate, 'aȝens my Lordys wyll / I wyll neuer groche (191–2); and, finally, is given by Abraham as an explanation for Isaac's deliverance:

Loo! Ysaac, my son, how thynke ȝe	
Be thys warke* that we haue wrogth*?	work; done
Full glad and blythe* we may be,	happy
Aȝens þe wyll of God þat we grucched nott,	
Vpon thys fayere hetth*.	heath

(Brome, 403–7)

---

[48] Woolf, *English Mystery Plays*, 153; David Mills, 'The Doctor's Epilogue to the Brome *Abraham and Isaac*: A Possible Analogue', *Leeds Studies in English*, n.s. 11 (1980), 105–10 (at 107).

[49] On the Doctor's approximation of a preacher's style, see Steenbrugge, *Drama and Sermon*, 72–5.

[50] Though see above, 216, and Ward, 'The E Museo 160 Manuscript', for the arguments that this particular play was copied to be read.

Neither Abraham or Isaac 'grucched' against God, and their forbearance is rewarded with God's promise to multiply their descendants. Similarly, the Doctor instructs that God will make amends to those who 'groche not a3ens' Him (456). But the play's articulation of patience as something that can only be explained as the opposite of resistance or complaint ensures the reality of human suffering is never forgotten. Seen from this perspective, the Doctor's final and conventional wish that 'Jesu ... Bryng vs all to heuyn-blysse' (465–6) does little to resolve the tension between doctrine and emotion that the play explores. In contrast to the Chester Expositor with whom I began this section, the Brome Doctor induces the reader to consider the various and problematic responses to the Abraham and Isaac story, and unlike the Expositor who functions to control the play's meaning, the Doctor seems more interested in extending its ambiguities.

Entry

Much has been written about entrances and exits in medieval drama, perhaps because it is the textual treatment of such stage business that definitively marks a text a play.[51] In this section, my focus is the thematic treatment of the idea of entry through a consideration of dramatizations of Christ's entrance into Jerusalem on Palm Sunday alongside Lydgate's *Triumphal Entry of Henry VI*. Lydgate's poem is a versified account of ten-year-old Henry VI's entry into London in February 1432, after two years spent in France, where he had been crowned king a few months earlier.[52] Pageants enacting the actions associated with the beginning of Holy Week survive from York, Chester, and N-Town and bear a close relationship to the Palm Sunday liturgy.[53] Presenting Christ as King coming to the gates of His city Jerusalem, they merit comparison with Lydgate's poetic account of Henry's triumphal entry, which, like all royal entries, borrows from the Palm Sunday procession. Civic liturgical procession, religious drama, and royal entry are here closely interdependent.

The *Entry to Jerusalem* plays enact Jesus's triumphal entry into the Holy City as recorded in all four Gospels (Matthew 21.1–11, Mark 11.1–11, Luke 19.28–44, and John 12.12–19). Greeted by the gathered crowds as the anointed royal figure of Jewish expectation, Jesus's entry fulfils the messianic prophecy in Zechariah 9.9 of a king who will enter Jerusalem on a donkey. All three plays depict Jesus as aware of His role in fulfilling this prophecy. In N-Town, Jesus follows the account of Matthew 21.1–3 and speaks to His disciples, asking

---

[51] For a recent overview, see Philip Butterworth, *Staging Conventions in Medieval English Theatre* (Cambridge, 2014), especially 78–90.

[52] Though once thought to have helped devise the pageants that marked the king's entrance, he is now better understood as tasked with their official commemoration. The poem is based on a Latin letter by one of the city's clerks. See Gordon Kipling, 'Lydgate: The Poet as Deviser', in Donka Minkova and Thersa Tinkle (eds), *Chaucer and the Challenges of Medievalism: Studies in Honor of H. A. Kelly* (Frankfurt, 2003), 73–101; H. N. McCracken, 'King Henry's Triumphal Entry into London, Lydgate's Poem, and Carpenter's Letter', *Archiv für das Studium der Neueren Sprachen und Literaturen*, 126 (1911), 75–102; and Claire Sponsler, *The Queen's Dumbshows: Lydgate and the Making of Early Theater* (Philadelphia, PA, 2014), especially 115–46.

[53] On this point see Eamon Duffy, *The Stripping of the Altars* (New Haven, CT, 1992), 23–8; and Pamela M. King, *The York Mystery Plays and the Worship of the City* (Woodbridge, 2006), 130–7. Only York treats the *Entry* as a standalone episode (play 25); the *Conspiracy* is treated in a separate pageant (play 26). In Chester the *Entry* is part of a sequence (play 14) that begins with Christ at the house of Simon the leper and ends with His cleansing of the Temple and Judas's conspiracy with Caiphas and Annas. In N-Town, it is part of the first Passion play, occurring immediately after the events of the Conspiracy, thereby offering a different order of events to the other two versions. In Towneley, since there is nothing between *Lazurus* (play 16) and the *Conspiracy* (play 17), the manuscript does not cover the Entry.

that they go to 'ȝon castle' (i.e., a village), find '[a]n asse' and a 'fole', '[v]nlosne þat asse and brynge it to me pleyne' (*N-Town*, 26.347–55).⁵⁴ Similarly, in Chester Jesus asks Peter and Philip to 'fetch ... an asse and a foale alsoe ... [and] bringe them hither anone' (*Chester*, 14.139–41). In York, Christ goes further:

Vnto ȝone* castell* þat is ȝou agayne*,	*yonder; village; before you*
Gois with gud harte and tarie noȝt,	
My comaundement to do be ȝe bayne*.	*willing*
Also I ȝou charge, loke it be wrought,	
þat schal ȝe fynde	
An asse þis feste, als ȝe had soght*.	*as you have sought*
ȝe hir vnbynde	
With hir foole, and to me hem bring,	
þat I on hir may sitte a space*,	*a while*
So þe prophi[tes] clere menyng	
May be fulfillid here in þis place:	
'Doghtyr Syon	
Loo, þi lorde comys rydand* an asse	*riding*
þe to opon.	
(*York*, 25.15–28)	

Here, Jesus's paraphrase of Matthew 21 is extended to include verses four and five of the gospel account, which directly invoke the messianic prophecy in Zechariah 9.9: '*exulta satis filia Sion iubila filia Hierusalem ecce rex tuus veniet tibi iustus et salvator ipse pauper et ascendens super asinum et super pullum filium asinae*' (Rejoice greatly, O daughter of Sion, shout for joy, O daughter of Jerusalem: behold thy king will come to thee, the just and saviour: he is poor, and riding upon an ass, and upon a colt, the foal of an ass).⁵⁵ By making Jesus gloss His own commands, having Him explain that they function to fulfil Old Testament prophecy, the author(s) give Him a role similar to that of the Chester Expositor, expounding meaning to His audience. But His words also cast him as the director of His own triumph, planning the nature of His own entry into the royal city. It is just one of a number of moments in the pageant where the fulfilment of prophecy is not only emphasized, but also used to determine the action.⁵⁶

The fulfilment of messianic royalty is also an implicit feature of all royal entries. In perhaps the single most influential critical work on the medieval civic triumph, Gordon Kipling has said of Henry VI's 1432 entry that its seven pageants create 'individual epiphanies' for the king that 'serve to reveal—indeed *manifest*—Henry's Christ-like identity'.⁵⁷ More recently, Claire Sponsler has argued that Lydgate mutes this messianic theme and accentuates a civic perspective that is likely to have chimed with those who commissioned

---

⁵⁴ Of the synoptic gospels, only Matthew has Jesus instruct his disciples to bring him an ass *and* a colt. Mark mentions only a colt; Luke describes the foal as a 'colt of an ass', but only demands that the juvenile animal be brought.

⁵⁵ The text in Matthew reads: '*Hoc autem totum factum est, ut adimpleretur quod dictum est per prophetam dicentem: Dicite filæ Sion: Ecce rex tuus venit tibi mansuetus, sedens super asinam, et pullum filium subjugalis*' ('Now all this was done that it might be fulfilled which was spoken by the prophet, saying: Tell ye the daughter of Sion: Behold thy king cometh to thee, meek, and sitting upon an ass, and a colt the foal of her that is used to the yoke'). None of the other synoptic gospels quote the prophecy from Zachariah 9.9, but it does appear in John 12.15.

⁵⁶ See, for instance *York*, 25.10, 47–9, and 153–4.

⁵⁷ Gordon Kipling, *Enter the King: Theatre, Liturgy, and Ritual in the Medieval Civic Triumph* (Oxford, 1998), 144.

the work.[58] But there are ways that Lydgate's celebration of London on behalf of its citizens can be seen to emphasize the entry's messianic associations:

> And lyke for Dauyd, afftyr his victorie,
> Reioyssed was alle Ierusalem,
> So this Citee with lavde, pris, and glorie*,   *honour, praise, and glory*
> For ioye moustred* lyke the sonne beem,   *assembled*
> To yeve ensample thur[u]h-out* the reem*;   *throughout; realm*
> Alle off assent*, whoso kan conseyve,   *All as one*
> Theyre noble kyng wern gladde to resseyve.
>   (*Triumphal Entry*, 22–8).

In this, the poem's fourth stanza, Lydgate likens the returning Henry to the biblical King David and London to the holy city of Jerusalem. As various critics have noted, the idea of London as a new Jerusalem was well established in the fifteenth century, but in this stanza Lydgate imagines 'Jerusalem' and 'this Citee' as figures of synecdoche that represent the civic citizenship.[59] Here, then, the city and her citizens are as one in their reception of the 'noble kyng' as a ruler analogous to Christ's royal forebear. These associations are explored further in Lydgate's account of the sixth pageant, which was presented at Cheapside Cross and featured a pedigree showing Henry's lineage from Saint Edward (England) and Saint Louis (France) and a Jesse tree showing Jesus's descent from David.[60] Jesse trees offer a visualization of the Advent prophecy found in Isaiah 11.1–2: '*Et egredietur virga de radice Jesse, et flos de radice ejus ascendet. Et requiescet super eum spiritus Domini*' (And there shall come forth a rod out of the root of Jesse, and a flower shall rise up out of his root. And the spirit of the Lord shall rest upon him). The visual twinning of Henry's and Christ's genealogies mark the returning king as 'the Christ-like Saviour, as the first king to come to rule not one but two kingdoms, and, like Christ, he comes to his kingdom as a child'.[61] The boy king who enters London does so as a flower risen from Jesse's root, welcomed by a city that is a manifestation of its citizens.

The York *Entry* play similarly foregrounds 'þe genolagye' and cites Moses, Jesse, David, and Solomon as proof of Christ's royal claim (*York*, 25.242); it is His 'modir kynne' (mother's lineage) that 'persuades the citizens to greet Him as King' (*York*, 25.241).[62] N-Town also invokes Christ's royal ancestry through the repeated epithet 'sone of Davyd' (*N-Town*, 26.454, 470), while a stage direction in Chester cites Matthew 21.9 and calls on the youths and citizens of Jerusalem to sing 'Hosanna, filio David!' (*Chester*, 14.209SD). According to Eyal Poleg, this single word, *hosanna*, stands 'out in biblical and liturgical accounts of Psalm Sunday … appearing twice in the Gospel lessons … seventeen times in antiphons and responsories' and repeated four times in the familiar hymn *Gloria laus*.[63] In Chester, the unity of the crowd and its identity with Jerusalem is exemplified in this moment of collective, liturgical song, which crowns the poetic welcome offered to Jesus by the Citizens and Boys. Over thirty-six lines, nine characters each recite four lines of tidings that are knit together through a recurrent *aaab*-rhyme:

---

[58] Sponsler, *The Queen's Dumbshows*, 133–5.
[59] For the comparison of Henry to David and London to Jerusalem, see Kipling, *Enter the King*, 5–16, 143–3.
[60] These pedigrees do not appear in the letter that served as Lydgate's source. See Richard Osberg, 'The Jesse Tree in the 1432 London Entry of Henry VI: Messianic Kingship and the Rule of Justice', *Journal of Medieval and Renaissance Studies*, 16 (1986), 213–32.
[61] Kipling, *Enter the King*, 145.
[62] Collier, *Poetry and Drama*, 232.
[63] Eyal Poleg, *Approaching the Bible in Medieval England* (Manchester, 2013), 46.

> PRIMUS PUER. Fellowes, I hard* my father saye   *heard*
> Jesu the prophet will come todaye.
> Thidder I read* we take the waye   *suggest*
> with branches in our hand.
>
> SECUNDUS PUER. Make wee myrth all that we maye
> pleasant to that lordes paye.
> 'Hosanna!' I read, by my faye*,   *faith*
> to synge that we founde*.   *as we have read*
>   (Chester, 14.201–8)

Matthew Sergi has argued that 'an ordering structure of half-stanzas or stanzas spoken in turn by bit players is a particular feature of the Chester cycle.'[64] Here, the *a*-rhyme and *b*-half rhyme (hand/founde) shared between the two Boys demonstrates the unity of those called to bear witness to Christ's entry. As in Lydgate's account of Henry VI's entry into London, the people *are* the city.

Collaborative stanzas are also a feature of the York *Entry*, where eight highly ornate celebratory stanzas welcome Christ to the city. Spoken by eight different citizens, each deploys the same 'Hayll' anaphora and makes use of decorative alliteration (rhyme rather than alliteration controls the underlying structure):

> Hayll, Dauid sone, doughty* in dede   *brave*
> Hayll, rose ruddy*, hayll, birrall* clere,   *red; beryl*
> Hayll, welle of welthe may make vs mede*,   *grant us reward*
> Hayll, saluer* of oure sores sere*,   *healer; many wounds*
> We wirschippe þe.
> Hayll, hendfull*, with solas sere*,   *worthy one; abundant joy*
> Welcome þou be.
>   (York, 25.503–9)

Here, the third Burgess welcomes Jesus with a series of epithets that emphasize His royal genealogy and highlight His sovereign virtues: He is brave and courageous and offers reward, healing, and comfort. Acclaiming Jesus as the ideal king and the citizens as His willing, obedient subjects, the play's Burgesses adopt language that is liturgical and paraliturgical in its order and phrasing. In addition to imagery derived from liturgical hymns (Christ is variously celebrated as the 'prince of pees' prophesied by Isiah [25.490], a flourishing flower that will never fade [25.496], a handsome knight [25.516], a gleaming lily, worthy of love [25.519], and a 'lampe of liff' [25.532]), the 'Hayll' stanzas also echo the form of Elevation lyrics, paraliturgical vernacular prayers designed specifically for lay use during the Mass. Comprised of a rhyming list of 'Hail' apostrophes, such lyrics were intended to be spoken in accompaniment with the clerical raising of the Eucharist, highlighting the standard lay encounter with the Host as a visual rather than an oral experience. An early fifteenth-century example from BL MS Royal 17 C XVII is typical. It begins 'Hayle Iesu! Godys Sone in forme of bred!' before going on to celebrate Christ as the embodiment of various virtues: 'Hayl Hope! Hale Fayth! Hayle Charyte! ... Hayle Lyfe! Hayl Merci! Hayle Hele! Hayle Pese and Pyte!'[65] Invoking prayers such as these, the York Burgesses hail Jesus

---

[64] Matthew John Sergi, 'Play Texts and Public Practice in the Chester Cycle, 1422–1607' (PhD Diss., University of California, Berkeley, 2011, 73).

[65] NIMEV 1052; the poem appears on fol. 98v but is reproduced here from Rossell Hope Robbins's transcription in his article 'Levation Prayers in Middle English Verse', *Modern Philology*, 40 (1942), 131–46.

in ways that anticipate the institution of the Eucharist as a sacramental remedy for all sin. Christ enters Jerusalem as conqueror, but He comes to be sacrificed and it is His sacrifice, repeated in the Eucharist, that redeems mankind.

In fact, as Pamela M. King has noted, the Burgesses' speeches are just one example of a great number of 'formal greetings in these texts of the York Cycle which superficially confirm to the formulae employed by Elevation prayers'.[66] Their form can also be felt in Lydgate's *Triumphal Entry*, which includes a lyric that welcomes the young king in terms that echo the epithets directed at Christ in both Elevation prayers and the dramatic texts that draw on them:

> 'Sovereyne Lorde, welcome to youre citee;
> Welcome, oure Ioye, and oure Hertis Plesaunce,
> Welcome, oure Gladnesse, welcome, our Suffisaunce*,   *Sufficiency*
> Welcome, welcome, riht welcome mote ye be'.
> (*Triumphal Entry*, 211–4)

Described by Lydgate as a 'roundell' (210), this eleven-line isolable lyric is identical with the form of the French *chanson* or *rondeau*: a four-line stanza rhyming *Abba* (where *A* is the refrain), a three-line stanza *abA* (where the final line, 'Sovereyene Lorde, welcome, welcome ye be' [217], combines the first half of the refrain with the second half of the *a*-line 'Welcome, welcome, riht welcome mote ye be'), and a five-line stanza *abbaA*.[67] But where *rondeaux* typically take secular love as their subject, Lydgate here celebrates Henry VI as a type of Christ, using paraliturgical language that associates him with the Eucharist. Henry is the people's joy, their heart's pleasure, gladness, and their sufficiency, just as Christ in the substance of the Eucharist is the 'ground ay of my goodness and my covernowre' (source of my goodness and my governor) and 'sustenans to my soule and my saveour' (my soul's sustenance and my saviour) for the author of one fifteenth-century Elevation lyric.[68] But where Elevation poems vocalize the individual supplicant's prayers ('*my* saveour'), the roundel, like the York Burgesses' welcome stanzas, articulates the collective hopes of the city and its citizens. The dramatic poetry of entry unites citizens around a stable image of the triumphant king made glorious through their recognition of his superb qualities.

Penance

Towards the end of the Croxton *Play of the Sacrament*, the play's Jews are shown first to be contrite; they are then directed by a bishop to make their sins known to a confessor; before finally being instructed to fast, pray, and do good work. Their actions fulfil the three parts of the sacrament of penance as understood by the late medieval church: 'for-þenkyng in herte' (contrition), 'shrifte of mouthe' (confession), and 'repentaunce' (satisfaction).[69] Recent critical discussion of fifteenth-century drama has noted its sacramental focus, which it has

---

[66] King, *Worship of the City*, 21. For other examples, see *York* 14.57–63, 16.309–44, and 17.320–73. The soldiers in the York *Crucifixion* subvert the form to mock Christ. See *York* 33.409–17.

[67] A sixteen-line welcome song with the refrain 'Soveraign lord, to your cite / With alle reverence welcome ye be' is included in English as part of the Latin letter on which Lydgate's poem is based. MacCracken describes Lydgate's version as 'an artistic revision'. McCracken, 'King Henry's Triumphal Entry', 98. For the Latin letter see London, Metropolitan Archives, Archives of the Corporation of London, MS Letter Book K, fols. 103v–4v (quotation at fol. 104).

[68] Ella Keats Whiting (ed.), *The Poems of John Audelay*, EETS, o.s. 184 (Oxford, 1931), 64, 8.55–6.

[69] Woodburn O. Ross (ed.), *Middle English Sermons, Edited from British Museum MS. Royal 18 B. xxiii.*, EETS, o.s. 209 (Oxford, 1940), 141.

interpreted in the light of contemporary religious controversy.[70] Fundamentally conservative in its outlook, biblical and moral drama has been shown to affirm orthodox teaching on all the sacraments, but especially those most hotly contested by Wycliffite reformers: the sacraments of the Eucharist and penance. In this section, I take a closer look at the performance of penance. Like the adapted Elevation lyrics considered in the previous section, dramatic treatment of this sacrament is inflected to reflect lay experience, adopting a vernacular theology that celebrates orthodox doctrine.

The Croxton *Play* is not the only play to dramatize the three stages of penance. As Charlotte Steenbrugge has noted, *Wisdom* offers 'by far the most, explicit, coherent and overtly orthodox representation in the surviving morality plays'.[71] Traditional teaching on the doctrine is nicely summarized by the titular character:

> By wndyrstondynge haue very contrycyon
> Wyth mynde of your synne* confessyon make,   *knowledge of sin*
> Wyth wyll yeldynge du satysfaccyon*;   *With a yielding will make recompense*
> Þan yowr soule be clene, I wndertake.
> (*Wisdom*, 973–6)

Wisdom here adopts the play's most common stanza-form; his lines are the first half of an eight-line *ababbcbc* stanza. But it is the second half of the stanza that shows how the play uses rhyme to cement its doctrinal message:

> ANIMA. I wepe for sorow, Lorde! I begyn awake,
> I that þis longe hath slumberyde in syne.
> *Hic recedunt demones**   *Here the demons exit*
> WYSDOM. Lo, how contrycyon avoydyth þe deullys blake!
> Dedly synne ys non yow within.
> (*Wisdom*, 977–80)

Here, Anima, the soul that requires cleansing, begins the process of repentance when she realizes how long she has been slumbering in sin. It is her awakening—her contrition—that exorcizes the demons who have possessed her. Rhyming 'syne' with 'within', the *c*-lines in this half-stanza emphasize contrition as an inward process, while the *b*-line rhymes across the stanza as a whole direct the contrite soul towards confession; it is the soul that is 'awake' that can 'confessyon make'.

The pains taken in *Wisdom* to highlight the importance of the connection between heartfelt contrition and auricular confession no doubt reflect contemporary controversy over the sacrament. The twenty-first decree of the Fourth Lateran Council (1215), *Omnis utriusque sexus* (all men and women), made annual confession a requirement for all Christians, thereby establishing the central role of the priest in orthodox doctrine. Without auricular confession there can be no priestly absolution. However, while the priest's absolution is necessary, his words remain useless unless the penitent is truly contrite. Where the Lollard response to this theological knot was to deny the role of the priest and emphasize instead 'contricioun [as] þe essencial parte of penance', dramatic treatment of the sacrament tends to highlight the importance of true contrition while simultaneously confirming

---

[70] The examples are too numerous to list but include: Steenbrugge, *Drama and Sermon*, especially ch.6; Charlotte Steenbrugge, 'Morality Plays and the Aftermath of Arundel's Constitutions', in King (ed.), *Research Companion*, 205–20; and Jay Zysk, *Shadow and Substance: Eucharistic Controversy across the Reformation Divide* (Notre Dame, IN, 2017).

[71] Steenbrugge, *Drama and Sermon*, 127.

the pivotal role of the priest.[72] For instance, in the Digby *Mary Magdalen* the integrity of the Magdalene's contrition is twice emphasized by Jesus, who is here imagined as the archetypal priestly confessor. It is 'wyth contrysson' that she 'hast mad a recumpens' thereby saving her soul 'from all dystresse' (701–2):

Woman, in contryssyon þou art expert	
And in þi sowle hast inward mythe*,	*inner strength*
That sumtyme were in desert*,	*the wilderness*
And from therknesse hast porchasyd lyth*.	*And has bought light from the darkness*
Thy feyth hath savyt* þe, and made þe bryth*!	*saved; bright*
Wherfor I sey to þe, 'Vade in pace'*.	*'Go in peace'*
(Digby *Mary Magdalen*, 686–91)	

Focusing on interior piety in contrast to outward religious expression, Christ, like Wisdom, stresses the importance of inward knowledge of sin. Moreover, just as Anima's heartfelt contrition causes her possessing demons to leave her, so Mary's 'expert' remorse results in an exorcism; following this speech a detailed stage direction instructs that '*Wyth þis word seuyn dyllys xall dewoyde from þe woman, and the Bad Angyll entyr into hell with thondyr*'.

While such dramatic demonstrations of true contrition successfully model the first stage of penance for a lay audience, in the face of Wycliffite assaults on the role of the priest in the sacrament, the orthodox church was especially insistent on the need for auricular confession. Though it would be wrong to suggest that all medieval drama functioned to promulgate orthodox teaching, in the context of fifteenth-century religious controversy the dramatic treatment of confession and absolution as priestly activities is particularly striking. In the Croxton *Play*, the Episcopus stresses 'Of synnys fo[r]gotyn take good avysement, / And knowlege them to yowr confessor full euyn' (874–5), reminding characters and audience members alike of the need to take careful thought of one's sins and make a full and exact confession to a priest. In *The Castle of Perseverance* the central importance of confession is signalled through the play's inclusion of a character by the same name:

CONFESCIO. Schryffte may no man forsake*.	*Every man must make confession*
Whanne Mankynde cryeth I am redy.	
Whanne sorwe* of hert þe hathe take	*sorrow*
Schryfte profytyth veryly*.	*Confession will profit him greatly*
(*Castle*, 1429–32)	

According to orthodox doctrine, the completion of any satisfaction enjoined by the priest in confession would free the soul from punishment after death. While Confescio does not here make explicit reference to satisfaction, he implies that the true profit to be gained from 'schryfte' is nothing less than eternal salvation; heartfelt confession by the contrite sinner to a priestly confessor can redeem the soul. However, while Humanum Genus is contrite (1381–9), does confess (1468–93), and is consequently absolved by Confescio (1494–1531), in the second half of the play he goes back to his sinful ways and dies unshriven. Though he is ultimately saved by God's mercy, the play is nonetheless careful to stress the consequences of overlooking the obligation to confess and make satisfaction. As Justicia warns, he who is 'ouyrlate' (too late) to confess, insufficiently contrite, and who fails to make satisfaction, ought to be 'dampne ... / to hell belyve' (3427, 3430).

---

[72] 'Sixteen Points on which the Bishops Accuse the Lollards', in Anne Hudson (ed.), *Selections of English Wycliffite Writings* (Cambridge, 1978), 21. While most Lollard texts deny priests the power to pronounce absolution, the majority concede that confession to a priest may be helpful. Nonetheless, they universally recognize the central importance of contrition before God.

Based on the fifteenth-century Dutch interlude *Elckerlijc*, the printed morality *Everyman* also makes effective use of personification allegory to teach orthodox sacramental doctrine. Everyman travels with Knowledge (of sin, i.e., contrition) to the 'House of Salvacyon' where 'that holy man Confessyon' dwells (540, 539). There, and in contrast to the *The Castle of Perseverance*, satisfaction is explicitly prescribed by Confession:

... a precyous jewell I wyll gyve thee	
Called Penaunce, voyder of adversytye*.	*remover of hardship*
Therwith shall your body chastysed be	
With abstynence and perseveraunce in Goddes servyce.	
... Knowlege, kepe hym in this vyage*,	*on this path*
And by that tyme Good Dedes wyll be with thee,	
But in any wyse be sure of mercy,	
For your tyme draweth fast*, and ye wyll saved be.	*approaches quickly*
Aske God mercy, and he wyll graunte truely.	
Whan with the scurge of Penaunce man doth hym bynde,	
The Oyle of Forgyvenes than shall he fynde.	
(*Everyman*, 557–72)	

By undertaking physical correction through use of a penitential scourge, Everyman learns that Good Deeds will recover and that, ultimately, he will be saved. The connection made here between confession, physical discipline, and absolution is not unique. As Ann Eljenholm Nichols has noted, 'scenes of expiation found in marginalia in English liturgical texts are sometimes triggered by the word *confessio* in the adjacent psalm, and the connection between flagellation and satisfaction is made explicit in the *Sherborne Missal* where such a scene is labelled *satisfacio*'.[73] It is Everyman's own expiatory scouring that enables Good Deeds to rise from the ground, allowing him, with Confession's blessing, to proceed directly to heaven.

The title-page to *Everyman* describes it as 'a treatise ... in maner of a morall playe' suggesting that its primary mode is instructive rather than dramatic. While a treatise can connote a work in verse or prose, it always refers to a text that expounds a theme, is of an informative character, or offers a disquisition on a circumscribed topic.[74] If the specified topic of *Everyman* is 'how þe hye fader of heuen sendeth dethe to sommon euery creature to come and gyue a counte of theyr lyues in this worlde', it is also true that it offers a thoroughgoing and detailed lesson on the sacrament of penance. It is a play that has a coherent and urgent message about salvation. In concluding this chapter, I turn to consider examples of moments or passages within fifteenth-century plays that seem to deviate from their central message or plot through their development of subplots. By focusing on the poetry of these set-pieces, their structural importance becomes newly apparent.

Subplots

The development of the subplot as a feature of British drama has often been attributed to the professional playhouse culture of the late sixteenth century.[75] However, the earliest

---

[73] Ann Eljenholm Nichols, *Seeable Signs: The Iconography of the Seven Sacraments, 1350–1544* (Woodbridge, 1994), 235–6.
[74] 'Tretis', *n.*1(a), MED.
[75] See, for instance, Richard Levin, *The Multiple Plot in English Renaissance Drama* (Chicago, 1971); and Norman Rabkin, 'The Double Plot: Notes on the History of a Convention', *Renaissance Drama*, 7 (1964), 55–69.

examples date back to the first half of the fifteenth century. Though sometimes treated as incidental, post hoc additions, the subplots in medieval drama typically use comedy in ways that reflect, comment on, and often nuance the meaning of the central plot. As such, they should be considered integral to the action, and where there is evidence for their later interpolation—as there is for the quack doctor episode in the Croxton *Play of the Sacrament*—their inclusion nonetheless contributes to the overall meaning and effect of the drama.[76] The earliest and perhaps most famous example is in the second of Towneley's two shepherds plays and features the madcap antics of the non-biblical sheep-stealer Mak. Critics have approached this episode in a variety of ways, noting its origins in European folklore,[77] its employment of the typological method,[78] and its socially significant use of a southern dialect.[79] I do not wish to rehearse these arguments here, but I do want to consider the similarities between the forms of verse adopted for this episode and the comic subplots found in both the Croxton *Play* and Henry Medwall's humanist drama *Fulgens and Lucres*. The *Second Shepherds' Play* is one of five pageants in the Towneley manuscript written entirely in what Charles Mills Gayley first identified as the distinctive stanza of the anonymous poet dubbed the 'Wakefield Master'.[80] This is a thirteener in which the rhyme scheme for the first eight lines (*abababab*) matches the cross-rhyming octave found in several other of the Towneley plays; the remaining five lines comprise of a *c*-rhyming 'bob' (i.e., a short, one-stress line) and a concluding quatrain rhyming *dddc*. In contrast to the quack doctor episode in the Croxton *Play*, which adopts stanza-forms not found elsewhere in the play, the consistent use of the Wakefield stanza throughout the *Second Shepherds' Play* would seem if nothing else to authenticate the subplot involving Mak as the work of the so-called Master.[81] Moreover, since the *Secunda Pastorum* is best understood as a revision of the earlier *First Shepherds' Play*, it is clear that the sheep-stealing plot is central to the

---

[76] Hardin Craig first suggested the scene featuring Brundyche and Colle (525–652) was a later interpolation, and this position was subsequently adopted by the play's EETS editor. See Hardin Craig, *English Religious Drama of the Middle Ages* (Oxford, 1955), 326–7; and Davis (ed.), *Non-Cycle Plays*, lxxv–lxxvi. In my book *The Drama of Reform: Theology and Theatricality, 1461–1553* (Turnhout, 2013), 22, I suggest 'there are good reasons for believing that the episode belongs to the play's original design'. For further discussion of the episode as integral to the original, see David Bevington, 'Staging and Liturgy in *The Croxton Play of the Sacrament*', in Wim Hüsken and Peter Happé (eds), *Staging Scripture: Biblical Drama, 1350–1660* (Leiden, 2016), 235–52; and Jillian Linster, 'The Physician and His Servant in the Croxton *Play of the Sacrament*', *Early Theatre*, 20.2 (2017), 31–48.

[77] Early accounts of these origins can be found in A. C. Baugh, 'Parallels to the Mak Story', *Modern Philology*, 15 (1918), 169–74; and Robert C. Cosbey, 'The Mak Story and Its Folklore Analogues', *Speculum*, 20 (1945), 310–17.

[78] A. C. Spearing has argued that 'the Wakefield Master has used the typological principle from which the structure of the cycle derives as a way of linking to the Nativity a secular plot which stands in an antitypical relationship to it'. Spearing, *Medieval to Renaissance*, 161. The interpretation of the sheep-stealing plot as a parody of the Nativity was first explored by Homer A. Watt, 'The Dramatic Unity of the "Secunda Pastorum"', in *Essays and Studies in Honor of Carleton Brown* (New York, 1940), 158–66. See also, Maris G. Fiondella, 'Derrida, Typology, and the *Second Shepherd's Play*: The Theatrical Production of Christian Metaphysics', *Exemplaria*, 6 (1994), 429–58.

[79] Lynn Forest-Hill, *Transgressive Language in Medieval English Drama* (London, 2000), especially 67; and Kathleen Irace, 'Mak's Sothren Tothe: A Philological and Critical Study of the Dialect Joke in the *Second Shepherd's Play*', *Comitatus*, 21 (1990), 38–51.

[80] Charles Mills Gayley, *Plays of Our Forefathers* (New York, 1907), 161–90. Following Mills Gayley's interpretation of the *frons* of the stanza as four run-on lines with both internal and end rhymes, all modern editions prior to Stevens and Cawley's EETS edition have transcribed this distinctive stanza in nine lines. However, I here follow Stevens and Cawley's rationale for describing it as a thirteener. See the introduction to their EETS edition, xxix–xxxi. See also, Martin Stevens, *Four Middle English Mystery Cycles: Textual, Contextual, and Critical Interpretations* (Princeton, NJ, 1987), 130–56.

[81] In the case of the Croxton *Play*, the distinct ballad stanza used for the scene with Brundyche and Colle is one reason why the episode has historically been identified as a later interpolation. See Craig, *English Religious Drama*, 326–7.

Wakefield Master's vision for the reworked pageant. Far more than comic relief then, the episode is integral to the play's approach towards and treatment of its theme.

The plot involving Mak begins and ends with music. Immediately prior to his entrance at line 274, the three Shepherds break into a three-part harmony; the episode ends with the music of the Angelus, whose singing of the *Gloria* serves to call the Shepherds to the Nativity. But music features within the subplot too, offering a neat illustration of the way the playwright uses parody to draw out the pageant's meaning. Having concocted a plan to conceal the stolen sheep by swaddling 'hym right / In my credyll', Mak's wife Gyll tells him to make their scheme more convincing by singing a lullaby (13.623–4):

Harken* ay* when thay call;	*Listen; now*
Thay will com onone*.	*soon*
Com and make redy all,	
And syng by thyn oone*;	*on your own*
Syng 'lullay' thou shall,	
For I must grone*,	*groan, i.e., as if in labour*
And cry outt by the wall	
On Mary and Iohn	
For sore.	
Syng 'lullay' on fast*	*quickly*
When thou heris at the last,	
And bot I play a fals cast*	*And if I am tricking you*
Trust me no more.	
(*Towneley*, 13.634–46).	

Gyll proposes that by singing a lullaby Mak will simultaneously warn his wife of the Shepherds' approach and convince them her labour is in earnest and the stolen sheep really a new-born child. Martin Stevens and A. C. Cawley have suggested that Mak is 'evidently intended to imitate the refrain of a lullaby carol', citing examples in Richard Leighton Greene's edition of *English Carols* that make use of burdens which include lulling words like 'lullay'.[82] These burdens typically take the form of cradle songs, often in the voice of Mary, as in this example from BL MS Sloane 2593: 'Lullay, myn lykyng, my dere sone, myn swetyng, / Lullay, my dere herte, myn owyn dere derlyng'.[83]

By having Mak sing a version of Mary's burden, his cradle song to quieten the bleating sheep is made to resemble the Virgin's soothing lullaby to her helpless child, thereby refining the parody inherent in this subplot in which the disguised sheep is clearly intended to invoke the Christ-child as the Lamb of God. Lullabies soothe, but they are also closely associated with lament, and as Kathleen Palti has noted, Middle English lullaby carols 'commonly anticipate the Passion and invoke the visual echoes between nativity scenes and pietas'.[84] Of course the torment that awaits this particular sheep-as-child is not the Passion, but rather its consumption as flesh, a fate to which Gyll mockingly alludes when she insists, 'If ever I you begyld, / That I ete this chylde' (*Towneley*, 13.774–5). Clearly, she is beguiling them; eating the stolen sheep is precisely the plan. And just as Mak is made to sing a song that is a type of lullaby carol, so too do Gyll's words unwittingly anticipate the

---

[82] Stevens and Cawley (eds), *The Towneley Plays*, 2.505. See also R. L. Greene (ed.), *The Early English Carols*, 2nd edn. (Oxford, 1977), 97–115. A burden is a chorus to be sung or considered as sung by the reader that occurs before the first stanza and is then repeated after each stanza. See Greene, *English Carols*, cxxxiii–cxlv.

[83] Greene, *English Carols*, 98.

[84] Kathleen Palti, 'Singing Women: Lullabies and Carols in Medieval England', *JEGP*, 110 (2011), 359–82 (at 376).

sacrament of the Eucharist, where Christ, the Lamb of God, is consumed under the form of bread.

If Mak sings a lullaby carol to warn Gyll that the Shepherds will shortly arrive, his song can also be taken as a Nativity carol that parodically anticipates the Angel's singing of the *Gloria* that brings the entire episode to a close. It is his singing that draws the Shepherds to his house as witnesses to a sham nativity that prefigures the Nativity. Moreover, in their response to it, the shepherds adopt the same musical terms ('hak' and 'crak') as they do for the Angel's rendition of the *Gloria* announcing the birth of Christ (compare 13.686, 688 with 13.947, 949). In terms not only of form but also of content then, the sheep-stealing plot is clearly crucial to the success of the *Second Shepherds' Pageant*.

The comic subplot in Henry Medwall's *Fulgens and Lucrece* is also central to the play's overall meaning, making use of a similar structural pattern in which the comic action 'precedes rather than follows the debate and thus changes the audience's response to the rhetoric'.[85] In this subplot, which is not present in Medwall's source, two nameless characters, A and B, discuss the play and anticipate the entry of the main characters (1–201); they then join the action by seeking employment with the two suitors of the main plot (347–409). In these roles they then attempt to win the love of Joan, a handmaid of the titular Lucres (859–1237), but when this contest backfires, they bring Part 1 to an end with some further discussion of the play (1325–1432). Like Part 1, Part 2 also begins and ends with A and B's commentary on the action (1–133, 808–921), while its middle section features their failed attempts to deliver love tokens to Lucres on behalf of their masters (134–355).

As this summary should make clear, A and B dominate throughout. The only scenes in which they do not play a substantial part are those in which a formal debate between the two noble suitors is planned (1, 1238–24) and executed (2, 405–751), though it seems clear that the contest between A and B over Joan in Part 1 prefigures and to some extent satirizes the debate between Cornelius and Gayus in Part 2. Joan's refusal of B foreshadows Lucres's rejection of his master Cornelius, while B's manhandling of Joan—she's forced at one point to cry, 'Tusshe, I pray you let me go' (1, 862)—anticipates Cornelius's identification of nobility with brute force (cf. 2, 771–94). Meanwhile, A's concerns about B's moral integrity (1, 1062–70) are matched by his master Gaius's questioning of Cornelius's way of living (2, 630–41), while Joan's objection to B's coarse language—she demands that he hold his tongue (1, 1058)—is echoed in Lucres's similar complaint about B's way of speaking when she asks 'No more thereof, I pray you! Suche wordis I hate' (2, 535). However, where the Mak plot in the *Second Shepherds' Play* serves to heighten the pageant's religious meaning, in *Fulgens* the comic plot featuring A and B threatens to overshadow the play's central message about true nobility. For, as Rick Bowers has argued, while they 'do indeed parody the stiff formality of ancient Rome and the old story of Fulgens and Lucres ... they do so by metatheatrical default as they instigate the real action of the play and find their way into the classical marriage debate though loop-holes of performance'.[86] For all their talk of rank and riches, virtue and honour, Cornelius and Gayus's high-minded debate is made to seem ridiculous in the light of A and B's knockabout comedy that exposes nobility itself as a kind of performance. Status in this play is simply a matter of how you dress, behave, and speak.

---

[85] Robert P. Merrix, 'The Function of the Comic Plot in *Fulgens and Lucrece*', *Modern Language Studies*, 7 (1977), 16–26 (at 17).
[86] Rick Bowers, 'How to Get from A to B: *Fulgens and Lucres*, Histrionic Power, and the Invention of the English Comic Duo', *Early Theatre*, 14.1 (2011), 45–59 (at 57).

The idea of status as performance is reinforced in this play through the allocation of different verse forms for characters of different ranks. The noble characters speak in rhyme-royal, a seven-line stanza rhyming *ababbcc*, which was made popular by Chaucer and is clearly Medwall's preferred stanza for formal speech. In the debate scene involving Gayus and Cornelius, this stanza functions as the main sense unit, with most speeches extending across a number of full stanzas. In contrast, the scenes involving A and B are mostly cast in tail-rhyme, with individual lines frequently shared between speakers:

> ANCILLA. Let me alone, with sorowe!
> B. Mary, so be hyt. But one worde:
> I wyll kys the or thou goo.
> ANCILLA. The devyllis torde*!   *turd*
> The man is madde I trowe*!   *believe*
> B. So madde I am that nedis I must
> As in this poynt have my lust*   *have my desire*
> How so ever I doo.
> ANCILLA. Parde, ye may do me that request,
> For why it is but good and honest.
>   (*Fulgens*, I, 996–1004)

The effect of this shared stanza is that the dialogue between B and Joan is made to feel more informal or extemporary than the debate scene between Lucres's suitors. However, allocating dialogue in this way does more than demonstrate Medwall's ability to maintain 'a high degree of natural vitality'.[87] As I have already suggested, collaborative stanzas can serve to signal the speakers' unity and are often used to mark moments of joy or celebration; here, however, it is clear that the sharing of stanzas operates rather differently. The interchange follows B's initial attempt to kiss Joan against her will and ends with him kissing her having won her reluctant consent. This action, which sees B force himself on Joan until she has little choice but to relent, is mirrored in the stanza's rhyme scheme. In Nelson's Tudor Interludes edition, B's 'I wyll kys the or thou goo' and Joan's 'The devyllis torde' are counted as two separate lines. Metrically this makes sense, but by reading Joan's words as ending B's line, she is able to assert control over the rhyme scheme, making the line rhyme with B's previous line 'Mary, so be hyt. But one worde', and thereby establishing a kind of inverted tail-rhyme (*abb* as opposed to *aab*) as the scheme for this stanza.[88] The following three lines follow this pattern, rhyming *acc*, but B's line 'How so ever I doo' rhymes with his earlier 'I wyll kys the or thou goo' and so overturns the *abb* pattern that Joan had earlier established. Her final couplet rounds off the stanza, but in so doing she is made to comply with B's new scheme.[89] In contrast to the use of collaborative stanza forms in the *Entry* plays, in this example the dispersal of the speakers' lines across the stanza show how form can be made to mirror content. Just as Joan first resists but ultimately capitulates to B's aggressive overtures, so the rhyme scheme shows her forced to accept B's control over the stanza.

*****

The surviving texts of fifteenth-century religious and moral drama include a wide variety of forms and genres, though the extant texts in manuscript and print are presumably only

---

[87] Nelson (ed.), *The Plays of Henry Medwall*, 26.
[88] Both the preceding and succeeding stanzas adopt the more typical *aab* arrangement of rhymes.
[89] The resultant stanza can therefore be described as follows: $ab\frac{c}{b}addcee$.

a small portion of what once must have existed. Auspices for these different types of drama varied too, from plays sponsored by city corporations and designed for pageant-wagon performance to single-authored interludes written for private performance. Early scholarly studies of this surviving corpus were preoccupied with the idea of medieval drama as 'pre-Shakespearean', but the lasting impact of twentieth-century scholarship has been to focus attention on staging. Interest in the actualities of playing has only intensified with the success of the *REED* (Records of Early English Drama) project, ongoing at the University of Toronto. In contrast to this approach, the work of this chapter has been to read the drama of the fifteenth century as poetry, arguing that the diversity of its forms and subject-matter is apiece with the experimentation of fifteenth-century verse more generally. The athleticism and invention found within the forms of fifteenth-century dramatic poetry should therefore not only serve to recuperate its critical reputation, but also bear witness to the remarkable dexterity of fifteenth-century readers and playgoers, whose tastes such forms evidently reflect.

CHAPTER 15
Science and Information

A. S. G. Edwards

The categories 'science' and 'information' discussed in this chapter lack the clarity of focus that will be apparent in other chapters in this volume. As will become evident, the materials involved here encompass verse dealing with a heterogeneous range of topics. As there has not previously been an attempt to provide any broad historical survey of verse that falls into these categories, and guides are few, this chapter is very much an outline rather than an exhaustive examination.[1] What follows will attempt an overview of relevant works or categories, but there is necessarily a degree of selectiveness in what is included. For some texts there are no reliable modern editions and for others no editions at all, factors that necessarily circumscribe discussion.

There are further problems. One is the accurate identification of what appropriately belongs in this chapter. At times, attempts to establish the scope of relevant material for inclusion here must avoid misunderstanding the nature of the evidence. For example, in the original *Index of Middle English Verse*, one entry is described as 'On the positions and courses of the planets'; it is hence a potential candidate for inclusion here.[2] Subsequent research has established that it is a paraphrase of lines from the widely circulating fourteenth-century devotional work, the *Prick of Conscience*, and therefore, on both chronological and generic criteria, outside the scope of this chapter.[3] Another poem is headed in its only manuscript 'The descryuyng of mannes membres', a title that suggests an informational approach to its subject.[4] But the poem is actually a carefully developed political allegory based on the parts of the body. Again, a poem titled 'þe huntyng of þe hare' turns out to be a comic poem about hunting, not a serious treatment of the subject.[5] Such examples point to the need for a proper understanding of the relevant literary contexts that are necessary to identify works that can be appropriately discussed in this chapter.[6]

---

[1] Since there are few reliable overviews of this field, bibliographical information here is fuller than is necessary or appropriate for other chapters. The most valuable specialist studies for present purposes are Robert M. Schuler, *English Magical and Scientific Poems to 1700: An Annotated Bibliography* (New York, 1979) and George R. Keiser, 'Works of Science and Information', in Albert E. Hartung (ed.), *A Manual of the Writings in Middle English 1050–1500*, 11 vols. (New Haven, CT, 1998), vol. 10. For a helpful, if necessarily brief, historical survey of some of the subjects discussed here, see Anke Timmerman, 'Scientific and Encyclopedic Verse', in Julia Boffey and A. S. G. Edwards (eds), *A Companion to Fifteenth-Century Poetry* (Cambridge, 2013), 199–211.

[2] Carleton Brown and Rossell Hope Robbins (New York, 1943), no. 2753.

[3] See Derek Britton, 'Unnoticed Fragments of the *Prick of Conscience*', *Neuphilogische Mitteilungen*, 80 (1979), 327–34; the correct identification appears as NIMEV 2753.

[4] NIMEV 4070; it is included in Schuler (no. 170); for the most recent edition, see Helen Barr (ed.), *The Digby Poems* (Exeter, 2009), 224–31.

[5] NIMEV 64; for an edition and analysis, see David Scott-Macnab, 'The Hunttyng of the Hare in the Heege Manuscript', *Anglia*, 128 (2010), 102–23.

[6] For example, there are a number of poems to do with medicine that fall within the scope of this chapter. There are also a number of poems that parody such treatments of the subject; see Denton Fox (ed.), *The Poems of Robert Henryson* (Oxford, 1981), 475–76 for further details.

An additional difficulty, at times, is the problem of dating works, of establishing with certainty that they were composed within the time-period of this volume. The relative brevity and lack of internal reference for many of these poems makes this a particular question. While a fifteenth-century date is probable for the great majority of the works discussed here, it is possible that some may have been composed earlier and recopied later, or that others may be from the early sixteenth century.[7] The lack of secure criteria for dating manuscripts very precisely on palaeographical grounds, when internal evidence is lacking, and the often complex patterns of textual transmission that they reflect can make cut-off dates hard to establish.[8]

There are other problems related to forms of transmission. Occasionally modern editing has obscured the proper understanding of the nature of a work. The *Liber cure cocorum*, a series of versified culinary recipes, in couplets, that survives in a single manuscript, has achieved an identity separate from its broader manuscript context, by being misleadingly edited as a distinct work.[9] It is clearly the final part of the antecedent work in this manuscript, also unique, *The Boke of Curtasye*.[10] In its complete form the manuscript offers a comprehensive overview of household administration. It needs to be understood in such terms.

In addition, it may be necessary to be aware of different forms of manuscript circulation. Sometimes relevant verse achieves more than one identity. For example, this stanza on spot removal appears as a separate poem in four manuscripts:

Of wyne awaye the molis* maye ye wasshe	*spots*
In mylkys white the fletynge oyle spot	
With lye* of benys make it klene & fresshe	*cleanser*
Wasshe with wyne the fervent ynke blotte	
All other thynge is clensed wele I wot	
With water clere purgied and made clene	
But these iij clensen wyne mylke & bene.[11]	

But it also forms part of a longer poem on instructions to laundresses.[12] Again, John Lydgate's 'A Pageant of Knowledge' a mini-encyclopaedic poem in thirty-nine rhyme royal stanzas, describes such topics as the seven estates, planets, virtues, artificial and liberal sciences and the signs of the zodiac, the elements, the complexions, times of the years, and aspects of the natural world. The separate stanzas on some of these topics sometimes circulated as distinct poems.[13] The disintegration of such a work into smaller informational nuggets is typical of broader processes of fifteenth-century manuscript transmission. The

---

[7] For example, as is discussed below, some alchemical verse survives in primarily post-fifteenth-century witnesses; some manuscripts were copied as late as the seventeenth century.

[8] An example of the difficulties of dating is the nearly thirty versions of poems on bloodletting listed under NIMEV 3848. Some of these have been dated to the fourteenth century and differ markedly from others in their textual form; for some examples and discussion of these see Linne R. Mooney, 'A Middle English Verse Compendium of Astrological Medicine', *Medical History*, 28 (1984), 406–19. On the other hand, other forms of works listed under this number have been identified as fifteenth-century and are discussed here.

[9] NIMEV 2361; it survives only in BL MS Sloane 1986, fols. 27–56v; it was edited under this title by Richard Morris (Berlin, 1862). For brief discussion of the problems of differentiating separate scientific and medical verse texts, see Laurel Means, 'Electionary, Lunary, Destinary, Questionary: Toward Defining Categories of Middle English Prognostic Material', *Studies in Philology*, 89 (1992), 367–403 (at 369–70).

[10] NIMEV 4152; BL MS Sloane 1986, fols. 12v–27; see J. O. Halliwell (ed.), *The Boke of Curtasye* (London, 1841). George R. Keiser was the first to point out the connection between the two works ('Works of Science', 3680).

[11] NIMEV 2668; I follow the version printed by Curt F. Bühler in his review of H. N. MacCracken's second volume of '*The Minor Poems of John Lydgate*' in *Review of English Studies*, 12 (1936), 237.

[12] NIMEV 4254; this poem is printed in H. N. MacCracken (ed.), *The Minor Poems of John Lydgate: Part 2: Secular Poems*, EETS, o.s. 192 (London, 1934), 723. The grounds for the attribution of this version to Lydgate are open to question.

[13] NIMEV 3651; extracts from it appear as NIMEV 576, 3503, 3504.

modern reader needs to be conscious of such processes and their potential relevance to the proper contextualization of a work.

But the largest problem for the modern reader in the material examined in this chapter is not likely to be bibliographical or textual. It is more likely to lie in the difficulty in understanding why many of the subjects treated here were felt appropriate for treatment in verse. The impulse to versification found unique expression in poems on such subjects as fencing,[14] heraldry,[15] and on rules of grammar,[16] for example. Such topics suggest something of the extensive range of subjects in the fifteenth century for which verse was felt an appropriate form, however limited the possibilities for distinctive poetic expression.[17]

The verses below offer advice about the points to consider when buying land:

> Who-so wil be wise in purchasing,
> consyder þe poyntes þat ben following:
> fyrst that the land be clere
> And that it stand in no daynger
> in the tytell of the seller
> Of no womans dower.
> Se whether yt be bond or free,
> and se the Relese of euery fefee*;   *debtor*
> Se that þe seller be of age,
> & yf the land be not in morgage ...
>   (1–10)[18]

This advice was evidently widely circulated: the poem (which runs to eleven couplets), is recorded in sixteen surviving manuscripts. Such an example raises an obvious question that has larger implications for this chapter: why was verse rather than prose seen as the appropriate expository medium for such guidance to the extent that it evidently was?

At its most basic level the purpose of some of the verse discussed here may have lain in its potential mnemonic usefulness. This quality can be seen particularly in some of the numerous shorter informational texts that survive. It can be illustrated by these deft lines on the construction of the body, where number and rhyme provide obvious memorial cues:

> XXXII teth that beþe full kene*,   *sharp*
> CC bonys and Nyntene,
> CCC vaynys sixty and fyve,
> Euery man haþe that is alyve.[19]

---

[14] NIMEV 3423; printed in T. Wright and J. O. Halliwell (eds), *Reliquiae Antiquae* (London, 1841–3), 1, 308–9.
[15] NIMEV 800; printed in F. J. Furnivall (ed.), *Queene Elizabethes Achademy*, EETS, e.s. 8 (London, 1869), 93–102.
[16] NIMEV 2252; printed in Wright and Halliwell (eds), *Reliquiae Antiquae*, 2.14.
[17] I should note one poem that might seem to have warranted inclusion here: NIMEV 4149. This work, 794 lines in couplets, appears uniquely in BL Royal 17 A I, fols. 1–32v and is titled there 'Constituciones artis geometrie secundum Euclidem'. See Douglas Knoop, G. P. Jones, and Douglas Hamer (eds), *The Two Earliest Masonic Mss.: The Regius Ms. (B.M. Bibl. reg. 17 AI), the Cooke Ms. (B.M. Add. ms. 23198)* (Manchester, 1938). This seems to be mainly an assemblage, in part from other works, of advice on conduct for masons and for worship in church, together with very brief discussion of the Seven Liberal Arts.
[18] NIMEV 4148; I follow here the version in Rossell Hope Robbins (ed.), *Secular Lyrics of the XIV and XVth Centuries*, 2nd edn (Oxford, 1955), no. 74, 70–1; I have transposed lines 4–5, a suggestion made privately by the late John Burrow.
[19] NIMEV 3572; Robbins (ed.), *Secular Lyrics*, no. 75, 71.

The following lines on how to find the date of Easter seem likely to have been similarly effective. They also circulated widely:

> In merche*, after þe fyrst C*,   *March, the seventh of March*
> Loke the prime* wher-euer he is be;   *new moon*
> The 3ᵈ sonday, full I-wysse,
> Ester day trewly yt ys.
> & yf þe prime on þe sonday be,
> rekyne þat sonday for one of þe thre.²⁰

Such examples demonstrate the expository qualities necessary for easy retention.

The formal limitations of such modest enumerative possibilities of verse quickly become apparent in less efficient hands, as here:

> I Wot a tre XII bowys betake,
> LII nestys beþe þat vp ymad;
> In euery nest beþ bryddys VII.
> I-thankyd be þe God of heuene
> And euery bryd with selcouth* name.²¹   *unusual*
>   (1–5)

These lines attempt to use the conceit of aspects of the tree to enumerate basic divisions of the year, months ('XII'), weeks ('LII') and days ('VII'). The coherence of conception is not matched by sustained execution. Both form and rhyme are imperfect, apart from lines 3–4. Since they are unique it is hard to be sure how much the inadequacies of form are the responsibility of scribe or author.

The lines also suggest that the composer was unskilled in verse composition. Such an inability to meet even the most elementary challenges of verse is demonstrated elsewhere when employing a more complex verse form, as in this attempt at a rhyme royal stanza on the complexions:

> Off yiftes large, in love hath grete delite,
> Iocunde and gladde, ay of laughyng chiere,
> Of ruddy color meynt* somdel with white;   *mingled*
> Disposed by kynde to be a champioun,
> Hardy I-nough, manly and bold of chiere.   5
> Of the sangwyne also it is a signe,
> To be demure, rigth curteys, and benynge.²²
>   (1–7)

The stanza form should rhyme *ababbcc*; but rhyme breaks down in line 4; in addition, lines 2 and 5 have the same rhyme word.

And, at times, while the principle of rhyme is clearly grasped, its application to verse form is erratically applied. In the following example, lines enumerating the names of birds, the shift from an opening monorhymed stanza of five lines to couplets may not have been occasioned by anything more than the limits of appropriate rhyme words:

---

²⁰ Robbins (ed.), *Secular Lyrics*, no. 70, 63; NIMEV 1502 records twenty-two manuscripts, to which should be added Cambridge, Magdalene College, MS Pepys 15, fol. 171.
²¹ NIMEV 1396; Robbins (ed.), *Secular Lyrics*, no. 69, 62.
²² NIMEV 2624; Robbins (ed.), *Secular Lyrics*, no. 77, 72; it survives in six manuscripts.

Today in the dawnyng
I hyrde þo fowles syng
The names of hem it likyt me to myng* *remember*
The parterygg the fesant and þe sterlyng
the quhayle & þe goldefyng and þe lapwing
the thrusch þe maueys* and þe wodewale *missel thrush, woodpecker*
the Jaye þe popynjaye and the nyghtyngale
the notthatch þe swallow and the semow* *seagull*
the chawȝe* the cucko þe rooke þe ravyn and the crow *chough/jackdaw*
Among all þe fowles þat maden gle
the rere mowse* and þe owle cowde I not see.²³ *bat*

Such examples of compositional uncertainty show the gap that could exist between even very modest aspirations to writing verse mnemonics and their successful execution. They could be multiplied.

Verses like these do demonstrate a clear memorial purpose, albeit not invariably successfully executed. The gap between intended function and imperfect execution can extend to encompass specific categories of material. Charms are particularly slippery. They lie both on the margins both of formal verse and of the material appropriate to this chapter. Many charms are both unique and irregularly rhymed, offering a series of ad hoc and crudely formed responses to situations or circumstances in which invocation of some form of higher authority was deemed appropriate.²⁴ This charm for travellers with its invocation of the Trinity is representative:

Here I ame and fourthe I mouste,
& in Iesus Criste is all my trust.
No wicked thing do me no dare,
nother here nor Elles whare.
The father with me; the sonne with me;
the holly gosste, & the trienete,
be by-twyxte my gostely Enime & me.
In the name of the father, & the sonne,
And the holly goste, Amen.²⁵

Some charms were more successful in achieving a form that seems to have enabled them to enjoy a developed tradition. A charm against bleeding, for example, is found in at least nineteen manuscripts.²⁶ Others had a wide circulation in various forms. The 'Flum Jordan' charm to staunch blood is an example:

Crist was born in Betlehem
and cristend in flom* Iordane *river*
and also þe flom stode als a stane,
stand þi blode, N. (neuen* his name) *give*
In nominee patris et filii et spiritus sancti. Amen²⁷

---

²³ NIMEV 3788.5; C. E. Wright, 'Middle English Parerga in a School Collection', *Review of English Studies*, n.s. 2 (1951), 114–120 (at 116).
²⁴ See, for example, NIMEV 1182 in Robbins (ed.), *Secular Lyrics*, no. 61, 58; NIMEV 1199 in Robbins (ed.), *Secular Lyrics*, no. 64, 60; NIMEV 2903 in Robbins (ed.), *Secular Lyrics*, no. 66, 6; and see also NIMEV 412.5, 417, 459, 605.5, 627.22, 627.3, 627.5, 860.5, 873.8, 992, 993, 1290, 1292, 1293.5, 1789.55, 1952.5, 2451.77, 2683.55, 3209.5, 3634.5, 3709, 4154.8.
²⁵ NIMEV 1199 in Robbins (ed.), *Secular Lyrics*, no. 64, 60.
²⁶ For details see NIMEV 1293.
²⁷ I quote the version (there are more than a dozen) in Douglas Gray, 'Notes on some Middle English Charms', in Beryl Rowland (ed.), *Chaucer and Middle English Studies: Studies in Honour of Rossell Hope Robbins* (London, 1974), 56–71 (at 62); this article remains the best general overview of the subject.

Here a blank space is left for the insertion of a specific name. This charm remained in manuscript circulation down to the seventeenth century. Copies can even be found in manuscripts owned by physicians. Other versions of it circulated in medieval Latin, French, and German.[28] It offers testimony to the enduring appeal—and perceived usefulness—of the verse charm over time.

Here, as elsewhere, the function of the charm is quasi magical. It relies on the power of address to create the appearance of authority, as in this charm against thieves, that begins:

I bitake þe*, holy gost, þis place here ysette,	*entrust you*
And þe fadir and þe sone, þeues for to lette*,	*prevent*
If any þeues here come my good awey to fette,	
The holy gost be hem byfore, and do hem for to lette* ...[29]	*obstruct*

The efficacy of the charm is established by its references to Christian powers, to the Trinity, and later to 'þe vertu of Mathew, Luke, Marke and Johan' and to 'seynt Bartholomew'. Yet these figures are not invoked in prayer, not named out of any spiritual purpose. Here they are called on to protect the material ('my good') in a way that moves towards the incantatory. In the manuscript in which this charm appears the charm is accompanied by instructions about signs to be made, presumably while the charm is recited. Similar literalizing of Christian authority comes in this charm against fever:

What manere of Ivell* thou be,	*evil*
In goddess name I coungere* the.	*conjure*
I coungere the with the holy crosse	
That Iesus was done on with fors.	
I conure the with nayles thre	
That Iesus was nayled vpon the tree.[30]	
(1–6)	

In this instance the authority that it invoked derives from the enumeration here of the instruments of Christ's Passion. After the 'holy crosse' and the 'nayles thre' of the Crucifixion, the charm goes on to describe the crown of thorns, Christ's blood, his five wounds, and Longinus's spear. These are concrete representations of suffering, elsewhere employed visually as meditative symbols of Christian faith, but here 'conjured' out of a belief in their immediate curative efficacy.

Charms, as a genre, demonstrate the naiveté of both conception and execution. Christian belief becomes superstition, the means of 'conjuring' as here. And they often demonstrate a flawed grasp of verse form. In such respects they establish the outer limits of the subject matter of this chapter. They offer articulations of primitive belief rather than any significant expression of information or knowledge.

If charms suggest a form that is shaped by barely literate levels of credulity there are other, more complex factors that contributed to other uses of verse for such informational

---

[28] NIMEV 624 records twelve manuscripts; there is a variant form at NIMEV 993.11. For a detailed study of this charm see T. M. Smallwood, '"God Was Born in Bethlehem ... ": The Tradition of a Middle English Charm', *Medium Ævum*, 58 (1989), 206–23.

[29] NIMEV 1285.66; edited in full by Gray, 'Notes on some Middle English Charms', 66.

[30] NIMEV 3911; see Robbins (ed.), *Secular Lyrics*, no. 65, 60–1 for the complete text. Charms against thieves are a recurrent category; see, for example, NIMEV 3771 in Robbins (ed.), *Secular Lyrics*, no. 63, 59 and NIMEV 1293.5, 1952.5, 4154.8.

purposes. The generations after the death of Chaucer in 1400 saw a developing sense of the potential of vernacular verse to expand the range of its subjects to encompass verse that was concerned with the transmission of various forms of knowledge. There are at least a couple of significant factors that seem to have shaped decisions to create verse compositions of this kind. One was the swiftly widening dissemination of Chaucer's works in the fifteenth century, and hence of the range of verse models they provided. Another was the apparent desire in some instances to create new verse forms of works that had achieved a developed prose circulation.

Both tendencies come together in John Walton's verse rendering of Boethius's *Consolation of Philosophy*, made in the early fifteenth century. This shows a clear awareness of Chaucer's late fourteenth-century prose version of this work, his *Boece*, from which he borrows. But Walton's version seems to have been more popular than Chaucer's, if numbers of surviving manuscripts are a valid indicator of its appeal. Chaucer's version survives in nine manuscripts and a single fragment; Walton's version survives complete in twenty-three manuscripts, as well as in a number of extracts; it is noteworthy that some of these extracts are wrongly ascribed to Chaucer.[31] Walton's translation suggests that the technical problems of verse composition were not necessarily an inhibiting factor either for author or audience. He demonstrates his metrical range by composing some parts of his work in rhyme royal stanzas, a form only recently introduced into English verse by Chaucer, and others in his eight-line 'Monk's Tale' stanzas (*ababbcbc*). His use of Chaucer's stanza forms and prose diction points to a confidence that they could be employed to extend the range of subjects explored in verse, notwithstanding the obvious potential challenges of balancing the constraints of rhyme, stanza form, and metre against the need to simultaneously convey complex content with appropriate expository clarity.[32]

A lot of the other verse that forms the subject of this chapter has a clear grasp of both form and function, even if some of its applications are limited. At times verse is employed contextually in relationship to a following lengthier prose text. It serves as a way of offering a summary of such prose content, thereby focusing the attention of the reader on the nature of what is to follow. These couplets that precede a prose version of Macer's herbal provide clear and succinct information about its subject matter:

> This booke is drawe by ffesyk* *compiled from a medical work*
> That Macer made for hem þat been seek*; *sick*
> Þe vertu of herbis it discryveth ryght wel
> And help of mannys helthe euery dele.[33]

Another example from a medical text again demonstrates this summarizing function:

---

[31] See NIMEV 1597 for details, and for discussion see A. S. G. Edwards, 'Reading John Walton's Boethius in the 15th and 16th Centuries', in Mary Flannery and Carrie Griffin (eds), *Spaces for Reading* (London, 2016), 35–49. On the Chaucer attributions see further, Julia Boffey, 'Proverbial Chaucer and the Chaucer Canon', *Huntington Library Quarterly*, 58 (1996), 37–48 and NIMEV 2820.

[32] Occasionally the indebtedness to Chaucer in the kinds of material discussed here involves a direct appropriation; for example, 'The Chance of Dice' (discussed below) appropriates a line from his *Legend of Good Women*; see A. S. G. Edwards, 'The Chance of Dice and The Legend of Good Women', *Notes and Queries*, n.s. 34 (1987), 295. And a poem on heraldry, NIMEV 800, borrows lines from the Knight's Tale (1116–17) in its discussion of coat armour; see F. J. Furnivall (ed.), *Queene Elizabethes Achademy*, EETS e.s. 8 (London, 1869), 94, lines 31–2.

[33] NIMEV 3578; for general discussion of this question, see George R. Keiser, 'Verse Introductions to Middle English Medical Texts', *English Studies*, 84 (2003), 301–17; quotation from 315; for other examples of verse preambles to medical texts, see NIMEV 533, 1605, 2368, 4182.

This booke hy3t* ypocras	is called
oon of þe beste syrgens þat euer was	
& galyen his felowe & socrates,	
to þis booke þai bere wytnesse	
ffor all þai were felowes in fer*:	together
while þai leved in erthe here	
Throu3he þe grace of heuene kynge	
Thay purchased hem medicynes to helpe mankynde	
Pray we for all to heuene kynge	
He 3eue her soulys good wonynge. Amen.[34]	

as does this prologue to a prose treatise on equestrian matters:

The boke of marchalsi here it xal* begunne	shall
3e þat wil wyth craft ony honour wynne	
Here 3e may lere of hors gret and smale	
How 3e schal her maladiis craftiliche hale*	heal
Also I wil 3ow telle owt of qwat cuntre	
3e mow good hors chosyn best for to be	
Bothe in werre and in pes wythowt ony fayle	
And how 3e shul hem chesyn be her good entayle*	quality
Of foles þat ben 3onge withowtyn lesing*	lie
Now I wyll 3ow telle of here kepyng	
How 3e xal* hem fede with hey and with corne	shall
And wyslych* hem kepe þat þei ben nowt lorn*	wisely, lost
Tyl þat þei ben of age and mightful at nede	
A kny3th vpon to ride at eueri dowti dede*[35]	brave deed

Such preambles can extend to announcements that offer considerable detail about content:

Here-in ben medycyns with-outhen fable*	lie
To hele al sores þat arn curable	
Of swerde, of knyf, & of arwe*—	arrow
Be wounde wyde or narow,	
Of spere, of quarel*, or dager, or darte ...[36]	crossbow bolt
(5–9)	

And so on for some thirty-two lines. The clarity and succinctness of such framing verse passages provides a helpful prefatory function.

Verse is also used to provide brief concluding summaries to a prose work. These can take the form of terse recapitulation: 'Here endys haukyng with medysyns and casting / And all that longys to goode hauke kepyng'.[37] This unique passage at the end of a manuscript of the prose hunting treatise, *The Master of Game*, offers a more extended example of this function:

---

[34] NIMEV 3577.55; printed in Henry Hargreaves, 'Additional Information for the Brown-Robbins "Index"', *Notes and Queries*, n.s. 16 (1969), 446, from Cambridge, Trinity College MS O. 1. 13, fol. 61v; I have relineated these lines here to reflect their verse form; they appear in three other manuscripts.

[35] NIMEV 3318; I have transcribed these lines in BL MS Harley 6398, fol. 1 from the facsimile in Frederick Smith, *The Early History of Veterinary Literature and Its Development* (London, 1919), 111. For a preamble to another hunting treatise, see NIMEV 202.

[36] NIMEV 3422; Robbins (ed.), *Secular Lyrics*, no. 103, 95–6; NIMEV records twenty-three manuscripts to which may be added one sold at Sotheby's, 30 December 2008, lot 30.

[37] NIMEV 1197.2.

> What man that wille of huntyng leere*   *learn*
> And in that science hymself avance
> he may therof fynde talkyng here
> ffor neither of songe harpe lute ne davnce
> He treteth he noght but of the ordenance
> Of alle gode hunting and who so lust it loke
> He shal it fynde compiled in this boke[38]

In addition, very occasionally, brief aphoristic verse passages are inserted into the body of prose instructional works.[39]

These examples suggest some of the limited possibilities of the use of verse around and within a predominant prose form of writing. There are a number of instances where the example of Walton's Boethius translation is replicated, where verse was more ambitiously employed to create a new form of a substantial work that has an established identity in prose. However, these instances often differ from Walton in that the verse form is much rarer than the prose one. For example, the contemporary popularity of Sir John Mandeville's *Travels* is evidenced by its survival in nearly forty manuscripts in a number of Middle English prose versions.[40] These manuscripts provide clear evidence of appeal as a source for information about geography and exploration, even though the author is fictitious and the treatment of its subject is based on others written sources, not on direct observation.

In contrast, only a single complete verse form of the work survives, in couplets, running to nearly three thousand lines.[41] 'Mavndevile' is invoked at the start:

> Som time in Engelonde was a knyght,
> A fers man boothe stronge and wyght.*   *brave*
> Sir Iohn Mavndevile was his name,
> And in Seinte Albones he was born ...
> A worþi sowdioure* forsothe was he   *soldier*
> And wel trauailid biyonde the see
> In many a dyuers kinges londe,
> As affter ye shal vndirstonde.
> For he was out of the londe here
> Holiche foure and thirti yere
> And euer he trauailid without wene
> The wondres of þis worlde to sene.
> And al þat he sawe he vndirtoke
> And euer he wrote it in a boke ...
>   (15–19, 23–32)

---

[38] NIMEV 3910.5; printed by Rossell Hope Robbins, 'A Middle English Diatribe Against Philip of Burgundy', *Neophilologus*, 39 (1955), 131–46 (at 134).

[39] For example, in the translation of Walter of Henley's treatise on husbandry; see NIMEV 2698, 4113.

[40] These are enumerated in M. C. Seymour, 'The English Manuscripts of *Mandeville's Travels*', *Transactions of the Edinburgh Bibliographical Society*, 4, part 5 (1966), 169–210.

[41] NIMEV 248.5; this survives in Coventry Archives & Research Centre PA325/1; it is edited by M. C. Seymour, *The Metrical Version of Mandeville's Travels*, EETS, o.s. 269 (London, 1973), the form cited here. The text was originally probably somewhat longer than what now survives; several leaves are lacking, and it breaks off abruptly without a clear ending. For discussion and analysis, see C. W. R. D. Moseley, 'The Metamorphoses of Sir John Mandeville', *Yearbook of English Studies*, 4 (1974), 14–16, and C. David Benson, *Imagined Rome: The City and its Stories in Middle English Poetry* (University Park, PA, 2019), 33–55.

The narrative uses various strategies to give the appearance of both authentic detail and references of relevance to the reader. It begins with a lengthy account of the city of Rome (62–462), 'þat same cite / Is chief of alle cristante / And also hede of holi church' (70–2). Here descriptive weight falls heavily on the enumerative, offering a gazetteer of the city's buildings and districts with emphasis on forms of material specificity, often on numbers and names. For example, the city walls are 'twoo and fourtie myle aboute' (151), with 'three hundred and ey3te and fourti toures' (159) and 'eighte and tene' (162) principal gates; within the city there were 'three and fourtie' (189) castles and 'seven thousand foure score and ten' (191) barbicans. At times, proper names pile up:

> And the paleis of Domician
> That is *ad micam auream**.   *to golden grain*
> And þe paleis also of Olimpias
> That seint Laurence rostid was.
> And þe paleis of Octovian,
> That place wel knoweth many a man.
> The paleis also of Veneris
> That *Scala Celi* nowe callid ys.*   *scale of heaven*
> The paleis of Camille is eke there by
> That nowe is called seinte Anthony ...
>   (263–72)

A variant of this enumerative technique is the simple list of items within a category, as here with precious stones:

> Amatistes, crisolites, and calcidoynes,
> Crapotines*, coteices*, and sardoynes,   *toad-stones, precious stones*
> Diamoundes, dianes* ful thik þere wore,   *black gems*
> Emeraudes, saphiris, and vermidore*,   *ruby*
> Peritotes* also and reflambines*,   *green gems, precious stones*
> And carbuncles that bright shines ...[42]
>   (327–32)

As the account moves beyond Rome, its longest single description, other narrative strategies are employed. In part, geography becomes Christianized, so that place acquires relevance through its relationship to the life of Christ and His disciples:

> ... That is þe cite of Peroun,
> For Ihesus Criste there rested hym
> Bifore þe castelle of Pilrym
>   (897–99)

This is particularly the case in the description of Jerusalem (934–1052) which is shaped by forms of association with New Testament history:

> At þe north gate þere as men geth
> There was seint Stephen stoned to deth. (936–7)
> There stant yitte þe same pilere
> That Criste was beten with scourgis kene. (963–4)
> In the south side of Iherusalem anone

---

[42] For other examples of this technique, see 2026–2030, 2406–12.

> Men shillen fynde the mount Syone
> There þat seint Peter, as seith the boke,
> Thries there oure lorde forsoke ... (1126–29)

The mode shifts again as description advances beyond the Holy Land, this time to stress the miraculous, the historical or the simply anecdotal:

> Nowe lesteneth and I shalle you telle
> A meracle and a grete meruelle (1384–5)
> And in Cisile there is also
> A wonder miracle amonge oþere moo. (1429–30)

Or in the account of the monk who carried away 'oo boorde' (1701) from Noah's ark (1699–1728). Or of the fate of the 'two and twenty kingis ... of þe iewis lynage' (2185–6) conquered by Alexander the Great (2181–2220). Sometimes there are several anecdotes woven together as in those figures associated with the 'oolde forleten castelle' (1549) whose different fates offer either untold riches or perpetual punishment depending on circumstance (1550–1611).

Although the poem ranges widely in its geographical scope 'Mandeville' never loses sight of his English audience and finds points of comparison or reference:

> ... And þere is a castelle realle fulle rich
> Is Engelonde is none hym liche ... (752–3)
> ... And king Coel hir fader was
> That made Colchester þat faire plas ... (974–5)
> ... Thoo stoones froo thens thei ham sette
> And here in Engelond thei ham sette
> Vppon the plaine of Salisbury ... (2133–5)
> ... In Engelonde groweth no better wolle*   *wool*
> Than þere wexeth vppon her solle ... (2902–3)

In such ways the poem seeks to maintain a connection between the foreign, hence exotic, nature of its subject and its envisioned readership. The range of its techniques makes it likely that it succeeded in its aims. But its lack of circulation suggests that the available prose forms limited its appeal.

There is another unique, but fragmentary, verse version of Mandeville's *Travels* that survives in eight-line ballade stanzas (*ababbcbc*).[43] It describes 'Mandeville's' visit to the 'Gret Caan of the Tartaris' (3) with whom 'he dwelt a ȝere and more' (86). It gives a vividly detailed account of the 'hed cety' (129) and of the burial practises for the Great Cham:

> Whan thay salle bery* the Gret Caane,   *bury*
> Mekylle* mete and drinke on the erth þay caste   *much*
> to fede hym after he be gane,
> for they thinke the saule it may nat faste.
> Than the body they bryng vnto þat place
> wher he salle ly, armet in his wede,
> in a tabernacle or a case.
>   (273–9)

---

[43] NIMEV 3117.6; this survives in BodL MS e Musaeo 160, fols. 109–14. It is edited by M. C. Seymour, 'Mandeville and Marco Polo: A Stanzaic Fragment', *AUMLA: Journal of the Australasian Universities Language and Literature Association*, 21 (1964), 42–50; quotations and line references here are from this edition.

The account breaks off shortly after this point. One may regret the loss of what might have followed. Even in its fragmentary form the poem indicates an ability to use its complex verse form to convey narrative and description with some skill.

There are various other verse writings related to travel and geography in the fifteenth century. The most extensive of these is William Wey's guide for pilgrims to the Holy Land incorporated into his prose Latin and Middle English *Itineraries*. This work survives in a single manuscript, BodL MS Bodley 565, composed in 352 lines in couplets.[44] It is based on Wey's observations on his pilgrimages to Jerusalem in the late 1450s and early 1460s. It is much less a descriptive guide to particular places and much more an enumeration of the specific implications of each site for New Testament events and figures. The significance of each site is defined in these terms, as in this account of the holy places of Jerusalem:

> Furthermore in that cyte
> Be pylgremagis both fayre and fre
> The fyrst tokening of all
> Ys at the corner of a wall
> There Jhesu met w^t hys modyr Marie
> Ther sorowyd together bothe he and she
> And ther the wymmen of Jerusalem
> Wept on Cryst when that he cam.
>
> (11)

The imprecision of spatial reference here ('at the corner of a wall … There … Ther … ther') is general. Very rarely does any specific detail emerge of about a place: 'a chapell, hit ys ryght lowe / Twenty pace downe as men hyt knowe' (10); 'a fayre rounde chapelle' (12) are the nearest Wey comes to any concrete information. Wey lacked the descriptive skill to illuminate his subject. It is difficult to believe that the aspiring pilgrim would have found the work very informative as a source for guidance about Rome and its environs.[45]

There are other instances of verse where it demonstrates a resistance to predominant prose models. The topics of horticulture and arboriculture provide further examples of this tendency. The most extensive example of a work of this kind is a version of Palladius' *De re agricultura*, composed in the fourth century. In its fullest form the Middle English version runs to over six and half thousand lines in rhyme royal stanzas, preceded by an alphabetical index.[46] The 'Prohemium' identifies the commissioner of the poem as Humfrey, duke of Gloucester (1390–447), later invoked by name, 'My blissed lord, mene y, the duc Homfrey' (85, line 454).[47] One of the surviving manuscripts, BodL MS Duke Humfrey d. 2, is extremely elaborately prepared, and appears to have been made for presentation to

---

[44] NIMEV 883; edited in G. Williams, *The Itineraries of William Wey* (London, 1857), 8–19; the text is cited by page number.

[45] There are a couple of other brief poems that include geographical information: NIMEV 3653, edited as 'The Divisions of the World', in Anthony Bale and Sebastian Sobecki (eds), *Medieval English Travel: A Critical Anthology* (Oxford, 2019), 145–50; and NIMEV 1083.5, a brief passage (eighteen lines, written as prose in John Capgrave, *Ye solace of pilgrimes, a description of Rome, circa A. D. 1450*, C. A. Mills (ed.) (London, 1911), 160–1).

[46] NIMEV 654, which records three manuscripts; the poem is edited as *The Middle-English Translation of Palladius De Re Rustica*, by Mark Liddell (Berlin, 1896); quotations here come from this edition, by page and line.

[47] The 'Prohemium' mentions (22, lines 89–104) Humfrey's bequest of books to Oxford, the first of which took place in 1439, the second in 1444; these dates provide the limits for the poem's composition.

Duke Humfrey.[48] There are indications that Humfrey had a close and active involvement in the preparation of the poem, seemingly correcting the text. At one point the author exclaims:

> And now my lord biholdith on his book.
> ffor sothe al nought, he gynnyth crossis make
> With a plummet and y noot whow his look,
> His cheer is straunge, eschaunge*. Almeest y quake,   *changeable*
> ffor ferd* y shrynke away, no leue y take.   *fear*
> (85, 480-4)

It is possible that the author may have been Humfrey's chaplain, Thomas Norton.[49] The 'Prohemium' is followed by a section headed 'Aier, Water, Lond, and Gouernaunce' and then by sections that follow the months of the year, from January to December. Each month has instructions for the appropriate tasks to be performed, often set out in considerable detail, in highly technical language. These are among the instructions for February:

> At places warme, in dayes lyth & drye,
> Is now the hilly londys vp to ere,*   *plough*
> Trimenstre* seed in erthe is now to strie*.   *three months, strew*
> Now wold also thy puls* be sowen there   *seeds*
> As thynne, & resolute, & faate hit were
> And namly dry. And whi? Lest luxurie*   *excess*
> And humor excessif go make hit dye.
> They may be sowe vntyl the mone be
> At dayes twelue. And forto make hem grete
> And uppe anoon, commixt* thou most hem see   *mix*
> With drie donge*, & theryn lette hem swete   *dung*
> Tyl* daies foure. As for oon aker* mete   *for, acre*
> A strik of hem, hit schal be so suffisid.
> And chicches* sowe afore as I deuysed.   *chickpeas*
> (87-8, 8-21)

Sometimes passages are descriptive as in this stanza on apple trees:

> As Marcial seith ypomelides*   *apple trees*
> Beth appul treen whos fruyt is lyk a serue*   *service tree*
> A commyn tre statured* doutelees, *   *of height*
> With whitly flour coloured, whos obserue.
> To worthy men the fruyt is worthy serue,
> ffor as he seith, hit is so tart and swete
> That wel is hym that with that fruyt may mete.
> (256, 22-8)

Infrequently the injunctions are as clear and succinct, as here:

> Pasturis ek in this mone is to brenne*   *burn*
> That busshus, ther they growith ouerhie
> And bisie beth the lond to ouerrenne,
> This brennyng may their stook & hem destrie.
> (197, 22-5)

---

[48] See the admirable discussion by A. C. de la Mare, 'Duke Humfrey's English Palladius (MS. Duke Humfrey d. 2)', *Bodleian Library Record*, 12 (1985-8), 39-51.

[49] The suggestion is made by D. R. Howlett, 'The Date and Authorship of the Middle English Verse Translation of Palladius *De re rustica*', *Medium Ævum*, 46 (1977), 245-52.

Such advice is occasionally interspersed with hints about household economy:

> If oil be foule, taak hoot salt alto grounde,
> And kest hit in, and diligently wrie*   *cover*
> And in a while al pure hit wole be fonde
> (250, 491–3)

It is not easy to envision the purposes that such a poem was intended to fulfil, the nature of Humfrey's own involvement, or the audience for which it was intended. The inclusion of an index suggests some practical purposes, but it is difficult to see who would choose such a work, in verse, and with a complex lexis, directly for practical purposes. This seems an especially curious undertaking in view of the wide availability of various related Middle English prose versions of *Godfridus super Palladium* and of Nicholas Bollard's *Tractatus* on the growing and grafting of trees.[50] It is possible that the work was conceived primarily for entirely different purposes, that had more to do with contemporary politics than a desire to disseminate information.[51] But it must stand, at least notionally, as a contribution to practical verse.

There are few other verse works on these matters. A poem of 196 lines in couplets gives a succinct survey of aspects of arboriculture, viticulture, planting seeds, sowing cabbage, parsley, and other kinds of herbs; it concludes with a discussion of planting saffron before breaking off abruptly.[52] The composition seems to be pragmatic and utilitarian. Verse possibly serves a memorial function in what, at times, is little more than a list: ' … Rose ryde, rose why3te, foxgloue and pympernold, / Holyhocke, coryawnder, pyony …' (179–80). The work is ascribed to 'Mayster Jon Gardener', a name that seems unlikely to indicate a real person. There is also a curious alliterative poem on plant names that survives uniquely in a schoolbook.[53]

There are also substantial prose traditions of writings on matters to do with hunting, most notably in the early-fifteenth-century translation of Gaston de Foix's *Livre de Chasse*, attributed to Edward, duke of York, *The Master of Game*, that survives in more than twenty manuscripts. The verse tradition is again more limited and is represented most extensively in printed form, in the 'boke of huntyng' that forms part of the *Book of St. Albans*, attributed spuriously to Dame Juliana Berners, published in St Albans in 1486 (STC 3308).[54] There are two manuscript versions that predate this edition.[55] In its printed form, the preface

---

[50] These works enjoyed an extensive prose tradition. For a (not necessarily complete) listing of the surviving manuscripts, see W. L. Braekman, 'Bollard's Middle English Book of Planting and Grafting and its Background', *Studia Neophilologica*, 57 (1985), 19–39 and David G. Cylkowski, 'A Middle English Treatise on Horticulture: Godfridus super Palladium', in Lister Matheson (ed.), *Popular and Practical Science of Medieval England* (East Lansing, MI, 1994), 301–29, both of which include editions of the relevant works.

[51] For some speculation about the relationship between patron, poem, and contemporary politics see A. S. G. Edwards, 'Duke Humfrey's Middle English Palladius Manuscript', in Jenny Stratford (ed.), *The Lancastrian Court* (Donington, 2003), 68–77.

[52] NIMEV 4146; edited in full from Cambridge, Trinity College MS O. 9. 38 in George Rigg, *A Glastonbury Miscellany of the Fifteenth Century* (London, 1968), 103–9; an incomplete version (not identified as such) appears in London, Wellcome Library MS 406, fols. 17–20; see A. Zettersten, *The Virtues of Herbs in the Loscombe Manuscript* (Lund, 1967), 22–6.

[53] NIMEV 1378.5; edited and discussed in Edward Wilson, 'An Unpublished Alliterative Poem on Plant-Names from Lincoln College, Oxford, MS. Lat. 129 (E)', *Notes and Queries*, n.s. 26 (1979), 504–8.

[54] Quotations here are from this version.

[55] See NIMEV 4064; this is printed by B. Danielsson, 'The "Kerdeston Library of Hunting and Hawking Literature": Early 15th C Fragments', in G. Tilander and C. A. Willemsen (eds), *Et Multum et Multa* (Berlin, 1971), 54–6. The fragmentary couplet version in London, Lambeth Palace Library MS 492, fols. 287–90v is printed and discussed by A. Zettersten, 'The Lambeth Manuscript of the "Boke of Huntyng"', *Neuphilologische Mitteilungen*, 70 (1969), 114–23. For discussion of the relationship between the different versions, see A. L. Binns, 'A Manuscript Source of the Book of St. Albans', *Bulletin of the John Rylands Library*, 33 (1950–1), 15–24 and on the place of

defines its audience as 'gentill men' or 'gentill personys' who are to be informed about 'the maner of hunting for all maner of bestys' (sig. ej). After some brief passages on such subjects as 'Bestys of venery', 'Bestys of the Chace', the roe deer, the boar, and the hare, the more extended sections of the work, in couplets, comprise exchanges between 'the mayster' and 'his man' about aspects of the hunt:

The mayster to his man makyth his Roys*	*boast*
That he knowith be kynde what the her* doys	*hare*
Att hunting euermore when he goys	
Quod the man to his maister that were good lore	
For to know what he doos the houndes before ...	
How many maner bestis yit mayster me tell	
Off venery Releuen by fryth* or by ffell	*wood*
To this quod the mayster I shall the answare ...	

The dialogic model is not the only form of address employed. Other portions of information about the hunt included here have a different audience, addressed from the outset as 'my dere chylde', 'my sonnys', 'my dere sonnys'. The shifts in address suggest that the work is a compilation from different sources, not a single coherently designed one, here cobbled together.[56]

Other verse categories of very different kinds are closely linked to prose works on the same subject. One such is lunaries, or moon books. They offer a series of verse prognostics according to the daily phases on the moon.[57] One announces that its purpose is to show 'what tyme is good to buy and to sylle' according to the aspect of each of the thirty days of the month. In fact, the scope of its advice is wider. Each day is treated in varying numbers of six-line stanzas (*aabccb*):

þe xxix day of þe mone	
Alle þyng ys good to done,	
And dremys ben ful goode.	
þat chyld turneþ to ioye and blysse,	
For Cryst þe day blesyd, y wys,	
þat for vs dayde* on þe rode[58]	*died*

Another lunary has been helpfully studied in relation to parallel prose versions.[59] It seems probable that, as with other versions of texts on the same subjects in prose and verse, the prose version preceded the verse.[60]

---

this work in the larger design of *The Boke of St. Albans*, see Rachel Hands, 'Juliana Berners and *The Boke of St. Albans*', *Review of English Studies*, n.s. 18 (1967), 373–86 (especially at 374, 378).

[56] Hunting and related matters do not seem to have achieved much other expression in verse; I am only aware of a single poem on hawking, NIMEV 3693, that survives uniquely in New Haven, CT, Beinecke Library MS 163, fols. 125–34, where it immediately precedes the prose *Master of Game*; for an edition see B. Danielsson (ed.), 'The Percy Poem on Falconry', *Stockholm Studies in Modern Philology*, 3 (1970), 5–60.

[57] For valuable discussion of verse lunaries, see Irma Taavitsainen, 'The Identification of Middle English Lunary MSS', *Neuphilologische Mitteilungen*, 88 (1987), 18–26, especially 21–2. Two related versions noted there are unpublished: NIMEV 970, NIMEV 3341, both in couplets. The work is occasionally titled 'The Thrytty Days of the Mone'.

[58] NIMEV 1171; edited by Willard Farnham, 'The Dayes of the Mone', *Studies in Philology*, 20 (1923), 70–82; references are to pages 73, 82.

[59] NIMEV 4264; for an edition of versions in both verse and prose, see Irma Taavitsainen, 'Storia Lune and its Paraphrase in Prose: Two Versions of a Middle English Lunary', in L. Kahlas-Tarkka (ed.), *Neophilologica Fennica* (Helsinki, 1987), 521–55.

[60] See, for example, Irma Taavitsainen, *Middle English Lunaries: A Study of the Genre* (Helsinki, 1988), 120–6; Professor Taavitsainen feels that the prose versions she discusses derive from the verse, but her evidence seems open to an alternative interpretation.

The range of forms of such prognosticatory verse is considerable. It ranges from fairly brief formulations, sometimes so gnomic as to be unintelligible beyond the audience for which they were composed, like these seemingly mnemonic lines on the seasons:

> Petyrs cheyre beynnethe Ver
> And Vrban begynnyth Somer
> Symphoryan begynneth harvest
> Clement begynnythe wynter,[61]

to those of considerable length, as with a series of Christmas Day prognostications, that enumerate the implications for each day of the week:

> Yf Cristemas day on A munday be,
> Grete wynter þat yere ye shull se;
> And full off wyndes lowde & felle ...
> Yf Cristemas day on a tuesday bee
> þat yere shull dye women grete plente
> And the wynter shall yeve grete mervell ...
>   (47–9, 59–61)[62]

Such prognostics include those that deal with the implications of different days, the so-called 'lucky' and 'unlucky' days.[63]

Lunaries and other prognostics are linked to temporal aspects of the natural world. Other verse works reflect related concerns that can again be juxtaposed with prose versions on the same topics. For example, there are writings in verse to do with herbs and plants. As with works on other topics, they are relatively infrequent in relation to their prose equivalents. A verse treatise on rosemary, however, survives in a number of manuscripts, some post-medieval.[64] *The Tretys of Diverse Herbis* also survives in a large number of manuscript forms. It presents a series of herbal recipes, in couplets. Discussion varies markedly in length and emphasis from manuscript to manuscript. Some of the versions are written as prose.[65] Most have not been edited, but those that have testify to the fluidity and adaptability of the text.[66]

---

[61] NIMEV 2750; printed in Rossell Hope Robbins, 'English Almanacks of the Fifteenth Century', *Philological Quarterly*, 18 (1939), 321–31 (at 322), an article that is still a helpful overview of this material.

[62] NIMEV 1905; Robbins (ed.), *Secular Lyrics*, no. 72; as noted above these prognostics are probably part of a longer work.

[63] A lengthy example, ninety lines in couplets, NIMEV 2131 is printed in Robbins (ed.), *Secular Lyrics*, no. 73, with a variant version, NIMEV 956, on 248–49; for other examples see NIMEV 1201.5, 1423, 1545, 4053. For an elegant illustration of the literary implications of unlucky days, see John C. Hirsh, 'Why Does The Miller's Tale Take Place on Monday', *English Language Notes*, 13 (1975), 86–90.

[64] NIMEV 3754; it survives in ten manuscripts. For an edition of an imperfect version, now London, Wellcome Library MS 406, see A. Zettersten (ed.), *The Virtues of Herbs in the Loscombe Manuscript* (Lund, 1967), 22–6; NIMEV 417.8 is part of NIMEV 3754 and should be deleted. For discussion of versions in both verse and prose, see George R. Keiser, 'A Middle English Rosemary Treatise in Verse and Prose', *American Notes and Queries*, n.s. 18 (2005), 9–18.

[65] One manuscript written in this way is discussed in Susan Powell, 'Another Manuscript of Index of Middle English Verse No. 2627', *Notes and Queries*, n.s. 34 (1987), 154–6.

[66] NIMEV 2627 records seventeen manuscripts; the textual complexities of the different forms are lucidly summarized by Keiser, 'Works of Science', 3642 [233], to which I am indebted. Two versions have been printed in full; see F. Holthausen, 'Medicinische Gedichte aus einer Stockholmer Handschrift', *Anglia*, 18 (1906), 307–31 (from Stockholm, Royal Library MS X. 90), and R. M. Garrett, 'Middle English Rimed Medical Treatise', *Anglia*, 34 (1911), 164–83 (from BL MS Add. 17866). Garrett (163–4) enumerates the extensive differences between these

Such works as lunaries and herbals for which frequent Middle English prose parallel forms exist may be contrasted with some verse renderings of medical materials of various kinds. Some of these suggest levels both of learning and poetic ingenuity as with a unique version of a Latin plague tract, in couplets, possibly intended to be useful as a mnemonic.[67] Also surviving uniquely is a poem on physiognomy, adapted from the corresponding section of a prose version of the *Secreta Secretorum*.[68] Some other expressions of medical matters in verse achieved a surprisingly wide range of forms and dissemination.[69] This may be, at least in part, because not all of them came from the pens of medical practitioners. Indeed, on the evidence of surviving copies, John Lydgate's *Dietary* was the most widely circulating text of this kind. It survives in various forms in over fifty manuscripts.[70] Thus it ranks just below Gower's *Confessio Amantis* and Langland's *Piers Plowman* in numbers of surviving copies. In the standard modern edition, the poem has twenty-one ballade stanzas. It begins with instructions for diet during times of plague:

> Ete nat gret flessh for no greedynesse
> And fro frutes hold thyn abstynence
> Poletis* & chekenys for ther tendirnesse,   *pullets*
> Ete hem with sauce ...'[71]
> (17–20)

before going on to advice about conduct ('With women aged flesshly have na a do', 29; 'Greedi souper & drynkyng late at eve / Causith of fflewme gret superfluyte' 73–4; 'Be clenly claad aftir thyn estat', 121). Little of the instruction Lydgate proffers is precise about aspects of diet or health. It offers generalities on aspects of well-being, physical and spiritual:

> Moderat foode yeueth* to man his helthe,   *gives*
> And all surfetis doth fro hym remewe*   *remove*
> And charite to the sowle is dewe
> (163–5)

The extensive circulation of the poem points to the appeal of such generalized observations particularly in manuscripts circulating among lay audiences.[72]

---

two versions. For some discussion of another manuscript of this work, New York, Morgan Library & Museum, MS Bühler 21, see Curt F. Bühler, 'A Middle English Medical Manuscript from Norwich', in MacEdward Leach (ed.), *Studies in Medieval Literature in Honour of Albert Croll Baugh* (Philadelphia, PA, 1961), 285–98 (at 288–92). In some manuscripts it also absorbs another collection of verse recipes that elsewhere circulate separately, NIMEV 1408; they occur together in the collections edited by Holthausen and Garrett noted above and in Bühler 21 and Cambridge, Trinity College MS R. 14. 36. An extract that circulated separately, NIMEV 2026.5, is in Robbins (ed.), *Secular Lyrics*, no. 80, 77.

[67] NIMEV 1190; for text and discussion see R. H. Bowers, 'A Middle English Mnemonic Plague Tract', *Southern Folklore Quarterly*, 20 (1956), 118–25.

[68] NIMEV 3339.99; printed and discussed by Joyce M. Sanderson, 'A Recently Discovered Poem in Scots Vernacular: "Complections of Man in Verse"', *Scottish Studies*, 28 (1987), 49–65.

[69] The survey by Rossell Hope Robbins, 'Medical Manuscripts in Middle English', *Speculum*, 45 (1970), 393–415, contains some useful material on verse in this field, although now inevitably rather dated.

[70] NIMEV 824 lists fifty-five, to which should be added a copy in a manuscript sold at Christie's, 27 January 2006, lot 501, now in a private collection; it is combined with NIMEV 4112 in BL MS Lansdowne 699 and elsewhere with other texts. See the valuable discussion by Jake Walsh-Morrissey, '"To al indifferent": The Virtues of Lydgate's *Dietary*', *Medium Ævum*, 84 (2015), 258–78.

[71] Quotations are from MacCracken (ed.), *The Minor Poems of John Lydgate*, 2.702–7.

[72] Walsh-Morrissey rightly points out the poem's 'diffuseness, aversion to technical jargon, unoriginality, and overt lack of sophistication' ('"To al indifferent"', 275).

Lydgate's *Dietary* is a case where author and subject demonstrate a symbiosis drawn from his manifest proficiency to write in verse on any subject, however seemingly intractable. His corpus also includes a verse 'Treatise for Lauandres* (*laundresses*)[73] and a poem on the properties of wine[74] as well as more extensive informational works, like 'A Pageant of Knowledge', discussed above. These poems, which form a small part of his *oeuvre*, point to the range of his adaptability and his willingness to give verse form to even the most unpromising of such informational works.

Lydgate's work can be best characterized as quasi-medical, a layman's guide that distils lore into accessible generalities. Other categories of writing in this field have a sharper focus, but are still explicitly aimed at a lay, unlearned audience.[75] One urinary tract announces its intention:

> Herknes of me, I lytyll spekyn
> For vrenes* I woll you tellyn   *urines*
> And turne Latin into Engglyche
> For simpull wyttes þat ar vnwyse.[76]

There were considerably greater challenges in attempting the rendering of any medical works of a more advanced kind, both because of the often ready availability of Middle English prose versions, sometimes illustrated, and also because of the general difficulties in rendering works with a high level of technical, usually Latin-derived vocabulary, into verse.

Yet some did achieve a surprising degree of accessibility and hence circulation. A poem on bloodletting survives in nearly thirty copies.[77] It begins in some manuscripts like this:

> Maistres! ye that vsen blode-lettynge,
> And therby geten youre lyuynge;
> Here May ye lerne wysdome goode,
> What plase that ye shall letten blode
> In man and in child ...
>   (1–5)

After this brisk start it proceeds to enumerate the points in the body from which blood may be drawn, moving from head to foot:

> Aboue the knokelles on the fete
> With ij veynes there þou may mete:
> Within sittith domestica,*   *internal organ*
> And withouten Siluatica.*   *a vein in the foot*
> Domestica clensith well
> The bleddir* within euery dell. *   *bladder*
> Siluatica, withouten do₃te,
> He clensith well frome the govte.
>   (69–76)

---

[73] NIMEV 4254; MacCracken (ed.), *The Minor Poems of John Lydgate*, 2. 723.
[74] NIMEV 4175; MacCracken (ed.), *The Minor Poems of John Lydgate*, 2. 724.
[75] For a helpful consideration of the questions involved for both medical texts and more broadly informational materials, see M. Teresa Tavormina, 'Three Middle English Verse Uroscopies', *English Studies*, 91 (2010), 591–622.
[76] NIMEV 1109.5; Tavormina (ed.) 'Three Middle English Verse Uroscopies', 597; I have emended the manuscript reading 'spelyn' in the opening line.
[77] NIMEV 3848; for an edition see Robbins (ed.), *Secular Lyrics*, no. 81, 77–80; quotations here are from this version. For an authoritative overview of Middle English verse on this subject, see Tony Hunt, 'The Poetic Vein: Phlebotomy in Middle English and Anglo-Norman Verse', *English Studies*, 77 (1996), 311–22.

Here the short, bouncy couplets serve as aids to both exposition and memory as they shape information into succinct forms. Other poems that fall into this loose category include several brief ones on the humours,[78] as well some more extended works.

There are more ambitious works that can be categorized as encyclopaedic in their scope. These raise unexpected questions about generic fluidity. That is, they demonstrate a modulation from one literary form to another. *The Court of Sapience* was composed in the second half of the fifteenth century, and runs to nearly two thousand lines, mainly in rhyme royal stanzas.[79] The work begins with the narrator taken in a dream to meet 'ladyes thre (148), Sapience, Intelligence and Science. Sapience, 'the moost soverayne' (154) of the three, initially instructs him by recounting a version of the widely circulating allegorical narrative of the Four Daughters of God, 'Mercy, Trouthe, Ryght, and Pease' (188), who offer the dreamer initial spiritual consolation.[80]

This account forms the first book of the work. In the second, longer book (903–2372), the narrator is guided by Sapience through her 'solempne mancyon' (905) with descriptions of her various courts. In the first court the narrator perceives first aspects of the natural world, starting with lapidary stones, before moving on to water (1107–97), fish (1198–1266), flowers and herbs (1267–323), trees (1324–86), birds (1387–435), animals (1436–70), the various human virtues (1471–533) followed by Theology, Philosophy, and their various categories (1534–721). The second court briefly describes the heavenly hierarchies (1688–721). The third court (1722–806) describes wisdom. The account then describes grammar (1807–41), dialectic (1842–90), rhetoric (1891–932), arsmetric (1933–74), geometry (1975–2016), music (2017–93), astronomy (2094–205), Christian faith (2206–310), hope (2311–373), before abruptly breaking off.

The wide range of topics is reflected in the sources on which the poem draws.[81] These include Bartholomaeus Anglicus, *De proprietatibus rerum* ('On the properties of things'). The influence of this work is most readily visible in the section on precious stones (953–1085), where, uniquely, the subject matter is organized in an alphabetic sequence that reflects the same organizing principle as in Bartholomaeus's work.[82] Other sources cited with varying degrees of frequency include works of Aristotle, Isidore of Seville, and Justinian. The aim of the poem seems to be to offer a general account of many aspects of the medieval world.

In terms of style and technique the *Court of Sapience* in distinctly uneven. It can be articulately responsive to aspects of the natural world, as in this appreciation of the beneficial qualities of water:

> ... That good water, that noble element,
> That ryver swete in his kynd moyst and cold,
> That is the holsome perfect nutryment
> To every thyng that is in erthe content:

---

[78] NIMEV 3157; printed in Robbins (ed.), *Secular Lyrics*, no. 76, 71–2; NIMEV 2624; printed in Robbins (ed.), *Secular Lyrics*, no. 77, 72–3.

[79] NIMEV 3406; three manuscripts survive as well as a substantive printed edition by Caxton (c1480) and a sixteenth-century copy from it made by the antiquary, John Stow; references are to E. Ruth Harvey (ed.), *The Court of Sapience* (Toronto, 1984).

[80] On the various medieval versions of this narrative, see Hope M. Traver, *The Four Daughters of God* (Philadelphia, PA, 1907).

[81] The fullest discussion is Curt F. Bühler, *The Sources of the Court of Sapience* (Leipzig, 1932).

[82] See Bühler, *The Sources of the Court of Sapience*, 41–7; there is otherwise only a single brief poem dealing with lapidaries, NIMEV 904; see Joan Evans and Mary S. Serjeantson (eds), *English Mediaeval Lapidaries*, EETS, o.s. 190 (1933), 60–2.

> To corne, herbe, tree, plant, and eche thyng lyvyng
> It geveth his drynk, and clenseth al foule thyng.
>
> (1107–12)

But it can swiftly modulate to the inertly enumerative:

> The whale, the dolphyn, and escaryus,*   (unidentified) fish
> The carabo,* and eke effimeron,*   crab, (unidentified) fish
> The cakodryl*, and uranoscopus,*   crocodile, stargazer fish
> The see-swyn,* and eke fascolyon,*   porpoise, (unidentified) fish
> The myllago* that fleith* the water on,   flying fish (?), flies
> The hamio* that dredeth ay the hooke,   (unidentified) fish
> With many moo,* whoso hath lust to loke.   more
>
> (1212–18)

As will be apparent, the work lacks a clear overall structure that connects its separate expository components into a coherent form. This is an obvious problem in the attempt to employ a quasi-encyclopaedic strategy which inevitably leads to a series of different kinds of versified lists only intermittently shaped around even the most elementary organizing principles (as with the section of precious stones).

The longest work in verse considered here is also encyclopaedic in scope. In its fullest version *Sidrac and Boccus* is just under thirteen thousand lines in couplets.[83] In one manuscript authorship is credited to 'Hughe of Campdene, / That þis boke hath þorogh sought / And vnto Englyssh ryme hit brought' (10928–30); nothing is known about him.[84] The text itself is a translation and versification of an Old French prose work, *Sidrac*. Insofar as conclusions are possible since a specific source manuscript has not been identified, there do not appear to be any significant additions to the source text.

Like *The Court of Sapience*, *Sidrac and Boccus* begins with a lengthy preamble that is concerned with the spiritual. It takes the form of a conversion narrative (1–1006). The king Bokkus seeks aid from King Traktabare against his enemy. The king sends 'his astronomyere, Sidrak … þe greet clerke' (229, 239) by whose advice Bokkus's enemies are defeated. After his victory Bokkus who 'was heþene and knew noght' (357) offers thanks and sacrifices to his pagan gods. But Sidrac who 'bileued on þe Trinite' (361) declines to do so and expounds his Christian beliefs. Bokkus seeks to kill Sidrac who is saved by a miracle but is then imprisoned and tortured, before converting Bokkus and then his people to Christianity. The preamble concludes by establishing the form of the rest of the work:

> þe king desired þan forto here
> Many þinges þat he wolde lere
> And preide Sidrak him telle shulde
> þinges þat he him axe wolde.
>
> (997–1000)

There then follows (1009–900) a versified enumeration of the questions that Bokkus poses to Sidrac, which is followed by the main text, a sequence of questions and their answers, in this form:

---

[83] NIMEV 772 and 2147; nine manuscripts survive of varying lengths and states of completeness and one substantive early printed edition (STC 3186). All references here are to T. J. Burton (ed.), *Sidrak and Bokkus*, 2 vols., EETS, o.s. 311–12 (Oxford, 1998), which prints parallel texts of the two main versions; line references here are to the longer version, edited from BL MS Lansdowne 793.

[84] See the discussion in Burton, 1, lxxvi–ii.

> *Ca° Primo*   The first þing þanne axede he:
> If God was euere and euere shal be.
> 'God had neuere begynnyng
> ... Ne neuere shal haue ending,
> And or þat heuen or erthe wroght
> Or any oþer þing to werk broght.
>   (1901–6)

The questions and their answers are divided in four books, the first three each of 100 chapters, the last of 112. There is also a different, sequential numeration into a series of (in its fullest form) 400 'questions' that in some manuscripts replaces the book divisions, but broadly corresponds to the chapter divisions. The questions and answers vary in length but are generally succinct, averaging less than thirty lines.[85] Here is a representative passage:

> 'Which is þe fairest beest þat is,
> As þinkeþ the wiþouten mys?'
> 'Hors is þe fairest beest in land
> And strengest and most helpand*   *useful*
> Wiþ horsis lordes ofte gete
> Londe and lyfe, drinke and mete;
> Hors in harowe and in plow
> And in carte is good inow;
> Hors beren men to and fro
> Þat elles on foote shulden goo:
> Þerfore is he þe beest fayrest
> And to manis bihoue* þe best'.   *man's advantage*
>   (11421–31)

The tone of calm certainty of such answers is a unifying aspect of the work. Doubt or nuance have no place in the expository techniques of *Sidrak and Bokkus*. Sometimes such authority is derived from, even if not asserted as, biblical and liturgical injunction:

> 'What manere of folke ben men holden to
> In þis worlde worshipe to do?'
> 'Euery man shal principaly
> Worship God, þat is an hy,
> Þat him made and shal vnmake
> Whanne he wole mannes lijf slake.
> A man shal shal his wyfe worship also,
> For oo body and flesshe þei ben boþe two ...
>   (6705–12)

But although the length of the work suggests an effort to be encyclopaedic in scope, it suffers from its failure to be encyclopaedic in form. The apparent fidelity to the original in the translation replicates its shapelessness.[86] Questions follow each other in seeming random fashion unshaped by any controlling principles of order or category of subject. It

---

[85] The longest is the answer to the question: '*Lyue any men in þe world mo / þan on erthe þat we on go?*' (3745–916).

[86] This shapelessness is demonstrated by the treatment of medicine. This is not treated in one place as a distinct subject, but scattered throughout the poem; see R. E. Nichols, 'Medical Lore from *Sidrak and Bokkus*: A Miscellany in Middle English Verse', *Journal of the History of Medicine and Allied Sciences*, 23, (1968), 167–172.

is hard to imagine how a medieval reader would have known what questions to ask and still less how to find the answers.

There are no prose equivalents in fifteenth-century composition to these verse works. They form part of a fairly small category of works that did establish a distinctive verse identity in their own terms. Alchemical verse provides both a striking and particularly problematic illustration of this tendency.[87] The identities of individual writers on the subject often remain shadowy and are perhaps wholly fictional at times. For example, a poem titled 'lapis philosophorum' ('of the philosopher's stone'), seventy-six lines in couplets, survives in at least twenty-five manuscripts.[88] It is occasionally ascribed to Richard Carpenter, who remains merely a name, as do others, like the otherwise unknown William Bolosse, credited with the composition of 'The marrow or pithe of alchymy'.[89]

The textual problems involved in alchemical verse are also considerable. Many works have an extended textual tradition that in some cases in largely post-medieval and sometimes reaching down to the seventeenth century. Others are unique and very short, usually limited to a few couplets and unpublished.[90] Some of these may possibly be excerpts from longer works that had passed into memorial tradition. Indeed, the whole field of alchemical verse is complex on textual, bibliographical, and attributional grounds.

These problems are linked to issues of style and technique. A typical example of such issues is the so-called 'Verses on the Elixir', ascribed in some texts to 'Pearce the Black Monke'. Nothing is known about the author, if that is what he is. And this work survives in at least thirty-five manuscripts, often varying markedly in length and content.[91] One version begins in the expository and instructional manner typical of the form:

> Take erth of erth erthes broder
> Water and erth it is non other
> And fire of therth that berith the price
> And of that erthe loke thou be wise
> The true elixir if ye list to make
> Erth out of erthe loke that ye take.[92]
>
> (1–6)

The key expository element is reiteration; the element 'erth' appears in various forms nine times; the one line in which the word does not appear contains the crucial term 'true elixir', the means of transforming base material so as to 'makith gold most riell / Euer to endure' (102–3).

This text, of which there are various forms, is linked in ways that are easy to define in summary to a number of other alchemical poems that either appear with it or as

---

[87] For a valuable overview and a number of editions of the more widely circulating texts, see Anke Timmerman, *Verse and Transmutation: A Corpus of Middle English Alchemical Poetry* (Leiden, 2013).

[88] NIMEV 2656; edited by Timmerman (*Verse*, 270–4); she also edits NIMEV 1558 and various poems not recorded there as part of Carpenter's corpus

[89] NIMEV 2826; this survives in six manuscripts.

[90] See, for example, NIMEV 703.5, 2354.5, 2729.5, 3452.5, 3616, 3618.

[91] NIMEV 3249 supplemented by Timmerman (*Verse*, 216–18). Nothing is known about the putative author. Another alchemical work in verse ascribed to him is NIMEV 3257, supplemented by Timmerman (*Verse*, 261), which was also evidently popular; nearly thirty manuscripts are recorded, only two of which are fifteenth century; edited by Timmerman (*Verse*, 263–5).

[92] I quote from the edition in Timmerman's *Verse* (220–3); she edits other versions at 224–32.

extracts from it, or seem conceived as supplements or addenda to it, or are related to it by manuscript context, again often in different forms and lengths; these are all anonymous.[93]

Understandably the details of how the alchemical processes might be carried out remain vague. At times, alchemical verse is little more than incantatory mumbo jumbo, as in these verses from the so-called 'Boast of Mercury:

> I am mercury the mighty flos florum
> I am most worthiest of all Singulorum
> I am sower of Sol and Lune and Mars
> I am genderer of Iovus of him be all wars.[94]
> (1–4)

Here repetition and a sprinkling of Latin provides the illusion of authority. The terminology here is probably intentionally opaque. The strategy of obfuscation seems an important element in the articulation of alchemical process, for obvious reasons.

Among the most widely circulating alchemical works was Thomas Norton's *The Ordinal of Alchemy*. This comprises 3102 lines in couplets in its most complete form, divided into a Preface (1–40, in Latin), Prohemium (1–180) and seven capitula (181–3102). There are more than thirty manuscripts, not all of them complete.[95] Little is known about Norton (?1433–1513/1514), who signs his name in an acrostic inserted into the opening phrases of the Prohemium and capitula i–iii of the poem. He seems to have lived in the Bristol area.[96] He tells that he began *The Ordinal* 'in the yere of Crist Ml. CCCC. Sevynty & sevyne' (3101). That he started it so late in the century may account for the fact that many of the surviving manuscripts date from the sixteenth century or even later.[97] Their number and chronological span are testimony to the enduring appeal of Norton's work.

Norton insists on the broadly based interest in alchemy 'of euery state which is within mankynde' (17), religious (21–4), royal and noble (25), 'merchantis' (27), and 'comon workmen' (29), as well as 'goldsmythis' (31), 'fremasons & tanners' (34), and 'staynours & glasiers' (35). His work draws on a considerable range of authorities, more than forty, including Chaucer, some of whom are frequently cited.[98]

Norton's overall approach to his subject is shaped by a mixture of the spiritual, the anecdotal, and the technical. Alchemy is initially defined as 'A wonderful science, secrete philosophie' (183), a 'holi arte' (228), 'holy Alchymye' (54, 264, 444). The very title is intended to recall 'the Ordinalle [that] to prestis settith owte / The seruyce of the dayes' (129–30). Norton claims that 'I hadde this arte bi grace fro hevyn' (137). He concludes by

---

[93] For example, NIMEV 1150.3, supplemented by Timmerman (*Verse*, 249) and edited (250–3); NIMEV 2666 greatly supplemented by Timmerman (*Verse*, 255), who records twenty-five manuscripts and several fragments, and edited at 257–9; NIMEV 4017 ascribed to Ripley ('probably erroneously' according to Timmerman; see *Verse*, 243), and edited by Timmerman (*Verse*, 245–47).

[94] NIMEV 1276, supplemented by Timmerman (*Verse*, 234–5), which survives in over thirty manuscripts; edited in various versions in Timmerman, *Verse*, 237–42.

[95] NIMEV 3772; all references are to John Reidy (ed.), *Ordinal of Alchemy*, EETS, o.s. 272 (London, 1975); the failure to provide notes or commentary in this edition is one of its more curious features.

[96] Reidy, in the Introduction to his edition (*Ordinal of Alchemy*, xxxvii–lii) gives an account of what little can be established about his life.

[97] Only two, BL MSS Add. 10302 and Sloane 1873, seem to be fifteenth century.

[98] Some of these are listed in Reidy's edition (*Ordinal of Alchemy*, 122–5). There are other sources mentioned in the poem not included there, for example, 'the boke de arbore' (1646), as well as others that Norton seems to have drawn on without acknowledgement, including Bartholomaeus Anglicus's thirteenth-century encyclopaedic work, *De Proprietatibus Rerum*, which he possibly knew in John Trevisa's late fourteenth-century Middle English prose translation; see Reidy, *Ordinal of Alchemy*, lxxii–iii.

seeing his work as a pilgrimage: 'Now haue I tagth you euiry thynge bi name / As men tech other the way to walsynghame' (3063-64; Walsingham was a popular pilgrimage site).

The potential expository challenges of a poem on a subject that has highly technical aspects of both language and method are considerable. Norton's meets them in part through the reiteration of key words that have conceptual significance. For example, in his longest chapter, chapter five (1383-2682), he deals in part with the four alchemical signs:

> It is no iape,* nother light to lerne   *joke*
> your principal Agent al sesons to discerne,
> which I tech yow to know be signes fowre,
> Bi coloure, sapoure,* odoure, and liqour.   *taste*
> (1763-6)

He then proceeds to enumerate the aspects of each of these signs, keeping each firmly before the reader:

> The nailis of hondis this *colour* wille be.
> The saphire *colour* that orient blewe,
> Like in *colour* to the heuynly hewe,
> Is moch fairere then wone *colour* to syght,
> For therin is more of Ayre, watir, & lyght,
> Then is in wone *colour*, & that bi manyfolde;
> wherefore such *colour* is more derer solde.[99]
> (1837-44; emphasis added)

This use of repetition as a way creating of expository focus recurs:

> *Liquour* is the conforte of this werke
> *Liquour* gevith evidence to a clerke
> Therbi to fastyn his Elementis,
> And also to loose theym for som ententis;
> *Liquour* conioynyth male with female wyfe,
> And causith dede thingis to resorte to lyfe;
> *Liquours* clansith with theire ablucion;*   *washing*
> *Liquours* to oure stone be chief nutricion.
> with-owte *liquours* no mete is goode
> *Liquours* conveith alle Alimente* & fode ...   *nutrition*
> (2185-94; emphasis added)[100]

There are other techniques used of a less ponderously expository kind that draw the reader into the implications of the subject. Norton introduces various 'exemples' (447, 548, 623, 685), or narrative passages. Chapter Two (541-1037) is largely devoted to cautionary tales about the dangers of alchemy, represented by the unhappy fates of a monk whose trust in his alchemical prowess leads to loss and fraud (541-620) or of 'bacon the frere' (625) who fruitlessly tried to build an illuminated bridge over the Thames (622-81) or of one 'Thomas Dalton' (917-1012) who was cruelly punished for his refusal to disclose the secret of alchemy. These accounts are crisply told and bring a level of immediacy to Norton's work.

[99] Compare the earlier use of 'colour(s)' in 1514-55, where the word appears nineteen times.
[100] A similar strategy of repetition occurs elsewhere; for example, the brief Chapter Four (1205-1380) has as its subject what is termed 'þe grose werk' of alchemy, the preliminary preparation of its materials; this phrase recurs, presumably as a memorial aid to the reader/user; see 1205, 1273,1285, 1321, 1323, 1332, 1350, 1375.

Norton stands apart from other alchemical versifiers both in his range of reference and his narrative skill, qualities that must have made his work more appealing and more accessible to its evidently wide audience.

The verse alchemical writings of George Ripley (d. c1490) are considerably more complex both in their range and the difficulties in clearly differentiating possible separate works that have circulated together in some instances.[101] Ripley was an Augustinian canon at Bridlington who by his own account had studied abroad in Italy and at Louvain university.[102] He seems to have been a prolific writer on alchemical topics in both English and Latin, and in verse and prose. The uncertainties about his canon and lack of full information about the manuscripts that may contain his works (of which there may be more than 200), together with the lack of modern editions of his works, make him difficult to discuss in any informed manner. His major English verse work was *The Compend* (or *Compound*) *of Alchemy*, composed c1470, which runs to about 2000 lines, mainly in rhyme royal stanzas. It is addressed to Edward IV and offers a general account of alchemical procedures.[103] It survives in various forms in some forty manuscripts, almost all of which are post-medieval.[104] Other poems are ascribed to Ripley with varying degrees of probability.[105] One distinctive aspect of Ripley's writings that invites consideration is their form; a number (some post-medieval) are copied into often elaborately decorated rolls, as a way perhaps intended of emphasizing their association with magic.[106] But Ripley's works, in our current state of knowledge, cannot be assessed in a very informed way. Indeed, any overall assessment of alchemical verse is difficult for the reasons I have already explained: the uncertainties about textual forms, the extended processes of transmission and the lack of full biographical contexts all create uncertainties that cannot be resolved in our current state of knowledge.[107]

Implicit in the nature of alchemical verse is the promise of future well-being through the creation of material wealth. Such concern with the future finds other forms of expression, in different ways. There are, for example, two lengthy poems on the consequences of throwing dice. One enumerates the fifty-six possible combinations of throwing three dice.[108] The other pronounces in vacuous terms on the consequences of the combinations of the three throws:

> Sisse*, kater*, deux,* tellis me tytt,   *six, four, two*
> þat þi loue has þe in despitt,
> Wit draw þi hert and gyf yt to plai
> ffor no man hold þat wyll away.[109]

---

[101] The bibliographical and textual problems of the Ripley corpus are very well discussed in Jennifer M. Rampling, 'The Catalogue of the Ripley Corpus: Alchemical Writings Attributed to George Ripley (d. ca. 1490)', *Ambix*, 57 (2010), 125–201, to which I am indebted.

[102] For Ripley's life I rely on the account by Anthony Gross in *ODNB*.

[103] These are summarized by Rampling in 'The Catalogue of the Ripley Corpus', 152.

[104] NIMEV 595, significantly enlarged by Rampling ('The Catalogue of the Ripley Corpus', 152-7). Brief extracts with commentary and notes are in Eleanor Prescott Hammond (ed.), *English Verse between Chaucer and Surrey* (Durham, NC, 1927), 252-7, 483-7. A previously unrecorded roll including both the *Compend* and other works ascribed to Ripley was sold at Christie's, 12 December 2017, lot 22.

[105] For example, NIMEV 1364.5, supplemented by Timmerman (*Verse*, 298); edited by Timmerman (*Verse*, 299); NIMEV 3721, 'attributed intermittently' to Ripley, according to Timmerman (see *Verse*, 286), who distinguishes and edits several versions (289–93).

[106] See further R. I. McCallum, 'Alchemical Scrolls Associated with George Ripley', in S. J. Linden (ed.), *Mystical Metal of Gold: Essays on Alchemy and Renaissance Culture* (New York, 2007), 161–88.

[107] See the discussion in Rampling's 'The Catalogue of the Ripley Corpus', especially 134 where Middle English alchemical verse is described as a 'problematic category'.

[108] NIMEV 803; edited by Eleanor Prescott Hammond, 'The Chance of the Dice', *Englische Studien*, 59 (1925), 1–16.

This is no more than persiflage, noteworthy chiefly for what it suggests about the existence of a credulous audience for such trivia. They illustrate the outermost range of material that can appropriately fall within the scope of this chapter.

Most of the verse discussed in this chapter is concerned to convey actual information, albeit with varying degrees of explicatory success. The range of its pragmatic employment described here rarely achieves any level of literary distinction. But it does demonstrate the ways in which verse became adopted as a form of exposition to an extent that is testimony to a widening sense of its utilitarian potential in the fifteenth century. While certainly not sweet, poetry does become pervasively useful.

---

[109] NIMEV 3694.3; edited by W. L. Braekman, 'Fortune Telling by the Casting of Dice', *Studia Neophilologica*, 52 (1980), 3–29 (quotation from 20); I have replaced the use of *y* there with thorn.

CHAPTER 16
Conduct Poetry

Matthew Giancarlo

Introduction: Practical Writing and Conduct Literature

The category of conduct includes such a wide range of subjects and genres that, even over the long development of 'conduct literature' from classical through medieval times, this generic designation was never definitely settled upon any particular literary form. Nonetheless works of conduct literature and conduct poetry share certain family resemblances. By the fifteenth century, texts about conduct that had been diffusely distributed in prior eras were consolidated and transmitted in synthesizing works and collected manuscripts. These were symptomatic of anxieties about behaviour, health and hygiene, education, class, and social order newly conceived but often re-expressed in familiar styles and simple terms. Despite its form in verse, conduct poetry of the fifteenth century might appear both ill-defined and sub-literary, practical and pragmatic but with very little artistic creativity or intellectual substance. Recent criticism has focused on conduct writings for testimony of developing gender roles and standards of social governance.[1] In these works, class and household relations are at their starkest, expressed in an amalgam of concerns with varying names: *norriture* or 'nurture', *manners, conduct, courtesy, governance, wisdom, regimen, thewis* or 'habits', *learning, demeanour,* and more, ranging from general moral and ethical guidance to intimate details of personal dress, behaviour, bodily movement, speech, physical order, and social interaction. The poeticizing of these concerns was a natural result of the need for easy and memorable transmission. But beyond that, it also reflects the changing environs of a growing social economy and widening literate audience, wherein people could put such things to verse for the kind of enjoyment derived from hearing socially reassuring and functional platitudes repeated back in artistic form.

For heuristic purposes, these forms can be grouped into three categories. The poetry of *nurture and manners* includes writings on basic bodily conduct and child-rearing, often overtly directed toward small children. But in the apparently paradoxical way of such writing—a feature characteristic even today of much 'children's literature'—it is actually more aimed at adults, to reinforce their sense of discipline for children through the repetition of familiar truths and accepted social standards. Similarly ideological but at a more

---

[1] Glenn D. Burger, *Conduct Becoming: Good Wives and Husbands in the Later Middle Ages* (Philadelphia, PA, 2018); Nicole D. Smith, *Sartorial Strategies: Outfitting Aristocrats and Fashioning Conduct in Late Medieval Literature* (South Bend, IN, 2012); Mark D. Johnston (ed.), *Medieval Conduct Literature: An Anthology of Vernacular Guides to Behaviour for Youths, with English Translations* (Toronto, 2009); Kathleen Ashley and Robert L. A. Clark (eds), *Medieval Conduct* (Minneapolis, MN, 2001); Claire Sponsler, *Drama and Resistance: Bodies, Goods, and Theatricality in Late Medieval England* (Minneapolis, MN, 1997); Nancy Armstrong and Leonard Tennenhouse (eds), *The Ideology of Conduct: Essays on Literature and the History of Sexuality* (London, 1987); Jonathan Nicholls, *The Matter of Courtesy: Medieval Courtesy Books and the Gawain-Poet* (Woodbridge, 1985), 7–74; Nicholas Orme, *From Childhood to Chivalry: The Education of the English Kings and Aristocracy 1066–1530* (London, 1984).

advanced level is the poetry of *conduct and courtesy,* the core mode of this genre. Conduct books and courtesy poems centre on the household and the individual as defined within it and through it, either by dominance or service: the proper lord, the 'good wife' and 'goodman' as well as the courteous servant, each a status inheritor within the household economy. Lastly, most broadly conceived are poems of *regimen and governance,* the fifteenth-century descendants of the long tradition of mirror writings, political *de regimine* treatises, collections of exempla and monitory moral verse. These have the strongest claim to be called 'high' imaginative literature, but it is important to remember their direct kinship to the practical conduct books and domestic guides, and they never completely leave these basic concerns behind. We can also see how the traditional three levels or realms of social governance—of the self, of the household, and of the kingdom—are generally reflected by these categories. Conduct poetry expressed ideals and criticisms of practical ethics at each level, with the conceptual overlap inherent in a world that still saw the conduct of 'the body politic' as directly analogous to the governance of a well-run household, and to the health and physical disciplining of the personal body.

Nurture and Manners

In several early volumes of the Early English Text Society publications, Frederick Furnivall and others collected a miscellany of conduct manuals and poems about the proper rearing of children and household management.[2] Handbooks of courtesy and conduct from across the fifteenth and sixteenth centuries are presented together, including many in verse such as John Russell's *Boke of Nurture* (c1460), 'The Babees Book' (c1475), and the *Boke of Curtasye* in BL MS Sloane 1586 (c1430), and more, together with numerous poems on the disciplining of children and youth.[3] They focus on 'facecia'/*facetias* or 'agreeable manners', practical courtesy and well-trained elegance in domestic settings especially, along with a strong sense of the moral and even aesthetic aspects of class-defined behaviour:

> But O, yonge Babees, whome bloode royalle
> With grace, Feture and hyhe habylite
> Hath enourmyd, on yow ys that I calle   *distinguished*
> To knowe this Book; for it were grete pyte,
> Syn that in yow ys sette sovereyne beaute,
> But yf vertue and nurture were with alle;
> To yow therfore I speke in specyalle ...[4]

The verse in 'The Babees Book' continues in high praise of 'governaunce, nurture, and honeste' (23) but with down-to-earth counsels: proper bowing, keeping your mouth shut especially when your lord is speaking, avoiding bad habits such as scratching your backside, cut your bread don't break it, don't pick your nose or your nails, don't speak with your mouth full, and so forth. These specific rules coincide with the general admonition

---

[2] Frederick J. Furnivall (ed.), *The Babees Book: Aristotle's A B C, Urbanitatis, Stans puer ad mensam, the lytille childrenes lytil boke, the bokes of nurture of Hugh Rhodes and John Russell, Wynkyn de Worde's Boke of Keruynge, the Booke of demeanor, the boke of curtasye, Seager's Schoole of vertue, &c. &c.: with some French & Latin poems on like subjects and some forewords on education in Early England,* EETS, o.s. 32 (London, 1868). References to shorter conduct works and lyrics collected in this volume are made by title and NIMEV number. On 'The Babees Book' see especially Deanna Delmar Evans, 'The Babees Book', in Daniel T. Kline (ed.), *Medieval Literature for Children* (New York, 2003), 79–92.
[3] NIMEV 1514, 1576, and 4152.
[4] Furnivall (ed.), *The Babees Book,* 1–9, lines 15–21.

to avoid behaving like low-class 'Felde men' or manual workers and to 'take delight in courtesy': 'But, swete children, haue al-wey your delyte / In curtesye, and in verrey gentylnesse, / And at youre myhte (*meat, meal*) eschewe boystousnesse' (180–2). As brief as it is, 'The Babees Book' is a good example of how close the standards of 'gentylnesse and of goode governaunce' were for both server and served, attendant and lord, and how central for the self-advancement of both (188; 216–17). As *The Boke of Curtasye* makes clear from the start, 'Qwo so wylle of curtasy lere / In this boke he may hit here! Yf thow be gentylmon, ȝomon (*yeoman*), or knaue, / The nedis nurture for to haue'.[5] Short poems such as 'The ABC of Aristotle'/'Learn or Be Lewed', 'Urbanitatis', 'The Young Children's Book'/'Dame Courtesy', and others all summarize and emphasize the same basic points, some in plain mnemonic forms and rudimentary verse.[6] Courteous behaviour is the virtuous ground and basis for all other hope of success: 'Who so euer wylle thryue or the[e] (*succeed*), / Must vertus lerne, & curtas be' ('The Young Children's Book', 1–2).

The earliest and most widely circulating of these poems in the fifteenth century was John Lydgate's popular and frequently copied poem *Stans puer ad mensam*, 'The Child Standing at the Table'.[7] This famous poem begins in the mode of a direct address to a 'dear child' or 'dear son', a pose common not just to verses of nurture and manners but to all the levels of conduct writing:

> My dere sone, first þiselff enable
> With al thyn herte to vertuous disciplyne
> Affore thy souereyn stondyng at the table,
> Dispose thy thouht affter my doctryne,
> To all norture thy corage do inclyne.
> First whane thou spekist be not reklees,
> Kepe feete & ffyngeris, hondis stille in pees ...
> (1–7)

In approximately a dozen rhyme-royal stanzas of lightly aureate poetry, Lydgate gives direct advice on everything from serving a lord at table to proper walking in town, attending to one's clothes and bodily cleanliness, proper eating, avoiding ribaldry, and generally behaving like a little gentleman. As Pearsall describes the poem, 'It manages to combine mnemonic advice about basic habits with an air of literary polish, and the literature of etiquette could hardly ask for more'.[8] The dual audience of this mode is indicated toward the end, when Lydgate breaks the frame of direct address to provide a few observations about the tractable nature of children:

> In childeris were* now myrthe, now debate,   *war*
> In her quarell is no greet vyolence;
> Now pley, now wepyng, selde in on estate,
> To her pleyntes yeve* no gret credence;   *give*
> A rod refourmeth al her insolence;
> In her corage no rancour doth abyde;
> Who spareth the yerde, al vertu set aside.
> (85–91)

---

[5] NIMEV 4152; Furnivall (ed.), *The Babees Book*, 299–327, ll.1–4.
[6] NIMEV 4155, 4153, 4127; see Furnivall (ed.), *The Babees Book*, 9–25, for these poems.
[7] NIMEV 2233, 1694, and related entries. H. N. MacCracken (ed.), *The Minor Poems of John Lydgate, Part II: The Secular Poems*, EETS, o.s. 192 (London, 1934), 739–44; see also Furnivall (ed.), *The Babees Book*, 26–33.
[8] Derek Pearsall, *John Lydgate* (London, 1970), 219.

The evocation of mildly turbulent childhood revels—provoking adult chastisement—is also characteristic of his autobiographical *Testament,* where he gives a humorously endearing sketch of his mis-spent boyhood.[9] Here the appeal to the familiar maxim 'spare the rod, spoil the child' is less interesting than the way Lydgate shifts from supposedly addressing youth—the 'yonge childer þat þe shal se or reede' (93)—to the real addressees: those copying, circulating, and reading the poem as adults and masters. And it is certainly notable how these humble conduct verses became such touchstones of this major fifteenth-century poet's *oeuvre*.

Lydgate's poems also highlight another important factor behind the prominence of conduct verse for a contemporary fifteenth-century audience: not just its specific behavioural or social advice, but its ethical and moral exhortations. Commonplaces, maxims, proverbs, and sentential rhymes are perdurable elements of folk literacy. Conduct writing of nurture presents an Aristotelian-style virtue ethics in these basic and forms, the no-nonsense, right-and-wrong admonitions to 'vertue' and 'learning': be learned or be lewd. The jingle 'ABC of Aristotle' provides an alphabetical list of the courteous virtues in a mean or *juste milieu*: '**A** To amerose *(amorous)*, to aunterose *(bold)*, ne argue not to myche / **B** to bolde, ne to besi, ne boorde *(joke, play)* not large / **C** to curteis, to cruel, ne care not to sore', and on through the alphabet, to conclude with the counsel 'For a mesurable meene is euere þe beste of alle'.[10] It was also a commonplace that courtesy comes from heaven and the first virtue is to learn courtesy, as it says in 'The Lytylle Childrenes Lytil Boke':

>Lytylle childrene, here ye may lere,
>Moche curtesy þat is wrytyne here;
>For clerkis that the vij arteȝ* cunne,   *the seven arts*
>Seyn þat curtesy from hevyn come
>Whan Gabryelle oure lady grette,
>And Eliȝabeth with mary mette.
>Alle vertues arne closide yn curtesye,
>And alle vices yn vylonye ...[11]

As all virtues partake of courtesy, all villainy arises from its defect. The fear of villainy and its punishment is the flip-side of this courteous coin. Not only guidance on how one should act, but dread of the shame for misbehaviour is ever-present: 'Þe bigynnynge of þi worschip is to drede schame'.[12] Such fear arises mainly from anxieties about proper speech and the various perils of mis-speaking, as catalogued in verses like 'Whate-ever thow sey, avyse thee welle!' which explicitly draw from the sentential traditions of Catonian maxims and Biblical wisdom poetry.[13] 'Symon's Lesson of Wysedome for all Maner Chyldryn' puts the matter directly as lessons of 'a wise man' and his books, applied with the proper caning stick or sharp spur:

>For, as the wyse man sayth and preuyth,
>A leve* chyld, lore he be-houyth;   *dear*

---

[9] NIMEV 2464; see H. N. MacCracken (ed.), *The Minor Poems of John Lydgate, Part I: The Religious Poems*, EETS, e.s. 107 (London, 1911), 329–62, especially lines 607–69.
[10] NIMEV 1920; Furnivall (ed.), *The Babees Book*, 11–12, ll.14–16, 35. See Martha Dana Rust, 'The "ABC of Aristotle"', in Kline (ed.), *Medieval Literature for Children*, 63–78.
[11] Furnivall (ed.), *The Babees Book*, 16–24, ll.1–8.
[12] 'Of the Manners to Bring One to Honour and Welfare' / 'Son I shall the show now take heed' (NIMEV 3195), in Furnivall (ed.), *The Babees Book*, 34–35, l.9.
[13] NIMEV 240; Furnivall (ed.), *The Babees Book*, 356–7.

> And as men sayth þat ben leryd,
> He hatyth þe chyld þat sparyth þe rodde;
> And as þe wyse man sayth yn his boke
> Off prouerbis and wysedomes, ho* wol loke,   *who(ever)*
> 'As a sharppe spore makyth an hors to renne
> Vnder a man that shold werre* wynne,   *war, battle*
> Ry3t so a 3erde may make a chyld
> To lerne welle hys lesson, and to be myld'.[14]

The poet concludes in direct address to his charges that if you don't misbehave, you won't be beaten: 'And þerfor, chyldere, loke þat ye do well, / And no harde betyng shall ye be-falle' (99–100). The ever-present threat of corporal punishment is viewed from the child's perspective in the carol now aptly-titled 'The Birched School Boy'/'The Schoolboy's Lament'.[15]

But it would be misrepresentative to cast all or even most of the books of nurture and manners as abusive in this way. Generally, they exhort children with practical and ethically positive guidance in a manner that takes for granted the intelligence and maturity of their young audience. These poems treat children like proper young adults. Indeed, at points, the open-eyed acknowledgement of one's position in life—in household service, or in some other sharply defined social hierarchy—is combined with a sense of high moral purpose, as in this passage from 'The Young Children's Book':

> Holy scryptour þus it seyth
> to þe þat Arte of cristen feyth,
> 'Yffe þou labour, þou muste ete
> That with þi hondes þou doyste gete':
> A byrde hath wenges forto fle,
> So man hath Armes labouryd to be.
> Luke* þou be trew in worde & dede,   *look*
> Yn Alle þi workes þan schall þou spede:
> Treuth wyt* neuer his master schame,   *commits (to)*
> Yt kepys hym out offe synne & blame.
> The weys to heuen þei bene þus tweyne,
> Mercy & treuthe, As clerkes seyne;
> Who so wyll come to þe lyfe of blysse,
> To go þe weys he may not mysse …[16]

Like a bird with wings made to fly, men have arms to labour, but also minds and spirits for learning the lessons of 'treuth'. Honest labour is made a propaedeutic and practice of truth, one that protects from shame. Thus, among the exhortations to keep one's nails clean and not to fart too loudly in the hallway, these weightier lessons also find their place.

---

[14] NIMEV 192; Furnivall (ed.), *The Babees Book*, 399–402, ll.87–96.
[15] NIMEV 1399; Furnivall (ed.), *The Babees Book*, 403–4.
[16] NIMEV 1920; Furnivall (ed.), *The Babees Book*, 17–25, ll.33–46. This work overlaps with 'The Lytylle Childrenes Lytil Boke'.

Conduct and Courtesy

Conduct books proper are more substantial and offer fascinating glimpses into the daily life of a late medieval household with its attendant behavioural expectations. In them we can also see cross-genre connections: they have the elements of penitentials, mummings, and romances, as well as lyrics and prose guides. The practical knowledge of service jobs is presented as the natural extension of general courtesy. In *The Boke of Curtasye*, for example, the moral and personal advice of the first two parts is joined in the third part with descriptions of the many household offices: porter, marshall, grooms and ushers, butler, steward, surveyor, chancellor, and so on through the ranks, with specific details, down to the number of cushions that the servants of the chamber should have ready for the lord upon retiring for the night, or how the ewerer or water-bearer should distribute the water for handwashing at mealtime.[17] This is practical poetry of considerable detail. We learn, for example, how the dish-setter or sewer (*fercularius*) should carry the covered silver dishes, being careful to avoid the semblance of 'tresoun' by uncovering any food, plus a little trick to make the job easier:

> This wyle þo squyer to kechyn shalle go,
> And brynges a bof* for assay þo;   *above, to the upper house*
> Þo coke assayes þe mete vngry3t*,   *readily*
> Þo sewer he takes and kouers on ry3t;
> Wo so euer he takes þat mete to bere,
> Schalle not so hardy þo couertoure rere,
> For colde ne hote, I warne 3ou alle,
> For suspecyon of tresoun as may befalle.
> Yf þo syluer dysshe wylle algate* brenne,   *repeatedly*
> A sotelté I wylle þe kenne,
> Take þe bredde coruyn and lay by-twene,
> And kepe þe welle hit be not sene;
> I teche hit for no curtayse,
> But for þyn ese ...
> (749–62)

Not for courtesy, but for ease: if the dish is burning hot, put a slice of bread—presumably older or stale bread not intended for the table—between it and your hands for protection. Books like this might themselves be seen as fulfilling an analogous function, offering practical guidance for working in the gilded world of household service without getting too burned.

In a similar vein, more extensive and interesting is John Russell's *Boke of Nurture* (also titled the *Boke of Kervyng & Nortur*).[18] This long prosy poem begins and ends with an autobiographical note of Russell's many years of service in the household of Humfrey, duke of Gloucester, the knowledge of which he wishes to share through good teaching. He does so in long-line verse of rough fourteeners:

> [A]n vsshere y Am / ye may beholde / to a prynce of highe degre,
> þat enioyethe to enfourme & teche / alle þo thatt wille thrive & thee,
> Of suche thynges as here-aftur shalle be shewed by my diligence
> To them þat nought Can / with-owt gret exsperience;

---

[17] NIMEV 4152; Furnivall (ed.), *The Babees Book*, 299–327, ll.479–86, 638–66.
[18] NIMEV 1514; Furnivall (ed.), *The Babees Book*, 117–99.

> Therefore yf any man þat y mete withe, þat for fawt of necligence,
> y wylle hym enfourme & teche, for hurtynge of my Conscience.
>
> (3-8)

This 'informing & teaching' is generally addressed to a 'dear son', a youth clearly older than the object of teaching in the verses of nurture but also unlearned and needing basic guidance. The book then presents a fictional frame story. One morning, 'As y rose owt of my bed, in a mery sesoun of may / to sporte me in a forest where sightes were fresche & gay' (13–14), the narrator encounters a young man out hunting, and he strikes up a conversation with him. The youth confesses his utter despondency—the narrator calls it 'wanhope' (30) or despair—at not having a secure position in household service: 'In certeyn, sir y haue y-sought Ferre & nere many a wilsom way / to gete mete (i.e., me to) a mastir; & for y cowd nouȝt, euery man seid me nay, / I cowd no good' (33–5). Hearing this, the narrator offers to instruct the youth and asks if he is interested in an array of jobs from low to high: servant, plowman, labourer, 'courtyour or a clark', merchant, mason, artificer, or 'Chamburlayn, or buttillere / pantere or karvere?' (37–40). The youth chooses the latter group, asking for instruction in the more distinguished household offices. The narrator agrees, and at this point the text launches into detailed specifics of the offices of a panter (pantry-keeper) and butler, as well as carver and chamberlain. Over the poem's 1200 lines, a wealth of information is shared about all manners of household service: wines and foods, carving and serving, table-setting and attendance, the proper ranks of estates, wardrobes and bathing and dressing, and the 'Symple Condicyons' (277) of cleanliness and good personal behaviour. At the end the narrator concludes on a wistful note, recalling his lifetime of service and how in his own youth 'y enioyed þese maters forseid / & to lerne y toke good hede' (1216). He asks for prayers for himself, his wife, his parents, and for his good lord 'duke vmfrey, duc of Glowcetur' as he looks toward his end (1229–34).

Beyond its utility as a training manual 'to know þe Curtesie of court' (1174), Russell's *Boke* also shows its connections to the genres of confessional guide or penitential treatise in its narrative framing. The young man in despair coming to learn from his priest-like elder is a familiar scene of confession, his lessons a catechism. The ill-governed youth appears like a figure out of Hoccleve's poetry, and his occasional responses reinforce this conflation of practical training with spiritual counsel. The humour aimed at cooks recalls Chaucer's Host's mocking of Roger of Ware and the Pardoner's comments on cooks' 'stampynge & gryndynge' (505–8). The lists of food and sample menus are reminiscent of similar lists found in verse romances. The *Boke* also contains copious advice for diet and health, what to eat (and when) and what to avoid. The behavioural standards are the same as in the shorter conduct verses for children, as are the directions for table manners. But now they are in a guide where the usher or marshall needs to know all the ranks of estates from 'the lady of low blode & degre' on up to 'blode royalle', and other weighty matters of distinction (1092–6). A guide like this, then, is liminal in literary as well as social space, simultaneously joining and distinguishing genres as it does persons. It also clearly delineates between in and out. Russell takes us from the despondent exclusion of a low-class youth out of the house, hoping to get in through service, to the busy and over-stuffed world of the late medieval great household such as the Duke of Gloucester headed, until his death in 1447. As such, it provides a detailed view of how those lucky enough to gain domestic employment both served and resembled their masters.

This kind of mirroring connects other styles of conduct poetry across the class divide. Gentry and bourgeois guides such as 'How the Good Wijf Tauȝt Hir Douȝtir' and 'How the Wise Man Tauȝt His Sone' originated from the long tradition of quasi-public guides for aristocratic and royal behaviour in the Anglo-French tradition, as well as clerical preaching materials.[19] There is thus some overlap with the *de regimine* and *Fürstenspiegel* 'mirrors for princes' genres, with the difference that these household conduct guides are geared toward the practical needs of gentry life. These poems originated in the mid-fourteenth century, but the surviving manuscripts indicate their widespread popularity in the 1500s.[20] 'How the Good Wijf Tauȝt Hir Douȝtir' in particular has gained attention as an English example of the Europe-wide genre of conduct manuals for women.[21] These cover the behaviours and attitudes expected of a demure bourgeois or gentry wife: religiosity, obedience to one's husband, cheerfulness, stability, chaste demeanour and bodily conduct, and a general seemliness:

> Be of semeli semblaunt, wijs, and oþer good maner,
> Chaunge not þi contynaunce for nouȝt þat þu may heere;
> Fare not as a gigge*, for nouȝt þat may bitide,   *a wanton girl*
> Lauȝe þou not to loude, ne ȝane* þou not to wide,   *yawn*
>   But lauȝe þou softe & myelde,
>   And be not of cheer to wielde,
>   Mi leue child.[22]

Generally avoiding bad behaviour 'as it were a strumpet' (82) is an overriding concern. Don't go out to public shows like wrestling matches or shooting competitions; don't drink too much; don't go gadding about town or waste your money in taverns; take no gifts; 'Aqweynte þee not with eche man þat gooþ by þe strete', and more (60–101; 88). Beyond their moralism, these bits of advice have a strongly practical cast, what Felicity Riddy has described as the 'bourgeois ethos' that was focused especially on young female behaviour.[23] Across its various versions the poem consistently emphasizes thrift—'for þo þat ben ofte drunke, / þrift is from hem sunke' (78–9)—and that those who stay at home minding their own business 'wexe soone riche' (84). Unsurprisingly, then, much of the treatise is devoted to how a good woman can successfully manage her household. Wives are expected to supervise the household staff with an easy but firm hand. If a job needs to be done urgently, the wife can help or even do it herself, and gain favour and praise for it: 'For manye handis & wight / Make an heuy worke light' (120–1). She should correct errors straightaway, keep the household keys close, pay wages promptly and fully, treat neighbours with charity and 'honest chere (169), and spend according to the means of her husband's wealth, neither overmuch nor too little (102–87). There is counsel about disciplining children, but this is a relatively minor concern limited to one stanza advising (predictably) that 'rebel' children be given a good flogging: 'take a smert rodde & bete hem on a rowe / Til þei crie mercy'

---

[19] NIMEV 671 and 1877 respectively. See Kathleen Ashley, 'The French *Enseignemenz a Phellipe* and *Enseignement a Ysabel* of Saint Louis', in Johnston (ed.), *Medieval Conduct Literature*, 3–22; Rebecca Barnhouse, *The Book of the Knight of the Tower: Manners for Young Medieval Women* (New York, 2006); Gina Greco and Christine Rose (eds), *The Good Wife's Guide (Le Ménagier de Paris): A Medieval Household Book* (Ithaca, NY, 2012).

[20] For analysis and context see especially Felicity Riddy, 'Mother Knows Best: Reading Social Change in a Courtesy Text', *Speculum*, 71 (1996), 66–86.

[21] Sponsler, *Drama and Resistance*, 50–74, and 'The English How the Good Wijf Taughte Hir Doughtir and How the Wise Man Taught His Sonne', in Johnston (ed.), *Medieval Conduct Literature*, 285–304.

[22] Quotations cited here are from the text in London, Lambeth Palace MS 853, from the mid-fifteenth century, as provided by Furnivall, (ed.), *The Babees Book*, 36–47, ll.53–9. Other manuscript versions are provided by Tauno F. Mustanoja (ed.), *The good wife taught her daughter, The good wyfe wold a pylgremage [and] The thewis of gud women* (Helsinki, 1948).

[23] Riddy, 'Mother Knows Best', 67.

(190–1). The wife's role is distinctly less motherly and more that of a household manager whose main concern is earning the blessings of 'þrift and þeedom' (*prosperity*) (209).

In contrast, the companion poem 'How the Wise Man Tauȝt His Sone' is comparatively anaemic. It covers less ground with less interest and vigour. Indeed, commonplaces about avoiding taverns, dicing, idleness, tale-bearing, staying up late, and the like are presented in an almost timorous manner. Several stanzas urge the 'sonne' not to choose a wife for money—this only creates problems later on—and that a good man does not range after 'newfangil' (115) changes or competition with neighbours.[24] Meekness is the best policy: 'þe more good þat þu hast, / þe raþer [b]ere þee meeke and lowe, / And booste not myche, it is but waast' (121-3). The poem even advises against seeking public office, for it will either set one against one's neighbours or it will force a man into dishonesty or malfeasance (41-8). In comparison to the advice for the daughter, that for the son stresses what he should not do in the public sphere and the ways he should restrain his desire for household aggrandizement. In the end all men die, and often a man's wealth is accumulated only to be enjoyed by the man who marries his wife after him (129-36). This rather depressing and unambitious conclusion perhaps indicates not just the different gender roles assumed by each treatise but also the particular temptations and limitations of male gentry life, especially the lower gentry. Compared to their female-orientated counterparts, fewer conduct books are directed at this class of men, which is certainly symptomatic of the greater restrictions placed on women of all classes and ages. But it also indicates how the more 'noble' books of this mode, regiminal treatises, were consumed by ambitious men of this rank. They habitually looked 'up' to see the style of conduct writing their class superiors were commissioning and reading, and evidence indicates they largely followed suit.[25] But for a humbler and more sober assessment of the domestic and social horizon of the gentry class, 'How the Wise Man Tauȝt His Sone' may actually give us a more realistic picture, one which resonates with other domestic English versions of regiminal writings from the fifteenth century.

A more substantial example of this middling style is the *Ratis Raving,* or 'Rate's Ravings'.[26] This under-studied poetic work is written in Lowland Scots English of the fifteenth century, and it provides a link between the service-orientated writings of nurture and the governance-orientated courtesy manuals and mirrors of noble conduct. It appears in a single composite manuscript in a sub-section with other instructive works in verse. The poem itself has four divisions that can stand alone but are joined by the same verse style and sentential focus: 'Ratis Raving', 'The Foly of Fulys and the Thewis of Wysmen', 'Consail and Teiching at the Vys Man Gaif his Sone', and 'The Thewis of Gudwomen', these last two obviously connecting the work with the 'advice to sons & daughters' trope.[27] In total the work spans over 3000 lines, with the first part accounting for over half at more than 1800 lines. The address of part one—to a 'dere sone' again—is structured like a secularized confessional manual following the elements of a syllabus, a connection that is made explicit later in the poem (723-30). After an opening appeal to the love and dread of God, moral admonitions and small exempla are keyed into the five senses, the seven cardinal virtues, an inventory of troublesome motivations (great joy, great fear, great sorrow/wanhope, great anger, and ignorance), humoral dispositions, and the traditional seven ages of man

---

[24] Furnivall, (ed.), *The Babees Book*, 48-52, l.115.
[25] Riddy, 'Mother Knows Best', 76-7.
[26] NIMEV 2235; J. Rawson Lumby (ed.), *Ratis Raving, and other Moral and Religious Pieces in Prose and Verse*, EETS, o.s. 43 (London, 1870).
[27] NIMEV 3154, 4100, 3362.

(infancy, youth, adolescence, young adulthood, maturity, old age, and dotage). In rough-and-ready four stress couplets, Rate's book provides basic moral and behavioural guidance according to the virtues with particular attention given to 'trouth' and honesty, along with frank advice about marriage, business, service, courtship, and self-governance.

The *Raving* is unique among conduct manuals for its stress on self-knowledge or awareness of one's own dispositions, put in the terms of prognostic astrology. This call to self-awareness strongly disposes the monitory cast of the poem (857–62). A man should know to eschew the desire 'to have gret thing in gouernynge' and be satisfied with 'leif in sympilte' (874–5), that is, a simple life in truth and loyalty (909–12). The marital advice is even-handed and irenic; in merchandizing or business, one should watch out for 'frysting' or trading on too much credit (925–1008). The advice on courtship is unromantic but sensible: beware of falling in love 'gyf þow wyll efter leif in pes' (1041), and if 'dam reson' and 'gud hop' do not bode success, leave your love behind (1043–53). Indeed, if the object of affection is too near kin or a married woman, the best thing 'war to lef of þe bygynyng' before things get complicated by the lady's enticing beauty: 'sice (*such*) are the perellus merouris / entisand ʒonge men til amouris' (1075, 1084–5). The review of the ages of man provides an anatomy of ethical growth, or its failure, in the conduct of each stage of life. Each age has its virtues and vices or tendencies and temptations. The central stage of maturity from the thirtieth to the fiftieth year, which should be the age 'of resone and discreccioune' (1415), is also the age where these virtues can go most awry, especially for men of higher status. Rate comments on the connection between age and the governance of 'stat'/'estate':

> For ay the vysar* that thai war,   *wiser, more mature*
> Thar gudlynes suld be the mare.
> And ay the gretar senʒory*   *seignory, lordship*
> Suld leid* thar stat mar mesour by;   *lead, govern*
> And gif that it war realtee,
> Of al thing rychtwys suld it bee …
> But now is ilkan*, of thir thre   *each (i.e. goodness, measure, righteousness)*
> Misgouernyt in thar degree …
>   (1470–5, 1480–1)

The propositions condensed here are shared by conduct books and regiminal treatises, and Rate's shift from one mode to the other is made possible by their conceptual overlap. The (male) age of ideal maturity should be the culmination of virtuous discipline and conduct, and the higher status one is, the better one should be in 'governance', both personal and public. 'Realtee' or royalty in particular should display 'righteousness' or justice, often called the apex of virtues. But what is seen more often is mis-governance, malice and malengine, 'tyrandry'/tyranny and felony, and so 'rycht and law is laid to sleip': right and law are put asleep (1496). Both biblical and contemporary examples teach this—the psalms of David, the contemporary example of 'Mortimer', Richard, duke of York—and those who fail in their duties are the ones who 'hurt the comon profyt' (1514–27, 1531, 1539). Admonishments about personal disposition thus slide naturally into critical assessments of the public realm and its governance, and of the ideals held to underlie the health of them both. The end of part one concludes, like Russell's *Boke of Nurture*, with a self-referential gesture, 'the quhilk is ratis raving cald / but for no raving I it hald' (1801–2).

The following three sections of Rate's work repeat and extend the familiar *topoi* of conduct advice and wisdom writing. Book two gives portraits of the wise and the foolish with the general physiognomic characteristics of each. There is continued strong emphasis on a virtuous mean of 'gud gouernyng' (202) and observing one's proper position. The final two sections on 'Consail and Teiching' to a son, and 'The Thewis off Gudwomen', advance these and other positions with some interesting details. To the son, for example, the advice is given not to avoid public office altogether—in contrast to 'How the Wise Man Tauȝt His Sone'—but specifically to avoid serving a tyrant prince: 'Desyr neuer kepinge of Justice, / In land quhar na law kepyt Is; / Na service office na maistry, / Wndyr princis that levis by tyrany' (279–82). Good will and good public virtue are advised towards all. The good woman is counselled to avoid pride, and if there is to be competition among neighbour wives, let it be for who can take the prize in thrift: 'In thrift stryf ay with thi nychtboure, / Qhua best can thryf but (*without*) dishonor' (81–2). Strict discipline for young women is advised but with at least some sense of gender equity insofar as correction should apply to both 'ȝunge lordis' and 'madenis' (213–18). There are sympathetic observations about the gendered impact of poverty, how it can drive women to do things they would not otherwise do (245–57). Parents should not defer to marry daughters in the hope of making an advantageous match, which, if it never comes, leaves a woman unable to provide for herself in her maturity:

> Thus mony gud maydyne oft tyme,
> For fault of mareag* in tyme,   *marriage*
> Ar tint* for fault of warldis gud;   *harmed, lost*
> thai can nocht wyne thar lyvis fud
> With trawaill, craft, and laborage ...
> (277–81)

As with the advice about the marriage of sons, these are strikingly pragmatic considerations. Parents and friends are made responsible not only for the proper disciplining of female conduct but also for controlling their own misdirected aspirations. Again, we can see how the 'gud thewis' or good conduct advised here has as much or more to do with that of the governors—parents and custodians and the like—as it does with youths. And while we have left behind the sphere of domestic service guides (there is no discussion in these manuals about such things as how to serve the water or set the tableware), their emphasis on truthful behaviour, decorous conduct, and knowing one's place is almost entirely the same. The shift across the class divide is a shift to an emphasis on ethical governance and regimen explicitly centred on the upper classes.

Regimen and Governance

Henry VI's accession to the English throne in 1422 at the age of nine months, and then his crowning as Henry II the King of France in 1431, motivated interest in regiminal works about the proper disciplining and upbringing of young princes and kings. But even before these events, regiminal books were an important part of the literary scene in England, and the moral and political poetry of the early fifteenth century shares traits characteristic of conduct verse in its humbler forms. These treatises and poems were also often significant political statements in their own right.[28] Works in the *De regimine* ('On Governance/Regimen') and 'mirrors for princes' or *Fürstenspiegel* traditions thus extend conduct writing to the third level of the conduct homology: as with the body, so with the household,

---

[28] For examples, see Jean-Philippe Genet (ed.), *Four English Political Tracts of the Later Middle Ages* (London, 1977), and Helen Barr (ed.), *The Digby Poems* (London, 2009). For general reference, see V. J. Scattergood, *Politics and Poetry in the Fifteenth Century* (London: 1971).

and so with the *civitas* or realm. Mirror books were composed and adapted in Latin, French, and English, and in the fifteenth century especially, with a freedom and diversity not characteristic of the genre in earlier periods. Many shorter political verses also gesture toward the tropes of conduct writing in this mode, expressing standards and rendering judgements about proper public and political behaviour.

Thomas Hoccleve's *Regiment of Princes*, probably composed in 1411, is an early example of the overlap of regiminal writing with poetical conduct writing, and of the striking creativity that could result.[29] Hoccleve's most important and most widely copied work, the *Regiment*, is in rhyme-royal stanzas of over 5000 lines, translating, adapting, and versifying earlier texts in this broad tradition: parts of the pseudo-Aristotelian *Secretum secretorum*, excerpts from the massive *De regimine principum* of Egidius Romanus, and bits from Jacob de Cessolis' *De ludo scaccorum* or 'On Chess', all of them important and widely circulated. The genre had also been practiced by his beloved predecessors Chaucer and Gower, both of whom he references directly. But the differences are more striking than the similarities, as Hoccleve's guide appeals much more directly to his political overlord (Henry Bolingbroke, the future Henry IV) and is more overt in servile self-presentation. The main section of the guide for princes combines familiar elements in an inventory of the virtues necessary for good governance: justice, piety, mercy, patience/sufferance, chastity, and the like. Hoccleve speaks *in propria persona* to give exhortations and exempla counselling his prince to temperance and virtue, both in self-rule and public governance. The rhyme-royal verse is cogent and generally good quality. But what makes the *Regiment* notable is its large autobiographical framing story—more than 2000 lines long—that ranges over a number of topics concerning governance and conduct. A pensive and anxious Hoccleve, weighed down by the anxieties of poverty, rises from his sleepless bed to take a walk outside, where he encounters 'a poore old hoor man' (122) and strikes up a long conversation. This talk with the wise old counsellor, who addresses Hoccleve as 'my sone' (143), quickly moves to an edifying discourse on 'governance':

> 'Right so, if thee list have a remedie
> Of thyn annoy that prikketh thee so smerte,
> The verray cause of thyn hid maladie
> Thow moot deskevere and telle out al thyn herte.
> If thow it hyde, thow shalt nat asterte
> That thow ne falle shalt in sum meschaunce;
> Forthy amende thow thy governance'.
>
> (260–6)

The scene is explicitly confessional. The old man's words advising the amendment of Hoccleve's conduct are echoed repeatedly as they discuss various subjects: heresy, presumptuous clothing, old age and poverty, wages and work, marriage and households, all suffused with Hoccleve's anxieties about the ill-temper of the times and his own bad situation.

The story also creates a multilevel mirroring between the old man and Hoccleve, and (later) between Hoccleve and his royal addressee of the *Regiment*, Prince Henry. Hoccleve recounts with regret his youthful bad conduct in passages reminiscent of his earlier poem '*La Male Regle*' ('The Ill-Governed'), and the old man too recalls his own mis-spent youth: 'O, where is now al the wantoun moneye / That I was maistir of and governour / Whan

[29] NIMEV 2229; Charles R. Blyth (ed.), Thomas Hoccleve, *The Regiment of Princes* (Kalamazoo, MI, 1999).

I kneew nat what povert was to seye?' (687–9). The men bewail the slipperiness of fortune in familiar Boethian terms, and their exchange certainly recalls the complaints of Boethius to Lady Philosophy. But it would be too limiting to see only the Boethian context here, as Hoccleve's self-portrait of mis-governance and misfortune derives equally from the admonitions of the conduct tradition. Indeed, in many instances, that more homely mode of writing appears to underwrite his practical choice of topics and his frankly un-philosophical conclusions: 'men han meryt aftir hir governance' (1484). As well, it supports the *Regiment*'s continual alignment of virtuous personal behaviour with household security and with the broader public weal. Lydgate's later and much more massive *Fall of Princes,* while proceeding from a different Boccaccian source and frame, has a similar alignment.

These generic influences and political elements contextualize the mid-century efflorescence of regiminal writings, translations, and hybrid works combining poetry and prose, Latin and English, especially in the work of writers affiliated with Sir John Fastolf. Specific books with strong conduct elements emerged as important source-texts. Following Hoccleve and Gower, in the fifteenth century there developed an apparent vogue for the *Secretum secretorum,* with several independent English translations and adaptations in prose.[30] It was this quasi-practical, quasi-mystical guidebook for rulers that Lydgate was translating into aureate verse as the 'Secrees of Old Philosoffres', possibly at the request of Henry VI, when he died in 1449, and that was completed by his successor Benedict Burgh.[31] For all the work's philosophical, alchemical, and physiognomic lore, its core modality as an advisory letter to a prince—supposedly an epistle from Aristotle to Alexander—was the main reason for its enduring popularity. Since the philosopher cannot counsel his prince in person, he sends his charge 'this pistil' with his secret teachings:

> In his exskus / this pistil to vncloose;
> And first Advertise / in Especial,
> Witt and Corage / and hym Silff dispoose,
> To leve al manerys / that be bestial,
> Vertues to folwe / that ben Inperyal;
> This is to seyne / first prudently discerne,
> Twen* vice and vertu / his peple to governe.   *between*
> (652–8)

The poem promises the secrets of virtuous self-rule and 'inperyal' governance, faux-gnostic teachings that appealed to eager aristocratic and bourgeois readers. Lydgate's last work has been described by its editor as 'scrappy, ill-ordered, and tedious to a remarkable degree even for him', but it was sufficiently popular to be issued in print in the early sixteenth century.[32] His successor Benedict Burgh also composed a poetic version of the Distichs

---

[30] Robert Steele (ed.), *Three Prose Versions of the Secreta Secretorum,* EETS, e.s. 74 (London, 1898); M. A. Manzalaoui (ed.), *Secretum Secretorum: Nine English Versions,* EETS, o.s. 276 (London, 1977).

[31] NIMEV 935; Robert Steele (ed.), John Lydgate and Benedict Burgh, *Lydgate and Burgh's Secrees of Old Philosoffres: A Version of the 'Secreta secretorum',* EETS, o.s. 66 (London, 1894). See Rory G. Critten, 'The Secrees of Old Philisoffres and John Lydgate's Posthumous Reputation', *Journal of Early Book Society,* 19 (2016), 31–64; Margaret Bridges, 'Lydgate's Last Poem', in Catherine Gaullier-Bougassas, Margaret Bridges, and Jean-Yves Tilliette (eds), *Trajectoires européennes du Secretum secretorum du Pseudo-Aristote (XIIIe–XVIe siècle)* (Turnhout, Belgium, 2015), 317–36.

[32] Steele (ed.), *Lydgate and Burgh's Secrees of Old Philosoffres,* xviii; DeWitt T. Starnes (ed.), *The Gouernaunce of Kynges and Prynces: The Pynson Edition of 1511* (Gainesville, FL, 1957).

of Cato, reflecting the equally strong mid-century vogue for Latinate wisdom literature.[33] Such florilegia and gatherings of the 'sayings of philosophers' were the upper-class equivalent to more humble proverb collections. Strong testimony of the continuing influence of the writings of Christine de Pizan is also evident in Stephen Scrope's elegant prosimetrum translation of the *Epistle of Othea*, which survives in several manuscripts, as well as an anonymous English prose translation of de Pizan's prose *Livre du Corps de Policie*, which is in the manuscript with *Rate's Ravings*.[34] As they were for Hoccleve, so also for these later English writers, de Pizan's works continued to be indispensable models for advisory literature in the later fifteenth century.

With these popular sources in mind, two poets from the mid- to later-fifteenth century stand out as notable: George Ashby and Peter Idley.[35] Like Hoccleve earlier in the century, both poets wrote large composite works made from familiar books in biographically framed arrangements. To take the earlier writer first, Peter Idley was a Lancastrian bureaucrat and regional Oxfordshire administrator who rose to the level of Esquire of Henry VI and Controller of the King's Works, in which office he remained until Henry's defeat in 1461. His primary work called *Instructions to His Son* is more rightly titled *Liber consolacionis et consilii*, the 'Book of Consolations and Counsels', the title that it carries in several manuscripts and that makes clear its debt to its primary source, Albertanus of Brescia's thirteenth-century Latin treatise of the same title.[36] This mis-naming is an understandable mistake drawn from a librarian's fly-leaf description of the work based on its opening address to 'my childe / That art yet yonge and somdele wylde'.[37] The 'wild child' is Idley's eldest son, Thomas, the ostensible addressee of the poem's first part. But as in other works addressed to a 'dear son', the pose is conventional, and indeed Idley draws this epistolary frame from his source-text as well. In English rhyme-royal stanzas of roughly four-beat lines, alternating with Latin extracts from Albertanus, Idley ranges over advice on conduct and governance in the mode characteristic of these mid-century works. Familiar platitudes are adapted, Englished, and embellished with Latin passages as a kind of text-and-gloss unit, all for the edification of a youth on the cusp of adult responsibilities. Idley advises his son to respect his elders and to value education and 'connyng' (32); he exhorts him to follow his father in the practice of law (and threatens disinheritance if he does not); and he gives a panoply of sober advice including guidance about clothing, cleanliness, proper speaking, moderate behaviour, seeking counsel, good marital relations, servants and neighbours, loyalty to one's king and country, and much more, poetically recasting Albertanus' Latin with relevant personal commentary.

The second part of Idley's work, which is over three times as long, moves from the personal counsels of the first part to a wider purview. While it maintains the fiction of an address to youth—'That like as þou growest firthir in age / So should þou grow to be more wyse and sage / And folow not ay youthes kynde' (3–5)—the work adapts Robert Mannyng's lengthy *Handlyng Synne* from the early fourteenth century, interspersed with

---

[33] NIMEV 854 and 3955; see Fraser James Dallachy, 'A Study of the Manuscript Contexts of Benedict Burgh's Middle English "Distichs of Cato"' (PhD thesis, University of Glasgow, 2012).

[34] The verse in the *Epistle* translation is NIMEV 2766 and 2700.66; see Curt F. Bühler (ed.), Stephen Scrope, *The Epistle of Othea*, EETS, o.s. 264 (London, 1970); and also Diane Bornstein (ed.), *The Middle English Translation of Christine de Pisan's 'Livre du corps de policie'*, MET 7 (Heidelberg, 1977).

[35] On both authors see John Scattergood, 'Peter Idley and George Ashby', in Julia Boffey and A. S. G. Edwards (eds.), *A Companion to Fifteenth-Century English Poetry* (London, 2013), 113–25.

[36] NIMEV 1540.

[37] Charlotte D'Evelyn (ed.), *Peter Idley's 'Instructions to His Son'* (Boston, 1935), l.6–7: citations from this edition are edited with reference to the manuscripts.

generous extracts from Lydgate's *Fall of Princes*. Again, these are adapted freely (and without identification of either source) together with occasional scriptural and sentential passages in Latin.[38] The work follows Mannyng's confessional syllabus with a selection of exempla for each item of the Ten Commandments, the Seven Deadly Sins, Sacrilege, the Seven Sacraments, and the Twelve Points of Shrift. None of the manuscript witnesses is complete and in fact they exhibit a remarkable range of excision, rearrangement, and overall adaptation, showing how flexible this mode was for its audiences.[39] In the present context, what stands out is the syncretic creativity with which Idley combines different genres from different times. Good 'governance' and proper 'reverence' are still key, dependent upon the bodily and political obedience of the young and impressionable (II, B, 78–84). The sins and their exempla provide a flexible means for exploring an inventory of moral pitfalls and the dangers of mis-rule. For example, in the treatment of the fourth sin, Sloth, familiar sentiments about the chastizing of children follow a Lydgatean lament for the 'fortune transitorie' (II, B, 1265) of earthly life:

> Also if it fortune the to have a childe,
> Looke thow chastise hym in tendre age,
> And suffre hym never to growe overwilde.
> Keepe hym cloos as a birde in a cage,
> For if he goo at large, he woll outrage
> And peraventure · [falle] to mischeif, sorow, and care.
> Therfore whoo lovyth the childe · he woll the rodde not spare.
>   (II, B, 1268–74)

Lydgatean *de casibus* moralism moves into conduct admonishment, in the setting of penitential guidance adapted from a clerical text from a century and a half prior, all filtered through a distinctly secular gentry sensibility. The dangers of lax discipline are exemplified in the following stories of 'The Tale of the Blaspheming Boy' and 'The Tale of Eli and his Sons', the latter a popular exemplum covering the spiritual and political sides of governance.[40] But it is variation in the lines immediately following 'spare the rod, spoil the child' that most directly if inadvertently reveal the double anxiety of regimen: 'Better were the childe to be unborn / Than unchastised and set in [no] governaunce … (II, B, 1275–6). The manuscripts' vacillation between 'governaunce' and 'no governaunce' neatly captures this dual significance in opposed but correlative meanings.[41] Woe to the child who has been ill-raised to bad conduct by *no* governance, that is, with no regimen or discipline; and woe to house, the land, the country where an unchastized child has been set *in* governance, that is, in a faulty political rule that is bound to fail. Here and throughout Idley's work, the

---

[38] See A. S. G. Edwards, 'The Influence of Lydgate's *Fall of Princes* c.1440–1559: A Survey', *Medieval Studies* 39 (1977), 424–39; Nigel Mortimer, *John Lydgate's 'Fall of Princes': Narrative Tragedy in its Literary and Political Contexts* (London, 2009), 244–51.

[39] For analysis, see Spencer Strub, 'Oaths and Everyday Life in Peter Idley's *Instructions*', *JEGP*, 119 (2020), 190–219; Yoshinobu Kudo, 'Reinstalling Clerical Authority, Juridical and Didactic: The Unique Rearrangements of Book II of Peter Idley's *Instructions to his Son* in London, British Library, Arundel MS 20', *Medium Ævum*, 88 (2019), 265–300; Matthew Giancarlo, 'Dressing up a "galaunt": Traditional Piety and Fashionable Politics in Peter Idley's "translacions" of Mannyng and Lydgate', in Vincent Gillespie and Kantik Ghosh (eds), *After Arundel: Religious Writing in Fifteenth-Century England* (Turnhout, 2012), 429–47.

[40] See, for example, Siegfried Wenzel, 'Eli and His Sons', *Yearbook of Langland Studies*, 13 (1999), 137–52.

[41] Of the six manuscripts, three have versions of 'no governance' (BL MSS Arundel 20, Add. 57335, Cambridge, Magdalene College MS Pepys 2030); two have 'governance' (BodL MS Laud Misc. 416, CUL MS Ee. 4. 37); and one (BodL MS Eng. Poet. d. 45) lacks the lines.

personal, domestic, and public spheres are addressed in a conservative critique of 'misrule' (1279) that repeatedly shifts among all three. Indeed, the familiar lament from Ecclesiastes 10.16, 'Woe to the land where the king is a child and whose princes feast in the morning', is one of the major theme-texts conjoining the conduct and regiminal modes in condemnation of mis-rule, and in the potential danger such condemnations could bring down upon a poet. Idley side-steps those threats through equivocation and through occasional appeals to that most fifteenth-century pose, dullness. After the first deposition of Henry VI in 1461, he appears to have retired from public life as his Lancastrian king went into exile and to eventual dethronement.

By that time, Idley's composite work was probably complete. In contrast, the troubles of Another loyal Lancastrian courtier, George Ashby, were just beginning. Ashby's *Active Policy of a Prince* and accompanying *Dicta & opiniones diversorum philosophorum* were written for prince Edward of Wales, possibly around the readeption of 1470–1 or earlier.[42] His 'A Prisoner's Reflections', dated to 1463, was written while he was a political prisoner in the Fleet, subject to the victorious Yorkists for two years or more.[43] Ashby is a connecting figure for much of the writing covered in this survey. As a Lancastrian administrator and signet clerk for Queen Margaret, he worked in the same governmental sphere as Peter Idley. In his early career he circulated in the royal household of Humfrey, duke of Gloucester, as he recalls from his youth in the 'Reflections':

> I gan remembre and revolue in mynde
> My bryngyng vp from chyldhod hedyrto,
> In the hyghest court that I coude fynd,
> With the kyng, quene, and theyr vncle also,
> The duk of Gloucetre, god hem rest do,
> With whom I haue be cherysshyd ryght well,
> In all that was to me nedefull euery dell.[44]

In this court he almost certainly knew—or at least interacted with—John Russell. In this reminiscence he sounds not too different from Russell's aspiring youth, lucky to have found a secure and 'cherysshyd' place in household service. Ashby's poetry exhibits Hoccleve's influence, not just in the general content of his *Fürstenspiegel* but in his posture as a 'failed beggar poet' whose servitude to the prince cathects his own anxieties of position and voice.[45] He appeals to the triumvirate of 'Maisters Gower, Chauucer & Lydgate / Primier poetes of this nacion' (*Active Policy*, 1–2), and his adaptation of the *Dicta Philosophorum* places him squarely in dialogue with the Fastolf circle. And where in Russell's *Boke of Nurture* the offices of 'courtyour or a clark' were listed among the household jobs one might aspire to, a man like Ashby may be what he had in mind. Signet clerks were effectively the servant-doubles of their masters, responsible for the conveyance and protection of their lords' textual selves in letters and documents.[46] Ashby's choices of texts to exemplify his own textual presence, then, make sense in this household service context, as well as in the wider literary environment.

---

[42] NIMEV 2130 and 738.
[43] NIMEV 437.
[44] Mary Bateson (ed.), *George Ashby's Poems*, EETS, e.s. 76 (London, 1899), 'A Prisoner's Reflections', 57–63. All three of Ashby's works are edited in this volume.
[45] Robert J. Meyer-Lee, 'Laureates and Beggars in Fifteenth-Century English Poetry: The Case of George Ashby', *Speculum*, 79 (2004), 688–726 (at 704).
[46] See Meyer-Lee, 'Laureates and Beggars', 716.

'A Prisoner's Reflections' appeals to the Boethian ideal of patience in undeserved political adversity, a conduct standard reaching from kings and queens right down to lowly clerks in Ashby's socially stratified formula:

> Right so kyng, Quene, Duke, Prynce and Emperoures,
> Erle, Baron, lord, knyght, and many squyers,
> Bysshop, Abbot, Pryour, and conquerours,
> And many gret estates and Rewlours,
> Clerkes, marchauntes and eke counseylours
> Haue be put in trouble and gret greuaunce
> For theyr soules helth by humble sufferaunce.
> (260–6)

While clerks and counsellors may rank with the bourgeois 'marchauntes' in status, they also connect to their superiors through this chain of loyal service and the ideal of humble sufferance in troubled times. The later *Active Policy* and accompanying *Dicta* similarly appeal to cross-class standards of conduct. As Prince Edward's nurture has been virtuous—'And so youre bringyng vp hath be right sad, / In all vertuous disposicioun / And to the honnour of god euer ladde' ('Active Policy', 113–15)—Ashby presumes to give him 'polletike' guidance to help avoid future troubles such as have beset the kingdom.[47] The prescription for this is, naturally, good governance, which includes the virtues of order, reason, truth, pity, justice, and courtesy native to it ('Active Policy', 310–23). The English verses are interspersed with Latin proof-texts, again like Idley and also Scrope, all advising good counsel convenable to both 'god and polleci' ('Active Policy', 643). His advice for cultivating dread and awe, and for the proper presentation of the sovereign 'countenance' or face, to 'auoide alwaies frownyng Cowntenance' ('Active Policy', 842–8), also recalls the *Secretum Secretorum*, as do many of the pithy versifications of the Latin dicta.

Ashby's book can hardly avoid cliché and repetitiveness, but by now it should be clear that this was not the standard by which conduct-discourse aspired to be judged. Clear sentential repetition was the point. And as we have seen from homely household manuals on up to counsel books addressed to the prince, the same advice was offered to 'children', again and again, to avoid the spectre of childish governance. To be worthy of obeisance, the prince must himself be obeisant and learn to serve:

> So he that hethe* childis condicion,   *has, possesses*
> Ys not acceptable to gouernaunce.
> For he that aught to haue subjeccion
> Of the people and verrey obeissaunce
> Must put hym selfe in witty assuraunce.
> As ye may oft see bi experience,
> He that shal reule must hau* gret diligence.   *have*
> ('Dicta Philosophorum', 36–42)

It seems unlikely that young prince Edward was ever in a position to benefit from such 'witty assurance' as Ashby provides here for his sovereign, before the latter's death at

---

[47] See generally Paul Strohm, *Politique: Languages of Statecraft between Chaucer and Shakespeare* (South Bend, IN, 2005), on the uses of 'politic'/*politique* and 'policy' in the period.

Tewkesbury in 1471 at the age of seventeen. Its assemblage of wisdom on governance and conduct nonetheless stands as a minor poetic monument, both to the perdurable aspirations of poets to influence the conduct of their princes, and to the cultural turning point apparent at the end of the fifteenth century. After this in the sixteenth century, both in England and on the continent, conduct books, courtesy manuals, and guides for princely regimen entered into a new modality with writers such as Thomas Elyot, Desiderius Erasmus, Baldassar Castiglione, Thomas More, and of course Niccolò Machiavelli. Remembering their English verse predecessors, and the lively context of conduct writing in which they were situated, helps to clarify both the humble origins and the broad appeal that these works had in their times, in diverse but related modes and at nearly all social levels.

CHAPTER 17
Love Visions and Love Poetry

Rory G. Critten

For C. S. Lewis, the fifteenth century saw a change in the medieval representation of love. Whereas the high Middle Ages had pitted private desires and public duties against each other in the great romances of Lancelot and Guinevere and Tristan and Isolde, a revalorization of marriage at the end of the period promised happier outcomes.[1] This chapter covers some of the same territory charted by Lewis, who was amongst the first critics to afford serious attention to the later Middle English love visions. It follows a development whereby, alongside poems that continue to describe men's experience of love after the fashion of Guillaume de Lorris's *Roman de la rose* (c1240), we start to find works that attempt to reach a resolution in matrimony of the tensions between desire and duty. It differs from Lewis and echoes some more recent commentators where it expresses doubt regarding the success of those attempts. Where their defence of marriage falls short, the texts addressed in this chapter invite contemplation in particular of women's experiences of love. Throughout the love poetry of the fifteenth century, Middle English writers increasingly evince frustration with traditional expressions of male desire and seek to develop new modes of writing that are capable of encompassing women's wants, including the possibility of women's same-sex desire. It is no coincidence, it will be argued, that the first long English poems in women's voices belong to this text type and period.

The chapter begins with an extended survey of the genre of poetry in English in which the new literary interest in love is most evident: the love vision. Particular attention will be afforded to the influence of Gower's *Confessio amantis* on the developments in love ideology that characterize fifteenth-century writing in this form. At its close, the chapter considers the great variety of shorter love lyrics that survive from the fifteenth century and the invention of the Middle English amorous verse sequence. While continental poetry could boast a long history of such cycles, poets writing in English were slow to take up this form. Fifteenth-century love poetry in English will thus be shown to innovate both where it departs from continental traditions and where it reapplies those traditions to create new literary possibilities.

The *Complaint of the Black Knight* and *Temple of Glass*

Because they demonstrate both the rich inheritance of the genre and its potential at the opening of the fifteenth century, Lydgate's love visions are an obvious place to begin this survey. They have tentatively been dated to the 1420s and are probably the earliest narrative

---

[1] See C. S. Lewis, *The Allegory of Love* (Oxford, 1936), especially 232–96.

poems that this chapter will treat.² Both works appear to have been popular: the *Complaint of the Black Knight* survives in nine manuscript copies and the *Temple of Glass* survives in ten, two of which are extracts, and one early print (1477? STC 17032).³ Of the two, the *Complaint* best illustrates the conventional parameters of the genre as Lydgate inherited it. In it, a love-sick narrator describes waking up one May morning and departing on a walk that takes him into a garden; there he drinks from a well and happens upon a wounded knight dressed in black and white. Surprised at his discovery, the narrator hides; overhears the knight complain of his unsuccess in love; returns home; and writes up his experience.

Lydgate's literary debts in the *Complaint* are manifold. The descriptions of the morning walk and the garden scene draw on a tradition going back to the *Roman de la rose*, and the meeting with the knight and the overheard complaint have clear parallels in the *Book of the Duchess* and in the poetry of Machaut, Froissart, and Oton de Granson.⁴ The poet's use of mythological references to adumbrate women's suffering in love also owes something to his fourteenth-century predecessors. Amongst the trees in the garden, the poet sees 'Daphene closed vnder rynde' (64; *rinde: bark*) and

> The philbert* eke* that lowe doth enclyne   *hazelnut tree; also*
> Her bowes grene to the erthe dovne
> Vnto her knyght icalled Demophovne.
> (68–70)

But aside from these allusions to the legends of Daphne and Phyllis, the *Complaint* concentrates overwhelmingly on the male experience of bad love. The knight complains that the one woman who could cure him only aggravates his wound. In a miniature allegory of court justice, he asserts the unfairness of his treatment: Truth has been put out by Falseness at a sham hearing presided over by Cruelty. He continues: he is like all those legendary lovers who deserved success but did not get it; love favours the false and love service goes unrewarded.

At the close of the *Complaint*, Lydgate offers a glimpse of a more equitable kind of love. The poet prays that before sunrise the next day, each of his readers will have been able to embrace his lady. He clarifies:

> I mene thus, that in al honeste,
> Withoute more, ȝe may togedre speke
> Whatso ye liste* at good liberte,   *Whatever you desire*
> That eche may to other her hert breke,*   *disclose their feelings*
> On Ielosie oonly to be wreke*   *avenged*
> That hath so longe of* malice and envie   *out of*
> Werred* Trouthe with his tiranye.   *Waged war on*
> (659–65)

Lovers are imagined here in easy conversation, but a limit is set to their interaction. They might embrace and speak 'in al honeste, / Withoute more'.

---

² On the uncertain dating of Lydgate's love visions, see Derek Pearsall, *John Lydgate (1371–1449): A Bio-bibliography* (Victoria, BC, 1997), 14.
³ NIMEV 1507 and 851; see John Norton-Smith (ed.), *John Lydgate: Poems* (Oxford, 1966). Lydgate's love visions are cited from this edition. Norton-Smith gives the *Complaint of the Black Knight* the title that it has in some early copies, the *Complaynt of a Loveres Lyfe*.
⁴ See Derek Pearsall, *John Lydgate* (London, 1970), 84–91; and Sue Bianco, 'New Perspectives on Lydgate's Courtly Verse', in Helen Cooney (ed.), *Nation, Court and Culture: New Essays on Fifteenth-Century English Poetry* (Dublin, 2001), 95–115 (at 97–102).

Any questions that this curious formulation might raise are swiftly passed over in the *Complaint*, whose dispatch is begun directly after the lines just cited. The idea of honest courtship receives fuller treatment in the *Temple of Glass*, although the tension that it comprises is not so much resolved as exposed there. In the *Temple*, Lydgate stakes out new ground for the love vision by taking as his subject the solution of one woman's amorous dilemma. It opens with the poet's transport to the temple of the title, on whose walls are depicted a multitude of legendary sufferers in love. The edifice is filled with visitors whose various love complaints are reported; amongst them are several women who lament that they have been married against their will, or that their lovers have tired of them.

One woman is singled out from the crowd and her complaint is given verbatim. At its heart is what appears to be an expression of unhappiness in marriage:

> For I am bounde to þing þat I nold:* *I would not be*
> Freli to chese þere lak I liberte,
> And so I want of þat myn herte would,
> The bodi is knyt,* alþouȝe my þouȝt be fre; *bound*
> So þat I most,* of necessite, *must*
> Myn hertis lust outward contrarie—* *outwardly oppose*
> Thogh we be on,* þe dede most varie. *Although we are one*
> (335–41)

Venus promises to remedy the woman's situation; provides her with a lover; and extracts from the lover a promise that his affection for the lady will remain 'grovndid opon honeste',

> That no wiȝt* shal, þurugh euil compassing,* *person; design*
> Demen amys of hir in no degre.
> For neiþer merci, reuþe,* ne pite *compassion*
> She shal not haue, ne take of þe non hede
> Ferþer þen longiþ vnto* hir womanhede. *pertains to*
> (870–5)

Venus finally joins the lovers in a golden chain and the poem ends with celebrations that are so loud that they wake the dreaming narrator.

Lydgate's debt to Chaucer in the *Temple of Glass* remains a perennial topic in criticism.[5] The influence of the French poets on the text has also received attention.[6] In contrast, the importance of Gower for Lydgate's concept of the love vision has been overlooked—but this seems crucial. In *Confessio Amantis*, Gower had developed at length a theory of 'honeste' love according to which the inevitable pangs of sexual desire might be restrained by reason and safely expressed in marriage.[7] Lydgate appears to allude to this idea in the *Complaint* and is keen to take it over more completely in the *Temple*. But he faces a problem. In *Confessio*, Amans's union with his lady is only ever a theoretical possibility and one which, famously, the poet eschews at the close of his work. In Lydgate's text, by contrast, the lady's conundrum is apparently resolved when she is united with her lover. Quite how satisfactory this remedy can be accounted is doubtful since Lydgate is stricter even than Gower. In the *Temple*, the necessity of abstinence is expressed more clearly than in the *Complaint*.

---

[5] Most recently, see Boyda Johnstone, 'Vitreous Visions: Stained Glass and Affective Engagement in John Lydgate's *The Temple of Glass*', *New Medieval Literatures*, 17 (2017), 175–200.
[6] See Susan Bianco, 'A Black Monk in the Rose Garden: Lydgate and the *Dit Amoureux* Tradition', *The Chaucer Review*, 34 (1999), 60–8.
[7] The classic exposition is J. A. W. Bennett, 'Gower's "Honeste Love"', in John Lawlor (ed.), *Patterns of Love and Courtesy: Essays in Memory of C. S. Lewis* (London, 1966), 107–21. Some of the tensions in this model are unpicked in Diane Watt, *Amoral Gower: Language, Sex, and Politics* (Minneapolis, MN, 2003).

'Abide awhile', Venus instructs the lover, 'and þan of þi desire / The time neigheth þat shal þe most delite' (1203–4; *the time neigheth*: the time will approach). The protagonists' final union is thus postponed.

One explanation for the inconclusive conclusion of the dream in the *Temple of Glass* is that it reflects a similar situation involving real people. There is a long history of readers pursuing this line of thought. One of the manuscripts transmitting the poem, now BodL MS Tanner 346, has annotations testifying to a curiosity regarding the lady's identity among its early readers. Next to lines 841–7 of that copy, where the lover expresses his desire for his lady's affection, someone has written '*hic vsque nescio quis*' (I still don't know who this is) (fol. 29v); and next to lines 970–6, where the knight begins his petition to the lady, an annotator asks exasperatedly 'who in all godly pity maye be[?]' (fol. 31v). Modern attempts to assign the poem to a particular occasion differ in their plausibility. Most recently, it has been suggested that the situation of the lady in the poem mirrors that of Jacqueline of Bavaria, countess of Hainault, who came to England in 1421 after repudiating her husband, John of Brabant; she was courted by Humfrey of Gloucester but could not marry him before obtaining the papal dispensation that came some time in 1422.[8]

This is the most satisfactory explanation currently available for the conclusion to the *Temple of Glass*, in which the lovers are instructed to content themselves temporarily with a chaste relationship. But, as the annotations to the Tanner manuscript demonstrate, this understanding was not available to all the poem's early readers. Although the dilemma expressed in the poem may have ended happily in reality, within the text, the long catalogue of unhappy lovers on the walls of the temple, the love complaints heard at Venus's court, and the lady's own complaint about her initial union all warn against the likelihood of an easy solution for the heroine (incidentally, whatever felicity Jacqueline enjoyed was short lived: already by 1428 her marriage to Humfrey had been declared void by pope Martin V and Humfrey had married one of her attendants, Eleanor Cobham). Indeed, it seems that the poem's optimistic ending can only be won at the expense of a shift in narrative focus. What began as a story set in motion by a woman's complaint to Venus is finally reframed as the celebration of a man's success in love: 'Thus is þis man to ioy and al plesaunce / From heuynes and from his peynes old / Ful reconsiled' (1285–7).

The *Kingis Quair*

It is perhaps not too much to claim that an air of unfinished business hung about the *Temple of Glass*. The textual history of the poem indicates that scribes as well as readers were keen to return to it. The manuscripts record different combinations of identifying mottoes for the lady, which suggests that the work could be repurposed, and the lady has a virulent complaint against jealousy that is transmitted in the earliest but not the later copies of the text, indicating that some reshaping of her character took place.[9] Lydgate's poem was also of interest to his poetic successors, one of whom was the author of the *Kingis Quair*.[10] Like the *Temple of Glass*, the *Quair* owes an important debt to Gower's notion of 'honeste' love, which here assumes a political cast. Like the *Temple* too, the *Quair* leaves a question mark

---

[8] See Julia Boffey, 'Shirley, Trinity College Cambridge MS R. 3. 20, and the Circumstances of Lydgate's *Temple of Glass*: Coterie Verse over Time', *Studies in the Age of Chaucer*, 38 (2016), 265–73.

[9] See John Norton-Smith, 'Lydgate's Changes in the *Temple of Glas*', *Medium Ævum*, 27 (1958), 166–72. The alterations that Norton-Smith identifies as authorial were more probably scribal.

[10] NIMEV 1215.

over the permanence of its actors' felicity despite its apparent determination to end on a high note.

The speaker of the *Kingis Quair* describes his capture in youth by his enemies; an almost eighteen-year imprisonment at their hands; his sight during that time of a beautiful woman; and, after a dream in which he secures the help of Venus, Minerva, and Fortune, his unification with that woman and final enfranchisement. Here the historical background implied by the narrative is easier to determine. The poem's plot maps readily onto the biography of the man who is identified as the author of the work in two paratextual attributions recorded in the only manuscript that now contains it, BodL MS Arch. Selden. B. 24. In a colophon, the second of the poem's two scribes identifies it as the work of '*Iacobus primus scotorum rex Illustrissimus*' (James I, the most illustrious king of the Scots) (fol. 211), and in a note preceding the opening of the poem, a later hand echoes this ascription, announcing 'the quair maid be King James of Scotland the first callit the kingis quair and maid quhan his majestee wes in Ingland' (fol. 191v). James I of Scotland (1394–1437) spent eighteen years in English captivity. He was delivered to Henry IV in 1406 by pirates who intercepted the ship that was to take him to France from Scotland, where his family feared for his safety. Negotiations for his release were completed in 1423 and his return to Scotland as its monarch followed upon his marriage in early 1424 to Joan Beaufort, a niece of cardinal Henry Beaufort and second cousin to Henry VI.[11]

Although the Selden manuscript is thought to have been compiled in the late fifteenth or early sixteenth century, it is normally assumed that James wrote the *Kingis Quair* sometime between his marriage to Joan in February and his murder in 1437.[12] Internal evidence in favour of an earlier date within that span has been found by critics who see the poem as an attempt to translate the potentially compromising experience of imprisonment into a source of authority for the new king.[13] An important aspect of this design is the prominence afforded to the triumphant description of James's union with his lady. Again, the Gowerian precedent is important. In the final tale of the *Confessio*, Apollonius of Tyre is said to derive his right to rule from his decision to wed 'honesteliche':

> Lo, what it is to be wel grounded:
> For he hath ferst his love founded
> Honesteliche as forto wedde,
> Honesteliche his love he spedde*   *advanced*
> And hadde children with his wif,
> And as him liste* he ladde his life.[14]   *as he desired*
> (VIII. 1993–8)

Success in marriage will lead to success on the throne: this is the claim being made for James, in line with the Gowerian model, which argued that a king's ability to govern depended on his capacity first to regulate his own private desires. It is not for nothing that Gower is listed—before Chaucer—as one of the poet's two 'maisteris dere' in the final stanza of the *Quair* (1373–4).[15]

---

[11] See the *ODNB* entry for James by M. H. Brown.
[12] See Julia Boffey (ed.), *Fifteenth-Century English Dream Visions: An Anthology* (Oxford, 2003), 90–93. The poem is cited from this edition.
[13] See Sally Mapstone, 'Kingship and *The Kingis Quair*', in Helen Cooper and Sally Mapstone (eds), *The Long Fifteenth-Century: Essays for Douglas Gray* (Oxford, 1997), 51–69. More recently, see too Joanna Martin, *Kingship and Love in Scottish Poetry, 1424–1540* (Aldershot, 2008), 19–29.
[14] Cited from G. C. Macaulay (ed.), *The English Works of John Gower*, EETS, e.s. 81, 82 (London, 1900–1).
[15] On the relationship between the *Kingis Quair* and *Confessio Amantis*, see further Joanna Summers, *Late-Medieval Prison Writing and the Politics of Autobiography* (Oxford, 2004), 74–81.

In the positive tones that mark the poem's allusion to James's marriage, Lewis famously heard something new. In the *Kingis Quair*, Lewis writes, 'the poetry of marriage at last emerges from the traditional poetry of adultery'. As such, he suggests, 'it is the first modern book of love'.[16] But the closing celebration of the poet's union with his lady in the *Kingis Quair* is undercut by references to the Ovidian legend of Philomela that run throughout the text. In that story, Philomela is brutally raped by Tereus, her sister Procne's husband, and, after avenging herself on Tereus by having him eat his son, Itys, is turned into the nightingale (*Metamorphoses*, VI. 412–674).

The first reference to this story comes towards the opening of the *Quair*, where the poet recalls how a chorus of nightingales put him in mind of love shortly before he first glimpsed his lady. That the birds are not merely part of the text's amorous décor is made clear when the poet shows himself imploring one of them to repeat its song for her 'for the love of Proigne, thy sistir dere' (380):

> Lift up thyne hert and sing with gude entent,
> And in thy notis suete the tresoun telle
> That to thy sister, trewe and innocent,
> Was kythit* by hir husband false and fell;*   *shown; treacherous*
> For quhois* gilt, as it is worthy wel,   *whose*
> Chide thir* husbandis that are false, I say,   *those*
> And bid thame mend, in the twenty deuil way!
> (386–92)

In *Troilus and Criseyde* (2. 64–70), Chaucer had invoked Philomela's legend at the moment where Pandarus begins to plot Troilus's union with his niece, thereby alluding to his heroine's vulnerability just as the love story is getting under way. Mention of the nightingale at this moment in the *Kingis Quair* might likewise encourage us to fear for the lady's future. But in the lines just cited, the poet attempts to redirect sympathy away from Philomela to her sister: Philomela is instructed to sing about Procne's woes as a wife.

An optimistic interpretation of this innovation would infer that the poet hereby demonstrates his awareness of the history of women's mistreatment by men, even within marriage, and that this awareness will allow him to craft a more equitable relationship with his own wife.[17] It might also be that the idiosyncratic use to which the Philomela story is put in the *Quair* is designed to the comic detriment of James, with a view to highlighting the erstwhile superficiality of his learning or the dizzying heights of his amorous enthusiasm. A parallel might be drawn with the poet's optimistic but fallacious use of Boethian philosophy to demonstrate the supposed security of his new-found good fortune.[18] The *Quair* offers a retrospective on its author's career and the poet is not averse to making himself risible in that perspective: the four stanzas in which he goes on to beg the nightingale to sing are clearly intended as a joke at his expense. Interpretations of this sort would be easiest to secure if James himself performed the poem. Such a scenario seems not unlikely given

---

[16] Lewis, *The Allegory of Love*, 237.

[17] See Elizabeth Robertson, '"Raptus" and the Poetics of Married Love in Chaucer's Wife of Bath's Tale and James I's *Kingis Quair*', in Robert M. Stein and Sandra Pierson Prior (eds), *Reading Medieval Culture: Essays in Honor of Robert W. Hanning* (Notre Dame, IN, 2005), 302–23.

[18] See further Lois E. Ebin, 'Boethius, Chaucer, and *The Kingis Quair*', *Philological Quarterly*, 53 (1974), 321–41, where a comparison with Chaucer's *Troilus* in Book IV of *Troilus and Criseyde* is explored.

what is known about the intimate and convivial settings in which poetry was enjoyed at fifteenth-century English and Scottish courts.[19]

Ultimately, the *Kingis Quair* would travel more widely. The most recent work on the text of the poem argues that it was issued twice, once for James's bride and her acquaintants in England, and a second time for 'a somewhat broader audience in Scotland'.[20] By the end of the century it had reached the household of Henry, Lord Sinclair (d. 1513), who appears to have commissioned the Selden manuscript, not earlier than c1489.[21] A sense of the reception that the *Quair* received in this context can be gleaned from the texts added to the book after its copying. These include Hoccleve's *Letter of Cupid*, in which the deity denounces men's mistreatment of women; the *Lay of Sorrow*, a complaint in a woman's voice about her abandonment by her lover; and the *Quare of Jelusy*, in which a poet's sympathy with a lady he spies weeping spills over into an emotional diatribe against jealousy.[22] Amongst a readership whose interest in women's experience of love is attested by these texts, the side-lining of Philomela's suffering in the *Kingis Quair* may have jarred. The owners of the Selden manuscript, who were relatives of James, can scarcely have been unaware of his grisly murder on the night of 21/22 February 1437; they may also have known about the difficult circumstances in which Joan herself died later in 1445.[23] At a remove from its subject, the *Quair* could lend itself to less hopeful readings not only of its protagonist's likely end but also of its central relationship.

Richard Roos's *Belle Dame Sans Merci* and the *Isle of Ladies*

The concern with women's experience of love that animates the *Temple of Glass* and, more subtly, the *Kingis Quair*, finds clearer treatment in contemporaneous poetry that explicitly envisages women's severance from love. The best example of writing of this sort in English is the Middle English *Belle Dame Sans Merci*, which is attributed to Sir Richard Roos (c1410–82) and dated to the mid fifteenth century.[24] In that poem, a knight whose own lady is dead relates a conversation that he overheard between another man and a woman who steadfastly refused to accept his love. The woman bats away every love commonplace that the man can muster in support of his case. He faults her eyes for his affliction, but she lays the blame with anyone who falls for a glance. He asks her why she disdains him, and she replies that she neither loves nor hates him, nor wishes to hear of his love for her. He suggests that his love will be fatal; she replies that his sickness is easy: 'but fewe people it causeth for to dye' (294).

---

[19] See Joyce Coleman, *Public Reading and the Reading Public in Late Medieval England and France* (Cambridge, 1996), 130–2.

[20] William A. Quinn, 'Red Lining and Blue Penciling *The Kingis Quair*', *Studies in Philology*, 108 (2011), 189–214 (at 190).

[21] See Julia Boffey, 'Bodleian Library MS Arch. Selden. B. 24 and Definitions of the "Household Book"', in A. S. G. Edwards, Vincent Gillespie, and Ralph Hanna (eds), *The English Medieval Book: Studies in Memory of Jeremy Griffiths* (London, 2000), 125–34.

[22] NIMEV 666, 482, 3627.5; see further Julia Boffey, 'The *Kingis Quair* and the Other Poems of Bodleian Library MS Arch. Selden. B. 24', in Priscilla Bawcutt and Janet Hadley Williams (eds), *A Companion to Medieval Scottish Poetry* (Cambridge, 2006), 62–74. For a complete account of the Selden MS and its contents, see Julia Boffey and A. S. G. Edwards (intro.), *The Works of Geoffrey Chaucer and* The Kingis Quair: *A Facsimile of Bodleian Library, Oxford, MS Arch. Selden. B. 24* (Cambridge, 1997), 1–60.

[23] See the *ODNB* entry for Joan by M. H. Brown.

[24] NIMEV 1086; see Dana M. Symons (ed.), *Chaucerian Dream Visions and Complaints* (Kalamazoo, MI, 2004). The text is cited from this edition.

Eventually, the would-be lover is forced to retire, and the narrator reports a rumour that he did in fact die shortly after the interview. Men are told not to boast of their affections or risk going unbelieved. Women are told not to be like the lady in the poem. As he comes to the close of his text, however, Roos seems to hedge his bets:

> And ye, ladies, or what astate ye be,
> Of whom worship hath chose his dwelling place,
> For Goddis love, doo no suche cruelté,
> Namly to hem that have deservyd grace.
> Nor in noo wise ne folow not the trace
> Of hire, that here is named rightwisly,*   *rightfully*
> Whiche, by reason, me semeth* in this cace,   *it seems to me*
> May be called la belle dame sanz mercy.
>   (821–8)

The French text from which Roos translates this poem, Alain Chartier's *Belle dame sans merci* (1424), is more straightforward in the last four lines of this stanza:

> Que ja nulle de vous ressemble
> Celle que m'oyez nommer cy,
> Qu'on appellera, ce me semble,
> La belle dame sans mercy!²⁵
>   (797–800)

(Let none of you resemble she whom you hear me name here, who shall be called, it seems to me, La belle dame sans merci).

The qualifiers added at the close of the English text—'rightwisly', 'by reason', 'in this case'—fill out the longer English line. At the same time, they indicate that the final judgement of the lady is pending. Chartier's *Belle dame* was a true *succès de scandale* that prompted a long series of responses whose earnestness is difficult to gauge.²⁶ Roos's version of the poem prepares it for an English audience; his principal innovation is the addition of a prologue in which he describes waking out of a half-sleep to the memory of his commission to write the work. By giving Chartier's poem the trappings of a love vision, Roos facilitated the extension of the *querelle de la belle dame* in England, where the text appears to have been popular: it survives in seven manuscript copies.²⁷

One other text that might briefly be mentioned here is the *Isle of Ladies*, which survives in two sixteenth-century manuscripts but which is thought to have been written in the fifteenth century.²⁸ The narrator of the *Isle* relates how he was transported in a waking dream to a mysterious island that was entirely enclosed in walls of glass. There were weathervanes in the form of songbirds and towers shaped like flowers. The sole inhabitants of the island

---

²⁵ Cited from J. C. Laidlaw (ed.), *The Poetical Works of Alain Chartier* (Cambridge, 1974). The translation is mine.
²⁶ See David F. Hult and Joan E. McRae (eds), *Le Cycle de la Belle dame sans mercy* (Paris, 2003).
²⁷ On Roos's translation, see further Ashby Kinch, 'A Naked Roos: Translation and Subjection in the Middle English *La Belle Dame Sans Mercy*', *JEGP*, 105 (2006), 415–45. More recently, see too Olivia Robinson, *Contest, Translation, and the Chaucerian Text* (Turnout, 2020).
²⁸ TM 1860; see Anthony Jenkins (ed.), *The Isle of Ladies or The Ile of Pleasaunce* (New York, 1980). The text is cited from this edition.

were women and their self-sufficiency is emphasized. Whoever was there might find their every need met:

> for flower, ne* tree,   *nor*
> Ne thinge wherein pleassaunce myght be,
> Ther fayled none for every wighte;*   *person*
> Had thay desyred day and nyghte
> Richesse, hele,* beawty, and ease,   *wellbeing*
> Withe everye thing that hem* might please,   *them*
> Thynke, and haue, hit* cost no more.   *it*
> (129–35)

The means by which the women are maintained in this condition are precarious, involving their queen in a treacherous voyage every seven years to retrieve three magic apples. The arrival of the dreamer is the first in a series of events that will see her reign toppled. While the poem ultimately relates the defeat of the women, the opening description of their independent existence and a concentration throughout on the strategies of resistance that they adopt makes the *Isle of Ladies* an engaging pendant to Roos's *Belle Dame Sans Merci*.[29]

The *Flower and the Leaf* and the *Assembly of Ladies*

The interest in women's experience of love that animates the late-medieval English love vision finds its fullest expression in two poems that are written in a woman's voice, both of which are dated to the third quarter of the fifteenth century: the *Flower and the Leaf*, which exists uniquely in an early print (1598; STC 5077) but was once included in the late fifteenth-century compilation that is now Warminster, Longleat House, MS 258; and the *Assembly of Ladies*, which survives in three manuscripts.[30] As these poems' early misattribution to Chaucer demonstrates, their premodern readers could interpret them as the work of a male author. More recent commentators have stressed the likelihood that the poems were written by women and explored the ramifications of taking their accounts of their authorship seriously.[31] While both works purport to offer an especially informed view on women's experience of love, they differ broadly in attitude and tone. One striking similarity between the texts is their more or less oblique treatment of women's same-sex desire.

In the *Flower and the Leaf*, an insomniac narrator wanders one spring morning into a marvellously constructed arbour that affords a view of the field behind it while shielding its occupant from vision without. From this vantage point, the arrival of a host of richly dressed ladies bearing chaplets of leaves upon their heads is observed. The women are followed by a company of men who also wear chaplets of leaves: trumpeters, kings of arms, heralds, knights, and henchmen. The men joust; meet the ladies; and, in pairs, the men and women go to dance and sing under a laurel tree. There then enters a company of men and women bearing chaplets of flowers. They also dance and sing, but their celebrations are

---

[29] See further Boyda Johnstone, '"Far semed her hart from obeysaunce": Strategies of Resistance in *The Isle of Ladies*', *Studies in the Age of Chaucer*, 41 (2019), 301–24.

[30] NIMEV 4026 and 1528; see Derek Pearsall (ed.), *The Floure and the Leafe and the Assembly of Ladies* (London, 1962). Both poems are cited from this edition.

[31] For example, see Ann McMillan, '"Fayre Sisters Al": *The Flower and the Leaf* and *The Assembly of Ladies*', *Tulsa Studies in Women's Literature*, 1 (1982), 27–42; and Alexandra A. T. Barratt, '*The Flower and the Leaf* and *The Assembly of Ladies*: Is There a (Sexual) Difference?', *Philological Quarterly*, 66 (1987), 1–24.

spoiled by a sudden blast of heat and a storm that leaves them bedraggled. The men and women who were protected under the laurel tree help the newer arrivals to recover. The leaf queen invites the flower queen to dine with her and, as they depart, both groups parade before the arbour in which the poet is hidden. The poet catches the attention of one of the departing leaf ladies and extracts from her a moralization of the scene.

For a reader of the poem (as opposed to an audience member who sees it performed by a woman), the revelation of the speaker's gender is delayed until the close of the text, where the departing leaf lady addresses her as 'doughter' (462). Earlier in the poem, the traditionally male associations of the place that this speaker occupies have been emphasized. We are told that her arbour was made by a man: 'he that tooke the cure / It to make, y trow, did all his peine' (62–3; *y trowe*: I trust). Indeed, the uniqueness of her situation is remarkable. Women are always being spotted in arbours in late-medieval literature; this is how the lady is first glimpsed in the *Kingis Quair*, for example. In the *Flower and the Leaf*, while the ladies of the leaf dance in the field, the speaker enjoys a privileged position:

> And, Got wot,* me thought I was wel bigone,* knows; situated
> For than I might avise hem,* one by one, scrutinize them
> Who fairest was, who coud best dance or sing,
> Or who most womanly was in all thing.
> (186–9)

It is difficult to think of another medieval poem that offers so clear an account of the pleasures of being a *voyeuse* of other women. It is characteristic of the indirect ways in which premodern texts imagine same-sex attraction that, for the private reader, this scene becomes visible only in retrospect.

Notwithstanding this innovative moment, a sense of belatedness hangs about the vision. The route that the speaker takes to her arbour is said to be 'forgrowen ... with grasse and weede' (45) and, when the departing leaf lady gives her moralization of the scene in the field, it transpires that all of its actors are dead.[32] The meanings attributed to the plants that the leaf women carry are of particular interest. The flower queen is said to be Diana, who carries a branch of *agnus castus*, a willow-like plant, in token of her virginity. Those amongst her followers who wore chaplets of the same plant likewise 'han kepte alway her maidenhede'; those wearing chaplets of laurel were 'hardy' and 'wan by deed victorious name'; and those wearing chaplets of woodbine 'never were / to love untrue in word, thought, ne dede' (472–90). By contrast, the adherents of the flower are said to have 'loved idelnes / and not delite of no busines' (536–7).

When she puts active and true-loving women on a par with virgins, the moralizing lady of the leaf achieves what is perhaps the most perfect iteration of the Gowerian ideal of chaste love that the fifteenth century has to offer.[33] But the couching of the moral in the *Flower and the Leaf* suggests that, like the actors in the field, the ideal might be a thing of the past. The ludic context in which the poem asks to be seen further discourages over-earnest interpretation. Late-medieval French and English poets, including Chaucer, refer to a 'game of love' in which participants took the part either of the flower or the leaf and

---

[32] For an alternative reading of these elements of the poem, see Paul Battles, 'In Folly Ripe, In Reason Rotten: The Flower and the Leaf and the "Purgatory of Cruel Beauties"', *Medium Ævum*, 72 (2003), 238–58.

[33] For a more sceptical reading, see Derek Pearsall, 'The *Flower and the Leaf* and the *Assembly of Ladies*: A Revisitation', in Anne Marie D'Arcy and Alan J. Fletcher (eds), *Studies in Late Medieval and Early Renaissance Texts in Honour of John Scattergood* (Dublin, 2005), 259–69.

argued for the superiority of their emblem; a participant might take either side: an outcome in favour of the leaf was not inevitable.³⁴ When the poet is finally identified as an adherent of the leaf at the end of the text, the primary purpose of the work as a playful 'move' to benefit that team is indicated. Certainly, the difference between the two companies, who engage in the same pursuits of song and dance, does not seem especially great, and the stakes are not high. In a break with convention, the narrator of this love vision is presented as perfectly content. It is a mystery why she cannot sleep at the outset 'for there nas erthly wight, / As I suppose, had more hearts ease / Then I' (19–21; nas: *was not*).

The equanimity of tone that defines the *Flower and the Leaf* is absent in the *Assembly of Ladies*, a poem that seems altogether less satisfied with medieval love traditions. In that work, the poem's speaker, who is identified as a woman at the outset, is attempting a maze one September afternoon when she is met by a man who asks why she is so pale. The speaker responds with a story about a dream that she had in an underground chamber at the heart of the labyrinth. Having fallen asleep there once, she was met by Perseveraunce, usher to lady Loiaulte, who had requested that the dreamer attend a council at her palace, Pleasaunt Regard. The dreamer and her fellowship should go there to present their petitions to Loiaulte and they should arrive wearing blue gowns that bear their personal mottoes. The narrator continues the story of her dream: en route to Plesaunt Regard, she interacts with different members of Loiaulte's all-woman household—Diligence, the dreamer's guide; Discretioun, Loiaulte's chief purveyor; Aqueyntaunce, her lodgings warden; and Contenaunce the porter—her petition is read out before Loiaulte along with the petitions of her companions and, although Perseveraunce had indicated that Loiaulte would be favourable to them, Loiaulte finally postpones her judgement in a brief speech, after which, the dreamer says, she awoke.

The *Assembly* is remarkable for the interest that it manifests in the workings of the late-medieval great house.³⁵ The dreamer's willingness to comply with the requirements of this world is not total, however. While she arrives at Pleasaunt Regard dressed in blue, her gown bears no motto, and she evades the enquiries that this omission excites. Her reluctance to overinvest in the scenario may be wise: Loiaulte's deferral of her judgement suggests her inability to resolve the problems brought before her. It may be that the poem develops a critique of the contemporary legal system.³⁶ The notion that some sort of trick is underfoot is indicated by the decoration of the chamber in which the petitions are read. Its walls are said to bear engravings of the stories of women disappointed in love: Phyllis, Thisbe, Cleopatra, Melusine, Anelida, and others. But these have been partly obscured by a hanging of 'umple', a kind of fine linen (471).

Nor is it clear that the dreamer's complaint falls within Loiaulte's remit. Her companions are shown to complain about a broken promise, service unrewarded, or unstable joy. But when the dreamer relays her own bill, it turns out that she seeks relief from another woman. Her complaint begins:

---

[34] See Pearsall (ed.), *The Floure and the Leafe*, 22–9.

[35] See further Janet M. Cowen and Jennifer C. Ward, '"Al myn array is bliew, what nedith more?": Gender and the Household in *The Assembly of Ladies*', in Cordelia Beattie, Anna Maslakovic, and Sarah Rees Jones (eds), *The Medieval Household in Christian Europe, c.850–c.1550: Managing Power, Wealth and the Body* (Turnhout, 2003), 107–26.

[36] See Wendy A. Matlock, '"And long to sue it is a wery thing": Legal Commentary in *The Assembly of Ladies*', *Studies in Philology*, 101 (2004), 20–37.

Nothyng so lief* as death to come to me	*dear*
For fynal end of my sorwes and peyne;	
What should I more desire, as seme ye—	
And ye knewe al aforne it for certeyne*	*if you knew fully all the circumstances*
I wote ye wold;* and for to telle yow pleyne,	*I know you would think so*
Without hir help that hath al thyng in cure*	*who has charge of everything*
I can nat thynk that it may long endure.	
(694–700)	

The 'hir' referred to here may be 'Loiaulte': the complaint has been related in response to a request from the man to whom the dream is being told.[37] But the bill is clearly introduced as a verbatim report: 'And thus it seyde, without any more' (693). Why would the dreamer refer to Loiaulte in the third person in a written submission to the lady?

If the dreamer's bill were encountered as a stand-alone lyric, we should have no trouble interpreting it as an expression of a man's thwarted love. In the context in which it appears in the *Assembly*, multiple readings are available. Perhaps this is an early expression of same-sex desire between women. Perhaps the dreamer requires another woman's help to secure the love of a man. Or perhaps the complaint is not about love at all: the dreamer may require a friend's help to get out of a different kind of fix. It has been pointed out that the bills read out in the *Assembly* might have to do not only with love but, more generally, with matters related to cohabitation at court or in a household.[38]

Expressions of same-sex desire hover on the edge of recognition in both the *Flower and the Leaf* and the *Assembly of Ladies*. In one sense this development is unsurprising. Where they focus attention on the knowability of women's desire, these women-voiced visions develop to the fullest extent a preoccupation that lies at the heart of the form. If they were not written by women, then they at least opened an imaginative space within which women's authorship could be conceived by future writers.[39] It is interesting to note that the connection between women and the dream vision would endure well into the early modern period. Long after male poets had abandoned the form, Elizabeth Melville chose it to express her Calvinist vision of hell, *Ane Godlie Dreame* (1603), and Rachel Speght used a literary dream to frame an allegorical story of her life, the *Mortalities Memorandum, with a Dreame Prefixed* (1621).[40]

Free-Standing Love Lyrics and Love Lyric Sequences

A variety of perspectives on the kinds of love explored in the love visions is afforded by a body of shorter, free-standing poems in Middle English that is both large and scattered.[41] One estimate puts the number of such poems at well over 400 and locates them in more

---

[37] So Barratt, 'The Flower and the Leaf and The Assembly of Ladies', 18–20.
[38] See Julia Boffey, '"Forto compleyne she had gret desire": The Grievances Expressed in Two Fifteenth-Century Dream-Visions', in Cooney (ed.), *Nation, Court and Culture*, 116–28 (at 122).
[39] See Liz Herbert McAvoy, 'Anonymous Texts', in Liz Herbert McAvoy and Diane Watt (eds), *The History of British Women's Writing, 700–1500* (Houndmills, 2011), 160–8 (at 167). On the potentially tactical anonymity of the *Assembly*, see too Simone Celine Marshall, 'The Anonymous Author of *The Assembly of Ladies*', *Neuphilologische Mitteilungen*, 114 (2013), 301–8.
[40] See Alexandra Barratt (ed.), *Women's Writing in Middle English*, 2nd edn. (London, 2010), 283.
[41] For a sample, see Thomas G. Duncan (ed.), *Medieval English Lyrics and Carols* (Cambridge, 2013), 188–213. The free-standing lyrics discussed are cited from this edition.

than 100 individual manuscripts.[42] An absolute formal distinction between the love visions and these shorter texts cannot be drawn since each of the visions includes lyric set pieces or cites lyric compositions. Where whole lyrics were intercalated, scribes could draw attention to this structural feature. Copyists of the *Temple of Glass* often marked up the lyric set pieces in that work, for example, and there is evidence to suggest that the balade with which Lydgate's lover woos his lady, beginning 'Princes of iouþe, and flour of gentilesse' (970), circulated independently.[43] In the *Flower and the Leaf*, the songs that the two companies sing are referred to by citations from their texts. It is useful to recall that these snippets are in French: '*Suse le foyle de vert moy ... / Seen & mon joly cueur en dormy*' (177–8; under the green May leaf my joyful heart went to sleep) and '*Si douce est la Margarete*' (350; the Marguerite is so sweet). Throughout the fifteenth century, the appeal of French love lyric remained strong.[44]

Like the love visions, the free-standing love lyrics are a rich resource for those considering late-medieval gender relations. Many of these poems manifest an interest in reliving men's experience of love pains. Lovers are shown begging a kiss (e.g., 'Gracius and gay'; complaining that they cannot see their ladies as freely as they would (e.g., 'Have godday, nou, Mergerete'); or worrying about their ladies' constancy (e.g., 'Thayr ys no myrth under the sky').[45] But even amongst these verses interesting perspectives are offered on women's roles. The speaker of 'Myn owne dere ladi fair and fre' complains that his jolly exterior does not reflect his inner turmoil but apparently receives some consolation from a confidante.[46] The poem concludes:

> Myself y wol myn arende bede;* *present my petition*
> The betur y hopë for te spede;* *be successful*
> Non so wel may do myn nede—* *do what I require*
> A woman so me tolde.
>
>   (13–16)

Other lyrics take a more obviously sceptical approach to the *topoi* of medieval love poetry. In 'Of my lady wel me rejoise I may', for example, Thomas Hoccleve parodies the traditional itemization of the lady's beauties.[47] This is the third in a sequence of lyrics in which Hoccleve shows first his request for the help of lady Money and then her negative response. Here the poet wreaks his revenge:

> Of my lady wel me rejoise I may!
> Hir golden forheed is ful narw and smal,
> Hir browës been lyk to dym reed coral,
> And as the jeet* her yën* glistren ay.*   *jet; eyes; always*
>
>   (1–4)

Hair might be golden, but a forehead should not be according to the standards of lyric beauty; nor should it be narrow. Lustreless red coral is unlikely ever to be an appealing shade and medieval poets do not traditionally single out black eyes for praise. Hoccleve

---

[42] See Julia Boffey, *Manuscripts of English Courtly Love Lyrics in the Later Middle Ages* (Cambridge, 1985).
[43] See David Fallows, 'Words and Music in Two English Songs of the Mid-15th Century', *Early Music*, 5 (1977), 38–43 (at 40–2).
[44] See Julia Boffey, 'The Manuscripts of English Courtly Love Lyrics in the Fifteenth Century', in Derek Pearsall (ed.), *Manuscripts and Readers in Fifteenth-Century England: The Literary Implications of Manuscript Study* (Cambridge, 1983), 3–14 (at 5–6).
[45] See respectively NIMEV 1010, 1121, 3534; Duncan (ed.), *Medieval English Lyrics*, 199–202.
[46] NIMEV 2185; Duncan (ed.), *Medieval English Lyrics*, 200.
[47] NIMEV 2640; Duncan (ed.), *Medieval English Lyrics*, 213.

goes on to lavish mock praise upon his lady's 'bowgy cheekës ... as softe as clay' (5; *bowgy*: *baggy*); her oversized nose and mouth; her body 'shape as a footbal' (19); and the parrot-like noise that she makes when she tries to sing.

'Of my lady wel me rejoise I may' draws clearly into focus the anti-feminist potential of the late-medieval love lyric, in which undying devotion often seems ready to tip into bitter resentment. This makes free-standing lyrics spoken in a woman's voice especially difficult to interpret. One such poem, 'Whatso men seyn', begins by expressing incredulity at men's promises of constancy in love and ends with the assertion that, since men are so untrustworthy, women should behave likewise:[48]

>   Then semëth me
>   Ye may well se
>   They be so fre
>   In every plase,
>   Hitt were peté
>   Butt they shold be
>   Begeled,* pardé,   *beguiled*
>   Withowtyn grase.*   *grace*
>   (25–32)

The poem survives uniquely in the Findern manuscript, CUL MS Ff. 1. 6, a book compiled from the late fifteenth into the sixteenth centuries into which several women's names have been written and that has been thought to contain some woman-authored texts.[49] One possibility is that 'Whatso men seyn' records a woman's playful resistance to men's wiles. But the evidence is susceptible to other readings. That women like to assume the moral high ground but are in fact no better than men is a commonplace in anti-feminist literature. Might this be a poem composed by a man (or a woman?) whose aim was to lampoon women? Was it copied (by a man? by a woman?) because its content was approved? or reproved? or enjoyed with ironic detachment? Where it illustrates the overlap between the discourses of proto- and anti-feminism, a poem like 'Whatso men seyn' invites its readers to reconsider the difference that gender makes not only to the experience of love but also to the expression of that experience in poetry.

'Whatso men seyn' neatly demonstrates the versatility of late-medieval secular lyric, a quality that is a hallmark of the genre and that was no doubt crucial to its success. While organized sequences of love lyrics were popular in other medieval European languages, especially French, there seems to have been little appetite for collections of Middle English amorous verse that were framed or grouped in ways that might direct their interpretation more narrowly.[50] Two interconnected sequences of Middle English love lyrics buck this trend, and it is with a consideration of these works that this chapter concludes. Both of the sequences have a strong French connection, but both also turn the love lyric to fresh ends in English.

The largest of the two sequences is Charles d'Orléans's *English Book of Love*, which brings together lyric and narrative poems to tell a story of their author's enamourment,

---

[48] NIMEV 3917; Duncan (ed.), *Medieval English Lyrics*, 211–12.
[49] See Sarah McNamer, 'Female Authors, Provincial Setting: The Re-Versing of Courtly Love in the Findern Manuscript', *Viator*, 22 (1991), 279–310.
[50] See Julia Boffey, '"Cy ensuent trois chaunceons": Groups and Sequences of Middle English Lyrics', in Graham D. Caie and Denis Renevey (eds.), *Medieval Texts in Context* (London, 2008), 85–95.

bereavement, and retirement from and return to love service.[51] The poems are thought to have been written by Charles during a period of captivity in England that extended from his capture at the Battle of Agincourt in 1415 to his release in 1440.[52] During this time, Charles also wrote poetry in French: about two thirds of the poems compiled in the *English Book of Love* have French parallels. That the author conceived of his English and French writings differently can be inferred from the arrangements that he made for their compilation. Just prior to his release, Charles ordered the production of at least two copies of his poetry.[53] Of these, one compiled the English verses organized in the fashion just described; that book is now BL MS Harley 682. In contrast, the copy of the French prison poetry disposed the works such that there remained space to include the poems that would be written into it after Charles's return to France. That book is now Paris, Bibliothèque nationale de France, MS fr. 25458.[54] In an odd sense, the *English Book of Love* might be considered the more 'French' of the two collections. In presenting himself as the compiler of a poetic sequence whose subject was ostensibly himself, Charles transferred into English the tradition of the *dit amoureux* that had been pioneered by his French predecessors Machaut and Froissart.[55]

Not only the disposition of the bilingual verses but also their texts differ across these two manuscripts. For example, in the French collection, balade 28 begins:

> En la nef de Bonne Nouvelle
> Espoir a chargié Reconfort
> Pour l'amener de par la belle
> Vers mon cueur qui l'ayme si fort.
> A joye puist venir au port
> De Desir, et pour tost passer
> La mer de Fortune, trouver
> Un plaisant vent venant de France,
> Ou est a present ma maistresse,
> Qui est ma doulce souvenance
> Et le tresor de ma lÿesse.
>
> (B28:1–11)

(In the ship of Good News Hope has loaded Comfort to send him from my lady to my heart who loves her (or him: Comfort) so much. May he come with joy to the port of Desire, and swiftly to pass the sea of Fortune, find a pleasant wind coming from France where my mistress is at present, who is my sweet thought, and the treasure of my happiness).

---

[51] See Mary-Jo Arn (ed.), *Fortunes Stabilnes: Charles of Orléans's English Book of Love* (Binghampton, 1994). The English poems are cited from this edition.

[52] For a convenient biography of Charles, see Arn (ed.), *Fortunes Stabilnes*, 12–38.

[53] See Mary-Jo Arn, 'Two Manuscripts, One Mind: Charles d'Orléans and the Production of Manuscripts in Two Languages', in Mary-Jo Arn (ed.), *Charles d'Orléans in England (1415–1440)* (Cambridge, 2000), 61–78.

[54] See Mary-Jo Arn and John Fox (eds), *Poetry of Charles d'Orléans and His Circle: A Critical Edition of BnF MS. fr. 25,458* (Turnhout, 2010). The French poems are cited from this edition; the translation is mine.

[55] See further Rory G. Critten, *Author, Scribe, and Book in Late Medieval English Literature* (Cambridge, 2018), 149–59; and Denis Renevey, '"Short song is good in ale": Charles d'Orléans and Authorial Intentions in the Middle English Ballade 84', in Julia Boffey and Christiania Whitehead (eds), *Middle English Lyrics: New Readings of Short Poems* (Cambridge, 2018), 201–10.

Here is the parallel English text. Since the language is especially tricky, I offer a full translation:

> Hoffa howe, myn hert! The schepe off Freche Teydyng
> Hope hath afresht with lusty Recomfort
> To cary to the fayrist borne lyvyng,
> Which is myn hertis lady and cheef resort,
> And if he may attayne the ioyfull port
> (In self passage, y mene, to his desere),
> The See of Fortune playn to his plesere,
> A ioly wind als blowyng into Fraunce
> Where now abidyng is my sovl maystres
> Which is the swete of all my remembraunce
> And hool tresoure of my worldly gladnes.
>   (1037–47)

(Heave ho, my heart! Hope has provisioned the ship of Fresh Tiding with happy Comfort, to carry [him] to the fairest born living, who is my heart's lady and chief source of comfort, provided he may attain the joyful port (in safe passage, I mean, according to his desire), the Sea of Fortune being smooth to his liking. [And provided he meets] a favourable wind too blowing into France where my unique mistress now abides, who is the sweetness of all my memories and the whole treasure of my worldly gladness.)

In the French version, the poet imagines his lady sending him a message into England, a pose that allows him to express his confidence in her affection. The mood of the passage is hortative ('*a joye puist venir au port*') and the verse is elegant and finely balanced (the enjambment in lines 5–8 is especially nicely handled). In contrast, the English version of the balade imagines the poet enthusiastically dispatching a message to his mistress. The tone is more colloquial ('Hoffa howe, my hert!'); the mood is conditional, encompassing the possibility of failure ('and if he may attayne the ioyfull port'); and the longer English line results in some ungainly padding (e.g., 'In self passage, y mene, to his desere'). These differences are replicated throughout the parallel corpora of Charles's French and English verse.

It may be that Charles's more emotional and less polished English self-image simply reflects his imperfect mastery of the language. But these aspects of the poet's English persona also seem likely to have had political significance. Amongst Charles's captors, reports of his tricky nature were frequent. Shortly before his release, for example, Humfrey of Gloucester wrote to his nephew, Henry VI, adducing Charles's 'grete subtilite and cauteleux disposition' as grounds for keeping him in England.[56] By presenting himself as an unsuccessful and unsubtle lover, the poet might have hoped to erode his reputation for political guile.[57] Consideration of the transmission history of Charles's poetry lends weight to this suggestion. Amongst the French poems that Charles wrote during his imprisonment there survives an exchange of balades between the poet and his continental ally, Philippe

---

[56] Cited from 'Rymer's Foedera with Syllabus: April-June 1440', in Thomas Rymer (ed.), *Rymer's Foedera*, vol. 10 (London, 1739–45), 763–76.
[57] See Rory G. Critten, 'The Political Valence of Charles d'Orléans's English Poetry', *Modern Philology*, 111 (2014), 339–64.

de Bourgogne, in which the two men plot Charles's liberation. These texts would seem to have been released into the continent early but withheld from the poet's English audience, to whom Charles presented a depoliticized version of his work in both French and English.[58] The sequencing of the poetry in Harley 682 can be seen as part of an attempt to project a particular image of the poet to his insular audience. Just as the author of the *Kingis Quair* mobilized the conventions of the love vision for the purposes of political self-advertisement, so the Middle English lyric might be turned to the purpose of public image making in Charles's *English Book of Love*.

The second, much smaller, Middle English love lyric sequence is transmitted in BodL MS Fairfax 16, a manuscript dating to *c*1450.[59] It comprises twenty rhyme royal poems; in combination, they tell a story of decreasing satisfaction. The opening poems express the lover's dedication to his lady (1); announce his service to her (2); and describe her beauties and virtues (3). After this, he runs into difficulties: he complains that he cannot see his lady (4, 14, 17); twice he must depart (5, 10); other obstacles are raised by men, perhaps rivals, whom he mentions glancingly (11, 12, 13); and he complains that deserving lovers such as himself are no longer properly rewarded:

> The world ys straunge, and now yt ys the guyse
> Who that doth best aqwyte hym in hys trouthe
> Shall sunnest* be foryet,* and that ys routhe*.[60]   *soonest; forgotten; a pity*
> (17. 424–6)

In the nineteenth poem, a speaker announces that he is compelled to praise the flower; he regrets that he lacks the skill of Chaucer, and attacks Lydgate for maligning love and women. Then, in the final text in the sequence, a 'parlement of love' is called at which Cupid hears complaints against Danger and promises to render judgement at a later date.

The authorship of the Fairfax Sequence remains a mystery, but there is one tantalizing clue. The eighth poem in the group, 'O thou Fortune, whyche has the governaunce',[61] also appears in Charles d'Orléans's manuscript, Bibliothèque nationale fr. 25,458, into which it was copied after Charles's return to his family home at Blois. Charles received many visitors from England there, one of whom was William de la Pole, duke of Suffolk (1396–1450), the man traditionally credited with writing 'O thou Fortune', and, by extension, the rest of the Fairfax poems. Although the case remains unsolved, William seems a likely enough author: he was known to Charles because he had been one of his keepers in England and he is credited with writing another group of French poems that survives in a manuscript copied by John Shirley.[62] Whoever wrote the Fairfax Sequence is to be credited with an ingenious anglicizing of the French form that it borrows. Much about the poems is drawn from the source that inspired French and English poets alike during the later Middle Ages, such as the reference to the game of the flower and the leaf and the 'parlement of love' with

---

[58] See Rory G. Critten, 'In France, In England, and Out of Europe: Locating Charles d'Orléans', *New Medieval Literatures*, 20 (2020), 174–215.

[59] See J. P. M. Jansen (ed.), *The 'Suffolk' Poems: An Edition of the Love Lyrics in Fairfax 16* (Groningen, 1989). The poems are cited from this edition.

[60] NIMEV 2295.

[61] NIMEV 2567.

[62] See further Derek Pearsall, 'The Literary Milieu of Charles d'Orléans and the Duke of Suffolk, and the Authorship of the Fairfax Sequence', in Arn (ed.), *Charles d'Orléans in England*, 145–56. On Shirley's attribution of French poetry to William, see too R. D. Perry, 'The Earl of Suffolk's French Poems and Shirley's Virtual Coteries', *Studies in the Age of Chaucer*, 38 (2016), 299–308.

which the sequence closes. But the references to Chaucer and Lydgate, as well as the decision to write in rhyme royal throughout, are features of the Fairfax Sequence that allow for its situation alongside other fifteenth-century works that sought to forge a native tradition. The Fairfax sequence is also anticipatory of subsequent developments in English writing. Together with Charles's *English Book of Love* it offers a foretaste of the lyric poetry of aristocratic introspection that would flourish in the sixteenth century.

CHAPTER 18
Chronicle and History

Andrew Galloway

Historical poetry in English presents a wide and well-populated range of forms and focuses between 1400 and 1500. In some ways this contrasts with its sparse though monumental legacy; long verse chronicles in England's two vernacular languages, French and English, began to appear within a century of the Norman Conquest, from Gaimar's *Estoire des Engleis* (c1136) and Wace's Anglo-Norman *Brut* (c1189) to Laȝamon's inventive English elaboration of Wace, *The Brut* (c1200–15), followed by another cluster from the period of Edward I and shortly after: Robert of Gloucester's English *Metrical Chronicle* (c1300), Pierre Langtoft's Anglo-Norman *Chronique* (c1307), and Robert Mannyng of Brunne's English *Chronicle* (c1338), which translated and combined Wace and Langtoft. By the fifteenth century the age of the long verse chronicle in Anglo-Norman (the 'French of England') was over. The English verse chronicle was also outmoded in some ways because of the rise of prose English history, especially the English prose *Brut*, nearly 200 copies of which survive. Initially translating the prose Anglo-Norman *Brut* (itself continued in various forms through the fourteenth century), the English prose *Brut* was continued to the mid-fifteenth century, merging and sharing continuations with prose English chronicles produced in and centred on London; John Trevisa's translation of Ranulph Higden's mid-fourteenth century *Polychronicon*, a monastic universal history, offered another option.[1] Yet in early fifteenth-century Scotland, Andrew Wyntoun wrote a 40,000-line verse universal history, the *Originall*, and near the end of the century Blind Hary produced an epic poem on *The Wallace*; in England, John Hardyng produced a long verse *Chronicle* in varying sizes for rapidly changing royal or would-be royal dedicatees from 1457 through 1465. Moreover, a plethora of short historical or political poems appeared, reporting on and slanting views of highly partisan recent events and figures, during a century of political, linguistic, and religious disruption. Historical poetry swelled in fifteenth-century England and, to a lesser extent, Scotland, encompassing epic, screed, chronicle, political caricature, 'tragedy', and allegorical satire. No European nation produced a similar range.

This, however, was in part the result of the earlier shift to prose vernacular history in France, Italy, and other European contexts, while in those regions vernacular poetry tended earlier than England to follow a classically influenced range of more 'lyrical' genres, whose properties were incompatible with historical narration. In continuing and even

---

[1] Friedrich W. Brie (ed.), *The Brut*, 2 vols., EETS, o.s. 131, 136 (London, 1906); see Lister Matheson, *The Prose Brut: The Development of a Middle English Chronicle* (Tempe, AZ, 1998); Mary-Rose McLaren, *The London Chronicles of the Fifteenth Century: A Revolution in English Writing* (Woodbridge, 2002); C. Babington and J. R. Lumby (eds), *Polychronicon Ranulphi Higden*, Rolls Series (London, 1865–86), which includes both Higden's Latin original and Trevisa's translation; John Taylor, *The Universal Chronicle of Ranulph Higden* (Oxford, 1966); A. S. G. Edwards, 'The Influence and Audience of the *Polychronicon*: Some Observations', *Proceedings of the Leeds Philosophical and Literary Society: Literary and Historical Section*, 17.6 (1980), 113–19.

expanding English historical poetry, fifteenth-century England and Scotland were anomalous. This lag, or late efflorescence, was the result both of residual traditions of earlier poetic histories—some of which, such as Robert of Gloucester's *Metrical Chronicle*, continued to be copied, updated, and continued in prose, while Wyntoun's *Originall* incorporated quantities of earlier Scottish vernacular history—and the demands of new political and historical circumstances.[2]

What follows frames this poetry in spans of political and national history, contexts meant to offer means to appreciate the poetic features as well as the historical and political perspectives of poems that were both topical and of enduring attention. These frames combine long verse 'chronicles' with short poems 'on contemporary conditions', although those are often categorically separated in guides, anthologies, and critical studies.[3] Combining these subgenres provides an opportunity for a more capacious perspective, showing both that long poems might represent more deeply settled political outlooks and that readers could derive literary or other interest from short 'political poetry' read long after the events it describes, when in fact most of the surviving copies were produced.

Lancastrian Reinventions: Henry IV

The century began with historiographical as well as historical revolution. Henry IV's usurpation of the throne in late September 1399, from his cousin Richard II, with only a weak claim of lineage, broke two centuries of varyingly successful primogeniture in royal lineage, foreshadowing a century of emphases on military conquest as the key to royal succession (Edward IV, Richard III, Henry VII).[4] This demanded new perspectives on the recent past. In parliament's official Latin 'Record and Process', also distributed as a separate pamphlet, Henry's declaration of two principles of his legitimacy was recorded, startlingly, in English: 'right line of þe blod', and 'help of my king and of my frendes'. Only after the archbishop of Canterbury's sermon opening parliament (on 1 Kings 9.17, 'This man shall reign over the people') did Henry add a third principle: 'conquest', though invoked negatively, not 'by waye of conquest' excet of 'thos persons that has ben agan the gude purpose and the commune profyt of the rewme'.[5]

---

[2] For some fifteenth-century reuses of Robert of Gloucester, see Richard Moll, *Before Malory: Reading Arthur in Later Medieval England* (Toronto, 2003), 198–216; Matthew Fisher, *Scribal Authorship and the Writing of History in Medieval England* (Columbus, OH, 2012), 178–87; Matheson, *Prose Brut*, 274. For Wyntoun, see below.

[3] See Rossell Hope Robbins, 'Poems Dealing with Contemporary Conditions', in Albert E. Hartung (ed.), *A Manual of the Writings in Middle English, 1050–1500*, 11 vols. (New Haven, CT, 1965), 5.1385–1536, 1631–1725; Edward Donald Kennedy, 'Chronicles and other Historical Writing', in Albert E. Hartung (ed.), *A Manual of the Writings in Middle English, 1050–1500*, 11 vols. (New Haven, CT, 1989), vol. 8. Rossell Hope Robbins's foundational anthology, *Historical Poems of the XIVth and XVth Centuries* (New York, 1959), excludes poems over 150 lines long (vii); in contrast, Antonia Gransden's Historical Writing in England, II: c1307 to the Sixteenth Century (London, 1982) discusses Hardyng's *Chronicle* (274–87) but disregards all short poems (as well as all historical writing from Scotland). John Scattergood's exemplary Politics and Poetry in the Fifteenth Century (London, 1971) emphasizes short 'political poetry', which Scattergood situates within his own narrative of the period's social and political history of England.

[4] See Edward Powell, 'Lancastrian England', in Christopher Allmand (ed.), *The New Cambridge Medieval History VII, c.1415–1500* (Cambridge, 1998), 457–76; Rosemary Stafford, 'Yorkist and Early Tudor England', in Allmand, (ed.), *New Cambridge Medieval History*, 477–95. Biographical dates and other basic information derive throughout from relevant entries in *ODNB*.

[5] David R. Carlson (ed.), *The Deposition of Richard II: The Record and Process of the Reconciliation and Deposition of Richard II (1399) and Related Writings* (Toronto, 2007), 58, 61.

The prose *Brut* similarly noted Henry's ascent 'be riȝt lyne' and by being 'chosen', with no mention of conquest.⁶ Chaucer, however, in his final months or days (he died on 25 October 1400) added an 'envoy' to his satiric begging poem 'To His Purse' addressed to

> O conquerour of Brutes Albyon,
> Which that by lyne and free eleccion
> Been verray kyng ...⁷

This grasped the moment's real innovation. But it left no (safe) room for narrative elaboration.

Two other English poems written around the same time offered longer accounts but as if from the final years of Richard's reign, thus avoiding the deposition itself. Both adopted the mode of allegory:

> The grene gras that was so long,
> Hit hath sclayn* a stede strong   *slain*
>   That worthy was and wyth*.   *strong*
> Wat kyng had that stede on holde,
> To juste on hym he myght be bold,
>   Als* schulde he go to fyth*.⁸   *Whenever, fight*

Thus the alliterative ballad, 'There is a busch that is forgrowe'. Sir Henry Green was the indigestible hay responsible for killing the 'stede strong', Richard, earl of Arundel, whose armorial bearing was a horse; Arundel had been executed in the 1397 'Revenge' Parliament. Green had assisted other parliamentary supporters of Richard, Sir John Bussy and Sir William Bagot, and these obscure figures became the evil trinity of all subsequent narratives. This poem's farmyard backdrop, which recalls ballads with sexual puns ('I have a gent cok crowit me day' or 'I have a newe gardyn and newe is begunne'), belies its grim judicial point; it closes with Green's and Bussy's executions at Henry's first parliament and Bagot's release under caution:⁹

> The grete bage* is so ytoron*   *i.e., Bagot, torn*
> Hit nyl holde neyther mele ne corne;
>   Hong hit up to drye!
> Wen hit is drye, then schalt thou se
> Yif hit wil amended be,
>   A beger* for to bye.   *beggar*
>   (79–84)

The early fifteenth-century alliterative allegory *Richard the Redeles*, uniquely preserved with a copy of *Piers Plowman*,¹⁰ extends the political drama of the period in which *Piers Plowman* was composed. Framed as if continuing *Piers Plowman* during one of that poem's waking interludes, it presents King Richard, 'that regned so riche and so noble ... be west'

---

⁶ *Brut*, 359; for various Latin chronicles to do with the issue of Henry's accession, see Chris Given-Wilson (trans.), *Chronicles of the Revolution, 1397–1400: The Reign of Richard II* (Manchester, 1993).
⁷ Larry D. Benson (general ed.), *The Riverside Chaucer*, 3rd edn. (Boston, 1987), lines 22–4.
⁸ NIMEV 3529; 'There is a Busch that is Forgrowe' (also called 'On King Richard Ministers'), in James M. Dean (ed.), *Medieval English Political Writings* (Kalamazoo, MI, 1996), lines 19–24.
⁹ Cf. NIMEV 1299, 1302. See Helen Barr (ed.), *The Piers Plowman Tradition: A Critical Edition of Pierce the Ploughman's Crede, Richard the Redeless, Mum and the Sothsegger and The Crowned King* (London, 1993), 269.
¹⁰ CUL MS Ll. 4. 14; James M. Dean (ed.), *Richard the Redeless and Mum and the Sothsegger* (Kalamazoo, MI, 2000); A. V. C. Schmidt (ed.), *William Langland: The Vision of Piers Plowman: A Critical Edition of the B-Text*, 2nd edn. (London, 1995).

on his late journey to Ireland (July 1399), while 'Henrri was entrid on the est half, / Whom all the londe loved' (Prol. 9–12): Richard's westward place recalls the setting sun, ironically reversing Richard's royal badge of a sun in splendor; Henry's eastern arrival is a new dawn. The poet, round-eyed, 'wuste not witterly what shulde fall' (27).

What follows is confusing. *Richard*'s scenes hint at the 1390 parliament, which condemned liveried private armies, and the 1397 'Revenge' parliament, when Richard insisted on convicting and executing those who had executed his advisors and followers in 1388. *Richard*'s temporal referents are densely layered by allegory and wordplay, conceits upon conceits. The animal avatars are followed by two bird parliaments, triggered when swarms of Richard's 'white hart' livery signs 'as hertis yheedyd and hornyd of kynde' drive everyone away or leave them 'stared for drede', until spotted by the 'eye of the Egle that our helpe brouute' (2.1–9). Figuring Henry as Eagle is both a political and literary usurpation. In *Richard*, Richard II is a partridge, whose 'nature' it is to steal the eggs and appropriate the nest of other birds. The hatchlings cry for their 'owen kynde dame' instead of the 'lurker' (3.55–8). Looking to the eagle, the 'nedy nestlingis' complain of 'busches' that 'noyed' them (75), invoking the predictable pun on Bussy, and complain 'with her billis, how they bete were' (73–8), punning on birds' and parliament's 'bills'.

Richard the Redeles offers seeming boldness in both literary and political domains. The author flaunts his cleverness by mocking an uncomprehending reader: 'Hicke Hevyheed, hard is thi nolle!' (3.66). This implies a standard of political savvy that reframes the rebuke of not knowing Christian doctrine in *Piers Plowman* when Holy Church scolds Will. 'Thow doted daffe! ... dulle are thi wittes. / To litel Latyn thow lernedest, leode, in thi youthe' (B.1.140–1). It seems doubtful, however, that the poet of *Richard* addressed actual parliamentarians, unlike Gower with his *Cronica tripertita*. Evaluating Richard II's fall was a safe way to dissect a courtly world gone awry for a readership widening beyond the court or parliament. This secularized pedagogy is consistent with other items in *Richard*'s manuscript, including astronomical and physiognomic treatises in English, elsewhere found in Latin, and an arithmetic treatise in English that, like the poem (4.53–4), mentions the exotic Arabic null.[11] This suggests a need to distinguish official propaganda from motifs taken up widely to indicate political loyalties, in a period when such declarations could be the difference between life or death. Even speculative words were risky.[12]

Other responses to these difficult years were anticlerical ones such as the diatribe with the post-medieval title 'The Plowman's Tale', delivered by an allegorical Pelican, which attacks proud clergy who 'han more myght in Englande here / Than hat the kynge and all hys lawes' (637–8).[13] The Pelican particularly vilifies monks, 'as proude as prynce in pall / In meate, and drynke, and all thynge' (999–1000).

If such stray Wycliffite poetry can be glimpsed among the political and historical writings of early fifteenth-century England, it hardly defines the consensus of English views. The Lancastrian regime made a point of introducing new secular powers for punishing heresy, starting with the king's role in commanding the burning of William Sawtre in 1399,

---

[11] See Andrew Galloway, '*Piers Plowman* and the Schools', *Yearbook of Langland Studies*, 6 (1992), 89–107 (at 103–4).

[12] See the cases in Isobel Thornley, 'Treason by Words in the Fifteenth Century', *English Historical Review*, 32 (1917), 556–61.

[13] 'The Plowman's Tale', in James Dean (ed.), *Six Ecclesiastical Satires* (Kalamazoo, MI, 1991), 51–101, which summarizes the complex problems of transmission and later adaptation that surround this text; see further Darryl Ellison, '"Take It as a Tale": Reading the *Plowman's Tale* as if it Were', *Chaucer Review*, 49 (2014), 77–101.

a position quickly formalized in 1401 in the statute *De heretico comburendo* (concerning the burning of heretics), which remained key to Lancastrian public postures.¹⁴ Given Lollards' efforts to make their sermons and other religious writings available in English, the king's parallel efforts to use English in official contexts or perhaps in patronage of English poetry like 'There is a Busch' and *Richard the Redeles*, made crushing Lollardy, the 'English heresy', all the more crucial. Royal efforts to invoke but control English poetry through historical narrative increased under Henry's son, Henry V. For a time those efforts were highly successful, though precisely because that success is so notable it is pertinent to bear in mind that even during the height of royal patronage of English historical poetry, England was not the only nation using English verse to write national history.

Wyntoun's Scotland

In the course of the fourteenth century both Scottish origin myths and documents prepared in support of Edward I's insistence on his role as Scotland's overlord were variously drafted into the historiographical war that accompanied hostilities between Scotland and England. By the fifteenth century, open war faded into occasional invasions, attacks, and ongoing Scottish military support for France.¹⁵ In 1408–*c*20, Andrew Wyntoun, prior of a house of Austin canons in Lochleven, Fife, wrote and repeatedly revised his 40,000-line octosyllabic verse *Originall* ('history of beginnings'), which achieved its scale partly by translating the kinds of Latin sources used in clerical 'universal histories' to provide a foundation of world history, such as Orosius and Martinus Polonus, followed by British history translated from Geoffrey of Monmouth.¹⁶ Wyntoun then completed his account by compiling and supplementing recent Scottish historical poetry in English, especially the fourteenth-century epic *The Bruce*, by John Barbour (1330–95), then sections of Barbour's lost *Oryginalle* (a history of the earlier origins of Stewarts in English verse), to which Wyntoun added long sections from another lost poem in English covering David II's and Robert II's reign, all smoothly integrated and modified by Wyntoun's own transitions, comments, and continuations, but noting where other poets began so that he 'walde vsurpe na fayme [*fame*] / Langer, na walde ber na blayme, / Þan he deserwit [*deserved*]' (8.2945–7).¹⁷

Wyntoun's work treats vernacular historical poetry as sources to be compiled in the clerical mode. But this invited clashes between standards of one kind of 'history' and another. Barbour, for example, blandly assured readers that everything he offered in *The Bruce* was true:

---

¹⁴ Peter McNiven, *Heresy and Politics in the Reign of Henry IV: The Burning of John Badby* (Woodbridge, 1987), 85–9.

¹⁵ See A. D. M. Barrell, *Medieval Scotland* (Cambridge, 2000), 92–136; Marjorie Drexler, 'Fluid Prejudice: Scottish Origin Myths in the Later Middle Ages', in Joel Rosenthal and Colin Richmond (eds), *People, Politics and Community in the Later Middle Ages* (Gloucester, 1987), 92–136; Emily Wingfield, *The Trojan Legend in Medieval Scottish Literature* (Cambridge, 2014), 10–15.

¹⁶ NIMEV 399; references to Wyntoun are to F. J. Amours (ed.), *The Original Chronicle of Andrew Wyntoun*, STS 50, 53, 54, 56, 57, 60, 6 vols. (Edinburgh, 1908–14), cited by book and line.

¹⁷ For the lost verse chronicle, see Stephen Boardman, 'Chronicle Propaganda in Fourteenth-Century Scotland: Robert the Steward, John of Fordun and the 'Anonymous Chronicle', *The Scottish Historical Review*, 76 (1997), 23–43.

Storys to rede ar delatibill*   *are delightful*
Suppos that thai be nocht bot fabill,   *Even if they are nothing except fable*
Than suld* storys that suthfast wer   *Therefore should*
And* thai war said on gud maner   *If*
Have doubill plesance in heryng ...[18]
(1.1–5)

Echoes show that Wyntoun had this in mind when opening his own ponderous work, but he struck notes of uncertainty, even at the prospect of translating prose Latin materials into English verse:

For storyis to heire ar delectable*,   *delightful*
Suppose þat sum be nocht bot fable;
And set* to þis I gif my will,   *In addition*
My wit I ken sa skant þartill   *I acknowledge is so feeble for this*
That I drede saire þame till offend   *sorely dread to offend those*
That can me and my work amend   *Who can amend*
Gif* I writ ouþer maire or lese*,   *If; either more or less*
Bot as* þe story beris* witness.   *Except as; bears*
(1.27–38)

Instead of Barbour's carefree confidence, Wyntoun started hemmed by doubts. On one side are standards of 'truth' that, as in many earlier Latin prose chroniclers, depended on fidelity to textual sources; on the other arise suspicions that, however 'dilectable', some vernacular sources 'be nocht bot fable'. On yet another side, readers who do not hear exactly the accounts they expect were ready to pounce.

These challenges probably arose less from lack of poetic talent than from efforts to address both secular readers, starting with his patron, the local lord John of Wemyss, and clerics.[19] The need for Scottish unity was surely felt during the long absence of James I, imprisoned in England for the first eighteen years of his reign (1406–24). Since Scotland 'had simply not yet developed ... the separation of the person of the king and the king's government',[20] this was a volatile period. But the real problem was Wyntoun's evasion of dogmatic nationalism. Wyntoun paralleled Fordun, author of the fourteenth-century Latin prose *Chronica*, in tracing the origins of the Scots to Greece and Egypt via Spain and Ireland, but his list of generations of Pictish kings using other sources indicated just how long the Picts had inhabited Scotland before the Scots (2.750–850), undermining Fordun's emphases on the rights of Scota, the Egyptian princess central to established views of Scottish origins. Wyntoun moreover traced the Irish not as the expeditioners of Scota but, according to Geoffrey of Monmouth's scheme of the colonization of 'Albion' by Brutus, as other descendants of the Trojans (2.770).[21] Wyntoun even invoked from Geoffrey of Monmouth the flight of the people of Albanact (ruler of Albania or Scotland) to the protection of his brother and overlord Locrine—a key element of the English case for overlordship. Yet Wyntoun made a subtle point while folding that into the origin stories. Since

---

[18] A. A. M. Duncan (ed. and trans.), *The Bruce* (Edinburgh, 1999).
[19] For Sir John Wemyss, see William Fraser, *Memorials of the family of Wemyss of Wemyss*, vol. 1 (Edinburgh, 1888), 44–58.
[20] Jenny Wormald, 'Scotland, 1406–1513', in Allmand (ed.), *New Cambridge Medieval History*, 514–31 (at 522).
[21] Michel D. Reeve (ed.) and Neil Wright (trans.), *The History of the Kings of Britain: An Edition and Translation of De gestis Britonum (Historia Regum Britanniae)* (Woodbridge, 2007), par. 23–4.

Albanact's people did not invite Locrine to their land but fled to enter Locrine's, Scotland was technically 'wast nere hande (*nearly waste*) lange eftyr (*after*) that eft (*still*), / Qwhil (*while*) Scottis and þe Peythitis were / In til it cummande (*coming into it*), as ȝhe sal here (*shall hear*)' (3.598–600). 'Waste', unoccupied land belonging to no one, carries legal force. Locrine at least would have no rights to such territory, whatever the relative rights of the Scots and Picts.

In spite of Wyntoun's moderate nationalism, his poem is an archive of Scottish literary antiquities. Narrating the momentous death of Alexander III (d. 1286), Wyntoun quoted in full a lament that remains one of the earliest surviving Scottish ballads:

> Þis sange was made of hym for þi:
> 'Qwhen Alexander our kynge was dede,
>   Þat Scotlande lede in lauche and le,
> Away was sons of alle and brede,
>   Off wyne and wax, of gamyn and gle.
> Our golde was changit in to lede.
>   Christ, borne in virgynyte,
> Succoure Scotland, and ramede,
>   Þat is stade in perplexite'.
>
> (7.2620–8)

The preservation of such a poem shows his connoisseurship of historical poetry. This is also evident in his reference to an alliterative poem on King Arthur made by 'Hucheon' (apparently the *Alliterative Morte Arthure*), noting that Hucheon's (and the *Alliterative Morte*'s) impossible reference to an 'emperor' Lucius could be explained on metrical grounds: 'þe cadence' required Hucheon to write 'emperoure' instead of 'procuratoure', which has at least the support of one passage in Geoffrey of Monmouth (5.4319–22). This is early vernacular philology, but also another instance of concern that poetry might include 'fable', a danger that remained part of Wyntoun's standards in assessing historical poetry.

Wyntoun ceased with an invitation for others to finish his work, a sign he wanted the genre to continue in the ambitious form he invented of universal Scottish vernacular history:

> Off þis tretice þe last ende
> Til bettyr þan I am*, I commende.   *To those better than I*
> (9.33–4)

Only prose continuations, however, appear in its manuscripts.[22] His only poetic follower was the bloodthirsty Blind Hary, who in his vehemently anti-English *The Wallace* (*c*1476–8) used Wyntoun's mention of William Wallace as his only internally dated scene (Wyntoun, 8.2029–48; *cf. Wallace*, 6.107–271).[23] While Wyntoun's work lay unprinted, *The Wallace* became the most frequently printed work of Scottish literature before the poems

---

[22] Three of the surviving nine copies of Wyntoun's poem include a terse prose continuation of Scottish history to 1482: Edinburgh, National Library of Scotland, Advocates' MSS 19. 2. 3 and 19. 2. 4; BL MS Royal 17 D XX.

[23] See Anne McKim (ed.), *The Wallace* (Edinburgh, 2003).

of Robert Burns. Burns thought it one of the two best books he ever read (the other was the life of Hannibal, whose hatred of Romans might have struck a similar chord).[24]

Mythic Henry V

Meanwhile, English kings had the resources to seek mythic status in their own time. A poem in nineteen eight-line stanzas, in BodL MS Digby 102, another manuscript that includes *Piers Plowman*, focuses on a royal coronation as an event of sacred summoning:

> Glade in God, call hom ȝoure herte!
> In ioye and blisse, ȝoure merþe encres,
> And kepe Goddis lawe in querte.
> Þes holy tyme, lete sorwe ases;
> Among oure self, God sende vs pes.
> Þerto, eche man be boun
> To letten fooles of here res*;   *rebellion*
> Stonde wiþ þe kyng, mayntene þe croun.[25]

It is filled with Easter liturgy and imagery. It may well refer to Henry V, since his coronation in 1413 was 9 April, two weeks before Easter (the manuscript dates from the first quarter of the century). It enacts as well as describes a 'now' of celebration, 'Þes holy tyme', which expands into a broad new dispensation of royal law and power. The opening line demands a pious act by pious listeners, but the next imperative demands repression of foolish rebellion ('res'). The final imperative, a refrain, is a battle-cry that would be at home at Agincourt or Rouen.

Topicality hovers over most of these lyrics though it is hard to see precise references. Most of the Digby poems invoke liturgical texts and religious lyrical traditions. But liturgy can be as topical as parliamentary discourse. Not only did Henry found the double monastery at Syon, he periodically ordered new liturgy, as when after a victory at sea near Harfleur in 1416 (when he reportedly heard that the soldiers were 'as eager as blood-brothers for one another's success') he instructed the clerks of his chapel to add hymns praising God, including an antiphon to St George, a saint otherwise celebrated at Easter.[26]

Henry V's reign conveys the impression of comprehensive royal promotion and control of historical writing. The subject of two biographies in Latin, one prose and one verse, Henry V was a more successful military figure than his father and a subtler propagandist, partly as beneficiary of the only non-controversial transfer of power through primogeniture of the fifteenth century. He expanded his father's occasional use of English for official communications into a regular custom, and Henry's presence or guidance is discernible in a number of English poems.[27]

The Crowned King features a direct spokesman to a king using parliamentary language recognizably contemporary with Henry's reign.[28] This 144-line alliterative poem is a vision,

---

[24] Those 'gave me more pleasure than any two books I ever read again ... the story of Wallace poured a Scotish prejudice in my veins which will boil along there till the flood-gates of life shut in eternal rest': J. DeLancey Ferguson and G. Ross Roy (eds), *The Letters of Robert Burns*, 2 vols., 2nd edn. (Oxford, 1985), 1.136.

[25] NIMEV 910; Helen Barr (ed.), *The Digby Poems: A New Edition of the Lyrics*, (Exeter, 2009), no. 12, 1–8.

[26] Frank Taylor and John S. Roskell (eds and trans), *Gesta Henrici Quinti: The Deeds of Henry the Fifth* (Oxford, 1975), 151–7.

[27] NIMEV 605; see Malcolm Richardson, 'Henry V, the English Chancery, and Chancery English', *Speculum*, 55 (1980), 726–50.

[28] Barr (ed.), *Piers Plowman Tradition*, 203–10.

but as with other Lancastrian dream-visions, it unfolds with sharp contemporary detail. The dreamer is seven miles outside Southampton, on the eve of Corpus Christi of 1415 (29 May); after a night in 'melodye and mirthes among my makes' reading 'romaunces and reuelyng', he falls asleep near dawn (20–8). In the subsequent vision a king asks parliament for a 'soleyn subsidie to susteyne his werres' (36). This too is tightly topical: having promised no further demands for subsidies in 1413 for relaunching the French wars, Henry V appealed a year later for an unprecedented ('soleyn') round of tenths and fifteenths as a war chest for his expedition to Harfleur and Agincourt; he would depart from Southampton.[29] The poem's economic focus includes the stipulation in the November 1414 parliament that the subsidy should be levied proportionate to wealth: 'they that rekened were riche by reson and skyle / Shuld pay a parcell for here poure neighbowres' (39–40).

The narrowly topical focus expands to larger advice. Although the waking narrator is a dissolute figure, his alter ego in the dream is a bold and eloquent 'clerk' who rises before parliament to address the king, like the truth-telling 'Goliard' in *Piers Plowman* who advises that king to live by law as well as impose it (*PP* Prol.139–45). But the clerk in *Crowned King* simply endorses the king's claim to apportion the requested subsidies by income, while noting how precious his subjects' loyalty is over any mere money:

> The loue of thi liegmen, that to thi lawe are bounde,
> Take hit for a tresour of hem that are true,
> That may the more availl in a myle wey
> Thanne moche of thy mukke that manhode loueth neuere.
> (61–4)

The clerk proceeds to discourse on rulership, though he rejects payment for such advice: 'to pike a thonk with plesaunce my profit were but simple' (48). Avoid flatterers (110); learn to read ('lere lettrewre in thy youthe, as a lord befalleth'; 113); practice fighting (123); avoid receiving gifts, but give gifts tactically to those who 'fele agrevel' (126); eschew covetousness (130–2).

It is possible to think of the poem as propaganda commissioned by Henry 'for home consumption' while Henry departed for Agincourt.[30] More recently, Jenni Nuttall situates the poem within a wider 'conversation' defining Lancastrian kingship, in which debates various arguments were made for the king to accept loyalty over cash, increasingly difficult to contribute to the king during the period's severe currency shortage.[31] Sharper warnings are implied as well. The poem's emphasis on exempting the poor from taxes recalls the risk of popular rebellion, like the poll taxes that led to the Peasants' Revolt of 1381. Such tax revolts (of which 1381 was merely the best known) were sometimes led by lower clergy, like the poem's narrator who is a dissolute, romance-reading goliard, revelling with others of his kind, 'frendes and felawes, fremde men (strangers) and other' (18). That his 'reuelyng' begins 'on Corpus Cristi even' (19) parallels the start of the 1381 revolt as well, exploiting the feast's opportunity for parodying authority.[32] Using the form of *Piers Plowman* adds to

---

[29] See Jenni Nuttall, *The Creation of Lancastrian Kingship* (Cambridge, 2007), 103–8.

[30] Derek Pearsall, 'Hoccleve's *Regement of Princes*: The Poetics of Royal Self-Representation', *Speculum*, 89 (1994), 386–410 (at 393).

[31] Nuttall, *The Creation of Lancastrian Kingship*.

[32] See Margaret Aston, 'Corpus Christi and Corpus Regni: Heresy and the Peasants' Revolt', *Past & Present*, 143 (1994), 3–47.

this message, since the rebels of 1381 repeatedly invoked that poem and its title figure; one chronicle even called a rebel leader 'Piers Plowman'.[33]

Poems on Agincourt (1415) were certainly sponsored by the royal court, though we need not assume all poetry on that battle was. The most famous is the 'Agincourt Carol', whose music survives (two voices in octave-separated unison except for the second line of the burden, where they harmoniously divide):

> There dukys & erlys, lorde & barone,
> Were take & slayne, & þat wel sone;
> And summe were ladde in-to lundone,
> With ioye and merthe & grete renone.
>   Deo gratias anglia   England, render thanks to God for the victory.
>   Redde pro victoria.[34]
>   (17–20)

This is preserved in two collections of religious carols, both monastic.[35] Amid such liturgical timelessness, the carol retains historical vestiges. It mentions, for instance, the French prisoners who were 'take & slayne, & þat wel sone', directly followed by the king's triumph. The prose *Brut* presents this as the battle's turning point, using language whose parallels suggest a common source: 'euery man scholde sle his prysoner þat he hadde take; ... and þus our King ... hadde þat day þe victory' (*Brut*, 379).

Those works embrace the military benefits of the executions, but this was not common practice, if only because it meant loss of ransoms. One *Brut* declares that the English mistook local French citizens watching the battle for French reinforcements, leading to Henry's execution order, '& þat was a myghty losse to Engelond, & a gret sorw to Fraunce' (*Brut*, 597). After the end of the house of Lancaster, the prisoners' executions were sharply criticized. John Hardyng's second, Yorkist version of his *Chronicle*, dedicated to King Edward IV, describes the order as 'fell and cruell'; to be sure, this is selective criticism, since Edward's own battles included executions of prisoners as at Towton (1461), when forty-two knights taken prisoner were executed.[36]

Little criticism is evident from Henry's own time, even in works outside likely royal control. A vigorous alliterative epyllion on Agincourt is partly preserved in a mid-century London chronicle, BL MS Cotton Cleopatra C IV, apparently assembled for personal use.[37] We know of this poem's existence only because the prose composer began directly quoting it after starting in hasty prose paraphrase:

> And in Aȝyngcorte felde owre kynge faught with þe Frensshmen þe Fryday tofore þe day of Symond and Jude ... þer men myght see a semble sade (*sombre conflict*), that turnyd many on to tene and tray (*affliction and grief*), for many a lorde þer ryght low lay, þat commen was of blod ful gent, By evensong tym, soþely (*truly*) to say; þere holpe us God omnipotent.

---

[33] M. V. Clarke and V. H. Galbraith, 'The Deposition of Richard II', *Bulletin of the John Rylands Library*, 14 (1930), 125–81 (at 164).
[34] NIMEV 2716; Robbins, *Historical Poems*, 91–2. For the music, see John Stevens (ed.), *Mediaeval Carols*, Musica Britannica IV (London, 2018), 6.
[35] See Stevens, *Medieval Carols*, for details.
[36] Charles Ross, *Edward IV* (New Haven, CT, 1974, 1997), 37.
[37] NIMEV 3213; TM 1462; see Charles Lethbridge Kingsford (ed.), *Chronicles of London* (Oxford, 1905), ix–x, 117–52; McLaren, *London Chronicles*, 45.

Stedes þer stumbelyd in þat stownde*,	*time of trouble*
þat stood stere stuffed under stele;	*strong encased in armour*
With gronyng grete þei felle to grownde,	
Her sydes federid* whan þei gone fele*.	*'feathered' (with arrows); fall*
Owr lorde þe kynge he foght ryght wele	
Scharpliche on hem his spere he spent,	
Many on seke* he mad þat sele*,	*hurt; on that occasion*
Þorow myght of god omnipotent.[38]	

The poem shows an ability to fill out a stanza with verbal variety if not precision. The preservation of this vigorous poem in a London commonplace book shows how the wider tradition of alliterative poetry, cultivated in the west and north, continued to circulate in the metropolis, as did *Piers Plowman*.

Looser ballads on Agincourt appear elsewhere. One is attributed in one copy to John Lydgate, but the poem shows none of his capabilities.[39] Its refrain epitomizes the poem's slack narrative and strained rhymes:

Oure kyng sente into France ful rathe*,	*quickly*
Hys bassatours* bothe faire and free;	*ambassadors*
His owne right to have;	
That is, Gyan and Normandie ...	
Wot* ye right wel that thus it was	*know*
Gloria tibi Trinitas*.[40]	*Glory to you, Trinity*

The poem's most stirring phrases are all found in the prose *Brut* (378), where, much as in the poem, Henry V asks at daybreak what time it is, leads a prayer, then charges into battle. The prose is tautly suspenseful, swiftly advancing the action; the poem requires twenty-four lines plus three refrains (stanzas 14–16) to convey the exchange. This suggests one kind of relationship between historical verse and prose: a poet's conversion of the *Brut*'s prose into ballade stanzas, inflating the results to fit available time or vellum. Other copies of this poem show the kind of textual degeneration associated with oral transmission over time: an eighteenth-century transcription of a lost copy presents it without refrain and in half the lines.[41]

Entirely different standards of concise precision of reportage are evident in John Page's *Siege of Rouen* treating the siege of 1418–19. Sometimes preserved half-absorbed into the *Brut*'s prose, though also independently, this poem was evidently finished before a ceasefire beginning 26 March 1420 preceding the Treaty of Troyes (which the poet would have mentioned), and certainly before the death of Gilbert Umfraville on 22 March 1421 (whom the poet compliments; 687).[42] Opening with well-worn minstrel tropes, the poet redefined that role as purveyor of eyewitness information:

Lystenythe vnto me a lytylle space,
And I shalle telle you howe hyt was:

---

[38] Kingsford, *Chronicles*, 120.
[39] NIMEV 969; Henry Noble MacCracken (ed.), *The Minor Poems of John Lydgate, Part I*, EETS, e.s. 107 (London, 1911), xlvii.
[40] From BL MS Harley 565, in Nicholas Harris Nicolas and Edward Tyrrell (eds), *A Chronicle of London from 1080 to 1483 Written in the Fifteenth Century* (London, 1827), 216–33. The lines here are unnumbered.
[41] BL MS Cotton Vitellius D XII, Part II; see Nicholas Harris Nicolas (ed.), *History of the Battle of Agincourt and of The Expedition of Henry V into France in 1415* (London, 1833), 303–25.
[42] NIMEV 979; Joanna Bellis (ed.), *The Siege of Rouen*, MET 51 (Heidelberg, 2015), xxxi.

And the better telle I may,
For at that sege with the kyng I lay ...
(19–22)

The detail bears this out. A chilling instance is the description of the poor expelled from the city to conserve its resources, then left without food or water in the ditch Henry had cut around the city because the English will not let them depart:

> Many a hundryd in a route,
> That hyt was pytte ham to see;
> Wemmen come knelyng on hyr kne
> With hyr chyldryn in hyr armys
> To socuvre* them from harmys,   *protect*
> Olde men knelynge them by,
> And made a dolfulle cry,
> And alle they sayden at onys thenne,
> 'Haue marcy vppon vs, ye Englysche men!'
> Oure men gaffe them of oure brede
> Thoughe they to us were neuere so quede*,   *hostile*
> And harme vnto them dyd they non
> But made them to the dyche gone.
> (538–50)

With its natural rhythms enhancing the poignancy, their situation becomes one of the poem's main focuses. But Page never ventured overall judgement, though he lingered over his eyewitness reportage. Describing a negotiation concerning the exiles, the narrative conveys a sense of awe in witnessing the powerful making history. The poet describes in detail the efforts by a group of Rouenese sent to resolve the problem, including their attempts to be noticed, their request to address the king, the delays and courtesies of every step. The narrative follows Umfraville as he stops to inform each of the king's three brothers of this request, 'tolde hem thys tydyngys alle in fere' (699), though his only 'tydyngys' are that the citizens wish a royal audience. The narrator prolonged his attention on Henry as if to capture every detail:

> Hys countenans dyd he not abate,
> But stylle he stode and in astate.
> Or* hym lyste to geue an answere,   *before*
> He sayde, 'Felowys, hoo put them there,
> Into the dyche of that cytte?
> I putte them not there and þat wot ye ...
> Let them fynde that they haue sought;
> They abode in the cytte whylys they mought'*.   *were able*
> (839–48)

The description takes as long as the experience. The fate of the outcasts, condemned to slow starvation, is treated poignantly: 'wommen holdyn in hyr armys, / Dede chyldryn, in hyr barmys, / And the chyldryn sokyng in the pappe / Within a dede womans lappe' (1007–10). No connection is made to the king's decision, whose argument is left to stand for itself.

Personal touches were part of the trend towards authorial individuality and self-inscription in all writing of this period. The anonymous *Gesta Henrici Quinti*, for instance, describing how Henry's army advancing on Agincourt was blocked by a river mentions the prayers of 'I who am writing, and many of the rest of the army'.[43] Writing in the ambit of Henry V seems particularly to have featured writers' personal experience, as if to emphasize authenticity and spontaneity, however guided by royal suggestion.

Hoccleve and Lydgate

The personal voice is particularly evident in the two most famous poets of Henry's reign. John Lydgate's connection to the royal family began c1408, when then-Prince Henry wrote to the abbot of St Edmunds requesting that a certain monk, J.L, continue his studies at Oxford.[44] Even before Henry's support of Lydgate's studies began paying off, Henry also drew poetic labour from Thomas Hoccleve, a former associate of Chaucer's who worked at the Privy Seal. The restocking of poetic supporters was timely. In 1408, John Gower, Lancastrian supporter par excellence, died, after several years of blindness; Henry IV was so ill that suggestions arose for him to transfer the crown to his son, although he did not die until 1413. The moment was ripe for Prince Henry to start to set his mark.[45]

Much of Hoccleve's poetry is topical: not only the extraordinary 2000-line self-dramatizing introduction to the *Regiment of Princes* (1411) but also the lyric on the reburial of Richard II in Westminster in 1413. In the latter, Hoccleve dwelled, rather incongruously, on Henry V's religious piety and orthodoxy; this was probably part of the anti-Wycliffite posture that Hoccleve emphasized for Henry, and implicitly himself. Hoccleve's anti-heretical posture is elaborated in his poem denouncing Sir John Oldcastle, the former captain in Henry's wars who fled charges of heresy while Henry journeyed to Harfleur and Agincourt in 1415:

> Looke how our cristen Prince, our lige lord,
> With many a lord & knyght beyond the Sea,
> Laboure in armes / & thow hydest thee![46]

Hoccleve's tone is regretful, while urging 'the ax or hamer of penance' (90); a combination that parallels Henry's efforts to persuade his old comrade in arms to renounce his Lollardy.[47] With Henry away on campaign, Hoccleve's offer of 'pitee' (3) to repenting sinners like Oldcastle is surprisingly authoritative. Hoccleve's final appeal for Oldcastle to 'humble ... thee' to the king (512) suggests a diplomat's message. Such appeals to Oldcastle would serve to confirm that the king was exhausting every means of rehabilitating his fellow soldier, though in the end Henry would lower the hammer of penance himself, ordering in 1417 the recalcitrant Oldcastle to be drawn, hanged, and burned, thus asserting beyond doubt Henry's own orthodoxy, which his long support of Oldcastle and still others might have called into question.[48]

---

[43] F. Taylor and J. S. Roskell (eds), *Gesta Henrici Quinti. The Deeds of Henry the Fifth* (Oxford, 1975), 66–7.
[44] Derek Pearsall, *John Lydgate (1371–1449): A Bio-bibliography*, English Literary Studies 71 (Victoria, BC, 1997), 56, item 8.
[45] See Christopher Allmand, *Henry V* (Berkeley, CA, 1992), 41–53.
[46] NIMEV 3407; F. J. Furnivall (ed.), *Hoccleve's Works: I. The Minor Poems*, EETS, e.s. 61 and 73, rev. reprint in one vol., by Jerome Mitchell and A. I. Doyle (Oxford, 1973), 24, lines 499–501.
[47] Taylor and Roskell (eds), *Gesta Henrici Quinti*, 183–5.
[48] McNiven, *Heresy and Politics*, 155, 224.

By then, however, Hoccleve seems himself to have been unwelcome at court. His capering self-satire in poems like the '*Male Regle de Thomas Hoccleve*' (c1405),⁴⁹ portraying his London and Westminster outings with his fellow clerks of the Privy Seal (including Hoccleve's small pleasures such as hearing boat-taxi operators call him 'maistir'), like the self-portraiture in the *Regiment of Princes* of his lack of coin and literary insecurities, is entertainingly unstable, but Hoccleve's suitability for courtly representation seems dubious after his descent into madness in 1414. Although he recovered by the end of the year, his 'þouȝtful maladie'⁵⁰ left him explaining and representing himself rather than the king, as when he explained how he scrutinized his face in the mirror before going out to be sure it presented a plausibly sane expression: 'This countinaunce, I am sure, and þis chere, / If I it forthe vse, is nothing repreuable' (168). His subsequent poems show him searching for a new patron.

Meanwhile, Lydgate was well launched with the massive *The Troy Book* (1412–20), commissioned by 'the eldest sone of the noble kyng' shortly before Henry IV's death.⁵¹ In his prologue, Lydgate elaborately presented the prince's purposes. Henry rejoiced in reading 'bokys of antiquite' for models of 'virtu', just as he sought that quality in 'pleies marcyal' (74–87). Reading ancient historical poetry was analogous to tournament training. Wider goals, especially inculcating nationalism, emerge as well in the prince's commission 'Of hem of Troye in englysche to translate':

> By-cause he wolde that to hyȝe and lowe
> The noble story openly wer knowe
> In oure tonge, aboute in euery age,
> And y-writen as wel in oure langage
> As in latyn and in frensche it is;
> That of the story þe trouthe we nat mys
> No more than doth eche other nacioun;
> This was the fyn* of his entencioun.   *aim*
> (110–18)

This agenda likely covered Henry's commission of Lydgate's *Siege of Thebes* as well (c1422), although that work lacks a dedication, perhaps because Henry died before it could be presented to him.

Henry V seems never to have tapped Lydgate for direct propaganda, discreetly left to the composers of the 'Agincourt Carol' and Henry's biographers. That changed with Henry's death in 1422. A long campaign ensued to bolster the legitimacy of Henry VI's dual crowns of France and England (according to the treaty of Troyes) after Charles VI's death a few months after Henry's. New coinage was immediately issued in France juxtaposing the shields of England and France. Spectacular civic entries confirmed Henry's kingships: Paris in 1431, London in 1432. There the eleven-year-old Henry VI was brought before a billboard in Cheapside depicting his lineage next to the tree of Jesse, linking him directly to Creation.⁵²

Lydgate was enlisted in this effort in 1426 by Richard Beauchamp, earl of Warwick, a close associate of the duke of Bedford. Lydgate was commissioned to translate a French

---

⁴⁹ NIMEV 2538.
⁵⁰ NIMEV 124; 'My Compleinte', from 'The Series', in Roger Ellis (ed.), *Thomas Hoccleve: My Compleinte and Other Poems* (Exeter, 2001), 21.
⁵¹ Henry Bergen (ed.), *Troy Book*, EETS e.s. 97, 103, 106, 126 (London, 1906–35), Prologue, lines 74, 95.
⁵² See J. W. McKenna, 'Henry VI of England and the Dual Monarchy: Aspects of Royal Political Propaganda, 1422–1432', *Journal of the Warburg and Courtauld Institutes*, 28 (1965), 145–62.

poem explaining Henry's lineage that Bedford had commissioned from a French poet, Laurence Calot, which was displayed in Notre Dame beside a banner showing entwining French and English royal genealogies from Saints Edward and Louis to Henry VI.[53] The prologue and epilogue of Lydgate's 'Title and Pedigree of Henry VI' are nearly as long (133 lines) as his translation of Calot's poem (193 lines). Lydgate's elaborate description of the commission itself shows the kind of care he took attending to Henry V's purposes in commissioning the *Troy Book*. His prologue also makes clear his sense of his own value in his monastic independence from the court. In his most conversational style, Lydgate's prologue explains his commission amid hopes for the king's felicitous future—'of age ny fyve yere ren, / Borne to be kyng of worthie reamys two', adding, 'And God graunt that it may be so' (29–32). The prayer was conventional, but it implied the new king's need to prove his worth. The epilogue unfolds an elaborate astronomical dating of Lydgate's commission: 20 July 1426, specified by the 'houses' and degrees of each planet: his commission seems the event being celebrated. Such digressions show that Lydgate could be Chaucerian whenever he wanted, and that royal lineages unfolded within a larger cosmos. Henry's true 'place' would emerge in God's time, however sped by human hopes

> That he may se his generacioun
> Vnto the forteth multiplicacioun*   *fourth generation*
> Victoriously for to regnen here,
> Aftir this lif aboue the sterres clere,
> God him graunt oonly of his grace
> Of mercy þer for to haue a place.
> (324–9)

A hint of alternate outcomes appears in the biblical 'unto the fourth generation', paralleling God's curse on 'those who hurt Me' (Deuteronomy 5.9, Exodus 20.5).

Probably in 1426 Lydgate also wrote a set of rhyme-royal stanzas on 'The Kings of England Sithen William the Conqueror', covering the reign of each king until Henry VI's double coronation; he might have written a poem celebrating the entry into London of Henry's new wife, Margaret of Anjou, as part of a treaty in 1444.[54] Lydgate's sideline in royal propaganda waned as he and the king grew older. He did not live to see hopes for Henry dashed. But Lydgate's hundreds of 'tragedies' of ancient kings and heroes in the *Fall of Princes* confirmed a pattern, established by Boccaccio and Chaucer, of contemplating the disasters of the powerful, raising questions of how character and historical 'fortune' intertwine.[55] One copy of his 'Kings of England Sithen William the Conqueror' uses Henry to exemplify not a triumphant recipient of 'title and pedigree' but a modern tragedy:

> in his youthe he had grete noblenes bothe in Englond and ffraunce.
> And in his last daies ther fell grete distaunce
> through his false counsell that was couetowse.
> he put downe from the Crowne by all the Comyns,
> So he Regned kynge here all-moste xxxix yeres.[56]

---

[53] NIMEV 3808; B. J. H. Rowe, 'King Henry VI's Claim to France: In Picture and Poem', *The Library*, 4th series, 13 (1933), 77–88.
[54] NIMEV 3632 and 882; and Robert Withington, 'Queen Margaret's Entry into London, 1445', *Modern Philology*, 13 (1915), 53–7 (not known to MacCracken).
[55] See Henry Ansgar Kelly, *Chaucerian Tragedy* (Woodbridge, 1997); Nigel Mortimer, *John Lydgate's Fall of Princes: Narrative Tragedy in Its Literary and Political Contexts* (Oxford, 2005).
[56] London, Lambeth Palace MS 306, fol. 18ᵛ; Linne R. Mooney, 'Lydgate's "Kings of England" and Another Verse Chronicle of the Kings', *Viator*, 20 (1989), 255–90 (at 259).

This copy of Lydgate's 'Kings of England' is accompanied by poems supporting Henry VI's Yorkist antagonists, Richard of York, his son Edward, and Richard Neville, earl of Warwick (the 'kingmaker').[57] It is one of at least thirty-six copies, plus a broadside, of Lydgate's poem, whose adaptability to new royal regimes and perspectives, and easily memorized format, made it a 'paragon' for political propaganda.[58] Its wide circulation shows an alternate legacy of Lydgate's historical poetry, beyond the sumptuous copies in noble houses that his ancient histories enjoyed. It also shows how inadequately Henry VI controlled his poetic image, particularly by comparison to his self-mythologizing father.

The Tragedy of Henry VI

Henry VI was often but distantly portrayed during his reign. The most moderate comments indicate a naively pious and extravagantly overgenerous, though elegant man, '*simplex et rectus*', in Abbot Whethamstede of St Alban's notoriously inscrutable comment. Hardyng, who dedicated his first version of his *Chronicle* (discussed below) to Henry, remarked he was an idiot; John Blacman, former precentor of Eton College which Henry founded and whose splendid architecture he helped design, described him as deeply pious. Richard III removed Henry's statue in York Minster because of popular veneration; an official effort at canonization followed, yielding Latin and English verse prayers to Henry in some late fifteenth and early sixteenth-century broadsheets.[59]

Henry's lack of interest in military adventure surely contributed to his indecipherability. An unusually pious Latin 'mirror of princes' was presented to Henry sometime after 1436 (BL MS Cotton Cleopatra A XIII), with discourses on humility, charity (with an explication of the herb 'trewlufe'), and, elaborately, peace. If the blessedly peaceful are the sons of God, those waging war are the devil's sons. Worldly men fight for earthly conquest, as the *exemplar* of Alexander makes clear: having conquered the globe, he ended in an eight-foot habitation.[60]

This hardly reflects the earlier program for the 'dual crowned' king, or the courtly faction under Henry's uncle, Duke Humfrey. Humfrey sought a renewal of war with France and above all the defense of Calais, against another faction led by his other uncle, John, duke of Bedford, regent of France, who tried to continue a stalemate with Charles VII by holding Normandy by treaty with Philip of Burgundy. Yet another faction, under the aging Cardinal Beaufort, John of Gaunt's 'natural' son thus Henry's great-uncle, pursued peace, to the contempt of Humfrey and knights like Sir John Fastolf. This knot around Henry, or rather its unravelling, was the background to a clutch of English poems from the late 1430s, shortly after a peace conference (summer 1435) between France, England, and Burgundy ended with nothing other than having driven Philip of Burgundy to abandon the English altogether, and league with Charles VII of France. A week later, Bedford died in Rouen, and the following year the French retook Paris (April 1436). In August 1436, Philip of Burgundy mustered Flemish troops and attacked Calais, of which Gloucester was then captain.

---

[57] (NIMEV 700) and 'The Receyvyng of Kyng Edward the IIIIth at Brystowe' (NIMEV 3880).
[58] Henry Noble MacCracken (ed.), *The Minor Poems of John Lydgate, Part II*, EETS, o.s. 192 (London, 1934), 710–16, 717–22. See Mooney, 'Lydgate's "Kings of England"', 263.
[59] Gransden, *Historical Writing*, 2.497–8; M. R. James (ed.), *Henry VI: A Reprint of John Blacman's Memoir* (Cambridge, 1919).
[60] *Tractatus de Regimine Principum ad Regem Henricum Septum*, in Jean-Philippe Genet (ed.), Four English Political Tracts of the Later Middle Ages, Camden Society 4th series, 18 (London, 1977), 40-173 (at 69).

The city's defences and the Flemings' lack of coordination caused the siege to fail even before Gloucester arrived from England, providing opportunity for celebrative poetry even amid so many other disasters. One poem, 'The Siege of Calais', uses a stanzaic *chanson d'aventure* frame, 'In Iuyll wan the sonne shone shene', to deflate Philip of Burgundy for his 'grete assemble in landes wide ... Of all the power and Chiualrie / Of Burgone and of Pykardie, / Of hanaude and holland'.[61] All the 'gonnes grete and ordinance' (37) are defeated by citizens great and small, from porters who 'kept full manly / The yates open' for the city's soldiers, to the 'worthy merchantes' and 'the gode comon / That had stuffed wel the town / With godes and vitaille' (81, 85–8). The lowly are the heroes. Women batter the siege machines with rocks, 'with stones stuffed euery scaffolde' (91). Even a dog, and an Irishman riding a nag, do their part. 'It was a sportfull sight' (123).

A more traditional 'Mockery of the Flemings', lambasting them for fleeing before Gloucester arrived, is preserved in a prose *Brut*.[62] The chronicler offered this as one of 'many rymes of þe fflemmynges ... here sette for a remembraunce' (*Brut*, 581–2). But parallel details in his prose suggest he found this particular poem useful for his own 'remembraunce'. Its couplets, with roughly thirteen syllables in each line, readily drop iambic stresses, approaching rhythmical prose, with figures again from all walks of life:

> Remembres eke on Goby, the watir-bailliffes dog,
> How he scarmysshed with you twyes vpon the day,
> And among you on þe sandes made many a fray.
> (32–4)

It is possible that Gloucester sponsored all these rowdy works, since they cohere in details. Gloucester generally continued Henry V's patronage of English poets, as his support of Lydgate through the *Fall of Princes* shows (finished c1348, roughly when these poems appeared). A more pacifist courtly faction, however, is represented by *The Libelle of Englyshe Polycye*, finished soon after the siege of Calais (which it mentions) but before news of the death of Emperor Sigismund, 9 December 1437.[63] This poem dovetails with Henry's 'mirror of princes' emphasizing charity and peace:

> In unité to live to Goddis pay.
> Whiche unité, pease, reste and charite
> He that was here cladde in humanite ...
> (1127–9)

Yet *Realpolitik* governs the *Libelle*'s argument. If the Flemings resist us, we can punish them by limiting access to our wool, 'For the lytell londe of Flaundres is / But a staple to other londes iwys' (115–16). Flanders supplied skilled labour and 'marchaundye' but few 'commoditees' (262)—a distinction fundamental not only to the economic theory of burgeoning capitalism, but also to the idea of economics as war by other means:

---

[61] NIMEV 1497; Robbins, *Historical Poems*, 14–18.
[62] NIMEV 4056.8; Robbins, *Historical Poems*, 83–6.
[63] NIMEV 3491; George Warner (ed.), *The Libelle of Englyshe Polycye: A Poem on the Use of Sea-Power, 1436* (Oxford, 1926), x. For a proposal that the author was William Lyndwood, keeper of the Privy Seal, see Sebastian Sobecki, 'William Lyndwood, the Privy Seal and the Form of *The Libelle of Englyshe Polycye*', *New Medieval Literatures*, 12 (2010), 251–88.

> Therefor if we wolde manly take on honde
> To kepe thys see fro Flaundres and fro Spayne
> And fro Scotelonde lych as fro Pety Bretayne,
> Wee schulde ryght sone have pease for all here bostes,
> For they muste nede passe by oure Englysshe costes.
>
> (271–5)

Scorn of 'bostes' distinguishes the temper of this poem from the battle poems. The *Libelle*'s voice is aggressive enough; after warning of the permanent loss of Calais, and praising Gloucester (who had no role in it) for the breaking of the recent siege, it scapegoats the Flemish:

> Wythoute Calise in ther buttere they cakked,
> Whan they flede home and when they leysere lakked
> To holde here sege; they wente lyke as a doo
> Wel was that Flemmynge that myght trusse and goo,
> For fere they turned back and hyede faste,
> Milorde of Gloucester made hem so agaste ...
>
> (290–5)

Bigotry against Flemings was a settled element of English responses to Flemish dominance in weaving and the cloth trade.[64] Here, all factions could agree. Protectionism was in fact imposed four months after the siege, on 8 December 1436, and presented, as in the *Libelle* and the battle poems, as retaliation for Burgundy's betrayal but targeting Flemish weavers and drapers operating in England. By 'advice and assent of the council', it was forbidden for any 'foreigner' to import linen, 'mader', or other goods from Flanders, 'after the notorious traitor, enemy and rebel calling himself duke of Burgundy ... did falsely fall away from the faith and allegiance' to England.[65] Bigotry's unifying powers were useful amid internal strife, during a reign in which both royalist history-fabricating and military action had achieved so little.

Civil War Poetry

Near the start of the civil wars launched by Richard, earl of Warwick, and Richard, duke of York, against the Lancastrians (now led by Margaret of Anjou, since Henry had slipped into his first long bout of insanity in 1453), topical poetry was sometimes enigmatic, and perhaps not only for us. In a London prose history in Latin, attributed to one John Benet, a poem in five stanzas is recorded and described as having been placed in the jaws of the heads of five dogs arranged in Fleet Street in 1456. In each stanza, the dog laments his fate:

> Whan lorschype fayleth gode felewschipe awaylth
> My mayster ys cruell and can no curtesye
> For whos offence here am y pyghte*   *set*
> Hyt ys no reson þt y schulde dyue
> For hys trespace & he go quyte.[66]

---

[64] See Bart Lambert and Milan Pajic, 'Immigration and the Common Profit: Native Cloth Workers, Flemish Exiles, and Royal Policy in Fourteenth-Century London', *Journal of British Studies*, 55 (2016), 633–57.

[65] *Calendar of Close Rolls: Henry VI, Vol. III, 1435–41* (London, 1937), 96.

A revolted passerby might wonder, who was his 'mayster'? Robbins argued that these laments complained against York (misidentified by Robbins as Edward) for betraying his servants. Alison Hanham more plausibly argues that the messages were meant ironically to represent laments by clerks from Inns of Court killed serving the king, mocked by legal colleagues who served the Yorkists.[67]

Proverbial sayings and animal fable were both established vehicles of political poetry, but the use of real animals was a grotesque and provocative innovation. Since Benet notes that this was in the aftermath of the first battle at St Albans in summer, 1455—when Warwick, Warwick's father, and Richard duke of York killed members of the king's party led by Edmund duke of Somerset—the display of actual violence in this poem's London 'publication' might have applied to either side. For that battle left York and his followers open to charges of treason for having attacked the king, but at this point, that was avoided by both the king and York. What aggression remained was suppressed. Shortly after the battle, a Chancery clerk wrote to a friend that 'all my lord of Warrwyk men, my lord of York, men, and also my lord of Salesbury men goo with harnez, and in harnes with strong wepon ... dayly vnto Westminster'. He added, however, that a recent bill required avoiding any mention of the battle, 'affermyng all thing doon there well doon, and nothing doon there neuer after this tyme to be spoken of; to the which bill mony a man groged (*complained*) fule sore'.[68] Obscure but savage satire was a predictable result.

Conflict and volatile loyalties between colleagues and family members was a persistent feature of the 'Wars of the Roses', driven less by competing dynastic claims than more immediate opportunities, loyalties, and grudges.[69] The John Talbot, first earl of Shrewsbury, who at Margaret's wedding gave her a lavishly illustrated book with an image of Henry's double lineage and a set of romances and political treatises,[70] died in France in 1453 fighting for the Lancastrians; yet his son, also John, sided with York and Warwick after the battle at St Albans in 1455. But the second John Talbot then returned to the king's side, dying at Northampton in 1460 when the king's party was soundly defeated and the king himself captured, after four of his chamber knights died trying to protect him, including Henry Stafford, first duke of Buckingham. One upshot of Northampton was Henry's agreement (the Act of Accord, 31 October 1460), to make York heir but leave Henry on the throne, but, like efforts to silence anger after the first battle of St Albans, this hardly put an end to the conflicts, as shown by the subsequent battles of Wakefield, when York was killed (December 1460), St Albans, again (February 1461), and Towton (March 1461), 'the bloodiest battle of the entire civil war'.[71]

Several moments seem folded into the most complex poem from the wars: the 'Battle of Northampton'.[72] Like the 'Five Dogs', this is an adroit manipulation of the genre of animal fable. All the figures are identifiable, either by heraldic association, or, if given human form, identified at first mention. The 'Berward' (bear-keeper) is 'Edward, yong of age' (22),

---

[66] NIMEV 2262.3; Robbins (ed.), *Historical Poems*, 189–90.
[67] Alison Hanham (trans.), *John Benet's Chronicle, 1399–1462* (New York, 2016), 60.
[68] Norman Davis (pts 1 and 2), and Richard Beadle and Colin Richmond (pt. 3) (eds), *Paston Letters and Papers of the Fifteenth Century*, EETS, s.s. 20-2 (London, 2004–5), 3.158, no. 1026.
[69] For this emphasis see R. L. Storey, *The End of the House of Lancaster* (Phoenix Mill, Gloucs, 1999).
[70] BL MS Royal 15 E VI; Rowe, 'King Henry VI's Claim', 80–1. For full facsimile, see http://www.bl.uk/manuscripts/FullDisplay.aspx?ref=Royal_MS_15_E_VI.
[71] Ross, *Edward IV*, 36.
[72] NIMEV 2609; Robbins (ed.), *Historical Poems*, 210–15.

that is, Edward, son of Richard of York, later Edward IV, just as 'the Hunt' is 'our Kyng', Henry VI:

Þe coriages berward put hym ferre in preese,	*courageous; himself far in chase*
To þe hunt, our Kyng, he hyed* hym ful fast;	*hastened*
The bere for all þe dogges wold not seese*,	*cease*
But hyed hym* sone afftre swyfftly in hast.	*hastened himself*
The dogges barked at hem ful fast,	*at them continually*
Þe buk set vp his hornes on hye;	*hunting horns and stag's horns*
Þe bererward, þei cryed, þei wold downe cast,	*they wished to*
The bere also, if that he come nye.	
The bereward asked no questioun why.	
But on þe dogges he set full rounde*;	*vigorously*
Þe bere made the dogges to cry,	
And with his pawme cast þeyme to grounde.	
The game was done in a litel stounde*,	*short time*
Þe buk was slayne, & borne away;	
A-gayne þe bere þan was none hounde,	
But he might sporte and take his play.	
But þe hunt he saued from harme þat day—	
He þouȝt neuer oþer in all his mynde—	*had no other intention*
He lowted* downe, & at his fote lay,	*bowed*
In token to hym that he was kynde*.	*well intentioned (gracious)*
The berward also, þe huntes frende,	
ffell downe on kne, saying with obedience:	
'Souereigne lord, thenk vs not vnkynde*,	*ungrateful (hostile)*
Nor take ye this in none offence ...'	
(41–64)	

The Bear is Warwick the 'kingmaker', whose seal and crest feature a bear with a branch or staff;[73] the Dog, Talbot, a name for a small hunting dog; the Buck, Sir Henry Stafford, first duke of Buckingham, an identification sealed by his role as the object of the allegorical hunting expedition led, surprisingly, by the Hunter, Henry VI, who was supported by Buckingham and Talbot, not their predator. The roles rearrange the figures' political positions while granting York piously loyal motives towards Henry VI: 'he lowted downe, & at his fote lay'. This appears to invoke York's posture not of 1460, when York began openly claiming the throne, but 1458, when York promised to the king's counsel, including Buckingham, in Star Chamber that he would travel to London only for 'all that that sholde or might be to the welfare of the king and of his subgettes'.[74] Given the capture of Henry VI at Northampton and the slaughter of Buckingham defending Henry in the king's tent, the poem might have been designed to show that Henry was one of them all along.

The poem is preserved with other materials that suggest prolonged rereading, next to four simpler poems on Yorkist victories in a manuscript that (in its original form) presents an anthology of simplified English poetry, including a truncated version of Chaucer's 'Steadfastness'; laments by Palamon, Emilye, and Arcite from Chaucer's 'Knight's Tale'; a simplified version of the romance *Roberd of Sisyle*; teacher's advice to 'dowȝteryn' and

---

[73] C. D. Ross (ed.), *The Rous Roll* (London, 1980), plate 1.
[74] *Calendar of the Patent Rolls: Henry VI*, vol. 6, 1452–61 (London, 1910), 143.

'sones'; and a story of an 'onhappy boye' whose naughtiness includes farting during sermons and putting fire under a horse's tail.⁷⁵ The collection, with its child's garden of Chaucer, seems designed for secular household education. One of the political poems features an acrostic on Warwick's name ('W. Wisdome *monstrat*') offering macaronic grammatical as well as ideological indoctrination.⁷⁶

Such poetry shows how partisan vernacular history was taught to the young as well as broadcast widely, though some poems in this set might not have remained timely for long. By 1470 Warwick joined Margaret of Anjou and helped restore Henry VI briefly to the throne; Warwick was later killed by Edward's forces. With the violence so unmanageable by agreements or silences, it is easy to understand the solution offered by the last long English verse chronicle of the Middle Ages, the *Chronicle* of John Hardyng: unifying the nation by inciting aggression focused elsewhere.

John Hardyng

When John Hardyng (c1378–c1465) completed the first version of his *Chronicle* for Henry VI in 1457, he was a corrodiary (secular retiree residing in a religious house) in the Augustinian priory of South Kyme, Lincolnshire, at the age of nearly eighty.⁷⁷ He was just entering his most productive years. As the nation underwent the turmoil of Henry's psychological and political collapse and Edward's rise, and before his death by 1465, Hardyng went on to revise the *Chronicle* substantially, condensing it to about half its 18,782 lines, while shifting dedications from Henry VI to Richard, duke of York, then, on Richard's death, to his son Edward, and finally to Edward IV. The fourteen copies of the revised version (both versions are in rhyme royal) present wide variants for grammatically independent single lines; this suggests Hardyng left those blank or with undecided alternates.⁷⁸ It is in any case easy to be sympathetic with his not entirely finishing a work whose royal (or prospectively royal) addressees kept changing so rapidly.

Hardyng was a former soldier and spy for Henry V, who commissioned him 'evydence to gette and to espy / Appurtenant unto hys monarchy' (dedication, 41–2), resulting in the documents from Scottish archives brought into his *Chronicle* as historically relevant. Most of those that have been discovered, however, were forged. His zeal for using history and documents for practical action carried over to his *Chronicle*, the sole surviving copy of whose initial version, presented to Henry VI, includes splendid genealogical illustrations of Edward III and a vivid and precise map of Scotland—the first full map of the country. That version declares his intention to provide the king a conspectus of England's history in order for the king to 'know the state of youre domynacioun' (dedication, 7) and regain it. It soon becomes clear that Hardying also wanted Henry VI to understand that his father,

---

⁷⁵ Rudolf Brotanek (ed.), *Middelenglische Dichtungen aus der Handschrift 432 des Trinity College in Dublin* (Halle, 1940); see Raluca Radulescu, 'Vying for Attention: The Contents of Dublin, Trinity College, MS 432', in Margaret Connolly and Raluca Radulescu (eds), *Insular Books: Vernacular Manuscript Miscellanies in Late Medieval Britain* (London, 2015), 121–43.

⁷⁶ NIMEV 3856.5; Robbins (ed.), *Historical Poems*, 380.

⁷⁷ NIMEV 710; For the first version of Hardyng's Chronicle, see James Simpson and Sarah Peverley (eds), *John Hardyng: Chronicle, Edited from British Library MS Lansdowne 204*, vol. 1 (Kalamazoo, MI, 2015), cited as *Chronicle¹*; for the second version see Henry Ellis (ed.), The Chronicle of John Hardyng (London, 1812) cited as *Chronicle²*.

⁷⁸ See A. S. G. Edwards, 'The Manuscripts and Texts of the Second Version of John Hardyng's Chronicle', in Daniel Williams (ed.), *England in the Fifteenth Century: Proceedings of the 1986 Harlaxton Symposium* (Woodbridge, 1987), 75–84.

Henry V, had died, leaving Hardyng 'nought rewarded aftyr hys intent' (dedication, 91). Hardyng's *Chronicle* is a manifesto, but also a begging poem, interwoven with strategic pleas to restore the nation's 'law' and unity.

Little about Hardyng's *Chronicle* seems archaizing, from his aggressively purposeful use of English historical claims to Scottish sovereignty, to his insertions of personal experiences in battles he described or documents he saw or collected, to his tendency for neologism ('vertuosite'; 'englaymed'; 'exercised'; 'laudified'; 'disformed'). But it is pertinent to recognize how archaic his work was in some ways. Hardyng based his work's information on the prose *Brut* but its form on the chronicles from the period of Edward I's expansive insular imperialism. Robert Mannyng's *Chronicle*, which translated Wace and Langtoft, was the least known of the older verse chronicles, but there are clear signs Hardyng knew and used it, perhaps discovering it because of their shared Lincolnshire clerical setting.[79] Mannyng's scorn of Scotland (e.g., 'grante me þat bone . þe Scottes sone . alle be confonded') would have been congenial.[80] So too would the idea of recovering an atavistic ideology of English greatness, even though the sense of English lordship over Scotland had gradually yielded to the assumption that Scotland was simply another nation, though, as the Scottish historical efforts show, the battle for and against English overlordship continued on parchment.[81]

Other political ideas pulled Hardyng towards his solution. For Hardyng, a weak king was dangerous to national unity and peace. This is clear in the first version in ancient Britain's disorder under four hostile kingdoms ruled by Clotane, Rudder, Pinner, and Stater, when 'every tirant than was a conqueroure / And lordes fayne subgyts bycome forfought' (2.1453–4). 'Defaute of law was cause of this myschefe', Hardyng observed:

> Wharefore unto a prynce acordyth right
> To kepe the pese with alle tranquilyté
> Within his reame to save his dygnyté.
>
> (2.1477–8)

In the revised version, rededicated to Richard duke of York (then, with Richard's death in 1460, to his son Edward), this becomes a constant theme. Rulers who valued the greater 'common profit' are more often and more explicitly identified: from King Constance's attention to the 'comon publick' (*Chronicle²*, 40.97), to the glorious instance of King Arthur, dedicated to the 'common profyt' (73.125), to King Ethelbert's dedication to the 'comon weale aboue all thyng' (115.214), to the more recent instance of Hardyng's first Yorkist dedicatee, Richard duke of York, who was (or implicitly ought to be) committed to 'the common wele to mayntene and amende' (233.401). Hardyng's remarks would challenge his royal readers to meet the standards of their predecessors—and to have as much energy as Hardyng himself. His final dedicatee, King Edward IV, is urged to reconcile with Henry VI, who—in another snapshot of 1465—is said to be then wandering in Scotland. Edward should give Henry the duchy of Lancaster to live on (addressing a common complaint that the former king and followers had drained the nation's wealth), and be

---

[79] See the references to Mannyng *passim* in the notes of *Chronicle¹*, definitively at 2.287n, 2.954–1016n. *Chronicle¹*, using the sole copy of Hardyng's first version, is cited by section and line; *Chronicle²* is cited by chapter and page.

[80] Idelle Sullens (ed.), *Robert Mannyng of Brunne: The Chronicle* (Binghamton, NY, 1996), 2.6841–52.

[81] See Michael Prestwich, 'England and Scotland During the Wars of Independence', in Michael Jones and Malcolm Vale (eds), *England and Her Neighbours, 1066–1453: Essays in Honour of Pierre Chaplais* (London, 1989), 181–98.

reconciled to the Percies (Lancastrian loyalists, but former patrons of Hardyng). In recapturing Henry, Edward should take the opportunity to destroy heretics, and, as Hardyng urged all his dedicatees, demolish the Scots. For 'truste it well, as God is nowe in heuen, / Ye shall neuer fynde the Scottes vnto you trewe' (240.414).

Hardyng's *Chronicle* cumulatively unfolds the vast scope of earlier English sovereignty, reaching back to King Arthur's supposed conquests (including Rome) and forwards to what rule of France ought to have brought the English. Like Arthur, English kings should by rights rule not only Wales, Scotland, Ireland, Rome, and Jerusalem, but also

> By papall bull, ye haue the right to Ireland,
> Gascowe, Paitowe and Normandye,
> Pountyf, Bebuile, Saunxie and Sauntignye,
> And all the lande beyond the Charente;
> Of Dangoleame, Dangolismoys & Luyrezyne,
> Of Caoure, Caourenno, Pyridor & Pirygunt countre,
> Of Rodis, Ronegeauis, Dagon, Dabonyse þe fine,
> Tharbe, Wigor & Gaure shoulde to you enclyne,
> With all the fraunchyses and all souerayntie,
> As hath the kyng of Fraunce in his degre.
> (*Chronicle²*, proheme, 21)

Against this hyperbole, Hardying made his real pitch: conquering Scotland, easier to take and govern, and at least a start on wider imperialism. Only three years were needed (*Chronicle²*, 240.414). Hardyng's envoy is rhyme royal stanzas describing 'the distaunce and miles of the tounes in Scotland, and þe waye how to conueigh an armie aswell by lande as water, into the chefest partes therof' (*Chronicle²*, 242.423–9).

As a military proposal, Hardyng's sturdily optimistic advice was naive at best, not only given England's financial and political depletion, but also in imagining a unified Scotland to be conquered at a stroke. Hardyng was more sophisticated in generating his legal claims. He wove into his history mentions of his clandestine acquisitions of charters and 'evidences' revealing Scottish kings' admissions that English kings were their sovereign lords, copies of which he noted having sent over the years to Henry V (170.305–6), Henry VI (proem 21), and Edward IV (178.317). Many of the actual documents survive, showing that Hardyng's were mostly forged, sometimes with elaborately forged cross-references.[82] Edward I's historiographical manipulations of 1291 might have seemed to sanction such efforts, and Hardyng's recurrent mentions of transferring documents to kings bolster his opening self-portrait as an individual spy and soldier heroically assisting the nation. The lack of noticeable military response or even literary encouragement by any of the kings to whom Hardyng presented his history suggest they agreed in finding it hopelessly archaic.

Yet Hardyng's invitation to imagine 'all the fraunchyses and all souerayntie' that England deserved, with his vivid map of Scotland laying bare his most immediate object of aggression, was an inspired fiction, and its manuscript and printed afterlife show that common readers were interested. In the 1460s, utopian nationalism was rare, perhaps possible only through a national poetic chronicle whose form harked back to the world of Robert Mannyng. Hardyng's proposal was both opposite to but also a conjoined version of the

---

[82] See Alfred Hiatt, *The Making of Medieval Forgeries: False Documents in Fifteenth-Century England* (London, 2004), 110–11.

disintegration of King Arthur's world chronicled by the prose *Morte Darthur* by Thomas Malory, another soldier-historian, which Malory began while Hardyng was still revising his *Chronicle*. Hardyng's *Chronicle* was another private citizen's contribution to a debate about England's longer future, by a historian passed over by the kings and lords who were more preoccupied, by the late century, with French prose histories and European courtly elegance than with vernacular populism.[83]

Stewart and Tudor Endings

In spite of the growth of printing and its boost to historical prose, historical poetry continued in the Scottish and English courts through the end of the century, and in a few cases more widely. At the Scottish court of James IV, William Dunbar unreeled brilliant occasional satires and celebrations, including a vulgarly scatological flyting with a Highland poet, Walter Kennedy, and a Chaucerian dream-vision celebrating the marriage in 1503 of James IV to Margaret Tudor, eldest daughter of Henry VII.[84] The marriage was the linchpin of the Anglo-Scottish treaty of Ayton (1497), and even if a later eruption of tensions led to Scottish incursions, then the battle of Flodden (1513), when the Scottish nobility including James IV were massacred, cultural connections between the two nations continued to increase.[85] Even Blind Hary's *Wallace*, which ends with Wallace's mock confession before execution in which he regrets not killing more Englishmen (12.1385–8), repurposed Chaucerian elements. Hary was the first poet in Scotland to use Chaucer's iambic pentameter, even emulating the complex nine-line stanzas of Chaucer's *Anelida and Arcite* (at 2.171–359) and eight-line stanza of 'the Monk's Tale' (6.1–104). Hary closed by adapting Chaucer's Franklin's false modesty concerning lack of rhetorical training:

> It is weill knawin I am a burel man.   *rustic*
> For her is said als gudly as I can;
> My spreyt felis na termys of Pernase ...[86]
> (12.1459–63)

Chaucerian appropriation was a general late fifteenth-century Scottish fashion; in Hary's virulently anti-'Saxon' case, this used the English master's tools as weapons against their owner.

In England, Henry VII drew Italian humanists to his court and employed a major French humanist scholar and poet, Bernard André (1450–1522), to tutor the then-prince of Wales, Arthur, and to produce official panegyric of Henry's deeds and family. Henry also provided a role to the English poet and scholar, John Skelton (1460–1529). Skelton for a few years tutored Henry's younger son, Henry, later Henry VIII, although Skelton was dismissed from court as soon as Prince Arthur died in 1502, and the younger son became the new Prince of Wales.

Skelton's poetic career flourished in the decades beyond this volume's scope, but his first datable poem, 'Upon the Dolorus Dethe and Muche Lamentable Chaunce of the Mooste

---

[83] On Edward IV's library of French histories and his emulation of Burgundian splendour, see Gordon Kipling, *The Triumph of Honour: Burgundian Origins of the Elizabethan Renaissance* (Leiden, 1977), 11–30. See also the observations on Edward's lack of interest in English writing in Ross, *Edward IV*, 266–7.
[84] 'Flyting of Dunbar and Kennedy', and 'Thistle and the Rose', in Priscilla Bawcutt (ed.) *The Poems of William Dunbar*, 2 vols. (Glasgow, 1998), 200–18, 163–8.
[85] John Guy, *Tudor England* (Oxford, 1988), 54.
[86] See *Franklin's Prologue*, V.716–28.

Honorable Erle of Northumberlande' (c1489), stands more directly in the long tradition of English historical poetry than his later flytings and allegorical satires.[87] The work laments the killing by a mob of the fourth earl of Northumberland, after a heavy royal tax roused the 'vilane hastarddis in ther furious tene' (24). What prompted Skelton's poem is debatable. André also wrote a Latin lament (in expert Sapphic meter) on Percy's death, denouncing the wild mob and urging the pious king (with the Virgin's encouragement) to reassert order; it is clear that Henry VII had reasons to weaken the independent northern lords like the Percies, furthering an aggressive program of expanding royal power through political and financial manipulation, by which, as the Italian papal emissary to England, Polydore Vergil, remarked, 'the king wished (as he said) to keep all Englishmen obedient through fear'.[88] It is sheer speculation that Henry actually engineered the death of the fourth earl of Northumberland, but there is no doubt that the king continued to hamper the recovery of power by the earl's young heir.[89] At the same time, the Percies were patrons of English poetry: Hardyng's career began in their household, and he picked them out for praise in his *Chronicle*; their patronage of English poetry included a verse chronicle of their family history written in the early sixteenth century, in a manuscript (BL MS Royal 18 D II) which includes a copy of Skelton's 'Dolorus Dethe', added to a collection including Lydgate's *Troy Book* and *Siege of Thebes*.[90] It is also a thoroughly conventional elegy in general structure.[91] But there are also grounds within Skelton's poem to support David Carlson's remark that Skelton's work was 'state propaganda not substantively different from André's'.[92]

One major difference from André's and other poems on the event is Skelton's focus not only on the 'vilane hastarddis' but also the complicity of Percy's 'awne servauntis of trust' (37): local 'knyghtis and squyers', who 'fled from hym for falshode or fere' (91). This adds a sharper edge of criticism than usual to the conventional features of the genre of lament. As A. S. G. Edwards's edition shows, the Percy verse chronicle similarly laments that the 'comonȝ' murdered 'ther own natural lord' while 'knyghtis and gentilmen ... To whom he have feeȝ ... Al sodenly from him fled' (271, 275–6). But Skelton drove home the claim of the local gentry's 'treson, agayn hym compassyd and wrought' (6) with a breadth of blame that would have struck fear in many families of the region. 'Men say', he remarked, that the local nobility were linked 'with a double chayn / And held with the commonns under a cloke' (75–6): 'barons, knightis squyers, one and alle, Togeder with servauntis of his famuly / Turnd ther backis and let ther master fall' (92–4). The poem blames for inaction even those not involved, putting on notice the entire 'nobelnes of the northe' (85).

Here is a flexing of poetic power like Skelton's later satires but novel in the long tradition of medieval lament for fallen lords and princes. Skelton's poem ends, as Scattergood indicates, conventionally enough with consolations and closing prayers, but its invitation for collective lament conveys a threat to punish every lord in the region, particularly those

---

[87] TM 683; John Scattergood (ed.), *The Complete English Poems of John Skelton*, rev. edn. (Liverpool, 2015), 23–8.

[88] André, '*Vita Henrici Septimi*', in James Gairdner (ed.), *Memorials of King Henry VII* Rolls Series (London, 1858), 48–9; Denys Hay (ed. and trans.), *The Anglia Historia of Polydore Vergil, 1485–1537*, Camden Society, third series, 74 (London, 1950), 127–8. See Guy, *Tudor England*, 53–79.

[89] M. E. James, 'Murder at Cocklodge', *Durham University Journal*, 57 (1965), 80–7; M. E. James, 'A Tudor Magnate and the Tudor State: Henry Fifth Earl of Northumberland', in *Society, Politics, and Culture: Studies in Early Modern England* (Cambridge, 1986), 48–90.

[90] A. S. G. Edwards, 'A Verse Chronicle of the House of Percy', *Studies in Philology*, 105 (2008), 226–44 (at 229 n.12).

[91] John Scattergood, *John Skelton: The Career of an Early Tudor Poet* (Dublin, 2014), 63–78.

[92] David R. Carlson (ed.), *The Latin Writings of John Skelton*, Studies in Philology, Texts and Studies (1991), 88:4, 2.

dependent on Percy 'in fee', whom the poem has already identified as conspirators. Skelton's closing counsel is fear:

> Wythe hevy chere, with dolorous hart and mynd,
> Eche man may sorow in his inward thought
> This lordis dethe ...
> More specially barons, and thos knightis bold,
> And all other gentelmen with hym enterteynd
> In fee, as menyall men of his houshold ...
> To sorouful weping thei ought to be constreynd ...
>   (176–88)

'Upon the Dolorus Dethe' might be casually read as poignant lamentation for a departed hero, but its invocation of the traditional genre of lament is also a recreation of that genre into a weapon of language. Before Skelton turned his withering invective openly on his fellow courtier Sir Christopher Garnesche, the killed king of Scotland James IV, Cardinal Wolsey, or the barmaid Eleanor Rumming, he turned it covertly on the bereaved neighbours and dependants of the murdered earl of Northumberland, using a poetic mode designed to offer sympathy to those mourning the dolorous death of a prince. Prose and print offered two challenges to the late revival of historical poetry, but the final blow would come from changes in poetics itself. André's continental literary standards led him to introduce Sapphic 'odes' amid prose Latin biography, suspending historical poetry's duties of narrative altogether; Skelton showed that the venerable genre of lament of prince's 'falls' could similarly be turned from describing action to becoming an act: twisting the knife in historical poetry's assassination of its own genre.

CHAPTER 19
Fictions of Antiquity

Venetia Bridges

The literary recuperation of the fifteenth century from an era of 'dullness' (in the modern sense) to a time of provocative literary production has been uneven.[1] Whilst prose romance and alliterative poetry (among other areas) have benefitted from renewed study, fifteenth-century verse romances are often overlooked, particularly those that are concerned with the ancient classical past.[2] Yet this little-studied corpus of 'fictions of antiquity' is an important part of late medieval literary landscapes in Britain as it highlights an interest in the distant past and the ways in which it might be retold for contemporary purposes. Not only raising familiar questions about the characteristics of romance as a genre at the end of the Middle Ages, it also provides an opportunity to investigate *translatio studii* or 'transfer of knowledge/learning' during the fifteenth century. This concept is a useful means of describing the habitual transference of inherited material between texts, languages, and regions characteristic of the later medieval period; it can also refer to the literary styles used in such transference.[3] This analysis will assume that *translatio studii* in the 'fictions of antiquity' is crafted, a response (deliberate or not) to texts and interpretative traditions inherited both from antiquity and from the medieval period itself.

These texts and traditions are just as important as the reworked classical material in understanding *translatio*, since earlier medieval authors' and genres' responses to classical material may affect fifteenth-century English poets' approaches.[4] In sum, analysing the nature of these poems' *translatio studii* necessitates considering a wider range of texts and traditions than antique material alone.

Fifteenth-century 'fictions of antiquity' include English-language narratives of Alexander the Great and Troy. However, these retellings of stories from prestigious classical traditions are joined by texts with more tangential relationships to classical antiquity, such as Charlemagne romances, Ovidian myths, and Chaucerian poetry. This study will begin by considering these prestigious traditions and then move on to discuss examples of these other texts.

---

[1] David Lawton's pivotal study, 'Dullness and the Fifteenth Century', *ELH*, 54 (1987), 761–99, challenged the idea that the century was 'a literary prolepsis of the Slough of Despond' (at 761) and enabled revisionist views about the period as 'provocative' to develop; see Andrea Denny-Brown, 'The Provocative Fifteenth Century', *Exemplaria*, 29 (2017), 267–79.

[2] The essays in Helen Cooper and Sally Mapstone (eds), *The Long Fifteenth Century: Essays for Douglas Gray* (Oxford, 1997), which are representative of key areas of study in the two decades since the book was published, demonstrate this; there is no essay dedicated to verse romances specifically. Where fifteenth-century verse romance is studied, the focus has not usually been on 'fictions of antiquity': see, for example, Nicola McDonald (ed.), *Pulp Fictions of Medieval England: Essays in Popular Romance* (Manchester, 2004), which does not discuss material inherited from classical narratives.

[3] See the overview in Venetia Bridges, *Medieval Narratives of Alexander the Great: Transnational Texts in England and France* (Cambridge, 2018), 19–22.

[4] See Derek Pearsall, 'The English Romance in the Fifteenth Century', *Essays and Studies*, 29 (1976), 56–83 (at 67), who observes 'a more self-consciously "literary" mode' within the genre by the fifteenth century.

Alexander the Great

Despite Chaucer's claim that Alexander's 'storie' is 'commune' by the later 1300s, the Macedonian's narrative is not found frequently in English until the following century, with only three extant works composed before 1400.[5] These texts, *Kyng Alisaunder* (c1300), the fragmentary *Alexander A* (c1340), and *Alexander and Dindimus/Alexander B* (c1350), are all romance works, demonstrating the fictional possibilities of Alexander's legendary life by the later Middle Ages. The Alexander verse romances produced during the fifteenth century highlight the range of poetic approaches available to romance authors. These texts—*The Wars of Alexander* (also known as *Alexander C*: before 1450), *The Buik of King Alexander the Conquerour* attributed to Sir Gilbert Hay (1460s) and the *Buik of Alexander* (c1438)—are respectively a Middle English alliterative poem, an Old Scots verse account in decasyllabic couplets, and another Old Scots verse romance in octasyllabic couplets.[6] Despite this variety, the narrative sources of all three works are the same texts: versions of the Latin prose *Historia de preliis* from the twelfth and thirteenth centuries, the twelfth-century Old French verse *Roman d'Alexandre*, and interpolated episodes including the *Voeux du Paon* and *Fuerre de Gadres* accounts. Their differences, therefore, may be less related to plot than to metre, form, and thematic emphasis in their *translatio studii*.

The *Historia de preliis* (from which the *Roman d'Alexandre*'s narrative is derived) recounts the Macedonian's life from birth to death, focusing not only on his extraordinary military achievements but also his encounters with the 'marvels' of the East (its people and animals). Despite its title, the Latin text (ultimately based on the Greek *Alexander Romance*) is generically akin to romance in its interest in such marvels, so that its retelling of the Alexander narrative is already inflected by romance features even before it influences fifteenth-century works.[7]

The Wars of Alexander

This 5800-line alliterative poem, which is missing the end and therefore the narrative of Alexander's death, survives in two manuscripts of the mid and later fifteenth century, which provides a *terminus ad quem* for *Wars*' composition of before c1450.[8] This study assumes a fifteenth-century date of composition without attempting to be more specific.

In a detailed study of Philip's dream of Alexander's conception, David Lawton observes that the *Wars*-poet's approach is informed as much by the stylistic habits of the alliterative

---

[5] Chaucer, 'The Monk's Tale', 2658, in Larry D. Benson (general ed.), *The Riverside Chaucer*, 3rd edn. (Boston, MA, 1987).

[6] These texts (respectively NIMEV 3947.3, NIMEV 3287.5, NIMEV 3923) are edited as follows: Hoyt N. Duggan and Thorlac Turville-Petre (eds), *The Wars of Alexander*, EETS, s.s. 10 (Oxford, 1989); John Cartwright (ed.), *The Buik of King Alexander the Conquerour*, 2 vols. (2 and 3), STS, 4th series 16 and 18 (Edinburgh, 1986, 1990); and R. L. Graeme Ritchie (ed.), *The Buik of Alexander*, 4 vols., STS, n.s. 17, 12, 21, and 25 (Edinburgh, 1921–29). The *Buik of Alexander* is not discussed here because it is not a complete narrative of Alexander's life.

[7] For an overview of the Greek *Alexander Romance* and its relationship to the *Historia*, see Bridges, *Medieval Narratives of Alexander*, 32–7.

[8] BodL MS Ashmole 44 was copied around 1450, and Dublin, Trinity College, MS 213 was written in the last quarter of the fifteenth century (Duggan and Turville-Petre, *Wars of Alexander*, ix–xii). However, the editors point out that the poem could have been composed at any point between c1350 and 1450.

tradition as it is by faithfulness to its Latin prose source.⁹ Donna Crawford further defines the alliterative expansionism noted by Lawton, characterizing it as 'adding elaborations and embellishments that glitter with the verbal artifice so characteristic of alliterative poetry'.¹⁰ This crafted, consciously literary style is characteristic of *Wars* more generally, naturally in its particularly ecphrastic passages but also in its battle accounts—'sone in scheuerand schidis schaftis ere brosten' (912, *soon spear-shafts are shattered into splintered fragments*)—and its descriptions of wildernesses—'a velans vale ... quare flaggis of þe fell snawe fell fra þe heuen' (4293–94; *a worthless valley ... where flakes of cruel snow fell from the sky*).¹¹ This sense of elaborate, expansive display relates not just to alliterative habits but also to romance as a genre. The relationship is suggested at the beginning of the poem, which consciously evokes a courtly setting reminiscent of *Sir Gawain and the Green Knight*, for example.¹² However, this setting is an explicitly literary context as well as a chivalric one, since in addition to wanting to hear 'of curtaissy, of kny3thode, of craftis of armys' (9, *of courtesy, of knighthood, of skill in arms*) the implied audience is depicted as enjoying 'þe lesing of sayntis' (4, *the tales of saints*) and as 'langinge of lufe lay[e]s to herken' (6, *longing to listen to stories of love*). This literary awareness, combined with the stylistic elaborations, makes it clear that romance as a genre is being deliberately invoked. Crucially, these romance features are fundamentally stylistic, adding depth and vivid detail (the 'splintered fragments' of shields and the 'flakes of cruel snow' in the lines quoted above, for example) in order to reinforce the chivalric universe of the narrative's setting, but not altering the parameters of the narrative in terms of plot. This characteristic romance setting makes it difficult to read Alexander in political-exemplary terms, since it locates the tale in a fictionalized universe defined by extraordinary chivalric deeds and therefore at some distance from easily identifiable historical parallels. Whilst Alexander is presented as morally ambiguous,¹³ *Wars*'s poetic approach does not seek to construct Alexander himself as an *exemplum*. Rather, it elaborates the narrative itself as a chivalric romance, aided by the expansive poetics of alliterative poetry (as briefly shown above). *Wars* therefore takes full advantage of the stylistic elaboration enabled by its alliterative form to construct a primarily romance-based form of *translatio*, demonstrating its awareness of the interpretative and literary traditions of the medieval genre (such as detailed descriptions of battles and vivid images of landscapes) as well as its Latin source material.

Buik of King Alexander the Conquerour

The Old Scots *Buik of King Alexander the Conquerour*, which in its surviving form is over 19,000 lines long, is attributed to Sir Gilbert Hay (*c*1403–after 1466), and was composed around 1460, soon after *Wars*, although the passage in which the authorial attribution

---

⁹ David A. Lawton, 'The Middle English Alliterative *Alexander A* and *C*: Form and Style in Translation from Latin Prose', *Studia Neophilologica*, 53 (1981), 259–68 (at 262–63). Donna Crawford also notes this faithfulness: 'Prophecy and Paternity in The Wars of Alexander', *English Studies*, 73 (1992), 406–16 (at 407).
¹⁰ Crawford, 'Prophecy and Paternity', 407.
¹¹ Peter Dronke discusses battle ecphraseis but focuses mainly on the episodes of Alexander's entry into Jerusalem and his encounter with Candace: see 'Poetic Originality in The Wars of Alexander', in Cooper and Mapstone (eds), *The Long Fifteenth Century*, 123–39.
¹² Crawford calls this a 'conventional opening', but the resemblance is still notable ('Prophecy and Paternity', 408); see for example 'Sir Gawain and the Green Knight', in Malcolm Andrew and Ronald Waldron (eds), *The Poems of the Pearl Manuscript*, rev. edn. (Exeter, 1987), 37–59.
¹³ Dronke, 'Poetic Originality', 137–8.

occurs at the end of the work is complicated by suggestion of later scribal revisions after Hay's death.[14] The *Buik* provides an important comparison with *Wars* and its treatment of Alexander's 'storie'.

The *Buik* survives in two manuscripts, BL MS Add. 40732 (c1530), and Edinburgh, National Archives of Scotland, MS GD 112/71/9 (c1580–90), both derived from a common original.[15] Both manuscripts were owned in the later sixteenth century by Duncan Campbell, seventh Laird of Glenorchy (1541–1631), but nothing is known about their earlier histories. The prologue and the conception of Alexander is lost in both witnesses, the text now starting with Philip's vision of his son's future. The sources of the *Buik* are the J2 version of the *Historia de preliis* and the *Roman d'Alexandre*, the presence of these suggested in the text by references to 'þe Lateine buik' (18,561, *the Latin book*) and the 'Frensche leid' in the epilogue (19,334, *the French tale*).[16]

The *Buik*'s 19,000 decasyllabic lines make it longer than both its sources, indicating an expansionist approach. The poet sometimes supplements his source with details to increase the vivid nature of the text's *descriptio*, for example in the descriptions of the East and the chivalric elaboration of battles.[17] Like *Wars*, this addition of details that emphasize the chivalric and fictionalized narrative world aligns the *Buik* with the generic habits of romance. However, Hay also incorporates a significant amount of other material, including that drawn from the *Secreta secretorum* (a letter of advice and information supposedly written by Aristotle to Alexander) and *Iter ad paradisum* (in which Alexander travels to the Earthly Paradise in the east, associated with the Biblical Garden of Eden) traditions, but also works of contemporary Scottish conduct literature, *The Thewis off Gudwomen* and the *Buke of Phisnomy*.[18] This expansive 'translatioun' (19,312) indicates a second distinct approach to *translatio* in the Scots romance.

Both the *Thewis* and the *Buke of Phisnomy* offer guidance to correct social and ethical behaviour, so their inclusion increases the text's sense of exemplarity, alongside Alexander's general presentation as 'a model of chivalry and *courtoisie*'.[19] Their presence widens

---

[14] Cartwright (ed.), *The Buik of King Alexander*, vol. 3. For a detailed analysis of the stages of the work's composition, see Emily Wingfield, 'The Composition and Revision of Sir Gilbert Hay's *Buik of King Alexander the Conquerour*', *Nottingham Medieval Studies*, 57 (2013), 247–86. See also John R. Cartwright, 'Sir Gilbert Hay and the Alexander Tradition', in Dietrich Strauss and Horst W. Drescher (eds), *Scottish Language and Literature: Medieval and Renaissance*, Scottish Studies, 4 (Frankfurt, 1986), 229–38 (at 229). For a dissenting view of the *Buik*'s authorship, see Matthew P. McDiarmid, 'Concerning Sir Gilbert Hay, the Authorship of *Alexander the Conquerour* and *The Buik of Alexander*', *Studies in Scottish Literature*, 28 (1993), 28–54, who concludes that the c1438 *Buik of Alexander* is by Hay, but that the *Buik of King Alexander the Conquerour* is the work of another anonymous author.

[15] Wingfield, 'Composition and Revision', 273. This contradicts Cartwright's opinion that the National Archives of Scotland copy (MS GD 112/71/9) (B) was made using the Additional MS (A): see Cartwright (ed.), *The Buik of King Alexander*, 2.xiii. The manuscripts are described briefly by Cartwright (2.vii–xvii) and considered more fully by Wingfield (267–76).

[16] The Latin prose *Historia de preliis Alexandri magni* (composed after the tenth century) exists in three different versions, J1, J2, and J3. J2 was composed not later than the second half of the twelfth century: see Alfons Hilka (ed.), *Historia Alexandri Magni (Historia de Preliis) Rezension J2 (Orosius-Rezension)*, 2 vols. (Meisenheim am Glan, 1976, 1977).

[17] See, for example, Alexander's entry into the Indian desert and his fight with Darius: Ritchie (ed.), *Buik of Alexander*, 4.10,830–32, 5950–93.

[18] See Joanna Martin, '"Of Wisdome and of Guide Governance": Sir Gilbert Hay and *The Buik of King Alexander the Conquerour*', in Priscilla Bawcutt and Janet Hadley-Williams (eds), *A Companion to Scottish Poetry* (Cambridge, 2006), 75–88 (at 77–8), and also Wingfield, 'Composition and Revision', 256–60, and ibid., 'The thewis off gudwomen: Female Advice in *Lancelot of the Laik* and *The Buik of King Alexander the Conqueror*', in Janet Hadley Williams and Derrick J. McClure (eds), *Fresche fontanis: Studies in the Culture of Medieval and Early Modern Scotland* (Newcastle, 2013), 85–96.

[19] Martin, 'Of Wisdome and of Guide Governance', 78.

the narrative's exemplary remit, since it allows love, an unusual feature of Alexander literature, to be included in this approach.[20] This is clear in the episode in which Alexander is tempted by a beautiful maiden who has only eaten venomous snakes and dragon's blood since childhood in order to kill him through contact during sexual intercourse.[21] Hay's elaboration of this episode emphasizes good counsel and kingly obedience, since Aristotle advises Alexander not to sleep with her for a few days, until 'hir maner of lyving men may se' (9312, *men may perceive her way of life*). She is caught eating her deadly food and her poisonous nature is confirmed by a 'presoner' who embraces and kisses her all night until in the morning he is 'swollen grete, / That his hert birst' (9335, 36, 39–40, *swollen [so] hugely/That his heart burst*). The result of Alexander's reliance upon Aristotle's advice is that the latter composes the 'Regiment' 'of princis gouernance' (9356, *of princes' guidance*) for Alexander's benefit. Thus the would-be love episode is not only advisory in itself, but is also clearly tied to issues of regal 'gouernance', linking the two passages and emphasizing the text's exemplary *translatio*.

However, this *translatio* is not constant throughout the text. Alexander is not a wholly positive figure despite Hay's interpolation of such episodes: the *Buik*'s attempts to present him as a chivalric *exemplum* are nuanced by criticism and moral ambiguity. Joanna Martin and Emily Wingfield both read this in terms of the political landscape of fifteenth-century Scotland, the former in terms of kingship (regicide and minority rule), and the latter in light of legal wrangling over earldoms.[22] In both analyses, the romance reflects aspirational guidance for rulers and the harsh realities of contemporary politics, contextualizing its exemplarity in this Scottish context.

The *Buik*, then, displays a variety of responses in its approach to Alexander's narrative, engaging both with poetics recognizable from romances and also with concepts of exemplarity that relate to political contexts.

Alexander *Translatio*

The texts analysed here demonstrate both a close knowledge of Alexander narratives derived from Latin and French medieval material, and also the interpretative habits of romance as a genre (including exemplarity, elaborate description, 'gouernance'). The varied emphasis placed on such habits in these works highlights the differing possibilities available to authors working within a single narrative tradition. Whether this variety is idiosyncratic or found in other 'fictions of antiquity' remains to be seen in future studies.

Troy

The early fifteenth century, a period described as the 'peak of interest' for Troy material in England, sees the composition of three substantial Troy narratives based on Guido delle Colonne's 1287 *Historia destructionis Troiae*.[23] This relatively short Latin prose

---

[20] Martin, 'Of Wisdome and of Guide Governance', 83.
[21] Cartwright, (ed.), *The Buik of King Alexander*, 3.9288–350.
[22] Martin, 'Of Wisdome and of Guide Governance', 86, and Wingfield, 'Composition and Revision', 252–56 (56).
[23] Władysław Witalisz, *The Trojan Mirror: Middle English Narratives of Troy as Books of Princely Advice* (Frankfurt, 2011), 44.

work, completed in 1287 by the Sicilian Guido delle Colonne, survives in about 150 manuscripts.[24] The English works deriving from it are the *Gest Hystoriale* or *The Destruction of Troy* (c1400), the *Laud Troy Book* (c1400), and Lydgate's *Troy Book* (1412–20).[25] The now-fragmentary c1400 Old Scots poem known as the *Scottish Troy Book* is also based on the *Historia*.[26] In addition to these works is the version of the fourteenth-century poem *The Seege or Batayle of Troye* found in BL MS Harley 525, a later fifteenth-century manuscript which has a different source.[27]

The Troy narrative had formed an important aspect of the literary landscape of medieval England since Geoffrey of Monmouth incorporated it into his *Historia regum Britannie* in the early twelfth century.[28] As a founding 'history' for the country and its ruling dynasties, it developed political importance, enabling claims of descent from ancient Rome as well as Troy. However, Guido's *Historia* and Geoffrey's work highlight that there was not a single tradition of Troy reception demonstrable in medieval Britain. James Simpson has pointed out the different emphases of the two works, seeing the *Historia regum Britannie* as an imperial text and the *Historia destructionis Troiae* as anti-imperialistic and 'relentlessly exemplarist'.[29] The different characters of the two key Troy texts indicate the variety possible within the fifteenth-century Troy narrative even before individual works' *translatio* is considered.

Guido's *Historia* begins with the story of the Golden Fleece and the first destruction of Troy before narrating the abduction of Helen and the subsequent war between Trojans and Greeks, including battles interspersed with truces and various erotic subplots (Troilus, Briseida, and Diomedes; Achilles and Polyxena), and the deaths of major heroes (Hector, Troilus, Achilles). The narrative then depicts Troy's betrayal to the Greeks by Aeneas and Antenor and its destruction, and ends with the fates of the Greeks. This structure is not new to Guido, since his source is Benoît de Sainte-Maure's *Roman de Troie* (c1165), but he significantly condenses the lengthy French narrative, reducing the number of battles and curtailing the descriptions of marvels.[30] This reduction may be an attempt to 'deromanticize' the *Historia* to make it seem a more historicist work, in line with Guido's additions of 'embellishments of his own that he conceives to be appropriate to an historical treatment of the story'.[31] However, these 'embellishments', which may be moralizing or encyclopaedic, frequently move the *Historia* away from historical narrative.[32] The *Historia* is therefore a composite text in its approach, since it unites elements of romance drawn from Benoît's

---

[24] A figure of 136 is given in Nathaniel Edward Griffin (ed.), Guido delle Colonne, *Historia destructionis Troiae* (Cambridge, MA, 1936), xi; a figure of about 150 is given in Mary Elizabeth Meek (trans.), Guido delle Colonne, *Historia destructionis Troiae* (Bloomington, IN, 1974), xi.

[25] Ibid. NIMEV 2129, 249, 2516; the last of these (Lydgate's *Troy Book*) is outside the remit of this chapter.

[26] NIMEV 298.5; see Emily Wingfield, *The Trojan Legend in Medieval Scottish Literature* (Cambridge, 2014), 89–120.

[27] NIMEV 3139; see Bridges, *Medieval Narratives of Alexander*, 225–34. For reasons of space, only the *Destruction* and the *Laud Troy Book* are discussed in detail here.

[28] For an extremely useful overview of the Trojan narrative's history in England, see Marilynn Desmond, 'Trojan Itineraries and the Matter of Troy', in Rita Copeland (ed.), *The Oxford History of Classical Reception in English Literature, Vol. 1: 800–1558* (Oxford, 2016), 251–68.

[29] James Simpson, 'The Other Book of Troy: Guido delle Colonne's *Historia destructionis Troie* in Fourteenth- and Fifteenth-Century England', *Speculum*, 73 (1998), 397–423 (at 397).

[30] Léopold Constans (ed.), *Roman de Troie*, 6 vols. (Paris, 1904–12).

[31] Meek (trans.), *Historia*, xiv.

[32] Examples are Cassandra's ethically-inflected prophecies and Medea's magical accomplishments; see Griffin (ed.), *Historia destructionis Troiae*, 79 (Bk 7, 'Troya forte minime defleuisset ... demulcent auditus'), and Meek (trans.), *Historia destructionis Troiae*, 78 (lines 489–94); Griffin (ed.), *Historia destructionis Troiae*, 16–17 (Bk 2, 'Fluuiorum autem decursus ... peritissimam non negetur'), and Meek (trans.), *Historia*, 14–15 (lines 186–234). C. David Benson, however, claims that 'Guido's purpose is never seriously theological or moral', as 'the apparently

Troie with more historical and reflective perspectives, and is hence more diverse than Simpson's term 'exemplarist' implies.

This overview of the *Historia*'s approach highlights the different, potentially competing impulses contained within the text, impulses that to some degree may inform the fifteenth-century Middle English works that draw on it. Although critical work relating to these Troy narratives has coalesced around the question of their relationship with history,[33] the following analysis reframes the question to focus on their interactions with romance.

Gest Hystoriale or the Destruction of Troy

This long alliterative poem (14,044 lines) is extant in a single manuscript, Glasgow, University Library, Hunterian MS 388 (V.2.8) copied by Thomas Chetham of Nuthurst, Lancashire, around 1540, in which authorship is ascribed to 'John Clerk'.[34] The late date of the manuscript within the alliterative tradition of Middle English poetry has caused debate over when the poem was composed, with possibilities ranging from the late fourteenth through to the sixteenth centuries.[35] Scholarly consensus has fixed on c1400 for its date, which parallels the 'peak of interest in Troy' in England noted above.[36] The manuscript's contents list indicates that the *Destruction* was made for a knight whose name is supposedly included at the end of Book Thirty-six (the final section), but no name is forthcoming.[37] However, a knightly patron (even if only in aspirational terms) indicates the kind of audience familiar from other romances: literate in English and interested in chivalric narratives.

The *Destruction* is notable as the only extant alliterative Middle English Troy poem, sharing this form (and perhaps its author) with the *Wars of Alexander*.[38] Its *translatio* is therefore governed to some extent by conformity to alliterative style.[39] Despite the formal difference between its Latin prose source (the *Historia destructionis Troiae*), and the alliterative mode, the *Destruction* stays notably close to its source: it is 'a more literal translation of Guido's *Historia* than any of the other Middle English versions of Guido'.[40] Yet its compression is not universal. For example, the Prologue begins with an invocation to God, 'maistur in magesté, maker of Alle' (*master in majesty, maker of all things*), which

---

moralistic passages Guido adds to Benoît are too rhetorical and contradictory to qualify as serious instruction': see Benson, *The History of Troy in Middle English Literature* (Woodbridge, 1980), 12.

[33] This is the approach taken by the most detailed comparison of the three works to date, David Benson's *History of Troy*. See Walter Wilflingseder, *The Motifs and Characters in the 'Gest Hystoriale of the Destruction of Troy' and in the 'Laud Troy Book'* (Frankfurt, 2007), 3–4, for a survey of critical opinions on the works in terms of history and romance.

[34] Edward Wilson, 'John Clerk, Author of The Destruction of Troy', *Notes and Queries*, n.s. 37 (1990), 391–6 (at 391).

[35] See Wilflingseder, *Motifs and Characters*, 3–4, McKay Sundwall, 'The *Destruction of Troy*, Chaucer's *Troilus and Criseyde* and Lydgate's *Troy Book*', *RES*, n.s. 26 (1975), 313–17, and Thorlac Turville-Petre, 'The Author of The Destruction of Troy', *Medium Ævum*, 57 (1988), 264–9.

[36] Wilflingseder, *Motifs and Characters*, 3–4, and Witalisz, *The Trojan Mirror*, 44. Alex Mueller refines the date to c1390 in 'Linking Letters: Translating Ancient History into Medieval Romance', *Literature Compass*, 4 (2007), 1017–29 (at 1018).

[37] Geoffrey A. Panton and David Donaldson (eds), *The 'Gest Hystoriale' of the Destruction of Troy: An Alliterative Romance translated from Guido de Colonna's 'Hystoria Troiana'*, 2 vols., EETS, o.s., 39 and 56 (London, 1869 and 1874), 1.lxx.

[38] Thorlac Turville-Petre considered the question of shared authorship and concluded it was unlikely ('Author', 267).

[39] D. A. Lawton, 'The *Destruction of Troy* as Translation from Latin Prose: Aspects of Form and Style', *Studia neophilologica*, 52 (1980), 259–70.

[40] Sundwall, 'The *Destruction of Troy*', 316.

is not found in Guido's version.⁴¹ Combined with another added idea that the narrative is 'breuyt into bokes for boldyng of hertes' (14, *recounted in books for encouragement of hearts*), this invocation gives the historical analysis of texts faithfully reproduced from Guido (Homer, Dares, Dictys) a subtly different inflection.⁴² The inclusion of religious anachronism and an ethical function ('boldyng of hertes') suggests that the poem may have a morally instructive dimension, an addition to Guido's Prologue. The factual and historicist narrative summary given by Guido is also expanded in line with explicit romance themes of courage and *aventure*, so that the participants (who in the Latin *Historia* are simply '*duces*' and '*reges*') have become 'Dukes full doughty (*brave*) and derffe (*daring*) Erles' who engage in 'dedis of were' (*deeds of war*), in other words romance knights.⁴³ Yet even in this slight amplification of the source, it is noticeable that there is not the same sense of verbal display as in parts of *The Wars of Alexander* (for example 912, 'scheuerand schidis'): there is little extraneous description and fewer multiple adjectives ('doughty' is an unusual example). These small amplifications emphasize the chivalric nature of knights through repetition (two references to dukes, for example) rather than through the adjectival elaboration seen in *Wars*, a difference that demonstrates the stylistic variation possible within alliterative poetry.

It is suggestive that this engagement with both history (in terms of the analysis of sources derived from Guido, 33–77) and the habits of romance is often perceived more widely in the *Destruction* in terms of opposition between the two literary modes, despite the fact that separating the two genres is inherently problematic.⁴⁴ Despite this apparent binary, the *Destruction*-poet's habit of condensing his source indicates that his approach still strongly prioritizes the historical account, notwithstanding the examples of moral and religious *translatio* seen in the prologue. The *Destruction* omits some of Guido's most learned digressions, for example those dealing with astronomical knowledge, geographical discussions, and comments on idolatry, and also reduces the length of its moralizing passages. The effect of these changes is to focus the work more consistently upon its narrative, making the historical tale more dominant.⁴⁵ It therefore seems apt to view the *Destruction* as a poem using a variety of intersecting modes of discourse, such as historical narrative, chivalric descriptions indebted to romance, moralization and religious references. However, it is ultimately a work whose strong emphasis on proximity to its source and tendency to condense rather than to amplify prioritizes the historical *translatio* of its narrative within this variety.

Laud Troy Book

The *Laud Troy Book* is also extant in a single manuscript, BodL MS Laud misc. 545, dating from about 1415; the poem itself is usually dated to around 1400, although this is not certain.⁴⁶ Written in couplets, it is another long work (18,664 lines) and is also

---

⁴¹ Panton and Donaldson (eds), '*Gest Hystoriale*', 1.1.
⁴² For a detailed analysis of the Prologue's historicity, see Mueller, 'Linking Letters', 1020–1.
⁴³ Griffin (ed.), *Historia destructionis Troiae*, 4–7 (Bk 5), and Meek (trans.), *Historia*, 2 (Prologue, lines 61–6); Panton and Donaldson (eds), '*Geste Hystoriale*', 1. 78–91.
⁴⁴ See Wilflingseder, *Motifs and Characters*, 3–4, for a survey of critical opinions.
⁴⁵ Benson, *History of Troy*, 48, 49, 46. This habit of concision separates the poem from its alliterative relation *The Wars of Alexander*, a reminder of the differences that may exist between poems that are formally similar.
⁴⁶ Wilflingseder, *Motifs and Characters*, 5, claims 'about 1400': James Simpson, 'The Other Book of Troy', opts for 'after 1343 and before the first quarter of the fifteenth century', 404–5.

based on Guido's *Historia*, although the author may in addition have known the *Roman de Troie*.[47] The two Troy poems therefore share a possible period of composition and a source, which might suggest their approach to *translatio* is similar despite the different demands of rhyming couplets and alliterative poetry.

The *Laud Troy Book* follows the same narrative as Guido and the *Destruction*, but it ends differently, without any of the details of the returning Greeks' fates or the lists of the dead and their killers that are found in both the Latin and the other Middle English poem. Instead, the *Laud Troy Book* draws to a close with a prayer to 'god that died vpon the tre', asking him to 'graunt vs alle his benysoun (*blessing*)' and particularly to 'he that this romaunce wroght (*created*) & made'.[48] This conventional Christian ending marks a different emphasis between the *Laud Troy Book* and the *Destruction* at this point, situating the 'romaunce' in an explicitly religious context. This is even more apparent at the beginning, where the first ten lines are an address to 'Alle-myghty god in trinite'. Although the *Destruction* also begins with an invocation to God, the *Laud Troy Book*'s religious prologue is longer and more involved, appealing to the Trinity and explicitly asking for 'the ioye of heauen' as well as God's presence at the beginning and end of the 'tale' (8, 5). This Christian frame of reference is not constant in the narrative, but it is noticeable for example that Polyxena calls 'so Crist me spede' (18,558, *so may Christ aid me*) when pleading in vain for her life. The import of the Prologue, ending, and instances such as this is to dilute the *Laud Troy Book*'s focus on historical narrative, distinguishing it from the more consistent interest in such narrative demonstrated in the *Historia* and the *Destruction*.

Calling the poem a 'romaunce', as at the end, might also indicate its perceived generic status, which seems to distinguish it from historical narrative. This generic status is supported by the Prologue's explicit invoking of 'romaunces' by the heroes' names: 'Many speken … Off Bevis, Gy (*Guy*), and of Gauuwayn (*Gawain*), / Off kyng Richard, & of Owayn (*Owain*)' (15–16). In line with this romance focus, Hector is defined not as a Trojan but as the 'worthiest wyght … that euere by-strod any stede' (*the worthiest man … that ever straddled any steed*), removing him from his historical period and situating him as the first hero of timeless chivalric virtue who 'alle prowes of knyghtes be-gan' (32, *initiated all knightly skill*). This removal from history is also indicated in his medieval status as one of the Nine Worthies, individuals juxtaposed from ancient and more recent eras. The romance focus on the hero exemplified by Hector, which is seen throughout the main narrative, reinforces the other parallels with the genre and contrasts with the usual non-individual approach of most Troy accounts.[49]

This deliberate romance opening distinguishes the *Laud Troy Book* from Guido and from the *Destruction*. However, despite the conscious interest shown in the genre, the poem's approach is not a simple opposition between history and romance. The second part of the prologue summarizes the narrative's major points in some detail, including aspects of chronology (81, 'how longe euery trewe (*truce*) laste') as well as chivalric achievements (76–77, 'alle the dedis as thei were / Of alle the lords that ther faught'), ending with the description of Dares and 'Dites' as eye-witnesses drawn from Guido. Like the *Destruction*, the *Laud Troy Book* here engages with historical and romance-inflected perspectives as

---

[47] Wilflingseder, *Motifs and Characters*, 1.

[48] J. Ernst Wülfing (ed.), *The Laud Troy Book, a romance of about 1400 AD*, 2 vols., EETS, o.s., 121 and 122 (London, 1902, 1903), 2.549 (18650–64).

[49] For a detailed discussion of this focus on the hero and on parallels with romance in the text generally, see Benson, *History of Troy*, 77–88.

part of its overall *translatio*: it is not a question of the poem being 'a serious work of history' 'beneath its romance trappings', but rather the text as an entwined synthesis of these perspectives, and others.[50]

Another perspective is seen in the section where the poet laments for Troy, which is not found in Guido's *Historia*, although there are moments of authorial lament present in the latter text.[51] In just over a hundred lines (9878–992), the Middle English poem predicts the fall of Troy and the deaths of Hector, Troilus, Hecuba, and Polyxena, and ends the passage with an address to the 'curteis Citeseyns' (9969, *courteous citizens*). It is telling that, although mourning the deaths of individuals, this is a collective tragedy of a well-established city (9905). This urban focus is an interesting hint of fifteenth-century perspectives on the Trojan conflict: although the context is a lyric lament for romance heroes, the emphasis is on the people of the city, the 'burgeis' who are both generous ('fre') with their '3ifftes' (*gifts*) and noble (9974–5). This emphasis perhaps reflects a more contemporary historicist moment of *translatio* in which the narrative is retold for the urban perspective/s of a fifteenth-century audience, in line with other romances like *The Seege or Batayle of Troye*; the idea that the city's 'burgeis' are defined by their fiscal generosity is perhaps a parallel to the *Seege*'s mercantile focus, and would be appropriate to the trade interests of many city-dwellers.[52] However, since there is only a single manuscript extant, the potential urban origins and reception of the *Laud Troy Book* have not been established.

Like the *Destruction*, the *Laud Troy Book* also condenses most of Guido's digressions and cuts the Greeks' returns to their homelands.[53] The decision to omit the Greeks' returns has significant effects. Whereas in Guido's *Historia* these returns balance the Trojan loss with punishment for the Greeks, making the text even-handed in its apportioning of disaster, the imbalance between the defeated Trojans and the victorious Greeks in the *Laud Troy Book* is stark. The text ends on a note of simultaneous destruction and victory, with Troy destroyed 'thorow strong tresoun' and the Greeks as 'conquerours' made rich with spoils.[54] This juxtaposition confuses the interpretation: is sympathy for the betrayed city or praise for the Greeks' acquisitions dominant here? The bourgeois interest in the city and its citizens' 'gifts' suggested above fits with either of these views. In any case, the end of the *Laud Troy Book* is left equivocal in its implications.

The *Laud Troy Book* is another work in which there are a variety of different perspectives and approaches to *translatio*. What C. David Benson calls its 'paradoxical nature' as the product of 'a surprisingly careful historian' who is also well-versed in romance should therefore not come as a surprise.[55] Both the *Laud Troy Book* and the *Destruction* demonstrate the intricacies of *translatio* in their use of a variety of modes of discourse, but the *Laud Troy Book*'s approach is more explicitly and thoroughly indebted to romance in this sense. This is perhaps partly the result of the latter's use of the rhyming couplets frequently identified with the genre.

---

[50] Benson, *History of Troy*, 67.
[51] See for example the lyric lament at the failure to come to a truce in book 29 (Griffin, *Historia destructionis Troiae*, 218–19, 'Sed O quam Priamo ... saluare non possunt'; Meek (trans.), *Historia*, 34–40, 210).
[52] See Nicola F. McDonald, '*The Seege of Troye*: "ffor wham was wakened al this wo?"', in Ad Putter and Jane Gilbert (eds), *The Spirit of Medieval English Popular Romance* (Harlow, 2000), 181–99.
[53] Benson, *History of Troy*, 68.
[54] Wülfing, *Laud Troy Book*, 2.41–2 (18937–8).
[55] Benson, *History of Troy*, 67.

Other Fictions of Antiquity

So far, this chapter has focused on what might be thought of as 'canonical' fictions of antiquity that derive ultimately from prestigious classical narrative traditions. What follows are brief analyses of works whose interactions with antiquity are not defined by these narrative traditions but more habitually by ancient settings or by the *translatio* of lesser-known tales. This creates the possibility that their performance of *translatio* may not be focused via the lens of textual or narrative traditions to the same extent as the stories of Troy and Alexander.

Ovidian Rewriting: *Amoryus and Cleopes*

Amoryus and Cleopes (1449) is a romance reworking of the tale of Pyramus and Thisbe by John Metham, a Norfolk-based poet who was part of an East Anglian literary network that included Lydgate, Bokenham, Capgrave, and Scrope.[56] His patrons, to whom he addresses his poem, were Sir Miles and Lady Katherine Stapleton of Ingham, Norfolk. The poem survives in a single manuscript, Princeton, NJ, University Library, MS Garrett 141.[57] The poem is notably metrically irregular (with between eight and seventeen syllables to a line and differing stanza lengths).[58]

The romance takes place in a broadly classical context in which Nero is the Roman emperor, but the tale is located in Persia, implicitly providing a sense of exoticism via this Eastern context. Although the main narrative derives from Book Four of Ovid's *Metamorphoses*, the first third of the poem is occupied by the destruction and rebuilding of the temple of Venus, complete with a magical sphere of the heavens operated by spirits.[59] At the temple's dedication, Amoryus and Cleopes (the renamed Pyramus and Thisbe) see each other for the first time, and the Ovidian story of the separated lovers and their communication via a wall begins, following its expected course (with some additions, such as Amoryus' fight with a dragon, 1177–542) until after both lovers are dead, when in a new twist they are resurrected by a Christian hermit and converted to Christianity, enabling the conversion of the Persians. The first third of the narrative thus sets the thematic scene for the triumphant conclusion, since it establishes the theme of pagan religion ultimately overcome by Christianity: the magical sphere is predicted to be destroyed at the hands of 'a crucyfyid man' (667).

As with much fifteenth-century poetry, *Amoryus and Cleopes* is heavily indebted to Chaucer, especially *Troilus and Criseyde*, but also potentially to the *Canterbury Tales*.[60] Roger Dalrymple reads the poem as an attempt 'to harmonise some of the central

---

[56] NIMEV 3320; see Stephen F. Page (ed.), *Amoryus and Cleopes* (Kalamazoo, MI, 1999); Roger Dalrymple, 'Amoryus and Cleopes: John Metham's Metamorphosis of Chaucer and Ovid', in Phillipa Hardman (ed.), *The Matter of Identity in Medieval Romance* (Cambridge, 2003), 149–62 (at 149).

[57] Carol M. Meale, 'Katherine de la Pole and East Anglian Manuscript Production in the Fifteenth Century: An Unrecognized Patron?', in Carol M. Meale and Derek Pearsall (eds), *Makers and Users of Medieval Books: Essays in Honour of A. S. G. Edwards* (Cambridge, 2014), 132–49 (at 133).

[58] Dalrymple, 'John Metham's Metamorphosis', 152. See, for example, 162–8, especially 165–6. Derek Pearsall claims that the poem's 'technical and metrical incompetence make it almost unreadable' ('The English Romance in the Fifteenth Century', 69).

[59] The tale of Pyramus and Thisbe is found in Book IV of the *Metamorphoses*, lines 55–166.

[60] For a study of the influence of *Troilus and Criseyde*, see Dalrymple, 'John Metham's Metamorphosis', and for that of Fragment V of the *Canterbury Tales*, see Jamie C. Fumo, 'John Metham's "straunge style": *Amoryus and Cleopes* as Chaucerian Fragment', *The Chaucer Review*, 43 (2008), 215–37.

antagonisms identifiable in Chaucer's great Trojan narrative, bringing conflicting conceptions of love, the pagan and the Christian, and competing models of tragic action into less inimical relationships', whereas Jamie C. Fumo sees it as influenced by the Squire's Tale and the Franklin's Tale, particularly in relation to religion, marvels, and magic, narrative style, and characterization.[61] Both critics perceive the poem to be skilled and detailed in its 'Chaucerianism' despite its irregular metrics. In addition to these thematic points, *Amoryus and Cleopes* resembles Chaucer's *Troilus and Criseyde* structurally in its book divisions and introductory prologues. However, the romance also displays a wider range of reference, drawing on 'legends of Alexander, *romans antiques*, Middle English popular romance, and hagiography'.[62] Lydgate is likewise important, not just his *Troy Book* but also his habit of elaborate descriptions and encyclopaedic knowledge, seen in the description of the magical sphere and a lengthy excursus about different kinds of dragons. *Amoryus and Cleopas* is therefore a 'learned' poem, displaying detailed knowledge of various literary genres and influences (Chaucer, romances, hagiography, Latin classics, encyclopaedic and scientific works) in line with the idea that the fifteenth century sees romance take on 'a more self-consciously "literary" mode'.[63]

Metham's pluralist approach to *translatio* is demonstrated in his addition of the dragon-slaying passage. Reminiscent of the story of Jason and Medea, in which Medea's knowledge and magical skill enable Jason to defeat various foes including a dragon, Metham uses it here for thematic emphasis. It allows Amoryus to show his courage and fighting skill, highlighting his chivalric worth as a romance hero, and it demonstrates the author's learning in its long description of different kinds of dragons. It also emphasizes feminine power, since Cleopas' knowledge of dragon-lore is vital to Amoryus' success, making her a partner in this enterprise, yet power that in contrast to Medea's is not threatening.[64] Finally, the success against the dragon balances the forthcoming encounter with the lion, which both Amoryus and Cleopes will lose; the two struggles against wild beasts highlight the power of Fortune and the inevitability of death, which underlines the contrasting certainty and joy of the conversion to Christianity. The dragon-slaying therefore extends emphases seen elsewhere in the narrative that demonstrate different kinds of *translatio*: that related to romance, to 'learning', to gender, and to Christianity. Metham's approach is thus a thematically integrated one, using a range of classical material and medieval interpretative and poetic habits to add nuance to his Ovidian tale.

Charlemagne Romance: The *Sowdon of Babylon*

The *Sultan* (or *Sowdon*) *of Babylon* is an early fifteenth-century romance set in Rome, with the city an active participant in the narrative.[65] It survives in a single manuscript, Princeton, NJ, University Library, MS Garrett 140. One of three Middle English Charlemagne romances that tell the story of Fierabras (the others are *Sir Ferumbras* and *Firumbras*, NIMEV 593.8 and 944.5), it is the only one to use stanzaic form instead of rhyming couplets and tail-rhyme, and is the sole narrative that prefaces its account with the destruction

---

[61] Dalrymple, 'John Metham's Metamorphosis', 151; Fumo, 'Chaucerian Fragment', 217.
[62] Fumo, 'Chaucerian Fragment', 216.
[63] Pearsall, 'The English Romance in the Fifteenth Century', 67.
[64] This thematic emphasis is in line with the joint dedication to the Stapletons, husband and wife.
[65] NIMEV 950; *The Sultan of Babylon*, in Alan Lupack (ed.), *Three Middle English Charlemagne Romances* (Kalamazoo, MI, 1990); Lupack claims the romance dates from 'the late fourteenth or early fifteenth century' (1).

of Rome at the hands of the titular sultan, Laban.[66] The city is depicted at a moment in a perfect Christian past—'While that Rome was in excellence / Of all realms in dignite' (17–18)—but is destroyed as an explicit result of sin (23). Rome is both an emblem of Christian perfection and a symbol of decline from that gold standard, a decline that here is due to sin. This theological construction of Rome thematizes the narrative that follows, which is one of Christian and 'Saracen' conflict and conversion.[67] This construction also problematizes the idea of Rome as an antique city, and therefore the nature of work as a classically-set 'fiction of antiquity'. Yet of course such fictions may rely on a vague sense of the past, in which Rome even as a Christian (and hence potentially a medieval) city symbolizes an indeterminate antiquity rather than a precise chronological moment. This imprecise historical positioning is generically habitual for romance, and *Sowdon*'s introduction further explicitly demonstrates generic awareness in assessing its sources as 'wryten in romaunce' (25). Rome in this sense is thus an apt setting for a 'fiction of antiquity' that is set in the post-classical era of medieval religious conflict. However, the introduction also displays a more intellectual genealogy, referring to other sources as 'bokes of antiquyté' (26) and 'cronycles' (28) derived from St Denis, the abbey credited with the foundation of royal French historiography.[68] This reference is a sign of informed historiographical knowledge, even if probably at several removes from the Middle English text.[69] Both history and romance are explicitly called on as sources for the events of Rome's destruction here, potentially doubling the generic authority of the reference, but perhaps also displaying anxiety about the status of romance: it is notable that only the books of antiquity are given an erudite ancestry, prioritizing historical writing. Again the *translatio* displayed here is varied, distancing the narrative from classical antiquity and a precise sense of the past in a mode habitual to romance, but also referring to historiography and thus a conscious sense of the past as seen in its ancient books.

Chaucerian Fanfiction: The *Tale of Beryn*

The *Tale of Beryn* and its Prologue (also known as 'The Canterbury Interlude') are preserved in a unique witness, Alnwick Castle, Northumberland, MS 455 (fols. 180–235), dated c1450–70, although the work itself was perhaps composed early in the fifteenth century by a Canterbury monk.[70] In rhyming couplets, it is an explicit reaction to the *Canterbury Tales*, describing the pilgrims' arrival at the city and the start of their journey back to London, and is integrated into a unique ordering of Chaucer's poem; it seems to have

---

[66] On these romances, see Marianne E. Ailes, 'Comprehension Problems and their Resolution in the Middle English Verse Translations of *Fierabras*', *Forum for Modern Language Studies*, 35 (1999), 396–407. Ana Grinberg points out that the Roman part is only in *Sowdon* ('The Lady, the Giant, and the Land: The Monstrous in *Fierabras*', *eHumanista: Journal of Iberian Studies*, 18 (2011), 186–92 (at 189)).

[67] See Emily Houlik-Ritchey, 'Troubled Conversions: The Difference Gender Makes in the *Sultan of Babylon*', *Literature Compass*, 5 (2008), 493–504, who argues convincingly that conversion of the non-Christian 'other' threatens the homosocial Christian body that it helps to define.

[68] On this, see Gabrielle M. Spiegel, *The Chronicle Tradition of St Denis* (Turnhout, 1978).

[69] Ailes, 'Comprehension Problems', 396.

[70] NIMEV 3926; John M. Bowers (ed.), *The Canterbury Interlude and Merchant's Tale of Beryn* in *The Canterbury Tales: Fifteenth-Century Continuations and Additions* (Kalamazoo, MI, 1992). Ben Parsons dates the poem to 'the second decade of the fifteenth century', following Derek Pearsall: Parsons, '"For my synne and for my yong delite": Chaucer, the *Tale of Beryn*, and the Problem of *adolescentia*', *Modern Language Review*, 103 (2008), 940–51 (at 940). The author is named in the manuscript as 'Filius ecclesie Thome', which could mean a Benedictine of the Canterbury house: for a survey of the possibilities, see Parsons, 'Problem of *adolescentia*', 940–1.

been copied as part of a careful edition of the *Tales* that aimed to complete that work, although as there are pages missing from the end of the witness the extent of this editorial programme is unknown.[71] Critical interest has focused mainly on the poem in relation to the *Tales*, with most attention paid to the Prologue, which details the would-be amorous adventures of the Pardoner with a Canterbury tapster in a fabliau-style narrative.[72] In the *Tale*, Beryn is charged with five different lawsuits in one day whilst visiting a foreign city where such legal chicanery is a national sport, including one in which he is accused of stealing a blind man's eyes, and is only rescued by a compatriot disguised as a fool who turns out to be even wilier in legal terms than the citizens. Despite this critical focus on the law, however, the *Tale* is also a 'fiction of antiquity', since the early part of its narrative is set in Rome. This little-discussed element of the poem aligns it with the other antique fictions in this chapter, and may demonstrate connections beyond its setting in terms of shared *translatio*.

The *Tale* begins with an idyllic description of Rome, which is the worthiest of all cities, wealthy, and supreme in honour, good fortune, and governance (735–37), but Rome's depiction is a more involved situation than this description reveals. The city's chronological placement is fluid, which complicates the *Tale*'s relationship with antiquity. The narrative begins in indeterminate 'old dawes' (733, *old days*), in which Rome was predominant over all nations whilst the emperor was alive (740). These 'old dawes' are not (as might be expected in context) the classical and pagan era, but a Christian past similar to that seen in *Sowdon*, as 'Rome was then obeyed in all Cristienté' (*Christianity*, 742). The nature of these 'old dawes' is clarified further in references to 'romaunces' and 'gestes' (746, *tales of deeds*), which situate the narrative in romance territory, as Karen Winstead notes.[73] Yet this Christian romance universe, set in timeless 'old dawes' of perfect obedience, is undercut as soon as it is established, as the poet introduces the familiar idea that 'all thing doth wast (*waste away*)' (744) before including Rome itself in this decline: 'No mervell is thoughe Rome be somwhat variabill / Fro honour and fro wele' (752–3, *it is not marvellous that Rome has altered in its honour and prosperity*).[74] This introduction of a historical perspective creates tension with the timelessness inherent in the 'romaunces', a tension that may be read in generic terms. This 'variabill' depiction of Rome complicates the following passage, which gives a version of Roman history moving from 'after Julius Cezar' (773) to the reign of the 'Doseperes' (the twelve Peers of Charlemagne, 776), Constantine III and his son 'Philippus Augustinus' (787), and ending with the era of the Seven Sages (789). This may seem 'a predictably mangled view of imperial history',[75] but in fact the references to imperial Roman rule combined with well-known romance figures integrate history with romance (or at least collapse any sense of a distinction between them). This mixed approach is familiar from other works' *translatio* discussed in this chapter, especially *Sowdon*, yet differs from them somewhat in the explicitness of its engagement; rejoicing in

---

[71] Key scholarship that discusses the relationship includes John M. Bowers, 'The *Tale of Beryn* and *The Siege of Thebes*: Alternative Ideas of *The Canterbury Tales*', *Studies in the Age of Chaucer*, 7 (1985), 23–50 (at 33–4), Elizabeth Allen, 'The Pardoner in the "dogges boure": Early Reception of the *Canterbury Tales*', *The Chaucer Review*, 36 (2001), 91–127 (at 114–15), Karen A. Winstead, 'The *Beryn*-writer as a Reader of Chaucer', *The Chaucer Review*, 22 (1988), 225–33, and Parsons, 'Problem of *adolescentia*'.

[72] On the Prologue as a fabliau, see Bradley Darjes and Thomas Rendall, 'A Fabliau in the Prologue to the *Tale of Beryn*', *Mediaeval Studies*, 47 (1985), 416–31; also Bowers, 'Alternative Ideas of *The Canterbury Tales*', 27–30. See also Richard Firth Green, 'Legal Satire in *The Tale of Beryn*', *Studies in the Age of Chaucer*, 11 (1989), 43–62, for an analysis of the legal context of the *Tale*.

[73] Winstead, 'Reader of Chaucer', 227.

[74] Winstead notes that these generic expectations are subverted as the tale develops ('Reader of Chaucer', 227).

[75] Parsons, 'Problem of *adolescentia*', 941.

its 'mangled view', the text happily juxtaposes figures, eras, and modes of discourse before embarking on the narrative proper.

This eclecticism diminishes somewhat as the *Tale* proceeds, since it occupies recognizable romance territory (youthful *enfances*, a sea voyage, and a shipwreck at a strange city), although the legal knowledge it displays is an unusual feature, and the fact that Beryn develops into an anti-hero supports the idea that the *Tale* subverts romance expectations.[76] The most notable moment of subversion happens when the fool Geffrey describes the marvels of the king Isope's castle, which Beryn does not experience as he is too afraid to enter (2707–804). This knowing contradiction of romance expectations (characterized as Chaucerian by Winstead) may indeed reflect Chaucer's writings' playful approach to generic interactions, as seen for example in the romance/fabliau relationships in Fragment I of the *Canterbury Tales*.[77] However, the generic awareness on which this contradiction depends also demonstrates how such play is predicated on a wider knowledge of inherited literary cultures. This knowledge relates this 'Chaucerian' fanfiction to the broader habits of fifteenth-century *translatio* observed in other texts discussed in this chapter.

Conclusion

All the texts discussed here, whether prestigious Troy narratives or lesser-known tales set in unspecified 'old dawes', rework their material using multiple perspectives and approaches, many of which are characteristic of romance as a genre. Their awareness of classical material itself is varied, from the *Buik of King Alexander* and the *Destruction*'s probable direct textual knowledge of their respective Latin sources to the vague sense of general antiquity seen in the *Sowdon of Babylon* and *Beryn*. Their engagement with romance is also varied, ranging from *Amoryus and Cleopas*'s 'self-consciously 'literary' mode'[78] with its learned material and sophisticated responses to Chaucer and Lydgate, to the *Destruction*'s implicit preference for greater historicity. Yet whatever the nature of their *translatio*, all these texts are conscious and crafted works, demonstrating neither dullness nor decay but rather a creative awareness of medieval literary traditions.

---

[76] Winstead, 'Reader of Chaucer', 227.
[77] The juxtaposed tales of the Knight, Miller, and Reeve all play with generic expectations between themselves and also individually: the Merchant's Tale is another example.
[78] Pearsall, 'The English Romance in the Fifteenth Century', 67.

CHAPTER 20
Fictions of Britain

Aisling Byrne

Engagement with the legendary British past takes a wide variety of forms in the fifteenth century. In chronicles, political prophecies, and material culture, figures such as King Arthur and Sir Guy of Warwick are used to both to bolster and undermine a range of royal, regional, and dynastic interests. The intensity of this interest may owe something to anxieties about political instability and civil war at home and territorial losses abroad. This pessimistic mood is discernible in the prose romances of the period.[1] Yet, many of the verse romances strike a rather different, more optimistic, note. Where fragmentation within a community or conflict between groups is depicted, these poems often resolve the situation through courtesy and piety. Such idealism can give the impression that these texts are problematically escapist, even by the standards of medieval romance, and may have contributed to the rather marginal position they have traditionally occupied in studies of English narrative. Perceptions of the inferior literary quality of many of these texts have also played a part in their relative neglect. Fifteenth-century verse romances that deal with the British past are poor relations on two counts. Firstly, they are often overshadowed by the great works of the end of the previous century: many of them can seem unsophisticated by comparison with *Sir Gawain and the Green Knight* or with Chaucer's forays into the genre. Secondly, in a period which saw the emergence of a significant body of romances in English prose, most notably Thomas Malory's *Le Morte Darthur*, the verse romances can also appear outmoded. This impression is enhanced by the fact that very few of these works were printed at an early point.[2]

Romances set in a legendary ancient Britain can be divided into two loose groups: longer translated works, often based on French narratives, and shorter pieces which have no obvious sources in other languages. A number of important features of the French Arthurian tradition enter Middle English in translations of this period.[3] The story of Lancelot and Guinevere's adulterous liaison does not feature prominently in an English-language text before the *Stanzaic Morte Arthur*, written in or around 1400.[4] About a generation later, Henry Lovelich offers the first account of the history of the Grail in English. In many

---

[1] On this quality of the prose romances, see Helen Cooper, 'Counter-Romance: Civil Strife and Father Killing in the Prose Romances', in Helen Cooper and Sally Mapstone (eds), *The Long Fifteenth Century: Essays for Douglas Gray* (Oxford, 1997), 141–62, and Megan G. Leitch, *Romancing Treason: The Literature of the Wars of the Roses* (Oxford, 2015).

[2] For an overview of romance in early print, see Carol M. Meale, 'Caxton, de Worde, and the Publication of Romance in Late Medieval England', *The Library*, 6th series, 14 (1992), 283–98.

[3] On innovations in romance of this period, see Helen Cooper, 'Romance After 1400', in David Wallace (ed.), *The Cambridge History of Medieval English Literature* (Cambridge, 1999), 690–719. For other overviews of the period which treat texts discussed in this chapter, see Derek Pearsall, 'The English Romance in the Fifteenth Century', *Essays and Studies*, n.s. 29 (1976), 56–83; Douglas Gray, *Later Medieval English Literature* (Oxford, 2008), Ch.15, 'Romances and Tales'; Barry Windeatt, 'The Fifteenth-Century Arthur', in Elizabeth Archibald and Ad Putter (eds), *The Cambridge Companion to the Arthurian Legend* (Cambridge, 2009), 84–102.

[4] NIMEV 1994. Larry D. Benson (ed.), *King Arthurs Death: The Middle English Stanzaic Morte Arthur and Alliterative Morte Arthure* (Kalamazoo, MI, 1994).

respects, Lovelich is the most ambitious translator of this period. His translations of two parts of the thirteenth-century *Lancelot-Grail Cycle*, the *L'Estoire de Merlin* and *L'Estoire del Saint Graal*, reproduce the content of his sources relatively faithfully. The two works come to 51,646 lines in total, despite the fact that the surviving copies of both are incomplete.[5] 'Translation', of course, is a term that can cover a very wide range of approaches. *The Knightly Tale of Golagros and Gawane* and the *The Jeaste of Sir Gawain* both appear to draw on episodes from the *First Continuation* of Chrétien de Troyes' *Perceval*, but they rewrite them radically.[6] Other translators reduce or amplify French sources, sometimes in ways that can alter the thematic emphasis of the text quite dramatically. The anonymous author of the *Stanzaic Morte* works from the final part of the *Lancelot-Grail Cycle* and reduces his leisurely and digressive French source to roughly one fifth of its original length. By contrast, the author of the Scots *Lancelot of the Laik* expands his source at numerous junctures, producing a poem which gives a good deal more prominence to the theme of right rule than the French original.[7] French influence on other verse texts seems minimal. Analogous material, where it is identifiable, is from the Middle English tradition. *The Greene Knight* offers a much briefer, and considerably less subtle, version of the narrative presented in *Sir Gawain and the Green Knight*, while both *The Wedding of Sir Gawain and Dame Ragnelle* and *The Marriage of Sir Gawain* follow the same basic plot as the 'Wife of Bath's Tale' and John Gower's 'Tale of Florent'.[8] Direct influence is difficult to prove in these cases, and these poems could well be based on widely-known story types or on common lost sources, rather than on each other. Other echoes are even fainter. The author of the *Awntyrs off Arthure* appears to draw on the *Alliterative Morte Arthure* at various points, but the central episodes in the romance have no obvious connection to this or to any other surviving texts.[9] Romance, of course, is a highly conventional genre. Although many of these texts cannot readily be classified as translations or adaptations, they still have many features in common, drawing as they do on the broad lexicon of shared motifs that characterize romance as a mode.[10]

Alongside new compositions, many works originating in earlier centuries remained in circulation. The great majority of surviving manuscripts of a work like *Sir Bevis of Hampton*, which was translated from Anglo-Norman in the early 1300s, date from the fifteenth century. Other texts were revised so heavily in this period that they have a good claim to be considered distinct versions of the works in question. For instance, *Of Arthour and of Merlin*, which first appears around 1330 in the Auchinleck Manuscript (Edinburgh, National

---

[5] NIMEV *842.5 and 2312. Ernst A. Kock (ed.), *Merlin: A Middle-English Metrical Version of a French Romance by Henry Lovelich*, EETS, e.s. 93, 112; and o.s. 185 (London, 1904, 1913, 1932); F. J. Furnivall (ed.), *The History of the Holy Grail by Henry Lovelich*, EETS, e.s. 20, 24, 28, 30 (London, 1874–8). For an account of English adaptations of the *Lancelot-Grail Cycle*, see Helen Cooper, 'The *Lancelot-Grail Cycle* in England: Malory and his Predecessors', in Carol Dover (ed.), *A Companion to the Lancelot-Grail Cycle* (Cambridge, 2003), 147–62.

[6] Ralph Hanna (ed.), *The Knightly Tale of Golagros and Gawane*, STS, 5th series 7 (Woodbridge, 2008); this work survives only in printed form (1508; STC 11984). Thomas Hahn (ed.), 'The Jeaste of Sir Gawain', in Thomas Hahn (ed.), *Sir Gawain: Eleven Romances and Tales* (Kalamazoo, MI, 1995), 393–418; the *Jeaste* is NIMEV *306.5.

[7] NIMEV 3466. Margaret Muriel Gray (ed.), *Lancelot of the Laik from Cambridge University Library MS*, STS, n.s. 2 (Edinburgh, 1912).

[8] *The Greene Knight* (NIMEV 1908), *The Wedding of Sir Gawain and Dame Ragnelle* (NIMEV 1908) and *The Marriage of Sir Gawain* (NIMEV 1819), are in Hahn (ed.), *Sir Gawain*, 313-35, 47–80 and 362–71.

[9] NIMEV 1566 and NIMEV 2322. Ralph Hanna III (ed.), *The Awntyrs off Arthure at the Terne Wathelyn: An Edition Based on Bodleian Library MS. Douce 324* (Manchester, 1974).

[10] See further, Helen Cooper, *The English Romance in Time: Transforming Motifs from Geoffrey of Monmouth to the Death of Shakespeare* (Oxford, 2004).

Library of Scotland, Advocates' MS 19. 2. 1), remerged in the fifteenth century in very different form.[11] Later copies of this romance all conclude much earlier in Arthur's career and are roughly five times shorter than the fourteenth-century version. The popularity of the 'matter of England' romance, *Guy of Warwick*, seems to have prompted the production of two new versions of the narrative in English, one surviving only in the seventeenth-century Percy Folio manuscript (*Guy and Colbrond*; BL MS Add. 27879) and the other a quasi-hagiography by John Lydgate. These versions not only rework the story, but they focus on a single episode from the romance: Guy's celebrated fight with the Danish giant, Colbrond.[12]

The verse forms used in these texts are eclectic. Many use tail-rhyme stanzas, a form that was already inextricably associated with popular romance when Chaucer was writing. However, their length can vary radically, from sixteen lines in *The Avowyng of Arthur* (NIMEV 1161) to six in *Guy and Colbrond* and the *Jeaste of Sir Gawain*. Another well-established form, the couplet, is employed across a wide range of texts, from Henry Lovelich's vast translations to the brief version of *The Carle of Carlisle* (NIMEV 1888) that survives in the Percy Folio. New alliterative compositions are few and far between in this period. *The Awntyrs off Arthure* seems to represent the tail end of the 'alliterative revival', and its use of alliteration and rhyme, as well as stanzas of nine long lines followed by a four-line 'wheel', recall the earlier *Sir Gawain and the Green Knight* more readily than works of the fifteenth century. An exception, and a significant chronological outlier, is the Scottish romance, *Golagros and Gawane*. Although it probably dates from the end of the 1400s, its stanza form is identical to that of the *Awntyrs* and its use is sustained over a work of nearly twice the *Awntyrs*' length. Another Scottish work, *Lancelot of the Laik*, also breaks the mould. Its exhibits the sort of aureation associated with Chaucer's writing, a style which, despite its profound influence on fifteenth-century English poetry, generally made very little impression on romance. *Lancelot of the Laik*'s use of pentameter couplets also follows Chaucerian precedent. It is probably no coincidence that the author of *Lancelot* adapts his French source in ways that draw the romance into sustained dialogue with other genres, including the dream vision and the 'mirror for princes'. The only other text in this group which employs Chaucer's 'high style' and a stanza form used (albeit fitfully) by Chaucer, the ballade, also crosses generic boundaries. This is John Lydgate's *Guy of Warwyk*, which, as we will see, has affinities with both chronicle and hagiography.[13]

Even by the standards of medieval romance these poems can be difficult to contextualize or date with precision.[14] A work like the *Stanzaic Morte* might just as readily be placed shortly before 1400 as shortly after. Matters are made particularly complicated by the fact that a significant proportion of these works survive only in much later manuscripts or in early print. Our sole copy of the *Stanzaic Morte* comes from a commonplace book (BL MS Harley 2252), copied about a century later than the text's probable date of composition. A

---

[11] NIMEV 1675 and 1162. O. D. Macrae-Gibson (ed.), *Of Arthour and of Merlin*, 2 vols., EETS, o.s. 268, 279 (Oxford, 1973, 1979).

[12] John W. Hales and Frederick J. Furnivall (eds), *Bishop Percy's Folio Manuscript: Ballads and Romances*, 3 vols. (London, 1867–8), 2.527–49; Pamela Farvolden (ed.), *Lydgate's Fabula Duorum Mercatorum and Guy of Warwyk* (Kalamazoo, MI, 2016). Lydgate's poem is NIMEV 875.

[13] NIMEV 875. On the generic affinities of the work, see A. S. G. Edwards, 'The *Speculum Guy de Warwick* and Lydgate's *Guy of Warwick*: The Non-Romance Middle English Tradition', in Alison Wiggins and Rosalind Field (eds), *Guy of Warwick: Icon and Ancestor* (Cambridge, 2007), 81–93.

[14] Helaine Newstead offers an overview of probable dates of composition in 'Arthurian Legends', in J. Burke Severs (ed.), *A Manual of the Writings in Middle English*, 11 vols. (New Haven, CT, 1967), 1.38–79, 224–56 (at 15–16).

good number of medieval romances dealing with the exploits of Gawain have only come down to us in the Percy Folio, a manuscript compiled in the middle of the seventeenth century. Very few of the authors of these texts are named in manuscript or print witnesses, and only one of these works is by a poet with a significant reputation, John Lydgate. Evidence of patronage is also limited. Incipits in the surviving manuscripts suggest that Lydgate's account of Guy's fight with Colbrond was produced for a member of the Earl of Warwick's family, but aristocratic patronage appears to have been the exception rather than the rule. The middle-ranking background of another named poet, Henry Lovelich, seems to have been much more typical of the audience for Middle English romance in this period. Lovelich was a member of the skinners' company and, by his own account, he translated *L'Estoire de Merlin* for his fellow guildsman, Henry Barton. For Lovelich, translation of the *Lancelot-Grail* material into English was also a process of social transformation. As Michelle Warren has noted, his *Merlin* represents 'a sustained effort to bend the aristocratic source to the civic milieu'.[15] The sole surviving manuscript of the *Stanzaic Morte* seems to have circulated in a similarly mercantile context; it was owned by the London mercer, John Colyns.[16] Outside urban areas, these works are most typically associated with gentry readers, like the Paston family, or Robert Thornton, who included the *Awntyrs off Arthure* in one of the large manuscripts he copied in the middle of the century.[17]

If the number of surviving manuscripts is an accurate indicator, fifteenth-century English-speaking audiences typically encountered Britain's ancient past in prose rather than in poetry. The prose *Brut*, with its sweeping account of the history and pseudo-history of the island, survives in more than 180 copies today. By contrast, most of the verse romances have come down to us in less than a handful of manuscripts and a particularly high proportion survive in unique copies only. Indeed, of the texts discussed here only three survive in multiple manuscripts: Lydgate's *Guy of Warwyk* (seven copies), the *Awntyrs off Arthure* (four copies) and the abbreviated *Of Arthour and of Merlin* (three copies). There is some evidence for the wider circulation of other works, but it is very limited: the *Stanzaic Morte* may now only survive in an early sixteenth-century copy, but it was clearly available to Thomas Malory in the mid-fifteenth century. Equally, a late fifteenth-century booklist from the household of Sir John Paston may well attest to lost medieval copies of *The Greene Knight* and *Guy and Colbrond*.[18] Even as printing gathers pace, however, pickings are slim. Prose romance predominates and the versions of verse romances that do make it into print in the fifteenth century tend to have been composed before 1400. It is not until 1508, when *Golagros and Gawane* is published in Edinburgh, that a fifteenth-century Arthurian verse romance appears in print. Two years later, Wynkyn de Worde printed the truncated *Of Arthur and of Merlin* (STC 17841).

Although there is little evidence that English verse romances circulated in large numbers, such works seem to have increased their geographical reach considerably in the fifteenth century. Two significant works, *Golagros and Gawane* and *Lancelot of the Laik*, originate in Scotland and form part of the late-medieval literary efflorescence associated with the Older

---

[15] Michelle R. Warren, 'Translation', in Paul Strohm (ed.), *Middle English* (Oxford, 2007), 51–67 (at 55).
[16] John J. Thompson, 'Postscript: Authors and Audiences' in W. R. J. Barron (ed.), *The Arthur of the English: The Arthurian Legend in Medieval English Life and Literature* (Cardiff, 2001), 371–95.
[17] On the gentry audience for romance, see Michael Johnston, *Romance and the Gentry in Late Medieval England* (Oxford, 2014).
[18] Norman Davis (ed.), *Paston Letters and Papers of the Fifteenth Century: Part 1*, EETS, s.s. 20 (Oxford, 2004), 516–18.

Scots dialect.[19] This period also saw the first sustained engagement with Middle English verse beyond the English-speaking world. Heavily adapted versions of *Guy of Warwick* were produced in Iberia in the first half of the fifteenth century. These works seem to derive from a fourteenth-century version of the romance, but the translators omit large portions of the narrative and focus on the same episode as the new Middle English versions of this period: the fight with the giant Colbrond.[20] Wynkyn de Worde's edition of *Of Arthour and of Merlin* was also translated into Dutch in the early decades of the sixteenth century—the only English-language Arthurian text translated into another vernacular in the medieval period.[21]

Fictive accounts of early Britain are central to a number of attempts to recover a 'usable past' amidst the conflicts and uncertainties of the era. The Welsh-born Henry VII was eager to encourage connections between his own biography and that of Arthur himself, an association he hoped to maintain into the next generation by naming his eldest son 'Arthur'. The earls of Warwick, particularly Richard Beauchamp (d. 1439), drew heavily on the cultural capital of their putative ancestor, Sir Guy of Warwick.[22] Although the romance relating his legend had been in circulation since the middle of the thirteenth century, the story gained particular prominence in the 1400s. As we have seen, John Lydgate's *Guy of Warwyk* has a direct connection with this milieu. An incipit that appears in two of the surviving manuscripts states the work was translated at the request of Richard's eldest daughter, Margaret, perhaps around the time of her marriage in 1425. It notes that Margaret 'is lenyally descendid' from Guy himself.[23] The emphasis on lineage is picked up in the main text of the poem where we are informed of how the succession of Guy's son to the earldom of Warwick was legally shored up after the hero's death. Guy's bloodline is not the only material connection between the past and the present. Lydgate notes that Colbrond's axe, which Guy used to kill him, was taken to Winchester Cathedral and could still be viewed at the time of the poem's composition. Further relics of the knight-hermit, in the form of his armour and sword, were displayed at Warwick Castle.[24] Other romances of this period may also draw connections between the ancient past and the late medieval present. *The Turke and Sir Gawain* seems likely to have some association with the Stanley earls of Derby, although the family is not mentioned explicitly in what survives of the poem.[25] The text is unique among Arthurian romances in focusing on the Isle of Man, and the title 'King of Man' is bestowed on Gawain's companion by King Arthur at the conclusion of the narrative. The romance imagines a sub-kingship for the Isle of Man of the sort that the Orkneys, Cornwall, and other regions enjoy in Geoffrey of Monmouth's *Historia Regum Britanniae*. Significantly, the title 'King of Man' was in use by the Stanley family at the time of the romance's composition, having been first conferred on Sir John Stanley (d. 1414).[26] The Percy Folio,

---

[19] On Scottish approaches to Arthur, see the contributions in Rhiannon Purdie and Nicola Royan (eds) *The Scots and Medieval Arthurian Legend* (Cambridge, 2005).
[20] Aisling Byrne, 'From Hólar to Lisbon: Middle English Literature in Medieval Translation, c.1286–c.1550', *Review of English Studies*, n.s. 71 (2020), 433–59 (at 446–7, 459).
[21] Byrne, 'From Hólar to Lisbon', 444–5, 459.
[22] Emma Mason, 'Legends of the Beauchamps' Ancestors: The Use of Baronial Propaganda in Medieval England', *Journal of Medieval History*, 10 (1984), 25–40 and Yin Liu, 'Richard Beauchamp and the Uses of Romance', *Medium Ævum*, 74 (2005), 271–87.
[23] Lydgate, *Guy of Warwyk*, 91.
[24] Liu, 'Richard Beauchamp', 271.
[25] NIMEV 1886, in Hahn (ed.), *Sir Gawain*, 340–58.
[26] Echoes of Sir John's own biography have been discerned in *Turke* by David A. Lawton in 'History and Legend: The Exile and the Turk', in P. C. Ingham and M. R. Warren (eds), *Postcolonial Moves* (New York, 2003), 173–94.

which contains the only surviving copy of the *Turke and Gawain*, also features a number of further texts which celebrate the Stanleys and their regional allies.[27] Other poems make rather more general references to contemporary practices or institutions. *The Greene Knight* concludes by noting that Knights of the Bath can trace their origins to the events described in the romance. *Sir Gawain and the Carle of Carlisle* seems to relate the origins of an episcopal, rather than a dynastic, succession—it traces the origins of the bishopric of Carlisle to a foundation by the titular Carl.[28]

The interest in historicity that marks a number of these poems also has generic implications. John Lydgate's account of Guy moves readily between history, romance, and hagiography. This is in part due to the nature of his source: a Latin prose chronicle attributed to one Gerald of Cornwall.[29] The poem opens with very un-romance-like degree of specificity:

> Fro Cristis birthe complet nyne hundrid yeer
> Twenty and sevene by computacioun,
> Kyng Ethelstan, as seith the cronycleer,
> Reynyng that tyme in Brutys Albyoun
> (107–24)

(Nine hundred and twenty-seven years had been completed from Christ's birth; King Athelstan, as the chronicler says, was reigning that time in Brutus' Albion ...)

However, the characteristic shape taken by fifteenth-century adaptations of the Guy narrative also aligns them with chronicle accounts. In omitting the knight's earlier exploits and focusing on the fight with Colbrond, these texts also present the point at which Guy's legend makes clearest contact with known history: the setting evokes wars with the Vikings and the event takes place in the reign of a historical monarch, Athelstan. Indeed, the episode was used to flesh out the account of Athelstan's reign in a number of chronicle accounts. A similarly porous boundary between history and romance is also in evidence in another verse work of the mid-fifteenth century, John Hardyng's *Chronicle*. The work includes a substantial summary of the history and quest of the Holy Grail—matter more typically confined to romances.[30]

While some writers locate legendary events in specific historical moments; others place events in concrete 'real world' locations. A number of the 'Gawain romances' have a particular investment in borderlands and disputed territories within Britain, and the events they relate often bring outlying territories under Arthur's centralized control.[31] Two texts from the Percy Folio, *King Arthur and King Cornwall* and, as we have seen, *The Turke and Sir Gawain*, present enemies of the Round Table from marginal British territories, Cornwall

---

[27] On this text and other Stanley-ite works in the Percy Folio, see Aisling Byrne and Victoria Flood. 'The Romance of the Stanleys: Regional and National Imaginings in the Percy Folio', *Viator*, 46 (2015), 327–51.

[28] The version of the same narrative preserved in the Percy Folio states that the Carl became the Earl of Carlisle. However, that earldom was in abeyance from 1323 to 1622, so it is possible that this particular reference may not be much earlier than the Percy Folio itself.

[29] This work is edited with an English translation in Farvolden (ed.), *Guy of Warwyk*, 148–56.

[30] NIMEV 710. James Simpson and Sarah Peverley (eds.), *John Hardyng, Chronicle: Edited from British Library MS Lansdowne 204* (Kalamazoo, MI, 2015). On Hardyng's engagement with romance, see Richard J. Moll, *Before Malory: Reading Arthur in Later Medieval England* (Toronto, ON, 2003), 67–97.

[31] On this group of texts, see Hahn's general introduction to his edition, *Sir Gawain*, and Roger Dalrymple, 'Sir Gawain in Middle English Romance', in Helen Fulton (ed.), *A Companion to Arthurian Literature* (Oxford, 2009), 265–77.

and the Isle of Man. Gawain's control of various Scottish territories was well established within the Arthurian tradition and prompts a territorial dispute in *The Awntyrs off Arthure*, a text written close to the Anglo-Scottish border, perhaps in Cumberland. This romance has a diptych-like structure. The first half describes an encounter with the ghost of Guinevere's mother. The second half of the narrative has more conventionally political concerns: a Scottish knight, Galeron of Galloway, arrives at court and complains that Arthur has deprived him of his lands and given them to Gawain:

> 'Mi name is Sir Galaron, withouten eny gile,
> Þe grettest of Galwey of greues and gylles,
> Of Connok, of Carrak, of Conyngham, of Kyle,
> Of Lonrik, of Lennex, of Loudan Hilles.
> Þou has wonen hem in werre with a wrange wile
> And geuen hem to Sir Gawayn - þat my hert grylles'.
> (417-22)

('My name is Galeron, in complete truth, the greatest [knight] of Galloway, of woods and ravines, of Comnock, of Carrick, of Cunningham, of Kyle, of Lanark, of Lennox and of Loudoun hills. You have won them in war unjustly and have given them to Gawain - this enrages my heart'.)[32]

In the combat that follows, Gawain only overcomes Galeron with great difficulty and is prevented from killing his opponent by the intervention of Guinevere and Galeron's lady. At the end of the romance, two separate grants of land are made. Firstly, Gawain cedes a range of lands to Galeron, listing them at similar length and in similar order to the other knight's original speech. To compensate and reward him for his magnanimity, Arthur offers Gawain further territories. Arthur's gift to Gawain confers a far broader range of lands upon him, including overseas possessions, transforming him from a regional lord into a pan-insular one:

> 'Here I gif Sir Gawayn, with gerson and golde,
> Al þe Glamergan londe with greues so grene,
> Þe worship of Wales at wil and at wolde,
> With Criffones Castelles curnelled ful clene;
> Eke Vlstur Halle to hafe and to holde,
> Wayford and Waterforde, wallede I wene;
> Two baronrées in Bretayne with burghes so bolde,
> Þat arn batailed abouȝt and bigged ful bene'.
> (664-71)

('Here I give Sir Gawain, with treasure and gold, all the lands of Glamorgan, with groves so green, the honour of Wales at his will and command, with Caerphilly Castle, crenelated

---

[32] Place names are copied with varying degrees of accuracy in the surviving manuscripts of the *Awntyrs* and pose many interpretative problems. See further, Rosamund Allen, 'Place-Names in *The Awntyrs off Arthure*: Corruption, Conjecture, Coincidence', in Bonnie Wheeler (ed.), *Arthurian Studies in Honour of P. J. C. Field* (Cambridge, 2004), 181-98. In translating this passage, I have used the place-name identifications offered by Andrew Breeze in his study, 'Place-Names and Politics in The Awntyrs off Arthure', *Journal of Literary Onomastics*, 7 (2019), at https://digitalcommons.brockport.edu/jlo/vol7/iss1/2.

cleanly; also Oysterlow Hall to have and hold, Wexford and Waterford, walled, I believe; two baronies in Brittany, with towns so bold, that are fortified all around and built very well.')[33]

Some of these locations are more readily identifiable than others, but it seems clear that lands in Wales are supplemented by locations in Ireland and Brittany.

The *Awntyrs* presents an Arthurian Britain drawn together by shared bonds of courtesy and liberality. The more coercive dimension of that power is by no means ignored in this romance, but the violent conquests of which Galeron complains have taken place 'off stage' and do not encroach unduly on the romance's idealized and bloodless resolution. Nonetheless, the readiness with which Arthur disposes of numerous locations in Britain and beyond underscores the reach of his imperial power. The unity of Arthur's ancient *imperium* is a point of emphasis in many of these texts. The opening lines of *The Greene Knight* offer a brief verbal map of a unified Arthurian Britain that is at once celebratory and nostalgic:

> List! wen Arthur he was King,
> He had all att his leadinge
>   The broad Ile of Brittaine.
> England and Scotland one was,
> And Wales stood in the same case,
>   The truth itt is not to layne.
>   (1–6)

(Listen! When Arthur was king, he had all the broad island of Britain under his leadership. England and Scotland were united, and Wales was in the same situation, the truth is not to be concealed.)

Both versions of the *Carle of Carlisle* also open in similar vein: enumerating the various regions of Britain and identifying Arthur as the ruler of all of them. In *The Turke and Sir Gawain*, the conquest of the Isle of Man functions in some ways as a mirror for the original settlement of Britain as related by Geoffrey of Monmouth. Gawain must overcome a group of giants in order to take control of the island. The story has many of the features of a foundation myth and parallels, in miniature, the Galfridian account of the giant-infested Albion, subjugated by Brutus.[34] However, for all their emphasis on Arthur's imperial reach, these poems rarely take us beyond the insular world. Although some of the 'Gawain romances' hint at the wider conquests of Arthur, none of them relate them at any length. The Older Scots romance *Golagros and Gawane* is unusual in setting its action on the continent and implies that Golagros, a lord living by the 'riche riuer of Rone' (1349), is unusual in not already being subject to Arthur. Arthur's European conquests are reported in the *Awntyrs*, but not described directly. In contrast to the *Alliterative Morte*, the *Stanzaic Morte* commences its account long after the Roman Wars have concluded. This insular focus is shared by non-Arthurian verse romances of this period. In directing their attention towards the later events in Guy of Warwick's life, the fifteenth century versions of his legend limit the geographical scope of their action to England. The adventures which took

---

[33] As above, the place names are from Breeze, 'Place-Names and Politics'.
[34] Byrne and Flood, 'Romance of the Stanleys'.

Guy across the continent in the earlier romances have disappeared in both Lydgate's text and in the Percy Folio *Guy and Colbrond*. In these poems, English engagement with the wider world is defensive, rather than aggressive; Guy's primary chivalric act is protecting his country from the invading Danes.

In most versions of the Guy story these Danes are, explicitly or implicitly, non-Christians. Indeed, where these poems place the history of Britain within a larger historical or geographical context, the focus is frequently religious, rather than political. *The Turke and Sir Gawain* presents the conquest of the Isle of Man as, in part, a religious conflict. Despite what we might expect, the 'Turk' of the title appears to be Christian, and the focus of religious animosity proves to be the giants who rule the Isle of Man. They are introduced as unequivocally pagan:

> The Turke said to Sir Gawaine
> 'Yonder dwells the King of Man,
>   A heathen soldan is hee.
> 'With him he hath a hideous rout
> Of giants strong and stout
>   And uglie to looke uppon'.
>   (128–33)

(The Turk said to Sir Gawain, 'Yonder, dwells the King of Man, he is a heathen sultan. He has a hideous group of strong and stout giants with him, who are ugly to look at'.)

'Soldan' is, of course, a term which evokes the Islamic world and is used of Muslim rulers in a range of romances from this period. It connects this local dispute on an island off Britain to wider conflicts. There was precedent for mapping large-scale contemporary religious conflicts onto the fictive history of Britain in romance: the thirteenth-century *King Horn* characterizes the antagonists as 'Saracens' and the Auchinleck *Of Arthur and of Merlin* stages a conflict between Arthur's Christian realm and the pagan kingdoms of Ireland and Denmark, again presented as 'Saracen'.[35] Gawain's encounter with heathen giants may reflect a wider preoccupation with religious conflict, particularly in the years following the fall of Constantinople in 1453.[36] Henry Lovelich's translation of the *L'Estoire del Saint Graal* situates the British past within the larger context of salvation history, rather than the contemporary wars with Muslim rulers. Lovelich's poem has a vast geographic sweep, moving from the eastern Mediterranean to its culminating action in ancient Britain, offering a sacred version of the *translatio imperii*. Although Lovelich is generally quite conservative in adapting his French source, his version is more concrete than the French in its use of British place names and, like Lydgate, he emphasizes the material continuity between the ancient past and the present day.[37] Towards the end of the narrative, in a rare deviation from his French source, Lovelich asserts that Joseph of Arimathea was buried at Glastonbury Abbey.[38] The Grail itself may have passed out of the world, but Joseph's own relics remain in England, forming a material link with both the British past and with the salvific events in Jerusalem to which he bore witness.

---

[35] Diane Speed, 'The Saracens of *King Horn*', *Speculum*, 65 (1990), 564–95.
[36] Cooper, 'Romance after 1400', 698–9.
[37] On Lovelich's tendency to localize the exotic, see Raluca L. Radulescu, *Romance and its Contexts in Fifteenth-Century England: Politics, Piety and Penance* (Cambridge, 2013), 134–5.
[38] Furnivall (ed.), *History of the Holy Grail*, 4. Ch. 54, 141–56.

The absorption of the 'other' into the Round Table is one of the most consistent features of these romances. The court's one-time-enemy, Galeron, becomes one of Arthur's knights at the close of the *Awntyrs*, regaining his lands, but submitting to Arthur. A broadly analogous reconciliation between an outsider and the Arthurian court occurs in *Golagros and Gawane*.[39] Gawain overpowers Golagros in single combat, but, as in the *Awntyrs*, force proves less conclusive than courtesy. Golagros refuses to surrender; however, he asks Gawain to feign defeat himself so as to spare him disgrace. Struck by his nobility, Gawain relents and returns to Golagros' castle as his prisoner. In gratitude, Golagros finally accompanies Gawain back to Arthur's camp and submits. In some works, political incorporation is paralleled by supernatural transformation. The Turk of the *Turk and Gawain* turns out to have been a knight, Sir Gromer, under enchantment. His installation as a sub-king of the Isle of Man parallels his transformation from a magical, exotic outsider to a chivalric insider. The Isle of Man itself has also been transformed in a similar way: once a wayward territory, ruled by giants, it is now part of the Arthurian realm.[40] Such accommodation has its limits, of course; there is no prospect of the giants being assimilated by the court in a similar way. Unlike Galeron and Gromer, they do not share the courteous ideology of Arthur and his knights. A similar emphasis on political incorporation and disenchantment marks the Percy Folio's *Greene Knight*. In this respect, the poem resembles other fifteenth century 'Gawain romances' more clearly than its celebrated analogue of the previous century. Where *Sir Gawain and the Green Knight* ends in Gawain's embittered rejection of this adversary's hospitality and his solitary return to court, *The Greene Knight* concludes in apparent reconciliation. In the Percy Folio text, not only does Gawain return to his host's castle after the revelations at the Green Chapel, they then travel on to Arthur's court together '[w]ith harts blyth and light' (497).[41] In the earlier poem, the final identity of Gawain's antagonist remains ambiguous—his appearance does not seem to change and he rides off into the distance. In the Percy Folio version, any uncertainties about the relationship between the natural and the supernatural evaporate as soon as interpersonal tensions have been resolved.

Courtly ideals, expressed through good manners and the maintenance of 'trawthe', are also the focus in a number of other 'Gawain romances': the two versions of *The Wedding of Gawain*, *The Avowyng of Arthur*, and both accounts of the *Carle of Carlisle*. The moral character of Gawain in *The Wedding of Gawain and Dame Ragnelle* and the Percy Folio *Marriage of Gawain* could not be further removed from Chaucer's unnamed rapist-knight in the analogous 'Wife of Bath's Tale'. Gawain is his conventional courteous self throughout both fifteenth-century poems and marries the loathly lady out of loyalty to Arthur, rather than in payment of any debt of his own. His wife is finally transformed into a young and beautiful woman by Gawain maintaining his customary manners in adverse circumstances, rather than through the dramatic change of heart outlined in Chaucer's text. As in other 'Gawain romances', transformation and reconciliation are brought about by courtesy, but the context here is intimate and domestic, rather than political and chivalric. The *Avowyng* is almost exemplum-like in its single-minded focus on the inviolability of oaths, even under intense provocation. Like the *Awntyrs* it has a two-part structure, the first, perhaps, more

---

[39] On similarities between these two texts, see further Randy P. Schiff, 'Borderland Subversions: Anti-Imperial Energies in *The Awntyrs off Arthure* and *Golagros and Gawane*', *Speculum*, 84 (2009), 613–32.
[40] See the discussion in Hahn (ed.), *Sir Gawain*, 338.
[41] *The Greene Knight*, in Hahn (ed.), *Sir Gawain*, 313–5.

conventional than the second. In the opening episode, Kay and a maiden are saved from a wandering knight by Gawain. The knight is sent to Arthur's court where he joins the Round Table. This episode has a good deal in common with the other 'Gawain romances'; however, Gawain is by no means the centre of attention in what remains of the poem. The supernatural aura dissipates, and the text turns to more quotidian application of courtly virtues. Four knights take vows, Arthur, Kay, Gawain, and Baldwin. Arthur promises to slay a great boar, Kay to ride through the forest and fight anyone he meets, and Gawain to keep vigil at the Tern Wadling. Baldwin, however, undertakes vows which test rather more interior virtues: he promises not to envy his wife, to refuse food to no one, and to have no fear of death. The distinctiveness of Baldwin's vows becomes immediately apparent when the poet describes the knights embarking on their quests:

> The King turnus to the bore;
> Gauan, wythoutun any more,
> To the tarne con he fore,
> To wake hit to day.
> Thenne Kay, as I conne roune,
> He rode the forest uppe and downe.
> Boudewynne turnes to toune
> Sum that his gate lay,
> And sethun to bed bownus he;
> (*Avowyng*, 149–57)[42]

(The king turns to find the boar; Gawain, without further delay, sets off for the Tern [Wadling] to keep vigil there until day. Then Kay, as I may tell, rode up and down through the forest. Baldwin turns to the town where his home lay and then he goes to bed.)

There could be few things less conventional in a romance than a knight turning 'to toune' and then 'to bed' to begin his quest, and the contrast is enhanced by the account of the others setting out into the wild. In a further subversion of romance norms, it is Arthur who provides the tests that Baldwin undergoes, rather than any challenger from beyond the court. Baldwin proves his fearlessness by defeating knights who attempt to prevent him coming to court. He proves his generosity by showing hospitality to a minstrel who Arthur sends to his house. Most strikingly, he declines to become jealous when Arthur has a knight lie in his wife's bed, observing that his wife must be allowed freedom in her decisions.

The two surviving versions of Gawain's encounter with the Carl of Carlisle focus on the courtesy owed a host.[43] Although the Carl of the title seems to lack the outward refinements of courtly life, he punishes Gawain's companions, Kay and Bishop Baldwin, for failing in courtesy to him. It emerges that he has killed previous guests who failed his tests. As in the *Avowyng*, the story features a series of elaborate trials: the first, a test of care for the host's horse, is straightforward enough. In the second test, the Carl bids Gawain throw a spear at him. Gawain obeys with such ferocity that he shatters the wall. The host then takes Gawain to his wife and asks him to kiss her three times, but to go no further than that. When Gawain succeeds, the Carl sends him to bed with his daughter. We are told that they 'play

---

[42] *The Avowyng of Arthur*, in Hahn (ed.), *Sir Gawain*, 119–68.
[43] *Sir Gawain and the Carle of Carlisle* in Hahn (ed.), *Sir Gawain*, 85–112; for the Percy Folio version, see Hales and Furnivall (eds), *Bishop Percy's Folio Manuscript*, 275–94.

togeydor' (486) all that night, subordinating the demands of chastity to those of obedience to the host. The version that now survives in the Percy Folio adds a fourth trial: the Carl asks Gawain to strike off his head. Gawain obliges and the Carl reveals himself to be a man of ordinary stature now freed from 'nigromancé' (405). The ending in both versions is marked by reconciliation and by the incorporation of an outsider into the Arthurian court: Gawain marries the Carl's daughter and the Carl himself is knighted by Arthur and joins the Round Table. The Carl's new-found chivalry is matched by his piety: he resolves to make amends for the guests he has killed by building a chantry chapel where masses will be said for their souls.

This connection between courtesy and religious piety, particularly spiritual care for the dead, is also a theme in *The Awntyrs off Arthur*. This text yokes two seemingly distinct episodes together. In many ways, the first of these is more like an extended exemplum than a romance: Gawain and Guinevere are riding in the forest when the hideous ghost of Guinevere's mother appears to them.[44] The ghost laments the loss of her physical beauty and urges her daughter to reflect on her own eventual death. She presents her own corrupt and withered body as a 'mirror' in which the living should contemplate their own ultimate end:

> For al þi fressh foroure,
> Muse on þy mirrour;
> For, king and emperour,
> Thus diȝt shul ye be.[45]
> (166–9)

(Despite all thy fresh furs, think on thy mirror [here]; since, king and emperor, shall be arrayed thus.)

Guinevere is enjoined to care for the poor since, when she is dead, '[þ]e praier of þe poer may purchas þe pes' (178, *the prayer of the poor may purchase peace for you*). She also commits to having masses said for the soul of her mother. The ghost condemns the absent Arthur himself in terms that are explicitly moral, warning that he is 'to couetous' (265) in his desire for conquest. Gawain responds to the ghost revelations by recognizing that he is also guilty of similar vanity:

> 'How shal we fare,' quod þe freke, 'þat fonden to fight,
> And þus defoulen þe folke on fele kinges londes,
> And riches over reymes withouten eny right,
> Wynnen worshipp in werre þorgh wightnesse of hondes?'
> (261–4)

('How shall we fare,' said the man, 'who undertake battle, and in that way oppress people in many kings' lands, and enter realms without any right, winning honour in war through strength of arms?')

---

[44] On the text's affinities with this mode, see David N. Klausner, 'Exempla and *The Awntyrs of Arthure*', *Medieval Studies*, 34 (1972), 307–25.
[45] Hanna (ed.), *Awntyrs*.

Gawain's words here strike at the heart of all the Arthurian world holds dear. Not only is political expansion called into question, but so too is the core chivalric notion of 'worshipp'. Tellingly the ghost offers no direct response. She merely relates Arthur's fortunes and his eventual downfall in a prophetic speech. The link between the encounter with the ghost and the second half of the *Awntyrs* describing Gawain's combat with Galeron is sufficiently weak that the work has sometimes been considered two distinct narratives. Indeed, the conversation between Guinevere and the ghost is so reminiscent of medieval devotional texts that, at times, the Arthurian setting can seem merely incidental. Nonetheless, despite their significant differences in tone and content, the two episodes cover common thematic ground. The *Awntyrs* seems to bring courtesy and piety together particularly neatly, paralleling the reconciliation of a political outsider through courtesy with the release of a soul from purgatory through prayer. Yet significant tensions between chivalric life and Christian priorities remain. Like *Sir Gawain and the Green Knight*, with which it has often been compared, this poem suggests the limits of chivalric ideology in the face of religious imperatives. It is rare for a short verse romance to stand back from its immediate context, however briefly, and consider the history of the Round Table in its doomed entirety. Although the *Awntyrs* reaches a conventionally happy conclusion, the ghost's detailed prophecy of the fall of the Round Table situates this work within a wider context where political tragedy is ultimately brought about by moral failing.

Piety and penance prove the only adequate responses to civil war and personal wrongdoing in the *Stanzaic Morte Arthur*. One of the rare instances where the English poet has added to, rather than contracted, his French source is in his description of a final meeting between Lancelot and Guinevere. In the *Lancelot-Grail Cycle*, Guinevere takes the habit and dies without ever seeing Lancelot again; however, the English poet introduces and elaborates a final encounter over the course of around 700 lines. The passage combines religious didacticism with intense affectivity. Guinevere swoons three times as Lancelot approaches the cloister. She urges him to leave her and to marry, but Lancelot refuses, vowing instead to enter religious life. The decision is expressed in terms which make it at once an act of penitence and a declaration of continued fidelity to their love. If they must be separated, then their lives will, at least, continue to mirror each other. To make the parallel explicit, Lancelot notes that he will join her in penance, in the same way he once joined her in pleasure:

> 'Brent to ben worthy I were,
> Yif I wolde take none such a life,
> To bide in penaunce, as ye do here,
> And suffer for God sorrow and strife;
> As we in liking lived in fere ...'[46]
> (3698–702)

('I would be worthy to be burned if I did not take on such a life, abiding in penance, as you do here, suffering sorrow and pain for God, as we lived in pleasure together ...')

Their unity in sorrow and penitence is confirmed by their shared emotional and physical response to their final parting. Where Guinevere had previously been the one to faint on seeing Lancelot, at their parting they both fall down swooning (3728). In renouncing any prospect of erotic reunion, the lovers are united in bodily pain and grief, as well as in

---

[46] Benson (ed.), *King Arthur's Death*.

their shared determination to turn to God. By the time of his own death, after seven years of penance and religious life, Lancelot has taken on many of the qualities of a saint. On the night he dies, one of his companions dreams that the knight has entered paradise, accompanied by 'angeles thirty thousand and seven' (3879).

Most versions of *Guy of Warwick* conclude in similarly hagiographical mood. As we have seen, objects associated with Guy take on a status similar to saint's relics and such was Guy's reputation for piety that his legend gave rise to at least one text of religious instruction, the *Speculum Gy de Warwyk*.[47] In omitting any account of Guy's exploits before his rejection of worldly glory and his departure from his wife and home, the fifteenth-century adaptations place particular emphasis on Guy's pious identity and take the story's unease with chivalric 'worshipp' to its logical conclusion. Like Lancelot, Guy dies a hermit in the wilderness and heavenly messengers attend the scene. An angel appears to Guy to inform him of his imminent death; in the Percy Folio's *Guy and Colbrond* this angel identifies himself as the Archangel Michael (551).[48] The reference to Michael is thematically apt and suggests comparison between this figure and Guy himself: Michael is the leader of the hosts of heaven in the war against Lucifer (Book of Revelation 12.7-9) and Guy defeats Colbrond, a 'devill out of Denmark' (41). Guy's wife dies shortly after him and they are buried together. This pattern of events, where separated lovers having lived lives of piety are united in death around the same time, also plays out in the *Stanzaic Morte*. The English poet reorders the events in his French source to produce this conclusion. In the French text, news of Guinevere's death is one of the catalysts for Lancelot's entry into religious life, but the poet of the *Stanzaic Morte* places her death many years later, around the same time as that of her former lover.

The most explicit summary of the values proposed by these verse romances appears in piece of prose from the 1480s. In prefacing his edition of Thomas Malory's *Morte Darthur* (STC 801), William Caxton presents the Arthurian past as plausibly historical, ideal, and instructive. He offers a catalogue of textual and material evidence for Arthur's career and those of his knights. He goes on to suggest that readers will find 'many joyous and playsant hystoryes and noble and renomed acts of humanité, gentylness, and chyvalryes' in Malory's work and he urges them to 'take the good and honest acts in their remembrance, and to follow the same' so that they may not only attain 'good fame and renomme in thys lyf' but 'everlastyng blysse in heven'.[49] In many respects, this interest in instruction is more evident in the poetic fictions of this period than in Malory's own text. On the surface, these verse accounts of ancient Britain seem characterized by their diversity, rather than by their similarities: they survive in a wide range of poetic forms and their style, tone, and plots can vary dramatically. However, they share a pronounced focus on conduct, whether courtly or religious. Several also draw their fabulous worlds into dialogue with known history and relate legendary individuals and events to contemporary objects and locations. These two impulses, the historicizing and the instructional, are, in some ways, connected. In a period when faith in the world-transforming capacities of courtesy and piety might be easily shaken, these poems present ideals of good conduct and piety as attainable in fact, as well as in fiction.

---

[47] Georgiana Lea Morrill (ed.), *Speculum Gy de Warewyke*, EETS, e.s. 75 (London, 1898). Discussed in Edwards, 'The *Speculum*'.
[48] Hales and Furnivall (eds), *Bishop Percy's Folio Manuscript*, 2.527-49.
[49] Caxton's prologue is edited in Stephen H. A. Shepherd (ed.), *Sir Thomas Malory, Le Morte Darthur* (New York, NY, 2003), 814-9 (at 817).

CHAPTER 21
Fictions of Christendom and Other Late Romances

Phillipa Hardman

The turn to prose romance with the rise of print production in the later fifteenth century coincided with a remarkable late flourishing of Middle English verse romance. In part, this can be seen in the prolific copying of older romances, provoking Derek Pearsall's claim that the fifteenth century 'is the great age of the fourteenth-century romance'.[1] As Pearsall argues, such scribal copying was often a more dynamic process than simple replication. Texts were regularly adapted to new circumstances and given new currency by being 'reworked and lightly modernised in their language'.[2] However, 're-composition', a term that has sometimes been given to this active process of enhanced recopying,[3] should perhaps be reserved for the different practice of another group of fifteenth-century verse romances: those that return to early French-language romances and *chansons de geste* to compose independent new English texts retelling well-known narratives in new forms. The fifteenth-century appetite for this kind of re-composition is particularly evident in two fields: heroic narratives of the defence of Christendom, and complex narratives of chivalric self-discovery and dynastic fulfilment; while alongside these reimagined traditional stories, newly invented narratives on similar themes attest to the continuing importance of verse as a medium for English romance.

The fifteenth century saw a proliferation of English texts dealing with the legendary history of Charlemagne and his Peers, part of a larger textual corpus traditionally known as the 'Matter of France'. Significantly, while readers in England had access to a wide range of the corpus in French-language texts, available in both insular copies and continental imports,[4] it was only three *chansons de geste*, centred on Charlemagne, Roland, and Oliver in conflict with Saracens in Europe, that were selected, sometimes repeatedly, for translation and adaptation into the inclusive medium of English. These texts, *La Chanson de Roland*, *Fierabras*, and *Otinel*, had an urgent topical appeal in the fifteenth century, for their focus on Saracen challenges to Charlemagne's power as Christian Emperor could be seen reflected in the perceived threat of imminent invasion of Europe by Ottoman Turks, giving the inherited material new life as what might be styled the 'Matter of Christendom'.

La Chanson de Roland tells a fictionalized version of the historical Charlemagne's only recorded military defeat at Roncevaux in 778, in which the Basque guerrilla fighters are transformed into massed armies of the Saracens of Spain. The earliest extant witness of

---
[1] Derek Pearsall, 'The English Romance in the Fifteenth Century', *Essays and Studies*, n.s. 29 (1976), 56–83 (at 58).
[2] Andrew King, 'Romance', in Julia Boffey and A. S. G. Edwards (eds), *A Companion to Fifteenth-Century English Poetry* (Cambridge, 2013), 187–98 (at 188).
[3] Pearsall, 'The English Romance', 58; Douglas Gray, *Later Medieval English Literature* (Oxford, 2008), 382.
[4] Phillipa Hardman and Marianne Ailes, *The Legend of Charlemagne in Medieval England: The Matter of France in Middle English and Anglo-Norman Literature* (Cambridge, 2017), 32–52.

the poem is a twelfth-century insular manuscript (BodL MS Digby 23), but there is no evidence of a Middle English translation until the fifteenth century. This English version, known as *The Song of Roland*, exists in an incomplete manuscript copy (BL MS Lansdowne 388, fols. 381–95v), and its four-stress couplet form with irregular alliteration has suffered in transmission.[5] However, what remains shows a striking programme of re-composition, abbreviating and reordering the inherited material to form a distinctly new work, shaped by new concerns. The poem shares the aesthetic of many Middle English popular romances, with its preference for condensed, linear narrative, prioritizing action and direct speech, and its focus on one individual hero.[6] In the process, it realigns the ethical and emotional direction of the material away from the feudal concerns of the French *chanson de geste*, and replaces the frequent identification of Charlemagne's Peers as 'Franceis' with their identity as 'the cristyn', to produce a story centred on Roland and his band of fellow-Christians, fatally betrayed to their Saracen enemies by Ganelon's treachery, but resolutely fighting as warriors for Christ. Before the battle, having refused to blow his horn for reinforcements, Roland sees the vast extent of the Saracen forces and weeps for the inevitable loss of his fellows, then urges his men to embrace their fate, looking towards their sacrificial death and the assurance of heavenly reward:

'... we shall supe ther* seintis be many,	*where*
And crist soulis fedithe*, this is no nay.	*feeds*
Think he suffrid for vs paynes sore,	
we shall wrek* hem with wepins þer for'.	*avenge*
(625–8)	

The poet has adapted a speech delivered by Bishop Turpin in the *chanson de geste*, replacing Turpin's reference to dying for the king with Roland's call to arms in revenge for Christ's suffering. In a similar alteration later, Turpin's words in the French text giving honour to Charlemagne for his valiant peers are adapted in the English poem to support Roland's new speech giving thanks to God for the peers' miraculous success:

Then callithe furthe turpyn, & tellithe son:	
'this lord that we serue, louythe* his own,	*loves*
that so few of his fellid so many'.	
(811–13)	

Faced by innumerable fresh Saracen forces, Roland again looks beyond death to the celestial feast: 'criste kep vs cristyn that ben here, / to serue your soper with seintis dere!' (962–3). While the unique copy of the romance breaks off just before the moment when, in the *chanson de geste*, Roland would belatedly sound his horn to summon Charlemagne's aid, the poet's foreshadowing interventions in the narrative clearly assume that readers and listeners are familiar with the story and have no doubt that the poem will end with the death of Roland and all the Christians in defence of Christendom.

In the aftermath of the disastrous defeat of the Christian coalition forces ranged against the Turkish armies of Sultan Bayezid I at Nicopolis in 1396, it is easy to imagine how readers might have felt an emotional connection to the representation of heroic Christian resistance, sacrifice, and sublimation in this account of Roland's leadership at Roncevaux.

---

[5] NIMEV 1132.5; 'The Song of Roland', in Sidney J. Herrtage (ed.), *The Sege of Melayne, Duke Rowland and Sir Otuell of Spayne, and The Song of Roland*, EETS, e.s. 35 (London, 1880); line references are to this edition.

[6] Phillipa Hardman, 'Roland in England: Contextualizing the Middle English *Song of Roland*', in Rhiannon Purdie and Michael Cichon (eds), *Medieval Romance, Medieval Contexts* (Cambridge, 2011), 91–104.

There is evidence that the parallel between the epic narrative and the current international situation was indeed felt at the time, for the chronicler Jean Froissart, writing soon after 1396, uses the archetypal story of Roncevaux to measure the catastrophe of Nicopolis (quoted here from Lord Berners' translation of 1523–5): 'sythe the batayle of Rounseualx, where as the xii. peres of Fraunce were slayne, crystendome receyued nat so great a dommage (*injury*)'.[7] Surveying the wider contemporary response to the defeat in France, Christopher Tyerman concludes: 'Nicopolis was transformed into a morality story of sin, redemption and heroism',[8] and reading *The Song of Roland* in light of this interpretation of events offers an insight into the process of compilation behind the romance. Materials from different sources have been combined, including an interpolation from the twelfth-century *Pseudo-Turpin Chronicle* that shows Charlemagne's knights on the eve of the battle, tricked by Ganelon, drunk on Saracen wine and seduced into sin with Saracen women (68–76). The *Pseudo-Turpin Chronicle* was one of the most popular of medieval narratives, and the moralistic import of this story would have been widely known.[9]

A few chapters earlier in Froissart's *Chronicles*, in a highly embellished account of the build-up to Nicopolis, the author presents the Turkish menace in terms of Christendom's worst fears, claiming that Bayezid threatened to invade Hungary 'and to go fro thens to the cytie of Rome, and wolde make his horse to eate otes vpon the high auter of Saynt Peter', his purpose being 'to dystroye crystendome'.[10] A similar note of heightened anxiety can be heard in two Middle English romances, *The Sege of Melayne* and *Duke Rowland and Sir Otuell of Spayne*, found together in a mid-fifteenth-century collection made by Robert Thornton of Yorkshire (BL MS Add. 31042, fols. 66v–94).[11] The careful structure of the compilation has often been commented on,[12] presenting a Salvation History of the world centred on the defining event of Christ's crucifixion, in which the two Charlemagne romances represent the latest stage of Christian response to that event through fighting God's enemies, figured as Saracens, heathens, or Turks.

The Sege of Melayne and *Duke Rowland and Sir Otuell of Spayne* are both written in tail-rhyme stanzas, perhaps on account of the potential equivalence between tail-rhyme stanzas and the *laisses* of *chansons de geste* as structural verse narrative units.[13] Both romances are centred on conflict between Charlemagne's knights and aggressive Saracen forces, set in Lombardy. The choice of this location in the thirteenth-century *Otinel* may recall Charlemagne's historical conquest of Lombardy in 774,[14] but its relative closeness to Britain provides a shocking immediacy. In *Rowland and Otuell* the Lombardy setting is far more

---

[7] Jean Froissart, in E. V. Utterson (ed.), *Sir John Froissart's Chronicles, translated by John Bourchier, Lord Berners*, 2 vols. (London, 1812), 2.669. See M le baron Kervyn de Lettenhove (ed.), *Oeuvres de Froissart*, 25 vols. (Brussels, 1867–77), 15: *Chroniques 1392–6* (1872), 316. Berners may have supplied the word 'crystendome' as the missing subject of this sentence in Froissart's text, or it may have been in his source manuscript.

[8] Christopher Tyerman, *God's War: A New History of the Crusades* (London, 2006), 857.

[9] *The Pseudo-Turpin Chronicle* (also known as *Historia Karoli Magni*) purports to be an eyewitness report of Charlemagne's legendary conquest of Spain. It circulated widely in both Latin and vernacular copies, including two fifteenth-century English translations, and was an important source for later chronicles and heroic literature.

[10] Utterson (ed.), *Chronicles*, 2. 636, 668; de Lettenhove (ed.), *Chroniques*, 15. 217, 310.

[11] NIMEV 234 and 1996.

[12] For a bibliography of scholarship, see Michael Johnston, 'Constantinian Christianity in the London Manuscript: The Codicological and Linguistic Evidence of Thornton's Intentions', in Susanna Fein and Michael Johnston (eds), *Robert Thornton and His Books: Essays on the Lincoln and London Thornton Manuscripts* (York, 2014), 177–204 (at 180, n.13).

[13] Herrtage (ed.), *The Sege of Melayne and Duke Rowland and Sir Otuell of Spayne*; and see Rhiannon Purdie, *Anglicising Romance: Tail-Rhyme and Genre in Medieval English Literature* (Cambridge, 2008), 9.

[14] The historical event was recorded in Jacobus de Voragine's *Legenda Aurea*, widely translated into medieval vernaculars.

prominent than in any previous version of the narrative. Otuel, sent as messenger by the Saracen Emperor, boasts that they have invaded the plains of Lombardy, Charlemagne's own territory, and slaughtered 50,000 Christian Lombards in a sustained massacre. *The Sege of Melayne* opens with outrages and killings perpetrated on the people of Lombardy by the Sultan Arabas. The conquest of Lombardy is the culmination of a campaign of war against Christendom in which Arabas has swept northwards through the Italian peninsula, destroying cities, overthrowing the pope in Rome, planting Saracen colonies in Tuscany, and desecrating churches. In each case, the Saracen invader demands that the Christians abandon their faith, embrace 'hethyn' belief, and be subject to the Sultan on pain of death:

> 'For-thi* hathe he sent the worde by mee,   *therefore*
> Þat þou schall vn-cristen bee
>   & leue* appon oure ley*'.   *believe, law*
>   (*Rowland and Otuell*, 217–19)
> 'And if he ne will noghte to oure lawe be sworne
> He sall be hanged or oþer morne*   *before another morning*
> And with wylde horse be drawen'.
>   (*Sege of Melayne*, 55–7)

Together, the two romances present a vivid parallel to the Turkish threat to Christendom imagined by Froissart.

The *Otinel* story was repeatedly adapted for insular readers, who no doubt appreciated its streamlined enactment of an archetypal fantasy in which Christian and Saracen champions meet in single combat, resulting in the defeat and subsequent conversion of the Saracen.[15] In the fifteenth century, this symbolic story proposed a reassuringly optimistic response to the danger posed to Christian homelands by the westward expansion of the Ottoman Empire. *Rowland and Otuell* is a new version of *Otinel*, independent of the two earlier Middle English romances,[16] and its rewriting of the inherited tradition includes a notable adaptation of the final battle that serves to intensify the parallel with contemporary concerns. The second half of the romance sees Otuel, now christened and one of Charlemagne's Peers, play a key role in the campaign to drive the Saracens out of Lombardy (which Otuel has been promised as his fief), and after many encounters between groups of Christians and Saracens, the enraged Sultan Garcy vows to destroy all Christians with his vast army, and battle commences. At first, 'Þe cristen men gan þe maystry (*upper hand*) wynn', but soon the Saracens force them back, and, uniquely, their success is here attributed to 30,000 Turkish foot-soldiers: 'thies fute men so staleworthe (*strong*) ware / þat oure Batells full ferre one bakke þay bare', fighting so effectively 'þat þay hade almoste won þe felde' (1426–61). The jeopardy for 'oure' army is sustained for a passage of twenty-four lines before they rally and push back against the Turks. Any reader who was aware of the crucial role played by the Turkish infantry in the defeat of the Christian forces at Nicopolis could identify keenly with 'oure folkes' (1528) as they battled the Turks,[17] and would be able to read the victory of Charlemagne's Christian forces as a satisfying fantasy corrective to the real disaster of 1396.

The Sowdone of Babylone offers a different staging of the threat to Christendom which, like *The Song of Roland*, includes a moralistic perspective that incriminates Christians as

---

[15] The fantasy gave rise to apocryphal images of Richard I unhorsing Saladin in single combat, seen on Chertsey floor tiles (London, British Museum, tiles 467, 468), and in the Luttrell Psalter (BL MS Add. 42130, fol. 82).
[16] *Otuel* (NIMEV 1103); *Otuel and Roland* (NIMEV 1106).
[17] Tyerman, *God's War*, 856.

well as Saracens.[18] It is the third Middle English verse romance derived ultimately from *Fierabras*, the twelfth-century French *chanson de geste* that also lies behind Caxton's prose *Lyf of Charles the Grete* (1485),[19] but is the only one based on the insular French tradition represented in BL MS Egerton 3028, where two texts together, *La Destruction de Rome* and *Fierenbras*, tell the whole story of the power struggle between Charlemagne and the Saracen Sultan of Spain. *The Sowdone of Babylone* opens with a new prologue expounding God's benevolent purposes for Man, thwarted by Man's sinfulness, and takes as its subject the example of Rome and 'for synne how it was shente' when a heathen Sultan destroyed it in an act of vengeance (1–24). Told in fast-moving quatrains, it begins with reciprocal atrocities carried out by Romans robbing the Sowdon's merchants, and Saracens sacking the city of Rome, whereupon Charlemagne vows revenge:

> 'I shalle him never leve I-wis
> Withinne walle ner withoute,
> I swere by god and seinte Denys,
> Tille I have sought him oute!'
> (759–62)

The Sowdon's son Ferumbras delivers a challenge to Charlemagne, leading to his combat with Oliver, his religious conversion and submission to Charlemagne, and (after many exploits of the Peers with the help of his resourceful sister Floripas) his joining the Peers in the conquest of Spain.

By the beginning of the fifteenth century, the Christian reconquest of Islamic Spain had been largely complete for a hundred years, but the English poet gives the story a new focus that brings it closer to contemporary concerns. The Saracen leader is here identified not as Sultan of Spain, but 'Sowdon of hie Babilon', who was 'born in Askalon' (Ashqelon), and although 'at þat tyme he soiorned' in the city of Agremore in Spain (30–5), his home was Babylon of Egypt (Cairo). The imagined geography of the story is thus extended eastwards, and at every opportunity the English poem (unlike the French) lists the Saracens summoned by the Sowdon's call to arms as coming from numerous named places in Africa, Asia, and elsewhere. Huge numbers of them embark in ships displaying the Sowdon's arms, and land on the Italian coast, where they immediately begin burning towns and churches and killing Christians: the same nightmare invasion as that invoked in *The Sege of Melayne*.

The Sowdone of Babylone omits all the further detail of these atrocities in the source. Similarly, when Ferumbras enters St Peter's in Rome there is none of the horror surrounding the scene in the French texts, where the pope is beheaded and the holiest of Christian relics are desecrated: Ferumbras simply walks in and takes the relics. It is not a case of English taste preferring spare narration, however, for the theft is followed by a long and detailed account of the rituals and feasting with which the Sowdon celebrated victory, and there are many other added passages describing cultural and religious practices of the Sowdon and his people in terms that suggest an anthropological interest in the lands of the East, perhaps informed by travel writing such as *The Book of John Mandeville*.[20] In one of these passages, the Sowdon has the king of Barbary buried 'by right of Sarsenye':

---

[18] NIMEV 950; Emil Hausknecht (ed.), *The Sowdone of Babylone*, EETS, e.s. 38 (London, 1881).
[19] *Ferumbras* (NIMEV 593.8); *Firumbras* (NIMEV 944.5).
[20] See Iain M. Higgins (ed. and trans.), *The Book of John Mandeville* (Indianapolis, IN, 2011).

> With brennynge fire and riche oynemente,
> And songe the Dirige of Alkaron,
> That bibill is of here laye*.   *belief*
> (*Sowdone*, 2269-71)

Iain M. Higgins comments on the 'openness to otherness' characteristic of *Mandeville*'s treatment of cultural difference: 'not only are other religious practices and beliefs presented as entertaining to hear about; they are sometimes also depicted as analogous to Christian ones', while customs and manners, 'if explained, are represented as rational'.[21] This seems to be precisely the attitude shown here, where the Koran and the Bible are put side by side and the funeral service is equated to the 'Dirige' (the Christian Office of the Dead); and equally when the poem explains that the Saracen custom of drinking animal blood is 'to egre (*excite*) here mode (*anger*) / Whan þai in werre to battayle goon' (1009-10). The poet's literary debts to Chaucer have long been recognized,[22] in added passages that help to invest the Sowdon with positive qualities of honour and knightly worthiness; this unusual presentation of Saracen customs may be part of the same attempt to reinterpret the inherited tradition with a more nuanced approach to the Saracen Other.

Readers of the romance, however, may have been more focused on the relentless escalation of hostilities between the Sowdon and Charlemagne, which are set out in a stylized pattern of reciprocal acts of violence and oaths of vengeance. The unique manuscript (Princeton, NJ, University Library, MS Garrett 140) is dated after 1450,[23] and it concludes with an elaborate calligraphic explicit summarizing the story: 'Here endithe the Romaunce of the Sowdon of Babyloyne and of Ferumbras his sone who conquerede Rome and Kynge Charles off Fraunce with xij. Dosyperes toke the Sowdon in the feelde And smote of his heede' (fol. 41). This suggests that in the later fifteenth century, and especially after the fall of Constantinople to the Ottoman Turks in 1453 and the Turkish siege of Belgrade in 1456, readers may have relished the comforting fantasy fiction of the Christian super-hero overcoming the would-be destroyer of Christendom with a final mighty blow.

The siege of Belgrade certainly seems to have retained a hold on the popular imagination, as witnessed by the evidence of three early-sixteenth-century printed editions of *Capystranus*, a heavily fictionalized tail-rhyme account of the siege, focused on the part played in historical fact by the Franciscan friar, Giovanni da Capistrano (1386-1456).[24] No manuscript survives, but the text probably dates from the later fifteenth century.[25] *Capystranus* explicitly presents its material as a sequel to the achievements of Charlemagne in defence of Christendom, and it shares many features with the 'Matter of Christendom' romances. The prologue recalls stories of knights of old fighting for God, 'As Charles dyde, that noble Kynge, / That hethen downe dyde brynge' (43-4). A whole stanza then summarizes Charlemagne's recovery of the Passion relics as told in the *Pseudo-Turpin Chronicle* and *Fierabras* and his killing of 'Turkes' and 'paynyms' in great numbers (46-56), before turning straight to the narrative moment when the Ottoman Sultan Mehmed II attacks Constantinople. The slaughter is described at great length, and while some details,

---

[21] Higgins, *Mandeville*, xxi.
[22] Hausknecht (ed.), *Sowdone*, xlvi.
[23] Carol M. Meale, 'Patrons, Buyers and Owners: Book Production and Social Status', in Jeremy Griffiths and Derek Pearsall (eds), *Book Production and Publishing in Britain, 1375-1475* (Cambridge, 1989), 201-38 (at 216-17).
[24] References to *Capystranus* are to Stephen H. A. Shepherd (ed.), *Middle English Romances* (New York, 1995), 391-408; for the printed editions see STC 14649 (c1515), STC 14649.5 (c1527), STC 14650 (c1530).
[25] Shepherd argues from evidence of textual corruption that it must have been composed some length of time before the earliest print (*Middle English Romances*, 391).

such as the Christians being greatly outnumbered, accord with historical evidence, others resemble tropes in romance, such as the destruction of crucifixes and images of the Virgin (77–81).[26] The Sultan's conquest of Constantinople is achieved, and his next target is Hungary, starting with the siege of Belgrade. The effect of the Sultan's guns on the city is vividly described (369–75), and, overwhelmed by Turkish reinforcements, Capystranus and his thousands of recruits are on the point of defeat, when the friar calls on God for help, referring to Charlemagne's prayer in similar circumstances: 'Thynke on the myracle that thou Charles sent / That for the dyde fight' (502–6). The friar's prayer is miraculously answered when 20,000 Christian soldiers rise from death to fight.

Capystranus is unusual in the topicality of its historical subject, but in its combination of religious fervour and extreme violence, and its choice of the tail-rhyme stanza, it shows a deep connection with the traditions of the Charlemagne romances. As in many of them, the narrative voice is fiercely partisan, rejoicing at Turkish losses, involving the reader with frequent asides in support of 'our' Christians, and calling on God to assist them and confound the Turks. The joy felt at Christian successes is conveyed with typically dark humour, such as when slaughter is figured as instruction in the Christian faith:

> There was scole maystres of the best;
> Many of them were brought to rest
> That wolde not lere theyr laye*!   *learn their creed*
> (423–5)

All these characteristics contribute to a markedly dramatic style of narration, with assurances of the truth of what 'you' hear, and plentiful use of direct speech:

> [The Turke] badde hym forsake Jhesu in haste—
> 'Or elles thou shalte have shame!
> Have done anone, and Hym defye ...'
> Valeryan answered, and sayd, 'Nay!
> Thou shalte never se that daye
> That I shall Hym forsake'.
> (167–9, 172–4)

These features are paralleled in the Middle English Charlemagne romances, attempting to replicate the effects of their French *chanson de geste* sources; equally, the use of tail-rhyme and various other verse forms in the English romances seems to constitute an ongoing experimental negotiation with the French *laisse*, seeking native verse equivalents for the standard verse form of the *chansons de geste*.[27] However, in a new composition such as *Capystranus*, the choice of verse rather than prose as narrative medium in the later fifteenth century merits discussion. *Capystranus* marks the division of its narrative with a traditional formula that constructs the presence of a social audience:

> For of this I fynde a Fytte*;   *narrative division*
> Ferther and ye wyll sytte,
> Herkyn and take good hede.
> (322–4)

---

[26] Compare *The Sege of Melayne*, 25–7.
[27] Other verse forms include rhymed quatrains, septenaries, and alliterative verse; alexandrines and octosyllabic couplets arranged in verse paragraphs. See Hardman and Ailes, *The Legend of Charlemagne*, 86–97.

It implies that the performance of verse narrative is a sociable act, that it creates community by involving narrator and attentive listeners in a shared fictive reality with its own consistent structure and rhythm. Even in a context of private reading, the imagined sound of metrical verse allows the reader to enjoy a virtual counterpart to the experience of social listening. This socializing capacity most likely played a part in the choice of verse as medium not only for the Matter of Christendom, but for narratives of all kinds.[28]

Medieval and early modern moral and spiritual writings often situate themselves in opposition to allegedly harmful fictions, especially romances. From the fourteenth to the sixteenth centuries, writers reiterated the view that young people were liable to be corrupted by reading romances of chivalry, and their lists can provide a helpful survey of the reading matter of the time. Juan Luis Vives' influential work on female education, translated by Richard Hyrd as *The Instruction of a Christen Woman* (1529), follows tradition in discussing 'What bokes be to be redde and what nat'. Vives condemns the availability of vernacular books that 'haue none other matter but of warre and love', and calls for a legal ban. To Vives' list of corrupting romances current in Spain, France, and Flanders, Hyrd adds his own list of regrettably popular reading matter in England, headed by three fifteenth-century romances: '*Parthenope, Genarides, Hippomadon*', together with old favourites '*William and Melyour, Libius and Arthur, Guy, Beuis*, and many other'.[29] *Partonope of Blois, Generides*, and *Ipomydon* have much in common: all are unusually long, complex love stories with episodic structures involving repeated separations in which the eponymous heroes demonstrate their worth in battles and tournaments. *Partonope* and *Ipomydon* both derive from twelfth-century French-language romances, and although no source for *Generides* is known to exist, a lost insular French romance very likely lies behind its combination of traditional topics and incidents.[30] All share with the earlier romances cited by Hyrd the assured appeal of some long-established narrative memes, and such perennial romance concerns as chivalric self-discovery and dynastic fulfilment, but they also speak to a newly fashionable interest in details of courtly life and manners. Despite Hyrd's censure, they are not concerned solely with 'warre and loue'; their elaborate plots also variously involve exotic locations, magic, hunting lore, self-fashioning and education, and courtesy and morality. As with the insular tradition of the Matter of Christendom, each of the three French romances has given rise to two or more Middle English versions, in different literary forms. Every one, freshly revisiting the inherited material, constitutes an independent work, and demonstrates the interplay of narrative tradition and cultural innovation typical of fifteenth-century poetry.

Ipomédon, Hue de Rotelande's idiosyncratic twelfth-century insular French romance, set in the Norman kingdoms of Sicily, Apulia, and Calabria, was clearly popular reading matter in England: five manuscript witnesses survive, but there is no evidence of a Middle English translation until the tail-rhyme *Ipomadon*, dated between c1390 and c1450.[31] *Ipomadon* offers an unusually close translation of Hue's poem, but with some omissions and

---

[28] Jocelyn Wogan-Browne similarly accounts for the fact that in the thirteenth century, insular French works continued to be written in verse alongside newly fashionable prose texts, by reference to the socializing function of verse ('Vernacular Knowledge in Thirteenth-Century England: Aesthetics and Power', Middle English Research Seminar, Oxford, 18 November 2020).

[29] *A Very Frutefull and Pleasant Boke Called the Instruction of a Christen Woman* (1529; STC 24856), Eiii–[Eiv]. The older romances named by Hyrd are: *William of Palerne* (NIMEV 3281.5); *Libeaus Desconus* (NIMEV 1690); *Guy of Warwick* (NIMEV 3145, 3146, 946); *Bevis of Hampton* (NIMEV 1993).

[30] Carol M. Meale, 'The Morgan Library Copy of *Generides*', in Maldwyn Mills, Jennifer Fellows, and Carol M. Meale (eds), *Romance in Medieval England* (Cambridge, 1991), 89–104 (at 92).

[31] NIMEV 2635; Rhiannon Purdie (ed.), *Ipomadon*, EETS, o.s. 316 (Oxford, 2001), liv.

changes of emphasis that reveal the different preoccupations of fifteenth-century readers. The English poem retains the initial focus on the heroine, 'the Fere' (the proud one), and her vow to love only the best knight in the world, but adds a new preface declaring that the romance is addressed to all 'that wote what love may meane' (*Ipomadon*, 3). As Rhiannon Purdie argues, the translation brings 'the theme of love into much sharper focus';[32] it also removes all the sexually explicit details, obscene humour, and misogynistic comments that give Hue's treatment of love its distinctly ironic perspective. As a result, the portrayal of women in *Ipomadon* is not compromised as it is in Hue's poem, and the characterization of the Fere is rendered more sympathetic by added details of her inner thoughts, such as her intent towards her beloved: 'Knyght in erthe but it were hee / Shuld neuer to wyff her wedde' (1764–5). Other changes serve to clarify the motives behind characters' actions, creating a more coherent plot (a process typical of Middle English romance adaptations), or to abbreviate battle scenes. On the other hand, scenes of courteous conversation are amplified, and descriptions of hunting etiquette are retained, along with details of courtly luxury, such as jewelled goblets and garments enriched with fur and embroidery, indicating what were probably the chief attractions of Hue's romance for fifteenth-century consumers. Three stanzas are devoted to the 'cupe sett wyth precyous stonys' (2649) that Ipomadon gives to Cabanus in token of friendship, demonstrating his noble largesse, and his courtly display is further evident in his dress:

> Ipomadon comys in to þe hall
> Clothed in a syrket off palle*   *outer garment of fine cloth*
> Purfelyed* wyth ermine,   *Trimmed*
> Bend abowte wyth orfrayes.   *adorned with embroidered bands*
> (2696–9)

The idea that courtliness had a high priority for fifteenth-century readers is supported by the context of the unique copy of *Ipomadon* in Manchester, Chetham's Library, MS 8009 (fols. 191–335v), a household compendium in which *Ipomadon* is paired with a courtesy manual. John Russell's *Boke of Nurture* is designed to teach the manners of the court to youths embarking on the kind of service 'that longys a gentill man to doo' (*Ipomadon*, 407), just as Ipomadon does when he arrives at the Fere's court. Russell advises the youth serving at the buttery: 'Be fayre of answere, redy to serue and also gentelle of chere, / and þan men wille sey "þere gothe a gentille officere"' (*Boke of Nurture*, 181–2),[33] and Ipomadon, on performing a generous act during his service at the buttery, is rewarded with the same recognition when all agree: 'It was a gentill dede', and the Fere acknowledges: 'This child is comyn of gentille blode' (*Ipomadon*, 485, 501). Romance expectations here neatly map on to didactic objectives.

An educational agenda clearly lies behind the process of re-composition that formed the couplet romance *The Lyfe of Ipomydon*,[34] an expert example of the medieval practice of *abbreviatio*. Hue's poem has not only been abridged to one-fifth of its original length: it has undergone radical restructuring. It begins not with La Fière (whose byname is here altered to 'the Eyre of Calabre'), but with the parentage, birth, infancy, and education of the hero, including new details in line with social norms: his christening, the employment of a nurse and ladies of the household to care for the young prince, and a clerk to teach him

---

[32] Purdie, *Ipomadon*, lxvi–lxvii.
[33] John Russell, 'The Boke of Nurture', in Frederick J. Furnivall (ed.), *The Babees Book*, EETS, o.s. 32 (London, 1868), 115–99.
[34] NIMEV 2142; Tadahiro Ikegami (ed.) *The Lyfe of Ipomydon*, 2 vols. (Tokyo, 1983, 1985).

to read and sing, as well as a knight to instruct him in matters of courtesy and chivalry. The subject of love is introduced in relation to Ipomydon's desirability, not the Lady's, as every female guest at his father's Whitsun feast is stricken to the heart by his 'feyre chere' (99–100). The poet creates a realistic scene of courtly leisure as the guests play and chat and the topic of the Calabrian heiress arises, at which point the information about her that formed the first part of Hue's poem is inserted. This careful rearrangement continues throughout the romance. Hue's long passages of interior monologue are cut: feelings are directly stated in dialogue or by the narration; incidents not essential to the plot are cut or elided; aspects of Hue's story are rationalized, as when Ipomydon asks his men to conceal his identity (228–34), or his mother's revelation that he has a half-brother is relocated to the last part of the narrative (1560–74). Most striking is the obliteration of the Lady's proud vow and of the hero's false reputation at her court for cowardice: here, the Lady seeks only to know if the 'strange squyer' comes of noble birth, and Ipomydon is scorned for his love of hunting only at King Mellyager's court. The result is an efficiently streamlined narrative true to its title: it tells the whole life of Ipomydon, with its focus on the hero's growth into the twin roles of husband of the heiress of Calabria and king of Apulia. One of the passages invented for this retelling speaks directly to the courtesy agenda. After accepting his offered service, the Lady asks Ipomydon to dine, but before he sits down, 'He saluted theym, grete & smalle, / As a gentillman shuld in halle' (303–4); an equivalent couplet marks his departure from the court: 'He went anone in to the halle / And toke his leue of grete and smalle' (467–8). These actions are exactly as prescribed in courtesy manuals and can be replicated in other romances such as *Sir Amadas*, aimed (as *Ipomydon* seems to be) at young readers.[35]

The manuscript in which the couplet *Ipomydon* survives (BL MS Harley 2252, fols. 54–84) is the early-sixteenth-century personal commonplace book of London merchant John Colyns, which he constructed around two 'found' pieces: booklet copies of *The Lyfe of Ipomydon* and the *Stanzaic Morte Arthur*, both produced some fifty years earlier in the same workshop.[36] The relationship of these two texts gives insight into fifteenth-century romance reading tastes and practices. The *Morte Arthur*, like *Ipomydon*, is translated from French with skilful techniques of abbreviation and reordering to produce a 'brilliant condensation', one-fifth the length of its source.[37] Evidently there was an enduring appetite for abridged, fast-paced new versions of classic romances from earlier centuries, for John Colyns's booklet was the copy for Wynkyn de Worde's print *The Lyfe of Ipomydon* (1522; 1527),[38] while the *Morte Arthur* was used by Sir Thomas Malory in his *Morte D'Arthur*, and Larry Benson argues that it may have influenced the way he 'condensed and modified the plots' of his French sources.[39] Like *Capystranus*, *Ipomydon* invokes the traditional expectation of social reading practices for verse romances: the poem uses conventional formulae, customized for this story, to divide the text into four evenly sized reading stints: 'Of child Ipomydon here is a space' (528); 'Latte hym go, God hym spede, / Till eftesone we of hym

---

[35] *Sir Amadas* is paired with a brief courtesy text that reinforces the message of the romance in Edinburgh, National Library of Scotland, Advocates' MS 19. 3. 1, fols. 84v–86v, and while this is not the case with *Ipomydon*, comparison may be made with a third fifteenth-century translation of Hue's poem, the prose *Ipomedon*, which is accompanied by two courtesy texts in a modestly prestigious vellum manuscript that passed through the hands of Richard of Gloucester (Warminster, Longleat House, MS 257).

[36] Carol M. Meale, 'The Middle English Romance of *Ipomedon*: A Late Medieval "Mirror" for Princes and Merchants', *Reading Medieval Studies*, 10 (1984), 136–91 (137).

[37] Introduction, in Larry D. Benson and Edward E. Foster (eds), *King Arthur's Death: The Middle English Stanzaic Morte Arthur and Alliterative Morte Arthure* (Kalamazoo, MI, 1994).

[38] STC 5732.5; STC 5733; see Carol M. Meale, 'Wynkyn de Worde's Setting-Copy for *Ipomydon*', *Studies in Bibliography*, 35 (1982), 156–71.

[39] Benson, *King Arthur's Death*, xviii.

rede' (1075-6); 'of Ipomydon here is a fytte' (1524), which work to create a milieu of shared enjoyment and anticipation.

The history of *Partonope of Blois* has a similar trajectory. The Middle English poem is based on the twelfth-century French romance *Partonopeu de Blois*, which survives in ten manuscript witnesses. Three are insular copies, including the one claimed to best represent the original form of the romance,[40] indicating that readers in England had access to the story in French long before the fifteenth-century English translation. *Partonope of Blois* closely follows the original French narrative: a role-reversed Cupid and Psyche plot (here it is the lady, Melior, who is the invisible lover, and the hero, Partonope, who is forbidden to try to see her) with an eventual happy ending, after adventures and a three-day tournament, in their marriage. For the most part, the English version reproduces the characterization and narratorial attitudes as well as the incidents and settings of the source, and mirrors its French octosyllabics in four-stress couplets. Nevertheless, there are changes that indicate fifteenth-century preferences. The English poem makes far more use of direct speech, creates new dramatic scenes, amplifies displays of sentiment, and strengthens the circumstantial and practical detail around events to create a thicker, more realistic narration, showing the same tendency seen in Chaucer's innovations in *Troilus*.[41] Chaucerian influence also touches the figure of the narrator in *Partonope*, when detachment replaces what the French poem portrays as the narrator's personal experience of love.[42] During the young couple's first sexual encounter, the English narrator refers repeatedly to the French source as if to deflect any blame for indelicacy, and seems anxious to reach the end of the episode:

> Off alle þys fere* make we a fine*. *business, end*
> Þe ffrenshe boke fulle welle In Ryme
> Tellethe hyt shortely, and noȝte in prose.[43]
> (1292-4)

Here, verse romance is preferred for its brevity to prose. One altered passage highlights the concern with the courtesy curriculum seen in *Ipomadon*: when Melior explains to Partonope what he must do to prepare for their marriage, the English version enhances her stress on chivalry and courtesy, advising that he 'be lowly to smale as welle as to grete', so all will say: '"Loo, yender goþe the welle of gentylnes"' (1855-7).

The Middle English *Partonope* exists in five manuscript witnesses from the mid to later fifteenth century:[44] an unusually high number for a romance, suggesting it was indeed popular with readers, as Hyrd complained. It was, of course, female readers about whom Vives and Hyrd were concerned, and evidence shows that 'women formed a significant portion of *Partonope of Blois*'s readership'.[45] Partonope's invocation of St Sytha (661), a saint popular with women in fifteenth-century England, would support the view that it was

---

[40] NIMEV 4132; and see Joseph Gildea and Leon P. Smith (eds), *Partonopeu de Blois*, 2 vols. (Villanova, PA, 1967-8), 2.2.

[41] B. A. Windeatt (ed.), *Troilus and Criseyde: A New Edition of 'The Book of Troilus'*, (London, 1984), 11.

[42] Brenda Hosington, 'Voices of Protest and Submission: Portraits of Women in *Partonopeu de Blois* and its Middle English Translation', *Reading Medieval Studies*, 17 (1991), 62-75 (at 69); King, 'Romance', 192-3; B. J. Whiting, 'A Fifteenth-Century English Chaucerian: The Translator of *Partonope of Blois*', *Mediaeval Studies*, 7 (1945), 40-54.

[43] A. Trampe Bodtker (ed.), *The Middle English Versions of Partonope of Blois*, EETS, e.s., 109 (London, 1912).

[44] BL MS Add. 35288, fols. 2-154; BodL MS Rawlinson poet. 14, fols. 8-92v; Oxford, University College, MS 188, fols. 1-91v; and two fragments: BodL MS Eng. poet. c. 3, fols. 6-7v; BodL MS Lat. misc. b. 17, fols. 157-158v.

[45] Amy N. Vines, 'A Woman's "Crafte": Melior as Lover, Teacher, and Patron in the Middle English *Partonope of Blois*', *Modern Philology*, 105 (2007), 245-70 (at 246, n.3).

composed with women in mind. But it seems another readership preferred an abridged and streamlined version of the narrative, for 308 lines remain of a shorter version in four-stress quatrains entitled *Pertinope*, consisting of the first 276 lines and a later fragment. *Pertinope*'s context in the Delamere Chaucer manuscript (New Haven, CT, Beinecke Library, MS Takamiya 32, fols. 164rb–165vb) suggests that it was afforded some prestige: the large vellum codex contains the *Canterbury Tales*, tales from Gower's *Confessio Amantis*, and popular moral texts such as the *Vision of Tundale*.[46]

There is no trace of a French source for *Pertinope*. Sif Rikhardsdottir argues that 'given the creative liberty with which English redactors approached their French sources, the notion that the text underwent the narrative reconfiguration in England is by no means an unlikely option', and points to its typical techniques of abbreviation and simplification, and also its 'delocalisation' rendering it available to a wider reading community.[47] As in the abbreviated *Ipomydon*, the story has been radically reordered, so that it begins not with Pertinope's history, but with the birth and education of Melior, her search for a husband, the discovery of Pertinope, and Melior's secret voyage to see him for herself. The reader no longer shares the hero's surprise when he experiences the magic ship and mysterious hospitality of the castle produced by Melior's enchantments. Nor is Melior a dangerously unseen presence for the reader: the poem repeatedly stresses the physical beauty of both hero and heroine in highly conventional lyrical formulae. Their sexual encounter is presented as uncomplicated mutual pleasure, and is immediately followed by Melior's generous provision for his year's travels: all indicates a simple test of the hero's constancy. The *Partonope* story shares many motifs with Breton lays, and it seems that this version has been remodelled on the pattern of the Middle English Breton lay: a short romance, typically dealing with love and magic and involving separation and reunion. The taste for such fiction persisted well beyond the fifteenth century, as shown by later manuscript copies and prints,[48] suggesting that the apparent archaism of *Pertinope*'s verse style was part of its appeal: claiming association with a valued romance tradition.

Generides differs from *Ipomadon* and *Partonope* in several ways: it has no extant source; the two Middle English versions, one in four-stress couplets and the other in rhyme royal, are distinct compositions, but both without abridgement; and the love story fails to give the complicated plot a structural device, such as La Fiere's vow or Melior's invisibility. It is difficult to summarize the narrative;[49] the producer of the unique copy of the couplet *Generides* in New York, Morgan Library & Museum, MS M 876, fols. 103v–152v, provides a 377-word prose summary, with an assurance that it will be 'more pleinlie declared' in the following book,[50] which claims to be based on a 'geste' translated from Latin into 'frensh

---

[46] NIMEV 4081. The volume has suffered damage, and six folios appear to be lost after *Pertinope*, but there was clearly a problem before any loss of further text, for the narrative disjunction between the opening section and the following lines (276–7) suggests either that the scribe was working from a fragmentary exemplar, or that he mistakenly copied text in the wrong order.

[47] Sif Rikhardsdottir, *Medieval Translations and Cultural Discourse: The Movement of Texts in England, France, and Scandinavia* (Cambridge, 2012), 119, 130–1.

[48] For example, *Sir Degaré* appears in BodL MS Douce 261, fols. 8–14v (1564); BL MS Add. 27879, 372–81 (The Percy Folio, c1650); and in four print editions dated 1512 to c1565: STC 6740, 6740.5, 6742, 6742.5.

[49] Derek Pearsall writes of the rhyme royal *Generydes*: 'It would be impossible to summarize its story briefly: let it suffice to say that it has a noble but easily outwitted hero, a beautiful but tearful heroine, a tyrannical father, a wicked steward, a treacherous queen, faithful servitors, pathetic love-scenes, and interminable battles, and that the action ranges over a vast remote region variously called India, Persia, Egypt' ('The Assembly of Ladies and Generydes', Review of English Studies, n.s. 12 (1961), 229–37 (at 229–30)).

[50] NIMEV 70; Frederick J. Furnivall (ed.), *A Royal Historie of the Excellent Knight Generides*, Roxburghe Club (London, 1865), 1.

ryme' at Hertford (23–8).⁵¹ There are traces of a lost, possibly insular French source: 'Vn romance de Generides' is listed among Richard II's books, and allusions in both courtly and moral fourteenth-century poems show the story was well known.⁵² The two versions agree on the plot, with its repeated deceptions and misunderstandings, and its large cast of characters, and they both fail to make anything of the exotic locations: 'Surre' might as well be Surrey as Syria. Derek Pearsall surmises that the couplet *Generides* is closer to the lost French original than the rhyme royal *Generydes*, pointing to its more bloodthirsty battle scenes, its frankness about sexual matters, and its freedom from moralizing.⁵³ The narrative style of *Generides*, with its traditional prologue and call to attention (1–32), the misogynistic tone of its narratorial digression on unfaithful wives (52–62), and its elaborate descriptions of jewelled artefacts (168–91; 291–326), recalls the characteristics of *Ipomédon* and *Partonopeu*, both of which attracted close fifteenth-century translations; but *Generides* apparently preserves features of the kind that the translator of *Ipomadon* omits, and makes no gesture towards a new Chaucerian model of romance, as seen in *Partonope of Blois*. It invites communal, episodic reading, with narratorial divisions, and resumés of previous events, and perhaps implies a conservative appetite among fifteenth-century readers for extravagant tales with recognizable romance memes, in the traditional narrative medium of couplet verse.

The rhyme royal *Generydes*,⁵⁴ on the other hand, not only adopts the verse form of *Troilus*, but seems at times to echo Chaucer's romance. The scene in Clarionas's bedroom, for instance, when she rebukes Generydes, then revives him from his swoon with a kiss, is remodelled to bring it closer to the similar scene in Criseyde's bedroom in *Troilus*. Like Troilus, Generydes pleads: 'of all this god wote I am full innocent' (4727; compare *Troilus*, 3.1084–5); and Clarionas makes peace: '"All is for geve," quod she' (4730), like Criseyde following Pandarus's advice (*Troilus*, 3.1106, 1129).⁵⁵ Like *Partonope*, *Generydes* expands opportunities for dialogue, often to emphasize the courteous behaviour on display, and no chance is missed to stress the chaste propriety of the lovers' long relationship.⁵⁶ A few new scenes enhance the focus on moral sentiment, as when Serenydes (uncharacteristically) confesses and repents of her wickedness (4892–909), or add emotional detail to the love story, as when Generydes gives Clarionas a little dog (4737–9). If *Generides* is addressed to the 'Worshipful sirres' invoked at the start of the story (33), perhaps, as Pearsall suggests, the remodelling in *Generydes* was intended to appeal to 'a predominantly female audience'.⁵⁷

---

⁵¹ Given the clear debt *Generides* owes to Hue's *Ipomédon*, it is not impossible that the author intended an allusion to Herefordshire, the home locality named by Hue in his sequel, *Prothesilaus*. 'Hereford' would scan better than 'Hertford'.
⁵² Meale, 'Morgan *Generides*', 90–2. *Generides* is mentioned in Gower, *Cinkante Balades*, 43. 19, in G. C. Macaulay (ed.), *The Complete Works of John Gower*, 4 vols. (Oxford, 1899), 1.372; *The Parlement of the Thre Ages*, 620–1, in Warren Ginsberg (ed.), *Wynnere and Wastoure and* The Parlement of the Thre Ages (Kalamazoo, MI, 1992).
⁵³ Pearsall, '*Assembly* and *Generydes*', 234–6.
⁵⁴ NIMEV 1515; W. Aldis Wright (ed.), *Generydes: A Romance in Seven-Line Stanzas*, EETS o.s. 55, 70 (London, 1878).
⁵⁵ Similarly, when Lucidas accepts Darel's ring, a new scruple is introduced: '"Ryng ne Writeng, as I remember canne, / I neuer yet resyuyd of noo gentilman"' (*Generydes*, 5076–7), perhaps modelled on Criseyde's demurral: '"scrit ne bille, | … Ne bring me noon"' (*Troilus*, 2. 1130–2).
⁵⁶ Pearsall, '*Assembly* and *Generydes*', 236.
⁵⁷ Pearsall, '*Assembly* and *Generydes*', 235.

Generydes survives in two manuscripts: Cambridge, Trinity College, MS O.5.2, fols. 1–37v, and Cambridge, Emmanuel College MS 405,[58] and three early sixteenth-century print editions.[59] Frank Stubbings describes the fragmentary paper MS 405 as a 'book of some dignity', with spacious layout and wide margins.[60] Trinity MS O.5.2 may be compared with Morgan MS M. 876, containing the couplet *Generides*, in that they are both prestigious vellum manuscripts for which programmes of illumination were planned, and in which the romance accompanies Lydgate's *Troy Book* and, in the Trinity MS, his *Siege of Thebes*. While the post-Chaucerian character of *Generydes* perhaps associates it with Lydgate's works, the prose preface to *Generides* in the Morgan MS presents the romance as exemplary history, a 'mirror for princes': 'a royal historie of the excellent knight Generides, king Aufreus son, king of Ynde ... and A goode cristen man, and a charitable to all maner of people' (1), echoed in the colophon: 'Here endeth the noble historie of the excellent Prince Generides, which by his mariage was Emperoure of Perse and of many a Region longyng therto, And bi heritage king of Ynde and of Surre' (312). There is no mention of Clarionas, nor does their love feature in the prose section headings added throughout; by contrast, the Trinity *Generydes* highlights the love story in the colophon: 'Explicit the boke of Generides and of his faire lady Clarionas' (223). The Morgan *Generides* invokes instead the prestige and royal associations explored by Carol Meale in relation to the lost French source;[61] besides the prologue, the 'advice to princes' theme is far more evident in this version's debate on law and justice versus royal power (2903–3246) than in *Generydes*, where a new love scene displaces the argument (1660–80). These differences produce two versions of the romance, catering to different readerships in fifteenth-century élite society.

The vitality of the verse romance form in the fifteenth century is further demonstrated in a new composition that merges inherited traditions with contemporary concerns. In *Sir Degrevant*, the courtly model offered by these fifteenth-century versions of French romance is realized in a shape adapted to the provincial English context of its origin, addressing the concerns of the gentry.[62] There is no trace of a source: *Sir Degrevant* is rooted in the traditional expectations of Middle English romance. But alongside its tail-rhyme form and alliterative phrases, its vocabulary shows an up-to-date adoption of French terminology across a wide range of topics: architecture, armour, costume, jewellery, horse trappings, contributing to a sophisticated blending of eclectic materials, in a sustained structure of contrasting narrative scenes that can be compared to the methods of *Sir Gawain and the Green Knight*.[63] *Sir Degrevant* survives in two non-professional domestic collections: Lincoln Cathedral Library, MS 91 (the Lincoln Thornton manuscript), fols. 130–8v, and CUL MS Ff. 1. 6 (the Findern manuscript), fols. 96–109v.[64] Michael Johnston

---

[58] Cambridge, Emmanuel College MS 405 is a set of nine fragments recovered from a sixteenth-century binding, containing thirty-six stanzas of *Generydes*. See Frank Stubbings, 'A New Manuscript of *Generydes*', *Transactions of the Cambridge Bibliographical Society*, 10 (1993), 317–40.

[59] STC 11721–11721.7, dated c1504, c1506, c1518 (Meale, 'Morgan *Generides*', 89).

[60] Stubbings, 'A New Manuscript', 318.

[61] Meale, 'Morgan *Generides*', 91–2.

[62] NIMEV 70; Michael Johnston, *Romance and the Gentry in Late Medieval England* (Oxford, 2014), 53.

[63] W. A. Davenport, '*Sir Degrevant* and Composite Romance', in Judith Weiss, Jennifer Fellows, and Morgan Dickson (eds), *Medieval Insular Romance: Translation and Innovation* (Cambridge, 2000), 111–31 (at 131); A. S. G. Edwards, 'Gender, Order and Reconciliation in *Sir Degrevaunt*', in Carol M. Meale (ed.), *Readings in Medieval English Romance* (Cambridge, 1994), 53–64 (at 56).

[64] The Thornton manuscripts were copied in the mid-fifteenth century by Robert Thornton of the prosperous minor gentry Thornton family residing at East Newton Manor in Ryedale, Yorkshire, probably for use within the family as a recreational, educational, devotional, and medical resource. The Findern manuscript (a collaborative, informal anthology of verse, chiefly secular and courtly) was compiled between the later fifteenth and early sixteenth centuries by the prominent gentry Findern family living at Findern, Derbyshire, and their social circle.

examines archival records of the families associated with these manuscripts to show that the conflict between Degrevant and the trespassing Earl speaks particularly to the kind of land disputes preoccupying such gentry families in the fifteenth century,[65] also reflected in the poem's precise legal terminology. The composite nature of the romance potentially gives it appeal to a wide readership within the family: the detailed account of Degrevant's virtuous way of life makes him a model for young gentlemen, while the unusual focus on positive female roles would attract female readers, as seems to be witnessed by the contemporary inscription of two women's names on the final page of the romance in the Findern manuscript: 'Elisabet Koton'; 'Elisabet frauncys' (fol. 109v).

What makes *Sir Degrevant* so convincing in its evocation of élite provincial life is not only the accumulation of specific details depicting Degrevant's manorial estate, Melidor's elegant costume and hair-style as she walks to church, Degrevant's fine horse-trappings, Melidor's painted chamber within the Earl's battlemented castle, the silken hangings of her bed, and the many dishes served at their private betrothal supper with spices, good wines, and spotless table linen. All this is brought to life by the imagined relationships of people in their social settings, as revealed in conversations expressing practical concerns. Melidor's mother argues cogently against the Earl's aggressive behaviour as neighbour and father; Melidor's maid speaks frankly of her satisfaction with the marriage Degrevant arranges for her; and Melidor and Degrevant conduct their love affair around Degrevant's grievance against her father with plain-speaking awareness of the situation. Negotiations by letter and message between Degrevant and the Earl alternate with episodes of violence in which household officers (butler, pantry-keeper, and marshall) take part as well as knights and archers; and Degrevant and Melidor's nine-month courtship (once she has made it clear there will be no union until her father's consent to their marriage is obtained) is depicted with unusual detail, from kissing on velvet cushions, to lying chastely together in bed. The alliterative sixteen-line tail-rhyme form proves very versatile: its short rhyming triplets can echo the cut and thrust of battle, or the rhythms of angry speech, but can also catch the lyrical accents of Degrevant's rhapsody when smitten by Melidor's beauty:

> 'My love is leliche ylyeght* *faithfully set*
> On a worthly wyeght.
> Ther is no berell so bryght,
>   Ne cristall so clere ...
> She ys precious in pall,
> Fere feyrest of all,
> Y say hur ones on a wall,
>   Y neighed* hur so nere.'[66] *approached*
>   (52–32, 541–44)

Sir Degrevant shows none of the Chaucerian influence detectable in *Partonope* and *Generydes*, but it achieves its own version of what John Burrow calls Chaucer's 'scenic art' in narrative, with its 'detailed notation of setting and behaviour',[67] while at the same time demonstrating a profound understanding of the resources of traditional verse romance.

---

[65] Johnston, *Romance and the Gentry*, 139–42; 188–92.
[66] *Sir Degrevant*, in Erik Kooper (ed.), *Sentimental and Humorous Romances* (Kalamazoo, MI, 2005).
[67] John Burrow, 'Old and Middle English', in Pat Rogers (ed.), *The Oxford Illustrated History of English Literature* (Oxford, 1987), 1–58 (at 44).

Like *Capystranus*, which draws on the heroic romances of Charlemagne to claim equivalent status for its narrative of contemporary heroes defending Christendom, *Sir Degrevant* exploits the materials of élite courtly romance to reflect the image of its fifteenth-century gentry owners and readers. The two romances bear witness both to the strength of the Middle English romance tradition and to its potential for development throughout the fifteenth century; while the many re-compositions of well-known earlier French texts—*chansons de geste* of holy war and courtly romances of love and chivalry—attest to a continuing and undiminished appetite for the classics of verse romance among different sections of the reading public.

CHAPTER 22
Popular Tales

Ben Parsons

There is a small number of fifteenth-century English comic narratives in verse. Most take place in a contemporary setting, and their plots usually revolve around cunning, slapstick, trickery, and humiliation. Beyond these recurring features, however, the poems are chiefly distinguished by the lack of critical attention they have received. Apart from the invaluable anthologies of Melissa Furrow, and the piecemeal efforts of earlier compilers, they have failed to attract the systematic editorial treatment given to comparable traditions in French or Dutch.[1] There are perhaps good reasons for this neglect. The texts are resistant to generalization, and their preservation scattered and haphazard: most survive in single copies, often in late manuscripts or early chapbooks. Yet despite the critical challenges they present, the texts have some importance as examples of fifteenth-century popular reading. Like the ballads which they resemble in several ways, they were popular in the fullest sense of the word, representing not only a demotic level of late medieval culture but gaining sufficient currency to endure beyond the Reformation.[2] In some cases they were still being published well into the eighteenth century, and read as pieces of entertainment rather than objects of purely antiquarian interest. Such extraordinary tenacity prompts questions about the resonances they had, and needs they fulfilled, for a public that clearly valued them.

When scholarship has paid attention to the texts, it has usually read them against the French fabliau.[3] Almost inevitably, it has either compared them to the earlier tradition or treated them as an offshoot or mirror of it. This identification is most visible at a taxonomic level. As soon as scholars began to catalogue the surviving body of medieval literature, they tended to equate the English texts with the French. Hence early twentieth-century commentators and editors commonly looked to the French genre when describing the English tales, labelling them 'English fabliaux' or 'fabliaux in English', a classification that still holds firm today.[4] Other critics have gone further still, organizing the texts into a coherent 'English fabliau tradition', rooted in and running parallel with the French corpus 'from

---

[1] Melissa Furrow (ed.), *Ten Fifteenth-Century Comic Tales* (New York, 1985); Melissa Furrow (ed.), *Ten Bourdes* (Kalamazoo, MI, 2013); George McKnight (ed.), *Middle English Humorous Tales in Verse* (Boston, MA, 1913); Frederick J. Furnivall (ed.), *Loose and Humorous Songs from Bishop Percy's Folio Manuscript* (London, 1868); Thomas Wright (ed.), *The Tale of the Basyn and The Frere and the Boy* (London, 1836); William Carew Hazlitt (ed.), *Remains of the Early Popular Poetry of England*, 3 vols. (London, 1864–6). On the French fabliau and Dutch boerde, see Willem Noomen and Nico van den Boogaard (eds), *Nouveau recueil complet des fabliaux* (henceforward *NCRF*), 10 vols. (Assen, 1983–98); C. Kruyskamp, *De Middelnederlandse boerden* (The Hague, 1957).

[2] On the popular ballad, its persistence, and the problems in identifying 'medieval' texts with confidence, see Douglas Gray, *Simple Forms: Essays on Medieval English Popular Literature* (Oxford, 2015), 71–88; Richard Firth Green, 'The Ballad and the Middle Ages', in Helen Cooper and Sally Mapstone (eds), *The Long Fifteenth Century: Essays for Douglas Gray* (Oxford, 1997), 163–84.

[3] On the characteristics and development of the fabliau, see Norris J. Lacy, *Reading Fabliaux* (Birmingham, AL, 1998); Roy Pearcy, *Logic and Humour in the Fabliaux* (Cambridge, 2007).

[4] G. Gregory Smith, 'Middle Scots Anthologies', in A.W. Ward and A. R. Waller (eds), *Cambridge History of English and American Literature*, 18 vols. (New York, 1907–21), 2.279–80.

an early period'.[5] Even for relatively recent criticism, the same frame of reference endures, and the idea that the English tales are 'fabliau or fabliau-like' in essence has solidified into received wisdom.[6]

Although this approach to the English poems has at times veered in some unhelpful directions, as Furrow has shown in her dismantling of its attendant 'myths', it has undeniable merit.[7] The fabliau is an obvious point of comparison for the English texts. Not only is it one of the most fertile and expansive comic traditions of the late Middle Ages, but it evidently circulated in England, if not in English. Fabliaux survive in Anglo-Norman versions in relative abundance, and a piece such as *Le jongleur d'Ely et le roi d'Angleterre* (c1300) shows how texts might even be customized for an English readership.[8] The fifteenth-century poems also hint at contact with the French pieces, sometimes evoking them as models, sometimes sources. Two examples are *Dane Hew Munk of Leicestre* and *Queen Eleanor's Confession*, both of which survive in Elizabethan printed editions that likely derive from originals created in the late Middle Ages.[9] The former tells the story of a lecherous monk whose corpse is furtively conveyed around nocturnal Leicester, mistaken for a living person, and repeatedly re-killed until he is 'once hanged and foure times slain'; the latter depicts Henry II disguising himself in a 'fryar's coat' to hear his queen's confession, only to learn of her infidelities and intent to kill him with 'poyson strong'.[10] Despite their emphatically English locations and characters, both mirror specific fabliaux closely.[11]

Another, more insistent link is provided by Chaucer. Chaucer's comic narratives are important prototypes for subsequent English tales. Some occur in manuscripts with material by Chaucer and his followers: *The Lady Prioress*, for instance, survives in a booklet with Lydgate's 'Ditty Against Haste', incorporated by John Stow into the Chaucerian compilation BL MS Harley 78.[12] Other tales show dependence on Chaucer's work to varying degrees. At one extreme is the *Mylner of Abyngton*, a retelling of the *Reeve's Tale* printed by de Worde in 1532–4(?) (STC 78); at the other is the earlier *Tale of the Basin*, which alludes to Chaucer's Absolon and Nicholas at several points, featuring an adulterous priest who can play 'gytryns, and synges wel' and who finds himself 'all baly-naked' after rising from bed to 'make watur'.[13] Chaucerian influence is in fact so pervasive that it even filters into narratives of an ostensibly non-literary, 'oral' cast. Two lyrics recorded in Oxford, Balliol College MS 354, 'Hogyn cam to bowers dore' and 'Alas sayd þe gudman', are most likely influenced by 'the Miller's Tale' and 'Wife of Bath's Prologue': although 'Hogyn' is usually treated as an independent analogue, its central figure looks like a deliberate conflation of John and

---

[5] Henry Seidel Canby, 'The English Fabliau', *PMLA*, 21 (1906), 200–14 (at 213); John Edwin Wells, *A Manual of The Writings in Middle English 1050–1400* (New Haven, CT, 1916), 177, 180.

[6] See Robert E. Lewis, 'The English Fabliau Tradition and Chaucer's "Miller's Tale"', *Modern Philology*, 79 (1982), 241–53; John Hines, *The Fabliau in English* (Harlow, 1993).

[7] Melissa Furrow, 'Middle English Fabliaux and Modern Myth', *ELH*, 56 (1989), 1–18.

[8] Susanna Fein (ed.), *The Complete Harley 2253 Manuscript*, 3 vols. (Kalamazoo, MI, 2015), 3.92–110; Anatole de Montaiglon and Gaston Raynaud (eds), *Recueil général et complet des fabliaux*, 6 vols. (Paris, 1872–90), 2.242–56.

[9] Elizabeth Carney, 'Fact and Fiction in "Queen Eleanor's Confession"', *Folklore*, 95 (1984), 167–70; Furrow (ed.), *Comic Poems*, 155–7.

[10] Furrow (ed.), *Ten Bourdes*, 73–80; Frederick Woods (ed.), *Oxford Book of English Traditional Verse* (Oxford, 1983), 1–3.

[11] *Queen Eleanor* follows much the same course as *Du chevalier qui fist sa fame confesse*, while *Dane Hew* reworks a story found in at least three thirteenth-century French versions; NCRF 4.227–43, 7.1–189.

[12] NIMEV 186; Seth Lerer, 'British Library Harley MS 78 and the Manuscripts of John Shirley', *Notes and Queries*, n.s. 37 (1990), 400–3.

[13] NIMEV 2658; see Hazlitt (ed.), *Remains of the Early Popular Poetry*, 3.100–18; Furrow (ed.), *Ten Bourdes*, 12–17.

Absolon, being an impotent 'old churl' tricked into kissing the 'ars' of his 'leman'; 'Alas' similarly reworks the battle between Alisoun and Jankyn as a 'lytill stryf' engineered by the 'sum-what shrew' wife, and even concludes with a blow 'on the ere'.[14] Given Chaucer's well-attested knowledge of the fabliaux, these debts provide another vital, albeit mediated link back to the French texts.

However, despite its basic validity, the tendency to read the poems exclusively in the light, or rather shadow, of the fabliau carries some serious problems. A key drawback is that using the French texts as an interpretive backdrop often leads to a curious diminution of the English pieces. More often than not, the fabliau serves as a yardstick for measuring the later poems, one against which they are usually found wanting. They are invariably seen as pale imitations of the boisterous French genre, a 'conservative' or 'orthodox' response to it that smooths over its notoriously 'rough surface'.[15] Cooke, Whiteford, and McKinley provide one example of this viewpoint, setting the English tales against 'the typical Old French fabliau' and finding them less 'explicit' and more supportive of 'orthodox morality' in comparison, but theirs is only one voice contrasting the tales with 'true fabliau' and stressing their commitment to 'conventional standards of decency' and relative hostility to 'deception'.[16] Studies of individual poems also follow the same lines: hence Darjes and Rendell detect a 'gingerly treatment of the earthier aspects of the genre' in the *Beryn Prologue*, while Robbins criticizes the *Mylner* for its 'sentimentality' and use of 'moral evaluation'.[17]

Needless to say, these appraisals do the tales something of a disservice. Again, they are not without foundation. It is true that the English texts tend to use comedy for practical or didactic rather than subversive ends: it might be said that they share a boundary with the overtly exemplary narratives Wells dubs 'pious tales', such as the repentance-stories *The Adulterous Falmouth Squire* and *Incestuous Daughter*, with which they occasionally appear in manuscripts.[18] But these judgements rest on two basic problems. Firstly, they tend to gloss over any distinctive features in the tales, framing them as deficiencies instead of characteristics that warrant analysis and discussion. Secondly, and more importantly, it is also questionable whether the fabliau is as dominant a model for the English poems as they assume. Despite the common ground between the two sets of texts, there are good reasons for disentangling them. The most obvious barrier is chronological. Even with Chaucer

---

[14] DIMEV 2035 and 96 respectively; see Roman Dyboski (ed.), *Songs, Carols, and other Miscellaneous Poems*, EETS, e.s. 101 (London, 1907), 110–12. On 'Hogyn', see Peter G. Beidler, 'Miller's Tale', in Robert Correale and Mary Hamel (eds), *Sources and Analogues of the Canterbury Tales*, 2 vols. (Woodbridge, 2005), 2.249–75.

[15] Peter Brown, 'Journey's End: the Prologue to the *Tale of Beryn*', in Julia Boffey and Janet Cowen (eds), *Chaucer and Fifteenth-Century Poetry* (London, 1991), 143–74 (at 166); Jerry Root, 'The Old French Fabliau and the Poetics of Disfiguration', *Medievalia et Humanistica*, n.s. 24 (1997), 17–32.

[16] Thomas D. Cooke (with Peter Whiteford and Nancy Mohr McKinley), 'Tales', in Albert E. Hartung (ed.), *A Manual of the Writings in Middle English 1050–1500*, 11 vols. (New Haven, CT, 1993), 9.3138–328, 3472–570 (at 3153); Hines, *Fabliau in English*, 256, 208; Marie Nelson and Richard Thomson, 'The Fabliau', in Laura C. Lambdin and Robert T. Lambdin (eds), *A Companion to Old and Middle English Literature* (Westport, CT, 2002), 281.

[17] The Beryn prologue is NIMEV 3926; see Bradley Darjes and Thomas Rendall, 'A Fabliau in the *Prologue to the Tale of Beryn*', *Mediaeval Studies*, 47 (1985), 416–31 (at 419); R. H. Robbins, 'The English Fabliau: Before and After Chaucer', *Moderna Språk*, 64 (1970), 231–44 (at 239).

[18] Wells, *Manual*, 165–76; Cooke (with Whiteford and Mohr), 'Tales', 3258–9. The *Falmouth Squire* and *Incestuous Daughter* (NIMEV 2052 and 1107) both appear in BodL MS Ashmole 61, whose contents are discussed below. A similar example is Lincoln Cathedral MS 91, compiled by the Yorkshire landowner Robert Thornton c1430–50, where the scurrilous story of an impotent 'olde horse' *Lyarde* (NIMEV 2026) and conversion tale *De miraculo beate Marie* (NIMEV 1722) appear on near-consecutive leaves. See Susanna Fein, 'The Contents of Robert Thornton's Manuscripts', in Susanna Fein and Michael Johnston (eds), *Robert Thornton and His Books: Essays on the Lincoln and London Thornton Manuscripts* (York, 2014), 13–65 (at 26–8); Melissa Furrow, 'A Minor Comic Poem in a Major Romance Manuscript: "Lyarde"', *Forum for Modern Language Studies*, 32 (1996), 289–302.

serving as a conduit, the French texts could only be at best a distant inspiration. Although they survive in impressive numbers, the fabliaux seem to have fallen out of vogue by the early fourteenth century, at least a century before comic narratives began to appear in English in significant numbers.[19] It is also clear that the two literatures were regarded in different terms by their readers and composers. Fabliaux were written and read as part of a cohesive and recognizable genre. They are invariably composed in octosyllabic couplets, generally brief, and define themselves with a consistent vocabulary, with many texts demanding '*escoutez le flabel*' or reflecting that they have '*dit le fablel*'.[20] The English tales, on the other hand, lack the same integrity as a genre. There is little sense that they are associated with any particular verse-form. The poems are in fact impressively varied, ranging from straightforward couplets (*Dane Hew, Freiris of Berwik*) to more intricate stanzaic schemes of six lines (*Sir Corneus, Iak and his Stepdame*), nine lines (*Tale of a Basin, Lady Prioress*), twelve lines (*King Edward and the Shepherd*), and even sixteen lines (*The Smyth Whych That Forged hym a New Dame*).[21] A few, such as the *Tournament of Tottenham*, even make use of ambitious forms borrowed from romance, rounding off each stanza with a bob-and-wheel quintain of the kind used in *Gawain and the Green Knight*.[22] More telling still is the vocabulary authors and copyists use when referring to the texts. Little consensus is apparent here: as well as the quotidien 'tale', writers and copyists variously identify them as 'bowrd', 'sport', 'song', 'fabula', 'trifull', 'gesttyng', and 'jest'. In short, the texts inhabit a more fluid and adaptable framework than that governing the fabliaux. They are a genre only in the loosest sense, less a group of narratological or formal requirements than a general tone or set of audience expectations.[23]

In terms of the materials they call on, the tales also point away from the fabliau and towards other areas of medieval culture. Several show a marked proximity with oral tradition.[24] Two key examples are *The Tale of a Basin* and *Iak and his Stepdame*, otherwise called the *Frere and the Boye*. The first revolves around a magic chamber pot, a 'vessell' to 'make watur in', that clings to anyone that touches it: in the course of the story, it is enchanted by a country parson in order to expose his brother's unruly wife and her priest, 'Sir John', who both grow 'dronken' at his brother's expense and even 'list to bedde' in his absence. In the second, the title-character gains a set of magical powers which enable him to humiliate his stingy stepmother and her ally, a friar: Jack's 'gyftes thre' consist of a 'bowe and bolte' that never miss their mark, a magic pipe with which he makes the friar dance in a bramble-patch, and the power to cause his stepmother to fart uncontrollably 'when she lokyth on me'. In either case, the central role given to spells and enchantment aligns the texts more closely with the folk-tale than the fabliau, since the French genre tends to treat the supernatural with pronounced scepticism.[25] Other details point to the same connection: in *Iak*, the very name of the central figure, and the fact that his 'steppemoder

---

[19] Keith Busby, 'Conspicuous by its Absence: the English Fabliau', *Dutch Quarterly Review*, 12 (1982), 30–41.
[20] 'Constant du Hamel', NCRF 1.29–126; 'De Gombert et des deus clers', NCRF 4.279–300.
[21] *Dane Hew* survives in a copy from 1560(?), STC 13257; the *Freiris of Berwik*, a late survival, is DIMEV 726; the remaining works listed are respectively NIMEV 219, 977, 2658, 2441, 988, 978.
[22] NIMEV 2615.
[23] Ardis Butterfield, 'Medieval Genres and Modern Genre Theory', *Paragraph*, 13 (1990), 184–201.
[24] See Derek Brewer, 'The International Medieval Popular Comic Tale in England', in Thomas J. Heffernan (ed.), *The Popular Literature of Medieval England* (Knoxville, TN, 1985), 131–47.
[25] Peter Goodall, 'An Outline History of the English Fabliau After Chaucer', *AUMLA: Australasian Universities Language and Literature Association*, 57 (1982), 5–23.

at home' is his chief antagonist, call on conventions of traditional storytelling still recognizable today.[26] The reliance of both texts on material of this kind is underscored by the indexes of traditional story-types and motifs compiled by Hans-Jörg Uther, Antti Aarne, and Stith Thompson, which show them weaving together multiple narrative elements from the vast, transcultural reservoir of folktale formulas.[27] Nor are they alone in this tendency. *The Lady Prioress* seems based in similar material: its story of how a senior nun rids herself of three unwanted suitors by tricking them into carrying out a fake burial rehearses a formula found across Europe and Asia.[28] Of course, none of this means that the tales can be described as purely oral in character, much as their nineteenth-century editors regarded them, like the ballads, as 'authentic ... traditionary poetry' with hallmarks of 'high and remote antiquity'.[29] As David Fowler in particular has stressed, the very appearance of the tales in written form places them at some remove from folk culture, a point further attested by their frequent metrical complexity.[30] But it does suggest that the fifteenth-century narratives looked to resources beyond the fabliau, and might not be grounded in the French form quite as closely as is often assumed. Even their occasional parallels with specific fabliaux might simply show both corpora relying on a common stock of story-types.

However, the most decisive point of departure between the English and French texts is the question of their audience. The exact readership of the French texts has long been a subject of debate. At various stages they have been linked with the lower gentry, with the royal court as '*une sorte de genre courtois*', and with '*clers marginaux*' or unbeneficed clerics in minor orders.[31] Some texts even seem to have been read by a range of social groups, judging from variation in their manuscripts.[32] The readership of the English texts, on the other hand, is more readily locatable. While there is evidence that they were known to a mixed constituency of readers, they seem to have had special appeal for the urban, middle-class group that can be broadly called 'mercantile'.[33] Where the compilers of the collections can be identified, most seem to belong to this approximate social band. Two well-known examples are BodL MS Ashmole MS 61 and Oxford, Balliol College MS 354. Both contain popular tales: the former *Sir Corneus*, *Sir Cleges*, and *The King and the Hermit*; the latter 'Good gossipis myn', an early text of *Iak and his Stepdame*, and a clutch of briefer narratives gathered under the collective heading in the table of contents (fol. 4) 'Dyueris

---

[26] Carl Lindahl, 'Jacks: The Name, The Tales, The American Traditions', in William Bernard McCarthy (ed.), *Jack in Two Worlds* (Chapel Hill, NC, 1994), xiii–xxxiv.

[27] Hans Jörg-Uther, *The Types of International Folktales* (Helsinki, 2004); Stith Thompson, The Motif-Index of Folk Literature, 2 vols. (Bloomington, IN, 1955–8). The former lists *Basin* as a specimen of tale-type 'ATU 571: All Stick Together', *Iak* as a hybrid of 'ATU 566: Three Magic Objects', and 'ATU 592: Dance Among the Thorns'. Thompson classifies the basin and its properties as motifs D1171.13, D1413.8, K1217, and Jack's powers as specimens of D1223, D1092, D2079.1, D1441.1, D1441.1, D1415.2.

[28] Furrow (ed.), *Ten Bourdes*, 55–63; W.A. Clouston, *Popular Tales and Fictions*, 2 vols. (Edinburgh, 1887), 2.436–52; J. A. Worp, *Geschiedenis van het drama en van het tooneel in Nederland*, 2 vols. (Groningen, 1903–7), 1.454–5. The *Types of International Folktales* lists *The Lady Prioress* as a variant of story-type 'ATU 1730: Entrapped Suitors', while Thompson lists her trickery as examples of the motifs K1218.1.3.2, K1214.1.1, K1218.3, K1218.4.

[29] Robert Jamieson, *Popular Ballads and Songs*, 2 vols. (Edinburgh, 1806), 1.ix; William Motherwell, *Minstrelsy: Ancient and Modern* (Glasgow, 1827), 9.

[30] David C. Fowler, *Literary History of the Popular Ballad* (Durham, NC, 1968), 5.

[31] Joseph Bédier, *Les fabliaux: études de littérature populaire* (Paris, 1893), 377; Per Nykrog, *Les Fabliaux* (Geneva, 1974), 18; Jean Charles Payen, *Littérature française: Le moyen age* (Paris, 1984), 147; Charles Muscatine, *Medieval Literature, Style and Culture* (Columbia, SC, 1999), 70.

[32] Jean Rychner, *Contribution à l'étude des fabliaux*, 2 vols. (Geneva, 1960) 1.32.

[33] See Malcolm Richardson, *Middle-Class Writing in Late Medieval London* (London, 2011); Pamela Nightingale, *A Medieval Mercantile Community: the Grocers' Company and the Politics and Trade of London* (New Haven, CT, 1995).

short tales & baletts'.³⁴ Both are self-evidently 'amateur' productions, put together by urban householders for private use. The Balliol manuscript was assembled between c1508 and c1536 by Richard Hill of Hillend, a freeman of the Merchant Adventurers and Grocers' Companies of London, and the Ashmole manuscript seems to have been compiled in the 1480s by a craftsman or tradesman resident in Leicester, known only by his signature 'Rate'. Whoever he may have been, Rate's social status is made clear by his inclusion of the *Debate of the Carpenters' Tools*, a piece so densely technical in its vocabulary that it would only be comprehensible to an artisanal reader.³⁵ Even when collections indicate possession beyond this social level, the evidence often proves uncertain, and can at times lead back in this direction. CUL MS Ff. 5. 48 is a case in point. The manuscript preserves the *Tale of the Basin*, *King Edward and the Shepherd*, one of three copies of the *Tournament of Tottenham*, and the only copy of its companion-piece the *Feest of Tottenham*; the manuscript's early owner is often assumed to be Gilbertus Pylkyngton, likely a priest at Lichfield, whose signature appears after one of the texts.³⁶ Nevertheless, Carol Meale offers a persuasive argument in favour of middle-class lay rather than clerical ownership, noting the variety of hands in the manuscript.³⁷ None of this means that the tales were exclusive to these circles, of course, but the readers that cared enough to collect them and copy them can generally be placed in this social bracket.

Their association with this public also explains why the poems were able to move relatively seamlessly into early commercial print, which after all served much the same market. A considerable number of pieces owe their survival to the press, evidently providing a reliable source of revenue for Tudor booksellers; their numbers steadily increase with the growth of the popular book-market during the sixteenth century. Some cases, such as *Dane Hew* and William Copland's c1565 edition of *The Smyth Whych That Forged hym a New Dame* (STC 22653.9), originally printed by de Worde in 1505 (STC 22653.5), show that printers were confident of the economic viability of tales even at some distance from their composition.³⁸ The urban public's continued enthusiasm for the texts is further shown by the fact that many became emblematic of middle-class tastes by the end of the sixteenth century. Puritan and university-trained writers often lump them together with other 'friuolous books' as examples of atavistic reading habits among bourgeois or provincial audiences: hence Arthur Dent, Thomas Nashe, Anthony Munday, and the author of the so-called Langham Letter, with its sardonic portrait of the Warwick mason 'Captain Cox', cite *Iak and his Stepdame* and several others when ridiculing 'vnexperienced and illiterated' tastes at this social level.³⁹ Despite their antipathy for pre-Reformation material, these witnesses show the extent to which print cemented the texts' association with a mercantile

---

³⁴ NIMEV 219, 1890, 1764, 1362, 977.

³⁵ David Reed Parker, *The Commonplace Book in Tudor London* (Lanham, MD, 1998), 37–85; Michael Johnston, *Romance and the Gentry in Late Medieval England* (Oxford, 2014), 115. See George Shuffelton, *Codex Ashmole 61: A Compilation of Popular Middle English Verse* (Kalamazoo, MI, 2008); Lynne Sandra Blanchfield, 'The Romances in MS Ashmole 61: An Idiosyncratic Scribe', in Maldwyn Mills, Jennifer Fellows, and Carol Meale (eds), *Romance in Medieval England* (Cambridge, 1991), 65–87. On the Debate (NIMEV 3461) and its likely occasion and primary readership, see Edward Wilson, 'The Debate of the Carpenter's Tools', *Review of English Studies*, n.s. 38 (1987), 445–70.

³⁶ Both the *Tournament* and *Feest* are NIMEV 2354; see Thomas H. Ohlgren, *Robin Hood: The Early Poems, 1465–1560* (Cranbury, NJ, 2007), 31, 36–7.

³⁷ Carol Meale, 'Romance and its Anti-type? *The Tournament of Tottenham*, The Carnivalesque and Popular Culture', in A. J. Minnis (ed.), *Middle English Poetry: Texts and Traditions* (Woodbridge, 2001), 103–27.

³⁸ For the *Smyth*, see Carl Horstmann (ed.), *Altenglische Legenden: Neue Folge* (Heilbronn, 1881), 322–8.

³⁹ Arthur Dent, *The Plaine Mans Path-way to Heauen* (1607; STC 6629), 373; Thomas Nashe, 'To the Gentlemen Students of Both Universities', in R. B. McKerrow (ed.), *Works*, 3 vols. (London, 1904–10), 3.314; Jonathan Rittenhouse (ed.), Anthony Munday, *Sir John Oldcastle* (London, 1984), 48; R. J. P. Kuin (ed.), *A Letter* (Leiden, 1983), 53–4.

readership. At the same time, they also testify to the tales' success in meeting the demands of these buyers and readers; if they were not effective in these terms, their enduring popularity with such a market would scarcely be possible.

The tales therefore lead us back to the late-medieval middle class from several directions, suggesting that they are in some measure an expression of its peculiar preoccupations. In fact, when approached in these terms, the tales become highly revealing. They shed light not merely on the literary appetites of this group, but also on the larger usages and expectations it asked of its reading. These concerns are perhaps most noticeable in their treatment of Chaucer. As we have already seen, some of the tales indicate a clear attraction to Chaucerian narrative, echoing the evidence of wills and other artefacts from the urban milieu.[40] However, they also hint at some dissatisfaction with aspects of his work. In revisiting his narratives, the tales tend to iron out their open-endedness, with many preferring clear-cut victors and victims to the ambiguity of their sources. Hence 'Alas sayd þe gudman' recasts the Wife of Bath as a manipulator of her 'stynkyng coward' husband, while the conclusion of the *Mylner of Abyngton* leaves the Simkin-character 'sicke in his bedde / All his life' as penalty for 'his falsehed'. Despite the reputation of the texts, these modifications are not strictly moralizations: grotesque, ribald, and especially slapstick elements remain conspicuously intact. But they do point to an audience with less inclination or leisure to use texts as prompts for exploratory debate. Despite its obvious interest in Chaucer, this readership seems to favour conclusion over discussion, suggesting a fundamental difference in reading practice between Chaucer's immediate circle and this later, secondary audience.[41]

Similarly telling is the texts' relationship with the romance. The romance genre is a recurrent point of reference in the tales. In fact, at times their use of romance motifs is so extensive that it compromises any sense of literary typology, and results in texts that cannot be comfortably placed in any single category. One such hybrid piece is *Sir Cleges*, which is remarkable for its generic uncertainty: although it calls on a number of romance trappings, it fixes them around an essentially comedic story of deception and counter-deception.[42] On the one hand, it is set in the 'tyme of Uter and Pendragoun', and asserts its protagonist's membership 'of the Ronde Tabull'; Cleges is in fact an incidental presence in a few vernacular romances, including the *Alliterative Morte Arthur* and *Awntyrs off Arthure*. On the other, it revolves around trickery. On his way to Uther's throne, Cleges is detained by the steward, porter, and usher, each of whom demand a third of his eventual reward from the king. Cleges is able to outwit and expose the three men, however: he requests 'nothyng bot strokes twelve' from his sovereign, and these are duly shared out among the servants.[43] Interesting though *Cleges* is, it is more usual for tales to evoke romance literature in a self-conscious, allusive way. Its devices and themes prove to be one of the most dependable comic resources in the tales, frequently being embedded in their humorous set-pieces. In the *Beryn Prologue*, for instance, when the Pardoner is caught up in a running battle in the kitchens of a hostelry, he stages his own low-rent equivalent of the standard arming of the

---

[40] F. J. Furnivall (ed.), *Fifty Earliest English Wills*, EETS, o.s. 78 (London, 1882), 139; V. A. Kolve, 'Chaucer and the Visual Arts', in Derek Brewer (ed.), *Geoffrey Chaucer* (Cambridge, 1974), 290–320 (at 292–3).

[41] Roger A. Ladd, 'The Mercantile (Mis) Reader in "The Canterbury Tales"', *Studies in Philology*, 99 (2002), 17–32.

[42] Derek Pearsall, 'The Development of Middle English Romance', in Derek Brewer (ed.), *Studies in Medieval English Romances: Some New Approaches* (Cambridge, 1991), 11–35 (at 15).

[43] Anne Laskaya and Eve Salisbury (eds), *The Middle English Breton Lays* (Kalamazoo, MI, 1995), 389.

hero, setting a cooking pan on his head and wielding 'a grete ladill' against his pursuers.[44] *Dane Hew* concludes on a similarly mock-heroic note, with its central figure making a final valiant charge in the vein of El Cid: Hew's much-abused corpse is at last tied to an old mare and sent galloping towards the pastures of his former monastery.[45]

What makes these currents significant is that their treatment, while self-evidently parodic, is not strictly speaking adversarial. On the contrary, they assume not merely a familiarity with romance convention on the part of their audience, but an interest in the chivalric culture which it served to propagate. This can be witnessed in a small set of poems which focus on Arthur and his court. Most suggestive is *Sir Corneus*, or 'The Cokwolds Daunce' as it was named by Hartshorne and Hazlitt.[46] *Corneus* focuses squarely on the theme of adultery, equipping Arthur with a magical drinking horn that will spill its contents 'yff any cokwold drynke of it'. Although the king uses it for his own amusement at feasts, sending any wronged husbands to eat at their own table wearing crowns of willow, when he himself drinks from it he is of course revealed as 'ther awne brother'.[47] Irreverent though the text is, its parody does not approach the material it ridicules from a dismissive or oppositional stance, of the kind famously outlined by Bakhtin.[48] Rather, it actively relies on the reader having existing, detailed knowledge of the Arthurian cycle: without such awareness, the humour and choice of theme would be unintelligible. As a result, the poem flags up the centrality of the romance in the literary diet of its readers, rather than expressing antagonism towards the genre.

This dimension of the texts is taken further still by two of the most sustained engagements with romance *topoi*, the interlinked poems *Tournament of Tottenham* and *Feest of Tottenham*.[49] Both seem to date from the 1420s or 1430s on the basis of documentary evidence, and they reveal some of the larger preoccupations that inform these borrowings. As their names suggest, they concern two of the most characteristic rituals of courtly life, although they transplant them to Tottenham, at this point a small rural community in Middlesex. Their humour is built around the substitution typical of medieval parody, since both replace various aspects of knightly culture with rustic analogues. In the *Turnament*, the 'kene conquerours' bear stereotypically plebeian forenames, such as Hawkyn, Tomkyn, and Perkyn, and strive for the hand of Tyb, daughter of a local reeve, whose father also offers a 'kowe', hen, mare, and 'spottyd sowe' to the victor; during the battle itself, 'schepe-skynnes' and 'mattes' are worn in place of armour, and flails are used as swords and bowls as shields. The *Feest* takes a more scatological tack. Its supposedly luxurious dishes are served from a 'muk cart' and include tarts baked with 'dongestekis' (manure); its dancing reaches a crescendo when Tyb 'late a fart / For stumbulyng at a stole'. Heraldry is also a recurring target across the pieces: the farmers carry banners made of rat-skins, emblazoned with plough-mauls and cowbells. Despite these playful extravagances, familiarity rather than hostility is again the rule. Both poems operate on the assumption that the audience is both aware of and interested in the chivalric practices they are evoking: they approach the butt of their jokes not as something beyond the horizons of the texts or their

---

[44] John M. Bowers (ed.), *Canterbury Tales: Fifteenth-Century Continuations and Additions* (Kalamazoo, MI, 1992), 75.
[45] Compare Paul Bancourt, 'Chansons de geste, roman, romance et fabliaux', in Danielle Buschinger and André Crépin (eds), *Comique, satire et parodie dans la tradition renardienne et les fabliaux* (Göppingen, 1983), 59–70.
[46] Charles Henry Hartshorne, *Ancient Metrical Tales* (London, 1829), 209–21; Hazlitt (ed.), *Remains of the Early Popular Poetry*, 1.35–49.
[47] Furrow (ed.), *Ten Bourdes*, 118–24.
[48] Furrow (ed.), *Ten Bourdes*, 132–8.
[49] Erik Kooper (ed.), *Sentimental and Humorous Romances* (Kalamazoo, MI, 2005), 181–95.

audience, but as part of the experience of both; indeed, A. Leslie Harris has shown that they demonstrate an 'up-to-date' awareness of recent trends in tourneying.[50] In particular, their focus on pageantry, on banqueting, heraldry, and war-games, shows that the texts are interested in knighthood as a mode of expression above all, privileging the performative aspects of courtly culture. This focus in turn speaks to a degree of social ambition among the readership, since these facets of knighthood are also its most imitable: in fact, the fundamental premise of the parody is that markers of nobility can be mimicked by figures outside the social elite, even if the mimicry is played for laughs. The point is, then, that the tales' teasing, satirical relationship with chivalric romance is not a hostile one, but stems from the priorities of its probable readership, and especially the 'ambition' and 'insecurity and mobility' long recognized as characteristic of this 'middle strata'.[51]

Aside from these concerns, the *Turnament* also highlights some of the other ways in which its core audience might utilize texts of this kind. The *Turnament* has a direct if ambiguous link to civic celebration. At Exeter, the receivers' account rolls for 1432–3 contain a cryptic reference to 'la Tornment de Totyngham' being staged for the entertainment of the mayor and city authorities at Rougemont castle.[52] Whether this alludes to some sort of performance of the text we have, or to the staging of a burlesque melée akin to the one it describes, it still indicates some tie to the ritual life of urban culture; even if the record and poem have no direct connection, they still call on a common vocabulary of comic images.[53] A number of other narratives seem to emanate from the same milieu. The amalgam of *Beryn* and its *Prologue* might owe its existence to a similar occasion if Peter Brown is correct to tie it to Canterbury's 1420 jubilee celebrations.[54] Thomas More's contribution to the literature, *A Mery gest how a sergeaunte wolde lerne to be frere*, first printed in 1516(?) (STC 18091), might also stem from urban banqueting, most likely the revels at Lincoln's Inn in the 1490s.[55] The contents of some texts allow similar connections to be inferred. Although it is not clear whether it was composed for an urban audience or the provincial gentry, *Sir Cleges* also shows links to seasonal revelry: its emphases on 'Crystynmes ... fest' and on its hero's love of minstrelsy make these origins clear.[56] *Sir Corneus* might also be seen in the same light, given the prominent roles that drinking and feasting play in its action. Both *Cleges* and *Corneus* are also consistent with the shift towards chivalry and away from liturgy that Sheila Lindenbaum finds in civic ritual during the early fifteenth century.[57] What seems to lie behind many of the poems, therefore, is the social activity of the guilds, confraternities, and other civic associations, or the analogous activities in the households of the lower gentry, and the celebration and conviviality that were such important means of generating cohesion among their members.[58]

---

[50] A. Leslie Harris, 'Tournaments and *The Tournament of Tottenham*', *Fifteenth Century Studies*, 23 (1996), 81–92.
[51] Sylvia L. Thrupp, *The Merchant Class of Medieval London, 1300–1500* (Ann Arbor, MI, 1962), 313.
[52] J. M. Wasson (ed.), *Records of Early English Drama: Devon* (Toronto, 1986), 93.
[53] Meale, 'Romance and its Anti-Type', 117.
[54] Brown, 'Journey's End', 148–50.
[55] Howard B. Norland, 'The Role of Drama in More's Literary Career', *Sixteenth Century Journal*, 13 (1982), 59–75. Compare a later text from More's circle, *Mery Iests of Wydow Edyth*, written by his servant Walter Smith in the 1520s, evidently as a household entertainment: Anne Lake Prescott, 'Crime and Carnival at Chelsea: Widow Edith and Thomas More's Household', *Moreana*, 100 (1989), 247–64.
[56] Linda Marie Zaerr, *Performance and the Middle English Romance* (Cambridge, 2012), 68–70.
[57] Sheila Lindenbaum, 'London Texts and Literate Practice', in David Wallace (ed.), *Cambridge History of Medieval English Literature* (Cambridge, 2002), 284–310.
[58] Paul S. Lloyd, *Food and Identity in England: Eating to Impress* (London, 2015), 73.

This celebratory context imprints itself on the tales at several levels. It is most readily detectable in the formal features they share, many of which seem to mark them for dramatic performance or quasi-dramatic recitation. Their strong emphasis on action, for instance, and their inclusion of dialogue between well-defined speaking personae, are both strikingly theatrical.[59] A piece such as 'Good gossipis myn' is at points almost indistinguishable from a formal play-text, and could easily be staged as a comic monologue or even dialogue. Not only does it incorporate a list of speakers, the old wives 'Elynore, Johan, and Margery, / Margret, Alis, and Cecely', but its simple story, involving one wife extorting 'a drawght of mery-go-down' from her peers with a sob-story of domestic abuse, is delivered almost wholly through direct speech: most stanzas begin with such directions as 'Anne bade', 'Alis with a lowde voys spak than', 'Margret meke saide', and so on.[60] But their affiliation with festivity leaves still stronger traces on the peculiar type of comedy they employ. Their mockery often seems to function in ways complementary to feasting itself, using laughter and ridicule to build social bonds and foster group identity. At the conclusion of *Cleges*, the punishment of the three servants is presented as a scene of unifying, communal mirth, one that explicitly brings together disparate elements in Uther's court. *Cleges* reports how the 'lordes lewghe, both old and yenge' at the servants being thrashed, using the spectacle of their punishment to elicit a shared response even among opposing parties: it also invites its readers or hearers to participate in the same process with their own laughter. The mockery of the *Turnament* and *Feest* works in a comparable but distinct way. Their caricature of the peasantry exploits the power of ridicule to draw defining boundaries between and around groups. By creating laughter at the expense of 'all the swete swynkers', and by characterizing them as their own discrete 'bachelery' with their own parallel rituals, it consolidates the viewers as a distinct body set apart from this other, imagined community. 'Good gossipis myn' performs much the same function: its clear strand of anti-feminism, which it shares with many of the poems in Hill's collection, reflects and reinforces the staunchly masculine environment of the guildhalls.[61] The unifying function of the two poems is further enhanced by the fact that both depict their rival groups as faulty in their own community-building. The peasants of the *Turnament* remain in violent opposition with one another, and the solidarity of the 'gossipis' crumbles after Anne fails to stand her round. Quite often, then, the texts seem to act much like the 'joke rites' described by Mary Douglas, a concept also used by Jean Goodich to discuss medieval urban drama.[62] Their humour is clearly deployed to foster 'fellowship' and 'contact' within a group, demarcating its limits by identifying and deriding outsiders, and declaring its internal unity through mutual participation in mockery and amusement.[63]

While celebration provides a suggestive context for many of the tales, others appear to have served somewhat different functions. *Iak and his Stepdame* in particular shows how comic narratives might have been put to less public uses. In some respects, this is the most important of the fifteenth-century tales; it is certainly the poem that circulated most freely.

---

[59] Compare Emily A. Ransom, 'The New Notbroune Mayd Vpon the Passion of Cryste: The Nutbrown Maid Converted', *English Literary Renaissance*, 45 (2015), 3–31.

[60] NIMEV 1362; see Dyboski (ed.), *Songs, Carols etc.*, 106–8.

[61] See further Susan E. Phillips, *Transforming Talk: The Problem with Gossip in Late Medieval England* (University Park, PA, 2007), 150–5.

[62] Jean N. Goodich, 'So I Thought as I Stood, To Mirth Us Among: The Function of Laughter in the Second Shepherds' Play', in Albrecht Classen (ed.), *Laughter in the Middle Ages and Early Modern Times* (Berlin, 2010), 531–46 (at 544).

[63] Mary Douglas, 'The Social Control of Cognition: Some Factors in Joke Perception', *Man*, 3 (1968), 361–76 (at 370).

It survives in four manuscripts, a printed edition of c1510 (STC 14522), and in Bishop Percy's copy from a lost exemplar.[64] A majority of medieval witnesses bear the hallmarks of mercantile or artisanal ownership: as well as Hill's collection, it occurs in BodL MS Rawlinson C. 86, a complex sequence of booklets that often 'hints at metropolitan provenance', containing the signatures of tradesmen involved in salting, ironmongery, goldsmithing, and scrivening.[65] *Iak* also attained an impressive longevity. There were at least eleven editions between 1545–1698, and no fewer than twenty-four chapbook editions between 1700–c1800; in 1680 it even gained a sequel.[66] Its place in the bloodstream of early modern culture can also be inferred from the volume of allusions it receives, from authors as diverse as Robert Burton, the parodist John Taylor, and the grammarian John Gibbon.[67] Most remarkably of all, it attained an international scope: in the early sixteenth century a Dutch-language version was twice printed at Antwerp and Amsterdam.[68] In this last case, transmission was no doubt the result of close commercial ties between England and the Low Countries, and underlines once again *Iak*'s special appeal to mercantile readers.

Clearly, this endurance speaks to the continued utility of the tale, and its ability to answer the requirements its core audience asked of it. There is in fact a case to be made for its near uniqueness in satisfying such needs. Nicholas Orme has suggested that the story might be approached as a rare early instance of a text intended for children, if not 'the only example' of a medieval story 'chiefly for the interest of the young'.[69] It is not difficult to imagine that the story might have particular value for a juvenile audience, given its protagonist 'butt yong of age', the latitude it gives him to disturb the niceties of the adult world, and its fantastical content; in fact, in the early modern period Barnabe Riche notes that *Iak* was put 'before me in my yonger daies' implicitly for its 'cunnyngly counterfeited' story, while Francis Kirkman remembers 'being hugely pleased' with it in his schooldays.[70] But the text's playful energies are not the only feature that would have made it suitable for youngsters. The manuscripts provide broad hints that early readers might have prized it for its educative potential as well. The poem often occurs in collections that show a marked

---

[64] Furrow (ed.), *Ten Bourdes*, 21–4.

[65] Julia Boffey and Carol Meale, 'Selecting the Text: Rawlinson C. 86 and Some Other Books for London Readers', in Felicity Riddy (ed.), *Regionalism in Late Mediaeval Manuscripts and Texts: Essays Celebrating the Publication of A Linguistic Atlas of Late Mediaeval English* (Cambridge, 1991), 143–69 (at 143, 157–8); Jeremy J. Griffiths, 'A Re-examination of Oxford, Bodleian Library, MS Rawlinson C.86', *Archiv für das Studium der Neuren Sprachen und Literaturen*, 219 (1982), 383–7.

[66] The standard bibliographies of STC and Wing record editions from Wynkyn de Worde (c1510; STC 14522), William Middleton (1545; STC 14522.5), Edward Allde (1589; STC 14522.7 and c1617; STC 14523), Elizabeth Allde (1626; STC 14524.3), Robert Sanders of Glasgow (1668; Wing F2205), and two late unsigned versions (1690; Wing F2205A, 1698; F2206). The Stationers' Register mentions three further imprints in 1558, 1569, and 1640 that are otherwise untraceable: Edward Arber, *Transcript of the Registers of the Company of Stationers*, 5 vols. (London, 1875–94), 1.22, 1.179, 4.481. Snyder and Smith's expanded *English Short-Title Catalogue* (currently online at the British Library) cite the later volumes, printed at locations as disparate as Newcastle, Wolverhampton, Derby, and Massachusetts. The earliest surviving edition of the sequel is *Here beginneth the second part of the fryer and the boy* (1680; Wing H1546C).

[67] Holbrook Jackson (ed.), Robert Burton, *Anatomy of Melancholy*, 2 vols. (London, 1964), 117; John Taylor, *Sir Gregory Nonsence his newes from no place* (1622; STC 23795), sig. A5; John Gibbon, *Unio dissidentium* (1680; Wing G653A), 1. See further Adam Fox, 'Popular Verses and their Readership in the Early Seventeenth Century', in James Raven, Helen Small, and Naomi Tadmor (eds), *The Practice and Representation of Reading in England* (Cambridge, 1996), 125–37 (at 135).

[68] G. Kalff, *Geschiedenis der Nederlandsche letterkunde*, 7 vols. (Groningen, 1906–12) 3.159–60. See further Elisabeth de Bruijn, 'To Content the Continent: The Dutch Narratives *Merlijn* and *Jacke* Compared to Their English Counterparts', *Tijdschrift voor Nederlandse Taal- en Letterkunde*, 133 (2017), 83–108.

[69] Nicholas Orme, 'Children and Literature in Medieval England', *Medium Ævum*, 68 (1999), 218–46 (at 234).

[70] Barnabe Riche, *True Report of a Late Practise Enterprised by a Papist* (1582; STC 21004), sig. Bi; Francis Kirkman, *Unlucky Citizen* (1673; Wing K638), 11.

interest in the training and deportment of the young.[71] Hence BodL MS Rawlinson C. 86 includes an extract from Peter Idley's *Instructions to His Son*, a series of sententious couplets outlining, amongst other qualities, 'þe properte of A gentilman', and the popular advisory poem *Stans puer ad mensam*.[72] In CUL MS Ee. 4. 35, the poem likewise appears close to the courtesy poem 'The Lytylle Childrenes Lytil Boke'.[73] In other words, the tale is often preserved in collections that reflect the household as a venue of instruction, among pieces that are concerned with imparting the behaviours and duties appropriate for middle-class sons.[74]

While the presence of such a rough-edged, scatological text in this company might be surprising, there are some striking ways in which Jack's story fits the general aims of the other texts. Although it is by no means a didactic poem, and no doubt owes its remarkable success to its ludic and boisterous qualities, its overall course serves to demonstrate the importance of good conduct, especially as it relates to the responsibilities of adult masculinity. Most obviously, Jack's ability to overcome his stepmother and the friar is presented as a reward for an act of charity: he only gains his powers after sharing his meal with a mysterious 'olde man' who 'was hungrid sore'. At the same time, however, it carries further implications. The 'gyftis thre' also equip him with the means to reimpose order on his household without compromising it himself. Both of his opponents in the text are invasive elements that have succeeded in disturbing the structure of his home. The stepmother's campaign against Jack is an assault not only on the boy but on the authority of his father, whose judgement she is able to compromise by convincing him, despite his reluctance, that his son is 'a shrewed lad'. The friar likewise, by aligning himself with the wife, recalls the idea of the *penetrans domos* or 'stealer into homes', a standard accusation lodged against mendicant orders in medieval polemic and satire.[75] Through his tricks, Jack is able to contain and expel these dual threats to the household and its order. Crucially, he is able to do so in ways that respect its rightful hierarchy, rectifying the oversights of his father without displacing or undermining him. *Iak and his Stepdame* therefore reflects and encourages one of the central responsibilities of the late medieval householder: not only does its preservation reflect the commitment householders had to the correct upbringing of their sons, but its story shows a boy attaining important facets of middle-class manhood.

Despite its unusual focus, *Iak* serves to highlight another purpose the mercantile readership might ask tales to perform. In fact, it is not alone in these concerns or approach. *The Tale of the Basin* is if anything even more explicit in the stress it lays on the proper exercise of paternal responsibility, even though its characters are all grown adults: the root cause of the problem is not the wife herself or her parasitic priest, but the fact that the parson's brother is 'a febull husbande', passively carrying out 'alle his wyves will' rather than assuming disciplinary authority, and lacking sufficient discretion to find the priest anything but 'gode and curtesse'. Other tales bring other educative functions into view, many of which could also conceivably be directed at the young. *How the plowman lerned his pater-noster*, surviving in an edition printed by de Worde ([1510], STC 20034) offers one

---

[71] See Janine Rogers, 'Courtesy Books, Comedy, and the Merchant Masculinity of Oxford Balliol College MS 354', *Medieval Forum*, 1 (2002), online.
[72] DIMEV 6137 and 2745, NIMEV 2233; see F. J. Furnivall (ed.), *Early English Meals and Manners*, rev. edn., EETS, o.s. 32 (London, 1876), 220; John Lydgate, in H. N. MacCracken (ed.), *The Minor Poems of John Lydgate Part II: Secular Poems*, EETS, o.s. 192 (London, 1934), 739–44.
[73] NIMEV 1920; Furnivall (ed.), *Early English Meals*, 265–73.
[74] See Rachel Moss, *Fatherhood and its Representations in Middle English Texts* (Cambridge, 2013), 47; Richardson, *Middle-Class Writing*, 132.
[75] Penn R. Szittya, *The Antifraternal Tradition in Medieval Literature* (Princeton, NJ, 1986), 39–41, 59–62.

such example.[76] Its central character is a miserly smallholder, made 'by his labour ryche' but with no knowledge of 'pater-noster nor aue'. His local priest cures him of both his ignorance and lack of charity at one stroke: he sends a sequence of 'fourty poore men' bearing names such as 'Pater', 'Noster', 'Qui-Es-In-Celis', and so on, to help themselves to his stocks of wheat, corn, and ale. When the smallholder complains to the priest the following day, and lists the names of the offenders 'on a rewe', he finds he has the prayer committed to memory. The text is therefore at one and the same time a dramatization of a lesson and a lesson in its own right: its vivid narrative is crafted to provide a mnemonic for readers unfamiliar with elementary Latin, a group that would naturally encompass youngsters.

However, what makes many tales remarkable is that their lessons in duty are sometimes less concerned with exercising authority than with urging a more cooperative, collaborative sense of governance. An interesting variation here is the 'Ballad of a Tyrannical Husband', preserved in Manchester, Chetham's Library MS 8009, whose handwriting and interest in courtesy texts point, once again, to a London mercantile compiler.[77] The ballad takes up a standard fabliauesque theme, the battle for supremacy between husband and wife, although pulls it away from the brutal aggression of *De sire Hain* ('Lord Hate') or *La dame escoillee* ('The castrated woman').[78] Instead of a pitched battle ending in physical dominance by one side or the other, it emphasizes mutual support and duty across the domestic hierarchy. Its two main characters are 'a good huswyfe, curteys and heynd' and 'an angry man': the two switch roles for a day after the husband demands 'what hast thou to doo, but syttes her at hame?'.[79] Although the poem is unfinished, its course can be reasonably inferred from its detailed list of the wife's responsibilities. The husband is obviously supposed to struggle with the food-preparation and child- and animal-care she must perform daily (after spending 'al nyght wakyng with our cheylde'), and thus gain a renewed appreciation of her industry. At a certain level, the text regards the couple's roles in the household as natural, even essentialist, a point that the husband's presumed failure to 'be howsewyfe and kype owr howse' underscores. It might even be designed to cement these roles in an active way: its comprehensive inventory of wifely duties—which includes such items as 'geve our chekyns met', 'bete and swyngylle flex', and 'clothe owreself and owr cheldren'—might imply that it was designed to instruct a young woman or man on proper household management, spelling out correct wifely and husbandly roles.[80] Nevertheless, even though it stresses the perils of transgressing behavioural norms, the text takes a nuanced approach towards them. As well as emphasizing collaborative interdependence in the home, its characterization of the husband as 'angry', compromised by his emotion and unreason, stresses that male authority is not absolute, but contingent on its own set of requirements and qualifications. To echo Barbara Hanawalt, its main point seems to be that 'patriarchal power' rests on the exercise of 'responsibility, restraint, and good judgment', rather than on unilateral submission.[81] Ultimately, therefore, the ballad shows the popular

---

[76] NIMEV 3182; Hazlitt (ed.), *Remains of Popular Poetry*, 1.209–16.

[77] NIMEV 3182; see Carol Meale, '*The Libelle of Englyshe Polycye* and Mercantile Literary Culture in Late-Medieval London', in Julia Boffey and Pamela King (eds), *London and Europe in the Later Middle Ages* (London, 1996), 181–227 (at 224); Jordi Sánchez-Martí, 'The Scribe as Entrepreneur in Chetham's Library MS 8009', *Bulletin of the John Rylands Library of the University of Manchester*, 85 (2003), 13–22.

[78] NRCF, 1.1–28, 8.1–125.

[79] Eve Salisbury (ed.), *The Trials and Joys of Marriage* (Kalamazoo, MI, 2002), 85–9.

[80] Conor McCarthy, *Marriage in Medieval England: Law, Literature, and Practice* (Woodbridge, 2004), 132; Rhiannon Purdie, 'Sexing the Manuscript: The Case for Female Ownership of MS Chetham 8009', *Neophilologus*, 82 (1998), 139–48.

[81] Barbara A. Hanawalt, 'Violence in the Domestic Milieu of Late Medieval England', in Richard W. Kaeuper (ed.), *Violence in Medieval Society* (Woodbridge, 2000), 197–214 (at 207, 214).

tale being used to convey some complex and subtle ideas, highlighting that its educational functions do not necessarily simplify its contents.

In sum, the most distinctive feature of the English tales is the free, often resourceful use they make of comedy and its varied potentialities. They show an obvious willingness to exploit humorous narrative to serve a range of ends, putting it to work in a number of different venues and making it generate multiple effects. In the public context of civic celebration, their ridicule is oriented towards community-building, tapping into the unifying power of laughter and the exclusionary power of derision; in the more private space of the household, instructive capacities instead come to the fore. Such versatility goes some way to explain why the tales prove so evasive when surveyed collectively, why they are so variable in form, metre, and terminology, and even why their preservation is so scattered. After all, the texts needed to be flexible in conception, given the range of functions asked of them, and the social meanings they were made to support. Ultimately, therefore, all of this brings us full circle, and underscores once again the inadequacy of reading the tales in light of the fabliau, and expecting the same cohesion of them. These English texts are clearly more than imperfect imitations of the French genre: they follow their own distinct sets of requirements, and respond to their own conditions and determinants. Measuring them against the fabliau, in short, only succeeds in obscuring their full complexity.

CHAPTER 23
Occasional Poetry, Popular Poetry, and the Robin Hood Tradition

Helen Phillips

While much is known of contexts and causes for occasional poetry, poetry we might deem 'popular' often presents puzzles: about origins, contexts, dates, primary audiences, whether what survives is a fragment or complete, sometimes whether it is religious or secular. Other puzzles concern how far texts are close to real-life poetry experienced in households, churches, the working day, taverns, and village greens, or are literary re-imaginings of those.

For both categories, there are questions of definition and inevitable overlaps with other categorizations of fifteenth-century poetry. What is certain is that both often had multimedia existence. Some popular religious verse may belong to solitude, some occasional texts address one person, but much was performed, spoken, or sung publicly, associated with music, dance, visual spectacle, acting, actions, or rituals, or with objects, including food and drink. Poetry played second fiddle to confectionary art at Henry VI's coronation banquet (see below), as Boar's Head lyrics did to roasted boar's heads with garlands, processions, singing, and music; and Plough Monday rhymes operated within powerful, interrelated parish institutions and festive rituals, as well as seasonal work practices. Grand occasional poetry contributed to the 'total-art' productions of civic pageantry or mummings for royalty and wealthy mercantile institutions. Popular poetry, even mere quoted fragments, can point us towards dance-songs, work-songs, Christmas festivities, charm-rituals to repel burglars or toothache, and summertime parish entertainments, whose sporting contests, special ales, costumed processions, and fund-raising were contexts for—and enter deeply into the content of—Robin Hood plays and ballads.

Occasional Poetry

'Occasional' poetry here includes verses for celebration of royal, civic, and institutional events; poems accompanying gifts; dedicatory texts, prefaces, and envoys; poems responding to major topical events; verse prophecies. Growing literacy meant that poetry that hailed, manipulated, and interpreted events was valued, commissioned, and often widely copied. The poetry for ephemeral occasions was likelier to be recorded. Though much occasional poetry was composed and received within elite culture, much reached wider audiences.

Lydgate's ballade stanzas (NIMEV 1929) for seven-year-old Henry VI's 1429 London coronation banquet accompanied sugar and pastry sculpture 'sotilte' figures of St Edward and St Louis (English and French royal saints, representing Henry's claim to both kingdoms); Henry V and the Emperor Sigismond (they had formed an alliance to fight infidels:

the message is about repressing Lollards); and England's St George with France's St Denis, presenting Henry to the Virgin, asking her blessing.¹ At the 1474 installation banquet for the new Bishop of Ely, John Morton, the subtleties' rhyme royal first commanded him:

> Think and thanke, Prelate of grate prise*,   *worthiness*
> That it hath pleased the habundant grace
> Of King Edward, in all his acts wise,
> Thee to promote hydar* to his please*,   *hither, place*
> This lytil Yle ...²   *i.e., Ely*

Following spectacular pageants celebrating Henry's Paris coronation, his February 1432 London entry included a giant, castles, angels, and three trees springing out of St Louis, St Edward, and Jesse. Lydgate's rhyme royal stanzas (a common form for royal entries) were posted beside pageants or, in an innovation that was much imitated, spoken or sung (NIMEV 3799).

For London's welcome to his queen in 1494, Henry VII ordered pageantry including 'a sight with angelles singinge and fresche balettes [*ballades*] thereon ... mad by the wysest doctours of this realme'.³ Royal entries drew on learned poets and also the expertise of cities accustomed to mounting mystery cycles. Queen Margaret viewed Coventry's plays in May 1457, while maintaining her Midlands Lancastrian power-base and coping with Henry VI's recurrent mental illness. In 1456 Coventry had honoured Margaret with thirteen pageants designed by John Wedurby of Leicester. Visually and verbally, these dramatized recognition that it was in Margaret's power and her young son that hopes for continued Lancastrian rule lay.⁴ Royal entries often drew parallels with the entries and advents of Christ into human life.⁵ Isaiah's speech (NIMEV 2781) likened Margaret to the Virgin and Prince Edward to the Christ-child: 'like as mankynde was gladdid by the birght of Ihesus / So shall þis empyre ioy the birthe of your bodye'.⁶ Pageants at various city locations presented prophets, patron saints, cardinal virtues, the Nine Worthies, and St Margaret, slaying a dragon, who assured Queen Margaret of her assistance. Jeremiah hailed Queen Margaret as 'Emprice, queen, princes, excellent in on person all iij'.⁷ Triune imagery and Christ-child prophecies reflected political reality: the regime depended on Margaret and the young prince as much as the king.

In 1474 Coventry welcomed the Yorkist Prince Edward and Queen Elizabeth. The pageants' rhyme-royal stanzas (NIMEV 3881) employed biblical prophetic and messianic tropes and the language of rightful dynasty: Coventry's joy at the 'right lyne of the Royall blode', now restored, voiced by figures representing King Richard II, Old Testament patriarchs, Edward the Confessor, and the Magi (complimenting the legendary ancestry of Elizabeth's mother, Jacquetta of Luxemburg, from one of them: Balthazar).⁸ Spectacles

---

[1] Rossell Hope Robbins (ed.), *Secular Lyrics of the XIVth and XVth Centuries*, 2nd edn. (Oxford, 1955), 98–9.
[2] DIMEV 5633; Anne Brannen, 'Intricate Subtleties: Entertainment at Bishop Morton's Installation Feast', *REED Newsletter*, 22 (1997), 2–11.
[3] Andrew Kirkman, *The Cultural Life of the Early Polyphonic Mass: Medieval Context to Modern Revival* (Cambridge, 2010), 92.
[4] R.W. Ingram (ed.), *Records of Early English Drama: Coventry* (Toronto, 1981), 29–44; J. L. Laynesmith, 'Constructing Queenship at Coventry: Pageantry and Politics at Margaret of Anjou's "Secret Harbour"', in Linda Clark (ed.), *Authority and Subversion*, The Fifteenth Century, 3 (Woodbridge, 2003), 137–47.
[5] Gordon Kipling, *Enter the King: Theatre, Literature and Ritual in the Medieval Civic Triumph* (Oxford, 1998), 19–27.
[6] Ingram (ed.), *Records*, 29–34 (30).
[7] Ingram (ed.), *Records*, 30.
[8] Ingram (ed.), *Records*, 53–5 (53).

included the mayor and leading citizens riding to welcome the royal party, highly aureate speeches, costly gifts, conduits running wine, and music (matching different pageants' themes) by the 'Waytes of the Cite', harp, lute, dulcimers, small pipes, organ, and singers representing the Children of Israel, casting flowers and sweetmeats. One pageant presented St George rescuing a princess from a dragon, her parents on a tower above, a scenario familiar to many spectators from the *Golden Legend* and fifteenth century visual representations. Dragons could be sensational: for Norwich's St George's Day, 1429, a man, paid 2s 4d, performed, using gunpowder, inside the dragon fighting St George.[9] George's Coventry speech celebrated God's gift of England as Our Lady's dowry, with George its 'proteccion perpetuall / Hit to defende from Enimies ffere & nere' (31–2).[10] St George, reputedly born at nearby Caludon Castle, was Coventry's pre-eminent saint. This royal entry, five days after St George's Day, incorporates elements from Coventry's traditional St George's Day 'Riding' in the city dignitaries' reception of their royal guests. Coventry's Cathedral, St George's Chapel, Holy Trinity Guild, and Priory had images and a relic, honoured annually in the Riding. The city's own traditions were being celebrated as well as royalty.

Poetry and imagery in fifteenth-century royal entries express an increasing aligning of English cities' administrations with the monarchy.[11] Coventry's 1474 stanzas repeatedly announce the prince is entering his 'chaumbr'. Coventry's motto was *Camera Principis* (prince's treasury-chamber), referencing Coventry property income received by princes of Wales, from the Black Prince on. Coventry's 1456 and 1498 welcomes to Prince Edward and Prince Arthur also used the trope.[12] York's 1486 poetry for Henry VII's reception, composed by Henry Hudson, spoke the language of victory while twinning Henry's triumph with the city's interests. Speeches (NIMEV 2214) by King David and York's mythical founder King Ebraucus articulated a message of royal entitlement jointly possessed by city and new king. David, beside a 'castell' filled with citizens arrayed in white and green (Tudor colours), handed Henry 'my swerd of victorie', beseeching him:

> Most prepotent prince of power Imperiall,
> Redowtid* in ich region of Cristes affiance*, *Feared, faith*

to bestow 'gracious complacence (*approval*)' upon this 'your Citie, not filid with dissavaunce (*defiled with deceit*) / Treu and bold to your blode'.[13] The politics of royal entries were frequently mutable and delicate: York had lavishly welcomed Richard III in 1483.[14]

Worcester, Hereford, and Bristol devised 1486 pageants too.[15] Each presented its own traditions and current concerns. Bristol, besides spectacles including a shipwrights' pageant, angled for help with its declining maritime economy (NIMEV 2200.5):

---

[9] Clifford Davidson, *Festivals and Plays in Late Medieval England* (Farnham, 2007), 32–6, 93–108.
[10] Ingram (ed.), *Records*, 55.
[11] Eliza Hartrich, *Politics and the Urban Sector in Fifteenth-Century England, 1413–1471* (Oxford, 2019), 177–80.
[12] Ingram (ed.), *Records*, 89–91.
[13] Alexandra F. Johnston and Margaret Rogerson (eds), *Records of Early English Drama: York*, 2 vols. (Toronto, 1979), 1.137–52 (at 150).
[14] Lorraine C. Attreed (ed.), *The York House Books, 1461–1490*, 2 vols., Richard III and Yorkist History Trust, (Stroud, 1991), 2.217. On the complexities, see C. E. McGee, 'Politics and Platitudes: Sources of Civic Pageantry, 1486', *Renaissance Studies*, 3 (1989), 29–34.
[15] John C. Meagher, 'The First Progress of Henry VII', *Renaissance Drama*, n.s. 1 (1968), 67–88.

> Bristow is fallen into decaye,
> Irrecuparable without* that a due remedy   *Irreparable unless*
> By you, there* hertes hope, and comfort in this distresse,   *their*
> Prouede bee* at your leysere conveniently,   *is forthcoming*
> To your navy and cloth making, wherby I gesse*   *on which I declare*
> The wele* of this towne standeth* in sikernesse.'[16]   *wealth, depends*

Henry, after a meeting with city leaders, promised assistance.

Worcester's problem was more frightening, having recently harboured rebel Humphrey Stafford. The Worcester speeches (NIMEV 3885.5) are, however, brilliantly subtle (written, I suggest, by the multi-talented John Alcock, Bishop of Worcester, Henry's current Chancellor and trusted advisor). First, a speaker representing Henry VI (d. 1471), already widely regarded as a murdered saint, exhorts Henry to 'embrace' merciful kingship, towards 'Your poore subiectes, liegemen, & Oratours (*petitioners*)'. Mercy is the pre-eminent quality of both kings and God. Worcester, 'Your oune Citie that neuer pollutede Was', acted out of 'Ignorance' and 'Is now defiled'. Worcester's sainted bishops, Oswald and Wulfstan, and the Virgin (all three the focus of massive pilgrimage at Worcester), each pray for the King, as does the Trinity, urging mercy.[17] A 'gate-keeper', *Janitor,* hails biblical and ancient heroes who, like Henry, surmounted adversity, exile, and danger, to bring security to their people. Reflecting perhaps Bishop Alcock's previous role as President of the Prince of Wales' Council of the Marches, the culminating acclamation declared Henry 'Cadwaladers blodde lynyally descending ... the fulfiller of the prophecye': the angelic prophecy to Cadwaladr, last British king, regarded by some as a saint, that a 'Mab Darogan', Son of Prophecy, another Welsh king, would regain the kingdom.[18] The Worcester texts cleverly position the monarch as the one receiving instructions, from sainted elders, and from God and Mary: to 'serve God in love and drede, / Having compassion of theym that hath nede'.[19] No one in Worcester faced punishment, and of the rebels only Humphrey Stafford was executed.

John Scattergood stresses a contemporary perception that the poet's role is to exalt the reputation of great men.[20] The provision of elaborately crafted verse, marking occasions of national, royal, civic, or individual importance, witnesses to belief in poetry's efficacy: for forging aristocratic and royal images, a national narrative, or a message of divine purposes at work in events. Henry VII mastered the art of using displays, clothes, processions, feasts, pageants—and poetry—as instruments of assertion, control, and national unification. The Garter was a tool for binding closer to the king the habitually factional, quasi-autonomous, magnates with regional power bases, and a uniting of political, ceremonial, and poetic instrumentality is displayed by rhyme royal stanzas (NIMEV 2526) for Henry's particularly lavish Garter celebrations for St George's Day, April 1488. The refrain is 'England now rejoysse, for joyous may thou bee / To see thy king so flowring in dignytie'. Its preliminary laudatory survey, back over Henry's achievements since 1485, rescuing England from 'great jeopardie', quashing regional insurrections, making 'al England ... to love and drede' him, winning international support—there are foreign ambassadors 'present keeping thy noble

---

[16] Emma Cavell (ed.), *The Heralds' Memoir 1486–1490: Court Ceremony, Royal Progress and Rebellion*, Richard III and Yorkist History Trust (Donington, 2009), 93–4, 96; David N. Klausner (ed.), *Records of Early English Drama: Herefordshire, Worcestershire* (Toronto, 1990), 407–9.

[17] Cavell, *Heralds' Memoir,* 83–9; Klausner (ed.), *Records,* 406–11 (at 407).

[18] Klausner (ed.), *Records,* 410. See Sydney Anglo, 'The British History in Early Tudor Propaganda', *Bulletin of the John Rylands Library,* 44 (1961), 17–48.

[19] Klausner (ed.), *Records,* 409.

[20] John Scattergood, 'Peter Idley and George Ashby', in Julia Boffey and A. S. G. Edwards (eds), *A Companion to Fifteenth-Century English Poetry* (Woodbridge, 2013), 113–26 (at 120–4).

feste'—finally gazes on today's scene, featuring harmonized Garter array, worn by the royal ladies of the Garter as well as the knights: 'O knightly order, clothed in robes with garter: / The quenes grace, thy moder in the same'.[21] The consolidation of Henry VII's control over the kingdom, in the two-and-a-half years since Bosworth, has its reflection in the tight design of this poem, its summary of royal achievement, and call to all England to rejoice.

Occasional verse often employs aureate diction, and classical and biblical figures. These tendencies are exemplified by Lydgate's 1420s mummings at Eltham and Bishopswood, and for London's Mercers and Goldsmiths. In the poetry of celebration, grandiloquence and obsequiousness were not, however, invariable. Carol Meale shows class and gender as 'important determinants in the language of patronage ... There is a hierarchy of address.'[22] A poet at York in 1486 addressed Henry as: 'Reuerende Rightwis Regent (*king*) of this Regalite (*kingdom*) ...', 'Moost prudent prynce of provid provision (*fulfilled prophecy*)', foretold by 'premordiall princes of this principalite (*foregoing rulers of this realm*)' (NIMEV 1186; 8–9, 2214–16).[23] In contrast, Lydgate's 1414 rhyme–royal poem upon Thomas Chaucer's departure on a diplomatic mission (NIMEV 2571), for a patron closer to a social equal, mingles erudite and simple styles. It grandly invokes saints and classical deities, beginning: 'O þow Lucyna, qwene and empyresse / Of waters alle, and of floodes rage', yet also speaks plainly:

> And for my part, I sey right as I thenk,
> I am pure sory and hevy in myn hert,
> More þan I expresse can wryte with inke ...[24]
> (71–3)

A distinguished Speaker of the Commons is here praised for informal, companionable, virtues: his 'passingly good chere (*hospitality*) with gentylesse' (28), friendship, generosity, and the 'plentyuous habounde' (34) of his wine (erstwhile Butler to the King, he doubtless had a knowledgeable cellar). Strikingly, William Dunbar's New Year gift poem for James IV (NIMEV 2267), c1500—'My prince in god gif þe guid grace, / Joy, glaidnes, confort and solace ...'—achieves, in unelaborate quatrains, a dignified compliment through simple words, including homely *hansel*, a 'first footing' gift, prognosticating fortune in the coming year, also hinting at reciprocal kingly appreciation—towards Dunbar.[25]

Occasional gifts, book dedications, and envoys typically display humility, even obsequiousness. Envoys frequently adapt Chaucer's 'Go Little Book' bidding (*Troilus and Criseyde*, V.1786–92) for their little treatise, little pamphlet, little quire, etc., often deferentially asking a reader to correct faults, a reflection of the literary world of patronage (the fifteenth century saw patronage and commissions greatly extended to English language writings). The brasher command that concludes Caxton's edition of the *Book of Curtesye*, c1477 (NIMEV 1919), to ignore envious disparagement once out in public, reflects a new literary economy where printed books compete for multiple anonymous purchasers.[26] The envoy to a psalter commentary (NIMEV 929), employing eight-line ballade stanzas, dramatizes its 'little book' going forth fearless, if once favoured with reading by judges, to other parts of the legal profession: 't'appere with support of theyme forto speede

---

[21] Cavell, *Heralds' Memoir*, 159–60.
[22] Carol M. Meale, 'The Patronage of Poetry', in Boffey and Edwards (eds), *Companion*, 7–20 (at 11).
[23] Johnston and Rogerson (eds), *Records*, 147, 148.
[24] H. N. MacCracken (ed.), *The Minor Poems of John Lydgate, Part II: Secular Poems*, EETS, o.s. 192 (London, 1934), 657–59.
[25] Robbins (ed.), *Secular Lyrics*, 91.
[26] Bernd Engler, 'Literary Form as Aesthetic Progress: The Envoy in England', *Yearbook of the Review of English and American Literature*, 7 (1991), 61–97.

(*be successful*) / to all th'ynnes of cowrte' (20–21), like a youth with influential sponsors. But its author insists it is 'goddes lawe' that will bring 'mede' (*reward*), and 'euer-lastyng blisse where rest is' (23–4).[27] The envoy to a comic poem (NIMEV 655), presenting two young men rejecting in turn many professions, apologizes (in denial of its deft aureation) for wearing no 'robys of rethoryk' but 'rusty roset (*russet*)' (155–6), a 'first mysshape cote of ynpullischyd speche', lacking dyed 'tungges purpurate' (162, 164).[28]

Historical poetry (see Chapter 18) is often occasional. Examples include poems on battles like those celebrating Towton and Northampton (NIMEV 1380, 2609), laments for kings, and epitaphs (see further Chapter 10). The lament for Edward IV, '*Miseremini mei*' (NIMEV 2192), employs mutability commonplaces including the proverbial image of this world as 'No sertayne butt a chery fere full of woo' (22), with original images like 'I haue pleyd my pagent & now am I past' (85).[29] Epitaphs often appear in manuscripts, including the haughty and magnificent epitaph of Humfrey, duke of Gloucester (NIMEV 3206), probably originally hung near his St Albans tomb and distributed to followers.[30] In the beautiful 'Ffare well, this world! I take my leve for euere' (NIMEV 769), in Oxford, Balliol College, MS 354, BL MS Lansdowne 762 and Cambridge, Trinity College, MS O. 2. 53, the deceased speaks as if poised between life and death, warning us against trusting this world: 'Speke softe, ye folk, for I am leyd aslepe! / I haue my dreme, in trust is moche treson (*confidence often proves treacherous*) (15–16).[31] Unlike the beauty and grandeur of some epitaphs and warnings about this world's transience in many, George, earl of Dunbar's epitaph (NIMEV 1206), three short couplets added in the margin of Fordun's *Scotichronicon*, alongside other Scottish historical material, in BL MS Add. 37223, constructs the earl himself as historical record. 'Heir lyis Erle George þe brytan', presumably linking him back to Brutus. It is followed by a brief summary of his genealogical links to three kings, his forty-eight-year tenure of the Dunbar title, and death-date in 1416.[32]

The taste across all classes for riddling and enigmatic verse (see further the next section) includes prophecies, which abounded in the fifteenth century, in prose and verse, in Latin, Welsh, and English. Prophecy is occasional poetry, sometimes clearly celebrating a specific royal or aristocratic exploit, veiled transparently in prophetic language, whose formulations could be reapplied to other occasions. Components are often mobile, extractable, and reused. Its origins include pan-European prophecy traditions rooted in biblical and classical prophecy and oracles, and, for Britain in particular, Geoffrey of Monmouth's *Prophecies of Merlin* (c1138), new poetic versions of which were still being composed in the fifteenth century, such as 'In the londe of more bretayngne' (NIMEV 1552). Political prophecy, rather than more generalized apocalyptic prophecy, dominated the English fifteenth-century surge in prophecy's popularity and influence.

A major fifteenth-century prophecy, 'When the cocke in the Northe hath bilde his nest ...' (NIMEV 4029), survives in twenty-three manuscripts.[33] In quatrains with much alliteration, possibly originating during the Percy-Glyndŵr-Mortimer insurgencies against

---

[27] Robbins (ed.), *Secular Lyrics*, 97.
[28] Henry Axel Person (ed.), *Cambridge Middle English Lyrics*, rev. edn. (Seattle, WA, 1962), 44–8.
[29] Carleton Brown (ed.), *Religious Lyrics of the XVth Century* (Oxford, 1939), 250–3.
[30] Rossell Hope Robbins (ed.), *Historical Poems of the XIVth and XVth Centuries* (New York, 1959), 180–3.
[31] Brown (ed.), *Religious Lyrics*, 236–7. Extant written copies are post-1500 but the text, wholly or partly, was apparently current by at least the 1480s: one stanza is recorded on three memorials to people who died in the 1480s, another fifteenth-century memorial includes two stanzas. Douglas Gray, 'A Middle English Epitaph', *Notes and Queries*, n.s. 8 (1961), 132–5, surmises the whole poem is fifteenth century.
[32] Robbins (ed.), *Secular Lyrics*, 119.
[33] Robbins (ed.), *Historical Poems*, 115–17.

Henry IV, it was later associated with Richard of York's opposition to Henry VI, and both Edward IV and Henry VII's claims to be fulfillers of Cadwaladr's prophecy. It foretells that 'a dredefull dragon (= originally Glyndŵr?) shall drawe hym from his denne / To helpe the lion (= originally Percy?) with all his myght ...' (9–10) and 'Than shall troy (i.e., London, "newe Troy") vntrew tremble þat days / ffor drede of a dede man, when þey here hym speke' (37–8). The 'dede man' could be read as Richard II, whom Henry IV's opponents had claimed might still be alive, or later Humfrey, duke of Gloucester, or Arthur returning.[34] Another example, in the more apocalyptic tradition, 'When the hills smoken / Thanne Babilon schall have an ende ...' (NIMEV 4036), foretells Doomsday and appears among an early fifteenth-century collection of sermons, in London, St Paul's Cathedral Library, MS 8. Prophecy's distinctive discourse, that includes its *when ... then ...* structure, its ciphers (the mole ... the mermaid ... a dead man rising ... the dragon ... the boar, etc.), and surreal scenarios, with puzzling introduction of place names, numbers, or letters, presents human and natural portents made stranger by insufficient context or connections. A form of participatory poetry, it challenges readers and hearers with destined looming disaster and sometimes hope, especially for a returning hero-king: traditions exploited for Richard, duke of York, Edward IV, Henry VII, and earlier for Henry V. Lesley Coote shows prophecy's contributions to a multimedia 1411–15 programme to promote Henry, including Hoccleve's *Regiment of Princes* and London's post-Agincourt pageantry.[35]

Fifteenth-century English verse prophecy may be composed in quatrains, couplets, irregular rhyme, and sometimes alliterative lines. Its gnomic phrasing and animal ciphers might suggest ancient, oral, or 'folk' origins. Yet the texts concern kings, magnates, and highest-level power struggles, they often use aristocratic heraldry, and have Latin and French analogues.[36] Prophecies, however, were familiar across social classes. Middle-class readers encountered them in histories, especially *Brut* chronicles, and Latin and English prophecy collections appear in many manuscripts (e.g., Dublin, Trinity College, MS 516; BL MS Cotton Rolls ii. 23). A wider public heard prophecies in public places. Parliamentary measures after Glyndŵr's rising banned minstrels who roused popular support through prophecies. Some friars' preaching did the same.[37] Perhaps codes are inherently subversive, and opaque vernacular prophecies were 'dangerous in the hands of the discontented and disaffected'.[38] A sermon condemned people's attention to prophecies by Thomas of Erceldoune and Robin Hood, while they disregarded God's prophets.[39] Prophecy poems claim authoritative authors, distant from the present-day world: Merlin, Taliesin, and, indeed, Robin Hood, named as author of a Welsh prophecy in Aberystwyth, National Library of Wales, MS Peniarth 53.[40] Its associated prophecies probably stimulated the popularity, and appearances in fifteenth- and early sixteenth-century manuscripts, of versions of the *Thomas of Erceldoune* romance (NIMEV 365).[41]

---

[34] Lesley A. Coote, *Prophecy and Public Affairs in Later Medieval England* (Woodbridge, 2000), 164–5, 198–200; Victoria Flood, *Prophecy, Politics and Place in Medieval England, From Geoffrey of Monmouth to Thomas of Erceldoune* (Cambridge, 2016), 155–91.
[35] Coote, *Prophecy*, 168–76.
[36] Flood, *Prophecy*, discusses arguments for elite readership, 2–3, 203–4.
[37] Coote, *Prophecy*, 164–6.
[38] Coote, *Prophecy*, 165.
[39] Coote, *Prophecy*, 166.
[40] Henry Lewis (ed.), *Peniarth 53*, Adysgrifau o'r Llawysgrifau Cymraeg 5 (Cardiff, 1927), 99–102.
[41] Ingeborg Nixon (ed.), *Thomas of Erceldoune*, Publications of the Department of English, University of Copenhagen, 9, 2 vols. (Copenhagen, 1980–3).

Prophecy's discourses invaded other fifteenth-century poetry: historical poems, like 'The Battle of Towton' (NIMEV 1380);[42] the lively 'Cronica' (NIMEV 3143.5), perhaps by priest John Benet, celebrating a 1451 sea-battle off Whitby;[43] romances (in the *Awntyrs off Arthure* (NIMEV 1566), Guenevere's mother's ghost prophesies Morded's treason and the demise of the Round Table); and also complaint poems, including (from NIMEV 3943):

When lordes wille is londes law,	
Prestes wylle trechery, and gyle hold soth saw*,	*considered truth-telling*
lechery callyd pryve solace*,	*private pleasure*
And robbery is hold no trespace—	
Then schal the lond of Albyon*	*England*
Torne in-to confusioun*![44]	*ruin*

This appears in numerous manuscripts. James Doig sees prophecy as gaining increasingly 'more popular and public influence', in the fifteenth and earlier sixteenth centuries.[45] Prophecy—occasional poetry, in its own idiosyncratic fashion—was also popular poetry.

Popular Poetry

'Popular' poetry means both poetry of non-elite culture and poetry widely enjoyed. Douglas Gray, whose *Simple Forms* and *Make We Merry, More and Less* are the pre-eminent guides to medieval popular literature, offers as basic definition that it is what the unsophisticated reader or hearer was given or chose for pleasure or instruction.[46] It was also usually literature familiar to everyone, whereas barriers of education, milieu, and elite cultural familiarities excluded many people from other types. 'Literate' and 'illiterate' denote a spectrum, not simple alternatives, but fifteenth-century popular literature remained in many respects oral culture, including, Gray stresses, 'the vast substratum of oral literature which has now disappeared, leaving only traces'.[47] Oral literary culture was frequently of high expertise and complexity.

For the nineteenth and much of the twentieth centuries, folk origins or contexts might have been prominent in any definition, connoting poetry born out of communities, rooted in ancient, possibly pre-Christian, cultures, and reflecting slow-changing 'traditional' societies. Folk seems now a less certain concept, while research into oral literature and mercantile, gentry, and working-class social and cultural history increasingly illuminates the literature and entertainments of late-medieval streets, taverns, cottages, village greens, and merchants' or gentry households. Research reveals how integrated local and seasonal festivities were within the institutions and structures (religious, secular, and economic) of parishes. And how important guilds, urban authorities, and merchant and gentry households could be in financing and putting on many kinds of entertainment, performance, and minstrelsy.

---

[42] Robbins (ed.), *Historical Poems*, 215–18.
[43] Rossell Hope Robbins, 'Victory at Whitby, A.D. 1451', *Studies in Philology*, 67 (1970), 495–504.
[44] Robbins (ed.), *Historical Poems*, 121.
[45] James A. Doig, 'The Prophecy of the "Six Kings to Follow John" and Owain Glyndŵr', *Studia Celtica*, 29 (1995), 257–68 (at 264).
[46] Douglas Gray, *Simple Forms: Essays on Medieval Popular Literature* (Oxford, 2015), 240; Douglas Gray and Jane Bliss (eds), *Make We Merry, More and Less: An Anthology of Medieval Popular Literature* (Cambridge, 2019), 1.
[47] Gray, *Simple Forms*, 2.

Clues to what might have been popular, in either sense, might include the survival of multiple copies, where the material seems non-elite, although some verifiably popular poems survive in a single manuscript. Sermons and chronicles describe some texts as popular. Variant versions could indicate long oral transmission, as can survivals, often greatly transformed, in post-medieval ballads, chapbooks, folksongs, or children's rhymes. Literary characters sometimes mention popular songs, like the thief Harvey Hafter in Skelton's *Bowge of Court* (1499), who mentions several titles including 'Heve and how, rombelow, Row the bote, Norman, rowe', a Thames boatmen's roundel, composed when John Norman initiated a river pageant upon becoming London Mayor, 1453.[48]

Presumably the contents of collections such as BL MS Sloane 2593, and BodL MS Eng. poet. e. 1, had wide appeal, and also texts that early printers judged a good investment to publish. Manuscript miscellanies created for middle-class individuals or households can suggest material congenial to such non-aristocratic audiences: often educational, family-orientated, and devout. Examples include BodL MS Ashmole 61; Edinburgh, National Library of Scotland, MS Advocates 19. 3. 1 (the Heege Manuscript); and Aberystwyth, National Library of Wales, MS Brogyntyn ii. 1 (*olim* Porkington 10).[49]

Popularity often lasted long. Indeed, even when a version is known or reliably conjectured to have existed before 1500, the only complete text of some popular medieval works may be a later source, such as the Percy Folio Manuscript, c1650 (BL MS Add. 27879), Richard Hill's commonplace book, Oxford, Balliol College, MS 354, c1503–36, and early printed books, including some Robin Hood ballads.

Allusions to peasants, their work, or rustic settings do not guarantee origins in such milieus. They might result from literate poets' inspiration from oral culture, from a higher-class audience's mocking amusement, and/or an aesthetic taste for bucolic charm. As examples, two carols in Cambridge, Gonville and Caius College, MS 383/603, about servant girls getting pregnant after enjoying a holiday and explicitly described sex, undoubtedly have such non-peasant origins, despite realistic details, like one girl's numerous chores. The other has the witty refrain:

> alas, alas, þe wyle*,   *time*
> þout y on no gyle,   *I didn't intend to do any wrong*
> alas, alas, þe wyle
> þat euer y cowde daunce,   *I ever knew how to dance*

as if the dance was the problem.[50] Similar lyrics with a specifically clerical seducer reflect literary traditions, of fabliaux and anticlerical satire.[51] Such lyrics' uneasy focalization through first-person female voices, and the sometimes coercive encounters, suggest a class- and gender-derived callousness. Images of lower-class license on holidays also recall

---

[48] John Scattergood (ed.), *The Complete English Poems of John Skelton*, rev. edn. (Liverpool, 2015), 44 (line 252); Charles Lethbridge Kingsford (ed.), *Chronicles of London* (Cambridge, 1905), 164.

[49] George Shuffelton (ed.), *Codex Ashmole 61: A Compilation of Middle English Popular Verse* (Kalamazoo MI, 2008); Phillipa Hardman (intro.), *The Heege Manuscript: A Facsimile of National Library of Scotland, MS Advocates 19.3.1* (Leeds, 2000).

[50] Robbins (ed.), *Secular Lyrics*, 22–5.

[51] Robbins (ed.), *Secular Lyrics*, 18–22.

complaints in popular 'Abuses of the Age' verses, that 'holiday' (*holy day*) is turned to 'gluttony', as in this fifteenth-century example (NIMEV 906):

> Wytte is treachery, loue is lechery,
> Play ys vileney, and holyday ys glotony ...[52]   *amusement loutishness*

Preachers sometimes cite popular poetry, often reinterpreting it religiously.[53] One, c1400, describes 'I sing of a maydyn' (NIMEV 1367) as sung '*communiter*', meaning widely sung or communally sung.[54] Like the Creed plays of York and elsewhere, fifteenth-century Creed-explaining poems were aids to popular education, important against Lollardy. Versified English religious teaching and prayers were undoubtedly valued. Gray points to Richard of Caistre's much copied 'Hymn' (NIMEV 1727) with its 'calm and gentle' tone as exemplifying such provision for lay people.[55] Saints legends were popular, and the *Freiris of Berwik*'s travelling friars 'Rycht wonder weill plesit' all the women in the town with their saints' legends (NIMEV 442.5).[56]

Versified proverbs, riddles, and charms were often copied and clearly appealed across social classes. Proverbs also appear frequently within poems of other genres, and riddles inspired some striking longer compositions. Best known is 'I have a yong suster' (NIMEV 1303), its lasting popularity confirmed by oral survivals into the nineteenth century. Its riddles include a cherry without a stone and a dove without a bone, finally emerging into the sunlight of the answer to how love can be without longing: 'Quan the maydyn hath that che (*she*) lovit'.[57] Another riddle poem (NIMEV 4169) depicts the 'foule fende' threatening sexual abduction if a girl cannot answer his riddles. She answers triumphantly, mixing piety and truths about life, as in 'Godys flesse ys betur than ys the brede, / Payne is strenger than ys the dede', in answer to the question 'What is better than bread? What is sharper than death?'[58] Walter Pollard of Plymouth copied this into his notebook, BodL MS Rawlinson D. 328, c1480, alongside eighty-seven proverbs, charms, educational, and religious texts. He included riddling religious verse: 'A God, and yet a man? / A Mayde, and yet a mother?' (NIMEV 37). Unlike secular riddles, this dismisses 'mans wit' to understand: it is enough to 'Believe, and leave to wonder'.[59]

Fifteenth-century verse tales in manuscripts, often in couplets or tail-rhyme, are doubtless the tip of an iceberg of popular entertainment.[60] They suggest quite a taste for inter-class social comedy. The still-hilarious *King John and the Bishop* in the Percy Folio Manuscript, and probably late medieval, celebrates a shepherd's cleverness in a riddle challenge, triumphing over Bad King John, and also the Archbishop of Canterbury, and Oxford and Cambridge scholars, ending up richly rewarded, vowing in future to bend his knee to no one.[61] Lower-class triumphs and some questioning of superiority conferred by birth appear elsewhere, including the *Squire of Low Degree* (STC 23111.5), whose hero wins

---

[52] Theodore Silverstein (ed.), *Medieval English Lyrics* (London, 1971), 144.
[53] Siegfried Wenzel, *Preachers, Poets and the Early English Lyric* (Princeton, NJ, 1986) is an authoritative study.
[54] Alan J. Fletcher, 'The Lyric in the Sermon', in Thomas Duncan (ed.), *Companion to the Middle English Lyric* (Cambridge, 2005), 189–209.
[55] Gray and Bliss (eds), *Make We Merry*, 40–1.
[56] Gray and Bliss (eds), *Make We Merry*, 178.
[57] Gray and Bliss (eds), *Make We Merry*, 262–3.
[58] Gray and Bliss (eds), *Make We Merry*, 256–8.
[59] Gray and Bliss (eds), *Make We Merry*, 264.
[60] Julia Boffey, 'Popular Verse Tales', in Boffey and Edwards, *Companion*, 213–23.
[61] Gray and Bliss (eds), *Make We Merry*, 258–62.

the king's daughter's hand.⁶² Numerous King and Subject narratives, including *John the Reeve* (NIMEV 989), c1440, *Rauf Coilȝear* (NIMEV 1541), c1450, *The King and the Hermit* (NIMEV 1764), c1500, and an episode in the *Gest of Robin Hood* (NIMEV 1915), c1495, depict an unrecognized monarch given hospitality by an independent-minded commoner, ending up bemused, bullied, and sometimes wiser, by the encounter and its comic aftermaths. Similar stories existed earlier: Alfred and the Cakes, for example, and Giraldus Cambrensis's tale of Henry II's incognito drinking bout with an afterwards embarrassed abbot. Fifteenth-century narratives present more boldness, with sometimes social complaints, from the commoner. More conservative, pro-monarch treatments return late in the century.⁶³ The king may find himself eating his own poached venison and meet his match in a physical contest. Sometimes kings offer the confident commoner a place at court, as in the *Gest of Robin Hood* and the later-recorded outlaw narrative *Adam Bell, Clim of the Clough and William of Cloudesley*, though there in less well integrated fashion: did this tale of violent Inglewood outlaws, known to have been popular by the 1430s, gain this conservative conclusion between then and its various printings, c1510—c1550?⁶⁴

Adam of Cobsam's *The Wright's Chaste Wife* (NIMEV 252), c1462, shows a carpenter's wife, during his lengthy absence on a job, repelling three higher-class would-be seducers, a lord, a steward, and a proctor (ecclesiastical legal administrator), locking each one up, agreeing to feed them only if they do women's work for her: preparing flax and spinning. The lord's wife laughs at her humiliated husband, takes him home, giving the carpenter's wife money he had brought. Foregrounding female solidarity and respect towards manual skills and workers, this ends praising good women and the White Rose of York.⁶⁵ The *Freiris of Berwik*, c1500, draws comedy from social pretensions, characters' disastrously divergent viewpoints, and perfectly judged timing and pace. It exhibits classic features of the fabliau: an everyday artisan setting, a stereotypical cast (lusty cleric, unfaithful wife, naive husband, clever trickster), ingenious plot twists mostly triggered by the lowest appetites—lust, deception, trickery, the pleasures of triumphing over others—and final slapstick come-uppance delivering a rough justice.⁶⁶

The Tournament of Tottenham (NIMEV 2615), c1455, offers a burlesque clash of chivalric and peasant worlds. Its first line promises chivalry, a tale of 'Of all these kene conquerours ...', but the combatants' names signal peasants: '... Tomkin, of Herry, / Of Hawkin, of Terry ...' (6–7).⁶⁷ They fight with flails, live in rural (though, interestingly, increasingly mixed socially) communities north of London: Islington, Highgate, Hackney, and Tottenham, and the comedy relishes farmyard details. Violent actions, many speeches, and reference to a song by six men suggest performative potential. A lost, probably similar, 'tornment de Totyngham' was acted at Rougement Castle, Exeter. Meale suggests the likely audience was middle-class urban tradesmen and the Exeter performance perhaps a

---

⁶² The earliest extant text is printed, c1520, but on linguistic grounds, critics concur with late fifteenth-century dating; see Erik Kooper (ed.), 'Introduction, *Squire of Low Degree*', in *Humorous and Sentimental Romances* (Kalamazoo, MI, 2005).

⁶³ Mark Truesdale, *The King and Commoner Tradition in Medieval and Early Modern Literature* (London, 2018).

⁶⁴ Stephen Knight and Thomas H. Ohlgren (eds), *Robin Hood and Other Outlaw Tales* (Kalamazoo MI, 1997), 80–168, 235–67; unless otherwise indicated, Robin Hood and outlaw texts are cited from this edition.

⁶⁵ Gray and Bliss (eds), *Make We Merry*, 191–9.

⁶⁶ Gray and Bliss (eds), *Make We Merry*, 178–89; Melissa M. Furrow (ed.), '"Freiris of Berwik" Introduction', in *Ten Bourds* (Kalamazoo MI, 2013).

⁶⁷ Kooper (ed.), *Sentimental and Humorous Romances*.

civic festivity.[68] Zaerr has illuminatingly explored and staged various performance possibilities.[69] *The Feest of Tottenham* (NIMEV 2354) depicts villagers cooking rural objects as if haute cuisine, a trope also common in nonsense poems (see below). The witty *Debate of the Carpenter's Tools* (NIMEV 3461) in Ashmole 61 shows similar potential for performance: in a series of speeches the tools, like his wife, criticize their master, who drinks too much. With its insider carpentry vocabulary, was it designed for a guild celebration?[70]

The Hunting of the Hare (NIMEV 64), c1470, in the Heege Manuscript, mocks peasants doing one of the defining activities of *gentils*: hunting. A yeoman and friends hunt a hare incompetently, then fight each other. Their names, Jack of the Wall, Davy of the Dale, etc., like the *Tournament's* shortened first names, are class-markers in the fifteenth century, the century of increasingly fixed surnames. So are elements of grossness like farts, brutish brawling, and wives taking injured fighters home in wheelbarrows. This picture of peasants' stupidity and self-inflicted injuries was perhaps created to entertain a gentry audience, the manuscript's first owners, the Derbyshire Sherbrooke family.[71]

A hunted hare is given a voice in the remarkable *Hunted Hare* (NIMEV 559). Beginning like a courtly lover's overheard lament, a hare complains about her ceaseless flight from attackers, both high and lowly. Its details contain countryside realities and sophisticated irony. The housewife whose kale she nibbles pulls out a stick, then sets two dogs on her. Sarcastically the hare expresses thanks to a 'genttylmane' who, for his own sporting reputation, will not immediately club the hare in her form but gives her an acre's space, before his greyhounds catch her. The hare finally acknowledges that her end is to be eaten with leeks.[72] An animal speaker facing death wryly with a joke on her lips fashions a thought-provoking transformation.

Everyday dramas of the cottage or manor-house hencoop inspired songs like 'The fals fox came vnto our croft' (NIMEV 3328). This uses popular poetry's favourite incremental structure, giving extra bite to its successive couplet rhymes, every time the fox gets away with yet another raid on 'our croft'.[73] 'The Fox and the Goose' (NIMEV 1622), whose folk-song survival indicates widespread popularity, works that fox-versus-farmer war equally brilliantly, giving the fox exaggeratedly human speech and attitudes.[74] Its refrain's greeting, '*Pax uobis* quod the fox …', conveys the same chilling bonhomie as the popular, ironically threatening, saying 'Good evyn, Good Robyn Hood', first recorded by Skelton, and adds its own hint of anti-friar satire that depicted friars as deceitful foxes.[75] Richard Firth Green points to popular traditions of monstrous animals, such as the massive Dun Cow, already associated with the earls of Warwick in the fifteenth century, and an adversary of Guy of Warwick in romances about Guy familiar in that century and the early modern period.[76] The comic Scots verse tale, *The Colkelbie Sow*, probably dating from c1450 to

---

[68] Carol M. Meale, 'Romance and its Anti-Type? *The Tournament of Tottenham*, the Carnivalesque, and Popular Culture', in Alastair J. Minnis (ed.), *Middle English Poetry, Texts and Traditions: Essays in Honour of Derek Pearsall* (Woodbridge, 2001), 103–27.
[69] Linda Marie Zaerr, 'The Tournament of Tottenham: Don't Tell the Dean', *This Rough Magic*, online journal (December 2018); 'Performance and the Middle English Romance', *Studies in Medieval Romance* (Woodbridge, 2012), 103–4.
[70] See text and commentary in Shuffelton (ed.), *Ashmole 61*, 456–60.
[71] Richard Firth Green, '*The Hunting of the Hare*: An Edition', in Anne Marie D'Arcy and Alan J. Fletcher (eds), *Studies in Late Medieval and Early Renaissance Texts in Honour of John Scattergood* (Dublin, 2005), 129–47.
[72] Robbins (ed.), *Secular Lyrics*, 107–10.
[73] Gray and Bliss (eds), *Make We Merry*, 225–7.
[74] Gray and Bliss (eds), *Make We Merry*, 224–5.
[75] See Gray, *Simple Forms*, 173.
[76] Green, 'The Hunting of the Hare', 131–2.

c1490, presents swine capable of attacking men (presented as fools), when one of their own species is threatened.⁷⁷ Are such transformations nightmares of hunted and domesticated animals striking back?

Nonsense poems also confirm popular delight in boundary crossings, especially human—animal, surreal 'impossibles', and up-side-down worlds. Children's rhymes include 'I saw a sparrow / Shoot an arrow / By a harrow / Into a barrow' (DIMEV 2259) and 'The krycket & þe greshope wentyn here to fy₃ght …' (NIMEV 3324), both rhymes set for Latin translation.⁷⁸ A poem combining nonsense tropes with the idioms of prophecy, 'When nettuls in wynter bere rosys rede / & thornys ber fygges naturally …' (NIMEV 3999) has a misogynist refrain: 'Than (*then*) put in a woman your trust & confydens'.⁷⁹ It includes herrings blowing hunting horns, crabs catching woodcocks, mice mowing corn with their tails, all typical of late-medieval nonsense poetry.

'Popular romance' is a necessarily inexact term. How far particular styles or subjects attracted specific social groups—such as lower- and middle-class, literate or illiterate, audiences—is a difficult question.⁸⁰ Romances share many tropes and styles in common with more obviously 'popular' forms. For example, evocations in written romances of oral minstrel delivery, like asking audiences to listen or requesting a drink, may indicate roots in oral culture or be somewhere between echoes of these and wholly literary formulas.

Manuscripts for non-aristocratic owners suggest the popularity among such audiences of both classic, romance storylines associated with the worlds of royalty and aristocrats—knightly combats, the fortunes of kingdoms, winning high-born brides—and romances that celebrate piety, family affection, and courageous, often penitential, responses to adversity: themes resonating throughout social classes. Yet, besides this evidence for middle-class tastes for sober godly heroes, a prose Lollard treatise, c1410, *The Dialogue between a Wise Man and a Fool,* complains that, if one tries to teach God's truth, people call instead for cheerful fictions of Guy of Warwick, Bevis of Hampton, Lybeaus Desconus, Robin Hood, or 'summe welfarynge man of here condiciouns & maners'—some dashing man of their type and exploits.⁸¹ Romances about the first three continued popular through the fifteenth and sixteenth centuries. Guy, Bevis, and Robin also star in ballads, and later chapbooks or broadsheet ballads, with wider and lower-class audiences. Ashmole 61 includes both swashbuckling, chivalric *Lybeaus Desconus* and *Erle of Tolous,* and sober *Sir Isumbras* and *Sir Cleges.*

Yet Lollard polemic is not objective socio-cultural research, and many fifteenth-century romances confirm the popularity of romances celebrating the strengths of Christian and family values and loyalty. An outstanding example is the skilful and engaging *Sir Cleges* (NIMEV 1890). This ignores the knight's former chivalric and seigneurial life, to focus on

---

⁷⁷ The only witness is from c1568; see Gregory Kratzmann (ed.), *Colkelbie Sow and the Talis of the Fyve Bestes* (New York, NY, 1983).

⁷⁸ Robbins, *Secular Lyrics,* 115. Also Joanna Bellis and Venetia Bridges, '"What shalt thou do when thou hast an English to make into Latin?": The Proverb Collection of Cambridge, St John's College, M F.26', *Studies in Philology,* 112 (2015), 68–92; Nicholas Orme, *Fleas, Flies and Friars: Children's Poetry from the Middle Ages* (Ithaca, NY, 2012).

⁷⁹ Robbins (ed.), *Secular Lyrics,* 103, 264.

⁸⁰ See Ad Putter and Jane Gilbert (eds), *The Spirit of Medieval English Popular Romance* (London, 2014), Introduction, 1–38, and Raluca L. Radulescu, *Romance and its Contexts in the Fifteenth Century: Politics, Piety and Penitence* (Woodbridge, 2013), 43–69.

⁸¹ See Helen Phillips, 'Reformist Polemics: Reading Publics and Unpopular Robin Hood', in Stephen Knight (ed.), *Robin Hood in Greenwood Stood: Alterity and Context,* (Turnhout, 2011), 87–117.

him, having lost his wealth through generosity, in now reduced circumstances, but sustained by other strengths: wifely support and God-fearing acceptance of adversity. The poem suits its Christmas setting, celebrating gifts, cheerfulness, devoutness, and family bonds. Husband and wife enjoy homely yuletide games with their children, with a nativity-like midwinter miracle in a humble setting: a fruit-bearing cherry tree at Christmas, makes possible a gift to the king, that rights their fortunes, perhaps recalling the Apocryphal Christ-child cherry-tree miracle celebrated in the *N-Town Play*, c1460–c1520.[82]

Often plots shifted between elite and popular genres and audiences. Thus, folktale motifs of Gawain encountering a shape-shifter loathly lady, who alternates between beauty and ugliness, inspired a 1299 court performance and the literary peaks of Chaucer's 'Wife of Bath's Tale' and *Sir Gawain and the Green Knight*, while the *Awntyrs off Arthure at the Terne Wathelyne* (NIMEV 1566), c1425, adapts the encounter to characteristically fifteenth-century preoccupations with Purgatory and masses for the dead. The motif appeared in non-elite ballads and numerous fifteenth-century Gawain romances which their editor Hahn considers popular, on the grounds of signs of oral dissemination, their very ordinary, shabby manuscripts, and their continuing early modern popularity. These include *Gawain and the Carle of Carlisle* (NIMEV 1888: a tail-rhyme form in Aberystwyth, National Library of Wales MS Brogyntyn ii.1 and a couplet version in the Percy Folio, BL MS Add. 27879), *The Wedding of Sir Gawain and Dame Ragnelle* (NIMEV 1916), and several more such romances in the Percy Folio.[83] Such diversity reveals not degradation but multilevel dissemination, both simultaneous and over time, a multimodality that increasing literacy preserved. It is also clear that audiences did not make much distinction between romances and popular tales, something well illustrated by the *Gest of Robin Hood*.

Extant verse perhaps occasionally preserves echoes of ordinary people's voices and environments—amusements or work contexts—in which they might have been heard. A fifteenth-century sermon in Cambridge, Jesus College, MS 13. Q. A, amidst imagery of the celestial city, with reference to the enclosure of an anchoress, Alice Huntington, quotes what was apparently a women's dance song (DIMEV 6175):

We schun* maken a ioly castel	shall
on a bank brysden a brymme*	beside a stream
schal no man comyn theryn	
but ȝyf* he kun swymme	unless
or buth be haue a both* of loue	if he has a boat
for to seykyn* ynnes.[84]	sail

The castle of love is an image in both mystical and courtly writings, but the preacher cites this as from '*cantico wlgari*', a common song.

Echoes from Plough Monday (the first Monday after Twelfth Night, the start of the agricultural year) illustrate the multiple contexts within which popular poetry might be performed and enjoyed. Plough Monday songs and the traditional shout 'God speed the

---

[82] Stephen Spector (ed.), *The N-Town Play: Cotton MS Vespasian D 8*, EETS, s.s. 11–12, (London, 1992), 2.469–70.

[83] Texts and invaluable introductions in Thomas Hahn (ed.), *Sir Gawain: Eleven Romances and Tales* (Kalamazoo, MI, 1995).

[84] Ralph Hanna, 'Verses in Sermons Again: The Case of Cambridge, Jesus College, MS 13.Q.A', *Studies in Bibliography*, 57 (2005-2006), 63–83; this warns about the interpretative complexities of trying to glean vernacular popular verse from clerical contexts.

plough' ('May God give success to the plough') were heard among activities that typically included a procession, disguised men pulling a decorated plough, the first ploughing of the year, dancing, drinking, and money-collecting, the proceeds of which went to communal 'Plough Light' church guilds. A fifteenth-century rhyme (NIMEV 964.5) in Cawston church (Norfolk) is a Plough Guild song:

> God spede the plow and send us ale corn enow
> Our purpose for to make: At crow of cok of þe plowlete* of Sygate: *ploughlight*
> Be mery and glade wat good ale þis work mad.

Such guilds, organizing seasonal festivals and fund-raising, typify the institutional roles and power, and the associated 'plebeian sociability', of skilled artisans in the parish.[85] 'God spede the plough', forms a refrain, for 'As I me walked' (NIMEV 363), a witty complaint about officials and clerics demanding money from farmers.[86]

Everyday work also features in nonsense poetry: sows wash kerchiefs, plash hedges, thresh in a barn, etc. An anti-misogynist carol, 'To onpreyse wemen yt were a shame' (NIMEV 3782), starts with two well-established rebuttals of misogyny—your mother and the Virgin were women—but continues with appreciation of routine women's work:

> A woman ys a worthy thynge—
> They do the washe and do the wrynge;
> 'Lullay, lullay', she dothe the synge,
> And yet she hath but care and woo.[87]
>   (5–8)

Echoes of women's lullabies appear in lyric refrains, 'lullay, lullay', 'baw, baw', etc., and in lullaby-influenced nativity carols.

Everyday voices, in this case singing in a tavern, are evoked too in 'Bring us in good ale' (NIMEV 549). Like much popular poetry its structure is incremental, building a bizarre sequence. Each kind of food proposed is rejected in favour of demands for yet more ale.[88] This, like other recorded drinking songs, comes perhaps from the authentic tavern repertoire (the seven-beat couplet lines readily suggest thumping tables) or a literary reformulation from that. Drinking, Christmas, and Boar's Head songs often imply group singing.[89] Convivial gatherings included songs about food and drink and also about men and women. Christmas and Hocktide festivities often included mock contests between the sexes, with paying of money fines or claims to establish which sex would have 'maystry' for the coming year, and, probably reflecting such communal amusements, the extant Holly and Ivy songs praise respectively men and women.[90]

---

[85] Eamon Duffy, *Saints, Sacrileges and Sedition: Religion and Conflict in the Tudor Reformations* (London, 2014), 86–8.
[86] James M. Dean (ed.), *Medieval English Political Writings* (Kalamazoo, MI, 1996).
[87] Gray and Bliss (eds), *Make We Merry*, 323–4; Robbins (ed.), *Secular Lyrics*, 31.
[88] Gray and Bliss (eds), *Make We Merry*, 9–10.
[89] Gray and Bliss (eds), *Make We Merry*, 3–5, 8–11, 45–50.
[90] Gray and Bliss (eds), *Make We Merry*, 45–7.

Robin Hood

A schoolchild's Latin translation exercise preserves this fragment:

> Robyn hod in scherewod stod
> Hodud and hathud, hosut and schod   *hatted, hosed*
> Ffour and thuynti arowis he bar In hits* hondus.[91]   *his*

So well-known was that first line (variants include 'greenwood' and 'Barnsdale': perhaps echoing a ballad introduction) it became a legal formula for unprovable assertions.[92] Despite evidence for Robin Hood's already well-established fourteenth-century popularity, the fifteenth century is crucial for showing us the extent and diversity of late-medieval Robin Hood traditions. Notwithstanding undoubted gaps in our knowledge of the fifteenth-century tradition, we have complete texts, numerous records of Robin Hood plays, and many fragments, sayings, allusions, and proverbs confirming the Scottish chronicler Bower's remark in his *Continuation* of Fordun's *Scotichronicon*, c1440, that 'the foolish populace are inordinately fond of celebrating [Robin Hood and Little John] in tragedies and comedies' and hearing minstrels sing about them, more than any other ballads. Bower dates Robin and John to 1266, among the 'disinherited', followers of Simon de Montfort. Andrew of Wyntoun's *Orygynale Chronicle*, c1420 dates them to 1283, as 'Waythmen commendit gud' (*admired hunters / forest outlaws*), operating in Inglewood and Barnsdale (Yorkshire).[93]

Portrayals of Robin, his comrades, and the nature and ideology of their activities constantly shift and extend. Searches for origins of the hero and the adventures found in Robin Hood poems among records of medieval men called Robert Hood prove generally unfruitful, though several were miscreants.[94] Definite historical roots, however, do exist: in British outlaw traditions, narratives about Hereward, Eustace the Monk, Fouke le Fitz Waryn, Dafydd ap Siancyn, William Wallace, the Inglewood outlaws, and others, part of international 'social bandit' traditions celebrating heroes who, despite law-breaking, are engaging, clever, and often defend a cause, as the 'good outlaw'. The same adventure can be attributed to several: Robin, Hereward, Wallace, and Eustace all disguise themselves as potters.

Most were well-born historical figures and their resistance part of national conflicts. Robin appears fictional. In extant fifteenth-century narratives he is a yeoman. He defies authority, targets travellers for robbery, and sometimes attacks powerful men administering authority corruptly or cruelly: the Sheriff, Sheriff's officer, and Abbot of St Mary's in York. He shows deep respect for the king (though which king is unclear) and the Virgin, who protects him, as in Marian miracles where she saves other less-than-perfect devotees.

The earliest Robin Hood play record is Exeter, 1426–7. Usually organized by churchwardens, raising money for parish needs and good causes by sale of special ale and the money-collecting activities of the actors dressed as Robin Hood—with obvious ironic links to the ballads and plays depicting muggings and robberies—performances are recorded from many places, mainly south-west England, the Thames valley, and north and north midlands, but also Norfolk (1441), Edinburgh (1492), and Wells (1498). The play text

---

[91] See International Robin Hood Bibliography: https://www.irhb.org/wiki/index.php/1401_-_Anonymous_-_Lincoln_Cathedral_MS_132
[92] Stephen Knight, *Robin Hood: A Complete Study of the English Outlaw* (Oxford, 1964), 16, 264.
[93] Knight and Ohlgren (eds), *Robin Hood*, 24–9.
[94] See further John Marshall, *Early English Performance: Medieval Plays and Robin Hood Games, Shifting Paradigms in Early English Drama Studies*, Philip Butterworth (ed.) (London, 2020).

(NIMEV 3118.4) in Cambridge, Trinity College, MS R. 2. 64, c1475, presents two episodes, a version of the Guy of Gisborne story and a fierce struggle over the Sheriff's attempts to imprison and hang the outlaws.

Real-life disorderly men often revelled in Robin Hood identifications. A chaplain turned robber in Surrey and Sussex, in 1417, assumed the name 'Friar Tuck'; Norfolk labourers, threatening to kill a judge in 1441, sang 'We arn Robynhodesman, war, war, war!'; rioters whose leader called himself Robin Hood marched to Willenhall to free an arrested man in 1497.[95]

Early Robin Hood ballads are mainly in *abcb* stanzas. In *Robin Hood and the Monk* (NIMEV 1534), CUL MS Ff. 5. 48, c1465, the outlaws are fierce, prepared to kill if necessary, yet at the same time Robin is devout and protected by the Virgin Mary. Robin's desire to hear Mass leads to his capture at church in Nottingham. Little John is arguably this ballad's real hero: Robin is rash, a bad loser about bets on their shooting match, which John won, and tries to lord it over John. John's clever plot rescues Robin (John gains twenty pounds and a court job offer from the deceived king in its course). At the denouement the king ruefully praises John's loyalty to his master. When Robin suggests John should become the band's master, John insists on equality—he and Robin are *fellows*.

Robin Hood and the Potter (NIMEV 1533), in CUL MS Ee. 4. 35, c1468, begins with a 'Robin Meets his Match' fight: a popular plot-pattern in Robin Hood ballads up to the nineteenth century. A bold potter refuses to pay money, fights well, and is welcomed into 'felishepe' by Robin, for his 'god yem[e]nrey' (90, 94). Disguised as the potter and trusting in Mary's protection, Robin comes to the attention of the Sheriff's wife, with whom he flirts, and the Sheriff. Invited to be their guest, he wins an archery contest, lures the Sheriff into Sherwood, and robs him. The last stanza asks God's blessing on 'all god yemanrey' (323), suggesting the social class of the expected audience.

The story in *Robin Hood and Guy of Gisborne* (in the Percy Folio, BL MS Add. 27879), already presented in the c1475 play, sees Robin, unrecognized, inveigling the Sheriff's officer, sent to capture him, into sporting contests, like those at the very parish festivities that surrounded Robin Hood plays. Successful—thanks to Mary—Robin beheads Guy, sticks his head on his bow ('thow hast beene a traytor all thy liffe', 165), exchanges clothes and weapons, and rescues John, earlier captured after a heroically uneven fight. This tale begins with Robin's nightmare about being attacked and the uncanny air increases with Guy's covering in a complete horse-skin, 'topp (*head*), and tayle, and mayne' (30). Conceivably a bizarre pagan survival, this may also, rather, mirror festive performers: horse guise is visually recorded among medieval entertainments and still challenges onlookers in the festive Welsh Mari Llwyd: a human clad in a horse-like cloak with horse's skull. *The Death of Robin Hood* (in the Percy Folio), a story told also in the *Gest*, probably existed by the mid fifteenth century. Robin meets an old woman foretelling his death and is murdered by the Prioress of Kirklees and her lover 'Red Roger'/'Syr Roger of Donkestere'.

The Gest of Robin Hood, printed by Pynson, c1495, followed by numerous sixteenth-century printings (STC 13688 etc.), a longer ballad with intricate plot, was possibly a distinctly literary creation, an *entrelacement* of adventures constructed specially for printing. Divided into fitts (sections) like some romances, it has romance-like features: Robin refuses dinner before a stranger-guest arrives; he and his men resemble a leader with his liveried retinue rather than equals; the king invites Robin to court. Robin finally, homesick

---

[95] Stephen Knight, *Robin Hood: A Complete Study of the English Outlaw* (Oxford, 1994), 108–9, 111–15, 263–7.

for greenwood life, returns and his men kneel in welcome. The main story, of Robin aiding, from his great wealth, a knight financially oppressed by an abbot, demonstrates him as the 'good outlaw': 'good Robyn Hode' as he is called more than once. He gives his men moral rules: they must not rob or attack 'no husbonde ... That tilleth with his ploughe', no 'gode yeman', nor any knight or squire 'That wol be a gode felawe', (51–6). The *Gest* ends praying for Robin, 'For he was a good outlawe / And dyde pore men moche god' (1823–4). *Robin Hood and the Potter*, where Robin is a lawless highway robber and a trickster delighting in bamboozling and robbing the Sheriff, nevertheless introduced him as 'corteys and fre' (*generous*, 10). The moral Robin and the lawless, violent robber, poacher, and, when necessary, slayer, were in a complicated tension with each other in the course of what we see of the fifteenth-century tradition, and that tension itself is undoubtedly related to the patterns of class, power, and politics within which this yeoman outlaw hero is presented.

The *Gest*'s dual courtly and yeoman affinities, rather than being fifteenth-century forerunners of the late sixteenth-century 'gentrifiction' of Robin, into Earl Robert of Huntington, probably mirror growing aspiration and confidence among skilled and mercantile 'middling' social groups—yeomen, urban tradesmen, and merchants. Such people's resentment at abuses of civil and clerical power would match the ballads' attitudes. Ohlgren notes the commercial discourse and parallels to 'mercantile self-fashioning' colouring the narratives of Robin and his men's exploits. One location for performance may have been guild entertainments.[96]

Difficult questions arise about performance: how far ballads were spoken, sung, or dramatized, and whether extant play-speeches indicate drama with extensive nonverbal action, most obviously fights.[97] There are many references to Robin Hood songs, now lost. 'Robin and Gandelyn' (NIMEV 1317), among songs and carols in BL MS Sloane 2593 (c1450), with its mysterious refrain 'Robyn lyth in grene wode bowndyn', references to 'gode Robyn', and shooting, venison, and greenwood, probably refers to him. A subtly allusive text, with a grim, frightening elegance, it possibly preserves a lost alternative narrative of Robin's death: at the hands of a boy, Wrennok. Green detects another lost tradition in the *Hermit and the Outlaw*, (NIMEV 260), c1450, whose unnamed outlaw becomes a penitent, but like Robin Hood has dashing vigour, wit, charm, archery skills—and bleeds to death.[98]

Proverbs, including 'Many men speak of Robin Hood who drew never in his bow', much recorded, and known to Chaucer, and numerous idioms ('Robin's Pennyworths', 'a Robin Hood mile', etc.) reveal a saturation of oral popular culture with the tradition. It appears in nonsense poems, like the Heege manuscript's 'The mone in þe morning ...' (NIMEV 3435; Edinburgh, National Library of Scotland, Advocates' MS 19. 3. 1), which includes 'reynall & robyn' ('Raynalde Grenelefe' is Little John's alias in the *Gest*), and 'Herkyn to my tale' (NIMEV 1116), where fish and animals frequently play instruments, including a sow who 'harpyd Robyn Howde'. This zany upside-down aura may reflect the tradition's sheer familiarity or perhaps 'Lord of Misrule' connections.

---

[96] Thomas H. Ohlgren and Lister M. Matheson (eds), *Robin Hood, The Early Poems, 1465–1560: Texts, Contexts, and Ideology* (Newark, DE, 2007), 68–96, 135–82; A. J. Pollard, *Imagining Robin Hood: The Late-Medieval Stories in Historical Context* (London, 2004); also Knight, *Complete Study*, 78–81; Gray, *Simple Forms*, 78–88.

[97] Stephen Knight, *Reading Robin Hood: Content, Form and Reception in the Outlaw Myth* (Manchester, 2015), 14–35.

[98] Richard Firth Green, 'The Hermit and the Outlaw: New Evidence for Robin Hood's Death?', in Helen Phillips (ed.), *Robin Hood: Medieval and Post-Medieval* (Dublin, 2005), 51–9.

Fifteenth-century merry men include Little John, Much, Friar Tuck, Scarlet/Scarlok, and Gilbert of the White Hand, some perhaps originally independent heroes. Theirs is a homosocial world; Robin honours all women, for Our Lady's sake, but without any aristocratic Lady Marian, sharing his greenwood exile: Robin's ladylike Marian only became firmly established after appearing in Anthony Munday's two 1590s *Robert Earl of Huntington* plays, which reconceived Robin as a high-minded earl, exiled by Prince John. The fifteenth century's combative Robin, defying lawful authority, enjoying trickster-like exploits, and 'Robin Meets His Match' fights with tradesmen, however, continued in innumerable ballads until the nineteenth century.

More than any other texts, late-medieval Robin Hood poetry actually represents the popular, presenting both merriment and that non-elite class identity expressed as 'gode yemanrey' and 'felishipe'. Greenwood poems also constitute visions of freedom—from everyday constraints, not just fictional Sheriff's prisons. Fifteenth-century ballads all have 'merey' summery openings, like this in *Robin Hood and the Potter*:

> In schomer, when the leves spryng,
> The bloschoms on every bowe,
> So merey doyt the berdys syng
> Yn wodys merey now.
> Herkens, god yemen,
> Comley, corteys, and god
> 						(*Potter*, 1–6).

The essence of popular poetry: celebrating pleasure and everyday communality.

PART IV
POETS

CHAPTER 24
John Lydgate

Robert R. Edwards

John Lydgate (*c*1370–1449/50) is the dominant figure in English poetry in the first half of the fifteenth century. Like Thomas Hoccleve, he presents himself as a disciple and thereby a successor and literary heir of Geoffrey Chaucer. Chaucer's themes, style, and phrasing suffuse Lydgate's poetry in a relation simultaneously deferential and rivalrous.[1] For writers in the fifteenth and sixteenth centuries, Lydgate, Chaucer, and John Gower comprise the founding triumvirate of English poets in a national vernacular literary tradition. Lydgate's poetry ranges widely over genres and topics, and serves an impressive array of royal, aristocratic, noble, ecclesiastical, and merchant patrons—men and women who exercised political, social, and cultural power in the first half of the fifteenth century. Lydgate has been described, with some justice, as a Lancastrian propagandist and unofficial court poet, especially in the early decades of the century.[2] At the same time, he establishes himself as an author different from Chaucer, who rhetorically disavows authorship, and Gower, who embraces it as a moralist.[3] Lydgate establishes instead a form of literary branding in which works bearing his signature are crafted for patrons, occasions, and coteries before they move, presumably carrying their prestige, into circulation among a wider, typically provincial audience.

In the Prologue to the *Siege of Thebes*, Lydgate inscribes this authorial signature in the narrative frame of a pseudo-apocryphal Canterbury tale, ostensibly the first one told on the return leg of the pilgrimage.[4] Chaucer's Host asks him 'First ȝoure name and of what contre' (87): 'I answerde "my name was Lydgate, / Monk of Bery"' (Prologue 92–3).[5] The Host's response—'Daun Iohn ... wel broke ȝe ȝoure name' (Prologue 96)—plays deftly on two senses of Middle English *brouken*: to do credit to his name and to use it to advantage.[6] Lydgate is an adaptive literary craftsman who remains grounded in Benedictine monastic tradition while meeting the requirements of genre and occasion; he writes in a 'stile counterfet' (*Troy Book*, 2.4715) that allusively and partially displays the expected contours of topic and genre, while retaining a margin for his invention. He is thus a poet

---

[1] A. C. Spearing, *Medieval to Renaissance in English Poetry* (Cambridge, 1985), 59–88.

[2] See, for example, Derek Pearsall, *John Lydgate* (London, 1970), 1; Paul Strohm, *England's Empty Throne: Usurpation and Its Aftermath, 1399–1422* (New Haven, CT, 1998), 173–95. Recent approaches connecting poets, sources, and patrons include R. D. Perry, 'Lydgate's Virtual Coteries: Chaucer's Family and Gower's Pacificism in the Fifteenth Century', *Speculum*, 93 (2018), 669–98; and Bridget Whearty, 'Chaucer's Death, Lydgate's Guild, and the Construction of Community in Fifteenth-Century English Literature', *Studies in the Age of Chaucer*, 40 (2018), 331–7.

[3] Robert R. Edwards, *Invention and Authorship in Medieval England* (Columbus, OH, 2017), 63–104. For an argument that Lydgate specifically rejects Chaucer's ambivalence, see Mary C. Flannery, *John Lydgate and the Poetics of Fame* (Cambridge, 2012).

[4] The 'authorial signature' described here differs from the unconscious patterning of function words in stylometry, as described in Maura Nolan, 'The Invention of Style', *Studies in the Age of Chaucer*, 41 (2019), 33–71 (at 54–5).

[5] Text quoted from Axel Erdmann and E. Ekwall (eds), *Lydgate's Siege of Thebes*, 2 vols, EETS, e.s. 108, 125 (London, 1911, 1930), 1.5.

[6] *MED*, s.v. 'brouken', v. 4a, 2a.

of displacement and belatedness, at the edge, to the side, or explicitly trailing behind the imaginative worlds he assembles from other sources. If on earlier appraisals Lydgate falls short of Chaucer's powers of characterization, description, wit, and voicing, we are in a position now to approach his poems for what they seek to accomplish, which is to establish the authority of clerical culture in the public arenas of Lancastrian England.[7] He does so by poetic self-inauguration, invention, and formal craft.

What we know of Lydgate's life derives from literary and documentary sources.[8] References in the *Siege of Thebes* (Prologue, 93) and *Fall of Princes* (8.191) place his birth around 1370 in the village of Lidgate (Suffolk). Lydgate entered the nearby Benedictine abbey of Bury St Edmunds sometime between 1382 and 1386. His *Testament*, written in the last decade of his life, records a spiritual change, roughly along the lines of Augustine's youthful pear tree episode (*Confessions* 2.4), before the age of fifteen (740–6).[9] Episcopal registers and letters dimissory (documents authorizing ordination) record that he was made an acolyte, then subdeacon in 1389, deacon in 1393, and priest in 1397. The scribe, anthologist, and secretary John Shirley (c1366–1456) placed Lydgate at Oxford, probably at Gloucester College, the Benedictine house.[10] A letter from Henry, Prince of Wales addressed to abbot William of Cratfield and the chapter at St Edmunds, written sometime between 1406 and 1408, asks permission for Lydgate to extend his stay at Oxford to further his studies in theology or canon law, as he wishes. Henry's letter praises Lydgate's intelligence, virtue, and good character ('*scen, vertue et bonne conversacion*').[11] Lydgate was present for the election of William of Exeter as the new abbot of St Edmunds in 1415. In 1423, he was elected prior of Hatfield Regis (Essex), a post he held, with absences, until 1434.[12] In 1426, he was in Paris in the service of John, duke of Bedford and Richard Beauchamp, earl of Warwick. On his return, he wrote a series of mummings and occasional pieces, for which Shirley claims his presence at Hertford Castle, London, and Windsor. In the undated poem 'God is Myn Helpere', he claims, 'I haue been offte in dyvers londys / And in many dyvers regiouns' (33–4), but there is no evidence of travel abroad except for the period in France.[13] Lydgate returned to Bury in 1434 and resided there until his death in 1449 or 1450.

Lydgate is the most prolific poet writing in English, the author of some 145,000 lines of verse. His major long poems—*Troy Book, Siege of Thebes, Fall of Princes, The Life of Our Lady*, the *Lives of Saints Edmund and Fremund*, and *The Life of Saint Alban and Saint Amphibal*—are the basis for his literary reputation. These are complemented by works of invention and formal achievement, such as his courtly dream visions, fables such as the *Churl and the Bird, Horse, Goose and Sheep*, saints' legends, and ancestral romances. Lydgate produced an extensive body of didactic poems and religious verse, some of them

---

[7] I take James Simpson's claim that both New Criticism and New Historicism consigned Lydgate to the same oblivion as one starting place for rethinking Lydgate's poetic enterprise; see Simpson, 'John Lydgate', in Larry Scanlon (ed.), *The Cambridge Companion to Medieval Literature* (Cambridge, 2009), 205–16 (at 206–7).
[8] For materials, see Derek Pearsall, *John Lydgate (1371–1449): A Bio-bibliography* (Victoria, BC, 1997). Biographical sketches in Lois Ebin, *John Lydgate* (Boston, 1985), 1–19; Pearsall, *John Lydgate*, 22–48; and Walter F. Schirmer, *John Lydgate: A Study in the Culture of the XVth Century*, trans. A. E. Keep (London, 1961).
[9] Text quoted from H. N. MacCracken (ed.), *The Minor Poems of John Lydgate*, 2 vols., EETS, e.s. 107 and EETS, o.s. 192 (London, 1911, 1934), 1.329–62.
[10] Pearsall, *John Lydgate*, 29, n.22.
[11] Pearsall, *John Lydgate (1371–1449): A Bio-bibliography*, 56.
[12] Sebastian Sobecki, 'The Earliest Record of John Lydgate at Hatfield Regis', *The Chaucer Review*, 54 (2019), 216–20, adds to documents in Pearsall, *John Lydgate (1371–1449): A Bio-bibliography*.
[13] MacCracken (ed.), *Minor Poems*, 1.28.

attaining wide circulation. The categories of secular and religious writing frequently overlap in his poems, as in the work of other fifteenth-century poets.[14] Lydgate was engaged as a translator for the *Danse Macabre* during his time in Paris and possibly for partial translations of Guillaume de Deguileville's *Pèlerinage de la vie humaine* and Évrart de Conty's *Les Échecs amoureux*. His occasional poems address public themes and events, particularly those surrounding Henry VI, and moments in the lives of patrons such as Thomas Chaucer or Humfrey, duke of Gloucester; they respond to requests for dynastic and devotional materials; a significant number accompany visual displays such as wall hangings and mural paintings or serve as paradramatic texts in mummings for court, municipal, and guild audiences. Shirley's manuscripts (BL MS Add. 16165; Cambridge, Trinity College, MS R. 3. 20; BodL MS Ashmole 59) and those derived from them (BL MSS Harley 2251 and 7333 and MSS Add. 29729 and 34360) preserve a number of Lydgate's minor poems with attributions usually considered reliable and information about context somewhat more suspect.[15] In his *Pastime of Pleasure* (1509), Stephen Hawes, who takes Lydgate as his master over Chaucer and Gower, mentions half a dozen major poems, adding to them the spurious *Court of Sapience* and *Assembly of Gods* and beginning a tradition of accumulated attributions by antiquarians over the next three centuries.[16] The modern assessment of Lydgate's canon begins with late-nineteenth- and early twentieth-century scholars.[17]

The major poems anchor the chronology of Lydgate's works; much of the rest must be inferred from the poems themselves or from the testimony of Shirley and John Stow, the sixteenth-century antiquary who had access to Shirley's manuscripts. Lydgate records Prince Henry's commission of *Troy Book* on Monday 31 October 1412 at 4 p.m. (Prologue 121–46) and completion of the poem in 1420 (5.3366–9).[18] Colophons in manuscripts of the *Life of Our Lady* credit Henry with 'the excitacion and styyryng' of the poem, and astronomical references indicate a date of 1421-2.[19] The *Siege of Thebes* incorporates an

---

[14] Anthony Bale, 'John Lydgate's Religious Poetry', in Julia Boffey and A. S. G. Edwards (eds), *A Companion to Fifteenth-Century English Poetry* (Cambridge, 2013), 73–85; Anke Bernau, 'Lydgate's Saintly Poetics', in Eva von Contzen and Anke Bernau (eds), *Sanctity as Literature in Late Medieval Britain* (Manchester, 2015), 151–71; Sebastian Sobecki, *Last Words: The Public Self and the Social Author in Late Medieval England* (Oxford, 2019), 127–58.

[15] A. S. G. Edwards, 'John Shirley and the Emulation of Courtly Culture', in John J. Thompson and Evelyn Mullaly (eds), *The Court and Cultural Diversity* (Cambridge, 1997), 309–17. For Shirley's manuscripts, see Margaret Connolly, *John Shirley: Book Production and the Noble Household in Fifteenth-Century England* (Aldershot, 1998); and A. S. G. Edwards, 'John Shirley, John Lydgate, and the Motives of Compilation', *Studies in the Age of Chaucer*, 38 (2016), 245–54.

[16] At the end of the antiquarian tradition, Joseph Ritson, *Bibliographia Poetica: A Catalogue of Engleish [sic] Poets, Of the Twelfth, Thirteenth, Fourteenth, Fifteenth, and Sixteenth Centurys, with a Short Account of Their Works* (London, 1802), 87, listing some 250 items in manuscript and printed editions, admits, 'It is, at the same time, highly probable that some of these pieces, mostly anonymous in the MS. copys [sic], are not by Lydgate; and that, on the other hand, he may be the author of many others in the same predicament'. For Josef Schick (ed.) *Lydgate's Temple of Glas*, EETS, e.s. 60 (London, 1891), cxlviii, Ritson's list is 'an Augean stable of disorder, glaring mistakes and inextricable confusion'.

[17] Schick (ed.), *Temple of Glas*, lxxxv–cxiii; MacCracken, *Minor Poems*, 2.v–lviii; Aage Brusendorff, *The Chaucer Tradition* (Oxford, 1925), 453–71; and Eleanor Prescott Hammond, *English Verse between Chaucer and Surrey* (Durham, NC, 1927), 97–102. MacCracken's canon is now supplemented and corrected by Alain Renoir and C. David Benson, 'John Lydgate', in J. Burke Severs, Albert E. Hartung, and Peter J. Beidler (eds), *A Manual of the Writings in Middle English 1050–1500*, 11 vols. (New Haven, CT, 2005), 6.1809–1920, 2071–175; Pearsall, *John Lydgate (1371–1449): A Bio-bibliography*, 50–2, 68–84; and NIMEV, index, 334.

[18] Text quoted from Henry Bergen (ed.), *Lydgate's Troy Book*, 4 vols., EETS, e.s. 97, 103, 106, 126 (London, 1906–8, 1935).

[19] Pearsall, *John Lydgate (1371–1449): A Bio-bibliography*, 19; Joseph A. Lauritis, Ralph A. Klinefelter, and Vernon F. Gallagher (eds), *A Critical Edition of John Lydgate's Life of Our Lady* (Pittsburgh, PA, 1961), 240, 8–10.

astronomical date (27 April 1421) and language from the Treaty of Troyes, suggesting completion of the poem before Henry's death on 31 August 1422. Pearsall identifies a 'laureate period' between the completion of these works and Lydgate's next major commission, *Fall of Princes* (1431–9) for duke Humfrey; for Lois Ebin, this is the period of his 'political poetry'.[20] The decade sees a brisk trade in occasional poems, commissions, and translations. It is also the most likely period for the composition of courtly poems such as *The Complaint of the Black Knight* and *The Temple of Glass*, which an earlier critical tradition assigned to a poetic apprenticeship before *Troy Book*.[21] Lydgate writes Humfrey's commission for *Fall of Princes* in 1431 into the poem (Prologue 421–34). In the eight years that Lydgate devoted to the *Fall*, he also produced the *Lives of Saints Edmund and Fremund* at the instigation of his abbot William Curteys to commemorate Henry VI's stay at St Edmunds from Christmas 1433 to Easter 1434. *Horse, Goose, and Sheep* can be dated on internal evidence after mid-1436. In 1439, Lydgate undertook a paid commission from John Whethamstede, abbot of St Albans, for another double life, *The Life of Saint Alban and Saint Amphibal*. Lydgate's final works include his *Testament* and *De Profundis*, an exposition of Psalm 129 ordered by Curteys 'At his chirche to hang it on the wal' (168).[22] Lydgate's collaborative translation with Benedict Burgh of the pseudo-Aristotelian *Secreta secretorum* ends with a marginal note of Lydgate's death at the line 'deth al consumyth, which may nat be denyed' (*The Secrees of Old Philosoffres*, 1491).[23]

'Þe Noble Worthi Fame of Conquerours'

The defining moment of Lydgate's poetic career is Henry's commission to write *Troy Book*. Lydgate's poem (30,117 lines) is a translation and amplification of Guido delle Colonne's *Historia destructionis Troiae* (composed in 1287), a Latin prose redaction of Benoît de Sainte-Maure's *Roman de Troie* (c1165). *Troy Book* recounts the full scope of the medieval Troy narrative from its remote causes in Jason's expedition to recover the Golden Fleece, which results in the destruction of Lamedon's original Troy, to the siege and destruction of Priam's rebuilt Troy, for which Hector's death is the centrepiece of the catastrophe, to the return journeys of the Greek heroes, culminating in the death of Ulysses.[24] Lydgate's poem aligns itself, rhetorically at least, with the tradition of pseudo-antique chronicle histories of the Trojan War. These claim their authority in the alleged eye-witness accounts of Dares's *De excidio Troiae historia* (fifth century CE) and Dictys's *Ephemeridos belli Troiani* (fourth century CE) rather than the fictions of Homer and other poets. Dares and Dictys are the sources for Benoît's poem, which significantly expands the scope of their narrative, recontextualizes it in medieval baronial culture, and transmits the classical 'Matter of Antiquity' as a vernacular *roman antique*.[25] Benoît's poem is not a direct source for Lydgate,

---

[20] Ebin, *John Lydgate*, 92.
[21] Schick (ed.), *Temple of Glas*, xcix–cxiii; but see Pearsall, *John Lydgate*, 84.
[22] Text quoted from MacCracken (ed.), *Minor Poems*, 1.77–84.
[23] Text quoted from Robert Steele (ed.), *Lydgate and Burgh's Secrees of old Philisoffres*, EETS, e.s. 66 (London, 1894), 48.
[24] C. David Benson, *The History of Troy in Middle English Literature: Guido delle Colonne's Historia Destructionis Troiae in Medieval England* (Woodbridge, 1980); and Sylvia Federico, *New Troy: Fantasies of Empire in the Late Middle Ages* (Minneapolis, MIN, 2003).
[25] Barbara Nolan, *Chaucer and the Tradition of the 'Roman Antique'* (Cambridge, 1992), 14–47. E. Bagby Atwood, 'Some Minor Sources of Lydgate's *Troy Book*', *Studies in Philology*, 35 (1938), 25–42, points out that Benoît is not a direct source.

and Guido does not acknowledge it as his source, but it sets the agenda for poetic invention by later writers.

The medieval Troy story begins the *translatio imperii* that leads Aeneas's great grandson Brutus to found Britain (1.824–36), and it provides as well an origin for chivalric culture, a mirror for princes, and models for aristocratic selfhood. Henry's reported intention in commissioning Lydgate's poem is to preserve the memory of 'verray kny3thod' (Prologue, 76) and 'the prowess of olde chiualrie' (Prologue, 78), pursuing the 'vertuous besynesse' (Prologue 84) of a radically militarized 'manhood' (Prologue, 85, 93).[26] Henry seeks a nationalistic English counterpart to the Latin and French narratives so that 'to hy3e and lowe / The noble story openly wer knowe / In oure tonge' (Prologue, 111–13) through his agency. Political and literary genealogies are intertwined in the patron's conception and the author's execution of the poem. Henry's descent from his father shows that 'The rotys vertu þus can the frute renewe' (Prologue, 98), and it promises orderly royal 'successioun' (Prologue, 103) to legitimate Lancastrian rule after Henry IV's usurpation.[27] For his part, Lydgate follows Guido as 'an auctour of ful hi3e renoun' (Prologue, 354) in the tradition of Dares and Dictys; he tacitly outdoes his 'maister' Chaucer by recounting the 'Troian gestes' (1.145), dismissed as 'a long digression' (1.143) in *Troilus and Criseyde*.[28] Lydgate's three-fold task is to translate (both to render and to relocate), compile (to combine multiple sources), and 'make' (to write competent verse based on Guido's prose).

Lydgate reshapes and reframes the materials designated by Henry and gives them polished formal expression. Claiming to preserve the 'substaunce' of Guido (Prologue, 359 and 5.3543), he restructures the divisions of the *Historia* into the five-book model of *Troilus and Criseyde*. He supplements the story with mythological and historical excursus, added speeches, descriptive passages, formal complaints, and moralisation. As an exemplary narrative, the Troy story conveys the ethical principles of aristocratic self-governance and the political lessons of statecraft in times of war. Lydgate adds a further dimension by aligning events in the classical story with their counterparts in the Old Testament to suggest a universal history fully legible only from the perspective of Christian history, for which a monastic writer is the most competent interpreter. The thematic focus of his poetic approach is the virtue of prudence, *recta ratio agibilium* ('right reason about things that can be done').[29] Prudence is concerned with deliberation about practical steps and foresight; it proves a guide but not a solution to mutability and especially to the precarity of epic heroism and kingship. As characters acknowledge in scenes of counsel and deliberation, the radical instability of Fortune requires some capacity to anticipate and weigh dangers and courses of action. But prudence can also miscarry, as when Lamedon refuses a layover to Jason and Hercules on their journey to Colchis and so inadvertently starts the war; or it can falter, as when Hector, overcome by the desire to pillage a dead king's armour, moves his shield and so falls victim to Achilles. For Lydgate the moralist-historian, incidental causes—what Benoît calls '*assez petit d'uevre*' (2831) and

---

[26] For the semantic range of memorial, see Robert J. Meyer-Lee, 'John Lydgate's Major Poems', in Boffey and Edwards (eds), *A Companion to Fifteenth-Century English Poetry*, 59–71 (at 60–2); and Meyer-Lee, 'The Memorial Form of John Lydgate's *Troy Book*', *Exemplaria*, 29 (2017), 280–95.

[27] The three claims for Lancastrian legitimacy—conquest, popular election, and succession—are enumerated in 'The Complaint of Chaucer to His Purse' (22–3).

[28] Text quoted from Larry D. Benson (general ed.), *The Riverside Chaucer* (Boston, 1987).

[29] Benson, *The History of Troy*, 119, 124–9.

Guido '*leues iniurie*' (Book Five)—can undo prudence.[30] So, too, can dissembling and simulation, which Agamemnon, for example, makes an instrument of prudence in counselling a distraught Menelaus to 'dissymble a wrong' (2.4373): 'who can ben peisible in his smerte, / It is a tokene he hath a manly herte' (2.4375–6). In Lydgate's moral lessons and exemplary action, prudence defines the tragic condition of the Troy story—a governing virtue for understanding and action working at times uncertainly within a foreclosed pagan history unredeemed by grace.

Lydgate devises a style to complement the elevation of his material and the complexity of his themes. Guido ostensibly (and improbably) 'hath no pere, / To rekne alle þat write of this matere' (Prologue, 367–8), but the poetic resources come from Chaucer—specifically, from Chaucer understood as a rhetorician chiefly concerned with eloquence.[31] For the narrative, Lydgate uses Chaucer's rhymed couplets in iambic pentameter and shifts to the other distinctive Chaucerian verse form, rhyme royal stanzas, in the Envoy. His prosody follows Chaucer's metrical patterns, including common variations such as headless lines, trochaic inversions, and triplets.[32] The broken-back line associated with Lydgate typically lacks an unstressed syllable at the start of the third foot, after a caesura. As in Chaucer's poetry, the line permits a variation of rhythm, marked emphasis, and semantic play, as in this couplet: 'And some of Troye, in conclusioun, / Iuparte nolde her lyues nor her toun' (3.4055–6). The Trojans in this passage reject the wager of self and city on single combat between Hector and Achilles 'in conclusioun'—definitively and at the end of their deliberations. Lydgate's aureate style in *Troy Book* and perhaps even more prominently in his religious poems amplifies the ornate diction of Chaucer's high style; it draws on Romance-Latinate vocabulary and features elaborate syntactical structures, some of them depending, as in the opening of *Troy Book* and *The Siege of Thebes*, on extended parallel constructions and on participles to replace finite verbs.[33]

Lydgate's poetic craft is fully on display when he amplifies set pieces from his sources, as in Priam's rebuilding of Troy in Book Two. Dares mentions Priam's reconstruction, and Benoît and Guido develop the description of the new city in successive stages. Lydgate's innovation is to amplify their topics and connect them thematically and ideologically. Benoît's workers ('*ovriers*', 2989) become Guido's experienced builders ('*peritis inhedeficandis artibus*', 46), whom Lydgate fashions not just as skilled artisans but artists with powers of reason, calculation, and imagination:

> He made seke in euery regioun
> For swiche werkemen as were corious*,   *ingenious*
> Of wyt inventyf, of castyng merveilous;
> Or swyche as coude* crafte of gemetrye,   *knew*
> Or wer sotyle in her fantasye ...
> (2.490–4)

---

[30] Texts quoted from Léopold Constans (ed.), *Le Roman de Troie par Benoît de Sainte-Maure*, 6 vols, SATF (Paris, 1906–12), 1.143; and Nathaniel Edward Griffin (ed.), *Historia Destructionis Troiae* (Cambridge, MA, 1936), 44.

[31] Nolan, 'The Invention of Style', 64–71, situates Lydgate's fashioning of his 'style' between Chaucer's ornate diction and Gower's plain style.

[32] For the taxonomy of Lydgate's metre, see Schick (ed.), *Temple of Glas*, lvi–lx.

[33] Phillipa Hardman, 'Lydgate's Uneasy Syntax', in Larry Scanlon and James Simpson (eds), *John Lydgate: Poetry, Culture, and Lancastrian England* (Notre Dame, IN, 2006), 12–35, argues that Lydgate's syntax incorporates deliberate stylistic devices and reflects an alignment with structural divisions in his poems.

Priam designs a second Troy 'At his devyse' (2.485) and organizes the work of his craftsmen as a civic poesis. Lydgate protests, 'I can no termys to speke of gemetrye' (2.552) or the individual crafts, but it is precisely those terms that embellish his account of the aesthetic, sensuous effects of Priam's military and civil engineering:

In þe frountel* of euery stretis syde,	*façade*
Fresche alures* with lusty hiȝe pynacles*,	*covered passages; turrets*
And moustryng* outward riche tabernacles*,	*facing; shrines*
Vowted* a-boue like reclinatories*,	*vaulted; canopied bed*
Þat called werne deambulatories* ...	*covered walkways*
(2.686–90)	

The carved, multicoloured, decorative surfaces of Troy parallel the rhetorical surfaces of the poem. Yet the guiding motive for amplification in both cases is the intellectual task of rational invention, expressed repeatedly through the figures of the builder's compass and the carpenter's square.

Priam invents and disposes the city to assert order and stability on the reclaimed foundations of Lamedon's ill-fortuned Troy. The massive city is laid out along straight lines (the length and breadth of each requires three days' journey) that allow the circulation of air along its broad avenues. The river Xanthus bisects the city to power grain mills, provide fish, and carry off waste. Craftsmen occupy their designated quarters in the city where they work 'at liberte' (2.710). In his social planning, Priam draws people from the countryside to repopulate Troy, as Benoît and Guido note, but Lydgate carries Priam's intent forwards to the creation of a polity: 'And hem þat wern afore to hym foreyns, / He hath in Troye maked citeȝeyns, / Ful discretly, liche as it is founde' (2.781–3). The headless third line in this passage, beginning with a stressed syllable, marks both Priam's attentive design and Lydgate's feigned textual authority. To the social and political order, Priam adds a cultural programme of martial and athletic feats, chess, games of chance, and performances of tragedy and comedy, much amplified in Lydgate's description. In Benoît and Guido, the *topographia* ends after a parallel description of Ilium, Priam's palace and stronghold, as Priam, confident in his achievements, returns to his grievance with the Greeks because of their attack on Lamedon and the abduction of Hesione. For Lydgate, this shift to war and vengeance merits an extended complaint, for it is a misapplication of the same quality of deliberation that rebuilt Troy: 'For Priam now in his entencioun / Cast & compaseth, revolvyng vp & dovn, / How strong he was of riches & meyne' (2.1095–7). His assessment, Lydgate warns, is a 'fantasye' (2.1102), and it reveals that Priam's twin project of building a city and a society merely deferred a larger catastrophe driven by an indwelling 'grayn of malys' (2.1071) that always remained beyond remedy and rational deliberation.

The dark vision of Trojan history, particularly in Guido's *Historia*, moves through the deaths of its heroes, the horrific vengeance exacted in the second fall of the city, and the fates that await most of the conquerors. Any escape from cycles of violence lies beyond the heroic narrative, in the generation of filial survivors who learn to make peace with each other—notably Achilleidos and Lamedon, the descendants of Achilles and Hector, and Ulysses's sons Telemachus and Telegonus—as each assumes the duties of kingship. Lydgate projects an equivalent resolution at the end of *Troy Book* in Henry's dual monarchy, adapting terms that recall Priam's indelible grievance: 'I mene þus, þat Yngelond and Fraunce / May be al oon, with-oute variaunce, / Oute of hertis old rancour to enchase (*drive out*)'

(5.3411–13). The prospect of Henry's marriage to Katherine of Valois seals the political union and potentially corrects the disastrous trade in women that provoked the Trojan war. For Lydgate the historian-moralist, however, the lesson of Troy remains unchanged (and prescient in the immediate context): 'For þer is nouþer prince, lord, nor king, / Be exaumple of Troye, like as ʒe may se, / Þat in þis lif may haue ful surete' (5.3576–8).

The Siege of Thebes is a companion piece to *Troy Book*, written in rhymed couplets, though with relatively more metrical variation within the pentameter lines. The poem has no identified patron, but Henry or Humfrey would be a likely dedicatee. Lydgate knows of Statius's *Thebaid* (1272 and *Troy Book* Prologue 230), but his immediate source is a French prose redaction that recounts the full narrative, from the dual founding of Thebes by Cadmus and Amphion to the Oedipus story, before centring on the fraternal strife between Eteocles and Polynices over succession to the throne and ending with Theseus's triumph over Creon and the destruction of the city. Lydgate's tale is at once a gesture of homage to Chaucer and a vehicle for authorial assertion, for he follows in the direction of the 'Knight's Tale' but claims a separate authority by telling the events that precede it. Though Chaucer is present from the opening lines of the Prologue, which imitate the General Prologue to the *Canterbury Tales*, and evoked throughout the poem in Lydgate's phrasing and allusions, he is not named until Theseus enters, precisely at the point where the Theban narrative and the 'Knight's Tale' intersect (4501).

As in *Troy Book*, Lydgate presents a *roman antique* that celebrates beneficent kingship and heroic virtues while reckoning their costs. The epideictic aim of the poem is a necessary preliminary to the didacticism. Love and truth are the 'moral postulates' that Lydgate chooses to exemplify rather than Statius's will to power.[34] Amphion builds Thebes by his eloquence and fosters the 'inward loue' (280) of his subjects. In a passage that veers from pentameter lines to conversational speech, Lydgate points the lesson that Adrastus's liberality cements bonds of allegiance and affection that sustain a monarch's rule:

> For loue is mor than gold or gret richesse;
> Gold faileth ofte loue wol abyde
> For lyf or deth be a lordys syde;
> And the tresour shortly, of a king
> Stondeth in loue abouen alle thing.
> Farwel lordshipe bothe morowe and Eve
> Specially whan loue taketh his leve!
> (2716–22)

Truth finds a compelling demonstration in Tydeus's mission to represent Polynices's claim on the alternating kingship of Thebes, which ends in Eteocles's disastrous effort to ambush him on his return to Argos. Lydgate asserts, 'By which ensample ʒe opynly may se / Ageynes trouthe falshed hath no myght' (2236). Tydeus emerges as a chivalric exemplar—'The beste knyght and most manly man' (4231)—in his friendship with Polynices and bravery in the assault on the city, and he remains largely untainted by the cannibalistic fury that denies him a hero's apotheosis in Statius.[35]

---

[34] Robert W. Ayers, 'Medieval History, Moral Purpose, and the Structure of Lydgate's *Siege of Thebes*', *PMLA*, 73 (1958), 463–74 (at 474).

[35] Lydgate cites Boccaccio (*Genealogie Deorum Gentium* 9.21) selectively for the presentation of Melanippus's head (4235–9). For the background, see Kyle Gervais, 'Tydeus the Hero? Intertextual Confusion in Statius, *Thebaid 2*', *Phoenix*, 69 (2015), 56–78.

The informing values of love and truth in the story, as critics point out, are continually open to violence and mischance.[36] Amphion overthrows Cadmus as the founder of the city. Oedipus kills Laius in a tournament 'of aventure' (580). The Theban nobles act prudently in sanctioning Oedipus's marriage to Jocasta and later endorsing the failed 'Couenaunt and conuencioun' (1929; cf.1696) for alternating kingship yearly between Eteocles and Polynices. The encomium on truth (1721–73) does not persuade Eteocles to honour his pledge to his brother. Adrastus miscalculates the power of the Greek force and the resistance shown by the Thebans under the rule of tyrants. Hypsipyle's aid to the Greeks occasions the death of Lycurgus's infant son. Jocasta's efforts to broker peace between her sons go awry when the escape of a tame tiger incites renewed battle. Eteocles, mortally wounded, treacherously kills his brother when Polynices tries to save him 'Of loue only handlyng hym ryght softe' (4287).

In recounting the full narrative of Thebes, Lydgate looks to causes beyond the obscure workings of Fortune, chance, and mutability, which shaped the Troy story. Doubleness and repetition drive Thebes's recursive history. The city has two founders. Oedipus is the son for both Laius and Polybus. Incest provides the controlling figure of repetition. The divided kingship of Thebes is replicated when Tydeus and Polynices first battle on the porch of Adrastus's palace and then marry his daughters, sharing jointly in the promise of being his heirs. The tyrant Creon, freely elected like Adrastus, succeeds the tyrant Eteocles. Two competing versions describe the razing of the city after Theseus's conquest. The point of recursive history, Lydgate understands, is that it offers no exit. Its origin lies in the original Fall: 'Lucyfer, fader of Envie, / The olde Serpent, he levyathan, / Was the first that euer werre gan' (4662-4). Its tragic witness is Adrastus, alone in his city at the end of the poem, bereft of companions. The victim is chivalric culture itself: 'For in the werre is non excepcioun / Of hegh estat nor lowh condicioun' (4645-6).

'Thuntrust off al Worldly Thyng'

Humfrey's commission to write *Fall of Princes* in 1431 returns Lydgate to the public and poetic themes of *Troy Book* and the *Siege*, though with a wider range of materials and a patron who sporadically intervenes to assert his authority. Lydgate's poem is a translation and adaptation of Laurent de Premierfait's second French translation of Giovanni Boccaccio's *De casibus virorum illustrium*, made for Jean de France, Duc de Berry and uncle of Charles VI, in 1409. Lydgate found in Laurent's translation the form of tragedy already familiar from Chaucer's 'Monk's Tale', which had earlier incorporated Boccaccio, Boethius, and the *Roman de la Rose* to produce biographical narratives of prominent characters from the Bible, classical antiquity, and contemporary history undone by changes in Fortune. *Fall of Princes* redacts Laurent's prose translation into rhyme royal stanzas, which are sometimes linked in elaborate syntactical structures or rhyming patterns; eight-line ballade stanzas, rhyming *ababbcbc*, are used occasionally in the envoys that punctuate the narratives and in several sections at the end of the poem. The verse forms thus connect the *materia* of individual tragedies to the stanza used in the tragedy of *Troilus* and to the

---

[36] James Simpson, '"Dysemol daies and fatal houres": Lydgate's *Destruction of Thebes* and Chaucer's *Knight's Tale*', in Helen Cooper and Sally Mapstone (eds), *The Long Fifteenth Century: Essays for Douglas Gray* (Oxford 1997), 16. Catherine Nall, *Reading and War in Fifteenth-Century England: From Lydgate to Malory* (Cambridge, 2012), 75–113, situates Lydgate's poem in the context of contemporary discussions of the ethics of waging war.

ballade stanza of Chaucer's 'Monk's Tale', which Lydgate had used earlier in both 'Lenvoye' and the words of the translator at the end of *Troy Book*.

The interests of patron and poet converge in Lydgate's translation in ways that complicate the political and literary succession joined earlier in *Troy Book*. Humfrey positions himself as the heir of his brother's ambitions, replacing Henry's theme of chivalric 'manhood' with a 'manheed' (1.400) based on 'Trouthe', the defence of orthodox religion against Lollards, and the cultivation of virtue through reading—the qualities that make a prince 'To knowe hymsilff' (1.419) and to govern wisely.[37] He adds the lustre of Italian humanist learning by having Lydgate insert Coluccio Salutati's version of the Lucretia story (2.1002–344) between an earlier mention of Chaucer's handling of Lucrece in the *The Legend of Good Women* (2.979–80) and Boccaccio's full treatment of the topic (3.932–1148). This is a gesture of policy that not only appropriates an authoritative political narrative, but also remakes it in a new intellectual fashion to match the Valois programme of translating classical authors for elite audiences, which Laurent advanced over his active career.[38] Accordingly, Lydgate introduces Humfrey by drawing a parallel between the fiction of Caesar's attending Cicero's lectures and Humfrey's love of learning.

For Lydgate, the poetic equivalent to Humfrey's ambition is a succession that sees Boccaccio as 'Myn auctour' (1.226), Laurent as a practical model of the poetic maker, and Chaucer as 'My maistir' (1.246). Chaucer as a writer of tragedies is the link, in turn, with Seneca, Cicero, Petrarch, and Boccaccio. Laurent, in his preface, furnishes an image that serves Lydgate particularly well by aligning translation with the process of poetic invention: '*Et aussi puest un potier casser et rumpre aulcun sien vaissel combien qu'il soit bien fait, pour lui donner aultre forme qui lui samble meilleur*' ('And also a potter can break and smash any of his vessels, no matter how well it is made, in order to give it another form that seems better to him').[39] Lydgate's rendering of the passage raises Laurent's artisan to 'Artificeres' (1.9), 'men off crafft' (1.15), and 'Expert maistres' (1.19) who freshen and 'Make olde thynges for to seeme newe' (1.28). From the standpoint of narrative technique, Lydgate adds distance and perspective by positioning *Fall of Princes* not as a direct rendering of Laurent or Boccaccio but as a report on Boccaccio's work as it unfolds in the procession of Fortune's victims. Lydgate's poem thus occupies a separate space for ethical commentary and for the continuous mediation between source texts and the idealized patron-reader, for whom Lydgate adds further sources (including *Troy Book* and the *Siege*), encyclopaedic lore, and moralisation as embellishment.

Within the poetics of invention and remaking borrowed from Laurent, one of the most fertile areas for Lydgate's poetic craft is the envoy. Humfrey insists that Lydgate append envoys to each narrative (2.141–61). Lydgate composes some of his most accomplished verse in these supplements to the exemplary tales of human failings, vice, and Fortune's mutability. Jenni Nuttall points out that the envoy breaks up the succession of narratives by locking in their meanings while providing an occasion for self-authorization; in it, the technical skill behind the poet's self-deprecation meets the accomplished reader able to

---

[37] Text quoted from Henry Bergen (ed.), *Lydgate's Fall of Princes*, 4 vols., EETS, e.s. 121–4 (London, 1924–7), 1.11.

[38] For Salutati and an anti-republican reading of the Lucretia story, see Nigel Mortimer, *John Lydgate's Fall of Princes: Narrative Tragedy in its Literary and Political Contexts* (Oxford, 2005), 61–78. Alessandra Petrina, *Cultural Politics in Fifteenth-Century England* (Leiden, 2004), 353, sees Humfrey as the heir to Henry's legacy.

[39] Text quoted from Patricia May Gathercole (ed.), *Laurent de Premierfait's 'Des Cas des nobles hommes et femmes'* (Chapel Hill, NC, 1968), 89.

recognize the formal achievements.⁴⁰ Although the frequency of envoys declines steadily and resumes only in the final book, the nearly seventy envoys that Lydgate adds stand as a counterpart to Boccaccio's disquisitions on topics such as pride, desire, poverty, women, poetry, rhetoric, and gluttony. Boccaccio's misogynistic excursus on women (*De casibus* 1.18 '*In mulieres*') is qualified by Lydgate's demurral that the rebuke 'nat touche hem that be weel gouernyd' (1.6734) and indirectly supported by his ironic, Ovidian envoy to widows (2.2199–233). In their manuscript and print transmission, the envoys, as excerpts, acquire an independent status as freestanding compositions.⁴¹

The celebrated envoy to Rome that closes Book Two is a lament that elaborates the *ubi sunt* motif to set Rome's power, monuments, and cultural achievements against their erasure in time:

> Where is the palace or royall mancion,
> With a statue clere of golde shining
> By Romulus wrought & set on that dongeon?
> Where is thy temple of christal bright shewing,
> Made half of gold, most richely moustryng
> Þe heauenly spheres, by compasse wrought & line,
> Which that long processe hath brought vnto ruine?
> (2.4481–7)

The repetition of 'processe' and 'ruyne' connects the final lines of the stanzas in the first half of Lydgate's envoy. The middle stanza offers a Christian remedy to the pride and presumption that carry Rome to the pinnacle of Fortune's wheel: 'Lefft up thyn herte onto that heuenli kyng' (2.4527). The refrain thereafter takes a new, redemptive direction: 'to saue the fro ruyne' (2.4529). In a distant echo, when he comes to Boccaccio's lament for the present state of Rome (*De Casibus* 8.17), Lydgate returns to the rhyme from the refrain: 'Now al attonis is turnid to ruyne!' (8.2534).

Lydgate consistently adopts the voice of the moralist-historian in his envoys, addressing 'Noble Princis'. He varies the tone, however, in several instances. Nero's depravity drives him to the point of wishing to remove his memory: 'Yif that I myhte, I wolde race his name / Out of this book' (7.782–3). Charles of Jerusalem, whose career pursues a similar course of early triumphs undone by avarice and lechery, elicits an elegiac tone in one of Lydgate's octaves:

> Lyk as Phebus in sum fressh morwenyng
> Aftir Aurora þe day doth clarefie,
> Fallith ofte that his briht shynyng
> Idirkid is with sum cloudi skie:
> A liknesse shewed in this tragedie,
> Expert* in Charlis, the stori doth weel preeue,   *Demonstrated*
> Youthe & age reknid ech partie,
> The faire day men do preise at eue.
> (9.2017–24)

---

⁴⁰ Jenni Nuttall, 'Lydgate and the Lenvoy', *Exemplaria*, 30 (2018), 35–48.
⁴¹ For extracts, see NIMEV 1168 (79); for the appearance in print culture, A. S. G. Edwards, 'Lydgate's *Fall of Princes*: Translation, Retranslation and History', in S. K. Barker and Brenda M. Hosington (eds), *Renaissance Cultural Crossroads: Translation, Print and Culture in Britain, 1473–1640* (Leiden, 2013), 21–34.

Here Lydgate's opening simile repeats the image used earlier in the narrative to express the apogee of Charles's rise under Fortune ('Lik Phebus shynyng in his mydday speere' 9.1969). Contrasting light and darkness and parsing out youth and age teach the expected lesson, but the echo prepares for a further effect. In a rare moment, Lydgate registers an affective component within exempla and proverbs, acknowledging the nostalgia and regret for the 'faire day' that continues to exercise attraction and emotional power despite the tragic outcome.

'Lo her the Guerdon that Thes Louers Haue'

Lydgate's courtly poems fit uneasily within any mapping of his poetic career, and there is no reason to assume that all or even many of the poems belong to a single concentrated period of writing. For some poems, Shirley's anecdotal remarks ascribe occasions ('Amerous balade by Lydegate made at departyng of Thomas Chauciers on þe kynges ambassade into Fraunce') and supply contexts ('Loo here begynneþe a balade whiche þat Lydegate wrote at þe request of a squyer þat serued in loves court').[42] More important, his rubrics posit a coherent and stable social world in which forms of expression and feeling remain available in courtly discourse, undisturbed by historical forces that might bear on Lydgate's immediate audience or his readers.[43] It is this underlying assumption of continuity and access that two of Lydgate's best courtly poems, *The Complaint of the Black Knight* and *The Temple of Glass*, exploit and complicate. Both poems ground themselves specifically in Chaucer's dream poetry, a body of work decades removed from Lydgate's poems in composition and original audience. Modern criticism insists that Lydgate's poems are as much a tissue of quotation and textual allusion as independent fictions set in a visionary landscape.[44] In this respect, the poems present themselves as consciously belated, faux originals. Consequently, they are performative works that foreground their sources and simulate for Lydgate's immediate audience and readers a comfortably familiar, if perhaps obsolescent, poetic heterocosm, Chaucerian and even Ricardian.

The Complaint of the Black Knight reprises and adapts Chaucer's *Book of the Duchess* in rhyme royal stanzas, and ends with two envoys in ballade stanzas. Formally, Lydgate follows his own practice in works like *Fall of Princes* rather than writing in Chaucer's tetrameter couplets. He provides the conventional furnishings from the pastoral tradition that underlies Chaucer's poem and its French sources, but with subtle shifts—'a parke, enclosed with a wal / In compass rounde' (39–40) open to all; raucous bird song, trees, bushes, and flowers vulnerable to 'al assaute of Phebus feruent fere' (55); mythological references (some of them foreboding, such as the allusions to Philomela, Daphne, and Phyllis), and a well that restores rather than beguiles the narrator-poet in the mirror of

---

[42] Texts from BL MS Add. 16165 and Cambridge, Trinity College, MS R. 3. 20 respectively; quoted from MacCracken (ed.), *Minor Poems*, 1.420 and 379.

[43] For a parallel to this thesis, centred on the material production of Lydgate's poems, see A. S. G. Edwards, 'John Shirley and the Emulation of Courtly Culture', who argues that the manuscripts provide a 'vicarious knowingness' and 'a form of social warrant' (316) for audiences that may not be fully integrated into aristocratic coteries.

[44] Seth Lerer, *Chaucer and His Readers: Imagining the Author in Late-Medieval England* (Princeton, NJ, 1993), 57–84; Larry Scanlon, 'Lydgate's Poetics: Laureation and Domesticity in the *Temple of Glass*', in Scanlon and Simpson (eds), *John Lydgate: Poetry, Culture, and Lancastrian England*, 61–97; William Rossiter, '"Disgraces the name and patronage of his master Chaucer": Echoes and Reflections in Lydgate's Courtly Poetry', in Kathleen A. Bishop (ed.), *Standing in the Shadow of the Master? Chaucerian Influences and Interpretations* (Newcastle upon Tyne, 2010), 2–27.

Narcissus.[45] As in the *Book of the Duchess*, Lydgate's persona identifies with the sorrow of the grieving protagonist and seeks 'the cause of his dedely woo' (149), which serves as the premise for the extended complaint. Lydgate makes a further adjustment by suppressing the exchange between Chaucer's man in black and the poem's narrator. To an extent, this brings Lydgate's work closer to the narrative personae of Machaut's *dits amoureux*; it also delineates the roles of the protagonist and narrator in the literary production of the poem: the black knight is the author of the complaint, while the narrator acts 'as doth a skryuener, / That can no more what that he shal write, / But as his maister beside dothe endyte' (194–6).[46] Like Chaucer's narrators in *Troilus* (2.13, 3.43) and *The Legend of Good Women* (Prologue F 69), Lydgate's persona makes no claim to possessing 'sentement' (197), the refined sensibility that distinguishes noble lovers, such as he imagines and invites for his audience. He casts himself as the medium to convey the complaint 'Worde be worde, as he dyd endyte' (600). In doing so, he reveals the aim of the poem. As he writes in the twilight that symbolizes a poetics of belatedness, he transcribes the lover's complaint 'your hertis to dysporte' (602). The poem is not a memorial or a mimetic fiction; it is a performance that mobilizes the commonplaces of courtly poetry for an imaginative recovery and participation.[47]

As Lydgate redirects the poem towards reception and social uses rather than representation, he constructs a paradox that reveals the ethical complexities of courtly writing. The crisis elaborated in the formal 'Compleynt' diverges from the self-cancelling themes of loss and betrayal that shape works like Ovid's *Heroides* or Chaucer's *Anelida and Arcite*.[48] It derives instead from the internal contradiction of a central value that underwrites courtly poetry: 'Thus for my trouthe Daunger doth me sterue' (250). Lydgate's protagonist faces the impossible dilemma of maintaining fidelity ('trouthe') in the face of resistance ('Daunger'). He is 'for Trouthe bounde' (289) to a beloved who freely exercises her will to reject his love and endorse the malign social forces of courtly life. His remedy lies beyond reach, in the unchanging source of his distress. Lydgate's ethical point is that the paradox is not just a trope of lyric or elegiac complaint but a structural element that remains in place. Returning yearly to repeat his May ceremony of complaint, the black knight embodies the recursive desire and moral stasis of the courtly mode, its self-sustaining aporia, which is also a point of imaginative access for poets and readers.

The Temple of Glass shares the themes of 'trouthe', desire, and will with the *Complaint of the Black Knight*, but it finds a different resolution to the dilemma of its protagonists. The model for the poem's setting and the opening descriptions of tragic classical and medieval heroines is Chaucer's *House of Fame*, augmented by descriptive passages from the *Parliament of Fowls* and the 'Knight's Tale'. Lydgate uses rhymed pentameter couplets for much of his narrative frame and rhyme royal stanzas for the complaints and petitions rehearsed by the two lovers and answered by Venus and for the final *balade* that recalls the ending of the *Parliament*. The poem exists in several textual states, though not separate versions,

---

[45] Text quoted from MacCracken (ed.), *Minor Poems*, 2.382–10.
[46] On reading behind Chaucer to his French sources, see Jamie C. Fumo, *Making Chaucer's* Book of the Duchess: *Textuality and Reception* (Cardiff, 2015), 138–9, who also likens the narrative situation in Lydgate's poem to a 'running commentary or a parallel-text translation' of the *Book of the Duchess*.
[47] For the shift from Chaucerian models to imitations, see Julia Boffey, '"Forto Compleyne She Had Gret Desire": The Grievances Expressed in Two Fifteenth-Century Dream-Visions', in Helen Cooney (ed.), *Nation, Court and Culture: New Essays on Fifteenth-Century English Poetry* (Dublin, 2001), 95–115.
[48] Lee Patterson, 'Writing Amorous Wrongs: Chaucer and the Order of Complaint', in James M. Dean and Christian K. Zacher (eds), *The Idea of Medieval Literature: New Essays on Chaucer and Medieval Culture in Honor of Donald R. Howard* (Newark, DE, 1992), 56.

and a further complaint has been added to it in the two earliest manuscripts.[49] Numerous proposals have been made to identify the couple whose supplication of Venus is the topic of the poem; the most likely pairing is Humfrey and Jacqueline of Hainault, whose marriage faced legal and political opposition and soon failed.[50]

Whatever the impetus for writing the poem, Lydgate takes the opportunity for a display of virtuosity. His poem incorporates set pieces such a catalogue of lovers, *ekphrases,* and idealized portraits of the protagonists; it teases out the grace notes of complaint and consolation, and inventories the minor genres of the courtly mode: bills, petitions, prayers, laments, supplications, and devices of narrative closure. Seth Lerer fashions *The Temple of Glass* as 'an allegory of reading an anthology' of Chaucer and Lydgate's minor poetry.[51] Yet the parallel structure that Lydgate gives the poem—the lady's complaint followed by the noble lover's—shows his invention in skilfully linking two different predicaments. In the earliest text of the poem, slander and jealousy oppress the lady; in the later version, she tells Venus, 'I am bounde to þing þat I nold; / Freli to chese þere lak I liberte' (335–6).[52] Both presumably refer to an oppressive husband or unwanted betrothal. The noble lover has a more familiar predicament; he is bound to love and serve 'That feyre fresshe wight in the temple yondre / Right nowe I saugh' (597–8). In her interviews with the protagonists, Venus promises relief to both, locks their hearts 'with my key of golde' (1245), and later binds them with a golden chain, but she enjoins them to exercise restraint and patience as well. Lydgate thus casts Venus in the role of a moralist, simultaneously invested in eros and regulation.[53] Seeing the lover's 'trouthe' (1075), the lady explicitly places Venus as a constraint on conduct and gratification: 'So am I bounde under hir dredful charge / Hir list t'obeye withouten varyaunce' (1090–1). In reshaping the lyrical-narrative vision, Lydgate replaces the stasis of elegiac complaint with a deferral of desire that nonetheless serves as a resolution: 'And thus hir hertis been bothe sette at rest / Withowten chaunge or mutabilitee' (1314-15). He has, in effect, recrafted aporia as satisfaction and a way of living within the predicaments of courtly culture.

'So Inly Spirituall'

Public, courtly, and civic works punctuate Lydgate's career; religious poetry is the constant, and it takes the form of translations, liturgical compositions, devotional pieces, anti-Lollard polemics, and hagiography.[54] Some of Lydgate's most accomplished poetry emerges from the intersection of religious topics and the elevated style of his secular writing. *The Life of Our Lady*, Lydgate's masterpiece in this mode, traces Mary's life from her birth to the presentation of Jesus in the temple (Luke 2.22–40) and incorporates the

---

[49] Discussion of the textual sources in Julia Boffey (ed.), *Fifteenth-Century English Dream Visions: An Anthology* (Oxford, 2003); text of the appended complaint in Schick (ed.), *Temple of Glas*, 59–67.

[50] Julia Boffey, 'Shirley, Trinity College Cambridge MS R.3.20, and the Circumstances of Lydgate's *Temple of Glass*: Coterie Verse over Time', *Studies in the Age of Chaucer*, 38 (2016), 265–73.

[51] Lerer, *Chaucer and His Readers*, 68.

[52] Texts in Boffey, *Fifteenth-Century English Dream Visions*, 41–2; and Schick (ed.), *Temple of Glas*, 13, respectively.

[53] Gower's portrayal of Venus at the end of the *Confessio Amantis* reflects the same commitments to love and order.

[54] Pearsall, *John Lydgate*, 256 enumerates the major categories of Lydgate's religious poetry as 'instructional works, paraphrases of hymns and psalms, prayers, poems on the Passion, Marian lyrics, and saints' lives'.

liturgical feasts of the Christmas calendar, ending with Candlemas.[55] The poem translates portions of the thirteenth-century pseudo-Bonaventuran *Meditationes Vitae Christi*, paralleling structural features from Nicholas Love's earlier prose rendering, *The Mirror of the Blessed Life of Jesus Christ*, and adding devotional, instructional, historical, and apocryphal materials from multiple sources to create a 'para-biblical' compilation.[56] Lydgate's verse is mostly in rhyme royal stanzas; the 'Magnificat', Mary's hymn of praise during her visit to Elisabeth (Luke 1.46–55), is rendered in amplified form in eight-line stanzas (2.981–1060); the allegory of the turtle dove is explained in one Latin stanza (6.295–301).

In compiling the Marian materials, whether at Henry's suggestion or by commission, Lydgate seeks to create a devotional and meditative work with the same poetic resources that he uses for his secular writing. The machinery of astral and classical allusions is applied to events in the biblical narrative. The modesty topos appears as Lydgate addresses facets of Mary's spiritual life in Nazareth: 'I am to Rude for to Rehersen, thaym all / For vnconyng' (1.869–70). As elsewhere (for example, in the later adaptation of St Bernard, 2.379–428), the poet's failing supposedly lies in both invention and craft: 'I dar nat, so high a style pace' (1.872). The most conspicuous repurposing of technique occurs when Lydgate turns to the Incarnation and finds 'the Retorykes swete' (2.1623) of Petrarch and Cicero dead and Chaucer 'nowe in his cheste' (2.1654) in much the same fashion as Chaucer's Clerk sees Petrarch 'deed and nayled in his cheste' (IV.29). The encomium of Chaucer as 'noble Rethor, poete of Brytayne' (2.1629) and laureate marks both Chaucer's end and one of many starting points for Lydgate's succession. Robert Meyer-Lee proposes that it is a point where the literary—the ensemble of Lydgate's devices and his aureate style of rhetorical elaboration and Latinate diction—emerges figuratively as an aesthetic and political counterpart to the Incarnation.[57] At a minimum, Lydgate's turn from the dead poet-rhetoricians and the Muses (2.1659) to Mary as a source of inspiration constitutes a moment in Lydgate's writing in which his materials seem to require more than the acquired, if frequently disowned, craft of making.[58]

In *The Life of Our Lady*, Lydgate redirects a number of familiar stylistic features. The linking of stanzas into larger units of discourse figures prominently, as does the variation of syntactical patterns and inversions.[59] The lyric portions of the poem receive particular elaboration. In the passage recounting Joseph's selection as Mary's husband, to take one example, the people who witness the miraculous sign of a dove alighting from Joseph's staff transform into a lyrical chorus 'with oo voys' (1.713):

> Blesside art thow; and blisside is thy chaunce;
> Thy fate is blesset and thyne aventure;

---

[55] Phillipa Hardman, 'Lydgate's *Life of Our Lady*: A Text in Transition', *Medium Ævum*, 65 (1996), 248–68, traces the structural patterns of Lydgate's poem, particularly the relation of Books 1-2 to Books 3-6, which see a movement from continuous narrative to topical organization.

[56] Katherine K. O'Sullivan, 'John Lydgate's *Lyf of Our Lady*: Translation and Authority in Fifteenth-Century England', *Mediaevalia*, 26 (2005), 169–201, makes the case for Love's structural influence at 180–4. I borrow the term 'para-biblical' from Michael G. Sargent, 'Nicholas Love's *Mirror of the Blessed Life of Jesus Christ*', in Elizabeth Solopova (ed.), *The Wycliffite Bible: Origin, History and Interpretation* (Leiden, 2017), 389–405 (at 390 n.1).

[57] Robert J. Meyer-Lee, 'The Emergence of the Literary in John Lydgate's *Life of Our Lady*', *JEGP*, 109 (2010), 322–48.

[58] Georgiana Donavin, 'The Light of the Virgin Muse in John Lydgate's *The Life of Our Lady*', in Georgiana Donavin and Anita Obermeier (eds), *Romance and Rhetoric: Essays in Honour of Dhira B. Mahoney* (Turnhout, 2010), 75–89.

[59] Pearsall, *John Lydgate*, 289–90, proposes that in some passages Lydgate disregards stanzas as units of meaning to blend 'the liturgical and the literary into a luminous rhetoric'.

> And blissed is thyne humble attendaunce;
> And thow art blisset so long to endure
> For to possede so fayre a creature,
> So goode, so holy, nowe in thy passed age,
> So clene a mayde to haue in mariage.
>
> (1.715–21)[60]

Amplifying the narrative from the Gospel of Pseudo-Matthew, the anaphora of the Beatitudes structures the opening lines of this stanza, including the characteristic inversion of word order (the repetition of 'blessed' recurs in a later meditative passage on Mary as the example of all virginity [1.820–54]). Latinate terms end each line and modulate the linguistic register. In the final four lines, using enjambment, Lydgate reaches a level of expression that stands at the boundary of linguistic order and semantic meaning. The phrase 'nowe in thy passed age' depends grammatically on 'thow are blisset', but Lydgate detaches it from its linguistic referent and positions it instead within the repeated phrases ('So goode, so holy ... / So clene a mayde') that describe not the receiver but the object of grace. Formally, the stanza requires a rhyme for the concluding couplet (age/mariage); Lydgate creates, in addition, a syntagmatic link between the contraries of age and youth that comprise the spiritual mystery of the episode.

The Lives of Saint Edmund and Saint Fremund, commissioned by Abbot Curteys to commemorate Henry VI's visit to St Edmunds, shares the strategies of poetic compilation and amplification with *The Life of Our Lady*. In some manuscripts, Lydgate's poem has a prologue of ten ballade stanzas, 'The Banner of St Edmund', celebrating Edmund as a king, martyr, and virgin.[61] The narrative, in rhyme royal stanzas, divides into three sections, devoted to Edmund's *vita* and *passio*; the resumption of Edmund's kingship by his nephew Fremund acting, like Edmund, as 'Cristis champion' (1415, 2546); and the miracles associated with Edmund, most memorably his posthumous vengeance on the Danish king Sweyn to whom he appears 'armyd lik a knyht / Conueied by an angel' (3077–8).[62] The poem ends with a prayer to Edmund in ballade stanzas and an envoy in rhyme royal stanzas. Lydgate shifts among genres and poetic modes such as hagiography, the mirror for princes (*Fürstenspiegel*), and romance, and adds supplementary materials on miracles and relics.[63] With this poem, he invents the free-standing double saints' life, whose material form is the deluxe presentation copy, including 118 miniatures, made for Henry (BL MS Harley 2278).[64] As poem and aesthetic object, the work serves a combination of memorial, institutional, didactic, propagandistic, and political aims.

Lydgate's opening announces an overlay of familiar poetic modes—'First to compile' (4) and then 'to translate and endite' (14). As in *The Life of Our Lady*, Lydgate looks beyond rhetorical craft to his protagonist as the source of 'grace' (12): 'Send doun of grace thi licour aureate / Which enlumynyth these rethoriciens / To write of martirs ther passiouns laureate' (141–3). The displacement of 'laureate' from a description of style to the quality of the martyrs' passions is one of many signs of the insistent literary

---

[60] Text quoted from Lauritis, Klinefelter, and Gallagher (eds), *The Life of Our Lady*; punctuation mine.
[61] NIMEV 530.
[62] Text quoted from Anthony Bale and A. S. G. Edwards (eds), *John Lydgate's 'Lives of Ss Edmund & Fremund' and the 'Extra Miracles of St Edmund'* (Heidelberg, 2009).
[63] Jennifer Sisk, 'Lydgate's Problematic Commission: A Legend of St. Edmund for Henry VI', *JEGP*, 109 (2010), 349–75, examines the divergent aims of hagiography and the mirror for princes.
[64] See A. S. G. Edwards (intro.), *The Life of St Edmund King and Martyr: John Lydgate's Illustrated Verse Life Presented to Henry VI: A Facsimile of British Library MS Harley 2278* (London, 2004).

engagement in Lydgate's writing. Chaucer's poetry echoes throughout, largely removed from citational context and serving as a source of phrasing and diction. Edmund's public life, which offers lessons in statecraft and royal devotion in resistance to tyranny, is a product of epideictic writing. The Danish invasion occurs as the consequence of a romance adventure undone by treachery and then supplanted by terror. Edmund turns from warrior to martyr in a conversion scene in which he abandons violence for charity and spiritual compassion for the Danish invaders about to slay him:

> He hadde a routhe that Goddis creature,
> Which rassemblid his liknesse and ymage,
> Sholde in helle eternal peyne endure,
> Thoruh mysbeleue for paganysme rage.
> (1450–3)

The complementary narrative of Fremund moves through a similar ensemble of poetic modes and genres. It follows, however, an opposite trajectory, as Fremund converts from a life of contemplation to epic heroism and miraculous victory before suffering his own martyrdom.

Edmund and Fremund illustrates in the sphere of religious and dynastic writing the elements that inform Lydgate's poetics. Commissions, such as Curteys's 'charge' (109) to translate the substance of Edmund's story out of Latin, authorize both composition and poetic self-definition. Source materials, in this case the chronicle accounts of the abbey, offer narratives and discursive structures that Lydgate reshapes in part and fills out with additions ranging from learned commentary to folk motifs. Despite his claims of inadequacy and disavowal, Lydgate writes in a stylistic register that accommodates classical epic, courtly dream visions, and hagiography. In both secular and religious poetry, Lydgate anticipates a context of reception in which patrons and audiences recognize the expectations of genre and topic as well as the innovations and revisions that he introduces. For much of his secular poetry, Lydgate exploits his poetic displacement, which opens up an area of critical reflection about the imaginative worlds he represents through his literary assemblages. In this respect, *Edmund and Fremund* sets an interesting problem for the 'Monk of Bery', who has been called to exercise his invention and formal craft for a significant state and institutional occasion. He must devise for his royal reader a narrative about patron-monarchs who balance war and piety and embrace martyrdom as political and spiritual triumph.

CHAPTER 25
Thomas Hoccleve

Sebastian Langdell

Thomas Hoccleve died at some point between 4 March and 8 May 1426.[1] Unlike his predecessor Chaucer, we do not know where Hoccleve's bones lie. Nor do we know the date (or year) of his birth. We date back to his birth, roughly, from what the 'Hoccleve' character says in his late poetic sequence, the *Series*: in the 'Dialogue' section of the *Series*, Hoccleve says he is 'Of age ... fifty wintir and three' (2.246).[2] If the 'Dialogue' was completed by early 1421, as is assumed based on historical references within the poem, and if the end-date of writing agrees with the moment of speaking in the poem—*and* if the poem's 'Hoccleve' equates with the historical Hoccleve—then the writer would have been born between 1367–8.[3] By May 1426, he would have been fifty-eight or fifty-nine years old.

By the end of his life, Hoccleve had produced what would become one of the most popular English vernacular poetic works of the later medieval period: the *Regiment of Princes*, which survives in over forty manuscripts.[4] He wrote another longer work, a sequence of poems now known as the *Series*, which travels alongside the *Regiment* in most manuscripts.[5] His poetic output also includes twenty-eight shorter pieces, all of which are preserved in two autograph manuscripts that Hoccleve produced in the final years of his life: 1422–6 (San Marino, CA, Huntington Library, MSS HM 111 and 744). The vast majority of Hoccleve's shorter poems (nineteen) exist only in the Huntington autographs.[6] These shorter poems testify to the range of poetic forms and subjects with which Hoccleve experimented: from roundels to rhyme royal, the *envoi* and the 'Cupid' poem, playful petitionary verse, *ars moriendi*, and Marian-devotional verse. His poetry—both shorter and longer—endures today for several reasons: for its formal experimentation; its forays into proto-autobiography; and its marshalling of Chaucerian conversational modes and the rhyme royal verse form into the literature of royal advice-giving and a broader spectrum of religious writing. Hoccleve's representation of Chaucer in his *Regiment of Princes* became, in itself, a foundational figure of moral and intellectual authority for English literary tradition. The Hoccleve narrator claims to have been acquainted with Chaucer (*Regiment*, 1867), and indeed the two writers would have travelled in the same circles in London and Westminster: Hoccleve worked by day as a clerk in the Office of the Privy Seal,

---

[1] See J. A. Burrow, *Thomas Hoccleve* (Aldershot, 1994), 29 for details.
[2] Thomas Hoccleve, *The Series*, in Roger Ellis (ed.), *'My Compleinte' and Other Poems* (Exeter, 2001).
[3] Burrow fixes May 1421 as the date by which Hoccleve would have completed a draft of the 'Complaint' and 'Dialogue'; see J. A. Burrow (ed.), *Thomas Hoccleve's Complaint and Dialogue* (Oxford, 1999), lix. See Burrow, *Thomas Hoccleve*, 2, for further discussion of Hoccleve's birthdate.
[4] See NIMEV 2229 for a full list of *Regiment* manuscripts.
[5] See Burrow, *Thomas Hoccleve*, 50–2. The only full copy of the *Series* unaccompanied by the *Regiment* is Hoccleve's autograph copy, Durham, University Library MS Cosin V. iii. 9.
[6] For a list of the contents and their non-autograph witnesses, see J. A. Burrow and A. I. Doyle (eds), *A Facsimile of the Autograph Verse Manuscripts: Henry E. Huntington Library, San Marino (California), MSS HM 111 and HM 744, University Library, Durham (England), MS Cosin V. III. 9*, EETS, s.s. 119 (Oxford, 2002), xii–xvii; on dating, see xx–xxi.

and was thoroughly enmeshed in London royal and bureaucratic circles at the turn of the fifteenth century.

Hoccleve's most popular work, the *Regiment of Princes*, is an advice-to-princes text, written to Prince Henry (the future Henry V) between 1410 and 1411. It is a 'plotmeel' (piecemeal) translation of Giles of Rome's *De regimine principum*, and also draws heavily on Jacob de Cessolis's *De ludo scaccorum* and the pseudo-Aristotelian *Secreta secretorum*.[7] The *Regiment* proper constitutes a series of exempla on virtues and various topics related to kingly conduct, and while Hoccleve's exposition remains mainly general throughout the text, he does sometimes tend towards the specific. The first 2,000 lines of the poem, by contrast, provide a metanarrative framework for the main text. This opening section is a first-person account by a narrator, identified as 'Hoccleve' in dialogue with an unnamed old man. In conversation with the old man, 'Hoccleve' discusses grievances both personal and political. Hoccleve's *Series*, composed later in his life, has a similar quasi-autobiographical frame. The opening sections of that work see 'Hoccleve' recounting an episode of mental illness and recovery (a 'wilde infirmite' (1.40)). The account also describes his attempts at social reintegration and considers the exemplary possibilities of his experience. The remaining three sections of the work follow a rather sporadic procession: two lively *Gesta Romanorum* tales sandwiching an *ars moriendi* treatise. The seemingly loose, spontaneous feeling of the *Series*, in which diverse texts arise out of an ongoing conversation between 'Hoccleve' and a friend, takes its cue from the French *dit* form.[8] The *dit* generally uses a conversation between two lovers as a platform for collecting previously written poems, as in Machaut's *Voir dit*. Hoccleve transposes this mode into a considerably more sombre key, moving it out of the realm of love and into the realm of mental (in)stability, contemporary politics, and *ars moriendi*.

Hoccleve's Formulary (a collection of specimen administrative documents), produced during the same four-year period (1422–6) as both his autograph manuscript of the *Series* (Durham, University Library MS Cosin V. iii. 9) and the Huntington 'shorter poem' manuscripts, speaks to the nature of Hoccleve's career as a professional scribe in the Office of the Privy Seal.[9] As with Hoccleve's birth, we calculate his start date at the Privy Seal from information given within his poetry: in the opening to the *Regiment*, we hear that 'Hoccleve' has been working at the Office of the Privy Seal for 'twenti yeer / And foure come Estren' (804–5), which, given a completion date of 1411 for the *Regiment*, would indicate a start date of Easter 1387, aged (roughly) twenty.[10] Hoccleve's Formulary compiles examples of documents to be used within the Privy Seal, and was assembled by Hoccleve for use in the training of future clerks. The fact that Hoccleve was assembling these documents at the same time that he saw fit to collect his shorter poetic pieces, written throughout his career, indicates a late preservative impulse on Hoccleve's part: a means of binding together his contributions to a burgeoning vernacular poetic tradition, as well as his contributions to the daily functions of king and kingdom.

Hoccleve's willingness to foreground a 'Hoccleve' persona in his poems, and to refer within his poems to the coordinates and qualities of what would seem to be his (Hocclevethe-author's) life, would appear to be a goldmine for the literary biographer. And yet to read through Hoccleve criticism since the Victorian era is to witness the variety of ways that the

---

[7] Thomas Hoccleve, in Charles R. Blyth (ed.), *The Regiment of Princes* (Kalamazoo, 1999), 2038–53, 2109–14.
[8] On the influence of the French *dit*, see John Burrow, 'Hoccleve and the Middle French Poets', in Helen Cooper and Sally Mapstone (eds), *The Long Fifteenth Century: Essays for Douglas Gray* (Oxford, 1997), 35–49.
[9] Hoccleve's Formulary is BL MS Add. 24062.
[10] Burrow, *Thomas Hoccleve*, 18.

information given by 'Hoccleve' is interpreted. To give but one example: do we take his declarations of dullness and insufficiency at face value, or read them rather as having a specific use, a stylistic function? What do we make of his professions of 'unkonnyng', and of insufficient wit or intelligence? For the late-nineteenth-century editor Frederick Furnivall, there was little need to distinguish between 'Hoccleve' and Hoccleve: the writer's professions of insufficiency informed his very personhood. In telling us he fell short, he was baring himself honestly to the reader—and Furnivall sees no reason to doubt such professions of inadequacy. Furnivall describes Hoccleve as a 'weak, sensitive, look-on-the-worst side kind of man'; 'he has the merit', Furnivall tells us, 'of recognizing his weakness, his folly, and his cowardice'.[11] Such a characterization has carried through Hoccleve scholarship to the extent that as late as the 1980s (and later), critics looked to Hoccleve for this token negativity, this admission of falling short: in Hoccleve, Malcolm Richardson saw 'a bungler, misfit, and perpetual also-ran'.[12] He was defined, if anything, by failure and by a willingness to offer up every detail of that failure.

More nuanced readings of Hoccleve have owed much to the arguments put forth in 'Dullness and the Fifteenth Century', in which David Lawton urges a more cautious reading of fifteenth-century poets' declarations of dullness: often such declarations can signal anything but, and Hoccleve's own confessions of dullness and insufficiency often arrive at those moments where the material approaches the politically hazardous.[13] Such avowals of inadequacy should not be taken on face value, but should rather be seen as indicative of the complexities of writing in a politically turbulent age. Consider, for instance, one such admission, in the midst of a poem that focuses on the reburial of Richard II in 1413:[14]

> My wit souffysith nat to peyse and weye
> With what honour he broght is to this toun,
> And with his queene at Westmynstre in th'abbeye
> Solempnely in toumbe leid adoun.
>
> (37–40)

(My intellect is insufficient to measure and weigh with what honour he is brought to this town and, with his queen, at Westminster Abbey solemnly laid down in a tomb.)

To extract from such a remark only an admission of the poet's dim-wittedness is to miss the textures of meaning that are alive in this poem: the resonance of a moment in which a king who has been deposed, dethroned, and killed is now unearthed and laid to rest again—not by hostile hands, but not by entirely 'friendly' ones either. How do we approach this moment? With what honour *is* he brought to this town? This point in the poem comes after Hoccleve has described the threat of heresy to the realm (the focus of most of the poem), and just after he has raised the question of what it would mean if the king himself was drawn towards heresy: 'What mighten folk of good byleeue seye, / If bent were our

---

[11] Frederick J. Furnivall and I. Gollancz (eds), revised by Jerome Mitchell and A. I. Doyle, *Hoccleve's Works: The Minor Poems*, EETS, e.s. 61, 73 (London, 1970), xxxviii.

[12] Malcolm Richardson, 'Hoccleve in His Social Context', *The Chaucer Review* 20 (1986), 313–22 (at 321). For more recent readings, see Lee Patterson's assessment of Hoccleve as 'a man filled with self-doubt and a sense of isolation who compensated by a brittle tavern gaiety', in '"What Is Me?": Self and Society in the Poetry of Thomas Hoccleve', *Studies in the Age of Chaucer* 23 (2001), 437–70 (at 469); and John M. Bowers, 'Thomas Hoccleve and the Politics of Tradition', *The Chaucer Review* 36 (2002), 352–69.

[13] David Lawton, 'Dullness and the Fifteenth Century', *ELH*, 54 (1987), 761–99.

[14] This is item eight in HM 111. See Furnivall and Gollancz (eds), *Minor Poems*, 47–9.

kynges affeccion / To the wrong part?' (25–7). Hoccleve uses the body of Richard II to make a simple point: any individual—including the king himself—can be fallible, anyone can err. Not content to stop at implicating Richard in this, Hoccleve gestures to the present monarch, Henry V. This is a good time for a bout of humility, perhaps, a good time to step back and claim a certain insufficiency of wit. A picture emerges not of a man suffering from a failure of nerve, but rather of a man willing to ask bold and inconvenient questions and willing to raise uncomfortable issues directly related to the state of the realm.

Few scholars today would argue that Hoccleve's professions of 'unkonnyng' are genuine, and written to be taken at face value. The point is that we should always be prepared for an authorial *pose* in Hoccleve, throughout Hoccleve's complex body of work. The boundary between person and persona should always be approached with caution, and with an eye towards asking why a given 'Hoccleve' is used in a given poem. It may be tempting, for instance, to see in the *Series* presentation of Hoccleve a defining portrait of the writer in his final years: solitary, wounded, weak, with his spirits (and prospects) dimming. But as John Burrow points out, one of Hoccleve's shorter poems, the 'balade … de bone conpagnie' written probably in April 1421, at the very time that Hoccleve was at work on the *Series*, sees Hoccleve anticipating a lively dinner party with friends and associates.[15] He writes to Henry Somer on behalf of the 'Court of Good Company', a dining club, reminding Somer of his duty to host the next dinner. The jovial tone of the letter—and the very idea of Hoccleve eagerly awaiting a dinner with friends—clashes with the sombre tone of the *Series*. Burrow sees in 'Good Company' 'a reminder of how little we know of the poet's social and private life', but the short poem is perhaps most striking in that it serves as something of a warning: not to take as the whole truth, the full picture, any 'Hoccleve' that comes our way.[16] In discussing the dissonance between these two late impressions of Hoccleve, Jenni Nuttall reminds us that Hoccleve's self-presentation can be 'partial and *purposeful*, temporary rather than defining' (italics mine).[17] And it is no doubt the *purpose* of Hoccleve's decision to foreground this particular image of himself in the *Series* that deserves further attention.

'Good Company' points up the extent to which the Hoccleve persona in the *Series*—as with the Hoccleve personae in 'Male Regle' and the *Regiment of Princes*—is contingent on seeing Hoccleve as solitary. The *Series*-Hoccleve takes from Chaucer's 'Geffrey' (and likely Langland's 'Will') the guise of the lone wanderer, often friendless, under fire from one interlocutor or another, and always searching. It is perhaps for this reason that 'Hoccleve' begins the *Regiment* lying sleepless in Chester's Inn, a rooming house for *unmarried* clerks, despite later admitting to being married and gesturing to his own 'poore cote' (*humble cottage*; 845).[18] Notably, in both the *Regiment* and the *Series* it is the surprise mention of Hoccleve's *wife* that tears at the illusion of solitude. Mentions of Hoccleve's wife serve as equivalents of the dissonance we tracked between the *Series* and 'Good Company': they underscore the place of the Hoccleve persona as a construct—inflected with historical details, no doubt, but manipulated, however slightly, to suit the purposes of the given poem. In the *Regiment*, Hoccleve waits until line 1450 to reveal that he is, in fact, married. By this point in the poem, the image of Hoccleve as a lone, underappreciated scribe is ingrained and indelible, and the mention of Hoccleve's married life arrives and fades like the aberration that it is. In the *Series*, we establish 'Hoccleve' as solitary first, wounded and abject,

---

[15] Burrow, *Thomas Hoccleve*, 28–9; printed in Furnivall and Gollancz (eds), *Minor Poems*, 64–6.
[16] Burrow, *Thomas Hoccleve*, 29.
[17] Jenni Nuttall, 'Thomas Hoccleve's Poems for Henry V: Anti-Occasional Verse and Ecclesiastical Reform', *Oxford Handbooks Online* (Oxford, 2015), 1–23 (at 3).
[18] On Chester's Inn, see Blyth (ed.), *Regiment*, note to lines 1–7.

and the mention of his being married arrives about 1100 lines into the work as a whole, close to the end of the 'Dialogue'. Hoccleve's interlocutor, the Friend, asks: 'Thomas, how is it twixt thee and thy feere (wife)?' Hoccleve responds, 'Wel, wel ... what list yow therof heere? / My wyf mighte haue hokir and greet desdeyn (contempt and great disdain) / If I sholde in swich cas pleye a soleyn' (2.739–42). Playing a 'soleyn'—a solitary individual—is of course what Hoccleve has been doing for the entirety of the poem thus far. Hoccleve cannot continue playing the role of 'soleyn' 'in swich cas'—that is, when he is asked about his wife—but the rest of the poem in fact depends upon the image of a solitary, wounded Hoccleve. These 'wife moments' serve as built-in reminders that Hoccleve is not entirely who he seems to be; 'Hoccleve' is not always Hoccleve.

These instances also invite the question of purpose: why is this particular 'Hoccleve' being foregrounded in the *Series*? Why is this instantiation of the Hoccleve persona necessary to the construction of *this* poem? Perhaps most obviously, Hoccleve is foregrounding a 'Hoccleve' who will resonate with the *imago*, the 'image of the dying man' who takes centre stage in the centre piece of the *Series*, Hoccleve's translation of the *ars moriendi* chapter from Henry Suso's *Horologium sapientiae*. In this work, divine Sapience instructs a disciple figure on the art of dying by asking him to summon to mind the image 'Of a man dyynge and talkyng with thee' (4.86). This is the only other text in the *Series*, besides the 'Complaint', that 'Hoccleve' declares himself intent on circulating.[19] 'Hoccleve' is created after the image of the Image—his friendless, abject, wounded state in the 'Complaint' fully resonant with the dying man in the Suso, who says, 'Forsake Y am. Frendshipe Y can noon fynde' (4.506; cf. 4.424–34).[20] The Image's description of his own soul as 'abiect, desolat, and forsake' (4.636) perfectly mirrors the mood of the Hoccleve persona in the 'Complaint' and 'Dialogue'. The psalmic voice is also central to this persona: in the 'Complaint', Hoccleve sums up his pain at being abandoned by those he used to know by quoting from the penitential psalms:

> As seide is in þe sauter miȝt I sey,
> *They þat me sy, fledden awey fro me.*
> Forȝeten I was al oute of mynde awey,
> As he þat deed was from hertis cherte.
> (1.78–81; italics mine)

(As it says in the Psalms, so might I say: 'Those that saw me, fled away from me'. I was all forgotten, out of mind, as one who is dead to the heart's kindness.)

Hoccleve translates here, in line 79, from Vulgate Psalm 30: *Qui videbant me foras fugierunt a me*. As David Lawton notes, it is 'important for Hoccleve's whole career to recognize him under the sign of the penitential psalms'.[21] Lawton underscores that the spirit of these lines is just as present in the opening to the *Regiment* as it is in the *Series*. And yet the mood is deepened in the *Series* by the specific circumstances of illness, recovery, and rejection. What is more, introducing 'Hoccleve' by having him inhabit the psalmic voice also enables Hoccleve to better tie his 'Complaint' to the Suso treatise. After the Image succumbs to death in that text, the disciple—in an allusion that has, to my knowledge, gone otherwise

---

[19] See 2.204–17.
[20] The Image asks the disciple to imagine a 'wrecchid vois' in purgatory saying this. It serves as a distillation of the Image's own message.
[21] David Lawton, *Voice in Later Medieval English Literature: Public Interiorities* (Oxford, 2017), 94.

unremarked—voices his astonishment by translating from Vulgate Psalm 21: 'Wher art thow now, o Sapience eterne? / *O, good lord, haast þou now forsaken me?*' (4.744–5; italics mine). The same line is of course voiced by Jesus himself on the cross: the disciple's response to the dying man echoing the final words of Jesus, God incarnate. When the dying man finally dies, the disciple calls out not for the dying man himself (who has been introduced and entertained throughout as an image), but rather for Sapience, divine wisdom, the poem's own instantiation of God/Christ.[22] It was Sapience who first spoke to the disciple, and Sapience who asked the disciple to fix in his mind the image of the dying man. When confronted with what he calls 'mazidnesse' (uncertainty; bewilderment) at whether the man has died 'in liknesse / Or in deede' (metaphorically or in real life), the disciple cries out to God—half in prayer, half in protest (4.743–56). The moment provokes a crisis of interpretation in the witness, which then leaves him refocusing his vision on the divine, in search of answers.

So too with 'Hoccleve'. The wounded man of the 'Complaint' gives way to the dying man of the 'Dialogue': the specific complaint of wits sundered gives way to more general descriptions of bodily disintegration, and the gaining approach of death ('Ripenesse of deeth faste vppon me now hastiþ', 2.247; see 2.245–59). And Hoccleve makes clear that he intends his self-presentation to be used as a 'spectacle', a lens through which he (and others) might better fathom the workings of God:

> ... For he in me hath shewid his miracle.
> His visitacioun is a spectacle
> In wiche that I biholde may and se,
> Bet þan I dide, how greet a lord is he.
> (2.95–8)

(For he has manifested his miracle within me. His visitation is a spectacle, through which I might behold and see, better than I had, how great a lord he is.)

Hoccleve argues that such a gift is transferable—that, indeed, he has a *duty* to disseminate this 'spectacle' to others (see 2.78–95). Hoccleve hereby makes his own aging body into a devotional image. And as he indicates in 'To Sir John Oldcastle', devotional images are to be used not as ends in themselves, but as mediums to be passed through en route to deeper, less-material understanding or action. In 'Oldcastle' Hoccleve also uses the metaphorical 'spectacle', underscoring the sense of sight being sharpened and enhanced by a devotional image:

> Right as a spectacle helpith feeble sighte
> Whan a man on the book redith or writ,
> And causith him to see bet than he mighte,
> *In which spectacle his sighte nat abit,*
> *But gooth thurgh*, and on the book restith it,
> The same may men of ymages seye:
> Thogh the ymage nat the seint be, yit
> The sighte vs myngith to the seint to preye.
> (417–24; italics mine)

---

[22] See 4.2–5; 4.26–7.

(Just as a spectacle helps weak eyesight, when a man reads or writes a book, and helps him to see better than he might otherwise (in which spectacle his eyesight does not stop, but rather passes through, and focuses on the book), so may men say of images: although the image itself is not the saint, the sight [of the image] reminds us to pray to the saint.)

The image—when the sight 'gooth thurgh'—can better facilitate spiritual understanding: in this case, it prompts the viewer to pray to a given saint; and in the *Series*, it affords a better understanding of 'how greet a lord is he [God]'.

What we might learn from engaging 'Hoccleve' as a devotional image—rather than a merely historical signifier, an end in itself—is partly signalled within the *Series* itself. 'Hoccleve' indicates that beholding this wounded image should bring the reader to realizations of God's ability to heal, and of the capacity for an otherwise unfortunate situation to prove to be, in fact, a blessing. By compiling his 'Hoccleve' with the *imago*, Hoccleve offers himself up as an extension of the *Series*' *ars moriendi*. The aging 'Hoccleve'—for whom 'the ni3t approcheþ'—can inspire the reader to take stock of his or her own life, and to prepare for the inevitable (2.245). The type of self-reflection and accounting that 'Hoccleve' hopes the Suso treatise will ultimately inspire in his readers (see 2.207–31) can be gained also from the image of Hoccleve presented in the 'Complaint' and 'Dialogue'. In some ways, Hoccleve makes the 'image of death' more tangible by presenting us with a life-like, believable Hoccleve, wounded and dying. We have consumed Hoccleve as *historical* before we have even begun to think of him as a construct, a mere image. We are left with our own meaning-making 'mazidnesse' (*uncertainty*): much as the disciple is left uncertain as to whether the Image has died 'in liknesse' or 'in deede', we as readers are left to parse figurative dying from actual dying, figurative melancholy from real, persona from person. And our own 'mazidnesse' can—as with the disciple—lead us to other truths. After we have read the Suso treatise, the 'Complaint' is simply a different text. We reflect on 'Hoccleve' there as not only a 'spectacle' through which we might see evidence of God's presence and mercy, but also as a more specific, believable, tactile representation of personal disintegration—a local habitation and a name for the 'image of a dying man'.

It has been suggested that the Suso treatise in the *Series* may well have existed before Hoccleve wrote the *Series*, and that the 'Complaint' and 'Dialogue' would have offered a framing mechanism for pre-existing texts—a practice that is in keeping with the French *dit* form that Hoccleve draws on extensively in the *Series*.[23] Indeed, one of Hoccleve's two autograph manuscripts of shorter poems includes a different version of the Suso treatise: it is the final item in MS HM 744. Orthographical and punctuation-based evidence suggests that this version predates the version found in the 'Durham manuscript', Hoccleve's autograph manuscript of the *Series*.[24] We should keep alive the possibility that Hoccleve translated the Suso first, and then sought to find a way to make the message all the more immediate by making it more deeply personal, by offering his own body as a site on which to inscribe the types of sacred truths usually found in literature officially labelled 'theological'. Indeed, part of Hoccleve's project in the *Series* appears to be blurring the boundaries between generic modes, so that the official theological treatise cannot help but reflect back on the 'autobiographical' opening, to the point that the two merge. Hoccleve already updates the Suso treatise by rendering it in rhyme royal verse, amplifying the imagery throughout, and

---

[23] Burrow (ed.), *Complaint and Dialogue*, lix–lx.
[24] Burrow (ed.), *Complaint and Dialogue*, 111–18; Sebastian J. Langdell, 'A Study of Speech-Markers in the Early- to Mid-Fifteenth-Century Hocclevian Manuscript Tradition', *Notes and Queries*, n.s. 59 (2012), 323–31.

enhancing the conversational dynamics of the poem.[25] The inclusion of the poem at the centre of the *Series* allows it to interact with the 'Complaint' and 'Dialogue', thereby facilitating an additional level of intra-poetic meaning-making. The *ars moriendi* text blends with the 'autobiographical' texts in a way that allows 'Hoccleve' himself to rise to the level of a model, a virtuous and didactic image.[26] Hoccleve's self-presentation tends this way, from details that would appear to be fixed in historical reality, to more general and didactic applications. We see this even within the span of a couple of stanzas in the 'Dialogue'— for instance, lines 2.246–59, in which the mention of his age (fifty-three; 2.246), gives way to a consideration of his failing faculties and quenched spirit (2.247–57), to more general and didactic pronouncements: 'Whan al is doon, al this worldes swetnesse / At ende torneth into bittirnesse' (2.258–9). Even in the earliest sections of the *Series*, 'Hoccleve' remains consistently aware of the capacity for his own disintegrating body to *mean*, to carry meaning beyond the frame.

Recent scholarship has signalled some of the places we might arrive when we use 'Hoccleve' as prescribed, as a lens meant to be gazed through en route to deeper realizations. One critical narrative builds on the date given for the restoration of Hoccleve's wits in the *Series*, and argues that the *Series* offers us, in part, a figure for the restoration of the English church after the scourge of heresy—a means of reflecting on the Council of Constance, and the church's attempts at communal reintegration and healing.[27] The Council of Constance (1414–18) brought together delegates from Italy, France, Germany, Spain, and England with the intention of reforming the church in 'head and members': this involved ending the papal schism, and confronting the problem of heresy in the contemporary church, in part by denouncing the views of the heresiarchs John Wyclif and Jan Hus. England was in a particularly sensitive position, having been home to the Wycliffite heresy: as such, English delegates sought to distance themselves from Wyclif, and to project a collective return to a state of ecclesiastical normality.[28] Heresy is a constant concern of Hoccleve's: poems such as 'To Sir John Oldcastle' and 'Knights of the Garter' confront the issue of Lollardy head-on, lamenting those who have drunk heresy's 'bittir galle' (bitter bile/drink) ('Garter', 14). The bitter taste of heresy gives way, elsewhere, to the olfactory: the whiff of a 'stinking' sin wafting through much of Hoccleve's devotional verse. When Hoccleve asks God to 'Graunte pardoun of our stynkyng errour' (152) in a poem written for Archbishop Henry Chichele's brother, Robert, it is difficult not to associate that stench with heresy, the prime ecclesiastical 'errour' of the day, the very problem that Archbishop Chichele would combat at the Council of Constance, and the problem that Hoccleve refers to repeatedly as an 'errour' throughout his works.[29] Most telling, however, is the word 'our': the phrase '*our* stynkyng errour' underscores Hoccleve's willingness to speak on behalf of the English church as a whole, and to admit a collective wound, a collective sin. The Robert Chichele poem

---

[25] On the amplification of imagery, see especially Steven Rozenski, '"Your Ensaumple and Your Mirour": Hoccleve's Amplification of the Imagery and Intimacy of Henry Suso's Ars Moriendi', *Parergon* 25 (2008), 1–16.

[26] If Hoccleve is adapting the *dit* mode in the *Series*, then one of the pre-existing 'texts' that he brings into the compilatory matrix is a rendition of himself.

[27] Vincent Gillespie, 'Chichele's Church: Vernacular Theology in England After Thomas Arundel', in Vincent Gillespie and Kantik Ghosh (eds), *After Arundel: Religious Writing in Fifteenth-Century England* (Turnhout, 2011), 3–42 (at 39–40); David Watt, *The Making of Thomas Hoccleve's Series* (Liverpool, 2013), 8–10.

[28] On the Council of Constance, see John Hine Mundy and Kennerly M. Woody (eds), *The Council of Constance: The Unification of the Church* (New York, 1961); Walter Brandmüller, *Das Konzil von Konstanz, 1414–1418*, 2 vols. (Paderborn, 1991).

[29] The ballade for Robert Chichele is collected in Ellis, '*My Compleinte*', 82–6 and in Furnivall and Gollancz (eds), *Minor Poems*, 67–72.

resonates with the first item in HM 744, 'Ad Patrem', in which a prayer to God encompasses Christ's wounded, dying body—and then a collective request for mercy, pitched in similar terms: 'Fadir and lord of mercy, on vs reewe / Þat for our *synnes stynken in thy sighte*' (134–5). It has a corollary, too, in 'Modir of lyf', HM 111, the poem that directly follows Hoccleve's 'Knights of the Garter', an address to Henry V and Emperor Sigismund on the need to combat heresy. 'Modir of lyf' engages the same lexicon, and in the light of these other poems reads as a script for the English church, wounded in the wake of heresy, the 'I' begging forgiveness: 'My soule is stuffid so with stynk of synne', the speaker says (17). And elsewhere:

> The more þat my gilt passith mesure,
> And *stynkith in thy sones sighte and thyn*,
> The gretter neede hath it of his cure
> And of thyn help.[30]
>
> (65–8)

(The more that my guilt builds beyond measure, and stinks in your son's sight and your own, the greater need it has of his attention and your help.)

The *Series* broadcasts from the other side of the stench: the narrative purports to be one of a body made whole, wholly healed and reformed by the grace of God. The problem is not so much begging forgiveness, but rather convincing others that the smell is entirely gone, 'bittir galle' flushed out—the 'greuous venim' voided (1.234). 'Hoccleve' tells his Friend that his 'seeknesse sprad was so wide' that he feels all the more compelled to broadcast widely news of his recovery: 'So wolde I nowe vppon þat othir side / Wist were howe oure lorde Ihesu … / Releued hath me sinful creature' (*So would I now have it known, on the other side, how our Lord Jesus has relieved me, sinful creature*; 2.58–63). As the English nation attempted to present itself at the Council of Constance as whole, newly reformed, void of the 'bittir galle' of heresy, here too 'Hoccleve' acknowledges that his narrative of recovery and mercy must be disseminated broadly to be believed.

That Hoccleve might be inviting a larger Christian 'body' into his own personal body in the *Series* should not by now be surprising. The *ars moriendi* subject is the Everyman, by definition—death doing its work as the great equalizer (a point made repeatedly in Lydgate's *Dance of Death*, the text that becomes the unofficial coda to the *Series* in all non-autograph manuscripts). But it is also a characteristically Hoccleovian move to foreground wounds and woundedness. At the heart of the *Regiment of Princes*, we encounter an exemplum involving a Roman soldier who bears his wounds before Caesar, as a means of moving him to compassion:

> 'My wowndes beren good witnesse ynow
> That I sooth seye, and lest yee leeve it naght,
> I shal yow shewe what harm have I caght,
> The doute out of your herte for to dryve.'
> He nakid him and shewid him as blyve.
>
> (3286–90)

---

[30] Printed in Furnivall and Gollancz (eds), *Minor Poems*, 43–6.

('My wounds bear good enough witness that I am telling the truth, and lest you don't believe it, I will show you what harm I have suffered, in order to drive the doubt from your heart.' He stripped himself naked and showed him [Caesar] quickly.)

I have argued elsewhere that this exemplum reflects a characteristically Hocclevian *modus operandi*: Hoccleve recognizes the ability of wounds to humanize and communicate, to exact sympathy.[31] It is a wounded Hoccleve who stumbles onto the scene in the opening lines of the *Regiment*: wounded mentally by the 'smert of thoght' (*pain of anxiety/melancholy*) with its 'mortel venym' (*lethal venom*) (106; 271); and also wounded physically, his eyes and back deteriorating after too many years of scribal labour, stooped over the 'sheepes skyn' (see 1013–29; '[*writing*] smertith him ful sore / In every veyne and place of his body' (1025–6)).

To read through Hoccleve's shorter poems is to witness how fully this wounded Hoccleve overlaps with images of a wounded Christ, and it summons to mind how sacred and secular wounds interrelate. Even the Caesar exemplum above subtly channels the story of Doubting Thomas: the soldier baring his wounds—'the *doute* out of your herte for to dryve'—echoes Christ appearing to the disciple Thomas and baring his wounds to help drive doubt from Thomas's heart.[32] In '*Ad Patrem*', images of Christ 'wowndid to the herte', waxing pale as death creeps in, lead to another request for mercy, wounds tied clearly (again) to compassion:[33]

> Beholde thy sones humanitee,
> And mercy haue on our seek feeblenesse.
> Beholde his toren membres, fadir free,
> And lat our substance in thyn herte impresse.
> (127–30)

(Behold your son's humanity, and have mercy on our frail feebleness. Behold his torn limbs, generous father, and let our substance sink into your heart.)

This poem, in turn, transitions into a prayer pitched to Christ himself—'*Ad filium*'—in which the speaker claims responsibility for, and inhabits, the wounds of Christ:[34]

> I am the wownde of al thy greuance.
> I am the cause of thyn occisioun
> And of thy deeth, dessert of thy vengeance.
> I am also verray flagicioun.
> I causid thee thy greuous passioun.
> Of thy torment I am solicitour,
> Thow, Goddes sone, our lord and sauueour.
> (8–14)

---

[31] Sebastian J. Langdell, *Thomas Hoccleve: Religious Reform, Transnational Poetics, and the Invention of Chaucer* (Liverpool, 2018), 193–4.
[32] Cf. John 20.27.
[33] See Furnivall and Gollancz (eds), *Minor Poems*, 275–9.
[34] See Furnivall and Gollancz (eds), *Minor Poems*, 279–81.

(I am the wound of all your injury. I am the cause of your slaughter and of your death, deserving of your vengeance. I am also true incitement. I caused your dreadful passion. Of your torment I am the instigator—you, God's son, our Lord and Saviour.)

Not content to merely align the wounds (and humanity) of Christ with the wounds (and humanity) of all mankind, the speaker claims responsibility for such wounds. The preoccupation with wounds is maintained throughout the Huntington 'shorter poems' manuscripts. Later in HM 744, we witness the Holy Spirit and Mary serving, respectively, as 'wowndes leche', and provider of a healing 'licour' that searches 'our wowndes greuous and sore' ('*Ad spiritum sanctum*', 45; '*Item de beata virgine*', 17–18).[35] The first item in HM 111, '*Conpleynte paramont*', follows Mary as she watches her son die on the cross, and the encounter itself is enough to sunder 'wit' from 'wight': 'Poore Marie,' she says to herself, 'thy wit is aweye' (217; cf. *Series* 1.207).[36] The 'wownde of deeth' prefigures a loss of self, a temporary voiding of 'wit' (53). The 'I' from her name (Maria) falls away with the death of her 'Ihesus', leaving her 'Mara' (*bitter*), and then 'marred'—inner death manifested in the marring of a name, a permanent shift in personhood (183–6; 218). The end of the poem reminds us that this is a means to a moral lesson: a closing reminder that 'al it was for your redempcioun' (245).

The wounded subject—'abiect, desolate, and forsake'—is nothing new for Hoccleve. Reaching beyond the *Series* means witnessing the various permutations of woundedness that Hoccleve examines: wounds as capable of fragmenting selfhood; wounds as evidence, tools for driving away doubt and exciting mercy; the magnifying of wounds to provoke healing processes both personal and communal; the meditation on wounded bodies for the sake of provoking self-reflection, prayer, and penitence. None of these readings of Hoccleve preclude the idea of an *actually* wounded Hoccleve, a historical Hoccleve with illness 'in deede'. They serve as a reminder that 'Hoccleve' contains multitudes. And reading 'Hoccleve' requires a certain negative capability—a willingness to dwell with the mysteries and unknowns that the persona invites, while taming that inner animal that wants to assign 'Hoccleve' wholly to Hoccleve, that wants to anchor the historical in the literary, once and for all.

We have already seen what Hoccleve is capable of achieving within the realm of religious writing. We have seen the innovative ways in which he explores genres of *ars moriendi*, Marian devotion, meditations on the wounded Christ, prayers for a wounded church, and admonitions against heresy. The *Regiment of Princes* poses the question of how to present such an authorial position for oneself, amid an atmosphere of heightened ecclesiastical scrutiny due to the threat of heresy.

In the opening section of the *Regiment of Princes*, 'Hoccleve' is approached by an unnamed old man, who notices something suspicious in Hoccleve's aspect, and sets about confirming Hoccleve's orthodoxy. The old man will later express interest in Hoccleve's occupation, his married life, his poetic ambitions—but the old man is more immediately concerned with establishing Hoccleve's orthodoxy, his good standing within the eyes of the church (see e.g., 372–3). The old man's identity is kept vague throughout this opening section, allowing him to be identified as a general medium for the English church's heightened scepticism amid the threat of heresy.[37] Hoccleve's weariness, his sleepless guise,

---

[35] See Furnivall and Gollancz (eds), *Minor Poems*, 281–3, 285–9.
[36] See Ellis (ed.), '*My Compleinte*', 53–60.
[37] At the end of their dialogue, the old man says he can be found daily at the 'Carmes messe' (Carmelite refectory), which has spurred the suggestion that he could be a Carmelite friar (2007). But this is never made explicit.

touched by the 'smert of thoght' (106), identify him—to the old man—as potentially dangerous. Perhaps the physical manifestation of his writerly afflictions (as expressed midway through their dialogue)—his stooped back and squinting eyes—indicate that he might be the *wrong* type of 'thoghtful wight', one of the heretics that Hoccleve denounces in 'Oldcastle', and chides for hiding in dark 'halkes [and] hernes' (*nooks* and *corners*)—those 'cursid caitifs, heires of dirknesse' (*cursed scoundrels, heirs of darkness*) (382; 15). The old man greets Hoccleve by telling him to 'be waar of thoght' (267), encouraging him to 'void' Thought's poison (203; 276), gesturing to the recent execution of the heretic John Badby, expounding on Badby's refusal to accept the orthodox definition of the Eucharist (281–322), holding forth on heretics more generally, and then asking Hoccleve: 'Sone, if God wole, thow art noon of tho / That wrappid been in this dampnacioun?' (372–3). Hoccleve reaches first for the dullness *topos*, signalling to the reader—as we saw above—that we are in truly hazardous territory:

> I thanke it God, noon inclinacioun
> Have I to laboure in probacioun
> Of His hy knowleche and His mighty werkis,
> *For swich mateere unto my wit to derk is.*
> (375–8; italics mine)

(I thank God that I have no inclination to labour in investigation of his high knowledge and his mighty works, for such material is too obscure for my intellect.)

'Hoccleve' then signals assent with the old man (and the church) by confirming his belief in the Eucharist, and declaring himself broadly in assent with 'Holy Writ' on 'alle othir articles of the feith' (379–85). Before the main text of the *Regiment* begins, 'Hoccleve' takes time to clarify that he is not a heretic.

The narrator's declaration of insufficient intellect here is countered by his admission, later on, that he had trained to be a priest but, upon getting married, abandoned the road to priesthood (1448–56). The very 'mateere' that 'Hoccleve' declares himself unfit to handle—'His mighty werkis' (377)—would have been the foundation of Hoccleve's priestly training. Like Langland's Will, 'Hoccleve' underwent priestly training, but his 'wyf' makes such training inappropriate; as a married man, he cannot advance within the church.[38] (In the *Piers Plowman* C.5 *apologia*, a passage often taken to be autobiographical for Langland, Will describes his life in similar terms, indicating that he underwent priestly training in his younger years, but that this was cut short; he also indicates elsewhere that he has a 'wyf'.)[39]

We do not have historical evidence that Hoccleve-the-author was in fact at one time on the road to priesthood, but we can say that the boundary between the clerical life and bureaucracy was more porous than one might now think—and Hoccleve's colleagues attest to this. Nicholas Bubwith, Keeper of the Privy Seal from March 1405—October 1406, advanced to the position of Bishop of Bath and Wells, and is notable for having been one of two English clergymen to commission a Latin translation of Dante's *Commedia*

For the old man's alignment with orthodoxy, and interest in confirming Hoccleve's orthodoxy, see lines 351–85. For further discussion, and for the church's scepticism, see Langdell, *Thomas Hoccleve*, Chs. 1 and 3.

[38] See 1447–56. On the Langlandian context here, see Langdell, *Thomas Hoccleve*, Ch. 4.
[39] Derek Pearsall (ed.), *Piers Plowman: A New Annotated Edition of the C-text* (Exeter, 2008), 5.1–108.

at the Council of Constance.⁴⁰ Bubwith's predecessor as Keeper of the Privy Seal, Thomas Langley, would go on to serve as Bishop of Durham.⁴¹ Hoccleve's apparent social circle also included clergymen: the 'Prentys and Arondel', referred to the 'Male Regle' in the context of drinking and merrymaking, both served as clerks of the King's Chapel. Prentys would rise to the position of Dean of St Stephen's, Westminster; and Arondel would become Dean of St George's, Windsor.⁴² The old man's sceptical gaze in the *Regiment* proceeds, one might think, not from this circle of friends (who may well have appreciated Hoccleve's writing), but from the climate of increasing suspicion surrounding the place of unlicenced preaching and instances of vernacular scriptural translation not sanctioned by the church. The Hoccleve-narrator's need to declare himself too dim-witted to entertain religious truths, despite the obvious evidence to the contrary, reflects the obstacles that face an early fifteenth-century writer who would want to claim an interstitial religious role—orthodox, no doubt, but not 'official'.

The old man's eventual authorization of Hoccleve as a 'safe pair of hands' in the *Regiment* comes in tandem with Hoccleve's creation of a new, hybridized Chaucer figure—a more conspicuously Christian Chaucer, who can in turn licence Hoccleve's poetic production.⁴³ The old man and Chaucer are the two figures for whom 'Hoccleve' uses the term 'my fadir' in the *Regiment*, and they are more alike, as constructs, than we often give them credit for. They are both clearly religious, official-seeming (without clarity on where that official status proceeds from), and conspicuously aligned with orthodoxy. Chaucer's own religious orthodoxy is anchored within the *Regiment* by the portrait that Hoccleve presents of him, towards the end of the work, in which Chaucer is seen grasping a rosary—an image bookended by (respectively) a prayer to the Virgin Mary, and an assault on Lollards.⁴⁴ This more conspicuously Christian version of Chaucer is introduced into the poem by the old man; 'Chaucer' is immediately commended by the old man, who functions in this poem as the voice of orthodoxy, sealing Chaucer's reputation as both orthodox and 'best of any wight' as soon as he appears on the page:

> 'What shal I calle thee, what is thy name?'
> 'Hoccleve, fadir myn, men clepen me.'
> 'Hoccleve, sone?' 'Ywis, fadir, that same.'
> 'Sone, I have herd or this men speke of thee;
> Thow were aqweyntid with Chaucer, pardee –
> God have his soule, best of any wight!
> Sone, I wole holde thee that I have hight'.
>   (1863–9)

('What shall I call you? What is your name?' 'Hoccleve, my father, men call me.' 'Hoccleve, son?' 'Indeed, father, the same.' 'Son, I have heard men speak of you. You were

---

⁴⁰ See David Wallace, *Premodern Places: Calais to Surinam, Chaucer to Aphra Behn* (Oxford, 2006), Ch. 3. For Bubwith's position in the Privy Seal, see S. Porter and I. Roy (eds), *Handbook of British Chronology*, 3rd edn. (London, 1986), 95.
⁴¹ Burrow and Doyle (intro.), *Facsimile*, xiv.
⁴² Watt, *Making*, 28–9.
⁴³ The phrase 'safe pair of hands' is borrowed from Gillespie, 'Chichele's Church', 42.
⁴⁴ See 4985–5012. The image of Chaucer is preserved in BL MS Harley 4866 (fol. 88). The image enjoys a long afterlife, with renditions made for later manuscripts, stand-alone portraits, and even the portrait created for Chaucer's tomb on the occasion of his reburial in 1556. For a survey of such images, see 'Appendix I' in Derek Pearsall, *The Life of Geoffrey Chaucer: A Critical Biography* (Oxford, 1992).

acquainted with Chaucer—God have his soul, best of any man! Son, I will keep my promise to you'.)

Hoccleve is named in this stanza (twice) for the first time in the poem. His status as named-author arrives hand-in-hand with his praise of Chaucer. With this stanza, Hoccleve's own journey from 'anonymous, potentially suspect writer' to 'named, orthodox writer' is complete. He has shed any aspect of the dark 'halkes' and 'hernes'. Chaucer serves as the validating model for Hoccleve: a figure who can represent at once orthodoxy, vernacular poetic pursuit, and general exemplarity ('best of any wight!').

Hoccleve's moral rendition of Chaucer, created within the *Regiment*, would go on to enjoy a long afterlife: it is by far the most successful of any Hocclevian *making*.[45] We are often less ready to see it as a Hocclevian invention because Hoccleve's introduction of *this* Chaucer into his poem relies on the simultaneous effacement of his own hand in its production. Chaucer enters the poem as if 'ready-made'. We might assume that Chaucer existed in this guise, with this reputation, prior to the *Regiment*. But an examination of references to Chaucer prior to the *Regiment* attests to the opposite.[46] John Walton's preface to his translation of Boethius's *Consolation of Philosophy* offers an instructive counterpoint. Walton wrote his translation c1410—at the exact time that Hoccleve was writing his *Regiment*.[47] Chaucer is not aligned with orthodox Christianity there, but is rather aligned with pagan stories. Walton initially speaks of Chaucer in positive terms, referring to him as 'floure of rethoryk / In Englisshe tong and excellent poete' (cf. Hoccleve's 'flour of eloquence'). But this initial praise finds a stumbling block as he attempts to reconcile the poetry of both Chaucer and Gower with Christianity:

> Noght liketh me to labour ne to muse
> Upon þese olde poysees derk,
> For Cristes feyth suche þing[es] schulde refuse;
> Witnes upon Ierom þe holy clerk.
> Hit schulde not ben a Cristen mannes werk
> Tho false goddes names to renewe,
> For he þat hath resayued Cristes merk,
> If he do so to Crist he is vntrewe.
> (2–3; stanza 6)

(I do not like to labour or muse upon these old obscure poems, for Christ's faith eschews such things. Take the word of Jerome, the holy clerk. It is not the work of a Christian man to renew the names of false gods. For he has received Christ's mark [in baptism], and so if he does so, he is untrue to Christ.)

These 'olde poysees derk' stand in contradistinction to Christianity—and to the aims of a Christian writer—in large part because they 'renewe' the names of 'false goddes' (i.e., classical/pagan gods). Walton will go on to specify what he means, using language that recalls *Troilus and Criseyde*: it is unnecessary to 'whette now þe dartes of cupide', he says, 'Ne for to bidde þat venus be oure gyde' (to whet the darts of Cupid, nor to ask that Venus

---

[45] On the afterlife of Hoccleve's Chaucer, see Langdell, *Thomas Hoccleve*, Conclusion.
[46] I explore the antecedents at length in Langdell, *Thomas Hoccleve*, Ch. 3.
[47] Mark Science (ed.), John Walton, *Boethius: De Consolatione Philosophiae*, EETS, o.s. 170 (London, 1927). On dating, see xliv.

be our guide).⁴⁸ Nor will he pray to any of the three furies; he will instead 'pray þat god of hys benignite / My spirit enspire wiþ hys influence' (pray that God, of his kindness, will inspire my spirit with his influence).⁴⁹ Walton's preface gives us one indication of how Chaucer fared differently outside of Hoccleve's able hands. In Hoccleve's hands, Chaucer is not relegated to a pagan past, but is integrated fully into the Christian present. Hoccleve's resident spokesman for orthodox Christianity (the old man) offers his highest approval as soon as Chaucer arrives on the scene. We are never in doubt. We never worry about being 'vntrewe' to Christ by praising Chaucer.

This representation of Chaucer reflects the type of writing Hoccleve is able to perform not only within the *Series* and the shorter poems (where the devotional vein is more conspicuous), but also within the body of the *Regiment* itself. We may feel that the *Regiment* presents itself as a 'political' text, and there is no doubt that, in offering advice on good leadership, Hoccleve engages in the political. But to suppose that the 'political' and the 'religious' would have been easily separated from each other at Hoccleve's time is anachronistic. The John Badby episode that opens the *Regiment* reflects this: Prince Henry and Archbishop Arundel were both instrumental in John Badby's execution for heresy; indeed, the situation afforded Prince Henry an opportunity to step into an intermediary role between king and church, inserting himself thoroughly into the proceedings as Arundel threatened Badby.⁵⁰ In the *Regiment*, it is Henry (not a priest) who arranges for the Eucharistic host to be presented to Badby as a last attempt at converting the heretic—and it is Henry who promises Badby both 'lyf' (306) and 'lyflode' (307) (income) should he recant and 'come unto our good byleeve ageyn' (305). The overlapping of 'religious' and 'secular' power comes to a head during Prince Henry's lifetime: Jeremy Catto notes that prior to 1400 'religion was outside the competence of the secular power'; whereas by the end of Henry V's rule, 'more than a century before the title could be used, Henry V had begun to act as the supreme governor of the Church of England'.⁵¹ In presenting himself as a hybrid authority—a religious writer nested within royal bureaucratic circles—Hoccleve presents himself (daringly) as a writer for the times. It is telling that a poem that opens with the execution of a heretic, resulting from a dispute over the meaning and presence of Christ's body (in the Eucharist), gives way to the author using Christ's body—and Christ's own examples—as the Prince's own private models of mercy, patience, and humility in the *Regiment* proper (see 3333–45; 3613–19). It is also telling that when Hoccleve's advice to Henry does become more specific in the *Regiment*, it comes as a plea to recognize the line between sacred and secular power, or to remember the explicitly *Christian* duties of a monarch. There is, for instance, Hoccleve's reminder to keep holy days sacred, and to not hold council meetings on holy days, lest you risk offending God (4964–77); and the final section of the *Regiment*, on 'Peace', where Hoccleve situates the championing of peace as a Christian imperative and rails against the ongoing war between England and France (5321–41).

Even Hoccleve's self-positioning with regard to Chaucer is situated within Christian devotional contexts. We have seen that Hoccleve's resident 'orthodox spokesman' (the old man) introduces Chaucer into the poem, and offers his immediate endorsement. Chaucer's surprise return at the end of the *Regiment* occurs in the stanzas immediately preceding

---

⁴⁸ See Science (ed.), *Boethius*, 3; stanza 7. Cf. the proem to Book Three of *Troilus and Criseyde*.
⁴⁹ See Science (ed.), *Boethius*, 3; stanza 8. Cf. the opening lines to *Troilus*, where the narrator prays to Tisiphone.
⁵⁰ Blyth (ed.), *Regiment*, 288–322.
⁵¹ Jeremy Catto, 'Religious Change Under Henry V', in G. L. Harriss (ed.), *Henry V: The Practice of Kingship* (Stroud, 1993), 97–115 (at 97, 115).

the final section, on 'Peace': it is here that Hoccleve presents his portrait of Chaucer.[52] Chaucer's prominently positioned rosary and devout black robe are often commented on—as are the stanzas that immediately follow, in which Hoccleve's image is likened to iconography, images of God and his saints. But Hoccleve's route *in* to the presentation stanzas is equally shrouded in the sacred: Hoccleve begins with his admonition against holding councils on holy days; this is followed by a stark reminder to Henry that any monarch is answerable to 'our lord God, king and commaundour / Of kynges alle' (4969–70), and that if the Prince disobeys God, he can only expect his own subjects to disobey him (4973–7); Hoccleve then presents Chaucer as a prime example of such virtuous advice-giving. Before we get to the portrait presentation stanzas, however, Hoccleve asks the Virgin Mary to serve as an 'advocat' for Chaucer (4984). A stanza is dedicated to the Virgin, conspicuously connecting Chaucerian virtue to Marian virtue ('O now thyn help and thy promocioun!'), which then leads to Hoccleve's aside that—by the way—he has 'heere [Chaucer's] liknesse / Do make', to 'putte othir men in remembrance / Of his persone' (4985–91; 4994–6). Hoccleve's choice to highlight here the intercessory, mediating function of the Virgin Mary—the Christian intercessor par excellence—is no coincidence. Hoccleve is indicating his own role as a virtuous go-between, a mediator, in conveying this vision of Chaucer. He does so by first gesturing towards Mary, 'mankyndes mediatrice' (as he refers to her elsewhere),[53] and then by highlighting his own mediating function in presenting Chaucer: his ability to 'do make' (cause to be made) the image of Chaucer gives him an intercessory role, rather than a purely active one. And he frames his own intercessory, intermediary position within a conspicuously Christian, Marian context. It is Mary's function as 'advocat', 'mene', and 'mediatrice' that Hoccleve highlights again and again in his shorter verse, and he takes care to align himself with this mediatory function as he presents his Chaucer to the reader.[54]

If 'Hoccleve' presents himself at times as a 'spectacle' (as in the *Series*), he is also a mediator, a virtuous intermediary. We see this in various forms throughout the shorter poems: as we have seen, in 'Good Company', Hoccleve serves as the intermediary between the other members of the supper club and Henry Somer, who would seem to be reluctant to fulfil his duties. In another ballade for Somer, Hoccleve reminds his recipient of funds eagerly awaited, not only for his own sake, but on behalf of his associates: 'We, your seruantes Hoccleue and Baillay, / Hethe and Offorde, yow byseeche and preye: / Haastith our heruest as soone as yee may! / For fere of stormes, our wit is aweye' (25–8).[55] That ballade closes with a 'chanceon' to Somer, continuing seasonal puns (spurred on by 'Somer' as summertime), evoking a similarly jovial mood to 'Good Company'—a begging poem that subsides into song.[56] We remember too that we see Hoccleve as one of many unnamed scribes who 'laboure in travaillous stilnesse' in the *Regiment* (1013), before we encounter him as a named and singular Hoccleve, a verse writer associated with the likes of Chaucer. Their pains and travails are his own, and in that communal portrait there is the sense of corporate identity, advocacy. This is heightened considerably in the *Regiment* proper as Hoccleve situates himself to advise a monarch. The voice that summons the strength to ask for money (or dinner) on behalf of his fellows, summons, in the *Regiment* proper, the tenacity to admonish the Prince on behalf of God and the people ('wynneth your peples

---

[52] 4985–5012.
[53] 'Oldcastle', 256.
[54] See, for instance, 'Modir of Lyf', 14; 'Modir of God', 40, 44, 83.
[55] See Furnivall and Gollancz (eds), *Minor Poems*, 59–61.
[56] See lines 33–40.

vois, / For peples vois is Goddes vois, men seyn' (2885-6)). Such a reading situates Hoccleve closer to the writer of *Crowned King*—which features a clerk who encourages the king to show reverence for the ultimate 'king', Christ, by treating his people more justly—or to the 'lunatik' in the Prologue to *Piers Plowman* who advises the king to 'lede thi lond so Leaute thee lovye, / And for thi rightful rulynge be rewarded in hevene!' (*rule thy realm so Loyalty may love thee, and for your rightful ruling be rewarded in heaven*) (B.126-7).[57]

It is important to register this aspect of Hoccleve's authorial stance because we can too easily assume that Hoccleve is merely elevating Chaucer to the heights of literary fame so that he can then claim the same mantle for himself. We might assume that Hoccleve invents this position for his master so that he can then inherit, usurp, or otherwise adopt it.[58] But Hoccleve himself makes no such claims to fame. Chaucer can enter the *Regiment* as 'flour of eloquence, / Mirour of fructuous entendement, / O universel fadir in science' (*flower of eloquence, mirror of fruitful intellect, O universal father in knowledge*), 'heir in philosophie / To Aristotle', and worthy to follow 'the steppes of Virgile in poesie' (1962-4, 2087-90); but Hoccleve never presumes to claim these roles for himself. Insofar as he operates politically, it is in the service of rallying the crown to respect Christian virtues, and working to mend the body of the church, to render it whole. His 'political' poetry has a virtuous aspect in its ability to speak on behalf of the less powerful, to emphasize tones of *vox populi vox Dei*. We come close to a statement of purpose, as regards his more political writing, in his earliest datable poem, the *Epistle of Cupid*, where the narrator asks:[59]

> Betrayen men nat remes grete and kynges?
> What wight is þat can shape a remedie
> Ageynes false and hid purposid thynges?
> Who can the craft tho castes to espye,
> But man whos wil ay reedy is t'applie
> To thyng þat sovneth into hy falshede?
> (85-90)

(Do men not betray great realms and kings? Which person can make a remedy against false, hidden, scheming things? Who has the skill to see such plots, except a man whose will is always ready to be applied to such things that concern high falsehood?)

Hoccleve recognizes the ability of the powerful to misuse their power, the capacity for wilfulness and treachery. He functions, however, within the inner circles of royal administration, and as such he understands the inner workings of such men, how wills might be bent. He is well positioned to 'shape a remedie / Ageynes false and hid purposed thynges'. This is the same Hoccleve who begins the '*Regiment* proper' by punning on chess moves, and admits that his years in civil service have taught him to be 'wys and waar' (*wise and crafty/prudent*).[60] It is the same Hoccleve who, in the '*Male Regle*', situates his ability to

---

[57] See *Crowned King* in Helen Barr (ed.), *The Piers Plowman Tradition* (London, 1993). For *Piers Plowman*: A. V. C. Schmidt (ed.), William Langland, *The Vision of Piers Plowman: A Complete Edition of the B-Text*, 2nd edn. (London, 1995).

[58] See for instance Ethan Knapp's discussion of 'poetic usurpation': *Bureaucratic Muse: Thomas Hoccleve and the Literature of Late Medieval England* (University Park, PA, 2001), 14, 123-4.

[59] The *Epistle* is dated, in its last stanza, to May 1402. (See Ellis (ed.), '*My Compleinte*', 93-107.) This poem is Hoccleve's translation of Christine de Pizan's *Epistre au dieu d'amours* (1399). Hoccleve condenses and restructures the poem considerably, heightening its applicability to contemporary English political events.

[60] See lines 2115-2121.

speak 'rownyngly' (*whisperingly; privately*) as an 'auauntage' (172, 169).[61] For those with ears to hear, Hoccleve's poetry advertises its own cautious stance—the layers of prudent positioning that enter into his persona, and his productions.

This more savvy, nimble Hoccleve is now coming to light. Jenni Nuttall has recently indicated how several of Hoccleve's 'political' poems, often read as officially sanctioned occasional verse, are in fact 'anti-occasional' and give no evidence of being officially requested—that is, they do nothing to underscore a role for Hoccleve as an 'official' poet or a Lancastrian 'spokesman', as has been assumed. Instead, they give Hoccleve a platform from which to critique royal authority and policy, often with a view to underscoring the rights of the church, and the need to focus on the spiritual health of the church and its communities.[62] As we have seen above, Hoccleve labours to create a para-ecclesiastical role for himself—an interstitial religious role—but he does so without claiming or seeking an 'official' title for himself. Jane Griffiths has indicated how Hoccleve uses his marginal glosses (themselves deeply understudied) as one element of engendering political critique and commentary—how his writerly savviness overlaps with *mise-en-page*, and with his training as a scribe.[63] David Lawton's work on voice has similarly redirected our attention to the scriptural tones in Hoccleve's voice, and also the spiritual boldness that it carries—how we might understand Hoccleve better in the context of Skelton, say, than Lydgate.[64] These recent developments join earlier appreciations of Hoccleve's position not as a follower, but rather as an intrepid innovator, for whom the sequence of 'firsts' is long: John Bowers claimed the Huntington holographs as 'the first collected poems in English'; Ethan Knapp sees in Hoccleve 'the dramatic first stirrings of vernacular autobiography', whereas Bernard O'Donoghue sees 'the earliest and inchoate exponent of a mixed kind of writing' that draws 'on conventional frameworks and apparently real experiences at the same time'; and Derek Pearsall credits Hoccleve, in his presentation of the Chaucer image, with the invention of English portraiture.[65] We are beginning to sharpen the lens through which we see Hoccleve: as a writer of unexpected boldness, of remarkable ingenuity and innovation, less a Lancastrian court poet, and more a virtuous intermediary, willing to ask difficult questions—and to place himself in potentially hazardous situations—for the sake of the common good.

---

[61] See Ellis (ed.), '*My Compleinte*', 64–76.
[62] Nuttall, 'Anti-Occasional', 4–11; 14.
[63] Jane Griffiths, '"In Bookes Thus Writen I Fynde": Hoccleve's Self-Glossing in the *Regiment of Princes* and the *Series*', *Medium Ævum*, 86 (2017), 91–107.
[64] Lawton, *Public Interiorities*, Ch. 4.
[65] John M. Bowers, 'Hoccleve's Huntington Holographs: The First "Collected Poems" in English', *Fifteenth-Century Studies* 15 (1989), 27–51 (at 27); Ethan Knapp, 'Bureaucratic Identity and the Construction of the Self in Hoccleve's *Formulary* and *La male regle*', *Speculum* 74 (1999), 357–76 (at 357); Thomas Hoccleve, Bernard O'Donoghue (ed.), *Selected Poems* (Manchester, 1982), 15–16; Pearsall, *Life of Geoffrey Chaucer*, 287–8.

CHAPTER 26
Robert Henryson

Joanna Martin

> ... quhen reson and perfyte sapience
> Playis apon the harp of eloquens,
> And persuadis our fleschly appetyte,
> To leif the thocht of this warldly delyte
> Than seisis of our hert the wicket will,
> Fra frawart language than the tong is still,
> Our synfull deidis fallis doun on sleip ...
>   (*Orpheus and Eurydice*, 507–13)[1]

(When reason and perfect sapience play on the harp of eloquence and convince our bodily appetite to leave the thought of this worldly delight, then the wicked will of our heart is calmed, the tongue ceases its perverse language, our sinful deeds fall down in sleep.)

In this passage from his adaptation of the classical myth of the harper Orpheus and his quest to rescue his beloved Eurydice, the Older Scots poet Robert Henryson (d. c1490) considers the nature and efficacy of eloquent language. Reason and wisdom, combined with eloquence, he suggests, pacify our wilful desires, just as a musician united with a harp brings forth harmonious music. Eloquence is persuasive, leading us away from deviant or ill-intentioned language, and from worldly concerns, and all the associated sins of uncontrolled appetite. Although Henryson's other major poems are set in the different contexts of Trojan history and animal fable, they yet share with *Orpheus and Eurydice* a preoccupation with how the eloquence of poetry might encourage readers to reasoned conduct, good judgement, and the wisdom of self-understanding, and away from subjection to their bodily desires. The thematic and stylistic coherence of the modest corpus associated with Henryson affords him a central place in fifteenth-century poetry, and this chapter explores the distinctive moral and ethical rhetoric which earns him this position in the eyes of his contemporaries and of later readers.

Little is known for certain about Henryson's life, but he is usually identified with an individual mentioned in the records of the University of Glasgow who was admitted to the institution in 1462, and who may have taught canon law there. Indeed, much of the surviving poetry attributed to Henryson employs formal legal registers and shows a concern with the administration of justice, befitting an author with just such a background. Other documentary evidence indicates that Robert Henryson was also a notary public and teacher. During the 1470s he was associated with the royal burgh of Dunfermline, Fife, where there was a large Benedictine abbey and grammar school. Three deeds of sasine (formal records of the transfer of property) in the chartulary of Dunfermline bear his signature.

---

[1] See Denton Fox (ed.), *The Poems of Robert Henryson* (Oxford, 1981), xiii–xv. References to Henryson's poems are to this edition.

Sixteenth-century printed editions of Henryson's best-known work, *The Morall Fabillis*, identify its author as 'Maister Robert Henrisone, scholemaister of Dumfermeling ...' (STC 185).[2]

As well as *The Morall Fabillis*, a collection of verse narratives in the tradition of Aesopian and Renardian beast writing, and *Orpheus and Eurydice*, Henryson is also the author of *The Testament of Cresseid*, a response to Book Five of Chaucer's *Troilus and Criseyde*, and of a number of shorter poems. All survive in witnesses that are significantly later than their likely date of composition: there are no holograph manuscripts of any of Henryson's works.[3] Nevertheless, the later witnesses indicate that Henryson's poetry was being read for more than a century after his own lifetime. The earliest copy of one of his poems is found in a compilation of Latin lecture notes, the Makculloch Manuscript, Edinburgh, University Library, MS La. III. 149 (Makculloch MS 205). The manuscript was compiled in 1477 in Leuven by Magnus Makculloch who was later clerk to Archbishop Scheves: around the turn of the sixteenth century the 'Prologue' and the first fable ('The Cock and the Jasp') of *The Morall Fabillis*, were added to the fly-leaves of the manuscript. One of Henryson's shorter religious poems makes a similar appearance as a casual sixteenth-century addition to an earlier manuscript: 'Forcy as deith is likand lufe' appears uniquely in Edinburgh, National Library of Scotland, Advocates' MS 34. 7. 3, the 'Gray Manuscript'. The manuscript itself is dated to the late fifteenth century, but the poem was added to it in the first third of the sixteenth century.

The next earliest witnesses of Henryson's poems are printed texts, suggesting that his work was popular enough by the early sixteenth century to have gained some commercial value. The moral poem 'Within a garth, vnder a rede rosere' (*The Praise of Age*), was printed by Scotland's first printers, Walter Chepman and Andro Myllar, in Edinburgh in 1508 (with *The Flyting of Dunbar and Kennedy* (STC 7348)). *Orpheus and Eurydice* was also issued by Chepman and Myllar in Edinburgh in 1508 (STC 186.5), with a complaint poem, 'Me ferlyis of this grete confusion' (*The Want of Wisemen*). Though this poem is not ascribed to a named author in the print, it appears in the later Bannatyne Manuscript (c1568, Edinburgh, National Library of Scotland, Advocates' MS 1. 1. 6) with an attribution to Henryson.[4] *Orpheus and Eurydice* is also contained in its longest and apparently most complete form in the Bannatyne Manuscript. It is likely that early printed texts of Henryson's poems made them accessible to sixteenth-century readers and manuscript compilers such as the notaries, John Asloan and George Bannatyne, and the laird, Richard Maitland. Asloan's manuscript collection of verse and prose (Edinburgh, National Library of Scotland, Advocates' MS 16500, c1530) contains *Orpheus* and once, according to its scribal contents list, also had six of *The Morall Fabillis*.[5] The Bannatyne Manuscript is a particularly important source for the shorter poems, containing the unique texts of *The Bludy Serk, The Garmont of Gud Ladies, Robene and Makyne*, and *Sum Practysis of*

---

[2] Douglas Gray, *Robert Henryson* (Leiden, 1979); John MacQueen, 'Henryson, Robert (d. c1490)', *ODNB*; Anthony Hasler, 'Robert Henryson', in Thomas Owen Clancy (ed.), *The Edinburgh History of Scottish Literature from Columba to the Union (until 1707)* (Edinburgh, 2007), 286–94.

[3] For the manuscripts of Henryson's poems, see Fox (ed.), *Poems*, xxxiv–cxxiv. Also Sally Mapstone, '*The Testament of Cresseid*, lines 561–7: A New Manuscript Witness', *Notes and Queries*, n.s. 32 (1985), 308–10; Whiting, 'A Probable Allusion to Henryson's Testament of Cresseid', *Modern Language Review*, 40 (1945), 46–7.

[4] Denton Fox does not include it in Henryson's canon. Neither is the poem included in the recent edition, D. J. Parkinson (ed.), *Robert Henryson: The Complete Works* (Kalamazoo, MI, 2010).

[5] Only *Orpheus* and one fable, 'The Two Mice', now remain in this imperfectly preserved codex. I. C. Cunningham, 'The Asloan Manuscript', in A. A. MacDonald, Michael Lynch, and Ian B. Cowan (eds), *The Renaissance in Scotland: Studies in Literature, Religion, History and Culture Offered to John Durkan* (Leiden, 1994), 107–35.

Medecyne, with attributions to Henryson. It also contains ten of the thirteen fables from *The Morall Fabillis*.[6] The Maitland Folio Manuscript (c1570–86, Cambridge, Magdalene College, Pepys Library, MS 2553), a household collection of verse compiled in the 1570s, also contains some of the shorter poems.[7]

Sixteenth-century printed editions of Henryson's *The Morall Fabillis* are not just an indication of the popularity of his poetry but are also of considerable textual value. The order in which we now read *The Morall Fabillis* is based not on the manuscript witnesses such as the Asloan or Banantyne manuscripts, but on the prints made in Edinburgh by Thomas Bassandyne (STC 185.5) and Henry Charteris (STC 185) in the 1570s. The text offered by these printers provides a carefully structured collection of fables probably reflecting authorial design.[8] Charteris also printed the *Testament of Cresseid* in 1593. These prints must both reflect and have further encouraged the popularity of Henryson's works several generations after his death. Indeed, it was from a print related to the Bassandyne print that a further manuscript version of the fables was made, now BL MS Harley 3865 (its title page bears the date 1571).

Henryson's poems had a life beyond Edinburgh too. *The Testament of Cresseid* appears to have been one of the most widely transmitted of Henryson's compositions, and again its earliest witness is a printed text: it was included in William Thynne's 1532 London edition of *The workes of Geffray Chaucer* (STC 5068), at the end of *Troilus and Criseyde*, although with no indication of its Scottish authorship. A single stanza from the poem was copied in the first half of the sixteenth century into The Book of The Dean of Lismore (Edinburgh, National Library of Scotland, Advocates' MS 72. 1. 37), a compilation of Gaelic, Latin, Scots, and English texts made by James McGregor, Dean of Lismore and notary public in Fortingall, Perthshire.

Style and Poetic Form

Henryson's poetry was well known in the first half of the sixteenth century to major Older Scots writers such as Gavin Douglas (d. 1513) and David Lyndsay (d. 1555).[9] The earliest reference to Henryson by one of his best-known poetic successors is, however, rather underwhelming. This is Dunbar's mention of Henryson in 'I that in heill wes and gladnes' (*The Lament for the Makars*), which was composed c1505–6.[10] The poem belongs to the 'dance of death tradition', and is a warning for 'all estaitis' (17), rich and poor, of the inevitability of death.[11] The poem abandons this main theme, however, to list the 'makaris'

---

[6] See Denton Fox and W. A. Ringler (intro.), *The Bannatyne Manuscript, National Library of Scotland, Advocates' MS. 1.1.6* (London, 1980), ix–xlv.

[7] Julia Boffey, 'The Maitland Folio Manuscript as a Verse Anthology', in Sally Mapstone (ed.), *William Dunbar the Nobill Poyet: Essays in Honour of Priscilla Bawcutt* (East Linton, 2001), 40–50.

[8] Roderick J. Lyall, 'Henryson's *Moral Fabillis*: Structure and Meaning', in Priscilla Bawcutt and Janet Hadley Williams (eds), *A Companion to Medieval Scottish Poetry* (Cambridge, 2006), 89–104; Sally Mapstone, 'Robert Henryson', in Larry Scanlon (ed.), *The Cambridge Companion to Medieval English Literature, 1100–1500* (Cambridge, 2009), 240–55 (at 246–7).

[9] See Janet Hadley Williams (ed.), *Sir David Lyndsay: Selected Poems* (Glasgow, 2000), xv; also Fox (ed.), *Poems*, 384–425, on the multiple references to *Orpheus and Eurydice* made by Douglas and Lyndsay. Most recently, see William Gillies and Kate McClune, 'The Purposes of Literature', in Nicola Royan (ed.), *The International Companion to Scottish Literature, 1400–1650* (Glasgow, 2018), 79–99 (at 89).

[10] References to Dunbar's poetry are to Priscilla Bawcutt (ed.), *The Poems of William Dunbar*, 2 vols., (Glasgow, 1998).

[11] See R. D. Drexler, '"Dunbar's Lament for the Makaris" and the Dance of Death Tradition', *Studies in Scottish Literature*, 13 (1978), 144–58; A. M. Kinghorn, 'Death and the *Makars: Timor mortis* in Scottish Poetry to 1600', *English Studies*, 60 (1979), 2–13.

(45; *poets*), who have gone to their graves. Dunbar begins his account of dead poets with Chaucer ('of makaris flour', 50), Lydgate, and Gower, before moving on to enumerate recently deceased Scottish writers. Little is said about the poetry of these makars beyond a few succinct remarks on their preferred genres or forms—'balat making and trigide' (59; *the writing of song and tragedy*), for example. Only the shadowy figure of 'Merseir', is treated in more detail: we are told that he 'did in luf so lifly write, / So schort, so quyk, of sentence hie' (73–5).[12] He writes of love vividly,[13] his style succinct ('schort'), but lively ('quyk'), his meaning ('sentence') lofty. Of Henryson, though, nothing more is noted than his quiet demise: death has 'In Dunfermelyne ... done rovne (*whispered*) / With maister Robert Henrisoun' (81–2). On what, then, did Henryson's reputation rest for his contemporaries and later readers? Was it on his 'lifly' manner of writing, or on his themes, his 'sentence hie' (*Lament*, 75)? Henryson's 'sentence' is the subject of the last section of this essay, but the next section considers formal aspects of Henryson's poetry in order to reflect on this question.

Style in the Shorter Poems

Like many late medieval poets, Henryson was acutely aware of the significance of stylistic choice, and of the close connection between the form of his writing and the meaning or 'sentence' that he wished to convey with it. The choice of stanza form is particularly significant for the communication of meaning in the condensed space afforded by the lyric or shorter poem, and Henryson's decisions about form are as carefully made as those of the technically brilliant and prolific Scots writer of the short poem, Dunbar. For example, Henryson's Annunciation poem, 'Forcy as deith is likand lufe', uses a complex form to mirror its elevated subject matter. It is composed in a twelve-line stanza with a tight rhyme scheme using only two rhymes (*ababbaabbaab*), and alternating lines of four and three stresses, similar to the twelve-line stanza used by Dunbar in his celebrated poem on the same subject, 'Hail Sterne Superne'.[14] One of the striking things about Henryson's poem, however, is that its complex stanza form is not matched by elevated diction and imagery, and the contrast between metrical ingenuity and a kind of lexical 'plain style' is a profound expression of the incarnation itself, a meeting of the divine and the human. So although Henryson's poem is a reworking of a Latin original, it does not over-use Latinate vocabulary or deploy the sorts of clever coinages characteristic, for example, of Dunbar's Annunciation poem which it resembles in stanza form. In Henryson's poem, Mary is a 'princes pure with-outyn peir' (27) and a 'quene' (72), but she is also presented in her humble role as handmaiden: she is simply that 'myld' (13; *the gentle one*). This noun carries the 'a' rhyme for the stanza, neatly encapsulating the key ideas of incarnation: the gentle Mary is 'a maid infild' (15) by God's word because she is 'fra syn exild' (18; *without sin*), unquestioningly obedient ('na thing begild', 22) to God's grace, and so her body offers the perfect chamber for her 'child' (23), Christ. The simple diction continues: she is 'that gay' (21; *the beautiful one*), 'that may maid moder suete' (47), and later a 'lady lele and lusumest' (61; *loyal and most lovable*, translating the Latin *domina dulcissima*), and 'blosum blith and bowsumest' (63;

---

[12] Compare David Lyndsay's *The Testament of the Papyngo*, line 19 where 'Mersar' appears in a list of poets with 'Henderson' (Henryson). See Hadley Williams (ed.), *Sir David Lyndsay*, 58. There are three 'ballatis of lufe' attributed to him in the Bannatyne Manuscript.

[13] See 'lyfly *adv.*', *Dictionary of the Scots Language* (Glasgow, 2004).

[14] See Bawcutt (ed.), *Poems of William Dunbar*, 1.83–5.

pleasant blossom and most obedient, for *mater clementissima*). Henryson's startling imagery is entirely his own and is combined with powerful alliterative patterns, and idiomatic collocations.[15] Thus, Gabriel tells Mary that God '... will tak rest and rufe' (10) in her, 'rufe' here meaning 'repose' but also playing on the use of 'ruf' to mean 'shelter'.[16] The Latin is adapted to describe God's love as a river of miracles: 'The miraclis ar mekle and meit (*many and great*) / Fra luffis ryuer rynnnis' (37–8).

For his short moral or admonitory poems, Henryson favours a popular eight-line ballade stanza, *ababbcbC*4, of the sort that his contemporaries would have recognized as highly suitable for sententious subjects.[17] In 'Allone as I went vp and doun' (*The Abbey Walk*) the narrator ponders a text about worldly transience that he finds 'writtin vpoun a wall' (6).[18] 'Wythin a garth, vnder a rede rosere' (*In Praise of Age*) is also a poem about worldly 'variance' (9), and is composed in a similar form, though with decasyllabic rather than octosyllabic lines (*ababbcbC*5). The same stanza form is used for 'O Eterne God of power infinyt' (*Ane Prayer for the Pest*), an extended penitential work; and for the two moral debate poems, *The Ressoning betuix Aige and Yowth* and *The Ressoning betuix Deth and Man*.

The precise moral instruction offered in Henryson's allegorical poem 'Wald my gud lady lufe me best' (*The Garmont (Garment) of Gud Ladies*) is well suited to its simple quatrain form (*a*4*b*3*a*4*b*3): each stanza focuses on one or two items of the lady's attire and the moral virtue(s) represented. The poem starts with the lady's 'hud' (*hood*) adorned with 'gouirnance so gud' (5–7), and moves on to consider her 'sark' (9; *shirt*), 'kirtill' (13; *dress*), and 'gown' (17), and even her neck ribbons and gloves. The patriarchal voice of the opening of the poem, 'Wald my gud lady lufe me best / And wirk eftir my will ...' (*If my good lady would love me best and behave according to my desires* ...), and the minute focus on the lady's body, is a combination likely to be an uncomfortable one for modern readers. However, the poem's diction sits ambiguously between the secular and religious, with every attribute represented by the clothing, even 'renowne' (18; *reputation*) and 'rewth' (28; *pity*), being as appropriate to the soul, perfectly chaste and humble, as to the idealized lady of love poetry.

Henryson's version of the popular 'Christ the Lover Knight' fable is more sophisticated in form than *The Garmont of Gud Ladies* but again shows a careful harnessing of form to subject matter and to the devotional exercise it encourages. It is composed in eight-line tail-rhyme stanzas, which, along with the poem's formulaic phrasing is, as Fox notes, 'characteristic of Scots Ballads'.[19] Indeed, Henryson uses the same form for his comic dialogue in the *pastourelle* tradition, *Robene and Makyne*. The poem offers a 'romance' narrative of the beautiful heir of a powerful king who is abducted by a hideous giant ('a fowll gyane', 18); she is rescued by a 'worthy prince that had no peir' (45) who is mortally wounded in the battle to free her. Henryson's poem is distinguished from many other versions of the story by its refusal to attribute any blame to the lady for her capture by the giant, or to indicate any tardiness in her response to the knight who claims her. Rather, the narrator offers vivid details of the giant's abhorrent form ('His nailis wes lyk ane hellis cruk (*hook*)', 27), and the lady's affecting dialogue with her knight (67–80). Her complaint, or 'mone' (65), leaves us with no doubt about her love for her rescuer, and her obedience to the knight's request

---

[15] A. A. MacDonald, 'The Latin Origins of Robert Henryson's Annunciation Lyric', in MacDonald et al. (eds), *The Renaissance in Scotland*, 45–65.

[16] The phrase 'roif and rest' also appears in *Robene and Makyne*, 49.

[17] See Bawcutt (ed.), *Poems of William Dunbar*, 2.301–2.

[18] For a Middle English version of the poem in the Vernon Manuscript, see 'By a way wandryng as I went', in Carleton Brown (ed.), rev. G. V. Smithers, *Religious Lyrics of the XIVth Century* (Oxford, 1952), 157.

[19] See Fox (ed.), *Poems*, 438.

that she keeps his bloody shirt to remind her of his sacrifice. Rhiannon Purdie has pointed out that 'Tail-rhyme, with its strong pious associations may ... have been used to temper or even redirect an audience's reception of a poem which was otherwise quite recognisably a romance'.[20] In Henryson's poem, though, the redirection is subtle and only formalized late in the text. The fact that the poem is a *contrafactum*, a sacred reinterpretation of a secular story, is made explicit in its final stanza, which likens the lady's love to our own obligations to God, and in the formal three-stanza *moralitas* which follows.[21]

The use of the same tail-rhyme stanza form as *The Bludy Serk* in *Robene and Makyne* is also part of the way in which Henryson shifts his reader's expectations. This poem is a moralized take on both the *pastourelle*, a form which usually concerned the attempted seduction and betrayal of a girl by her social superior, and on the comic genre of the 'peasant wooing'.[22] In Henryson's poem, however, the maiden, Makyne, is the wooer, fixing her affections on a reluctant shepherd. The poem's comedy is subtle: Robene's rejection of Makyne's amorous advances because he has to tend his sheep is dully dutiful. Her passionate wooing is humorously couched in instructional diction: she offers 'reid' (34; *advice*) and recommends that he learns an 'A B C' (18) in 'luivs lair' (17; *the school of love*), as she offers her 'hairt all haill, / Eik and [her] maidinheid' (35–6). When Robene eventually changes his mind, he finds that Makyne has become pious and a source of proverbial wisdom, rather than amatory advice. She dismisses his advances, reminding him that he made 'play' (109) of her pain, and determines to 'mend' (112) her ways. The poem rescues the seduced and abandoned maiden of the *pastourelle* by turning her into an exemplum—not unlike Henryson's Cresseid, as we shall see—of moral growth.

The Annunciation poem shows Henryson's engagement with a Latinate devotional tradition, while *The Bludy Serk*, *The Abbey Walk*, and *Robene and Makyne* belong to vernacular genres or rework insular sources. Of a more regional character though is Henryson's use of alliterative traditions often associated with (though not completely confined to) the North West Midlands, the North of England, and Scotland.[23] The medical burlesque, *Sum Practysis of Medecyne*, may take its parodic theme from French and English dramatic analogues, but it specifically uses the thirteen-line stanza with its alliterative long lines, each containing three alliterating stressed syllables, with a wheel (*ababababcdddc*), which was employed by other Older Scots poets of comic poetry and flytings.[24] The comedy of Henryson's dramatic monologue is generated by its scatology, obscure diction, and imagery, and the barrage of sound which emerges from the alliterative lists in which the improbable and unappealing medical remedies for a range of ailments are assembled. In

---

[20] Rhiannon Purdie, *Anglicising Romance: The Tail-Rhyme and Genre in Medieval English Literature* (Cambridge, 2008), 6.

[21] The poem appears in the Bannatyne Manuscript, with *Orpheus and Eurydice* and some of *The Morall Fabillis*, with a marginal gloss describing it as 'Fable VII'. See Fox and Ringler (intro.), *The Bannatyne Manuscript*.

[22] See Evelyn S. Newlyn, 'Tradition and Transformation in the poetry of Robert Henryson', *Studies in Scottish Literature*, 18 (1983), 33–58; Alessandra Petrina, 'Deviations from Genre in Robert Henryson's "Robene and Makyne"', *Studies in Scottish Literature*, 31 (1999), 107–20.

[23] See Thorlac Turville-Petre, *Description and Narrative in Middle English Alliterative Poetry* (Liverpool, 2018), 1–2.

[24] See Nicola Royan, 'The Alliterative Awntyrs Stanza in Older Scots Verse', in J. A. Burrow and Hoyt N. Duggan (eds), *Medieval Alliterative Poetry: Essays in Honour of Thorlac Turville-Petre* (Dublin, 2010), 185–94; Andrew W. Kline, 'Scots Take the Wheel: The Problem of Period and the Medieval Scots Alliterative Thirteen-Line Stanza', *Studies in Scottish Literature*, 43 (2017), 15–21. Also see Denton Fox, 'Henryson's "Sum Practysis of Medecyne"', *Studies in Philology*, 69 (1972), 453–60.

this example, a few plausible ingredients (bile and stale urine) are combined with the thoroughly bizarre (a goose's clucking and a drake's penis):

> *Recipe* thre ruggis of the reid ruke,
> The gant of ane gray meir, the claik of ane gus,
> The dram of ane drekters, the douk of ane duke,
> The gaw of ane grene dow, the leg of ane lows,
> Fyve vnce of ane fle wing, the fyn of ane fluke,
> With ane sleiffull of slak that growis in the slus ...
>
> (40–5)

(*Take* three tugs of the red rook, the yawn of a grey mare, the cry of a goose, the dram of a drake's penis, the cluck of a duck; the bile of a young dove, the leg of a louse, five ounces of a fly's wing, the fin of a flounder, with a sleeve full of algae that grows in the mire ...)

This remedy is entitled 'Dia longum' and is a bath for the testicles ('ba cod', 49)—an aphrodisiac—which is designed to prevent the patient from sleeping.[25]

The four stanzas of the poem which contain the remedies are each carefully structured. The list of ingredients occupies the first seven or eight lines of the stanza, and is followed by some instructions on the preparation and application of the mixture. The wheel to each stanza, with its distinct rhyming pattern, sums up the efficacy of the drug. The end of the last wheel is comically appropriate, parodying the proverb 'A mirk mirror is a manes minde',[26] to underscore the obscurity of the text and uselessness of its recommended concoctions: 'It is ane mirk mirrour / Ane vthir manis ers' (90–1; *Another man's arse is a cloudy mirror*).

Even alliteration which is used for ornamental ends or for emphasis in Henryson's verse (so-called stylistic alliteration) can be so pronounced as to approach the sort of structural alliteration evidenced in *Sum Practysis*. In *The Ressoning Betuix Aige and Yowth*, much of the diction belongs to the tradition of alliterative verse. Phrases such as 'firth and feildis' (2; *wood and fields*), or 'stark and sterne' (59; *strong and resolute*) are well-attested alliterative collocations; others, such as 'grvme on grund' (21), 'berly berne' (57), are common alliterative variations on 'man'. This passage shows the use of three more alliterative synonyms—'senȝour', 'bairne', and 'freik on fold':

> This senȝeour sang, bot with a sobir stevin;
> Schakand his berd, he said, 'My bairne, lat be.
> I wes within thir sexty ȝeiris and sevin
> Ane freik on fold bayth frak, forsy and fre;
> Als glad, als gay, als ȝung, als ȝaip as ȝe'.
>
> (25–9)

(This man sang, but with a sober voice; shaking his beard, he said, 'My son, let it be. I was under the age of sixty-seven, a man active, strong and noble; as good, as happy, as young, as eager as you'.)

---

[25] Fox, 'Henryson's 'Sum Practysis of Medecyne', 459.
[26] E. Beveridge (ed.), *Fergusson's Scottish Proverbs from the Original Print of 1641 together with a larger MS collection of about the same period, hitherto unpublished*, STS, 2nd series, 15 (Edinburgh, 1942), proverb 70.

Form and Style in the Longer Poems

Metrical and stylistic ingenuity also characterize Henryson's longer poems, *The Morall Fabillis*, *The Testament of Cresseid*, and *Orpheus and Eurydice*. These narrative works are composed mainly in a seven-line rhyme royal stanza ultimately derived from Chaucer's poetry and a fashionable staple of fifteenth-century poets which testified to their knowledge and inheritance of the artistry of the great English master.[27] Henryson certainly knew the works of 'worthie Chaucer glorious' (*Testament*, 41), but his approach to them is sceptical and independent: as his narrator asks in *The Testament of Cresseid*, 'Quha wait gif (*knows if*) all that Chauceir wrait was trew?' (*Testament*, 64). While Chaucer used rhyme royal stanzas in poetry which dealt with moral, religious, and philosophical themes (for example *The Parliament of Fowls*, 'The Man of Law's Tale', and *Troilus and Criseyde*), Henryson responds to this impulse with his own innovations. As in other Older Scots poems, moments of significance, moral seriousness, or complaint, are marked in his poems by a shift from rhyme royal to a longer stanza.[28] For example, the *moralitas* (moralization) to the 'The Two Mice' is entirely in ballade form, and so metrically distinct from the fable: three eight-line stanzas, rhyming *ababbcbc*, with a partial refrain. In this second fable of the collection, the country mouse narrowly escapes the claws of Gib Hunter the Cat as she dines on 'Ane plait of grottis and ane disch full off meill' (282), rejecting the luxurious but dangerous world of her sister the 'burges mous' (342) for the simplicity of her own quiet existence.[29] The narrator of the *moralitas* is gentle to begin with, addressing his audience as 'Freindis' (365), but then introduces stern apostrophe ('O wantoun man', 381) to urge us to reject gluttony and turn to self-scrutiny and contentment with 'small possessioun' (372), a phrase repeated in the final line of each stanza.

The switch in stanza form from rhyme royal to ballade stanza is used again in the final fable of *The Morall Fabillis*, 'The Paddock and the Mouse', another narrative about greed. This fable is the bleakest of the collection. A 'lytill mous' (2778) trying to cross the river to reach food is deceived by the ugly and cunning 'paddock' (*toad*) who tries to drown her in a 'wretchit battell' in the water (2897). The struggling creatures are plucked from the river and eaten by a kite—a 'gredie gled' (2906), both the pitiable and the reprehensible meeting the same fate. The *moralitas* to this dark tale is distinguished by its opening address to 'My brother' (2910) which is made in three ballade stanzas (*ababbcbc*). The rhyme royal stanzas resume at line 2934 as the narrator interprets the fable's meaning, character by character, but the ballade section is closely focused on self-governance. Each of the three stanzas concludes with a partial refrain, repeating the word 'marrow' (2917, 2925, 2933; *friend*), and forms of the verb 'matche' (*associate*), to warn of the dangers of entering into association with untrustworthy people, particularly those who use deceptive language—'that speiks fairlie vnto the', with 'silkin toung' and 'ane hart of crueltie' (2921–2). The theme of duplicitous language, of those who use words for their own selfish or immoral ends,

---

[27] David Lawton, 'Dullness and the Fifteenth Century', *ELH*, 54 (1987), 761–99.

[28] For example, 'The Lay of Sorrow' and 'The Lufaris Complaynt' in BodL MS Arch. Selden. B. 24, where nine-line decasyllabic stanzas are twice replaced with a sixteenth-line stanza for moments of intense melancholy. See Kenneth G. Wilson (ed.), 'The Lay of Sorrow and the Lufaris Complaynt: An Edition', *Speculum*, 29 (1954), 709–26.

[29] On the fable's sources, see William Calin, 'Robert Henryson, Morall Fabillis', in *The Lily and the Thistle: The French Tradition and the Older Literature of Scotland* (Toronto, 2013), 84–102 (at 87).

is central to *The Morall Fabillis*: while in 'The Two Mice' the town mouse's comforting 'wordis hunny sweit' (315) are simply foolish, the paddock's are deliberately and cruelly obfuscating.

Henryson's use of different stanza forms in these two moralities should be understood in the context of a range of other hermeneutic strategies used in the morals to individual fables. Indeed, there are no rules or formulae for successfully decoding the moralities of Henryson's fables: his aim is to keep the audience interpretively alert through variety.[30] The strategies of the moralities include startling contradictions in the ways that recurring characters or details are explained, challenging re-readings of apparently obvious details in the narratives, and an ever-changing narratorial voice and presence. For example, the *moralitas* to 'The Fox and the Wolf' is surprisingly short and selective in the details it reinterprets—only the fox's conduct receives attention. In the gloss to 'The Trial of the Fox', the lion king is interpreted as the world, worshipped by those in power, but in 'The Lion and the Mouse' he is a king or emperor. The *moralitas* of 'The Sheep and the Dog' allows the oppressed protagonist of the narrative to reappear in the gloss and offer over twenty lines of complaint based on Psalm 44. The *moralitas* to the next fable, 'The Lion and the Mouse', remains part of the narrative, specifically of the narrator's vision, rather than a waking reflection on the significance of the dream.

Orpheus and Eurydice was copied into the Bannatyne Manuscript in a sequence of beast fables, indicating the scribe's attention to genre: the narrator invites the reader to view the classical narrative as a 'feynit fable' (416) and indeed the scribe writes in the margin that it is 'Fable VI', also penning '*Moralitas*' clearly above the gloss. Like the two of *The Morall Fabillis* just discussed, Henryson differentiates the *moralitas* from the narrative by varying its poetic form and thus giving additional emphasis to the strenuous and detailed re-reading of the foregoing narrative that it offers. Most of the *moralitas* is written in decasyllabic couplets, while much of the foregoing story (and the final two stanzas of the *moralitas*) is in rhyme royal. Based closely on Nicholas Trivet's Commentary on Boethius's *Consolation of Philosophy*, the morality explains the classical story as being concerned with the struggles between the 'part intellectiue / Of mannis saul and vnder-standing' and 'sensualitee' (428–30), reason and desire.[31] We have to understand Eurydice both as 'oure affection' (431), which is vulnerable to temptation, and 'gude vertewe (435)', which aspires to purity, 'Quhilk besy is ay to kepe oure myndis clene' (437). Orpheus is 'our ressoun' (610) capable of contemplation and virtue, but always vulnerable to the pull of worldly lust.

An important moment in the narrative itself is also marked by a change of stanza form—Orpheus's lament on the abduction of Eurydice by the 'quene of fary' (125). Here the rhyme royal stanzas are replaced by five ten-line stanzas (*aabaabbcbc*) which are described as 'sangis lamentable' (184). The longer stanzas enact the outpouring of sorrow and anger, pausing the narrative, and formalizing Orpheus's grief. As noted above, stylistic alliteration is a characteristic of Henryson's verse, and here it is used to give the metrically distinct

---

[30] Much attention has been paid to the matter of the tale-*moralitas* relationships in *The Morall Fabillis*. For example, Stephan Khinoy, 'Tale-Moral Relationships in Henryson's *Morall Fabillis*', *Studies in Scottish Literature*, 17 (1982), 99–115; Arnold Clayton Henderson, 'Having Fun with the Moralities: Henryson's Fables and Late Medieval Fable Innovation', *Studies in Scottish Literature*, 32 (2001), 67–87.

[31] See Ian Johnson, 'Reading Robert Henryson's *Orpheus and Eurydice*: Sentence and Sensibility', in Ian Johnson and Alessandra Petrina (eds), *The Impact of Latin Culture on Medieval and Early Modern Scottish Writing* (Kalamazoo, MI, 2018), 175–98; Thomas Rutledge, 'Robert Henryson's *Orpheus and Eurydice*; A Northern Humanism?', *Modern Language Review*, 38 (2002), 396–411; Alessandra Petrina, 'Robert Henryson's *Orpheus and Eurydice* and its Sources', *Fifteenth Century Studies*, 33 (2008), 198–217.

complaint added intensity. Other rhetorical devices cluster together in the additional space provided by the longer stanzas. Orpheus's apostrophe personifies his harp, and the final line of each of the longer stanzas forms an *ubi sunt* refrain. Here is the third of the ten-line stanzas, which dwells on this trope of loss in a passage of particularly dense alliteration, with the repetition of consonants sometimes extending over two lines:

> Fair weill, my place; fair weile, plesance and play;
> And welcome, woddis wyld and wilsome way,
> My wikit werd in wildernes to wair!
> My rob ryall and all my riche array,
> Changit sall be in rude russat of gray;
> My diademe in till ane hat of hair;
> My bed sall be with bever, broke, and bair,
> In buskis bene, with mony bustous bes
> Withoutin sang, sayng with siching sair,
> 'Quhar art thow gane, my luf Erudices?'
> (154–63)

(Farewell my residence, farewell pleasure and play; and welcome wild woods and lonely paths, my unfortunate lot to endure in the wilderness. My royal robe and my fine clothing will be exchanged for course grey cloth. My bed will be with the beaver, badger and bear, in the thicket's shelter with many violent beast, without song, saying with painful sighs, 'Where have you gone, my love, Eurydice.)

While Orpheus's complaint may elicit the reader's sympathy, it is introduced in such a way as to associate it with a dangerous lack of rationality. Before the complaint begins, Orpheus is said to be 'inflammit all in ire, / And rampand (*raging*) as ane lyoun ravenus' (120–1). His complaint ('mone') is made as in a state of near-madness—he is 'Half out of mynd ...' (129). His rampaging temper is evidence of his inability to control himself as the sorrow bursts out in complaint, and at the end of the narrative section of the poem we see him still drawing on the Chaucerian, even Petrarchan, language of love, in a state of dejected self-pity, unable understand the reason for his final loss of his queen: 'Quhat art thou lufe? How sall I thee dyffyne? / Bitter and suete, cruel and merciable' (401–2).

The practice of using a longer, distinctive stanza form for complaint, and to guide our response to that complaint, is found in *The Testament of Cresseid* too, as Cresseid bemoans the leprosy that has been inflicted on her as a divine punishment for her blasphemy and infidelity, 'In ane dark corner of the hous allone' (405). Once again rhyme royal gives way to longer stanzas of lament, this time composed in nine lines, using only two rhymes (*aabaaabbab*), across seven stanzas. As in Orpheus's complaint, apostrophe and extensive alliteration indicate the speaker's isolation, distress, and lack of reason. The rhetorical questioning and the *ubi sunt* convention are also used as Cresseid compares her present social isolation to her previous enjoyment of privilege and material pleasures, her high 'estatit' (437): 'Quhair is thy chalmer wantounlie besene (*luxuriously furnished*) ... ?' (416). Like Orpheus, Cresseid is preoccupied with her misfortunes ('wickit is thy weird', 412), rather than with recognizing her responsibility for them: the only lesson she is able to draw from her misery is that 'Fortoun is fikkill' (469). She is said to be 'chydand' (*arguing*) with 'hir drerie destenye' (470) just as Orpheus was 'chydand on with lufe' (413): the consistency of Henryson's moral lexis across his longer works is striking, as this small example indicates.

Description, Register, Rhetoric

Henryson is a master of different registers, from the idiomatic and the proverbial, to the learned and technical. He can move seamlessly form Orpheus's courtly appeal to Venus ('Wate ye noucht wele I am your avin trewe knycht?', 206) to the highly technical account of the music of the spheres heard by the poet as he embarks on his journey to find his queen. Specialist musicological diction distinguishes this heavenly music from that emitted by Orpheus's own 'dulfull' (134) harp, which does not comfort him for his loss. Orpheus's exposure to the music of the spheres is part of his relearning of harmony and proportion. These lines describe harmonic intervals, and draw on Pythagorean theories of music, derived from Macrobius.[32]

> Thare lerit he tonys proportionate,
> As duplar, triplar, and epetritus;
> ...
> And of thir sex, suete and dilicius,
> Ryght consonant, fyve hevynly symphonyis
> Componyt ar, as clerkis can deuise.
> (226–32)

(There he learnt the proportionate tones such as the duplar, triplar and epitritus ... and of these six, sweet and delicious, [and] very harmonious, five heavenly symphonies are composed, as scholars describe.)

Henryson has also been praised for the 'iconographical richness' of his descriptions.[33] Rhetoricians favoured descriptive set pieces that focused on people, time, and place and *The Morall Fabillis* is punctuated by several structurally significant descriptive episodes on these themes.[34] The 'Parliament of Animals' which assembles before the 'wild lyoun' (878) king in the fifth fable, 'The Trial of the Fox', is one such example. This passage (887–921) is a catalogue drawing on bestiaries and heraldic treatises. Alliteration and internal rhyme ('The da, the ra, the hornit hart, the hynd', 900) bind the lists of creatures as the immense and fantastical (the 'warwolff, and the pegase perilous', 889) are brought together with the small and familiar from the Scottish farmyard and landscape ('The gukit gait (*goat*), the selie scheip, the swyne', 905), The episode serves to introduce the lion king, who will, by the central fable, become the focus for Henryson's exploration of justice: its combination of the strange and the familiar, the noble heraldic beast and the lowly blind 'mowdewart' (915; *mole*), mirrors the fable's perennial and yet highly topical themes about the corruption of justice and abuse of the weak.

Further descriptive passages mark out the importance of 'The Lion and the Mouse' in the collection. The prologue to this central fable (and it is the only one to have its own prologue) contains both a description of a burgeoning June landscape from the framing

---

[32] This passage has received much comment. See for example, John MacQueen, *Complete and Full with Numbers: The Narrative Poetry of Robert Henryson* (Amsterdam, 2006), 255–60.
[33] Priscilla Bawcutt, 'Henryson's "Poeit of the Auld Fassoun"', *Review of English Studies*, n.s. 32 (1981), 429–34 (at 429). On this passage also see Jill Mann, 'Chaucer, Henryson and the Planetary Deities', in Ruth Morse and Barry Windeatt (eds), Chaucer Traditions: Studies in Honour of Derek Brewer (Cambridge, 1990), 91–106.
[34] James Goldstein, 'Vernacular Eloquence: reading Older Poetry Rhetorically', in his *The English Lyric Tradition: Reading Poetic Masterpieces of the Middle Ages and Renaissance* (North Carolina, 2018), 10–40; Turville-Petre, *Description and Narrative*, 16.

devices of the French *chanson d' aventure* and the description of the attire and demeanour of the authority figure.[35] The latter is 'maister Esope, poet lawriate' (1377) whose presence allows Henryson to introduce a debate on the value and purpose of poetry into the collection. The *chanson d'aventure* opening is also echoed in the opening to the next fable, 'The Preaching of the Swallow', where it is preceded by a rumination on divine providence and creation. This descriptive passage serves to show the contrast between the imperfect royal justice exposed in 'The Trial of the Fox', 'The Sheep and the Dog' and 'The Lion and the Mouse' with the 'profound wit off God omnipotent' (1623). God's perfection is impossible to comprehend for 'mannis saull ... febill and ouer small' (1644), but some inkling of it is communicated through the wonders of creation:

> 3yt neuertheles we may haif knawlegeing
> Off God almychtie be his creatouris,
> That he is gude, fair, wyis and bening.
> (1650–1)

(Yet nevertheless we may gain knowledge of Almighty God, that he is good, beautiful, wise and benign, through his creations.)

From the firmament and planets 'makand harmonie and sound' (1660), to the fish and fowl, creation demonstrates God's benignity. Each season is described in one rhyme royal stanza, except for winter, which is ominously accorded twice the space given to other times of year: the description of winter's severe weather anticipates the dark ending to the fable. The 'wickit' (*cruel*) winds have 'to-rent and reuin (*torn*) in pecis small' the 'garment' of summer (1694–5); the birds change their song to 'murning' and are 'neir slane' with cold (1697–8); the dales are 'drounit' (1699) with puddles; animals withdraw to their burrows 'for dreid' (1704). In the space of five stanzas the whole cycle of the year turns until we are back to the spring where the narrator embarks on his woodland walk, marvelling at the industrious labourers in the fields and listening to bird song. The cycle is again repeated in the course of the fable, as the birds, observed by the narrator, watch the sowing of hemp seed in spring, and repeatedly fail to take the swallow's advice first to eat the seed, then seedlings, to prevent the nets being made. In autumn the fowler harvests his crop and his wife spins the lint into threads for net making. Then, 'The wynter come, the wickit wind can blaw' (1832), and the 'famischit' (1867) birds are caught as they scratch around for food and bludgeoned to death.

Amongst the most memorable uses of description in Henryson's poetry is his portrayal of the planetary deities in *The Testament of Cresseid*. Appearances, clothes, gestures, and objects are used to delineate each threatening presence in a way that presages the sentence they pass on the accused. Saturn's face is a study in frosty old age, wrinkled ('fronsit', 155), leaden in colour, nose dripping, lips blue, voice hoarse, as defaced as Cresseid's will become by the leprosy ('spottis blak', 339) bestowed on her by Cynthia's 'bill' (332). The ireful Mars is depicted waving a 'roustie sword' (188), his face 'Wrything' (189) in anger, 'reid' ... 'with grislie glowrand ene' (191). Venus's appearance merits the longest description: she comes to the parliament for two reasons—both 'Hir sonnis querrell for to defend, and mak / Hir awain complaint' (219–20). She is Fortune-like,

---

[35] The *chanson d' aventure* typically depicted a narrator walking in a spring landscape. See P. E. Bennett, 'Chansons de Geste and Chansons d'aventures: Recent Perspectives on the Evolution of a Genre', *French Studies*, 66 (2012), 525–35.

> ... cled in ane nyce array,
> The ane half grene, the vther half sabill blak,
> With hair as gold kemmit and sched abak;
> Bot in hir face semit greit variance,
> Quhyles perfyte treuth and quhyles inconstance.
>
> Vnder smyling scho was dissimulait,
> Prouocatiue with blenkis amorous,
> And suddanely changit and alterait,
> Angrie as ony serpent vennemous ...
>   (220–8)

(... dressed in extravagant clothing, one half green, the other black as sable; with golden hair combed and pushed back; but in her face there seemed to be great variance, sometimes perfect truth and sometimes inconstancy. Under her smiles she was dissimulating, provocative with amorous blinking, and suddenly changed and altered, as angry as a venomous serpent.)

Her parti-coloured clothes reflect the opposing hews of youth and mourning; her enigmatic face and shifting expressions, which encourage 'lust' (her glances, 'Prouocatiue with blenkis amorous'), are recalled in Troylus's erotic memory of Cresseid's own 'amorous blenking' (503). Like the hungry mouse in 'The Paddock of the Mouse' who understood the significance of the toad's ugly 'fronsit face' and 'runkillit (*wrinkled*) cheikis' (2819–20) we need to read the details of these faces correctly. Unlike the mouse, we need to act on our readings.

Poet and Reader

Amongst the planets in the *Testament* is Mercury, depicted as a writer, reporting and performing, giving merriment to others, and bookishly rehearsing approved rhetorical strategies in so doing.[36]

> With buik in hand than come Mercurius,
> Richt eloquent and full of rethorie,
> With polite termis and delicious,
> With pen and ink to report all reddie,
> Setting sangis and singand merilie
>   (239–44)

(Then with book in hand came Mercy, very eloquent and full of rhetoric, with polished and delightful words, with pen and ink ready to write, composing songs and singing merrily.)

Mercury is pointedly referred to as 'Lyke to ane poeit of the auld fassoun' (245), a poet of the past. Exactly how Henryson saw his own role as a poet in relation to tradition is the subject of the Prologue to *The Morall Fabillis* which contains his most extensive discussion of the

---

[36] For an interpretation of Mercury's headgear and its possible association with the Crown of Laurels, see Bawcutt, 'Henryson's "Poeit of the Auld Fassoun"'.

nature and value of poetry, and of the relationship between poet and audience. Although at first glance its succession of metaphors and similitudes is conventional, closer attention shows that it is also taxing, providing an introduction both to the collection and to the way we are to read it, sorting through interpretive complexities, our judgement swayed and expectations often confounded.[37] Sally Mapstone has pointed out that 'Henryson's poetry actively engages the reader in the formation of the reading experience and in the interpretive act of reading correctly'.[38] This involvement is demanding of even the most agile mind. The prologue opens with the narrator defending the value of 'fein3eit (*invented*) fabils of ald poetre' (1). These fables, he explains, are not 'grunded vpon truth' (2) but nevertheless give pleasure to their audience. The adjectives are drawn from traditional discussions of 'rhetore' (3; *rhetoric*) and most immediately echo the prologue to the fables of Gualterus Anglicus: fables offer pleasure because—like Mercury's books in the *Testament*—they are written in polished (2; *polite*) and 'sweit' (*delectable*) words or 'termes' (3). However, the use of 'fein3eit' in the opening line of the prologue is unsettling. The collocation 'fein3eit fabils' is conventional, and it at first merely draws attention to the entertaining imaginary worlds of poetry. But later in the collection 'fein3eit' takes on the sense of dangerous dissimulation. As the fox, a master of rhetoric himself, attempts to flatter the cock in the second fable, the narrator describes him as 'This fen3eit foxe, fals and dissimulate' (460); the deceitful paddock of the last fable, also a master of specious language, is described as a 'fein3eit' friend (2925). In the prologue to 'The Lion and The Mouse', Aesop, 'poet lawriate' (1377), asks the narrator, '... quhat is it worth to tell ane fein3eit taill,/ Quhen haly preiching may na thing auaill?' (1389–90). The use of 'fein3eit' to describe any kind of utterance is troubling elsewhere in Older Scots poetry. For example, in Dunbar's 'Off Februar the fyiftene nycht', the personification of 'Invy' (*Envy*) is said to be the leader of flatterers, backbiters and liars: he presides over 'mony freik dissymlit / With fein3eit wirdis quhyte' (47; *many dissimulating individuals with feigned fair-seeming words*), including those that frequent the courts of kings.[39]

The first stanza of the Prologue continues to challenge our expectations. The promise that fictional fables will bring pleasure is followed by a stern reprimand in the stanza's last couplet: fables were invented to admonish as much as entertain—'to repreif (*reprove*) the of thi misleuing' (6). The rest of the prologue encourages caution further through a series of rhetorical twists and turns. After the promise of pleasure, the next figure used in the prologue explains that reading poetry is actually rather difficult. It is like a rough ('bustious') ground, which has to be worked before it will yield a nourishing crop.[40] It is the reader, not the poet, who has to take on the role of labourer trying to get a harvest from his reading:

> In lyke maner as throw a bustious eird,
> Swa it be laubourit with grit diligence,
> Springis the flouris and the corne abreird,

---

[37] The Prologue's theme of interpretation has long been appreciated. See for example, Gregory Kratzmann, 'The Poetics of the "Feinyeit Fabill": Chaucer and the Middle Scots Poets', in R. S. D. Jack and Kevin McGinley (eds), *Of Lion and Of Unicorn: Essays on Anglo-Scottish Literary Relations in Honour of Professor John MacQueen* (1993), 16–38. Also see James Simpson, '"And That Was Litel Nede': Poetry's Need in Robert Henryson's *Fables* and *Testament of Cresseid*", in Christopher Cannon and Maura Nolan (eds), *Medieval Latin and Middle English Literature: Essays in Honour of Jill Mann* (Woodbridge, 2011), 193–21.

[38] Mapstone, 'Robert Henryson', 245.

[39] Compare Fortune's 'fein3eit' face' in David Lyndsay's *Testament of the Papyngo*, line 195.

[40] DOST cites Henryson's poem as evidence for the sense 'fertile'. Fox disagrees. See 'bustuous *adj.*', *Dictionary of the Scots Language*; Fox, *Poems*, 189.

> Hailsum and gude to mannis sustenence;
> Sa springis thair ane morall sweit sentence
> Oute of the subtell dyte of poetry,
> To gude purpois, quha culd it weill apply.
>   (8–14)

(Just as through a rough ground, if it is worked with care, springs the flowers and corn in young shoots, wholesome and beneficial for man's sustenance, so there springs a sweet moral meaning out of the subtle style of poetry, for good ends, whoever can apply it well.)

The adjective 'sweit', used here of the 'sentence' or meaning of poetry, links the stanza to the first stanza, where it is the artistry of the fable rather than its truth value that was 'sweit'. The Latinate quality of 'diligence' is more appropriate to mental than physical or agricultural exertion. The adjective 'subtell', applied to the 'dyte of poetry', and has connotations of the hidden and difficult and we also learn that the goodness of the poetry really emerges in the way in which the reader responds to it.

The next stanza continues with the traditional imagery of nourishment, the sentence of poetry being like wholesome food. The adjective 'sueit' reappears, again describing the meaning to be found in poetry, not the poet's rhetorical art. The simile of the nut, with its 'hard and teuch' shell (15) which has to be broken to reach the edible kernel within, echoes the idea of the rough ground which has to be broken in order to bring forth crops. The image is an ancient one,[41] and well suited to Henryson's purpose here: it also foreshadows the themes of the second fable, 'The Two Mice', where simple nuts and peas carefully stored prove to be more sustaining than the abundant food of the town mouse.

However, having spent ten lines exhorting the reader to diligence in pursuit of hidden and valuable meanings, Henryson's narrator takes a different course again reminding us that serious subjects, as his sources had stated, are best combined with humour. Instead of work we are encouraged to find ways of amusing ourselves: 'And clerkis sayis, it is richt profitabill / Amangis ernist to ming ane merie sport' (18–19). The following stanza introduces a new image, that of the bow which is always bent growing slack ('vnsmart', 23) to describe the mind that is always studying becoming dulled with the effort. Where in stanza 2 'diligence' (9) was encouraged, now the 'diligent' (24) mind is in danger of missing the point. Yet, later in the fables levity can have disastrous consequences. In 'The Wolf and the Wether' the young sheep disguises himself as a dog in order to defend his flock; when his pretence is discovered by the wolf, it is cast as 'bourding in ernist' (2560), a joke made in seriousness. He attempts to excuse himself by playing down the 'earnest' ('I bot playit, be gracious me till', 2577) and is doubly condemned. He is eaten for his trouble, and the narrator glosses his conduct as presumption, showing a lack of self-knowledge.

The next contradiction of the Prologue comes in the form of an apparently conventional modesty topos. Where previously the sweet terms of rhetoric had been recommended as the way to convey and discover sweet moral sentence, now the narrator claims not to be able to write in the way he had celebrated as so profitable. Indeed, his 'translatioun' (32) is to be composed in unsophisticated or 'hamelie language' and 'termes rude' (36) because of his failure to comprehend 'eloquence' and 'rethorike' (37–8), those qualities described at the start of the prologue as so important to poetry's moral efficacy. This disclaimer is comic, particularly as it is immediately followed by a passage of dense Latinate diction

---

[41] Fox (ed.), *Poems*, 190.

(39–49). However, it is yet another of the narrator's challenging, and now familiar, changes in direction which prove to be training for our reading of the fables to follow.

The ensuing fables constantly revisit the meta-literary language of the prologue to make the reader highly conscious of his or her act of interpretation. For example, in the *moralitas* to 'The Cock and the Fox' we are reminded that fables are 'ouerhellit with typis figurall' (*covered with figurative forms*), and the 'sentence' lies 'Vndir thir fenʒeit termis textuall' (586–9). The *moralitas* to 'The Trial of the Fox' uses a common metaphor for understanding the processes of getting the value from poetry:

> Richt as the mynour in his minorall
> Fair gold with fyre may fra the leid weill wyn.
> Richt so vnder ane fabill figurall
> Sad sentence men may seik, and efter fyne,
> As daylie dois the doctouris of deuyne,
> That to our leuing full weill can apply
> And paynt thair mater furth be poetry.
> (1097–1103)

(Just as the miner of ore may win fine gold from lead by the means of fire, so under the figurative fable, men can seek and afterwards find a serious meaning, as doctors of divinity do daily, which can be applied to our way of living, and their substance can be depicted by means of poetry.)

This image considerably increases the stakes set out in the Prologue with its rough earth to plough and nuts to crack. The process of finding profound meaning in a text is as demanding as extracting a precious metal from ore: the reader of fables and writers of poetry alike are elevated here to the status of the 'doctouris of deuyne', scholars who employ exegesis to fully understand the significance of biblical texts.

In addition to this, the individual narratives repeatedly show us the benefit of exercising caution in our approach to texts, appreciating their power and unpredictability. In some of the more optimistic moments in the collection, texts offer correction to the unwise, sometimes in comically literal ways. In the 'Trial of the Fox', the fox is sent by the lion king to bring the old mare to the parliament of beasts. When the fox arrives, accompanied by the wolf, the mare tells him that she has a year-long 'respite' from attending sessions (1009), which he is then invited to read. A 'respite' is both a privilege granted under royal prerogative, and specifically the text that sets this out, which is how it is imagined here.[42] The document is, the mare informs her visitors, 'vnder my hude, weill hid' (1018). The fox, always more cunning than his fable rival, protests that he cannot 'spell' (*read*), but that the wolf can. The wolf 'blindit with pryde' at Lowrence's description of him as 'ane nobill clerk' (1011), stoops to read the respite and is rewarded with a hoof in the head. When the mare asks Lowrence to 'luke on my letter' (1027) he is wise enough to refuse. The mare's letter is not given any attention in the *moralitas* to this fable, which is one of the most perplexing of the collection, deliberately inverting its sources to represent the lion as the world, the wolf as sensuality, the fox as temptations, and the mare as the religious who remove themselves from the world in penance and contemplation. But in the fable itself we see a powerful instance of the text subduing the proud. What it does not do, of course, is have any effect

---

[42] See 'respit *n.*', *Dictionary of the Scots Language*.

on the behaviour of the fox who is soon found eating the fattest of a 'trip off lambis' (1044) on his way back to the parliament.

There are repeated examples in *The Morall Fabillis* of authoritative texts failing to have their desired effect on their intended audience. While the shared wisdom of the proverb may sometimes be reliable, proverbs are equally likely to be manipulated to serve self-interest. For example, the toad in 'The Paddock and Mouse' who deceptively counters the mouse's Latin proverb with his own vernacular one as she correctly reads its ugly and dangerous 'fronsit' (2819) face: '"Thow suld not iuge ane man efter is face"' (2839). Even more troubling is the misappropriation of biblical text and methods of preaching based on them. We are prepared for this by Aesop's pessimism about preaching in 'The Lion and the Mouse' and by the Swallow's failed efforts to warn the birds with her 'helthsum document' (1769) which is delivered with all the rhetorical methods of sermonizing: she cites her authorities ('clerkis sayis', 1755), appeals to her audience, exhorts with apostrophe, imperatives, and proverbs in five separate appeals to the birds across the year, but fails to gain their attention.

In the penultimate fable, 'The Wolf and the Lamb', we have a particularly bleak example of the abuse of biblical text. In this narrative, the 'selie lamb' (2637), is accused by the Wolf of contaminating a stream by drinking from it. He attempts to convince the Wolf that the 'accusation / failȝeis fra treuth and contrair is to ressoun' (2642–3) only to receive an additional charge based on the crimes his father supposedly committed. The lamb responds by reminding the Wolf of 'quhat Halie Scripture sayis / Endytit with the mouth off God almycht' (2665), recalling Ezekiel 18. The Wolf counters this with another Old Testament text, Exodus 20.5: 'I am the Lord thy God, mighty, jealous, visiting the iniquity of the fathers upon the children ...' (2671–7). His usurping of the voice of God immediately reveals his own sinfulness, and attentive readers might additionally be able to counter his use of the text with other teachings from the Old Testament (for example, Deuteronomy 24.16) which confirm the lamb's position. Nevertheless, the lamb is decapitated, his pitiful bleating being the last we hear of him.

If *The Morall Fabillis* draws attention to the difficulties of using different kinds of texts in the way their author intended, and to the text's vulnerability to misappropriation, the question remains as to whether poetry is exempt from this kind of misuse, at the top of a hierarchy of texts because of its ability to shape the reader, through its combination of earnest and game as modelled in the Prologue, into an attentive audience. This question is never satisfactorily answered in the fables, but we cling on, like the narrator of 'The Lion and the Mouse', to the fact that fables are 'morall' (1401) and though 'thay fenȝeit be, / Ar full of prudence and moralitie' (1380–1). The fables leave us with the strong impression that even if texts can be misused, readers may yet learn to be nimble enough to negotiate these misappropriations in order to find profound meaning.

The emphasis on skilful reading in *The Morall Fabillis* dominates *The Testament of Cresseid*. The opening of the *Testament* is well-known for its questioning of literary truth, as the narrator juxtaposes the accounts of 'ane quair ... / Writtin be worthie Chaucer' (40–41) and 'ane vther quair' which tells of Cresseid's 'fatall destenie' (61–2).[43] The end of the poem is equally significant in its meta-literary emphasis. It brings three textual moments together

---

[43] This moment has received much critical attention. Most recently see W. H. E. Sweet, 'The "Vther Quair" as the *Troy Book*. The Influence of Lydgate on Henryson's *Testament of Cresseid*', in Joanna Martin and Emily Wingfield (eds), *Premodern Scotland: Literature and Governance, 1420–1587. Essays for Sally Mapstone* (Oxford, 2017), 58–73.

to balance their opposing claims and allow the reader to form his or her own ethical judgement of the narrative's significance. The first 'text' is Cresseid's own testament through which she disposes of her body and remaining goods appropriately: 'with paper scho sat doun, / And on this maneir maid hir testament' (575–6). Her final bequest is of her spirit to Diana, who is to be recognized as the goddess of chastity as she is in Dunbar's *The Goldyn Targe*—'the goddesse chaste of woddis grene' (76). This bequest resonates with what we have witnessed of Cresseid's growing self-understanding in the succession of complaints she is given as Henryson returns to her the voice which has faded out of Chaucer's poem. The first of these complaints comes immediately after she wakes from her 'doolie dreame' (344) to discover her leprosy (lines 351–7) and laments the 'fraward langage' (352) of her blasphemy; the second formal complaint has been addressed above. The third comes after her meeting with Troylus and just before she composes her testament. It is marked out by a distinctive refrain in three of its rhyme royal stanzas, 'O fals Cresseid and trew knicht Troilus' (546, 553, 560), which summarizes Cresseid's rueful self-analysis and recognition of her inconstancy, and leads to her concluding statement of acceptance, 'Nane but myself as now I will accuse' (574). Where her long complaint was addressed to 'ladyis fair of Troy and Grece', this second complaint is addressed more generally to all 'Louers' (560) to be mindful of their conduct, stressing the importance of self-scrutiny and self-governance for all.

However, the next two textual moments position their audience specifically as female and read as much more limited accounts of the poem. The first of the pair is scripted by Troylus. It offers an interpretation of Cresseid which does not and cannot take account of her inner journey that we as readers have been privileged to witness. This text is the inscription on Cresseid's tomb:

> Sum said he maid ane tomb of merbell gray,
> And wrait hir name and superscriptioun,
> And laid it on hir graue quhair that scho lay,
> In goldin letteris, conteining this ressoun:
> 'Lo, fair ladyis, Cresseid of Troy the toun,
> Sumtyme countit the flour of womanheid,
> Vnder this stane, lait lipper, lyis deid.
>
> (602–9)

(Some said he made a tombstone of grey marble and placed it on her grave where she lay, and wrote her name and inscription on it in golden letters, with this lesson: 'Observe, fair ladies, Cresseid of the town of Tory, once regarded as the flower of femininity and lately a leper, lies dead under this stone.)

This affords Cresseid two identities which are entirely associated with her physical body—a once-beautiful woman and a leper. The lesson is specifically aimed at women but is not one of any profundity: female beauty is transitory. Troylus's personal interpretation of Cresseid's life is equally incomplete: 'Scho was vntrew, and wo is me thairfoir' (602). Our final text—the story itself—is presented by the narrator as of relevance only to 'worthie wemen' (610). It is described as a 'ballet schort' (610; *short poem*) that will admonish them and exhort them to good conduct. Like Troylus's epitaph, this text is an incomplete reading of Cresseid's experience and its significance.

As the ending of *The Testament of Cresseid* shows, Henryson is not a poet of straightforwardly didactic or instructional verse. He prefers, as here, to make us navigate multiple perspectives in order to exercise our own moral judgements and to distinguish between right and wrong, perhaps even to recognize that these categories are not absolute. He is deeply invested in the power of poetry to encourage us towards reading with discrimination. Poetry, like the music of Orpheus's harp, has the power to lead 'oure desire' to make peace with our 'reson', but it does not alone guarantee moral perfection. Both its creator and its audience might still be tempted to glance backwards in doubt and temptation.

CHAPTER 27
William Dunbar

Pamela M. King

Singling William Dunbar (1460?–1513 x 30) out for special treatment in a literary history of late medieval poetry in English is moderately contentious. Dunbar wrote not in Middle English but in Scots, a separate language, not simply an extreme dialect. Moreover, when Scots is treated as a linguistic entity, the period from the middle of the fifteenth century has been re-labelled 'Early Modern' in the trajectory from Old Northumbrian. Dunbar is accordingly now recognized as a Renaissance poet, on linguistic as well as cultural grounds.[1] His claim to be included in the present context, however, remains valid, as, although the term 'Scots Chaucerians' has long been abandoned, in the specific milieu in which he wrote he self-identifies as a heritor of Chaucer's work. Although older Scots culture can claim at least as much influence from other countries on the Continent as it can from England, the micro-cultural moment when Dunbar was writing was one of political rapprochement between England and Scotland, albeit precarious, because of the marriage between James IV of Scotland and Margaret Tudor, the English princess and daughter of Henry VII. 'Maister' William Dunbar, known to be in holy orders, is probably the man of that name who graduated from the University of St Andrews in 1479, suggesting that he was born around 1460. Nothing is known about his parentage, but it is surmised circumstantially that he was a lowlander. He does not enter public record until 1500, at which point his long service in the royal household of James IV commenced. Dunbar, like his near contemporary Gavin Douglas, is consequently part of the moment of Scottish history which was to end, as did their surviving writing, at the Battle of Flodden in 1513.[2] Dunbar uniquely has left 'vignettes of court life' of 'exaggerated clarity' from this fleeting moment. It is thought he died around 1520.[3]

We have not inherited a secure canon of Dunbar's work, nor any reliable chronology. His poetry seems to have been transmitted piecemeal, as the character of the eighty-four poems—often known by eighteenth and nineteenth-century titles—now accepted as the canon suggest.[4] The earliest surviving witnesses to any of his poems were printed in Edinburgh by Walter Chepman and Andrew Myllar in 1507–8 (STC 7347–9, 7350).[5] Others appear in the Aberdein Sasine Register (Aberdeen, City Charter Room, The Town

---

[1] The arguments are succinctly expressed in Joanna Kopaczyk, 'The Language of William Dunbar: Middle Scots or Early Modern Scots?' *European Journal of English Studies*, 18 (2014), 21–41.

[2] For further biographical detail see Denton Fox, 'The Chronology of William Dunbar', *Philological Quarterly*, 39 (1960), 413–25; Douglas Gray, 'William Dunbar', in M. C. Seymour (ed.), *Authors of the Middle Ages*, 3 (Aldershot, 1996), 179–94.

[3] Sally Mapstone, 'Was there a Court Literature in Fifteenth-Century Scotland?' *Studies in Scottish Literature*, 26 (1991), 410–22 (at 410).

[4] All eighty-four are published in the two-volume critical edition by Priscilla Bawcutt (ed.), *The Poems of William Dunbar*, 2 vols. (Glasgow, 1998). All citations in the present essay refer to this edition; poems are identified parenthetically in round brackets, followed when relevant by line numbers.

[5] Edinburgh. National Library of Scotland Sa.6 (1)–(11), digitized at https://digital.nls.uk, and see William Beattie (ed.), *The Chepman and Myllar Prints* (Edinburgh, 1950); Catherine van Buuren, 'The Chepman and Myllar Texts of Dunbar', in Sally Mapstone (ed.), *William Dunbar, 'The Nobill Poyet'* (East Linton, East Lothian, 2001), 24–39 (at 24).

House), the Asloan Manuscript (Edinburgh, National Library of Scotland, MS 16500, after 1513), but chiefly in the much later Bannatyne Manuscript (Edinburgh, National Library of Scotland, Advocates' MS 1. 1. 6, c1568) and the Maitland Folio (Cambridge, Magdalene College, Pepys Library, MS 2553, between 1570 and 1586).[6] Both of the latter are miscellanies of poetry. George Bannatyne, who copied over forty of Dunbar's poems into his large collection, groups all its contents according to generic categories, offering some insight into near-contemporary readings. The canon is, however, largely a product of later editions, beginning with the influential collection of older Scots verse published by Allan Ramsay in 1724, entitled *The Ever Green*.[7]

An imaginative opportunity for the historian and critic is to be found in the instability of the texts, and the difficulties they present to editors. The poems, mostly short, probably circulated initially on single sheets amongst coteries in the court of James IV. They had a material specificity, albeit friable by its nature, which enriches and informs their reading. All eighty-four cannot be done justice to in what follows. The subject matter includes devotional panegyric (nos. 1, 10, 16, 58), political satire and complaints on contemporary society (nos. 2, 11, 13, 20, 43, 55, 74, 75, 80), burlesque (nos. 3, 57, 70), invective against and tributes to contemporary individuals (nos. 4, 19, 23, 27, 29, 48, 56, 65, 72, 73, 76), petitions and compliments to the king, queen and other patrons (nos. 5, 9, 15, 22, 30, 36, 37, 54, 61, 62, 63, 64, 66, 67, 68, 79, 84), moral exhortation and excoriation (nos. 6, 12, 14, 17, 18, 21, 26, 31, 32, 41, 42, 44, 45, 46, 47, 49, 51, 53, 77, 78, 81, 82, 83), poems of love and the erotic (nos. 7, 24, 25, 34, 38, 40, 50, 69, 71), occasional poems (nos. 8, 28, 52, 59), as well as personal reflection on the inadequacy of the poet (no. 35). Yet so many of the poems manipulate, mix, or defy conventional categories; almost all are indissolubly of their moment. Here the aim is to discuss a selection of the best known alongside some that are less often attended to in detail, while giving some general view of the range of subject and style embodied in the whole.[8]

First some general observations: Dunbar's metres and lexicon are distinctive, and interdependent. He writes mostly rhymed verse, favouring eight- or five-line stanzas, although his longest poem, 'The Tretis of the Tua Mariit Wemen and the Wedo' (no. 3), is in unrhymed alliterative verse. Aural linkages, through alliteration and assonance, are more striking than any attempts at strict patterns of stress. In the poem beginning 'In secreit place ...' (no. 25), a young woman responds to the advances of her lover thus:

Quod scho: 'My clype*, my vnspaynit gyane*,	*clumsy lump, unweaned giant*
With moderis mylk ȝit in ȝour mychane*	*? mouth*
My belly huddrun*, my swete hurle bawsy*,	*? fat person, ?? (obscure)*
My hwwny gukkis*, my slawsy gawsy*,	*honey fool; ? plump dear*
Ȝour mvsing* waild perse ane harte of stane*	*complaining, stone*
Tak gud confort, my grit heidit slawsy*,	*? big-headed dear one*
Full leif* is me ȝour graceless gane*.	*dear, ugly mug*

---

[6] Details of the manuscript witnesses are in Bawcutt (ed.), *Dunbar*, 1.4–10. See also W. A. Craigie (ed.), *The Asloan Manuscript: A Miscellany in Prose and Verse*, 2 vols., STS n.s. 14, 16 (Edinburgh, 1923, 1925); Denton Fox and William A. Ringler (intros.), *The Bannatyne Manuscript. National Library of Scotland Advocates' MS 1. 1. 6*, (London, 1980); Julia Boffey, 'The Maitland Folio Manuscript as a Verse Anthology', in Mapstone (ed.), '*The Nobill Poyet*', 40–50.

[7] See further A. S. G. Edwards, 'Editing Dunbar: The Tradition', in Mapstone (ed.), '*The Nobill Poyet*', 51–68.

[8] Bibliographical information can be found in Bawcutt (ed.), *Dunbar*, 1.4–10; and some additional material in John Conlee (ed.), *William Dunbar: The Complete Works* (Kalamazoo, MI, 2004).

Although there are a number of hapax legomena in the stanza, probably derived from low-life sexual street-slang, which obscure exact understanding, aural patterns convey exactly where the dialogue is heading, playing on repetitions of syntax, syllables, and back vowels.

At the opposite end of Dunbar's virtuoso stylistic range, the opening stanza of his panegyric to Margaret Tudor (no. 15, 1–8) may serve to demonstrate the same characteristic:

> Gladethe, thoue queyne of Scottis regioun,
> ȝing* tendir plaunt of plesand pulchritude*,   *Young, beauty*
> Fresche flour of ȝouthe, new germyng* to burgeoun,   *budding*
> Our perle of price, our princes fair and gud
> Our charbunkle* chosin of hye imperial blud,   *carbuncle/ruby*
> Our rois riale* most reuerent vnder crovne,   *royal rose*
> Ioy be and grace onto thi selcitud*,   *majesty*
> Gladethe, thoue queyne of Scottis regioun.

In these lines, rhetorical considerations outweigh any attempt at metrical regularity, so that the aural qualities of the stanza inhere in the repetition of the apostrophe in the first and last lines, as well as the three lines beginning 'Our', which is followed by the alliterating epithets, 'perle of price', 'charbunkle chosin', and 'rois riale'. In the second line, the notably stumbling metrical effect created to accommodate the double alliteration on 'p' and 'l', and of the word 'pulchritude', meaning beauty, also seems of secondary importance. Many of the poems have refrains.[9] As both examples demonstrate, the range of his vocabulary is extraordinary, drawing on the full available lexicon of both Middle English and Scots, including short-lived ephemeral street talk.[10]

One of Dunbar's signature techniques, which testifies to his attention to the polished surface of his work, is aureation, that is the lexical 'gilding', or the embellishment of high-style poetry by the use of numerous latinate words. These words are not simply the higher register latinate forms available in the common vocabulary of literary English or Scots, for example the use of 'request' as a synonym for 'ask', but are coinages, often custom-made for the context. They are polysyllabic and create sonorous feminine endings when used as rhyme words, such as 'matutyne' and 'cristallyne' in the first stanza of 'The Goldyn Targe' (no. 59, 3–4). Aureate diction accompanies classical allusion, as in the list of the passengers who alight from the ship in this poem (e.g., 118–126). The alighting from the ship is framed, however, within French-derived conventional settings and *topoi* (see also e.g., 69, 14). The combination fashions distinctive poetry of the high style. In the stanza from no. 15 quoted above, a good example of the aureate style, 'pulchritude' rhymes with 'selcitud', more often spelled 'celcitud', meaning 'loftiness', a coinage from '*caelum*', the Latin word for the sky, but with connotations of heavenliness as in the commoner 'celestial'. Here the imagery is drawn from the biblical, the 'perle of price' of Matthew 13.45–6, and a description of heaven, reinforced by the lapidary 'charbunkle', the ruby, but also from French romance in the density of flower imagery, such as 'plaunt', 'flour', and 'rois'. These fields of imagery are sustained and developed through the rest of the poem.

Dunbar was in holy orders, so it is perhaps fitting to commence our review of individual poems with a dazzling showpiece of the high style, 'Hale, sterne superne …' (no. 16). A. A. MacDonald's account of the poem is apt, seeing Dunbar as retaining 'complete control of his subject through the tight discipline of a virtuoso stanza-form'. The lyric is 'technically dazzling, and has the poet's signature attention to surfaces', exploiting 'the chiming

---

[9] For further information about Dunbar's stanza forms and metres, see Bawcutt (ed.), *Dunbar*, 1.14–15.
[10] See further Priscilla Bawcutt, *Dunbar the Makar* (Oxford, 1992), Ch.9: 'Language at Large'.

harmonies of internal rhyme'. The substance of the poem is formed of a convincingly exhaustive string of epithets for the Virgin cast in the form of an extended version of the angelic greeting of the Annunciation (Luke 1.28), the opening words of which are repeated macaronically, *Ave Maria gratia plena*, as the ninth line of each stanza. Each twelve-line stanza has two end-rhymes which alternate throughout, echoed in a number of internal rhymes in the odd-numbered lines:

> Haile, ȝhyng*, benyng* fresche flurising*,   *young, mild, blossom*
> Haile, Alphais habitakle*,   *Alpha's dwelling*
> Thy dyng* offspring maid ws to syng   *worthy*
> Befor his tabernacle.
> All thing maling* we dovne thring*   *evil, drive*
> Be sicht of his signakle*,   *sign of the cross*
> Quhilk* king ws bring vnto his ryng*,   *which, kingdom*
> Fro dethis dirk vmbrakle*.
>   (13–24) (see below)

Bawcutt has remarked rather dismissively, 'Such metrical ingenuity was highly characteristic of late medieval Marian lyrics',[11] but surely in Dunbar's case it is the lexical as well as the metrical endeavour that pushes form to its limits. Again in the second stanza, quoted above, rhyming the commonplace 'tabernacle' with the ingenious 'Alphais habitakle', that is Alpha's dwelling, where God is defined as the alpha and the omega, 'signakle', meaning the sign (of the cross), and 'vmbrakle' (shadow), demonstrates a degree of strenuous ingenuity applied to refresh commonplace images. The poem is all surface, but whether it is thus superficial, a show-off piece of rhetorical wizardry, or a marker of the speaker's devotion, is beyond the competence of textual criticism, and ultimately for the reader to decide.

Dunbar wrote a number of works which were labelled as *ballats* in the Bannatyne manuscript. He refers to himself as one able to write only 'ballattis brief' in 'Schir, ȝit remember ...' (no. 68, 48), and 'ballat wyse complaine', in 'This hinder nycht ...' (no. 75, 69). The term was, however, used more permissively than modern understandings suggest, and seems to have held a particular connection with performance.[12] One of the themes that will recur in what follows is the fundamentally performative nature of much of Dunbar's work, not only in the attention to the tenor and aurality in his own voice, as in 'Hale sterne superne', but in the creation of distinct and sometimes multiple voices for other 'players'.

Amongst Dunbar's poems in the Bannatyne manuscript is one that is categorized amongst 'ballettis mery'. It is commonly headed in modern editions as 'The Lament for the Makars' (no. 21), and, with its refrain from the Office of the Dead, *Timor mortis conturbat me* ('Fear of death disturbs me'), it seems far from merry. In it Dunbar plays games of genre metamorphosis, using the model of estates' satire to shape what begins as a complaint and grows into elegy. In it he lists other poets alive and dead, making it a major source for understanding his vision of the literary tradition of which he was part. It is certainly a 'ballett', or ballad, understood in our contemporary sense as having a performative element, as it is informed by the iconographic tradition of the Dance of Death, in which a personification of death carries off dancing-partners who are representatives of the 'estates'

---

[11] Bawcutt (ed.), *Dunbar*, 2.322.
[12] The *Dictionary of the Older Scottish Tongue* cites sixteen examples of 'ballat' prior to 1700, of which nine make specific reference to a performance context (https://www.dsl.ac.uk/entry/dost/ballat). See also Sarah Carpenter, 'Plays and Playcoats: A Courtly Interlude Tradition in Scotland', *Comparative Drama*, 6 (2012), 475–96.

of medieval society. It is also, however, a lament, and a metaphorical funeral procession, or pageant, as a quarter of its lines are the repeated liturgical response, *Timor mortis conturbat me*, though the 'me' also serves to refer back to its deeply personal opening:

> I that in heill* wes and gladnes[s]   *health*
> Am trublit now with gret seiknes,
> And feblit* with infirmite.   *enfeebled*
> (1–3)

It is a *memento mori* (a penitential work of art reminding the viewer or reader to remember their own death), an immortalizing tribute to dead authors, and an implicitly self-validating exercise inscribing the author into their number. As a meditation upon death it reflects the same sentiments as the short 'Quat is this lyfe bot ane straucht way to deid' (no. 21, 51) but exposes in its complexity the string of mortality clichés—the turning wheel of fortune, the briefness of pain or pleasure in this life as opposed to eternal joy or torment—that make up that poem.

'The Lament for the Makars' draws upon the pan-European, late medieval tradition of the Dance of Death but, perversely, involves little dancing. The history of the Dance is well attested; it first occurs in France in the fourteenth century, and the most influential illustrated version in England was commissioned for the Pardon Churchyard at St Pauls' in the City of London in 1430. It occurs in English poetry in the version by John Lydgate.[13] The closest version to Dunbar in date and proximity survives in Rosslyn Chapel, the extraordinary building project just outside Edinburgh, undertaken by the king's close associate William Sinclair (1410–84), first earl of Caithness and last earl (Jarl) of Orkney, Baron of Roslin, and finished in the poet's lifetime.[14] The scenes in the chapel show Death as a skeleton, sometimes to the left of his victim, sometimes to the right, so that the overall effect is like a ring dance. The victims are, so far as can be discerned, estates types which more or less align with those mentioned in the poem (no. 21, 5–11). There is a knight, and a baby taken 'on the moderis breist sowkand' (26) as the mother appears in the scene and the baby is spread-eagled upside down, its ankle clutched in Death's bony grasp. There are military figures which Dunbar represents as a champion and captain (29–0). The 'lady ... full of bewte' is there, in a splendid kennel hood (31). And there are figures in long gowns and clerical headgear, one holding a book, which are equivalent to the clerk, magicians, astrologers, rhetoricians, logicians, theologians, medical practitioners, surgeons, and physicians (37–44).[15]

Whatever his source of inspiration, be it literary or visual, the focus of Dunbar's poem comes to lie elsewhere. The occupations Dunbar's Death seizes move from singulars, 'the bab', 'the lady', to the negatively generalized 'no lord', 'na clerk' (33–4), and thence to the plural, 'art magicianis and astrologgis ...' (37–42). Thus he uses this simple shift from singular to plural to pull away from the individuated estates types of other versions of the Dance and to write a very different poem. The remainder of the poem lists all the 'makars', that is writers, who have been snatched by death. The dead makars follow on from a list of 'estates' heavily weighted in favour of the three higher faculties of the medieval university,

---

[13] See Sophie Oosterwijk, 'Of Dead Kings, Dukes and Constables: the Historical Context of the *Danse Macabre* in Late Medieval Paris', *Journal of the British Archaeological Association*, 161 (2008), 131–62.

[14] R. D. Drexler, 'Dunbar's "Lament for the Makaris" and the Dance of Death Tradition', *Studies in Scottish Literature*, 13 (1978), 144–58 (at 149), suggests the connection, but unaccountably alleges that want of space shows Death only once, and crouching. See https://www.rosslynchapel.com/visit/things-to-do/explore-the-carvings [accessed 1 February, 2020].

[15] Author's observations of the carvings in situ, 28 January 2020.

Theology, Medicine, and Law, all of which required the qualifying Master of Arts, demonstrating that no amount of learning is guarantee of immortality, that lives are just 'padȝenis' (*pageants*; 46). Dunbar thus invokes what will become the Shakespearian trope that any life is the performance of an actor who 'struts and frets his hour upon the stage' (*Macbeth*, 5.5, 2382) but also, perhaps, the allied trope that in listing the makars in a poem, 'So long lives this and this gives life to [me]' (*Sonnet* 18, line 14).

Staying with the unusual concatenation of religious observation and dancing, the poem beginning 'Off Februar the fyiftene nycht ...' (no. 47) evokes a conventional dance of the seven deadly sins, set as a dream which the narrator experienced on Ash Wednesday, 'Full lang befoir the dayis lycht' (2), 'Off schrewis that wer nevir schrevin' (7), that is those who had failed to engage in the sacrament of penance on the eve of Lent, the Church's major fast leading up to Holy Week. For Dunbar, it offers an opportunity to satirize the abuses of the age, in an eccentric dream vision that blends the allegorical with the carnivalesque. 'Mahoun' (the name given to the devil) instructs gallants to prepare a 'gyis' (10, 26), that is a disguising, and cast off their latest French garments. The dancing gallants, led by the personification of each sin, wear outlandish costumes, many of which have puzzled commentators, but which may reflect those familiar from court entertainments such as would have taken place on the eve of Lent. For example, Pride wears a fashionable bonnet on the side of his head, and all around him spread the 'organ-pipe pleats' of his fashionable base coat, while from the back he is naked and covered in hair like a wild man.[16]

Once the sins have all entered the dance, the audience is reminded that there is no music, as there are no minstrels (or poets) in hell. But a minstrel who is also a murderer is found and then a highland bagpiper (although in the carvings in Rosslyn Chapel, the bagpipe appears amongst the angelic choir, the bagpipe tends to be associated with the lower body in art). Mahound calls for a 'heland padȝane' (*Highland pageant*), so McFadyan the piper is called up from his northern nook. He is surrounded by 'Erschemen' (Irish or Scottish Gaels are undistinguished in the term), of whom hell is full, and they make such a loud noise that Mahoun is moved to smother them with smoke (109–20).[17] When this is accomplished, the sins embark on another kind of entertainment, the mock tournament. The combatants are a tailor and a soutar (shoemaker), characters who will later turn up as burlesque representatives of the third estate in Sir David Lyndsay's *Ane Satyre of the Thrie Estaits*.[18] Each is described according to the stock abuses associated with his trade, and each, in this piece of mock-aristocratic theatrical sport, rides under a banner. Guild banners were common in processions at the period, bearing emblems of the trade and emulating the heraldry of the chivalric class. The scatological details of the ensuing combat cause the narrator to laugh so heartily at the scene that he wakes himself up. The poem is truly Bakhtinian in its evocation of the types of carnival activity typical of the season.

---

[16] Bawcutt (ed.), *Dunbar*, 2.262.

[17] Dunbar's contempt for the Gaelic-speaking highlander reflects the historic, and periodically explosive, animosity in late medieval and Renaissance Scotland between the 'civilised', Scots-speaking peoples of the east and lowlands, and the Gaelic-speaking 'wild' Scots of the west and north which had been an unwelcome distraction for the Stewart monarchy throughout the poet's lifetime.

[18] Lyndsay's long morality play is commonly considered to be the only early play in Scots. Archival records suggest, however, that it is purely the sole surviving complete script. See, for example, the fragment 'Droiches part in the play', and other traces, cited in Sarah Carpenter, 'Scottish Drama until 1650', in I. Brown (ed.), *The Edinburgh Companion to Scottish Drama*, The Edinburgh Companions to Scottish Literature (Edinburgh, 2011), 6–21.

A third poem on the subject of dancing takes us straight into the royal court. 'Sir Ihon Sinclair begowthe to dance ...' (no. 70) is of its moment. Courtly dancing gained new prominence, and was more extensively recorded, during the period when Dunbar was writing. A specialized vocabulary for dancing emerged, and two Italian treatises were in circulation, offering instruction and choreographies of dances to be learnt: *De la arte di ballare et danzare,* by Domenico da Piacenza *c*1425 and Guglielmo Ebreo's *De Pratica seu Arte Tripudii* (*c*1455).[19] Exhibition dances performed by experts involved extreme moves, such as women moving as if on wheels, while men engaged in vigorous leaping. Social dancing sought to emulate these achievements, giving rise to the unfortunate result which Dunbar satirizes in his poem.

Sir John Sinclair is expected to perform well 'for he was new cum owt of France' (2). Sinclair does not appear to have learnt much in France, however, for 'the an futt yeid ay onrycht and to the tother wald nocht gree' (*one foot went always the wrong way, and would not agree with the other*) (4–5). He is ridiculed off the floor. Maistir Robert Schau looked good at first, but then he staggered like a horse that was hobbled above the knee (9–12). Dunbar, who is participant as well as observer, 'hoppet lyk a pillie wanton' (*a randy cock*) for the love of Maesteres Musgraeffe, but lost his slipper in his enthusiasm (25). Maesteres Musgraeffe, of course, dances with 'guid conwoy and contenance' (32). Guglielmo's treatise emphasizes how the dancer must respond to the space available, but also to the sound-world of a specific situation. The same steps should be adapted to reflect for example, the shawm as opposed to the lute, reflecting its 'air', that is, its distinctive 'voice'. The dance described by Dunbar, however, is unfortunately accompanied by inadvertent bodily noises: while Dame Dounteboir danced 'bisselye / An blast of wind son from hir slippis' (40–1).

All the dancers in the poem have been identified as real members of the court of James IV.[20] The final one, who danced with all the grace of a mastiff, and who adds unfortunate bodily odours to the overall sensory experience evoked by the poem, is James IV's, and latterly Queen Margaret's, long-standing wardrobe official, James Dog, whose surname was an open goal for a court satirist, and who is further the butt of the paired poems, 'The wardraipper of Wenus Boure ...' (no. 72) and 'O gracious princes guid and fair' (no. 73).[21] In the first of these, the refrain 'Madam ʒe heff a dangerous dog' is ironic, as 'danger' in Old Scots and English was understood as reluctance and meanness as well as the power to cause harm. Dunbar refers to the attitude with which Dog distributed the clothing allowance which the poet, as a member of the royal household, was entitled to. He is as surly giving out a doublet, as if it were a 'futt syde frog' (*full-length gown*) (no. 72, 3). He barks and 'girnis', and treats the poet as if he is going to bite him when he produces the queen's written grant, even if he is spoken to in a friendly way. He is a mastiff fit to protect the wardrobe from the legendary giant Gogmagog,[22] but really quite unsuitable. The queen is advised to replace him with a lapdog.

---

[19] Jennifer Nevile, *The Eloquent Body: Dance and Humanist Culture in Fifteenth-Century Italy* (Bloomington IN, 2004), 59 *et passim*. I am grateful here to the illuminating conversations and the unpublished work of Dr Frances Eustace, then a postgraduate student at the University of Bristol, a bassoonist and former dance therapist, who greatly enriched my reading of this poem.

[20] For detailed identification see Bawcutt (ed.), *Dunbar*, 2.459–61.

[21] See further John Burrow, 'Dunbar and the Accidents of Rhyme', *Essays in Criticism*, 63 (2013), 20–8.

[22] The giant seems to be an amalgam of the British giant Goemagot, the Moslem sultan, and biblical figures Gog and Magog. See further Bawcutt (ed.), *Dunbar*, 2.463.

The satire is sustained in this extended metaphor throughout the short poem, yet its target is transparently a long-standing official of mean disposition. The follow-up poem is an ironic apology for the first, claiming, according to the refrain, 'He is na dog, he is a lam' (no. 73, 4 etc.). In fact he is such a lamb that his wife can break his bones and cuckold him when she chooses. Bawcutt refers to a further potential level of satire in the second poem, as another court official and contemporary who appears in the Treasurers' Accounts for the period is one James Lam.[23] This reference remains obscure to the modern reader, further underscoring the fact that Dunbar wrote for a coterie audience.

Unfortunate physical attributes and silly names delight the court satirist, but not as much as ridiculous aspiration. The poem, 'As ȝung Awrora with cristall haile ...' (no. 4) concerns a true event, the occasion on which John Damian, dilatory abbot of Tongland and alchemist extraordinaire to the court of James IV, attempted to fly. The poem is not a documentary account, though there is a corroborative narrative in John Leslie's later *De origine moribus rebus gestis Scotorum* (1578) that suggests that it is based on a real experiment.[24] Dunbar's poem instead, as a perverted dream vision, is another example of his manipulation of genres, a gleeful array of inflated rhetorical figures and mythological parallels simply to mock the aspiring aeronaut, setting the whole account within a nightmare. Damian is thus a child of the devil rather than a mere negligent cleric, an imposter physician who killed all his patients. He is accused of never going to Mass, but rather exchanging the incense and liturgy of matins for the smoke of the smithy used in his experiments in alchemy. Finally the protagonist takes on plumage: 'A fedrum on he tuke' (60) in order to fly to Turkey.

The poem's exuberant shift into bird lore borrows from the tradition of Chaucer's *Parliament of Fowls*, but most nearly from the Scots *Buke of the Howlat*—from which Dunbar also borrows the conventions of alliterative verse to great comic effect—as the birds debate what this creature might be.[25] Their avian flights of fancy speculate that he is Daedalus, the Minotaur, Vulcan, or Saturn's cook. Every imaginable bird then attacks him in different parts of his body: they 'nybbillit him with noyis and cry'. Inevitably the cackling of the triumphant birds wakes the dreamer, bringing on his curses. The ill-fated abbot is returned for another twist of the knife in the dream poem beginning 'Lucina schyning in silence of the nycht' (no. 29), which opens with a highly conventional complaint against Fortune. Dame Fortune's answering rebuke offers the consolation that the narrator's fate will not be as extreme as that of a flying abbot. The narrator confesses that he awoke thinking what a silly dream he had had until he discovered that there really was an abbot who intended to fly.

At the other extreme from satirical attacks on the court was the requirement upon all courtiers known to be poets to offer the source of patronage, in Dunbar's case the king and queen themselves, sycophantic flattery and sage advice. The ideal vehicle for this activity is

---

[23] Bawcutt (ed.), *Dunbar*, 2.463.
[24] Dunbar, *Poems*, Bawcutt (ed.), 2.296.
[25] The earlier poem, by Richard Holland, is dated with reasonable degrees of precision to c1448. Holland is paired with John Barbour, who wrote the late fourteenth-century epic verse chronicle and first major surviving work in Old Scots, *The Brus*, in Dunbar's 'I that in heill wes and gladnes ... (nos. 21, 61). *The Buke of the Howlat*, dedicated to Elizabeth Douglas, the 'Dove of Dunbar', draws on the plural and complex Scots Aesopian tradition. It is written in an elaborate thirteen-line stanza, employing both alliteration and rhyme, with a section similar to the English 'bob and wheel' that has a long ninth line instead of a 'bob'. In the poem, redolent with heraldic imagery and contemporary satire, an owl is caught in a trap of his own making: in its quest for more beautiful plumage, it is eventually stripped of his feathers, '... degradit fra grace for his gret pryde' (952). See Ralph Hanna (ed.), *Richard Holland: The Buke of the Howlat*, STS, 5th series, 12 (Woodbridge, 2014).

the model of the pseudo-Aristotelian *Speculum principis,* or 'mirror for princes'.[26] Dunbar, inevitably, seems to have regarded working in this genre as the perfect opportunity to take a side-swipe at others of his fellow courtiers: the warning against taking bad counsellors—a conventional feature of the genre—takes over the whole exercise. The poem opening 'Schir, ʒe haue mony seruitouris' (no. 67) begins with a seemingly innocuous list of all the officers that attend upon the monarch, from churchmen to apothecaries. The choice to alliterate many of the names of the occupations in groups of three in each line, in this poem of rhymed couplets of iambic tetrameters, is a playful tour de force which both belittles them further as items on a list, and prepares for what will follow. The poet, he claims, is unworthy to hold a place amongst them (25–34). The stanza which, after an elaborate statement of false modesty, describes what he is prepared to do, rising to the heights of rhyming on polysyllabic latinate words:

> ... Als haill* in everie circumstance,   *wholly*
> In forme, in mater and substance,
> But* wering* or consumptioun,   *without, wearing out*
> Roust, canker or corruptioun,
> As ony of thair werkis all ...
>   (29–33)

to end on 'Suppois that my rewarde be small' (34). The poem then heads off on another alliterating list of all the unprofitable hangers-on that cling to the court, from the hypocrites and flatterers conventional to the *speculum principis,* to shoulderers and shovers, taking in the French and the Irish. The list is then animated by the evocation of a scene of them all crowding in and making a din. The narrator in his second short and personal passage (73–8) confides that he cannot understand how all of these are rewarded when he is not, something that drives him into a rage and brings on fits of melancholy. In fact, we realize that this is not a poem directed at the king at all, but a poem about Dunbar himself, carrying the veiled threat to those hangers-on of the power of the pen: 'Als lang in mynd my work sall hald ... But wering or consumption' (*As long as my work be held in mind without being worn away or destroyed,* 27, 30). The poems beginning 'Schir, ʒit remember as befoir ...' (no. 68) and 'To speik of science, craft or sapience' (no. 82) offer some of the same criticisms of court functionaries.

A further courteous but witty reminder of the poet's own worth is offered in the short poem beginning 'I thocht lang quhill sum lord come hame' (no. 22). Its refrain, 'Welcome, my awin lord thesaurair', welcomes the Lord Treasurer back to Edinburgh, avowing that he, Dunbar, has never lost faith in eventually being paid, despite 'my wage wantit quhill ʒuill' (22)—having been in arrears since Christmas. Court life, it seems, was one long battle for attention, to get the clothing due from Dog at the wardrobe, and to extract payment from the Treasury. Although not as subtle as the poem known as 'The Complaint of Chaucer to his Purse', in which the addressee is wittily made the empty purse, Dunbar's poem is a perfectly pitched and dry reproach.[27]

In another poem of similar purpose, 'Schir for ʒour grace, bayth nicht and day' (no. 63), Dunbar begs not directly for money, but for a benefice, another variety of royal preferment

---

[26] The genre originates in the advice allegedly written for Alexander the Great by Aristotle. English redactions in the period covered in the present volume include Thomas Hoccleve's *Regiment of Princes,* and John Lydgate's *Fall of Princes.*

[27] See further John Burrow, 'Dunbar's Art of Asking', *Essays in Criticism,* 65 (2015), 1–11.

which provides the courtly cleric with a source of income and few necessary accompanying duties. In this begging letter he wishes, in the repeated refrain, that James were 'Iohn Thomsounis man', a proverbial expression for a man ruled by his wife.[28] Dunbar's use of the expression is either affectionate or audacious, but the context makes clear that he is suggesting that the king is not dominated by his wife, and the poet wishes that the rose, English Margaret, would soften the thistle, James. The obscure reference to vowing on the swan in the same poem (19) may refer to Edward I's 1306 ceremony in which all 267 men knighted attended a banquet at which the king swore upon two swans to march against the Scots, thus another reference to the desired domination of the Scot, James, by the English Margaret. The licence Dunbar seems to enjoy, or to assume, in all these poems differentiates them from their nearest English comparators, but this may speak less of cultural difference than of the media of initial reception, Dunbar's piece conceivably having been circulated relatively informally amongst a very small circle of favoured courtiers, and not in a presentation manuscript.

The affected fury that brings 'Schir, ȝe hauye mony seruitouris' (no. 67) to its abrupt close expresses an inability to restrain himself further from intemperate attack. 'My mynd so fer is set to flyt/That of nocht ellis I can endyt' (79–80). The 'flyting' is a formalized exchange of insults in verse, a genre found in *Beowulf*, in medieval Norse and Gaelic poetry, as well as in Chaucer's *Parliament of Fowls,* and in the *Buke of the Howlat.* It is in the Stewart court in Scotland, however, that the form is truly performative: instead of mythological and fictional characters, and birds, trading insults, flytings are presented in the voices of real people attacking one another. Dunbar's 'Flyting of Dunbar and Kennedie' (no. 65), and the 'Flyting betwixt Montgomerie and Polwart', written for the court of James VI in 1572, are well known examples of the genre.[29] Whether the 'Flyting of Dunbar and Kennedie' was written by both poets, or by Dunbar alone has long been contested, as has its tone.[30] W. H. Auden read it as 'sheer high-spirited fun', in contrast to the 'morose or kinky' poetry of his own age.[31] Bannatyne heads the poem 'The Flyting of Dunbar and Kennedie. Heir efter followis iocund and mirrie' (f. 147); others, notably Tom Scott in his critical book about Dunbar's poetry, have found it repellent.[32]

'Gude maister Walter Kennedy', lying 'in poyt of dede' in the 'Lament for the Makars' (no. 21, 89–90) is Walter Kennedy (?1455–1518) a graduate of Glasgow University and an examiner for the Faculty of Arts, a writer praised by Gavin Douglas (c1474–1522) and David Lindsay (c1490–1555), but few of whose works survive.[33] 'Quinting' (no. 65, 2) seems to have been a genuine collaborator; other poets mentioned in the poem, Stobo and Ross, were probably dead by the time the 'Lament' was written. Hard to date, the 'Flyting' reinforces the sense that Scotland was a culture, in which, unsurprisingly, 'makars' knew one another personally, exchanged ideas, and engaged in some rivalry, genuine or playful.

---

[28] The *Dictionary of the Scots Language* (https://www.dsl.ac.uk) notes 'Origin not known. Jamieson suggested *Joan Thomson's man*, but, although the masc. and fem. forms were not at differentiated, there is no evidence for it'. Dunbar's use is the earliest known reference.

[29] Sally Mapstone, 'Invective as Poetic: The Cultural Contexts of Polwarth and Montgomerie's *Flyting*', *Scottish Literary Journal*, 26 (1999), 18–40.

[30] The question is explored in Douglas Gray, 'Rough Music: Some Early Invectives and Flytings', *Yearbook of English Studies*, 14 (1984), 21–43, and the chapter on 'Flytyng' in Bawcutt, *Dunbar the Makar*, 220–56. It is included as part of the Kennedy canon in Nicole Meier (ed.), The Poems of Walter Kennedy, STS, 5th series, 6 (2008), 88–179 (with discussion in the Introduction, xcvii–cxvii).

[31] W. H. Auden, *Ode to the Medieval Poets*: see *Poetry*, November 1971, 63–4.

[32] Tom Scott, *Dunbar: A Critical Exposition of the Poems* (Edinburgh, 1966), 175.

[33] See Meier (ed.), *The Poems of Walter Kennedy*, 88–179.

Dunbar affects here reluctance to 'flyte', not being a 'baird' (no. 65, 17). To be a 'bard' was to belong to the oral Gaelic tradition, an insult later to be directed at Kennedy, taunted for 'Erchry' ('Gaelic') (107). Kennedy's lands were in Carrick in the south-west, still part of Gaeldom. This triggers much of the invective: he is dirty, a thief, and impoverished, all markers of the 'uncivilised' Scot. A Lowland arse makes a better sound than Highland poetry, and the presumably plaid-clad Kennedie lacks breeches to stop his testicles from jingling (104, 119). Woven into the invective from Dunbar's voice is a virtuoso display of highly imaginative, insulting, and obscene epithets, often alliterating within the formal stanza of eight decasyllables, rhyming *ababbccb*; for example:

> Revin*, raggit ruke*, and full of rebaldrie*,   *raven, rook, obscenity*
> Skitterand* scorpioun, scauld* in scurrilitie,   *shitting, scold*
> I se the haltane* in they harlotrie   *haughty*
> And in to vthir science* no thing slie*,   *knowledge, skilled*
> Of every vertew woyd, as men may sie.
> (57–1)

In rhetorical terms they are the obverse of the epithets for the Virgin Mary displayed in 'Haill Sterne Superne' (no. 16). Amongst the most colourful are 'wanfukkit funling' (38; *misbegotten foundling*); 'cuntbittin crawdoun' (50; *pox-ridden coward*); 'gluntoch' (99; *knobbly knees*); 'sueir swappit swanky'(130; *lazy drunken fellow*); 'nyse nagus nipcaik' (177; *pernickety stingy miser*); 'skyttand skarth' (194; *shitting cormorant*); 'wraiglane wasp' (195; *wriggling wasp*); 'ostyr dregar' (242; *oyster dredger*); and 'flay fleggar' (242; *flea frightener*). There is no attempt at unified imagery in this accumulation of descriptors, unless it is a general animalism. The thrust lies rather in the caricature of Kennedy as a skinny, dirty, disreputable thief, a Hollywood highlander straight from central casting, who in Edinburgh is derided in the streets by fishwives and chased by dogs (231–2, 226). The demotic register does not preclude a liberal sprinkling of biblical and classical references, apparently randomly selected to add a patina of learning to the attack. The voice attributed to Kennedy in the rejoinder opens with invective but takes another route into mock etymology and monstrous genealogy. The Lowlander, Dunbar, from Cockburnspath (a coastal village eight miles south of the town of Dunbar) is an eastern borderer, so as good as English and from a long line of traitors to Scotland. Amongst the many insults which cannot be further explored here, Dunbar is compared to Tutiuillus (513), the devil who gathered idle language in his bag, and a caricature that Dunbar, if he wrote the whole poem, might have enjoyed applying to himself, proud of his signature lexical profligacy.

Dunbar could praise as extravagantly as he could insult. His address to Margaret Tudor, beginning 'Gladethe, thoue queyne of Scottis regioun' (no. 15) addresses James IV's queen in aureate terms further burnished by their interchangeability with standard figures found in hymns to the Virgin Mary, such as 'Hale sterne superne' (no. 16). The queen, like the Virgin, is compared to the pearl of price from Matthew 13.45–6. Margaret is also, like the Virgin, a rose, but this rose is red and white (25), the royal rose of the Tudors, signalling the alliance of York and Lancaster. Precious stone imagery, drawing on the resources of the medieval lapidary, abounds as Margaret is compared through indefinite superlatives in the repeated formulaic 'Mor blitht ...', 'More deir ...' of the final stanza, to the beryl, diamond, sapphire, emerald, and ruby, a veritable 'gem of ioy' (34–9). Poems like this, emblazoning the attributes of the beautiful lady, derive squarely from the French and English lyric tradition, in which there is a consistent cross-over between compliments to aristocratic ladies and addresses to the Virgin.

Further extravagant courtly praise of the 'rose red and white' appears also in a poem which appears to be a highly conventional and transparent dream vision, compiled from Chaucerian exemplars, 'Quhen Merche wes with variand windis past' (no. 52), also known as 'The Thristell and the Rose'. A sluggard dreamer is roused by Dame Nature to welcome in the May and to witness her ceremony of crowning the lion king of beasts, exhorting him to 'Exerce iustice with mercy and conscience, / And lat no small beist suffir skaith na skornis' (106–7), to treat apes and unicorns alike even-handedly. The eagle is crowned king of the birds and similarly exhorted. Both lion and eagle are transparently symbols for James IV, and Nature's advice an oblique *speculum principis*. When the flowers are called forth the red and white rose is crowned queen, audaciously above the lily, probably not the Virgin Mary this time but the *fleur de lis* of France. No advice is offered to the queen, or agency, but another objectifying panegyric to her beauty. Predictably, all the birds make such a noise celebrating this multiple coronation that they wake the dreamer.

There is more to say here, however, bringing us back to the performative nature of all Dunbar's work. This poem has a demonstrable connection with an actual event, in this case the wedding of James IV to Margaret Tudor, and knowledge of that context considerably illuminates not only the poem but our understanding of the stylized and ekphrastic way in which cultural events interrelate within the decorum of the broader court culture. Sarah Carpenter has aptly described it as '… an imaginative, literary re-conception of the marriage … The poem survives for us purely as a literary text; but it is intimately adapted to the network of material performances of heraldic images that embodied and expressed the marriage.'[34] Dunbar's achievement is to take the static heraldic description of the alliance found in the panegyric written by Walter Ogilvie, a member of the Scots delegation to Henry VII to seal the betrothal in 1502, and to turn it into what Carpenter calls 'a theatrical encounter'. Actual historical events are animated in the world of the poem by action, dialogue, argument, and song. Carpenter points out that the end of the poem is a hymn in praise of the Rose, interspersed as direct speech in narrative (159–82) and echoing a song with music written for performance at Margaret's entry into Edinburgh:

> Young tender plant of pulcritud
> Descendyd of Imperyall blode
> Freshe fragrant floure of ffayre hede shene
> Welcum of scotlond to be quen
> Welcum the rose bothe rede & whyte
> Welcum the floure of oure delyte.[35]

The correlation between the heraldic description and the poem suggests that, if Dunbar's poem was not part of the event, it related to it at a remove. It also relates, more obscurely, to the disguising celebrating the marriage of Arthur and Katherine of Aragon which was put on for the Scottish delegation in London, and at which the circumstantial evidence for Dunbar's presence is strong.[36] The details of this disguising survive, and the affinity of

---

[34] Sarah Carpenter, '"Gelly with tharmys of Scotland England": Word, Image and Performance at the Marriage of James IV and Margaret Tudor', in Janet Hadley Williams and J. Derrick McClure (eds), *Fresche fontanis: Studies in the Culture of Medieval and Early Modern Scotland* (Cambridge, 2013), 165–77.

[35] Carpenter, 'Gelly', 172, quoting BL MS Royal App. 58, fol. 17v, published in Kenneth Elliott, *Now fayre, fayrest off every fayre (for three voices): welcome song for Margaret Tudor on her marriage to James IV of Scotland, 1503, Musica Scotica* (Glasgow, 2003).

[36] See the account quoted in Carpenter, 'Gely', 172.

the event with Dunbar's poem as an animated symbolic and heraldic show, is evident.[37] Moreover, Margaret was accompanied to Scotland by musicians and a troupe of players, and John Leland records that on the third day after the marriage the court was treated to a performance of 'sum moralite' by 'Johne Inglysche and hys companyons' after supper.[38] There is no evidence of any dialogue in the event, but Gordon Kipling has pointed out that English disguisings frequently attempted to recreate the scenarios of late medieval dream visions.[39] Dunbar seems to reverse the process, reimagining the model of court disguisings in the form of the dream vision.

The poem beginning 'Ryght as the sterne of day begouth to schyne', often known as 'The Goldyn Targe' (no. 59), similarly seems to draw on the conventions of court disguising. It has given rise to bafflement, specifically whether the imaginary content of this 'dream vision' is a 'real' or a theatrical event, and a case, therefore, of double artifice.[40] Dunbar's modes and genres redeployed for engaging with, or reflecting on, pageantry are various: for example in the poem about the Queen's entry into Aberdeen beginning 'Blyth Aberdeane, thow beriall of all tounis' (no. 8), a retrospective account of events becomes a eulogy addressed to the city in the form of an apostrophe. In 'The Goldyn Targe' he chooses dream vision again. The poem has no proven connection with a particular pageant, but arguably there are even more internal clues to a probable relationship than can be found in the 'Thrissel and the Rose' (no. 52). The poem opens with a narrator entering a rose garden, where he falls asleep. Thus far it is conventional, but there are clues to the poet's manipulation of the dream vision genre from the start, as the waking landscape is replete with images of superlative artificiality: the sun is a 'goldyn candill' with 'cristallyne' beams (4–5); the field is 'anamalit' (13); the birds sing their liturgical hours like angels (10). As is frequently pointed out, the scene, described in aureate vocabulary, is all surfaces. The cumulative effect of imagery and the absence of verbs that might suggest real activity, all contribute to the sense of a theatrical show rather than a 'real' event, however stylized.

James IV was a king who enjoyed an ostentatious show according to numerous testimonies.[41] His military exploits are also legendary, particularly the construction of two naval white elephants, the 'Great Michael' and the 'Margaret'. It has been suggested that James's enthusiasm for ships and guns accounts for the inclusion of a ship in 'The Golden Targe', but this is surely simplistic.[42] Rather the ship in the poem paradoxically seems to suggest the monarch's attitude to his real ships, more as toys than as serious military machines, presaging the series of showy military disasters which ended at Flodden. The ship in the poem approaches thus:

---

[37] Gordon Kipling, 'Henry VII and the Origins of Tudor Patronage', in Guy Fitch Lytle and Stephen Orgel (eds), *Patronage in the Renaissance* (Princeton, NJ, 1981), 152–55.

[38] See Sarah Carpenter, '"To thexaltacyon of noblesse": a Herald's Account of the Marriage of Margaret Tudor and James IV', *Medieval English Theatre*, 29 (2009 for 2007), 104–20.

[39] Gordon Kipling, *The Triumph of Honour: Burgundian Origins of the Elizabethan Renaissance* (Leiden, 1977), 107–9.

[40] What follows is heavily influenced by my own reading of the poem, notwithstanding the intervening decades, in 'Dunbar's *The Golden Targe*: A Chaucerian Masque', *Studies in Scottish Literature*, 19 (1984), 115–131. In the rich critical literature the poem has attracted, contrary arguments that find in the poem deeper psychological explorations of the experience of falling in love are also worth exploring. These include William Calin's convincing demonstration of how the poem deploys Guillaume de Lorris's *Roman de la Rose* as an intertext; see The Lily and the Thistle: The French Tradition and the Older Literature of Scotland (Toronto, 2014), 54–60.

[41] See for example Ayala's Description of James IV of Scotland from G. A. Bergenroth (ed.), *Calendar of Letters, Despatches and State Papers Relating to the Negotiations Between England and Spain. Vol. 1, 1485–1509* (London, 1862), 169–79, and Scott, *Dunbar*, 1–21.

[42] Frank Shuffleton, 'An Imperial Flower: Dunbar's *The Golden Targe* and the Court Life of James IV of Scotland', *Studies in Philology*, 72 (1975), 193–207 (at 200–1).

>   A saill, als quhite as blossum vpon spray,
>   Wyth merse* of gold brycht as the stern of day,   *top-castle*
>   Quhilk tendit to* the land full lustily,   *approached*
>   As falcoun swift desyrouse of hir pray.
>
>   (51–4)

It does not drop anchor, but it 'tendit to the land' where its passengers disembark unimpeded; a courtly spectacle rather than a war machine. These features may be dreamlike, but they also could describe a piece of theatrical machinery at a disguising. The ship's departure, on the other hand, involves explosions:

>   In twynklyng of ane eye to schip thai went,
>   And swyth* vp saile vnto the top thai stent,   *quickly, stretched*
>   And with swift course atour* the flude thai frak*;   *over, move quickly*
>   Thai fyrit gunnis with powder violent,
>   Till that the reke* raise to the firmament,   *smoke*
>   The rochis all resownyt wyth the rak*.   *explosion*
>
>   (235–40)

Artillery fire was not uncommon in pageantry, as Dunbar observed in his address to Aberdeen: 'Gryt was the sound of the artelyie' (no. 8, 15). Such a stage machine would doubtless have surprised and impressed this king. Robert Lyndsay of Pitscottie's laconic chronicle account of the launching ceremony of James's two real ships, at which he fired golden cannon balls, amply illustrates the elision of power and the theatre of power characteristic of this monarch.[43] Elaborate ships as elements of stage machinery in pageants are also commonplace, as is recalled by Aurelius in Chaucer's 'Franklin's Tale', who also has trouble distinguishing spectacle from reality.[44]

The integration of court poets into court societies devoted to ostentatious display, a feature of fifteenth-century courtly culture in England and Scotland, inspired a number of ekphrastic texts.[45] In 'The Goldyn Targe', Dunbar strips the dream vision of all its psychologically penetrating elements and all its internal debates. He presents the reader instead with a reluctant lover-dreamer, a mere eavesdropper who is met by a list of barely differentiated assailants. There is no mediator between the dreamer and the world of his dream and no explicit opposition between the two courts from whom the attack emanates. These factors combine to make the poem a curious representative of the genre, but they are more clearly reminiscent of a series of challengers, or balanced teams, meeting a champion, endeavouring to win a prize, in a staged contest. Pageantry may also be used to explain the surprising concision with which Dunbar describes the allegorical characters which people the dream: where costume and heraldic devices are involved, attributes and groupings are sufficient identifiers.[46] We know that indoor disguisings in Edinburgh were integral to the royal marriage celebrations, although Leland was less detailed in his descriptions than he was of tournaments and royal entries,[47] and other difficulties presented by the poem can be resolved when it is read in a performative context. Two courts of assorted gods and

---

[43] Aeneas J. G. Mackay (ed.), Robert Lindsay of Pitscottie, *Historie and Chronicles of Scotland*, STS, 1st Series 43 (Edinburgh, 1899), 251–2.

[44] 'The Franklin's Tale', 1142–5.

[45] Richard Firth Green, *Poets and Princepleasers: Literature and the English Court in the Late Middle Ages* (Toronto, 1980), 119–20.

[46] See further Glynne Wickham, *Early English Stages 1300–1669* (London, 1959), 1.45.

[47] Cf. the detail of indoor events in the English court when Prince Arthur married Katherine of Aragon, certainly reported in Scotland. Pageant cars that appeared first in the tournament later appeared in the disguising,

goddesses disembark from the ship without any apparent rhetorical utility.[48] The second court plays no part in action except blowing Eolus' horn to break up the conflict. If, however, the courts are seen as the audience at a tournament, made up of interested parties on either side, they become opposing parties of supporters. In short, reading 'The Goldyn Targe' in a performative context, alongside Dunbar's other works which were more demonstrably written to accompany or reflect on court shows, can dispose of many of the adverse criticisms the poem has attracted when read purely as a late dream vision.[49] The poem has, refracted through the imagined disguising and expressed through the dream vision, the dual function of parodying the matter of courtly artifice surrounding the battle of the sexes, while mimicking its manner.

We end with, and can barely do justice to, Dunbar's longest surviving poem. The 'Tretis of the Tua Mariit Wemen and the Wedo' (no. 3) draws together many of the distinctive features observed in all the preceding: rhetorical exercises turned to contemporary and satirical ends; the adaptation of late medieval conventionalized genres such as the dream vision, the complaint and the panegyric; the manipulation of register through the whole Scots lexicon, and the relinquishing of the narratorial voice to other dramatized voices which make for a performative text. The poem may superficially be read as concerned with the gap between appearance and reality. This game is carried through at a meta-textual level, as the opening suggests a conventional *locus amoenus* (beautiful place), complete with abundant vegetation and birdsong, while the 'thre gay ladeis', sitting in a 'grene arbour' (16) whose voices will occupy the majority of the poem will, like the setting, turn out not to be what they appear. Despite the setting, this is not a dream landscape, and the narrator is wide awake, concealed from view in a hedge and listening to what ensues. The time of year, midsummer, the proliferation of thorny plants which scratch the eavesdropping narrator, and a number of suspect details in the idealized landscape and descriptions of the three speakers are placed for readers adept at identifying early clues to things that will later prove significant.[50]

As the dialogue begins (41), rhetorically the poem not only moves into a lower register, but moves closer to the patterns of real speech. The succession of questions, if not the tone, with which the widow opens evokes the conventional *demande d'amour* (question of love), *débat* (love-debate), or *jugement* (judgment of lovers' conundrum), all familiar from French love poetry. The voice of the first respondent immediately enters with an attack upon arranged marriage, as 'agane the law of luf, of kind, and of nature' (58), a sentiment squarely within the courtly tradition—except that this wife's protestations, drawing incongruously on the *chanson de mal mariée* (song of the badly married), are founded not on the frustration of true love so much as the curbing of her sexual freedom. Her satisfaction with her husband's sexual prowess lasted all of a month (80) before she began to cast about for a replacement.

The wife's description of how she would dress up in her finery and put herself about at fairs transports the reader to the world evoked in another of Dunbar's poems, that beginning 'In secreit place'[51] (no. 25) where again the narrator is an eavesdropper, this time on

---

including the 'ship' of William de la Ryvers; Wickham, *Stages*, 1.44 and 209, and Carpenter, '"To thexaltacyon of noblesse"'.

[48] E. Allen Tilley, 'The Meaning of Dunbar's *The Golden Targe*', *Studies in Scottish Literature*, 10 (1973), 220–31 (at 228).

[49] See, for example. Denton Fox, 'Dunbar's *Golden Targe*', *ELH*, 26 (1959), 311–34.

[50] For detailed analysis here, see the notes in Bawcutt (ed.), *Dunbar*, 2.286–95.

[51] The poem is noted for the first recorded use of 'fukkit' (see further P. Bawcutt, 'Credit to Dunbar', *Times Literary Supplement*, 27 March 2020, 8).

a sexual transaction performed as a dialogue between a young man who is 'townysche, peirt and gukit' (10; *stupid*) and a cunning woman. Amongst the compliments and insults traded here, the man compares the object of his affection to a 'capirculʒoun' (43; *a large grouse*) and to 'crowdie mowdie' (46; *mouldy soft cheese*), while she says he is as 'sweit as ony vnʒoun' (52). She gives way to him when he gives her an apple. The poem serves to demonstrate Dunbar's knowledge of Edinburgh nightlife, but is really just a game of rhyming, alliterating incongruities.

There is much of this aural and lexical game in the 'Tretis of the Tua Mariit Wemen and the Wedo' (no. 3), once the women embark on the descriptions of their husbands and their behaviour. The first as described by his young wife is a January figure, drawn from Chaucer's 'Merchant's Tale'. He has the same slack skin and bristly face, but Dunbar moves revulsion up a notch as he is described in vernacular Scots redolent with comparisons drawn from the world of animals and vermin, and with more explicit sexual references. The wife moves into *complainte* mode, and, as she wishes for a different fate, the prevalence of conditional verbs describing her wished-for situation is notable.

As this first young wife completes her account, the party passes round a cup of strong wine (148–9). This ritual action recurs (239, 505), as each of the others completes her account, further suggesting a performative imaginary for the exchange. That is reinforced as the second wife begins her account of her ill match by assuring the others that she will speak openly as 'ther is no spy neir'. This device foregrounds the double audience of the eavesdropping narrator and of ourselves. In poetry such a device is simple irony, but in the courtly interlude of Dunbar's time, decisions about whether to acknowledge and include the audience, or to pretend they are not there, are commonly used for strategic effect.

The husband she describes has been a 'hur (*whore*) maister' (168) and is 'waistit apon wemen' (178), that is worn out from his sexual profligacy. No longer interested in, or capable of, sexual activity, he nonetheless maintains the rakish appearance of a womanizer (180). Animal imagery is graphic, as his wife tells us: 'He dois as a dotit dog that damys (*urinates*) on all bussis, / And liftis his leg apone loft, thocht he nought list pische' (186–7). She claims that she is worse off than the first speaker, as an old man is an old man, whereas she is married to a lusty shadow (191). Like the first woman her voice then moves into the realms of fantasy as she recalls the way she used to behave, tricking men into what might be described as 'date rape'. She wishes her husband on to a sexually fastidious woman whom he would be sure not to bother.

Again the party laughs uproariously, despite the embittered tone of the preceding account, takes more drink, and makes way for the voice of the widow herself who offers her own account. The two wives' accounts have taken the form of a mock confessional, owing not a little to the Prologue to Chaucer's 'Wife of Bath's Tale', while the widow's voice now takes on the tenor of a parodic and knowingly false preacher, more like Chaucer's Pardoner than the Wife of Bath. Like the Pardoner she opens with a frank confession of her duplicity.[52] The focus in her account is not on spiritual hypocrisy, however, but on the social hypocrisy of the aspirant classes. The widow's 'lesson' is summed up as, 'Be of your luke like innocentis, thought ye haif evill myndis ...' (267).

The widow has had two husbands. The first was a physically repellent old man, so she took a discreet young lover. The second husband was a middle-aged merchant. She despised him for being her inferior in stature and rank, but incongruously part-quoting the

---

[52] See further P. Bawcutt, '"Tretis of the Tua Mariit Wemen and the Wedo" 185–87 and Chaucer's Parson's Tale', *Notes and Queries*, n.s. 11 (1964), 332–3.

female falcon in Chaucer's 'Squire's Tale', 'pity renneth soone in gentile herte' (479),[53] she claims she remained with him because of the gentility of her social status: 'For neuer bot in a gentill hert is generit ony [t]ruth' (316). Her account is followed by a bird image, but not of the courtly falcon but of Chanticleer, as she compares herself to a cockerel crowing over the final subjugation of this husband (325–6). Thus begins her account of the uncourtly gender reversal she effected in the marriage, gradually bullying her husband more and more: 'I maid that wif carll to werk all womenis werkis, / And laid all manly materis and mensk in this eird' (351–2). He is wealthy, so she encourages him to sweeten her, unsuccessfully, with expensive gifts and clothes that she stored so that she could use them to win his successor, and, when he was dead, she got rid of the children of his first wife, his friends, and relations, for the benefit of her own sons. She cuckolded him, and, when he did demand to sleep with her, she imagined he was someone else. She buried her woes with him, although she makes a show of sorrow for form's sake, and extols the benefits of the life of a rich widow.

As a proto-feminist, the widow's promotion of psychological abuse is not an attractive blueprint, and certainly for Dunbar's audience she personifies the worst male fears of the unnatural topsy-turvydom of the masterful woman. The poem sustains another level of reading here, however, as she also presents as a shape-shifter, shrouded in her widow's weeds, sometimes using a wet sponge to feign tears. Dunbar borrows the description of her peeping through her black veiling like the new moon through cloud from Chaucer's description of Criseyde (*Troilus and Criseyde*, 1. 70–5), but Dunbar's is the more arresting, and chilling, image:

> And as the new mone all pale oppressit with change,
> Kythis* quhilis* her cleir face throw cluddis of sable,   *shows, at times*
> So keik* I throw my clokis, and castis kynd lukis   *peep*
> To knychtis and to cleirkis and cortly personis.
>   (432–6)

There is a dark undertow to the widow's sermon, but Dunbar backs away from any really serious spiritual question.

The poem, like Chaucer's 'Merchant's Tale', presents problems of tone, but without any separation of narrative voice from authorial voice. It can be read as a piece of casual nihilism, as a piece of fun that sets out to impress its audience by shocking them, or as an experiment in misogyny offensive to modern sensibilities. It is certainly an adept close and creative reading of Chaucer, full of literary wit for the connoisseur of genre and rhetoric, and a grotesque-burlesque performance piece. In the end it returns to the *locus amoenus* setting, and to midsummer's day. Midsummer's day is the feast of Saint John the Baptist who lost his head at the hands of another legendarily manipulative woman.

Biographical criticism of any author so far removed in time as Dunbar, and who has left scant life-records, is limited and probably fallacious. Yet for the fifteenth century the general reflexivity enjoyed between art and life had a complementary effect in inspiring authors to write themselves into their texts. James I of Scotland does so in *The Kingis Quair*, and Thomas Hoccleve in a quite different way contrives to write his mental disturbance. Dunbar writes so much about traceable real people in the court circles in which he moved, and animates them in arrestingly performative verse, that it is hard not to construct him

---

[53] The same line appears in 'The Knight's Tale' (1761), 'The Merchant's Tale' (1986), and *The Legend of Good Women* (G 491, F 503).

imaginatively as a player in his own game. His voice at times has something in common with Skelton's paranoid Drede in *The Bowge of Court*, though is, perhaps, not quite so insecure.[54] He does not suffer from Gavin Douglas's writing blocks confided in the prologues to the *Eneydos*, but he on the other hand does not appear to have ever attempted a project of comparable ambition. He does suffer from headaches, and fears death, and in the poem beginning, 'Schir, ʒit remember as befoir' (no. 68), another petition to the monarch, he pleads,

> Thocht I in courte be maid refuse*   *rejected*
> And haue few vertewis for to ruse,   *boast of*
> ʒit am I cum of Adame and Eve
> And fane wald leif as vtheris dois.
> Exces of thocht dois me mischeif.
> (36–40)

'Exces of thocht' must surely resonate with any writer-commentator on his or her times. Dunbar's thought is not only that of one in holy orders, whose religious verse gives us no reason to believe that his devotion is at all cynical, but is that of a wicked imagination that does not suffer fools at all, while bending to the decorum of court life and its attendant hierarchies and necessary need for measured sycophancy. He proves himself extraordinarily well read, particularly identifying his own tradition with the English legacy of Chaucer, refracted through some humanist influences,[55] but chiefly through his own Lowland Scottishness and its word-hoard, as well as its antipathy for everything to do with Gaeldom. His work is often read as embellished or, to use his own term 'anamalit' (no. 59, 257; *enamelled*) with the implication of superficiality, but this is surely a misreading. The court milieu in which Dunbar wrote was enthusiastically dedicated to expressing its realities through display, self-consciously performing its everyday life. Dunbar's poetry performs itself through genre manipulation, through rhetorical flourish, through its signature aureation. Its metatextual and ekphrastic turns are saved from an in-growing logocentricity by its compelling exchange not with reality but with the contemporary performing arts.

---

[54] See further A. S. G. Edwards, 'Dunbar, Skelton and the Idea of Court Poetry in the Early Sixteenth Century', in Jennifer and R. H. Britnell (eds), *Vernacular Literature and Current Affairs in the Early Sixteenth Century: France, England and Scotland* (Aldershot, 2000), 121–34.

[55] As well as the works of Erasmus, the writings of Poggio and Lorenzo Valla and of Jacques Lefèvre of Etaples have been identified as having wide influence on late fifteenth- and early sixteenth-century Scottish writers and thinkers. See further John Durkan, 'The Beginnings of Humanism in Scotland', *The Innes Review*, 4 (1953), 5–24.

PART V
CONTINUITY AND CHANGE

CHAPTER 28
Transitions: After the Fifteenth Century

Jane Griffiths

The late fifteenth and early sixteenth centuries were a rich, yet challenging time to be a poet in England or Scotland. The genres—and indeed the languages—of late-medieval writing in England were strikingly heterogenous. There was a large body of popular literature, a large body of romance, both native and adapted from the French, a large body of religious and didactic writing, and a dramatic tradition that included elements of all of these.[1] Even at the very end of the fourteenth century, it made sense for Gower to write in French and Latin as well as in English, and macaronic writing (writing in which two or more languages are combined) was common until well into the sixteenth century, not least in sermons and popular carols and lyrics.[2] Poetry was almost the default medium for conveying all kinds of information, for all kinds of narration, and for religious and historical enquiry. A poet was a writer, not a figure of symbolic or national importance.

Yet over the course of the late fourteenth and fifteenth centuries, this changed. A vernacular poetic tradition was established—largely, though not exclusively, through John Lydgate's extensive series of responses to Chaucer's writing. This both located Chaucer as the founder of that tradition and determined the way in which it should be understood; on the one hand, Lydgate redeployed Chaucerian genres, tropes, and verse-forms, while on the other, he moved far from Chaucer's practice by positing the poet as moral instructor and conscience of the nation, and by forging a distinctive aureate vocabulary with which to describe the poet's work.[3] He thus not only perpetuated many of the features of Chaucer's writing, but—unlike Chaucer—shaped them into a very nearly explicit poetics which his successors, in turn, might either engage with or reject, but which they could not readily ignore.

The works of poets including Gavin Douglas (c1476–1522), Alexander Barclay (c1484–1552), Stephen Hawes (c1475–c1510), and Robert Copland (fl. 1505–47), as well as those of John Skelton (c1463–1529), all show clear traces of this legacy, whilst also being marked by elements of resistance to it. Challenges to Lydgate's understanding of the poet as educator and record-keeper arose from political, cultural, religious, and technological changes alike. Lydgate's own positioning of himself as *de facto* laureate—poet to the king as well as instructor of the nation—had not been without difficulties, but for poets attached to the later courts of Henry VII and Henry VIII, these became still more pronounced. Both

---

[1] See further Eleanor Prescott Hammond, *English Verse between Chaucer and Surrey* (Durham, NC, 1927); Corinne Saunders (ed.), *A Companion to Medieval Poetry* (Oxford, 2010); for popular poetry specifically, see Douglas Gray, *Simple Forms* (Oxford, 2015).

[2] See further Elizabeth Archibald, 'Macaronic Poetry', in Saunders (ed.), *Companion*, 277–88; Siegfried Wenzel, *Preachers, Poets and the Early English Lyric* (Princeton, NJ, 1986).

[3] See further Lisa H. Cooper and Andrea Denny-Brown (eds), *Lydgate Matters: Poetry and Material Culture in the Fifteenth Century* (New York, 2008); Lois Ebin, *Illuminator, Makar, Vates: Visions of Poetry in the Fifteenth Century* (Lincoln, NE, 1988); A. S. G. Edwards, 'Beyond the Fifteenth Century', in A. S. G. Edwards and Julia Boffey (eds), *A Companion to Fifteenth-Century Poetry* (Cambridge, 2013), 225–36; Robert J. Meyer-Lee, *Poets and Power from Chaucer to Wyatt* (Cambridge, 2007), 49–87.

monarchs made conscious use of poets and rhetoricians for propaganda purposes, and the very openness with which they did so led to rivalry for preferment, whilst also exacerbating the potential for conflict between, on the one hand, a poet's duty to (or dependence on) his king and, on the other hand, his Lydgatean task of defending moral and civic virtue.[4] Matters were further complicated by the increased currency of humanist ideas and practices from the late fifteenth century onwards. In particular, a new emphasis on classical Latin texts not only as repositories of knowledge, but also as stylistic exempla, threatened the position of English as an adequate literary language just at the point when a vernacular poetic tradition seemed to have been securely established.

Moreover, the roughly concurrent introduction of the printing press in England, as well as the influx into the country of books printed on the Continent, made the contrast between the two strikingly visible. Prominent among the latter were classical texts with elaborate paratextual apparatus, most notably extensive commentaries, with all the claims to authority those entailed. Yet William Caxton (1415x25–1492), Wynkyn de Worde (d. 1534/5), and their immediate successors were exploring print publication in a very different way, attempting to work out, in practice, what an English press might be for: transmission of the vernacular heritage in the form of Chaucer's and Lydgate's works, or in the form of popular romance; production of explicitly useful works such as grammatical and mathematical treatises; circulation of polemic; perhaps even publication of editions to rival those classical texts—or all of the above.[5] As the sixteenth century progressed, the increasing prevalence of print and its capacity to reach large audiences also became instrumental as an agent of the Reformation, as seen in the printing of Bibles as well as of religious—predominantly Protestant—satire and polemic.[6]

Not all the authors with which this chapter is concerned lived to see that development, but all except Douglas confronted the questions of what the printing press could do for them and what it might do *to* them: specifically, how it might affect their relationship with their readers. And those took their place among other questions with which poets of this period quite directly and explicitly engaged. How should they locate themselves in a vernacular poetic tradition when the contexts in which they were writing were so different from those of their predecessors? How should they position themselves in relation to their contemporaries? How, and what, should they communicate? Cumulatively, such questions created a sense of pressure that resulted in a variety of experiments with poetic form and poetic voice, as well as an imaginative engagement with print. A recurrent feature in works of this period is an emphatic first-person presence: they frequently include a portrait of the poet *as* poet (or, in Copland's case, as printer), sitting over a blank page or grappling with previous pages that are insufficiently blank. One particularly telling example is found in Robert Henryson's *Testament of Cresseid* (late fifteenth-century), which begins with a vivid fictionalization of the way the poem came into being on a cold Scottish night. A Henryson-like narrator huddles by the fire to read first Chaucer's *Troilus and Criseyde*,

---

[4] See further Richard Firth Green, *Poets and Princepleasers: Literature and the English Court in the Late Middle Ages* (Toronto, 1980); Antony J. Hasler, *Court Poetry in Late-Medieval England and Scotland* (Cambridge, 2011); Meyer-Lee, *Poets and Power*.

[5] For the mutual dependency of literary and technological developments, see William Kuskin, *Symbolic Caxton: Literary Culture and Print Capitalism* (Notre Dame, IN, 2008), and cf. Lotte Hellinga, *William Caxton and Early Printing in England* (London, 2010).

[6] See Elizabeth Eisenstein, *The Printing Press as Agent of Change: Communications and Cultural Transformations in Early Modern Europe* (Cambridge, 1979).

then an unnamed 'vther quair' (61), and questions the veracity of both.⁷ Although the concerns about the authority of previous writing are broadly conservative ones—themselves inherited from Chaucer—the precise details we are given about the narrator stoking the fire and pouring a drink against the cold make them seem real and pressing ones. The scene is characteristic of the way that poets of the later fifteenth century make visible the extent to which the act of writing occurs in the present: reading them, it is clear that they did not realize that they were dead, white, and male, but instead were fully and humanly engaged in the difficult business of putting words on paper, not knowing whether they would succeed in doing so to their own satisfaction or to that of their readers. We see this made playfully explicit in many of Skelton's works, with their multiple envoys, as well as in his almost obsessive revision of his own writings.⁸ It is near-explicit, too, in Henryson's dream-like encounter with Aesop in his *Fables*, in the course of which Aesop voices Henryson's own doubts about the effectiveness of writing for instruction (1388–90). But it also informs Hawes's rewriting of a single narrative in three different forms, bringing it closer and closer to autobiography, and John Audelay's frequent reference to the process of writing, as when he states that: 'This boke I made with gret dolour / When I myght not slep ne have nor rest'.⁹ The concerns with process and communication that underpin each of these episodes are emblematized, in early printed texts, by the use of author portraits as frontispieces. Although these are stock images, not accurate representations of the authors concerned, they tend to emphasize the intimate connection between writer and book. The poet is frequently shown at a lectern, in act of putting pen to paper; the effect is to draw attention to the physical human labour (and time-taking process) that preceded the making of the finished, printed book that the reader holds in his hand.¹⁰

Gavin Douglas

Gavin Douglas, one of the younger sons of the Earl of Angus and Bishop of Dunkeld, is best known as author of *The Palis of Honoure* (c1501) and the *Eneados* (completed 1513). At first sight these works appear to have little in common: the former is a dream vision in the mould of Chaucer's *House of Fame*; the latter is the first full translation of the *Aeneid* into English, including not only Virgil's twelve books, but also the apocryphal thirteenth book by the Italian Mappheus Vegius (from 1428), who wrote in Latin in an imitation of Virgil's style. But although the *Palis* is an exercise in an established vernacular genre, while the *Eneados* is a monumental work of classical reception, closer inspection shows the two to be connected in ways that reveal the experimental nature of Douglas's writing.

Douglas's framing of the *Eneados* stresses both the magnitude and the sheer difficulty of his work of translation. The Prologue that he adds to Book One, for example, asserts

---

⁷ NIMEV 285; in Denton Fox (ed.), *Robert Henryson: The Poems* (Oxford, 1981). All quotations from Henryson's works will be taken from this edition.
⁸ Skelton's *Speke Parrot* is the most be-envoyed of his poems, but his habit of emendation is deeply engrained. See further Seth Lerer, *Chaucer and his Readers: Imagining the Author in Late-Medieval England* (Princeton, NJ, 1993), 199–202.
⁹ NIMEV 1200; John Audelay, 'Epilogue to the Counsel of Conscience', in Susanna Fein (ed.), *John the Blind Audelay, Poems and Carols* (Kalamazoo, MI, 2009), 484–5 (at 145).
¹⁰ See Cynthia J. Brown, *Poets, Patrons, and Printers: Crisis of Authority in Late-Medieval France* (Ithaca, NY, 1995), 99–151; cf. Martha Driver, *The Image in Print: Book Illustration in Late-Medieval England and Its Sources* (London, 2004), 77–114; Alexandra Gillespie, '"These proverbes yet do last": Lydgate, the Fifth Earl of Northumberland and Tudor Miscellanies from Print to Manuscript', *Yearbook of English Studies*, 33 (2003), 215–32.

the detailed attention that he has paid to Virgil's text, and the fidelity with which he has attempted to capture its meaning; in particular, he distinguishes his work from William Caxton's *Eneydos* (1490), stressing its distance from Virgil's work (1.Prol. 138–43); Caxton's source was not the *Aeneid* itself, but a French prose version, the *Liure des Eneydes*.[11] Famously, Douglas also acknowledges the challenges inherent in attempting a faithful translation, discussing the very different connotations of apparently straightforward equivalents such as '*homo*' and 'man' (gloss to 1.Prol. 367). Such attention to detail, combined with Douglas's rhetorical claims of fidelity to his source, have led the *Eneados* to be heralded as the first humanist translation of Virgil into English: one that reflects what was, in England and Scotland, a relatively recent interest in classical texts as works to be studied as complete entities, rather than as storehouses of material to be excerpted and adapted into new forms. Yet there are nonetheless pronounced continuities between Douglas's translation practices and those of his predecessors, and—despite his professions of fidelity—Douglas makes significant alterations to his source.[12]

The Prologues and marginal glosses in which Douglas lays bare the process of translation are prominent among these alterations.[13] So too are those points where vernacular poetic traditions inform his work. One notable instance of the latter occurs in the highly aureate humility topos at the beginning of the Prologue to Book One:

> Lawd, honour, praysyngis, thankis infynyte
> To the and thy dulce ornat fresch endite*,   *honeyed, ornate, engaging writing*
> Maist reuerend Virgill, of Latyn poetis prynce,
> Gem of engine* and flude* of eloquens,   *jewel of invention, stream*
> Thow peirless perle, patroun* of poetry,   *origin*
> Royss*, regester*, palm, lawrer* and glory,   *rose, remembrancer, laurel*
> Chosyn charbukkill*, cheif flour and cedyr tre,   *carbuncle (a precious stone)*
> Lantarn, laid stern*, myrrour and A per se*,   *lode star, first of all (poets)*
> Maister of maisteris, sweit sours and spryngand well.
>   (1.Prol. 1–9)

On first reading, it seems that Douglas praises Virgil as the origin of eloquence, by comparison with whom he himself, 'with rude engyne and barrand emptyve brayn' (1.Prol. 20) can do no more than 'contryfate' his source. Yet the style of his verse belies its content. In a unique nine-line stanza form, he not only combines end rhyme with alliteration, but also performs an impressive feat of amplification by piling up terms of praise, deploying a specifically poetic vocabulary to do so. The cluster of terms related to precious stones ('gem', 'perle', 'charbukkill', 'rose') and the three adjectives in the phrase 'dulce ornat fresch endyte' all echo words and phrases used during the fifteenth century—in particular by Lydgate—to describe aureate poetry: the ornate, polished artefacts created by laureate and would-be laureate poets.[14] By redeploying terms that had been used for the past century

---

[11] All quotations from the *Eneados* will be taken from Gavin Douglas, in David F. C. Coldwell (ed.), *Virgil's Aeneid*, 4 vols., STS 25, 27, 28, and 30 (Edinburgh, 1957–64).

[12] See further Emily Wilson, 'The First British *Aeneid*: A Case Study in Reception', in William Brockliss (ed.), *Reception and the Classics: An Interdisciplinary Approach to the Classical Tradition* (Cambridge, 2012), 108–23; cf. also Priscilla Bawcutt, *Gavin Douglas* (Oxford, 1976), 69–163; A. E. C. Canitz, 'From *Aeneid* to *Eneados*: Theory and Practice of Gavin Douglas' Translation', *Medievalia et Humanistica*, 19 (1991), 81–100; Nicola Royan, 'Gavin Douglas's Humanist Identity', *Medievalia et Humanistica*, 41 (2016), 119–36.

[13] For the Prologues, see Bawcutt, *Douglas*, 164–91; A. E. C. Canitz, 'The Prologue to the *Eneados*: Gavin Douglas' Directions for Reading', *Studies in Scottish Literature*, 25 (1990), 1–22; Lois Ebin, 'The Role of the Narrator in the Prologues to Gavin Douglas' *Eneados*', *The Chaucer Review*, 14 (1980), 353–65. For the glosses, see Jane Griffiths, *Diverting Authorities: Experimental Glossing Practices in Manuscript and Print* (Oxford, 2014), 81–102.

[14] See Ebin, *Illuminator, Makar, Vates*.

by vernacular poets, both to canonize their predecessors and to describe their own poetic endeavour, Douglas recasts Virgil as a proto sixteenth-century vernacular writer, viewing the *auctor* (that is, a classical writer of unimpeachable literary and moral authority) through the lens of his own practice before he has even begun the work of translation.

Implicitly positioning Douglas as an author of equivalent standing to Virgil, the opening lines are just one instance of a recurrent emphasis on his ownership of the translation. They anticipate the way in which Douglas makes visible his presence in the work, not only speaking in the first person in several of the glosses, but also inscribing himself within the body of the text as character, rather than as commentator. In the Prologue to Book Seven, for example, he gives a virtuoso description of the intense cold of a Scottish winter's night, followed by an account of his own difficulty in sleeping and his attempt to keep warm by curling up: 'I crosyt me, syne bownyt for to sleip' (7.Prol. 97). Waking reluctantly the following morning, he sees 'Virgill on a lettron stand' (7.Prol. 143: Virgil on a lectern) and determines to continue his translation:

To writ onone* I hynt* a pen in hand,	*at once, took*
Fortil perform* the poet grave and sad,	*in order to translate*
Quham sa fer furth or than begun I had,	
And wolx ennoyt* sum deill in my hart	*grew rather irritated*
Thar restit* oncompletit sa gret a part.	*remained*
And to my self I said: 'In gud effect	
Thou mon draw furth*, the 3ok lyis on thy nek.	*must continue*
(7.Prol. 144–9)	

This self-portrait is remarkable for the way its vividly realized image of a man curled up in bed against the cold collapses the distance between the 1500s and the present day—and also for the way it recalls and subverts a Chaucerian dream vision trope: unlike Chaucer's, Douglas's insomniac narrator finally sleeps without first reading a book, and without dreaming—but then, on waking in the grey light of dawn, sees the book that he has been failing to read still stubbornly at hand. Presenting Douglas's *Eneados* not as a monumental, achieved artefact, but as a work in progress (or rather, as a work whose lack of progress is causing its author considerable irritation), it confirms what is suggested by Douglas's discussions of the translation process: that he is not claiming to create a text whose authority lies in its timeless, immutable meaning, but rather investigating the processes by which meaning is made: he claims ownership precisely because Virgil's meaning *is* subject to change, and he is currently engaged in the business of changing it. His acknowledgement that his translation was begun 'sa fer furth, or than' (so long before the 'now' in which he writes this particular prologue) locates it firmly in real time, and as something that *takes time*. It provides a glimpse of the poet at work comparable to that found in an encounter with the earliest surviving manuscript of the text, that in Cambridge, Trinity College, MS O. 3. 12, which includes corrections and revisions in Douglas's own writing: physical traces of times when he 'hynt ane pen in hand' (wielded a pen).[15]

Like the terms in which he praises Virgil in the opening lines, Douglas's compellingly immediate first-person presence owes much to his vernacular predecessors. Chaucer's influence is particularly significant: it makes its way into the *Eneados* via *The Palis of Honoure*, a dream vision that directly reflects both the *House of Fame* (1379–80)—with which it shares questions about the value of literary endeavour and a challenging, frequently comic

---

[15] See further Griffiths, *Diverting Authorities*, 97–8.

journey to a rocky allegorical outpost—and the Prologue to the *Legend of Good Women* (1380–7). In the latter, Douglas's dreamer-narrator not only (like Chaucer's in the *House of Fame*) invites us to identify him with the author, but does so in terms that directly anticipate those of the *Palis*.[16] Just as the dreamer in Chaucer's Prologue is commanded by the God of Love to write the legends as penance for having slandered women in his previous writings (F Prologue 537–67; G Prologue 525–43), Douglas's dreamer is commanded by Venus to compose a ballad in her praise as penance for having sung a song scorning love, and also to perform 'the nixt resonabil command / Quhilk I him charge' (997–8: the next reasonable command I give him).[17] Thus, when he re-encounters Venus and she gives him 'ane buik' whose contents are unspecified, but which she commands him to put into rhyme, and which we are told we will hear more of 'sumtyme efter' (1757), the implication is that it is the *Aeneid*: with Venus's commission, the unnamed narrator of the *Palis* takes on the identity of the future author of the *Eneados*. The effect—despite the apparent unlikeness of the two works—is to posit one as prequel to the other. The *Palis* thus prepares the ground for the way in which Douglas's self-portraits within the *Eneados* turn its poet-translator into a secondary hero. By presenting membership of the Court of Rhetoric as one way of gaining admission to a Palace of Honour governed by Mars (God of War), the *Palis* implies what the *Eneados* makes explicit: that poetic and physical service of the state are equivalents, and that authorship is a form of civic endeavour. Taken together, Douglas's two works show him writing within the tradition of poetry as public service, whilst at the same time demonstrating how he fuses this humanist influence with a vernacular poetic one.

Unlike the works of his English contemporaries such as Skelton, Barclay, and Hawes, Douglas's works were circulated exclusively in manuscript during his lifetime. When they were printed, posthumously, in 1553, it was in a form that seems—at first sight—nicely to reflect his interest in asserting his ownership of his works. The title pages of the 1553 editions of *The Palis of Honoure* (STC 7073) and the *Eneados* (STC 24797) both use his social and religious standing to confer authority on his literary work: that to the *Palis* announces that it was 'Compeled (created) by Gawyne douglas Byshope of Dunkyll', while that to the *Eneados* proclaims that the book consists of 'The .xiii. Bukes of Eneados of the famose Poete Virgill Translatet out of Latyne verses into Scottish metir, bi the Reuerend Father in God, Mayster Gawin Douglas Bishop of Dunkel & vnkil to the Erle of Angus'. The way the text of the *Eneados* is presented, with extensive glossing, similarly seems to reaffirm its status. Yet closer inspection reveals that these glosses are radically different from Douglas's detailed reflections on the processes of translation and reception in his own marginal comment. Douglas's pen-portraits of himself at work on the text and explicit discussions of the difficulty of translation show his understanding of authorship to be inextricably bound up

---

[16] For *The House of Fame*, see Piero Boitani, *Chaucer and the Imaginary World of Fame* (Cambridge, 1984); Sheila Delany, *Chaucer's House of Fame: The Poetics of Skeptical Fideism* (Chicago, IL, 1972); Jesse M. Gellrich, *The Idea of the Book in the Middle Ages: Language, Theory, Mythology, and Fiction* (Ithaca, NY, 1985), 167–201; Vincent Gillespie, 'Lunatics, Lovers and Poets: Compact Imaginations in Chaucer and Medieval Literary Theory', in Martin Procházka and Jan Čermák (eds), *Shakespeare between the Middle Ages and Modernism: From Translator's Art to Academic Discourse* (Prague, 2008), 11–39. For Douglas's response to it, see Chelsea Honeyman, 'The Palice of Honour: Gavin Douglas' Renovation of Chaucer's House of Fame', in Kathleen A. Bishop (ed.), *Standing in the Shadow of the Master? Chaucerian Influences and Interpretations* (Newcastle-upon-Tyne, 2010), 65–81. The precise questions the two poems address are notably different; whereas Chaucer calls into doubt the very possibility of authentic fame or reputation, Douglas is concerned with the way reputation or honour might best be achieved.

[17] All quotations from the *Palis* are taken from David Parkinson (ed.), *The Palis of Honoure* (Kalamazoo, MI, 1992).

with the business of writing: the embodied, time-consuming acts of thinking and putting pen to paper. In contrast, the 1553 edition presents both author and text as monuments: just as Douglas is frozen in place on the title-page, as an authority divorced from the man engaged in the struggle of making the work, so too the glosses propose the meaning of the text as immutable, emphasizing the general, sententious teaching that may be drawn from it, rather than its historical particularity.[18] By implying that Douglas's translation contains a universality equivalent to that of Virgil's original, the glosses credit Douglas and his work with an authority equivalent to that of Virgil—yet the 1553 edition belies the very means by which, for Douglas, that authority is achieved. The poet's own transformation of texts and print's transformation of the figure of the poet witness very different kinds of transition in the way authorship was viewed.

Alexander Barclay

Whereas Douglas's work as poet was entirely separate from both his aristocratic status and his prestigious career as churchman, Barclay (a clergyman and would-be courtier) attempted to make his poetry and his career coterminous. Basing his understanding of what a poet should be and do largely on Lydgate's laureate poetics, he sought to achieve recognition as a writer whose work was of national significance. Although he never achieved institutional endorsement in such a role—as Robert Meyer-Lee has argued, his 'Lydgatean ideal of the noble place and function of poetry and the poet … was patently unrealizable in the early Tudor court'—both the form and the content of his writing nonetheless show him assuming it unilaterally.[19] In particular, his close involvement with the printing of his works, and their innovative layout, indicate that print was central to his exploration of what it meant to be a poet.

Barclay's first work, *The Ship of Fools* (1509; STC 3545), clearly demonstrates his desire to be recognized as a poet of moral and intellectual stature. Its sheer scale is impressive. Barclay did not merely amplify his source-text, Jacob Locher's 1497 Latin version of Sebastian Brant's *Das Narrenschiff* (1494), but collaborated with the printer Richard Pynson (active 1491–1529) to create a book whose layout reveals the magnitude of his ambition.[20] As well as Barclay's English verse, it contains Locher's Latin: the two are printed alternately, with Barclay's version of each chapter following the original.[21] Locher's work itself is encyclopaedically didactic, providing extensive classification and dissection of fools by type, with each chapter headed by a lively, illustrative woodcut and surrounded by source glosses. In Barclay's treatment, both comprehensiveness and didacticism become yet more pronounced: he adds new fools within many of the chapters, as well as contributing envoys in which the reader is directly exhorted to avoid the kinds of behaviour that have just been anatomized. Moreover, many of these amplifications are explicitly identified as Barclay's:

---

[18] See further Griffiths, *Diverting Authorities*, 91–7.
[19] Meyer-Lee, *Poets and Power*, 193; cf. Hasler, *Court Poetry*, 88–98.
[20] See David R. Carlson, 'Alexander Barclay and Richard Pynson: A Tudor Printer and His Writer', *Anglia*, 113 (1995), 283–302 (at 297–301); for modification of some of Carlson's conclusions, see John Colley, 'Branding Barclay: The Printed Glosses and Envoys to Alexander Barclay's *Shyp of Folys* (1509)', *Philological Quarterly*, 99 (2020), 147–70. I am grateful to the author for allowing me to read this article prior to publication.
[21] For Barclay's treatment of Locher's text, see Brenda Hosington, 'Sebastian Brant's *Das Narrenschiff* in Early Modern England: A Textual Voyage', in Lynne Bowker (ed.), *Lexicography, Terminology, and Translation: Text-Based Studies in Honour of Ingrid Meyer* (Toronto, 2006), 146–56.

chapter headings draw attention to his authorship of a large number of the envoys, and marginal glosses claim several of Barclay's additions elsewhere in the text as his own.[22]

As John Colley has argued, these glosses and envoys both contribute to a sustained and often playful endeavour, throughout the *Ship*, to emphasize the extent to which Barclay refashions the text, laying the foundations for Pynson's subsequent efforts to brand him as a latter-day Lydgate.[23] Yet even as the *Ship's mise-en-page* materially embodies the way Barclay envisaged his work as poet, it also makes it noticeably difficult to read. The sequential printing of Latin and English means that a monolingual reader must skip over large portions of text to reach those that are comprehensible, whilst a bilingual reader encounters each type of folly twice over. In addition, the pages are strikingly crowded: the glosses that surround Locher's Latin not only recur alongside the English text, but are in many cases expanded, with citation glosses becoming source glosses that quote the relevant passage as well as providing a reference for it, and source glosses being lengthened to quote more of the source.[24] The woodcuts that accompany each new chapter appear not at the beginning of the relevant passage of Latin, but between Barclay's translation of the chapter heading and the rest of his translation of that passage, with the Latin chapter heading printed alongside each woodcut.[25] This means that they appear *after* the Latin they supposedly introduce, and also that woodcut and Latin together prevent continuous reading of Barclay's translation. Further, although Latin and English are typographically distinguished by the use of Roman and Black Letter respectively, this does not simply provide a navigational aid, but also adds to the visual busy-ness of the pages. Viewed in its entirety, the layout of the *Ship* appears to be an entirely genuine and not entirely successful experiment in the new medium of print: one that is highly regimented in principle, yet in practice is always bursting its boundaries.[26]

In Barclay's later works, too, he and Pynson continued to experiment with bilingual layout, moving to a more readily legible parallel text format.[27] But it is a work printed in monolingual form, Barclay's *Eclogues* (c1509–14), that most clearly reveals Barclay's intense engagement with vernacular poetic tradition and the poetics that that entails.[28] His source-texts are three eclogues by Aenius Sylvius Piccolomini (1405–64; created Pope Pius II in 1458) and two by the Carmelite Mantuan (1447–1516); since Piccolomini's eclogues focus on the miseries of court life and one of Mantuan's on the lack of patronage for poets, they readily enable Barclay to reflect on the position of poets at the early Tudor court, and

---

[22] See further Colley, 'Branding Barclay'.

[23] Colley, 'Branding Barclay', 155–60.

[24] For example, three of the glosses to the Latin chapter 'De malis consultoribus', 'Salustius. L.ij.ff.de ori.iu', 'Virgilius', and 'Salustius priusque incipias consulto' (sig. c.i) become, in the English version of the chapter 'Of evyl Counsellours', respectively: 'Salustius vel. catclinario. Dilecti quibus corpus annis infermum ingenium sapientia validum erat reip. consultabant hij &c', 'Virgilius. nec curare deum crevis mortalia quemquam', and 'Salustius priusque incipias consulto et ubi consulueret mature opus est facto' (sig. c.ii).

[25] See Edward Hodnett, *English Woodcuts, 1480–1535* (London, 1973), 379–87, nos. 1824–1932.

[26] As Meyer-Lee notes, a quirk of Barclay's translation is the way he stresses his presence in the text by 'consistently violating the formal boundary between chapter and envoy, embedding details in the former that align the narratorial "I" with his own' (*Poets and Power*, 195): like the form of the text, its content is less under control than initially appears.

[27] Barclay refers to the parallel text format as '*meo more*' ('my habitual practice'), in Greg Waite (ed.), *The Famous Cronycle of the Warre Which the Romayns Had Agaynst Jugurth*, EETS, o.s. 244 (2014), 14. See further Daniel Wakelin, 'Possibilities for Reading: Classical Translations in Parallel Texts ca. 1520-1558', *Studies in Philology*, 105.4 (2008), 463–86 (especially 474–9).

[28] For the dating of the *Eclogues*, see Beatrice White (ed.), *The Eclogues of Alexander Barclay*, EETS o.s. 175 (1928), lvi–lx.

on his own lack of position specifically. His attacks on his intermittently more successful contemporary Skelton, in particular, suggest that this was a cause of grievance; although he writes in the Prologue to his *Eclogues* that he has no desire to be known as laureate (103–10), his assertion of indifference is belied by his very invocation of Skelton's title even as he denies having any interest in claiming it himself.

Moreover, there are signs within the *Eclogues* that Barclay had thoroughly internalized Skelton's work. In his third Eclogue, for example, in a passage with no direct equivalent in his source-text, the courtier-shepherd Coridon declares:

I was so drenched* with dreames, a dread so sore,	*beset*
I trowe* neuer man was troubled so before.	*believe*
Me thought that in the court I taken was in trap,	
And there sore handled, God geue it an ill hap*.	*curse it!*
Me thought the scullions* like fendes of their looks*	*serving-men, looking like devils*
Came some with whittels*, some other with fleshhokes.	*cloaks*
Me thought that they stoode* eche one about me thicke	*crowded about me*
With knives ready for to flay me quicke.	
So had I (sleeping) as much of feare and dreade,	
As I should (waking) haue lost my skin in deede.²⁹	
(13–22)	

This representation of the struggle for courtly preferment in intensely physical terms owes much to Skelton's *Bowge of Court* ([1499?]; STC 22597), whose narrator finds himself increasingly harried until:

Me thoughte I see lewde* felawes here and there	*rough*
Came for to slee me of mortall entente.	
And as they came, the shypborde faste I hente*,	*I grabbed the edge of the ship*
And thoughte to lepe; and even with that woke,	
Caughte penne and ynke, and wroth this lytell boke.³⁰	
(528–32)	

Barclay's use of the passive structure 'me thought' and his transition, at the moment of attack, from sleeping to waking, clearly echo Skelton's, while the knives perceived by his speaker recall the knife engraved with the word 'Myscheve' which Skelton's Dyssymulation keeps hidden in his sleeve. In light of these verbal echoes, Barclay's use of the word 'dreade' twice within ten lines reinforces the Skeltonic allusion, bringing to mind Skelton's eponymous narrator. Rivalry finds expression not just through Barclay's use of a persona comparable to Skelton's—each of them writing within the tradition that shows how a virtuous man has no place at court—but also through his use of something so closely resembling Skelton's voice that it is as if their identities merge.

Such specific emulation is not the only indication of Barclay's intense engagement with vernacular poetic tradition, however. In his fourth Eclogue in particular, Barclay explicitly addresses his vernacular heritage more generally. His version of Mantuan's depiction of a poet's struggle to find patronage is greatly amplified, not least by his introduction of an elegy for Sir Edward Howard (1476/7–1513), in which he shows the naval commander overcoming a series of allegorical vices in order to enter the equally allegorical tower of Honour and Virtue. Merely the presence of this tower confirms that the tradition in which

---

²⁹ All quotations from the *Eclogues* will be taken from White (ed.), *Eclogues*.
³⁰ All quotations from Skelton's works will be from John Scattergood (ed.), *John Skelton: The Complete English Poems*, 2nd edn. (Liverpool, 2015).

Barclay seeks to locate himself is a vernacular one. Its immediate source is likely to have been Jean Lemaire de Belges' elegy for his patron Pierre II of Bourbon, the 'Temple dhonneur et de vertus' (1503), but it also aligns Barclay's work with an English poetic tradition of allegorical edifices—particularly towers and temples—that goes back at least as far as Chaucer, and that was reaffirmed by later authors including Lydgate and the anonymous author of the mid-fifteenth century *Court of Sapience*, as well as by Barclay's own contemporaries: Douglas (in *The Palis of Honoure*), Skelton (in *A Garlande of Laurell*), and Hawes (in *The Pastime of Pleasure* and *The Conforte of Lovers*).[31]

It is significant, then, that it is precisely in this elegy that Barclay switches from the rhyming couplets that characterize both the rest of this Eclogue and his other Eclogues, to a verse form with more authoritative connotations: the eight-line stanza commonly known ballade or Monk's Tale stanza.[32] Just as, in the *Ship of Fools*, his use of rhyme royal speaks directly to his poetic self-fashioning, so too does the change of verse form in the fourth Eclogue. In the *Ship*, rhyme royal is one of the means, together with the glosses and chapter headings drawing attention to Barclay's presence in the text, by which Barclay invites comparison of his work with Lydgate's *Fall of Princes*, as both verse form and paratexts mirror those of the earlier work.[33] In the fourth Eclogue, use of the Monk's Tale stanza similarly invokes a vernacular poetic tradition: as Jenni Nuttall argues, it is based on the Italian *ottava rima* stanza used by Boccacio in his *Teseida* and *Filostrato*, and it was adopted not only by Chaucer, but also by Lydgate in the envoys to the *Fall of Princes*, as well as by Benedict Burgh for the envoys to the *Dicta Catonis*, and by Osbern Bokenham for his prologues to the *Legends of Holy Women*.[34] In Barclay's *Eclogue*, too, the switch to the Monk's Tale stanza signals a change in the type of address, from shepherds' dialogue to formal set piece, and from 'reported speech' to a piece of writing that was constructed with the printed page in mind. The point of transition is very marked: the speaker Minalcas accedes to his companion's request for a lament for Howard's death with a rather halting rhyme:

> Nowe harken Codrus, I tell mine elegy,
> But small is the pleasure of dolefull armony*.   *miserable song*
> (821–2)

This is followed by a formal title, set in a larger type size and seemingly designed to resemble a printed title-page rather than constituting a speech act: 'The description of the Tovvre *of vertue and honour, into the which* the noble Hawarde contended *to enter by worthy actes of* chiualry'. Only then does Minalcas resume, under the heading 'Minalcas speaketh', and in striking elevated diction as well as in Monk's Tale stanza:

---

[31] For Lemaire as source for Barclay, see White (ed.), *Eclogues*, 258–62; for allegorical buildings in vernacular poetry of the fourteenth and fifteenth centuries, see Christiania Whitehead, *Castles of the Mind: A Study of Medieval Architectural Allegory* (Cardiff, 2003), 143–260.

[32] See further Jenni Nuttall, http://stylisticienne.com/two-four-six-eight-a-stanza-to-appreciate/ [accessed 31 July 2020].

[33] See further Meyer-Lee, *Poets and Power*, 193–4, and cf. Mark Rankin, 'Sebastian Brant's *Shyp of Folys* at the Accession of Henry VIII', in James Willoughby and Jeremy Catto (eds), *Books and Bookmen in Early Modern Britain: Essays Presented to James P. Carley* (Toronto, 2018), 64–79 (at 73, 78).

[34] Jenni Nuttall, http://stylisticienne.com/two-four-six-eight-a-stanza-to-appreciate/ [accessed 31 July 2020].

> High on a mountayne of highness maruelous,
> With pendant* cliffs of stones harde as flent,   *overhanging*
> Is made a castell or toure moste curious,
> Dreadefull vnto sight, but inward excellent.
> Such as would enter finde paynes and torment,
> So harde is the way vnto the same mountayne,
> Stregyth*, hye, and thorny, turning and different,   *challenging*
> That many labour for to ascende it in vayne.
> (823–30)

Verse form and diction are both consonant with the contents of the elegy: in it, Barclay not only mourns the passing of Howard, but also engages closely with the laureate poet's task of recording and memorializing the deeds of his society's great men, by praising a soldier who fought in 'His princes quarell with right and equitie ... / Till death abated his bolde audacitie' (972, 974). Indeed, when the Eclogue's poet-figure Minalcas declares that his business is to record those who come to the tower 'For marciall actes with crownes laureate' (862), he explicitly uses the word 'laureate' in a way that links the endeavours of the soldier with those of the poet. These are not just presented—as in Douglas's *Palis*—as equivalently valid forms of service to the state, but are shown to be codependent. Literally, the 'crownes laureate' are the triumphal garlands with which military victors are bedecked, but the term 'laureate' inevitably also calls to mind the sense in which Skelton used it, recalling the laurels with which former poets such as Petrarch and Mussato had been crowned, for literary achievement specifically in service of the state.[35] The failure of Minalcas's potential patron, Codrix, to reward him for his labour thus becomes not just an abstract refusal, but a very specific failure to recognize the mutual obligations that bind patrons and poets; Minalcas's position clearly reflects the way in which Barclay perceived his own. As Meyer-Lee has argued, Barclay attempts throughout the *Eclogues* to invoke his status as cleric as an alternative source of authority to the court that is failing to provide.[36] It reinforces what is implied by his choice of a verse form that aligns him with his vernacular heritage.

Barclay's writing, then, shows him adapting available tropes and genres both to reflect on the poet's position in society and to attempt himself to achieve a position that formally recognized his usefulness. Although not all of his experiments were entirely successful, either practically or poetically, they nonetheless show a poet actively engaged in rethinking the poetic traditions at his disposal. Specifically, they reveal his attempt to reconcile inherited Lydgatean assumptions about the value of poetry with the impossibility, at the early Tudor court, of achieving recognition as laureate guide to princes. More positively, they show him working out ways—most notably experiments with the new medium of print—through which he might reach an alternative audience.

Stephen Hawes

For Stephen Hawes, too, poetry and print are inextricably linked. In his case, however, this is less for the self-fashioning opportunities print presents than for the idea of permanence that he associates with it. In each of his major works, from *The Example of Vertu* ([c1504];

---

[35] See further J. B. Trapp, 'The Owl's Ivy and the Poet's Bays: An Enquiry into Poetic Garlands', *Journal of the Warburg and Courtauld Institutes*, 21 (1958), 227–55.
[36] Meyer-Lee, *Poets and Power*, 198–204.

STC 12945) to *The Conforte of Lovers* ([c1510]; STC 12942.5), Hawes devotes a great deal of time and space to his complex theory of poetry. At its core is the belief that poetry is coterminous with allegory: in the dedication to *The Pastime of Pleasure* ([c1506]; STC 12948), for example, Hawes writes of the way that Lydgate 'cloked the trouthe / of all his scryptures' with 'clowdy fygures' (35, 34), and continues with a humility topos that conveys his poetics in a nutshell, even as he professes his own inability:

> The lyght of trouthe/I lacke connynge to cloke
> To drawe a curtayne/I dare not to presume
> Nor hyde my mater/with a mysty smoke
> My rudenes connynge/dothe so sore consume
> Yet as I maye/I shall blowe out a fume
> To hyde my mynde/vnderneth a fable
> By couert colour/well and probable[37]
>
> (36–42)

> (I lack poetic ability to cloak the light of truth.
> I dare not presume to draw an allegorical veil
> Nor hide my subject in misty smoke
> Because my want of wit so completely destroys poetic ability.
> But in so far as I'm able, I shall create an allegory
> To hide my mind under a fable,
> Using a false appearance that is effective and engaging.)

The terms 'cloke', 'curtain', 'smoke', 'fume', 'fable', and 'colour' each encapsulate Hawes's core belief that poetry consists of fictions that serve a greater truth. Over the course of his writing, however, the way in which he discusses the relationship between outward form and inner verity becomes increasingly complex, as he formulates a theory in which 'the lyght of trouthe' is not just conveyed covertly in the poet's words, but validated by appearing in print.

This theory inflects Hawes's already idiosyncratic experiment with genre. His three main surviving works form a series of allegorical romances, in which he effectively treats the same material over and over again; they witness an evolving experiment with the adaptation of chivalric romance, pilgrimage of life, dream vision, and encyclopaedia into a form of life-writing. Whereas the 'I'-speaker in Barclay's *Ship of Fools* and *Eclogues*, like that of Douglas's *Eneados*, represents the author at work on the text, negotiating between his source text and his readers, Hawes figures himself with increasing explicitness as the questing hero of his strangely hybrid spiritual, moral, and highly personal romances: whereas *The Example of Vertu* is a more or less straightforward exercise in the genre of the pilgrimage of life, the life presented in the *Pastime* is explicitly that of a poet, and that in the *Conforte* is demonstrably the life of the poet Stephen Hawes. Hawes is not just concerned with allegory on a narrative level, however; rather, the life that is allegorized serves to define the purpose of poetry. Drawing on a profoundly emotional as well as intellectual engagement with the work of his English predecessors, most particularly Lydgate, Hawes attempts to remake the

---

[37] All quotations will be taken from Stephen Hawes, in W. E. Mead (ed.), *The Pastime of Pleasure*, EETS, o.s. 173 (London, 1928).

genres he inherits into an adequate expression of everything he knows and everything he is, giving the impression of working at the limits of what it is possible to say.

In the *Pastime*, written while Hawes was at court as Groom of the Chamber to Henry VII, it is the struggle to define poetry itself that dominates. When, at the outset of his quest, Hawes's protagonist Grand Amour comes to a crossroads, he does not choose the 'streght waye / of contemplacyon' (85), but rather 'the waye / of worldy dygnyte / Of the actyfe lyfe' (93–4). Viewed in light of Hawes's earlier *Example of Vertu*, where the protagonist's life is an allegory of spiritual development, the choice seems a surprising one—and although it gradually becomes apparent that, like Douglas in *The Palis of Honoure*, Hawes is invoking the commonplace that poetry is a valid route to fame, his treatment of it is unconventional. As is indicated by the name of his protagonist, Grand Amour, the *Pastime* is not concerned with poetry as public service, but rather presents it as a means for Amour to achieve the purely private goal of marriage with La Belle Pucelle. Even after Amour's death, when personifications of Death, Fame, Time, and Eternity debate the value of his achievements, what is at stake is his *personal* reputation: although Fame mentions an impressive series of historical figures (ranging from Hector of Troy to Julius Caesar and King Arthur) in support of her desire to preserve Amour's name, the expected argument—that the writings of poets have preserved the rulers' reputations—is made subsidiary to her assertion that poets—including Amour—deserve to be honoured equally with kings and warriors; she even refers to Amour as 'my *knyght* in specyall' (5589, my emphasis).

Hawes's description of Amour's education in the Liberal Arts affirms that his interest is in the poet as writer, rather than the poet in society. His lengthy discussion of the art of rhetoric (701–1295), in particular, not only conflates it with poetry, but functions as a strange, interior handbook of how to forge the 'truth' that, for Hawes, is poetry's defining feature.[38] What is particularly striking about his analysis of the creative process is the way he maps each of the five parts of rhetoric onto one of the inner wits (the component parts or faculties of the mind, including fantasy, imagination, reason, and memory). It becomes apparent that his 'trouthe' is not a given, but the product of the poet's mental processes, through which subject-matter and the expression of it become inextricably fused.[39] It also appears that the product of the composition process, the finished book, serves as physical memorial to both the matter it contains and the intellectual endeavour by which it was brought into being. Hawes's presentation of the poet's memory as a storehouse of images that provide the material for his writing is, in itself, entirely conventional, aligning Hawes with models of mind and theories of composition that have their roots in classical rhetorical treatises, and that remained standard throughout the medieval period.[40] Yet his choice of the word 'enprynted' (1261) to describe the way those images are lodged in the writer's mind not only suggests that he conceives them in strikingly concrete terms, but also indicates why he attached great significance to the printing of his works. Although the term was in use before the invention of the printing press, in the more general sense of 'impressed', for Hawes the opportunity to print his works appears to have been an opportunity to make

---

[38] For the distinction between poetry and rhetoric, see Gillespie, 'Lunatics', 14–25; for Hawes's treatment of rhetoric, see Rita Copeland, 'Lydgate, Hawes, and the Science of Rhetoric', *Modern Language Quarterly* 53 (1992), 57–82 (at 76–80).

[39] See further Jane Griffiths, *John Skelton and Poetic Authority: Defining the Liberty to Speak* (Oxford, 2006), 140–2.

[40] See Mary Carruthers, *The Book of Memory: A Study of Memory in Medieval Culture*, 2nd edn. (Cambridge, 2008).

them the outward and visible signs of the poet's inner invisible mental storehouse—and thus a material manifestation of his 'truth'.[41]

The Conforte of Lovers shows how this might work in practice. Written after the accession of Henry VIII, at a time when Hawes had lost his position at court, and after Wynkyn de Worde had printed all of Hawes's previous works, the poem is both a dream vision and an exercise in symbolic life-writing, centred on a poet who speaks of his fellow-courtiers as 'woulues' who 'dyde me touse and rent' (163), who accused him specifically of disloyalty to the king, and who prevented him from writing (135).[42] In response to these accusations, the poet mounts a defence in which he attempts to show that his inner 'truth', or poetic ability, and his outer 'truth', or loyalty, are coterminous, and to establish that combined 'truth' as at once the source, the product, and the validation of his writing. As appears from the scene in which his protagonist encounters the lady he is courting, the way in which his established relationship with de Worde enables him to envisage his writing as, literally, *printed* writing, is key to that defence. The names of the protagonists are identical to those in the *Pastime*—Grand Amour and La Belle Pucelle—and the correspondence is clearly not accidental. Although the Pucelle of the *Conforte* appears at first not to recognize Amour, she goes on to declare:

> Of late I sawe aboke of your makynge
> Called the pastyme of pleasure/whiche is wondrous
> For I thynke and you had not ben in louynge
> Ye coude neuer haue made it so sentencyous*.   *full of meaning*
> (785–88)

This is an extraordinary statement. First, it implies that the Grand Amour who died at the end of the *Pastime* was also its author, and thus that his death was a fiction; the second implication is that this new work, the *Conforte*, is not a work of fiction, but true to life. One consequence is that the *Conforte* is established as a work of cryptic yet highly specific court satire, in which Grand Amour's tribulations figure Hawes's own. Another is that the book, as physical realization of Amour's (or Hawes's) words, is shown to function as guarantee of his integrity: for Pucelle, its literary value, or sententiousness, is a sign that his love was true.

The sudden invocation, within the *Conforte*, of the *Pastime* as physical artefact affirms a still more important aspect of Hawes's poetics. The implication is that the poet's endeavour of writing truth acquires significance only when his words are, quite literally, given material representation in the outside world: it is this that gives the 'truth' its talismanic power. Indeed, Hawes implies that such physically *present* words not only cloak existing truths, but have the power to shape future ones:

> In many placys/I se by prophecy
> As in the storyes/of the olde buyldynge
> Letters for my lady/depeynted wonderly

---

[41] See further Seth Lerer, *Chaucer and his Readers: Imagining the Author in Late-Medieval England* (Princeton, NJ, 1993), 176–93.

[42] All quotations from the *Conforte* will be taken from Stephen Hawes, in Florence W. Gluck and Alice B. Morgan (eds), *The Minor Poems*, EETS o.s. 271 (London, 1974). For Hawes and de Worde, see A. S. G. Edwards, 'Poet and Printer in Sixteenth Century England: Stephen Hawes and Wynkyn de Worde', *Gutenberg Jahrbuch* (1980), 82–8, and 'From Manuscript to Print: Wynkyn de Worde and the Printing of Contemporary Poetry', *Gutenberg Jahrbuch* (1991), 143–8. Cf. also Seth Lerer, 'The Wiles of a Woodcut: Wynkyn de Worde and the Early Tudor Reader', *Huntington Library Quarterly*, 59 (1996), 381–403.

And letters for me/besyde her meruayllously
Agreynge well/vnto my bokes all
In dyuers placys/I se it in generall.

(281–94)

(In many places, I see by prophecy:
For example, in the storeys of the old building
There are letters representing my lady, strangely painted,
And letters representing me beside her, as if by miracle—
Which corresponds perfectly with all my books.
I see this same thing in many places.)

Amour suggests not only that the 'letters ... depeynted' on old buildings 'memorialize' his *future* with Pucelle, but also that, in doing so, they agree with what is recorded in his own books. This effect of overdetermination recurs when, towards the end of his quest, Amour enters a tower where he finds three mirrors that reflect his past, present, and future, each accompanied by a 'scrypture' engraved in the wall in letters of gold. Cumulatively, these predict Amour's ultimate vindication as a poet who is divinely inspired, and thus incapable of writing anything other than 'truth'. Their power, however, derives not only from their status as engravings within the poem's fiction, but also from the way they are re-recorded in the pages of the *Conforte*. Although the poem ends inconclusively, with Amour waking from his dream at the point where it seems he is about to win La Belle Pucelle, the implication is that, since its words are impressed or 'enprynted', the events it memorializes will come to pass: that is, that by writing it, Amour (or Hawes) is altering the course of the future.[43] For Hawes, then, print serves as a way of reimagining what poetry is and does. Far from being a vehicle for disseminating an already completed text, print is a medium that he thinks *through*, and thinks *with*.

Robert Copland

An equally imaginative response to print is found in the work of Robert Copland. Unlike the other writers considered here, he was a printer first and a poet second: an apprentice to Wynkyn de Worde, with whom he continued a close association even after setting up his own print-shop in 1514, acting as editor for de Worde and taking on some of his work.[44] Although he composed a number of original, stand-alone poems in English—*The Seuen Sorowes that Women Haue When Theyr Husbandes Be Deade* ([written c1526]; STC 5734), *Iyl of Braintfords Testament* ([c1535]; STC 5730), and *The Hye Way to the Spyttell Hous* ([c1536]; STC 5732)—the majority of his writings take the form either of translations from the French, or of prefaces and envoys to works printed either by himself or by de Worde. His total output gives the impression of extreme professional busy-ness, and of complete immersion in both the literature and print culture of the time: in addition to being a printer, he was active as a translator of French literature, with a highly diverse output that included

---

[43] For Hawes and divine inspiration, see further Jane Griffiths, 'The Object of Allegory: Truth and Prophecy in Stephen Hawes's *Conforte of Lovers*', in Mary Carr, Kenneth Clarke, and Marco Nievergelt (eds), *On Allegory: Some Medieval Aspects and Approaches* (Newcastle, 2008), 132–54.

[44] For Copland's biography, see Mary C. Erler (ed.), *Poems* (Toronto, 1993), 3–10. All quotations from Copland's poems will be taken from this edition.

romances, monumental works such as the *Secrete of Secretes* (1528; STC 770), the first English translation of a treatise on classical memory arts, *The Art of Memory* ([c1545]; STC 24112), surgical treatises, devotional and dance manuals, and a navigational guide.⁴⁵ These translations were printed either by de Worde or, subsequently, by Copland himself; they show him creating the matter which he then put into circulation.

Copland's prologues and epilogues indicate just how conscious he was of the contribution that he was making to the production of books in London and of the practical difficulties attendant on that production—but also how he sought to frame that contribution as part of a developing vernacular poetic tradition. His paratexts clearly respond to the writing of his English poetic predecessors and contemporaries. His intermittent use of aureate language indicates familiarity with Lydgate, and his full-length works show clear signs of French influence—for example in his adaptation of the mock-testament in *Jyl of Braintford* and fool-list satire in *Hye Way*—but equally striking, and less predictable, are the echoes of his contemporaries. Thus, as Erler has argued, Copland's envoy to the 1528 *Secrete of Secretes* echoes Hawes's envoy to his *Conuersyon of Swerers*, and part of *The Kalendar of Shepherdes* seems to parody his theory of allegory.⁴⁶ In addition, one of the passages (18c) that Copland adds to William Walter's translation of *Guystarde and Sygysmonde* (de Worde, 1532; STC 3183.5) echoes Barclay's *Ship of Fools* in the terms in which it discusses fortune, while the categorisation of fools throughout *Hye Way* also suggests a project similar to Barclay's, if not his direct influence.

Skelton's influence is more pervasive; it appears at the level of the individual word in Copland's references to a ship as a 'bonaventure' in *The Rutter of the Sea* (1528; STC 11550.6) and *Hye Way*, echoing the name of the ship in Skelton's *Bowge of Court*, but also in entire passages. The opening of Copland's prologue to the *Seuen Sorowes*, for example, startlingly echoes the supplicants to the Queen of Fame in Skelton's *Garlande of Laurell* (491-511):

>With what newes? or here ye any tidings
>Of the pope, or the Emperour, or of kynges
>Of martyn Luther, or of the great Turke
>Of this and that, and how the world doth worke.
>...
>
>With haue ye the takyng of the Frenche kyng
>Or what conceytes haue ye of laughing
>Haue ye the balade called maugh murre
>Or bony wenche, or els go from my durre
>Col to me, or hey downe dery dery
>Or a my hert, or I pray you be mery
>   (*Seuen Sorowes*, passage 12b, 5-8, 13-18)⁴⁷

The satirical loss of grammatical coherence is clearly Skeltonic, while the urgent question 'What newes?' is an echo of *Why Come Ye Nat to Court?* (233). Skeltonic, too, is the way the

---

⁴⁵ See further Mary Erler, 'Copland [Coplande], Robert [Roberte] (*fl.* 1505–1547)', *ODNB*.

⁴⁶ Copland, in Erler (ed.), *Poems*, 14, 156–7. The Hawes parody in *The Kalendar of Shepherdes* occurs in passage 3e, 1–2.

⁴⁷ The titles given here appear to be those of contemporary ballads; for details, see Erler (ed.), *Poems*, 111.

last lines run together a series of song titles—as witness Skelton's 'Agaynst a Comely Coystrowne', for example. Elsewhere, combinations of verse form and of rhyme words show how fully Copland had internalized Skelton's writing: in *The Rosarye of Our Lady in Englysshe*, for example, the assertion that Mary's name 'can neuer dye / But euermore renewe / In goodnesse and vertewe' (19–21) seems to echo Skelton's praise of Jane Scrope in *Phyllyp Sparowe*, 'She floryssheth new and new / In beaute and vertew' (896-7), while the poem's short lines and use of only two rhymes per stanza may also have been influenced by the equally short lines and long rhyme-leashes of the verse form to which Skelton gave his name: the Skeltonic. The dead man's lament in Copland's translation of the *Kalendar of Shepherdes* (1516; STC 22409) owes a yet more substantial debt to Skelton:

> Man loke and se
> Take hede of me
> How thou shalte be
> Whan thou art deed
> Drye as a tree
> Wormes shall ete the
> Thy grete beaute
> Shall be lyke leed
> ... Now entende
> For to amende.
> (passage 3c, 1–8, 17–18)

These lines are formally quite different from the equivalent lines in both Copland's source and the roughly contemporary translation of it published by Pynson in 1506—but their resemblance to Skelton's 'Upon a deedmans hed (a skull)' is striking; they even end with the word that Skelton too very often deploys by way of conclusion: amend.[48] Cumulatively, Copland's echoes of Skelton amount almost to discipleship.[49]

Copland's responsiveness to his contemporaries is also apparent in the way he echoes their statements concerning the value of poetry, in particular Barclay's recurrent emphasis on the moral profit that is to be gained from it (for example in his envoy to *The Secrete of Secretes* (1528; STC 770), 15–21). Yet he is capable of complicating this inherited position; in his Prologue to *The Castell of Pleasure* (1518, STC 18476), in particular, he parodies it outright. Here, he first praises the author, William Neville, for his 'good entent' and the 'labour dylygent' with which he has managed:

> Bookes to endyte of maters ryght vncouthe — *quite unfamiliar*
> Ensample gyuynge to all suche as pretende
> In tharte of loue theyr myndes to condescende — *to devote their minds to*
> (passage 4a, 1, 3, 10–12)

---

[48] As Erler has observed (*Poems*, 142), the sole surviving manuscript witness to Skelton's *Speke Parrot* (BL MS Harley 2252) was also Copland's copy-text for his edition of *Ipomydon*; it is in *Speke Parrot* that Skelton uses 'amend' with particularly pointed emphasis (274–7; 353–6).

[49] Copland's French envoys to *The Castell of Pleasure* also recall Skelton's use of macaronic envoys, particularly those to *A Garlande of Laurell*; like Skelton's, they include a dedication to Henry VIII—but more importantly, their code-switching and their breathless accumulation of loosely connected matter mirrors Skelton's reluctance ever to stop writing (see further Lerer, *Chaucer and his Readers*, 193–208, especially 200–1). Erler rightly describes them as witnessing 'hectic energy' (*Poems*, 12): a quality Copland and Skelton share.

Even here, the mismatch between (on the one hand) Copland's aureate diction and his praise of the author's morality and (on the other hand) the book's subject-matter—the art of love—suggests that the praise should not be taken at face value. That suspicion is confirmed when the speaker abruptly switches tone:

> Yet ben there many that lytell regarde
> Your pleasures castell/inhabyte with Beaute
> And I am sure wold gyue but small rewarde
> For this your labour/and studyous dyte
> But had ye compiled some maner subtylte
> Lucre to gete/theyr neyghbour to begyle
> They wolde alowe it a perfyte dyscrete style
> (passage 4a, 15–21)

> (But there are many who have little regard
> For your Castle of Pleasure, inhabited by beauty,
> And I am sure would give little praise or money
> For your work on it, and your studious practice.
> But if you had written some kind of crafty guide
> To getting rich or cheating their neighbour,
> They would consider it a fine piece of writing.)

The stanza puns almost outrageously on the two senses of profit, even blurring the distinction between writing that instructs in how to get lucre and writing whose own purpose is 'lucre to gete'; the implication is that the moral position personified by Barclay is simply untenable for a printer whose business is to make a living.[50] It thus makes explicit a play on words that underlies many of Copland's references to 'profit', even when the pun is potential rather than actual. Copland's repeated self-representation, within his prologues, as a practical man and a man of business entails an emphatic focus on the realities of textual production and (especially) marketing.[51] By dramatizing the dilemmas of the publisher, he adapts an established paratextual convention—the use of prologues and envoys to frame a printed text—in a way that draws the reader's attention to the medium in which the text is transmitted as well as to its content. He is an early adopter of what Rachel Stenner has identified as the 'typographic imaginary': a series of self-reflexive tropes and practices through which authors (and printers) reveal a marked self-consciousness about both the potential and the limitations of print.[52]

One way this manifests in practice is Copland's frequent use of the sixteenth-century trope (common in publishers' prefaces, in particular) which asserts the perfection of the printed text; in his envoy to the *Assemble of Foules* (1530; STC 5092), for example, he declares that print has rescued Chaucer's poem 'frome ruynous domage' by liberating it from ripped and worm-eaten mouldy green manuscripts to preserve it 'in snowe wyte paper' (passage 16b, 10–11). Yet Copland also betrays a clear awareness that a printed text's appearance of perfection may be misleading; thus, in the envoy to *The Secrete of Secretes*, he

---

[50] See Erler (ed.), *Poems*, 13, and cf. Kathleen Tonry, *Agency and Intention in English Print, 1476–1526* (Turnhout, 2016), 17–70.

[51] See further Rachel Stenner, *The Typographic Imaginary in Early Modern English Literature* (London, 2018), 89–95.

[52] See Stenner, *Typographic Imaginary*, 2–5.

inventively reworks a commonplace when, rather than suggesting that his readers should separate the text's sententious corn from its fictional weeds, he suggests that the 'weeds' are typographical errors (passage 13b, 22–7). Copland's self-consciousness about writing specifically for print is also in evidence in his frequent use of a first person speaker, not only in his prologues (as in *The Castell of Pleasure*), but also in his marginal glosses, and even within the text itself. In *Guystarde and Sygysmonde*, for example, his presence is that of the translator; like Barclay and Lydgate before him, he makes additions to his source text, and signals these through paratextual directions that take the form of rubrics such as 'R. Coplande to these louers in the effect of theyr loue' and 'R. Coplande by exclamacyon to fortune'. Such identification of new material as original to the translator suggests that he also shared his predecessors' concern to present himself as author—or, at the very least, that he had inherited the *form* of such claims to authority, as a trope.

Elsewhere, in his stand-alone poems, Copland appears as character rather than as author, actively performing the mediation between text and reader that is implied by the paratexts in his translations. In *Hye Way*, as interlocutor of the spital house porter who lists the kinds of fool who seek lodging there, his main role is to serve as facilitator of the poem's satire. Yet because the prologue too is spoken in Copland's voice, its re-emergence in the body of the text blurs the boundaries between paratext and poem and between fiction and reality. In *Iyl of Braintford*, the effect of such playful experimentation with the boundaries between different parts of the text is still more striking: here 'Robert Copland the auctor' appears both in the short story that forms the prologue, curiously enquiring after the origin of the saying 'ye shall haue a fart / Of Iyll of Brantford for your paine (*trouble*)' (20–1), and in the story told in the body of the text, of the composition of Iyl's testament and her bequest of 'xxvi. farts and a half' (colophon, 175). Like Hawes, Copland creates slippage between truth and fiction—but unlike Hawes, he is more interested in playful fictions than in poetic truth.

In his engagement with the idea of print, too, Copland is both like and unlike Hawes. Both are extremely interested in the way in which print affects the meaning of a text. But whereas Hawes is greatly invested in print's permanent impressions, Copland is interested in the potential contradiction inherent in representing the spoken word on the printed page. Such an interest is not peculiar to print, of course: both Hoccleve's and Lydgate's works, among others, anticipate it in poems written for manuscript. Yet in Copland's hands the trope is developed in ways that *are* print-specific, fostered by his awareness of the materiality of the text and by his intimate working knowledge of the processes of print production. As Stenner has noted, the layout of Copland's dialogues bears a striking resemblance to printed drama of the period, yet many speeches incorporate a multiplicity of voices; in *Hye Way*, for example, the porter ventriloquizes a large number of the beggars he encounters, while in the prologues to *The Castell of Pleasure* and *Seuen Soroues*, the Copland figure voices the clamour of demands that are made of printers.[53] Because the emergence of these secondary voices is not indicated in the layout of the text, there is a marked contrast between the seeming clarity of the printed page and the Babel it attests; the effect is a kind of reversal of that seen in Barclay's *Ship of Fools*, where the confusion of the page belies Barclay's drive to categorize and anatomize. Such mismatches draw attention to the illusory nature of print's 'perfect' finished state just as Copland's envoy to the *Seuen Sorowes* does. Like later self-consciously *printed* texts such as William Baldwin's *Beware the Cat* ([c1553]; STC 1245) and *Mirror for Magistrates* (1559; STC 1248), or

---

[53] Stenner, *Typographic Imaginary*, 85–9.

Thomas Nashe's *Pierce Penilesse his supplication to the diuell* (1592; STC 18371) and *Haue with you to Saffron-walden* (1596; STC 18369), Copland's prologues present the finished printed text as if it were mutable: like the spoken words it records, a fluid and continuous act of creation.[54] Copland thus makes strikingly visible the conditions of writing at the time, dramatizing the process of turning both written and spoken words into a printed artefact.

Conclusion

The contrast between the vignette, in the *Eneados*, of Douglas taking up his pen in solitude to work on a single epic, and Copland's habitual self-portrayal as an almost frenetically socialized printer of miscellaneous texts might seem to suggest that print entirely altered the way poets conceived of themselves during the first twenty years of the sixteenth century. That would be a misrepresentation, however. With the exception of Douglas, the writers of this period were closely linked through their reading of and responses to one another's works, by personal contact, and frequently also through the printers who published them. All in different ways engage with overlapping questions about how to formulate the position of the poet at court, the position of the poet in the text, and the potential of print to reshape the way the poet envisages both his work as writer and the physical manifestations of that work. Central to their thinking about these questions is their shared vernacular poetic heritage. Even as they sought actively to define themselves in a contemporary context, they did so to a very large extent by referring back to their predecessors.

---

[54] For Baldwin, see Stenner, *Typographic Imaginary*, 110–27; for Nashe, see Neil Rhodes, 'On Speech, Print, and New Media: Thomas Nashe and Marshall McLuhan', *Oral Tradition*, 24 (2009), 373–92; cf. also Griffiths, *Diverting Authorities*, 123–48, 175–204.

Bibliography

Anonymous primary works are listed under the first significant word of the title when the first word is the definite or indefinite article. Post-medieval collections of primary texts are entered under the name of the editor, as are works for which the title is not demonstrably medieval.

The following abbreviations are used:

EETS: Early English Text Society; cited by series: e.s. (extra series), o.s. (original series) s.s. (supplementary series), by volume number(s) and date(s).
MED: *Middle English Dictionary*, ed. Robert E. Lewis, et al. (Ann Arbor, MI, 1952–2001).
MET: Middle English Texts (Heidelberg), cited by series number.
STS: Scottish Text Society, cited by series, volume number(s) and date.
DIMEV: Linne Mooney et al., *A Digital Index of Middle English Verse* (online).
NIMEV: J. Boffey and A. S. G. Edwards, *A New Index of Middle English Verse*. London, 2005.
ODNB: H.C.G. Matthew and Brian Harrison (eds) *Oxford Dictionary of National Biography*. Oxford, 2004 (also online, with supplements).
STC: A. W. Pollard and G. R. Redgrave, revised and enlarged by W. A. Jackson, and F. S. Ferguson, completed by Katharine F. Pantzer, *A Short-Title Catalogue of Books Printed in England, Scotland, & Ireland and of English Books Printed Abroad 1475–1640*. 3 vols. 2nd edn. London, 1976–91.
Wing: Donald G. Wing, *A Short-Title Catalogue of Books Printed in England, Scotland, Ireland, Wales, and British America, and of English Books Printed in Other Countries, 1641–1700*. 4 vols. 2nd edn. New York, 1972–98.

Ackerman, Robert W. '*The Debate of the Body and the Soul* and Parochial Christianity'. *Speculum*, 37 (1962), 541–65.
Ailes, Marianne E. 'Comprehension Problems and their Resolution in the Middle English Verse Translations of *Fierabras*'. *Forum for Modern Language Studies*, 35 (1999), 396–407.
Alan of Lille. Winthrop Wetherbee (ed. and trans.). *Literary Works*. Cambridge, MA, 2013.
Alexander, The Prose Life of. J. S. Westlake (ed.). EETS, o.s. 143. London, 1913.
Allen, Elizabeth. 'The Pardoner in the "dogges boure": Early Reception of the *Canterbury Tales*'. *The Chaucer Review*, 36 (2001), 91–127.
Allen, Hope Emily. 'The Desert of Religion: Addendum'. *Archiv für das Studium der neueren Sprachen und Literatur*, 127 (1911), 388–90.
Allen, Rosamund. 'Place-Names in *The Awntyrs off Arthure*: Corruption, Conjecture, Coincidence'. In Bonnie Wheeler (ed), *Arthurian Studies in Honour of P. J. C. Field*. Cambridge, 2004. 181–98.
Allmand, Christopher. *Henry V*. Berkeley, CA, 1992.
Allmand, Christopher. *The De Re Militari of Vegetius: The Reception, Transmission and Legacy of a Roman Text in the Middle Ages*. Cambridge, 2011.
Anderson, M. D. *Drama and Imagery in English Medieval Churches*. Cambridge, 1963.
Anglo, Sydney. 'The British History in Early Tudor Propaganda'. *Bulletin of the John Rylands Library*, 44 (1961), 17–48.
Anne, The Middle English Stanzaic Versions of the Life of Saint. Roscoe E. Parker (ed.). EETS, o.s. 174. London, 1928.
Appleford, Amy. *Learning to Die in London, 1380–1540*. Philadelphia, PA, 2015.
Appleford, Amy, and Nicholas Watson. 'Merchant Religion in Fifteenth-Century London: The Writings of William Litchfield'. *The Chaucer Review*, 46 (2011), 203–22.
Arber, Edward (ed.). *Transcript of the Registers of the Company of Stationers*. 5 vols. London, 1875–94.

Archambo, Shelley Batt. 'The Development of the English Carol through the Fifteenth Century'. *Choral Journal*, 27 (1986), 28–31.
Archibald, Elizabeth. 'Macaronic Poetry'. In Corinne Saunders (ed.), *A Companion to Medieval Poetry*. Oxford, 2010. 277–88.
Armstrong, Nancy and Leonard Tennenhouse (eds). *The Ideology of Conduct: Essays on Literature and the History of Sexuality*. London, 1987.
Arn, Mary-Jo (ed.). *Charles d'Orléans in England (1415–1440)*. Cambridge, 2000.
Arn, Mary-Jo. 'Two Manuscripts, One Mind: Charles d'Orléans and the Production of Manuscripts in Two Languages'. In Mary-Jo Arn (ed.), *Charles d'Orléans in England (1415–1440)*. Cambridge, 2000. 61–78.
Arn, Mary-Jo. 'Charles of Orleans and the Poems of BL MS, Harley 682'. *English Studies*, 74 (1993), 222–35.
Arthour and of Merlin, Of. O. D. Macrae-Gibson (ed.). EETS, o.s. 268, 279. London, 1973, 1979.
Ashby, George. Mary Bateson (ed.). *George Ashby's Poems*. EETS, e.s. 76. London, 1899.
Ashe, Laura. 'The "Short Charter of Christ": An Unpublished Longer Version, from Cambridge University Library, MS Add. 6686'. *Medium Ævum*, 72 (2003), 32–48.
Ashley, Kathleen. 'The French *Enseignemenz a Phellipe* and *Enseignement a Ysabel* of Saint Louis'. In Mark D. Johnston (ed.), *Medieval Conduct Literature: An Anthology of Vernacular Guides to Behaviour for Youths, with English Translations*. Toronto, 2009. 3–22.
Ashley, Kathleen and Robert L. A. Clark (eds). *Medieval Conduct*. Minneapolis, MIN, 2001.
Asloan Manuscript, The: A Miscellany in Prose and Verse. W. A. Craigie (ed.). STS, n.s. 14, 16. Edinburgh, 1923, 1925.
Aston, Margaret. 'Corpus Christi and Corpus Regni: Heresy and the Peasants' Revolt'. *Past & Present*, 143 (1994), 3–47.
Atkin, Tamara. *The Drama of Reform: Theology and Theatricality, 1461–1553*. Turnhout, 2013.
Atkin, Tamara. 'Playbooks and Printed Drama: A Reassessment of the Date and Layout of the Manuscript of the Croxton *Play of the Sacrament*'. *Review of English Studies*, n.s. 60 (2009), 194–205.
Attreed, Lorraine C. (ed.). *The York House Books, 1461–1490*. 2 vols. Stroud, 1991.
Attridge, Derek. *The Rhythms of English Poetry*. London, 1982.
Atwood, E. Bagby. 'Some Minor Sources of Lydgate's *Troy Book*'. *Studies in Philology*, 35 (1938), 25–42.
Audelay, John. *John the Blind Audelay, Poems and Carols (Oxford, Bodleian Library MS Douce 302)*. Susanna Fein (ed.). Kalamazoo, MI. 2009.
Audelay, John. Ella Keats Whiting (eds). *The Poems of John Audelay*. EETS, o.s. 184. London, 1931.
Awyntrs off Arthure at the Terne Wathelyn. Ralph Hanna III (ed.). Manchester, 1974.
Ayers, Robert W. 'Medieval History, Moral Purpose, and the Structure of Lydgate's *Siege of Thebes*'. *PMLA*, 73 (1958), 463–74.
Baker, Donald C. and John L. Murphy, 'The Late Medieval Plays of MS Digby 133: Scribes, Dates, and Early History'. *Research Opportunities in Renaissance Drama*, 10 (1967), 153–66.
Bale, Anthony. 'From Translator to Laureate: Imagining the Medieval Author'. *Literature Compass*, 5 (2008), 918–34.
Bale, Anthony. 'John Lydgate's Religious Poetry'. In Julia Boffey and A. S. G. Edwards (eds), *A Companion to Fifteenth Century English Poetry*. Cambridge, 2013. 73–85.
Bale, Anthony. 'A Norfolk Gentlewoman and Lydgatian Patronage: Lady Sibylle Boys and her Cultural Environment'. *Medium Ævum*, 78 (2009), 394–413.
Bale, Anthony and Sebastian Sobecki (eds). *Medieval English Travel: A Critical Anthology*. Oxford, 2019.
Bancourt, Paul. 'Chansons de geste, roman, romance et fabliaux'. In Danielle Buschinger and André Crépin (eds), *Comique, satire et parodie dans la tradition renardienne et les fabliaux*. Göppingen, 1983. 59–70.
Bannatyne Manuscript, The. National Library of Scotland Advocates' MS 1. 1. 6. Denton Fox and William A. Ringler (intro.). London, 1980.
Barbour, John. *The Bruce*. A. A. M. Duncan (ed. and trans.). Edinburgh, 1999.

Barnhouse, Rebecca. *The Book of the Knight of the Tower: Manners for Young Medieval Women*. New York, 2006.
Barr, Beth Allison. 'Gendering Pastoral Care: John Mirk and His *Instructions for Parish Priests*'. In J. S. Hamilton (ed.), *Fourteenth Century England, IV*. Woodbridge, 2006. 93–108.
Barr, Helen (ed.). *The Digby Poems*. Exeter, 2009.
Barr, Helen (ed.). *The Piers Plowman Tradition*. London, 1993.
Barratt, Alexandra A. T. '*The Flower and the Leaf* and *The Assembly of Ladies*: Is There a (Sexual) Difference?'. *Philological Quarterly*, 66 (1987), 1–24.
Barratt, Alexandra (ed.). *Women's Writing in Middle English*, 2nd edn. London, 2010.
Barrell, A. D. M. *Medieval Scotland*. Cambridge, 2000.
Barthes, Roland. 'The Death of the Author'. In Stephen Heath (trans.), *Image-Music-Text*. New York, 1977. 142–8.
Batt, Catherine. 'The *Epistre au dieu d'Amours* and *The Letter of Cupid*: Christine de Pizan, Thomas Hoccleve, and Vernacular Poetics'. In Catherine Batt, Jonathan Hsy, and René Tixier (eds), *'Booldly bot meekly': Essays on the Theory and Practice of Translation in the Middle Ages in Honour of Roger Ellis*. Turnhout, 2018. 427–44.
Battles, Paul. 'In Folly Ripe, In Reason Rotten: *The Flower and the Leaf* and the 'Purgatory of Cruel Beauties'. *Medium Ævum*, 72 (2003), 238–58.
Baugh, A. C. 'Parallels to the Mak Story'. *Modern Philology*, 15 (1918), 169–74.
Bawcutt, Priscilla. 'Credit to Dunbar'. *Times Literary Supplement*, 27 March 2020, 8.
Bawcutt, Priscilla. *Dunbar the Makar*. Oxford, 1992.
Bawcutt, Priscilla. 'Henryson's "Poeit of the Auld Fassoun"'. *Review of English Studies*, n.s. 32 (1981), 429–34.
Bawcutt, Priscilla. 'Tretis of the Tua Mariit Wemen and the Wedo' 185–87 and Chaucer's Parson's Tale'. *Notes and Queries*, n.s. 11 (1964), 332–3.
Bazire, Joyce. 'Mercy and Justice'. *Neuphilologische Mitteilungen*, 83 (1982), 178–91.
Bazire, Joyce. '"Mercy and Justice": The Additional 31042 Version'. *Leeds Studies in English*, n.s. 16 (1985), 259–71.
Beadle, Richard. 'Monk Hyngham's Hand in the Macro Manuscript'. In Richard Beadle and A. J. Piper (eds), *New Science out of Old Books: Studies in Manuscripts and Early Printed Books in Honour of A. I. Doyle*. Aldershot, 1995. 315–41.
Beadle, Richard. 'Occupation and Idleness'. *Leeds Studies in English*, n.s. 32 (2001), 7–47.
Beadle, Richard. 'The Origins of Abraham's Preamble in the York Play of *Abraham and Isaac*'. *Yearbook of English Studies*, 11 (1981), 178–87.
Beadle, Richard, and Anthony Smith. 'A Carol by James Ryman in the Holkham Archives'. *Review of English Studies*, n.s. 71 (2020), 850–66.
Bédier, Joseph. *Les fabliaux: études de littérature populaire*. Paris, 1893.
Beidler, Peter G. 'Miller's Tale'. In Robert Correale and Mary Hamel (eds), *Sources and Analogues of the Canterbury Tales*. 2 vols. Woodbridge, 2005. 2.249–75.
Bellis, Joanna. '"Fresch Anamalit Termes": The Contradictory Celebrity of Chaucer's Aureation'. In Isabel Davis and Catherine Nall (eds), *Chaucer and Fame: Reputation and Reception*. Cambridge, 2015. 143–63.
Bellis, Joanna. *The Hundred Year War in Literature, 1337–1600*. Cambridge, 2016.
Bellis, Joanna and Venetia Bridges. '"What shalt thou do when thou hast an English to make into Latin?". The Proverb Collection of Cambridge, St John's College MS M.F.26'. *Studies in Philology*, 112 (2015), 68–92.
Bennett, J. A. W. 'Gower's "Honeste Love"'. In John Lawlor (ed.), *Patterns of Love and Courtesy: Essays in Memory of C. S. Lewis*. London, 1966. 107–21.
Bennett, J. A. W. (ed.). *Devotional Pieces in Verse and Prose from MS Arundel 285 and MS Harleian 6919*. STS, 3rd series, 23. Edinburgh, 1955.
Bennett, P. E. 'Chansons de Geste and Chansons d'aventures: Recent Perspectives on the Evolution of a Genre'. *French Studies*, 66 (2012), 525–35.
Benson, C. David. 'A Chaucerian Allusion and the Date of the Alliterative *Destruction of Troy*'. *Notes and Queries*, n.s. 21 (1974). 206–7.

Benson, C. David. *The History of Troy in Middle English Literature.* Woodbridge, 1980.
Benson, C. David. *Imagined Rome: The City and its Stories in Middle English Poetry.* University Park, PA, 2019.
Benson, Larry D. (ed.). *King Arthurs Death: The Middle English Stanzaic Morte Arthur and Alliterative Morte Arthure.* Indianapolis, IN, 1994.
Benson, Larry D. 'The Order of *The Canterbury Tales*'. *Studies in the Age of Chaucer*, 3 (1981), 77–120.
Bergenroth, G. A. (ed.), *Calendar of Letters, Despatches and State Papers Relating to the Negotiations Between England and Spain. Vol. 1, 1485–1509.* London, 1862.
Bernardus de cura rei famuliaris, with Some Early Scottish Prophecies. Joseph Rawson Lumby (ed.). EETS, o.s. 42. London, 1870.
Bernau, Anke. 'Lydgate's Saintly Poetics'. In Eva von Contzen and Anke Bernau (eds), *Sanctity as Literature in Late Medieval Britain.* Manchester, 2015. 151–71.
Beveridge, E. (ed.). *Fergusson's Scottish Proverbs from the Original Print of 1641 together with a larger MS collection of about the same period, hitherto unpublished,* STS, 2nd series, 15. Edinburgh, 1942.
Bevington, David. 'Staging and Liturgy in *The Croxton Play of the Sacrament*'. In Wim Hüsken and Peter Happé (eds), *Staging Scripture: Biblical Drama, 1350–1660.* Leiden, 2016. 235–52.
Bianco, Sue. 'A Black Monk in the Rose Garden: Lydgate and the *Dit Amoureux* Tradition'. *The Chaucer Review*, 34 (1999), 60–8.
Bianco, Sue. 'New Perspectives on Lydgate's Courtly Verse'. In Helen Cooney (ed.), *Nation, Court and Culture.* 2001. 95–115.
Binns, A. L. 'A Manuscript Source of the Book of St. Albans'. *Bulletin of the John Rylands Library*, 33 (1950–1), 15–24.
Bitterling, Klaus. 'An Abstract of John Mirk's "Instructions for Parish Priests"'. *Notes and Queries*, n.s. 24 (1977), 146–8.
Blacman, John. M. R. James (ed.) *Henry VI: A Reprint of John Blacman's Memoir.* Cambridge, 1919.
Blake, N. F. *Caxton: England's First Publisher.* London, 1976.
Blake, N. F. 'De Worde, Wynkyn'. *ODNB.* 2004.
Blake, N. F. *The English Language in Medieval Literature.* London, 1977.
Blake, N. F. 'The Literary Language'. In N. F. Blake (ed.), *1066–1476.* Vol. 2 in Richard M. Hogg (ed.), *The Cambridge History of the English Language.* Cambridge, 1992. 500–41.
Blake, N. F. 'Manuscript to Print'. In Jeremy Griffiths and Derek Pearsall (eds), *Book Production and Publishing in Britain 1375–1475.* Cambridge, 1989. 403–32.
Blake, N. F. 'Rhythmical Alliteration'. *Modern Philology*, 67 (1969), 118–24.
Blake, N. F. *William Caxton and English Literary Culture.* London, 1991.
Blanchfield, Lynne Sandra. 'Rate Revisited: the Compilation of the Narrative Works in MS Ashmole 61'. In Jennifer Fellows, Rosalind Field, Gillian Rogers, and Judith Weiss (eds), *Romance Reading on the Book: Essays on Medieval Narrative Presented to Maldwyn Mills.* Cardiff, 1996. 208–20.
Blanchfield, Lynne Sandra. 'The Romances in MS Ashmole 61: An Idiosyncratic Scribe'. In Maldwyn Mills, Jennifer Fellows, and Carol M. Meale (eds), *Romance in Medieval England.* Cambridge, 1991. 65–87.
Blatt, Heather. *Participatory Reading in Late-Medieval England.* Manchester, 2018.
Blayney, M. S. (ed.). *Fifteenth-Century English Translations of Alain Chartier's Le Traite de l'Esperance and Le Quadrilogue Invectif.* EETS, o.s. 270, 281. Oxford, 1974 and 1980.
Blayney, Peter M. W. *The Stationers' Company and the Printers of London 1501–1557.* 2 vols. Cambridge, 2013.
Blurton, Heather, and Hannah Johnson. 'Reading the *Prioress's Tale* in the Fifteenth Century: Lydgate, Hoccleve, and Marian Devotion'. *The Chaucer Review*, 50 (2015), 134–58.
Boardman, Stephen. 'Chronicle Propaganda in Fourteenth-Century Scotland: Robert the Steward, John of Fordun and the 'Anonymous Chronicle'. *The Scottish Historical Review*, 76 (1997), 23–43.
Boccaccio, Giovanni. *Tutte le opere di Giovanni Boccaccio.* Vittore Branca (ed.). 10 vols. Milan, 1964–98.
Boccaccio, Giovanni. Virginia Brown (ed. and trans). *Famous Women.* Cambridge, MA, 2001.

Boethius. *Theological Tractates.* F. Stewart, E. K. Rand, and S. J. Tester (eds and trans). Cambridge, MA, 1973.

Boffey, Julia. 'Audelay's Carol Collection'. In Susanna Fein (ed.), *My Wyl and my Wrytyng: Essays on John the Blind Audelay.* Kalamazoo, MI, 2009. 218–29.

Boffey, Julia. 'Bodleian Library MS Arch. Selden. B. 24 and Definitions of the "Household Book"'. In A. S. G. Edwards, Vincent Gillespie, and Ralph Hanna (eds), *The English Medieval Book: Studies in Memory of Jeremy Griffiths.* London, 2000. 125–34.

Boffey, Julia. 'Chaucerian Prisoners: The Context of the *Kingis Quair*'. In Julia Boffey and Janet Cowen (eds), *Chaucer and Fifteenth-Century Poetry.* London, 1991. 84–102.

Boffey, Julia. '"Cy ensuent trois chaunceons": Groups and Sequences of Middle English Lyrics'. In Graham D. Caie and Denis Renevey (eds), *Medieval Texts in Context.* London, 2008. 85–95.

Boffey, Julia. 'The Early Reception of Chartier's Works in England and Scotland'. In Emma Cayley and Ashby Kinch (eds), *Chartier in Europe.* Cambridge, 2008.

Boffey, Julia. 'English Dream Poems of the Fifteenth Century and Their French Connections'. In Donald Maddox and Sara Sturm-Maddox (eds), *Literary Aspects of Courtly Culture: Selected Papers from the Seventh Triennial Congress of the International Courtly Literature Society.* Cambridge, 1994. 113–21.

Boffey, Julia (ed.). *Fifteenth-Century English Dream Visions: An Anthology.* Oxford, 2003.

Boffey, Julia. '"Forto compleyne she had gret desire": The Grievances Expressed in Two Fifteenth-Century Dream-Visions'. In Helen Cooney (ed.), *Nation, Court and Culture.* 2001. 116–28.

Boffey, Julia. 'The *Kingis Quair* and the Other Poems of Bodleian Library MS Arch. Selden. B. 24'. In Priscilla Bawcutt and Janet Hadley Williams (eds), *A Companion to Medieval Scottish Poetry.* Cambridge, 2006. 62–74.

Boffey, Julia. 'The Maitland Folio Manuscript as a Verse Anthology'. In Sally Mapstone (ed.), *William Dunbar the Nobill Poyet: Essays in Honour of Priscilla Bawcutt.* East Linton, 2001. 40–50.

Boffey, Julia. 'The Manuscripts of English Courtly Love Lyrics in the Fifteenth Century'. In Derek Pearsall (ed.), *Manuscripts and Readers in Fifteenth-Century England: The Literary Implications of Manuscript Study.* Cambridge, 1983. 3–14.

Boffey, Julia. *Manuscripts of English Courtly Love Lyrics in the Later Middle Ages.* Cambridge, 1985.

Boffey, Julia. 'Middle English Lyrics and Manuscripts'. In Thomas G. Duncan (ed.), *A Companion to the Middle English Lyric.* Cambridge, 2005. 1–18.

Boffey, Julia. 'Proverbial Chaucer and the Chaucer Canon'. *Huntington Library Quarterly*, 58 (1996), 37–48.

Boffey, Julia. 'Shirley, Trinity College Cambridge MS R. 3. 20, and the Circumstances of Lydgate's *Temple of Glass*: Coterie Verse over Time'. *Studies in the Age of Chaucer*, 38 (2016), 265–73.

Boffey, Julia. 'Short Texts in Manuscript Anthologies: The Minor Poems of John Lydgate in Two Fifteenth-Century Collections'. In Stephen G. Nichols and Siegfried Wenzel (eds), *The Whole Book: Cultural Perspectives on the Medieval Miscellany.* Ann Arbor, MI, 1996. 69–82.

Boffey, Julia, and A. S. G. Edwards. '"Chaucer's Chronicle", John Shirley, and the Canon of Chaucer's Shorter Poems'. *Studies in the Age of Chaucer*, 20 (1998), 201–18.

Boffey, Julia and A. S. G. Edwards (eds). *A Companion to Fifteenth-Century English Poetry.* Cambridge, 2013.

Boffey, Julia and A. S. G. Edwards. *A New Index of Middle English Verse.* London, 2005.

Boffey, Julia and A. S. G. Edwards. '*The Squire of Low Degree* and the Penumbra of Romance Narrative in the Early Sixteenth Century'. In Elizabeth Archibald, Megan G. Leitch, and Corinne Saunders (eds), *Romance Rewritten: The Evolution of Middle English Romance. A Tribute To Helen Cooper.* Cambridge, 2018. 229–40.

Boffey, Julia and A. S. G. Edwards. 'Towards a Taxonomy of Middle English Manuscript Assemblages'. In Margaret Connolly and Raluca Radulescu (eds), *Insular Books: Vernacular Manuscript Miscellanies in Late Medieval Britain.* London, 2015. 263–80.

Boffey, Julia and A. S. G. Edwards (intro.). *The Works of Geoffrey Chaucer and The Kingis Quair: A Facsimile of Bodleian Library, Oxford, MS Arch. Selden. B. 24.* Cambridge, 1997.

Boffey, Julia and Carol Meale. 'Selecting the Text: Rawlinson C. 86 and Some Other Books for London Readers'. In Felicity Riddy (ed.), *Regionalism in Late Mediaeval Manuscripts and Texts:*

Essays Celebrating the Publication of A Linguistic Atlas of Late Mediaeval English. Cambridge, 1991. 143–69.

Boffey, Julia and John J. Thompson. 'Anthologies and Miscellanies: Production and Choice of Texts'. In Jeremy Griffiths and Derek Pearsall (eds), *Book Production and Publishing in Britain*. Cambridge, 1988. 279–315.

Boffey, Julia and Christiania Whitehead (eds). *Middle English Lyrics: New Readings of Short Poems*. Cambridge, 2018.

Boke of Curtasye, The. J. O. Halliwell (ed.). London, 1841.

Bokenham, Osbern. Mary S. Serjeantson (ed.). *Legendys of Hooly Wummen*. EETS, o.s. 206. London, 1938.

Bokenham, Osbern. *Lives of Saints*. Simon Horobin (ed.). Vols. I, II. EETS, o.s. 356, 359. Oxford, 2020, 2022.

Bolton, J. L. *The Medieval English Economy 1150–1500*. London, 1980.

Bornstein, Diane (ed.). *The Middle English Translation of Christine de Pisan's 'Livre du corps de policie'*. MET 7. Heidelberg, 1977.

Bourchier, John, Lord Berners (trans). *Sir John Froissart's Chronicles*. E. V. Utterson (ed.). 2 vols. London, 1812.

Bourdieu, Pierre 'The Field of Cultural Production, or: The Economic World Reversed'. Richard Nice (trans.). *Poetics*, 12 (1983), 311–56.

Bowers, John M. 'Hoccleve's Huntington Holographs: The First "Collected Poems" in English'. *Fifteenth-Century Studies*, 15 (1989), 27–51.

Bowers, John M. 'Thomas Hoccleve and the Politics of Tradition'. *The Chaucer Review*, 36 (2002), 352–69.

Bowers, John M. '*The Tale of Beryn* and *The Siege of Thebes*: Alternative Ideas of *The Canterbury Tales*'. *Studies in the Age of Chaucer*, 7 (1985), 23–50.

Bowers, Rick. 'How to Get from A to B: *Fulgens and Lucres*, Histrionic Power, and the Invention of the English Comic Duo'. *Early Theatre*, 14.1 (2011), 45–59.

Bowers, R. H. 'A Middle English Mnemonic Plague Tract'. *Southern Folklore Quarterly*, 20 (1956), 118–25.

Bowers, R. H. (ed.). *Three Middle English Religious Poems*. Gainesville, FL, 1963.

Boyd, Beverly (ed.). *The Middle English Miracles of the Virgin*. San Marino, CA, 1964.

Boyle, Leonard E. 'The Fourth Lateran Council and Manuals of Popular Theology'. In Thomas J. Heffernan (ed.), *The Popular Literature of Medieval England*. Knoxville, TN, 1985. 30–43.

Bradshaw, Henry and Carl Horstmann (ed.). *The Life of Saint Werburge of Chester*. EETS, o.s. 88. London, 1887.

Braekman, W. L. 'Bollard's Middle English Book of Planting and Grafting and its Background'. *Studia Neophilologica*, 57 (1985), 19–39.

Braekman, W. L. 'Fortune Telling by the Casting of Dice'. *Studia Neophilologica*, 52 (1980), 3–29.

Brandmüller, Walter. *Das Konzil von Konstanz, 1414–1418*. 2 vols. Paderborn, 1991.

Brannen, Anne. 'Intricate Subtleties: Entertainment at Bishop Morton's Installation Feast'. *REED Newsletter*, 22 (1997), 2–11.

Brantley, Jessica. *Reading in the Wilderness: Private Devotion and Public Performance in Late Medieval England*. Chicago, IL, 2007.

Brantley, Jessica. 'Reading the Forms of *Sir Thopas*'. *The Chaucer Review*, 47 (2013), 416–38.

Brayer, Edith and Anne-Françoise Leurquin-Labie (eds). *La Somme le Roi par Frère Laurent*. Paris, 2008.

Bredehoft, Thomas A. 'Ælfric and Late Old English Verse'. *Anglo-Saxon England*, 33 (2004), 77–107.

Breeze, Andrew. 'Place-Names and Politics in *The Awntyrs off Arthure*'. *Journal of Literary Onomastics*, 7 (2019), 12–27.

Brewer, Derek. 'The International Medieval Popular Comic Tale in England'. In Thomas J. Heffernan (ed.), *The Popular Literature of Medieval England*. Knoxville, TN, 1985. 131–47.

Bridges, Margaret. 'Lydgate's Last Poem'. In Catherine Gaullier-Bougassas, Margaret Bridges, and Jean-Yves Tilliette (eds), *Trajectoires européennes du Secretum secretorum du Pseudo-Aristote (XIIIe–XVIe siècle)*. Turnhout, 2015. 317–36.

Bridges, Venetia. *Medieval Narratives of Alexander the Great: Transnational Texts in England and France.* Cambridge, 2018.
Britton, Derek. 'Unnoticed Fragments of the *Prick of Conscience*'. *Neuphilologische Mitteilungen*, 80 (1979), 327–34.
Brotanek, Rudolf (ed.). *Mittelenglische Dichtungen aus der Handschrift 432 des Trinity College in Dublin.* Halle, 1940.
Brown, Carleton (ed.). G.V. Smithers (revised). *Religious Lyrics of the XIVth Century.* 2nd edn. Oxford, 1952.
Brown, Carleton (ed.). *Religious Lyrics of the XVth Century.* Oxford, 1939.
Brown, Carleton and Rossell Hope Robbins. *The Index of Middle English Verse.* New York, 1943.
Brown, M. H. 'James I (1394–1437), king of Scots'. *ODNB.* 2004.
Brown, M. H. 'Joan (née Joan Beaufort) (d. 1445), queen of Scots, consort of James I 1394–1437. *ODNB.* 2004.
Brown, Michelle P. 'The Role of the Wax Tablet in Medieval Literacy: A Reconsideration in Light of a Recent Find from York'. *British Library Journal*, 20 (1994), 1–16.
Brown, Peter. 'Journey's End: The Prologue to the *Tale of Beryn*'. In Julia Boffey and Janet Cowen (eds), *Chaucer and Fifteenth-Century Poetry.* London, 1991. 143–74.
Brusendorff, Aage. *The Chaucer Tradition.* Oxford, 1925.
Brut, The. Friedrich W. Brie (ed.). EETS, o.s. 131, 136. London, 1906.
Buckle, Alexandra. 'Fit for a King: Music and Iconography in Richard Beauchamp's Chantry Chapel'. *Early Music*, 38 (2010), 3–20.
Bühler, Curt F. 'Review of H. N. MacCracken (ed.), *The Minor Poems of John Lydgate*'. *Review of English Studies*, 12 (1936). 236–38.
Bühler, Curt F. 'A Middle English Medical Manuscript from Norwich'. In MacEdward Leach (ed.), *Studies in Medieval Literature in Honour of Albert Croll Baugh.* Philadelphia, PA, 1961. 285–98.
Bühler, Curt F. *The Sources of the Court of Sapience.* Leipzig, 1932.
Buik of Alexander, The. R. L. Graeme Ritchie (ed.). STS, n.s. 17, 12, 21, and 25. Edinburgh, 1921–29.
Buik of King Alexander the Conquerour, The. John R. Cartwright (ed.). STS, 4th series, 16. Edinburgh, 1986, 1990.
Burger, Glenn D. *Conduct Becoming: Good Wives and Husbands in the Later Middle Ages.* Philadelphia, PA, 2018.
Burnley, J. D, and Graham Williams. 'Language'. In Peter Brown (ed.), *A New Companion to Chaucer.* Hoboken, NJ, 2019. 227–42.
Burnley, J. D. 'Lexis and Semantics'. In N. F. Blake (ed.), *1066–1476.* Vol. 2 in Richard M. Hogg (ed.), *The Cambridge History of the English Language.* Cambridge, 1992. 409–99.
Burnley, J. D. 'Scogan, Shirley's Reputation and Chaucerian Occasional Verse'. In G. Lester (ed.), *Chaucer in Perspective: Middle English Essays in Honour of Norman Blake* (Sheffield, 1999). 28–46.
Burrow, J. A. *Thomas Hoccleve.* Aldershot, 1994.
Burrow, J. A. *Medieval Writers and Their Work: Middle English Literature 1100–1500.* Oxford, 1982.
Burrow, John. 'Dunbar and the Accidents of Rhyme'. *Essays in Criticism*, 63 (2013), 20–8.
Burrow, John. 'Dunbar's Art of Asking'. *Essays in Criticism*, 65 (2015), 1–11.
Burrow, John. 'Hoccleve and the Middle French Poets'. In Helen Cooper and Sally Mapstone (eds), *The Long Fifteenth Century: Essays for Douglas Gray.* Oxford, 1997.
Burrow, John. 'Old and Middle English'. In Pat Rogers (ed.), *The Oxford Illustrated History of English Literature.* Oxford, 1987. 1–58.
Burton, Robert. *Anatomy of Melancholy.* London, 1964.
Busby, Keith. 'Conspicuous by its Absence: The English Fabliau', *Dutch Quarterly Review*, 12 (1982), 30–41.
Buschinger, Danielle. '*Le Livre des faits d'armes et de chevalerie* de Christine de Pizan et ses adaptations anglaise et haut-alémanique'. *Comptes rendus des séances de l'Académie des Inscriptions et Belles-Lettres*, 155 (2011), 1073–92.
Butler, Judith. *Gender Trouble: Feminism and the Subversion of Identity.* New York, 1990.
Butler, Michelle M. 'The Borrowed Expositor'. *Early Theatre*, 9 (2006), 73–90.

Butterfield, Ardis. *The Familiar Enemy: Chaucer, Language, and Nation in the Hundred Years War*. Oxford, 2009.
Butterfield, Ardis. 'Lyric and Elegy in *The Book of the Duchess*'. *Medium Ævum*, 60 (1991), 33–60.
Butterfield, Ardis. 'Medieval Genres and Modern Genre Theory'. *Paragraph*, 13 (1990), 184–201.
Butterfield, Ardis. 'Rough Translation: Charles d'Orléans, Lydgate and Hoccleve'. In Emma Campbell and Robert Mills (eds), *Rethinking Medieval Translation: Ethics, Politics, Theory*. Cambridge, 2012. 204–25.
Butterworth, Philip. *Staging Conventions in Medieval English Theatre*. Cambridge, 2014.
Butterworth, Philip and Katie Normington (eds). *Medieval Theatre Performance: Actors, Dancers, Automata and Their Audiences*. Cambridge, 2017.
Byrne, Aisling. 'From Hólar to Lisbon: Middle English Literature in Medieval Translation, c.1286–c.1550'. *Review of English Studies*, n.s. 71 (2020), 433–59.
Byrne, Aisling and Victoria Flood. 'The Romance of the Stanleys: Regional and National Imaginings in the Percy Folio'. *Viator*, 46 (2015), 327–51.
Cable, Thomas. *The English Alliterative Tradition*. Philadelphia, PA, 1991.
Cable, Thomas. 'Foreign Influence, Native Continuation, and Metrical Typology in Alliterative Lyrics'. In Judith Jefferson and Ad Putter (eds), *Approaches to the Metres of Alliterative Verse*. Leeds, 2009. 219–34.
Cable, Thomas. 'Middle English Meter and its Theoretical Implications'. *Yearbook of Langland Studies*, 2 (1988), 47–69.
Cable, Thomas. 'Standards from the Past: The Conservative Syllable Structure of the Alliterative Revival'. *Tennessee Studies in Literature*, 31 (1989), 42–56.
Caie, Graham D. '"I do not wish to be called auctour, but the pore compilatour": The Plight of the Medieval Vernacular Poet'. *Miscelánea*, 29 (2004), 9–21.
Calendar of Close Rolls: Henry VI, Vol. III, 1435–41. London, 1937.
Calendar of the Patent Rolls: Henry VI, Vol. 6, 1452–61. London, 1910.
Calin, William. *The Lily and the Thistle: The French Tradition and the Older Literature of Scotland*. Toronto, 2013.
Camargo, Martin. 'Chaucer and the Oxford Renaissance of Anglo-Latin Rhetoric'. *Studies in the Age of Chaucer*, 34 (2012), 173–207.
Camp, Cynthia Turner. *Anglo-Saxon Saints' Lives as History Writing in Late Medieval England*. Cambridge, 2015.
Campbell, T. P. *Tapestry in the Renaissance. Art and Magnificence*. New York, 2002.
Canby, Henry Seidel. 'The English Fabliau'. *PMLA*, 21 (1906), 200–14.
Cannon, Christopher. 'Form'. In Paul Strohm (ed.), *Oxford Twenty-First Century Approaches to Literature: Middle English*. Oxford, 2007. 177–90.
Cannon, Christopher. 'The Late Fourteenth-Century Renaissance of Anglo-Latin Rhetoric'. *Philosophy and Rhetoric*, 45 (2012), 107–33.
Cannon, Christopher. *The Making of Chaucer's English: A Study of Words*. Cambridge, 1998.
Canterbury Tales: Fifteenth-Century Continuations and Additions. John Bowers (ed.). Kalamazoo, MI, 1992.
Capgrave, John. Karen A. Winstead (ed). *John Capgrave: The Life of Saint Katherine*. Kalamazoo, MI, 1999.
Capgrave, John. Cyril Smetana (ed.). *The Life of St Norbert*. Toronto, 1977.
Capgrave, John. C. A. Mills (ed.). *Ye solace of pilgrimes, a description of Rome, circa A. D. 1450*. London, 1911.
Carleton-Williams, E. 'Mural Paintings of the Three Living and Three Dead in England'. *Journal of the British Archaeological Association*, 3rd series, 7 (1942), 31–40.
Carlson, David R. 'Chaucer, Humanism and Printing: The Conditions of Authorship in Fifteenth-century England'. *University of Toronto Quarterly*, 64 (1995), 274–88.
Carlson, David R. 'The Chronology of Lydgate's Chaucer References'. *The Chaucer Review* 38 (2004), 246–54.
Carlson, David R. 'The Civic Poetry of Abbot John Whethamstede of St Albans (+1465)', *Mediaeval Studies*, 61 (1999), 205–42.

Carlson, David R. (ed.). *The Deposition of Richard II: The Record and Process of the Reconciliation and Deposition of Richard II (1399) and Related Writings*. Toronto, 2007.
Carlson, David R. 'The Latin Writings of John Skelton'. *Studies in Philology*, 88 (1991), 1–125.
Carlson, David R. 'The Occasional Poetry of Pietro Carmeliano'. *Aevum*, 61 (1987), 495–502.
Carlson, David R. 'Woodcut Illustrations of the *Canterbury Tales*, 1483–1602'. *The Library*, 6th series, 19 (1997), 25–67.
Carney, Elizabeth. 'Fact and Fiction in "Queen Eleanor's Confession"'. *Folklore*, 95 (1984), 167–70.
Carpenter, Christine. 'The Beauchamp Affinity: A Study of Bastard Feudalism at Work'. *English Historical Review*, 95 (1980), 514–32.
Carpenter, Christine. *Locality and Polity: a Study of Warwickshire Landed Society, 1401–1499*. Cambridge, 1992.
Carpenter, Sarah. '"Gelly with tharmys of Scotland England": Word, Image and Performance at the Marriage of James IV and Margaret Tudor'. In Janet Hadley Williams and Derrick J. McClure (eds), *Fresche fontanis: Studies in the Culture of Medieval and Early Modern Scotland*. Cambridge, 2013. 165–77.
Carpenter, Sarah. 'Plays and Playcoats: A Courtly Interlude Tradition in Scotland'. *Comparative Drama*, 6 (2012), 475–96.
Carpenter, Sarah. 'Scottish Drama until 1650'. In I. Brown (ed.), *The Edinburgh Companion to Scottish Drama*. Edinburgh, 2011. 6–21.
Carpenter, Sarah. '"To thexaltacyon of noblesse": A Herald's Account of the Marriage of Margaret and James IV'. *Medieval English Theatre*, 29 (2009 for 2007), 104–20.
Carr, A. D. 'Sir Lewis John—a Medieval London Welshman'. *Bulletin of the Board of Celtic Studies*, 22 (1966–8), 260–70.
Cartwright, John R. 'Sir Gilbert Hay and the Alexander Tradition'. In Dietrich Strauss and Horst W. Drescher (eds). *Scottish Language and Literature: Medieval and Renaissance*. Scottish Studies, 4. Frankfurt, 1986. 229–38.
Catto, Jeremy. 'Religious Change Under Henry V'. In G. L. Harriss (ed.). *Henry V: The Practice of Kingship*. Stroud, 1993. 97–115.
Catto, Jeremy. 'The Triumph of the Hall in Fifteenth-century Oxford'. In Ralph Evans (ed.), *Lordship and Learning: Studies in Memory of Trevor Aston*. Woodbridge, 2004. 209–23.
Cavell, Emma. 'Henry VII, The North of England, and the First Provincial Progress of 1486'. *Northern History*, 39 (2002), 187–207.
Cavell, Emma. *The Heralds' Memoir, 1486–1490: Court Ceremony, Royal Progress and Rebellion*. Donington, 2009.
Caxton, William (trans). *The Doctrinal of Sapience*. J. Gallagher (ed.). MET 26. Heidelberg, 1993.
Caxton, William. Henry Oskar Sommer (eds). *The Recuyell of the Historyes of Troye, Translated by William Caxton*, 2 vols. London, 1894.
Chambers, E. K. and Frank Sidgwick (eds). *Early English Lyrics*. London, 1907.
Champion, Matthew. *Medieval Graffiti: The Lost Voices of England's Churches*. London, 2015.
Chartier, Alain. *The Poetical Works of Alain Chartier*. J. C. Laidlaw (ed.). Cambridge, 1974.
Chartier, Roger. 'Jack Cade, the Skin of a Dead Lamb, and the Hatred for Writing'. *Shakespeare Studies*, 34 (2006), 77–89.
Chaucer, Geoffrey (?). *The Romaunt of the Rose*. Charles Dahlberg (ed.). Norman, OK, 1999.
Chaucer, Geoffrey. *The Poetical Works of Geoffrey Chaucer: A Facsimile of Cambridge University Library MS Gg. 4. 27*. M. B. Parkes and Richard Beadle (intro.). 3 vols. Cambridge, 1979–80.
Chaucer, Geoffrey. *The Riverside Chaucer*. Larry D. Benson (general ed.). 3rd edn. Boston, MA, 1987.
Chaucer, Geoffrey. *Troilus and Criseyde: A New Edition of 'The Book of Troilus'*. B. A. Windeatt (ed.). London, 1984.
Chepman and Myllar Prints, The: Nine Tracts from the First Scottish Press, Edinburgh, 1508. William Beattie (intro.). Edinburgh, 1950.
Chester Mystery Cycle, The. R. M. Lumiansky and David Mills (eds). EETS, s.s. 3, 9. Oxford, 1974, 1986.
Christianson, C. Paul. *A Directory of London Stationers and Book Artisans 1300–1500*. New York, 1990.

Christianson, C. Paul. 'London's Late Medieval Manuscript-book Trade'. In Jeremy Griffiths and Derek Pearsall (eds), *Book Production and Publishing in Britain, 1375–1475*. Cambridge, 1989. 87–108.

Christianson, C. Paul. 'The Rise of London's Book-Trade'. In Lotte Hellinga and J. B. Trapp (eds), *The Cambridge History of the Book in Britain, Volume III: 1400–1557*. Cambridge, 1999. 128–47.

Christie, Sheila. 'The Chester Cycle'. In Thomas Betteridge and Greg Walker (eds), *The Oxford Handbook of Tudor Drama*. Oxford, 2012. 21–35.

Cicero. *De inventione: De optimo genere oratorum*. H. Hubbell (ed.). Cambridge MA, 1949.

Clarke, M. V. and V. H. Galbraith. 'The Deposition of Richard II'. *Bulletin of the John Rylands Library*, 14 (1930), 125–81.

Clouston, W.A. *Popular Tales and Fictions*. 2 vols. Edinburgh, 1887.

Coldiron, Anne E. B. *Printers without Borders: Translation and Textuality in the Renaissance*. Cambridge, 2015.

Coldiron, Anne E. B. 'A Survey of Verse Translations from French Printed Between Caxton and Tottel'. In Ian F. Moulton (ed.), *Reading and Literacy: in the Middle Ages and Renaissance*. Turnhout, 2004. 63–84.

Coldiron, Anne E. B. 'Translation's Challenge to Critical Categories: Verses from French in the Early English Renaissance'. *The Yale Journal of Criticism*, 16 (2003), 315–44

Cole, Kristin Lynn. 'The Destruction of Troy's Different Rules: The Alliterative Revival and the Alliterative Tradition'. *JEGP*, 109 (2010), 162–76.

Coleman, Joyce. 'Aurality'. In Paul Strohm (ed.), *Middle English: Oxford Twenty-First Century Approaches to Literature*. Oxford, 2007. 68–85.

Coleman, Joyce. 'Lay Readers and Hard Latin: How Gower May Have Intended the *Confessio Amantis* to Be Read'. *Studies in the Age of Chaucer*, 24 (2002), 209–35.

Coleman, Joyce. *Public Reading and the Reading Public in Late Medieval England and France*. Cambridge, 1996. 130–2.

Coleman, Joyce. 'Where Chaucer Got His Pulpit: Audience and Intervisuality in the *Troilus and Criseyde* Frontispiece'. *Studies in the Age of Chaucer*, 32 (2010), 103–28.

Colgrave, Bertram. 'The St Cuthbert Paintings on the Carlisle Cathedral Stalls'. *Burlington Magazine*, 23 (1938), 17–19.

Colledge, Edmund. 'The Augustine Screen in Carlisle Cathedral'. *Augustiniana*, 36 (1986), 65–99.

Colledge, Edmund. 'Caxton's Additions to the *Legendi Sancti Augustiniani*', *Augustiniana*, 34 (1984), 198–212.

Collier, Richard. *Poetry and Drama in the York Corpus Christi Play*. Hamden, CT, 1979.

Colonne, Guido delle. *Historia destructionis Troiae*. Nathaniel Edward Griffin, (ed.). Cambridge, MA, 1936.

Colonne, Guido delle. *Historia destructionis Troiae*. Mary Elizabeth Meek (trans.). Bloomington, IN, 1974.

Conlee, John W. (ed.). *Middle English Debate Poetry: A Critical Anthology*. East Lansing, MI, 1991.

Connolly, Margaret. 'Compiling the Book'. In Alexandra Gillespie and Daniel Wakelin (eds), *The Production of Books in England 1350–1500*. Cambridge, 2011. 129–49.

Connolly, Margaret. *John Shirley: Book Production and the Noble Household in Fifteenth- Century England*. Aldershot, 1998.

Connolly, Margaret and Raluca Radulescu (eds). *Insular Books: Vernacular Manuscript Miscellanies in Late Medieval Britain*. London, 2015.

Constans, Léopold (ed.). *Roman de Troie par Benoît de Sainte-Maure*. 6 vols. Paris, 1904– 12.

Cook, Megan L. '"Here taketh the makere of this book his leve": The *Retractions* and Chaucer's Works in Tudor England'. *Studies in Philology*, 113 (2016), 32–54.

Cook, Megan L. *The Poet and the Antiquaries*. Philadelphia, PA, 2019.

Cooke, Thomas D. with Peter Whiteford and Nancy Mohr McKinley. 'Pious Tales: Miracles of the Virgin'. In Albert E. Hartung (ed.), *A Manual of the Writings in Middle English, 1050–1500*. 11 vols. New Haven, CT, 1993. 9.3138–328, 3472–570.

Cooney, Helen (ed.). *Nation, Court and Culture: New Essays on Fifteenth-Century English Poetry*. Dublin, 2001.

Cooper, Helen. 'Counter-Romance: Civil Strife and Father Killing in the Prose Romances'. In Helen Cooper and Sally Mapstone (eds), *The Long Fifteenth Century: Essays for Douglas Gray*. Oxford, 1997. 141–62.
Cooper, Helen. *The English Romance in Time: Transforming Motifs from Geoffrey of Monmouth to the Death of Shakespeare*. Oxford, 2004.
Cooper, Helen. 'The *Lancelot–Grail Cycle* in England: Malory and his Predecessors'. In Carol Dover (ed.), *A Companion to the Lancelot-Grail Cycle*. Cambridge, 2003. 147–62.
Cooper, Helen. 'Romance After 1400'. In David Wallace (ed.), *The Cambridge History of Medieval English Literature*. Cambridge, 1999. 690–719.
Cooper, Helen and Sally Mapstone (eds). *The Long Fifteenth Century: Essays for Douglas Gray*. Oxford, 1997.
Cooper, L. H. and A. Denny-Brown (eds). *The 'Arma Christi' in Medieval and Early Modern Culture, with a Critical Edition of 'O Vernicle'*. Farnham, 2014.
Coote, Lesley A. *Prophecy and Public Affairs in Later Medieval England*. Woodbridge, 2000.
Copeland, Rita. *Rhetoric, Hermeneutics, and Translation in the Middle Ages: Academic Traditions and Vernacular Texts*. Cambridge, 1991.
Copeland, Rita and Ineke Sluiter (eds), *Medieval Grammar and Rhetoric: Language Arts and Literary Theory, AD 300–1475*. Oxford, 2009.
Cornelius, Ian. 'The Accentual Paradigm in Early English Metrics'. *JEGP*, 114 (2015), 459–81.
Cornelius, Ian. '*The Lay Folks' Catechism*, Alliterative Verse, and *Cursus*'. *Review of English Studies*, n.s. 70 (2018). 14–36.
Cornelius, Ian. *Reconstructing Alliterative Verse: The Pursuit of a Medieval Meter*. Cambridge, 2017.
Cornelius, Roberta D. *The Figurative Castle: A Study in the Mediaeval Allegory of the Edifice with Especial Reference to Religious Writings*. Bryn Mawr, PA, 1930.
Cornell, C. '"Purtreture" and "Holsom Stories": John Lydgate's Accommodation of Image and Text in Three Religious Lyrics'. *Florilegium*, 10 (1988–91), 167–78.
Court of Sapience, The. E. Ruth Harvey (ed.). Toronto, 1984.
Cosbey, Robert C. 'The Mak Story and Its Folklore Analogues'. *Speculum*, 20 (1945), 310–17.
Coulton, George G. 'Medieval Graffiti, Especially in the Eastern Counties'. *Cambridge Antiquarian Society Communications* 19 (1914–15), 53–62.
Cowen, Janet M. and Jennifer C. Ward. '"Al myn array is bliew, what nedith more?": Gender and the Household in *The Assembly of Ladies*'. In Cordelia Beattie, Anna Maslakovic, and Sarah Rees Jones (eds), *The Medieval Household in Christian Europe, c.850–c.1550: Managing Power, Wealth and the Body*. Turnhout, 2003. 107–26.
Cowen, Janet (ed.), *On Famous Women: The Middle English Translation of Boccaccio's 'De Mulieribus Claris'*. MET 52. Heidelberg, 2015.
Craig, Hardin. *English Religious Drama of the Middle Ages*. Oxford, 1955.
Crane, Susan. 'The Writing Lesson of 1381'. In B. Hanawalt (ed.), *Chaucer's England*. Minneapolis, MIN, 1992. 201–21.
Crawford, Donna. 'Prophecy and Paternity in *The Wars of Alexander*'. *English Studies*, 73 (1992), 406–16.
Cressy, David. *Literacy and the Social Order: Reading and Writing in Tudor and Stuart England*. Cambridge, 1980.
Critten, Rory G. *Author, Scribe, and Book in Late Medieval English Literature*. Cambridge, 2018.
Critten, Rory G. 'Imagining the Author in Late Medieval England and France: The Transmission and Reception of Christine de Pizan's *Epistre au dieu d'Amours* and Thomas Hoccleve's *Letter of Cupid*'. *Studies in Philology*, 112 (2015), 680–97.
Critten, Rory G. 'Locating Charles d'Orléans: In France, England and out of Europe', *New Medieval Literatures*, 20 (2020), 174–215.
Critten, Rory G. 'The Political Valence of Charles d'Orléans's English Poetry'. *Modern Philology*, 111 (2014). 339–64.
Critten, Rory G. '*The Secrees of Old Philisoffres* and John Lydgate's Posthumous Reputation'. *Journal of Early Book Society*, 19 (2016), 31–64.

Cunningham, I. C. 'The Asloan Manuscript'. In A. A. MacDonald, Michael Lynch, and Ian B. Cowan (eds), *The Renaissance in Scotland: Studies in Literature, Religion, History and Culture Offered to John Durkan*. Leiden, 1994. 107–35.
Culler, Jonathan. *Theory of the Lyric*. Boston, 2015.
Curtis, Cathy. 'Richard Pace's De fructu and Early Tudor Pedagogy'. In Jonathan Woolfson (ed.), *Reassessing Tudor Humanism*. London, 2002. 43–77.
Cylkowski, David G. 'A Middle English Treatise on Horticulture: *Godfridus Super Palladium*'. In Lister Matheson (ed.), *Popular and Practical Science of Medieval England*. East Lansing, MI, 1994. 301–29.
Dallachy, Fraser James. 'A Study of the Manuscript Contexts of Benedict Burgh's Middle English "Distichs of Cato"'. PhD thesis, University of Glasgow, 2012.
Dalrymple, Roger. '*Amoryus and Cleopes*: John Metham's Metamorphosis of Chaucer and Ovid'. In Phillipa Hardman (ed.), *The Matter of Identity in Medieval Romance*. Cambridge, 2003. 149–62.
Dalrymple, Roger. 'Sir Gawain in Middle English Romance'. In Helen Fulton (ed.), *A Companion to Arthurian Literature*. Oxford, 2009. 265–77.
Dance of Death, The. Florence Warren and Beatrice White (eds). EETS, o.s. 181. London, 1931.
Danielsson, B. 'The "Kerdeston Library of Hunting and Hawking Literature": early 15th c fragments'. In G. Tilander and C. A. Willemsen (eds), *Et Multum et Multa*. Berlin, 1971. 54–56.
Danielsson, B. 'The Percy Poem on Falconry'. *Stockholm Studies in Modern Philology*, 3 (1970), 5–60.
Darjes, Bradley and Thomas Rendall. 'A Fabliau in the Prologue to the Tale of Beryn'. *Mediaeval Studies*, 47 (1985), 416–31.
Davenport, W. A. *Fifteenth-Century English Drama*. Cambridge, 1982.
Davenport, W. A. '*Sir Degrevant* and Composite Romance'. In Judith Weiss, Jennifer Fellows, and Morgan Dickson (eds), *Medieval Insular Romance: Translation and Innovation*. Cambridge, 2000. 111–31.
Davidson, Clifford. *Festivals and Plays in Late Medieval England*. Farnham 2007.
Day, Mabel. 'Fragment of an Alliterative Political Prophecy'. *Review of English Studies*, 15 (1939), 61–66.
De Bruijn, Elisabeth. 'To Content the Continent: The Dutch Narratives Merlijn and Jacke Compared to Their English Counterparts'. *Tijdschrift voor Nederlandse Taal- en Letterkunde*, 133 (2017), 83–108.
Deguileville, Guillaume de. *Le pèlerinage de l'âme*. J. J. Stürzinger (ed.). London, 1895.
Deguileville, Guillaume de. *Le pèlerinage Jhésu Crist*. J. J. Stürzinger (ed.). London, 1897.
Deguileville, Guillaume de. *Le pèlerinage de vie humaine*. J. J. Stürzinger (ed.). London, 1893.
Denny-Brown, Andrea. 'Charles d'Orléans' Aureation'. In R. D. Perry and Mary-Jo Arn (eds), *Charles D'Orléans' English Aesthetic: The Form, Poetics, and Style of Fortunes Stabilnes*. Cambridge, 2020. 211–35.
Denny-Brown, Andrea. 'The Provocative Fifteenth Century'. *Exemplaria*, 29 (2017), 267–79.
Dent, Arthur. *The Plaine Mans Path-way to Heauen*. London, 1607.
Desmond, Marilynn. 'Trojan Itineraries and the Matter of Troy'. In Rita Copeland (ed.), *The Oxford History of Classical Reception in English Literature*. Vol. 1: *800–1558*. Oxford, 2016. 251–68.
D'Evelyn, Charlotte, and Frances A. Foster. 'Saints' Legends'. In J. Burke Severs (ed.), *A Manual of the Writings in Middle English, 1050–1500*. 11 vols. New Haven, CT, 1970. 2.410–57, 553–649.
Devil's Parliament, The and the Harrowing of Hell and Destruction of Jerusalem. C. W. Marx (ed.). MET 25. Heidelberg, 1993.
Dexler, R. D. '"Dunbar's Lament for the Makaris" and the Dance of Death Tradition'. *Studies in Scottish Literature*, 13 (1978), 144–58.
Dodd, Gwilym. 'Trilingualism in the Medieval English Bureaucracy: The Use—and Disuse—of Languages in the Fifteenth-Century Privy Seal Office'. *Journal of British Studies*, 51 (2012). 253–83.
Dockray-Miller, Mary (ed.). *Saints Edith and Æthelthryth: Princesses, Miracle Workers, and Their Late Medieval Audience. The Wilton Chronicle and the Wilton Life of St Æthelthryth*. Turnhout, 2009.
Dodsworth, Roger and John William Clay (eds). *Yorkshire Church Notes, 1619–1631*. Yorkshire Archaeological Society, Record Society series 34. Leeds, 1904.

Doglio, Maria Luisa. *L'exemplum nella novella latina del Quattrocento*. Turin, 1975.
Doig, James A. 'The Prophecy of the "Six Kings to Follow John" and Owain Glyndŵr'. *Studia Celtica*, 29 (1995), 257–68.
Donaldson, E. Talbot. 'Idiom of Popular Poetry in the *Miller's Tale*'. In *Speaking of Chaucer*. London, 1970. 13–29.
Donatelli, Joseph M. P. (ed.). *Death and Liffe*. Cambridge, MA, 1989.
Donavin, Georgiana. 'The Light of the Virgin Muse in John Lydgate's *The Life of Our Lady*'. In Georgiana Donavin and Anita Obermeier (eds), *Romance and Rhetoric: Essays in Honour of Dhira B. Mahoney*. Turnhout, 2010. 75–89.
Douglas, Gavin. Priscilla Bawcutt (ed.), *The Shorter Poems of Gavin Douglas*, STS, 5th series, 2. Edinburgh, 1967.
Douglas, Gavin. David F. C. Coldwell (ed.). *Virgil's Aeneid*, 4 vols. STS, 3rd series, 25, 27, 28, 30. Edinburgh, 1957–64.
Douglas, Mary. 'The Social Control of Cognition: Some Factors in Joke Perception'. *Man*, 3 (1968), 361–76.
Doyle, A. I. 'Stephen Dodesham of Witham and Sheen'. In P. R. Robinson and Rivkah Zim (eds), *Of the Making of Books: Medieval Manuscripts, their Scribes and Readers: Essays Presented to M. B. Parkes*. Aldershot, 1997. 94–115.
Doyle, A. I. 'An Unrecognized Piece of *Piers the Ploughman's Creed* and Other Work by its Scribe'. *Speculum*, 34 (1959), 428–36.
Doyle, A. I. 'The Work of a Late Fifteenth-Century Scribe, William Ebesham'. *Bulletin of the John Rylands Library*, 39 (1957), 298–325.
Doyle, A. I. and M. B. Parkes. 'The Production of Early Copies of the *Canterbury Tales* and the *Confessio Amantis* in the Early Fifteenth Century'. In M. B. Parkes and Andrew G. Watson (eds), *Medieval Scribes, Manuscripts and Libraries: Essays Presented to N. R. Ker*. London, 1978. 163–210.
Drexler, Marjorie. 'Fluid Prejudice: Scottish Origin Myths in the Later Middle Ages'. In Joel Rosenthal and Colin Richmond (eds). *People, Politics and Community in the Later Middle Ages*. Gloucester, 1987. 92–136.
Drexler, R. D. 'Dunbar's "Lament for the Makaris" and the Dance of Death Tradition'. *Studies in Scottish Literature*, 13 (1978), 144–58.
Drimmer, Sonja. *The Art of Allusion: Illuminators and the Making of English Literature, 1403–1476*. Philadelphia, PA, 2019.
Driver, Martha W. *The Image in Print: Book Illustration in Late Medieval England and its Sources*. London, 2004.
Driver, Martha W. 'Pageants Reconsidered'. In Carol M. Meale and Derek Pearsall (eds), *Makers and Users of Medieval Books: Essays in Honour of A. S. G. Edwards*. Cambridge, 2014. 34–47.
Driver, Martha W. 'Mapping Chaucer: John Speed and the Later Portraits'. *The Chaucer Review*, 36 (2002), 228–49.
Dronke, Peter. 'Poetic Originality in *The Wars of Alexander*'. In Helen Cooper and Sally Mapstone (eds), *The Long Fifteenth Century: Essays for Douglas Gray*. Oxford, 1997. 123–39.
Duffell, Martin J. *Chaucer's Verse Art in its European Context*. Tempe, AZ, 2018.
Duffell, Martin J. '"The craft so long to lerne": Chaucer's Invention of the Iambic Pentameter'. *The Chaucer Review*, 34 (2000), 269–88.
Duffy, Eamon. *Saints, Sacrileges and Sedition: Religion and Conflict in the Tudor Reformations*. London, 2014.
Duffy, Eamon. *The Stripping of the Altars*. New Haven, CT, 1992.
Dugdale, William. *Monasticon Anglicanum*. John Caley, Henry Ellis, and Bulkeley Bandinel (eds). 6 vols. London, 1830.
Duggan, Hoyt N. 'Extended A-Verses in Middle English Alliterative Poetry'. *Parergon*, 18 (2000), 53–76.
Duggan, Hoyt N. 'Final *-e* and the Rhythmic Structure of the B-Verse in Middle English Alliterative Poetry'. *Modern Philology*, 81 (1988), 119–45.
Duggan, Hoyt N. 'The Shape of the B-Verse in Middle English Alliterative Poetry'. *Speculum*, 61 (1986), 564–92.

Dunbar, William. *The Poems of William Dunbar*. Priscilla Bawcutt (ed.). 2 vols. Glasgow, 1998.
Dunbar, William. *William Dunbar: The Complete Works*. John Conlee (ed.). Kalamazoo, MI, 2004.
Duncan, Thomas G. (ed.). *A Companion to the Middle English Lyric*. Cambridge, 2005.
Duncan, Thomas G. (ed.). *Late Medieval English Lyrics and Carols, 1400–1530*. London, 2000.
Duncan, Thomas G. (ed.). *Medieval English Lyrics, 1200-1400*. London, 1995.
Duncan, Thomas G. (ed.). *Medieval English Lyrics and Carols*. Cambridge, 2013.
Durkan, John. 'The Beginnings of Humanism in Scotland'. *The Innes Review*, 4 (1953), 5–24.
Durkan, John. *Scottish Schools and Schoolmasters, 1560-1633*. Woodbridge, 2013.
Dyboski, Roman (ed.). *Songs, Carols, and other Miscellaneous Poems*. EETS, e.s. 101. London, 1907.
Dyboski, R. and Z. M. Arend (eds), *Knyghthode and Bataile: A XVth Century Verse Paraphrase of Flavius Vegetius Renatus' Treatise 'De re militari'*. EETS, o.s. 201. London, 1935.
Dyer, Christopher. *Desert Villages Revisited*. Hatfield, 2010.
Easthope, Antony. 'Problematizing the Pentameter'. *New Literary History*, 12 (1981), 475–92.
Ebin, Lois A. 'Boethius, Chaucer, and *The Kingis Quair*'. *Philological Quarterly*, 53 (1974), 321–41.
Ebin, Lois A. *Illuminator, Makar, Vates: Visions of Poetry in the Fifteenth Century*. Lincoln, NE, 1988.
Ebin, Lois. *John Lydgate*. Boston, MA, 1985.
Echard, Siân. 'Pre-Texts: Tables of Contents and the Reading of John Gower's *Confessio Amantis*'. *Medium Ævum*, 66 (1997), 270–87.
Echard, Siân. *Printing the Middle Ages*. Philadelphia, PA, 2008.
Edsall, M. A. '*Arma Christi* Rolls or Textual Amulets? The Narrow Roll Format Manuscripts of "O Vernicle"'. *Magic, Ritual, and Witchcraft*, 9 (2014), 178–209.
Edwards, A. S. G. 'Beinecke 661 and Early Fifteenth-Century Manuscript Production'. *Beinecke Studies in Early Manuscripts, Yale University Library Gazette*, 66, Supplement, (1991), 181–96.
Edwards, A. S. G. '*The Chance of Dice* and *The Legend of Good Women*'. *Notes and Queries*, n.s. 34 (1987), 295.
Edwards, A. S. G. 'The Circulation and Audience of Bokenham's *Legendys of Hooly Wummen*'. In A. J. Minnis (ed.), *Late Medieval Religious Texts and their Transmission*. Cambridge, 1994. 157–67.
Edwards, A. S. G. (ed.). *A Companion to Middle English Prose*. Woodbridge, 2004.
Edwards, A. S. G. 'Duke Humfrey's Middle English Palladius Manuscript'. In Jenny Stratford (ed.), *The Lancastrian Court*. Donington, 2003. 68–77.
Edwards, A. S. G. 'Dunbar, Skelton and the Idea of Court Poetry in the Early Sixteenth Century'. In Jennifer and R. H. Britnell (eds), *Vernacular Literature and Current Affairs in the Early Sixteenth Century: France, England and Scotland*. Aldershot, 2000. 121–34.
Edwards, A. S. G. 'Editing Dunbar: The Tradition'. In Sally Mapstone (ed.), *William Dunbar, 'The Nobill Poyet': Essays in Honour of Priscilla Bawcutt*. East Lothian, 2001. 51–68.
Edwards, A. S. G. 'Fifteenth-Century English Collections of Female Saints' Lives'. *Yearbook of English Studies*, 33 (2003), 131–41.
Edwards, A. S. G. 'Fifteenth-Century Middle English Verse Author Collections'. In A. S. G. Edwards, Vincent Gillespie, and Ralph Hanna (eds), *The English Medieval Book: Studies in Memory of Jeremy Griffiths*. London, 2000. 101–12.
Edwards, A. S. G. 'Gender, Order and Reconciliation in *Sir Degrevaunt*'. In Carol M. Meale (ed.), *Readings in Medieval English Romance*. Cambridge, 1994. 53–64.
Edwards, A. S. G. 'The Influence and Audience of the *Polychronicon*: Some Observations'. *Proceedings of the Leeds Philosophical and Literary Society: Literary and Historical Section*, 17, pt. 6 (1980), 113–19.
Edwards, A. S. G. 'The Influence of Lydgate's *Fall of Princes* c.1440–1559: A Survey'. *Medieval Studies* 39 (1977). 424–39.
Edwards, A. S. G. 'John Lydgate's *Lives of Ss Edmund and Fremund*: Politics, Hagiography and Literature'. In Anthony Bale (ed.), *St Edmund, King and Martyr: Changing Images of a Medieval Saint*. Woodbridge, 2009. 133–44.
Edwards, A. S. G. 'John Shirley and the Emulation of Courtly Culture'. In Evelyn Mullally and John Thompson (eds), *The Court and Cultural Diversity*. Cambridge, 1997. 309–17.
Edwards, A. S. G. 'John Shirley, John Lydgate, and the Motives of Compilation'. *Studies in the Age of Chaucer*, 38 (2016). 245–54.

Edwards, A. S. G. (intro.). *The Life of St Edmund King and Martyr: A Facsimile of British Library MS Harley 2278*. London, 2004.
Edwards, A. S. G. 'Lydgate's *Fall of Princes*: Translation, Retranslation and History'. In S. K. Barker and Brenda M. Hosington (eds), *Renaissance Cultural Crossroads: Translation, Print and Culture in Britain, 1473–1640*. Leiden, 2013. 21–34.
Edwards, A. S. G. 'The Manuscripts and Texts of the Second Version of John Hardyng's Chronicle'. In Daniel Williams (ed.), *England in the Fifteenth Century. Proceedings of the 1986 Harlaxton Symposium*. Woodbridge, 1987. 75–84.
Edwards, A. S. G. 'McGill MS 143 and the Composition of Lydgate's *Fall of Princes*'. *Florilegium*, 33 (2019 for 2016), 45–62.
Edwards, A. S. G. 'Middle English Inscriptional Verse Texts'. In John Scattergood and Julia Boffey (eds), *Texts and their Contexts: Papers from the Early Book Society*. Dublin, 1997. 26–43.
Edwards, A. S. G. 'The Middle English Translation of Claudian's *De Consulatu Stilichonis*'. In A. J. Minnis (ed.), *Middle English Poetry: Texts and Traditions. Essays in Honour of Derek Pearsall*. Woodbridge, 2001. 267–78.
Edwards, A. S. G. 'Northern Magnates and their Books'. *Textual Cultures*, 7 (2012), 176–86.
Edwards, A. S. G. 'Poetic Language in the Fifteenth Century'. In Corinne Saunders (ed.), *A Companion to Medieval English Poetry*. Chichester, 2010. 520–37.
Edwards, A. S. G. 'Reading John Walton's Boethius in the 15th and 16th Centuries'. In Mary Flannery and Carrie Griffin (eds), *Spaces for Reading*. London, 2016. 35–49.
Edwards, A. S. G. 'The *Speculum Guy de Warwick* and Lydgate's *Guy of Warwick*: The Non–Romance Middle English Tradition'. In Alison Wiggins and Rosalind Field (eds), *Guy of Warwick: Icon and Ancestor*. Cambridge, 2007. 81–93.
Edwards, A. S. G. *Stephen Hawes*. Boston, 1983.
Edwards, A. S. G. 'A Verse Chronicle of the House of Percy'. *Studies in Philology*, 105 (2008), 226–44.
Edwards, A. S. G. and Derek Pearsall. 'The Manuscripts of the Major English Poetic Texts'. In Jeremy Griffiths and Derek Pearsall (eds), *Book Production and Publishing in Britain*. Cambridge, 1988. 257–78.
Edwards, Graham R. and Philippe Maupeu (eds and trans). *Le livre du pèlerin de vie humaine*. Paris, 2015.
Edwards, Robert R. *Invention and Authorship in Medieval England*. Columbus, OH, 2017.
Eighteen Anglo-Norman Fabliaux. Ian Short and Roy Pearcy (eds). Anglo-Norman Text Society 14. London, 2000.
Ellenberger, Bengt. *The Latin Element in the Vocabulary of the Earlier Makars, Henryson and Dunbar*. Lund Studies in English, 51. Lund, 1977.
Elliott, Kenneth. *Now fayre, fayrest off every fayre (for three voices): Welcome Song for Margaret Tudor on her Marriage to James IV of Scotland, 1503*. Glasgow, 2003.
Ellis, Roger (ed.). *The Medieval Translator: The Theory and Practice of Translation in the Middle Ages*. Cambridge, 1989.
Ellis, Roger (ed.). *Oxford History of Literary Translation into English. Vol. 1: to 1550* Oxford, 2008.
Ellison, Darryl. '"Take It as a Tale": Reading the *Plowman's Tale* as if it Were'. *The Chaucer Review*, 49 (2014), 77–101.
Enders, Jody (ed.). *A Cultural History of Theatre in the Middle Ages*. London, 2019.
Engler, Bernd. 'Literary Form as Aesthetic Progress: The Envoy in English'. *Yearbook of the Review of English and American Literature*, 7 (1991). 61–97.
English Mediaeval Lapidaries. Joan Evans and Mary S. Serjeantson (eds). EETS, o.s. 190. London, 1933.
Epp, Garrett P. J. '"Corectyd & not playd": An Unproductive History of the Towneley Plays'. *Research Opportunities in Renaissance Drama*, 43 (2004), 38–53.
Epstein, Robert. 'Eating their Words: Food and Text in the Coronation Banquet of Henry VI'. *Journal of Medieval and Early Modern Studies*, 36 (2006), 355–77.
Erler, Mary C. 'Copland, Robert'. *ODNB*. 2004.
Evans, Deanna Delmar. '*The Babee's Book*'. In Daniel T. Kline (ed.), *Medieval Literature for Children*. New York, 2003. 79–92.

Everyman and its Dutch Original, Elckerlijc. Clifford Davidson, Martin W. Walsh, and Ton J. Broos (eds). Kalamazoo, MI, 2007.

Ewan, Elizabeth. 'Hamperit in ane hony came': Sights, Sounds and Smells in the Medieval Town'. In Edward J. Cowan, and Lizanne Henderson (eds), *A History of Everyday Life in Medieval Scotland.* Edinburgh, 2011. 109–44.

Ewan, Elizabeth. 'Schooling in the Towns, c.1400–c.1560'. In R. D. Anderson (ed.), *The Edinburgh History of Education in Scotland.* Edinburgh, 2015. 39–56.

Fallows, David. 'Words and Music in Two English Songs of the Mid-15th Century'. *Early Music,* 5 (1977), 38–43.

Farnham, Willard. 'The Dayes of the Mone'. *Studies in Philology,* 20 (1923), 70–82.

Federico, Sylvia. *New Troy: Fantasies of Empire in the Late Middle Ages.* Minneapolis, MIN, 2003.

Fein, Susanna. 'The Contents of Robert Thornton's Manuscripts'. In Susanna Fein and Michael Johnston (eds), *Robert Thornton and His Books: Essays on the Lincoln and London Thornton Manuscripts.* Woodbridge, 2014. 13–65.

Fein, Susanna. 'The Early Thirteen-Line Stanza: Style and Metrics Reconsidered'. *Parergon,* 18 (2000), 97–126.

Fein, Susanna. 'English Devotions for a Noble Household: The Long Passion in Audelay's *Counsel of Conscience'.* In Vincent Gillespie and Khantik Ghosh (eds), *After Arundel: Religious Writing in Fifteenth-Century England.* Turnhout, 2011. 325–42.

Fein, Susanna. '*Haue Mercy of Me* (Psalm 51): An Unedited Alliterative Poem from the London Thornton Manuscript'. *Modern Philology,* 86 (1989), 223–41.

Fein, Susanna. 'John Audelay and James Ryman'. In Julia Boffey and A. S. G. Edwards (eds), *A Companion to Fifteenth-Century Poetry.* Cambridge, 2013. 127–41.

Fein, Susanna (ed.). *Moral Love Songs and Laments.* Kalamazoo, MI, 1998.

Fein, Susanna (ed.). *'My Wyl and My Wrytyng': Essays on John the Blind Audelay.* Kalamazoo, MI, 2009.

Fein, Susanna (ed.). *Poems and Carols (Oxford, Bodleian Library MS Douce 302).* Kalamazoo, MI, 2009.

Fein, Susanna and Michael Johnston (eds). *Robert Thornton and his Books: Essays on the Lincoln and London Thornton Manuscripts.* Woodbridge, 2014.

Fein, Susanna, David Raybin, and Jan Ziolowski (eds and trans). *The Complete Harley 2253 Manuscript.* 3 vols. Kalamazoo, MI, 2014–15.

Fenster, Thelma S. and Mary C. Erler (eds), *Poems of Cupid, God of Love: Christine de Pizan's Epistre au dieu d'Amours and Dit de la Rose; Thomas Hoccleve's The Letter of Cupid.* Leiden, 1990.

Field, Rosalind. 'Romance'. In Roger Ellis (ed.). *Oxford History of Literary Translation into English.* Vol. 1: to 1550. Oxford, 2008. 296–331.

Findern Manuscript, The: Cambridge University Library MS Ff. 1. 6. Richard Beadle and A. E. B. Owen (intro.). London, 1978.

Finlayson, John. 'Alliterative Narrative Poetry: The Control of the Medium'. *Traditio,* 44 (1988), 419–51.

Fiondella, Maris G. 'Derrida, Typology, and the *Second Shepherd's Play*: The Theatrical Production of Christian Metaphysics'. *Exemplaria,* 6 (1994), 429–58.

Fisher, John H. 'Chancery and the Emergence of Standard Written English in the Fifteenth Century'. *Speculum,* 52 (1977), 870–99.

Fisher, John H. 'A Language Policy for Lancastrian England'. *PMLA,* 107 (1992), 1168–80.

Fisher, Matthew. *Scribal Authorship and the Writing of History in Medieval England* Columbus, OH, 2012.

Flannery, Mary C. *John Lydgate and the Poetics of Fame.* Cambridge, 2012.

Fletcher, Alan J. 'The Lyric in the Sermon'. In Thomas Duncan (ed.), *A Companion to the Middle English Lyric.* Cambridge, 2005. 189–209.

Fletcher, Alan J. 'The N-Town Plays'. In Richard Beadle (ed.), *The Cambridge Companion to Medieval English Theatre.* Cambridge, 1994. 163–88.

Fletcher, Alan J. *Preaching, Politics and Poetry in Late-Medieval England.* Dublin, 1998.

Fletcher, Bradford York and A. L. Harris. 'A Northampton Poetic Miscellany of 1455–56'. *English Manuscript Studies 1100–1700*, 7 (1998), 216–35.
Flood, John L. '"Safer on the battlefield than in the city": England, the "Sweating Sickness", and the Continent'. *Renaissance Studies*, 17 (2003), 147–76.
Flood, Victoria. *Prophecy, Politics and Place in Medieval* England, *From Geoffrey of Monmouth to Thomas of Erceldoune*. Cambridge, 2016.
Floure and the Leafe, The, The Assembly of Ladies, The Isle of Ladies. Derek Pearsall (ed.). Kalamazoo, MI, 1990.
Floyd, J. 'St George and the "Steyned Halle": Lydgate's Verses for London Armourers'. In L. Cooper and A. Denny-Brown (eds), *Lydgate Matters: Poetry and Material Culture in the Fifteenth Century*. Basingstoke, 2008. 139–64.
Flügel, Ewald. 'Kleinere Mitteilungen aus Handschriften'. *Anglia*, 14 (1892), 463–97.
Flügel, Ewald. 'Eine mittelenglische Claudian-Übersetzung (1445) (Brit. Mus. Add. Ms. 11814)'. *Anglia*, 28 (1905), 255–99, 421–38.
Forest-Hill, Lynn. *Transgressive Language in Medieval English Drama*. London, 2000.
Forni, Kathleen (ed.). *The Chaucerian Apocrypha: A Selection*. Kalamazoo, MI, 2005.
Fort, Margaret D. 'The Metres of the Brome and Chester *Abraham and Isaac* Plays'. *PMLA*, 41 (1926), 832–39.
Foss, David B. 'John Mirk's *Instruction for Parish Priests*'. *Studies in Church History*, 26 (1989), 131–40.
Foucault, Michel. 'What Is an Author?'. In Donald F. Bouchard (ed.), Donald F. Bouchard and Sherry Simon (trans), *Language, Counter-Memory, Practice: Selected Essays and Interviews*. Ithaca, NY, 1977. 113–38.
Fowler, David C. *The Life and Times of John Trevisa, Medieval Scholar*. Seattle, WA, 1995.
Fowler, David C. *Literary History of the Popular Ballad*. Durham, NC, 1968.
Fowler, J. T. (ed.). *The Life of St Cuthbert in English Verse*. Surtees Society, 88. Edinburgh, 1891.
Fox, Adam. *Oral and Literate Culture in England 1500–1700*. Oxford, 2000.
Fox, Adam. 'Popular Verses and their Readership in the Early Seventeenth Century'. In James Raven, Helen Small, and Naomi Tadmor (eds), *The Practice and Representation of Reading in England*. Cambridge, 1996. 125–37.
Fox, Denton. 'The Chronology of William Dunbar'. *Philological Quarterly*, 39 (1960), 413–25.
Fox, Denton. 'Dunbar's *Golden Targe*'. *ELH*, 26 (1959), 311–34.
Fox, Denton. 'Henryson's "Sum Practysis of Medecyne"'. *Studies in Philology*, 69 (1972), 453–60.
Fraser, William. *Memorials of the Family of Wemyss of Wemyss*. Edinburgh, 1888.
Froissart, Jean. M le baron Kervyn de Lettenhove (eds). *Oeuvres*. 25 vols. Brussels, 1867–77.
Frulovisi, Tito Livio. Cristina Cocco (eds). *Hunfreidos*. Florence, 2014.
Frye, Northrop. 'Intoxicated with Words'. In Robert D. Denham (ed.), *Northrop Frye's Uncollected Prose*, Toronto. 2015. 61–74.
Fryer and the boy, Here beginneth the second part of the. London, 1680.
Fumo, Jamie C. *Making Chaucer's* Book of the Duchess: *Textuality and Reception*. Cardiff, 2015.
Fumo, Jamie C. 'John Metham's "straunge style": *Amoryus and Cleopes* as Chaucerian Fragment'. *The Chaucer Review*, 43 (2008), 215–37.
Frederick J. Furnivall (ed.), *The Babees Book: Aristotle's A B C, Urbanitatis, Stans puer ad mensam, the lytille childrenes lytil boke, the bokes of nurture of Hugh Rhodes and John Russell, Wynkyn de Worde's Boke of Keruynge, the Booke of demeanor, the boke of curtasye, Seager's Schoole of vertue, &c. &c.: with some French & Latin poems on like subjects and some forewords on education in Early England*. EETS, o.s. 32 (London, 1868).
Furnivall, Frederick J. (ed.). *Bishop Percy's Folio Manuscript: Loose and Humorous Songs*. London, 1864.
Furnivall, Frederick J. (ed.). *Early English Meals and Manners*. Rev. edn. EETS, o.s. 32 London, 1876.
Furnivall, Frederick J. (ed.). *Fifty Earliest English Wills*. EETS, o.s. 78. London, 1882.
Furnivall, Frederick J. (ed.). *Political, Religious, and Love Poems*. EETS, o.s. 15. London, 1866, re-edited 1903.

Furnivall, Frederick J. (ed.). *Queene Elizabethes Achademy*. EETS, e.s. 8. London, 1869.
Furnivall, Frederick J. (ed.). *A Royal Historie of the Excellent Knight Generides*. Roxburghe Club. London, 1865.
Furnivall, Frederick J. and Katharine B. Locock (eds). *The Pilgrimage of the Life of Man*. 3 vols. EETS, o.s. 78, 83, 92. London, 1899–1904.
Furrow, Melissa. 'A Minor Comic Poem in a Major Romance Manuscript: "Lyarde"'. *Forum for Modern Language Studies*, 32 (1996), 289–302.
Furrow, Melissa. 'Middle English Fabliaux and Modern Myth'. *ELH*, 56 (1989), 1–18.
Furrow, Melissa (ed.). *Ten Bourdes*. Kalamazoo, 2013.
Furrow, Melissa (ed.). *Ten Fifteenth-Century Comic Tales*. New York, 1985.
Galloway, Andrew. 'Middle English Prologues'. In David F. Johnson and Elaine Treharne (eds), *Readings in Medieval Texts: Interpreting Old and Middle English Literature*. Oxford, 2005. 288–305.
Galloway, Andrew. '*Piers Plowman* and the Schools'. *Yearbook of Langland Studies*, 6 (1992), 89–107
Garbàty, Thomas. 'Wynkyn de Worde's "Sir Thopas" and Other Tales'. *Studies in Bibliography*, 31 (1978), 57–67.
Garmonsway, G. N. and R. R. Raymo. 'A Middle English Metrical Life of Job'. In Arthur Brown and Peter Foote (eds), *Early English and Norse Studies Presented to Hugh Smith in Honour of his Sixtieth Birthday*. London, 1963. 77–98.
Garrett, R. M. 'Middle English Rimed Medical Treatise'. *Anglia*, 34 (1911), 164–83.
Gaullier-Bougassas, Catherine, Margaret Bridges, and Jean-Yves Tilliette (eds). *Trajectoires européennes du 'Secretum secretorum' du Pseudo-Aristote (XIIIe–XVIe siècle)*. Turnhout, 2015.
Gayk, Shannon. '"Ete this book": Literary Consumption and Poetic Invention in John Capgrave's *Life of St Katherine*'. In Shannon Gayk and Kathleen Tonry (eds), *Form and Reform: Reading Across the Fifteenth Century*. Columbus, OH, 2011. 88–109.
Gayk, Shannon. *Image, Text, and Religious Reform in Fifteenth-Century England*. Cambridge, 2010.
Genet, Jean-Philippe. 'English Nationalism: Thomas Polton at the Council of Constance'. *Nottingham Medieval Studies*, 28 (1984), 60–78.
Genet, Jean-Philippe (ed.). *Four English Political Tracts of the Later Middle Ages*, Camden Society 4th series, 18. London, 1977.
Genette, Gérard and Marie Maclean. 'Introduction to the Paratext'. *New Literary History*, 22 (1991), 261–72.
Gerould, Gordon Hall. 'The Legend of St Wulfhad and St Ruffin at Stone Priory'. *PMLA*, 32 (1917), 323–37.
Gerould, Gordon Hall. '"Tables" in Medieval Churches'. *Speculum*, 1 (1926), 439–40.
Gervais, Kyle. 'Tydeus the Hero? Intertextual Confusion in Statius, *Thebaid* 2'. *Phoenix*, 69 (2015), 56–78.
'*Gest Hystoriale' of the Destruction of Troy, The: An Alliterative Romance translated from Guido de Colonna's 'Hystoria Troiana'*. Geoffrey A. Panton and David Donaldson (eds). EETS, o.s. 39, 56. London, 1869, 1874.
Gesta Henrici Quinti: The Deeds of Henry the Fifth. Frank Taylor and John S. Roskell (eds and trans). Oxford, 1975.
Giancarlo, Matthew. 'Troubling the New Constitutionalism: Politics, Penitence, and the Dilemma of Dread in the Digby Poems'. *JEGP*, 110 (2011), 78–104.
Giancarlo, Matthew. 'Authorship'. In Marion Turner (ed.), *A Handbook of Middle English Studies*. Malden, MA, 2013. 137–54.
Giancarlo, Matthew. 'Dressing up a "galaunt": Traditional Piety and Fashionable Politics in Peter Idley's "translacions" of Mannyng and Lydgate'. In Vincent Gillespie and Khantik Ghosh (eds), *After Arundel: Religious Writing in Fifteenth-Century England*. Turnhout, 2012. 429–47.
Gibbon, John. *Unio dissidentium*. London, 1680.
Gibson, Gail McMurray. 'The Macro Manuscripts and the Making of the Morality Play'. *Papers of the Bibliographical Society of America*, 113 (2019), 255–95.
Gibson, Gail McMurray. 'The Macro Play in Georgian England'. In Tamara Atkin and Laura Estill (eds), *Early British Drama in Manuscript*. Turnhout, 2019. 311–28.

Giles, Kate, Antony Masinton, and Geoff Arnott. 'Visualizing the Guild Chapel, Stratford- upon-Avon: Digital Models as Research Tools in Buildings Archaeology'. *Internet Archaeology*, at https://intarch.ac.uk/journal/issue32/1/toc.html.

Giles, Kate and Jonathan Clark. 'The Archaeology of the Guild Buildings of Shakespeare's Stratford-upon-Avon'. In J. R. Mulryne (ed.), *The Guild and Guild Buildings of Shakespeare's Stratford: Society, Religion, School and Stage*. Farnham, 2012. 135–70.

Gillespie, Alexandra. *Print Culture and the Medieval Author: Chaucer, Lydgate, and their Books 1473–1557*. Oxford, 2006.

Gillespie, Alexandra. 'Poets, Printers, and Early English Sammelbände'. *Huntington Library Quarterly*, 67 (2004), 189–214.

Gillespie, Vincent. 'Chichele's Church: Vernacular Theology in England after Thomas Arundel'. In Vincent Gillespie and Kantik Ghosh (eds), *After Arundel: Religious Writing in Fifteenth-Century England*. Turnhout, 2011. 3–42.

Gillespie, Vincent. 'Medieval Hypertext: Image and Text from York Minster'. In P. R. Robinson and Rivkah Zim (eds), *Of the Making of Books: Medieval Manuscripts, their Scribes and Readers. Essays Presented to M. B. Parkes*. Aldershot, 1997. 206–29.

Gillespie, Vincent. 'Moral and Penitential Lyrics'. In Thomas Gibson Duncan (ed.), *A Companion to the Middle English Lyric*. Cambridge, 2005. 68–96.

Gillespie, Vincent. 'Religious Writing'. In Roger Ellis (ed.), *The Oxford History of Literary Translation in English, Volume One: To 1500*. Oxford, 2008. 234–83.

Gillespie, Vincent. 'Vernacular Theology'. In Paul Strohm (ed.), *Middle English: Oxford Twenty-First Century Approaches to Literature*. Oxford, 2007. 401–20.

Gillespie, Vincent and Kantik Ghosh (eds). *After Arundel: Religious Writing in Fifteenth Century England*. Turnhout, 2011.

Gillies, William and Kate McClune. 'The Purposes of Literature'. In Nicola Royan (ed.), *The International Companion to Scottish Literature, 1400–1650*. Glasgow, 2018. 79–99.

Given-Wilson, Chris (trans.). *Chronicles of the Revolution, 1397–1400: The Reign of Richard II*. Manchester, 1993.

Golagros and Gawane, The Knightly Tale of. R. Hanna (ed). STS, 5th series, 7. Woodbridge, 2008.

Goldstein, James R. '"Betuix pyne and faith": The Poetics of Compassion in Walter Kennedy's *Passioun of Crist*'. *Studies in Philology*, 110 (2013), 482–505.

Goldstein, James R. 'Vernacular Eloquence: reading Older Poetry Rhetorically'. In *The English Lyric Tradition: Reading Poetic Masterpieces of the Middle Ages and Renaissance*. Chapel Hill, NC, 2018. 10–40.

Goodall, Peter. 'An Outline History of the English Fabliau After Chaucer'. *AUMLA. Australasian Universities Language and Literature Association*, 57 (1982), 5–23.

Goodich, Jean N. 'So I Thought as I Stood, To Mirth Us Among: The Function of Laughter in the Second Shepherds' Play'. In Albrecht Classen (ed.), *Laughter in the Middle Ages and Early Modern Times*. Berlin, 2010. 531–46.

Görlach, Manfred. *The Textual Tradition of the South English Legendary*. Leeds Texts and Monographs, n.s. 6. Leeds, 1974.

Gower, John. G. C. Macaulay (ed.). *The Complete Works*. 4 vols. Oxford, 1899–1901.

Gower, John. G. C. Macaulay (ed.). *The English Works of John Gower*. EETS, e.s. 81, 82. London, 1900–1.

Gower, John. R. F. Yeager (ed. and trans.). *John Gower: The French Balades*. Kalamazoo, MI, 2011.

Gradon, Pamela. *Form and Style in Early English Literature*. London, 1971.

Gransden, Antonia. *Historical Writing in England, II: c1307 to the Sixteenth Century*. London, 1982.

Gray, Douglas (ed.). *English Medieval Religious Lyrics*. Rev. edn. Exeter, 1992.

Gray, Douglas. *Later Medieval English Literature*. Oxford, 2008.

Gray, Douglas. 'A Middle English Epitaph'. *Notes and Queries*, n.s. 8 (1961), 132–5.

Gray, Douglas. 'Notes on Some Middle English Charms'. In Beryl Rowland (ed.), *Chaucer and Middle English Studies: Studies in Honour of Rossell Hope Robbins*. London, 1974. 56–71.

Gray, Douglas. *Robert Henryson*. Leiden, 1979.

Gray, Douglas. 'Rough Music: Some Early Invectives and Flytings'. *Yearbook of English Studies*, 14 (1984), 21–43.
Gray, Douglas. *Simple Forms: Essays on Medieval English Popular Literature*. Oxford, 2015.
Gray, Douglas. *Themes and Images in the Medieval Religious Lyric*. London, 1972.
Gray, Douglas. 'William Dunbar'. In M. C. Seymour (ed.), *Authors of the Middle Ages*. Vol. 3. Aldershot, 1996. 179–94.
Gray, Douglas and Jane Bliss (eds). *Make We Merry, More and Less: An Anthology of Medieval English Popular Literature*. Cambridge, 2019.
Greco, Gina and Christine Rose (eds). *The Good Wife's Guide (Le Ménagier de Paris): A Medieval Household Book*. Ithaca, NY, 2012.
Green, Monica (ed.). *Pandemic Disease in the Medieval World: Rethinking the Black Death*. [The Medieval Globe, i.] Kalamazoo, MI, 2014.
Green, Richard Firth. *Poets and Princepleasers: Literature and the English Court in the Late Middle Ages*. Toronto, 1980.
Green, Richard Firth. 'The Ballad and the Middle Ages'. In Helen Cooper and Sally Mapstone (eds), *The Long Fifteenth Century: Essays for Douglas Gray*. Oxford, 1997. 163–84.
Green, Richard Firth. 'The Hermit and the Outlaw: New Evidence for Robin Hood's Death?'. In Helen Phillips (ed.), *Robin Hood: Medieval and Post-Medieval*. Dublin, 2005. 51–9.
Green, Richard Firth. '*The Hunting of the Hare*: An Edition'. In Anne Marie D'Arcy and Alan J. Fletcher (eds), *Studies in Late Medieval and Early Renaissance Texts in Honour of John Scattergood*. Dublin, 2005. 129–47.
Green, Richard Firth. 'Legal Satire in *The Tale of Beryn*'. *Studies in the Age of Chaucer*, 11 (1989), 43–62.
Greene, Richard L. (ed.). *The Early English Carols*. Oxford, 2nd edn. 1977.
Greene, Richard L. 'A Middle English "Timor Mortis" Poem'. *Modern Language Review*, 28 (1933), 234–38.
Griffith, David. 'English Commemorative Inscriptions: Some Literary Dimensions'. In Caroline M. Barron and Clive Burgess (eds), *Memory and Commemoration in Medieval England*. Donington, 2010. 251-70.
Griffith, David. 'A Newly Identified Verse Item by John Lydgate at Holy Trinity Church, Long Melford, Suffolk'. *Notes and Queries*, n.s. 58 (2011), 364–67.
Griffiths, Jane. '"In Bookes Thus Writen I Fynde": Hoccleve's Self-Glossing in the *Regiment of Princes* and the *Series*'. *Medium Ævum*, 86 (2017), 91–107.
Griffiths, Jeremy. '*Confessio Amantis*: The Poem and its Pictures'. In A. J. Minnis (ed.), *Gower's Confessio Amantis: Responses and Reassessments*. Cambridge, 1983. 163–77.
Griffiths, Jeremy. 'A Re-examination of Oxford, Bodleian Library, MS Rawlinson C.86'. *Archiv für das Studium der Neuren Sprachen und Literaturen*, 219 (1982), 381–8.
Grinberg, Ana. 'The Lady, the Giant, and the Land: The Monstrous in *Fierabras*'. *eHumanista: Journal of Iberian Studies*, 18 (2011), 186–92.
Gross, Anthony. 'Ripley, George (d. c.1490)'. *ODNB*. 2004.
Grossi, Joseph. 'Cloistered Lydgate, Commercial Scribe: British Library Harley 2255 Revisited'. *Medieval Studies*, 72 (2010), 313–61.
Guddat-Figge, Gisela. *Catalogue of Manuscripts Containing Middle English Romances*. Munich, 1976.
Gunton, Simon. *The History of the Church of Peterburgh*. London, 1686.
Guy, John. *Tudor England*. Oxford, 1988.
Gwara, Joseph J. and Mary Morse. ' A Birth Girdle Printed by Wynkyn de Worde'. *The Library*, 7th series, 13 (2012), 33–62.
Hales, John W. and Frederick J. Furnivall (eds). *Bishop Percy's Folio Manuscript: Ballads and Romances*. 3 vols. London, 1867-8.
Halliwell, J. O. (ed.). *Early English Miscellanies in Prose and Verse*. London, 1855.
Hallmundsson, M. Newman. 'Chaucer's Circle: Henry Scogan and his Friends'. *Medievalia et Humanistica*, n.s. 10 (1981), 129–39.
Hammond, Eleanor Prescott. 'The Chance of the Dice'. *Englische Studien*, 59 (1925), 1–16.

Hammond, Eleanor Prescott. *English Verse between Chaucer and Surrey*. Durham, NC, 1927.
Hammond, Eleanor Prescott. 'On the Order of the Canterbury Tales: Caxton's Two Editions'. *Modern Philology*, 3 (1905), 159–78.
Hammond, Eleanor Prescott. 'A Scribe of Chaucer'. *Modern Philology*, 27 (1929–30), 27–33.
Hammond, Eleanor Prescott. 'Two British Museum Manuscripts (Harley 2251 and Adds 34360): A Contribution to the Bibliography of John Lydgate'. *Anglia*, 28 (1905), 1–28.
Hammond, Eleanor Prescott. 'Two Tapestry Poems by Lydgate: The *Life of St George* and the *Falls of Seven Princes*'. *Englische Studien*, 43 (1910–11), 10–26.
Hanawalt, Barbara A. 'Violence in the Domestic Milieu of Late Medieval England'. In Richard W. Kaeuper (ed.), *Violence in Medieval Society*. Woodbridge, 2000. 197–214.
Hands, Rachel. 'Juliana Berners and *The Boke of St. Albans*'. *Review of English Studies*, n.s. 18 (1967), 373–86.
Hanham, Alison (trans.). *John Benet's Chronicle, 1399–1462*. New York, 2016.
Hanna, Ralph. 'Alliterative Poetry'. In David Wallace (ed.), *The Cambridge History of Medieval English Literature*. Cambridge, 1999. 488–512.
Hanna, Ralph. '*The Bridges at Abingdon*: An Unnoticed Alliterative Poem'. In Michael Calabrese and Stephen H. A. Shepherd (eds), *Yee? Baw for Bokes. Essays on Medieval Manuscripts and Poetics in Honor of Hoyt N. Duggan*. Los Angeles, CA, 2013. 31–44.
Hanna, Ralph. 'English Bible Texts before Lollardry and their Fate'. In Fiona Somerset, Jill C. Havens, and Derrick G. Pitard (eds), *Lollards and Their Influence in Late Medieval England*. Woodbridge, 2003. 141–53.
Hanna, Ralph. 'The Index of Middle English Verse and Huntington Library Collections: A Checklist of Addenda'. *Papers of the Bibliographical Society of America*, 74 (1980), 235–58.
Hanna, Ralph. 'The Sizes of Middle English Books ca.1390–1430'. *Journal of the Early Book Society*, 18 (2015), 181–91.
Hanna, Ralph. 'Verses in Sermons Again: The Case of Cambridge, Jesus College, MS 13.Q.A'. *Studies in Bibliography*, 57 (2005–2006), 63–83.
Hanna, Ralph. 'The Versions and Revisions of *Piers Plowman*'. In Andrew Cole and Andrew Galloway (eds), *The Cambridge Companion to Piers Plowman*. Cambridge, 2013. 33–49.
Hanna, Ralph and Thorlac Turville-Petre. 'The Text of the *Alliterative Morte Arthure*: A Prolegomenon for a Future Edition'. In Susanna Fein and Michael Johnston (eds), *Robert Thornton and his Books: Essays on the Lincoln and London Thornton Manuscripts*. Woodbridge, 2014. 131–55.
Hanson, Kristin. 'From Dante to Pinsky: A Theoretical Perspective on the History of the Modern English Iambic Pentameter'. *Rivista di Linguistica*, 9 (1996), 53–97.
Harcourt, Charles Gordon Vernon. *Legends of Saint Augustine, Saint Antony, and Saint Cuthbert Painted on the Back of Stalls in Carlisle Cathedral*. Carlisle, 1868.
Hardison, O. B., Jr. *Prosody and Purpose in the English Renaissance*. Baltimore, MY, 1989.
Hardman, Phillipa. 'Lydgate's *Life of Our Lady*: A Text in Transition'. *Medium Ævum*, 65 (1996), 248–68.
Hardman, Phillipa. 'Lydgate's Uneasy Syntax'. In Larry Scanlon and James Simpson (eds), *John Lydgate: Poetry, Culture, and Lancastrian England*. Notre Dame, IN, 2006. 12–35.
Hardman, Phillipa. 'Roland in England: Contextualizing the Middle English *Song of Roland*'. In Rhiannon Purdie and Michael Cichon (eds), *Medieval Romance, Medieval Contexts*. Cambridge, 2011. 91–104.
Hardman, Phillipa and Marianne Ailes (eds). *The Legend of Charlemagne in Medieval England: The Matter of France in Middle English and Anglo-Norman Literature*. Cambridge, 2017.
Hardt, Hermann von der (ed.). *Magnum oecumenicum Constantiense Concilium de universali Ecclesiae reformatione*. 6 vols. Frankfurt, 1697–1700.
Hardyng, John. H. Ellis (ed.), *The Chronicle of John Hardyng*. London, 1812.
Hardyng, John., James Simpson and Sarah Peverley (eds). *John Hardyng, Chronicle: Edited from British Library MS Lansdowne 204*. Vol. 1. Kalamazoo, MI, 2015.
Hargreaves, Henry. 'Additional Information for the Brown-Robbins "Index"'. *Notes and Queries*, n.s. 16 (1969), 446.

Harper, Carrie A. 'A Comparison Between the Brome and Chester Plays of *Abraham and Isaac*'. In *Studies in English and Comparative Literature Presented to Agnes Irwin*. Boston, 1910. 31–73.
Harris, A. Leslie. 'Tournaments and The Tournament of Tottenham'. *Fifteenth Century Studies*, 23 (1996), 81–92.
Hartrich, Eliza. *Politics and the Urban Sector in Fifteenth-Century England, 1413–1471*. Oxford, 2019.
Hartshorne, Charles Henry (ed.). *Ancient Metrical Tales*. London, 1829.
Harvey, M. W. *Jack Cade's Rebellion*. Oxford, 1991.
Hary. Anne McKim (ed.). *The Wallace*. Edinburgh, 2003.
Hasler, Antony J. *Court Poetry in Late Medieval England and Scotland: Allegories of Authority*. Cambridge, 2011.
Hasler, Antony J. 'Robert Henryson'. In Thomas Owen Clancy (ed.), *The Edinburgh History of Scottish Literature from Columba to the Union (until 1707)*. Edinburgh, 2007. 286–94.
Hatcher, John. 'Mortality in the Fifteenth Century: Some New Evidence'. *The Economic History Review*, n.s. 49 (1986), 19–38.
Hatfield, Edmund. *Here begynneth ye lyf of Saynt Ursula after ye cronycles of englonde*. London, c1510.
Hawes, Stephen. William Edward Mead (eds), *The Pastime of Pleasure*. EETS, o.s. 173. London, 1928.
Hawes, Stephen. Florence W. Gluck, and Alice B. Morgan (eds). *Stephen Hawes: The Minor Poems*. EETS, o.s. 271. London, 1974.
Hazlitt, William Carew (ed.). *Remains of the Early Popular Poetry of England*. 3 vols. London, 1864–6.
Heege Manuscript, The: A Facsimile of National Library of Scotland MS 19. 3. 1. Phillipa Hardman (introd.). Leeds, 2000.
Hellinga, Lotte. 'Manuscripts in the Hands of Printers'. In J. B. Trapp (ed.), *Manuscripts in the Fifty Years after the Invention of Printing*. London, 1983. 3–11.
Hellinga, Lotte. *William Caxton and Early Printing in England*. London, 2010.
Henderson, Arnold Clayton. 'Having Fun with the Moralities: Henryson's Fables and Late Medieval Fable Innovation'. *Studies in Scottish Literature*, 32 (2001), 67–87.
Henry, Avril. 'The Dramatic Functions of Rhyme and Stanza Patterns in *The Castle of Perseverance*'. In O. S. Pickering (ed.), *Individuality and Achievement in Middle English Poetry*. Cambridge, 1997. 147–83.
Henryson, Robert. Denton Fox (ed.). *The Poems of Robert Henryson*. Oxford, 1981.
Henryson, Robert. D. J. Parkinson (ed.). *Robert Henryson: The Complete Works*. Kalamazoo, MI, 2010.
Heroic Women from the Old Testament in Middle English Verse. Russell A. Peck (ed.). Kalamazoo, MI, 1991.
Heyman, Paul, Leopold Simons, and Christel Cochez. 'Were the English Sweating Sickness and the Picardy Sweat Caused by Hantaviruses?'. *Viruses*, 6 (2014), 151–71.
Heyworth, Gregory and Daniel E. O'Sullivan, with Frank Coulson (eds). *Les Eschéz d'Amours: A Critical Edition of the Poem and its Latin Glosses*. Leiden, 2013.
Hiatt, Alfred. 'Beyond a Border: The Maps of Scotland in John Hardyng's *Chronicle*'. In Jenny Stratford (ed.), *The Lancastrian Court: Proceedings of the 2001 Harlaxton Symposium*. Donington, 2003. 78–94.
Hiatt, Alfred. *The Making of Medieval Forgeries: False Documents in Fifteenth-Century England*. London, 2004.
Hicks, M. 'Chantries, Obits and Almshouses: The Hungerford Foundations, 1325–1478'. In C. M. Barron and C. Harper-Bill (eds), *The Church in Pre-Reformation Society*. Woodbridge, 1985. 123–42.
Higden, Ranulf. C. Babington, and J. R. Lumby (eds). *Polychronicon Ranulphi Higden*. 9 vols. Rolls Series. London, 1865–86.
Higgins, Iain M. (ed. and trans.). *The Book of John Mandeville*. Indianapolis, IN, 2011.
Hill, Eugene D. 'The Trinitarian Allegory of the Moral Play of *Wisdom*'. *Modern Philology*, 73 (1975), 121–35.
Hills, R. L. *John Tate, England's First Papermaker*. London, 1993.

Hilmo, Maidie. 'The Clerk's Unscholarly Bow: Seeing and Reading Chaucer's Clerk from the Ellesmere MS to Caxton'. *Journal of the Early Book Society*, 10 (2007), 71–105.

Hindley, K. S. 'Eating Words and Burning Them: The Power of Destruction in Medieval English Charm Texts'. In C. Kühne-Wespi, P. Oschema, and J. F. Quack (eds), *Zerstörung von Geschriebenem: historische und transkulturelle Perspektiven*. Berlin, 2019. 359–72.

Hindley, K. S. 'The Power of Not Reading: Amulet Rolls in Medieval England'. In S. G. Holz, J. Peltzer, and M. Shirota (eds), *The Roll in England and France in the Late Middle Ages: Form and Content*. Berlin, 2019. 289–306.

Hines, John. *The Fabliau in English*. Harlow, 1993.

Hirsh, John C. (ed.). *Medieval Lyric: Middle English Lyrics, Ballads and Carols*. Malden, MA, 2005.

Hirsh, John C. 'Why Does The Miller's Tale Take Place on Monday'. *English Language Notes*, 13 (1975), 86–90.

Historia Alexandri Magni (Historia de Preliis) Rezension J2 (Orosius-Rezension). Alfons Hilka (ed.). 2 vols. Meisenheim am Glan, 1976, 1977.

Historye of the Patriarks, The. Mayumi Taguchi (ed.). MET 42. Heidelberg, 2010.

Hoccleve, Thomas. *Thomas Hoccleve: A Facsimile of the Autograph Verse Manuscripts*. J. A. Burrow and A. I. Doyle (intro.). EETS, s.s. 19. Oxford, 2002.

Hoccleve, Thomas. *Hoccleve's Works: The Minor Poems*. Frederick J. Furnivall and I. Gollancz (eds) and Jerome Mitchell and A. I. Doyle (rev. eds). EETS, e.s. 61, 73, reprinted in one vol. London, 1970.

Hoccleve, Thomas. *Thomas Hoccleve: The Regiment of Princes*. Charles R. Blyth (ed.). Kalamazoo, MI, 1999.

Hoccleve, Thomas. *'My Compleinte' and Other Poems by Thomas Hoccleve*. Roger Ellis (ed.). Exeter, 2001.

Hoccleve, Thomas. *The Regiment of Princes*. Frederick J. Furnivall (ed.), *Hoccleve's Works*: III. *The Regement of Princes*. EETS, e.s. 72. London, 1897.

Hoccleve, Thomas. Burrow, J. A. (ed.), *Thomas Hoccleve's Complaint and Dialogue*. EETS, o.s. 313. Oxford, 1999.

Hoccleve, Thomas. Bernard O'Donoghue (ed.), *Selected Poems*. Manchester, 1982.

Hodnett, Edward. *English Woodcuts 1480–1535*. Rev. edn. London, 1973.

Holland, Richard. Ralph Hanna (ed.), *The Buke of the Howlat*. STS, 5th series, 12. Woodbridge, 2014.

Holthausen, F. 'London Lickpenny'. *Anglia*, 43 (1919), 61–68.

Holthausen, F. 'Medicinische Gedichte aus einer Stockholmer Handschrift'. *Anglia*, 18 (1906), 307–30.

Holton, Amanda. *The Sources of Chaucer's Poetics*. Aldershot, 2008.

Horobin, Simon. 'Charles d'Orléans, Harley 682, and the London Booktrade'. In R. D. Perry and Mary-Jo Arn (eds), *Charles d'Orléans's English Aesthetic*. Cambridge, 2020. 245–64.

Horobin, Simon. *Chaucer's Language*. 2nd edn. Basingstoke, 2013.

Horobin, Simon. 'A Manuscript Found in the Library of Abbotsford House and the Lost Legendary of Osbern Bokenham'. *English Manuscript Studies 1100–1700*, 14 (2008), 132–62.

Horobin, Simon. 'Politics, Patronage, and Piety in the Work of Osbern Bokenham'. *Speculum*, 82 (2007), 932–49.

Horobin, Simon. 'The Scribe of Bodleian Manuscript Digby 102 and the Circulation of the C-Text of *Piers Plowman*'. *Yearbook of Langland Studies*, 24 (2010), 89–112.

Horobin, Simon. 'Thomas Hoccleve: Chaucer's First Editor?', *The Chaucer Review*, 50 (2015), 228–50.

Horrox, Rosemary. *The Black Death*. Manchester, 1994.

Horstmann, Carl (ed.). *Altenglische Legenden: Neue Folge*. Heilbronn, 1881.

Horstmann, Carl (ed.). *The Life of St Werburge of Chester by Henry Bradshaw*. EETS, o.s. 88. London, 1887.

Horstman, Carl. 'Nachträge zu den Legenden. 7. Romanze von Christi Auferstehung aus Ms. Ashmol. 61, fol. 138'. *Archiv für das Studium der neueren Sprachen und Literatur*, 79 (1887), 441–7.

Horstmann, Carl (ed.). 'Thomas Beket, Epische Legende, von Laurentius Wade (1497)'. *Englische Studien*, 3 (1880), 409–69.

Hosington, Brenda. 'Partonopeu de Blois and its Fifteenth-Century English Translation: A Medieval Translator at Work'. In Roger Ellis (ed.), *The Medieval Translator: Volume II*. London, 1991. 231–52.

Hosington, Brenda. 'Voices of Protest and Submission: Portraits of Women in *Partonopeu de Blois* and its Middle English Translation'. *Reading Medieval Studies*, 17 (1991), 62–75.

Houghton, Josephine. 'Deguileville and Hoccleve Again'. *Medium Ævum*, 82 (2013), 260–8.

Houlik-Ritchey, Emily. 'Troubled Conversions: The Difference Gender Makes in the *Sultan of Babylon*'. *Literature Compass*, 5 (2008), 493–504.

Houston, R. A. *Literacy in Early Modern Europe: Culture and Education, 1500–1800*, 2nd edn. Oxford, 2013.

Howlett, D. R. 'The Date and Authorship of the Middle English Verse Translation of Palladius *De re rustica*'. *Medium Ævum*, 46 (1977), 245–52.

Hübner, Walter. 'The Desert of Religion'. *Archiv für das Studium der neueren Sprachen und Literatur*, 126 (1911), 58–74.

Hudson, Anne. 'The Debate on Bible Translation, Oxford 1401'. *English Historical Review*, 90 (1975), 1–18.

Hulme, William Henry (ed.). *The Middle-English Harrowing of Hell and Gospel of Nicodemus*. EETS, e.s. 100. London, 1907.

Hult, David F. and Joan E. McRae (eds). *Le Cycle de la Belle dame sans mercy*. Paris, 2003.

Hult, David F. (ed. and trans.). *The Debate of the 'Romance of the Rose'*. Chicago, 2010.

Hume, Cathy. '*The Storie of Asneth*: A Fifteenth-century Commission and the Mystery of its Epilogue'. *Medium Ævum*, 82 (2013), 44–65.

Hunt, Tony. 'The Poetic Vein: Phlebotomy in Middle English and Anglo-Norman Verse'. *English Studies*, 77 (1996), 311–22.

Husband, T. B. and J. Hayward (intro.). *The Secular Spirit: Life and Art at the End of the Middle Ages*. New York, 1975.

Huws, Daniel. 'Porkington 10 and its Scribes'. In Jennifer Fellows, Rosamond Field, Gillian Rogers, and Judith Weiss (eds), *Romance Reading on the Book*. Cardiff, 1996. 188–207.

Idley, Peter. Charlotte D'Evelyn (eds). *Peter Idley's 'Instructions to His Son'*. Boston, 1935.

Ingram, R.W. (ed.). *Records of Early English Drama: Coventry*. Toronto, 1981.

Inoue, Noriko. 'A New Theory of Alliterative A-Verses'. *Yearbook of Langland Studies*, 18 (2004), 107–32.

Inoue, Noriko and Myra Stokes. 'The Caesura and the Rhythmic Shape of the A-Verse in the Poems of the Alliterative Revival'. *Leeds Studies in English*, n.s. 40 (2009), 1–26.

Ipomadon. Rhiannon Purdie (ed.). EETS, o.s. 316. Oxford, 2001.

Ipomedon, in drei englischen Bearbeitungen. E. Kölbing (ed.). Breslau, 1889.

Ipomydon, The Lyfe of. Tadahiro Ikegami (ed.). 2 vols. Tokyo, 1983, 1985.

Irace, Kathleen. 'Mak's Sothren Tothe: A Philological and Critical Study of the Dialect Joke in the *Second Shepherd's Play*'. *Comitatus*, 21 (1990), 38–51.

Isle of Ladies, The or The Ile of Pleasaunce. Anthony Jenkins, (ed.). New York, 1980.

Jacob, E. F. '"Florida Verborum Venustas": Some Early Signs of Euphuism in England'. *Bulletin of the John Rylands Library*, 18 (1933), 264–90.

James, M. E. 'Murder at Cocklodge'. *Durham University Journal*, 57 (1965), 80–7.

James, M. E. *Society, Politics, and Culture: Studies in Early Modern England*. Cambridge, 1986.

James, M. R. 'Lives of St Walstan'. *Norfolk Archaeology Society Papers*, 19 (1917), 238–67.

James-Maddocks, Holly. ' Illuminated Caxtons and the Trade in Printed Books'. *The Library* 7th series, 22 (2021), 291–315.

Jamieson, Robert. *Popular Ballads and Songs*. 2 vols. Edinburgh, 1806.

Jansen, J. P. M. (ed.). *The 'Suffolk' Poems: An Edition of the Love Lyrics in Fairfax 16*. Groningen, 1989.

Johnson, Eleanor. *Staging Contemplation: Participatory Theology in Middle English Prose, Verse, and Drama*. Chicago, IL, 2018.

Johnson, Ian. *The Middle English Life of Christ: Academic Discourse, Translation, and Vernacular Theology*. Turnhout, 2013.

Johnson, Ian. 'Prologue and Practice: Middle English Lives of Christ'. In Roger Ellis (ed.), *The Medieval Translator: The Theory and Practice of Translation in the Middle Ages*. Cambridge, 1989. 69–85.
Johnson, Ian. 'Reading Robert Henryson's *Orpheus and Eurydice*: Sentence and Sensibility'. In Ian Johnson and Alessandra Petrina (eds), *The Impact of Latin Culture on Medieval and Early Modern Scottish Writing*. Kalamazoo, MI, 2018. 175–98.
Johnson, Ian R. 'Walton's Sapient Orpheus'. In Alastair J. Minnis (ed.), *The Medieval Boethius: Studies in the Vernacular Translations of 'De Consolatione Philosophiae'*. Cambridge, 1987. 139–68.
Johnston, Alexandra F. 'The Towneley Plays: Huntington Library MS HM 1'. In Tamara Atkin and Laura Estill (eds), *Early British Drama in Manuscript*. Turnhout, 2019. 55–70.
Johnston, Alexandra F. and Margaret Rogerson (eds). *Records of Early English Drama: York*. 2 vols. Toronto, 1979.
Johnston. Mark D. (ed.). *Medieval Conduct Literature: An Anthology of Vernacular Guides to Behaviour for Youths, with English Translations*. Toronto, 2009.
Johnston, Michael. 'Constantinian Christianity in the London Manuscript: The Codicological and Linguistic Evidence of Thornton's Intentions'. In Susanna Fein and Michael Johnston (eds), *Robert Thornton and His Books: Essays on the Lincoln and London Thornton Manuscripts*. Woodbridge, 2014. 177–204.
Johnston, Michael. *Romance and the Gentry in Late Medieval England*. Oxford, 2014.
Johnston, Michael. 'Two Leicestershire Romance Codices: Cambridge, University Library MS Ff. 2. 38 and Oxford, Bodleian Library MS Ashmole 61'. *Journal of the Early Book Society*, 15 (2012), 84–99.
Johnstone, Boyda. '"Far semed her hart from obeysaunce": Strategies of Resistance in *The Isle of Ladies*'. *Studies in the Age of Chaucer*, 41 (2019), 301–24.
Johnstone, Boyda. 'Vitreous Visions: Stained Glass and Affective Engagement in John Lydgate's *The Temple of Glass*'. *New Medieval Literatures*, 17 (2017), 175–200.
Jonker, M. A. 'Estimation of Life Expectancy in the Middle Ages'. *Journal of the Royal Statistical Society. Series A (Statistics in Society)*, 146 (2003), 105–117.
Jörg-Uther, Hans. *The Types of International Folktales*. Helsinki, 2004.
Kalff, G. *Geschiedenis der Nederlandsche letterkunde*. 3 vols. Groningen, 1906–12.
Kamath, Stephanie A. Viereck Gibbs. *Authorship and First-Person Allegory in Late Medieval France and England*. Cambridge, 2012.
Katharine of Alexandria, The Life of St. Carl Horstmann, (ed.). EETS, o.s. 100. London, 1893.
Keen, Maurice. *English Society in the Later Middle Ages 1348–1500*. Harmondsworth, 1990.
Keiser, George R. 'A Middle English Rosemary Treatise in Verse and Prose'. *American Notes and Queries*, n.s. 18 (2005), 9–18.
Keiser, George R. 'Practical Books for the Gentleman'. In Lotte Hellinga and J. B. Trapp (eds), *The Cambridge History of the Book in Britain, III: 1400–1557*. Cambridge, 1999. 470–94.
Keiser, George R. 'Serving the Needs of Readers: Textual Division in Some Late-Medieval English Texts'. In Richard Beadle and A. J. Piper (eds), *New Science out of Old Books: Studies in Manuscripts and Early Printed Books in Honour of A. I. Doyle*. Aldershot, 1995. 207–26.
Keiser, George R. 'Verse Introductions to Middle English Medical Texts'. *English Studies*, 84 (2003), 301–17.
Keiser, George R. 'Works of Science and Information'. In Albert E. Hartung (ed.), *A Manual of the Writings in Middle English 1050–1500*. 11 vols. New Haven, CT, 1998. Vol. 10.
Kekewich, Margaret Lucille, Colin Richmond, Anne F. Sutton, Livia Visser-Fuchs, and John L. Watts (eds). *The Politics of Fifteenth-Century England: John Vale's Book*. Stroud, 1995.
Kelly, Henry Ansgar. *Chaucerian Tragedy*. Woodbridge, 1997.
Kennedy, Edward Donald. 'Chronicles and other Historical Writing'. In Albert E. Hartung (ed.), *A Manual of the Writings in Middle English, 1050–1500*. 11 vols. New Haven, CT, 1989. Vol. 8.
Kennedy, Ruth. 'Strong-Stress Metre in Fourteen-Line Stanza Forms'. *Parergon*, 18 (2000), 127–55.
Kennedy, Walter. Nicole Meier (ed.), *The Poems of Walter Kennedy*. STS, 5th series, 6. Cambridge, 2008.

Khalaf, Omar. 'An Unedited Fragmentary Poem by Anthony Woodville, Earl Rivers in Oxford, Bodleian Library, MS Bodley 264'. *Notes and Queries*, n.s. 58 (2011), 487–90.

Khinoy, Stephan. 'Tale-Moral Relationships in Henryson's *Morall Fabillis*'. *Studies in Scottish Literature*, 17 (1982), 99–115.

Kinch, Ashby. 'Chartier's European Influence'. In Daisy Delogu, Emma Cayley, and Joan E. McRae (eds), *A Companion to Alain Chartier (c.1385–1430): Father of French Eloquence*. Leiden, 2015. 279-302

Kinch, Ashby. 'A Naked Roos: Translation and Subjection in the Middle English *La Belle Dame Sans Mercy*'. *JEGP*, 105 (2006), 415–45.

King, Andrew. 'Romance'. In Julia Boffey and A. S. G. Edwards (eds), *A Companion to Fifteenth-Century English Poetry*. Cambridge, 2013. 187–98.

King, Pamela M. 'The Coventry Playbooks'. In Tamara Atkin and Laura Estill (eds), *Early British Drama in Manuscript*. Turnhout, 2019. 33–54.

King, Pamela M. 'Dunbar's *The Golden Targe*: A Chaucerian Masque'. *Studies in Scottish Literature*, 19 (1984), 115–31.

King, Pamela M. (ed.). *The Routledge Research Companion to Early Drama and Performance*. London, 2017.

King, Pamela M. *The York Mystery Plays and the Worship of the City*. Woodbridge, 2006.

King, Pamela M., Meg Twycross, and Greg Walker (eds). '"The Best Pairt of our Play": Essays Presented to John J. McGavin'. *Medieval English Theatre* 37–8 (2016–17).

Kinghorn, A.M. 'Death and the *Makars*: Timor mortis in Scottish Poetry to 1600'. *English Studies*, 60 (1979), 2–13.

Kingsford, Charles Lethbridge (ed.). *Chronicles of London*. Oxford, 1905.

Kipling, Gordon. *Enter the King: Theatre, Liturgy, and Ritual in the Medieval Civic Triumph*. Oxford, 1998.

Kipling, Gordon. 'Henry VII and the Origins of Tudor Patronage'. In Guy Fitch Lytle and Stephen Orgel (eds), *Patronage in the Renaissance* (Princeton, NJ, 1981). 117–64.

Kipling, Gordon. 'Lydgate: The Poet as Deviser'. In Donka Minkova and Theresa Tinkle (eds), *Chaucer and the Challenges of Medievalism: Studies in Honor of H. A. Kelly*. Frankfurt, 2003. 73–101.

Kipling, Gordon. *The Triumph of Honour: Burgundian Origins of the Elizabethan Renaissance*. Leiden, 1977.

Kirkman, Andrew. *The Cultural Life of the Early Polyphonic Mass: Medieval Context to Modern Revival*. Cambridge, 2010.

Kirkman, Francis. *Unlucky Citizen*. London, 1673.

Klausner, David N. 'Exempla and *The Awntyrs of Arthure*'. *Medieval Studies*, 34 (1972), 307–25.

Klausner, David N. (ed.). *Records of Early English Drama: Herefordshire, Worcestershire*. Toronto, 1990.

Kline, Andrew W. 'Scots Take the Wheel: The Problem of Period and the Medieval Scots Alliterative Thirteen-Line Stanza'. *Studies in Scottish Literature*, 43.1 (2017), 15–21.

Kline, Daniel T. (ed.). *Medieval Literature for Children*. New York, 2003.

Knapp, Ethan. 'Bureaucratic Identity and the Construction of the Self in Hoccleve's *Formulary* and *La male regle*'. *Speculum*, 74 (1999), 357–76.

Knapp, Ethan. *Bureaucratic Muse: Thomas Hoccleve and the Literature of Late Medieval England*. University Park, PA, 2001.

Knight, Stephen. *Reading Robin Hood: Content, Form and Reception in the Outlaw Myth* Manchester. 2015.

Knight, Stephen. *Robin Hood: A Complete Study of the English Outlaw*. Oxford, 1994.

Knoop, Douglas, G. P. Jones, and Douglas Hamer (eds). *The Two Earliest Masonic Mss.: The Regius Ms. (B.M. Bibl. reg. 17 AI), the Cooke Ms. (B.M. Add. ms. 23198)*. Manchester, 1938.

Knox, Philip. *The Roman de la Rose and Fourteenth-Century English Poetry*. Oxford, 2021.

Kolve, V. A. 'Chaucer and the Visual Arts'. In Derek Brewer (ed.), *Geoffrey Chaucer*. Cambridge, 1974. 290–320.

Kopaczyk, Joanna. 'The Language of William Dunbar: Middle Scots or Early ModernScots?' *European Journal of English Studies*, 18 (2014), 21–41.

Kratzmann, Gregory (ed). *Colkelbie Sow and The Talis of the Fyve Bestes*. New York, 1983.
Kratzmann, Gregory. 'The Poetics of the "Feinyeit Fabill"': Chaucer and the Middle Scots Poets'. In R.S.D. Jack and Kevin McGinley (eds), *Of Lion and Of Unicorn: Essays on Anglo-Scottish Literary Relations in Honour of Professor John MacQueen*. Edinburgh, 1993. 16–38.
Kreuzer, James R. 'Thomas Brampton's Metrical Paraphrase of the Seven Penitential Psalms: A Diplomatic Edition of the Version in MS Pepys 1584 and MS Cambridge University Ff 2. 38 with Variant Readings from All Known Manuscripts'. *Traditio*, 7 (1951), 359–403.
Krochalis, Jeanne. '*Magna Tabula*: The Glastonbury Tablets'. *Arthuriana* 15 (1997), 93–118; 16. (1998), 41–27.
Krochalis, Jeanne. 'The Newberry Stations of Rome'. In M. V. Hennessy (ed.), *Tributes to Kathleen L. Scott. English Medieval Manuscripts: Readers, Makers and Illuminators*. London, 2009. 129–37.
Kruyskamp, C. *De Middelnederlandse boerden*. The Hague, 1957.
Kudo, Yoshinobu. 'Reinstalling Clerical Authority, Juridical and Didactic: The Unique Rearrangements of Book II of Peter Idley's *Instructions to his Son* in London, British Library, Arundel MS 20'. *Medium Ævum*, 88 (2019), 265–300.
Kuczynski, Michael P. *Prophetic Song: The Psalms as Moral Discourse in Late Medieval England*. Philadelphia, PA, 1995.
Kuhn, Sherman M. 'Was Ælfric a Poet?' *Philological Quarterly*, 52 (1973), 643–62.
Kurvinen, Auvo. 'Mercy and Righteousness'. *Neuphilologische Mitteilungen*, 73 (1972), 181–91.
Kurvinen, Auvo. 'The Source of Capgrave's Life of St Katharine of Alexandria'. *Neuphilologische Mitteilungen*, 61 (1960), 268–324.
Kwakkel, Erik. 'A New Type of Book for a New Type of Reader: The Emergence of Paper in Vernacular Book Production'. *The Library*, 7th series, 4 (2003), 219–48.
Lacy, Norris J. *Reading Fabliaux*. Birmingham, AL, 1998.
Ladd, Roger A. 'The Mercantile (Mis) Reader in "The Canterbury Tales"'. *Studies in Philology*, 99 (2002), 17–32.
Laing, M. 'John Whittokesmede as Parliamentarian and Horse Owner in Yale University Library, Beinecke MS 163'. *Journal of the Spanish Society for Medieval English Language and Literature*, 17 (2010), 1–72.
Lake, Prescott Anne. 'Crime and Carnival at Chelsea: Widow Edith and Thomas More's Household'. *Moreana*, 100 (1989), 247–64.
Lambert, Bart and Milan Pajic. 'Immigration and the Common Profit: Native Cloth Workers, Flemish Exiles, and Royal Policy in Fourteenth-Century London'. *Journal of British Studies*, 55 (2016), 633–57.
Lamont, M. '"Genealogical History" and the English Roll'. In *Medieval Manuscripts, Their Makers and Users: A Special Issue of Viator in Honor of Richard and Mary Rouse*. Turnhout, 2011. 245–61.
Lancelot of the Laik from Cambridge University Library MS. Margaret Muriel Gray (ed.). STS, n.s. 2. Edinburgh, 1912.
Langdell, Sebastian J. 'A Study of Speech-Markers in the Early- to Mid-Fifteenth-Century Hocclevian Manuscript Tradition'. *Notes and Queries*, n.s. 59 (2012), 323–31.
Langdell, Sebastian J. *Thomas Hoccleve: Religious Reform, Transnational Poetics, and the Invention of Chaucer*. Liverpool, 2018.
Langham, Robert. *A Letter*. R. J. P. Kuin, (ed.). Leiden, 1983.
Langland, William. Derek Pearsall (ed.). *Piers Plowman: A New Annotated Edition of the C-text*. Exeter, 2008.
Langland, William. Derek Pearsall and Kathleen Scott L. (intro.). *Piers Plowman. A Facsimile of Bodleian Library Oxford MS Douce 104*. Cambridge, 1992.
Langland, William. A. V. C. Schmidt (ed.). *The Vision of Piers Plowman: A Critical Edition of the B-Text*, 2nd edn. London, 1995.
Lass, Roger. 'Phonology and Morphology'. In N. F. Blake (ed.), *1066–1476*. Vol. 2 in Richard M. Hogg (ed.), *The Cambridge History of the English Language*. Cambridge, 1992. 23–155.
Late Medieval Religious Plays of Bodleian MSS Digby 133 and E Museo 160, The. Donald C. Baker, John L. Murphy, and Louis B. Hall Jr. (eds). EETS, o.s. 283. Oxford, 1982.

Laud Troy Book, The, a Romance of About 1400 AD. J. Ernst Wülfing (ed.). EETS, o.s. 121, 122. London, 1902, 1903.
Lawler, Traugott. 'On the Properties of John Trevisa's Major Translations'. *Viator*, 14 (1983), 267–88.
Lawton, David A. 'The Bible'. In Roger Ellis (ed.), *The Oxford History of Literary Translation in English: Volume 1 To 1550*. Oxford, 2008. 193–233.
Lawton, David A. '*The Destruction of Troy* as Translation from Latin Prose: Aspects of Form and Style'. *Studia Neophilologica*, 52 (1980), 259–70.
Lawton, David A. 'Dullness and the Fifteenth Century'. *ELH*, 54 (1987), 761–99.
Lawton, David A. 'History and Legend: The Exile and the Turk'. In P. C. Ingham and M. R. Warren (eds). *Postcolonial Moves*. New York, 2003. 173–94.
Lawton, David A. 'Literary History and Scholarly Fancy: The Date of Two Middle English Alliterative Poems'. *Parergon*, 18 (1977), 17–25.
Lawton, David A. 'The Middle English Alliterative *Alexander A* and *C*: Form and Style in Translation from Latin Prose'. *Studia Neophilologica*, 53 (1981), 259–68.
Lawton, David A. 'The Unity of Middle English Alliterative Poetry'. *Speculum*, 58 (1983), 72–94.
Lawton, David A. 'Voice after Arundel'. In Vincent Gillespie and Kantik Ghosh (eds), *After Arundel: Religious Writing in Fifteenth-Century England*. Turnhout, 2011. 133–51.
Lawton, David A. *Voice in Later Medieval English Literature: Public Interiorities*. Oxford, 2017.
Lawton, Lesley. 'The Illustration of Late Medieval Secular Texts' In Derek Pearsall (ed.), *Manuscripts and Readers in the Fifteenth Century*. Cambridge, 1983. 41–69.
Lay Folks Mass Book, The. Thomas Frederick Simmons (ed.). EETS, o.s. 71. London, 1879.
Laynesmith, J. L. 'Constructing Queenship at Coventry: Pageantry and Politics at Margaret of Anjou's "Secret Harbour"'. In Linda Clark (ed.). *Authority and Subversion*. Woodbridge, 2003. 137–47.
Lee, B. S. 'Lucidus and Dubius: A Fifteenth-Century Theological Debate and its Sources'. *Medium Ævum*, 45 (1976), 79–96.
Leitch, Megan G. *Romancing Treason: The Literature of the Wars of the Roses*. Oxford, 2015.
Leneghan, Francis. 'Introduction: A Case Study of Psalm 50.1–3 in Old and Middle English'. In Tamara Atkin and Francis Leneghan (eds), *The Psalms and Medieval English Literature: From the Conversion to the Reformation*. Cambridge, 2017. 1–33.
Lerer, Seth. 'British Library Harley MS 78 and the Manuscripts of John Shirley'. *Notes and Queries*, n.s. 37 (1990), 400–3.
Lerer, Seth. *Chaucer and His Readers: Imagining the Author in Late-Medieval England*. Princeton, NJ, 1993.
Lerer, Seth. *Inventing English: A Portable History of the Language*. New York, 2007.
Lerer, Seth. 'The Rhetoric of Fame: Stephen Hawes's Aureate Diction'. *Spenser Studies*, 5 (1984), 169–84.
Lester, Geoffrey (ed.). *The Earliest English Translation of Vegetius' 'De re militari'*. MET 21. Heidelberg, 1988.
Levin, Richard. *The Multiple Plot in English Renaissance Drama*. Chicago, 1971.
Lewis, C. S. *The Allegory of Love: A Study in Medieval Tradition*. Oxford, 1936.
Lewis, Henry (ed.). *Peniarth 53*. Adysgrifau o'r Llawsgrifau Cymraeg, 5. Cardiff, 1927.
Lewis, Robert E. 'The English Fabliau Tradition and Chaucer's "Miller's Tale"'. *Modern Philology*, 79 (1982), 241–55.
Lewis, Robert E. and Angus McIntosh. *A Descriptive Guide to the Manuscripts of the Prick of Conscience*. Oxford, 1982.
Libelle of Englyshe Polycye: A Poem on the Use of Sea-Power, 1436. George Warner (ed.). Oxford, 1926.
Liddell, Mark (ed.). *The Middle-English Translation of Palladius De Re Rustica*. Berlin, 1896.
Liddy, Christian D. 'Urban Enclosure Riots: Risings of the Commons in English Towns, 1480–1525'. *Past & Present*, 226 (2015), 41–77.
Lindahl, Carl. 'Jacks: The Name, The Tales, The American Traditions'. In William Bernard McCarthy (ed.), *Jack In Two Worlds*. Chapel Hill, NC, 1994. xiii–xxiv.
Lindenbaum, Sheila. 'London Texts and Literate Practice'. In David Wallace (ed.), *Cambridge History of Medieval English Literature*. Cambridge, 2002. 284–310.

Lindsay, Robert of Pitscottie. *Historie and Chronicles of Scotland.* Aeneas. J.G. Mackay (ed.). STS, 1st series, 43. Edinburgh, 1899.
Linster, Jillian. 'The Physician and His Servant in the Croxton *Play of the Sacrament*'. *Early Theatre*, 20 (2017), 31–48.
Liszka, Thomas R. 'The *South English Legendaries*'. In Heather Blurton and Jocelyn Wogan-Browne (eds), *Rethinking the South English Legendaries.* Manchester, 2011. 23–41.
Liu, Yin. 'Richard Beauchamp and the Uses of Romance'. *Medium Ævum*, 74 (2005), 27–87.
Livingston, Michael (ed.). *The Middle English Metrical Paraphrase of the Old Testament.* Kalamazoo, MI, 2011.
Lloyd, Paul S. *Food and Identity in England: Eating to Impress.* London, 2015.
Lorris, Guillaume de and Jean de Meun. *Le Roman de la Rose.* Félix Lecoy (ed.). 3 vols. Paris, 1965–70.
Louis, Cameron (ed.). *The Commonplace Book of Robert Reynes of Acle: An Edition of Tanner MS 407.* New York, 1980.
Love, Nicholas. *Nicholas Love's Mirror of the Blessed Life of Jesus Christ: A Critical Edition.* Michael G. Sargent (ed.). New York, 1992.
Lovelich, Henry. E. A. Kock (ed.). *Henry Lovelich's Merlin.* EETS, e.s. 93, 112, o.s. 185. London, 1904, 1913, 1932.
Lovelich, Henry. F. J. Furnivall (ed.). *The History of the Holy Grail by Henry Lovelich.* EETS, e.s. 20, 24, 28, 30, 95. London, 1874–1905.
Lucas, Peter J. *From Author to Audience: John Capgrave and Medieval Publication.* Dublin, 1997.
Lupack, Alan (ed.). *Lancelot of the Laik and Sir Tristrem.* Kalamazoo, MI, 1994.
Luttrell, C. A. 'Three North-West Midland Manuscripts'. *Neophilologus*, 42 (1958), 38–50.
Lyall, Roderick J. 'Henryson's *Moral Fabillis*: Structure and Meaning'. In Priscilla Bawcutt and Janet Hadley Williams (eds), *A Companion to Medieval Scottish Poetry.* Cambridge, 2006. 89–104.
Lydgate, John. Pamela Farvolden (ed.). *Lydgate's Fabula Duorum Mercatorum and Guy of Warwyk.* Kalamazoo, MI, 2016.
Lydgate, John. Henry Bergen (eds). *Fall of Princes.* 4 vols. EETS, e.s. London, 1924, 1927.
Lydgate, John. J. E. van der Westhuizen (eds). *John Lydgate: The Life of Saint Alban and Saint Amphibal.* Leiden, 1974.
Lydgate, John. Anthony Bale, and A. S. G. Edwards (eds). *John Lydgate's 'Lives of Ss Edmund & Fremund' and the 'Extra Miracles of St Edmund'.* MET 41. Heidelberg, 2009.
Lydgate, John. Joseph A. Lauritis, R. A. Klinefelter, and V. F. Gallagher (eds). *A Critical Edition of John Lydgate's Life of Our Lady.* Pittsburgh, PA, 1961.
Lydgate, John. Henry Noble MacCracken (ed.). *The Minor Poems of John Lydgate: Part I: Religious Poems; Part II: Secular Poems.* 2 vols. EETS, e.s. 107, EETS, o.s. 192. London, 1911, 1934.
Lydgate, John. Claire Sponsler (ed.). *John Lydgate: Mummings and Entertainments.* Kalamazoo, MI, 2010.
Lydgate, John. Axel Erdmann, and E. Ekwall (eds). *Lydgate's Siege of Thebes.* 2 vols. EETS e.s. 108, 125. London, 1911, 1930.
Lydgate, John. Josef Schick (eds). *Lydgate's Temple of Glas.* EETS e.s. 60. London, 1891.
Lydgate, John. Henry Bergen (ed.). *Lydgate's Troy Book.* 4 vols. EETS e.s. 97, 103, 106, 126. London, 1906, 1908, 1910, 1935.
Lydgate, John, and Benedict Burgh. Robert Steele (eds). *Lydgate and Burgh's Secrees of Old Philisoffres.* EETS e.s. 66. London, 1894.
Lydgate, John and Benedict Burgh. DeWitt T. Starnes (intro). *The Gouernaunce of Kynges and Prynces: The Pynson Edition of 1511.* Gainesville, FL, 1957.
Lynch, Kathryn L. 'Dating Chaucer'. *The Chaucer Review*, 42 (2007), 1–22.
Lyndsay, David. Janet Hadley Williams (ed.). *Sir David Lyndsay: Selected Poems.* Glasgow, 2000.
Macro Plays, The. Mark Eccles (ed.). EETS, o.s. 262. Oxford, 1969.
Mankind. Kathleen M. Ashley and Gerard NeCastro (eds). Kalamazoo,MI, 2010.
McCallum, R.I. 'Alchemical Scrolls Associated with George Ripley'. In S. J. Linden (ed.), *Mystical Metal of Gold: Essays on Alchemy and Renaissance Culture,* (New York, 2007). 161–88.
McCarthy, Conor. *Marriage in Medieval England: Law, Literature, and Practice.* Woodbridge, 2004.

McAvoy, Liz Herbert. 'Anonymous Texts'. In Liz Herbert McAvoy and Diane Watt (eds), *The History of British Women's Writing, 700–1500*. Houndmills, 2011. 160–68.

MacCracken, Henry Noble. 'King Henry's Triumphal Entry into London, Lydgate's Poem, and Carpenter's Letter'. *Archiv für das Studium der Neuen Sprachen und Literaturen*, 126 (1911), 75–102.

MacCracken, Henry Noble. 'Lydgatiana III: The Three Kings of Cologne'. *Archiv für das Studium der neueren Sprachen und Lliteraturen*, 129 (1912), 50–68.

MacCracken, Henry Noble. 'A Meditation upon Death, for the Tomb of Ralph, Lord Cromwell (c.1450), Lord Treasurer of England'. *Modern Language Notes*, 26 (1911), 85–6.

MacCracken, Henry Noble. 'Notes Suggested by a Chaucer Codex'. *Modern Language Notes*, 23 (1908), 212–14.

McRae, Joan E. (ed.), *Alain Chartier: The Quarrel of the Belle Dame Sans Mercy*. London, 2004.

McRae, Joan E. 'A Community of Readers: The Quarrel of the *Belle Dame Sans Mercy*'. In Daisy Delogu, Emma Cayley, and Joan E. McRae (eds), *A Companion to Alain Chartier (c.1385–1430): Father of French Eloquence*. Leiden, 2015. 200–22.

McDiarmid, Matthew P. 'Concerning Sir Gilbert Hay, the Authorship of *Alexander the Conquerour* and *The Buik of Alexander*'. *Studies in Scottish Literature*, 28 (1993), 28–54.

MacDonald, A. A. 'The Latin Origins of Robert Henryson's Annunciation Lyric'. In A.A. MacDonald, Michael Lynch, and Ian B. Cowan (eds), *The Renaissance in Scotland: Studies in Literature, Religion, History and Culture Offered to John Durkan*. Leiden, 1994. 45–65.

MacDonald, A. A. 'Lyrics in Middle Scots'. In T. G. Duncan (ed.), *A Companion to the Middle English Lyric*. Cambridge, 2005. 242–62.

McDonald, Nicola F. (ed.). *Pulp Fictions of Medieval England: Essays in Popular Romance*. Manchester, 2004.

McDonald, Nicola F. '*The Seege of Troye*: "ffor wham was wakened al this wo?"'. In Ad Putter and Jane Gilbert (eds), *The Spirit of Medieval English Popular Romance*. Harlow, 2000. 181–99.

McGee, C.E. 'Politics and Platitudes: Sources of Civic Pageantry, 1486'. *Renaissance Studies*, 3 (1989), 29–34.

McGerr, Rosemarie Potz (ed.). *The Pilgrimage of the Soul: A Critical Edition of the Middle English Dream Vision*. Vol. 1. Garland Medieval Texts, 16. New York, 1990.

McGovern-Mouron, A. 'The *Desert of Religion* in British Library Cotton Faustina B VI, pars II'. In James Hogg (ed.), *The Mystical Tradition and the Carthusians*, Analecta Cartusiana, 130. 9. Salzburg, 1996. 149–62.

McKenna, J. W. 'Henry VI of England and the Dual Monarchy: Aspects of Royal Political Propaganda, 1422–1432'. *Journal of the Warburg and Courtauld Institutes*, 28 (1965), 145–62.

Mackenzie, W. Roy. 'A Source for Medwall's *Nature*'. *PMLA*, 29 (1914), 189–99.

McLaren, Mary-Rose. *The London Chronicles of the Fifteenth Century: A Revolution in English Writing*. Woodbridge, 2002.

McMillan, Ann. '"Fayre Sisters Al": *The Flower and the Leaf* and *The Assembly of Ladies*'. *Tulsa Studies in Women's Literature*, 1 (1982), 27–42.

McMillan, Samuel F. 'Trailing an Unreasonable *Rose*: Authorship in John Lydgate's *Reson and Sensuallyte*'. *Modern Philology*, 116 (2018), 95–120.

McNiven, Peter. *Heresy and Politics in the Reign of Henry IV: The Burning of John Badby*. Woodbridge, 1987.

MacQueen, John. *Complete and Full with Numbers: The Narrative Poetry of Robert Henryson*. Amsterdam, 2006.

MacQueen, John. 'Henryson, Robert (d. c.1490), Poet'. *ODNB*. 2004.

McNamer, Sarah. 'Female Authors, Provincial Setting: The Re-Versing of Courtly Love in the Findern Manuscript'. *Viator*, 22 (1991), 279–310.

Machan, Tim William. 'Robert Henryson and Father Aesop: Authority in the Moral Fables'. *Studies in the Age of Chaucer*, 12 (1990), 193–214.

Maidstone, Richard. *Richard Maidstone's Penitential Psalms*, ed. from Bodl. MS Rawlinson A 389. Valerie Edden (ed.). MET 22. Heidelberg, 1990.

Malo, Robyn. *Relics and Writing in Late Medieval England*. Toronto, 2013.

Malory, Thomas. James W. Spisak (eds). *Caxton's Malory*. 2 vols. Berkeley, CA, 1983.
Malory, Thomas. Stephen H. A. Shepherd, (eds). *Le Morte Darthur*. New York, 2003.
Manly, J. M. and Edith Rickert. *The Text of the Canterbury Tales*. 8 vols. Chicago, 1940.
Mann, Jill. *Feminizing Chaucer*. Woodbridge, 2002.
Mann, Jill. 'Chaucer, Henryson and the Planetary Deities'. In Ruth Morse and Barry Windeatt (eds), *Chaucer Traditions: Studies in Honour of Derek Brewer*. Cambridge, 1990. 91–106.
Mannyng, Robert. Idelle Sullens, (eds). *Robert Mannyng of Brunne: The Chronicle*. Binghamton, NY, 1996.
Mapstone, Sally. 'Invective as Poetic: The Cultural Contexts of Polwarth and Montgomerie's *Flyting*'. *Scottish Literary Journal*, 26 (1999), 18–40.
Mapstone, Sally. 'Kingship and *The Kingis Quair*'. In Helen Cooper and Sally Mapstone (eds), *The Long Fifteenth-Century: Essays for Douglas Gray*. Oxford, 1997. 51–69.
Mapstone, Sally. 'Robert Henryson'. In Larry Scanlon (ed.), *The Cambridge Companion to Medieval English Literature, 1100–1500*. Cambridge, 2009. 240–55.
Mapstone, Sally. '*The Testament of Cresseid*, lines 561-7: A New Manuscript Witness'. *Notes and Queries*, n.s. 32 (1985), 308–10.
Mapstone, Sally. 'Was there a Court Literature in Fifteenth-Century Scotland?' *Studies in Scottish Literature*, 26 (1991), 410–22.
Mare, A. C. de la. 'Duke Humfrey's English Palladius (MS. Duke Humfrey d. 2)'. *Bodleian Library Record*, 12 (1985-8), 39–51.
Marks, Richard. 'Picturing Word and Text in the Late Medieval Parish Church'. In Linda Clark, Maureen Jurkowski, and Colin Richmond (eds), *Image, Text and Church, 1380–1600. Essays for Margaret Aston*. Toronto, 2009. 162–203.
Marks, Richard. *Stained Glass in England during the Middle Ages*. Abingdon, 1993.
Marks, Richard and P. Williamson (eds). *Gothic Art for England, 1400–1557*. London, 2003.
Marshall, John. *Early English Performance: Medieval Plays and Robin Hood Games, Shifting Paradigms in Early English Drama Studies*. Philip Butterworth (ed.) London, 2020.
Marshall, Simone Celine. 'The Anonymous Author of *The Assembly of Ladies*'. *Neuphilologische Mitteilungen*, 114 (2013), 301–08.
Martin, Joanna (ed.). *The Findern Manuscript: A New Edition of the Unique Poems*. Liverpool, 2020.
Martin, Joanna. *Kingship and Love in Scottish Poetry, 1424–1540*. Aldershot, 2008.
Martin, Joanna. '"Of Wisdome and of Guide Governance": Sir Gilbert Hay and *The Buik of King Alexander the Conquerour*'. In Priscilla Bawcutt and Janet Hadley-Williams (eds), *A Companion to Scottish Poetry*. Cambridge, 2006. 75–88.
Martin, Joanna. 'Responses to the Frame Narrative of John Gower's *Confessio Amantis* in Fifteenth- and Sixteenth-Century Scottish Literature'. *Review of English Studies*, n.s. 60 (2009), 561–77.
Martindale, J. H. 'Notes on the Deanery, Carlisle'. *Cumberland and Westmoreland Antiquarian and Archaeological Society Transactions*, series 2.7 (1907), 185–206.
Marx, C. W. *The Devil's Rights and the Redemption in the Literature of Medieval England*. Cambridge, 1995.
Marx, C. W. 'The *Gospel of Nicodemus* in Old English and Middle English'. In Zbigniew Izydorczyk (ed.), *The Medieval Gospel of Nicodemus: Texts, Intertexts, and Contexts in Western Europe*. Tempe, AZ, 1997. 207–59.
Marx, William. 'St Ursula and the Eleven Thousand Virgins: The Middle English *Legenda Aurea* Tradition'. In Jane Cartwright (ed.), *The Cult of St Ursula and the 11,000 Virgins*. Cardiff, 2016. 143–62.
Mason, Emma. 'Legends of the Beauchamps' Ancestors: The Use of Baronial Propaganda in Medieval England'. *Journal of Medieval History*, 10 (1984), 25–40.
Matheson, Lister. *The Prose Brut: The Development of a Middle English Chronicle*. Tempe, AZ, 1998.
Matthew of Vendôme. Franco Munari (ed.). *Mathei Vindocinesis: Opera*. 3 vols. Rome, 1977–88.
Matthew of Vendôme. Roger Parr (trans.). *Ars versificatoria: The Art of the Versemaker*. Milwaukee, WI, 1981.
Matlock, Wendy A. '"And long to sue it is a wery thing": Legal Commentary in *The Assembly of Ladies*'. *Studies in Philology*, 101 (2004), 20–37.

Matsuda, Takami. *Death and Purgatory in Middle English Didactic Literature*. Cambridge, 1997.
Meagher, John. C. 'The First Progress of Henry VII'. *Renaissance Drama*, n.s. 1 (1968), 67–88.
Meale, Carol M. 'Amateur Book Production and the Miscellany in Late Medieval East Anglia: Tanner 407 and Beinecke 365'. In Margaret Connolly and Raluca Radulescu (eds), *Insular Books: Vernacular Manuscript Miscellanies in Late Medieval Britain*. London, 2015. 156–73.
Meale, Carol M. 'Caxton, de Worde, and the Publication of Romance in England'. *The Library*, 6th series, 14 (1992), 283–98.
Meale, Carol M. '"Gode Men / Wiues Maydnes and Alle Men": Romance and its Audiences'. In Carol M. Meale (ed.), *Readings in Medieval English Romance*. Cambridge, 1994. 209–25.
Meale, Carol M. 'Katherine de la Pole and East Anglian Manuscript Production in the Fifteenth Century: An Unrecognized Patron?'. In Carol M. Meale and Derek Pearsall (eds), *Makers and Users of Medieval Books: Essays in Honour of A. S. G. Edwards*. Cambridge, 2014. 132–49.
Meale, Carol M. '*The Libelle of Englyshe Polycye* and Mercantile Literary Culture in Late-Medieval London'. In Julia Boffey and Pamela King (eds), *London and Europe in the Later Middle Ages*. London, 1996. 181–227.
Meale, Carol M. 'The Middle English Romance of *Ipomedon*: A Late Medieval "Mirror" for Princes and Merchants'. *Reading Medieval Studies*, 10 (1984), 136–91.
Meale, Carol M. 'The Morgan Library Copy of *Generides*'. In Maldwyn Mills, Jennifer Fellows, and Carol M. Meale (eds), *Romance in Medieval England*. Cambridge, 1991. 89–104.
Meale, Carol M. 'The Patronage of Poetry'. In Julia Boffey and A.S.G. Edwards (eds), *A Companion to Fifteenth-Century Poetry*. Woodbridge, 2003. 7–20.
Meale, Carol M. 'Patrons, Buyers and Owners: Book Production and Social Status'. In Jeremy Griffiths and Derek Pearsall (eds), *Book Production and Publishing in Britain, 1375–1475*. Cambridge, 1989. 201–38.
Meale, Carol M. (ed.), *Readings in Medieval English Romance*. Cambridge, 1994.
Meale, Carol M. 'Romance and its Anti-type? The Tournament of Tottenham, The Carnivalesque and Popular Culture'. In A. J. Minnis (ed.), *Middle English Poetry: Texts and Traditions*. Woodbridge, 2001. 103–27.
Meale, Carol M. 'Wynkyn de Worde's Setting-Copy for *Ipomydon*'. *Studies in Bibliography*, 35 (1982), 156–71.
Means, Laurel. 'Electionary, Lunary, Destinary, Questionary: Toward Defining Categories of Middle English Prognostic Material'. *Studies in Philology*, 89 (1992), 367–403.
Medwall, Henry. Alan H. Nelson (eds). *The Plays of Henry Medwall*. Cambridge, 1980.
Memorials of King Henry VII. James Gairdner (ed.). Rolls Series. London, 1858.
Meredith, Peter. 'A Reconsideration of Some Textual Problems in the N-Town Manuscript (BL MS Cotton Vespasian D VIII)'. *Leeds Studies in English*, n.s. 9 (1977), 35–50.
Meredith, Peter. 'Manuscript, Scribe and Performance: Further Looks at the N-Town Manuscript'. In Paula Neuss (ed.), *Aspects of Early English Drama*. Cambridge, 1983. 109–28.
Merlin: A Middle-English Metrical Version of a French Romance by Herry Lovelich. Ernst A. Kock (ed.). EETS, e.s. 93, 112, o.s.185. London, 1904, 1913, 1932.
Merrix, Robert P. 'The Function of the Comic Plot in *Fulgens and Lucrece*'. *Modern Language Studies*, 7 (1977), 16–26.
Metham, John. Stephen F. Page (ed.). *Amoryus and Cleopes*. Kalamazoo, MI, 1999.
Metham, John. Hardin Craig (eds), *The Works of John Metham*. EETS, o.s. 132. London, 1916.
Metrical Life of Christ, The, ed. from MS BM Add. 39996. Walter Sauer (ed.). MET 5. Heidelberg, 1977.
Metrical Version of Mandeville's Travels, The. M. C. Seymour (ed.). EETS, o.s. 269. London, 1973.
Meyer-Lee, Robert J. 'The Emergence of the Literary in John Lydgate's *Life of Our Lady*'. *JEGP*, 109 (2010), 322–48.
Meyer-Lee, Robert J. 'John Lydgate's Major Poems'. In Julia Boffey and A. S. G. Edwards (eds), *A Companion to Fifteenth-Century English Poetry*. Cambridge, 2013. 59–71.
Meyer-Lee, Robert J. 'Laureates and Beggars in Fifteenth-Century English Poetry: The Case of George Ashby'. *Speculum*, 79 (2004), 704.

Meyer-Lee, Robert J. 'The Memorial Form of John Lydgate's *Troy Book*'. *Exemplaria*, 29 (2017), 280–95.
Meyer-Lee, Robert J. *Poets and Power from Chaucer to Wyatt*. Cambridge, 2007.
Meyer-Lee, Robert J. and Catherine Sanok (eds). *The Medieval Literary: Beyond Form*. Cambridge, 2018.
Meyers, Walter E. 'Typology and the Audience of the English Cycle Plays'. In Hugh T. Keenan (ed.), *Typology and English Medieval Literature*. New York, 1992. 261–73.
Middle English Breton Lays, The. Anne Laskaya and Eve Salisbury (eds). Kalamazoo, MI, 1995.
Middle English Humorous Tales in Verse. George McKnight (ed.). Boston, 1913.
Medieval English Political Writings. James M. Dean (ed.). Kalamazoo, MI, 1996.
Middle English Romances. Stephen H. A. Shepherd (ed.). New York, 1995.
Middle English Sermons, Edited from British Museum MS. Royal 18 B. xxiii. Woodburn O. Ross (ed.). EETS, o.s. 209. Oxford, 1940.
Mills, David. 'Brought to Book: Chester's Expositor and His Kin'. In Philip Butterworth (ed.), *The Narrator, the Expositor, and the Prompter in European Medieval Theatre*. Turnhout, 2007. 307–25.
Mills, David. 'The Doctor's Epilogue to the Brome *Abraham and Isaac*: A Possible Analogue'. *Leeds Studies in English*, n.s. 11 (1980), 105–10.
Mills Gayley, Charles. *Plays of Our Forefathers*. New York, 1907.
Millward, Celia (ed.). *La Estorie del Evangelie: A Parallel-Text Edition*. MET 30. Heidelberg, 1998.
Minnis, A. J. *Medieval Theory of Authorship: Scholastic Literary Attitudes in the Later Middle Ages*. 2nd edn. Philadelphia, PA, 2010.
Minnis, A. J. *Translations of Authority in Middle English Literature: Valuing the Vernacular*. Cambridge, 2009.
Minnis, A. J. and A. B. Scott (eds). *Medieval Literary Theory and Criticism c1100–c1375: The Commentary Tradition*. Oxford, 1988.
Mirk, John. Edward Peacock (ed.). *Instructions for Parish Priests by John Myrc*. EETS, o.s. 31. London, 1902.
Mirk, John. Gillis Kristensson (ed.). *John Mirk's Instructions for Parish Priests Edited from MS Cotton Claudius A II and Six Other Manuscripts*. Lund, 1974.
Mirk, John. Susan Powell (eds). *John Mirk's Festial Edited from British Library MS Cotton Claudius A. II*. 2 vols. EETS, o.s. Oxford, 2009, 2011. 334–5.
Moll, Richard J. *Before Malory: Reading Arthur in Later Medieval England*. Toronto, 2003.
Monckton, Linda. 'Fit for a King? The Architecture of the Beauchamp Chapel'. *Architectural History*, 47 (2004), 25–52.
Montaiglon, Anatole and Gaston Raynaud de (eds). *Recueil général et complet des fabliaux*. 6 vols. Paris, 1872–90.
Mooney, Linne R. 'A Holograph Copy of Thomas Hoccleve's *Regiment of Princes*'. *Studies in the Age of Chaucer*, 33 (2011), 263–96.
Mooney, Linne R. 'Lydgate's "Kings of England" and Another Verse Chronicle of the Kings'. *Viator*, 20 (1989), 255–90.
Mooney, Linne R. 'A Middle English Verse Compendium of Astrological Medicine'. *Medical History*, 28 (1984), 406–19.
Mooney, Linne R. 'Verses upon Death and Other Wall Paintings Surviving in the Guild Hall, Stratford-upon-Avon'. *Journal of the Early Book Society*, 3 (2000), 182–90.
Mooney, Linne R, and Estelle Stubbs. *Scribes and the City: London Guildhall Clerks and the Dissemination of Middle English Literature 1375–1425*. York, 2013.
Moran, James. *Wynkyn de Worde: Father of Fleet Street*. 2nd rev. edn. London, 1976.
More, St Thomas. A. S. G. Edwards, Katherine Gardiner Rodgers, and Clarence H. Miller (eds). *The Yale Edition of the Complete Works of St Thomas More. Volume 1, English Poems, The Life of Pico, The Last Things*. New Haven, CT, 1997.
More, St Thomas. George M. Logan, Robert M. Adams, and Clarence H. Miller (eds). *Utopia*. Cambridge, 1995.
Morey, James H. *Book and Verse: A Guide to Middle English Biblical Literature*. Urbana, IL, 2000.

Morey, James H. 'Peter Comestor, Biblical Paraphrase, and the Medieval Popular Bible'. *Speculum*, 68 (1993), 6–35.
Morgan, Edwin. 'Dunbar and the Language of Poetry'. *Essays in Criticism*, 11 (1952), 138–56.
Morris, Richard (ed.). *The Boke of Curtasye*. Berlin, 1862.
Morse, M. 'Two Unpublished English Elevation Prayers in Takamiya 56'. *Journal of the Early Book Society*, 16 (2013), 269–77.
Morse, M. '"Thys moche more ys oure lady mary longe": Takamiya 56 and the English Birth Girdle Tradition'. In S. Horobin and L. Mooney (eds), *Middle English Texts in Transition. A Festschrift Dedicated to Toshiyuki Takamiya on his 70th Birthday*. Woodbridge, 2014. 199–219.
Morte Arthure. Edmund Brock (ed.). EETS, o.s. 8. London, 1865.
Morte Arthure, A Critical Edition. Mary Hamel (ed.). New York, NY, 1984.
Morte Arthur, Le: A Critical Edition. P. F. Hissiger (ed.). The Hague, 1975.
Mortimer, Nigel. *John Lydgate's Fall of Princes: Narrative Tragedy in Its Literary and Political Contexts*. Oxford, 2005.
Moseley, C. W. R. D. 'The Metamorphoses of Sir John Mandeville'. *Yearbook of English Studies*, 4 (1974), 5–25.
Moss, Rachel. *Fatherhood and its Representations in Middle English Texts*. Cambridge, 2013.
Mosser, Daniel W. 'Longleat House MS 30, T. Werken, and Thomas Betson'. *Journal of the Early Book Society*, 15 (2012), 319–31.
Mosser, Daniel W. 'The Manuscript Glosses of the *Canterbury Tales* and the University of London's Copy of Pynson's [1492] Edition: Witness to a Lost Exemplar'. *The Chaucer Review*, 41 (2007), 360–75.
Motherwell, William. *Minstrelsy: Ancient and Modern*. Glasgow, 1827.
Mouron, Anne. *The Desert of Religion*: A Textual and Visual Compilation'. In Marleen Cré, Diana Denissen, and Denis Renevey (eds), *Late Medieval Devotional Compilations in England*. Turnhout, 2020. 385–409.
Mueller, Alex. *Translating Troy: Provincial Politics in Alliterative Romance*. Columbus, OH, 2013.
Mueller, Alex. 'Linking Letters: Translating Ancient History into Medieval Romance'. *Literature Compass*, 4 (2007), 1017–29.
Mum and the Sothsegger. Mabel Day and Robert Steele (eds). EETS, o.s. 199. London, 1936.
Munby, Julian. 'Richard Beauchamp's Funeral Car'. *Journal of the British Archaeological Association*, 155 (2002), 278–87.
Munday, Anthony. *Sir John Oldcastle*. Jonathan Rittenhouse (ed.). London, 1984.
Mundy, John Hine and Kennerly M. Woody (eds). *The Council of Constance: The Unification of the Church*. New York, 1961.
Muscatine, Charles. *Medieval Literature, Style and Culture*. Columbia, SC, 1999.
Mustain, James K. 'A Rural Medical Practitioner in Fifteenth-Century England'. *Bulletin of the History of Medicine*, 46 (1972), 469–76.
Mustanoja, Tauno F. (ed.). *The good wife taught her daughter, The good wyfe wold a pylgremage [and] The thewis of gud women*. Helsinki, 1948.
Myklebust, Nicholas. 'The Problem of John Metham's Prosody'. In Ad Putter and Judith A. Jefferson (eds), *The Transmission of Medieval Romance: Metres, Manuscripts and Early Prints*. Cambridge, 2018. 149–69.
Mynors, R. A. B. 'A Fifteenth-century Scribe: T. Werken'. *Transactions of the Cambridge Bibliographical Society*, 1 (1949–53), 97–104.
Nafde, Aditi. 'Gower from Print to Manuscript: Copying Caxton in Oxford, Bodleian Library, MS Hatton 51'. In Martha Driver, Derek Pearsall, and R. F. Yeager (eds), *John Gower in Manuscripts and Early Printed Books* (Cambridge, 2020). 189–200.
Nafde, Aditi. 'Laughter Lines: Reading the Layouts of *Sir Thopas*'. *Pecia*, 16 (2015), 143–51.
Nall, Catherine. *Reading and War in Fifteenth-Century England: From Lydgate to Malory*. Cambridge, 2012.
Nall, Catherine. 'William Worcester reads Alain Chartier: Le *Quadrilogue invectif* and its English Readers'. In Emma Cayley and Ashby Kinch (eds), *Chartier in Europe*. Cambridge, 2008. 105–18.
Nashe, Thomas. R.B. McKerrow (ed.). *Works*. 3 vols. London, 1904–10.

Nelson, Ingrid. *Lyric Tactics: Poetry, Genre and Practice in Later Medieval England*. Philadelphia, PA, 2017.
Nelson, Marie and Richard Thomson. 'The Fabliau'. In Laura C. Lambdin and Robert T. Lambdin (eds), *A Companion to Old and Middle English Literature*. Westport, CT, 2002. 255–76.
Nevile, Jennifer. *The Eloquent Body: Dance and Humanist Culture in Fifteenth-Century Italy*. Bloomington IN, 2004.
Newhauser, R. G. and A. G. Russell. 'Mapping Virtual Pilgrimage in an Early Fifteenth-Century *Arma Christi* Roll'. In L. H. Cooper and A. Denny-Brown (eds), *The 'Arma Christi' in Medieval and Early Modern Culture, With a Critical Edition of 'O Vernicle'*. Farnham, 2014. 83–112.
Newlyn, Evelyn S. 'Tradition and Transformation in the Poetry of Robert Henryson'. *Studies in Scottish Literature*, 18 (1983), 33–58.
Newstead, Helaine. 'Arthurian Legends'. In J. Burke Severs (ed.), *A Manual of the Writings in Middle English 1050–1500*. 11 vols. New Haven, CT, 1967. 1.38–79, 224–56.
Nicolas, Nicholas Harris and Edward Tyrrell, (eds). *A Chronicle of London from 1080 to 1483 Written in the Fifteenth Century*. London, 1827.
Nicolas, Nicholas Harris (ed.). *History of the Battle of Agincourt and of The Expedition of Henry V into France in 1415*. London, 1833.
Nichols, Ann Eljenholm. 'O Vernicle'. In L. H. Cooper and A. Denny-Brown (eds), *The 'Arma Christi' in Medieval and Early Modern Culture, With a Critical Edition of 'O Vernicle'*. Farnham, 2014. 308–91.
Nichols, Ann Eljenholm. '"O Vernicle": Illustrations of an *Arma Christi* Poem'. In M. V. Hennessy (ed.), *Tributes to Kathleen L. Scott. English Medieval Manuscripts: Readers, Makers and Illuminators*. London, 2009. 139–69.
Nichols, Ann Eljenholm. *Seeable Signs: The Iconography of the Seven Sacraments, 1350–1544*. Woodbridge, 1994.
Nichols, R. E. 'Medical Lore from *Sidrak and Bokkus*: A Miscellany in Middle English Verse'. *Journal of the History of Medicine and Allied Sciences*, 23 (1968), 167–72.
Nicholls, Jonathan. *The Matter of Courtesy: Medieval Courtesy Books and the Gawain-Poet*. Woodbridge, 1985.
Nielsen, Henrik Thiil. *International Robin Hood Bibliography*: https://www.irhb.org/wiki/index.php/Bibliography.
Nightingale, J. *Beauties of England and Wales*. 19 vols. in 26 parts. London, 1801–15.
Nightingale, Pamela. *A Medieval Mercantile Community: The Grocers' Company and the Politics and Trade of London*. New Haven, CT, 1995.
Nitzsche, Jane Chance. *The Genius Figure in Antiquity and the Middle Ages*. New York, NY, 1975.
Nixon, Ingeborg (ed.). *Thomas of Erceldoune*. 2 vols. Publications of the Department of English, University of Copenhagen 9. Copenhagen, 1980, 1983.
Nolan, Barbara. *Chaucer and the Tradition of the 'Roman Antique'*. Cambridge, 1992.
Nolan, Maura. 'The Invention of Style'. *Studies in the Age of Chaucer*, 41 (2019), 33–71.
Nolan, Maura. 'Performing Lydgate's Broken-Backed Meter'. In Susan Yager and Elise E. Morse-Gagné (eds), *Interpretation and Performance: Essays for Alan Gaylord*. Provo, UT, 2013. 141–59.
Non-Cycle Plays and Fragments. Norman Davis (ed.). EETS, s.s. 1. Oxford, 1970.
Non-Cycle Plays and the Winchester Dialogues: Facsimiles of Plays and Fragments in Various Manuscripts and the Dialogues in Winchester College MS 33. Norman Davis (intro.). Leeds, 1979.
Noomen, Willem and Nico van den Boogaard (eds). *Nouveau recueil complet des fabliaux*, 10 vols. Assen, 1983–98.
Noonan, Sarah. 'Private Reading and the Rolls of the *Symbols of the Passion*'. *Journal of the Early Book Society*, 15 (2012), 289–301.
Norland, Howard B. 'The Role of Drama in More's Literary Career'. *Sixteenth Century Journal*, 13 (1982), 59–75.
Norton-Smith, John. 'Lydgate's Changes in the *Temple of Glas*'. *Medium Ævum*, 27 (1958), 166–72.
Norton, Thomas. John Reidy (ed.). *Ordinal of Alchemy*. EETS, o.s. 272. London, 1975.
N-Town Play, The: Cotton MS Vespasian D.8. Stephen Spector (ed.). EETS, s.s. 11, 12. Oxford, 1991.
Nuttall, Jenni. *The Creation of Lancastrian Kingship*. Cambridge, 2007.

Nuttall, Jenni. 'Lydgate and the Lenvoy'. *Exemplaria*, 30 (2018), 35–48.
Nuttall, Jenni. 'Margaret of Anjou as Patron of English Verse?: The *Liber Proverbiorum* and the *Romans of Partenay*'. *Review of English Studies*, n.s. 67 (2016), 636–59.
Nuttall, Jenni. 'Thomas Hoccleve's Poems for Henry V: Anti-Occasional Verse and Ecclesiastical Reform'. *Oxford Handbooks Online*. Oxford, 2015. 1–23.
Nykrog, Per. *Les Fabliaux*. Geneva, 1974.
Ohlgren, Thomas H. 'The "Marchaunt" of Sherwood: Mercantile Ideology in *A Gest of Robyn Hode*'. In Thomas Hahn (ed.), *Robin Hood in Popular Culture: Violence, Transgression and Justice*. Cambridge, 2000. 175–90.
Ohlgren, Thomas H. *Robin Hood: The Early Poems, 1465–1560*. Cranbury, NJ, 2007.
Ohlgren, Thomas H. and Lister M Matheson (eds). *Robin Hood, the Early Poems: Texts, Contexts, and Ideology*. Newark DE, 2000.
Olsan, L. T. 'The Corpus of Charms in the Middle English Leechcraft Remedy Books'. In J. Roper (ed.), *Charms, Charmers and Charming, International Research on Verbal Magic*. London, 2009. 214–37.
Oosterwijk, Sophie. 'Of Dead Kings, Dukes and Constables: The Historical Context of the *Danse Macabre* in Late Medieval Paris'. *Journal of the British Archaeological Association*, 161 (2008), 131–62.
Oosterwijk, Sophie. 'Of Corpses, Constables and Kings: The *Danse Macabre* in Late Medieval and Renaissance Culture'. *Journal of the British Archaeological Association*, 157 (2004), 61–90.
Oosterwijk, Sophie. and S. Knöll (eds). *Mixed Metaphors: The Danse Macabre in Medieval and Early Modern Europe*. Newcastle upon Tyne, 2011.
Orgel, Stephen. 'Textual Icons: Reading Early Modern Illustrations'. In Jonathan Sawday and Neil Rhodes (eds), *The Renaissance Computer: Knowledge Technology in the First Age of Print*. London, 2000. 57–91.
Orléans, Charles d'. Jean-Claude Mühlethaler (ed.). *Ballades et rondeaux*. Paris, 1996.
Orléans, Charles d'. Mary-Jo Arn (ed.). *Fortunes Stabilnes: Charles of Orleans's English Book of Love*. Binghamton, NY, 1994.
Orléans, Charles d'. Mary-Jo Arn and John Fox (eds). *Poetry of Charles d'Orléans and His Circle: A Critical Edition of BnF MS. fr. 25458*. Turnhout, 2010.
Orme, Nicholas. 'Children and Literature in Medieval England'. *Medium Ævum*, 68 (1999), 218–46.
Orme, Nicholas. *Fleas, Flies and Friers: Children's Poetry from the Middle Ages*. Ithaca, NY, 2012.
Orme, Nicholas. *From Childhood to Chivalry: The Education of the English Kings and Aristocracy 1066–1530*. London, 1984.
Orme, Nicholas. *Medieval Children*. New Haven, CT, 2001.
Orme, Nicholas. *Medieval Schools*. New Haven, CT, 2006.
Osberg, Richard. 'The Jesse Tree in the 1432 London Entry of Henry VI: Messianic Kingship and the Rule of Justice'. *Journal of Medieval and Renaissance Studies*, 16 (1986), 213–32.
O'Sullivan, Katherine K. 'John Lydgate's *Lyf of Our Lady*: Translation and Authority in Fifteenth-Century England'. *Mediaevalia*, 26 (2005), 169–201.
Ovid. *Metamorphoses: Volume I: Books 1–8*. Frank Justus Miller (trans.) and G. P. Goold (rev.). Cambridge, MA, 1916.
Page, John. Joanna Bellis (ed.). *The Siege of Rouen*. MET 51. Heidelberg, 2015.
Palladius. Robert H. Rodgers (ed.). *Opera*. Leipzig, 1975.
Palmer, Barbara D. 'Recycling the "Wakefield Cycle": The Records'. *Research Opportunities in Renaissance Drama*, 41 (2002), 88–130.
Palti, Kathleen. 'Singing Women: Lullabies and Carols in Medieval England'. *JEGP*, 110 (2011), 359–82.
Parkes, M. B. 'The Literacy of the Laity'. In David Daiches and Anthony Thorlby (eds), *Literature and Western Civilization: The Medieval West* (London, 1973). 555–77.
Parkes, M. B. 'The Provision of Books'. In P. R. Robinson (ed.), *Pages from the Past: Medieval Writing Skills and Manuscript Books*. Aldershot, 2013. 407–83.
Parkes, M. B. 'Richard Frampton: A Commercial Scribe, c.1390–c.1420'. In P. R. Robinson (ed.), *Pages from the Past: Medieval Writing Skills and Manuscript Books*. Abingdon, 2012. 113–24.

Parsons, Ben. '"For my synne and for my yong delite": Chaucer, the *Tale of Beryn*, and the Problem of *adolescentia*'. *Modern Language Review*, 103 (2008), 940-51.
Partenay, The Romans of, or of Lusignen. W. W. Skeat (ed.). EETS, o.s. 22. London, 1866.
Partonope of Blois, The Middle English Versions of. A. Trampe Bödtker (ed.). EETS, e.s. 109. London, 1912.
Partonopeu de Blois. Joseph Gildea and Leon P. Smith (eds). 2 vols. Villanova, PA, 1967-68.
Pascual, Rafael J. 'Ælfric's Rhythmical Prose and the Study of Old English Metre'. *English Studies*, 95 (2014), 803-23.
Paston Letters and Papers of the Fifteenth Century. Norman Davis, Richard Beadle and Colin Richmond (eds). EETS, s.s. 20-22. London, 2004-5.
Patterson, Lee. '"What Is Me?": Self and Society in the Poetry of Thomas Hoccleve'. *Studies in the Age of Chaucer*, 23 (2001), 437-70.
Patterson, Lee. 'Writing Amorous Wrongs: Chaucer and the Order of Complaint'. In James M. Dean and Christian K. Zacher (eds), *The Idea of Medieval Literature: New Essays on Chaucer and Medieval Culture in Honor of Donald R. Howard*. Newark, DE, 1992. 56-ADD.
Payen, Jean Charles. *Littérature française: Le moyen age*. Paris, 1984.
Payne, M. T. W. 'Caxton the Businessman: A New Glimpse', *The Library*, 7th series, 17 (2016), 103-14.
Pearcy, Roy. *Logic and Humour in the Fabliaux*. Cambridge, 2007.
Pearsall, Derek. 'The *Assembly of Ladies* and *Generydes*'. *Review of English Studies*, n. s. 12 (1961), 229-37.
Pearsall, Derek. 'Chaucer and Lydgate'. In Ruth Morse and Barry Windeatt (eds). *Chaucer Traditions: Studies in Honour of Derek Brewer*. Cambridge, 1990. 39-53.
Pearsall, Derek. 'The Development of Middle English Romance'. In Derek Brewer (ed.), *Studies in Medieval English Romances: Some New Approaches*. Cambridge, 1991. 11-35.
Pearsall, Derek. 'The English Romance in the Fifteenth Century'. *Essays and Studies*, 29 (1976). 56-83.
Pearsall, Derek (ed.). *The Floure and the Leafe and the Assembly of Ladies*. London, 1962.
Pearsall, Derek. 'The *Flower and the Leaf* and the *Assembly of Ladies*: A Revisitation'. In Anne Marie D'Arcy and Alan J. Fletcher (eds), *Studies in Late Medieval and Early Renaissance Texts in Honour of John Scattergood*. Dublin, 2005. 259-69.
Pearsall, Derek. 'Hoccleve's *Regement of Princes*: The Poetics of Royal Self-Representation'. *Speculum*, 89 (1994), 386-41.
Pearsall, Derek. 'The Idea of Englishness in the Fifteenth Century'. In Helen Cooney (ed.), *Nation, Court and Culture: New Essays on Fifteenth-Century Poetry*. Dublin, 2001. 15-27.
Pearsall, Derek. *John Lydgate*. London, 1970.
Pearsall, Derek. *John Lydgate (1371-1449): A Bio-bibliography*. Victoria, BC, 1997.
Pearsall, Derek. *The Life of Geoffrey Chaucer: A Critical Biography*. Oxford, 1992.
Pearsall, Derek. 'The Literary Milieu of Charles d'Orléans and the Duke of Suffolk, and the Authorship of the Fairfax Sequence'. In Mary-Jo Arn (ed.), *Charles d'Orléans in England*. Cambridge, 2000. 145-56.
Pearsall, Derek. 'The Metre of the *Tale of Gamelyn*'. In Ad Putter and Judith A. Jefferson (eds), *The Transmission of Medieval Romance: Metres, Manuscripts and Early Prints*. Cambridge, 2018. 33-49.
Pearsall, Derek. *Old English and Middle English Poetry*. London, 1977
Perkins, Nicholas. *Hoccleve's 'Regiment of Princes': Counsel and Constraint*. Cambridge, 2001.
Perkins, William. *A Reformed Catholike; Or, A Declaration Shewing How Neere We May Come to the Present Church of Rome In Sundrie Points Of Religion: And Wherein We Must Euer Depart From Them*. Cambridge, 1598.
Perry, Ryan. 'The Clopton Manuscript and the Beauchamp Affinity: Patronage and Reception Issues in a West Midlands Reading Community'. In Wendy Scase (ed.), *Essays in Manuscript Geography: Vernacular Manuscripts of the English West Midlands from the Conquest to the Sixteenth Century*. Turnhout, 2007. 131-59.

Perry, R. D. 'The Earl of Suffolk's French Poems and Shirley's Virtual Coteries'. *Studies in the Age of Chaucer*, 38 (2016), 299–308.
Perry, R. D. 'Lydgate's Virtual Coteries: Chaucer's Family and Gower's Pacificism in the Fifteenth Century'. *Speculum*, 93 (2018), 669–98.
Person, Henry Axel (ed.). *Cambridge Middle English Lyrics*. Seattle, 1952, rev. ed. 1962.
Petrarch, Francis. Mark Musa (ed. and trans.). *The Canzoniere, or Rerum vulgarium fragmenta*. Bloomington, IN, 1999.
Petrarch, Francis. F. N. M. Diekstra (ed.). *A Dialogue Between Reason and Adversity: A Late Middle English Version of Petrarch's De Remediis*. Assen, 1968.
Petrarch, Francis. Edward Wilson and Daniel Wakelin (eds). *A Middle English Translation from Petrarch's Secretum*. EETS, o.s. 351. Oxford, 2018.
Petrina, Alessandra. 'Boccaccio in Kent: le peregrinazioni di Guiscardo e Ghismonda'. In Giuseppe Sertoli, Carla Vaglio Marengo, and Chiara Lombardi (eds), *Comparatistica e intertestualità: Studi in onore di Franco Marenco*. Alessandria, 2010. 217–26.
Petrina, Alessandra. *Cultural Politics in Fifteenth-century England*. Leiden, 2004.
Petrina, Alessandra. 'Deviations from Genre in Robert Henryson's "Robene and Makyne"'. *Studies in Scottish Literature*, 31 (1999), 107–20.
Petrina, Alessandra. 'The Humanist Petrarch in Medieval and Early Modern England'. *Journal of Anglo-Italian Studies*, 12 (2013), 45–62.
Petrina, Alessandra. 'The Middle English Translation of Palladius's *De Agricultura*'. In René Tixier, Rosalynn Voaden, Roura Sanchez, and Jennifer Rytting (eds), *The Medieval Translator 8*. Turnhout, 2003. 317–28.
Petrina, Alessandra. 'Robert Henryson's *Orpheus and Eurydice* and its Sources'. *Fifteenth- Century Studies*, 33 (2008), 198–217.
Phillips, Helen. 'Chaucer and Deguileville: The ABC in Context'. *Medium Ævum*, 62 (1993), 1–19
Phillips, Helen. *Imagining Robin Hood: The Late Medieval Stories in Historical Context*. London, 2004.
Phillips, Helen. 'Reformist Polemics: Reading Publics and Unpopular Robin Hood'. In Stephen Knight (ed.), *'Robin Hood in Greenwood Stood': Alterity and Context in the English Outlaw Tradition*. Turnhout, 2011. 87–117.
Phillips, Susan E. *Transforming Talk: The Problem with Gossip in Late Medieval England*. University Park, PA, 2007.
Pickering, O. S. 'Poetic Style and Poetic Affiliation in the *Castle of Perseverance*'. *Leeds Studies in English*, n.s. 29 (1998), 275–91.
Pickering, O. S. 'Saints' Lives.' In A. S. G. Edwards (ed.), *A Companion to Middle English Prose*. Cambridge, 2004. 249–70.
Pickering, O. S. 'The *Temporale* Narratives of the *South English Legendary*'. *Anglia*, 91 (1973), 425–55.
Pickering, O. S. 'An Unpublished Middle English Resurrection Poem'. *Neuphilologische Mitteilugen*, 74 (1973), 269–82.
Pilgrimage of the Lyfe of the Manhode, The. Avril Henry (ed.). EETS, o.s. 288, 292. Oxford, 1985, 1988.
Pizan, Christine de. Sumner Willard and Charity Cannon Willard (eds). *The Book of Deeds of Arms and of Chivalry*. University Park, PA, 1999.
Pizan, Christine de. Renate Blumenfeld-Kosinski and Earl Jeffrey Richards (eds and trans). *Othea's Letter to Hector*. Toronto, 2017.
Poleg, Eyal. *Approaching the Bible in Medieval England*. Manchester, 2013.
Poletti, Federico. 'Fortuna letteraria e figurativa della "Ghismonda" (*Dec.* IV, 1) fra Umanesimo e Rinascimento'. *Studi sul Boccaccio*, 32 (2004), 101–44.
Pollnitz, Aysha. *Princely Education in Early Modern Britain*. Cambridge, 2015.
Pons-Sanz, Sara María. *The Language of Early English Literature: From Cædmon to Milton*. Basingstoke, 2014.
Porter, Elizabeth. 'Gower's Ethical Microcosm and Political Macrocosm'. In Alastair Minnis (ed.). *Gower's Confessio amantis: Responses and Reassessments*. Cambridge, 1983. 135–62.
Porter, S. and I. Roy (eds). *Handbook of British Chronology*. 3rd edn. London, 1986.

Potter, Robert. *The English Morality Play: Origins, History, and Influence of a Dramatic Tradition*. London, 1975.
Powell, Edward. 'Lancastrian England'. In Christopher Allmand (ed.), *The New Cambridge Medieval History VII, c.1415–1500*. Cambridge, 1998s. 457–76.
Powell, Susan. 'All Saints' Church, North Street, York: Text and Image in the *Pricke of Conscience* Window'. In Nigel J. Morgan (ed.), *Prophecy, Apocalypse and the Day of Doom*. Donington, 2004. 292–316.
Powell, Susan. 'Another Manuscript of Index of Middle English Verse No. 2627'. *Notes and Queries*, n.s. 34 (1987), 154–6.
Powell, Susan. 'John Audelay and John Mirk: Comparisons and Contrasts'. In Susanna Fein (ed.). *My Wyl and My Wrytyng: Essays on John the Blind Audelay*. Kalamazoo, MI, 2009. 86–111.
Premierfait, Laurent de. Patricia May Gathercole (ed.). *Laurent de Premierfait's 'Des Cas des nobles hommes et femmes'*. Chapel Hill, NC, 1968.
Prestwich, Michael. 'England and Scotland During the Wars of Independence'. In Michael Jones and Malcolm Vale (eds), *England and Her Neighbors, 1066–1453: Essays in Honour of Pierre Chaplais*. London, 1989. 181–98.
Pribyl, Kathleen. *Farming, Famine and Plague: The Impact of Climate in Late Medieval England*. Cham, 2017.
Prick of Conscience. Ralph Hanna and Sarah Woods (eds). *Richard Morris's 'Prick of Conscience'*. EETS, o.s. 342. Oxford, 2013.
Pritchard, Violet. *English Medieval Graffiti*. Cambridge, 1967.
Puddephat, W. 'The Mural Paintings of the Dance of Death in the Guild Chapel of Stratford-upon-Avon'. *Transactions of the Birmingham Archaeological Society*, 76 (1958), 29–35.
Purdie, Rhiannon. *Anglicising Romance. The Tail-Rhyme and Genre in Medieval English Literature*. Cambridge, 2008.
Purdie, Rhiannon. 'The Implications of Manuscript Layout in Chaucer's *Tale of Sir Thopas*'. *Forum for Modern Language Studies*, 41 (2005), 263–74.
Purdie, Rhiannon. 'Sexing the Manuscript: The Case for Female Ownership of MS Chetham 8009'. *Neophilologus*, 82 (1998), 139–48.
Purdie, Rhiannon, and Nicola Royan (eds). *The Scots and Medieval Arthurian Legend*. Cambridge, 2005.
Putter, Ad. 'The Language and Metre of *Pater Noster* and *Three Dead Kings*'. *Review of English Studies*, n.s. 55 (2004), 498–526.
Quatrefoil of Love, The. Israel Gollancz and Magdalene M. Weale (eds). EETS, o.s. 195. London, 1935.
Quinn, William A. 'Red Lining and Blue Penciling *The Kingis Quair*'. *Studies in Philology*, 108 (2011), 189–214.
Quixley, John. 'Quixley's Ballades Royal (? 1402)'. Henry Noble MacCracken (ed.). *Yorkshire Archaeological Journal*, 20 (1909), 33–50.
Rabkin, Norman. 'The Double Plot: Notes on the History of a Convention'. *Renaissance Drama*, 7 (1964), 55–69.
Radegunde, Life of. London, c1525.
Radulescu, Raluca L. *Romance and its Contexts in Fifteenth-Century England: Politics, Piety and Penance*. Cambridge, 2013.
Radulescu, Raluca L. 'Vying for Attention: The Contents of Dublin, Trinity College, MS 432'. In Margaret Connolly and Raluca Radulescu (eds), *Insular Books: Vernacular Manuscript Miscellanies in Late Medieval Britain*. London, 2015. 121–43.
Rampling, Jennifer M. 'The Catalogue of the Ripley Corpus: Alchemical Writings Attributed to George Ripley (d. ca. 1490)'. *Ambix*, 57 (2010), 125–201.
Ransom, Emily A. 'The New Notbroune Mayd Vpon the Passion of Cryste: The Nutbrown Maid Converted'. *English Literary Renaissance*, 45 (2015), 3–31.
Ratis Raving, and other Moral and Religious Pieces in Prose and Verse. J. Rawson Lumby (ed.). EETS, o.s. 43. London, 1870.

Raymo, Robert R. 'Works of Religious and Philosophical Instruction'. In Albert E. Hartung (ed.), *A Manual of the Writings in Middle English 1050–1500*. 11 vols. New Haven, CT, 1986. 7.2255–378, 2467–582.
Reames, Sherry. 'Origins and Affiliations of the Pre-Sarum Office for Anne in the Stowe Breviary'. In John Haines and Randall Rosenfeld (eds), *Music and Medieval Manuscripts: Paleography and Performance*. Farnham, 2004. 349–68.
Reed Parker, David. *The Commonplace Book in Tudor London*. Lanham, MD, 1998.
Reichl, Karl. 'James Ryman's Lyrics and the Ryman Manuscript: A Reappraisal'. In Lucia Kornexl and Ursula Lenker (eds), *Bookmarks from the Past*. Frankfurt, 2003. 195–227.
Reichl, Karl. 'The Middle English Carol'. In T. G. Duncan (ed.), *A Companion to the Middle English Lyric*. Cambridge, 2005. 150–70.
Reichl, Karl. 'Orality and Performance'. In Raluca L. Radulescu and Cory James Rushton (eds), *A Companion to Medieval Popular Romance*. Cambridge, 2009. 132–49.
Renevey, Denis. '"Short song is good in ale": Charles d'Orléans and Authorial Intentions in the Middle English Ballade 84'. In Julia Boffey and Christiania Whitehead (eds), *Middle English Lyrics: New Readings of Short Poems*. Cambridge, 2018. 201–10.
Renoir, Alain and C. David Benson. 'John Lydgate'. In Albert E. Hartung (ed.), *A Manual of the Writings in Middle English 1050–1500*, 11 vols. New Haven, CT, 1980. 6.1809–1920, 2071–175.
Reson and Sensuallyte. Ernst Sieper (ed.). EETS, e.s. 84, 89. London, 1901.
Reeve, Michael D. (ed.) and Neil Wright (trans.). *The History of the Kings of Britain: An Edition and Translation of De gestis Britonum (Historia Regum Britanniae)*. Woodbridge, 2007.
Revell, Peter. *Fifteenth-Century English Prayers and Meditations: A Descriptive List of Manuscripts in the British Library*. New York, 1975.
Richardson, Malcolm. 'Henry V, the English Chancery, and Chancery English'. *Speculum*, 55 (1980), 726–50.
Richardson, Malcolm. 'Hoccleve in His Social Context'. *The Chaucer Review*, 20 (1986), 313–22.
Richardson, Malcolm. *Middle-Class Writing in Late Medieval London*. London, 2011.
Riche, Barnabe. *True Report of a Late Practise Enterprised by a Papist*. London, 1582.
Riddy, Felicity. 'Mother Knows Best: Reading Social Change in a Courtesy Text'. *Speculum*, 71 (1996), 66–86.
Rigg, George. *A Glastonbury Miscellany of the Fifteenth Century*. London, 1968.
Riggio, Milla Cozart (ed.). *The Play of Wisdom: Its Texts and Contexts*. New York, 1998.
Rikhardsdottir, Sif. *Medieval Translations and Cultural Discourse: The Movement of Texts in England, France, and Scandinavia*. Cambridge, 2012.
Riley, Henry T. (ed.). *Annales Monasterii S. Albani*, 2 vols. Rolls Series 28. London, 1870–1.
Ringler, William A. Jr (ed.), *Bibliography and Index of English Verse in Manuscript 1501–1558*. London, 1992.
Ritson, Joseph. *Bibliographia Poetica: A Catalogue of Engleish [sic] Poets, Of the Twelfth, Thirteenth, Fourteenth, Fifteenth, and Sixteenth Centurys, with a Short Account of Their Works*. London, 1802.
Robbins, Rossell Hope. 'The *Arma Christi* Rolls'. *Modern Language Review*, 34 (1939), 415–21.
Robbins, Rossell Hope. 'English Almanacs of the Fifteenth Century'. *Philological Quarterly*, 18 (1939), 321–31.
Robbins, Rossell Hope. 'The English Fabliau: Before and After Chaucer'. *Moderna Sprak*, 64 (1970), 231–44.
Robbins, Rossell Hope (ed.). *Historical Poems of the XIVth and XVth Centuries*. New York, 1959.
Robbins, Rossell Hope. 'John Crophill's Ale-Pots'. *Review of English Studies*, n.s. 20 (1969), 181–9.
Robbins, Rossell Hope. 'Levation Prayers in Middle English Verse'. *Modern Philology*, 40 (1942), 131–46.
Robbins, Rossell Hope. 'Medical Manuscripts in Middle English'. *Speculum*, 45 (1970), 393–415.
Robbins, Rossell Hope. 'A Middle English Diatribe against Philip of Burgundy'. *Neophilologus*, 39 (1955), 132–46.
Robbins, Rossell Hope. 'Poems Dealing with Contemporary Conditions'. In Albert E. Hartung (ed.), *A Manual of the Writings in Middle English, 1050–1500*. 11 vols. New Haven, CT, 1965. 5.1385–536, 1631–725.

Robbins, Rossell Hope (ed.). *Secular Lyrics of the XIV and XVth Centuries*. 2nd edn. Oxford, 1955.
Robbins, Rossell Hope. 'The *Speculum misericordie*'. *PMLA*, 54 (1939), 935–66.
Robbins, Rossell Hope 'Victory at Whitby, A.D. 1451'. *Studies in Philology*, 67 (1970), 495–504.
Robbins, Rossell Hope. 'Wall Verses at Launceston Priory'. *Archiv für das Studium der neueren Sprachen und Literatur*, 200 (1963), 338–43.
Robert of Knaresborough, The Metrical Life of St. Joyce Bazire (ed.). EETS, o.s. 228. London, 1953.
Roberts, P. D. 'Some Unpublished Middle English Lyrics and Stanzas in a Victoria Public Library Manuscript'. *English Studies*, 54 (1973), 105–18.
Robertson, Elizabeth. 'Kissing the Worm: Sex and Gender in the Afterlife and the Poetic Posthuman in the Late Middle English "A Disputacion betwyx the Body and Wormes"'. In Jane E. Burns and Peggy McCracken (eds), *From Beasts to Souls: Gender and Embodiment in Medieval Europe*. Notre Dame, IN, 2013. 121–54.
Robertson, Elizabeth. '"Raptus" and the Poetics of Married Love in Chaucer's Wife of Bath's Tale and James I's *Kingis Quair*'. In Robert M. Stein and Sandra Pierson Prior (eds), *Reading Medieval Culture: Essays in Honor of Robert W. Hanning*. Notre Dame, IN, 2005. 302–23.
Robertson, Kellie. *Nature Speaks: Medieval Literature and Aristotelian Philosophy*. Philadelphia, PA, 2017.
Robin Hood and Other Outlaw Tales. Stephen Knight and Thomas H. Ohlgren (eds). Kalamazoo, MI, 1997.
Robinson, Olivia. *Contest, Translation, and the Chaucerian Text*. Turnout, 2020.
Rogers, Janine. 'Courtesy Books, Comedy, and the Merchant Masculinity of Oxford Balliol College MS 354'. *Medieval Forum*, 1 (2002), online.
Rold, Orietta da. *Paper in Medieval England*. Cambridge, 2020.
Rooney, Kenneth. *Mortality and Imagination: The Life of the Dead in Medieval English Literature*. Turnhout, 2011.
Root, Jerry. 'The Old French Fabliau and the Poetics of Disfiguration'. *Medievalia et Humanistica*, n.s. 24 (1997), 17–32.
Roscow, G. H. *Syntax and Style in Chaucer's Poetry*. Cambridge, 1981.
Rosewell, Roger. *Medieval Wall Paintings*. Woodbridge, 2008.
Ross, Charles. *Edward IV*. New Haven, CT, 1974.
Ross, C. D. (ed.). *The Rous Roll*. London, 1980.
Rossiter, William. '"Disgraces the name and patronage of his master Chaucer": Echoes and Reflections in Lydgate's Courtly Poetry'. In Kathleen A. Bishop (ed.), *Standing in the Shadow of the Master? Chaucerian Influences and Interpretations*. Newcastle upon Tyne, 2010. 2–27.
Rowe, B. J. H. 'King Henry VI's Claim to France: In Picture and Poem'. *The Library*, 4th series, 13 (1933), 77–88.
Royan, Nicola. 'The Alliterative Awntyrs Stanza in Older Scots Verse'. In J. A. Burrow and Hoyt N. Duggan (eds), *Medieval Alliterative Poetry: Essays in Honour of Thorlac Turville-Petre*. Dublin, 2010. 185–94.
Rozenski, Steven. '"Your Ensaumple and Your Mirour": Hoccleve's Amplification of the Imagery and Intimacy of Henry Suso's *Ars Moriendi*'. *Parergon*, 25 (2008), 1–16.
Rundle, David. 'Filippo Alberici, Henry VII and Richard Fox: The English Fortunes of a Little-Known Italian Humanist'. *Journal of Warburg and Courtauld Institutes*, 68 (2005), 137–55.
Rundle, David. 'From Greenwich to Verona: Antonio Beccaria, St Athanasius and the Translation of Orthodoxy'. *Humanistica*, 5 (2010), 109–19.
Rundle, David. 'The Unoriginality of Tito Livio Frulovisi's *Vita Henrici Quinti*'. *English Historical Review*, 123 (2008), 1109–31.
Rust, Martha Dana. 'The "ABC of Aristotle"'. In Daniel T Kline (ed.), *Medieval Literature for Children*. New York, 2003. 63–78.
Rutledge, Thomas. 'Robert Henryson's *Orpheus and Eurydice*; A Northern Humanism?'. *Modern Language Review*, 38 (2002), 396–411.
Rychner, Jean. *Contribution à l'étude des fabliaux*, 2 vols. Geneva, 1960.
Rymer, Thomas (ed.). *Foedera*. 10 vols. London, 1739–45.

Sajavaara, Kari (ed.), *The Middle English Translations of Robert Grosseteste's Chateau d'Amour*. Helsinki, 1967.
Salisbury, Eve (ed.). *The Trials and Joys of Marriage*. Kalamazoo, MI, 2002.
Salter, Elizabeth. *Nicholas Love's "Myrrour of the Blessed Lyf of Jesu Christ"*. Analecta Cartusiana, 10. Salzburg, 1974.
Sánchez-Martí, Jordi. 'The Scribe as Entrepreneur in Chetham's Library MS 8009'. *Bulletin of the John Rylands Library of the University of Manchester*, 85 (2003), 13–22.
Sánchez-Martí, Jordi. 'Reading Romance in Late Medieval England: The Case of the Middle English *Ipomedon*'. *Philological Quarterly*, 83 (2004), 13–39.
Sanderson, Joyce M. 'A Recently Discovered Poem in Scots Vernacular: "Complections of Man in Verse"'. *Scottish Studies*, 28 (1987), 49–65.
Sanok, Catherine. *New Legends of England: Forms of Community in Late Medieval Saints' Lives*. Philadelphia, PA, 2018.
Sanok, Catherine. 'Saints' Lives and the Literary After Arundel'. In Vincent Gillespie and Kantish Ghosh (eds), *After Arundel: Religious Writing in Fifteenth-Century England*. Brepols, 2011. 269–86.
Sargent, Michael G. 'Nicholas Love's *Mirror of the Blessed Life of Jesus Christ*'. In Elizabeth Solopova (ed.), *The Wycliffite Bible: Origin, History and Interpretation*. Leiden, 2017). 389–405.
Saupe, Karen (ed.). *Middle English Marian Lyrics*. Kalamazoo, MI, 1997.
Sawyer, Daniel. 'Codicological Evidence of Reading in Late Medieval England, with Particular Reference to Practical Pastoral Verse'. DPhil thesis. University of Oxford, 2016.
Scanlon, Larry. 'Lydgate's Poetics: Laureation and Domesticity in the *Temple of Glass*'. In Larry Scanlon and James Simpson (eds), *John Lydgate: Poetry, Culture, and Lancastrian England*. Notre Dame, IN, 2006. 61–97.
Scase, Wendy. *Literature and Complaint in England, 1272–1553*. Oxford, 2007.
Scase, Wendy (ed.). *The Vernon Manuscript: A Facsimile Edition of Oxford, Bodleian Library MS. Eng. Poet. A. 1*. Bodleian Digital Texts, 3. Oxford, 2011.
Scahill, John. *Middle English Saints' Legends*. Cambridge, 2005.
Scattergood, John. 'The Date and Composition of George Ashby's Poems'. *Leeds Studies in English*, n.s. 21 (1990), 167–76.
Scattergood, John. *John Skelton: The Career of an Early Tudor Poet*. Dublin, 2014.
Scattergood, John. *The Lost Tradition: Essays on Middle English Alliterative Poetry*. Dublin, 2000.
Scattergood, John. 'Peter Idley, George Ashby'. In Julia Boffey, and A. S. G. Edwards (eds), *Companion to Fifteenth-Century English Poetry*. London, 2013. 113–25.
Scattergood, John. 'Two Unrecorded Poems from Trinity College, Dubin, MS 490'. *Review of English Studies*, n.s. 38 (1987), 46–9.
Scattergood, V. J. *Politics and Poetry in the Fifteenth Century*. London, 1971.
Schiff, Randy P. 'Borderland Subversions: Anti-Imperial Energies in *The Awntyrs off Arthure* and *Golagros and Gawane*'. *Speculum*, 84 (2009), 613–32.
Schleich, Gustav (ed.). *Die mittelenglische Umdichtung von Boccaccios 'De claris mulieribus'*. Leipzig, 1924.
Schmidt, A. V. C. *The Clerkly Maker: Langland's Poetic Art*. Cambridge, 1987.
Schirmer, Walter F. *John Lydgate: A Study in the Culture of the XVth Century*, trans. A. E. Keep. London, 1961.
Schuler, Robert M. *English Magical and Scientific Poems to 1700: An Annotated Bibliography*. New York, 1979.
Scott, Kathleen L. *Later Gothic Manuscripts, 1390–1490*. 2 vols. London, 1996.
Scott, Kathleen L. 'Lydgate's *Lives of SS Edmund and Fremund*: a Newly Located Manuscript in Arundel Castle'. *Viator*, 13 (1982), 335–66.
Scott, Tom. *Dunbar: A Critical Exposition of the Poems*. Edinburgh, 1966.
Scott-Macnab, David. '*The Hunttyng of the Hare* in the Heege Manuscript'. *Anglia*, 128 (2010), 102–23.
Scrope, Stephen. Curt F. Bühler (ed.). *The Epistle of Othea*. EETS, o.s. 264. London, 1970.

Searle, William George (ed.). *Christ Church Canterbury*, Cambridge Antiquarian Society, octavo publications 34. Cambridge, 1902.
Secretum Secretorum: Nine English Versions Manzalaoui, M. A. (ed.). EETS, o.s. 276. London, 1977.
Secreta Secretorum, Three Prose Versions of the. Steele, Robert (ed.). EETS, e.s. 74. London, 1898.
Sege of Melayne, The, Duke Rowland and Sir Otuell of Spayne, and The Song of Roland. Sidney J. Herrtage (ed.). EETS, e.s. 35. London, 1880.
Selections of English Wycliffite Writings. Anne Hudson (ed.). Cambridge, 1978.
Sentimental and Humorous Romances. Erik Kooper (ed.). Kalamazoo, MI, 2005.
Sergi, Matthew. ' Play Texts and Public Practice in the Chester Cycle, 1422-1607'. PhD Diss. University of California, Berkeley, 2011.
Sergi, Matthew. 'Un-Dating the Chester Plays: A Reassessment of Lawrence Clopper's "History and Development" and MS Peniarth 399'. In Tamara Atkin and Laura Estill (eds), *Early British Drama in Manuscript*. Turnhout, 2019. 71-102.
Sergi, Matthew *Practical Cues and Social Spectacle in the Chester Plays*. Forthcoming, Chicago, 2020.
Severs, J. Burke. 'The Relationship Between the Brome and Chester Plays of *Abraham and Isaac*'. *Modern Philology*, 42 (1945), 137-51.
Seymour, M. C. 'The English Manuscripts of *Mandeville's Travels*'. *Transactions of the Edinburgh Bibliographical Society*, 4, part 5 (1966), 169-210.
Seymour, M. C. 'Mandeville and Marco Polo: A Stanzaic Fragment'. AUMLA: *Journal of the Australasian Universities Language and Literature Association*, 21 (1964), 42-50.
Shailor, Barbara. *Catalogue of Medieval and Renaissance Manuscripts in the Beinecke Rare Book and Manuscript Library Yale University, Volume II: MSS 251-500*. Binghamton, NY, 1987.
Sharp, Thomas. *A Dissertation on the Pageants or Dramatic Mysteries Anciently Performed at Coventry*. Coventry, 1825.
Sharp, Thomas (ed.), *The Pageant of the Sheremen and Taylors*. Coventry, 1817.
Sheingorn, Pamela. 'Typology and the Teaching of Medieval Drama'. In Richard Emmerson (ed.), *Approaches to Teaching Medieval English Drama*. New York, 1990. 90-100.
Shuffelton, George (ed.). *Codex Ashmole 61: A Compilation of Popular Middle English Verse*. Kalamazoo, MI, 2008.
Shuffelton, George. 'Is There a Minstrel in the House? Domestic Entertainment in Late Medieval England'. *Philological Quarterly*, 87 (2008), 51-76.
Shuffleton, Frank. 'An Imperial Flower: Dunbar's *The Golden Targe* and the Court Life of James IV of Scotland'. *Studies in Philology*, 72 (1975), 193-207.
Sidrak and Bokkus. T. J. Burton (ed.). EETS, o.s. 311-12. Oxford, 1998.
Silverstein, Theodore (ed.). *Medieval English Lyrics*. London, 1971.
Simpson, James. '"And That Was Litel Nede": Poetry's Need in Robert Henryson's *Fables* and *Testament of Cresseid*'. In Christopher Cannon and Maura Nolan (eds), *Medieval Latin and Middle English Literature: Essays in Honour of Jill Mann*. Woodbridge, 2011. 193-21.
Simpson, James. 'Chaucer as a European Writer'. In Seth Lerer (ed.), *The Yale Companion to Chaucer*. New Haven, CT, 2005. 55-86.
Simpson, James. '"Dysemol daies and Fatal houres": Lydgate's *Destruction of Thebes* and Chaucer's *Knight's Tale*'. In Helen Cooper and Sally Mapstone (eds), *The Long Fifteenth Century: Essays in Honour of Douglas Gray*. Oxford, 1997. 15-33.
Simpson, James. '"For al my body ... weieth nat an unce": Empty Poets and Rhetorical Weight in Lydgate's *Churl and the Bird*'. In Larry Scanlon and James Simpson (eds). *John Lydgate: Poetry, Culture, and Lancastrian England*. Notre Dame, IN, 2006. 129-46.
Simpson, James. '"Gaufred, deere maister soverain": Chaucer and Rhetoric'. In Suzanne Akbari and James Simpson (eds). *The Oxford Handbook to Chaucer*. Oxford, 2020. 126-46.
Simpson, James. 'Human Prudence versus the Emotion of the Cosmos: War, Deliberation and Destruction in the Late Medieval Statian Tradition'. In Andrew Lynch, et al. (eds), *Emotions and War*. London, 2015. 98-116.
Simpson, James. 'John Lydgate'. In Larry Scanlon (ed.), *The Cambridge Companion to Medieval Literature*. Cambridge, 2009. 205-16.

Simpson, James. 'Killing Authors: Skelton's Dreadful *Bouge of Court*'. In Kathleen Tonry and Shannon Gayk (eds), *Form and Reform: Reading the Fifteenth Century*. Columbus, OH, 2011. 180–96.

Simpson, James. 'The Other Book of Troy: Guido delle Colonne's *Historia destructionis Troiae* in Fourteenth- and Fifteenth-Century England'. *Speculum*, 73 (1998), 397–423.

Simpson, James. 'The Power of Impropriety: Authorial Naming in *Piers Plowman*'. In Kathleen M. Hewett-Smith (ed.), *William Langland's* Piers Plowman: *A Book of Essays*. New York, 2001. 145–65.

Simpson, James. *Reform and Cultural Revolution, 1350–1547*. Oxford, 2002.

Simpson, James. 'Saving Satire after Arundel: John Audelay's *Marcol and Solomon*'. In Ann Hutchison and Helen Barr (eds), *Text and Controversy from Wyclif to Bale, Essays in Honour of Anne Hudson*. Turnhout, 2005. 387–404.

Simpson, James. *Sciences and the Self in Medieval Poetry: Alan of Lille's Anticlaudianus and John Gower's Confessio amantis*. Cambridge, 1995.

Simpson, James. 'Trans-Reformation English Literary History'. In Kristen Poole and Owen Williams (eds), *Early Modern Histories of Time: The Periodizations of Sixteenth- and Seventeenth-Century England*. Philadelphia, PA, 2019. 88–101.

Sir Gawain: Eleven Romances and Tales. Thomas Hahn (ed.). Kalamazoo, MI, 1995.

Sir Gawain and the Green Knight. Israel Gollancz, (ed.), Mabel Day and Mary S. Serjeantson, intro. EETS, o.s. 210. London, 1940.

Sir Gawain and the Green Knight. Malcolm Andrew and Ronald Waldron (eds). *The Poems of the Pearl Manuscript*. Rev. edn. Exeter, 1987.

Sisk, Jennifer. 'Lydgate's Problematic Commission: A Legend of St. Edmund for Henry VI'. *JEGP*, 109 (2010), 349–75.

Six Ecclesiastical Satires. James Dean (ed.). Kalamazoo, MI, 1991.

Skeat, W. W. (ed.). *Chaucerian and Other Pieces*. Oxford, 1897.

Skemer, D. C. 'Amulet Rolls and Female Devotion in the Late Middle Ages'. *Scriptorium*, 55 (2001), 197–227.

Skemer, D. C. *Binding Words: Textual Amulets in the Middle Ages*. Philadelphia, PA, 2006.

Skemer, D. C. 'Words Not Written in Stone: John Shirwood's Epitaph for a Canon of Exeter Cathedral'. In Colum P. Hourihane (ed.), *Manuscripta illuminata: Approaches to Understanding Medieval and Renaissance Manuscripts*. Princeton, NJ, 2014. 108–43.

Smallwood, T. M. 'Conformity and Originality in Middle English Charms'. In J. Roper (ed.), *Charms, Charmers and Charming. International Research on Verbal Magic*. London, 2009. 87–99.

Smallwood, T. M. '"God Was Born in Bethlehem ... ": The Tradition of a Middle English Charm'. *Medium Ævum*, 58 (1989), 206–25.

Smallwood, T. M. 'The Transmission of Charms in English, Medieval and Modern'. In J. Roper (ed.), *Charms and Charming in Europe*. Basingstoke, 2004. 11–31.

Smith, Frederick. *The Early History of Veterinary Literature and Its Development*. London, 1919.

Smith, G. Gregory. 'Middle Scots Anthologies'. In A.W. Ward and A. W. Verrall (eds), *Cambridge History of English and American Literature*, 18 vols. New York, 1907–21.

Smith, Jeremy J. 'Charles d'Orléans and His Finding of English'. In R. D. Perry and Mary-Jo Arn (eds), *Charles D'Orléans' English Aesthetic: The Form, Poetics, and Style of Fortunes Stabilnes*. Cambridge, 2020. 182–210.

Smith, Nicole D. *Sartorial Strategies: Outfitting Aristocrats and Fashioning Conduct in Late Medieval Literature*. South Bend, IN, 2012.

Sobecki, Sebastian. 'Bureaucratic Verse: William Lynwood, the Privy Seal, and the Form of *The Libelle of Englyshe Polycye*'. *New Medieval Literatures*, 12 (2011), 251–88.

Sobecki, Sebastian. 'The Earliest Record of John Lydgate at Hatfield Regis'. *The Chaucer Review*, 54 (2019), 216–20.

Sobecki, Sebastian. *Last Words: The Public Self and the Social Author in Late Medieval England*. Oxford, 2019.

South English Ministry and Passion, The, ed. from St John's College, Cambridge, MS B.6. O. S. Pickering (ed.). MET 16. Heidelberg, 1984.

Sowdone of Babylone, The. Emil Hausknecht (ed.). EETS, e.s. 38. London, 1881.
Spalding, Mary Caroline. *The Middle English Charters of Christ.* Bryn Mawr, PA, 1914.
Spearing, A. C. *Medieval Autographies: The 'I' of the Text.* Notre Dame, IN, 2012.
Spearing, A. C. *Medieval to Renaissance in English Poetry.* Cambridge, 1985.
Speculum Gy de Warewyke. Georgiana Lea Morrill (ed.). EETS, e.s. 75 London, 1898.
Speed, Diane. 'The Saracens of *King Horn*'. *Speculum*, 65 (1990), 564–95.
Spencer, Alice. *Language, Lineage and Location in the Works of Osbern Bokenham.* Newcastle upon Tyne, 2013.
Spiegel, Gabrielle M. *The Chronicle Tradition of St Denis.* Turnhout, 1978.
Sponsler, Claire. *Drama and Resistance: Bodies, Goods, and Theatricality in Late Medieval England.* Minneapolis, MIN, 1997.
Sponsler, Claire. *The Queen's Dumbshows: Lydgate and the Making of Early Theater.* Philadelphia, PA, 2014.
St. Erkenwald. Henry L. Savage (ed.). New Haven, CT, 1926.
Stadolnik, Joe. 'The Brome *Abraham and Isaac* and Impersonal Compilation'. In Tamara Atkin and Laura Estill (eds), *Early British Drama in Manuscript.* Turnhout, 2019. 19–32.
Stafford, Rosemary. 'Yorkist and Early Tudor England'. In Christopher Allmand (ed.), *New Cambridge Medieval History.* Cambridge, 1998. 477–95.
Staley, Lynn. *Island Garden: England's Language of Nation from Gildas to Marvell.* South Bend, IN, 2012.
Staley, Lynn. 'The Penitential Psalms: Conversion and the Limits of Lordship'. *Journal of Medieval and Early Modern Studies*, 37 (2007), 221–69.
Stanzaic Life of Christ, A, Compiled from Higden's Polychronicon and the Legenda Aurea Edited from MS. Harley 3909. Frances A. Foster (ed.). EETS, o.s. 166. London, 1926.
Starkey, David. 'The Age of the Household: Politics, Society and the Arts c.1350–c.1550'. In Stephen Medcalf (ed.). *The Later Middle Ages.* London, 1981. 225–90.
Statutes of the Realm. T. E. Tomlins, et al. (eds.). 11 vols. London, 1810-1828.
Steenbrugge, Charlotte. *Drama and Sermon in Late Medieval England: Performance, Authority, Devotion.* Kalamazoo, MI, 2017.
Steenbrugge, Charlotte. 'Morality Plays and the Aftermath of Arundel's Constitutions'. In Pamela M. King (ed.), *The Routledge Research Companion to Early Drama and Performance.* London, 2016. 205–20.
Steiner, Emily. '*Piers Plowman*, Diversity, and the Medieval Political Aesthetic'. *Representations*, 91 (2005), 1–25.
Stevens, John (ed.) *Mediaeval Carols.* Musica Britannica IV. London, 2018. NB Date??
Stevens, Martin. *Four Middle English Mystery Cycles: Textual, Contextual, and Critical Interpretations.* Princeton, NJ, 1987.
Stevenson, Allan. 'Tudor Roses from John Tate'. *Studies in Bibliography*, 20 (1967), 15–34.
Stockwell, Robert P. and Donka Minkova. 'The Partial-Contact Origins of English Pentameter Verse: The Anglicization of an Italian Model'. In Dieter Kastovsky and Arthur Mettinger (eds), *Language Contact in the History of English.* Frankfurt, 2001. 337–62.
Storey, R. L. *The End of the House of Lancaster.* Phoenix Mill, Gloucs, 1999.
Stow, John. Charles Lethbridge Kingsford (ed.). *A Survey of London.* 2 vols. Oxford, 1908.
Stratford, Jenny. *The Bedford Inventories.* London, 1993.
Strohm, Paul. 'Hoccleve, Lydgate and the Lancastrian Court'. David Wallace (ed.), *The Cambridge History of Medieval English Literature.* Cambridge, 1999. 640–61.
Strohm, Paul. *England's Empty Throne: Usurpation and the Language of Legitimation 1399–1422.* New Haven, CT, 1998.
Strohm, Paul. *Politique: Languages of Statecraft between Chaucer and Shakespeare.* South Bend, IN, 2005.
Strub, Spencer. 'Oaths and Everyday Life in Peter Idley's *Instructions*'. *JEGP*, 119 (2020), 190–219.
Stubbings, Frank. 'A New Manuscript of *Generydes*'. *Transactions of the Cambridge Bibliographical Society*, 10 (1993), 317–40.
Sugano, Douglas. '"The game wel pleyd in good a-ray": The N-Town Playbooks and East Anglian Games'. *Comparative Drama*, 28 (1994), 221–34.

Summers, Joanna. *Late-Medieval Prison Writing and the Politics of Autobiography*. Oxford, 2004.
Sundwall, McKay. 'The *Destruction of Troy*, Chaucer's *Troilus and Criseyde* and Lydgate's *Troy Book*'. *Review of English Studies*, n.s. 26 (1975), 313–17.
Sutherland, Annie. *English Psalms in the Middle Ages 1300–1450*. Oxford, 2015.
Sutherland, Annie. 'Performing the Penitential Psalms in the Middle Ages'. In Almut Suerbaum and Manuele Gragnolati (eds), *Aspects of the Performative in Medieval Culture*. Berlin, 2010. 15–37.
Swanson, Robert N. 'Gens secundum cognationem et collectionem ab alia distincta? Thomas Polton, two Englands, and the challenge of medieval nationhood'. Gabriela Signori and Birgit Studt (eds), *Das Konstanzer Konzil als europäisches Ereignis: Begegnungen, Medien und Rituale*. Ostfildern, 2014. 57–87.
Sweet, W. H. E. 'The "Vther Quair" as the *Troy Book*. The Influence of Lydgate on Henryson's *Testament of Cresseid*'. Joanna Martin and Emily Wingfield (eds), *Premodern Scotland: Literature and Governance, 1420–1587. Essays for Sally Mapstone*. Oxford, 2017. 58–73.
Symons, Dana M. (ed.). *Chaucerian Dream Visions and Complaints*. Kalamazoo, MI, 2004.
Szittya, Penn R. *The Antifraternal Tradition in Medieval Literature*. Princeton, NJ, 1986.
Taavitsainen, Irma. 'The Identification of Middle English Lunary MSS'. *Neuphilologische Mitteilungen*, 88 (1987), 18–26.
Taavitsainen, Irma. *Middle English Lunaries: A Study of the Genre*. Helsinki, 1988.
Taavitsainen, Irma. 'Storia Lune and its Paraphrase in Prose: Two Versions of a Middle English Lunary'. L. Kahlas-Tarkka (ed.), *Neophilologica Fennica* (Helsinki, 1987). 521–55.
Tavormina, M. Teresa. 'Three Middle English Verse Uroscopies'. *English Studies*, 91 (2010), 591–622.
Taylor, Andrew. *The Songs and Travels of a Tudor Minstrel: Richard Sheale of Tamworth*. Woodbridge, 2012.
Taylor, Andrew. 'Vernacular Authorship and the Control of Manuscript Production'. In Michael Johnston and Michael Van Dussen (eds), *The Medieval Manuscript Book: Cultural Approaches*. Cambridge, 2015. 199–213.
Taylor, Frank and John S. Roskell (eds). *Gesta Henrici Quinti: The Deeds of Henry the Fifth*. Oxford, 1975.
Taylor, John. *Sir Gregory Nonsence his newes from no place*. London, 1622.
Taylor, John. *The Universal Chronicle of Ranulph Higden*. Oxford, 1966.
Taylor, Karla. 'Writers of the Italian Renaissance'. Roger Ellis (ed.). *Oxford History of Literary Translation into English. Vol. 1: to 1550*. Oxford, 2008. 390–406.
Thielmans, Marie-Rose. *Bourgogne et Angleterre, relations politiques et économiques entre les Pays-Bas bourguignons et l'Angleterre 1435–1467*. Brussels, 1966.
Thompson, Anne B. *Everyday Saints and the Art of Narrative in the South English Legendary*. Aldershot, 2003.
Thompson, John J. *The Cursor Mundi: Poem, Texts and Contexts*. Medium Ævum Monograph, 19. Oxford, 1998.
Thompson, John J. 'Literary Associations of an Anonymous Middle English Paraphrase of Vulgate Psalm L'. *Medium Ævum*, 57 (1988), 38–55.
Thompson, John J. *Robert Thornton and the London Thornton Manuscript*. Woodbridge, 1987.
Thompson, John J. 'Postscript: Authors and Audiences'. In W. R. J. Barron (ed.), *The Arthur of the English: The Arthurian Legend in Medieval English Life and Literature*. Cardiff, 2001. 371–95.
Thompson, John J. 'Textual Instability and the Late Medieval Reputation of Some Middle English Religious Literature'. *Text: Transactions of the Society for Textual Scholarship*, 5 (1991), 175–94.
Thompson, Stith. *The Motif-Index of Folk Literature*. 2 vols. Bloomington, IN, 1955–8.
Thornley, Isobel. 'Treason by Words in the Fifteenth Century'. *English Historical Review*, 32 (1917), 556–61.
Thornton Manuscript, The (Lincoln Cathedral MS 91). Derek Brewer and A. E. B. Owen (intro.). London, 1975.
Three Alliterative Saints' Hymns: Late Middle English Stanzaic Poems. Ruth Kennedy (ed.). EETS, o.s. 321. Oxford, 2003.
Three Middle English Charlemagne Romances. Alan Lupack (ed.). Kalamazoo, MI, 1990.
Thrupp, Sylvia L. *The Merchant Class of Medieval London, 1300–1500*. Ann Arbor, 1962.

Tilley, E. Allen. 'The Meaning of Dunbar's *The Golden Targe*'. *Studies in Scottish Literature*, 10 (1973), 220–31.
Timmerman, Anke. 'Scientific and Encyclopedic Verse'. Julia Boffey and A. S. G. Edwards (eds), *A Companion to Fifteenth-Century Poetry*. Cambridge, 2013. 199–211.
Timmerman, Anke. *Verse and Transmutation: A Corpus of Middle English Alchemical Poetry*. Leiden, 2013.
Tokunaga, Satoko. 'Wynkyn de Worde's Lost Manuscript of the *Canterbury Tales*: With New Light on HRC MS 46'. *The Chaucer Review*, 50 (2015), 30–54.
Towneley Plays, The. Martin Stevens, and A. C. Cawley (eds). EETS, s.s. 13,14. Oxford, 1994.
Towneley Cycle, The: A Facsimile of Huntington MS HM 1. A. C. Cawley and Martin Stevens (eds). San Marino, CA, 1976.
Trapp, J. B. 'Verses by Lydgate at Long Melford'. *Review of English Studies*, n.s. 6 (1955), 1–11.
Traver, Hope M. *The Four Daughters of God*. Philadelphia, PA, 1907.
Trevisa, John. *The Governance of Kings and Princes: John Trevisa's Middle English Translation of the 'De Regimine Principum' of Aegidius Romanus*. David C. Fowler, Charles F. Briggs, and Paul G. Remley (eds). New York, 1997.
Trevisa, John. 'Trevisa's Original Prefaces on Translation: A Critical Edition'. Ronald Waldron (ed.). In Edward D. Kennedy, Ronald Waldron, and Joseph S. Wittig (eds), *Medieval English Studies Presented to George Kane*. Wolfeboro, NH, 1988. 285–95.
Trigg, Stephanie. *Congenial Souls: Reading Chaucer from Medieval to Postmodern*. Minneapolis, MIN, 2002.
Truesdale, Mark. *The King and Commoner Tradition in Medieval and Early Modern Literature*. London, 2018.
Turville-Petre, Thorlac. 'The Author of *The Destruction of Troy*'. *Medium Ævum*, 57 (1988), 264–9.
Turville-Petre, Thorlac. *Description and Narrative in Middle English Alliterative Poetry*. Liverpool 2018.
Turville-Petre, Thorlac. 'Some Medieval English Manuscripts in the North-East Midlands'. In Derek Pearsall (ed.), *Manuscripts and Readers in Fifteenth-Century England*. Cambridge, 1983. 125–41.
Turville-Petre, Thorlac. '"Summer Sunday", "De Tribus Regibus Mortuis", and "The Awntyrs off Arthure": Three Poems in the Thirteen-Line Stanza'. *Review of English Studies*, n.s. 25 (1974), 1–14.
Tyerman, Christopher. *God's War: A New History of the Crusades*. London, 2006.
Utley, Francis Lee. 'Dialogues, Debates, and Catechisms'. In Albert E. Hartung (ed.), *A Manual of the Writings in Middle English 1050–1500*. 11 vols. New Haven, CT, 1972. 3.669–745, 829–902.
Vale, Malcolm. *The Princely Court*. Oxford, 2001.
Van Buuren, Catherine. 'The Chepman and Myllar Texts of Dunbar'. In Sally Mapstone (ed.), *William Dunbar, 'The Nobill Poyet'*. East Linton, East Lothian, 2001. 24–39.
Van Dorsten, J. A. 'The Leyden Lydgate Manuscript'. *Scriptorium*, 14 (1960), 315–25.
Van Dussen, M. 'Tourists and *Tabulae* in Late-Medieval England'. In F. Somerset and N. Watson (eds), *Truth and Tales: Cultural Mobility and Medieval Media*. Columbus OH, 2015. 238–54.
Vegetius. *Epitoma Rei Militaris*. Oxford, 2004.
Vergil, Polydore. Denys Hay (ed. and trans.). *The Anglia Historia of Polydore Vergil, 1485–1537*. Camden Society, 3rd series, 74. London, 1950.
Vines, Amy N. 'A Woman's "Crafte": Melior as Lover, Teacher, and Patron in the Middle English *Partonope of Blois*'. *Modern Philology*, 105 (2007), 245–70.
Vinsauf, Geoffrey. Margaret F. Nims (trans.). *The Poetria Nova*. Toronto, 1967.
Visser-Fuchs, Livia. '"Honour is the Reward of Virtue": The Claudian Translation Made for Richard, Duke of York, in 1445'. *The Ricardian*, 18 (2008), 66–82.
von Contzen, Eva. 'Narrating Vernacular Sanctity: The *Scottish Legendary* as a Challenge to the "Literary Turn" in Fifteenth-century Hagiography'. Eva von Contzen and Anke Bernau (eds), *Sanctity as Literature in Late Medieval Britain*. Manchester, 2015. 172–90.
von Contzen, Eva. *The Scottish Legendary: Towards a Poetics of Hagiographic Narration*. Manchester, 2016.
Waite, Greg. 'Skelton and the English Language'. In Sebastian Sobecki and John Scattergood (eds), *A Critical Companion to John Skelton*. Cambridge, 2018. 139–62.

Wakelin, Daniel. 'The Carol in Writing: Three Anthologies from Fifteenth-Century Norfolk'. *Journal of the Early Book Society*, 9 (2006), 25–49.

Wakelin, Daniel. *Humanism, Reading, and English Literature 1430–1530*. Oxford, 2007.

Wakelin, Daniel. 'The Occasion, Author and Readers of Knyghthode and Bataile'. *Medium Ævum*, 73 (2004), 260–72.

Wallace, David. *Premodern Places: Calais to Surinam, Chaucer to Aphra Behn*. Oxford, 2006.

Walling, Amanda. 'Feminizing Aureation in Lydgate's *Life of Our Lady* and *Life of Saint Margaret*'. *Neophilologus*, 101 (2017), 321–36.

Walsh-Morrissey, Jake. '"To al indifferent": The Virtues of Lydgate's *Dietary*'. *Medium Ævum*, 84 (2015), 258–78.

Walsingham. *Of this chapel se here the fundacyon*. London. c1496.

Walter, Melissa. 'Performance Possibilities for the Chester Expositor, 1532–1575'. *Comitatus*, 31 (2000), 175–95.

Walton, John. Mark Science (ed.). *Boethius: De Consolatione Philosophiae*. EETS, o.s. 170. London, 1927.

Warner, Laurence. *Chaucer's Scribes*. Cambridge, 2018.

Warren, Michelle R. 'Translation'. In Paul Strohm (ed.), *Middle English*. Oxford, 2007. 51–67.

Wars of Alexander, The. Hoyt N. Duggan and Thorlac Turville-Petre (eds). EETS, s.s. 10. Oxford, 1989.

Warton, Thomas. *The History of English Poetry from the Close of the Eleventh to the Commencement of the Eighteenth Centuries*, 3 vols. London, 1774–81.

Wasson, J.M. (ed.), *Records of Early English Drama: Devon*. Toronto, 1986.

Watson, Nicholas. *Balaam's Ass: Vernacular Theology Before the English Reformation*. Philadelphia, PA, forthcoming.

Watson, Nicholas. '"A Clerke schulde haue it of kinde for to kepe counsell"'. In Vincent Gillespie and Kantik Ghosh (eds), *After Arundel: Religious Writing in Fifteenth-Century England*. Turnhout, 2011. 563–89.

Watson, Nicholas. 'Censorship and Cultural Change in Late-Medieval England: Vernacular Theology, the Oxford Translation Debate, and Arundel's Constitutions of 1409'. *Speculum*, 70 (1995), 822–64.

Watson, Nicholas. 'Theories of Translation'. In Roger Ellis (ed.). *Oxford History of Literary Translation into English. Vol. 1: to 1550*. Oxford, 2008. 76–8.

Watt, David. *The Making of Thomas Hoccleve's Series*. Liverpool, 2013.

Watt, David. 'Thomas Hoccleve's *La Male Regle* in the Canterbury Cathedral Archives'. *Opuscula: Short Texts of the Middle Ages and Renaissance*, 2 (2012), 1–11

Watt, Diane. *Amoral Gower: Language, Sex, and Politics*. Minneapolis, MIN, 2003.

Watt, Homer A. 'The Dramatic Unity of the "Secunda Pastorum"'. In *Essays and Studies in Honor of Carleton Brown*. New York, 1940. 158–66.

Weever, John. *Ancient Funerall Monuments within the United Monarchie of Great Britaine*. London, 1631.

Weiskott, Eric. 'Alliterative Meter after 1450: *The Vision of William Banastre*'. In Lindy Brady and M. J. Toswell (eds), *Early English Poetic Culture and Meter: The Influence of G. R. Russom*. Kalamazoo, MI, 2016. 149–79.

Weiskott, Eric. '*The Ireland Prophecy*: Text and Metrical Context'. *Studies in Philology*, 114 (2017), 245–77.

Wellesley, Mary. 'Textual Lyricism in Lydgate's *Fifteen Joys and Sorrows of Mary*'. In Julia Boffey and Christiania Whitehead (eds), *Middle English Lyrics*. 2018. 122–37.

Wells, John Edwin. *A Manual of the Writings in Middle English 1050–1400*. New Haven, CT, 1916.

Wells, Minnie E. 'The Age of Isaac at the Time of the Sacrifice'. *Modern Language Notes*, 54 (1939), 579–82.

Wenzel, Siegfried. 'Eli and His Sons'. *Yearbook of Langland Studies*, 13 (1999), 137–52.

Wenzel, Siegfried. *Preachers, Poets, and the Early English Lyric*. Princeton, 1986.

Wey, William. G. Williams (ed.). *The Itineraries of William Wey*. London, 1857.

Whearty, Bridget. 'Chaucer's Death, Lydgate's Guild, and the Construction of Community in Fifteenth-Century English Literature'. *Studies in the Age of Chaucer*, 40 (2018), 331–7.

Whitehead, Christiania. *Castles of the Mind: A Study of Medieval Architectural Allegory*. Cardiff, 2003.
Whitehead, Christiania. 'The Middle English Religious Lyric'. In T. G. Duncan, (ed.), *A Companion to the Middle English Lyric*. Cambridge, 2005. 96–119.
Whitehead, Christiania. 'Regional, and with Attitude: The Middle English Metrical Life of St Cuthbert'. In Catherine Batt and René Tixier (eds), *Booldly bot meekly: Essays on the Theory and Practice of Translation in the Middle Ages in Honour of Roger Ellis*. Turnhout, 2018. 115–32.
Whiting, B. J. 'A Fifteenth-Century English Chaucerian: The Translator of *Partonope of Blois*'. *Mediaeval Studies*, 7 (1945), 40–54.
Whiting, B. J. 'A Probable Allusion to Henryson's *Testament of Cresseid*'. *Modern Language Review*, 40 (1945), 46–7.
Whiting, B. J., and H. W. Whiting. *Proverbs, Sentences and Proverbial Phrases from English Writings Mainly Before 1500*. Cambridge, MA, 1968.
Wickham, Glynne. *Early English Stages 1300–1669*. 3 vols. London, 1959.
Wilflingseder, Walter. *The Motifs and Characters in the* Gest Hystoriale of the Destruction of Troy *and in the* Laud Troy Book, Studies on themes and motifs in literature, 93. Frankfurt, 2007.
Wilkins, David (ed.). *Concilia Magnae Britanniae et Hiberniae*. 4 vols. London, 1737.
Wilkins, Ernest Hatch. *Studies in the Life and Works of Petrarch*. Cambridge, MA, 1955.
William of Palerne, The Romance of. Walter W. Skeat (ed.). EETS, e.s. 1. London, 1867.
Williams, Arnold. 'Typology and the Cycle Plays: Some Criteria'. *Speculum*, 43 (1968), 677–84.
Williams, M. E. *Civic Treasures of Bristol*. Bristol, 1984.
Williams, W. H. (ed. and trans.). *Book of Chess*. New York, 2008.
Willoughby, J. M. W. (ed.), *The Libraries of Collegiate Churches*, 2 vols. London, 2013.
Wilmart, Dom A. 'Les compositions d'Osbert de Clare en l'honneur de sainte Anne'. In *Auteurs spirituels et textes dévots du moyen age Latin*. Paris, 1932. 261–86.
Wilson, Edward. 'The Debate of the Carpenter's Tools'. *Review of English Studies*, n.s. 38 (1987). 445–70.
Wilson, Edward. 'An Unpublished Alliterative Poem on Plant-Names from Lincoln College, Oxford, MS. Lat. 129 (E)'. *Notes and Queries*, n.s. 26 (1979), 504–8.
Wilson, Kenneth G. 'The Lay of Sorrow and the Lufaris Complaynt. An Edition'. *Speculum*, 29 (1954), 708–26.
Wilson, R. M. *The Lost Literature of Medieval England*. 2nd edn. London, 1974.
Windeatt, Barry. 'Chaucer and Fifteenth-Century Romance: *Partonope of Blois*'. In Ruth Morse and Windeatt (eds), *Chaucer Traditions*. Cambridge, 1990. 62–80.
Windeatt, Barry. 'The Fifteenth-Century Arthur'. In Elizabeth Archibald and Ad Putter (eds), *The Cambridge Companion to the Arthurian Legend*. Cambridge, 2009. 84–102.
Windeatt, Barry. 'Geoffrey Chaucer'. In Roger Ellis (ed.). *Oxford History of Literary Translation into English. Vol. 1: to 1550*. Oxford, 2008. 137–48.
Wingfield, Emily. 'The Composition and Revision of Sir Gilbert Hay's *Buik of King Alexander the Conquerour*'. *Nottingham Medieval Studies*, 57 (2013), 247–86.
Wingfield, Emily. '*Lancelot of the Laik* and the Literary Manuscript Miscellany in 15th- and 16th-century Scotland'. In Margaret Connolly and Raluca Radulescu (eds), *Insular Books: Vernacular Manuscript Miscellanies in Late Medieval Britain*. London, 2015. 209–20.
Wingfield, Emily. 'The thewis off gudwomen: Female Advice in *Lancelot of the Laik* and *The Buik of King Alexander the Conqueror*'. In Janet Hadley Williams and Derrick J. McClure (eds). *Fresche fontanis: Studies in the Culture of Medieval and Early Modern Scotland*. Newcastle, 2013.
Wingfield, Emily. *The Trojan Legend in Medieval Scottish Literature*. Cambridge, 2014.
Winkless, D. 'Medieval Sudeley. Part II etc'. *Family History*, 10 (1977), 21–39.
Winstead, Karen A. 'The *Beryn*-writer as a Reader of Chaucer'. *The Chaucer Review*, 22 (1988), 225–33.
Winstead, Karen A. *John Capgrave's Fifteenth Century*. Philadelphia, PA, 2007.
Winstead, Karen A. 'John Capgrave and the Chaucer Tradition', *The Chaucer Review*, 30 (1996), 389–400.
Witalisz, Władysław. *The Trojan Mirror: Middle English Narratives of Troy as Books of Princely Advice*, Studies in English Medieval Language and Literature, 29. Frankfurt, 2011.

Withington, Robert. 'Queen Margaret's Entry into London, 1445'. *Modern Philology*, 13 (1915), 53–7.
Wogan-Browne, Jocelyn, Nicholas Watson, Andrew Taylor, and Ruth Evans (eds), *The Idea of the Vernacular: An Anthology of Middle English Literary Theory, 1280–1520*. University Park, PA, 1999.
Woodforde, Christopher. *The Norwich School of Glass-Painting in the Fifteenth* Century. London, 1950.
Woods, Frederick (ed.). *The Oxford Book of English Traditional Verse*. Oxford, 1983.
Woolf, Rosemary. 'The Effect of Typology on the English Medieval Plays of Abraham and Isaac'. *Speculum*, 32 (1957), 805–25.
Woolf, Rosemary. *The English Mystery Plays*. London, 1972.
Woolf, Rosemary. *The English Religious Lyric in the Middle Ages*. Oxford, 1968.
Wormald, Jenny. 'Scotland, 1406–1513'. In Christopher Allmand (ed.), *New Cambridge Medieval History* (Cambridge, 1998). 514–31.
Worp, J.A. *Geschiedenis van het drama en van het tooneel in Nederland*. 2 vols. Groningen, 1903–7.
Wright, C. E. 'Middle English Parerga in a School Collection'. *Review of English Studies*, n.s. 2 (1951), 114–20.
Wright, Herbert G. *Boccaccio in England: From Chaucer to Tennyson*. London, 1957.
Wright, Herbert G. (ed.), *Early English versions of the tales of Guiscardo and Ghismonda and Titus Gisippus from the Decameron*. EETS, o.s. 205. London, 1937.
Wright, Sylvia. 'The Author Portraits in the Bedford Psalter Hours: Gower, Chaucer and Hoccleve'. *British Library Journal*, 18 (1992), 190–201.
Wright, Thomas (ed.). *The Tale of the Basyn and The Frere and the Boy*. London, 1836.
Wrigley, E. A., R. S. Davies, J. E. Oeppen, and R. S. Schofield. *English Population History from Family Reconstitution 1580–1837*. Cambridge, 1997.
Wyntoun, Andrew. *The Original Chronicle of Andrew Wyntoun*. F. J. Amour (ed.). 6 vols. STS 50, 53, 54, 56, 57, 63. Edinburgh, 1903–14.
Yakovlev, Nicolay. 'The Development of Alliterative Metre from Old to Middle English'. DPhil thesis, University of Oxford, 2008.
York Plays, The: A Critical Edition of the York Corpus Christi Play as Recorded in British Library Additional MS 35390. Richard Beadle (ed.). EETS, s.s. 23, 24. Oxford, 2009, 2013.
Wynnere and Wastoure and *The Parlement of the Thre Ages*. Warren Ginsberg (ed.). Kalamazoo, MI, 1992.
Yorkshire Writers: Richard Rolle of Hampole, an English Father of the Church and His Followers. Carl Horstman (ed.). 2 vols. London, 1895–6.
Youngs, Deborah. *Humphrey Newton (1466–1536): An Early Tudor Gentleman*. Woodbridge, 2008.
Zaerr, Linda Marie. *Performance and the Middle English Romance*. Cambridge, 2012.
Zaerr, Linda Marie. 'The Tournament of Tottenham: Don't Tell the Dean'. *This Rough Magic*, December 2018, online.
Zeeman, Nicolette. 'The Schools Give a License to Poets'. In Rita Copeland (ed.), *Criticism and Dissent in the Middle Ages*. Cambridge, 1996. 151–80.
Zettersten, Arne. 'The Lambeth Manuscript of the "Boke of Huntyng"'. *Neuphilologische Mitteilungen*, 70 (1969), 114–23.
Zettersten, Arne. 'On the Aureate Diction of William Dunbar'. In Michael Chesnutt et al. (eds), *Essays Presented to Knud Schibsbye: On his 75th birthday 29 November 1979*. Copenhagen, 1979. 51–68.
Zettersten, A. (ed.). *The Virtues of Herbs in the Loscombe Manuscript*. Lund, 1967.
Zieman, Katherine. 'Compiling the Lyric: Richard Rolle, Textual Dynamism and Devotional Song in London, British Library, Additional MS 37049'. In Julia Boffey and Christiania Whitehead (eds), *Middle English Lyrics: New Readings of Short Poems*. Cambridge, 2018. 158–73.
Zupitza, Julius. 'Anmerkungen zu Jacob Rymans Gedichten. II Tiel'. *Archiv für das Studium der neueren Sprachen und Literaturen*, 93 (1894), 369–98.
Zupitza, Julius. 'Die Gedichte de Franziskaners Jakob Ryman'. *Archiv für das Studium der neueren Sprachen und Literaturen*, 89 (1892), 167–338
Zysk, Jay. *Shadow and Substance: Eucharistic Controversy across the Reformation Divide*. Notre Dame, IN, 2017.

Manuscript Index

Abbotsford House Library, Abbotsford Legendary, 189
Aberdeen, City Charter Room, The Town House (Aberdein Sasine Register), 461–462
Aberystwyth, National Library of Wales, Brogyntyn ii. 1 (*olim* Porkington 10), 122, 175, 177 n.111, 393, 398
Aberystwyth, National Library of Wales, Peniarth 53, 391
Aberystwyth, National Library of Wales, Peniarth 392D (Hengwrt Manuscript), 86–87
Aberystwyth, National Library of Wales, Peniarth 399, 215
Alnwick Castle, Northumberland, 79, 148 n.38
Alnwick Castle, Northumberland, 455, 338–339
Asloan Manuscript *see* Edinburgh, National Library of Scotland, Advocates Library 16500
Auchinleck Manuscript *see* Edinburgh, National Library of Scotland, Advocates' 19. 2. 1

Bannatyne Manuscript *see* Edinburgh, National Library of Scotland, Advocates Library 1. 1. 6

Cambridge
  Corpus Christi College 61, 23
  Corpus Christi College 80, 118–119
  Emmanuel College 405, 368
  Gonville and Caius College 383/603, 393
  Jesus College, 13. Q. A, 398
  Magdalene College, Pepys Library 15, 241 n.20
  Magdalene College, Pepys Library 1584, 165 n.39
  Magdalene College, Pepys Library 2030, 278 n.41
  Magdalene College, Pepys Library 2553 (Maitland Folio Manuscript), 443–444, 461–462
  Trinity College, O. 1. 13, 244 n.34
  Trinity College, O. 2. 53, 390
  Trinity College, O. 3. 12, 485
  Trinity College, O. 3. 58, 203–204 n.50
  Trinity College, O. 5. 2, 368
  Trinity College, O. 9. 26, 144 n.23
  Trinity College, O. 9. 38, 251 n.52
  Trinity College, R. 3. 20, 117, 197 n.14, 285 n.8, 409, 418 n.42
  Trinity College, R. 3. 21, 124–125 n.89, 190, 197 n.14
  Trinity College, R. 2. 64, 400–401
  Trinity College R. 14. 36, 253 n.66
  CUL Add. 2585, 124
  CUL Ee. 1. 12, 115, 203–204
  CUL Ee. 4. 35, 382, 401
  CUL Ee. 4. 37, 278 n.41
  CUL Ff. 1. 6 (Findern Manuscript), 122–123, 295, 368–369
  CUL Ff. 2. 38, 119–120, 165 n.39
  CUL Ff. 5. 48, 376, 401
  CUL Gg. 4. 27, 114, 136
  CUL Ll. 4. 14, 302 n.10
  CUL Mm. 4. 42, 103, 116 n.33
Chicago, IL, Newberry Library, 32, 146 n.30

Delamere Manuscript *see* New Haven, CT, Beinecke Library, Takamiya 32
Dublin, Trinity College, 213, 327 n.8
Dublin, Trinity College, 432, 120–121, 151 n.54, 216, 319–320
Dublin, Trinity College Library 490, 115 n.23, 204 n.51
Dublin, Trinity College, 516, 391
Dublin, Trinity College, 652, 218 n.31
Durham, University Library, Cosin V. iii. 9, 116, 424–425

Edinburgh, National Archives of Scotland, GD 112/71/9, 329
Edinburgh, National Library of Scotland, Advocates Library, Abbotsford Manuscript, 114
Edinburgh, National Library of Scotland, Advocates Library 1. 1. 6 (Bannatyne Manuscript), 443–444, 462
Edinburgh, National Library of Scotland, Advocates Library 18. 7. 21, 202–203 n.
Edinburgh, National Library of Scotland, Advocates Library 19. 2. 1 (Auchinleck Manuscript), 342–343, 349
Edinburgh, National Library of Scotland, Advocates Library 19. 2. 3, 306 n.22
Edinburgh, National Library of Scotland, Advocates Library 19. 2. 4, 306 n.22
Edinburgh, National Library of Scotland, Advocates Library 19.3.1 (Heege Manuscript), 120–121, 203–204 n.52, 364 n.35, 393, 402
Edinburgh, National Library of Scotland, Advocates Library 34. 7. 3, 443
Edinburgh, National Library of Scotland Advocates Library 72. 1. 37 (Book of The Dean of Lismore), 444
Edinburgh, National Library of Scotland, Advocates Library 16500 (Asloan Manuscript), 443–444, 461–462
Edinburgh, University Library, La. III. 149 (Makculloch 205), 443
Ellesmere Manuscript *see* San Marino, CA, Huntington Library, EL 26 C 9

Findern Manuscript *see* CUL Ff. 1. 6

Glasgow, University Library, Hunterian 388 (V. 2. 8), 332

Heege Manuscript *see* Edinburgh, National Library of Scotland, Advocates' 19. 3. 1
Hengwrt Manuscript *see* Aberystwyth, National Library of Wales, Peniarth 392D

Leiden, University Library Vossius Germ. Gall. Q. 9, 124
Lincoln Cathedral 91 (Lincoln Thornton manuscript), 45 n.62, 120, 123, 151, 180–181, 190–191, 211 n.84, 368–369, 373 n.18
Lincoln Cathedral 132, 400 n.91
Lincoln Thornton manuscript *see* Lincoln Cathedral 91
London
  London Thornton Manuscript *see* BL Add. 31042
  BL Add. 5465, 204 n.49
  BL Add. 5665, 204 n.49
  BL Add. 10302, 260 n.97
  BL Add. 10304, 60 n.98
  BL Add. 10305, 215 n.7
  BL Add. 11814, 5 n.14, 58–59 n.90, 114
  BL Add. 16165, 117, 409, 418 n.42
  BL Add. 17866, 253 n.66
  BL MS Add. 20059, 50
  BL Add. 24062, 116, 425 n.9
  BL Add. 27879 (Percy Folio), 140 n.4, 342–343, 366 n.48, 393, 398, 401
  BL Add. 29729, 99, 136 n.23, 409
  BL Add. 31042 (London Thornton Manuscript), 120, 142, 165, 177 n.111, 204 n.52, 357–358
  BL Add. 34360, 117–118 n.39, 408–409
  BL Add. 35288, 365 n.44
  BL Add. 35290, 214–215, 218 n.31
  BL Add. 37049, 151, 172 n.88, 175–176, 207–212
  BL Add. 37223, 390
  BL Add. 40732, 329
  BL Add. 42130, 358 n.15
  BL Add. 57335, 278 n.41
  BL Add. 88947, 251 n.55
  BL Arundel 20, 278 n.41
  BL Arundel 38, 116
  BL Arundel 83, 152 n.59
  BL Arundel 168, 114 n.15
  BL Arundel 285, 167
  BL Arundel 327, 105, 114
  BL Cotton Augustus A IV, 119
  BL Cotton Cleopatra A XIII, 315
  BL Cotton Cleopatra C IV, 309–310
  BL Cotton Faustina B VI, 172 n.88
  BL Cotton Nero C XII, 150 n.50
  BL Cotton Tiberius A IV, 136
  BL Cotton Tiberius A VII, 124
  BL Cotton Titus A XXXI, 174
  BL Cotton Vespasian D VIII, 215 n.4, n.11, 218 n.31
  BL Cotton Vitellius D XII, 310 n.41
  BL Cotton Rolls ii. 23, 391
  BL Egerton 3028, 358–359
  BL Egerton 3307, 204 n.49
  BL Harley 43, 21
  BL Harley 78, 372–373
  BL Harley 525, 331
  BL Harley 542, 87
  BL Harley 565, 310 n.40
  BL Harley 682, 55, 73 n.61, 124, 295–298
  BL Harley 1735, 121–122
  BL Harley 1782, 18 n.20
  BL Harley 2013, 215 n.7
  BL Harley 2124, 215 n.7
  BL Harley 2250, 78
  BL Harley 2251, 117–118 n.39, 409
  BL Harley 2252, 343–344, 364–365, 497 n.48
  BL Harley 2255, 113 n.13, 197 n.14
  BL Harley 2278, 113, 422
  BL Harley 3865, 444
  BL Harley 5396, 120–121
  BL Harley 6398, 245 n.35
  BL Harley 7333, 118–119, 409
  BL Lansdowne 204, 71 n.52, 115–116, 320 n.77, 346 n.30
  BL Lansdowne 205, 151 n.51
  BL Lansdowne 388, 355–356
  BL Lansdowne 699, 124, 254 n.70
  BL Lansdowne 793, 257 n.83
  BL Royal 15 E VI, 318 n.70
  BL Royal 17 A I, 240 n.17
  BL Royal 17 C XVII, 174 n.93, 228–229
  BL Royal 17 D VI, 116
  BL Royal 17 D XVIII, 116 n.31
  BL Royal 17 D XX, 306 n.22
  BL Royal 18 B XXIII, 229 n.70
  BL Royal 18 D II, 154 n.72, 323–324
  BL Royal App 58, 472 n.35
  BL Sloane 1586, 265
  BL Sloane 1873, 260 n.97
  BL Sloane 1986, 239 n.9
  BL Sloane 2593, 204, 234, 393, 402
  BL Yates Thompson 13, 152 n.59
London, Dulwich College MS 22, 161 n.17
London, Lambeth Palace Library 306, 314–315
London, Lambeth Palace Library 344, 124
London, Lambeth Palace Library 406, 251 n.52
London, Lambeth Palace Library 491, 123
London, Lambeth Palace Library 492, 251–252
London, Lambeth Palace Library 853, 176, 177 n.111, 271–272
London, Lambeth Palace Library 935, 151 n.49
London, Metropolitan Archives, Archives of the Corporation of London, Letter Book K, 229 n. 68
London, St Paul's Cathedral Library 8, 390–391

MANUSCRIPT INDEX 553

London, Wellcome Library 406, 251 n.52, 253 n.64
London, Wellcome Library 632, 145

Macro Plays *see* Washington DC, Folger Shakespeare Library, V. a. 354
Maitland Folio Manuscript *see* Cambridge, Magdalene College, Pepys Library 2553
Manchester, Chetham's Library 8009, 190 n.51, 363, 383–384
Manchester, John Rylands University Library, Eng. 1, 119
Melbourne, State Library of Victoria *096/G94, 66–67
Melrose, Scotland, *see* Abbotsford
Minneapolis, MN, Minnesota University Library, Z.822.N.81, 181–182
Montreal, PQ, McGill University Library, McGill 143, 113 n.13

New Haven, CT, Beinecke Library 163 (Wagstaffe Miscellany), 121–122, 252 n.56
New Haven, CT, Beinecke Library 283, 119 n.49
New Haven, CT, Beinecke Library 365, 120–121, 216, 218 n.31
New Haven, CT, Beinecke Library 661, 116–117 n.34
New Haven, CT, Beinecke Library, Takamiya 32 (Delamere Manuscript), 365–366
New Haven, CT, Beinecke Library, Takamiya 38, 115
New Haven, CT, Beinecke Library, Takamiya 56, 145
New Haven, CT, Beinecke Library, Takamiya 112, 145–146 n.28
New York, Columbia University Library, Plimpton Add. 4, 145–146
New York, Morgan Library & Museum, Bühler 21, 254 n.66
New York, Morgan Library & Museum, G 39, 146 n.29
New York, Morgan Library & Museum, M 486, 146 n.28
New York, Morgan Library & Museum, M 876, 362 n.30, 366–368
New York Public Library, Spencer 193, 148 n.37

Oxford
BodL Arch. Selden. B. 24, 122–123, 286, 288, 449 n.28
BodL Arch. Selden. B. 26, 204 n.49–n.50
BodL Ashmole 44, 327 n.8
BodL Ashmole 48, 140 n.4
BodL Ashmole 59, 117, 197 n.14, 409
BodL Ashmole 61, 119–120, 142, 181, 373 n.18, 375–376, 393
BodL Bodley 175, 215 n.7
BodL Bodley 264, 24–25 n.51
BodL Bodley 315, 154 n.73
BodL Bodley 565, 249
BodL Bodley Rolls 5, 148 n.38
BodL Digby 23, 355–356
BodL Digby 102, 3, 7, 83, 97–98, 104, 118, 163–164, 195–197, 307

BodL Digby 133, 214 n.4, 215–217, 218 n.31
BodL Douce 104, 125
BodL Douce 261, 366 n.48
BodL Douce 302, 50 n.33, 83, 99–100, 115, 174 n.96, 194–195 n.3, 201, 203–204, 210 n.81, 212
BodL Douce 322, 125 n.89
BodL Douce 324, 123, 341–342 n.9
BodL Duke Humfrey d. 2, 249–251
BodL e Musaeo 160, 216, 248 n.43
BodL Eng. poet. a. 1 (Vernon Manuscript), 161
BodL Eng. poet. c. 3, 366 n.44
BodL Eng. poet. d. 45, 278 n.41
BodL Eng. poet. e. 1, 203–204 n.49, 393
BodL Fairfax 16, 298–299
BodL Firth d. 14, 147 n.34
BodL Hatton 51, 136
BodL Hatton 73, 124
BodL Hearne's Diaries 38, 124
BodL Lat. misc. b. 17, 366 n.44
BodL Lat. misc. c. 66, 154 n.73
BodL Laud misc. 545, 333–334
BodL Laud misc. 416, 278 n.41
BodL Lyell 34, 141 n.6
BodL Marshall 135, 148 n.38
BodL Rawlinson A. 389, 164–165 n.33
BodL Rawlinson C. 86, 381–382
BodL Rawlinson C. 506, 144 n.24
BodL Rawlinson D. 328, 394
BodL Rawlinson poet. 14, 365 n.44
BodL Rawlinson poet. 225, 181
BodL Tanner 346, 285
BodL Tanner 407, 121
Oxford Balliol College, 354, 251 n.53, 372–373, 375–376, 381–382 n.71, 390, 393
Oxford Lincoln College, Lat. 129 (E), 251 n.53
Oxford, Magdalen College, 213, 133 n.18
Oxford, University College, 188, 365 n.44

Paris, Bibliothèque nationale, fr. 25458, 55, 295–296, 298–299
Percy Folio, *see* BL Add. 27879
Porkington 10 *see* Aberystwyth, National Library of Wales, Brogyntyn ii. 1
Princeton NJ, Princeton University Library, Garrett 140, 337–338, 360
Princeton, NJ, Princeton University Library, Garrett 141, 115, 336
Princeton, NJ, Princeton University Library, Taylor 5, 133 n.18
Princeton, NJ, Princeton University Library, Taylor 9, 123
Princeton, NJ, Princeton University Library, Taylor 22, 21 n.34

San Marino, CA, Huntington Library, EL 26 C 9 (Ellesmere Manuscript), 86–87, 111–112, 124–125
San Marino, CA, Huntington Library, HM 1, 215

San Marino, CA, Huntington Library, HM 2, 215 n.7
San Marino, CA, Huntington Library, HM 111, 106, 116, 424–425, 432, 434
San Marino, CA, Huntington Library HM 142, 124
San Marino, CA, Huntington Library, HM 744, 116, 424–425, 434
San Marino, CA, Huntington Library, HM 1086, 144 n.23
San Marino, CA, Huntington Library, HM 26054, 146 n.30
Stockholm, Royal Library, X. 90, 253 n.66

Vernon Manuscript *see* BodL Eng. poet. a. 1
Wagstaffe Miscellany *see* New Haven, CT, Beinecke Library 163
Warminster, Wiltshire, Longleat House 30, 124
Warminster, Wiltshire, Longleat House 257, 364 n.35
Warminster, Wiltshire, Longleat House, 258, 290
Washington DC, Folger Shakespeare Library, V.a.354 (Macro Plays), 217, 218 n.31
Winchester, Winchester College 33, 176

Index

This is primarily an index of names, titles and places although other matters are sometimes included. Entries are normally under the first significant word, not under the definite or indefinite article. Individual saints appear under their names, not *St*. Initial *I-* for *J-* is indexed under *J-*.

'ABC of Aristotle', 154, 265–267
Aberdeen, 473–474
Aberdeen University, 21
Abingdon, bridge, 153–154
Abraham and Isaac, 121, 216, 220–225
abuses of the age, 154–155, 394, 466
Adam of Cobsam, *The Wright's Chaste Wife*, 395
Adulterous Falmouth Squire, 120, 373
'Against the Night Goblin', 144
Ælfric, 89
Aesop, 443, 454–455, 468 n.25, 482–483
Agincourt, Battle of, 2–4, 18, 73, 296, 307–313, 390–391
'Agincourt Carol', 309, 313
Alan of Lille, *Anticlaudianus*, 39 n.41, 63–64
Alcock, John, bishop, 388
Alexander A, 328 n.9
Alexander and Dindimus/Alexander B, 327
Alexander the Great, 248, 326–330
Alexander III, King of Scotland, 306
Alisaunder, King, 81, 327
Amys, Thomas and Margery, 155
André, Bernard, 323–325
Anne, St, Life of, 121, 190, 191–192, 203
Annunciation, 50, 168, 191, 206, 445, 448, 464
Anthony Hermit, St, 153
Antichrist, 214–216
Anwykyll, John, 21
Aquinas, Thomas, 196
Aristotle, 39, 256, 276, 329–330, 440
    see also 'ABC of Aristotle'
Arma Christi, 125, 145–146, 211 n.84
Armourers' company, 148–150
ars moriendi, 424–425, 428, 430–432, 434
Arthur, Prince, 323, 387
Arthur, King, 306, 321–322, 342–354, 378, 391, 493
    (see also *Awntyrs off Arthure, Avowyng of Arthur, Alliterative Morte Arthure, King Arthur and King Cornwall, of Arthur and of Merlin, Stanzaic Morte Arthur*)
Arundel, Richard, earl of, 302
Arundel, Thomas Archbishop of Canterbury, 195–197, 221, 438
Arundel's Constitutions, 31, 42, 160, 170–171
Ashby, George, 5, 25, 88, 277
    Active Policy of a Prince, 40, 99–100, 102, 103, 279, 280–281
    Dicta & opiniones diversorum philosophorum, 100, 279
    A Prisoner's Reflections, 40, 107, 280
Asneth, Storie of, 163
Assemble of Foules: see Chaucer, *Parliament of Fowls*
Assembly of Gods, The, 129–137, 409
Assembly of Ladies, The, 290–293
Athelstan, King, 346
Audelay, John, 6–9, 76, 100, 104–105, 115, 174, 194–195, 209, 483
    carols, 202–203
    'Childhood'/*Cantalena de puericia*, 83–84
    De tribus regibus mortuis/Three Dead Kings, 81–82
    liturgical sequence, 201–202
    Marcolf and Solomon, 42–43, 50
Augustine, St (of Canterbury), 153
Augustine, St (of Hippo), 59, 166, 174
    City of God, 66
    Confessions, 96, 408
aureation, aureate style, 30–31, 50, 59, 63–70, 153, 179, 186, 190, 192, 195, 266, 276, 343, 387, 389, 412, 422, 463–464, 471, 473, 478, 481, 484, 496, 498
Avowyng of Arthur, The, 88, 89, 343, 350–352
Awntyrs off Arthure, The, 81, 174–175, 341–344, 346–353, 377–378, 392, 398

'Babees Book', The, 265–266
Badby, John, 435, 438
Bagot, Sir William, 302
Bakhtin, Mikhail, 378, 466
'Balat set uppone the yates of Caunterbury', 141
ballade, 142, 152–153, 198, 199, 439–440
Baldwin, William, *Beware the Cat*, 499
ballade stanza, 5, 8, 156, 194, 213–214, 248, 254, 310, 343, 385–386, 389–390, 415–416, 418, 422, 446, 449–450, 490
Balzac, Honoré de, 93
Banastre, William, *Vision of*, 80
Banester, Gilbert, *Tale of Guiscardo and Ghismonda*, 60
Barbour, John, 304–305
Barclay, Alexander, 105, 481–482, 487–91
    Castle of Labour, 130

Barclay, Alexander, (*Continued*)
  Eclogues, 488–491
  Ship of Fools, 137, 487–488
Barthes, Roland, 91–93
Bartholomaeus Anglicus, *De proprietatibus rerum*, 256, 260 n.98
Barton, Henry, 118–119, 343–344
Barton Turf (Norfolk), parish church, 155
Bassandyne, Thomas, 444
Bawburgh (Norfolk), parish church, 150
Beauchamp family, 5
Beauchamp, Richard, 13th Earl of Warwick, 24, 117, 146–147, 313–314, 345, 408
Beaufort, Henry, Cardinal, 286, 315
Beaufort, Joan, countess of Westmorland, 116
Beaufort, Joan, queen of Scotland, 35, 286
Beccaria, Antonio, 25
Benet, John, 317–318, 392
Benoît de Sainte-Maure, *Roman de Troie*, 331–332, 410–413
Beowulf, 470
Berkeley, Elizabeth, 5, 53–54
Berkeley, Lord Thomas, 47, 54, 57
Bernard, St, of Clairvaux, 166–167, 421
Berners, Juliana, Dame, 251–252
Berners, Lord, 357
Berthelet, Thomas, 131, 133, 134, 139
Beryn, Tale of, 18, 338–340, 373, 377–379
Bevis of Hampton, 129–131, 137, 139, 334, 342–343, 397
'Birched School Boy', 268
birds, poem on the names of, 241
birthing girdle, 145
Black Death, 15
Blacman, John, 315
Blanche of Lancaster, 51
Blind Hary *see* Hary
Blomfylde, Miles, 217–218
Boar's Head lyrics, 385, 399
'Boast of Mercury', 260
Boccaccio, Giovanni, 29, 59
  Decameron, 59–60
  De casibus virorum illustrium, 4–5, 56–60, 101–102, 314, 415
  De mulieribus claris, 4–5, 59–60
  Filostrato, 36
  Teseida, 36
'Bochas', 101–102
Boethius, *Consolation of Philosophy*, 5, 21, 35, 53–54, 62, 62, 106, 244, 275–276, 415–416, 437, 450
bloodletting, poem on, 255–256
Bohun, Humphrey de, earl of Hereford and Essex, 78
Boke of Curtasye, The, 239, 265–266, 269
Bokenham, Osbern, 5–7, 49, 58, 88, 99, 115, 336
  Legendys of Hooly Wummen, 49, 105, 114, 180, 182–183, 490
    'Life of St Anne', 182
    'Life of St Audrey', 188
    'Life of St George', 182
    'Life of St Margaret', 178–179, 189
    'Life of St Mary Magdalene', 185
    'Life of St Winifred', 188
Bollard, Nicholas, *Tractatus*, 251
Bolosse, William, 259
Bonaventure, St, 92–93
Book of Good Counsel to the Scots King, 131
Book of St. Albans, 251–252
Boteler family, 148
Boughton (Oxfordshire), church of St Mary, 151
Bourgchier, Isabella, Countess of Eu, 185
Bower, Walter, *Scotichronicon*, 13, 400
Bradshaw, Henry, 6
  Life of St Werburge, 105–106, 188
Brampton, Thomas, 164–165
Brandon, Charles, duke of Suffolk, 137
Brant, Sebastian, *Narrenschiff*, 130, 487–488
Breton lays, 366
Brewers' Company, 118
Bridget, St, 208
'Bring us in good ale', 399
Bristol, civic insignia, sword, 143
Brome (Suffolk), 120–121, 215–216, 222–225
Bruni, Leonardo, *Fabula Tancredi*, 60
Brut, 13, 118, 141, 188, 300, 302, 309–310, 316, 321, 344, 391
Bubwith, Nicholas, 435–436
Buik of Alexander, 327, 328–330, 340
Buke of Phisnomy, 329–330
Buonaccorso da Montemagno, *De vera nobilitate*, 218
Burgh, Benedict, 98–99, 122
  translation of *Disticha Catonis*, 490
  'Secrees of Old Philosoffres', 57, 276, 409–410
Burgh, Thomas, 114
Burns, Robert, 306–307
Burton, Robert, 381
Bury St Edmunds, Benedictine house, 113, 124–125, 127, 150, 204, 217, 408
Bussy, Sir John, 303

Caen, 21
Calais, 2, 17, 27, 315–317
'Calais, Siege of', 316
Calot, Laurence, 146–147, 313–314
Cantlow, John, prior of Bath abbey, 153
Capgrave, John, 7, 49, 99, 113–115, 179, 189, 336
  Life of St Katherine, 49–50, 105, 114, 189
  Life of St Norbert, 49–50, 114
'Captain Cox', 376–377
Capystranus, 129, 360–361, 364, 370
Carlisle, 123, 153–154, 346
Carlisle abbey, Prior's Tower, 153
Carmeliano, Pietro, 21
Carpenter, Richard, 259
Castiglione, Baldassar, 281
Castle of Love, A, 171
Castle of Perseverance, 217, 231, 232
Castillon, Battle of, 2

Caxton, William, 17–18, 26, 55, 91, 96, 125–126, 128–139, 354, 482
  Book of Curtesye, 389
  Book of fayytes of armes and of chyualrye, The, 57
  Eneydos, 484
  Lyf of Charles the Grete, 359
  Recuyell of the Historyes of Troye, 128
chancery English, 47–48
chanson d'aventure, 163, 173, 316, 452–453
chanson de geste, 56, 355–359, 361, 370
Chanson de Roland, La, 355–356
Charlemagne, 56, 174, 326, 337, 339–340, 355–361, 370
Charlemagne romances see Duke Rowland and Sir Otuell of Spain, The Sege of Melayne, The Song of Roland, The Sowdone of Babylone
Charles V, King of France, 47–48, 421,
Charles VI, King of France, 313, 415
Charles VII, King of France, 21, 315
Charles d'Orléans (Charles of Orleans), 4, 8, 18, 24, 55, 73, 87, 124, 295–299
  English Book of Love, 295–298
  'En la nef de Bonne Nouvelle', 296–297
  'Hoffa howe, myn hert! The schepe off Freche Teydyng', 297
  'O thou Fortune, whyche has the governaunce', 298–299
Charles of Jerusalem, 417
charms, 7, 121, 143–145, 156, 242–244, 394
Charter of Christ, 161, 168–170
Charteris, Henry, 444
Chartier, Alain,
  La Belle dame sans merci, 54, 289
  Querelle de la belle dame, 54
  Quadrilogue Invectif, 54
  Traité de l'espérance, 54
Chastising of God's Children, The, 135
Chaucer, Geoffrey, 1–5, 8–9, 18, 28–32, 38, 40, 45, 48, 58, 59–66, 70, 72–74, 76, 79–80, 85–88, 93–94, 96, 99–102, 105, 111–112, 117, 122–125, 179, 185, 197–198, 211, 243–244, 260, 275, 284–286, 290, 291, 298–299, 312, 314, 317, 336–337, 340, 341, 343, 360, 369, 372–373, 377, 402, 407, 411, 414, 416, 420, 421, 424–425, 427, 436–441, 444–445, 458–459, 461, 468, 481, 482–483, 490
  'ABC', 51, 179, 198
  Anelida and Arcite, 128, 323, 419
  Boece, 35, 53–54, 117, 244
  Book of the Duchess, 29–30, 33, 34, 82–83, 418–419
  Canterbury Tales, 21, 35–37, 62, 76, 111–113, 125–139, 179, 197–198, 336–340, 365–366, 407–408, 414
    'Clerk's Tale', Prologue, 63, 421
    'Cook's Tale', 270
    'Franklin's Tale', 323, 337, 474
    'Knight's Tale', 35–36, 106, 319–320, 414, 419–420
    'Manciple's Tale', 38
    'Man of Law's Tale', 95, 449
    'Melibee', 94, 112, 134, 138
    'Merchant's Tale', 476, 477
    'Miller's Tale', 62, 372–373
    'Monk's Tale', 36, 53–54, 179, 244, 323, 327 n.5, 415–416
    'Nun's Priest's Tale', 38
    'Pardoner's Tale', Prologue, 40, 270, 476
    'Parson's Tale', 112, 131–132, 134–135, 173
    'Reeve's Tale', 372
    'Retraction', 127, 134–135
    'Squire's Tale', 337, 476–477
    'Tale of Sir Thopas', 89, 135–136, 138
    'Wife of Bath's Prologue,' 476
    'Wife of Bath's Tale', 40, 342, 350, 372–373, 377, 398
  'Canticus Troili', 59
  'Complaint of Mars', 131
  'Complaint of Venus', 131
  'Complaint to Pity', 34
  dream poetry, 418, 485
  'Envoy to Bukton' 131
  House of Fame, 29–34, 93, 95–96, 106, 126, 128, 130, 419–420, 483, 485–486
  'Lak of Steadfastness', 319
  Legend of Good Women, 29–30, 33, 52, 416, 419, 486
  lyrics, 76
  Parliament of Fowls, 29–30, 34, 76, 85–86, 125–126, 128–130, 419–420, 449, 468, 498–499
  'To His Purse' 302, 469
  Troilus and Criseyde, 3, 23–24, 36, 37, 43–44, 65, 76, 85–86, 113, 126, 128–130, 137, 198, 287, 336–337, 365, 367, 389, 411–15, 419, 437, 443, 444, 449, 459, 477, 482–483
  'Truth', 123
  works, 114, 131, 136, 444
Chaucer, Thomas, 409
Chaundler, Thomas, 21
Chaworth, Sir Thomas, 119
Cheapside Cross, 227
Chepman, Walter, 131, 443, 461
Chester, 166, 188
Chester plays, 214–216, 219–228
Chester's Inn, 427
Chetham, Thomas, 332
Chevalere Assigne, 81
Chevy Chase, 140
Chichele, Henry, 159, 195, 200, 431–432
Chichele, Robert, 431–432
Chrétien de Troyes, Perceval – First Continuation, 342
Christ, Metrical Life of, 161, 167
Christ, Stanzaic Life of, 166–167, 168
Christ's Burial, 216
Christ's Passion, instruments of, 145–146, 243
Christ's Resurrection, 216
Cicero, 35, 73, 102, 416, 421
Clim of the Clough and William of Cloudesley, 395
Conty, Évrart de, Les Échecs amoureux, 53, 409

'Cryst þat was born in bedlem', 144
Christopher, St, 181–183
Clanvowe, John, 85–87, 122
Claudian, *De consulatu Stilichonis*, 5, 58–59, 114
Clement of Llanthony, *Unum ex Quattuor*, 166
Clopton, John, 152–153
cloth, painted, 148
Col, brothers Gontier and Pierre, 52
Colkelbie Sow, 396–397
Colyns, John, 344, 364–365
Comestor, Peter, *Historia Scholastica*, 162, 166
Conduct books, 264–265, 269, 280–281
Constance, Council of, 18, 159, 431–432, 436
Conversion of St Paul, 216–217
Cook, Sir Thomas, 118
Copland, Robert, 131, 481–482, 495–500
    Art of Memory, 496
    Assemble of Foules, Prologue to, 498–499
    Castell of Pleasure, Prologue, 497–500
    Guystarde and Segismonde, verses in, 498–499
    Hye Way to the Spyttell Hous, 495, 499
    Iyl of Braintfords Testament, 495, 499
    Kalendar of Shepherdes, 496–497
    Rosarye of Our Lady in Englysshe, 497
    Secrete of Secretes, 497–498
    Seuen Sorowes that Women Haue When Theyr Husbandes Be Deade, 495
Copland, William, 376
Corpus Christi play, 214–216
Court of Sapience, 256–257, 409, 490
Courtesy poems, 265, 269
Coventry, 6, 15, 27, 214–215, 386–387
Coventry carol, 206
Coventry plays, 215–216
Croo, Robert, 215–216
Crophill, John, 121–122
Crowned King, The, 3, 79–80, 307–308
Croxton Play of the Sacrament, 84–85, 216–217, 219–220, 229–234
Cursor Mundi, 160–162
Curteys, William, 113, 150, 188, 410, 422, 423
Cuthbert, St, 153
Cuthbert, St, Metrical Life of, 187–189

Dafydd ap Siancyn, 400
Dane Hew Munk of Leicestre, 372–374, 376–378
Dance of death, 152, 432, 444–445, 464–465
Dante Alighieri, 29, 33, 35, 39
    Commedia, 435
Dares, *De Excidio Troiae*, 333, 334, 410–411, 412
David, King, 227, 387
David II, King of Scotland, 304
De heretico comburendo, 304
Death and Life, 79–81, 174–175
Death of Robin Hood, 401
Debate between Mercy and Righteousness, 177
Debate of the Carpenter's Tools, 396
Deguileville, Guillaume de,
    Pèlerinage poems, 51

Pèlerinage de l'âme, 66
Pèlerinage de vie humaine, 51–52, 409
Deschamps, Eustache, 48
'descryuyng of mannes members', 238
Desert of Religion, 125, 172–173, 211
Desputisoun bitwen þe Bodi and þe Soule, 175
Destruction of Troy, 43–45, 81, 330–332
Devil's Parliament, 169–170, 171
Dialogue between a Wise Man and a Fool, 397
Dialogue between Reason and Adversity, 59
Dialogus inter Corpus et Animam, 175
dice, poems on, 262
Dictys, *Ephemeridos Belli Troiani*, 333, 410
Disputacion bitwyx the Body and Wormes, 175–176
dit amoureux, 296
Dodesham, Stephen, 116–117
Doom, Fifteen Tokens of, 151
Douglas, Archibald, earl of Moray, 5
Douglas, Gavin, 74, 444, 461, 470, 478, 481
    Eneados, 74–75, 483–487, 492, 500
    Palis of Honoure, 483, 485–487
Dublin 'Pale', 2
Duke Rowland and Sir Otuell of Spayne, 357–358
Dunbar, George, earl of, 390
Dunbar, William, 5, 9, 27, 88, 445–446, 461–478
    'Apon the Midsummer Ewin, merriest of nichtis' (*The Tretis of the Tua Mariit Wemen and the Wedo*), 131, 475–477
    'As ȝung Awrora with cristall haile', 468
    'Blyth Aberdeane, thow beriall of all tounis', 473
    'Gladethe, thoue queyne of Scottis regioun', 463, 471
    'Hale, sterne superne, hale, in eterne' (*Ane Ballat of our Lady*), 463–464, 471
    'I that in heill we and gladnes' (*Lament for the Makars*), 14, 444–445, 464–466, 470
    'I thocht lang quhill sum lord come hame', 469
    'In secret place this hyndir nycht', 462–463, 475–476
    'My prince in god gif þe guid grace, 389
    'O gracious princes guid and fair', 467
    'Off Februar the fyiftene nycht', 455, 466
    'Quhen Merche wes with variand windis past' (*The Thristell and the Rose*), 323, 472–473
    'Renownit, ryall, right reuerend and serene' (*The Ballad of Bernard Stewart*), 131
    'Ryght as the stern of day begouth to schyne' (*The Goldyn Targe*), 74–75, 131, 463, 473–475
    'Schir for ȝour grace, bayth nicht and day', 469–470
    'Schir Iohine the Ros' (*The Flying of Dunbar and Kennedy*), 131, 323, 443–444, 458–459, 470–471
    'Sir Ihon Sinclair begowthe to dance', 467–468
    'Schir, ȝe haue mony seruitouris', 468–470
    'Schir, ȝit remember ...', 464, 469
    'Schir, ȝit remember as befoir', 469, 478
    'The wardraipper of Wenus Bour', 467
    'This hinder nycht, half sleiping as I lay', 464
    'To speik of science, craft or sapience', 469

Dunfermline, 20, 442–443
Durham priory, 153
Duxford (Cambs), St John's church, 154

East Anglia, 49, 68–69, 99, 113–114, 124, 214–217, 336
East Newton, Yorkshire, 120
Easter, poem on date of, 241
Ebraucus, King, 387
Ebreo, Guglielmo *De Pratica seu Arte Tripudii*, 467
Edith, St, 187
Edmund of Abingdon, *Speculum Ecclesie*, 160
Edmund, duke of Somerset, 318
Edward the Confessor, King of England, 386–387
Edward III, King of England, 17, 48, 320–321
Edward IV, King of England, 3, 24–25, 31, 71, 115–116, 141, 262, 301, 309, 318–322, 390–391
Edward, duke of York, *Master of Game, The*, 245, 251–252
Edward of York, later Edward IV, 103
Edward, Prince of Wales (son of Henry VI), 40, 103, 279–281, 386–387
Edward, St, 385
Egidius Romanus, *De Regimine Principum*, see Giles of Rome
Eleanor of Aquitaine, 55
'Elixir, Verses on the', 259–260
Elizabeth, Queen, 386–387
Elckerlijc, 217–218, 232
Elyot, Thomas, 281
Entry to Jerusalem plays, 225–226
epitaphs, 150–151, 154–156, 390
Erasmus, Desiderius, 281
Erkenwald, St, 43, 78, 81
Erle of Tolous, 119–120, 397
'Erthe upon erthe', 151, 155
Estoire de Merlin, 342, 344
Estorie del Evangelie, La, 161
Estoire del Saint Graal, 56, 342, 349
Eton College, 19–20, 315
Eustace, St, 119
Eustace the Monk, 400
Everyman, 217–220, 232
Évrart de Conty, *Eschéz Amoureux*, 53, 408–409
Exeter, 379, 385, 400–401

fabliau, 32, 62, 180–181, 196–197, 338–340, 371–375, 383–384, 395
'Farewel my frends the tide abideth no man', 155
Fastolf, Sir John, 276, 279, 315
Feest of Tottenham, 375–376, 378–380, 396
Fierenbras, 359
'Fifteen Oes', 145–146
First Shepherds' Play, 232–234
Firumbras, 337–338
Flodden, battle of, 323, 461, 473
Flower and the Leaf, The, 8, 290, 294, 298
Foix, Gaston de, *Livre de Chasse*, 251–252
Fordun, John of, *Chronica*, 305–306

Formande, Richard, 153
Foucault, Michel, 91–93, 96, 108
Fouke le Fitz Waryn, 400
Four Daughters of God, 168, 171, 177, 256
Fourth Lateran Council, 171, 230–231
'Fox and the Goose', 396
Freiris of Berwik, 374, 394, 395
Frere and the Boye see *Iak and his Stepdame*
Friar Daw's Reply, 89
Froissart, Jean, 21, 283, 296, 357–358
Frulovisi, Tito Livio, 25
Fuerre de Gadres, 327
Furnival, Lord, 108

Gaimar, *Estoire des Engleis*, 300
Game and Play of the Chess, 138
Gascoigne, George, *Certayne Notes of Instruction Concerning the Making of Verse or Ryme in English*, 77
Gawain-poet, 31, 43, 95
Gawain romances, 346–351, 398
Gawain and the Carle of Carlisle, Sir, 343, 346, 348, 398
Gawain and the Green Knight see *Sir Gawain and the Green Knight*
Gaytryge, John, *Lay Folks' Catechism*, 89, 173–174
Generides, 362, 366–367
Generydes, 129, 366–368, 369
Geoffrey of Monmouth, *Historia Regum Britanniae*, 304, 306, 331, 345, 348–349, 390
Geoffrey of Vinsauf, *Poetria Nova*, 179
George, St, 307, 386–389
Gerald of Cornwall, 346
Gerson, Jean, 52
Gest Hystoriale see *Destruction of Troy*
Gesta Henrici Quinti, 311–312
Gest of Robin Hood, 395, 398, 401–402
Gesta Romanorum, 425
Gibbon, John, 381
Giles of Rome, *De Regimine Principum*, 57, 425
Giraldus Cambrensis, 395
Glasgow University, 167
Glastonbury Abbey, 349
Godfray, Thomas, 131
Godfridus super Palladium, 251
Godstow, Benedictine nunnery, 143
Golden Legend, 387
Golagros and Gawane, The Knightly Tale of, 342–345, 348–350
'Good gossipis myn', 375
Gower, John, 4, 8, 9–10, 30, 38, 41, 45, 62, 85–87, 106, 111–112, 123, 129–130, 133–135, 137, 275–276, 284–286, 291–292, 312, 407, 417, 437, 444–445, 481
  Confessio Amantis, 1–3, 23, 38–39, 95–96, 113, 118, 122, 123–125, 128, 131, 133–134, 136, 139, 254, 282, 284–285, 286, 366

Gower, John (*Continued*)
    Cronica tripertita, 303
    'Tale of Florent', 39, 342
    Traitié pour les amantz marietz, 88
'Gracius and gay', 294
graffiti, 154
Granson, Oton de, 283
Gray, William, 124
Great Bardfield (Essex), church of St Mary the Virgin, 154
Great Ormsby (Norfolk), parish church, 154–155
Green, Sir Henry, 302
Greene Knight, The, 342, 344, 346, 348, 350
Gregory, 166–167
Grimestone, John, 203 n.42
Grocers' company, 143
Grosseteste, Robert
    Chateau d'amour, 161, 171
    Templum Domini, 172
Gualterus Anglicus, 454–455
Guido delle Colonne, *Historia destructionis Troiae*, 44, 65, 93, 330–331, 410
Guy and Colbrond, 342–344, 348–349, 354
Guy of Warwick, 345–346, 348–349, 354, 396–397
Guy of Warwick, 130, 139, 341–345

Harfleur, 307–308, 312
Hatfield, William, *Life of St Ursula*, 188
Hatfield Regis, 408
Hardyng, John, *Chronicle*, 6, 71–73, 115–116, 125, 300, 309, 315, 320–323
Harrowing of Hell and the Destruction of Jerusalem, The, 169
Hary, *The Wallace*, 3, 300, 306–307, 323
'Have godday, nou, Mergerete', 294
Hawes, Stephen, 73–75, 107–108, 137, 409, 481, 483, 486, 490, 491–495, 499
    Conforte of Lovers, 130, 489–492, 494
    Conuersyon of Swerers, 496
    Example of Virtue, The, 130
    Pastime of Pleasure, 73, 130, 409, 490–492, 493, 495
Hay, Sir Gilbert, *Buik of King Alexander the Conquerour*, 327–328
Heege, Richard, 121, 393, 396, 402,
Henry II, King of England, 55, 274, 372, 395
Henry IV, King of England, 2, 9, 23, 33, 42, 108, 275, 286, 301–304, 312, 313, 390–391, 411,
Henry V, King of England, 2–3, 17–18, 31, 58, 97, 164, 194–197, 304, 307, 314, 316, 320–322, 385, 391, 425, 427, 432, 438
Henry VI, King of England, 2, 3, 20, 24–25, 31, 33, 48, 57, 71, 87, 103, 105, 113, 115, 141, 142, 146, 188, 197, 203, 219, 225, 226–229, 274–279, 286, 297, 313–315, 317, 319–322, 385–386, 388, 391, 409–410, 422
Henry VII, King of England, 3, 9, 15, 18, 24–25, 27, 31, 73, 107, 137, 148, 301, 323–324, 345, 386, 387–390, 391, 461, 472, 481–482, 493

Henry VIII, King of England, 25, 148, 323, 481–482, 494
Henry, prince of Lancaster, 116
Henryson, Robert, 9, 10, 20, 37–38, 88, 442–460, 482–483
    Abbey Walk, The, 446–448
    Annunciation poem, 445–447
    Bludy Serk, The 443, 447
    'Christ the Lover Knight', 446–447
    Garmont of Gud Ladies, 443–444, 446–447
    'Lion and the Mouse, The', 450, 452–453, 455, 458
    Morall Fabillis, 37–38, 443–444, 449–450, 452, 454–455, 458–459
    Orpheus and Eurydice, 131, 442, 443, 444, 449, 450
    Praise of Age, 443, 446
    Prayer for the Pest, 446
    Ressoning betuix Aige and Yowth, 446, 448
    Ressoning betuix Deth and Man, 446
    Robene and Makyne, 443, 446–447
    'Sheep and the Dog, The', 450, 453
    Sum Practysis of Medecyne, 443–444, 447
    Testament of Cresseid, 8, 37, 443, 444, 447, 449, 451, 453, 454, 458–60, 483–484
    Traitie of Orpheus see Orpheus and Eurydice
    'Trial of the Fox, The', 450, 452–453, 457
    Want of Wisemen, The, 443
Henrysson family, 151
Hereward, 400,
Hertford, 22, 366–367
Hertford Castle, 142, 408
Hessle family, 151
Heydon (Norfolk), church of SS Peter and Paul, 151
Higden, Ranulf, *Polychronicon*, 47, 166, 300
Hill, Richard, 376, 380–381, 393
Hilton, Walter, 190
Historia de preliis, 327, 329
Hoccleve, Thomas, 1–3, 9, 18, 26, 35, 38, 39–41, 46, 48, 61–62, 65–67, 77–78, 85–88, 98–100, 116, 117–118, 122–123, 312, 407, 424–441
    'Ad patrem', 431–434
    'Ars moriendi', 424–425, 428–432
    'Balade ... de bone compagnie' ('Good Company'), 427–428, 439–440
    Balade on the Reburial of Richard II at Westminster, 312, 426
    'Balade to the Virgin and Christ', for Robert Chichele, 431–432
    'Conpleynte paramont' (Complaint of the Virgin), 434
    Formulary, 116, 425
    'Male Regle', 39, 106–108, 313, 440–441
    'Miracle of the rosary', 185–186
    'Modir of lyf', 432
    'Mother of God', 66
    'Lament of the Virgin', 51
    Letter (Epistle) of Cupid, 52, 288, 298, 424, 440
    'Of my lady wel me rejoise I may', 294–295

Regiment of Princes, 3, 28–29, 38, 39–40, 57, 61, 63, 86–87, 93–95, 101, 113, 116, 118, 125, 275–276, 312–313, 391, 424–425, 427, 432–441
  'To Sir John Oldcastle', 312, 429–430
  Series, 39, 424–425, 427–432, 438–439
Holland, Richard, *Buke of the Howlat*, 5, 72–73, 81, 131
Holloway, Somerset, chapel of St Mary Magdalen, 153
Homer, 93, 333, 410
Honorius Augustodunensis, *Elucidarium*, 176
'How the Good Wijf Tauȝt Hir Douȝtir', 270–271
How the plowman learned his pater noster, 129–130, 382–383
'How the Wise Man Tauȝt His Sone', 272–274
Howard, Sir Edward, 489–490
'Hucheon', 306
Hudson, Henry, 387
Hue de Rotelande, *Ipomédon*, 362–363, 367
Hughe of Campdene, 257
Humanism, 4–5, 58, 59
Humfrey, duke of Gloucester, 24–26, 33, 58, 249–250, 269, 270, 279, 390–391, 408–409
Hundred Years War, 2, 4, 48
Hunted Hare, The, 396
'Hunting of the Cheviot', 140
Hunting of the Hare, The (þe hunttyng of þe hare), 238, 396
Hus, Jan, 431
Hyngham, Thomas, 217
Hyrd, Richard, *Instruction of a Christen Woman*, 362, 365

Idley, Peter, 277, 280
  Instructions to His Son, 277–279, 280, 382
Incestuous Daughter, 373–374
Infancy of Jesus, 215–216
Inglewood outlaws, 395, 400
Ipomadon, 362–363, 365, 366–367
Ipomydon, 56, 362–365, 366
Ireland Prophecy, 78, 80, 90
Isidore of Seville, 256
Isle of Ladies, The, 288–290
Iter ad Paradisum, 329

Jack Cade's Rebellion, 15–16
Jacob de Cessolis, *Book of Chess*, 56–57
  De ludo scaccorum, 275, 425
Iak and his Stepdame, 374–377, 380–382
Jack Upland, 76, 88, 89
Jacqueline of Bavaria, countess of Hainault and Duchess of Gloucester, 285, 420
Jacquetta of Luxemburg, 386–387
James I, King of Scotland, 9
  Kingis Quair, 24–25, 35, 87, 106, 122–123, 285–288, 291, 298, 305–306, 477
James IV, King of Scotland, 5, 323, 325, 389, 461–462, 467, 468, 471–473
Jean de Meun, *Roman de la Rose*, 52, 54, 415–416

Jean de Montreuil, 52
Jeaste of Sir Gawain, The, 342, 343
'Ihesu that was in bedelem borne', 144
Job, Metrical Life of, 164
Johan, Lewis, 22, 24, 26
'John Clerk', 43–44, 332
John, duke of Bedford, 24, 36–37, 103, 116, 146–147, 313–315, 408
John, lord of Wemyss, 305
John of Gaunt, duke of Lancaster, 33
John the Baptist, alliterative life of, 184
John the Evangelist, alliterative life of, 184, 190, 191–192
John the Reeve, 395
Jongleur d'Ely et le roi d'Angleterre, le, 372
Joseph of Arimathea, 167, 169, 349
Josephus, 93, 221–222
Jousts of the Month of May, 137
Justinian, 256

Kalendar of Shepherdes, 496
Katherine, of Aragon, 472–473
Katherine, Queen of England, Katherine of Valois, 414
Katherine, St, alliterative hymn to, 146, 148
Katherine, St, life of, 105, 181, 183
Kennedy, Walter, *Passioun of Christ*, 167, 171
Killing of the Children, 216–217
King and the Hermit, The, 375–376, 395
King Edward and the Shepherd, 374–376
Kings of England, anonymous verses on, 147
King's Printer, 130
Knolles, Thomas, 155
Knyghthode and Bataile, 57–59
Kyng Alisaunder, 327

Lady Prioress, The, 372–375
'Lamentacioun of our lady for sweryng', 151
Lancelot of the Laik, 56, 341–344
Lancelot-Grail Cycle, 344, 351–353
Langland, William, *Piers Plowman*, 8, 41, 42, 76, 79–80, 95, 111, 113, 123, 125, 254, 427, 435
Langley, Thomas, 436
Langtoft, Pierre, *Chronique*, 300, 321
'lapis philosophorum', 259
Laud Troy Book, 331, 333–335
Launceston priory, Cornwall, 154
Laurent, Friar, *Somme le Roi*, 172–173
Lay of Sorrow, 288
Laȝamon, *Brut*, 300
'Learn or Be Lewed', 266
Leconfield, East Yorkshire, 154
Lefèvre, Raoul, 128–129
Legenda Aurea, 153, 166–167, 188
Leland, John, 91, 473–475
Lemaire de Belges, Jean, 490
Leslie, John, *De Origine Moribus Rebus Gestis Scotorum*, 468
Lestrange, Richard, Lord, 105, 115, 201

Lewis, C. S., 282
Libelle of Englyshe Polycye, 4, 87, 316–317
Liber cure cocorum, 239
Liber Proverbiorum, 70–71
Lichfield, 376
Lichfield, William, *Complaint of God*, 121, 176
Lidgate (Suffolk), 408
Little Gest of Robin Hood, 129, 130
Locher, Jacob, 487–488
London, St Antolin's Church, 155
London, St Paul's Cathedral, Pardon churchyard, 152, 465
Long Melford, Suffolk, Holy Trinity Church, 152–153
Lorris, Guillaume de, *Roman de la rose*, 282
Louis, St, 227, 314, 385–386
Love, Nicholas, *Mirror of the Blessed Life of Jesus Christ*, 160, 421
Lovelich, Henry, 341–342, 343, 344
   Merlin, 118–119
   History of the Holy Grail, 56, 118–119, 125, 349
Lucidus and Dubius, 176
Ludolphus of Saxony, *Meditationes Vitae Christi*, 167
lunary (lunaries), 121, 252–254
Lybeaus Desconus, 119, 397
Lydgate, John, 3, 5, 6–10, 26, 32, 38, 40, 45, 46, 48, 49–53, 56–60, 63, 66, 68, 73, 74, 78, 85, 87, 91, 95–96, 98, 101, 105, 107, 113–114, 117–118, 122–126, 128, 150–151, 174, 179, 184, 185, 189, 191, 195, 197–201, 207–208, 210, 278, 298, 310, 312, 336–337, 340, 349, 368, 407–423, 441, 445, 481–482, 488, 490–492, 496, 497
   'Ballade at the Reverence of Our Lady', 152–153
   'Ballade on a New Year's Gift of an Eagle, Presented to King Henry VI', 142–143
   Bycorne and Chychevache, 6, 149–150
   Churl and the Bird, 38, 43, 125, 128–130, 408
   Complaynt of a Loveres Lyfe (Complaint of the Black Knight), 131, 282–284, 410, 418–419
   Dance of Death (Danse Macabre), 152, 409, 432, 465
   De profundis clamavi, 150, 410
   Dietary, 254–255
   'Ditty Against Haste', 372–373
   Fall of Princes, 4–5, 33, 58–60, 101–103, 113, 119, 124–125, 130, 275–276, 314, 316, 323–324, 408–410, 415–418, 490
   Guy of Warwyk, 343–346
   Horse, Goose and Sheep, 125, 128–130, 137, 408
   'Lamentacioun of Our Lady Maria', 152–153
   'Legend of Dan Joos', 190
   Life of Our Lady, 7, 49, 65, 113, 120–121, 124–125, 128–129, 190, 192, 199, 408–410, 420–422
   Life of Saint Alban and Saint Amphibal, 188, 408, 410
   'Life of St Anne' 186–187
   Life of St George, 148–149, 182
   'Life of St Giles', 183–184, 186, 189–190
   'Life of St Margaret', 49, 178–179, 182
   Lives of Saints Edmund and Fremund, 105, 113, 124–125, 188, 408–410, 422–423
   Mumming at Bishopswood, 389
   Mumming at Eltham, 389
   Mumming for Goldsmiths, 389
   Mumming for Mercers, 389
   'Pageant of Knowledge', 239–240, 255
   Pilgrimage of the Life of Man, 51–52, 124, 409
   Prayers on Christ's Passion, 149–150
   'Prayer to St Thomas of Canterbury', 150
   Procession of Corpus Christi, 220
   'Secrees of Old Philosoffres', 57, 276–277, 409–410
   Siege of Thebes, 2, 35–37, 87, 96, 106, 113, 116–117, 123, 125, 129–130, 313, 368, 407–410, 412, 414
   Sotelties for Henry VI, 142–143, 385–386
   Stans Puer ad Mensam, 125, 128–129, 266–267, 382
   Temple of Glass, 34, 117, 125, 128–130, 283, 284–285, 288, 294, 410, 418, 420
   Testament, 152–153, 267, 408–410
   Thomas Chaucer, poem on, 389
   'Title and Pedigree of Henry VI', 313–314
   Translation of Laurence Calot's poem on Henry VI, 146–147, 313–314
   'Treatise for Lauandres', 255
   Triumphal Entry of Henry VI, 219, 225–229
   Troy Book, 3, 36, 44, 56–57, 63, 65, 101–102, 113, 119, 123, 125, 313–314, 337, 368, 407–416
   Verses on the kings of England, 146–147, 314–315
Lyndsay, David, 444–445
   Ane Satyre of the Thrie Estaits, 466
Lyndsay, Robert, 474
'Lytylle Childrenes Lytil Boke', 267, 382

McGregor, James, 444
Macer, herbal, 244–245
Machiavelli, Niccolò, 281
Macro, Cox, 217
Machaut, Guillaume de, 95, 283, 296, 419, 425
Maidstone, Richard, *Penitential Psalms*, 124, 161, 164–165
Makculloch, Magnus, 443
Mallarmé, Stéphane, 93
Malory, Thomas, *Le Morte Darthur*, 323, 341, 344, 354, 364
Mandeville, Sir John, *Travels*, 246–249, 359–360
Mankind, 69, 213, 217, 219–220
Mannyng, Robert, 322–323
   Handlyng Synne, 277–278
   Chronicle, 300, 321
Mantuan, 488
Mappheus Vegius, 483
Margaret, St, 121, 181, 189, 386
Margaret of Anjou, 5, 25, 70, 103, 279, 314, 317, 320, 386
Margaret Tudor, 323, 461, 463, 467, 470, 471, 473
Marriage of Sir Gawain, 342
'Marrow or pithe of alchymy, The', 259

Martinus Polonus, 304
Mary de Pratis, St, abbey, Leicester, 118
Mary Magdalen, 172
Mary Magdalen, Life of, 185
Mary Magdalen, play of, 216, 219, 230–231
Mary Magdalen, St, chapel of, 153
Mary of Egypt, 172
Mary, Virgin, 65–66, 68, 151, 164, 388, 401, 420–421, 434, 439, 471, 472, 497
Matthew of Vendôme, *Ars versificatoria*, 63
Maykin, Robert, 127
mazer, 143
Medwall, Henry, 6–7, 235
   Fulgens and Lucrece, 217–218, 233–236
   Nature, 217–218
Melton, Robert, 121
'Merseir', 445
Metham, John, 68–69, 88, 99
   Amoryus and Cleopes, 5, 115, 336–337
Metrical Paraphrase of the Old Testament, Middle English, 161–162
Michael, St, Archangel, 354
Middleton, Jane and Thomas, 156
Milton, John, 78, 108
Mirk, John, *Instructions for Parish Priests*, 173–174
Mirror for Magistrates, 499
Mirror of the World, 128
'Mockery of the Flemings', 316
Montague, Thomas, 52
moon books *see* lunaries
More, Thomas, 281
   Mery gest how a sergeaunte wolde lerne to be frere, 379
   Pageant verses, 149
   Utopia, 15
Morgan, Edwin, 74–75
Morte Arthure, Alliterative, 43, 45, 81, 120, 139, 306, 342
Morte Arthur, Stanzaic, 56, 341–344, 348, 353–354, 364
Morton, John, Bishop of Ely, Archbishop of Canterbury, 6, 143, 218, 386
motto(es), 143, 285, 292, 387
Mum and the Sothsegger, 42, 76, 79–80
Myllar, Androw, 131, 443–444, 461
Mylner of Abyngton, 372–373, 377
'Myn owne dere ladi fair and fre', 294
Myrour of Lewed Men, 171–172

Nashe, Thomas, 376
   Pierce Penilesse his supplication to the diuell, 500
   Haue with you to Saffron-walden, 500
Nevill, Thomas, 150–151
Neville, Cecily, 114
Neville, Richard, earl of Warwick, 315
Neville, William, 497
Newcastle, 215–216
Newton, Humphrey, 154

Nicodemus, Gospel of, 168–169, 177
Nicodemus, Stanzaic Version of the Gospel of, 169
Nine Worthies, 121, 334, 386
Northampton, 120–121, 216, 318–320, 390
Northern Homily Cycle, 161
Northern Passion, The, 119, 161
Norton, Thomas, ?chaplain, 250
Norton, Thomas (alchemical author), *The Ordinal of Alchemy*, 260–262
Norwich, 26–27, 215, 387
Norwich, church of St John Maddermarket, 155
Notary, Julian, 131
N-Town plays, 215, 222, 225–227, 398

Occupacyon and Ydelnes, 176
Of Arthour and of Merlin, 342–345, 349
Ogilvie, Walter, 472
Oldcastle, Sir John, 2, 196–197, 312, 429, 431, 435
Oon of Foure, 166
Opus agriculturae, 58
Origen, 223–224
Orosius, 304
Otinel, 355
Ovid (also Ovidian), 29, 34, 39, 326, 417
   Heroides, 419
   Metamorphoses, 287, 336–337
Owain Glyndŵr, 2, 17, 390–391
Owayne Miles, 121

Page, John, *Siege of Rouen*, 4, 310, 311
pageant(s), 27, 121, 140, 149, 215–216, 219, 225, 226–227, 233–235, 386–389, 466, 474
Palladius, *De re agricultura, On Husbondrie*, 58, 70, 249–251
Paris, 17, 26, 99, 137, 313, 315, 386, 408–409
Paris, church of Holy Innocents, 152
Parliament of the Three Ages, 80
Partenay, Romans of, 56, 70–71
Partonope of Blois, 56, 362, 365–367, 369
Pascon agun Arluth, 18
Paston, family, 344
Paston, Sir John, 344
'Pearce the Black Monke', 259
Peasants' Revolt (1381), 15, 308–309
Pecham, John, 159, 170–173, 177
Penitential Psalms, 124, 161, 163, 165, 205, 428
   see also Maidstone, Richard
Pepysian Gospel Harmony, 166
Percy, Henry, fourth earl of Northumberland, 3, 323–325
Percy Chronicle, 148, 324
Percy family, 148, 154
Peterborough Abbey, 153
Petrarch, Francis, 29, 33, 59–60, 63, 101–102, 416, 421, 451, 491
   De Remediis Utriusque Fortunae, 59
   Rerum Vulgarium Fragmenta (*Canzoniere*), 59
   Secretum, 59
Pety Job, 163–164, 165

Philip of Burgundy, 315–316
Piacenza, Domenico da, *De la arte di ballare et danzare*, 467
Piccolomini, Aenius Sylvius, 488–489
Pierce Penilesse his supplication to the diuell, 499–500
Piers the Plowman's Creed, 42, 79, 118
Pigott, 150–151
Pilgrimage of the life of the Manhode, 46, 124
Pisan *see* Pizan
Pizan, Christine de, 52–53, 95–96
    Epistle of Othea, 53, 125, 277
    Epistre au dieu d'Amours, 52
    Livre des faits et d'armes et decs chevalerie, 57
    Livre du Corps de Policie, 277
'Plowman's Tale', 303
Pole, William de la, duke of Suffolk, 117, 298–299
Pollard, Walter, 394
Polton, Thomas, bishop of Chichester, 16–17
Premierfait, Laurent de, *Des cas des nobles hommes et femmes*, 57, 415–417
Prick of Conscience, 111, 123, 151, 238
Privity of Privities, 115
prognosticatory verse, 252–253
Prophecies of St Thomas of Canterbury, 80
Pseudo-Bonaventure, 49
Pseudo-Matthew, Gospel of, 422
Pseudo-Turpin Chronicle, 357, 360–361
Pylgremage of the Sowle see Pilgrimage of the Soul
Pylkyngton, Gilbertus, 376
Pynson, Richard, 105–106, 127, 130, 134–139, 188, 401, 487–489, 497
Pyramus and Thisbe, 336

Quare of Jelusy, 288
Quatrefoil of Love, 161, 170
Queen Eleanor's Confession, 372
Querelle de la Rose, 54
Quixley, 88

Ramsay, Allan, 462
Rastell, John, 131, 218
Rastell, William, 218
'Rate', 119–120
Ratis Raving, 272–274
Rauf Coilȝear, 395
Recuyell of the Historyes of Troye, 128
Remembraunce of the Passioun of Our Lord Jesu Criste, A, 168
Reson and Sensuallyte, 53–54, 217–218
Resurrection and Apparitions, 168
Reynard the Fox, 137
Reynes, Robert, 121
Rhodes, 2
Rich, Edmund, St, 209 n.74
Richard II, King of England, 2, 301–303, 312, 367, 386, 391, 426–427
Richard III, King of England, 3, 17, 31, 301, 315, 387
Richard, duke of York, 5, 58, 71, 114–115, 185, 273, 317–318, 320–321, 391

Richard de Caistre, 124, 394
Richard Coeur de Lion, 129
Richard the Redeles, 42, 79–80, 302–304
riddle poems, 394
Ridgewell (Essex), church of St Lawrence, 154
Ripley, George, *Compend of Alchemy, The*, 262
Robert II, King of Scotland, 304
Robert of Gloucester, *Metrical Chronicle*, 300–301
Robert of Knaresborough, *Life of*, 188
'Robin and Gandelyn', 402
Robin Hood, 129–130, 385, 391, 393, 395, 397–398, 400–403
Robin Hood and Guy of Gisborne, 400–401
Robin Hood and the Monk, 401
Robin Hood and the Potter, 401–403
Rolle, Richard, 163, 172, 190, 210–211
    Ego dormio, 210
rolls, genealogical, 146–147
Roman d'Alexandre, 327, 329
Roman de la Rose see Lorris, Guillaume de, and Meun, Jean de
Rome, 101, 235, 247, 249, 322, 331, 337–339, 357–360, 417
Romford, Essex, church of St Edward the confessor, 155
Roos, Sir Richard, *La Belle Dame Sans Merci*, 54–55, 122, 288–290
rosemary, treatise on, 253
Rosslyn Chapel, 465–466
Rougement Castle, Exeter, 395–396
Rowland and Otuell, 358
Ruffin, St, 150–151
Russell, John, *Boke of Nurture*, 265, 269–270, 273, 279, 363
Rutter of the Sea, 496
Ryman, James, 6–9, 115, 195, 204

Saham, Robert, 127
Salisbury cathedral, Hungerford chapel, 152
Sammelband, 128
Sawtre, William, 303–304
'Schoolboy's Lament', 268
Scogan, Henry, 22–23, 62–63, 85
Scottish Troy Book, 331
Scrope, Jane, 497
Scrope, Stephen, 280, 336
    Epistle of Othea, 53, 125, 277
Second Shepherds' Play, 219, 233–235
Secreta Secretorum, 254, 329, 410, 425
Seege or Batayle of Troye, 331, 335
Sege of Melayne, The, 141–142, 357–359
Seneca, 102, 416
Senhouse, Simon, prior of Carlisle, 153
Shakespeare, William, 77–78, 85,
    Macbeth, 466
Shirley, John, 22–24, 99, 117–118, 298–299, 408–409, 418
Shirwood, John, 21
Sidrac and Boccus, 257–259

Siege of Jerusalem, The, 118
Sigismund, Emperor, 316, 432
Sinclair, Henry, 3rd lord, 122–123, 288
Sinclair, Sir John, 467
Sinclair, William, Earl of Caithness, 465
Sinner's Lament, The, 119
Sir Amadas, 364
Sir Cleges, 119–120, 377, 379–380, 397–398
Sir Corneus, 374
Sir Degaré, 366 n.48
Sir Degore, 129
Sir Degrevant, 368–370
Sir Eglamour of Artois, 129, 131
Sir Ferumbras, 337–338
Sir Gawain and the Carl of Carlisle, 346
Sir Gawain and the Green Knight, 77, 139, 327–328, 341–343, 350, 353, 368, 398
Sir Isumbras, 119
Sir Orfeo, 119
Skelton, John, 3, 8, 25, 74, 105, 107–108, 323–324, 396, 441, 481, 483, 486, 489, 491, 497
  'Agaynst a Comely Coystrowne', 496–497
  Bowge of Court, 126, 130, 393, 478, 489, 496
  'Eleanor Rumming', 325
  Garlande of Laurell, 107–108, 490, 496
  Garnesche, Christopher, 325
  Phyllyp Sparowe, 497
  'Upon a deedmans hed', 497
  'Upon the Dolorus Dethe and Muche Lamentable Chaunce of the Mooste Honorable Erle of Northumberlande', 3, 323–325
  'Why Come Ye Not to Court', 496
'Smerte', *Epitaffe on the moste noble & valyaunt Iasper late duke of Beddeforde*, 126
Smyth Whych That Forged hym a New Dame, The, 374, 376
Somer, Henry, 427, 439–440
'sotelties', 142–143, 149
Soul and Body, 175
Southwark, St Mary Overie, 88
Sowdon of Babylon, 337–338, 339–340, 358–360
Spalding, Richard, 'Life of St Katherine', 184, 186–187, 189
speculum principis, 469, 472
Speed, John, 136
Spofforth, North Yorkshire, All Saints' church, 156
St Andrews University, 21, 461
Stafford, Henry, duke of Buckingham, 318–319
Stafford, Humphrey, 388
Stafford family, 5, 150–151
stained glass, 151
Stamford, Lincolnshire, 146
Stapleton, Lady Katherine, 336
Stapleton, Miles, Sir, 5, 115, 336
Stephen's, St, Westminster, 436
Stone Priory, Staffordshire, 150
Story of Resurrection, 168
Stow, John, 87, 154–155, 372–373, 409–410

South English Legendary, 111, 160, 161, 166, 177, 179–180
Speculum Gy de Warwyk, 354
Speculum misericordie, 173
Speculum vitae, 172–173
Spenser, Edmund, 98, 212
Squire of Low Degree, 129–130, 394–395
Stanley, Earls of Derby, 345–346
Stanzaic Morte Arthur, see *Morte Arthur, Stanzaic*
Statius, *Thebaid*, 93, 414
Stratford-upon-Avon, guild chapel, 151–152, 155
'Such as ye be, such wer we', 155
Sudeley Castle, Gloucestershire, 148
Sudeley family, 148
Surigone, Stefano, 18
Surrey, Henry Howard, earl of, 78, 86, 90
Suso, Henry, *Horologium sapientiae*, 428–431
'Symon's Lesson of Wysedome for all Maner Chyldryn', 267

tableaux vivants, 142–143
tables, 150–151
Talbot, John, earl of Shrewsbury, 318
Tale of the Basin, 372–374, 376, 382–383
tapestry, 148
Taylor, John, 381
'Te deum laudamus', 68
'Thayr ys no myrth under the sky', 294
'There is a busch that is forgrowe', 302
Thewis off Gudwomen 272–274, 329
Thomas of Erceldoune, 391
Thoresby, John, 173–174
Thornton, Robert, 56, 120–122, 142, 151, 190, 344, 357
Three Kings of Cologne, 120
Three living and the three dead, 152, 174–175
Thynne, William, 131, 444
'Timor mortis conturbat me', 14, 18, 155, 203, 464
Tournament of Tottenham, 374, 376, 378–379, 395–396
Towneley plays, 214–215, 219–220, 232–236
Towton, Battle of, 103, 309, 318, 390, 392
translatio studii, 326, 327
Trevisa, John, 47
  De proprietatibus rerum see Bartholomaeus Anglicus
  Dialogue between a Lord and a Clerk, 47
  Polychronicon, 47, 300
Trivet, Nicholas, 450
Troy, 36, 71, 326, 330–335, 411–414
Troyes, Treaty of, 2, 310, 313, 409–410
Turke and Sir Gawain, The, 345–349

Umfraville, Gilbert, 310–311
Undo Youre Dore see *Squire of Low Degree*
Upland's Rejoinder, 89
'Urbanitatis', 266
urinary tract, 255
Urswick, Thomas, 21

Vale, John, 118
Vegetius, *De Re Militari*, 57
Vergil, Polydore, 324
Veronica, 145–146
Virgil, *Aeneid*, 29, 33, 35, 44, 73–74, 93, 440, 483–487
Virtues of the Mass, 174
Vision of Tundale, 121, 366,
Voeux du Paon, 327

Wace, *Brut*, 300, 321
Wade, Laurence, *Life of Thomas Becket*, 188–189
Wagstaffe miscellany, 121–122
Wakefield, 215, 318
Wakefield Master, 31, 233–234
Wallace, William, 3, 300, 306–307, 323, 400
wall-paintings, 151–152
Walsingham, 188, 260–261
Walstan, St, 150–151
Walter, William, *Guystarde and Sygysmonde*, 496
Walton, John, *Consolation of Philosophy*, 5–6, 53–54, 58, 62, 63, 87, 244, 246, 437–438
Wars of Alexander, 43–45, 328, 332
Warton, Thomas, 1, 9, 30
Watson, Henry, 130
Waynflete, William, 20
Wedding of Gawain and Dame Ragnelle, The, 342, 350–351, 398
Weever, John, 154–155
Welles, Sir John, mayor of London, 143
Wensley, North Yorkshire, Holy Trinity church, 152
'Werken, T.', 124
Westminster, 5, 15, 17, 26–27, 116, 312, 313, 318, 424
Wey, William, *Itineraries*, 249
'Whatso men seyn', 295
Whethamstede, John, 18, 188, 315, 410
Whittocksmead, John, 121
'Whoo soo hym be thowgh', 151

William of Cratfield, 408
William of Exeter, 408
William of Pagula, *Oculus sacerdotis*, 173–174
William of Palerne, 43, 78, 362 n.29
William of Tours, *Contemplation of Sinners*, 126
William the Conqueror, 147–148, 150–151, 314
Winchester, 176
Winchester Cathedral, 345
Wingale, John, 114
Winner and Waster, 40, 43
Wisdom, 213–214, 216–217, 230–231
'With wiel my herte is wa', 154
Wolsey, Thomas, Cardinal, 325
Woodville, Anthony, earl Rivers, 24–25,
Worcester, 387–388
Worde, Wynkyn de, 129–130, 135–138, 176, 188, 344–345, 364, 372, 376, 382–383, 482, 494–496
Worksop Abbey (Notts.), 150–151
Wressle, East Yorkshire, 154
Wyatt, Thomas, 59–60, 78, 90
Wyclif, John, 46–47, 160, 431
Wycliffite Bible, 46–49, 159–160
Wyer, Robert, 131
Wykeham, William, 20
Wyntoun, Andrew, 6
    Originall, 300–301, 304–306

'Yerly be þe morowe in a somer-tyde', 141
York, 6–7, 15, 16, 22, 27, 120, 151, 214–216, 219, 225, 389, 394
York, All Saints' church, North St, 151
York cycle, 214, 229
York *Entry* play, 227, 235
York Minster, 150 n.47, 315
York, St Mary's Abbey, 400
'Young Children's Book', 266, 268